HUDDERSFIELD'S ROLL OF HONOUR 1914–1922

J. MARGARET STANSFIELD

EDITOR
Reverend Paul Wilcock BEM

Published by University of Huddersfield Press

University of Huddersfield Press
The University of Huddersfield
Queensgate
Huddersfield HD1 3DH
Email enquiries university.press@hud.ac.uk

First published 2014
Text © The Authors 2014
Images © as attributed

Every effort has been made to locate copyright holders of materials included and to obtain permission for their publication.

The publisher is not responsible for the continued existence and accuracy of websites referenced in the text.

All rights reserved. No part of this book may be reproduced in any form or by any means without prior permission from the publisher.

A CIP catalogue record for this book is available from the British Library.
ISBN 978-1-86218-126-7

Designed and printed by

JMP
113 Lidget Street
Lindley
Huddersfield HD3 3JR
www.wearejmp.co.uk

COVER IMAGE:
Trench map of Bullecourt in 1918
Courtesy of the Trustees of the Duke of Wellington's Regiment Museum and Archives.

Reverend Paul Wilcock BEM is the Director of the Arms and Armour Research Institute at the University of Huddersfield. He is a Trustee of the Huddersfield Drill Hall, the Duke of Wellington's Regiment Museum and of the Huddersfield War Memorial Trust.

CONTENTS

Foreword – HRH The Duke of York KG	v
Maps	vi
Orders of Battle	viii
Introduction – Reverend Paul Wilcock BEM	xi
Roll of Honour	1
War Memorials and Rolls of Honour	503
Personal Tribute – Martin Middlebrook	505
Acknowledgements	507

FOREWORD

BUCKINGHAM PALACE

I am honoured to have been invited to write the foreword to this work commemorating service personnel from Huddersfield who gave their lives during the First World War.

As Patron of the University of Huddersfield, this book provides a fitting tribute at the beginning of the four years in which we commemorate the First World War. The University is now a major part of the town and I am proud that it has made the publication of this work possible.

3,439 people are listed in the book of which 1,304 are men who died fighting with the Duke of Wellington's Regiment. This is particularly important as 'The Dukes' are one of the antecedent regiments of the Yorkshire Regiment for whom I am Colonel-in-Chief.

This publication represents the lifetime work of Margaret Stansfield, who sadly passed away at the end of 2012. Margaret spent thirty years compiling the 3,439 biographical entries giving a poignant insight into the background, working lives and families of those who selflessly left Huddersfield to fight for their country, never to return. In some cases they lie in marked graves in their field of conflict, in some they are remembered only on memorials in the theatre where they fell. Now these brave souls will be remembered in the pages of this book researched, published and printed in the town they loved so dearly.

I commend this book to you, not only as an important historical resource but also as a constant reminder of the ultimate price paid by so many a century ago.

HRH The Duke of York KG

THE SOMME

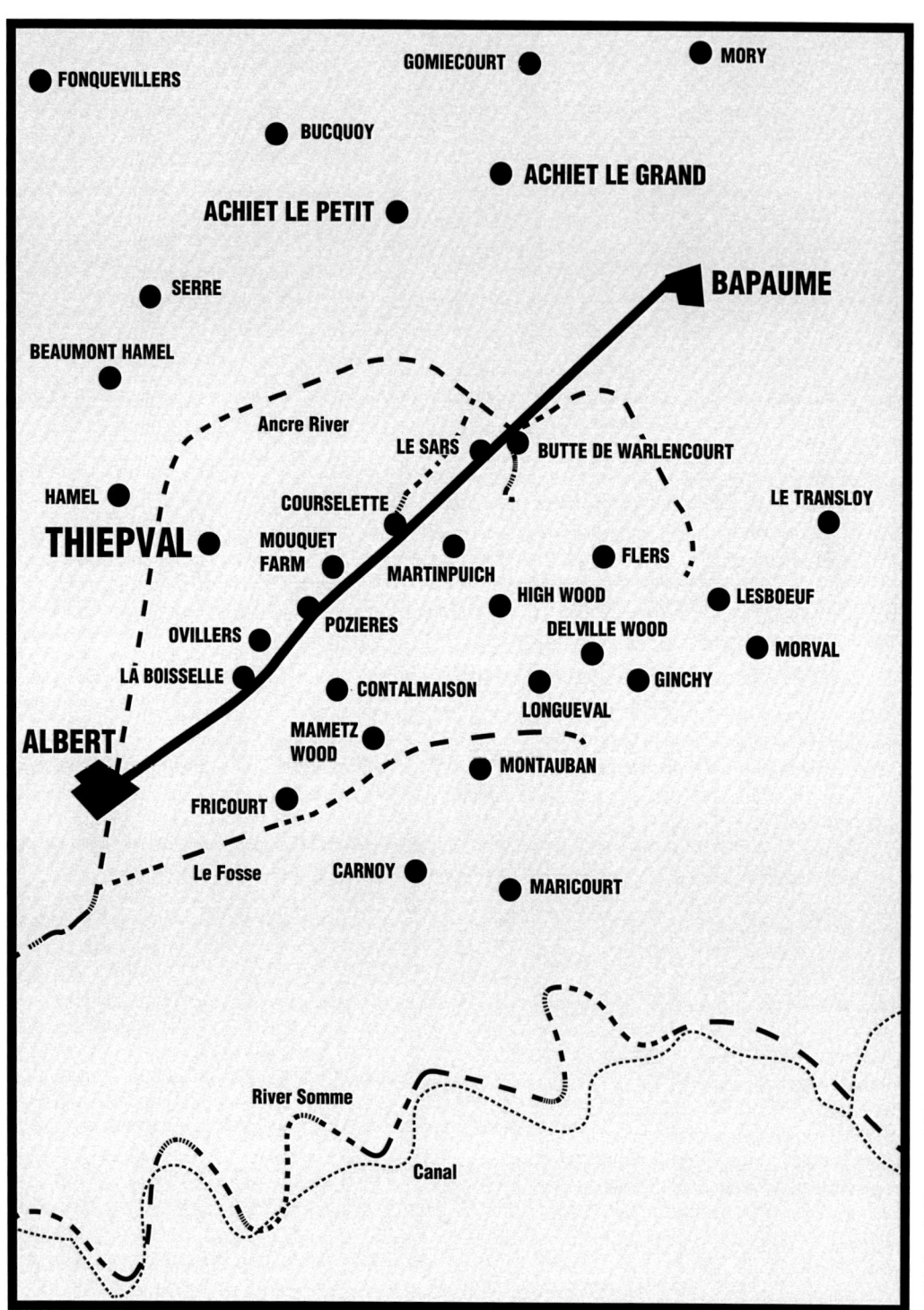

YPRES SALIENT

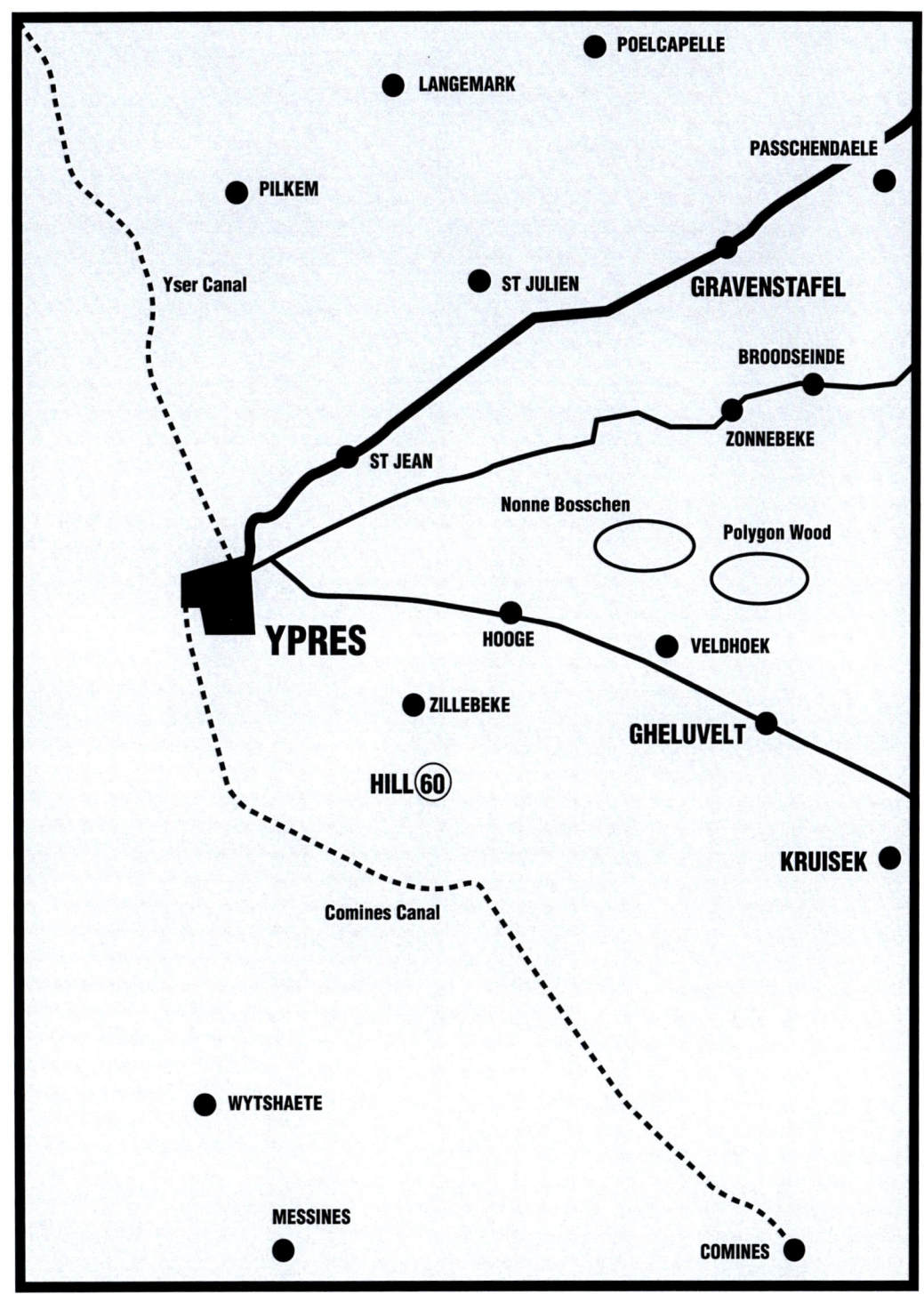

ORDERS OF BATTLE

MANY OF THE UNITS FEATURED IN THIS BOOK WERE PART OF THE TWO WEST RIDING DIVISIONS, AS LISTED BELOW.

49TH (WEST RIDING) INFANTRY DIVISION

146TH (WEST RIDING) BRIGADE

1/5th Battalion, The Prince of Wales's Own (West Yorkshire Regiment)

1/6th Battalion, The Prince of Wales's Own (West Yorkshire Regiment)

1/7th (Leeds Rifles) Battalion, The Prince of Wales's Own (West Yorkshire Regiment)

1/8th (Leeds Rifles) Battalion, The Prince of Wales's Own (West Yorkshire Regiment) (until January 1918)

147TH (2ND WEST RIDING) BRIGADE

1/4th Battalion, The Duke of Wellington's (West Riding Regiment)

1/5th Battalion, The Duke of Wellington's (West Riding Regiment) (until January 1918)

1/6th Battalion, The Duke of Wellington's (West Riding Regiment)

1/7th Battalion, The Duke of Wellington's (West Riding Regiment)

148TH (3RD WEST RIDING) BRIGADE

1/4th Battalion, The King's Own Yorkshire Light Infantry

1/5th Battalion, The King's Own Yorkshire Light Infantry (until February 1918)

1/4th (Hallamshire) Battalion, The York and Lancaster Regiment

1/5th Battalion, The York and Lancaster Regiment

PIONEERS

19th (Service) Battalion (3rd Salford), Lancashire Fusiliers (from August 1916)

HUDDERSFIELD'S ROLL OF HONOUR 1914–1922

62ND (2ND WEST RIDING DIVISION)

185TH BRIGADE (2/1ST WEST RIDING)

1/5th Battalion, The Devonshire Regiment (joined June 1918)

1/8th Battalion, The West Yorkshire Regiment (joined January 1918)

2/5th Battalion, The West Yorkshires (joined March 1915, left August 1918)

2/6th Battalion, The West Yorkshires (joined March 1915, left January 1918)

2/7th Battalion, The West Yorkshires (joined March 1915, left June 1918)

2/8th Battalion, The West Yorkshires (joined March 1915, left February 1918)

2/20th (County of London) Battalion, The London Regiment (joined August 1918)

186TH BRIGADE (2/2ND WEST RIDING)

5th Battalion, The Duke of Wellington's Regiment (joined January 1918)

2/4th Battalion, The Duke of Wellington's (joined March 1915)

2/5th Battalion, The Duke of Wellington's (joined March 1915, left January 1918)

2/6th Battalion, The Duke of Wellington's (joined March 1915, disbanded January 1918)

2/7th Battalion, The Duke of Wellington's (joined March 1915, left as a cadre June 1918)

2/4th Battalion, The Hampshire Regiment (joined June 1918)

187TH BRIGADE (2/3RD WEST RIDING)

5th Battalion, The King's Own Yorkshire Light Infantry (joined February 1918)

2/4th Battalion, The King's Own Yorkshire Light Infantry (joined March 1915)

2/5th Battalion, The King's Own Yorkshire Light Infantry (joined March 1915, absorbed February 1918)

2/4th (Hallamshire) Battalion, The York and Lancaster Regiment (joined March 1915)

2/5th Battalion, The York and Lancaster (joined March 1915, disbanded February 1918)

In January 1918, as the result of heavy casualties and in anticipation of a major German Offensive following the collapse of Russia, the British Army underwent a major reorganisation with each Infantry Brigade being reduced from four Battalions to three. Many Battalions were amalgamated, releasing soldiers to reinforce other units, and many Battalions were switched between Brigades and Divisions. The 62nd Division was particularly affected by these changes.

HUDDERSFIELD'S ROLL OF HONOUR 1914–1922

INTRODUCTION

In March, 2013, I received a call asking if a gentleman could visit the Arms and Armour Research Institute to seek advice on the publication of a book. Mr Alan Stansfield arrived clutching a large ring binder along with a box full of newspaper cuttings and photographs. Alan recounted a lifetime's work, 'The Project' as he called it, undertaken principally by his late wife, Margaret, to document all the soldiers from Huddersfield who had lost their lives during the First World War. There began the final chapter in a 30 year-long journey to honour the fallen of Huddersfield in this published Roll of Honour.

As the account unfolded it became clear that Margaret's work encompassed many hours spent in Huddersfield Library, along with visits to war memorials, archives and a significant series of trips to the battlefields themselves. It also became clear that this was one of the occasions when, as a University, we should support the publication, creating an enduring memorial in the year of the 100th Anniversary of the beginning of what had once been described as 'the war to end all wars'.

In carrying out this research Margaret aimed to document the fallen of Huddersfield. However, defining that presented its own issues. Did it mean those born in Huddersfield or those who lived in Huddersfield when they joined up? In practice both are included and without doubt there will be omissions and possibly even inclusions of those who, based on today's boundaries, are not strictly in Huddersfield. However, the important factor is not whether they are included or not, dependent upon an arbitrary line on a map, but that they are remembered. So in geographical terms Margaret erred on the side of inclusion. I have endeavoured to remain completely faithful to Margaret's original text, however ultimately this work will exist in electronic form and should any further information be discovered, it can be included at a later date.

Margaret worked hard to ensure the information in her work was as accurate as possible but it was not without its challenges. Her sources included the Commonwealth War Graves Commission (CWGC), the publication 'Soldiers Died in the Great War 1914–1919', regimental archives, family correspondence and records supplied after the war to local libraries to enable the erection of war memorials. One constant challenge in works such as this is the spelling of individual names. Margaret took an informed decision to use the Commonwealth War Graves Commissions database and in editing the volume I have followed her lead. The issue is best illustrated by Private Joseph Batty. On two memorials in Huddersfield he is listed as Battye. His birth certificate reads 'Battye' as it is on his father's marriage certificate. His baptism certificate records his surname as 'Batty'. On the 1901 Census he is recorded as 'Batty'; on the 1911 Census it is 'Battye'. Hence in this, and in several other cases, Margaret took an executive decision which I have chosen to abide by. As well as some variations in spelling there is a further anomaly which must be considered when searching for a relative among Great War casualty lists. For a variety of reasons soldiers and seamen did not always give their real names. Sometimes this was because they were fleeing some personal crisis at home or sometimes to avoid identification as being too young to join up. There are many tragic examples of soldiers who lied about their age to serve their country. In some cases they paid the ultimate price.

This publication records the fallen from the beginning of the conflict in 1914 through to 1922. These casualties were not of course restricted to those serving on the front line. Although the majority of the service personnel listed were killed as a result of enemy action, some died in accidents, such as Louie

Fethney, an Assistant Inspector of Munitions, who, in May, 1918, at the age of 20, died in an explosion at the Naval Munitions Factory, Crosland Moor.

Personnel from all the armed services are commemorated in this book. The vast majority are soldiers but those serving with the Royal Navy, Merchant Navy, Royal Flying Corps (latterly the Royal Air Force) and Royal Naval Air Service appear, along with one nurse, Ada Stanley, who died in 1915.

Most of the deaths commemorated in this book took place on the Western Front, though the campaign in the Dardanelles in 1915 and early 1916 claimed many lives, particularly the landing at Suvla Bay in August 1915. There were of course, a number of those listed who lost their lives at sea, however, as a unit, it is the Duke of Wellington's Regiment which features most prominently, mainly as a result of this part of Yorkshire being their primary recruiting ground.

The assassination of Archduke Franz Ferdinand of Austria in Sarajevo was the spark that began the sequence of events that would eventually lead to war. War was declared on 4th August 1914 and the British Expeditionary Force (BEF) began to embark for France. The BEF was a small army comprising 80,000 men initially formed into two Corps. The 2nd Battalion the Duke of Wellington's Regiment formed part of the 13th Brigade, 5th Div, 2nd Corps, arriving in France on 16th August and crossing the Belgian frontier to deploy in St. Ghislain six days later. The Battle of Mons was the first engagement of the war with the BEF outnumbered three to one. Nevertheless they succeeded in halting the German advance long enough to prevent the French Fifth Army from being outflanked. Many of the casualties listed in 1914 are from the 'Dukes', such as Private James Edwin Lunn of the 2nd Battalion, who lost his life during the retreat from Mons on 23rd August.

During 1915 the number of casualties continued to rise. Part of this was due to the arrival in April of that year of the 49th (West Riding) Division, which comprised units from the Duke of Wellington's Regiment, The West Yorkshire Regiment, the King's Own Yorkshire Light Infantry and the Yorkshire and Lancashire Regiment. Significant numbers of these men were recruited from Huddersfield. The Division was created from members of the pre-war Territorial Force who had volunteered for overseas service. A reference which appears frequently is *Hill 60*. The 2nd Battalion of the 'Dukes' was heavily involved in these engagements at the southern edge of the Ypres Salient. The entry for Private Thomas Boyle includes a moving letter to his uncle from his Company Sergeant Major detailing his death and giving reassurance, as so many of these letters do, that he did not die in any pain. Some of the casualties listed suffered from the effects of gas and it was during this phase of the war that this dreadful weapon was first used, to devastating effect.

Of course there are many soldiers from Huddersfield represented in other units. The Machine Gun Corps, as it developed, recruited from within the ranks of the existing Infantry battalions which were called upon to provide the most suitably qualified men. This was also the case with the fledgling Royal Flying Corps. Soldiers were given the opportunity to transfer, such as 2nd Lieutenant Charles William Brook, who joined the 8th Battalion of the Duke of Wellington's Regiment as a Private soldier, eventually qualified as a pilot but tragically died in a flying accident.

The Battle of the Somme in 1916 is arguably the most well known engagement of the war. The 10th Battalion of the West Yorkshire Regiment suffered one of the highest instances of casualties and there are frequent references in this book to Thiepval, and the Schwaben Redoubt where the engagement was at its fiercest. Of those listed as killed in 1916, more than half were soldiers from the Duke of Wellington's Regiment. Visitors to the cemeteries in this area will recognise the cap badges of both these units, in significant numbers, on the regimented rows of white headstones. The entry for 2nd Lieutenant Frank Thornton, of the 7th Battalion, East Yorkshire Regiment, provides a vivid account of the action which ultimately led to his death on the 1st July. Lieutenant Robert Huntriss Tolson, of the 15th Battalion, West Yorkshire Regiment – 'The Leeds Pals' – died the same day, tragically followed by his brother, Lieutenant James Martin Tolson, who died of wounds near Cambrai only a few days before the war ended. The Tolson brothers were commemorated by the establishment of the Tolson Memorial Museum In 1919. Their uncle, Legh Tolson gave Ravensknowle Hall to Huddersfield Corporation as a museum in memory of his two nephews. The museum was formally opened on 27 May, 1922.

The year 1917 witnessed the highest number of casualties, principally due to the engagements at Arras, the Third Battle of Ypres (known more commonly as Passchendaele) and Cambrai. The significant number of deaths of Huddersfield men in 1917, almost double the number of 1916, is accounted for partly by the arrival of the 62nd (2nd West Riding) Division. This Division was made up mostly of men

INTRODUCTION

serving in either the Prince of Wales Own Regiment of Yorkshire (The 'West Yorks') or the 'Dukes'. There were significant fatalities among these units. Two unsuccessful offensives at Bullecourt to the south east of Arras, in April and May of 1917 still remain one of the darkest memories of the war. The map on the front cover of the book is part of the trench map used during this battle. The Roll of Honour in the Huddersfield Drill Hall records many names of soldiers who died here. Among them is Private Lewis Townend of the 2/5th Battalion, Duke of Wellington's Regiment. A member of Huddersfield Amateur Operatic Society as well as his church choir, he has no known grave but, like so many of his comrades who died at Bullecourt, is commemorated on the Memorial to the Missing in Arras.

The campaigns of 1918 began slowly and a series of German offensives in the Spring caused crippling losses to all of the locally recruited Battalions. It was, however, the last gasp of the German onslaught and the incredibly successful response of the British and Dominion Divisions, supported by the arrival of American forces, eventually ground down the exhausted German forces leading to the Armistice in November. Depleted German medical services and freezing conditions had a devastating effect on those who were held in Prisoner of War camps. Many detainees, already weakened by wounds or sickness, died before they were able to return home to their loved ones.

While the war raged on land, naval engagements claimed many lives. The most famous engagement, the Battle of Jutland, was fought over two days between 31st May and 1st June, 1916. The magnitude of fatalities in this conflict assumed horrific proportions. Ordinary Seaman Wilfred Haigh from Skelmanthorpe died on board the battle cruiser *HMS Indefatigable*. The ship was hit in the first few minutes and went down with only two of the crew of 2,019 surviving. Boy 1st Class Thomas Quarmby, from Crosland Hill, died on board *HMS Queen Mary* which sank with the loss of 1,266 men. In total five Huddersfield men died at Jutland, however a further four died on board the destroyer *HMS Partridge* on 12th December 1917, the full account of which is in the entry for Able Seaman Donald Haigh. It appears to have been a tragic coincidence that these four men from Huddersfield perished together in a small vessel so far from home.

In the biographical entries there are a number of references to locations of memorials and graves. It was determined early in the conflict, that those killed in action would be buried in the theatre of war rather than repatriated. In many cases therefore there is a headstone and a grave location and if known it is listed. In some cases however the casualty has no known grave. There are many reasons for this not least that on occasion burials took place in the heat of battle and soldiers were buried where they fell. While every attempt was made to mark these, subsequent shelling and the constantly moving battle lines meant that they were often lost. These soldiers are commemorated on one of the many Memorials to the Missing such as those at Thiepval, The Menin Gate at Ypres and the Memorial at Arras. Even today in both France and Belgium the bodies of soldiers are still being uncovered. Where they can be identified they are buried in marked graves, where they cannot, they too are recorded on a Memorial to the Missing. They are always re-buried with full military honours, whether identified or not, and, wherever possible, members of the soldiers' families are invited to attend the burials. The cemeteries that are scattered across the Western Front contain many headstones commemorating soldiers who are not able to be identified, often with the simple inscription *'Known only unto God'*. Those who were lost at sea are commemorated in many coastal towns around the country though there are large Memorials to the Missing in Portsmouth, Plymouth and Chatham.

Locally there are many War Memorials in villages across Huddersfield and in churches, churchyards, schools, and clubs. After the war every attempt was made to record those who had lost their lives and lists were sent to local libraries. For a variety of reasons however, sometimes administrative and sometimes economic, they were not recorded. As a result there are soldiers listed here who are commemorated in several places. There are some, like Pioneer James Starkey of the Royal Engineers, who are only commemorated in this volume.

Perhaps one of the most poignant memorials is in the Huddersfield Drill Hall. As one walks into the Hall and gazes to the right, there are two huge edifices commemorating soldiers of both the 5th and 7th Battalions of The Duke of Wellington's Regiment. The impact is powerful and causes visitors to stand and contemplate the immense sacrifice made by these men. Their heritage is maintained as the Drill Hall is currently home to Corunna Company of the 4th Battalion The Yorkshire Regiment.

During the conflict there were a number of gallantry medals awarded to local men and during the war a decision was taken to also award campaign medals. These are illustrated in the centre pages of this book. The gallantry awards represent an acknowledgement of particularly gallant or brave conduct. The most well-known, the Victoria Cross, was not granted to any of the Huddersfield fallen, although one recipient, 40989 Pte E Sykes VC who died in 1949, is buried in Lockwood Cemetery. Nevertheless, there are over seventy other examples of gallantry awards. In cases where the serviceman was awarded the medal on more than one occasion, a bar was affixed to the medal ribbon. After the war the campaign medals were issued and these are the medals most frequently owned by family members today. There were three representing campaign service, which are illustrated with descriptions of the criteria for receiving them.

In many of the entries in this book there are included excerpts from letters. These are often deeply moving and represent an attempt by a senior officer or colleague to bring some small comfort to the family having received the stark and somewhat formal notification of the death of a loved one. It is hard to comprehend the shock to a family as this notification arrived. As the war went on there were few who had not experienced such a loss or at least were close to someone who had. There are two examples in this book of multiple members of a family being killed. Sergeant Stephen Hargill Lee DCM and Bar 2/5th Duke of Wellington's Regiment who enlisted on the day war broke out in 1914 and was killed on the 7th November 1918, just four days before the Armistice. He was awarded the DCM for *'conspicuous gallantry and devotion to duty'*. His brother Private Henry Lee of the Army Cyclists Corps died of wounds on the 20th October 1917, his older brother Private John Lee of the 1st Royal Montreal Regiment had emigrated to Canada and enlisted in 1914. He was killed by a German sniper while recovering a wounded German soldier on the 29th May 1915. The trauma for their parents Henry and Ada can barely be imagined.

The letters themselves are a brave attempt to soften the blow. They also provide an insight into the day to day horrors of the engagements with the enemy and the effect on colleagues. This letter from Major W U Rothery to the parents of Private John William Wagstaff, 1/7th Battalion Duke of Wellington's Regiment, depicts a slightly formal but nonetheless compassionate response:

'I am extremely sorry to inform you that your son was killed yesterday. He was in charge of the bombers and after a successful sniping shot he received a bullet through the head. I saw him immediately afterwards and death was instantaneous. He was buried in our cemetery last night by the Brigade Chaplain and his grave will be marked with a cross. His death is a blow to me as he was one of the very few old members of the Milnsbridge Company and I knew him intimately. He was a good soldier and will be a great loss to the Company. I am afraid I can say nothing which will comfort you but it will be some satisfaction to you to know that he gave his life whilst actually fighting for his country.'

Sadly, this is not the only letter in this book from Major Rothery to the family of one of his men.

There are recurring themes in the letters reflecting the love for the soldier's family and often a reassurance that in death the comrade had felt no pain. This moving letter from Lance Corporal Foulkes to the wife of Private George William Smith, 1/5th Duke of Wellington's Regiment ably demonstrates the thought and effort that went into writing to loved ones:

'He was killed almost instantly. I remained with him in the last moments and succoured him as a comrade should. You may take great consolation in the fact that his last thoughts and words were of his dear wife and little ones until God called to him. As his Section Commander I deeply regret the loss of your husband as he was a steady, reliable man whom everyone could get along with and I can assure you that the men both of the section and platoon will keenly feel the loss of such a good comrade. You may take consolation also in the fact that he died a soldier's death, facing the foe and bore himself splendidly throughout the great crisis.'

Some of the letters also reflect the sorrow felt by those writing. This is particularly evident in a letter from a comrade of Corporal Samuel Earnshaw of 'C' Battery (Holme Valley) 168 Brigade Royal Field Artillery. It seems Corporal Earnshaw had taken it upon himself to try to repair a telephone wire and when he did not return his comrades went to search for him. The poignancy of the account is striking and warrants its recounting in full:

INTRODUCTION

'I hardly know how to start this letter, but I feel that I must write and express to you the regrets and sympathy not only of myself but of the whole Battery in your sad bereavement. I know quite well how you will miss Sammy for I know how we miss him out here. In fact it is very difficult to realise that we shall not see him again. I thought I should like to write to you tonight not only to express my sympathy but also to tell you as much as possible how Sammy met his death. Unfortunately no one can tell you how or where he was killed as he was alone at the time but as I was one of the search party who found him perhaps I can tell you as much as anyone can. The last time I saw Sammy was on the afternoon of the 11th November when he was leaving the Battery for Signal Headquarters. As usual he stopped and had a few cheery words with me and then went on his way. From what I can gather he left the Signal Headquarters some hours later and returned to the Battery which however he never reached. We found him about a mile away from the Battery. Evidently he had decided to overhaul one of the telephone wires on his way back to the Battery for we found him laid beside the wire which was some distance from his usual way back. You will be glad to know as we were that he must have died instantaneously as he was wounded through the head and heart. Poor lad – he died as he would have wished to have died, doing his duty and working to the last. He will be missed by all of us for I can safely say that there isn't a man in the Battery whom he had not helped sometime or other even if only been by his cheery smile.'

The archives of the Duke of Wellington's Regiment provide an enduring insight into the final thoughts of one Huddersfield soldier and the effect of his death.[1]

The following letters concern the death of Private Charles Langrick, 1/5th Battalion (Huddersfield Territorials). Charles was the second son of Mr L Langrick, Headmaster of the Armitage Bridge National School. The last letter written by Private Langrick to his father on August 20th, two days before he met his death, seems to contain a strange presentiment of what would happen to him a few hours later. The letter reads as follows,

'Dear Dad, Very many happy returns of your birthday, as you say, and to my great surprise as I had always looked upon you as one young and energetic. It is now 23 years since you took up your duties at Armitage Bridge. May you be spared another 23 years to do your duty there and may the evening of your career be abundantly blessed with all the things of life that are best, will always be my prayer.

I am not at all surprised at the Company's action and think they have behaved splendidly towards their staff. Their expenses are sure to have been very heavy.

We are safe again in the trenches and supports, but keep looking forward to a rest. Vernon (Mr Langrick's eldest son) and myself are quite well and all the boys from home are likewise. Poor Samson Taylor's loss was a great shock to us as it was so unexpected and sudden. Always my dear Dad, my thoughts are with you and often in the still hours of the night I can imagine myself at home leading the old life. And then the magnitude of the cross which has been laid upon us all comes home to us with every thought and I hope we shall be able to bear it and not in vain. Well, Dad, I must close now as the shadows are falling and it is almost impossible to write but, as I finish, the song comes into my mind, 'Dusk and the shadows are falling.'
Yours loving son, Charles.

The London, Liverpool and Globe Insurance Company, by whom he was employed, had paid him full wages since the commencement of the war and at the close of the first twelve months intimated that they would now pay half wages. The following is a copy of Private Langrick's last letter written on August 21st to Mrs A M Wheatley, wife of Captain Wheatley,

'Dear Madam, On behalf of, and as a Private of, No 15 Platoon, I beg to tender to you their heartiest thanks for the present of sweetcakes which arrived today. We have been out of the trench just now for a couple of days and are resting in a place about a mile from the firing line,

---

1   Originating from the *Huddersfield Examiner* 1st September 1915

so we were able to eat the cake in comfort surrounded by four walls for the first time for a few months. We often have exciting times but, except for accidents which nobody can help, great care is exercised and we hope that the majority, if not all of us, will be spared to come home. Our life here consists of trench work and spells of rest and, whilst resting, we often amuse ourselves by impromptu concerts and every item, whether serious or comic, is treated to salvoes of applause. In fact, we may be said to be like a huge family with our Captain as our head. When we survey our surroundings we feel thankful that old England has been spared such scenes and are determined that it shall ever be thus. When feeling a little doleful presents such as we have received today cheer us up and so, you may guess, Madam, how much your gift is appreciated. We all hope that Captain Wheatley has had a pleasant leave and that it will not be long before he is able to return finally. With renewed thanks, I am, dear Madam, respectfully yours, C Lindley Langrick.*

Charles was wounded in the neck by a sniper and died on the 23rd August 1915. Second Lieutenant N Rippon, 15th Platoon, D Company, 1/5th Battalion DWR, wrote to his parents:

'Dear Mr and Mrs Langrick, Please allow me to offer my deepest sympathy with you in the death of your son who was wounded in the neck on Sunday, August 22nd, and died in the Clarence Hospital at 7.15 pm on August 23rd. Immediately your son had been attended to I rang up his brother, Sergeant Vernon Langrick, and everything possible was done for him, but the wound proved fatal. He was a thoroughly good soldier and a splendid fellow to get on with. I am greatly indebted to him for the tremendous lot of work he did for me. He could speak French fluently and always wrote all the letters on behalf of the Platoon. I can assure you his loss is felt by all the Officers, NCOs and men of D Company. I sincerely hope you will be able to take some little consolation from the fact that he died a brave man's death fighting for his King and Country and also he will have a nice little grave in a hospital cemetery instead of just behind the trenches. Again, expressing our united sympathy with you in your great loss.'

Second Lieutenant Rippon himself did not survive the war. A member of the famous family of motor engineers and coachbuilders he was killed in action on 18th November, 1915. Finally, in a further letter of sympathy, Platoon Sergeant G H Senior writes,

'He was the life and soul of his platoon and we miss his cheery smile and joke very keenly for he was a marvel of high spirits. Even when lying wounded he had to have his joke. You can understand the blank it leaves in our platoon, we don't feel like the same platoon and you have our deepest sympathy in your heavy loss. Hoping this will in some way help you to bear it.'

In the absence of any other comfort these letters may have brought some closure to the grieving families. In some cases however there were no letters and indeed no memorial until much later. This sorrowful state of affairs simply serves to underscore the value of Margaret's work in compiling these entries.

The reader will be able to pursue many of the names in this book and find further details in local churches, war memorials and in archives. For some it will be the beginning of a search that will shed light onto an otherwise dimly lit page of family history. There will be those who, as a result of the information here, follow in the footsteps of Margaret and her husband, Alan, as they walk quietly through rows of headstones, seeking a particular name or Regiment close to a French, Belgian or Turkish battlefield.

There will, however, be those commemorated here for whom this book will be the only memorial of an enduring sacrifice that took them far away from their families and friends, who lived in the warm and friendly town of Huddersfield, to the horrors of a battleground in a distant foreign land. The dedicated pilgrimage undertaken by Margaret has brought the stories of these local servicemen and one woman, together to ensure that we will always remember those from this town who paid the ultimate price.

Reverend Paul Wilcock BEM

ABBY, ALBERT. Private. No 53069. 1/4th Duke of Wellington's Regiment. Born Huddersfield 1886. Son of John M. and Hannah Abby, 22 Ash Grove Road, Huddersfield (1901 Census). Married Miranda Harrison in 1908. Lived 27 Slades Road Golcar, father of 3 children. Employed at Messrs John Crowther and Sons, woollen spinners, Milnsbridge. Enlisted July 1918. Embarked for France after the signing of the Armistice and had only been there for three days when he was killed whilst clearing the battlefield, 10.12.1918, aged 32 years. Buried **DOUAI BRITISH CEMETERY.** Grave location:- Row C, Grave 34. ROH:- St. John's Church, Golcar.

ACKROYD, ARTHUR. Private. No 254457. Labour Corps. Formerly No 12444 Duke of Wellington's Regiment. Born Clayton West. Husband of Mary Ackroyd, High Street, Clayton West. Enlisted Huddersfield. Died at home, 21.2.1918, aged 41 years. Buried **ALL SAINTS CHURCHYARD, HIGH HOYLAND.** Grave location:- in South-West part. ROH:- Clayton West/High Hoyland War Memorial.

ACKROYD, DOUGLAS. Private. No 59183. 15/17th Battalion West Yorkshire Regiment (Leeds Pals). Son of Crowther and Harriet Ackroyd, 3 Middle Haigh House, Lindley, Huddersfield. Born Fixby, Huddersfield. Enlisted Huddersfield. Killed in action, 17.9.1918, aged 19 years. Has no known grave. Commemorated on the **PLOEGSTEERT MEMORIAL TO THE MISSING.**

ACKROYD, WALTER. Private. No 202407. 2/4th Battalion Duke of Wellington's Regiment. Born Huddersfield. Killed in action, 25.11.1917, at the Battle of Cambrai. Has no known grave. Commemorated on the **CAMBRAI MEMORIAL TO THE MISSING.** ROH:- St. Philip's Church, Birchencliffe.

ADAMSON, JOE WILLIE. Private. No 40202. 10th Battalion Northumberland Fusiliers. Formerly No 32249 Durham Light Infantry. Born Underhill, Holmfirth. Son of Mr E. J Adamson, Church Terrace, Berry Brow. Employed by Messrs Brook and Woodhouse, woollen and worsted manufacturers, Queen's Mill, Huddersfield. Enlisted February 1916. Had been in France for seven weeks when he was killed by a sniper on 10.11.16, aged 20. Buried in **RAILWAY DUGOUTS (TRANSPORT FARM) BURIAL GROUND.** Grave location:- Plot 6, Row O, Grave 27. ROH:- Armitage Bridge War Memorial.

ADAMSON, WILLIAM BURGESS. Acting Sergeant. No 3/11505. 9th Battalion Duke of Wellington's Regiment. Born Scarborough. Son of Benjamin and Ann Adamson. Came to Huddersfield three years before the outbreak of war. Lived 5 Cross Grove Street, Huddersfield. Husband of Lilian Adamson. Employed by Mr G. S. Jarmaine of Dalton. Enlisted September 1914. Had served in the Boer War. Killed in action, 15.8.1917. Buried in **BROWN'S COPSE CEMETERY.** Grave location:- Plot 4, Row A, Grave 55.

ADDERLEY, FRANK. Private. No 46524. 24th (Tyneside Irish) Battalion Northumberland Fusiliers. Formerly No 37342 Durham Light Infantry. Son of Mrs Stringer, 12 Malvern Road, off Newsome Road. Attended Stile Common School, Primrose Hill. Employed as a woollen piecer at Messrs Walter Sykes, woollen and worsted manufacturers, Zetland Mills, Huddersfield. Enlisted 14.5.1916. Killed in action at King Crater, near Roclincourt, two and quarter miles north north east of Arras, 9.4.17, aged 27 years. Buried **ROCLINCOURT VALLEY CEMETERY.** Grave location:- Plot 2, Row B, Grave 4.

ADDY, FRED. Private. No 98551. 2nd Battalion Machine Gun Corps. Brother-in-law of E. A. Priestley, The Royal Hotel, Newsome Road, Huddersfield. Died 17.11.1918, aged 38 years. Buried **ETAPLES MILITARY CEMETERY.** Grave location:- Plot 50, Row D, Grave 4.

ADDY, NORMAN. Private. No 205535. 212th Area Employment Company, Labour Corps. Formerly No 205535 Duke of Wellington's Regiment. Son of Arthur and Eliza Addy of Bank Bottom, Shelley. Employed by Firth Brothers at Bank Bottom Mill. Died from bronchial pneumonia on 24.9.1918, aged 27 years. Buried in **LONGUENESSE (St. OMER) SOUVENIR CEMETERY.** Grave location:- Plot 5, Row E, Grave 26. ROH:- Emmanuel Church, Shelley.

ADDY, WILLIE ISHMAEL. Private. No 30/346. 12/13th Battalion Northumberland Fusiliers.

Born Holmfirth. Lived 20, Townend Road, Holmbridge. Worked at Albion Mills, Meltham. Enlisted in 1916. Killed in action, 28.3.1918. Has no known grave. Commemorated on the **POZIERES MEMORIAL TO THE MISSING.** ROH:- Holme and Holmbridge War Memorial.

ADSETTS, WILLIE. Private. No 48320. 2nd Battalion Lancashire Fusiliers. Son of Mr and Mrs A. Adsetts, 119, Wakefield Road, Huddersfield. Born 29th January, 1899. Educated at Moldgreen Board School. Employed by Mr W. T.. Johnson, cloth finisher, Moldgreen. Attended Moldgreen United Methodist Sunday School. Enlisted 10.3.1917. Killed in action, 28.3.18, aged 19. Has no known grave. Commemorated on the **ARRAS MEMORIAL TO THE MISSING.** ROH:- Christ Church, Moldgreen.

AINLEY, ARTHUR EDWARD. Private. No 2287. 44th Battalion Australian Infantry, Australian Imperial Force. Born Huddersfield. Lived Outlane. Attended Bethel United Methodist Church, Outlane. Son of William and Jane Ainley, 327 Perth Street, Subiaco, Western Australia. Native of Ballarat, Victoria, Australia. Worked in Australia as a storekeeper. Sailed from Fremantle, Western Australia, on the 'Port Macquarie' on the 13th October, 1916. Killed in action, 10.6.1917, aged 24 years. Buried **MESSINES RIDGE BRITISH CEMETERY.** Grave location:- Special Memorial 6. ROH:- Bethel United Methodist Church, Outlane, Huddersfield.

AINLEY, DAVID. Private. No 38361. 2nd Battalion West Yorkshire Regiment. Son of Richard and Alice Ainley, 79, Barcroft Road, Close Hill, Huddersfield. Born 22.2.1898. Attended Newsome Church of England School. Worked as a woollen warehouseman. Enlisted 25.10.16. Killed in action, 16.8.1917. Has no known grave. Commemorated on the **TYNE COT MEMORIAL TO THE MISSING.** ROH:- St. John's Church, Newsome.

AINLEY, ELLERY P. Private. No 3/10588. 2nd Battalion Duke of Wellington's Regiment. Son of Mr Shaw Ainley, 16, Lowergate, Longwood. Employed as a piecer at Messrs C. and J. Hirst's Mill, Longwood. Enlisted on August 4th, 1914. Killed in action at the Battle of Arras on 11.4.17, aged 22 years. Has no known grave. Commemorated on the **ARRAS MEMORIAL TO THE MISSING.** ROH:- St. Mark's Parish Church, Longwood.

AINLEY, FRED. Private. No 18063. 2nd Battalion Duke of Wellington's Regiment. Born 9.8.1894. Son of John and Ellen Ainley, 20 Rose Street, St Andrew's Road, Huddersfield. Educated at St Andrew's and Rashcliffe Church of England Schools. Employed as a cloth finisher for Messrs John Lee Walker and Sons, of Deighton. Was a member of the Ramsden Street Men's Own Class. Enlisted January 1916. Killed in action at the Battle of the Somme on 12.10.16, aged 22 years. Has no known grave. Commemorated on the **THIEPVAL MEMORIAL TO THE MISSING.** (Brother of Private **WILLIE AINLEY**, killed in action, 9.4.1917, q.v.). ROH:- Northumberland Street Primitive Methodist Church and School.

AINLEY, FRED. Private. No 23974. 10th Battalion Duke of Wellington's Regiment. Born Golcar. Son of William and Emma Ainley, 2 Bolster Moor, Golcar. Attended Clough Head Council School and Sunnybank Baptist Chapel. He was one of a family of ten children, five boys and five girls. Employed as a weaver by Messrs Ben Hall and Sons, Milnsbridge. Enlisted April 1916. Killed by a shell on 5.1.1917, aged 23 years, Buried in **MENIN ROAD SOUTH MILITARY CEMETERY.** Grave location:- Plot 1, Row Q, Grave 8. (Brother of Private **JOSEPH AINLEY**, who died of wounds, 24.5.1917, q.v.). ROH:- St. John's Church, Golcar.

AINLEY, HEFFORD WILLIAM ERNEST. Lieutenant. 168th Brigade Royal Field Artillery. Born 26.6.1883 at Kirkheaton. Son of John Shaw and Emma Louisa Ainley of Martin Bank, Somerset Road, Huddersfield. Attended Giggleswick School. Worked as a woollen manufacturer, first at the mill established by his grandfather, Mr Hefford Ainley, and then with Messrs John Taylor Limited, Colne Road. He married the daughter of Mr Joseph Hopkinson and lived at 'Overstrand', Sunnybank Road, Edgerton, and had one child. Enlisted 25.7.1916. (*Died on the night of Sunday 4.2.17 from pneumonia supervening on burns. Lieutenant Ainley had gone behind the wagon lines for rest and was sleeping with a few fellow officers in a bivouac of timber, corrugated iron and canvas. During the night this building in some way caught fire. The other officer was overcome and* *rendered insensible whilst Lieutenant Ainley who dragged his friend to a place of safety was badly burned about the hands and feet and also about the head. He was removed as quickly as possible to a Casualty Clearing Station and every attention was paid to him. He appeared to be progressing very favourably with the burns but pneumonia set in and he passed away very quietly on Sunday as stated – 'Huddersfield Weekly Examiner' 9.2.1917).* Buried **PUCHEVILLERS BRITISH CEMETERY.** Grave location:- Plot 3, Row C, Grave 4. ROH:- St. Stephen's Church, Lindley; Memorial in St. John's Old Churchyard, Kirkheaton.

AINLEY, HERBERT McARTHUR. Private. No 3185. 1/5th Battalion Duke of Wellington's Regiment. Born 4.3.1894. Son of Law and Margaret Ainley, 24 Regent Road, Edgerton, Huddersfield. Educated at Hillhouse Board School. Worked as a cloth manufacturer at Bay Hall Mills. Enlisted 4.9.1914. Killed in action, 17.11.1915, aged 21 years. Commemorated on the **MENIN GATE MEMORIAL TO THE MISSING.** ROH:- Fartown and Birkby War Memorial; Gledholt Wesleyan Church; Huddersfield Drill Hall.

AINLEY, JOCK. Private. No 235329. 1/7th Battalion Duke of Wellington's Regiment. Son of the late Mr Sam Ainley and Mrs Joe Bower (formerly Ainley), 20 Bankfield Terrace, Outcote Bank, Huddersfield. Worked at Messrs Elliott, Hallas and Sons Limited, Kirkgate. Killed in action, 1.11.1918, aged 21 years. Buried in **FAMARS COMMUNAL CEMETERY EXTENSION.** Grave Location:- Grave 25. ROH:- Huddersfield Drill Hall.

AINLEY, JOHN HIRST. 2nd Lieutenant. The Rifle Brigade. Born 19.2.1899. Son of Mr and Mrs Hirst Ainley, Woodlands, Lindley Moor. Educated at Huddersfield College School and Oundle Public School, which he left in July, 1916. He was killed on 21.6.1918 at Hinges near Bethune, while waiting beside a wounded man until the stretcher-bearers arrived, aged 19. Buried at **LE VERTANNOY BRITISH CEMETERY, BETHUNE.** Grave location:- C, 22. ROH:- Bethel United Methodist Church, Outlane; Huddersfield College School; Memorial plaque in Stainland Church.

AINLEY, JOSEPH. Gunner. No 140919. 3rd Divisional Ammunition Column Royal Field Artillery. Born Golcar. Son of William and Emma Ainley, 2 Bolster Moor, Golcar. Educated at Clough Head Council School and attended Sunnybank Baptist Chapel. He was one of a family of ten children, five boys and five girls. Employed as a weaver by Messrs Whitwam and Company, Ramsden Mill, Golcar. Enlisted May, 1916, and embarked for France in September. Died of gunshot wounds to abdomen at the 19th Casualty Clearing Station, 4.5.1917, aged 27. Buried in **DUISANS BRITISH CEMETERY.** Grave location:- Plot 3, Row N, Grave 48. (Brother of Private **FRED AINLEY,** killed in action, 5.1.1917, q.v.). ROH:- St. John's Church, Golcar.

AINLEY, JOSEPH, MM. Corporal. No 15981. 8th Battalion Duke of Wellington's Regiment. Son of John Thomas and Clara Ainley, 13 Whiteley Street, Milnsbridge. Worked for Messrs Crowther Brothers, Stanley Mills, Milnsbridge. Served in Egypt, Gallipoli and France. Killed in action, 11.8.1917, aged 21 years. Has no known grave. Commemorated on the **MENIN GATE MEMORIAL TO THE MISSING.** ROH:- Milnsbridge War Memorial.

AINLEY, WILFRED. Sergeant. No L/25719. 153rd Brigade Royal Field Artillery. Born 14.2.1882. Son of Mrs Sarah Ann Ainley, Whiteley Street, Milnsbridge. Attended Milnsbridge Baptist School. Married to Mary Jane Ainley, 3 Reeder's Yard, Cross Grove Street, Huddersfield and had five children. Worked as a labourer for Mr J. Charlesworth, East Parade. Played football for the Milnsbridge and Fartown clubs. Enlisted 3.5.1915. Killed in action 25.4.1918. Buried in **BRANDHOEK NEW MILITARY CEMETERY No 3.** Grave location:- Plot 1, Row O, Grave 4. ROH:- Milnsbridge War Memorial.

AINLEY, WILLIAM. Private. No 241832. 2/5th Battalion Duke of Wellington's Regiment. Only son of Mr and Mrs Clarence Ainley, 36 Third Avenue, Myrtle Road, Golcar. Worked as a weaver for Messrs Titus Calverley and Sons, Milnsbridge. Attended St John's Parish Church, Golcar and was a member of the Golcar Central Liberal Club. Enlisted 22.3.16 and embarked for France on January 10th, 1917. Killed by a shell at the Battle of Cambrai 27.11.1917. Has no known grave. Commemorated on the **CAMBRAI MEMORIAL TO THE MISSING.** ROH:- St John's Church, Golcar; Huddersfield Drill Hall.

AINLEY, WILLIE. Private. No 307740. 1/7th Battalion Duke of Wellington's Regiment. Born 18.7.1892. Son of John and Ellen Ainley, 20, Rose Street, Turnbridge. Attended St. Andrew's Church of England School, Huddersfield. Worked as an under twisting overlooker for Messrs A. Dawson and Sons, Aspley Mills. Enlisted 9.2.1916 and was wounded on 3.7.1916. Returned to France on 3.12.1916. Killed in action, 9.4.17, aged 24 years. Buried in **St. VAAST POST MILITARY CEMETERY.** Grave location:- Plot 4, Row F, Grave 8. (Brother of Private **FRED AINLEY**, who was killed in action 12.10.16 q.v.). ROH:- Northumberland Street Primitive Methodist Church and Sunday School; Huddersfield Drill Hall.

ALLAN, JOHN. Private. No 305672. Duke of Wellington's Regiment. Born 31.7.1877 at West Richmond Street, Edinburgh. Worked as a sheet-metal worker. Married to Mrs Jemima Allan, 17 Mills Row, Castlegate, Huddersfield. 3 children. Enlisted 25.9.1914. Died 11.1.1921 at 17 Mills Row, Castlegate from valvular disease of the heart and tuberculosis.

ALLEN, ALURED THOMAS STEWART. Private. No 17265. 11th Battalion Royal Inniskilling Fusiliers. Born Enniskillen, County Fermanagh, 1.7.1895. Lived Pretoria Street, Slaithwaite. Reported missing, presumed killed, on the first day of the Battle of the Somme 1.7.1916. Has no known grave. Commemorated on the **THIEPVAL MEMORIAL TO THE MISSING.** ROH:- St. James Church, Slaithwaite; Slaithwaite War Memorial.

ALLEN, FRANK. Private. No 241785. 2/5th Battalion Duke of Wellington's Regiment. Born New Mill. Son of Mr and Mrs Ben Allen. Peter's Farm, Binn, Marsden. Worked as a weaver at Bank Bottom Mills, Marsden. Enlisted 1916. Embarked for France January, 1917. Killed in action at the Battle of Bullecourt, 3.5.1917, aged 30. Has no known grave. Commemorated on the **ARRAS MEMORIAL TO THE MISSING.** ROH:- Marsden War Memorial; Huddersfield Drill Hall.

ALLEN, HILDRED, MM. Sergeant. No 305544. 2/7th Battalion Duke of Wellington's Regiment. Son of Mr and Mrs Thomas Allen, 1 Station Terrace, Longwood and formerly of 12 Sandwell Street, Hill Top, Slaithwaite. Worked at the Globe Worsted Company. Attended St James's Church Sunday School, Slaithwaite. Was a member of the Slaithwaite Cricket and Bowling Club. Enlisted 31.8.1914. Embarked for France 10.1.1917. Had been twice wounded. Awarded the Military Medal in August, 1917. Died from suffocation by charcoal fumes from a brazier whilst sleeping in his dugout, 18.5.1918, aged 21 years. Buried in **BIENVILLERS MILITARY CEMETERY.** Grave location:- Plot 16, Row D, Grave 10. ROH:- St Mark's Parish Church, Longwood; St James Church, Slaithwaite; Huddersfield Drill Hall; Slaithwaite War Memorial.

ALLEN, JOHN W. Private. No 7223. 1st Battalion East Yorkshire Regiment. Born Honley. Died 3.1.1920. Buried in **HONLEY CHURCH BURIAL GROUND.** Grave location:- 63, 595. ROH:- Honley War Memorial.

ALLEN, THOMAS HARRY. Sapper. No 342707. 157th Field Company Royal Engineers. Lived 99a Storths, Moldgreen, Huddersfield. Died from the effects of war service, at home, on 28.11.1919. Buried in **ALMONDBURY CEMETERY.** Grave Location:- A, 'C', 12.

ALLEN, WILLIE. Lance Corporal. No 17/931. 15/17th Battalion (Leeds Pals) West Yorkshire Regiment. Born 15.6.1896. Son of Mr and Mrs Tom Allen, 34 Industrial Street, Primrose Hill. Worked as a teamer on the railways. Enlisted 5.1.1915. Killed in action, 19.7.1918, aged 22 years. Commemorated on the **PLOEGSTEERT MEMORIAL TO THE MISSING.**

ALLOTT, WILFRED CORNELIUS. Private. No 15196. 10th Battalion Duke of Wellington's Regiment. Born 25.1.1887 at Tinmill near Wortley. Son of Mrs Grace Allott, 29 Norman Road, Birkby. Worked as a labourer at the Huddersfield Gasworks. Enlisted 8.1.1915. Killed in action 20.9.1917, aged 30 years. Buried in **HOOGE CRATER CEMETERY.** Grave location:- Plot 9, Row D, Grave 1. ROH:- St. Cuthbert's Church, Birkby; Fartown and Birkby War Memorial; Huddersfield Corporation Roll.

ALVEY, PATRICK. Private. No 10067. 1st Battalion Duke of Wellington's Regiment. Born Huddersfield. Died in India, 19.12.18. Buried in **DAGSHAI CEMETERY, INDIA.** Commemorated on the **KIRKEE 1914-1918 MEMORIAL, INDIA.**

AMBLER, ALBERT. Private. No 23777. 5th Battalion Cameron Highlanders. Born 30.6.1893 at Stanley near Wakefield. Attended Stanley School. Worked as a brick worker for Messrs B. Elliott and Sons, Lepton. Husband of Emily Ambler, 12, Trevelyan Street, Moldgreen. Enlisted 15.11.1915. Died of wounds, 26.5.1918, aged 24 years. Buried in **CAESTRE MILITARY CEMETERY.** Grave location:- Plot 1, Row B, Grave 29. ROH:- Christ Church, Moldgreen.

AMBLER, NOAH. Private. No 268374. 9th Battalion Duke of Wellington's Regiment. Born 7.10.1889 at Netherton, Huddersfield. Son of Josh Ambler. Attended Stile Common Council School, Primrose Hill. Worked as a violinist at the Empire Picture House. Married, with one child. Lived at 11, Newsome Road. Killed in action, 12.10.18, aged 29 years. Buried in **SELRIDGE BRITISH CEMETERY.** Grave location:- Plot 2, Row D, Grave 8. ROH:- St. Paul's Church, Southgate, Almondbury; Almondbury War Memorial.

AMBROSE, WILLIAM. Lance Corporal. No 6224. 2nd Battalion Oxford and Bucks. Light Infantry. Born Caversham, Berkshire. Lived Pond Cottages, Moldgreen. Married, with one child. Employed by the Huddersfield Corporation Tramways Department in the track repair section. Enlisted at the beginning of the war. Was reported missing for over one year before his wife received official notice that he had been killed in action at the Battle of Loos, 25.9.1915. (One of four brothers, three of whom were killed and the other was a Prisoner of War in Germany). Commemorated on the **LOOS MEMORIAL TO THE MISSING.** ROH:- Christ Church, Moldgreen.

ANDERSON, JOE. Private. No 204476. 10th Battalion Duke of Wellington's Regiment. Born Holmfirth. Educated at Wooldale Lane Bottom School and attended Wooldale Townend Primitive Methodist Sunday School. Was a member of Holmfirth Harriers. Married in June 1914. Left a widow, (Edith) and a boy, aged two years. Worked as a millhand in the finishing department of Messrs James Lancaster and Sons, Mytholm Bridge. Embarked for France in May, 1917. Died of wounds in No.13 Casualty Clearing Station, Belgium, 20.9.1917, aged 22 years. Buried in **LIJSSENTHOEK MILITARY CEMETERY.** Grave location:- Plot 23, Row B, Grave 14. ROH:- Underbank War Memorial.

ANDREW, JOSEPH. Private. No 38767. 7th Battalion York and Lancaster Regiment. Born Huddersfield. Married. Lived 17 Thomas Street, Huddersfield. Worked as a labourer for Messrs Elliot, Hallas and Sons Limited, Beast Market, Huddersfield. Killed in action 25.8.1917, aged 29 years. Buried in **BARD COTTAGE CEMETERY.** Grave location:- Plot 4, Row D, Grave 37.

ANNIS, ALBERT WILLIAM FREDERICK (BERT). Able Seaman. No SS/7020. Royal Navy – serving on board *HMS Vehement*. Born 21st July, 1897. Son of Mr and Mrs Albert Annis of Finchley, London. From the age of 13 years lived with Mrs John Sykes, 5 Victoria Terrace, Golcar. Before joining the Navy, in 1916, was employed as a piecer at Messrs John Lockwood and Sons Limited, Milnsbridge. Attended St. John's Church and Sunday School, Golcar and was a member of the Golcar Conservative Club. Drowned at sea, the destroyer he was serving on being sunk by an enemy mine, on 2.8.1918, aged 21 years. Commemorated on the **PLYMOUTH NAVAL MEMORIAL TO THE MISSING.** ROH:- St. John's Church, Golcar.

APPLEYARD, HAROLD HARRY. Private. No 41514. 24th (Tyneside Irish) Battalion Northumberland Fusiliers. (Formerly No 19881 Duke of Wellington's Regiment). Born 30.12.1889 at Hebble Bridge, Bradford Road, Huddersfield. Son of Mrs Mary Hannah Appleyard, 'The Miner's Arms,' Fartown. Worked in the warehouse of Messrs Whitwam and Schofield, Lion Arcade. Was treasurer of the Great Northern Street Chapel Young Men's Bible Class. Enlisted 8.4.1916. Killed at the Battle of Arras, 28.4.1917, aged 28 years. Commemorated on the **ARRAS MEMORIAL TO THE MISSING.** ROH:- Great Northern Street Congregational Church; Fartown and Birkby War Memorial.

APPLEYARD, HAROLD. Private. No 242661. 1/6th Battalion West Yorkshire Regiment. Son of William and Sarah Appleyard of Marsh. Enlisted Leeds. Killed in action, 9.10.17, aged 24 Buried in **TYNE COT CEMETERY, PASSCHENDAELE.** Grave Location:- Plot 28, Row B, Grave 16. ROH:- Marsh War Memorial.

ARAM, HERBERT EDGAR. Private. No 8079. 1st Battalion South Wales Borderers. Born Storths, Moldgreen. Attended Lockwood National School. Worked as a carter for the London and North Western Railway Company. Married to Elizabeth Aram three days before he enlisted. Lived 19, Violet Street, Turnbridge. Enlisted 5.8.1914. Captured by the Germans and died as a Prisoner of War on 2.11.14, aged 29 years. Buried in **HARLEBEKE NEW BRITISH CEMETERY.** Grave location:- Plot 15, Row A, Grave 5. ROH:- Marsh War Memorial; London and North Western Railway Roll.

ARCHARD, FREDERICK JOHN. Private. No 2798. 1/5th Battalion Duke of Wellington's Regiment. Son of Mr and Mrs J. G. Archard, Springdale Hall, Longroyd Bridge. Employed by Messrs Netherwood and Dalton, printers, Huddersfield. Served in the Territorials before the war. Embarked for France in April, 1915. Hit in the head by a German sniper's bullet while repairing a damaged parapet, 22.8.1915, aged 23 years. Commemorated on the **MENIN GATE MEMORIAL TO THE MISSING.** ROH:- St Stephen's Church, Rashcliffe; Huddersfield Drill Hall.

ARMFIELD, RALPH. Private. No 34258. Leicestershire Regiment; transferred to No 41593 Lincolnshire Regiment. Awarded the Victory and British War Medal. ROH:- Denby Dale and Cumberworth War Memorial.

ARMISTEAD, RICHARD (DICK). Private. No 241717. 2/5th Battalion Duke of Wellington's Regiment. Born Rochdale. Attended Crow Lane Board School, Milnsbridge. Husband of Kathleen Armistead, 23 Spring Street, Huddersfield. Killed in action at the Battle of Bullecourt, 3.5.1917. Commemorated on the **ARRAS MEMORIAL TO THE MISSING.** ROH:- Parkwood Methodist Chapel; St. Mark's Parish Church, Longwood; Crow Lane Board School, Milnsbridge.

ARMITAGE, ALBERT. Private. No 18048. 2nd Battalion Duke of Wellington's Regiment. Son of Mr and Mrs Walter Armitage, Bank Bottom, Shelley. Worked for Messrs Firth Brothers, Bank Bottom Mill. Was a member of the Shelley Brass Band. Enlisted in January, 1915. Embarked for France in 1916 and was wounded in the same year. Died of wounds at No 19 Casualty Clearing Station, Etrun, near Arras, 28.3.1918, aged 24 years. Buried in **DUISANS BRITISH CEMETERY.** Grave location:- Plot 5, Row F, Grave 47. ROH:- Emmanuel Church, Shelley.

ARMITAGE, ALBERT HENRY. Private. No 202482. 1/4th Battalion King's Own Yorkshire Light Infantry. Born Colne Bridge, Huddersfield. Son of William and Clara Armitage, 94 Gledhill Terrace, off Heckmondwike Road, Dewsbury. Died of wounds, 13.5.1918, aged 21 years. Buried **BOULOGNE EASTERN CEMETERY.** Grave location:- Plot 9, Row B, Grave 74.

ARMITAGE, ALLAN. Private. No 28503. 23rd (Tyneside Irish) Battalion Northumberland Fusiliers. Born Meltham. Son of John and Clara Armitage, Mill Moor, Meltham. Attended Meltham Wesleyan Church, was a Sunday School teacher there and a Band of Hope worker. Enlisted April, 1916, and embarked for France 10.8.1916. Killed in action, 27.9.1916, aged 19 years. Buried in **RATION FARM MILITARY CEMETERY.** Grave location:- Plot 2, Row C, Grave 4. ROH:- St. Bartholomew's Church, Meltham.

ARMITAGE, ARTHUR EDWARD. Lance Corporal. No 29126. 7th Battalion Yorkshire Regiment. Born Schofield's Yard, Moldgreen 29.8.1892. Son of Mr and Mrs Thomas William Armitage, 30, Smithy Lane, Moldgreen. Attended Moldgreen Council School. Worked as a dyer for Messrs. J. Holroyd and Company, Seed Hill, Huddersfield. Was a member of St. Michael's (Somerset Road) Young Men's Bible Class. Enlisted 27.3.1916. Died from gunshot wounds to abdomen at No 19 Casualty Clearing Station, Etrun, near Arras 22.7.1917. Buried in **DUISANS BRITISH CEMETERY.** Grave location:- Plot 3, Row N, Grave 48. ROH:- Moldgreen; Christ Church, Moldgreen; Almondbury War Memorial.

ARMITAGE, ARTHUR WILLIAM. Rifleman. No C/7762. 18th Battalion Kings Royal Rifle Corps. Born Lepton 25.4.1883. Attended

Moldgreen Council School. Worked as a milkhand for Messrs Rhodes and Brierley, Kirkheaton. Married, with six children. Lived 44 Fleming House Lane, Dalton. Enlisted November, 1916. Killed in action at the Battle of Flers, 15.9.1916, aged 34 years. Buried in **BULLS ROAD CEMETERY**. Grave location:- Plot 2, Row G, Grave 3. ROH:- St. John's Church, Kirkheaton.

ARMITAGE, EDWARD STONEY. 2nd Lieutenant. 76th Army Brigade Royal Field Artillery. Formerly Private, Honourable Artillery Company. Born 42 Blacker Road, Birkby, 29.3.1898. Son of James Willie and Maude Annie Armitage, 7 Water Street, Huddersfield. Educated at Mr Wild's College School, Huddersfield, and Drax Grammar School, Selby. Worked as an apprentice in the manufacturing sector before enlisting on 24.7.1916. Was given a commission in June, 1917. Killed in action, 29.8.1918. Buried in **DOUCHY-LES-AYETTE BRITISH CEMETERY**. Grave location:- Plot 4, Row E, Grave 8. ROH:- Huddersfield Parish Church; Huddersfield College School; Fartown and Birkby War Memorial.

ARMITAGE, ERNEST. Private. No 3180. 1/5th Battalion Duke of Wellington's Regiment. Born Grafton Place, Huddersfield, 30.4.1891. Son of Mr Albert Armitage. Lived with his Aunt, Mrs Peace, 16 West Parade, Huddersfield. Attended Trinity Church School, Huddersfield. Worked as a stockbroker's clerk for Messrs Robert Ramsden and Company, Byram Arcade. Played tennis with Paddock Tennis Club. Enlisted October 1914. Embarked for France April, 1915. Died of appendicitis at No 13 General Hospital, Boulogne, 25.11.15. Buried in **BOULOGNE EASTERN CEMETERY**. Grave location:- Plot 8, Row C, Grave 60. ROH:- All Saints Church, Paddock; Huddersfield Drill Hall.

ARMITAGE, FRANK. Private. No 2390. 1/5th Battalion Duke of Wellington's Regiment, attached 147th Coy. Machine Gun Corps. Born Holmfirth. Son of Sarah Ann Armitage and the late John Armitage of Holmbridge. Attended Holmbridge Church Sunday School. Was employed by Messrs W. Greenwood and Sons, Perseverance Mills. Enlisted in the local Territorials six months before the outbreak of the war. Embarked for France in April, 1915. Killed at the Battle of the Somme 3.9.1916, aged 20 years. Commemorated on the **THIEPVAL MEMORIAL TO THE MISSING**. ROH:- Holme and Holmbridge War Memorial; Huddersfield Drill Hall.

ARMITAGE, FRED. Private. No 2459. 2/5th Battalion Duke of Wellington's Regiment. Son of Thomas and Elizabeth Armitage, Cinderhills, Holmfirth. Worked as a piecer at Messrs Woodhead's Mill, Thongsbridge. Enlisted August, 1914. Contracted pneumonia whilst in training and spent periods in Huddersfield Royal Infirmary and Holmfirth Military Cottage Hospital. Transferred to 2/5th Battalion in training at Thoresby Park, Nottinghamshire. Admitted to the Doncaster Royal Infirmary suffering from meningitis. Died 17.6.15, aged 17 years. Buried with full military honours at **St. JOHN'S CHURCHYARD, UPPERTHONG**. Grave location:- Row H, Grave 8. ROH:- Underbank War Memorial; Huddersfield Drill Hall.

ARMITAGE, GEORGE. Private. No 43060. 9th Battalion King's Own Yorkshire Light Infantry. (Formerly No 28885 Northumberland Fusiliers). Born Scammonden. Lived 'Swan Inn', Crimble, Slaithwaite. Was employed at Messrs W and E. Crowther Limited. Attended Deanhead Church in his younger days. Was a member of Upper Slaithwaite Working Men's Club. Embarked for France December, 1916. Killed in action 9.4.1917, aged 34 years. Buried in **COJEUL BRITISH CEMETERY**. Grave location:- Row D, Grave 42. ROH:- St. James' Church, Slaithwaite; Slaithwaite War Memorial; Pole Moor Churchyard Memorial.

ARMITAGE, HARRY. Private. No 203561. 2/5th Battalion Duke of Wellington's Regiment. Born Crosland Moor 22.2.1892. Son of John and Elizabeth Armitage, 87 College Street, Crosland Moor. Attended Crosland Moor Council School. Worked as a gardener at the Crosland Moor Institution. Was a playing member of the Crosland Moor Public Handbell Ringers. Attended St. Barnabas Church, Crosland Moor. Enlisted February, 1916. Died of multiple wounds and loss of blood through having a leg amputated at 34th Casualty Clearing Station, 2.11.18. Buried in **GREVILLERS BRITISH CEMETERY**. Grave location:- Plot 17, Row D, Grave 16. ROH:- St. Barnabas Church, Crosland Moor;

United Methodist Church, Crosland Moor; Huddersfield Drill Hall.

ARMITAGE, HARRY. Private. No 23/368. 2nd Battalion Durham Light Infantry. Born Holmfirth. Lived 43 Southern Road, Milnsbridge. Was employed as a labourer at Longwood Gasworks. Was a member of the Milnsbridge Brotherhood and full member of the Cartworth Moor Wesleyan Sunday School. Killed in action, 21.1.1917, aged 20 years. Buried in **CAMBRIN CHURCHYARD EXTENSION.** Grave location:- Row T, Grave 23. ROH:- Milnsbridge War Memorial.

ARMITAGE, HARRY (HENRY) VINCENT. Private. No 241006. 2/5th Battalion Duke of Wellington's Regiment. Son of Mr and Mrs Willie Armitage, Old Post Office Yard, Shelley. Worked at Messrs. Stringer and Jagger's Colliery, Emley Moor. Enlisted. February 1915. Killed in action at the Battle of Bullecourt, 3.5.1917, aged 21 years. Commemorated on the **ARRAS MEMORIAL TO THE MISSING.** ROH:- Emmanuel Church, Shelley; Huddersfield Drill Hall.

ARMITAGE, HERBERT. Driver. No 149553. 30th Divisional Ammunition Column Royal Field Artillery. Born Lockwood. Son of Fred and Emma Armitage, 5 Bank Terrace, Armitage Bridge. Worked at Newsome Mills. Enlisted 1916. Died of wounds at No 38 Casualty Clearing Station, Haringhe, Belgium, 25.4.1918. Buried in **HARINGHE (BANDAGHEM) MILITARY CEMETERY.** Grave location:- Plot 3, Row E, Grave 44. Brother of Private **WILFRED ARMITAGE,** died of wounds 9.12.1916, q.v.). ROH:- Armitage Bridge War Memorial.

ARMITAGE, JAMES. Gunner. No 174031. 'C' Battery, 93rd Brigade Royal Field Artillery. Born 26.10.1880 at Fields Chapel Row, Lepton. Son of Robert and Eliza Armstrong. Attended Moldgreen Council School. Husband of Venitta Armstrong, 25 Grove Street, Huddersfield. Worked as a weaver for Messrs Dyson Hall and Company, Greenside, Dalton. Was Secretary for the Tandem Homing Society. Enlisted 21.9.1916. Killed in action near Poperinghe, Belgium, 1.9.1917, aged 36 years. Commemorated on the **TYNE COT MEMORIAL TO THE MISSING.**

ARMITAGE, JOHN FITTON. Private. No 202151. 1/4th Battalion Northumberland Fusiliers. Born Kirkburton. Son of the late Darius and Sarah Ann Armitage. Killed in action, 22.3.1918, aged 37 years. Commemorated on the **POZIERES MEMORIAL TO THE MISSING.** ROH:- All Hallows Parish Church, Kirkburton; commemorated on his parents' headstone in Kirkburton Churchyard.

ARMITAGE, THOMAS EDWARD. Private. No 301964. 2nd Battalion Royal Scots (Lothian Regiment). Born Linthwaite. Son of Mr and Mrs Tom Armitage, Pleasant View, Manchester Road, Linthwaite. Worked in the Jovil branch of the Linthwaite Co-operative Society Limited. Attended the Slaithwaite Wesleyan Chapel and Sunday School. Enlisted October 1916. Embarked for France May 1917. Wounded 4.9.1917. Admitted into hospital in Exeter, October 1917, suffering from a gunshot wound on the right side of the chest and the right arm. Pleurisy subsequently set in and in December he underwent an operation on the arm. He improved and was able to go out but collapsed and died, 27.2.1918. As the cause of death was obscure a post-mortem examination was held and this revealed a clot of blood in the pulmonary artery. The cause of death was Pulmonary Embolism due, not to the wounds, but to the length of illness. Buried in **LINTHWAITE WESLEYAN METHODIST BURIAL GROUND.** Grave location:- near East boundary. ROH:- Linthwaite War Memorial.

ARMITAGE, VINCENT. Private. No 42240. 6th Battalion Leicestershire Regiment. (Formerly No 46761 South Staffordshire Regiment). Son of Ben and Louisa Armitage, Bank Bottom. Shelley. Worked at Messrs Wallaces Limited, St. John's Road, Huddersfield. Killed in action, 28.5.1918, aged 19 years. Commemorated on the **SOISSONS MEMORIAL TO THE MISSING.**

ARMITAGE, WALTER EDWARD. Sergeant. No G/14597. 7th Battalion East Kent Regiment. Born West End, Skelmanthorpe. Son of the late Mr C. S. Armitage and Mrs Roebuck, 19 Frederick Street, Crosland Moor. Attended the National School, Skelmanthorpe and Higher Grade College, Huddersfield. Was in business as a butcher at Crosland Moor. Enlisted 21.9.1916. Killed in action, 26.8.1918, aged 19 years. Buried in **DANTZIG ALLEY CEMETERY.** Grave location:- Plot 8, Row H, Grave 10. ROH:- St. Barnabas Church, Crosland Moor.

ARMITAGE, WILFRED. Private. No 4953. 4th Battalion Seaforth Highlanders. Born Holmfirth. Son of Fred and Emma Armitage, 5 Bank Terrace, Armitage Bridge. Attended Armitage Bridge Church. A keen violinist. Employed at Armitage Bridge Mills. Wounded 8.12.1916 and died the following day, 9.12.1916, in No 49 (West Riding) Casualty Clearing Station, aged 19 years. Buried in **CONTAY BRITISH CEMETERY.** Grave location:- Plot 8, Row E, Grave 1. (Brother of Private **HERBERT ARMITAGE** died of wounds 25.4.1918 q.v.). ROH:- Armitage Bridge War Memorial; Armitage Bridge Mills Roll.

ARMITAGE, WILLIAM. Lance Corporal. No 270123. 16th Battalion The Royal Scots (Lothian Regiment). Born Kirkburton. Son of Henry and Annie Armitage, Mount Pleasant, Kirkburton. Apprenticed to Messrs Broadhead and Graves, Manufacturers, Kirkheaton. Enlisted April 1916. Embarked for France, January, 1917. Wounded, 9.4.1917, and died of gunshot wounds in No 3 General Hospital, Le Treport, 23.4.1917, aged 23 years. Buried in **MONT HUON MILITARY CEMETERY.** Grave location:- Plot 3, Row F, Grave 10B. ROH:- All Hallows Parish Church, Kirkburton.

ARMITAGE, WILLIE. Private. No 25449. 5th Battalion Yorkshire Regiment. Born 12.9.1894 at Battyeford, Mirfield. Son of Albert and Jessie Armitage. Educated at St. Saviour's School, Ravensthorpe, Dewsbury, and Christ Church School, Moldgreen. Lived 68 Storths, Moldgreen. Worked as a cotton piecer. Enlisted November 1915 Captured by the Germans and died as a Prisoner of War, 21.10.18, aged 24 years. Buried in **GLAGEON COMMUNAL CEMETERY EXTENSION.** Grave location:- Plot 2, Row C, Grave 9. ROH:- Almondbury War Memorial.

ARMITAGE, WILLIE. Rifleman. No C/7912. 18th Battalion King's Royal Rifle Corps. Born Upperthong. Son of Mr George Armitage. Lived Victoria, Holmfirth. Educated at St. John's School. Married, with one son. Worked as a tailor, firstly for Mr Herbert Battye and then for Mr Alex Peace of Holmfirth. Member of the St. John's Institute billiard team. Enlisted November 1915. Embarked for France May 1916. Killed in action, 10.10.1916, aged 31 years. Buried in **WARLENCOURT BRITISH CEMETERY.** Grave location:- Plot 3, Row D, Grave 27. ROH:- Upperthong War Memorial.

ARMITAGE, WILLIE. Acting Bombardier. No 120363. 58th Brigade Royal Field Artillery. Born 10.1.1894. Son of Mr and Mrs Herbert Armitage, Grange Terrace, Marsden. Employed at the Globe Worsted Company, Slaithwaite. Deputy organist at the Marsden Wesleyan Chapel and accompanist in the Sunday School. Was a member of the Marsden Adult School Institute. Enlisted 1.11.1915. Embarked for France 4.11.16. Suffered severe shell wounds to the abdomen on 10.1.17 (his birthday) and was taken to No 4 Casualty Clearing Station. Two letters were sent to his parents at Marsden from the Sister in charge advising them of his critical condition and he died on 12.1.1917, aged 23. Buried in **VARENNES MILITARY CEMETERY.** Grave location:- Plot 1, Row F, Grave 42. ROH:- Marsden War Memorial.

ARMSTRONG, WILFRED. Sapper. No R/289166. Royal Engineers. Born Huddersfield. Lived 9 Somerset Place, Moldgreen, Huddersfield. Married. Died at home from appendicitis and malaria on 29.4.1920.

ARNOLD, JOHN DENIS. Private. No 32838. 1/4th Battalion Duke of Wellington's Regiment. Born 14.1.1899 at Middleton Villa, Swinton near Rotherham. Son of Mrs Harrilena Arnold, 11 Marsden Road, Huddersfield. Educated at Swinton National School. Was employed in the wool blending department at Messrs George Mallinson and Sons Limited of Linthwaite. Secretary of the Men's Class in connection with Buxton Road Wesleyan Church. Enlisted 17.9.1917. Died of wounds to spine, 15.4.18, at No 64 Casualty Clearing Station. Buried in **MENDINGHEM MILITARY CEMETERY.** Grave location:- Plot 9, Row E, Grave 37. ROH:- St.Barnabas Church, Crosland Moor.

ARNOLD, P. Staff Sergeant. No 143880. Royal Engineers. Died 26.9.1919. Buried in **EDGERTON CEMETERY.** Grave location:- 11B, 116.

ASHURST, SHORROCK. Private. No 205120. 1/7th Battalion Duke of Wellington's Regiment. Born Barrow-in-Furness. Lived with his wife and child at Bellmount House, Luck Lane, Marsh. Was in business as a draper at New Street and formerly in King Street. Killed by a shell, 9.10.17, aged 36. Commemorated on the **TYNE COT MEMORIAL TO THE MISSING.** ROH:- All Saints Church, Paddock; Huddersfield Drill Hall.

ASHTON, JOHN BROWNHILL. Driver. Royal Field Artillery. Lived Thongsbridge. Before enlistment worked as a farmhand, firstly for Mr Herbert Wood of Kilnhouse Bank and then for Mr Joseph Wood of Hagg Farm. He was then employed by Mr Herbert Mellor of Mytholm Bridge. Enlisted in December 1914. He served in France and Belgium for over three years until May 9th, 1918, when he was discharged. After discharge he worked for the Glasgow Corporation for three weeks when an attack of pneumonia proved fatal and he died in the Royal Infirmary, Glasgow, aged 28 years (at the end of May 1918). ROH:- Hade Edge War Memorial.

ASHWORTH, EDWIN. Guardsman. No 28758. 3rd Battalion Grenadier Guards. Born, 7.2.1890, at 14 Hawk Street, Huddersfield. Son of James Armitage. Attended Huddersfield Parish Church School and Paddock Council Schools. Worked as a Confidential Clerk. Enlisted 1.1.1917. Reported killed in action at the Battle of Cambrai, 27.11.1917. Commemorated on the **CAMBRAI MEMORIAL TO THE MISSING.** ROH:- St. Mark's Parish Church, Longwood and also commemorated on his parents' headstone in Edgerton Cemetery.

ASPIN, WILLIAM P. Private. No 21108. 7th Battalion King's Own Yorkshire Light Infantry. Born Clayford, Kent. Lived Kirkheaton. Died of wounds, 16.9.1915. Buried **SAILLY-sur-la-LYS CANADIAN CEMETERY.** Grave location:- Plot 2, Row F, Grave 133. ROH:- St. John's Church, Kirkheaton.

ASPINALL, FREDERICK (FREDDIE). Private. No 71465. 17th Battalion Sherwood Foresters. (Formerly No 31669 North Staffordshire Regiment). Born Wooldale. Son of William and Ellen Aspinall, 74 Sunny Brow, Wooldale. Attended Lane Congregational Sunday School. Worked for Mr Fred Lawton, Bridge Mills. Enlisted November 1916. Reported missing, 4.8.17, aged 19. Commemorated on the **MENIN GATE MEMORIAL TO THE MISSING.** (Brother Private **HARRY ASPINALL**, killed in action, 9.9.1916, q.v.). ROH:- Wooldale War Memorial.

ASPINALL, HARRY. Rifleman. No R/19769. 2nd Battalion King's Royal Rifle Corps. Born Wooldale. Son of William and Ellen Aspinall, 74 Sunny Brow, Wooldale. Attended Lane Congregational Sunday School. Worked for Mr Fred Lawton, Bridge Mills. Enlisted 28.2.1916. Reported missing on 9.9.1916 and afterwards presumed to have been killed on that date. He was 23 years of age. His parents received the following information from a comrade of their son who wrote, *'On September 9th Rifleman Aspinall was in a bombing raid with me in front of Le Sars. We were occupying one portion of a trench and the Germans held the other end. About 25 of us went over the barricade and took about seventy yards from the Germans and after we had finished Rifleman Aspinall was missing. He was not in the part of the trench we captured so he must have gone further up and I fear he was killed.'* Buried in **CATERPILLAR VALLEY CEMETERY.** Grave location:- Plot 2, Row F, Grave 8. (Brother of Private **FREDDIE ASPINALL**, killed in action, 4.8.1917, q.v.). ROH:- Wooldale War Memorial.

ASTIN, FRANK. Private. No 63547. 2nd Battalion Kings Own Yorkshire Light Infantry. Born Daisy Lea, Outlane. Son of James William and Matilda Astin, 11 Slack, Outlane. Attended Outlane Council School. Worked as a cloth finisher for Messrs Edward Sykes, Gosport Mills, Outlane. Enlisted 21.11.1918. Killed in action, 30.9.1918, aged 18 years. Commemorated on the **VIS-en-ARTOIS MEMORIAL TO THE MISSING.** ROH:- St. Mark's Parish Church, Longwood.

ASTON, HENRY NORMAN. Captain. 3rd Battalion York and Lancaster Regiment. Born 31.5.1891 at 69 Blacker Road, Huddersfield. Son of the late Alderman Aston JP and Mrs Mary E. Aston of Stonegarth, 174 Halifax Old Road, Huddersfield. Educated at Almondbury Grammar School. Carried on the business of his late father as an oil merchant in Market Street in partnership with his brother-in-law, Mr Wild. Enlisted 20.3.1915; Gazetted 2nd Lieutenant. Wounded in the thigh at the Battle of Loos, 29.9.1915. Suffered severe shell shock at the Battle of Messines, 7.6.1917. After convalescence served in London, being attached to the RAF. Died from influenza and pneumonia at the 2nd London Hospital, Chelsea, 6.11.1918, aged

27 years. Buried with full military honours at **EDGERTON CEMETERY, HUDDERSFIELD.** Grave location:- 19, 'C', 28. ROH:- Almondbury Grammar School; St. Andrew's Church, Leeds Road, Huddersfield; Fartown and Birkby War Memorial.

ATKINSON, ALBERT. Private. No 3679. 1/5th Battalion Duke of Wellington's Regiment. Born Holmbridge. Son of Herbert and Emily Atkinson, 'Roseleigh,' Hinchliffe Mill. Worked for Messrs H and S. Butterworth, Lower Mill. Embarked for France April, 1915. Killed in action, 14.11.1915, aged 19 years. Buried in **TALANA FARM CEMETERY, BELGIUM.** Grave location:- Plot 4, Row F, Grave 4. *His parents received a letter from Sergeant VERNON MILLS LANGRICK who wrote, 'It is my unpleasant and painful duty to have to inform you of the death of your son. He was killed by a Maxim gun whilst on a working party. The heartfelt sympathy of myself and the platoon are with you in your sudden loss. He was a quiet, inoffensive lad and had made himself quite popular amongst his comrades. It is a pity his life was cut short so young but on the other hand he died a hero's death for the sake of his King and Country and you can always face the world and say that your son had not shirked his duty in his country's hour of need. We are burying him tonight in a little graveyard behind the firing line. Hoping that in time the bitter pang of sorrow will gradually wear away.'* ROH:- Holme and Holmbridge War Memorial; Huddersfield Drill Hall.

ATKINSON, CLAUDE. No 24702. Lance Sergeant. 9th Battalion Duke of Wellington's Regiment. Son of John and Louisa Atkinson, 61 Halifax Old Road, Huddersfield. Employed by Mr Thomas Canby, finisher. Killed in action, 25.8.1918, aged 23 years. Commemorated on **VIS-en-ARTOIS MEMORIAL TO THE MISSING.** ROH:- Fartown and Birkby War Memorial.

ATKINSON, EDWARD ERNEST. Private. No 242308. 1st Battalion West Yorkshire Regiment. Born Leeds. Lived Lepton. Son of Edward and Emily Etta Atkinson. Died of wounds (gas) on 28.4.1918. He was 23 years of age. Buried **BOULOGNE EASTERN CEMETERY.** Grave location:- Plot 9, Row B, Grave 11. ROH:- Lepton Parish Church.

ATKINSON, FRED. Private. No 301805. 1/8th Battalion Durham Light Infantry. Born 4 Fieldhouse Road, off Cassel Street, Huddersfield, 8.1.1892. Son of Mrs M. Atkinson, 46 Thistle Street, Leeds Road. Attended St. Andrew's School. Worked as a tuner for Messrs T. and H. Blamires. Enlisted 1.6.1916. Embarked for France 4.10.1916. Mother received a letter from a Corporal of his platoon informing her that her son was wounded in a charge and died in his arms whilst he was being taken back to the trench on 5.11.1916. Age 24 years. Commemorated on the **THIEPVAL MEMORIAL TO THE MISSING.** ROH:- St Andrew's Church, Leeds Road.

ATKINSON, FREEMAN CLEMENT. Lance Corporal. No 11033. 9th Battalion King's Own Yorkshire Light Infantry. Born Sheffield. Son of George Atkinson, 22 Midland Street, Sheffield. Married to Lily Atkinson, 52 Moorend Road, Lockwood. Two children. Worked as an engine cleaner for the London and North Western Railway Company. Enlisted November 1913. Killed on the first day of the Battle of the Somme 1.7.1916 at Fricourt. Age 23 years. Commemorated on the **THIEPVAL MEMORIAL TO THE MISSING.** ROH:- Emmanuel Church, Lockwood.

ATKINSON, GEORGE. Private. No G/66870. 32nd Battalion Royal Fusiliers. Formerly No 31551 Duke of Wellington's Regiment. Born Slaithwaite. Lived 27 Chapel Street, Slaithwaite. Employed by Messrs George Cock Limited, Longfield Dyeworks, Linthwaite. Embarked for France in May, 1917. Killed instantly by a shell, 31.7.1917, aged 33 years. Buried in **VOORMEZEELE ENCLOSURE 1 and 2, BELGIUM.** Grave location:- Plot 1, Row E, Grave 31. ROH:- St. James Church, Slaithwaite; Slaithwaite War Memorial.

ATKINSON, GEORGE WILLIAM. Able Seaman. No Tyneside Z/9371. Royal Naval Volunteer Reserve. *HMS Egmont*, RN Depot (Port Said). Eldest son of Mrs John Atkinson, 94 West End Road, Golcar. Worked as a weaver at Messrs Ben Hall and Sons, Milnsbridge. Connected with Golcar Baptist Chapel and a member of the Young Men's Bible Class. Enlisted in the Navy in March, 1916. Accidentally drowned at sea, 8.8.1918, aged 26 years. Buried in **PORT SAID WAR MEMORIAL CEMETERY, EGYPT.** Grave location:- Plot L, Grave 7. ROH:- St. John's Church, Golcar; Golcar Baptist Chapel.

ATKINSON, HERBERT. Private. No 21876. 10th Battalion West Yorkshire Regiment. Son of Mr and Mrs Arthur Atkinson of Hinchliffe Mill. Worked as a millhand in the finishing room of Messrs Whiteley and Green, Hinchliffe Mill. Attended Hinchliffe Mill Wesleyan School. Keen on athletics and cycling. Enlisted August 1915. Died of wounds at No 56 Casualty Clearing Station 2.11.1916, aged 21 years. Buried in **GROVE TOWN CEMETERY.** Grave location:- Plot 2, Row F, Grave 40. ROH:- Holme and Holmbridge War Memorial.

ATKINSON, JOHN WHITEHEAD. Sergeant. No 20264. 2nd Battalion Yorkshire Regiment. Born Upperthong. Son of Thomas and Lily Atkinson, Greenhill Bank, New Mill. Educated at New Mill National School. Attended the Sunday School and was a chorister in the New Mill Parish Church choir. Worked as a butcher, firstly for Mr Fred Brook of Holmfirth and then for Mr James Taylor of Crosland Moor. Enlisted 1.2.1915. Embarked for France October, 1915. Was killed by shellfire, 26.5.1918, at 5.50pm, aged 23 years. Buried in **St. PATRICK'S CEMETERY, LOOS.** Grave location:- Plot 2, Row A, Grave 13. (Brother to Gunner **RANDAL ATKINSON**, killed in action 25.4.1917 q.v.). ROII:- New Mill Working Men's Club; Fulstone War Memorial; also commemorated on memorial in St David's Churchyard, Holmbridge.

ATKINSON, MARSDEN, MSM. Staff Sergeant. No M2/021751. Army Service Corps. Born Shaw Mills near Pateley Bridge, Yorkshire, on 12.12.1880. Educated at Spring Grove Council School. Lived at 142 Brierley Wood, Marsden Road, Huddersfield, before moving to Cheetham Hill, Manchester. Worked as a motor engineer. Married. Enlisted November 1914. Killed by a shell near the Cloth Hall, Ypres, 12.4.1918. Buried in **YPRES RESERVOIR CEMETERY.** Grave location:- Plot 3, Row E, Grave 24.

ATKINSON, RANDAL. Gunner. No 117807. 256th Siege Battery Royal Garrison Artillery. Born Holmfirth. Son of Thomas and Lily Atkinson, Greenhill Bank, New Mill. Worked as a butcher for Councillor Luther Firth of Holmfirth. Married Miss Helena Child, eldest daughter of Mr and Mrs W. Child of Wooldale. Enlisted August 1916. Embarked for France in February, 1917. Killed by a shell which killed six other men, 25.4.1917, aged 19 years. Buried in **FEUCHY BRITISH CEMETERY.** Grave location:- Plot 1, Row B, Grave 21. (Brother of Private **JOHN WHITEHEAD ATKINSON**, killed in action, 26.5.1918 q.v.). ROH:- New Mill Working Men's Club; Fulstone War Memorial; also commemorated on memorial in St. David's Church, Holmbridge.

ATKINSON, WILLIAM GLADSTONE. Marine Engineer. Born Huddersfield. Brother of Mr H. S. Atkinson, 9 Marsh Grove Road, Huddersfield. Married. Enlisted 4.8.1914. Serving on board *HMS Alfred H Read* (Pilot Patrol boat No 1). Pilot boat engaged in Mersey defence when accidentally shot on board,15.10.1917.

ATKIN, MARK. Private. No 6666. 1/14th (County of London) Battalion (London Scottish). Son of Amos and Jane Elizabeth Atkin of West Cliffe Lodge, Denby Dale. Killed in action on the first day of the Battle of the Somme, 1.7.1916, aged 18 years. Commemorated on the **THIEPVAL MEMORIAL TO THE MISSING.** ROH:- Denby Dale and Cumberworth War Memorial.

AVERY, EDGAR. Private. No 29615. 2nd Battalion Duke of Wellington's Regiment. Born Berry Brow, Huddersfield, 3.11.1897. Son of Edwin and Mary Avery, 64 Parkgate, Berry Brow. Attended Berry Brow Council School. Worked as a farmer's assistant at Lower Park Farm, Berry Brow. Enlisted 3.10.1916. Reported wounded and missing near Monchy, east of Arras, 31.8.1918, aged 20 years. Commemorated on the **VIS-en-ARTOIS MEMORIAL TO THE MISSING.** ROH:- Armitage Bridge War Memorial.

BACKHOUSE, CHARLES. Private. No 2547. 1/5th Battalion Duke of Wellington's Regiment. Born Thurstonland. Son of James and Sarah Backhouse of Brockholes. (later of Leeds). Attended Brockholes Wesleyan Church and was secretary of the Wesley Guild. Embarked for France in April, 1915. Was badly wounded by shrapnel on the morning of 1.7.1915. Was on his way to his dugout to prepare a meal when a shell burst near him and he was struck on the head. Was taken to a dressing station where he died a week later, on 11.7.15. Age 26 years. Buried in **FERME-OLIVER CEMETERY, ELVERDINGHE, BELGIUM.** Grave location:- Plot 1, Row J, Grave 8. ROH:- Thurstonland War Memorial; Brockholes War Memorial; Huddersfield Drill Hall. A letter was received by Private Backhouse's sister from Captain Eastwood (Captain, 1/5th Battalion Duke of Wellingtons' Regiment, '*It is with very great regret that I have to break the news to you that your brother Charles has died from his wounds received the other day. I wish to offer you my deepest sympathy in your great loss. I may say I feel it as keenly as anyone possibly can seeing that he has been my orderly for nine months and in close contact with me all the time. I am the one who knew his worth more than anyone else. He was the most faithful, clean, good natured boy in the whole battalion. He never ceased to look after me and I trusted him with all my private affairs and money so you can tell how I appreciated him. All the Company feel his loss very much indeed and they all have a good word for him. He was wounded just outside my dugout whilst doing his duty. He was a brave lad and shells did not frighten him and it was a most unfortunate thing that he was wounded by a shell. I am so far away from the hospital that I shall not be able to attend his funeral. I should have liked to have done so for my own feelings and also yours. Let this be an example to the Holmfirth young men and those who have not joined yet. I trust that the death of a noble young man like your brother are the means of the slacker coming forward to avenge his death. He was a lad to be proud of and I cannot praise him too highly. May you seek comfort in the fact that came forward to do his duty in this great war and that duty he did nobly and well and may God comfort you in your trouble is all that I his Officer whom he served so well can say.*'

BAGGS, SAMUEL. Rifleman. No C/7365. 18th Battalion King's Royal Rifle Corps. Born Yeadon near Leeds, 14.4.1892. Son of Mr and Mrs George Henry Baggs, 344 Wakefield Road, Huddersfield. Attended Guiseley Council School. Worked as a woollen spinner for Messrs Rhodes and Brierley of Kirkburton. Enlisted 30.10.1915. Embarked for France in May, 1916. Killed in action at the Battle of Flers, 15.9.1916, aged 24 years. Buried in **BULLS ROAD CEMETERY, FLERS.** Grave location:- Plot 3, Row C, Grave 2. ROH:- St John's Church, Kirkheaton.

BAGLEY, JAMES. Private. No 107377. 2/5th Battalion Sherwood Foresters. Born Morley, Leeds. Son of John Bagley (stationmaster at Marsden Station) and Jane Bagley, East Lea, Marsden. Reported missing, presumed killed in action, 14.4.1918, aged 19 years. Commemorated on the **PLOEGSTEERT MEMORIAL TO THE MISSING.** ROH:- Marsden War Memorial.

BAILEY, ALBERT. Private. No 25552. 13th Battalion Yorkshire Regiment. Born Huddersfield. Son of Mrs Haveland, 6 Upperhead Row, Huddersfield. Killed in action, 13.4.1918, aged 27 years. Buried in **RATION FARM CEMETERY, LA CHAPELLE d'ARMENTIERES.** Grave location:- Plot 7, Row B, Grave 4.

BAILEY, ALBERT. Private. No 267406. 1/6th Battalion Northumberland Fusiliers. Born Underbank, Holmfirth. Son of John and Emma Bailey of Underbank. Attended Holmfirth Parish Church where he was a sidesman and a singer. Was a member of the Holmfirth Harriers. Enlisted in the Royal Field Artillery during the summer of 1916. Embarked for France on Boxing Day, 1916. Transferred to the Northumberland Fusiliers. Came home on leave at the beginning of 1918 but became ill and died in Royds Hall Hospital on 6.2.1919, at the age of 23 years, after being in hospital practically the whole of the time. Buried in **HOLY TRINITY BURIAL GROUND, HOLMFIRTH.** Grave location:- N, 5. ROH:- Underbank War Memorial.

BAILEY, ARTHUR WILLIAM. Private. No 67294. 6th Battalion Machine Gun Corps, (Formerly No 29406 Duke of Wellington's Regiment). Born Thornhill Lees near Dewsbury, 7.6.1882. Son of William and Harriet Bailey, 300 Lee Hall Road, Thornhill Lees, near Dewsbury. Educated at Walker's Endowed School, Thornhill. Worked as a gardener. Married to Florence Bailey, 19 Croft House Lane, Marsh. Enlisted September 1916. Taken prisoner by the Germans on the 21.3.1918 and died of diphtheria, 19.6.1918, aged 36. Buried in **VIS-en-ARTOIS BRITISH CEMETERY.** Grave location:- Plot 9, Row C, Grave 14. ROH:- Gledholt Wesleyan Church.

BAILEY, F. Private. No 21915. 6th Battalion Kings Own Scottish Borderers. Born Crimble, Slaithwaite. 4.12.1893. Son of Mrs G.H. Bailey,

81 Longwood Gate, Longwood. Educated at Slaithwaite National School. Employed as a spinner by Messrs Taylor, Livesey and Company Limited, Paddock. Attended Paddock United Methodist Church and Sunday School. Enlisted 21.10.1915. Left for France on 2.2.1916. Killed in action, 17.4.1916, aged 23 years. Buried in **TANCREZ FARM CEMETERY.** Grave location:- Plot 1, Row A, Grave 6. ROH:- Parkwood Methodist Church and St. Mark's Parish Church, Longwood. His mother received the following letter from Sergeant A. B. Fleming of the same Regiment who said that Private Bailey was in a working party under the charge of Sergeant Fleming when he was shot by a sniper. ' *He fell into my arms and I did all I possibly could for him but it was of no avail. He only lived two minutes. He did not suffer much and died in my arms. I know it is hard indeed for you to bear such a great loss but keep up your heart and rest contented for he died a hero's death doing his duty. He was liked by all who knew him and you have the sympathy of all the N.C.O's and men.*'

BAILEY, FRANCE. No 28506. Private. 2nd Battalion Northumberland Fusiliers. Born Slaithwaite. Son of Mr and Mrs Jim Bailey, 8 New House, Moorside, Slaithwaite. Connected with the Shred Church and Sunday School. Enlisted April 1916. Went out to Salonica, Greece, in June 1916. Killed in action, 31.10.1916, aged 20 years. Buried in **STRUMA MILITARY CEMETERY, GREECE.** Grave location:- Plot 6, Row G, Grave 4. ROH:- Slaithwaite War Memorial; Pole Moor Baptist Church; St. James Church, Slaithwaite.

BAILEY, HERBERT. Private. No 352242. Training Reserve, transferred to 160th Company Labour Corps. Born Fewston near Harrogate. Educated at Thorpe Board School, Idle, Bradford. Worked as a spinner. Husband of Florence Edith Bailey, 184 Blackmoorfoot Road, Crosland Moor, Huddersfield. Enlisted 22.6.1916. Killed in action near Cambrai, 22.12.17. Buried **RIBECOURT ROAD CEMETERY.** Grave location:- Plot 1, Row D, Grave 2. (Brother of Private **LEONARD BAILEY**, killed in action, 27.1.1918 q.v.). ROH:- St. Barnabas Church, Crosland Moor.

BAILEY, JAMES. Gunner. No 173943. 'A' Battery, 45th Brigade Royal Field Artillery. Son of Mr and Mrs Albert Bailey, St. George's Road, Scholes, Holmfirth. Married 1915. Lived at Totties. Worked as a weaver for Messrs Kaye and Stewart of Lockwood. Educated at Hepworth Church School and was a scholar and teacher at Scholes Primitive Methodist Sunday School. Enlisted 1916. Killed by a shell at Ypres, Belgium, 15.8.1917, aged 29 years. Buried in **MENIN ROAD SOUTH MILITARY CEMETERY, YPRES.** Grave location:- Plot 2, Row E, Grave 22. ROH:- Hepworth and Scholes; Hepworth Church. A letter was received by the widow from a comrade of Gunner Bailey telling her of his death:- '*It is with the deepest sympathy I have to write to tell you that your husband was killed on the 15th August. He did not suffer I can tell you. I found him one of the very best of pals and he was already to cheer us up. I cannot tell you how sorry I am for I have lost a good friend. I hope you do not take it to heart as he always did his best.*'

BAILEY, JAMES. Private. No 30690. 2nd Battalion Yorkshire Regiment. Born 3.7.1897 at 37 York Street, Huddersfield. Son of Mrs Martha Bailey, 3 Dent's Yard, Quay Street. Educated at Huddersfield Parish Church School. Married. Living at 2 Tindall's Yard, Hawk Street, Huddersfield. Employed as a cloth finisher of khaki cloth at the works of Mr Murgatroyd, Leeds Road. Enlisted June, 1916. Embarked for France October, 1916. Killed in action, 2.4.1917. Buried in **HENIN COMMUNAL CEMETERY EXTENSION.** Grave location:- Plot 2, Row C, Grave 22. ROH:- Huddersfield Parish Church.

BAILEY, LEONARD. Private. No 307683. 1/8th Battalion West Yorkshire Regiment. Born Fewston near Harrogate. Educated at Thorpe Board School, Idle, Bradford. Lived 'Ivy House Inn', Crosland Moor. Worked as a moulder. Was wounded at Ypres, 5.12.1917. Died of wounds at No 24 General Hospital, Etaples, 27.1.1918. Buried in **ETAPLES MILITARY CEMETERY.** Grave location:- Plot 31, Row F, Grave 12A. (Brother of Private **HERBERT BAILEY** killed in action, 22.12.1917 q.v.). ROH:- St. Barnabas Church, Crosland Moor.

BAILEY, LAWRENCE. Private. No 32137. 9th Battalion Border Regiment. Lived St. Helens Gate, Almondbury. Enlisted 1916. Saw active service in Salonica, Greece. Invalided home September, 1918, after several attacks of malaria.

Died at home, 20.2.1919, aged 25 years. Buried with full military honours in **ALMONDBURY CEMETERY**. Grave location:- U, 'C', 79. ROH:- Almondbury War Memorial.

BAILEY, THOMAS DISMORE. Private. No 3189. 'B' Coy, 1/5th Battalion Duke of Wellington's Regiment. Born Field Street, Marsh, 29.12.1895. Son of Samuel and Selina Bailey of 5, Holme Place, Grasscroft Road, Marsh. (Samuel Bailey was employed as coachman by Mr J H Sykes, 'Bryancliffe,' Edgerton, Huddersfield). Educated at Holy Trinity Church School, Huddersfield. He was a member of the choir at Holy Trinity Church. Worked as a tailor's cutter for Messrs Bairstow, Sons and Company. Enlisted 6th October, 1914. Embarked for France April, 1915. Was a stretcher-bearer in the Ambulance Section. Was shot by a sniper whilst going out to rescue a wounded comrade, 14.6.1915, aged 19 years. Buried **RUE-DAVID MILITARY CEMETERY, FLEURBAIX**. Grave location:- Plot 1, Row B, Grave 13. ROH:- Holy Trinity Church, Huddersfield; Huddersfield Drill Hall. His parents received the following letter from their son's Commanding Officer, Captain J. E Eastwood, who wrote, *'We had just one man badly wounded, and your son, as a stretcher-bearer, was attending to him, when I heard that we had another man wounded higher up in the trenches, so your son set off to attend to him, and while doing so was shot dead on the spot.'* Lieutenant A L McCally of the R.A.M.C wrote:- *'As you know, I have not been very long in charge of the Ambulance Section, but I have heard nothing but praise of your son from Sergeant Flood and his late comrades. He was always willing to do his share of whatever was in hand, and the fact of his at once going out to a dangerous place to help a wounded man shows that he had the very highest conception of what his duty was.'*

BAILEY, WALTER. Private. No 241879. 2/5th Battalion Duke of Wellington's Regiment. Born Golcar. Son of Mary Bailey, 16 Brook Terrace, Slaithwaite and the late John William Bailey. Employed as a weaver at Crimble Mills, Slaithwaite. Was a well known cricket and football player. Enlisted 24.5.1916. Embarked for France January, 1917. Reported missing, presumed killed, at the Battle of Bullecourt, 3.5.1917, aged 37 years. His body was found lying out on the battlefield sixteen weeks later, on the 24.8.1917. Commemorated on the **ARRAS MEMORIAL TO THE MISSING**. ROH:- St. John's Church, Golcar; St. James Church, Slaithwaite; Slaithwaite War Memorial; Huddersfield Drill Hall.

BAILEY, WALTER PERCIVAL. Lance Corporal. No 38205. Yorkshire Regiment. Born New Mill, Holmfirth. Lived 16 Rock Terrace, Brockholes. Married, with one child. Employed by Messrs Taylor and Lodge, Rashcliffe Mills, Huddersfield. Formerly connected with New Mill Parish Church and a playing member of the Brockholes Bowling Club. Enlisted September 1916. Killed in action at the Battle of Arras, 24.4.1917. Commemorated on the **ARRAS MEMORIAL TO THE MISSING**. ROH:- Honley War Memorial; Brockholes War Memorial.

BAILEY, WILFRED. Private. No 52856. 13th Battalion Durham Light Infantry. Formerly No 5794 Manchester Regiment. Born Hill Top, Lindley 5.8.1887. Son of Charles Henry Bailey, 82 Cowrakes Road, Lindley. Educated at Oakes Council School. Employed at Messrs Martin, Sons and Company, Limited, Wellington Mills, Lindley, as a cloth weaver. Married. Lived at 17 Burn Road, Birchencliffe. Attended Salendine Nook Baptist Chapel. Was a member of Paddock Cricket Club and also treasurer for the Lindley Conservative Club. Enlisted May 1916. Killed in action at Cameron House, Polygon Wood, Belgium, 20.10.1917, aged 30 years. Commemorated on the **TYNE COT MEMORIAL TO THE MISSING**. ROH:- Salendine Nook Baptist Church; St. Philip's Church, Birchencliffe.

BAILEY, WILLIAM. Private. No 32586. 21st Battalion Northumberland Fusiliers. Husband of Nellie Bailey, 11 Norman Road, Birkby. Died at home, 29.11.1919, aged 27 years. Buried in **EDGERTON CEMETERY, HUDDERSFIELD**. Grave location:- 11, 141G.

BAINES, GEORGE. Lance Corporal. No 15442. 9th (Service) Battalion West Yorkshire Regiment. Born School Street, Old Town, Barnsley. 10.8.1886. Married to Clara Baines and lived at 36 Leymoor Bottom, Longwood. Worked as a blacksmith's striker. Enlisted 10.10.1914. Killed in action between Scimitar Hill and Sulajik,

Suvla, at Gallipoli on 9.8.1915. He was 29 years of age. Commemorated on the **HELLES MEMORIAL TO THE MISSING, GALLIPOLI.** ROH:- Longwood War Memorial.

BAIRSTOW, FRANK. Private. No 216720. 1st Canadian Mounted Rifles. Born Huddersfield. Son of Mr and Mrs S. Bairstow of Huddersfield. Emigrated to Canada in 1908. Was living in Winnipeg, Canada, prior to the outbreak of the war. Reported wounded and missing on April 10th, 1917, and afterwards presumed to have been killed on that date. He was 37 years of age. Has no known grave. Commemorated **VIMY RIDGE MEMORIAL TO THE MISSING.** ROH:- St. John the Evangelist Church, Birkby; Fartown and Birkby War Memorial.

BAIRSTOW, GEORGE. Private. No 3026. 1/5th Battalion Duke of Wellington's Regiment. Born Grimscar, Huddersfield, 6.11.1895. Son of Ernest and Hannah M Bairstow, 'The Winnats', 22 Edgerton Grove Road, Huddersfield. Educated at Almondbury Grammar School. Was learning the bookselling business at Messrs Coates and Bairstow, Station Street, Huddersfield. Enlisted 4.9.1914. Embarked for France April, 1915. Was struck on the head by a shell splinter or a shrapnel bullet after leaving the trench to fetch water for breakfast on 31.7.1915, aged 20 years. Buried in **BARD COTTAGE CEMETERY, BELGIUM.** Grave location:- Plot 1, Row A, Grave 39. ROH:- St. Cuthbert's Church, Birkby; St. John's Church, Birkby; Almondbury Grammar School; Huddersfield Drill Hall; Fartown and Birkby War Memorial.

BAKER, TOM. Private. No 305801. 1/7th Battalion Duke of Wellington's Regiment. Born Marsden. Lived with his sister, Mrs Bacon, 17 Gladstone Buildings, Marsden. Employed as a feeder at Readycarr Mills. Enlisted November 1914. Accidentally drowned whilst on active service in France, 21.10.1917, aged 27 years. Buried in **TROUVILLE COMMUNAL CEMETERY.** Grave location:- in Military plot. ROH:- Marsden War Memorial; Huddersfield Drill Hall.

BALDERSTONE, HERBERT. Private. No 19884. 2nd Battalion Duke of Wellington's Regiment. Born Wood Street, Longwood, 24.4.1884. Educated at Goitfield Board School, Longwood. Employed as a woollen weaver by Messrs B. Crosland of Oakes. Enlisted March 1916. Reported missing at the Battle of Arras, 3.5.1917. Commemorated on the **ARRAS MEMORIAL TO THE MISSING.** ROH:- Longwood Wesleyan Church; St. Marks Parish Church, Longwood.

BALLANTYNE, PHILIP HUGH. Lieutenant. 4th Battalion Seaforth Highlanders. Born Ripponden near Halifax. Second son of Annie Ballantyne, The School House, New Mill. Educated at Heath Grammar School, Halifax. Worked for the Metropolitan Asylums Board, London. Enlisted October 1914. Was granted a commission in February, 1917. Was wounded at Messines Ridge and at the Battle of Cambrai. Killed in action, 28.10.1918, aged 27 years. Commemorated on the **VIS-en-ARTOIS MEMORIAL TO THE MISSING.** ROH:- New Mill Working Men's Club; Fulstone War Memorial.

BALL, WILLIAM HENRY. Private. No 10629. 9th Battalion Duke of Wellington's Regiment. Born Rotherham. Only son of William Henry and Agnes Ball of Cockley Hill, Kirkheaton. Enlisted in the Regular Army in 1913. Prior to that was employed at Lodge Mill Colliery Lepton. Killed in action at the Battle of the Somme, 2.8.1916, aged 21 years. Commemorated on the **THIEPVAL MEMORIAL TO THE MISSING.** ROH:- St. John's Church, Kirkheaton; Lepton Parish Church.

BALMFORD, ARNOLD. Private. No 24963. 1/5th Battalion Duke of Wellingtons' Regiment. Born Longwood 8.6.1895. Son of John Alfred and Edith Balmford, Stonegarth, 174 Halifax Old Road. Educated at the Huddersfield Municipal Secondary School and the Huddersfield Technical College. Completed his education in Brussels. A keen musician and a bass vocalist of great promise. Enlisted July 1915. Was wounded February, 1916. On return to France was transferred to the 2nd Battalion Duke of Wellington's Regiment. Killed in action at the Battle of Arras, 3.5.1917, aged 21. Commemorated on the **ARRAS MEMORIAL TO THE MISSING.** ROH:- Fartown and Birkby War Memorial; Huddersfield Drill Hall.

BALMFORD, WILLIE. Private. No 24638. 9th Battalion Duke of Wellington's Regiment. Born Cleveland Road, Marsh. Attended Crosland Moor Council School. Employed by Messrs Firth and Wilson, wholesale grocers. Married. Wife living at 3 Devonshire Street, Swan Lane, Lockwood. Enlisted 11.10.1915. Killed in action at Monchy-le-Preux, near Arras, 25.4.1917, aged 28 years. Commemorated on the **ARRAS MEMORIAL TO THE MISSING.** ROH:- St. Barnabas Church, Crosland Moor; Milton Independent Church.

BALMFORTH, ERNEST. Lance Corporal. No 10644. 10th Battalion Duke of Wellington's Regiment. Born Whitehead Lane, Huddersfield 15.2.1893. Son of William and Mary Ann Balmforth, 20 Whitehead Lane, Primrose Lane. Lived with his grandmother at Northbank, Somerset Road. Worked as a blacksmith at Kirkburton. Enlisted in the King's Own Yorkshire Light Infantry, 9.10.1913 but was later transferred to the Duke of Wellington's Regiment. Wounded at La Bassée, 24.10.1914, and returned to the front in June, 1916,. Killed in action 25.9.1916, aged 23 years. Commemorated on the **THIEPVAL MEMORIAL TO THE MISSING.** ROH:- St. Paul's Church, Southgate; Almondbury War Memorial.

BALMFORTH, JOE. Rifleman. No R/15269. 9th Battalion King's Royal Rifle Corps. Born Shaw, Oldham. Lived Meltham. Killed in action at the Battle of Flers, 15.9.1916. ROH:- St. Bartholomew's Church, Meltham.

BALMFORTH, MITCHELL. Corporal. No TR/24034. 10th Battalion East Yorkshire Regiment. Born Lockwood. Son of Joseph and Hannah Balmforth, 17 Bland Street, Lockwood. Employed as a worsted weaver. Husband of Elsie Balmforth, 41 Frederick Street, Crosland Moor (later of 76 St Annes Road East, St. Annes-on-Sea, Lancashire. Enlisted 22.6.1916. Was accidentally killed, 14.9.1917, whilst riding a bicycle near Rugeley Camp, aged 32. He collided with a motor car whilst turning a nasty curve in the road. The funeral took place at Milnsbridge Church, with full military honours, after the body was brought to Huddersfield from Rugeley Camp. Buried in **ST. LUKE'S CHURCHYARD, MILNSBRIDGE.** Grave location:- 1, South, D, 13. ROH:- Mount Pleasant Chapel, Lockwood; Memorial in Lockwood Cemetery.

BAMFORD, WILLIE. Corporal. No 238122. 1st Battalion Northumberland Fusiliers. Son of John Willie and Martha Bamford. Husband of Alice S. Bamford, 6 Bank End, Heath House, Golcar. Died at home, 25.1.1919, aged 36 years. Buried in **ST. LUKE'S CHURCHYARD, MILNSBRIDGE.** Grave location:- 1, South, B, 6. ROH:- St. John's Church, Golcar; Milnsbridge War Memorial.

BAMFORTH, ARTHUR STANLEY. Gunner. No 293646. 136th Heavy Battery Royal Garrison Artillery. Born Marsden. Son of Mr and Mrs Frank Bamforth, Manse Side, Marsden. Employed as principal assistant at Marsden Gasworks. Attended Marsden Congregational Church. Was secretary of the Marsden Liberal Club and a playing member of the Marsden Cricket Club. Enlisted October 1915. Had been in France over two and a half years. Died from pleurisy following an attack of gas poisoning, received from an enemy gas shell a fortnight before, at the 72nd General Hospital, Trouville, 14.11.1918. His parents received a telegram from the hospital informing them of his critical condition and intimating that, if they desired, passes would be prepared for them to go to France to see their son. They at once left Marsden, arriving in London the following morning. Whilst awaiting instructions a further telegram arrived to say that their son had died, whereupon the parents immediately returned home. Buried in **TOURGEVILLE MILITARY CEMETERY,** aged 29 years. Grave location:- Plot 7, Row A, Grave 18. ROH:- Marsden War Memorial; Marsden Liberal Club.

BAMFORTH, CHARLEY. Private. No 41931. 12th Battalion Manchester Regiment. (Formerly No 31670 North Staffordshire Regiment). Born Slaithwaite. Son of Mr and Mrs C. Bamforth, 123 Woodsome Glen, Slaithwaite. Employed as a weaver by Messrs Pearson Brothers, Commercial Mills, Slaithwaite. Closely associated with Lingards Wood Bottom Sunday School where he was a teacher. Enlisted 2.11.1916. Embarked for France March, 1917. Died of wounds, 25.8.1917, aged 19 years. Buried in **LEVEL CROSSING CEMETERY, FAMPOUX.** Grave location:- Plot 1, Row E,

Grave 8. ROH:- Slaithwaite War Memorial; St. James Church, Slaithwaite.

BAMFORTH, EDGAR. Private. No 5880. 19th (County of London) Battalion (St. Pancras). Formerly No C/7668 18th Battalion King's Royal Rifle Corps. Born 7 Henry Street, Huddersfield, 8.2.1897. Son of Willie and Edith Alice Bamforth. Educated at Spring Grove Council School. Worked as a bottler for Messrs Seth Senior and Sons, Cross Church Street. Attended Huddersfield Parish Church. Enlisted in the King's Royal Rifle Corps, 15.11.1915, but was transferred to the London Regiment in May, 1916, and embarked for France at the end of that month. Killed in action at High Wood during the Battle of the Somme, 15.9.1916, aged 19 years. Commemorated on the **THIEPVAL MEMORIAL TO THE MISSING.** ROH:- Huddersfield Parish Church.

BAMFORTH, FRANK. Private. No 25020. 8th Battalion Duke of Wellington's Regiment. Born Slaithwaite. Second son of Mr and Mrs George Bamforth, Union Street, Slaithwaite. Employed in the office of the Globe Worsted Company Limited, Slaithwaite. Was a member of the Slaithwaite Cricket Club and of the Conservative Club. Enlisted February 1916, training at Clipstone Camp. Sailed for France on Christmas Day, 1916. Killed in action, 27.8.1917, aged 26 years. Buried in **POELCAPELLE BRITISH CEMETERY, BELGIUM.** Grave location:- Plot 34, Row E, Grave 20. ROH:- Slaithwaite War Memorial; St. James Church, Slaithwaite.

BAMFORTH, FRED. Private. No 235269. 10th Battalion York and Lancaster Regiment. Formerly No 4970 Duke of Wellington's Regiment. Born Slaithwaite. Son of Mr James Bamforth, Wilberlee, Slaithwaite. Employed as a weaver by Messrs John Crowther and Sons, Milnsbridge. Was a member of the Slaithwaite Cricket and Bowling Club. Was also a keen member of the Conservative Club. Enlisted March, 1916, into the Duke of Wellington's Regiment. Was posted to the York and Lancaster Regiment as a Lewis gunner and drafted to France in May, 1917. Killed in action, 12.8.1917, aged 23 years. Buried in **OOSTTAVERNE WOOD CEMETERY, WYTSCHAETE, BELGIUM.** Grave location:- Plot 2, Row B, Grave 6. ROH:- St. James Church, Slaithwaite; Slaithwaite War Memorial.

BAMFORTH, GEORGE. Private. No 241783. 2/5th Battalion Duke of Wellington's Regiment. Born Marsden. Son of Mr Samuel Bamforth, 7 Hawthorne Terrace, Carrs Road, Marsden. Was employed as a weaver by Messrs Crowther, Bruce and Company Limited. Enlisted 1916. Embarked for France January, 1917. Killed in action at the Battle of Bullecourt, 3.5.1917, aged 35 years. Commemorated on the **ARRAS MEMORIAL TO THE MISSING.** ROH:- Marsden War Memorial; Huddersfield Drill Hall.

BAMFORTH, HAROLD. Driver. No L/25524. 'A' Battery 168th (Huddersfield) Brigade Royal Field Artillery. Born Marsden. Only son of Mr and Mrs Arthur Bamforth, The Liberal Club, Marsden. Was employed in the pattern room by Messrs Joseph Dyson at Elm Ing Mills, Milnsbridge. Attended Marsden Parish Church being a member of the choir and a teacher in the Sunday School. Was a member of the Liberal Club. Enlisted May, 1915, and crossed over to France at the end of the year. Came home on his only leave, September 1917. Was seriously wounded in the chest on the 19.1.1918 and taken to the No 3 Canadian Casualty Clearing Station at Remy Siding, Belgium. Died of his wounds, 20.1.1918, aged 20 years. Buried in **LIJSSENTHOEK MILITARY CEMETERY, BELGIUM.** Grave location:- Plot 27, Row F, Grave 1. His parents received a letter from the Chaplain to the Forces, conveying the information that their son, after being admitted to hospital, got steadily worse, the end coming very peacefully while he was unconscious. The letter continues, *'I know what this means to you. He did his best to get better and every possible care was given to him but the effect of the wound in his chest rendered all aid futile. The last time I spoke to him that day he seemed cheerful and patient. You have lost a brave and devoted son and even in your grief you will be proud as you remember his faithful loyalty.'* ROH:- Marsden War Memorial; Marsden Liberal Club.

BAMFORTH, HERBERT. Lance Corporal. No 26487. 2nd Battalion South Wales Borderers. Born Marsden. Son of Mr and Mrs Frank Bamforth of Troaves, Marsden. Both parents died when Herbert was in his early teens. Worked as an assistant for Mr Dan Lunn, butcher, Marsden. Left the district and joined the army.

After his military service had expired he found employment as a farm bailiff for a clergyman near Aberystwyth. Re-enlisted in the autumn of 1915. Served under the assumed name of BANKS. Died of wounds at a main dressing station at Louvencourt, 29.6.1916, aged 37 years. Buried in **LOUVENCOURT MILITARY CEMETERY**. Grave location:- Plot 1, Row B, Grave 42.

BAMFORTH, JACK. Private. 2/5th Marine Battalion American Marines. Born Prickleden, Holmfirth. Son of Mr and Mrs Harry Bamforth, 249 West 178th Street, New York, United States of America. Was aged six or seven when the family emigrated to the USA. Before enlistment was in the postcard business with his father. Enlisted 3rd May, 1917. Killed in action 15.6.1918, aged 20 years. Buried **HILLSIDE CEMETERY, COURTLAND MANOR** (on the Hudson River, just north of New York).

BAMFORTH, JAMES. Ordinary Seaman. No J/5880. Royal Navy *HMS Marmion*. Born Slaithwaite. Son of Walker and Mary Hannah Bamforth, 15 Booth Banks, Slaithwaite. Employed as a beamer by Messrs Crowther, Bruce and Company, New Mills, Marsden. Attended the West Slaithwaite Church Sunday School and the Upper Slaithwaite School. Enlisted 19.9.16. Was drowned, aged 20, when *HMS Marmion* (on convoy duty) was in collision with *HMS Tirade* in atrocious weather off the Shetland Isles, 21.10.1917. Commemorated on the **PLYMOUTH NAVAL MEMORIAL TO THE MISSING**. ROH:- St. James Church, Slaithwaite; Slaithwaite War Memorial.

BAMFORTH, JOHN WILLIAM RICHARD. Private. No 6134. 1/4th Battalion Duke of Wellington's Regiment. Born Slaithwaite. Son of William and Alice A. Bamforth, 25 Hill Top, Slaithwaite. Employed as a teamer by Mr Albert Schofield of Slaithwaite. Attended St James' Church and Sunday School. Enlisted May, 1916, and embarked for France early in December, 1916. Was admitted to Etaples Base Hospital suffering from diphtheria where he died ten days later, 23.2.1917, aged 20. Buried in **ETAPLES MILITARY CEMETERY**. Grave location:- Plot 21, Row H, Grave 2A. His parents received a letter from the Sister-in-charge who wrote, '*Your son was very plucky and he was extremely anxious that you should not worry about him.*'

ROH:- St. James Church, Slaithwaite; Slaithwaite War Memorial.

BAMFORTH, NORMAN HANSON. Private. No 31687. 13th Battalion York and Lancaster Regiment. Formerly No 3362 Duke of Wellington's Regiment. Born Barton Road, Crosland Moor, 1.10.1890. Son of Mrs E. Bamforth. Educated at Crosland Moor Council School. Was employed as a pattern weaver at Messrs John Crowther and Sons, Union Mills, Milnsbridge. Married. Living at 273 Blackmoorfoot Road, Crosland Moor. Enlisted 6.11.1914. Embarked for France in April, 1915, and was wounded in November, 1915. Killed in action, 12.4.1918, aged 28 years. Commemorated on the **PLOEGSTEERT MEMORIAL TO THE MISSING**. ROH:- St. Barnabas Church, Crosland Moor; United Methodist Church, Crosland Moor.

BAMFORTH, NORMAN LOCKWOOD. Private. No 242343. 2/6th Battalion West Yorkshire Regiment. Born Primrose Hill 29.11.1885. Son of Mr and Mrs Harry Bamforth, 142 Albert Street, Lockwood. Educated at Mount Pleasant Council School. Was employed as a healder and twister but after war broke out worked as a moulder's labourer for Messrs William Whiteley and Sons, Lockwood. Was a member of the Lockwood Conservative Club bowling team. Enlisted 12.10.1916. Killed at the Battle of Cambrai, 22.11.1917, aged 32 years. Commemorated on the **CAMBRAI MEMORIAL TO THE MISSING**. ROH:- Mount Pleasant Chapel, Lockwood; Emmanuel Church, Lockwood; Memorial in Almondbury Cemetery.

BAMFORTH, RONALD. Private. No 235852. 2/4th Battalion King's Own Yorkshire Light Infantry. Formerly No 268826 Duke of Wellington's Regiment. Born Slaithwaite. Only son of William Henry and Ellen Jane Bamforth, 'Coverdale', Howgate Road, Slaithwaite. Assisted his father in the business of card nailer and emery roller maker. So essential was his work of card nailer to local manufacturers that they secured three month's leave from military duties. Was a teacher at the Slaithwaite Church Sunday School, and a member of the Conservative Club and the tennis club. Embarked for France, 5.3.1918. Killed in action, 6.4.1918, aged 24 years. Buried in **BIENVILLERS MILITARY CEMETERY**.

Grave location:- Plot 13, Row A, Grave 11. ROH:- St. James Church, Slaithwaite; Slaithwaite War Memorial.

BAMFORTH, SAM. Private. No 242022. 2/5th Battalion Duke of Wellington's Regiment. Born Stainland. Son of Mr James Bamforth, Green Top, Marsden. Was employed at Clough Lea Mill, Marsden. Enlisted 1915. Embarked for France January, 1917. Killed in action, 22.7.1918, aged 39. Commemorated on the **SOISSONS MEMORIAL TO THE MISSING.**

BAMFORTH, THOMAS HENRY. Private. No 301971. 9th Battalion The Royal Scots (Lothian Regiment). Born Golcar. Son of Mr and Mrs George Bamforth, 122 Scar Lane, Milnsbridge. Married. Living at 31 Scar Wood Terrace, Milnsbridge. Employed as a weaver by Messrs B. and J. Whitwam and Sons Limited. Was a member of the Milnsbridge Socialist Club. Was in Canada until Christmas, 1915. Enlisted 3.10.1916. Embarked for France, 9.6.1917. Killed in action, 3.8.1917, aged 31 years. Commemorated on the **MENIN GATE MEMORIAL TO THE MISSING.**

BAMFORTH, THOMAS JAMES. Private. No 202497. 5th Battalion King's (Liverpool Regiment). Born Slaithwaite. Younger son of the late Edward and Mary Bamforth, Moorside, Slaithwaite, and was employed by the Slaithwaite Urban District Council. Formerly lived with his married sister, Mrs Swindell, Moorside, Slaithwaite. Moved to Southport in 1909. Single. Attended Pole Moor Baptist Chapel and Sunday School. Brother of Joe Bamforth, Ivy Cottage, Dirker, Marsden. Killed in action, 1.5.1917, aged 41 years. Buried in **CITE BONJEAN MILITARY CEMETERY, ARMENTIERES.** Grave location:- Plot 8, Row B, Grave 5. ROH:- Slaithwaite War Memorial; Pole Moor Baptist Church.

BAMFORTH, TOM SYKES. Corporal. No 533641. 15th (County of London) Battalion (P.W.O. Civil Service Rifles). Born Slaithwaite. Son of M. H. and J. Bamforth of Pasford House, Slaithwaite. Husband of Ellen Bamforth of 'Hillbrae'. 18 Wood Street, Slaithwaite. Killed in action, 23.3.1918, aged 37 years. Buried in **FINS NEW BRITISH CEMETERY.** Grave location:- Plot 8, Row E, Grave 20. ROH:- St. James Church, Slaithwaite; Slaithwaite War Memorial.

BAMFORTH, WALKER. Able Seaman. No J/50849. Royal Navy, *HMS Partridge*. Born Slaithwaite. Stepson of Rose Helena Bamforth, 12 Waterside, Slaithwaite. Employed as a joiner in the spinning department of the Slaithwaite Spinning Company Limited. Attended Slaithwaite Parish Church. Enlisted in the Navy in March 1916. *HMS Partridge*, along with the Pellew and four armed trawlers, were escorting a convoy of one British and five neutral ships on 12.12.1917, which were proceeding to Norway when they were attacked by a German naval force in the North Sea. Reported missing in the North Sea, 12.12.1917, aged 24 years. Commemorated on the **PORTSMOUTH NAVAL MEMORIAL TO THE MISSING.** (Three other men from Huddersfield were drowned when *HMS Partridge* was sunk on 12.12.1917. They were Ordinary Seaman **FRED DRANSFIELD**, Able Seaman **DONALD HAIGH**, and Ordinary Seaman **SHEARD WINDLE** q.v.). ROH:- St. James Church, Slaithwaite; Slaithwaite War Memorial.

BAMFORTH, WILLIE. Private. No 43027. Depot Battalion King's Own Yorkshire Light Infantry. Formerly No 32/6069 Training Reserve Northumberland Fusiliers. Born Marsden, 22.8.1893. Attended Paddock Church of England School. Employed as a labourer at the United Indigo and Chemical Company Limited, Longroyd Bridge. Husband of Rebecca Bamforth, 8 Longroyd Bridge, Huddersfield. Enlisted 26.4.1916. Wounded Ypres August, 1917, and at Rheims, 23.7.1918. Died in Royds Hall War Hospital, Huddersfield, of bronchial-pneumonia, 16.11.1918, aged 25. Buried in **St. BARTHOLOMEW'S CHURCHYARD, MARSDEN.** Grave location:- South, 30, 32. ROH:- All Saints Church, Paddock.

BANBURY, JAMES. Private. No 12557. 8th Battalion Duke of Wellington's Regiment. Born Huddersfield. Son of William and Mary Banbury. Employed as a badge porter by the London and North Western Railway Company. Killed in action at the Dardenelles during the attack on Isamail Oglu Tepe on 21.8.1915, aged 20 years. The Official History of the Gallipoli campaign records that *'the Battalion, with the 9th Battalion West Yorkshire Regiment, were hurried forward to capture the first objective, but they swung left-handed, ending up in a position north of Helman Chair. An attempt was then made to assault a* *communication trench, but this turned out to be a heavily defended fire trench. The enemy's resistance could not be overcome; and the troops fell back towards the southern slopes of Green Hill.' The War Diary records 'high casualties'. Held position under heavy artillery fire until relieved (23rd).* Commemorated on the **HELLES MEMORIAL TO THE MISSING, GALLIPOLI.** ROH:- Lancashire and North Western Railway Company.

BANBURY JAMES E. Private. No 12677. 8th Battalion Duke of Wellington's Regiment. Died of wounds at home, 23.6.1917. Buried in **EDGERTON CEMETERY, HUDDERSFIELD.** Grave location:- 66, 84G.

BANKS, JOHN ROBERT. Private. No 241511. 2/5th Battalion Duke of Wellington's Regiment. Born Sheffield, enlisted Huddersfield. Died as a Prisoner of War in Germany, 12.9.1917. Buried in **HAMBURG CEMETERY, OHLSDORF, GERMANY.** Grave location:- Plot 1, Row E, Grave 2. ROH:- St. Stephen's Church, Rashcliffe.

BARBER, EDGAR. Private. No 4663. 1/5th Battalion Duke of Wellington's Regiment. Son of Mrs Ruth Barber, Flush House, Holmfirth. Was employed as a shoemaker by Mr John Wagstaffe of Holmfirth. Attended Holmbridge Parish Church. Enlisted December 1915. Embarked for France August, 1916. Reported missing, presumed killed, 3.9.1916, Buried in **MILL ROAD CEMETERY.** Grave location:- Plot 1, Row I, Grave 9. ROH:- Holme and Holmbridge; Huddersfield Drill Hall.

BARBER, SAMUEL. Rifleman. No R/15155. 10th Battalion King's Royal Rifle Corps. Born Heckmondwike. Husband of Annie Barber, 3 Hill Terrace, Clough Lane, Paddock. Employed as a core maker by Messrs Whiteleys. Attended Queen Street Mission. Enlisted 23.8.1915 at Chester. Killed in action, 3.9.1916, aged 32 years. Buried in **BERNAFAY WOOD CEMETERY.** Grave location:- Row M, Grave 56. ROH:- St. Stephen's Church, Rashcliffe.

BARBER, WILLIAM. Private. No 32055. 10th Battalion Duke of Wellington's Regiment. Born Widnes. 1.11.1893. Lived 12 Folly Road, Cowcliffe. Married, with one child. Employed as a boiler fireman by Messrs. L B Holliday and Company. Killed in action in Italy, 11.9.1918. Buried in **CAVALLETTO BRITISH CEMETERY, ITALY.** Grave location:- Plot 1, Row F, Grave 2. ROH:- Fartown and Birkby War Memorial.

BARDEN, FRED. Private. No 21961. 8th Battalion King's Own Scottish Borderers. Born Thunderbridge, Kirkburton. Son of Godfrey Barden. Attended the Methodist New Connection, Shelley. Embarked for France February, 1916. Was wounded in the head in June, 1916, and was in hospital for eight weeks. Was killed a few days after he resumed his duties. Killed in action, 10.8.1916, aged 22 years. Has no known grave. Commemorated on the **THIEPVAL MEMORIAL TO THE MISSING.** ROH:- Emmanuel Church, Shelley.

BARDEN, PERCY. Rifleman. No C/7918. 13th Battalion King's Royal Rifle Corps. Born Almondbury. Lived 70 New Road, Salford, Lockwood. Married, with two children. A member of the Milton Church P.S.A. Was employed in the dyehouse at Westfield Cotton Company, Dalton. Reported missing, presumed killed, 10.4.1917, aged 29 years. Has no known grave. Commemorated on the **ARRAS MEMORIAL TO THE MISSING.** ROH:- Emmanuel Church, Lockwood.

BARDSLEY, WILLIAM MATTHEW. Lance Corporal. No 10679. 23rd Battalion Royal Fusiliers. Born Glasgow, 3.12.1884. Son of Joshua and Emma Bardsley. Educated at Rossall Public School. Lived at Cowlersley House, Milnsbridge. Married. Worked as an analytical chemist. Enlisted April 1916. Reported missing in action at Beaumont Hamel, 13.11.1916, aged 31. Buried in **SERRE ROAD CEMETERY NO 2.** Grave location:- Plot 2, Row C, Grave 29. ROH:- St. Barnabas Church, Crosland Moor; Milnsbridge War Memorial.

BARKER, CHARLES VICTOR. Private. No 203571. 2/5th Battalion Duke of Wellingtons' Regiment. Born Seacombe, Cheshire. Enlisted Huddersfield. Lived Kirkheaton. Killed at the Battle of Cambrai, 20.11.1917. Has no known grave. Commemorated on the **CAMBRAI MEMORIAL TO THE MISSING.** ROH:- St. John's Church, Kirkheaton; Huddersfield Drill Hall.

BARKER, FRANK LESLIE. Private. No 21579. No 4 Company, 5th Battalion, 2nd Brigade, 1st Canadian Expeditionary Force. Born South End Farm, South Crosland, 22.6.1893. Son of Hector and Martha Barker, 26 Prince Royd, Birchencliffe. Educated at South Crosland Church School and Spring Grove Council School. Emigrated to Canada. Single. Was working as a cowboy at Moose Jaw when war was declared. Enlisted August 1915. Killed in action 'in a little village near Festubert', 22.5.1915, aged 22. Has no known grave. Commemorated on the **VIMY RIDGE MEMORIAL TO THE MISSING CANADIAN FORCES.** ROH:- South Crosland and Netherton. (Brother of Private **GEORGE BARKER**, q.v.).

BARKER, GEORGE. Private. No 18173. 2nd Battalion (Eastern Ontario) Regiment. Born Sun End Farm, South Crosland, 31.8.1891. Son of Hector and Martha Barker, 26 Prince Royd, Birchencliffe. Educated at South Crosland Church School and Spring Grove Council School. Emigrated to Canada. Single. Enlisted August 1914. Reported missing, presumed killed, between the 22nd and 26th April, 1915, near Hill 60, aged 23. Has no known grave. Commemorated on the **MENIN GATE MEMORIAL TO THE MISSING.** ROH:- South Crosland and Netherton. (Brother to Private **FRANK LESLIE BARKER** q.v.).

BARKER, GEORGE WHITWELL. Private. No 23443. 8th Battalion Duke of Wellington's Regiment. Born Linthwaite. Husband of Mabel Barker, 18 Pogg Hall, Upper Clough, Linthwaite. Employed as a weaver by Messrs George Mallinson and Sons Limited. Was a member of the Linthwaite Cricket Club. Killed in action, 28.8.1917, aged 31 years. Has no known grave. Commemorated on the **TYNE COT MEMORIAL TO THE MISSING.** ROH:- Linthwaite War Memorial.

BARKER, JOHN WILLIAM WRIGHT. Private. No 28452. Royal Army Medical Corps. Born Hall Bower, Huddersfield, 1.7.1887. Husband of Mary Alice Barker, 50 Cowcliffe Hill, Birkby. Was employed as a labourer at Hopkinsons. Enlisted 16.11.1914. Died in Royds Hall War Hospital of Pernicious Anaemia, Influenza and Bronchial Pneumonia, 24.10.1918, aged 31 years. Buried in **ALMONDBURY CEMETERY.** Grave location:- M, 'C', 181. ROH:- St. Hilda's Church, Cowcliffe; Fartown and Birkby War Memorial.

BARKER, LEONARD. Private. No 40757. 2/5th Battalion South Staffordshire Regiment. Formerly No 31516 Duke of Wellington's Regiment. Born Linthwaite. Son of Mr and Mrs Charles Barker, 1 Coldwell Street, Linthwaite. Was employed by Messrs Charles Lockwood and Sons Limited. Was a member of the Linthwaite Liberal Club and a playing member of the Linthwaite Cricket Club. Enlisted 3.4.1917. Went over to France in July, 1917. Died of wounds, 30.11.1917, aged 19. Buried in **ORIVAL WOOD CEMETERY.** Grave location:- Plot 2, Row A, Grave 27. ROH:- Linthwaite War Memorial.

BARKER, SAM OXLEY. Private. No 240744. 2/5th Battalion Duke of Wellington's Regiment. Born Seacombe, Cheshire. Lived Kirkheaton. Adopted son of Miles and Alice Milner of 'Claremont,' Water Royd Lane, Mirfield. Died of wounds, 20.5.1918, aged 32 years. Buried in **BAGNEUX BRITISH CEMETERY.** Grave location:- Plot 2, Row C, Grave 6. ROH:- Huddersfield Drill Hall.

BARLOW, ERNEST. Private. No 3285. 1/5th Battalion Duke of Wellington's Regiment. Lived Thurstonland. Was employed as a farmer's man for Mr James Atkinson of Bottoms, Holmfirth. Engaged to be married. Enlisted in the Holmfirth Territorials at the outbreak of the war. Died of wounds, 10.7.1915. Buried in **FERME-OLIVER CEMETERY, ELVERDINGHE, BELGIUM.** Grave location:- Plot 1, Row J, Grave 5. ROH:- Holme and Holmbridge; Huddersfield Drill Hall; Thurstonland War Memorial.

BARNICOT, JOHN LIVINGSTONE. 2nd Lieutenant. 3rd Battalion Lincolnshire Regiment. Born Shelley 14.12.1897. Son of Richard Ashworth Barnicot and Lucy Gertrude Barnicot, Woodside, Grimscar, Huddersfield. Grandson of Mr John Barnicot of Wood Lea, Shepley and Mr Livingstone Middlemost of Sedgefield. Educated at Clive House School, Colwyn Bay and Marlborough Public School. From the Officers' Training Corps of Marlborough School he obtained a commission in the Lincolnshire Regiment on 12.6.1915. For nine months he was attached to Headquarters Staff at an East coast town but joined his Regiment in France in

September, 1916. Accidentally shot by a British sentry only eight days after his 19th birthday at Vermelles, 22.12.1916. Buried in **VERMELLES BRITISH CEMETERY.** Grave location:- Plot 5, Row F, Grave 33. ROH:- Emmanuel Church, Shelley; Fartown and Birkby War Memorial.

BARRACLOUGH, CHARLES KILNER. Private. No 103293. 204th Company Machine Gun Corps. Formerly No M2/264118 Army Service Corps. Born Upper Denby 18.5.1883. Educated at Upper Denby National School. Employed as traveller by Mr G. H. Inman, Mineral Water Manufacturer. Married. Lived 114 Eldon Road, Marsh. Was on the committee of Marsh Conservative Club and a member of the Manchester Order of Oddfellows. Attended Holy Trinity Church, Huddersfield. Killed in action at the Battle of Passchendaele, 8.10.1917. Has no known grave. Commemorated on the **TYNE COT MEMORIAL TO THE MISSING.** ROH:- Marsh War Memorial; Holy Trinity Church.

BARRACLOUGH, FRANK. Private. No 267713. 2/6th Battalion Duke of Wellington's Regiment. Born Bradford. Enlisted Huddersfield. Died in Royds Hall War Hospital, 28.10.1917, aged 32 years. Buried with full military honours in **EDGERTON CEMETERY, HUDDERSFIELD.** Grave location:- 11B, 125.

BARRACLOUGH, GEORGE W. 2nd Lieutenant. 6th Battalion Duke of Wellington's Regiment. Born Almondbury. Son of Superintendent H. Barraclough of the West Riding Constabulary of Dewsbury, formerly of Huddersfield. Educated at Almondbury Grammar School. Was in the employ of Mr J. E. Crowther at the Bank Bottom Mills. Killed in action at Havrincourt, 29.9.1918, aged 22 years. Buried in **GRAND RAVINE BRITISH CEMETERY, HAVRINCOURT.** Grave location:- Row C, Grave 13.

BARRACLOUGH, HARRY. Private. No 241631. 6th (City of Glasgow) Battalion Highland Light Infantry. Born Almondbury. Son of Emma J. Barraclough, 148 Ashes Lane, Almondbury. Employed as a cellarman at the Huddersfield Railway Station restaurant. Killed in action, 7.7.1918, aged 21 years. Buried in **LA TARGETTE BRITISH CEMETERY.** Grave location:- Plot 4, Row A, Grave 5. ROH:- Almondbury War Memorial.

BARRACLOUGH, IRVIN. Private. No 15210. 10th Battalion Duke of Wellington's Regiment. Born Holmfirth. Son of Mrs Heppinstall, 41 Cliffe, Holmfirth. Educated at Netherthong School. Employed as a millhand at Washpit Mills. Enlisted 18.1.1915. Reported missing, presumed killed, 30.7.1916, aged 22 years. Has no known grave. Commemorated on the **THIEPVAL MEMORIAL TO THE MISSING.** ROH:- Wooldale War Memorial. His mother received a last letter from him dated 27.7.1916, '*You must keep smiling Mother, better days are in store.*' In November, 1916, she received a letter and a small book from a chum of her son, Private **ERNEST A. CROOKES,** who wrote, '*You will no doubt be a bit surprised to have a letter from me but I thought I would write and let you know all I know of Irvin's death. I dare not write before as I was not sure what had happened to him. I made many enquiries in his Company about him and from what I can make out he was one of the many lads who went over the top one night when we were in that terrible fighting and failed to return. But the strange part of it is that I had made enquiries about him the night after we came out and they told me he was wounded. Then we were ordered back into the line again in a bit of a hurry and I happened to be walking in a trench which I had never been in before and what should I pick up but his small book which I enclose. I was dumbstruck when I saw the name and it seems a man in another regiment which we relieved had found his body somewhere in the line and had taken his letters etc. to forward on to you. That was what one of our fellows told me who had seen the letters in the man's possession and I think he must have dropped the book out whilst he was showing these letters to this fellow. It seemed very strange that the book should be there for me to find and after that I made sure Irvin was killed. It was a blow to me and I hope you will accept my deepest sympathy in your sad bereavement. He was the only friend I had who came from up our way and when we saw one another we always used to ask each other if we had anything fresh from home and talk over old times. I have thought since what lucky beggars we were who came through those few weeks we were there as it was too terrible for words. The sights we saw were awful and I don't think words can describe them. I suppose it was God's will that he should go under. I must apologise for not writing sooner but I was in some doubt about him.*'

BARRAS, ALEXANDER EDWARD. Gunner. No 96691. 59th Battery Royal Field Artillery. Born Fountain Yard, Leeds Road, Huddersfield. 24.11.1878. Educated at Spring Grove Council School. Worked as a motor tyre repairer. Attended St. Paul's Church, Southgate. Married, with six children. Lived 22 Bradley Street, Huddersfield. Enlisted 29.8.1914. Killed in action, 15.8.1917, aged 39 at Potijze, one and a half miles north east of Ypres. Has no known grave. Is commemorated on the **MENIN GATE MEMORIAL TO THE MISSING.** ROH:- St. Paul's Church, Southgate, Huddersfield.

BARRETT, HOLDSWORTH. Corporal. No 30847. 94th Company Machine Gun Corps. Formerly No 3/17789 Duke of Wellington's Regiment. Born Netheroyd Hill 16.5.1894. Son of Albert and Elizabeth Barrett, 35 Woodhouse Avenue, Fartown. Educated at Cowcliffe National School and Hillhouse Board School. Served his apprenticeship as a newspaper compositor with the 'Huddersfield Examiner.' Was organist at Netheroyd Hill Congregational Church and a teacher in the Sunday School. Enlisted January 1916. Killed by a shell in the trenches at Oppy Wood near Gavrelle, 19.5.1917, aged 23 years. Has no known grave. Commemorated on the **ARRAS MEMORIAL TO THE MISSING** ROH:- Netheroyd Hill Church; Fartown and Birkby War Memorial.

BARRETT, JOHN PATRICK. Private. No 29587. 8th Battalion Duke of Wellington's Regiment. Born Dock Street 8.6.1898. Son of Thomas and Alice Barrett, 12 Dock Street, Huddersfield. Attended St. Patrick's School. Worked as a tailor's presser. Enlisted 2.10.16. Killed in action at Passchendaele, 28.8.1917, aged 19. Has no known grave. Commemorated on the **TYNE COT MEMORIAL TO THE MISSING.**

BARRETT, LEONARD. Private. No 241939. 1/7th Battalion Duke of Wellington's Regiment. Born Meltham. Son of William and Emily Barrett of Owler Bars, Meltham. Employed by Albion Mills, Meltham. Killed in action, 29.4.1918, aged 25 years. Has no known grave. Commemorated on the **TYNE COT MEMORIAL TO THE MISSING.** ROH:- St. Bartholomew's Church, Meltham; Huddersfield Drill Hall.

BARRITT, NORMAN GOMERSALL. Private. No 41515. 24th (Tyneside Irish) Battalion Northumberland Fusiliers. Formerly No 19941 Duke of Wellington's Regiment. Born 'Paden Aaron', Kirkheaton, 31.5.1893. Son of Joe and Alice Barritt. Educated at Bradley Church School. Before enlistment lived at 'Paden Aaron', Colne Bridge, Bradley. Single. Was in business as a farmer and butcher and in the Sewage Works Department of Huddersfield Corporation. Enlisted 1.4.1916. Was critically injured near Armentieres, 24.10.1916. Taken to the 2nd Australian Casualty Clearing Station where he died on the 25.10.16, aged 23. Buried in **TROIS-ARBRES CEMETERY, STEENWERCK.** Grave location:- Plot 1, Row B, Grave 17. ROH:- St. John's Church, Kirkheaton; St. Thomas's Church, Bradley; Huddersfield Corporation Roll.

BARROWCLOUGH, BENJAMIN. Rifleman. No 81360. 1/8th Battalion West Yorkshire Regiment. Formerly No 52405 Duke of Wellington's Regiment. Born Kirkburton. Husband of Martha Ann Barrowclough of Beckett, Kirkburton. Killed in action, 20.10.1918, aged 27 years. Buried in **BELLE VUE BRITISH CEMETERY, BRIASTRE.** Grave location:- Row A, Grave 4. ROH:- All Hallows Parish Church, Kirkburton.

BARROW, JOHN WILLIAM. Private. No 29591. 8th Battalion Duke of Wellington's Regiment. Born Lepton. Parents living at Spa Bottom, Lepton. Married. Wife living at 33 Ravensknowle Road, Dalton. Attended St Helen's Church, Fenay Bridge. Employed by Mr James Tetlow, painter and decorator, of Aspley. Reported wounded and missing at the Battle of Passchendaele 27.8.17. Has no known grave. Is commemorated on the **TYNE COT MEMORIAL TO THE MISSING.** ROH:- Lepton Parish Church; Christ Church, Moldgreen.

BARROW, SIDNEY. Private. No 38393. 2nd Battalion Lincolnshire Regiment. Born 27.8.1898. Was the only son of Mr and Mrs Jack Barrow, 25 Fisher's Fold, Longroyd Bridge. Educated at St. Thomas's Church of England School, Longroyd Bridge. Was employed as a teamer by Messrs Hall Brothers of Lockwood. Single. Killed in action at Gouzeacourt, south of Cambrai, 29.9.1918, aged 20. Has no known grave. Commemorated on the **VIS-en-ARTOIS MEMORIAL TO THE MISSING.** ROH:- St. Thomas's Church, Longroyd Bridge.

BARROW, STANLEY. Private. No 24640. 9th Battalion Duke of Wellington's Regiment. Lived 47 Armitage Road, Birkby. Employed as a clerk in the Huddersfield Industrial Society's offices. Enlisted October 1916. Died from gunshot wounds to the head at No 46 Stationary Hospital, Etaples, 29.4.1917, aged 35 years. Buried in **ETAPLES MILITARY CEMETERY**. Grave location:- Plot 18, Row C, Grave 4. ROH:- Fartown and Birkby War Memorial.

BARROW, WILLIAM HENRY. Private. No 241751. 2/5th Battalion Duke of Wellington's Regiment. Born Paddock 16.10.1884. Son of George I. Barrow, 21 Branch Street, Paddock. Educated at Paddock Council School. Employed as a plasterer by Mr G. H. Day of Milnsbridge. He was a playing member of the Paddock Cricket Club and a member of Paddock Conservative Club. Enlisted 17.3.1916. Reported missing, presumed killed, at the Battle of Bullecourt on 3.5.1917. Has no known grave. Commemorated on the **ARRAS MEMORIAL TO THE MISSING**. ROH:- All Saints Church, Paddock; Huddersfield Drill Hall.

BARTLEY, THOMAS. Private. No 10879. 2nd Battalion Durham Light Infantry. Born Wavertree, Liverpool. Both parents deceased. Lived with Mr and Mrs George Fretwell, 3 Back Lane, Holmfirth. Employed as a taxi cab driver for Mr Walter Haigh of Holmfirth. Enlisted in the Regular Army in 1910 and had served in India. Died at No 10 Stationary Hospital, St Omer, of wounds received in action, 17.10.1914. Buried in **LONGUENESSE (St. OMER) SOUVENIR CEMETERY**. Grave location:- Plot 1, Row A, Grave 5. ROH:- Holmfirth War Memorial.

BASTOW, HARRY. Gunner. No 741306. 34th Brigade Royal Field Artillery. Born Huddersfield. Died of wounds, 25.9.1918. Buried in **TERLINCTHUN BRITISH CEMETERY**. Grave location:- Plot 5, Row B, Grave 24. ROH:- St. Bartholomew's Church, Meltham.

BATCH, CHARLES WILLIAM. Private. No 30/349. 13th Battalion Northumberland Fusiliers. Born Ramsey, Huntingdon. Educated at Ramsey School. Living at 9 Siggott Street, Longwood, before enlistment. Worked as a teaser. Enlisted 10.5.1916. Missing, presumed killed, at Fontaine-les-Croisilles, near Bullecourt, on 16.6.1917, aged 28, Has no known grave. Commemorated on the **ARRAS MEMORIAL TO THE MISSING**. ROH:- St. Mark's Church, Longwood; Salendine Nook Baptist Chapel.

BATES, ARTHUR. Private. No 41932. 12th Battalion Manchester Regiment. Formerly No 3/31667 North Staffordshire Regiment. Born 1 Brian Street, Lindley 1897. Son of Mrs G. Ellam. Employed by Messrs Joseph Sykes Brothers Limited, Acre Mills, Lindley. Enlisted 13.9.1916. Reported missing, presumed killed, 9.9.1918, aged 21 years. Has no known grave. Commemorated on the **VIS-en-ARTOIS MEMORIAL TO THE MISSING**.

BATES, DONALD. Lance Sergeant. No 241660. 6th Battalion King's Liverpool Regiment. Born Huddersfield. Son of Norris and Ellen Bates of Edgerton Road, South Shore, Blackpool. Reported missing, presumed killed at the Battle of Cambrai, 30.11.1917, aged 25 years. Has no known grave. Commemorated on the **CAMBRAI MEMORIAL TO THE MISSING**. (Brother of Private **NORMAN BATES**, who died of sickness in Mesopotamia, 29.6.17, q.v.) ROH:- Memorial in Salendine Nook Churchyard, 46E.

BATES, ERNEST. See 'HARGREAVES, HOLMES' the true family name.

BATES, FRED. Guardsman. No 21465. 2nd Battalion Coldstream Guards. Born Towngate, Newsome 10.11.1896. Only son of Mrs Ellen Bates of Newsome. Educated at Newsome School. Was in business on his own account as a carrier. Married, with one child. Died of wounds at No 19 Casualty Clearing Station, 19.9.1918. Buried in **SUNKEN ROAD CEMETERY, BOISLEUX-ST-MARC**. Grave location:- Plot 2, Row D, Grave 13. ROH:- St. John's Church, Newsome.

BATES, HAROLD. Private. No 8862. 2nd Battalion Manchester Regiment. Born Halifax. Son of Mr H.B. Bates, 50 May Street, Crosland Moor. Employed by Messrs W. and P. Holroyd, painters and decorators, High Street, Huddersfield. Had served three years with the Colours and had been a reservist for nine years. Called up at the outbreak of the war. Killed in action at Wulverghem, Belgium, 11.1.1915. Buried in **RATION FARM (La PLUS) DOUVE**

ANNEXE, PLOEGSTEERT. Grave location:- Plot 1, Row A, Grave 8. ROH:- St. Barnabas Church, Crosland Moor.

BATES, JAMES ARTHUR. Private. No 31710. 12th Battalion Durham Light Infantry. Born 2 Bottomley's Yard, Upperhead Row, Huddersfield, 12.5.1888. Educated at St. Patrick's School. Employed by Messrs Calvert and Company, Folly Hall as an iron dresser. Lodged with his married sister, Mrs McEvoy, and his brother, George Bates, at 64 Upperhead Row. Enlisted 30.3.1915. Reported missing, presumed killed, on Passchendaele Ridge, 18.5.1917, aged 37 years. Has no known grave. Commemorated on the **MENIN GATE MEMORIAL TO THE MISSING.**

BATES, NORMAN. Private. No 3462. 1/5th Battalion Duke of Wellington's Regiment. Born Newsome 21.9.1892. Son of Ellen Bates, 110 West End, Newsome. Educated at Kirkheaton National School. Employed as a joiner by Messrs Sunderland of Lockwood Scar. Enlisted 13.11.1914. Killed by a sniper, 17.11.1915, aged 23 years. Buried in **TALANA FARM CEMETERY.** Grave location:- Plot 4, Row F, Grave 11. ROH:- Huddersfield Drill Hall; St. John's Church, Newsome. His mother received a letter from his cousin, Private Stanley Dean, also serving in the Duke of Wellington's Regiment, describing the manner of his death, *'He had just received a parcel and was saying 'I have got some fags' when he put his head above the top of the trench and got hit.'*

BATES, NORMAN. Acting Corporal. No A/257233. Army Service Corps.(Canteens). Born Huddersfield. Son of Norris and Ellen Bates, 22 Edgerton Road, North Shore, Blackpool. Died of sickness in Mesopotamia, 29.6.17. Buried in **BASRA WAR CEMETERY.** Grave location:- Plot 4, Row H, Grave 11. (Brother of Private **DONALD BATES**, killed in action, 30.11.1917, q.v.). ROH:- Memorial in Salendine Nook Churchyard.

BATLEY, ARTHUR. Private. No 14478. 12th Battalion West Yorkshire Regiment. Born Holmfirth. Son of Thomas and Annie Batley of Hinchliffe Mill. Educated at Dobb School and attended the Hinchliffe Mill Wesleyan Sunday School, where he was a member of the choir. Worked as a costumier on his own account in Leeds. Enlisted August 1914. Embarked for France August, 1915. Killed in action, 5.4.1917, at the Battle of Arras, aged 23 years. Buried in **FAUBOURG D'AMIENS CEMETERY, ARRAS.** Grave location:- Plot 2, Row O, Grave 27. ROH:- Holme and Holmbridge War Memorial.

BATTEYE, ALBERT. Private. No 48004. 13th Battalion The Royal Inniskilling Fusiliers. Formerly No 38142 West Yorkshire Regiment. Born Hinchliffe Mill. Son of Mr and Mrs J.W. Battye. Educated at St. John's National School. Employed by Mr Arthur Charlesworth. Played football with the Hinchliffe Mill AFC. Attended Hinchiffe Mill Wesleyan Church, being a member of the choir and the bible class. Married, with one daughter. Enlisted 1916. Suffered from a severe attack of trench feet in the summer of 1917. Killed in action 27.8.1918. Buried in **NIEPPE-BOIS (RUE De BOIS) BRITISH CEMETERY, VIEUX-BERQUIN.** Grave location:- Row D, Grave 24. ROH:- Wooldale War Memorial.

BATTY, NORMAN. Private. No G/52504. 2nd Battalion Middlesex Regiment. Formerly No 39018 York and Lancaster Regiment. Born Scissett. Enlisted in Pontefract. Killed in action, 31.7.1917. Has no known grave. Commemorated on the **MENIN GATE MEMORIAL TO THE MISSING.** ROH:- Scissett War Memorial; Clayton West and High Hoyland War Memorial.

BATTYE, ALBERT EDWARD. Private. No 2291. 10th (Prince of Wales' Own Royal) Hussars. Born Dalton 7.2.1889. Son of Tom and Emma Battye, 42 Springwood Street, Milnsbridge. Educated at St Paul's Church School and Spring Grove Council School. Single. Enlisted 10.3.1908 and at the outbreak of war was stationed in South Africa with his regiment. Recalled to England, they left for France on 6.10.1914. Reported missing, presumed killed, 13.5.1915, near Ypres. Has no known grave. Commemorated on the **MENIN GATE MEMORIAL TO THE MISSING.** (Brother of Private **HARRISON BATTYE**, who died at home, 10.12.1920, q.v.).

BATTYE, BOOTH. Private. No 79609. 1/9th Battalion Durham Light Infantry. Son of Edward and Sarah Battye, 33 Green Hill Bank Road, New Mill, Holmfirth. Employed as a weaver by Messrs Graham and Pott Limited, Kirkbridge Mills,

New Mill. Single. Taken prisoner by the Germans, 27.5.1918, and died in Germany as a Prisoner of War,. 29.10.1918, aged 23 years. His sister, Mrs G.W. Edinburgh, received a postcard from him, dated October 20th, 1918, saying that he was a Prisoner of War and not ill or wounded. An appeal for information was made in the Holmfirth Express, on 11.1.1919, as to his whereabouts but it was not until 8.3.1919, after many enquiries had been made, that the War Office informed the family that he had died on 29.10.1918. Buried in **WORMS (HOCHHEIM HILL) CEMETERY, GERMANY.** (The names are carved on a screen wall in the Allied Plot). ROH:- New Mill Working Men's Club; Fulstone War Memorial.

BATTYE, CHARLES ALFRED. Private. No 91514. 1/4th Battalion Northumberland Fusiliers. Formerly No 468694 Labour Company. Born Holmfirth. Son of Mr and Mrs S. Battye of Upperbridge, Holmfirth. Educated at Upperthong National School. Attended St. John's Sunday School and was a member of the Young Men's Institute. Employed by Councillor Luther Firth, of Upperbridge, as a butcher and also by Mr Joseph Stockwell of Victoria Square, Holmfirth. Enlisted May 1917. Died in the VAD Hospital at Hornsea of septic pneumonia at 1.30pm on 8.11.1918, aged 19 years. Buried with full military honours, **ST JOHN'S CHURCHYARD, UPPERTHONG.** Grave location:- 1, north of Church, 18. ROH:- Holmfirth War Memorial.

BATTYE, DAN. Private. No 241696. 2/5th Battalion Duke of Wellington's Regiment. Born Marsden. Lived 9 Sandhurst Cottages, Marsden. Employed as a weaver by Messrs Crowther, Bruce and Company Limited, Marsden. Attended Marsden Wesleyan Church and Sunday School. A member of the Marsden Liberal Club. Enlisted March 1916. Embarked for France January, 1917. Missing, presumed killed, at the Battle of Bullecourt, 3.5.1917, aged 27 years. Has no known grave. Commemorated on the **ARRAS MEMORIAL TO THE MISSING.** ROH:- Marsden Liberal Club; Huddersfield Drill Hall; Marsden War Memorial.

BATTYE, HARRISON. Private. Army Service Corps. (Motor Transport). Born Long Lane, Dalton 16.2.1888. Son of Tom and Emma Battye, 42 Springwood Street, Milnsbridge. Educated at St. Paul's Church School. Employed as a motor driver. Married. Enlisted February 1915. Died at home, 42 Springwood Street, from the effects of gas poisoning, 10.12.1920. Buried **EDGERTON CEMETERY, HUDDERSFIELD.** (Brother of Private **ALBERT EDWARD BATTYE**, killed in action, 13.5.1915, q.v.).

BATTYE, HARRY. Rifleman. No C/7452. 18th Battalion King's Royal Rifle Corps. Born Deanbridge, Holmfirth. Lived 16 Bank Street, Jackson Bridge. Employed by Messrs Vickermans of Thongsbridge. Killed in action at Flers during the Battle of the Somme, on 15.9.1916, aged 19 years. Has no known grave. Commemorated on the **THIEPVAL MEMORIAL TO THE MISSING.** ROH:- New Mill Working Men's Club; Hepworth and Scholes War Memorial.

BATTYE, HERBERT. Rifleman. No C/7662. 3rd Battalion King's Royal Rifle Corps. Born Hinchliffe Mill. Son of George Armitage and Ann Battye, Lower Water Side, Holmbridge. Educated at Dobb Council School. Attended Hinchliffe Mill Wesleyan Sunday School. Employed in the textile trade at Messrs Whiteley and Green's mill, Hinchliffe Mill. Enlisted 17.11.1915. Served in Salonica where he was wounded. In hospital in Malta for several months suffering from malaria. Arrived home at Holmbridge to convalesce on Saturday, 31.5.1918, but died very suddenly, 5.6.1918, aged 24 years. Buried **HOLY TRINITY BURIAL GROUND, HOLMFIRTH.** Grave location:- South East, E, 77. ROH:- Holme and Holmbridge War Memorial.

BATTYE, JOHN. Private. No 19416. 2nd Battalion Duke of Wellington's Regiment. Born Kirkburton. Son of Mr Edgar Battye, Tatt Row, Kirkburton. Enlisted 2.3.1916. Killed in action, 12.10.16, aged 29 years. Has no known grave. Commemorated on the **THIEPVAL MEMORIAL TO THE MISSING.** ROH:- All Hallows Parish Church, Kirkburton.

BATTYE, JOHN WALLACE. Private. No 25430. 13th Battalion East Yorkshire Regiment. Son of Mrs Andrew Battye, 48 Back Lane, Holmfirth. Was employed as a willeyer at Firth Brothers of Shepley. Enlisted 1916. Embarked for France, 5.6.1916. His mother received a message that he had been taken a Prisoner of War on 13.11.1916, but was going on fine. Died of shrapnel wounds to the back as a Prisoner of War at Stettin,

Germany, 1.12.1916, aged 30 years. Buried **BERLIN SOUTH-WESTERN CEMETERY, STAHNSDORF, GERMANY.** Grave location:- Plot 5, Row A, Grave 5. ROH:- Holmfirth War Memorial.

BATTY, JOSEPH. Private. No 241823. 2/5th Battalion Duke of Wellington's Regiment. Born Thurlestone. Son of Mr and Mrs Jonas Batty, Upper House Farm, Hepworth. Was Superintendent at Crow Edge Wesleyan School and a member of the Chapel there. Killed in action at the Battle of Bullecourt, 3.5.1917, aged 41. Has no known grave. Commemorated on the **ARRAS MEMORIAL TO THE MISSING.** ROH:- Hepworth and Scholes War Memorial; Hepworth Parish Church; Huddersfield Drill Hall.

BATTYE, WALTER. Private. No 241773. 2/5th Battalion Duke of Wellington's Regiment. Born Holme. Son of Mr and Mrs George Battye. Educated at Holme Council School. Attended Holme Sunday School. Employed as a weaver at Digley Mills. Enlisted 18.3.1916. Embarked for France, 17.1.1917. Reported missing, presumed killed, at the Battle of Bullecourt, 3.5.1917. Has no known grave. Commemorated on the **ARRAS MEMORIAL TO THE MISSING.** ROH:- Holme and Holmbridge War Memorial; Huddersfield Drill Hall.

BATTYE, WILLIE. Gunner. No 32463. 168th (Holme Valley) Battery Royal Field Artillery. Son of Joseph and Sarah A. Battye of Totties, Thongsbridge; husband of Lizzie Battye of Totties, Thongsbridge. Killed by a piece of shrapnel, 29.6.1916, aged 30. Buried in **BOUZINCOURT COMMUNAL CEMETERY EXTENSION.** Grave location:- Plot 2, Row C, Grave 19. ROH:- Wooldale War Memorial. His widow received the following letter from Sergeant Champion of the same battery, *'As fellow comrades of your dear husband we write to extend our deepest sympathy to you in the loss of such a dear friend. He has now gone but never will his kind actions and deeds be forgotten. He was held in the highest esteem by all, but with the lads of his own section he was like a brother. Always so calm and steadfast in his duties, always willing to extend a helping hand. He was truly a friend to everyone in his battery and his loss is one that will be hard to replace. He worked like a man among men and as such no man was ever more respected. It may be comforting to you our dear friend to know that he passed away with very little pain. He died a brave soldier and to the last possessed a calmness which was always characteristic of him. We wish to extend to you and yours our deepest and sincerest sympathy and hope that you will find a comfort in knowing that he died a noble death whilst doing his duty bravely.'*

BAXTER, ERNEST. Private. No 267440. 1/6th Battalion Duke of Wellington's Regiment. Son of Joseph and Naomi Townend, 71 Coronation Terrace, Handel Street, Golcar. Employed as a mason, firstly by Messrs W. and H. Firth, contractors of Golcar, and then at the erection of Captain L. B. Holliday's new works at Deighton. Was a prominent member of the Golcar Conservative Club and attended St. John's Church, Golcar. Enlisted 1.3.1916. Embarked for France on Whit Wednesday, 1916. Killed by a shell whilst on church parade, 13.5.1917, aged 29 years. Buried in **St. VAAST POST MILITARY CEMETERY, RICHEBOURG L'AVOUE.** Grave location:- Plot 4, Row H, Grave 1. ROH:- St. John's Church, Golcar.

BAXTER, FRED. Private. No 1987. 7th Battalion King's Own Yorkshire Light Infantry. Born Linthwaite. Lived 8 Slantgate, Linthwaite. Employed by Messrs Shaw and Hirst of Crosland Moor. Was a member of the Slaithwaite Brass Band. Died from pleurisy and pneumonia at Etaples Base Hospital, 22.12.1917, aged 32 years. Buried in **ETAPLES MILITARY CEMETERY.** Grave location:- Plot 31, Row D, Grave 1. ROH:- Linthwaite War Memorial.

BAXTER, FRED, MM. Lance Sergeant. No 306015. 1/7th Battalion Duke of Wellington's Regiment. Son of Mr and Mrs William H. Baxter of Linthwaite; husband of Ann Baxter, 10 Spring Buildings, Hoyle House, Linthwaite. Employed as a weaver at Messrs Ben Hall and Company, Milnsbridge. Embarked for France in January, 1917. Was awarded the Military Medal in June, 1917. Killed in action, 11.10.1918, aged 37 years. Buried in **WELLINGTON CEMETERY.** Grave location:- Plot 2, Row C, Grave 4. ROH:- Linthwaite War Memorial; Huddersfield Drill Hall.

BAXTER, FRED. Corporal. No 241360. 2/5th Battalion Duke of Wellington's Regiment. Lived

38 New North Road, Crimble, Slaithwaite. Married. Employed by Messrs John Haigh, oil merchants, Slaithwaite. Enlisted October 1915. Embarked for France January, 1917. Died of wounds to arm and thigh, 7.5.1917, aged 43 years. Buried in **St. SEVER CEMETERY EXTENSION, ROUEN.** Grave location:- Block P, Plot 2, Row J, Grave 12A. ROH:- Huddersfield Drill Hall; St. James Church, Slaithwaite; Slaithwaite War Memorial.

BAXTER, GERALD WILLIAM. 2nd Lieutenant. 10th Battalion Manchester Regiment. Son of Mr W.K. Baxter, solicitor, of Netherton. Educated at Huddersfield College School. Before enlisting was studying economics at Huddersfield Technical College. Was an enthusiastic football and tennis player and a member of the Technical College football club and the Netherton Tennis Club. Enlisted in the Artists' Rifles Cadet Battalion. Commissioned into the Manchester Regiment in April, 1917, and embarked for France in June, 1917. Killed at Passchendaele, 9.10.1917, aged 19 years. Has no known grave. Commemorated on the **TYNE COT MEMORIAL TO THE MISSING.** ROH:- South Crosland and Netherton; Huddersfield College School.

BAXTER, HARTLEY. Private. No DM2/179140. 363rd Motor Transport Company Army Service Corps. Born Linthwaite. Son of Fred and Elizabeth Baxter, Broad Oak, Linthwaite. As a boy was a chorister in the Linthwaite Church choir and, later, a fine bass singer. Enlisted 1916. Was killed whilst driving his motor lorry in France, 17.4.1918, aged 29 years. Buried in **VARENNES MILITARY CEMETERY.** Grave location:- Plot 1, Row M, Grave 25. ROH:- Linthwaite War Memorial.

BAXTER, JOE. Rifleman. No 63774. 8th Battalion West Yorkshire Regiment. Born Linthwaite. Son of George Henry and Sarah Ann Baxter, 124 Radcliffe Road, Crimble, Slaithwaite. Killed in action near Rheims, France, 27.7.1918, aged 18 years. Buried in **COURMAS BRITISH CEMETERY.** Grave location:- Plot 2, Row G, Grave 10. ROH:- Linthwaite War Memorial; St. James Church, Slaithwaite; Slaithwaite War Memorial.

BAXTER, JOHN CARTER. Private. No 201781. 18th Battalion Northumberland Fusiliers.

Husband of Lily Ann Baxter, 42 Spoutfield Terrace, Station Road, Golcar. Severely wounded in the shoulder whilst serving in France in June, 1918. Received treatment at Beech Street Military Hospital, Paddock. Towards the end of October, 1918, he contracted influenza, which developed into pneumonia, and he died on Saturday morning, 16.11.1918, at Beech Street Military Hospital, Paddock, aged 35 years. Buried with full military honours at **St. JOHN'S CHURCHYARD, GOLCAR.** Grave location:- H, south of Church, 9. ROH:- St. John's Church, Golcar.

BAXTER, JOHN WILLIAM. Private. No 5/3274. 1/5th Battalion Duke of Wellington's Regiment. Lived Kirkheaton. Son of Mr and Mrs John Baxter of Upper Heaton, Kirkheaton. Employed as a labourer by the London and North Western Railway Company. Attended Upper Heaton Wesleyan Church. Enlisted in August, 1914, and embarked for France in April, 1915. Died of wounds, 7.9.1916, aged 21 years. Buried in **ACHIET-LE-GRAND COMMUNAL CEMETERY EXTENSION.** Grave location:- Beaumetz-les-Cambrai Communal Cemetery Memorial 1. ROH:- Huddersfield Drill Hall; London and North Western Railway Company Roll.

BAXTER, PERCY. Private. No 52754. 1/4th Battalion Duke of Wellington's Regiment. Son of John Mayband and Lizzie Baxter of Linthwaite; husband of Grace H. Baxter, 70 Sykes Buildings, Crimble, Slaithwaite. Employed in the milling and scouring department at Messrs W. and E. Crowther, Brook Mills, Slaithwaite. Went over to France after the signing of the Armistice. Died in No 42 Casualty Clearing Station from wounds sustained by the bursting of a shell whilst clearing the battlefield, 10.12.1918, aged 32 years. Buried in **DOUAI BRITISH CEMETERY.** Grave location:- Row C, Grave 31, (Served with Private **ALBERT ABBY** q.v.). ROH:- St. James Church, Slaithwaite; Slaithwaite War Memorial.

BEADON, BASIL HERBERT EDWARDS. Captain and Adjutant. 1/7th Battalion Royal Welsh Fusiliers. Born 11th January, 1887, at Longley Hall, Huddersfield. Son of Frederick W. Beadon (the Land Agent in Huddersfield of the Ramsden estate) and Elizabeth Eleanore Beadon. Educated at Almondbury Grammar School, Cheltenham College and

Sedbergh Public School. He was brought up on the Ramsden Estate, then on the Duke of Buccleuch's Rugby estate and, finally, on Lord Hothfield's Skipton property, and then went to Mr Naylor-Leyland's Kerry's Montgomeryshire estate, as sub-agent. He returned to the Ramsden estates, as assistant to his father, in 1912. He had joined the Warwickshire Yeomanry in 1908, and, on leaving the county, passed into the 7th Battalion Royal Welsh Fusiliers, in July 1910, in which he was appointed Lieutenant on 18th July, 1913, and Captain and Adjutant on 21st November, 1914. Was a playing member of the Huddersfield Old Boys' Rugby Union Football Club. Married to Margaret, daughter of Mr Anthony Maynard, of Newton Hall, Durham. One daughter, Joan, born 1st February, 1915. Enlisted 11.8.1914. Killed at the Battle of Suvla Bay, Gallipoli, 1.8.1915, aged 27 years. Had only been in Gallipoli for one day when he was killed. According to a letter received by his father, he was wounded in the morning of the 10th August, 1915, but was able to remain in the fighting line throughout the day. In the evening he had just concluded a consultation with his Colonel and was turning to speak to another officer when he was shot by a sniper and killed instantly. Has no known grave. Commemorated on the **HELLES MEMORIAL TO THE MISSING**. *Following her husband's death Mrs Beadon was granted a gratuity of £250 and an annual pension of £100. Their daughter was given a gratuity of £83 6s 8d and an annual pension of £24. Captain Beadon's will was written by Capel, Cure and Ball, solicitors, 6 Clements Inn, Strand, London, WC, on March 1st, 1915. The Executor was Anthony Charles Hutton Maynard and his estate was valued at £1,042 19s 8d.* ROH:- Huddersfield Parish Church; Christ Church, Woodhouse Hill; Lowerhouses War Memorial; Almondbury Grammar School. Waterloo R.U.F.C. Roll; Almondbury War Memorial; Skipton War Memorial.

BEANLAND, JOEL. Private. No 22979. 8th Battalion York and Lancaster Regiment. Born Liversedge. Son of William and Mary Ellen Beanland; husband of Mary Zilpah Beanland of Scott Hill, Clayton West, Huddersfield. Killed in action, 27.4.1916, aged 34 years. Buried in **ALBERT COMMUNAL CEMETERY EXTENSION**. Grave location:- Plot 1, Row C, Grave 24. ROH:- Clayton West and High Hoyland War Memorial.

BEARDSELL, ALBERT. Private. No 240351. 1/5th Battalion Duke of Wellington's Regiment. Born 5 Garden Street, Lockwood 12.4.1893. Son of the late John and Sophia Beardsell. Educated at Rashcliffe Church School. Lived with his sister, Mrs Emily Mosley, 96 Nursery Terrace, Newsome Road, Huddersfield. Employed as a woollen shrinker by Messrs John Crowther and Sons. Attended St. Matthew's Church, Primrose Hill, and was in the cricket, athletic and football clubs of that church. Enlisted 7.8.1914. Embarked for France April, 1915. Wounded in November, 1915, and returned to France at the end of May, 1916. Reported wounded and missing, 3.9.1916, aged 23. Has no known grave. Commemorated on the **THIEPVAL MEMORIAL TO THE MISSING**. ROH:- St. Matthew's Church, Primrose Hill; St. John's Church, Newsome; Huddersfield Drill Hall.

BEARDSELL, DONALD. Private. No 241842. 12th Battalion Highland Light Infantry. Born Holme, Holmfirth. Son of Mr and Mrs B. Beardsell, Field Head, Holme. Educated at Holme Council School and a scholar at Holme Sunday School. Employed by Messrs Whiteley and Green, Hinchliffe Mill Mills. Enlisted May 1916. Invalided home on account of disease. Treated at various hospitals, including Holmfirth Auxiliary Hospital. Returned to duty in Ireland and Scotland and then returned to France in the Spring of 1918. Died of wounds, 9.8.1918, aged 23 years. Buried in **ARNEKE BRITISH CEMETERY**. Grave location:- Plot 3, Row C, Grave 10. ROH:- Holme and Holmbridge War Memorial; Huddersfield Drill Hall.

BEARDSELL, FREDDIE. Private. No 242045. 1/5th Battalion Duke of Wellington's Regiment. Lived Burnlee, Holmfirth. Son of Mr and Mrs Dennis Beardsell, Burnlee, Holmfirth. Educated at Dobb School and the Wesleyan School at Hinchliffe Mill. Employed as a spinner at Yew Tree Mill, Hinchliffe Mill. Embarked for France May, 1916. Reported missing, presumed killed, in the attack on the Schwaben Redoubt, 3.9.1916. Buried in **MILL ROAD CEMETERY**. Grave location:- Plot 1, Row C, Grave 23. ROH:- Upperthong War Memorial; Huddersfield Drill Hall.

BEARDSALL, HARRY. Drummer. No 101. 1/7th Battalion Duke of Wellington's Regiment. Born Marsden. Son of Mr and Mrs James Beardsell, Oliver Lane, Marsden. Joined the local Territorials, as a bugler, at the age of 14 and served continuously until his death at the age of 22. As a time-expired man, was expecting a month's leave at the end of May, 1916, and had arranged to marry Miss Violet Anne Hansom, daughter of Mr and Mrs Hansom, 21 Gatehead, Marsden, on 11.6.1916. He was greatly disappointed when his leave was cancelled. Killed in action, 4.7.1916, aged 22 years. Has no known grave. Commemorated on the **THIEPVAL MEMORIAL TO THE MISSING.** ROH:- Marsden War Memorial; Huddersfield Drill Hall.

BEARDSELL, NORMAN. Private. No TR5/102016. 52nd T.R. Battalion Northumberland Fusiliers. Born Crosland Moor, 14.11.1899. Son of Arthur and Mary E. Beardsell, 35 Charles Street, Crosland Moor. Educated at Crosland Moor Council School. Employed as a woollen piecer. Enlisted 3.5.1917. Died at home, 35 Charles Street, Crosland Moor, of tuberculosis, 2.5.1919, aged 20. Buried in **LOCKWOOD CEMETERY.** Grave location:- D, 117. ROH:- St. Barnabas Church, Crosland Moor; United Methodist Church, Crosland Moor. (Brother of **PERCY HOWARD BEARDSELL**, died 17.11.1917, q.v.).

BEARDSELL, PERCY HOWARD. Private. No 41590. Northumberland Fusiliers. Born Lockwood, 21.6.1892. Son of Arthur and Mary E. Beardsell, 35 Charles Street, Crosland Moor. Educated at Crosland Moor Council School. Employed as a scourer and miller. Enlisted 7.2.1915. Died at home, 35 Charles Street, Crosland Moor, of dysentery, 17.11.1917, aged 24. Buried in **LOCKWOOD CEMETERY.** Grave location:- D, 117. ROH:- St. Barnabas Church, Crosland Moor; United Methodist Church, Crosland Moor. (Brother of **NORMAN BEARDSELL**, who died 2.5.1919, q.v.).

BEARDSHAW, HARRY. Private. No 45816. 12th/13th Battalion Northumberland Fusiliers. Born Leeds Road, Huddersfield, 26.6.1891. Educated at Beaumont Street Board School. Married. Living at 15 Bradford Road, Huddersfield. Employed as a woollen tenter at Bay Hall Mills. Enlisted 21.6.1916. Killed in action, 21.8.1918, aged 27 years. Buried in **QUEENS CEMETERY BUCQUOY.** Grave location:- Plot 3, Row B, Grave 13.

BEARDSLEY, ISAAC. Private. No 14528. 10th Battalion Duke of Wellington's Regiment. Born Swinton, near Mexborough, Yorkshire. Had lived in Golcar for four years and lodged with Mr Eli Whitwam, 7 Leymoor Road, Golcar. Employed as a weaver by Messrs George Mallinson and Sons, Linthwaite. Attended Golcar Baptist Reading Room and Golcar Parish Church. Enlisted 9.11.1914. Killed in action, 26.10.15, aged 23 years. Has no known grave. Commemorated on the **PLOEGSTEERT MEMORIAL TO THE MISSING.** ROH:- Golcar Baptist Church; Longwood War Memorial. His sister received the following letter from Lieutenant G R C Heale, 10th Battalion Duke of Wellington's Regiment:- *'You will have been informed by the War Office of the sad loss you have sustained in the death of your brother. He died in action and was killed during an exceptionally heavy shellfire raid, two hundred high explosive shells having being sent within fifty yards from where he and others were working. The Royal Engineers Officer who was there spoke in the highest terms of the conduct of the men during that terrible ordeal and your brother was killed when on his way to stand to arms to repel an expected attack. I have always considered him the best man in the platoon and it was always a matter of regret that he would not accept promotion. He was an exemplary soldier and by his good conduct and constant cheerfulness he earned the goodwill and respect of all the Officers, N.C.O's and men of the Company. His loss is a great blow to me, his death must have been absolutely instantaneous and it must be a comfort to you to know that he suffered no pain. Please accept my sincere sympathy and consolation in your terrible loss. I am yours very truly.'*

BEASLEY, GEORGE. Gunner. No L/25396. 'D' Battery, 110th Brigade Royal Field Artillery. Son of Alfred and Mary Beasley of Port Talbot, South Wales. Husband of Eva Beasley, 7 Shore Bank, off Commercial Street, Huddersfield. Employed as a patent glazier. Enlisted April, 1915. Killed in action, 24.3.1918. Has no known grave. Commemorated on the **ARRAS MEMORIAL TO THE MISSING.**

BEAUMONT, ARTHUR. Private. No 1706. 5th Battalion Australian Imperial Force. Born Oldham. Son of Abraham and Christina Beaumont of Rashcliffe, Huddersfield. Employed as a brass finisher by Messrs J Hopkinson of Birkby before emigrating to Australia. Enlisted soon after the outbreak of war and served in Gallipoli, where he contracted Enteric Fever. After making a recovery he was drafted to France. Killed in action, 18.8.1916, aged 21 years. Has no known grave. Commemorated on the **VILLERS-BRETONNEUX MEMORIAL TO THE MISSING**. ROH:- Cowcliffe Wesleyan Church, Huddersfield.

BEAUMONT, ARTHUR. Private. No 240686. 1/5th Battalion Duke of Wellington's Regiment. Born Honley. Son of George and Ada Beaumont, 74 Far Reins, Honley. Died at home, 19.2.1919, aged 27 years. Buried in **HONLEY CHURCH BURIAL GROUND**. Grave location:- 36, 3931. ROH:- Huddersfield Drill Hall; Honley War Memorial.

BEAUMONT, CHARLES. Driver. No 129524. 'C' Battery 102nd Brigade Royal Field Artillery. Born Lindley, 8.8.1895. Son of Mrs Emma Beaumont, 13 Holly Bank Road, Lindley. Educated at Lindley National School. Employed by Messrs Liddle and Brierley, Stanley Mills, Marsh, as a warehouseman. Attended St. Stephen's Church, Lindley, and was a choirboy there for some years. Enlisted 4.3.1915. Killed in action near Ypres, 25.6.1917, aged 31 years. Buried in **DICKIEBUSCH NEW MILITARY CEMETERY EXTENSION**. Grave location:- Plot 3, Row D, Grave 43. ROH:- St. Stephen's Church, Lindley.

BEAUMONT, DYSON. Private. No 46735. 13th Battalion Northumberland Fusiliers. Born Longwood Gate, 7.2.1895. Son of Joe and Betsy Beaumont, 7 Spark Street, Longwood. Educated at Goitfield School. Employed as a clerk by the Longwood Finishing Company. Was a member of the Longwood Wesleyan Choir and the Liberal Club. Enlisted 12.6.1916. Killed in action, 16.6.1917, aged 22 years. Has no known grave. Commemorated on the **ARRAS MEMORIAL TO THE MISSING**. ROH:- Longwood Wesleyan Chapel; St. Mark's Parish Church, Longwood; Longwood War Memorial.

BEAUMONT, EDGAR HAMBY. Private. No 235241. 2nd Battalion Duke of Wellington's Regiment. Son of Mr and Mrs Joe Beaumont of Wilshaw, Meltham. Employed by Messrs Josiah France Limited of Honley. Enlisted October 1915. Killed in action, 28.3.1918, aged 22 years. Has no known grave. Commemorated on the **ARRAS MEMORIAL TO THE MISSING**. ROH:- St. Bartholomew's Church, Meltham; Wilshaw Church, Meltham.

BEAUMONT, EDWIN. Private. No 203577. 1/4th Battalion Duke of Wellington's Regiment. Born Taylor Hill 14.2.1891. Son of Mr and Mrs Benson Beaumont, 57 Newsome Road, Berry Brow. Educated at Berry Brow Council School. Employed as a scourer by Messrs Vickerman and Sons, Limited, Taylor Hill. Single. Enlisted 1.7.1916. Killed in action at Erquinghem, near Armentieres, 10.4.1918, aged 27 years. Has no known grave. Commemorated on the **TYNE COT MEMORIAL TO THE MISSING**. ROH:- Armitage Bridge War Memorial.

BEAUMONT, ERIC GORDON. Sergeant. No 15225. 8th Battalion Duke of Wellington's Regiment. Son of Albert and Emily Beaumont, Richmond House, 2 Richmond Avenue, Fartown. Employed as a commercial traveller by Messrs William Preston and Company, woollen merchants, Station Street, Huddersfield. Enlisted August 1914. Killed in action at the Dardenelles, 21.8.1915, aged 21 years. Has no known grave. Commemorated on the **HELLES MEMORIAL TO THE MISSING, GALLIPOLI**. ROH:- Christ Church, Woodhouse Hill; Fartown and Birkby War Memorial; commemorated on headstone in Kirkheaton Cemetery.

BEAUMONT, FREDERICK WILLIAM. Private. No 30200. 26th Battalion (Tyneside Irish) Northumberland Fusiliers. Son of Chadwick and Mary Emma Beaumont, 35 Wood Street, Longwood. Attended Crow Lane Board School, Milnsbridge. Employed by the Hillhouse Cooperative Stores and had also worked at the Longwood, Paddock and Golcar branches. Attended Salendine Nook Baptist Church and Sunday School. Was a member of the Milnsbridge Liberal Club. Enlisted April 1916. Mentioned in despatches. Had served in France for seven months when he was wounded and died at Wimereux, 27.10.1917, aged 25 years. Buried in **WIMEREUX COMMUNAL CEMETERY.** Grave location:- Plot 6, Row E, Grave 31A. ROH:- Salendine Nook Baptist Church and a memorial in the churchyard, 509E; St. Mark's Parish Church, Longwood; Crow Lane Board School, Milnsbridge.

BEAUMONT, GEORGE HENRY. Private. No 268685. 2nd Battalion West Yorkshire Regiment. Married. At the time of enlistment lived at 175 Halifax Road, Birchencliffe. Worked as a dyer's labourer. Enlisted 16.10.1916. Reported missing, presumed killed, 16.1.1918. Has no known grave. Commemorated on the **TYNE COT MEMORIAL TO THE MISSING.** ROH:- St. Philip's Church, Birchencliffe.

BEAUMONT, GEORGE WILLIAM. Private. No 3067. 1/5th Battalion Duke of Wellington's Regiment. Born Holmfirth. Son of Hirst and Harriet Ann Beaumont, 3 Hightown, Holmfirth. Employed by Messrs A. Thornton and Sons, Limited, Honley, in the finishing room. Enlisted August 1914. Embarked for France April, 1915. Reported missing, presumed killed, on 3.9.1916, aged 23. Buried in **MILL ROAD CEMETERY.** Grave location:- Plot 9, Row D, Grave 1. ROH:- Holmfirth War Memorial; Huddersfield Drill Hall. After various enquiries had been made in official and other quarters, his parents received the following letter from Lieutenant Brown, in February 1917, *'I regret to inform you that nothing has been heard of him since September 3rd, 1916. I think it is almost certain that he has not passed through any of our hospitals or you would have heard before this. I am afraid your only hope of his being alive is that he may be a prisoner and possibly wounded. I trust you will get definite news of him. please accept my heartfelt sympathy with you in your trouble.'* (Brother of Private **HARRY BEAUMONT,** died of pneumonia, 27.5.1915, q.v.).

BEAUMONT, HAROLD. Private. No 72500. 23rd Battalion Machine Gun Corps. Formerly No 9517 West Yorkshire Regiment. Born Holmfirth. Son of John and Harriet Beaumont of Holmfirth. Died of wounds, 23.11.1917, aged 30 years. Buried in **NINE ELMS BRITISH CEMETERY, POPERINGHE, BELGIUM.** Grave location:- Plot 9, Row F, Grave 10.

BEAUMONT, HAROLD. Private. No 12979. 1st Battalion King's Own Royal Lancaster Regiment. Born Sowood. Son of Willie and Sarah Elizabeth Beaumont of Longwood. Killed in action, 2.11.1918, aged 21 years. Buried in **PRESEAU COMMUNAL CEMETERY EXTENSION.** Grave location:- Row B, Grave 9.

BEAUMONT, HARRY. Rifleman. No R/ 19757. 20th Battalion King's Royal Rifle Corps. Son of Brook and Ellen Beaumont of Choppards Buildings, Holmfirth. Employed in the finishing department of Messrs J. Watkinson and Sons Limited, Washpit Mills. Attended Hade Edge Wesleyan Church, being Superintendent of the Sunday School and a member of the choir. Enlisted 26.1.1916. Wounded, 9.9.1916, and came back to England, receiving treatment in Lancashire. Returned to France after three month's treatment. Killed in action, 12.3.1917, aged 22 years. Buried in **FAUBOURG D'AMIENS CEMETERY, ARRAS.** Grave location:- Plot 2, Row F, Grave 25. ROH:- Hade Edge War Memorial.

BEAUMONT, HARRY. Private. No 21/726. 2/5th Battalion West Yorkshire Regiment. Born Meltham. Enlisted Huddersfield. Killed in action, 20.7.1918, near Rheims. Has no known grave. Commemorated on the **SOISSONS MEMORIAL TO THE MISSING.** ROH:- St. Bartholomew's Church, Meltham.

BEAUMONT, HARRY. Private. No 3552. 2/5th Battalion Duke of Wellington's Regiment. Born Holmfirth. Son of Hirst and Harriet Beaumont, New Fold, Holmfirth. Employed as a plasterer's labourer by Mr John Haigh. Enlisted December 1914. Died of pneumonia at Thoresby Camp, Ollerton, Nottinghamshire, 27.5.1915, aged 25 years. Buried with full military honours in **St. JOHN'S CHURCHYARD, UPPERTHONG.** Grave location:- B, north of Church, B, 27. (Brother of Private **GEORGE WILLIAM BEAUMONT,** killed in action, 3.9.1916, q.v.). ROH:- Holmfirth War Memorial; Huddersfield Drill Hall.

BEAUMONT, HARRY. Private. No 200727. 1/5th Battalion Durham Light Infantry. Formerly No 33016 Northumberland Fusiliers. Born Matlock Place, 11.11.1892. Son of Thomas Beaumont, 43 Park Road West, Crosland Moor.

Educated at Crosland Moor Church School. Employed as a weaver. Enlisted 24.4.1916. Killed in action, 24.3.1918. Has no known grave. Commemorated on the **POZIERES MEMORIAL TO THE MISSING.** ROH:- St. Barnabas Church, Crosland Moor; United Methodist Church, Crosland Moor; 'Rising Sun' Public House, Crosland Hill.

BEAUMONT, HENRY. Private. No 17793. 2nd Battalion Duke of Wellington's Regiment. Born South Crosland. Son of Mr J.H. Beaumont of Big Valley, Berry Brow. Employed by Messrs Jordan and Munro, The Kirkgate Press, Huddersfield. Attended Armitage Bridge Church and was a member of the choir. Reported wounded and missing, 12.10.1916, aged 21 years. Has no known grave. Commemorated on the **THIEPVAL MEMORIAL TO THE MISSING.** ROH:- Armitage Bridge War Memorial.

BEAUMONT, HENRY. Private. No 27655. 92nd Company Machine Gun Corps. Formerly No 17792 Duke of Wellington's Regiment. Born Somerset Yard, Moldgreen, 13.7.1895. Son of Joseph and Louisa Beaumont, 19 Violet Street, Turnbridge. Educated at Huddersfield Parish Church School. Employed as a dyer by Mr Arthur Dyson of Aspley Mills. Attended the Rock Mission and was a member of Turnbridge Working Mens' Club. Enlisted 20.1.1916. Killed in action, 17.5.1917, near Arras. Buried in **BAILLEUL ROAD EAST CEMETERY.** Grave location:- Plot 1, Row J, Grave 13. ROH:- Turnbridge War Memorial.

BEAUMONT, HENRY. Private. No 3/3463. 1st Battalion King's Own Yorkshire Light Infantry. Born 23 Manchester Street, Huddersfield, 8.9.1886. Son of William and Gerthina Beaumont. Educated at Spring Grove Council School. Employed as a teamer by Messrs C. and J. Hirst of Longwood. Married. Lived 8 Parkin's Yard, Salford, Lockwood. Enlisted 1.1.1915. Reported missing, presumed killed, 8.5.1915, aged 29 years. Has no known grave. Commemorated on the **MENIN GATE MEMORIAL TO THE MISSING.** ROH:- Emmanuel Church, Lockwood.

BEAUMONT, HENRY. Private. No 35693. 2nd Battalion King's Own Yorkshire Light Infantry. Born Huddersfield. Married. Lived 72 Armitage Street, Primrose Hill. Was in business as a window cleaner and a member of the Primrose Hill Cricket Club before enlisting. Died of wounds, 6.7.1917, aged 26 years. Buried in **COXYDE MILITARY CEMETERY.** Grave location:- Plot 1, Row C, Grave 32.

BEAUMONT, HERBERT. Private. No 5536. 1/5th Battalion Duke of Wellington's Regiment, attached 2/10th Battalion King's Own Yorkshire Light Infantry. Born Hepworth. Son of Hannah Wibberley and stepson of George Wibberley of Greengate, Holmbridge. Employed as a weaver at Clarence Mills, Holmbridge. Was a playing member of the Holmbridge Football Club. Enlisted March 1916. Embarked for France in July, 1916. Wounded on 27.9.1916 and lay out in No Man's Land for two days before he was found. Died of gunshot wounds to the chest, 10.10.1916, aged 21 years. Buried in **ABBEVILLE COMMUNAL CEMETERY EXTENSION.** Grave location:- Plot 1, Row H, Grave 11. ROH:- Holme and Holmbridge War Memorial; Hade Edge War Memorial; Huddersfield Drill Hall.

BEAUMONT, HERBERT. Private. No 53411. 2/9th Battalion The King's (Liverpool) Regiment. Born Snow Lea, Longwood, 16.3.1892. Son of Arthur and Emma Beaumont, Rose Bank, New Hey Road, Longwood. Educated at Goitfield Council School, Longwood. Employed by Messrs J. Hopkinson and Company Limited, Birkby, as a brass finisher. Enlisted 3.2.1917. Gassed in Gommecourt Wood and died at the Base Hospital at Rouen of the effects of gas, 16.5.1918, aged 20 years. Buried in **St. SEVER CEMETERY EXTENSION, ROUEN.** Grave location:- Block P, Plot P, Row 11. Grave 2B. ROH:- Longwood Wesleyan Chapel; Longwood War Memorial.

BEAUMONT, HERBERT. Private. No 400317. 1/5th Battalion Manchester Regiment. Formerly No 4929 Lancashire Fusiliers. Born Moorfield Farm, Crosland Moor, 14.6.1889. Son of Thomas Albert and Sarah Jane Beaumont, 21 Hawthorne Terrace, Crosland Moor. Educated at Crosland Moor Board School and Higher Grade School, Huddersfield. Married. At the time of enlistment was working as a tailor in Manchester and living at 20 Wardley Street, Walkden, near Manchester. Enlisted 29.6.1916. Killed in action in Havrincourt Wood, near Cambrai, 27.9.1918, aged 29 years. Buried in **RIBECOURT ROAD CEMETERY.** Grave location:- Plot 4, Plot B, Grave 10. ROH:- Crosland Moor Wesleyan Church; St. Barnabas Church, Crosland Moor.

BEAUMONT, HUBERT HAVELOCK. Private. No 40795. 23rd Battalion (Tyneside Scottish) Northumberland Fusiliers. Son of James and Mary Alice Beaumont, 145 Shamrock House, Manchester Road, Milnsbridge. Was apprenticed to Mr Timothy Wood, Mill Furnisher, Queen Street, Huddersfield, but later worked for Mr F. H. Hampshire of Holmfirth. Attended Milnsbridge Baptist Chapel, was a member of the Holmfirth Liberal Club and formerly a member of Milnsbridge Liberal Club. Enlisted 29.2.1916. Embarked for France in July, 1916. Killed in action, 24.10.1917, aged 25 years. Buried in **POELCAPELLE BRITISH CEMETERY.** Grave location:- Plot 42, Row E, Grave 12. ROH:- Milnsbridge War Memorial; commemorated in Salendine Nook Baptist churchyard, 139E.

BEAUMONT, JAMES HUTCHINGS. Lieutenant. 2/7th Battalion Duke of Wellington's Regiment. Son of John and Bertha E. Beaumont, Dogley Villa, Kirkburton. Educated at Almondbury Grammar School. Employed by Messrs Marriott and Moss of Halifax. Commissioned in February, 1915. Died of wounds at Boulogne Base Hospital, 24.6.1917, aged 22 years. Buried in **BOULOGNE EASTERN CEMETERY.** Grave location:- Plot 7, Row B, Grave 24. ROH:- Almondbury Grammar School; All Hallows Church, Kirkburton; commemorated on headstone in Kirkburton Cemetery.

BEAUMONT, JOHN ARTHUR. Private. No 5966. 19th (County of London) Battalion (St. Pancras). Formerly No C/7244 King's Royal Rifle Corps. Born Birchencliffe, 22.4.1895. Son of Joshua and Mary A. Beaumont (stepmother), Bridgefield House, 145 Leeds Road, Huddersfield. Educated at Huddersfield Parish Church School and Lindley National School. Employed as a cloth finisher at Messrs John Lee Walker of Deighton. Enlisted 14.10.1915. Killed in action, 15.9.1916, on the Somme, aged 21 years. Has no known grave. Commemorated on the **THIEPVAL MEMORIAL TO THE MISSING.** ROH:- St. Andrew's Church, Leeds Road, Huddersfield.

BEAUMONT, JOHN VICTOR. Private. No 62496. 5th Battalion King's Own Yorkshire Light Infantry. Formerly No 93787 8th T.R. Battalion. Born Meltham. Son of Wilson and Hannah Beaumont of Green Hey, Meltham. Killed in action, 2.9.1918, aged 18 years. Buried in **VAULX HILL CEMETERY.** Grave location:- Plot 2, Row F, Grave 27. ROH:- St. Bartholomew's Church, Meltham.

BEAUMONT, LAWRENCE. Private. No 24367. 4th Battalion North Staffordshire Regiment. Formerly No 3/20577 Duke of Wellington's Regiment. Born Lindley. Son of Hiram and Ellen Beaumont of Huddersfield. Lived 129 Scar Lane, Milnsbridge. Killed in action, 23.10.1918. Buried in **STACEGHEM COMMUNAL CEMETERY, HARLEBEKE.** Grave location:- Row A, Grave 8. ROH:- Longwood War Memorial.

BEAUMONT, LEWIS. Private. No 242023. 2/5th Battalion Duke of Wellington's Regiment. Son of Tom and Annie Beaumont, 6 Upper Hagg, Thongsbridge. Employed at Rock Mills Dyehouse and was a member of the Brockholes Church Young Men's Class. Killed in action at the Battle of Bullecourt, 3.5.1917, aged 22 years. Has no known grave. Commemorated on the **ARRAS MEMORIAL TO THE MISSING.** ROH:- Netherthong and Thongsbridge War Memorial; Huddersfield Drill Hall; Brockholes War Memorial.

BEAUMONT, LLOYD. Corporal. No 11846. 8th Battalion The Yorkshire Regiment. Born Birkby, Huddersfield. Son of Wright and Lucy Beaumont, 35 Ruthven View, Leeds. Died of wounds, 10.1.1917, aged 24 years. Buried in **WIMEREUX COMMUNAL CEMETERY.** Grave location:- Plot 2, Row C, Grave 3. ROH:- Fartown and Birkby War Memorial.

BEAUMONT, STANLEY. Private. No 40197. 9th Battalion Duke of Wellington's Regiment. Born Paddock, Huddersfield. At the time of enlistment was living at Battyeford near Mirfield where he worked as a miner at the King's Head Pit. Volunteered to serve early in the war but was not then allowed to leave his work. Killed in action, 4.11.1918, aged 20 years. Buried **ROMERIES COMMUNAL CEMETERY EXTENSION.** Grave location:- Plot 7, Row B, Grave 4.

BEAUMONT, STANLEY. Signaller. No 241434. 1/5th Battalion Duke of Wellington's Regiment. Born Oakes. Son of Mr and Mrs Lockwood Beaumont, 7 Arnold Terrace, Reinwood Road, Lindley. Educated at Oakes Council School and the Higher Grade School, Huddersfield. Employed as a warehouseman by Messrs Bairstow, Sons and Company Limited. Attended the Lindley Zion Methodist Church and was a member of the Paddock Institute. Enlisted 8.2.1916. Killed in action at Passchendaele, 7.10.1917, aged 24 years. Has no known grave. Commemorated on the **TYNE COT MEMORIAL TO THE MISSING.** ROH:- Lindley Zion Methodist Church; St. Stephen's Church, Lindley; Huddersfield Drill Hall; commemorated in Salendine Nook Baptist Chapel yard D188.

BEAUMONT, TOM. Private. No 29159. 5th Battalion The Yorkshire Regiment. Born Honley, Son of Mr and Mrs John Beaumont, 58 George Street, Milnsbridge. Employed as a finisher by Messrs Titus Calverley and Sons Limited, Milnsbridge. Was a member of Milnsbridge Socialist Club. Enlisted 28.3.1916. Embarked for France, 17.7.1916. Wounded in action and was in hospital for five months. Returned to France, 5.3.1917. Reported missing, presumed killed, at the Battle of Arras, 23.4.1917, aged 24 years. Has no known grave. Commemorated on the **ARRAS MEMORIAL TO THE MISSING.** ROH:- Milnsbridge War Memorial.

BEAUMONT, TOM. Private. No 41068. 2nd Battalion West Yorkshire Regiment. Born Outlane Moor. Son of James Wilton and Elizabeth Ellen Beaumont, 22 Grove Street, Hill Top, Slaithwaite. Attended Pole Moor Baptist Chapel. Employed as a weaver by the Colne Valley Tweed Company. Was a member of the Upper Slaithwaite Bandroom. Enlisted in the Northumberland Fusiliers, 5.6.1916, and was with them until 4.10.1916, when he was transferred to the West Yorkshire Regiment. Killed in action, 7.3.1917, aged 28 years. Has no known grave. Commemorated on the **THIEPVAL MEMORIAL TO THE MISSING.** ROH:- Clough Head Methodist Church; St. James Church, Slaithwaite; Slaithwaite War Memorial; Pole Moor Baptist Church.

BEAUMONT, WILLIAM. Private. No 16029. 8th Battalion Duke of Wellington's Regiment. Son of Oliver and Mary Jane Beaumont of Oldfield's Square, Lockwood Road, Huddersfield. Married. Lived Junction Street, Coventry. Killed in action, 14.6.1917, aged 33 years. Buried in **R.E. FARM CEMETERY, WYTSCHAETE.** Grave location:- Plot 2, Row C, Grave 5.

BEAUMONT, WILLIAM. Private. No 44999. 2nd Battalion York and Lancaster Regiment. Born Almondbury. Married. Lived 2 Back Wood Terrace, Primrose Hill. Employed by Messrs J. and E. Morton., Milnsbridge. Reported missing, presumed killed, 21.3.1918, aged 24 years. Has no known grave. Commemorated on the **ARRAS MEMORIAL TO THE MISSING.** ROH:- Almondbury War Memorial; Fartown and Birkby War Memorial.

BEAUMONT, WILLIAM EDWARD. Private. No 98452. 55th Company Machine Gun Corps. Born Hawthorn Terrace, Crosland Moor, 5.6.1894. Son of Mrs Clara Helena Beaumont, 35 Barton Road, Crosland Moor. Educated at Crosland Moor Board School. Attended Crosland Moor United Methodist Church and Sunday School. Employed as a grocer's assistant. Enlisted 15.1.1917. Killed in action, 10.10.1917, aged 23 years. Buried in **BARD COTTAGE CEMETERY.** Grave location:- Plot 5, Row A, Grave 21. ROH:- St. Barnabas Church, Crosland Moor; United Methodist Church, Crosland Moor.

BEAUMONT, WILLIAM HENRY. Private. No 291781. 1/7th Battalion Northumberland Fusiliers. Lived with his sister, Mrs Fawcett at 23 Wakefield Road, Moldgreen. Employed by Mr Wortley, hay and straw merchant. Enlisted 1915. Reported missing, presumed killed, 26.10.1917, aged 38 years. Buried in **CEMENT HOUSE CEMETERY, LANGEMARCK, BELGIUM.** Grave location:- Plot 14, Row D, Grave 12.

BECKETT, ALFRED. Private. No 42120. 2/6th Battalion South Staffordshire Regiment. Born Stocksbridge, Yorkshire. Son of Mrs Annie Elizabeth Firth (formerly Beckett), of Yew Tree, Holmfirth. Attended Holmbridge Parish Church and was a member of the choir. Enlisted 1917. Reported missing, presumed killed, 21.3.1918, aged 19 years. Has no known grave. Commemorated on the **ARRAS MEMORIAL TO**

THE MISSING. ROH:- Holme and Holmbridge War Memorial.

BECKWITH, WILLIE. Private. No 30/393. 12th/13th Battalion Northumberland Fusiliers. Born Southwark, London. Son of John and Sarah Beckwith, 6 Bankgate, Slaithwaite. Employed as a butcher by the Huddersfield Cooperative Society. Attended the Carr Lane Methodist Church, Slaithwaite. Engaged to Constance of the Albion Hotel, Buxton Road. Enlisted May 1916. Embarked for France August, 1916. Wounded in the right leg by a bullet on 28.5.1918 and died in the No 6 Canadian Hospital at Troyes on 11.6.1918, aged 24 years. Buried in **PERREUSE CHATEAU FRANCO BRITISH NATIONAL CEMETERY.** Grave location:- Plot 1, Row A, Grave 48. ROH:- Carr Lane Methodist Church; St. James Church, Slaithwaite; Slaithwaite War Memorial.

BEDFORD, GEORGE. Private. No 24641. 9th Battalion Duke of Wellington's Regiment. Lived Kirkheaton. Son of Jane Etchell (formerly Bedford) of Fields Place, Kirkheaton. Reported missing, presumed killed, 25.4.1917, aged 19 years. Has no known grave. Commemorated on the **ARRAS MEMORIAL TO THE MISSING.** ROH:- St. John's Church, Kirkheaton.

BEDFORD, JOHN EDWARD. Private. No 5285. 2/5th Battalion Duke of Wellington's Regiment. Born Jubilee Lane, Linthwaite, 28.1.1897. Son of Robert Bedford. Educated at Crosland Moor Council School. Employed as a greengrocer. At the time of enlistment was living at 8 Stoney Battery, Crosland Moor. Enlisted 25.2.1916. Killed in action, 28.2.1917. Has no known grave. Commemorated on the **THIEPVAL MEMORIAL TO THE MISSING.** ROH:- 'Rising Sun' Public House, Crosland Moor; St. Thomas's Church, Longroyd Bridge; Huddersfield Drill Hall.

BEECROFT, ALBERT HENRY. Corporal. No 31312. 18th Battalion Manchester Regiment. Born Marsh 5.3.1881. Educated at Holy Trinity Church Schools. At the time of enlistment was living at 16 Buckingham Street, Moss Side, Manchester. Employed as a commercial traveller. Enlisted May 1915. Killed in action at Guillemont, 30.7.1916. Has no known grave. Commemorated on the **THIEPVAL MEMORIAL TO THE MISSING.**

BEEDLES, ROBERT. Private. No 7454. 6th Battalion King's Shropshire Light Infantry. Born Montgomery, Wales, 21.9.1884. Son of Mr R. Beedles of Frolic Street, Newtown, Montgomery, Wales. Educated at Newtown Council School, Montgomery. Married. Employed as a woollen fettler. At the time of enlistment, on 14.9.1914, was living at 61 Gledhill's Yard, Moldgreen. Died of pneumonia in Etaples Base Hospital, 23.4.1918, aged 34 years. Buried in **ETAPLES MILITARY CEMETERY.** Grave location:- Plot 32, Row B, Grave 6A.

BEEVER, GEORGE HENRY. Sergeant. No 16748. 12th Company Machine Gun Corps. Formerly No 14187 Duke of Wellington's Regiment. Born Cumberworth. Married Miss Hanwell of Lower Hagg, Holmfirth, at Holmfirth Parish Church in 1913. Lived Lane Head, Shepley. Employed at Messrs Hampson's Quarries. Played football with the Shepley, Hepworth and Cumberworth teams. Killed in action on the first day of the Battle of the Somme, 1.7.1916, aged 25 years. Has no known grave. Commemorated on the **THIEPVAL MEMORIAL TO THE MISSING.** ROH:- Shepley War Memorial.

BEEVER, GLADSTONE. Private. No 24050. 2nd Battalion York and Lancaster Regiment. Born Denby. Employed by Messrs Z. Hinchliffe and Sons Limited, Denby Dale. Embarked for France in June, 1916. Killed in action, 15.9.1916. Has no known grave. Commemorated on the **THIEPVAL MEMORIAL TO THE MISSING.** ROH:- Denby Dale and Cumberworth War Memorial.

BEEVER, HARRY. Private. No 45290. 13th Battalion York and Lancaster Regiment. Formerly No 59384 West Yorkshire Regiment. Born Holmfirth. Son of John and Elizabeth Beever of Burnlee, Holmfirth. Educated at Park Head Day and Sunday Schools. Employed by Messrs W. H. and J. Barber, Clarence Mills, Holmbridge. Enlisted 1.9.1917. Trained at Catterick and later at Whitley Bay, leaving there on 30.3.1918. Arrived in France, 1.4.1918. Reported missing, 12.4.1918, aged 18 years. Buried in **LE GRAND BEAUMART BRITISH CEMETERY, STEENWERCK.** Grave location:- Plot 2, Row G, Grave 9. ROH:- Upperthong War Memorial.

BEEVER, JOHN. Wireless Officer. Mercantile Marine. *SS Connemara*. Born Huddersfield

15.7.1894. Son of John and Emily M Beever, Woodland Mount, Bradford Road, Huddersfield. (His father was a uniform maker and hearth-rug manufacturer at Brook Street Mills.) Educated at Fartown Grammar School and Huddersfield Technical College where he studied woollen design. But his great love was the study of wireless apparatus and he erected a large wireless plant at his home. At the outbreak of war he attempted to enlist in both the Army and Navy but was rejected on numerous occasions as he was medically unfit. Twice offered a commission in the Royal Naval Air Service but again was rejected on medical grounds. Ultimately he succeeded in joining the L. and L.W. Passenger boat service as a wireless operator, 4.2.1915. Died at post on duty after sending out an SOS. on *SS Connemara* after she was sunk in a collision off the Irish Coast. Drowned 3.11.1916. Buried in **EDGERTON CEMETERY, HUDDERSFIELD.** ROH:- Christ Church, Woodhouse Hill; Fartown and Birkby War Memorial.

BEEVERS, FRANK. Private. No 42618. 8th Battalion The Yorkshire Regiment. Born 16 Great Northern Street, Huddersfield in December 1886. Educated at Beaumont Street Council School. Was a partner in the firm of Messrs A. Beevers and Sons, painters and decorators. Enlisted 15.5.1916. Reported missing, presumed killed, 7.10.1917, aged 31 years. Has no known grave. Commemorated on the **TYNE COT MEMORIAL TO THE MISSING.** ROH:- Huddersfield Parish Church; St. Andrew's Church, Leeds Road, Huddersfield.

BEIGHTON, GEOFFREY. Private. No 36984. 4th Battalion North Staffordshire Regiment. Born Longwood Road, 8.12.1898. Son of Mr and Mrs William Beighton, 10 Royds Hall, Paddock. Educated at Paddock Council School and Paddock Wesleyan Sunday School. Employed by Messrs Sam Hirst and Sons, Bridge Croft Mills as a cloth finisher. Was a member of Longwood Harriers and the Huddersfield Swimming Club. Enlisted 1.3.1917. Died of wounds on the way to hospital, 29.11.1917, aged 19 years. Buried in **MINTY FARM CEMETERY, St. JAN, BELGIUM.** Grave location:- Plot 2, Row A, Grave 6. ROH:- All Saints Church, Paddock; Shared Church, Paddock. Commemorated on his parents' headstone in Edgerton Cemetery, Huddersfield. (Brother **HAROLD BEIGHTON**, died of wounds at the Dardenelles, 11.12.15 q.v.).

BEIGHTON, HAROLD. Private. No 16669. 8th Battalion Duke of Wellington's Regiment. Formerly Trooper in the 2nd Dragoon Guards (Queens Bays). Born Burncross, Sheffield, 28.9.1890. Son of William and Elizabeth (*nee* Horsfall) Beighton, 10 Royds Hall, Paddock. Educated at Paddock Council School and Huddersfield Higher Grade School. Employed as a butcher by Messrs John Wilkinson and Sons, butchers, Kirkgate Market, Huddersfield. Single. Enlisted, 30.8.1914, in the 2nd Dragoon Guards but was later transferred to the Duke of Wellington's Regiment. Went out to the Dardenelles in August, 1915. Died of a gunshot wound in the left groin at No 26 Casualty Clearing Station on 11.12.15, aged 25 years. Buried in **HILL 10 CEMETERY, SUVLA, GALLIPOLI.** Grave location:- Plot 3, Row C, Grave 3. ROH:- St. Mark's Parish Church, Longwood; All Saints Church, Paddock; Marsden Conservative Club. Commemorated on his parents' headstone in Edgerton Cemetery, Huddersfield. (Brother of **GEOFFREY BEIGHTON**, died of wounds, 29.11.1917, q.v.).

BEIGHTON, HAROLD. Corporal. No 14552. 10th Battalion Duke of Wellington's Regiment. Born Manchester. From the age of three lived with his uncle, Mr Joe Beighton of Hawthorne Terrace, Marsden. Employed as a weaver at Bank Bottom Mills, Marsden. Was an enthusiastic player of football taking the position of centre half in the Marsden United team. Played cricket with the Marsden Second Eleven. Was also a member of the Marsden Conservative Club, taking a great interest in the game of billiards. Enlisted 6.11.1914. Went over to France, 26.8.1915. Died of gunshot wounds to the chest and abdomen at the South Midland Casualty Clearing Station, 6.10.1916, aged 28 years. Buried in **DERNANCOURT COMMUNAL CEMETERY EXTENSION.** Grave location:- Plot 3, Row F, Grave 47. ROH:- Marsden War Memorial. His Uncle received the following letter from stretcher-bearer S. Swallow, *'Just a few lines as I thought it my duty as a great chum of your nephew to write to you. He was wounded on the night of the 4th October. No one was more sorry than I when he came back over the parapet and said to me 'Dick, I am hit.' So I attended* *to him straight away but the worst was then to come for as I was taking him to the dressing station which was two miles away we had to go across open country owing to the condition of the trenches. So we were exposed both to the shell fire and machine gun fire and the Germans didn't forget to shell us either. When we started from the trenches with your nephew on the stretcher the shells were bursting all around us and at the finish they covered us up with clay and I had to wriggle myself from underneath and then free your nephew. I shall never forget that day – it was hell on earth.'*

BELLARBY, REGINALD. Private. No 28834. 13th Battalion The Yorkshire Regiment. Born 26.1.1896. Son of Mr and Mrs Tom Bellarby, 42 Prospect Street, Huddersfield. Educated at Lindley Church School. Employed by Messrs Alfred Crowther (Huddersfield Limited), plumbers merchants. Enlisted January, 1916, and had been in France for three months. Killed in action, 2.11.1916, aged 20 years. Has no known grave. ROH:- St. Thomas's Church, Longroyd Bridge.

BELLINGHAM. GEORGE T. Private, No 4123 Royal West Kent Regiment, transferred to No (469307) 366th Reserve Employment Company Labour Corps. Husband of Florence Bellingham, 49 Lockwood Road, Huddersfield. Died in hospital in London on 5.3.1918, aged 42 years. Buried in **LOCKWOOD CEMETERY, HUDDERSFIELD.** Grave location:- D, 110. ROH:- St. Stephen's Church, Rashcliffe.

BELL, FRED. Gunner. No 66709. 'A' Battery, 103rd Brigade, Royal Field Artillery. Born Scissett. Son of Annie Bell of High Bridge, Scissett, Huddersfield. Killed in action, 21.10.1917, aged 26 years. Buried in **LA CLYTTE MILITARY CEMETERY, RENINGHELST.** Grave location:- Plot 3, Row E, Grave 18. ROH:- Scissett War Memorial.

BELL, JOHN CUMMING. Lance Corporal. No S/11588. 1st Battalion Black Watch. Born Huddersfield 6.1.1897. Son of Thomas and Isobel E. Bell, 2 Trinity Place, Huddersfield. Educated at Huddersfield College School and Rugby Public School. Enlisted September, 1915, in the 11th Battalion Black Watch and went in a draft to the 1st Battalion in France in January, 1916. Was promoted to Lance Corporal in June, 1916. He fought in the Battle of the Somme from July to September, 1916, and for his gallantry was recommended for the Military Medal. In the capture of a crater in High Wood he was killed instantaneously on 3.9.1916, aged 19 years. Has no known grave. Is commemorated on the **THIEPVAL MEMORIAL TO THE MISSING.** ROH:- Huddersfield College School. His father received the following letter from the Officer Commanding his son's Company, *'In the action on August 17th–18th when in 'No Man's Land', your son volunteered to go forward with me to find 'A' Company, which we believed to be in the German line and eventually he saved me from walking into the German line in mistake for our own. He behaved in such a brave and creditable way that I recommended him for the Military Medal, but he was killed before the award could be made.'*

BELL, ROBERT ALFRED. Private. No 64881. 22nd Battalion (Tyneside Scottish) Northumberland Fusiliers. Formerly No TR/5/5696 Territorial Reserve. Born Cleckheaton, 26.3.1899. Son of Charlie and Barbara Ann Bell, 6 Scholes Square, Northgate, Huddersfield. Educated at Beaumont Street Board School. Employed as a crane driver by Sir Robert McAlpine. Enlisted 11.4.1917. Reported missing, presumed dead, 11.4.1918, aged 19 years. Buried **CABARET ROUGE BRITISH CEMETERY.** Grave location:- Plot 20, Row D, Grave 22.

BELL, WILLIAM. Sergeant. No 5/1695. 1/5th Battalion Duke of Wellington's Regiment. Born Bradford 6.10.1892. Son of Mrs Ada Foster, 9 Back Spring Street, Upperhead Row, Huddersfield. Educated at St. Paul's Church School, Huddersfield. Employed as a labourer by the London and North Western Railway Company. Enlisted in the Territorials in June, 1911. Killed in action, 17.11.1915, aged 23. Buried in **ARTILLERY WOOD CEMETERY.** Grave location:- Plot 2, Row A, Grave 13. ROH:- St. Paul's Church, Southgate; Huddersfield Drill Hall. London and North Western Railway Company Roll.

BENNETT, WYLIE. Private. No 1201. 1/7th Battalion Duke of Wellington's Regiment. Born Marsden. Son of Mr and Mrs Harry Bennett, formerly of Marsden but lived in Shepherd's Bush, London, from 1912. Grandson of Mrs Sexton of Carrs Road, Marsden. Employed by Mr J. E. Crowther at Bank Bottom Mills. Engaged to Miss Lily Hirst of Sandhurst Cottages, Marsden. Was a member of the local Territorials before the outbreak of war. Died of wounds at Rouen Base Hospital, 25.9.1915, aged 20 years. Buried in **St. SEVER CEMETERY, ROUEN.** Grave location:- Plot A, Row 11, Grave 15. ROH:- Huddersfield Drill Hall; Marsden War Memorial.

BENSON, IRVINE. Rifleman. No 1403. 1st Battalion King's Royal Rifle Corps. Born Huddersfield. Son of John and Hannah Benson. Died whilst a Prisoner of War, 30.3.1915, aged 33 years. Buried in **TINGLEV CHURCHYARD, TONDER, DENMARK.**

BENSON, MARRIOTT. Colour Sergeant. No 6970. No 5 Company, 2nd Battalion King's Own Yorkshire Light Infantry, attached Sherwood Foresters. Born Dewsbury. Lived 73 Spring Mill, Milnsbridge. Husband of J. F. P. Benson. Killed in action at the Battle of Loos, 13.10.1915, aged 29 years. Has no known grave. Commemorated, **LOOS MEMORIAL TO THE MISSING.**

BENSON, PERCY. Private. No 240423. 2nd Battalion Duke of Wellington's Regiment. Son of Joe and Ellen Benson. husband of Edith S. Benson, 33 Silver Street, Moldgreen. Employed by Messrs Thomas Broadbent and Sons Limited, engineers, and was a church officer at St. Michael's Church, Somerset Road. He was a member of the Huddersfield Operatic Society and of the Huddersfield and District Light Opera Society. Killed in action, 31.8.1918, aged 25 years. Buried in **VIS-en-ARTOIS BRITISH CEMETERY.** Grave location:- Plot 1, Row E, Grave 47. ROH:- Almondbury War Memorial.

BENTLEY, CHARLES EDWARD. Lance Corporal. No 4107. 2/5th Battalion Duke of Wellington's Regiment. Husband of Alice Maria Bentley, 54 Fleming House Lane, Dalton, Huddersfield. Regimental Postman. Found drowned in the flood dykes at Mansfield Woodhouse near Clipstone Camp, 30.1.1916, aged 41 years. Buried **KIRKHEATON CEMETERY.** Grave location:- 'C', 450. ROH:- St. John's Church, Kirkheaton; Huddersfield Drill Hall.

BENTLEY, GEORGE. Private. No 4419. 1/5th Battalion Duke of Wellington's Regiment. Married. Lived 40 Eldon Road, Marsh, Huddersfield. Employed as a gardener at Greenhead Park and was a member of the Ramsden Street Chapel Brotherhood. Enlisted 9.8.1915. Embarked for France in January, 1916. Killed by a shell, 15.11.1916, aged 26 years. Buried in **FONCQUEVILLERS MILITARY CEMETERY.** Grave location:- Plot 1, Row J, Grave 28. ROH:- Marsh War Memorial; Huddersfield Drill Hall.

BENTLEY, IRVIN. Private. No 241708. 2/5th Battalion Duke of Wellington's Regiment. Born New Mill, 28.9.1890. Educated at New Mill Church School. Employed by Messrs John Crowther and Sons, Union Mills, Milnsbridge, as a woollen piecer. Married. Lived 5 Blamires Yard, Swan Lane, Lockwood. Enlisted 16.3.1916. Reported missing, presumed killed, at the Battle of Bullecourt, 3.5.1917, aged 26 years. Has no known grave. Commemorated on the **ARRAS MEMORIAL TO THE MISSING.** ROH:- Emmanuel Church, Lockwood; Huddersfield Drill Hall.

BENTLEY, TOM. Captain and Adjutant. 2/5th Battalion Duke of Wellington's Regiment. Born Ravensthorpe. Dewsbury in November, 1888. Son of Mr Tom Bentley of Poplar Villas, Huddersfield. Educated at Hillhouse Council School and was awarded a Holroyd scholarship, which was held later at Fartown Grammar School. Employed as a woollen designer with Messrs Marshall, Kaye and Marshall Limited, woollen manufacturers, Ravensthorpe. Formerly a volunteer and, at the outbreak of the war, was a Sergeant but later received a commission. Married. Died of wounds in France, 4.5.1917, aged 28 years. Buried in **ACHIET-LE-GRAND COMMUNAL CEMETERY EXTENSION.** Grave location:- Plot 1, Row A, Grave 5. ROH:- Fartown and Birkby War Memorial; Huddersfield Drill Hall.

BERRY, ALBERT. Private. Deal/15243 (S) Royal Marine Labour Corps (Dunkerque). Lived 2 Bath Street, Lockwood, Huddersfield. Died 23.10.1918. Buried in **DUNKERQUE TOWN CEMETERY.** Grave location:- Plot 4, Row D, Grave 7. ROH:- St. Stephen's Church, Rashcliffe.

BERRY, ARTHUR. Driver. No L/29245. 168th (Huddersfield) Brigade Royal Field Artillery. Born Meltham 7.1.1897. Son of the late Solomon Berry of Meltham. Educated at Meltham National School and Huddersfield Technical College. Employed by Messrs Needhams of Birkby as an apprentice chemist. Single. Died of wounds, 7.2.1917. Buried in **BERTRANCOURT MILITARY CEMETERY.** Grave location:- Plot 2, Row A, Grave 20. ROH:- St. Bartholomew's Church, Meltham.

BERRY, BENJAMIN, DCM. Sergeant. No 26747. 'D' Battery, 71st Brigade Royal Field Artillery. Lived Cliffe Villa, Shepley. Educated at Penistone Grammar School. Played football with the Shepley team. Was studying farming near Doncaster when war broke out. Awarded the DCM. The following citation is from the London Gazette, dated 12.3.1917,– *'For conspicuous gallantry in action. He displayed great courage and determination in extinguishing a fire in a gun-pit during a heavy hostile bombardment. He set a splendid example to all ranks.'* Killed in action, 9.8.1917, aged 22 years. Buried in **POTIJZE CHATEAU GROUNDS CEMETERY.** Grave location:- Plot 1, Row B, Grave 8. ROH:- Shepley War Memorial.

BERRY, EDGAR. Private. No 50598. 12th Battalion West Yorkshire Regiment. Born Shepley. Son of James and Mary Ann Berry, of Greenside, Shepley; husband of Ada Berry of 2 Royal Terrace, Scar Lane, Milnsbridge. Employed by Mr Jubb, of Denby Dale, as a painter and decorator. Enlisted December 1916. Killed in action, 3.5.1917, aged 37. Has no known grave. Commemorated on the **ARRAS MEMORIAL TO THE MISSING.** ROH:- Shepley War Memorial.

BERRY, ERNEST ANDREW. Sapper. Royal Engineers. Formerly Duke of Wellington's Regiment. Born Commercial Crescent, Commercial Street, 6.6.1883. Son of Andrew and Sarah Ann Berry. Educated Spring Grove Council School. Employed as a tailor's presser. Husband of Eleanor Berry, 12 Barrow Buildings, Moldgreen. Enlisted 10.12.1915. Died in the Royal Infirmary, Huddersfield, 17.10.1919, of tuberculosis, enteritis and peritonitis.

BERRY, FRED. Private. No 268555. 1/7th Battalion Duke of Wellington's Regiment. Born 51 Oak Road, Bradley, 15.12.1896. Educated at Bradley Church of England School. Employed at Messrs Learoyd Brothers as a textile worker. Married. Killed in action 9.4.1917. Buried in **St. VAAST POST MILITARY CEMETERY, RICHEBOURG L' AVOUE.** Grave location:- Plot 4, Row G, Grave 1. ROH:- St. Thomas's Church, Bradley; Learoyd Brothers; Huddersfield Drill Hall.

BERRY, JOHN EDWARD. Private. No 17584. 2/4th Battalion Duke of Wellington's Regiment. Born Barnsley. Lived Milnsbridge. Died of wounds, 22.11.1917. Buried in **ROCQUIGNY-EQUANCOURT ROAD BRITISH CEMETERY.** Grave location:- Plot 2, Row D, Grave 30. ROH:- Longwood War Memorial.

BERRY, JOHN WILLIE. Private. No 333411. 9th (Glasgow Highland) Battalion Highland Light Infantry. Born Honley. Son of John and Clara Berry, Owen Terrace, Bradshaw Road, Honley. Employed at Rock Mills, Brockholes. Attended Woodroyd United Methodist Church. Embarked for France June, 1917. Killed in action, 25.9.1917, aged 20. Has no known grave. Commemorated on the **TYNE COT MEMORIAL TO THE MISSING.** ROH:- Honley War Memorial.

BERRY, JOSEPH, MM. Private. No 240283. 1/7th Battalion Duke of Wellingtons' Regiment. Born 35 Lockwood Road, Huddersfield 11.6.1898. Son of the late Arthur and Annie Berry. Educated at Rashcliffe Church School, Huddersfield. Employed as an engineering apprentice by Messrs David Brown and Sons Limited, Park Works, Lockwood. Single. Enlisted 4.8.1914. Awarded the Military Medal in September 1918. Seriously wounded with gunshot wounds to the lungs and chest on 10.10.1918 and died at a Casualty Clearing Station on 13.10.1918, aged 20 years. Buried in **BUCQUOY ROAD BRITISH CEMETERY.** Grave location:- Plot 4, Row F, Grave 41. ROH:- St. Stephen's Church, Rashcliffe; Huddersfield Drill Hall.

BERRY, REGINALD. 2nd Lieutenant. 4th Battalion, attached 2nd Battalion, South Staffordshire Regiment. Born Lockwood 9.7.1888. Son of Walter Sydney and Annie Berry, 'Clareville,' New Hey Road, Huddersfield. Educated at Huddersfield Higher Grade School.

Employed as a junior partner in the firm of Messrs Walter Berry and Sons, yarn and wool merchants, 41 Market Street, Deighton Mill, Huddersfield. Joined the Sheffield University Officers Training Corps in January, 1915. Was Gazetted 2nd Lieutenant in South Staffordshire Regiment in March, 1915, and was sent out to Jersey for five months training. Embarked for France in August, 1915, and served there for nine months. He was killed on the night of 30.5.1916, when leading a bombing party in an attack against a trench recently taken by the Germans at Vimy Ridge. He was 27 years of age. Buried at **CANADIAN CEMETERY No 2, NEUVILLE St. VAAST.** Grave location:- Plot 3, Row A, Grave 8. ROH:- New North Road Baptist Church.

BERRY, WALTER. Private. No 19301. 7th Battalion York and Lancaster Regiment. Born Hanson Lane, Lockwood, 19.12.1890. Son of Alfred and Clara Berry, 10 Thomas Street, Thornton Lodge, Huddersfield. Educated at Mount Pleasant Council School. Attended Mount Pleasant Wesleyan Sunday School and Church, Lockwood. Employed as an iron moulder by Mr James Bailey of Meltham. Enlisted 29.8.1914. Killed in action, 29.12.1916, aged 26 years. Buried in **GUARDS' CEMETERY, LESBOEUFS.** Grave location:- Plot 10, Row T, Grave 5. ROH:- St. Stephen's Church, Rashcliffe; Mount Pleasant Chapel, Lockwood.

BERRY, WILFRED. Lance Corporal. No 3257. 1/5th Battalion Duke of Wellington's Regiment. Born 4 Meltham Road, Lockwood. Son of Harry and Sarah Ann Berry, 4 Meltham Road, Lockwood. Educated at Mount Pleasant Council School. Employed as a cloth finisher by Messrs Vickerman and Sons Limited of Taylor Hill. Attended Mount Pleasant Wesleyan Sunday School. Enlisted 14.11.1914. Killed in action, 3.9.1916. Has no known grave. Commemorated on the **THIEPVAL MEMORIAL TO THE MISSING.** ROH:- Emmanuel Church, Lockwood; Mount Pleasant Chapel, Lockwood; Huddersfield Drill Hall.

BERRY, WILLIAM. Private. No 39822. 11th Battalion Leicestershire Regiment. Born Meltham. Killed in action, 22.3.1918. Has no known grave. Commemorated on the **ARRAS MEMORIAL TO THE MISSING.** ROH:-. St. Bartholomew's Church, Meltham.

BEST, BENJAMIN. Private. No 9467. 1st Battalion Duke of Wellington's Regiment. Born Upperthong, Holmfirth, 12.11.1887. Son of George and Martha Best. Educated at Spring Grove Board School, Huddersfield. Employed as a bootmaker before enlisting on 26.8.1908. Died in Ambala, India, from heat-stroke, 1.7.1915, aged 27 years. Commemorated **KARACHI 1914-1918 WAR MEMORIAL, PAKISTAN.**

BETTS, TALBOT. Gunner. No 326420. 287th Siege Battery Royal Garrison Artillery. Formerly Duke of Wellington's Regiment. Born Holmfirth. Son of Mr and Mrs J. T. Betts of Huddersfield Road, Holmfirth. Employed by Messrs. B. Mellor and Sons at Albert Mills. Married, with one child, who was three weeks old on the day his father was killed. Was a member of the local Territorials who were mobilised at the beginning of the war, 4.8.1914. Invalided home and, when he returned to France on 27.7.1917, was transferred to the Royal Garrison Artillery. A fortnight later he was killed on 12.8.1917. Eleven men were sleeping in a dugout when a shell came over the top, six were killed and four were wounded, only one escaping injury. Buried in **THE HUTS CEMETERY, DICKEBUSCH, BELGIUM.** Grave location:- Plot 2, Row D, Grave 1. ROH:- Holmfirth War Memorial; Hepworth and Scholes War Memorial.

BEVERLEY, VINCENT ROEBUCK. Private. No 23812. Depot Battalion King's Own Yorkshire Light Infantry. Born Kirkburton. Son of Christopher and Lilly Beverley, 64 George's Road, Heaton Norris, Cheshire. Died of sickness, contracted whilst a Prisoner of War, on 14.2.1919, aged 27. Buried **CHRIST CHURCH CHURCHYARD, HEATON NORRIS, CHESHIRE.** ROH:- All Hallows Parish Church, Kirkburton.

BICKERDIKE, FRANK. Private. No 1800. 1/5th Battalion Duke of Wellington's Regiment. Born 24 Hope Street, Turnbridge, Huddersfield, in July 1891. Son of the late Tom Alexander Bickerdike (who lost his life in an accident at St. Andrew's Church in October, 1914) and Martha Bickerdike. Lived with his mother at 1 Lily Street, Turnbridge. Educated at Huddersfield Parish Church School. Employed at the Huddersfield Cooperative Society's painting department. Attended Northumberland Street and Ramsden Street Bible Classes and the Turnbridge Working

Men's Club. With his brother, Fred, had been a member of the local Territorials for four years before the outbreak of the war. Killed in action, 23.8.1915, aged 24 years. Has no known grave. Commemorated on the **MENIN GATE MEMORIAL TO THE MISSING.** ROH:- Northumberland Street Primitive Methodist Church and School; Christ Church, Moldgreen; Huddersfield Drill Hall. His mother received the following letter from her son, Private **FRED BICKERDIKE**, who was also serving in France, *'It is with deep regret that I have to write this, for our Frank has been killed this morning by a bullet. I went at once but he was unconscious till he died. We have to be thankful that he had no pain. I know this will be a great shock to you but you must try and bear up for there are thousands of mothers who have given their sons for the country. The Commanding Officer and his Company send their best sympathy and so do all his friends for Frank was one of the best. Do not get depressed, remember it is the fortune of war.'*

BIGGIN, FRANK. Private. No 21163. Depot Battalion King's Own Scottish Borderers. Lived Square Hill. Died 5.12.1918. Buried in **KIRKHEATON CEMETERY.** Grave location:- 'C', 1276.

BILSON, HAROLD DAVID. Eng. Sub Lieutenant. Royal Naval Reserve. *HMS Sarnia.* Born Holmfirth. Son of David and Fanny Bilson of Holmfirth. Husband of Lillian Alice Bilson (whom he married on 18.5.1918). Killed in action involving a submarine in the Mediterranean, 12.9.1918, aged 32 years. Commemorated on the **PORTSMOUTH NAVAL MEMORIAL.**

BILTCLIFFE, JOHN WAREING. Acting Bombardier. No 1440. 1/2nd East Lancashire Royal Field Artillery. Born Diggle. Lived Marsden. Second son of George and Ada Biltcliffe of 52 Brantfell Road, Blackburn and formerly of Marsden. Was in business with his father as a butcher before joining the forces on 2.2.1915. On Sunday, 23.1.1916, his horse fell on him whilst in training at Uckfield, Sussex. He was admitted to hospital in Brighton where he died of his injuries on 29.1.1916, aged 20 years. Buried in St. **BARTHOLOMEW'S CHURCHYARD, MARSDEN.** Grave location:- SE, 7, 21.

BILTCLIFFE, PERCY. Lance Corporal. No 19447. Coldstream Guards. Born Huddersfield. Killed in action, 13.4.1918. Has no known grave. Commemorated on the **PLOEGSTEERT MEMORIAL TO THE MISSING.**

BILTCLIFFE, PERCY. Lance Corporal. No 305486. 2/7th Battalion Duke of Wellington's Regiment. Born Marsden. Son of Rachel and the late Thomas Biltcliffe, 3 Argyle Street, Marsden. Employed as a woollen piecer by Messrs Crowther, Bruce and Company. Enlisted August, 1914, and went over to France in January, 1917. Killed in action at the Battle of Bullecourt, 3.5.1917, aged 21 years. Has no known grave. Commemorated on the **ARRAS MEMORIAL TO THE MISSING.** ROH:- Huddersfield Drill Hall; Marsden War Memorial.

BINNS, MARK ROWLAND. Gunner. No 96705. Royal Field Artillery. Born Peterborough. Son of Mr and Mrs T. Binns of Craig Street, Peterborough. Lived with his sister at 33 Midland Street, Huddersfield. Was employed as a stableman for three years on the London and North Western Railway at Huddersfield. Enlisted September 1914. Wounded in his right leg, 1.6.1915, and died of septicaemia in Birmingham War Hospital on 14.6.1915, aged 24. Buried with full military honours in **PETERBOROUGH CEMETERY.** ROH:- St. Andrew's Church, Leeds Road; Fartown and Birkby War Memorial; London and North Western Railway Company Roll.

BINTCLIFFE, JOHN HENRY. Private. No 306909. 2/7th Battalion Duke of Wellington's Regiment. Son of Zillah Bintcliffe of Greengate Head, Outlane. Attended the Wesleyan Sunday School, Outlane, and was also a member of the United Mutual Improvement Society and the Wesleyan Institute. Employed as a woollen weaver by Messrs C. and J. Hirst, Longwood. Enlisted 27.3.1916. Died of septic poisoning, 18.2.1918, aged 25 years. Buried in **AUBIGNY COMMUNAL CEMETERY EXTENSION.** Grave location:- Plot 3, Row C, Grave 23. ROH:- Huddersfield Drill Hall.

BIRCH, CHRISTOPHER SMITH. Private. No 29045. 10th Battalion Duke of Wellington's Regiment. Born Upperthong. Son of Mrs W.S. Birch of Victoria Street, Holmfirth. Educated at Holmfirth Wesleyan Day School. On leaving school he entered the postal service, first being attached to the telegraph department and then he became a postman in both the Holmfirth and Thongsbridge Post Offices. Before enlistment, on 17.8.1916, worked for his grandfather Mr Christopher Dawson, baker and confectioner. Had just been offered a commission when he was killed at the Battle of Passchendaele, 18.10.1917, aged 32 years. Buried in **TYNE COT CEMETERY**. Grave location:- Plot 45, Row H, Grave 13. ROH:- Holmfirth War Memorial.

BIRCHLEY, FREDERICK. Guardsman. No 12164. 3rd Battalion Grenadier Guards. Born Swanscombe, Greenhithe, Kent. Son of George Edd. and Sarah Birchley, 2 Break North Hill, Swanscombe, Greenhithe, Kent. Employed as a labourer until he enlisted in the Grenadier Guards, on 17.4.1905, for a three year period. On the 29.9.1906, he extended his service, staying with the Guards until 17.4.1912. He was then transferred to the Army Reserve list. On 28.6.1913, he married Ada Alice Shillito at St. Helen's Church, Leeds. One week later, on 4.7.1913, he joined the Huddersfield Borough Police force. Called to the colours on 5.8.1914. On 29.9.1914, Ada Birchley gave birth to their daughter, Grace Ellen. He embarked for France on 26.7.1915. Killed in action during the period 14th to 17th September, 1916, during the Battle of the Somme. Has no known grave. Commemorated on the **THIEPVAL MEMORIAL TO THE MISSING**. ROH:- Huddersfield Police Headquarters; Huddersfield Corporation Roll.

BIRDSALL, WILFRED. Private. No 23596. 9th Battalion Duke of Wellington's Regiment. Born 63 New Street, Paddock, 24.6.1897. Son of the late Tobias and Isabella Mona Birdsall. Educated at Paddock National School. Attended South Street Primitive Methodist Sunday School and Chapel. Employed as a basket maker. Enlisted 10.8.1916. Embarked for France, 4.12.1916. Was killed in action at Guedecourt, 25.12.1916, aged 19 years. Has no known grave. Commemorated on the **THIEPVAL MEMORIAL TO THE MISSING**. ROH:- South Street Methodist Chapel; All Saints Church, Paddock.

BIRKS, ARNOLD. Private. No 2826. 1/5th Battalion Duke of Wellington's Regiment. Born Holmfirth 9.8.1890. Son of Mr and Mrs William Brown, 10 Yews Hill Road. Educated at Mount Pleasant School, Lockwood. Employed as a pattern maker by Messrs E. M. Browns, East Parade, Huddersfield. Married. At the time of enlistment was living at 2 Thornton Road, Longroyd Bridge. Enlisted in the Territorials at the age of 17 and had completed his five years service. Re-enlisted at the outbreak of war. Killed in action at Pilkem Ridge, near Ypres, 17.8.1915, aged 25 years. Has no known grave. Commemorated on the **MENIN GATE MEMORIAL TO THE MISSING**. ROH:- St. Stephen's Church, Rashcliffe; St. Thomas's Church, Longroyd Bridge; Huddersfield Drill Hall.

BIRMINGHAM, JOHN WILLIAM. Private. No 5/3463. 1/5th Battalion Duke of Wellington's Regiment. Born Huddersfield 7.8.1895. Foster son of Mrs Firth, 6 Castlegate, Huddersfield. Educated at St. Patrick's School. Employed as an oiler at Albion Mills, Firth Street, Huddersfield. Single. Enlisted 6.11.1914. Killed in action at the Battle of the Somme, 4.7.1916, aged 20 years. Buried in **CONNAUGHT CEMETERY**. Grave location:- Plot 1, Row D, Grave 3. ROH:- Huddersfield Drill Hall.

BIRMINGHAM, THOMAS. Private. No 50007. 2nd Battalion Lancashire Fusiliers. Born High Street, Huddersfield, 7.2.1900. Son of William and Florence Birmingham, 10 Watergate, Huddersfield. Educated at St. Patrick's School, Huddersfield. Employed as a general labourer by Messrs L. B. Holliday and Company, of Deighton. Single. Enlisted 29.6.1917. Reported missing, presumed killed, 28.3.1918, aged 18 years. Has no known grave. Commemorated on the **ARRAS MEMORIAL TO THE MISSING**.

BIRRELL, BERNARD. Private. No 52008. King's Own Yorkshire Light Infantry. Died at home, 22.12.1918. Buried in **EDGERTON CEMETERY, HUDDERSFIELD**. Grave location:- 11B, 116. ROH:- St. Stephen's Church, Lindley.

BLACKBURN, FRED. Lance Corporal. No 23147. 13th Battalion The Yorkshire Regiment. Born Taylor Hill, Huddersfield. Son of David And Eleanor K. Blackburn, 65 Barcroft Road, Close Hill, Huddersfield. Educated at Berry Brow Council School and Huddersfield College. Employed as a weaver by Messrs Kaye and Stewart of Lockwood and formerly was a grocer's assistant at the Close Hill Cooperative Stores. Attended Taylor Hill Primitive Methodist Church and Sunday School. Enlisted 6.8.1915. Killed in action, 19.7.1916, aged 26 years. Buried in **MAROC BRITISH CEMETERY, GRENAY, FRANCE**. Grave location:- Plot 1, Row J, Grave 32. ROH:- St. John's Church, Newsome; Taylor Hill Primitive Methodist Church.

BLACKBURN, JOHN WILLIE. Private. No 65100. 1st Battalion Northumberland Fusiliers. Formerly No 32043 Duke of Wellington's Regiment. Born Brighouse. Lived Commercial Road, Skelmanthorpe. Married, with three children. Employed by Messrs Stringer and Son, Emley Moor Collieries. Killed in action, 23.8.1918, aged 38 years. Buried in **RAILWAY CUTTING CEMETERY, COURCELLES-LE-COMTE**. Grave location:- Row A, Grave 34. ROH:- St. Aidan's Church, Skelmanthorpe.

BLACKBURN, JOSEPH WILLIAM. Lance Corporal. No DM2/207576. Army Service Corps. Born Leys, Longwood, 14.7.1893. Son of Albert and Mary Blackburn, 14 Parkwood Road, Longwood. Educated at Goitfield Board School, Longwood. Was employed as a dyer by Messrs. Wadsworth, Lees and Company Ltd., Leymoor Dyeworks. Single. Attended Longwood Wesleyan Chapel and had acted as assistant secretary at the Sunday School. Enlisted 31.8.1916. Died at home whilst on leave, of pneumonia, following influenza and bronchitis on 11.2.1919, aged 25 years. His demobilisation papers arrived the same day. Buried in **LONGWOOD WESLEYAN BURIAL GROUND**. Grave location:- north part. ROH:- Longwood Wesleyan Chapel; St. Mark's Parish Church, Longwood.

BLACKBURN, PERCY WILLIAM. Gunner. No 83782. 243rd Siege Battery Royal Garrison Artillery. Born Linthwaite. Son of Job and Anne Blackburn of 5 Flathouse, Linthwaite. Employed as a weaver by Mr J E Crowther at Bank Bottom Mills. Was a member of the Slaithwaite United Harriers. Single. Enlisted 20.5.1916. Killed in action, 7.9.1917, aged 24 years. Buried in **BLEUET FARM CEMETERY, BELGIUM**. Grave location:- Plot 1, Row H, Grave 52. ROH:- Linthwaite War Memorial.

BLACKBURN, STANLEY. Private. No 36812. 1/6th Battalion Durham Light Infantry. Born Huddersfield. Lived St. John's Road, Birkby. Killed in action, 31.5.1918. Has no known grave. Commemorated on the **SOISSONS MEMORIAL TO THE MISSING**. ROH:- Fartown and Birkby War Memorial.

BLACKBURN, WILLIAM MORRIS. Private. No 241846. 2/5th Battalion Duke of Wellington's Regiment. Born New Mill, 18.12.1878. Son of John William and Elizabeth Blackburn, 140 Ash Brow Road, Fartown. Assisted his father in his business as a plumber. Was a member of the bible class at Christ Church, Woodhouse. Enlisted 23.3.1916. Killed in action at the Battle of Bullecourt, 3.5.1917, aged 39 years. Has no known grave. Commemorated on the **ARRAS MEMORIAL TO THE MISSING**. ROH:- Huddersfield Drill Hall; Fartown and Birkby War Memorial

BLACKSTONE, FRANK. Gunner. No 29378. 'D' Battery 64th Brigade Royal Field Artillery. Born Marsden. 10.9.1898. Son of Charles T. and Sarah J. Blackstone, 94 Willow Lane, Birkby. Educated at St. Thomas's Church of England School, Longroyd Bridge. Single. Died of wounds, 14.5.1918, at No 8 Stationary Hospital, Wimereux, aged 19 years. Buried in **BOULOGNE EASTERN CEMETERY**. Grave location:- Plot 9, Row B, Grave 80. ROH:- St Thomas's Church, Longroyd Bridge; Fartown and Birkby War Memorial.

BLAKELEY, JAMES EDWARD, MM. Sergeant. No 305907. 2/5th Battalion Duke of Wellington's Regiment. Lived 2 Lane, Lingards, Slaithwaite. Enlisted at the outbreak of the war. Had served four and a half years with the Colours. Awarded the MM, 16.7.1918. Came home from France with the Cadre of the 1/5th Battalion Duke of Wellington's Regiment a week before he died of pneumonia, on 14.5.1919, aged 22 years. Buried with full military honours in **SLAITHWAITE CEMETERY**. Grave location:- B, 3, 111. ROH:- St. James Church, Slaithwaite; Slaithwaite War Memorial; Huddersfield Drill Hall.

BLAKEY, HAROLD. Private. No 204537. 1/4th Battalion Duke of Wellington's Regiment. Born 10.11.1897. Son of Joe Smith Blakey, 481 Bradford Road, Huddersfield. Educated at Hillhouse Council School, Huddersfield. Employed as a joiner's apprentice. Enlisted 15.1.1915. Killed in action, 6.10.1917, at Passchendaele. Buried in **TYNE COT**

CEMETERY. Grave location:- Plot 34, Row G, Grave 22. ROH:- St. Hilda's Church, Cowcliffe; Christ Church, Woodhouse Hill; Fartown and Birkby War Memorial.

BLAKEY, JAMES. Private. No 1789. 1/7th Battalion (Colne Valley Territorials) Duke of Wellington's Regiment. Born Bradford. Had lodged with Mrs Warrington, Warrington Terrace, Marsden, for three years before enlistment. Employed by Mr J.E. Crowther Bank Bottom Mills, Marsden as a cloth presser. Killed in action, 29.10.1915, aged 25 years. Buried in **TALANA FARM CEMETERY.** Grave location:- Plot 3, Row D, Grave 3. ROH:- Huddersfield Drill Hall; Marsden War Memorial.

BLAKE, JAMES. Private. No 45815. 12th Battalion Northumberland Fusiliers. Born Huddersfield. Lived with his sister, Mrs K. Sykes, at 17 Castlegate, Huddersfield. Employed as a labourer by British Dyes Limited. Attended St. Joseph's Church, Huddersfield. Killed in action at the Battle of Arras, 12.4.1917, aged 25 years. Has no known grave. Commemorated on the **ARRAS MEMORIAL TO THE MISSING.**

BLAND, THOMAS WILLIAM. Private. No 40758. 2nd Battalion South Staffordshire Regiment. Son of Mr and Mrs Herbert Bland of Far Dene, Kirkburton. Employed as a groom by Major Holliday. Enlisted in 1916. Killed in action, 28.9.1918, aged 20 years. Buried in **ORIVAL WOOD CEMETERY, FLESQUIERES.** Grave location:- Plot 1, Row B, Grave 34. ROH:- All Hallows Parish Church, Kirkburton.

BLEZARD, ARTHUR. Private. No 269334. 2/5th Battalion Duke of Wellington's Regiment. Born 22 Silver Street, Moldgreen. Son of Mr James Blezard, 156 Wakefield Road, Moldgreen. Educated at Moldgreen Council School. Employed as a labourer. Enlisted 4.8.1917. Killed in action, 10.4.1918, north west of Bapaume. Buried in **DOUCHY-LES-AYETTE BRITISH CEMETERY.** Grave location:- Plot 2, Row E, Grave 21. ROH:- Christ Church, Moldgreen; Huddersfield Drill Hall.

BODKER, JOHN GEORGE. Lieutenant. York and Lancaster Regiment, attached 2/5th Battalion Duke of Wellington's Regiment. Son of the late Mrs Bodker of Folkestone and son in law of Mr Tom Bentley of Halifax Old Road. Commenced his business career with Messrs W. Holmes and Company Limited, engineers of Turnbridge and later served with a firm of colliery proprietors in Durham. Enlisted in a Territorial battalion and obtained his commission in February, 1915. Married and living at 132 Halifax Old Road. Killed in action at the Battle of Cambrai, 20.11.1917, aged 25 years. Buried in **RUYAULCOURT MILITARY CEMETERY.** Grave location:- Row F, Grave 9. ROH:- Huddersfield Drill Hall; Fartown and Birkby War Memorial.

BOLTON, CHARLES EDWARD. Private. No 41413. 26th Battalion (Tyneside Irish) Northumberland Fusiliers. Formerly No 17776 Duke of Wellington's Regiment. Born Huddersfield 18.2.1894. Son of Charles M. and Ada Bolton, 16 South Street, Huddersfield. Educated at St. Paul's Church of England School. Employed as a traveller for Messrs. Snowden's, confectioners, of Huddersfield. Was a member of the Huddersfield Permanent Orchestra where he played the violin. Attended the Hillhouse P.S.A. and the Ramsden Street Congregational Church. Single. Enlisted 20.1.1916. Killed in action, 19.12.1916, aged 22 years. Buried in **RATION FARM MILITARY CEMETERY, ARMENTIERES.** Grave location:- Plot 3, Row B, Grave 3.

BOND, WILLIAM ARTHUR, MC and Bar. Captain and Flight Commander. King's Own Yorkshire Light Infantry, attached to 40th Squadron Royal Flying Corps. Born Chesterfield 27.6.1890. Son of Arthur and Elizabeth Bond, 'Sherwood,' Tennyson Avenue, Chesterfield and formerly of Milnsbridge. Educated at Clay Cross and Netherthorpe Grammar Schools. Was on the sub-editorial staff of the Huddersfield Examiner and afterwards joined the Paris staff of the Daily Mail. Enlisted in August, 1914, as a Private in the 20th Hussars. Was commissioned into the King's Own Yorkshire Light Infantry and was afterwards transferred to the Royal Flying Corps. Married in January, 1917, to Miss Aimee McHardy. Reported missing on 22.7.1917, when his aeroplane was seen to go down out of control near Lens, aged 28. Has no known grave. Commemorated on the **ARRAS FLYING SERVICES MEMORIAL.** ROH:- New North Road Baptist Church. The Major of his unit, in a letter, described him as *'a wonderful pilot and a magnificent patrol leader.'*

BONSER, HENRY. Private. No 41126. 1st Battalion Worcestershire Regiment. Formerly No 31651 North Staffordshire Regiment. Born Cumberworth. Son of the late Mr W Bonser and Mrs Bonser of Grasscroft, Almondbury. Husband of Lily Bonser, 22 Back Industrial Street, Primrose Hill. Employed as a dairyman by the Huddersfield Cooperative Dairies Limited. Attended the Huddersfield Mission. Enlisted 6.11.1916. Reported missing, presumed killed, 1.4.1918. Has no known grave. Commemorated on the **POZIERES MEMORIAL TO THE MISSING.** ROH:- Almondbury War Memorial.

BOOTH, ARNOLD. Private. No 24343. 9th Battalion Duke of Wellington's Regiment. Son of Mrs Susannah Booth, 19 Thornhill Road, Longwood. Killed in action at the Battle of Arras, 25.4.1917, aged 30 years. Has no known grave. Commemorated on the **ARRAS MEMORIAL TO THE MISSING.** ROH:- St. Mark's Parish Church, Longwood.

BOOTH, EDWIN SYKES. Gunner. No 174036. 3rd Battery, 45th Brigade Royal Field Artillery. Born Crosland Moor, 5.12.1882. Son of Silas and Charlotte Booth, 75 Thorn Road, Thornton Lodge, Huddersfield. Educated at Mount Pleasant Council School. Employed as a warehouseman by Messrs William Cumming and Company, Railway Street. Attended Thornton Lodge Wesleyan Church and Sunday School and was a member of the choir. Was also member of Lockwood Conservative Club. Married. At the time of enlistment was living at 115 North Street, Lockwood. Enlisted 21.9.1916. Died of wounds at the 2nd Canadian Casualty Clearing Station, 27.11.1917, aged 36 years. Buried in **LIJSSENTHOEK MILITARY CEMETERY.** Grave location:- Plot 26, Row A, Grave 13A. ROH:- Lockwood Baptist Church; St. Stephen's Church, Rashcliffe.

BOOTH, EMMANUEL. Gunner. Royal Field Artillery. Born Honley Moor, 29.9.1877. Educated Primrose Hill School. Employed as a cotton piecer by Messrs Whiteleys of Huddersfield. Single. Enlisted 5.8.1914 . Died in Storths Hall Mental Asylum of General Paralysis of the Insane, 16.10.1917.

BOOTH, FRANK. Ordinary Seaman. No J/50575. Royal Navy. *HMS Anchusa.* Born Bradley, 1.10.1894. Son of George H. and Mary Hannah Booth, 47 Coal Pit Lane, Outlane. Educated at Bradley School. Employed as cloth finisher by Messrs Joseph Hoyle and Son, Longwood. Single. Enlisted in the Navy in 1916. Killed in action involving a submarine off the north coast of Ireland, 16.7.1918, aged 23. Commemorated on the **PLYMOUTH NAVAL MEMORIAL TO THE MISSING.** (Brother of Privates **WILLIE and SELWYN BOOTH,** both killed in action, q.v.).

BOOTH, FRANK. Private. No 29119. 123rd Company Machine Gun Corps. Formerly No C/7275 King's Royal Rifle Corps. Born Bradford Road, Huddersfield, 28.2.1897. Son of Norman Booth, 142 Junction Road, Leek, Staffordshire. Educated at schools in the Gorton area of Manchester. Lived with his grandfather at 21 Burbeary Road, Lockwood. Employed firstly at Huddersfield Technical College and then as a clerk in the textile office of Mr Allan Gee. Enlisted in 1916. Killed in action at the Battle of Passchendaele, 23.9.1917, aged 20 years. Buried **KEMMEL No1 FRENCH CEMETERY.** Grave location:- Plot 2, Row B, Grave 9. ROH:- Emmanuel Church, Lockwood; Moldgreen War Memorial; memorial in Lockwood Cemetery.

BOOTH, FREDERICK STEPHEN. Private. No G/52850. 'B' Company, 9th Battalion Royal Fusiliers. Formerly 10/ 57074 103rd Territorial Reserve Battalion. Born West Hartlepool. Son of John and Ellen Booth, 4 Carriage Drive, Lockwood, Huddersfield. Reported missing, presumed killed, at the Battle of Arras on 3.5.1917, aged 21 years. Has no known grave. Commemorated on the **ARRAS MEMORIAL TO THE MISSING.** ROH:- commemorated on headstone in Lockwood Cemetery.

BOOTH, GEORGE. Lance Corporal. No 40801. 23rd Battalion (Tyneside Scottish) Northumberland Fusiliers. Born New Mill. Son of Mr James Booth of Totties, Holmfirth. Employed in the warehouse at Ford Mill, Holmfirth. Attended Scholes Primitive Methodist Chapel, being Sunday School Superintendent, a member of the choir and a lay preacher. He was a keen cricketer, playing for the Holmfirth team and winning the gold medal of the Huddersfield and District league for the best bowling. When he pleaded a conscientious objection to warfare the Holmfirth Tribunal granted him a non-combatant certificate. But when he reported himself to Halifax Barracks, however, he felt that he could not avail himself of the privilege granted to him by the tribunal and he enlisted on 5.5.1916, going into training at North Shields. Embarked for France in July 1916. Died of wounds, 7.6.1917, aged 25 years. Buried in **BAILLEUL ROAD EAST CEMETERY.** Grave location:- Plot 5, Row B, Grave 11. (Brother of Private **PERCY BOOTH,** who died of wounds, 20.7.1916, q.v.). ROH:- Wooldale War Memorial.

BOOTH, GEORGE ERNEST. Private. No 7700. 2nd Battalion Duke of Wellington's Regiment. Born Moores Buildings, Lowerhead Row, Huddersfield, 6.4.1880. Educated at Beaumont Street Council School, Huddersfield. Employed as a labourer by the London and North Western Railway at the Huddersfield Goods Station. Married, with four children. Was a reservist and had served for three years in India. Rejoined on 5.8.1914. Killed in action at Hill 60 on 18.4.1915, aged 31 years. Has no known grave. Commemorated on the **MENIN GATE MEMORIAL TO THE MISSING.** ROH:- Huddersfield Parish Church; London and North Western Railway Company Roll.

BOOTH, GEORGE HENRY. Private. No 28460. 31st Battalion Machine Gun Corps. Formerly No 16880 East Lancashire Regiment. Born Huddersfield, 15.11.1893. Son of Tom and Annie Booth, 19 Trinity Street, Huddersfield. Educated at Holy Trinity Church of England School. Employed by Mr J W Hobson as a tobacconist's traveller. Enlisted October 1914. Went to the Dardenelles and France. Died of wounds, 28.3.1918, aged 24 at Etaples Base Hospital. Buried in **ETAPLES MILITARY CEMETERY.** Grave location:- Plot 33, Row C, Grave 21A. (Brother of Private **HERBERT BOOTH,** killed in action, 6.11.1917, q.v.). ROH:- Holy Trinity Church, Huddersfield.

BOOTH, GEORGE HERBERT. Private. No 301950. 2/7th Battalion Durham Light Infantry. Formerly No 6083 Duke of Wellington's Regiment. Son of Mrs John Booth of Underbank. Educated at Netherthong National School. Married, with two children. Lived at Liphill Bank. Employed by Messrs. W. H. and J. Barber, Clarence Mills, Holmbridge. Enlisted July 1916. Killed in action, 2.4.1918, aged 26 years. Has no known grave. Commemorated on the **POZIERES MEMORIAL TO THE MISSING.** His wife received a letter from a friend of her husband who wrote, *'I saw him just before he went into action and shook hands with him. He was quite cheerful. We knew we were in for a hot time but I did not think it would be the last time I should ever see him. The news that he had been killed was a great shock to me because he was the only pal I had out here whom I knew. Of course I have some good pals in the Regiment. Well I am glad to tell you we have got out of it and I think I am a lucky chap.'* ROH:- Upperthong War Memorial.

BOOTH, HAROLD. Driver. No 115750. 'A' Battery, 55th Brigade, Royal Field Artillery. Born Brighouse. Son of Henry Lawton and Annie Maria Booth, 39 Springdale Street, Huddersfield. Educated at Mount Pleasant Council School, Huddersfield. Employed as a warehouseman by Messrs James McDonald and Company, Wood Street, Huddersfield. Attended St. Thomas's Church and was a member of the Young Men's Bible Class. Enlisted 28.10.1915 and went out to India in the following July. Was later drafted to Mesopotamia where he died of dysentery on 16.1.1918, aged 21 years. Buried in **BAGHDAD (NORTH GATE) WAR CEMETERY.** Grave location:- Plot 16, Row J, Grave 4. ROH:- St. Thomas's Church, Longroyd Bridge; St. Stephen's Church, Rashcliffe; memorial in Lockwood cemetery.

BOOTH, HARRY. Private. No 39664. 8th Battalion Bedfordshire Regiment. Formerly No DM2/230987 Army Service Corps. Born Berry Brow, 18.2.1898. Son of Alfred and Annie Booth, 31 School Lane, Berry Brow, Huddersfield. Educated at Berry Brow Council School. Employed at British Dyes as a motor driver and was connected with Salem United Methodist Church, Berry Brow. Single. Enlisted 9.10.16. Accidentally killed behind the lines near Bethune, 25.6.1917, aged 19 years. Buried in **PHILOSOPHE BRITISH CEMETERY, MAZINGARBE.** Grave location:- Plot 2, Row R, Grave 9. ROH:- Armitage Bridge War Memorial; memorial in Almondbury Cemetery.

BOOTH, HERBERT. Private. No 32436. 1/4th Battalion South Lancashire Regiment. Formerly Motor Transport Section, Army Service Corps. Son of Mrs Booth, 19 Trinity Street, Huddersfield. Educated at Holy Trinity Church of England School, Huddersfield and was in the choir at Trinity Church. Employed by Mr R. A. Bell, wholesale druggist, as a motor driver. Enlisted 19.4.1915. Killed in action, 6.11.1917, aged 28. Has no known grave. Commemorated on the **THIEPVAL MEMORIAL TO THE MISSING.** (Brother of Private **GEORGE HENRY BOOTH,** died of wounds, 23.3.1918, q.v.). ROH:- Holy Trinity Church, Huddersfield.

BOOTH, JAMES FREDERICK. Private. No 240799. 1/7th Battalion (Colne Valley Territorials) Duke of Wellington's Regiment. Born Salendine Nook, 8.11.1895. Son of Mr and Mrs Albert Booth, 19 Bank End, Greenhead Lane, Dalton. Educated at Lepton Council School. Employed by Messrs Haighs, St. John's Road, Huddersfield as a tailor's cutter. Enlisted October 1914. Reported wounded and missing, presumed killed, 12.4.1918, aged 22 years. Buried in **CABARET ROUGE BRITISH CEMETERY.** Grave location:- Plot 20, Row D, Grave 27. ROH:- Huddersfield Drill Hall; Almondbury War Memorial.

BOOTH, JOHN. Private. No 241147. 1/5th Battalion Duke of Wellington's Regiment. Lived Rowley Hill, Lepton. Employed as a collier by Messrs Swift and Netherwood. Killed in action, 3.9.1916, aged 19 years. Buried in **MILL ROAD CEMETERY.** Grave location:- Plot 1, Row E, Grave 23. ROH:- Lepton Parish Church; Huddersfield Drill Hall.

BOOTH, LAWRENCE EWART. Private. No 2314. 1/7th Battalion Duke of Wellington's Regiment. Born 19 Lowergate, Longwood 13.5.1898. Son of Harry Booth (foreman of the London and North Western Railway Company Goods Station, Longwood). Lived 51 Crow Lane Terrace, Milnsbridge. Educated at Paddock Council School and Crow Lane Board School, Milnsbridge. Apprenticed to Messrs A. Dawson and Sons, butchers, Milnsbridge. Attended the Paddock Congregational Church and also St. Michael's Mission Church, Milnsbridge. Single. Enlisted 7.10.1914. Embarked for France April 1915. Shot by a sniper in the trenches, 27.5.1915, aged 17 years. Buried in **RUE-DAVID MILITARY CEMETERY, FLEURBAIX.** Grave location:- Plot 1, Row B, Grave 15. ROH:- Shared Church, Paddock; St. John's Church, Golcar; Crow Lane Board School, Milnsbridge; Huddersfield Drill Hall.

BOOTH, LEWIS. Private. No 38160. 17th Battalion West Yorkshire Regiment. Born Wooldale. Son of George Henry and Elizabeth Booth; husband of Ann Booth of Hollin Gleave, New Mill. Employed by Messrs Cooper and Liversedge, dyers, of Honley as a stoker. Taken prisoner by the Germans on 21.8.1917. Died of pneumonia at Cassel, Germany, on 21.4.1918, aged 35 years. Buried in **NIEDERZWEHREN CEMETERY, CASSEL, GERMANY.** Grave location:- Plot 8, Row F, Grave 7. ROH:- New Mill Working Men's Club; Fulstone War Memorial

BOOTH, MAURICE. 1st Class Stoker. No SS/110814. Royal Navy. *HMS Lion.* Born Marsden. Son of Moses Booth, 15 Mount Road, Marsden. Employed as a weft man by Messrs Crowther, Bruce and Company Limited, New Mills, Marsden. Single. Had completed five years active service in the Navy on 12.3.1915 but had seven years to serve in the Reserve so he was kept on service. Had served on board *HMS Lion* since she was first commissioned. Killed in action at the Battle of Jutland, 31.5.1916, aged 26 years. Commemorated on the **PLYMOUTH NAVAL MEMORIAL TO THE MISSING.** ROH:- Marsden War Memorial.

BOOTH, OLIVER. Private. No 91486. Royal Army Medical Corps. Born Quarmby, Huddersfield, 14.4.1898. Son of Mr and Mrs Albert Booth, 19 Bank End, Greenhead Lane, Dalton. Educated at Lepton Council School and Huddersfield Technical College. Was a pupil teacher under the Huddersfield Education Committee. Single. Enlisted November 1916. Died in Worksop Hospital, of pneumonia, 31.10.1918. Buried in **ALMONDBURY CEMETERY.** Grave location:- Row C, Grave 67. ROH:- Almondbury War Memorial; Huddersfield Corporation Roll.

BOOTH, PERCY. Private. No 2816. 1/5th Battalion Duke of Wellington's Regiment. Born Totties, Thongsbridge. Son of James and Eliza Booth. Educated at Wood Lane Bottom School and attended Scholes Primitive Methodist Church. Employed as a millhand in the finishing department at Glendale Mills. Enlisted in Huddersfield, 5.9.1914, training at Clipstone Camp and later at Doncaster. Embarked for France April, 1915. Died of wounds at Rouen, 20.7.1916, aged 20 years. Buried in **St. SEVER CEMETERY, ROUEN.** Grave location:- Plot A, Row 16, Grave 38. ROH:- Wooldale War Memorial; Huddersfield Drill Hall. His parents received the following letter from the Rev. W. E. Harper, a Church of England Chaplain at No 1 Stationary Hospital at Rouen, *'It is with the deepest sympathy that I have to tell you of the death of your son who died of wounds in this hospital at 1.30am on 20.7.1916. His wound was in the left knee and the leg had to be amputated to try to save him but he passed away unconsciously and without pain. He is to be buried tomorrow in St. Sever's Cemetery, Rouen. May God comfort you in your grief over the loss of a brave and gallant son.'* (Brother of Lance-Corporal **GEORGE BOOTH,** who died of wounds, 7.6.1917, q.v.).

BOOTH, PHILIP JOHN, MC. Lieutenant. 2nd Battalion Royal Scots Fusiliers. Son of James John and Alice Elizabeth Booth of Whitegates, Netherton. Educated Uppingham Public School; left December 1913. Granted his commission from the Royal Military College, Sandhurst. Embarked for France in June 1916. Served in France with 2nd Battalion The Cameronians (Scottish Rifles). Awarded the Military Cross in September, 1917, for *'conspicuous gallantry and devotion to duty at a critical moment. He took command of his company under direct fire of a hostile machine gun which, had killed his Company Commander, and assaulted the position, capturing the gun and killing its team. He then led his company to their final objective under heavy fire and it was entirely owing to his gallantry and determined energy that his men were able to hold their ground and repulse the hostile counter attacks which were continually against them throughout the day'*. (London Gazette 9th January, 1918). Died of pneumonia, 2.3.1920, aged 23. Buried in **HAIDAR PASHA CEMETERY, ISTANBUL.** Grave location:- Plot 1, Row J, Grave 12.

BOOTH, ROLAND HARTLEY. Boy 1st Class. No J/24104. Royal Navy. *HMS Hawke.* Born Huddersfield, 1897. Son of Arthur Newsome and Ruthetta Booth, 177 Newsome Road, Huddersfield. Educated at Almondbury Grammar School. Enlisted in the Royal Navy in 1913. Killed in action involving a submarine in the North Sea, 15.10.1914, aged 17 years. Has no known grave. Commemorated on **PORTSMOUTH NAVAL MEMORIAL TO THE MISSING.** ROH:- Almondbury Grammar School; St. John's Church, Newsome.

BOOTH, SELWYN. Corporal. No 241401. 2/5th Battalion Duke of Wellington's Regiment. Born Bradley 14.5.1896. Son of Mr and Mrs Booth, 47 Coal Pit Lane, Outlane. Was a chorister at St. Mary's Church, Outlane. Employed by Messrs Crowthers, Stanley Mills, Milnsbridge, prior to enlisting on 2.11.1915. Single. Reported missing, presumed killed, at the Battle of Cambrai, 27.11.1917, aged 21 years. Has no known grave. Commemorated on the **CAMBRAI MEMORIAL TO THE MISSING.** ROH:- Huddersfield Drill Hall. (Brother of Privates **WILLIE AND FRANK BOOTH,** killed in action, q.v.).

BOOTH, THOMAS ROGER. Private. No 24863. 8th Battalion Duke of Wellington's Regiment. Born Holmfirth. Son of Hirst and Harriet Booth of Ward Place, Holmfirth; husband of Sarah Booth (later Jessop), Old Yew, Holmbridge, Huddersfield. Educated at Choppards School and the Wesleyan Sunday School. Employed as a fettler at Dover Mills and later at Vickermans of Thongsbridge. A keen football player and cricketer. Killed by shellfire, 10.6.1917, aged 32 years. Buried in **DERRY HOUSE CEMETERY No 2, WYTSCHAETE, BELGIUM.** Grave location:- Plot 1, Row A, Grave 7. ROH:- Cartworth War Memorial; Huddersfield Drill Hall.

BOOTH, TOM. Lance Corporal. No 5863. 2nd Battalion Duke of Wellington's Regiment. Born Rastrick, Brighouse. Educated at Rastrick Schools. Husband of Anni Booth, 10 Folly Road, Cowcliffe. Employed as a warehouseman. Enlisted 5.8.1914. Killed in action, near Ypres, 8.11.1914, aged 36 years. Has no known grave. Commemorated on the **MENIN GATE MEMORIAL TO THE MISSING.** ROH:- St. Hilda's Church, Cowcliffe; Christ Church, Woodhouse Hill; Fartown and Birkby War

Memorial; Brighouse War Memorial; St. Matthew's Church, Rastrick.

BOOTH, WALTER. Private. No 47369. 22nd Battalion (Tyneside Scottish) Northumberland Fusiliers. Born Holmfirth. Enlisted Halifax. Killed in action, 21.3.1918. Has no known grave. Commemorated on the **ARRAS MEMORIAL TO THE MISSING.**

BOOTH, WILFRED. Lance Corporal. No 21/962. 21st Battalion West Yorkshire Regiment. Born Industrial Street, Primrose Hill, Huddersfield. Son of George and Mary Elizabeth Booth, 46 Kilner Bank, Moldgreen. Employed as a packer by Messrs Broadbent and Groves Limited, Kirkheaton. Attended the Buxton Road Wesleyan Young Men's Class. Single. Killed in action at Arras, 6.5.1917, aged 22 years. Buried in **St. NICOLAS BRITISH CEMETERY.** Grave location:- Plot 1, Row J, Grave 2.

BOOTH, WILLIE. Private. No 10/3839. 2nd Wellington Battalion New Zealand Expeditionary Force. Born Bradley, Huddersfield, 23.8.1892. Son of George Hay and Mary Booth, 47 Coal Pit Lane, Outlane. Was formerly a scholar, church councillor and sidesman at St. Mary's Church, Outlane. Emigrated to New Zealand. Single. Before enlistment was living at Riverside Farm, Normanby Road, Manai, Taranaki, New Zealand. Enlisted 15.11.1915. Killed in action, 15.6.1916, aged 23 years. Buried in **CITE BONJEAN MILITARY CEMETERY.** Grave location:- Plot 2, Row B, Grave 40. (Brother of Privates **SELWYN AND FRANK BOOTH,** killed in action, q.v.). ROH:- St. Mark's Parish Church, Longwood.

BOOTH, WILLIE. Private. No 41733. 2nd Battalion Wellington Regiment New Zealand Expeditionary Force. Born Holmfirth. Son of Richard and Emily Booth. Educated St. John's School, Holmfirth. Was a joiner by trade. Went out to New Zealand in 1908. Single. Killed in action, 22.7.1918, aged 32 years. Buried in **SERRE ROAD CEMETERY No 1.** Grave location:- Plot 5, Row C, Grave 13.

BOOTHROYD, ALFRED. Private. No 3/9796. 1st Battalion Northumberland Fusiliers. Born Lepton 30.9.1870. Educated at Lepton National School. Employed as a labourer at the Leeds Road Fireclay Works at Field House. Married, with one child. Enlisted October 1914. (Had also served in Egypt and was present at the fall of Omdurman and subsequently served all through the South African War). Killed in action at the Battle of the Somme, 18.8.1916, aged 45 years. Has no known grave. Commemorated on the **THIEPVAL MEMORIAL TO THE MISSING.** ROH:- Christ Church, Woodhouse Hill.

BOOTHROYD, DENNIS ALLEN. Private. No 17772. 2nd Battalion Duke of Wellington's Regiment. Born Honley. Son of Allan and Eliza Boothroyd, Lake Cottage, Honley. Employed by Messrs Liversedge, dyers, Leeds Road, Huddersfield. Attended Honley Primitive Methodist Church and was a member of the choir. Enlisted January 1916. Reported missing, presumed killed, 12.10.1916, aged 25 years. Has no known grave. Commemorated on the **THIEPVAL MEMORIAL TO THE MISSING.** ROH:- Honley War Memorial.

BOOTHROYD GAMALIEL. Private. No 23419. Durham Light Infantry. Son of Mr Gamaliel Boothroyd of Pog Ing, Holmfirth. Educated at Wooldale Council School and Townend Primitive Methodist Sunday School. Assisted his father with his yeast business. Enlisted June 1916. Went across to France in October, 1916, after training at Hornsea. In June, 1917, was severely wounded in the left thigh and left hand. He remained in hospital until May, 1918, when he was invalided out of the army. Died in Holmfirth Auxiliary Hospital from tuberculosis of the lungs and spine, 20.10.1918, aged 29 years. Buried in **CHRIST CHURCH CHURCHYARD EXTENSION, NEW MILL.** ROH:- Wooldale.

BOOTHROYD, GEORGE CLEMENT. Lance Corporal. No 28792. 2nd Battalion Duke of Wellington's Regiment. Born Denby. Son of John and Emily Boothroyd of Lower Denby. Died of wounds, 9.2.1917, aged 28 years. Buried in **BRAY MILITARY CEMETERY.** Grave location:- Plot 1, Row D, Grave 32. ROH:- Denby Dale and Cumberworth War Memorial.

BOOTHROYD, HARRY. Private. No 269184. 1/7th Battalion Duke of Wellington's Regiment. Born Swan Lane, Lockwood 16.3.1882. Son of George Boothroyd. Husband of Edith Annie Boothroyd, 63 Blackhouse Road, Fartown. Employed by Messrs T. and H. Blamires Limited,

Leeds Road. Was a member of the Bradley Mills Bowling Club. Enlisted 17.3.1917. Killed in action, 14.4.1918, aged 36 years. Has no known grave. Commemorated on the **TYNE COT MEMORIAL TO THE MISSING.** ROH:- Christ Church, Woodhouse Hill; Huddersfield Drill Hall; Fartown and Birkby War Memorial; memorial in Lockwood Cemetery.

BOOTHROYD, HERBERT. Private. No 2168. 4th Battalion Hampshire Regiment. Born Sheepridge, Huddersfield, 26.6.1885. Son of Law and Ann Boothroyd, 52 Bentley Street, Lockwood. Educated at Mirfield Grammar School. Employed as a school teacher. Enlisted 16.9.13. Died at home, 52 Bentley Street, Lockwood, of Chronic Nephritis on 14. 11. 1920, aged 35. Buried in **LOCKWOOD CEMETERY.** Grave location:- D, 'C', 143C. ROH:- Lockwood Baptist Church; Emmanuel Church, Lockwood.

BOOTHROYD, HILDRED. Lance Corporal. No 52006. 6th Battalion Somerset Light Infantry. Born Netherton, 30.7.1893. Son of Walker and Martha Boothroyd, 17 Burbeary Road, Lockwood. Educated at Netherton Wesleyan School and Mount Pleasant Council School. Employed as a reedmaker by Mr Walter Ellis of Commercial Street, Huddersfield. Single. Enlisted 25.6.1917. Died of pneumonia in Bradford War Hospital, 20.11.1918, aged 25 years. Buried with full military honours in **EDGERTON CEMETERY, HUDDERSFIELD.** Grave location:- 47, 90. (On his headstone is inscribed: 'his sister died of a broken heart on 29.11.1918 age 16'). ROH:- Emmanuel Church, Lockwood; Mount Pleasant Chapel, Lockwood.

BOOTHROYD, JOE. Private. Royal Inniskilling Fusiliers. Born Almondbury, 29.1.1881. Educated at Almondbury Central National School. Employed as a warehouseman in astrakhan and plush manufacture. Husband of Nellie Boothroyd, 55 Northgate, Almondbury. Enlisted 4.5.1917. Died in Huddersfield Royal Infirmary 'of the effects of war', 4.7.1920. ROH:- Almondbury War Memorial.

BOOTHROYD, NORMAN. Private. No 29840. 9th Battalion Duke of Wellington's Regiment. Born Crosland Moor. Son of Friend and Caroline Boothroyd, 3 Barton Road, Crosland Moor.

Attended Crosland Moor Wesleyan Chapel. Employed in the teazing department of Messrs Gledhill Brothers, Longroyd Bridge. Single. Enlisted 30.11.1916. Had only been in France for five weeks when he died from a wound to the right thigh at No 24 Casualty Clearing Station on 13.5.1917, aged 25 years. Buried in **AUBIGNY COMMUNAL CEMETERY.** Grave location:- Plot 3, Row J, Grave 15. ROH:- St. Barnabas Church, Crosland Moor; Crosland Moor Wesleyan Church; memorial in Lockwood Cemetery.

BOOTHROYD, RICHARD. Private. No PO/18942. 6th Battalion Royal Marine Light Infantry. Born Shepley 5.11.1898. Son of Clement and Frances Boothroyd, Yew Tree Villas, Station Road, Shepley. Enlisted 8.10.1915. Died of wounds at Svyatnavalok, North Russia, 27.8.1919. Buried in **MURMANSK NEW BRITISH CEMETERY** and also commemorated on **THE BROOKWOOD RUSSIA MEMORIAL IN BROOKWOOD MILITARY CEMETERY, SURREY.** ROH:- Shepley War Memorial. A letter was written on Canadian YMCA headed note paper from Richard's Company Captain to Mrs Boothroyd, *'I very much regret having to write to announce the death of your son Private Boothroyd. We managed to get him back to the doctor who did everything he could for him. Unfortunately the only way we could get him back to Svyatnavlok was by country carts where I am afraid he was rather badly shaken up. Nevertheless he was very cheery when we arrived and everybody thought there was quite a chance for him. He got worse during the night and died in the early morning. He was buried here on the 29th at Svyatnaolok Church. I wish I had a camera here but unfortunately I have none. Major Laing, myself and all the subalterns join me in offering you our deepest sympathy in your bereavement. If there is anything else I can do for you please let me know.'*

BOOTHROYD, PERCY. Private. No 241924. 2/5th Battalion Duke of Wellington's Regiment. Born Birkby 28.5.1893. Son of T S and E Boothroyd, 12 Armitage Road, Birkby. Educated at Hillhouse School. Employed as a lithographic machine minder. Married. At the time of enlistment, on 10.12.1915, was living at 17 Broomfield Terrace, Broomfield Road. Killed in action at the Battle of Bullecourt, 3.5.1917. Has no known grave. Commemorated on the **ARRAS**

MEMORIAL TO THE MISSING. ROH:- Huddersfield Drill Hall; Fartown and Birkby War Memorial.

BOOTHROYD, THOMAS RAYMOND. Private. No 241865. 2/5th Battalion Duke of Wellington's Regiment. Born 34 Kaye Lane, Almondbury 24.12.1896. Son of Wright Boothroyd, 7 Fenay Lane, Almondbury. Educated at Central National Schools, Almondbury. Employed as a van man. Single. Enlisted 16.2.1916. Wounded at Cambrai, 4.12.1917. Died of pneumonia at 7 Fenay Lane, Almondbury, 19.1.1920. Buried in **ALMONDBURY CEMETERY.** Grave location:- L, 'C', 222. ROH:- Almondbury War Memorial.

BOOTHROYD, WILLIAM. Lance Corporal. No 36657. 7th Battalion East Lancashire Regiment. Born Honley. Son of Charles Henry and Sarah Boothroyd; husband of May Boothroyd. Died of tuberculosis at home, 29.1.1919, aged 29 years. Buried in **HONLEY CHURCH BURIAL GROUND.** Grave location:- 122, 4529. ROH:- Honley War Memorial.

BOOTHROYD, WILLIAM M. R. Lance Corporal. Machine Gun Corps. Formerly Duke of Wellington's Regiment. Son of Mr and Mrs Joe Boothroyd, Town Head, Honley. Employed by the Honley Cooperative Society. Enlisted in the Duke of Wellington's Regiment at 16 years of age. He fought at Gallipoli, where he was wounded, and afterwards served in Egypt and France. Taken prisoner by the Germans on 21.3.1918. Died at the Prisoner of War Camp at Stendal, Germany. ROH:- Honley War Memorial.

BOOTHROYD, WILLIE. Private. No 39006. 14th Battalion Machine Gun Corps. Formerly No 14401 Duke of Wellington's Regiment. Born Huddersfield. Lived Bradshaw Road, Honley. Died 21.9.1918. Buried in **St. SOUPLET BRITISH CEMETERY.** Grave location:- Plot 1, Row E, Grave 31. ROH:- Crosland Moor Wesleyan Church.

BORTHWICK, JOHN EDWIN. Private. No 9877. 9th Battalion King's Own Yorkshire Light Infantry. Born York. Lived Clayton West. Killed in action, 5.10.1917. Has no known grave. Commemorated on the **TYNE COT MEMORIAL TO THE MISSING.** ROH:- Clayton West and High Hoyland War Memorial.

BOSTOCK, WILLIE. Private. No 10643. 2nd Battalion Duke of Wellington's Regiment. Born Huddersfield. Lived at Whitworth's Buildings, Lascelles Hall, Kirkheaton. Had been in the Army a few years before the outbreak of the war. Had been three times invalided home. Killed in action, 3.5.1917, aged 25 years. Has no known grave. Commemorated on the **ARRAS MEMORIAL TO THE MISSING.** ROH:- St. John's Church, Kirkheaton.

BOTTERILL, ALFRED ROSE. Private. No 23953. 10th Battalion Duke of Wellington's Regiment. Born Bishop Wilton. Yorkshire. Lived at The Knowle, Shepley. Employed by Messrs Firth Brothers. Keenly interested in rabbits and had been a successful exhibitor. Enlisted March, 1916, and embarked for France on 14.9.1916. Killed in action, 5.10.1916, aged 19 years. Has no known grave. Commemorated on the **THIEPVAL MEMORIAL TO THE MISSING.** ROH:- Shepley War Memorial.

BOTTOMLEY, ARCHIE. Gunner. No 366222. 20th Siege Battery (North Scottish) Royal Garrison Artillery. Born Upperthong. Son of George and Janet Bottomley, 6 Cooperative Terrace, Meltham. Married, with one child. Employed as a tuner in the spooling department at Meltham Mills. Died of wounds, 12.9.1917, aged 30 years. Buried in **TALANA FARM CEMETERY.** Grave location:- Plot 3, Row I, Grave 6. ROH:- St. Bartholomew's Church, Meltham.

BOTTOMLEY, FRANK. Bombardier. Royal Field Artillery. Lived Old Lane, Hinchliffe Mill, Holmfirth. Employed at Farrar's Dyeworks, Honley. Played cricket with the Holmbridge and Cartworth Moor teams. Was a member of the Hinchliffe Mill brass band. Attended Hinhcliffe Mill Wesleyan Chapel. Married, with three children. Enlisted August 1916. Saw service in Damascus and Mesopotamia. Returned home on 5.1.1920. Died at home on 27.1.1920, aged 31 years. Buried **HINCHLIFFE MILL WESLEYAN CHAPEL.**

BOTTOMLEY, LEWIS. Private. No 268580. 1/7th Battalion Duke of Wellington's Regiment. Born Marsden. Son of John and Ellen Bottomley of Ardwick, Manchester and late of Fern Lea, Marsden. Educated at Marsden National School and Longwood Grammar School. Attended Marsden Parish Church where he was a choirboy. Was a member of the Marsden Conservative Club. Employed in the family firm of Messrs J. and J. Bottomley as a contractor. A keen cricketer and football player. Enlisted in October, 1914, at the age of 16 years. Killed in action, 29.4.1918, aged 20 years. Has no known grave. Commemorated on the **TYNE COT MEMORIAL TO THE MISSING.** ROH:- Huddersfield Drill Hall; Marsden War Memorial; Marsden Conservative Club; memorial in Marsden Churchyard; St. Mark's Parish Church, Longwood.

BOTTOMLEY, LEWIS. Private. No S/18016. 1st Battalion Cameron Highlanders. Born Crosland Moor, 23.6.1887. Educated at Crosland Moor Board School. At the time of enlistment was employed as a weaver at Peebles, Scotland. Single. Enlisted 3.5.1915. Killed in action on the Somme, 18.8.1916, aged 29 years. Has no known grave. Commemorated on the **THIEPVAL MEMORIAL TO THE MISSING.** ROH:- St. Barnabas Church, Crosland Moor; United Methodist Church, Crosland Moor.

BOTTOMLEY, MICHAEL STANLEY. Gunner. No 32879. 'C' Battery 88th Brigade Royal Field Artillery. Born Victoria Street, Lockwood, 1893. Son of Dyson and Catherine Bottomley. Educated Huddersfield Parish Church School. Employed as a porter at Huddersfield Railway Station. Single. Killed in action, 22.4.1918, aged 28 years. Has no known grave. Commemorated on the **TYNE COT MEMORIAL TO THE MISSING.** ROH:- Christ Church, Moldgreen.

BOTTOMLEY, WILLIAM. Private. No G5/71038. London Regiment. Born Marsden. Son of George Bottomley, 13 Sandhurst Cottages, Marsden. Married. Living at Victoria Terrace, Marsden. Employed as a spinner at Ready Carr Mill, Marsden. Was a member of the Conservative Club and attended Marsden Parish Church. He was a member of Marsden Brass Band. Enlisted April 1917. Embarked for France, 30.9.1917. Missing in action, 26.10.1917, aged 25 years. Commemorated on **TYNE COT MEMORIAL TO THE MISSING.** ROH:- Marsden War Memorial.

BOTTRILL, CHRISTOPHER THOMAS. Sergeant. No 6837. 16th Battalion (1st Manchester Pals) Manchester Regiment. Born Shelley. Lived Chorlton-cum-Hardy. Killed in action on the first day of the Battle of the Somme, 1.7.1916, aged 25 years. Has no known grave. Commemorated on **THIEPVAL MEMORIAL TO THE MISSING.** ROH:- Emmanuel Church, Shelley; commemorated on his parents' headstone in churchyard.

BOULTON, ARTHUR FREDERICK. Private. No 11340. 10th Battalion Duke of Wellington's Regiment. Born Dodsroyd, Berry Brow, 7.8.1890. Son of Arthur Frederick Boulton, 19 Scholes Road, Birkby. Educated at St. Paul's Church School. Employed as a labourer by Messrs William Whiteley and Sons Limited, Prospect Ironworks, Lockwood. Single. Lived with his sister Mrs Tom Berry at 63 Lightcliffe Road, Crosland Moor. Enlisted 27.8.1914. Served in the Dardenelles. Killed whilst acting as a stretcher-bearer, 18.10.1917, aged 27 years. Has no known grave. Commemorated on the **TYNE COT MEMORIAL TO THE MISSING.** ROH:- St. Barnabas Church, Crosland Moor.

BOWER, CHARLES FREDERICK. Private. No 241714. 2/5th Battalion Duke of Wellington's Regiment. Born Dale Street, Chapel Hill, Huddersfield, 20.12.1893. Educated at Spring Grove Council School. Employed as a labourer. Enlisted in 1915. Reported missing, presumed killed, at the Battle of Cambrai, 27.11.1917. Has no known grave. Commemorated on the **CAMBRAI MEMORIAL TO THE MISSING.** (Brother of **HERBERT BOWER**, killed in action, 11.11.1914, q.v.). ROH:- Huddersfield Drill Hall.

BOWER, EDWARD. Private. No 20239. 1/7th Battalion Duke of Wellington's Regiment. Born Meltham. Son of Isabella Bower of Green End, Meltham. Died of wounds, 2.1.1918, aged 30 years. Buried in **LIJSSENTHOEK MILITARY CEMETERY.** Grave location:- Plot 26, Row D, Grave 13. ROH:- Huddersfield Drill Hall; St. Bartholomew's Church, Meltham.

BOWER, HAROLD. Private. No 39658. 8th Battalion King's Own Yorkshire Light Infantry. Born Linthwaite. Husband of Ada Bower. Lived High House Green, Linthwaite. Attended Holthead General Sunday School. Employed as a weaver by Messrs Charles Lockwood and Sons, Blackrock Mills, Linthwaite. Enlisted 13.9.1916 and trained at North Ferriby. Embarked for France, 13.12.1916. Killed in action, 7.6.1917, aged 33 years. Has no known grave. Commemorated on the **MENIN GATE MEMORIAL TO THE MISSING.** ROH:- Linthwaite.

BOWER, HARRY. Private. No 25244. 15th Battalion Sherwood Foresters. Born Lindley 11.4.1897. Son of Mrs Bower, 48 Ramsden Street, Huddersfield. Educated at Holy Trinity Church of England School, Huddersfield. Employed as a collier. Married. Living at 11a Bradford Road, Huddersfield. Enlisted April 1916. Reported missing, presumed killed, 28.3.1918. Has no known grave. Commemorated on the **POZIERES MEMORIAL TO THE MISSING.**

BOWER, HERBERT. Private. No SD/3889. 11th Royal Sussex Regiment. Formerly Army Cyclist Corps. Born Golcar. Had served in the South African War in the R.A.M.C. as a stretcher-bearer. Married, with three children. Had worked for four years as a porter at Crosland Moor Workhouse until leaving the district to take up a similar position at Worcester Workhouse. Enlisted in June 1915. Killed in action, 21.10.1916, aged 36 years. Has no known grave. Commemorated on the **THIEPVAL MEMORIAL TO THE MISSING.**

BOWER, HERBERT. Private. No 6714. 2nd Battalion Duke of Wellington's Regiment. Born Dale Street, Chapel Hill, Huddersfield. Educated at Rashcliffe Church School. Employed as a labourer. Enlisted 4.8.1914. Killed in action, 11.11.1914. Has no known grave. Commemorated on the **MENIN GATE MEMORIAL TO THE MISSING.** (Brother of Private **CHARLES FREDERICK BOWER**, killed in action, 27.11.1917, q.v.).

BOWER, JAMES. Guardsman. No 21039. Coldstream Guards. Born Holmfirth. Son of William Henry and Emily Bower of Gully, Holmfirth. Educated at Holmfirth National School and Underbank Wesleyan School. Employed at Rock Mills. Was a member of Underbank Harriers. Enlisted 16.12.1916. Had been in France for six weeks when he was wounded on 30.11.1917. Died of wounds at No 55 Casualty Clearing Station, 2.12.17, aged 19 years. Buried **TINCOURT NEW BRITISH CEMETERY.** Grave location:- Plot 3, Row B, Grave 14. ROH:- Underbank War Memorial.

BOWER, JOHN THOMAS. Private. No 3024. 1/7th Battalion Duke of Wellington's Regiment. Born Damside Road, Huddersfield, 7.7. 1892. Son of Mr and Mrs John Bower, 2 Graham's Yard, Milford Street, Huddersfield. Educated at St. Paul's School. Employed as a cleaner by the Huddersfield Corporation Tramways Committee. Husband of Ida Bower, The Fold, Netherton. Enlisted 2.6.1915. Wounded in the spine in September, 1916, which left him paralysed in both legs. He was brought to Royds Hall War Hospital, Huddersfield in January, 1917, and died there on 27.4.1918, aged 26 years. Buried with full military honours in **EDGERTON CEMETERY, HUDDERSFIELD.** Grave location:- 11B, 116. ROH:- South Crosland and Netherton War Memorial; Huddersfield Drill Hall; Huddersfield Corporation Roll.

BOWER, J. Battery Sergeant Major. No 35906. Royal Field Artillery. Died at home, 28.1.1917. Buried in **St. BARTHOLOMEW'S CHURCHYARD, MARSDEN.** Grave location:- south, 17, 38.

BOWER, LEWIS. Lance Corporal. No 40229. 10th Battalion Northumberland Fusiliers. Born Honley. Son of Mrs F. Bower, 312 Vicarage Road, Longwood. Employed as a weaver by Messrs Hirst and Mallinson Limited, Cliffe End Mills, Longwood. Reported wounded and missing, 20.9.1917, aged 26. Buried in **YPRES RESERVOIR CEMETERY.** Grave location:- Plot 11, Row D, Grave 35. ROH:- St. Mark's Parish Church, Longwood. (Brother of Private **NORRIS BOWER,** who died of wounds, 9.6.1918 q.v.).

BOWER, NORRIS. Corporal. No 10828. 9th Battalion Duke of Wellington's Regiment. Born Honley. Son of Mrs F. Bower, 312 Vicarage Road, Longwood. Enlisted August 1914. Died of wounds, 9.6.1918, aged 24 years. Buried **ACHEUX BRITISH CEMETERY.** Grave location:- Plot 1, Row D, Grave 35. ROH:- St. Mark's Parish Church, Longwood. (Brother of Private **LEWIS BOWER,** reported missing, 20.9.1917, q.v.).

BOWKER, JOHN. Corporal. No TR5/22512. 21st Battalion West Yorkshire Regiment. Born Settle. He was a Police Constable and had served at Elland, Lane End, Holmfirth and Denby Dale. Had served with the East Lancashire Regiment in the Boer War. Had been gassed in the recent fighting in France and this was followed by muscular rheumatism. Married, with two children. Died at Rugeley Camp, Staffordshire, from the effects of gas poisoning, 10.7.1917, aged 30 years. Buried in **ELLAND CEMETERY**. Grave location:- 'U', A, 1480. ROH:- Scissett War Memorial.

BOWMAN, HARRY. Private. No 32263. 25th Battalion (Tyneside Irish) Northumberland Fusiliers. Born Honley. Son of John and Ellen Bowman, 28 Cliffe Wood Terrace, Neiley, Honley. Employed at Neiley Mills. Attended Woodroyd United Methodist Church. Enlisted June, 1916, and embarked for France the following November. Killed in action, 21.3.1918, aged 25 years. Has no known grave. Commemorated on the **ARRAS MEMORIAL TO THE MISSING**. ROH:- Honley War Memorial; Brockholes War Memorial.

BOYLE, THOMAS. Private. No 3/10910. 2nd Battalion Duke of Wellington's Regiment. Born Huddersfield 10.2.1876. Was a nephew of Mr Patsy Boyle of The Star Inn, Rosemary Lane, Huddersfield. Educated at St. Patrick's School. A widower, with children living at North's Yard, Northgate. Employed as a chemical labourer. Had served in the Boer War and re-enlisted at the outbreak of the present war. Killed at Hill 60, 5.5.1915. Has no known grave. Commemorated on the **MENIN GATE MEMORIAL TO THE MISSING**. Mr Boyle received the following letter from CSM Harrington of 'A' Company:-*'Just a few lines as I thought you would like to know the circumstances attending poor Tommy's death. Of course you know he died as many another good lad has died out here. We were holding a position in front of Hill 60 when the Germans got in on our left and it was during the time we were driving them back that he got hit in the groin. He was not killed outright and fought hard for his life but I think the bullet must have gone into his stomach. Anyhow he passed peacefully away after about an hour. Of course it does not follow that because a man is hit with a rifle bullet he died in pain and I think Tommy must have passed away peacefully because he seemed so resigned and he told me not to bother with him any longer as he said he was done for. A gap has been made in this Company that will be hard to fill. He was the life and soul of us all and was just as happy in the trenches as he was out of them. He has been sorely missed. I was his Platoon Sergeant at the time and I can only say he died like a man. I hope you will accept this my deepest sympathy in your sad bereavement.*

BOYTON, GEORGE. Private. No 17300. 1st Battalion Royal Welsh Fusiliers. Born Cheltenham, Gloucestershire. Son of Mrs Davies, (formerly Boyton), 61 Whitehead Lane, Primrose Hill, Huddersfield. Educated at Chippenham High School. Employed as a pattern maker. Enlisted 6.11.1914. Reported missing, presumed killed, 16.5.1915, aged 22. Has no known grave. Commemorated on the **LE TOURET MEMORIAL TO THE MISSING**. ROH:- Gospel Mission, Huddersfield.

BRACKENBURY, HAROLD. Private. No 33222. 6th Battalion York and Lancaster Regiment. Formerly No 31383 Duke of Wellington's Regiment. Born Thongsbridge. Son of Mrs J. Brackenbury, 33 Deanhouse. Educated at Netherthong National School. Attended the Wesleyan Church, Netherthong. Employed at Albion Mills, Thongsbridge. Was a member of the Burnlee Association football club. Enlisted March, 1917, and left for France on 20.6.1917. Had been home on leave a few weeks before he died and in his last letter to his mother he wrote *'It felt hard leaving home.'* Died of wounds, 1.10.1918, aged 20. Buried **CHAPEL CORNER CEMETERY, SAUCHY-LESTREE**. Grave location:- Row C, Grave 12. ROH:- Netherthong and Thongsbridge War Memorial; Netherthong Working Men's Club.

BRADBURY, LEWIS. Private. No 44787. 7th Battalion Lincolnshire Regiment. Born Marsden. Son of Mrs Harriet Bradbury, Eastwood Mount, Mount Road, Marsden. Employed as a minder at New Mills, Marsden. Attended the Wesleyan Church and Adult Bible Class. Enlisted May, 1917, and embarked for France in March, 1918. Killed in action, 7.6.1918, aged 19 years. Buried in **AUCHONVILLERS MILITARY CEMETERY**. Grave location:- Plot 2, Row L, Grave 8. ROH:-

Marsden War Memorial; commemorated on memorial in Marsden Churchyard.

BRADBURY, NORRIS. Private. No 28913. 10th Battalion Northumberland Fusiliers. Born Paddock, Huddersfield. Killed in action, 3.6.1917. Buried in **RAILWAY DUGOUTS (TRANSPORT FARM) BURIAL GROUND.** Grave location:- Plot 4, Row E, Grave 13. ROH:- All Saints Church, Paddock.

BRADLEY, CROWTHER SPENCER. Private. No 39535. 1st Battalion West Yorkshire Regiment. Born Huddersfield. Lived Lockwood. Husband of Sarah Bradley of Leeds. Killed in action, 24.9.1918, aged 40 years. Buried **CHAPELLE BRITISH CEMETERY, HOLNON, FRANCE.** Grave location:- Plot 1, Row E, Grave 6.

BRADLEY, EDGAR. Gunner. No L/25455. 'D' Battery, 250th Brigade Royal Field Artillery. Born Paddock 17.8.1894. Son of William Walter and Harriet Bradley, 101 Longwood Road, Longwood. Educated at Paddock Council School. Attended Paddock United Methodist Church. Employed as a clerk. Enlisted 5.5.1915. Killed in action, 19.11.1917, aged 23 years. Buried in **SOLFERINO FARM CEMETERY.** Grave location:- Plot 2, Row B, Grave 23. ROH:- St. Mark's Parish Church, Longwood; Shared Church, Paddock.

BRADLEY, ERNEST. Private. No 25786. 6th Battalion King's Own Yorkshire Light Infantry. Born Taylor Hill Road, Huddersfield, 13.8.1896. Son of Albert and Mary Ann Bradley, 21 Falcon Street, Close Hill. Educated at Berry Brow Council School. Employed as a finisher by Messrs Kaye and Stewart. Attended Taylor Hill Primitive Methodist Sunday School. Enlisted 10.11.1915. Killed in action near Delville Wood during the Battle of the Somme, 19.8.1916, aged 20 years. Buried in **LONDON CEMETERY AND EXTENSION.** Grave location:- Plot 4, Row F, Grave 6. ROH:- St. John's Church, Newsome; Taylor Hill Primitive Methodist Church.

BRADLEY, FRANK. Private. No 4717. 1/5th Battalion Duke of Wellington's Regiment. Born Castlegate, Huddersfield, 10.3.1898. Son of Mrs Elizabeth Bradley, 22 Union Street, Huddersfield. Educated at the Huddersfield Parish Church School. Employed by Messrs T. and H. Blamires Limited, Leeds Road, Huddersfield, as a tailor's cloth presser of khaki uniforms. Enlisted 8.2.1916. Reported missing, presumed killed, 3.9.1916, aged 18 years. Has no known grave. Commemorated on the **THIEPVAL MEMORIAL TO THE MISSING.** ROH:- Huddersfield Parish Church; Huddersfield Drill Hall; commemorated on parents' headstone in Edgerton Cemetery, Huddersfield.

BRADLEY, FRANK. Private. No 2087. 1/5th Battalion Duke of Wellington's Regiment. Born Huddersfield. Lived with his brother, Mr P. Bradley, at 22 St Peter's Street, Huddersfield. Was in the employ of Messrs Benjamin Crook and Sons Limited, leather curriers, Fitzwilliam Street, and he previously worked on the Huddersfield Corporation Tramways. Embarked for France in April, 1915. He was injured by shrapnel in the head, thigh and hand, never regaining consciousness, and he died a few hours later on 9.5.1915, aged 32 years. Buried in **SAILLY-sur-la-LYS CANADIAN CEMETERY.** Grave location:- Plot 2, Row B, Grave 45. ROH:- Huddersfield Drill Hall.

BRADLEY, GEORGE HUBERT. First Class Air Mechanic. No 403127. 1st Aeroplane Supply Depot Repair Park Royal Air Force. Formerly Duke of Wellington's Regiment. Son of Fred and Ada Bradley of Newlands View, Thongsbridge. Educated at Netherthong National School and was also a scholar at Thongsbridge Sunday School. Employed as a weaver by Messrs James Watkinson and Sons, Bridge Mills, Holmfirth. Enlisted 4.8.1914. Embarked for France April, 1915, with the local Territorials ('F' Company, 1/5th Battalion Duke of Wellington's Regiment). Accepted into the RAF in July, 1917. Died of wounds, 23.9.1918, aged 22 years. Buried in **TERLINCTHUN BRITISH CEMETERY.** Grave location:- Plot 4, Row C, Grave 26. ROH:- Netherthong and Thongsbridge War Memorial.

BRADLEY, HARRY. Private. No 241518. 2/5th Battalion Duke of Wellington's Regiment. Born Elland. Son of James and Sarah Bradley; husband of the late Sarah Ann Bradley. One child. Sister lived at The Brown Cow Inn, Holywell Green, Halifax. Lodged with Mrs Armitage, 72 George Street, Milnsbridge. Employed by Mr Sam Hirst, cloth finisher of Milnsbridge. Enlisted 4.3.1916. Embarked for France in January, 1917. Taken prisoner at the Battle of Bullecourt and died in captivity, 19.5.1917, aged 33 years. Buried in **MONS COMMUNAL CEMETERY**. Grave location:- Plot 4, Row B, Grave 8. ROH:- Huddersfield Drill Hall; Longwood War Memorial; Elland War Memorial.

BRADLEY, JAMES. Private. No 202906. Northumberland Fusiliers. Born Moor End, Lockwood in 1888. Educated at Crosland Moor Board School. Married. Employed as a milk dealer. At the time of enlistment, on the 8.8.1916, was living at 199 Manchester Road, Huddersfield. Died at home on 6.12.1921 of debility from wounds, acute bronchitis and heart failure.

BRADLEY, JOE. Private, No 22512, 2nd Battalion Duke of Wellington's Regiment. Born Huddersfield 5.7.1892. Son of William and Eliza Ann Bradley, 14 William Street, Huddersfield. Educated at Beaumont Street Council School. Employed by Messrs Alfred Crowther Limited, Northumberland Street, Huddersfield as a teamer and warehouseman. Played football with Northumberland Street football club. Husband of Lily Bradley, 64 Market Street, Paddock. Enlisted at the outbreak of the war. Killed in action near Armentieres, 8.8.1918, aged 27 years. Buried in **GONNEHEM BRITISH CEMETERY**. Grave location:- Row H, Grave 4. ROH:- Great Northern Street Congregational Chapel; All Saints Church, Paddock. (Brother of Private **WILLIAM BRADLEY**, died of wounds, 15.5.1915, q.v.).

BRADLEY, LEWIS. Private. No 29/570. 12/13th Battalion Northumberland Fusiliers. Born Moldgreen, Huddersfield 28.12.1886. Son of Mrs Mary Iredale, 27 High Royd Lane, Moldgreen. Educated at Moldgreen Council School. Employed as a teamer by Messrs John Bray and Company, Rock Street, Huddersfield. Single. Enlisted 16.5.1916. Taken prisoner by the Germans on 27.5.1918. His mother received a postcard from him dated 17.7. 1918, to say that he was in fine spirits. It was not until 8.2.1919 that his mother knew that he died in Langensalza Camp, Germany of pneumonia on 9.11.1918, aged 32 years. Buried in **NIEDERZWEHREN CEMETERY, CASSEL, GERMANY**. Grave location:- Plot 4, Row C, Grave 1. ROH:- Christ Church, Moldgreen.

BRADLEY, NORMAN. Private. No 241938. 2/5th Battalion Duke of Wellington's Regiment. Born Berry Brow, Huddersfield, 21.7.1891. Son of George and Clara Bradley, 61 Newsome Road South, Berry Brow. Educated at Berry Brow Council School. Had served his apprenticeship as a draper with Messrs Whitfield Brothers, Manchester Road, Huddersfield, and then worked for two and a half years at Brighouse Cooperative Stores. At the time of enlistment was employed in the drapery department at Honley Cooperative Stores. Attended both St. Paul's Church and Armitage Bridge Church and was a member of the Berry Brow and Armitage Bridge Conservative Club. Single. Enlisted 27.3.1916. Was accidentally killed on 3.4.1917, aged 25. Buried in **POZIERES BRITISH CEMETERY**. Grave location:- Plot 2, Row D, Grave 26. ROH:- Huddersfield Drill Hall; Armitage Bridge War Memorial; commemorated on his parents' headstone in Newsome Churchyard.

BRADLEY, WILLIAM. Private. No 5/1683. 1/5th Battalion Duke of Wellington's Regiment. Born Huddersfield 19.6.1890. Son of William and Eliza Ann Bradley, 14 William Street, Huddersfield. Educated at Beaumont Street Council School. Employed as a blacksmith's striker. Single. Enlisted 4.8.1914. Died of wounds, 15.5.1915, aged 25 years. Buried in **MERVILLE COMMUNAL CEMETERY**. Grave location:- Plot 3, Row B, Grave 8. ROH:- Great Northern Street Congregational Chapel; St. Andrew's Church, Leeds Road; Huddersfield Drill Hall. (Brother of Private **JOE BRADLEY**, killed in action, 8.8.1918, q.v.).

BRADSHAW, HARRY. Corporal. No 32846. 1st Battalion Lincolnshire Regiment. Born 31 Chapel Street, Berry Brow, Huddersfield. Son of Joseph and Mary Hannah Bradshaw, 50 Chapel Street, Berry Brow. Educated at Berry Brow Council School. Employed as a power loom tuner at Messrs John Brook and Sons, Armitage Bridge Mills. Was a member of Holmfirth Harriers and the Lockwood Cricket Club. Single. Enlisted 29.4.1916. Wounded three times. Killed in action, 21.8.1918, aged 28 years. Buried **QUEENS CEMETERY, BUCQUOY**. Grave location:- Plot 2, Row H, Grave 11. ROH:- Armitage Bridge War Memorial; Armitage Bridge Mills.

BRAHNEY, JACK. Private. No 203093. 2/4th Battalion Duke of Wellington's Regiment. Born 22 Thomas Street, Huddersfield, 24.8.1899. Son of Mr and Mrs John Brahney, 9 Willow Lane East, Huddersfield. Educated at Huddersfield Parish Church School. Employed as a motor mechanic by the Karrier Car Works, Colne Road. Single. Enlisted 1916. Killed instantly by shrapnel in the temple, 20.7.1918, aged 20 years. Has no known grave. Commemorated on the **LOOS MEMORIAL TO THE MISSING.** ROH:-. St. Andrew's Church, Leeds Road, Huddersfield; Fartown and Birkby War Memorial.

BRAIN, FREDERICK WILLIAM. Private. No 6966. 6th Battalion Northamptonshire Regiment. Born Earls Barton, Northampton 1.6.1886. Son of William Henry Brain, Hide Park, Earls Barton, Northampton. Educated at Earls Barton Church School. Employed as a guard on the London and North Western Railway. Husband of Blanche Brain, 27 Northumberland Street, Huddersfield. Called up as a Reservist at the outbreak of war. Took part in the retreat from Mons and was wounded at the beginning of the fighting around Ypres in November, 1914. Died of wounds received at the Battle of the Somme, 2.8.1916, at No 2 Stationary Hospital, Abbeville. Buried in **ABBEVILLE COMMUNAL CEMETERY.** Grave location:- Plot 6, Row G, Grave 4. ROH:- London and North Western Railway Roll.

BRAMWELL, JOSEPH. Private. No 40933. 10th Battalion (Hull Commercials) East Yorkshire Regiment. Son of Francis and Hannah Bramwell, Choppards Farm, Holmfirth. Educated firstly at Hepworth Church National School, (where he also attended the Sunday School) and then at Hade Edge Council School. Attended Choppards Sunday School. Employed by Mr Fred Lawton at Bridge Mills, Holmfirth and assisted his father on the family farm. Enlisted May 1917. Was wounded in the hand in March, 1918, and returned to England for treatment. Went back to France in September, 1918. Died of wounds in the 3rd Canadian Hospital at St. Omer, 6.11.1918, aged 20. Buried **LONGUENESSE SOUVENIR (St. OMER) CEMETERY.** Grave location:- Plot 5, Row E, Grave 45. ROH:- Cartworth War Memorial.

BRAWN, ERNEST. Private. No 30440. 2/5th Battalion Royal Warwickshire Regiment. Formerly No 3/31749 South Staffordshire Regiment. Born Shelley. Son of Mr J. Brown, Woodend Farm, Thurstonland. Employed as a grocer's assistant by Mr Percy Hopwood of Bank Bottom, Shelley. Enlisted February 1917. Died of wounds at No 8 Casualty Clearing Station, 20.11.1917, aged 19 years. Buried **DUISANS BRITISH CEMETERY.** Grave location:- Plot 6, Row D, Grave 43. ROH:- Emmanuel Church, Shelley; Thurstonland War Memorial.

BRAWN, GEORGE HERBERT. Guardsman. No 22549. 2nd Battalion Coldstream Guards. Formerly No 3864 1st Life Guards and No 73 Household Battalion. Son of Mr James Brawn of Barkhouse, Shelley. Employed by Messrs G. and W. Moseley, shopkeepers and farmers, of Shelley. Died of wounds at Le Treport, 2.9.1918, aged 25 years. Buried in **MONT-HUON MILITARY CEMETERY.** Grave location:- Plot 7, Row E, Grave 3B. ROH:- Emmanuel Church, Shelley.

BRAY, ALFRED. Private. No 12687. 10th Battalion Lancashire Fusiliers. Born Halifax. Son of Mr and Mrs Henry Bray, Badger Hey, Marsden. Brother of Mrs S. Firth, Pinewood Grove, Marsden. Employed as a quarryman. Had served in the Royal Navy. Before enlistment was living at 20 Coldhurst Street, Oldham. Married, with two children. Enlisted 11.12.1914. Killed in action, 22.12.1915, aged 33 years. Has no known grave. Commemorated on the **MENIN GATE MEMORIAL TO THE MISSING.**

BRAY, CHARLES CHRISTOPHER. Private. No 26497. 2nd Battalion King's Own Yorkshire Light Infantry. Born Upper Batley 30.1.1916. Son of Charles and Emma Bray, 25 Upper Bleasdale Avenue, Birkby. Educated at Spring Grove Council School. Employed as a baker and confectioner. Single. Enlisted 18.11.1915. Reported missing, 18.11.1916, aged 21. Buried in **WAGGON ROAD CEMETERY, BEAUMONT HAMEL.** Grave location:- Row A, Grave 22.

BRAY, FRED. Private. No 39601. 2/4th Battalion King's Own Yorkshire Light Infantry. Brother of Mrs M. A. Kemp, 316 Vicarage Road, Longwood. A very tragic incident affecting the life of the late soldier was the accidental burning to death of his wife in September, 1917, whilst descending the bedroom stairs at their home at Leymoor, Golcar. This disaster was brought about by a lighted taper which she carried slipping and igniting her flannelette nightdress. He was a senior partner in the firm of Messrs Bray and Smith, rag grinders, Leymoor, Golcar.

Was a member of the Longwood Conservative Club. Embarked for France in January, 1917. Killed in action, 1.6.1918, aged 38 years. Buried **BIENVILLERS MILITARY CEMETERY.** Grave location:- Plot 21, Row B, Grave 2. ROH:- St. John's Church, Golcar.

BRAY, FRED. Private. No 241964. 2/5th Battalion West Yorkshire Regiment. Born Parkgate, Berry Brow 8.4.1896. Son of George and Elizabeth Bray, 'The Boot and Shoe Inn,' Scholes, Thongsbridge. Educated at Berry Brow Council School and Hillhouse Higher Elementary School. Attended Berry Brow Wesleyan Church. Employed as a clerk by Messrs John Sutcliffe and Sons, Richmond Mills, Fitzwilliam Street, Huddersfield. Single. At the time of enlistment was living at 12 Caldercliffe Road, Berry Brow. Enlisted 2.3.1916. Had recently received a certificate from the General Officer Commanding his Division for distinguished conduct in the field. Killed in action, 24.5.1918, aged 22 years. Buried **GOMMECOURT BRITISH CEMETERY No 2.** Grave location:- Plot 4, Row H, Grave 21/22. ROH:- Armitage Bridge War Memorial. (Brother of Private **LEWIS BRAY,** who died in Egypt, 10.12.1919, q.v.).

BRAY, HARRY. Driver. No 223380. 24th Battery, 38th Brigade Royal Field Artillery. Born Holmfirth. Son of Ben and Lucy A. Bray, of Hill Top, Cinderhills, Holmfirth. Educated at Holmfirth National School and was also a member of the Underbank Wesleyan School. A keen footballer and cricket player for the local teams. Employed by the Hinchliffe Mill Cooperative Society, being formerly manager of the Underbank stores and, before enlistment, manager at the Holmfirth branch. Enlisted April 1917. Married. Embarked for France in October, 1917. Died of pleurisy and pneumonia at Etaples Base Hospital, 16.4.1918, aged 30 years. Buried in **ETAPLES MILITARY CEMETERY.** Grave location:- Plot 29, Row D, Grave 10A. ROH:- Underbank War Memorial.

BRAY, JAMES ARTHUR. Gunner. No 13340. 383rd Siege Battery Royal Garrison Artillery. Born Lindley 16.11.1885. Son of Fred Bottom and Ann Bray, 14 Lidget Street, Lindley. Educated at Lindley Church Schools. Employed as a woollen warehouseman by Messrs O. Rayner and Company, West Parade, Huddersfield. Enlisted 12.12.1916. Died of pneumonia in Jerusalem, 7.11.1918, aged 32 years. Buried **JERUSALEM WAR CEMETERY.** Grave location:- Row W, Grave 20. (Brother of Private **WILLIE BRAY,** who died, 31.5.1916, q.v.). ROH:- Lindley Zion Methodist Chapel; St. Stephen's Church, Lindley.

BRAY, LEWIS. Private. No 103321. 33rd Battalion Machine Gun Corps. Born 12 Bond Street, Brighouse. Son of George William and Elizabeth Bray, 'The Boot and Shoe Inn', Scholes, Thongsbridge. Educated at Berry Brow Council School. Attended Berry Brow Wesleyan Church. Employed as a cloth finisher. At the time of enlistment was living at 12 Caldercliffe Road, Berry Brow. Single. Enlisted 30.1.1917. Served in France and Italy. Taken seriously ill at Haifa and died at Kantara, Egypt, 10.12.1919, aged 22 years. Buried in **KANTARA WAR CEMETERY.** Grave location:- Plot B, Grave 100. (Brother of Private **FRED BRAY,** killed in action, 24.5.1918, q.v.).

BRAY, LISTER. Lance Corporal. No 203005. 1/4th Battalion King's Own Yorkshire Light Infantry. Son of Mr T. J. Bray of Hall Ing, Honley. Employed by Messrs Thorntons, Crossley Mills. Attended with Woodroyd United Methodist Church. Married, with one child. Enlisted September, 1914, and was wounded in 1916. Killed in action, 9.10.1917, at the Battle of Passchendaele, aged 26 years. Has no known grave. Commemorated on the **TYNE COT MEMORIAL TO THE MISSING.** ROH:- Armitage Bridge War Memorial; Honley War Memorial; Brockholes War Memorial.

BRAY, NORMAN. Lance Corporal. No B/201873. 1/8th London Regiment The Rifle Brigade. Formerly No T/307972 Army Service Corps. Born Honley, Huddersfield. Son of John and Martha Bray. Lived with his sister, Miss S.A. Bray, 15 Church Street, Honley. Employed by Messrs Taylor and Lodge . Died of wounds, 25.7.1918, aged 33 years. Buried **PERNOIS BRITISH CEMETERY.** Grave location:- Plot 3, Row A, Grave 10. ROH:- Honley War Memorial.

BRAY, TED. Gunner. No 194355. 154th Siege Battery Royal Garrison Artillery. Born Golcar. Son of John and Alice Bray, of Knowle Road, Golcar. husband of Maria Varley Bray of Longcroft, Golcar. Was in business as a stonemason. Enlisted January 1918. Killed in action, 4.6.1918, aged 31 years. Buried **HAGLE DUMP CEMETERY, BELGIUM.** Grave location:- Plot 1, Row B, Grave 1. ROH:- St. John's Church, Golcar; Golcar Baptist Church.

BRAY, WALTER BOOTH. Private. No 23585. 2/7th Battalion Duke of Wellington's Regiment. Born Thongsbridge, Huddersfield. Educated at Netherthong National School. Employed by Messrs T. Dyson and Sons, Deanhouse Mills. Was a member of the Netherthong Working Men's Club and the Free Gardener's Society. A keen footballer and cricketer. Married. Enlisted in January 1917. Killed in action, 27.3.1918. Buried **POMMIER COMMUNAL CEMETERY.** Grave location:- Grave 1. ROH:- Netherthong and Thongsbridge War Memorial; Netherthong Working Men's Club; Huddersfield Drill Hall; also commemorated on a memorial in All Saints Churchyard, Netherthong.

BRAY, WILLIE. Private. No 5485. 2/5th Battalion Duke of Wellington's Regiment. Born Lindley 12.9.1890. Son of Fred Bottom and Ann Bray, 14 Lidget Street, Lindley. Educated at Lindley Church Schools. Employed as a cloth warehouseman. Enlisted 20.3.1916. Died at Fargo Hospital, Salisbury Plain, of thrombosis. Buried with full military honours, 31.5.1916, in **LINDLEY (ZION) METHODIST CHAPEL YARD.** Grave location:- in south-east part. (Brother of Private **JAMES ARTHUR BRAY**, who died in Jerusalem, 8.11.1918, q.v.). ROH:- Lindley Zion Methodist Chapel; St. Stephen's Church, Lindley; Huddersfield Drill Hall.

BRAY, WILLIS. Private. No 21/271. 21st Battalion West Yorkshire Regiment. Born Honley. Son of Fred and Alice Mary Bray, of Bradshaw Road, Honley. Employed by Messrs Holdroyd and Sons, joiners, of Honley. Attended Honley Parish Church and was a member of the bible class. Enlisted December 1915. Embarked for France in July, 1917, and came home on leave in December, 1917. Killed in action, 27.3.1918, aged 28 years. Buried **MINDEL TRENCH BRITISH CEMETERY.** Grave location:- Row D, Grave 19. ROH:- Honley War Memorial.

BRAYSHAW, ERNEST. Private. No 203309. 1/4th Battalion Duke of Wellington's Regiment. Born 20 Back Union Street, Huddersfield. Son of Thomas William and Annis Brayshaw, 11 Great Northern Street, Huddersfield. Educated at Beaumont Street Council School. Employed by Messrs T. and H. Blamires Limited as a cloth finisher. Enlisted 5.4.1916. Wounded on 11.10.1918 and died in 1st Australian Hospital, Rouen, after having his leg amputated below the knee on 25.10.1918. Buried in **St. SEVER CEMETERY EXTENSION, ROUEN.** Grave location:- Block S, Plot S, Row KK, Grave 2. ROH:- Great Northern Street Congregational Chapel; St. Andrew's Church, Leeds Road, Huddersfield.

BRENNAN, MARTIN HENRY. Private. No 241113. 2/5th Battalion Duke of Wellington's Regiment. Born Huddersfield 27.8.1877. Educated at St. Patrick's School. Employed at British Dyes as a boilermaker. Married, with four children. At the time of enlistment, was living at 7 Hirst's Yard, Thomas Street, Huddersfield. Enlisted 30.4.1915. Killed in action, 7.8.1917, aged 40 years. Buried **QUEANT ROAD CEMETERY, BUISSY.** Grave location:- Plot 3, Row H, Grave 13. ROH:- Huddersfield Parish Church; Huddersfield Drill Hall; commemorated on his parents' headstone in Edgerton Cemetery.

BRETT, LEONARD. Lance Corporal. No 8332. 2nd Battalion Leinster Regiment. Born Halifax. Lived Stile House, Scammonden. Killed in action at Ypres, 15.8.1915, aged 26 years. Buried in **POPERINGHE NEW MILITARY CEMETERY.** Grave location:- Plot 1, Row G, Grave 9.

BRICK, LLEWELLYN. Private. No 242446. 1/5th Battalion Duke of Wellington's Regiment. Born 75 Wellington Street, Oakes, Huddersfield, 10.9.1893. Son of Austin and Clara Brick. Educated at Oakes Council School. Employed as a machine tenter by Messrs Joseph Sykes Brothers of Acre Mills, Lindley. Single. Enlisted 4.9.1914. Embarked for France in April, 1915. Was wounded in the thigh by shrapnel in August, 1915, whilst water carrying. Treated at the Royal Herbert Hospital, Woolwich. Reported missing 3.9.1916, aged 23, in the attack on the Schwaben Redoubt. Buried **MILL ROAD CEMETERY.** Grave location:- Plot 1, Row E, Grave 19. ROH:- Oakes Baptist Church; St. Stephen's Church, Lindley; Huddersfield Drill Hall.

BRIDGE, JAMES. Private. No 3/11469. 9th Battalion Duke of Wellington's Regiment. Born Bury. Lived Church Terrace, Holmfirth.

Employed at the Valley Dyeworks, Holmfirth. Enlisted in 1915. Died of wounds, 27.4.1916. Buried **BAILLEUL COMMUNAL CEMETERY EXTENSION.** Grave location:- Plot 2, Row D, Grave 152. ROH:- Holmfirth War Memorial.

BRIER, WILLIAM. Private. No 956. 21st Battalion West Yorkshire Regiment. Born Marsh, Huddersfield 23.6.1892. Son of Mr and Mrs Sam Brier, 45 Broomfield Road, Marsh. Employed by Mr Ainley, joiner, of Crosland Moor. Attended Gledholt Wesleyan Sunday School. Single. Enlisted 16.2.1916. Died of wounds near Arras, 6.5.1917, aged 23 years. Buried **FAUBOURG D'AMIENS CEMETERY, ARRAS.** Grave location:- Plot 4, Row G, Grave 10. ROH:- Marsh War Memorial; Gledholt Wesleyan Church; Holy Trinity Church, Huddersfield.

BRIERLEY, FRANK MM. Sergeant. No 11990. 10th Battalion Duke of Wellington's Regiment. Born Huddersfield 3.1.1897. Son of Mr and Mrs Joe Brierley, 142 Longwood Road, Longwood. Educated at Paddock Council School. Attended Paddock United Methodist Church. Employed as a driller by Messrs J. Hopkinson and Sons Limited of Birkby. Single. Enlisted 25.8.1914. Had served in France and the Dardenelles. Awarded the Military Medal on 1.9.1918 for 'invaluable assistance in the reorganisation of his platoon under very heavy fire.' Killed in action in Italy, 27.10.1918, aged 21 years. Buried **TEZZE CEMETERY, ITALY.** Grave location:- Plot 4, Row B, Grave 13. ROH:- St Mark's Parish Church, Longwood; Shared Church, Paddock.

BRIERLEY, HIRAM. Private. No 204188. 1/4th Battalion Duke of Wellington's Regiment. Born Lepton. Married, with four children and living at Botany, Lepton. Employed as a twister by Messrs. R. Mitchell and Company, Spa Mills, Lepton. Killed in action, 11.4.1918, aged 36 years. Has no known grave. Commemorated on the **TYNE COT MEMORIAL TO THE MISSING.** ROH:- Lepton Parish Church.

BRIERLEY, WILFRED. Private. No 202632. 1/4th Battalion King's Own Yorkshire Light Infantry. Son of Dyson Brierley, of Wellhouse, Golcar; husband of Edith Brierley, 28 Crossley Place, Linthwaite. Killed in action, 13.4.1918, aged 34. Has no known grave. Commemorated on the **TYNE COT MEMORIAL TO THE**

MISSING. ROH:- St. John's Church, Golcar; Linthwaite War Memorial.

BRIERLEY, WILLIAM. Private. No 394. 1/7th Battalion Duke of Wellington's Regiment. Born Longwood. Son of the late Mr and Mrs Roland Brierley, 202 Cliffe End, Longwood. Was employed by Messrs John Lockwood and Sons Limited, Holme Mills, Golcar as a piecer. Was a member of the Cliffe End Working Men's Club. Had served with the local Territorials for some years before the outbreak of war. Embarked for France in April, 1915, and had been home on leave in June, 1916. Reported missing, presumed killed, 3.9.1916, aged 24 years. Has no known grave. Commemorated on the **THIEPVAL MEMORIAL TO THE MISSING.** ROH:- St. Mark's Parish Church, Longwood; Huddersfield Drill Hall.

BRIERS, THOMAS. Lance Corporal. No 3/6757. 1st Battalion Bedfordshire Regiment. Born Eye Green, Northamptonshire. Lived 504 Carlton Terrace, Leeds Road, Huddersfield. Employed at the Huddersfield Corporation Waterworks and had previously worked at the goods station. Had been in Huddersfield for about four years. Was called up at the outbreak of war. Killed in action, 27.5.1915, aged 22 years. Has no known grave. Commemorated on the **MENIN GATE MEMORIAL TO THE MISSING.** ROH:- Christ Church, Woodhouse Hill; Huddersfield Corporation Roll.

BRISCOE, HORACE. Private. No 9812. 1st Battalion 'The Queens,', (Royal West Surrey) Regiment. Born Huddersfield. Son of Mrs Briscoe of Huddersfield. Died of wounds, 15.10.1915, aged 23 years. Buried in **ABBEVILLE COMMUNAL CEMETERY.** Grave location:- Plot 3, Row B, Grave 12.

BROADBENT, GEORGE HENRY. Rifleman. No 307156. 1/8th Battalion West Yorkshire Regiment. Born Upperthong. Employed by Messrs Howarth and Harpin, butchers, of Huddersfield. Married in June, 1915. Husband of Annie Broadbent, 33 Town End, Wooldale. Enlisted June, 1916. Embarked for France September, 1916. Killed in action at the Battle of Passchendaele, 9.10.1917, aged 27 years. Has no known grave. Commemorated on the **TYNE COT MEMORIAL TO THE MISSING.** ROH:- Wooldale War Memorial.

BROADBENT, HARTLEY TOLSON. Gunner. No 11177. 'D' Battery, 150th Brigade Royal Field Artillery. Born Moldgreen 3.9.1897. Son of Willie and Kathleen Evelyn Broadbent, 11 Thornton Lodge, Crosland Moor. Educated at Primrose Hill and Crosland Moor Council Schools. Employed as a clerk by Messrs David Brown and Sons, Park Works, Crosland Moor. Single. Enlisted 20.4.1916. Embarked for France in November, 1916. Killed in action, 24.7.1917, aged 19 years. Buried in **BRANDHOEK MILITARY CEMETERY**. Grave location:- Plot 2, Row N, Grave 15. ROH:- St. Barnabas Church, Crosland Moor; St. Stephen's Church, Rashcliffe.

BROADBENT, HERBERT LIONEL (BERTIE). Private. No 7/2240. 1/7th Battalion Duke of Wellington's Regiment. Born 5.1.1899. Son of Superintendent A. Broadbent, Deputy Chief Constable of Huddersfield, and Mrs Broadbent of 6, Woodthorpe Terrace, Bankfield Road, Huddersfield. Educated at St. Thomas's Church of England School, Longroyd Bridge. Employed as an apprentice in the wire-drawing department at Messrs Joseph Sykes Brothers Limited, Acre Mills, Lindley. Single. Enlisted September 1914. Trained at Riby and Doncaster. Embarked for France in April, 1915. Killed in action near Ypres, 30.7.1915, aged 16 years. Buried in **COLNE VALLEY CEMETERY**. Grave location:- Row D, Grave 7. ROH:- St. Thomas's Church, Longroyd Bridge; Huddersfield Drill Hall.

BROADBENT, JACK. Private. No 3908. 1st Battalion Northumberland Fusiliers. Born Honley Wood Bottom 6.9.1894. Son of Mr J. Broadbent, 210 Leeds Road, Huddersfield. Educated at St. Andrew's Church School. Employed as a minder. Killed in action 16.6.1915. Has no known grave. Commemorated on the **MENIN GATE MEMORIAL TO THE MISSING**.

BROADBENT, JAMES. Private. No 20003. 1st Battalion King's Own Scottish Borderers. Born Liverpool. Son of Thomas and Margaret Broadbent; husband of Elizabeth Broadbent of Jackson Bridge, New Mill. Killed in action at Beaumont Hamel, 1.7.1916, aged 32 years. Has no known grave. Commemorated on the **THIEPVAL MEMORIAL TO THE MISSING**. ROH:- New Mill Working Men's' Club; Fulstone War Memorial.

BROADBENT, JIM. Lance Corporal. No 37986. 34th Battalion Machine Gun Corps. Formerly No 3026 Duke of Wellington's Regiment. Son of Mrs Broadbent, 26 Lipscombe Street, Milnsbridge. Educated Crow Lane Board School, Milnsbridge. Employed by the Longwood Gas Company. Single. Enlisted soon after war broke out. Died at Rouen Base Hospital from the effects of mustard gas, 29.7.1918, aged 22 years. Buried in **St. SEVER CEMETERY EXTENSION, ROUEN**. Grave location:- Block Q, Plot 4, Row E, Grave 8. ROH:- St. Mark's Parish Church, Longwood; Crow Lane Board School, Milnsbridge.

BROADBENT, JOHN FRANKLIN. Private, No 306241. 1/7th Battalion Duke of Wellington's Regiment. Born Marsden. Was the eldest son of a family of eight children of Augustus Henry Broadbent, 22 Ottiwells Terrace, Marsden. Employed as a piecer by Messrs Robinson Brothers, Clough Lea Mill, Marsden. Attended Marsden Adult School and Marsden Parish Church. Single. Played football with the Marsden Villa AFC. Enlisted 15.9.1915. Killed in action in the attack on the Schwaben Redoubt, 3.9.1916, aged 21 years. Has no known grave. Commemorated on the **THIEPVAL MEMORIAL TO THE MISSING**. ROH:- Huddersfield Drill Hall; Marsden War Memorial.

BROADBENT, NORMAN. 1st Class Stoker. No SS/108049 (RFR/DEV/B/5636) Royal Naval Division (Howe Battalion). Born Paddock 25.5.1890. Son of the late William and Mary Ellen Broadbent, 22 Salford, Lockwood. Educated at Lockwood Church Schools. At the time of enlistment, was living at 22 Salford, Lockwood. Married. Enlisted in the Royal Naval Volunteer Reserve in February, 1910. In August, 1914, he was mobilised from the Royal Fleet Reserve and, in October 1914, he served at the siege of Antwerp. Killed in action at the Third Battle of Krithia, Gallipoli, on 4.6.1915, aged 25 years. Has no known grave. Commemorated on the **HELLES MEMORIAL TO THE MISSING, GALLIPOLI**. ROH:- Emmanuel Church, Lockwood. (Brother of Private **WILFRED BROADBENT**, killed in action, 9.4.1918, q.v.).

BROADBENT, REUBEN. Farrier Sergeant. No L/29255. 'A' Battery, 155th Brigade Royal Field Artillery. Born Somerset Bridge, Moldgreen, 2.9.1880. Educated at Beaumont Street Council

School. Employed as a stoker at the Huddersfield Corporation Gasworks. Husband of Annie Broadbent, 5 Hawk Street, Huddersfield. Father of six children. Had served throughout the South African War. Enlisted May 1915. Killed in action near Cambrai, 3.10.1918, aged 37 years. Buried in **CHAPEL CORNER CEMETERY, SAUCHY-LESTREE.** Grave location:- Row A, Grave 24.

BROADBENT, STANLEY. Private. No 24992. 10th Battalion Duke of Wellington's Regiment. Born Almondbury. Only son of Albert and Louisa Broadbent, 185 Westgate, Almondbury. Employed by Messrs Dugdale Brothers, Northumberland Street, Huddersfield. Attended Almondbury Church and was the Sunday School Secretary. Was a member of the Conservative Club. Embarked for France in January, 1917. Killed in action, 20.9.1917, aged 23 years. Buried in **TYNE COT CEMETERY.** Grave location:- Plot 58, Row C, Grave 13. ROH:- Almondbury War Memorial.

BROADBENT, WILFRED. Private. No 5/4438. 1/5th Battalion Duke of Wellington's Regiment. Born Field Gate, Leeds Road, Huddersfield, 12.10.1886. Educated at Beaumont Street Board School. Employed by Messrs James Haigh Limited, dyers and finishers, Colne Road, Huddersfield. Married, with two children. Enlisted 8.8.1915. Killed by a German sniper, 9.8.1916, a year and a day after he enlisted. Buried **CONNAUGHT CEMETERY, THIEPVAL.** Grave location:- Plot 3, Row J, Grave 2. ROH:- Huddersfield Drill Hall.

BROADBENT, WILFRED. Private. No 129197. 55th Battalion Machine Gun Corps. Born Paddock 6.6.1886. Son of the late William and Mary Ellen Broadbent, 22 Salford, Lockwood. Educated at Lockwood Church Schools. Employed as a wood sawer's assistant. Husband of Elsie Broadbent, 20 Swan Lane, Lockwood. Enlisted 9.8.1917. Reported missing, presumed killed, 9.4.1918, aged 31 years. Has no known grave. Commemorated on the **LOOS MEMORIAL TO THE MISSING.** (Brother of Private **NORMAN BROADBENT**, killed in action in the Dardenelles, 4.6.1915, q.v.). ROH:- Emmanuel Church, Lockwood.

BROADBENT, WILLIAM. Sergeant. No 3/10686. 8th Battalion Duke of Wellington's Regiment. Born Sheffield 1.1.1876. Educated at Newsome School. Employed as a dyer's labourer. Married. Enlisted 10.8.1914. Died at home, 108 Lockwood Road, of consumption on 10.3.1917, aged 41 years. Buried in **LOCKWOOD CEMETERY.** Grave location:- A, 'U', 117.

BROADHEAD, ARTHUR. Private. No 2823. 1/5th Battalion Duke of Wellington's Regiment. Born Kirkheaton. Son of Irvy and the late Alice Broadhead, St. Mary's Fold, Kirkheaton. Shot in the jaw and died in No 10 Casualty Clearing Station (Remy Siding), 5.8.1915, aged 24 years. Buried in **LIJSSENTHOEK MILITARY CEMETERY.** Grave location:- Plot 1, Row C, Grave 14. ROH:- St. John's Church, Kirkheaton; Huddersfield Drill Hall.

BROADHEAD, JOHN ELLIS. Gunner. No 117358. 394th Siege Battery Royal Garrison Artillery. Born Huddersfield. Son of George and Elizabeth Ann Broadhead of Denby; husband of Ellen Ann Broadhead. Died of malaria in Palestine, 13.10.1918, aged 42 years. Buried in **RAMLEH WAR CEMETERY, PALESTINE.** Grave location:- Plot Z, Grave 56.

BROADHEAD, WILLIE. Private. No PO/1439 (S) Royal Marine Light Infantry 2nd Royal Marine Battalion Royal Naval Division. Born Kirkheaton. Son of Mrs E. A. Broadhead and the late W. Broadhead of Blue Slates, Kirkheaton. Employed as a presser by Messrs T. and H. Blamires Limited, of Leeds Road, Huddersfield. Was a member of Kirkheaton Church Sunday School and later attended Moldgreen Congregational Sunday School. A keen footballer. Enlisted February 1916. Killed in action on 8.2.1917, aged 22, when the advance line came under heavy fire from the enemy's artillery and a shell bursting in the post in which he was stationed killed him instantly. Has no known grave. Commemorated on the **THIEPVAL MEMORIAL TO THE MISSING.** ROH:- St. John's Church, Kirkheaton.

BROOK, ARTHUR. Private. No 11966. 2nd Battalion Duke of Wellington's Regiment. Born Shepherd Lane, Deighton, 22.6.1892. Son of Nancy Brook, 1 Woodhouse Avenue, Fartown. Educated at Deighton Board School. Employed by Messrs J. Hopkinson and Company, Birkby, as a labourer. Single. Enlisted 24.8.1914. Killed at

Hill 60, 5.5.1915, aged 22 years. Has no known grave. Commemorated on the **MENIN GATE MEMORIAL TO THE MISSING.** ROH:- Christ Church, Woodhouse Hill; Fartown and Birkby War Memorial.

BROOK, ARTHUR. Private. No 235314. 4th Battalion Lincolnshire Regiment. Formerly No 205207 West Yorkshire Regiment. Born 3 Union Street, Lindley 4.9.1879. Son of Hannah Brook and the late Benny Brook. Educated at Lindley Church of England School. Worked in his late father's business as a painter and decorator. Was a member of Lindley Conservative Club and attended St. Stephen's Church, Lindley. Married, with one child. Living at 23 Victoria Street, Lindley. Enlisted 17.4.1917. Wounded at Bullecourt, 21.3.1918, and died in 13th General Hospital, Boulogne, of his wounds on 3.4.1918, aged 40. Buried in **BOULOGNE EASTERN CEMETERY.** Grave location:- Plot 1, Row I, Grave 179. ROH:- St. Stephen's Church, Lindley.

BROOK, ARTHUR. Private. No 241793. 2/5th Battalion Duke of Wellington's Regiment. Born Meltham. Lived Meltham. Killed in action at the Battle of Bullecourt, 3.5.1917. Has no known grave. Commemorated on the **ARRAS MEMORIAL TO THE MISSING.** ROH:- St. Bartholomew's Church, Meltham; Helme Parish Church; Huddersfield Drill Hall.

BROOK, ARTHUR CHARLES. 2nd Lieutenant. 5th Battalion Manchester Regiment. Born 18.6.1884. Eldest son of Mr Arthur Brook of HM Treasury and of Ruth Mary Brook of Woodhouse, Weybridge, Surrey, and a nephew of Mr T. Julius Hirst of Meltham Hall and of Mr C. L. Brook of Harewood Lodge. Educated at The Grange, Folkestone, and at Rugby Public School from 1898 to 1903. In 1903 he entered Exeter College, Oxford. After taking his BA degree he joined the firm of Messrs Jonas Brook and Brothers, cotton thread manufacturers, of Meltham Mills, of which he became a director in 1912. Lived at Helme Lodge, near Meltham, and was a Church Warden at Helme Church. Husband of Sydney Harriet (nee Darlington) Brook. They were married on 8.7.1909 in the Parish Church in Douglas, Lancaster. Father of Ruth Blanche Mary (born 29.5.1910) at Manor Croft, Helme Edge. He was passionately fond of horticulture and he acted as President of the Meltham Mills Flower Show. He was a good all round sportsman. Enlisted at the outbreak of the war in the 5th Battalion Manchester Regiment and proceeded with them to Egypt in September, 1914. On 4.5.1915, he landed with his battalion in the Dardenelles. During the attack by the Manchester's on the Turkish trenches below Achi Baba he was directing his men, who were taking ammunition under heavy fire to the captured trenches, when he was shot and killed instantaneously on 4.6.1915, aged 30 years. Buried in **REDOUBT CEMETERY, HELLES, GALLIPOLI.** Grave location:- Plot 12, Row A, Grave 20. ROH:- St. Bartholomew's Church, Meltham; Helme Parish Church. *2nd Lieutenant Brook's will was written by Fisher and Company, solicitors, of John William Street, Huddersfield. His will was granted probate on 11.10.1915 and his estate valued at £3,606 5s 2d.*

BROOK, BENJAMIN. Private. No 301786. 1/8th Battalion Durham Light Infantry. Formerly No 29373 Northumberland Fusiliers. Son of Emor and Martha Ann Brook, 34 Woodhead Road, Holmfirth. Employed in the teazing and fettling department at Messrs H. and S. Butterworth, Lower Mills, Holmfirth. Attended St. John's Church and Sunday School, Holmfirth. Enlisted 6.6.1916. Reported missing, presumed killed, 15.11.1916, aged 26. Has no known grave. Commemorated on the **THIEPVAL MEMORIAL TO THE MISSING.** ROH:- Holmfirth.

BROOK, CHARLES. Private. No 27788 8th Battalion East Yorkshire Regiment. Formerly No 41431 Durham Light Infantry. Born Holmfirth. Lived Longley Lane, Holmfirth. Educated at Hade Edge Council School. Employed by Messrs Davies and Company, dyers of Holmfirth. Married, with four children. Enlisted 30.8.1916. Embarked for France in November, 1916. Reported missing, presumed killed, 26.9.1917, aged 31 years. Has no known grave. Commemorated on the **TYNE COT MEMORIAL TO THE MISSING.** ROH:- Hade Edge War Memorial.

BROOK, CHARLES DOUGLAS. Lance Corporal. No M2/077850. 30th Ammunition Sub Park, Army Service Corps. Born 11.12.1892. Son of Tom and Emma Brook, 11 South Parade, Huddersfield. Educated at Fartown Grammar School. Was a prominent member of the

YMCA and also a member of the Huddersfield Swimming Club. Employed by Messrs Vickers, Sons and Maxim Limited, of Barrow, as an engineer. Enlisted 5.11.1914. Died as the result of accidental injuries at No 7 Casualty Clearing Station, 5.9.1916. Buried **MERVILLE COMMUNAL CEMETERY EXTENSION.** Grave location:- Plot 1, Row A, Grave 9. His youngest brother, Private **GEORGE WILLIAM BROOK**, attended the funeral. (Brother of Private G. W. Brook, who was commissioned into the Duke of Wellington's Regiment and died, 12.11.1918, q.v.). ROH:- Huddersfield Parish Church.

BROOK, CHARLES WILLIAM. 2nd Lieutenant. Royal Flying Corps. Formerly Private 8th Battalion Duke of Wellington's Regiment. Born Crosland Moor 18.1.1891. Son of George William and Ida Brook, Birkhouse Cottage, Crosland Moor. Educated at Crosland Moor National School, Spring Grove Board School and Huddersfield Higher Grade School. Single when joining the forces but married on 26.12.1917 and his wife (Hilda) lived at Glenview, Bank Bottom, Shelley. Enlisted on 27.8.1914. as a Private and quickly gained the rank of Sergeant. He saw service in the landing at Suvla Bay, Gallipoli, and was invalided home, suffering from wounds and dysentery, in August, 1915. He embarked for France in March, 1916, and was in the Battle of the Somme. In December, 1916, he was recommended for a commission and, after undergoing training at Gailes, Scotland, was Gazetted Second Lieutenant on 30.5.17. In September he joined the Royal Flying Corps and completed his training as a pilot. He came home on leave a week before he was killed, returning to Winchester awaiting orders for service overseas. Killed in a flying accident at Winchester on 26.3.1918, aged 27 years. Buried in **LOCKWOOD CEMETERY, HUDDERSFIELD.** Grave location:- A, 471. ROH:- St. Barnabas Church, Crosland Moor; Lockwood Baptist Church; Shelley War Memorial.

BROOK, CHARLEY. Private. No 240947. 2/5th Battalion Duke of Wellington's Regiment. Born 16 Wood Street, Moldgreen, 16.11.1894. Son of Thomas and Charlotte Brook, 7 West Place, Dalton. Educated at Moldgreen Church Schools. Employed as a butcher. Enlisted 20.1.1915. Died 15.7.1918 of bronchial pneumonia, aged 23 years. Buried in **MARISSEL FRENCH NATIONAL CEMETERY.** Grave location:- Grave No 663. ROH:- Christ Church, Moldgreen; Huddersfield Drill Hall.

BROOK, COLONEL. Private. No 204216. 1/4th Battalion Duke of Wellington's Regiment. Son of Mabel Brook, 168 Blackmoorfoot Road, Crosland Moor. Educated at Crosland Moor Council School. Employed as a stonemason at Linthwaite and had worked for a time for Messrs Robert McAlpine and Sons. Was a member of the Working Men's Club and played football with the local team. Married, with two children and, at the time of enlistment, was living at 48 Barton Road, Crosland Moor. Enlisted 29.9.1916. Embarked for France in April, 1917. Suffered severe gunshot wounds to the chest at Nieuport, 5.8.1917, and died in the 39th Casualty Clearing Station on 10.8.1917, aged 35 years. Buried in **ADINKERKE MILITARY CEMETERY.** Grave location:- Row C, Grave 7. ROH:- St. Barnabas Church, Crosland Moor; United Methodist Church, Crosland Moor.

BROOK, ESNOR. Private. No 241788. 2/5th Battalion Duke of Wellington's Regiment. Born Golcar in 1880. Son of Mr and Mrs Joe William Brook of Slantgate, Kirkburton. Employed as a woollen spinner by Messrs W. Singleton and Company, Brook Mills, Kirkburton. Enlisted March 1916. Died of septic poisoning on 17.6.1917, in Hamelin Internment Camp, Germany, where he had been held as a wounded Prisoner of War, aged 36 years. Buried in **NIEDERZWEHREN CEMETERY, CASSEL, GERMANY.** Grave location:- Plot 10, Row F, Grave 17. ROH:- All Hallows Parish Church, Kirkburton; Huddersfield Drill Hall.

BROOK, FRANK. Private. No 44025. 1st Battalion South Lancashire Regiment. Born 52 Cross Lane, Marsh, 21.1.1890. Son of Joseph and Hannah Brook, 20 Eldon Road, Marsh. Educated at Holy Trinity Church of England School. At the time of enlistment was working in St. Helens, Lancashire, as a cost clerk. Married. Enlisted 10.11.1917. Died in Port Said Military Hospital of influenza, 29.12.1919, aged 30. Buried in **PORT SAID WAR MEMORIAL CEMETERY, EGYPT.** Grave location:- Plot R, Grave 4. ROH:- Holy Trinity Church; St. Mark's Parish Church, Longwood.

BROOK, FREDERICK WILLIAM. Private. No 57613. 11th Battalion West Yorkshire Regiment. Born Victoria Road, Lockwood, 19.5.1888. Son of Lewis and Wilhelmina Brook, of Lockwood. Employed as a tramcar cleaner at the Corporation tramway shed, Great Northern Street, Huddersfield. Married, with two children and, at the time of enlistment, was living at 44 Moorbottom Road, Crosland Moor, Huddersfield. Enlisted 11.7.1917. Died of wounds to face, right hand and abdomen on 4.7.1918, in Italy, aged 30. Buried **CAVALLETO BRITISH CEMETERY, ITALY**. Grave location:- Plot 1, Row A, Grave 3. ROH:- St. Stephen's Church, Rashcliffe; Huddersfield Corporation Roll.

BROOK, GEORGE WILLIAM. 2nd Lieutenant. 5th Battalion Duke of Wellington's Regiment. Born 20.9.1894. Son of Tom and Emma Brook, 11 South Parade, Huddersfield. Educated at Fartown Grammar School and Huddersfield Technical College. Before enlistment, was learning the business of manufacturing with Messrs J. Heywood and Sons, Marsh Mills. Was a member of the Huddersfield YMCA and the Huddersfield Swimming Club. Enlisted as a Private in August, 1914, and embarked for France in April, 1915. Was once wounded and, after training at Fermoy, Ireland, he received his commission with the Duke of Wellington's Regiment, in March 1918. Died at home, 11, South Parade, Huddersfield from pneumonia contracted on active service, 12.11.1918, aged 25 years. Buried in **St. PAUL'S CHURCHYARD, ARMITAGE BRIDGE**. (Brother of 2nd Lieut. **CHARLES DOUGLAS BROOK**, who died, 5.9.1916, q.v.). ROH:- Huddersfield Parish Church; Huddersfield Drill Hall.

BROOK, HAROLD. Private. No 62284. 2nd Battalion West Yorkshire Regiment. Born Blackpool. Lived 30 Royds Terrace, Marsden. Reported missing, presumed killed, 24.4.1918, aged 18 years. Has no known grave. Commemorated on the **POZIERES MEMORIAL TO THE MISSING**. ROH:- Marsden War Memorial.

BROOK, HAROLD. Private. No 307759. 1/7th Battalion Duke of Wellington's Regiment. Born 24.9.1897. Son of Mr George Brook, plumber, 14 Thornton Road, Crosland Moor. Educated at St. Thomas's Church of England School. Employed by Messrs Wilson, Travis and Company, packing case makers, of William Street, Huddersfield. Single. Gassed at Nieuport and died on 30.7.1917, aged 19 years. Buried in **COXYDE MILITARY CEMETERY**. Grave location:- Plot 3, Row A, Grave 6; ROH:- St. Thomas's Church, Longroyd Bridge; Huddersfield Drill Hall.

BROOK, HAROLD CYRIL. Private. No 302123 2nd Battalion The Royal Scots (Lothian Regiment). Born Lindley. Son of Albert and Emily Isabella Brook, 9 Sandhill Cottages, Marsden. Employed as a woollen minder at Holme Mills, Marsden. Was a member of Longwood Church choir and attended Lingards Church Sunday School, Slaithwaite. Killed in action, 18.9.1918, aged 20 years. Buried in **MORCHIES AUSTRALIAN CEMETERY**. Grave location:- Row C, Grave 11, ROH:- Marsden War Memorial.

BROOK, HARRY. Gunner. No 161698. 308th Siege Battery Royal Garrison Artillery. Born Holmfirth. Educated at Holmfirth National School. Employed by Messrs J. Bower and Sons, Dover Mills, Holmfirth. Was a member of the Hepworth Brass Band, playing both the euphonium and the cornet. Married, with one child. Lived Kippax Row, Underbank, Holmfirth. Enlisted May 1917. Killed in action, 4.11.1917. Buried in **MENIN ROAD SOUTH CEMETERY, YPRES**. Grave location:- Plot 3, Row K, Grave 35. ROH:- Underbank War Memorial. His wife received the following letter from a comrade, *'You ask me about your poor husband's death. It as hard for me to write it as it is to tell you as we were the best of chums. Well on November 4th, Sunday morning at 7.30am, Harry and a young man named Denham went to the cookhouse to get breakfast ready for the men on the guns, only about two hundred yards behind, when Fritz sent a high explosive shell over. This dropped close to them and killed them both instantaneously, hitting poor Harry in the stomach and the other poor fellow in the face. We carried them about two miles on stretchers and they were put away very nice and comfortable under the circumstances. Along with several of our chums we had service over them and they are buried in the military cemetery at Ypres. I am sure that he did not suffer any pain as it was all over in a second and that is a lot better than lying in agony for days and then go.'*

BROOK, HARRY. Sergeant. No 240082. 2/5th Battalion Duke of Wellington's Regiment. Born 58 Great Northern Street, Huddersfield. Son of Pearson and Emily Brook, 85 Hillhouse Lane, Huddersfield. Educated at Beaumont Street Board School. Employed as a warehouseman by Messrs M. Haigh, Sykes and Company, St. John's Road, Huddersfield. Enlisted July 1911. Killed in action at the Battle of Bullecourt, 3.5.1917, aged 21. Has no known grave. Commemorated on the **ARRAS MEMORIAL TO THE MISSING.** ROH:-. St. Andrew's Church, Leeds Road, Huddersfield; Huddersfield Drill Hall; Fartown and Birkby War Memorial.

BROOK, HARRY. Sergeant. No 305197. 1/7th Battalion Duke of Wellington's Regiment. Born Marsden. Lived 35 Royds Terrace, Marsden. Employed in the warehouse at Bank Bottom Mills, Marsden. Had been out in France since 1914. Killed in action, 7.10.1917, aged 23 years. Has no known grave. Commemorated on the **TYNE COT MEMORIAL TO THE MISSING.** ROH:- Huddersfield Drill Hall; Marsden War Memorial.

BROOK, HARRY. Private. No 49686. 1/9th Battalion The King's (Liverpool Regiment). Formerly No 30180 Duke of Wellington's Regiment. Son of Mrs Clara Brook of Delph Terrace, Manchester Road, Milnsbridge; husband of Sarah Brook of 'Casa Nova,' 334 Manchester Road, Milnsbridge. Employed as a twister's overlooker by Messrs John Crowther and Sons, Milnsbridge. Killed in action, 31.7.1917, aged 26 years. Has no known grave. Commemorated on the **MENIN GATE MEMORIAL TO THE MISSING.** ROH:- Milnsbridge War Memorial.

BROOK, HENRY. Private. No 241451. 2/5th Battalion Duke of Wellington's Regiment. Born Southport, son of the late Francis and Ellen Brook of Southport. Lived Lockwood Scar, Huddersfield. Killed in action, 29.3.1918, aged 27 years. Has no known grave. Commemorated on the **ARRAS MEMORIAL TO THE MISSING.** ROH:- Huddersfield Drill Hall.

BROOK, HERBERT, MSM. Corporal. No 441158. Royal Army Medical Corps. Born 30 Violet Street, Halifax 10.12.1891. Son of Richard and Mary Brook, 91 Northgate, Huddersfield. Educated at Beaumont Street Board School; Huddersfield Higher Grade School and Bangor College. Was a school teacher in Sheffield before enlisting on 18.6.1915. Was on holiday at Cologne when war was declared. Single. Was demobilised at the beginning of February, 1919, but was taken ill on the journey home. Died from influenza and pneumonia at home, 91 Northgate, Huddersfield, on 19.2.1919, aged 27. He had recently been awarded the Meritorious Service Medal for clerical work in the 4th Army Headquarters. Buried **EDGERTON CEMETERY, HUDDERSFIELD.** Grave location:- 46, 130G. ROH:- Great Northern Street Congregational Chapel; St. Andrew's Church, Leeds Road; Fartown and Birkby War Memorial.

BROOK, HERBERT. Private. No 10617. 2nd Battalion Duke of Wellington's Regiment. Born Brighouse. Son of Mrs Brook, confectioner, 29 Bankwell Road, Milnsbridge. Died of wounds, 28.3.1915, aged 21. Buried in **CLACTON CEMETERY, ESSEX.** Grave location:- C, 259. ROH:- Milnsbridge. (Brother of Private **JOHN AMOS BROOK,** killed in action, 23.4.1917, q.v.).

BROOK, HERBERT WILSON. Private. No 131828. 50th Machine Gun Depot, Machine Gun Corps. Born Thongsbridge, Holmfirth, Huddersfield. Lived Thongsbridge. Killed in action, 11.9.1918. Buried **HARLEBEKE NEW BRITISH CEMETERY, BELGIUM.** Grave Location:- Plot 19, Row B, Grave 8. ROH:- Wooldale.

BROOK, HILDRED. Private. No 3/10601. 2nd Battalion Duke of Wellington's Regiment. Born Meltham. Son of the late Sam and Lydia Ann Brook. Lived Mill Moor, Meltham. Killed in action on the first day of the Battle of the Somme, 1.7.1916, aged 26 years. He had been previously wounded and gassed at Hill 60 in May, 1915. Buried in **EUSTON ROAD CEMETERY.** Grave location:- Plot 1, Row A, Grave 53. ROH:- St. Bartholomew's Church, Meltham.

BROOK, HORACE. Private. No 241564. 2/5th Battalion Duke of Wellington's Regiment. Born 59 Baker Street, Oakes, Huddersfield, 24.9.1893. Son of John William Brook, 61 Baker Street, Oakes. Educated at Oakes Board School. Employed as a scourer and miller by Messrs T. and H. Blamires Limited, Leeds Road, Huddersfield. Died of wounds, 13.9.1918, aged 24 years. Buried in **SUNKEN ROAD CEMETERY, BOISLEUX-ST-MARC.** Grave location:- Plot 2, Row A, Grave 5. ROH:- Oakes Baptist Church; St. Stephen's Church, Lindley; Huddersfield Drill Hall.

BROOK, HORACE, MM. Corporal. No 27585. 'C' Company, 37th Battalion Machine Gun Corps. Formerly No 17782 Duke of Wellington's Regiment. Born Jacob's Row, Lockwood. Son of Mrs E. E. Brook, 408 Blackmoorfoot Road, Crosland Moor. Educated at Mount Pleasant and Spring Grove Council Schools. Employed as a shop assistant in a booksellers and stationers. Single. Enlisted 20.1.1916. Awarded the Military Medal in May, 1918. Killed in action, 24.8.1918, aged 25 years. Buried in **ACHIET-LE-GRAND COMMUNAL CEMETERY EXTENSION.** Grave location:- Plot 3, Row K, Grave 28. ROH:- Rehoboth Baptist Chapel; 'Rising Sun' Public House, Crosland Hill; St. Barnabas Church, Crosland Moor.

BROOK, IRVING. Private. No 241058. 2/5th Battalion Duke of Wellington's Regiment. Son of Mr and Mrs S. W. Brook of Muslin Hall, Thongsbridge. Employed at Kirkbridge Mills. Captured by the Germans at Bullecourt, 3.5.1917, and was severely injured in the jaw. An operation was performed which was not successful and he was repatriated to England and treated on G3 Ward, King George's Hospital, London, where he underwent another operation. He died suddenly on 21.6.1918, aged 24 years. Buried in **LYDGATE PRESBYTERIAN CHAPEL YARD, HOLMFIRTH.** Grave location:- near South-East corner. 427. ROH:- Wooldale War Memorial; Huddersfield Drill Hall.

BROOK, JAMES. Private. No 21/712. 1/5th Battalion West Yorkshire Regiment. Born Kirkburton. Son of Mr and Mrs Tom Brook of Bank End, Kirkburton. Employed by Mr W. Armitage of Springfield Mills. Enlisted February 1915. Killed in action, 23.9.1918, aged 22 years. Has no known grave. Commemorated on the **VIS-en-ARTOIS MEMORIAL TO THE MISSING.** ROH:- All Hallows Parish Church, Kirkburton; Shelley War Memorial.

BROOK, JOE. Private. No 202154. 1/4th Battalion Northumberland Fusiliers. Born Marsden. Son of Japheth and Mary Brook of Clough Lea, Marsden. Employed as a spinner at Bank Bottom Mills, Marsden. Enlisted in June, 1916, and went over to France in October, 1916. Died of wounds, 27.3.1918, aged 30. Buried in **St SEVER CEMETERY EXTENSION, ROUEN.** Grave location:- Block P, Plot 7, Row C. Grave 9B. ROH:- Marsden War Memorial. His mother received the following letter from the Sister in charge of an ambulance train, *'He seemed to have no pain as he was more or less unconscious from the time he boarded the train until he died. We did all we could but his case was hopeless. His body was taken to Rouen.'*

BROOK, JOHN AMOS. Private. No SR/6974. 16th Battalion Middlesex Regiment. Born Halifax. Son of Mrs Brook, confectioner, 29 Bankwell Road, Milnsbridge. Formerly employed in an engineering works in London. Killed in action, 23.4.1917, aged 25 years. Has no known grave. Commemorated on the **ARRAS MEMORIAL TO THE MISSING.** ROH:- Milnsbridge War Memorial. (Brother of Private **HERBERT BROOK,** who died of wounds, 28.3.1915, q.v.).

BROOK, JOHN ARTHUR. Private. No 305213. 2/5th Battalion Duke of Wellington's Regiment. Born Golcar. Lived 327 Radcliffe Road, Crimble, Slaithwaite. Son of Mr T. Brook. Employed as a piecer by Messrs Pogson and Company and attended the Crimble Congregational Mission Church. Was a member of Slaithwaite Liberal Club. Embarked for France in January, 1916. Killed by a bursting shell in France on 28.9.1918, whilst making his way to a dressing station after being wounded in the chin. Aged 22 years. Buried in **GRAND RAVINE BRITISH CEMETERY, HAVRINCOURT.** Grave location:- Row A, Grave 13. ROH:- St. James Church, Slaithwaite; Slaithwaite War Memorial; Huddersfield Drill Hall.

BROOK, LEONARD STARKEY. Private. No 14234. 1st West Riding Divisional Cyclist Company. Formerly No 2406 Duke of Wellington's Regiment. Born Paddock, Huddersfield, 25.2.1897. Son of John and Mary Ellen Brook, 12 May Street, Crosland Moor. Educated at Paddock and Crosland Moor Church Schools. Employed as a printer. Enlisted 24.2.1914. Died of a perforated gastric ulcer in No 2 Canadian Casualty Clearing Station, 16.6.17, aged 20 years. Buried in **LIJSSENTHOEK MILITARY CEMETERY.** Grave location:- Plot 14, Row F, Grave 14. ROH:- St. Barnabas Church, Crosland Moor.

BROOK, NORMAN. Private. No 267682. 2/6th Battalion Duke of Wellington's Regiment. Son of Benjamin and Sarah Hannah Brook, 81 Britannia Road, Milnsbridge. Employed as a night feeder by Messrs B. and J. Whitwam and Sons Limited, Stanley Mills, Milnsbridge. Attended Golcar Providence United Methodist Sunday School. Enlisted, 5.11.1915, and embarked for France in February, 1917. Reported missing, presumed killed, at the Battle of Bullecourt, 3.5.1917, aged 21 years. Has no known grave. Commemorated on the **ARRAS MEMORIAL TO THE MISSING.**

BROOK, RAYMOND TYAS. Private. No 42003. 10th Battalion Northumberland Fusiliers. Formerly No 23407 Leicestershire Regiment. Born Hepworth. Son of John and Clara Lockwood Brook of 46 St. George's Road, Scholes, Holmfirth. Attended Scholes Primitive Methodist Sunday School and Hepworth Parish Church. Employed in the finishing room at Washpit Mills, Holmfirth. Enlisted May 1916. Embarked for France in the first week of October, 1916. Killed in action in Italy, 27.10.1918, aged 21 years. Buried **TEZZE BRITISH CEMETERY, ITALY.** Grave location:- Plot 3, Row D, Grave 3. ROH:- Hepworth and Scholes War Memorial; Hepworth Parish Church. His parents received the following letter from Private F. F. Halstead, who belonged to the same Company, giving an account of how Raymond met his death. *'I feel the loss very much as he was a good pal but we have one consolation in knowing that he suffered no pain as a bullet from an enemy machine gun hit him in the head. It happened just as we had crossed the river and started the advance on the 27.10.1918. He was killed at my side as we had to lie down on the ground while the machine gun was firing but your dear son had the misfortune to be hit so once again I express my deepest sympathy as a better pal never lived.'*

BROOK, THOMAS WALTON. Private. No 305362 The Tank Corps. Formerly No 301389 Staffordshire Yeomanry. Son of Walter Ernest and Hannah Brook of Upperheaton, Kirkheaton. Employed by Messrs Jarmaine and Sons. Killed in action, 3.10.1918, aged 19 years. Has no known grave. Commemorated on the **VIS-en-ARTOIS MEMORIAL TO THE MISSING.** ROH:- St. John's Church, Kirkheaton.

BROOK, TOM. Private. No 14408. 2nd Battalion Duke of Wellington's Regiment. Born Meltham. Lived Meltham Mills. Employed by Messrs Floyd of Netherthong. Single. Enlisted November 1914. Served in the Dardenelles and was invalided home. Embarked for France in August, 1916. Reported missing, presumed killed, 12.10.1916, aged 32. Buried in **GUARDS' CEMETERY, (LESBOEUFS).** Grave location:- Plot 6, Row AA, Grave 7. ROH:- St. Bartholomew's Church, Meltham.

BROOK, WILFRED STEEL. Private. No 38417. 7th Battalion The Yorkshire Regiment. Formerly No 5/36399 10th Territorial Reserve Battalion. Born Thornhill, Longwood, 31.8.1918. Educated Longwood National Church School. Lived with his sister, Mrs George Walker, at 21 Ballroyd, Longwood. Employed as a dyer's labourer by Messrs C. and J. Hirst and Sons Limited of Longwood. Attended Longwood Parish Church. Single. Enlisted 28.3.1916. Embarked for France on 13.11.1916. Died of wounds on his way to a Casualty Clearing Station near St. Quentin, 25.4.1917, aged 35 years. Has no known grave. Commemorated **ARRAS MEMORIAL TO THE MISSING.** ROH:- St, Mark's Parish Church, Longwood.

BROOK, WILLIAM HANSON. Lance Corporal. 8th Battalion King's Royal Rifle Corps. Born Sands Terrace, Leeds Road, Huddersfield, 6.12.1898. Son of William and Phoebe Brook, Wigan House, 182 Deighton Road, Huddersfield. Educated at Deighton Council School and the Secondary School, New North Road, Huddersfield. Employed as a pupil teacher at Deighton Council School. Single. Was a member of the Huddersfield troop of boy scouts and also a member of the Sheepridge and Deighton Liberal Club. Enlisted 29.12.1915. Died at Ljungbyhed, Sweden, of pneumonia on the way home from Parchim Camp, Germany, on 6.1.1919, aged 20 years. Buried in **RISEBERGA CHURCHYARD, SWEDEN.** ROH:- Christ Church, Woodhouse Hill.

BROOK, WILLIAM MATTHEWMAN. Corporal. No 66037. 321st Siege Battery Royal Garrison Artillery. Born 12 Hey Lane, Lowerhouses, Huddersfield 24.8.1893. Son of the late Matthewman and Mrs Brook, Hey Farm, Lowerhouses. Educated at Lowerhouses and Deighton Schools and Huddersfield Higher Grade

School. Employed by the Huddersfield Industrial Society at the Rashcliffe branch as a grocer's assistant. Single. Enlisted 7.11.1915. Killed in action near Poperinghe, Belgium, 24.7.1917, aged 22 years. Buried in **VLAMERTINGHE NEW MILITARY CEMETERY.** Grave location:- Plot 3, Row H, Grave 17. ROH:- Lowerhouses War Memorial; Almondbury War Memorial.

BROOK, WILLIE. Private. No 498079, 257th Area Employment Company, Labour Corps. Son of Amos and Eliza Brook of Dale Street, Longwood, Huddersfield; husband of Caroline Brook, 262 Longwood Road, Longwood. Died in Germany, 2.3.1920, aged 36. Buried in **COLOGNE SOUTHERN CEMETERY, GERMANY.** Grave location:- Plot 6, Row C, Grave 6.

BROOK, WILLIE. Private. No 28468. 1/5th Battalion Loyal North Lancashire Regiment. Formerly No 48502 The Yorkshire Regiment. Born 34 Northumberland Street, Huddersfield. Son of Mr Alfred Brook, 34 Clayton's Yard, Northumberland Street, Huddersfield. Educated at Beaumont Street Council School. Employed as a moulder by Messrs J. Hopkinson and Company Limited, of Birkby. Enlisted December 1917. Died of wounds near St. Pol, France, 31.8.1918, aged 19 years. Buried in **LIGNY-sur-CANCHE BRITISH CEMETERY.** Grave location:- Row B, Grave 18.

BROOK, WILLIE. Private. No 242073. 1/5th Battalion Duke of Wellington's Regiment. Born Hurstpond, Outlane, 29.12.1894. Son of Fred and Elizabeth Brook, 43 Coal Pit Lane, Outlane. Educated at Outlane Council School. Employed as a twister-in for Messrs Waterhouse and Sons Limited, Parkwood Mills, Longwood. Attended the Mount Wesleyan Mission and was a member of Outlane Cricket Club. Attested under the Derby scheme on February 28th, 1916, and joined the forces on 1.4.1916. Reported missing, presumed killed, 3.9.1916, aged 20. Has no known grave. Commemorated on the **THIEPVAL MEMORIAL TO THE MISSING.** ROH:- Outlane Trinity Methodist Church; Bethel United Methodist Church, Outlane; Huddersfield Drill Hall.

BROOK, WILLIAM. Private. No 52521. 1st Battalion West Yorkshire Regiment. Formerly No 31965 Duke of Wellington's Regiment. Lived Carrs Farm, Lindley. Was employed as a teamer by Messrs James Hawkyard of Upper Edge, Elland. Reported missing, presumed killed, 21.3.1918. Has no known grave. Commemorated on the **ARRAS MEMORIAL TO THE MISSING.** ROH:- St. Philip's Church, Birchencliffe

BROOKE, EDWARD, DSO. Lieutenant Commander. Royal Navy. *HMS Strongbow.* Born 25.8.1885 in Ecclesfield. Son of the late Edward Burkall Brooke and Gertrude Sykes Brooke of Thorpe, Almondbury, and grandson of the late Mr Edward Brooke of Oakleigh House, Edgerton. Joined the Navy on 30.7.1902. Was married on 20.3.1913, at St. John's Cathedral, Hong Kong, to Miss Helene Sarah Sherris. Severely wounded in convoy action, 17.10.1917. Was formerly in command of *HMS Sprightly* and was mentioned in despatches for his work at the Battle of Jutland. Awarded the DSO, 7.8.1918. The official citation reads;- '*in command of HMS Strongbow. Fought a gallant action against overwhelming odds in endeavouring to protect a convoy. He was seriously wounded during the engagement.*' Died at home, 10.2.1919, aged 33. Buried in **ALMONDBURY CEMETERY.** Grave location:- K, 'C', 30.

BROOKE, FRANK. Lance Bombardier. No 82171. 'A' Battery, 52nd Brigade Royal Field Artillery. Born Golcar. Son of John and Kate Brooke, 32 Townend, Golcar. Employed by his brother, Mr J.W. Walker, woollen manufacturer, at Springdale Mills, Longroyd Bridge. Attended St. John's Church, Golcar and was a member of the St. John's Institute and Golcar Conservative Club. Enlisted, 4.8.1914, at the age of 16. He took part in the Dardenelles campaign, served for 12 months in Egypt and for two years in France. Wounded during the first battle of the Somme, in 1916, during the fight for Beaumont Hamel. Was at home on leave in August, 1918. Died of wounds, 4.9.1918, aged 20 years. Buried in **FAUBOURG D'AMIENS CEMETERY, ARRAS.** Grave location:- Plot 7, Row F, Grave 7. ROH:- St. John's Church, Golcar.

BROOKE, JAMES WILLIE. Driver. No L/25470. 168th (Huddersfield) Brigade Royal Field Artillery. Born Moldgreen, Huddersfield, 5.8.1880. Educated at Stile Common Board School. Employed as a dyer by Messrs Dyson, Hall and Company, Greenside, Dalton. Husband of Mary Jane Brooke, 7 Fleming House Lane, Waterloo, Dalton. Enlisted May 1915. Embarked for France in December, 1915. Died of wounds received near Ypres, 28.12.1917, aged 37 years. Buried in **BLEUET FARM CEMETERY, ELVERDINGHE, BELGIUM.** Grave location:- Plot 2, Row B, Grave 51. ROH:- St. John's Church, Kirkheaton.

BROOKE, JOHN. Driver. No 222994. 17th Divisional Ammunition Column, Royal Field Artillery. Son of Mr and Mrs Dan Brooke, of Dunsley, Holmfirth. Husband of Mary Annie Brooke, Sunnyside Cottages, Ford Gate, Holmbridge. Employed at Albion Mills, Thongsbridge. Enlisted 29.3.1917. Killed in action, 25.3.1918, aged 28 years. Has no known grave. Commemorated on the **ARRAS MEMORIAL TO THE MISSING.** ROH:- Holme and Holmbridge War Memorial.

BROOKE, JOSHUA. Private. No 409. 21st Battalion West Yorkshire Regiment. Son of Joseph and Ann Brooke, Marsh Road, Scholes Holmfirth. Employed in the mill warehouse of Mr Waterhouse of Lockwood. Was Secretary of Mount Tabor United Methodist School and a member of the choir. Enlisted 1915. Had become ill and had undergone two operations. Died at Etaples Base Hospital, 2.12.1916, aged 23 years. Buried in **ETAPLES MILITARY CEMETERY.** Grave location:- Plot 20, Row D, Grave 8. ROH:- Hepworth and Scholes War Memorial; Hepworth Parish Church.

BROOKS, ALBERT EDWARD. Private. No 202983. 1/4th Battalion Duke of Wellington's Regiment. Lived Spa Bottom, Lepton. Employed by Messrs Ben Elliott and Sons at the Lodge Mill Colliery. Killed in action, 29.4.1918, aged 21. Buried in **LA CLYTTE MILITARY CEMETERY.** Grave location:- Plot 5, Row C, Grave 3. ROH:- St. John's Church, Kirkheaton; Lepton Parish Church.

BROOKS, FREDERICK. Private. No 15325. 24th Battalion (Oldham Pals) Manchester Regiment. Born East Hagbourne, Berkshire. Son of George and Ellen Brooks. Lived Bankfield, Manchester Road, Marsden. From boyhood had been brought up by his Uncle, Mr Howson of Marsden. Employed as a weaver at Bank Bottom Mills, Marsden. Was a member of the Adult Sunday School and the Socialist Institute. Enlisted 12.5.1915. Embarked for France, 12.11.1915. Received a gunshot wound to the head whilst engaged in bomb throwing on 2.7.1916. After first aid had been given he was taken to the Base Hospital at Rouen where he died of his injuries on 12.7.1916, aged 24. Buried in **St. SEVER CEMETERY, ROUEN.** Grave location:- Plot A, Row 28, Grave 8. ROH:- Marsden War Memorial.

BROTHERTON, RICHARD. Guardsman. No 6015. Coldstream Guards. Born St. Peter's, Lincoln. Lived 2 King Street, Lindley. Was a Police Constable with the Huddersfield Borough Police force. Enlisted in August, 1914, and embarked for France with the British Expeditionary Force. Reported missing, presumed killed, at the 1st Battle of Ypres, 29.10.1914. Has no known grave. Commemorated on the **MENIN GATE MEMORIAL TO THE MISSING.** ROH:- St. Stephen's Church, Lindley; Huddersfield Corporation Roll; Huddersfield Police Headquarters.

BROWN, ARNOLD. Private. No 30357. 30th Company Labour Corps. Formerly 17th Battalion York and Lancaster Regiment. Born Milnsbridge. Son of Joe Brown of High House Green, Linthwaite. Husband of Mrs Brown, 284 Buxton Road, Macclesfield, Cheshire. Died of disease, 19.10.1918, aged 29 years. Buried in **MONT HUON MILITARY CEMETERY.** Grave location:- Plot 7, Row K, Grave 4a.

BROWN, HARRY, MM. Private. No 100192. 24th Battalion Royal Fusiliers. Born Holmfirth. Son of Frederick and Ruth E. Brown, 10, Dewhurst Road, Fartown, Huddersfield. Educated at Holmfirth and Woodhouse Church of England Schools. Employed as a porter by Mr H. Hardy, of Birkby, in his paper warehouse. Enlisted May 1917. Embarked for France in April 1918. Awarded the Military Medal 1.10.1918 for 'bravery and resourcefulness during an attack on an enemy defensive system'. Killed during the attack on 1.10.1918, aged 19 years. Buried in **ANNEUX BRITISH CEMETERY.** Grave location:- Plot 2, Row H, Grave 12. ROH:- Christ Church, Woodhouse Hill; Fartown and Birkby War Memorial.

BROWN, HARRY. Private. No 5542. 1/5th Battalion Duke of Wellington's Regiment. Born

Holmfirth. Lived Longley, Holmfirth. Employed Messrs. Watkinson and Sons at Washpit Mills, Holmfirth. A keen cricketer, playing with the Cartworth Moor and Choppards teams. Was one of 29 cousins serving in the forces, being the sons of seven brothers. Had been at the front just seven weeks when reported missing, presumed killed, in the attack on the Schwaben Redoubt on 3.9.1916, aged 32 years. Has no known grave. Commemorated on the **THIEPVAL MEMORIAL TO THE MISSING.** ROH:- Holmfirth; Huddersfield Drill Hall.

BROWN, HARRY HAMER. Private. No 46093. 2nd Battalion York and Lancaster Regiment. Formerly No 22668 Duke of Wellington's Regiment. Born Bradford. Son of Mrs A. Brown, 13 Shackleton Fold, Whitehall Road, Leeds. Came to Huddersfield when he was six years old. Lodged with Mr J. W. Littlewood, 12 Drawer's Row, Berry Brow. Employed by Messrs Shaw Brothers, Firth Street, Huddersfield. Wounded in head and right hand, 16.10.1918, and died of wounds, aged 19, at No 72 General Hospital, Trouville on 16.1.1919. Buried in **TOURGEVILLE MILITARY CEMETERY.** Grave location:- Plot 7, Row C, Grave 12. ROH:- Armitage Bridge War Memorial.

BROWN, JOHN THOMAS. Lance Corporal. No 9738. 1st Battalion The King's (Liverpool Regiment). Born Huddersfield 2.10.1883. Foster son of Mrs Heath, 'Wells Tavern,' Northgate, Huddersfield. Educated at St. Joseph's School, Huddersfield. Employed as a tramway conductor by the Huddersfield Corporation Tramways Department. Married. Living at 24 Portland Street, Huddersfield. Enlisted 4.8.1914. Killed in action during the Battle of the Somme, 8.8.1916. Has no known grave. Commemorated on the **THIEPVAL MEMORIAL TO THE MISSING.** ROH:- Huddersfield Corporation Roll.

BROWN, JOHN WILLIAM. Private. No 242857. 1/5th Battalion York and Lancaster Regiment. Born 15 Castlegate, Huddersfield, 26.11.1897. Son of John William and Ada Brown, 23 Zetland Street, Huddersfield. Educated at the Huddersfield Parish Church School and was a member of the pierrot troupe at the school. Employed as a hairdresser by Mr John Hoyle at his hairdressing saloon in Beast Market, Huddersfield. Single. Enlisted 9.9.1916. Gassed at Nieuport, 19.7.1917, and died of the effects of gas poisoning at Le Treport, 9.8.1917, aged 19 years. Buried in **MONT HUON MILITARY CEMETERY, LE TREPORT.** Grave location:- Plot 3, Row B, Grave 9a. ROH:- Huddersfield Parish Church.

BROWN, VINCENT FRANK. Gunner. No 68484. 32nd Siege Battery Royal Garrison Artillery. Born Preston. Son of Frank and Sarah Hannah Brown, 2 Sussex Street, Salford, Manchester. Lived Grange Cottages, Marsden. Employed as a weaver by Messrs Crowther Bruce and Company Limited. Was a member of the Marsden Socialist Club. Single. Embarked for France in July, 1916. Killed in action, 9.4.1918, aged 31 years. Buried in **ROYAL IRISH RIFLES GRAVEYARD, LAVENTIE.** Grave location:- Plot 3, Row C, Grave 9. ROH:- Marsden War Memorial.

BROWN, WILLIAM FRANCE. Corporal. No 248080. 29th Battalion Durham Light Infantry. Born Slaithwaite. Son of James Robert and Ann Brown of New House, Moorside, Slaithwaite. Killed in action, 19.9.1918, aged 24 years. Buried in **TYNE COT CEMETERY.** Grave location:- Plot 59, Row E, Grave 31. ROH:- St. James Church, Slaithwaite; Slaithwaite War Memorial; Pole Moor Baptist Church.

BRUCE, NORMAN VICTOR. Gunner. No 231391. 108th Brigade HQ, Royal Field Artillery. Born Harrogate. Son of Robert and Elinor Bruce of 102 Huddersfield Road, Holmfirth. husband of Louie Bruce of South Lane, Holmfirth. Educated at Holmfirth National School. Worked at Rock Mills for a time and then joined the West Riding Constabulary and worked as a clerk at the Depot in Wakefield. Married at Holmfirth Parish Church, 9.4.1917, and enlisted on the following Monday. Killed instantly by a piece of shrapnel, 27.3.1918, aged 25 years. Has no known grave. Commemorated on the **POZIERES MEMORIAL TO THE MISSING.** ROH:- Holmfirth. (Brother of Private **ROBERT VERNON BRUCE,** who was killed on 9.4.1917, his brother's wedding day, q.v.).

BRUCE, ROBERT VERNON. Sergeant. No 235225. 2nd Battalion Duke of Wellington's Regiment. Son of Robert and Elinor Bruce, 102 Huddersfield Road, Holmfirth. Attended Holmfirth Parish Church. Employed in the office of Messrs Farrar and Company, Thirstin Dyeworks, Honley. Killed in action on the first day of the Battle of Arras. He was a member of a British attacking party who had cleared four lines of German trenches and had also cleared the enemy out of the village beyond when, according to information, Sergeant Bruce saw a British soldier lying wounded in an exposed position. In order to bandage the poor fellow who was lying in distress he crept out into the open but a German bullet killed him instantly. Killed in action, 9.4.1917, aged 26 years. Has no known grave. Commemorated on the **ARRAS MEMORIAL TO THE MISSING.** ROH:- Holmfirth War Memorial. (Brother of Private **NORMAN VICTOR BRUCE,** killed in action, 27.3.1918, q.v.).

BRUNTON, ALBERT SAMUEL. Private. No 92202. 1st Battalion Royal Fusiliers (Posted to 1st London Regiment). Formerly No 128012 Royal Flying Corps. Born 1.10.1899. Son of Herbert Helm Brunton and Mary Brunton, 24 Fenton Square, Manchester Road, Huddersfield. Educated at Spring Grove Council and Hillhouse Schools. Employed as a mechanical dentist by Mr Frost of Bradford Road, Huddersfield. Single. Killed in action, 26.8.1918, aged 18 years. Buried in **SUMMIT TRENCH CEMETERY, CROISILLES.** Grave location:- Plot 2, Row A, Grave 2. ROH:- St. Thomas's Church, Longroyd Bridge.

BUCKLEY, ARNOLD. Gunner. No 142068. 289th Siege Battery Royal Garrison Artillery. Born Longwood 24.6.1894. Son of John Denton and Lavinia Buckely, 161 Longwood Gate, Longwood, Huddersfield. Educated at Goitfield Board School. Prior to enlistment was employed as manager by Mr Shaw Hardcastle in his drapery business in Halifax and formerly worked for Messrs Kaye and Monnington of King Street, Huddersfield. Attended Lockwood Baptist Sunday School. Enlisted 26.4.1916. Embarked for France February, 1917. Killed in action near Ypres, 31.5.1917, aged 23 years. Buried in **VLAMERTINGHE MILITARY CEMETERY.** Grave location:- Plot 7, Row C, Grave 22. ROH:- Salendine Nook Baptist Church (memorial in the churchyard 514E); Longwood War Memorial. (Brother of Private **DONALD BUCKLEY,** reported missing, presumed killed, 28.4.1917, q.v.).

BUCKLEY, DONALD. Private. No 35063. 24th Battalion (Tyneside Irish) Northumberland Fusiliers. Born Longwood 12.2.1898. Son of John Denton and Lavinia Buckley, 161 Longwood Gate, Longwood. Educated at Goitfield Board School. Had worked at Rushworths Limited, Westgate, Huddersfield, but at the time of enlistment was employed by his father in his drapery business. Attended the Lockwood Baptist Sunday School and was a member of the North Ward Liberal Club. Enlisted October, 1916, and embarked for France at about the same time as his brother. Reported missing, presumed killed, 28.4.1917, aged 19 years. Has no known grave. Commemorated on the **ARRAS MEMORIAL TO THE MISSING.** ROH:- Salendine Nook Baptist Church and a memorial in the churchyard 514E; Longwood War Memorial. (Brother of Private **ARNOLD BUCKLEY,** killed in action, 31.5.1917, q.v.).

BUCKLEY, FRED. Private. No 241695. 9th Battalion Duke of Wellington's Regiment. Born Linthwaite. Son of John and Mary Buckley of Barber Row, Linthwaite. Employed as a weaver by Messrs George Mallinson and Sons. Attended the Linthwaite Wesleyan Sunday School. Enlisted March, 1916, and embarked for France about Christmas time of the same year. Came home on leave in September, 1918, and was killed in action, 12.10.1918, aged 34 years. Buried **SELRIDGE BRITISH CEMETERY.** Grave location:- Plot 2, Row D, Grave 10. ROH:- Linthwaite War Memorial.

BUCKLEY, JAMES IRVIN. Private. No 29/612. 12/13th Battalion Northumberland Fusiliers. Born Outlane 6.11.1917. Son of Nancy Buckley, 204 Longwood Road, Longwood. Educated at Longwood Board School. Employed as a weaver. Enlisted on Easter Wednesday, 1916. Reported missing, presumed killed, 4.10.1917, aged 30. Has no known grave. Commemorated on the **TYNE COT MEMORIAL TO THE MISSING.** ROH:- Bethel United Methodist Church, Outlane; St. Mark's Parish Church, Longwood.

BUCKLEY, JOE. Private. No 31956. 2nd Battalion South Staffordshire Regiment. Born Linthwaite. Son of Ernest and Sarah Buckley of Golcar. Husband of Ivy Buckley, of White Hart, Towngate, Marsden. Employed as a foreman spinner and scribbling engineer at Messrs Gledhill

Brothers, woollen manufacturers, of Lockwood. Enlisted November 1916. Served as a stretcher-bearer. Wounded in the right arm and both legs on 27.11.1917. Taken to Etaples Base Hospital, where his right leg was amputated. Died of his wounds, 11.12.1917, aged 26 years. Buried **ETAPLES MILITARY CEMETERY.** Grave location:- Plot 31, Row C, Grave 10a. ROH:- St. John's Church, Golcar; Marsden War Memorial.

BUCKLEY, JOSEPH MITCHELL. Private. No 240551. 1/6th Battalion Duke of Wellington's Regiment. Born Clayton West. Son of G G and Emily Buckley. Died of wounds, 9.5.1918, aged 31 years. Buried in **BOULOGNE EASTERN CEMETERY.** Grave location:- Plot 9, Row B, Grave 60. ROH:- Clayton West and High Hoyland War Memorial.

BUCKLEY, LEONARD. Private. No 14231. 9th Battalion Duke of Wellington's Regiment. Born Netherthong. Son of Mr and Mrs R Buckley. Educated at Netherthong Church Day School. Attended Netherthong United Methodist Church. Employed as a tuner by Messrs Vickerman and Sons, Thongsbridge Mills. Enlisted shortly after the outbreak of the war. Wounded whilst repairing telephone wires. Died of wounds, 25.4.1916, aged 25 years. Buried in **BAILLEUL COMMUNAL CEMETERY EXTENSION.** Grave location:- Plot 2, Row D, Grave 156. ROH:- Netherthong and Thongsbridge War Memorial; Netherthong Working Men's Club.

BUCKLEY, WALTER. Private. No 202574. 1st Battalion Royal Scots Fusiliers. Born Huddersfield. Brother of Mr L Buckley, 45 Scholes Road, Birkby. Lived 18 Little Carr Green, Dalton. Employed as a tenter by Messrs Edwin Walker and Company Limited, Field Mills, Leeds Road, Huddersfield. Was a violinist in the Huddersfield String Orchestra. Died of wounds, 16.9.1918, aged 21. Buried **ABBEVILLE COMMUNAL CEMETERY EXTENSION.** Grave location:- Plot 4, Row F, Grave 3. ROH:- St. Andrew's Church, Huddersfield; Christ Church, Moldgreen.

BUCKLEY, WALTER. Private. No 93885. 51st Battalion Northumberland Fusiliers. Son of Samuel and Ada Alice Buckley, 6 Back Union Street, Northgate, Huddersfield. Died at home, 20.4.1921, aged 20 years. Buried in **EDGERTON CEMETERY, HUDDERSFIELD.** Grave location:- 15B, 90C.

BULL, HARRY. Private. No 240575. 2/5th Battalion Duke of Wellington's Regiment. Born Lane End, Dalton, 21.9.1897. Son of Richard and Georgina Bull, 48 Thistle Street, Huddersfield. Educated at St. Andrews Church of England School, Leeds Road, Huddersfield. Employed as a brass finisher by Messrs. J. Hopkinson and Company, of Birkby. Enlisted 21.9.1914. Reported missing presumed killed, at the Battle of Bullecourt, 3.5.1917. Has no known grave. Commemorated on the **ARRAS MEMORIAL TO THE MISSING.** ROH:- St. Andrew's Church, Leeds Road, Huddersfield; Huddersfield Drill Hall.

BULLAS, SAMUEL SCHOFIELD. Private. No 204347. 2nd Battalion Duke of Wellington's Regiment. Born Bacup. Fifth son of Mrs Joseph Bullas, 96 New Lane, Bacup. Lived 53 Northumberland Street, Huddersfield. Employed by British Dyes Limited. Was a member of the Royal Antediluvian Order of Buffaloes. Enlisted March, 1917, and embarked for France in June, 1917. Killed in action, 10.10.1917, aged 24. Has no known grave. Commemorated on the **TYNE COT MEMORIAL TO THE MISSING.**

BULLAS, THOMAS. Private. No 32044. 1/5th Battalion North Staffordshire Regiment. Born 19.3.1899. Son of Mr and Mrs Fred Bullas, 65 Manchester Road, Huddersfield. Educated at St. Paul's Church of England School, Huddersfield. Employed by Messrs John Crowther and Sons of Milnsbridge as a piecer. Enlisted in November, 1916, and embarked for France in March, 1917. Reported missing presumed killed, 1.7.1917, aged 19 years. Has no known grave. Commemorated on the **ARRAS MEMORIAL TO THE MISSING.** ROH:- St. Paul's Church, Southgate, Huddersfield; St. Thomas's Church, Longroyd Bridge.

BURCH, HARRY, MM. Corporal. No 16578. 2nd Battalion Duke of Wellington's Regiment. Formerly No 8000 Dragoons. Born Amberley, Gloucestershire. Lodged with Mrs Bradley, 3 Austin's Yard, Upperhead Row, Huddersfield. Employed as a goods porter by the London and North Western Railway Company at Huddersfield Goods Yard. Enlisted at the outbreak of the war and embarked for France on 4.2.1916. Was awarded the Military Medal on 1.9.1916 for 'gallant conduct under fire.' Died of wounds at 2/2nd London Casualty Clearing Station, 13.10.1916, aged 32. Buried in **GROVE TOWN CEMETERY, MEAULTE.** Grave location:- Plot 1, Row L, Grave 10. ROH:- London and North Western Railway Roll.

BURGESS, BROOKE. Private. No 29/652. 9th Battalion Northumberland Fusiliers. Born Wooldale. Son of John and Elizabeth Burgess of Wooldale. Employed by Messrs Lancasters, of Mythom Bridge. Enlisted 17.5.1916. Embarked for France, 31.8.1916. Died of gunshot wounds to the head at 2/2nd London Casualty Clearing Station, 10.11.1916, aged 19 years. Buried **GROVE TOWN CEMETERY, MEAULTE.** Grave Location:- Plot 2, Row H, Grave 41. ROH:- Holmfirth War Memorial. (Brother of Private **JOSEPH BURGESS**, who died of wounds at sea, 10.8.1915 q.v.).

BURGESS, JOSEPH. Private. No 1917. 7th Battalion Australian Imperial Force. Born Wooldale. Son of John and Elizabeth Burgess of Wooldale. Was well known in local athletic circles as a skilful gymnast. Emigrated to Australia in May, 1914. Enlisted in the A.I.F. on January 14th, 1915, in Melbourne, Victoria. Went to the Dardenelles. Died of wounds at sea, 10.8.1915. Has no known grave. Commemorated on the **LONE PINE MEMORIAL TO THE MISSING, GALLIPOLI.** ROH:- Holmfirth War Memorial. (Brother of Private **BROOKE BURGESS**, who died of wounds, 10.11.1916, q.v.).

BURHOUSE, HENRY JOE. Lance Corporal. No 41888. 7th Battalion Leicestershire Regiment. Son of James William and Mary Burhouse. Lived 106 Yews Hill Road, Lockwood. Died in Germany as a Prisoner of War, 6.11.1918, aged 20 years. Buried **BERLIN SOUTH WESTERN CEMETERY, STAHNSDORF, GERMANY.** Grave location:- Plot 18, Row B, Grave 5.

BURKE, GEORGE. Private. No 936. 1/7th Battalion Duke of Wellington's Regiment. Enlisted Huddersfield. Killed in action, 20.12.1915. Has no known grave. Commemorated on the **MENIN GATE MEMORIAL TO THE MISSING.**

BURKE, S. Gunner. No L/32570. 9th Reserve Battery Royal Field Artillery. Died at home, 5.6.1916. Buried **EDGERTON CEMETERY, HUDDERSFIELD.** Grave location:- 60, 117G.

BURKE, THOMAS. Rifleman. No 43621. 16th Battalion The County of London Regiment, attached to the King's Royal Rifle Corps. Born Huddersfield. Killed in action, 17.6.1918. Buried in **DAINVILLE BRITISH CEMETERY.** Grave location:- Plot 1, Row F, Grave 11.

BURKITT, TOM. Lance Corporal. No 2594. No 9 Platoon, 'C' Company, 1/5th Battalion Duke of Wellington's Regiment. Born Knutsford, Cheshire, 19.3.1893. Son of Mrs Adah Burkitt, 56 Northgate, Almondbury. Educated at Almondbury Church of England School. Employed as a tailor's fettler at Messrs Bairstow's clothing factory, Fitzwilliam Street, Huddersfield. Single. Had served four years with the local Territorials. Although his mother was a widow, he said that as a trained man he could not stand aside and he must go along with his elder brother, who was in the Ambulance Section of the same Regiment. Enlisted 12.8.1914. Embarked for France April, 1915. Killed in action near Bois Grenier, 25.6.1915, aged 22 years. Buried **RUE DAVID MILITARY CEMETERY, FLEURBAIX.** Grave location:- Plot 1, Row B, Grave 8. His mother received the following letter from Lieutenant J. M. Haigh, of 'C' Company, *'I regret to have to inform you that your son, Lance Corporal T. Burkitt, was killed last night. He died doing his duty as a soldier and a man. A bullet struck him in the back. He was taken to hospital but died very soon afterwards. The funeral took place at 11am today. There are some things which are difficult to say but your son deserves the highest tribute and praise. I have never met a braver man, nor one in whose character there was more to admire. It is a noble thing that he has done. Please accept our deepest sympathy with you in your great loss.'* ROH:- Huddersfield Drill Hall; Almondbury War Memorial.

BURLEY, ARTHUR. Private. No 5887. 1/6th Battalion Durham Light Infantry. Born 6 Moorbottom Road, Thornton Lodge, Huddersfield. Son of Mr and Mrs Fred Burley, 23 Hill Top, Paddock. Educated at St. Thomas's Church of England School, Longroyd Bridge. Attended Thornton Lodge Wesleyan Sunday

School. Employed at Priestroyd Mills as a woollen piecer. Single. Enlisted 3.7.1916. Embarked for France in November, 1916. Died of wounds at No 46 Casualty Clearing Station on 16.1.1917. Buried **DERNANCOURT COMMUNAL CEMETERY EXTENSION.** Grave location:- Plot 4, Row G, Grave 14. ROH:- All Saints Church, Paddock.

BURNLEY, ALBERT. Private. No 66347. 240th Company Machine Gun Corps. Formerly No 29319 Duke of Wellington's Regiment. Born Kirkheaton, Huddersfield. Lived Greenwood's Buildings, Kirkheaton. Husband of Clara Burnley. Employed by British Dyes Limited. Killed in action, 16.9.1917, aged 33 years. Buried in **HESBECOURT COMMUNAL CEMETERY.** Grave location:- No 6. ROH:- St. John's Church, Kirkheaton.

BURNLEY, HARRY RAYMOND. Sergeant. No 1859. 1/5th Battalion Duke of Wellington's Regiment. Born Boroughbridge. Son of the late Mr Joseph Burnley, St. Wilfred's Hotel, Ripon, and Mrs Burnley of Golcar Brow, Meltham. Employed by Messrs J. Hopkinson of Birkby. Enlisted August 1914. Embarked for France April, 1915. Died of wounds at No 17 Casualty Clearing Station (Remy Siding), 11.11.1915, aged 20. Buried in **LIJSSENTHOEK MILITARY CEMETERY.** Grave location:- Plot 4, Row B, Grave 7. (Brother of Private **JOE BURNLEY,** who died of wounds, 26.8.1918, q.v.). ROH:- St. Bartholomew's Church, Meltham; Huddersfield Drill Hall.

BURNLEY, HERBERT. Lance Corporal. No 15/160. 15th Battalion (Leeds Pals) West Yorkshire Regiment. Born Huddersfield. Son of Walter and Fanny Burnley. Killed in action, 1.7.1916, aged 27 years. Buried in **EUSTON ROAD CEMETERY.** Grave location:- Plot 1, Row A, Grave 51. ROH:- Longwood War Memorial.

BURNLEY, JOE, DCM. Private. No 242043. 6th Battalion Leicestershire Regiment. Formerly No 2367 Duke of Wellington's Regiment. Born Ripon. Son of the late Mr Joseph Burnley, St. Wilfred's Hotel, Ripon, and Mrs Burnley, 56 Quarmby Road, late of Golcar Brow, Meltham. Had served in the army for five years and had come home on time expired leave at Whitsuntide, 1918. Died of gunshot wounds to abdomen in No 3 Casualty Clearing Station, Gezaincourt, 26.8.1918, aged 20 years. One week after his death he was awarded the DCM for 'gallantry and devotion to duty on the field of battle.'. Buried **BAGNEUX BRITISH CEMETERY.** Grave location:- Plot 6, Row B, Grave 3. ROH:-. St. Bartholomew's Church, Meltham; Longwood War Memorial. (Brother of Private **HARRY RAYMOND BURNLEY,** who died of wounds, 11.11.1915, q.v.).

BURROWS, EDWARD HORACE. Private. No 142565. 62nd Battalion Machine Gun Corps. Formerly No 32426 Duke of Wellington's Regiment. Son of Thomas and Mary Burrows, 43 Arnold Street, Birkby. Employed by Messrs J. Hopkinson, of Birkby. Was a member of the Birkby Baptist Young Men's Bible Class. Embarked for France just before Christmas, 1917. Died of pneumonia at Etaples Base Hospital, 6.4.1918, aged 20 years. Buried in **ETAPLES MILITARY CEMETERY.** Grave location:- Plot 33, Row D, Grave 12. ROH:- Fartown and Birkby War Memorial; Slaithwaite War Memorial.

BURROWS, RICHARD. Lance Corporal. No 47288. 19th Battalion Manchester Regiment. Born Ardwick, Manchester. Son of Richard and Hannah Burrows of Ardwick; husband of Adelaide Burrows, 166 Nook, Newsome Road, Huddersfield. Killed in action, 7.9.1917, aged 31 years. Buried in **MESSINES RIDGE CEMETERY.** Grave location:- Memorial 2.

BURTON, CHARLES. Lance Corporal. No 32955. 1/4th Battalion King's Own Yorkshire Light Infantry. Born East View, off Croft House Lane, Marsh, 31.10.1889. Son of Tom Heeley and Evalina Burton, 1 Clara Street, Fartown. Educated at St. John's School, Hillhouse. Employed by the Maypole Dairy Company, Dewsbury, as a grocer's assistant. Enlisted June 1916. Reported missing, presumed killed, 14.4.1918. Has no known grave. Commemorated on the **TYNE COT MEMORIAL TO THE MISSING.** ROH:- St. John's Church, Birkby; Fartown and Birkby War Memorial; also commemorated on parents' headstone in Edgerton Cemetery, Huddersfield.

BURTON, FREDERICK WILLIAM. Private. No 528122. 14th (County of London) Battalion (London Scottish). Born Marsh 9.7.1888. Son of Joe Burton, 4 Lowergate, Longwood. Educated at Holy Trinity Church of England School. Employed as a undertuner. Enlisted 15.12.1915. Killed in action, 21.8.1918, aged 30 years. Has no known grave. Commemorated on the **TYNE COT MEMORIAL TO THE MISSING**. ROH:- Longwood War Memorial.

BURTON, HAROLD. Private. No 4144. 1/5th Battalion King's Own Yorkshire Light Infantry. Enlisted Cawthorne, Barnsley. Killed in action, 4.7.1916. Has no known grave. Commemorated on the **THIEPVAL MEMORIAL TO THE MISSING**. ROH:- Clayton West and High Hoyland War Memorial.

BURTON, NORMAN. Private. No 181378. 18th Battalion (2nd Bradford Pals) West Yorkshire Regiment. Born Clayton West. Enlisted Bradford. Killed in the attack on Serre on the first day of the Battle of the Somme 1.7.1916. Has no known grave. Commemorated on the **THIEPVAL MEMORIAL TO THE MISSING**. ROH:- Clayton West and High Hoyland War Memorial.

BUSHBY, JOHN. Private. No 23/337. 19th Battalion Durham Light Infantry. Born Marsden. Son of Alfred and Martha Bushby, 6 Green Bower, Marsden. Employed by Messrs Crowther, Bruce and Company Limited, Marsden, Reported missing, presumed killed, 28.7.18, aged 36. Has no known grave. Commemorated on the **TYNE COT MEMORIAL TO THE MISSING**. ROH:- Marsden War Memorial.

BUTLER, CYRIL FRANK. 2nd Lieutenant. 112th Brigade Royal Field Artillery. Born Settle 19.8.1894. Son of Mr and Mrs Butler, 'Paragon Hotel,' Westgate', Huddersfield. Educated at Skipton Grammar School, where he was schools champion for 1910, 1913 and 1914. Went to Ripon and St. John College, York, where he was a student. Played for Skipton Rugby Union Club and later for York, Huddersfield and Halifax Northern Union clubs at three-quarter back. He was also a keen runner and fine athlete. Enlisted, 4.1.1916, in the Royal Horse Artillery as a Gunner. Died of wounds near Rheims, 8.6.1918. Buried **MARFAUX BRITISH CEMETERY**.

Grave location:- Plot 7, Row D, Grave 1. ROH:- Huddersfield Parish Church.

BUTLER, GEORGE. Gunner. No 111910. 'A' Battery, 186th Brigade Royal Field Artillery. Born 6 Brian Street, Lindley, 11.10.1895. Son of Fred and Keziah Butler, 144 Lime Tree Avenue, Eldon Road, Marsh. Educated at Oakes Council School. Employed by Mr A. Willis as a tailor's cutter. Attended Marsh United Methodist Church and was a Sunday School teacher there. Was a member of Marsh United Harriers. Enlisted 29.12.1915. Killed in action, near Poperinghe, 27.6.1917, aged 21 years. Buried in **POPERINGHE NEW MILITARY CEMETERY**. Grave location:- Plot 2, Row A, Grave 30. ROH:- Marsh War Memorial.

BUTLER, WILLIAM AUDSLEY. 2nd Lieutenant. 3rd Battalion South Staffordshire Regiment, attached 1/8th Royal Warwickshire Regiment. Born Huddersfield. Only son of Mr F. C. Butler, Cranwich Road, Stamford Hill, London, who was formerly factory inspector for Huddersfield. Educated at Huddersfield College School and later at Huddersfield Technical College and London University, where he received a war degree of BSc in engineering. Was commissioned in July, 1915, and embarked for France in June, 1917. Killed in action, 16.11.1916, aged 22 years. Buried in **ADANAC MILITARY CEMETERY**. Grave location:- Plot 3, Row F, Grave 25. ROH:- Huddersfield College School.

BUTTERWORTH, CHARLES HERBERT. Private. No 204475. 1/4th Battalion Duke of Wellington's Regiment. Born Meltham. Son of Mr and Mrs J. C. Butterworth of Golcar Brow, Meltham. Educated at Meltham Church Schools. Employed by the Meltham Spinning Company. Mobilised with the local Territorials in August, 1914. Killed in action, 10.4.1918, aged 20 years. Has no known grave. Commemorated on the **TYNE COT MEMORIAL TO THE MISSING**. ROH:- St. Bartholomew's Church, Meltham.

BUTTERWORTH, ERNEST. Private. No 2165. 1/7th Battalion Duke of Wellington's Regiment. Born Holmfirth. Son of Alfred H and Alice A Butterworth, Park Ryding, Holmfirth. Attended Holmfirth Wesleyan Church and was an active member of the Holmfirth Liberal Club. Assisted his father in the business of Messrs H. and S.

Butterworth, woollen manufacturers, Lower Mills, Holmfirth. Enlisted with the local Territorial battalion at the outbreak of the war. Shot through the head and died instantenously, 12.7.1915, aged 26 years. Buried in **COLNE VALLEY CEMETERY**. Grave location:- Row D, Grave 14. ROH:- Holmfirth War Memorial; Upperthong War Memorial; Huddersfield Drill Hall. (Brother of 2nd Lieutenant **NORMAN BUTTERWORTH**, killed in action, 9.5.1917, q.v.).

BUTTERWORTH, NORMAN. 2nd Lieutenant. 5th Battalion Manchester Regiment, attached 70th Squadron Royal Flying Corps. Born Holmfirth. Son of Alfred H and Alice A Butterworth, Park Ryding, Holmfirth. Educated at Holmfirth Wesleyan Day School, later became a boarder at Fulneck School, Pudsey, and finished his schooling in Switzerland. He became associated with the business of Messrs Armitage and Rhodes of Ravensthorpe and was one of the partners in the firm when war broke out. He enlisted in November, 1915, a few months after his brother Ernest was killed, and obtained a commission in the 5th Battalion Manchester Regiment. He embarked for France in October, 1916, attached to the 17th Battalion Manchester Regiment. Then he returned to England and went through training for the Royal Flying Corps, returning to France on 5.4.1917. On 9.5.1917, some British aircraft went over the German lines and they were attacked by a large number of German planes. There was a long and close fight in which two German machines were shot down and two others driven down. Norman was hit during the combat and killed instantenously. The machine was very badly damaged and became almost uncontrollable and only by very fine piloting was it possible for the machine to return. Killed in action whilst flying, 9.5.1917, aged 24 years. Buried in **BRAY MILITARY CEMETERY**. Grave location:- Plot 2, Row G, Grave 16. ROH:- Upperthong War Memorial. (Brother of Private **ERNEST BUTTERWORTH**, killed in action, 12.7.1917, q.v.).

BYRNE, HENRY. Private. No 8648. 2nd Battalion Royal Dublin Fusiliers. Born Dublin. Brother of Mrs Murphy, 7 Burns Head Yard, Thomas Street, Huddersfield. Lived 9 Swallow Street, Huddersfield. Employed as a labourer by Messrs John Sykes and Sons, Turnbridge. Killed at Hill 60 on 26.4.1915. Has no known grave. Commemorated on the **MENIN GATE MEMORIAL TO THE MISSING.**

BYRAM, THOMAS RICHARD. Lance Corporal. No 241875. 2/5th Battalion Duke of Wellington's Regiment. Born Greenfield. Lived 23 Royds Terrace, Binn Road, Marsden. Employed as a weaver at New Mills, Marsden. Was a member of Saddleworth Handbell Ringers and also played the violin. Married. Enlisted March 1916. Embarked for France January, 1917. Wounded in the head and died instantly, 20.7.1918, aged 39 years. Buried **COURMAS BRITISH CEMETERY**. Grave location:- Plot 2, Row D, Grave 7. ROH:- Huddersfield Drill Hall.

CAINE, DAVID. Private. No 17/940. 17th Battalion West Yorkshire Regiment. Born Jarrow. Living at Moldgreen. Employed as a labourer. Married. Enlisted at the outbreak of the war. Killed in action, 30.7.1916. Has no known grave. Commemorated on the **THIEPVAL MEMORIAL TO THE MISSING.** ROH:- Christ Church, Moldgreen.

CAINE, FREDERICK, MM. Sergeant. No 240244. 1/5th Battalion Duke of Wellington's Regiment. Born Huddersfield. Second son of Mr and Mrs Dennis Caine, 17 Dock Street, Huddersfield. Attended St. Patrick's Church. Employed by Messrs J. Lumb and Sons Limited, Folly Hall, Huddersfield. Awarded the Military Medal 9.12.1916. Killed in action at the Battle of Passchendaele, 9.10.1917, aged 22 years. Has no known grave. Commemorated on the **TYNE COT MEMORIAL TO THE MISSING.** (Brother of Private **THOMAS CAINE**, killed in action, 20.1.1917, q.v.). ROH:- Huddersfield Drill Hall.

CAIN, JAMES EDWARD, MM. Acting Bombardier. No L/25688. 'D' Battery, 168th (Huddersfield) Brigade Royal Field Artillery. Born Hyde Cheshire. Husband of Emily Ann Caine, Church Green, Kirkburton. Employed as a miner by Messrs Swift and Netherwood, Lepton Collieries. Awarded the Military Medal on 17.9.1917, *'for standing to the guns for 16 hours after all his companions had been gassed.'* Killed in action, 30.10.1917, aged 31. Buried **MINTY FARM CEMETERY, St. JAN, BELGIUM.** Grave Location:- Plot 2, Row B, Grave 19. ROH:- All Hallows Church, Kirkburton.

CAINE, THOMAS. Corporal. No 3321. 1/5th Battalion Duke of Wellington's Regiment. Born Huddersfield. Lived 5 Water Royd, Turnbridge, Huddersfield. Employed as a labourer by Mr A. Graham, contractor, of Colne Road, Huddersfield. Attended St. Patrick's Church. Married, with five children, the youngest of whom was born a fortnight before her father was killed. Enlisted at the outbreak of the war and embarked for France in April, 1915. Killed in action, 20.1.1917, aged 30 years. Buried **HUMBERCAMPS COMMUNAL CEMETERY EXTENSION.** Grave location:- Plot 1, Row C, Grave 14. (Brother of Private **FREDERICK CAINE MM,** killed in action, 9.10.1917, q.v.). ROH:- Huddersfield Drill Hall.

CALKIN, ELLIS. Private. No 241355. 2/5th Battalion Duke of Wellington's Regiment. Lived 19 Colne Street, Aspley, Huddersfield. Employed by Messrs T. Liversidge and Sons, Canal Dyeworks, Huddersfield. Married, with four children. Accidentally shot 9.9.1917. Buried **St. HILAIRE CEMETERY, FREVENT.** Grave location:- Plot 3, Row A, Grave 27. ROH:- St. Paul's Church, Southgate, Huddersfield; Huddersfield Drill Hall.

CALLAGHAN, CHARLES HENRY, MM, MSM. Sergeant. No 45400. 'D' Battery, 256th Brigade Royal Field Artillery. Born Albion Street, Huddersfield, 11.8.1887. Son of Mrs J. Callaghan, Park Side House, Maple Street, Huddersfield, and the late Inspector Callaghan of the Huddersfield Borough Police Force. Educated at Spring Grove Council School. Prior to enlistment was working in Glasgow as a plumber and glazier. Single. Enlisted January 1896. Awarded the Military Medal for 'bravery in the field' in April, 1917. Wounded near Cambrai on 13.5.1917. Treated in Hove Hospital, England for hip wound and amputation of left leg. Died of wounds at Hove, 30.12.1917, aged 30. Buried in **EDGERTON CEMETERY, HUDDERSFIELD.** Grave location:- 11B, 116. ROH:- Mount Pleasant Chapel, Lockwood.

CALVERLEY, HAROLD. Private. No 30418. 1st Battalion King's Own (Royal Lancaster Regiment). Born Lillands Lane, Brighouse, 3.8.1895. Educated at Moldgreen Council School. Worked as licensed hawker. Married. At the time of enlistment, was living at 281 Wakefield Road, Moldgreen. Enlisted 3.8.1916. Reported missing, presumed killed, near Poelcapelle, Belgium, 9.10.1917, aged years. Has no known grave. Commemorated on the **TYNE COT MEMORIAL TO THE MISSING.** ROH:- St. Andrew's Church, Huddersfield; Christ Church, Moldgreen.

CALVERLEY, PHILIP HENRY. Private. No 3/2100. 'B' Company, 1st Battalion King's Own Yorkshire Light Infantry. Born Crumpsall, Manchester, 29.12.1893. Son of William Henry and Eva Calverley, 89 Luck Lane, Marsh. Educated at Paddock Council School. Attended Paddock United Methodist Church. Employed as a clerk in the Huddersfield office of the Royal Insurance Company. Was a teacher and active worker in the Marsh United Methodist Sunday School, where he was also secretary of the Band of Hope and Plan Secretary to the Christian Endeavour Society. Was also secretary and treasurer for the Marsh United Harriers of which he was an active member. Enlisted 31.8.1914. Trained at Sutton-on-Humber and, afterwards, at Winchester and passed his firing course at Strensall and Hornsea. Embarked for France on 14.1.1915. Killed in action between Zonnebeke and Zillebeke, Belgium, on 8.5.1915, aged 21 years. Has no known grave. Commemorated on the **MENIN GATE MEMORIAL TO THE MISSING.** ROH:- All Saints Church, Paddock; Shared Church, Paddock; commemorated in Salendine Nook Baptist Chapel yard, D312.

CALVERT, FRANK. Private. No 72004. 1/5th Battalion Devonshire Regiment. Born Fartown 22.11.1898. Son of Mrs E. D. Calvert, 20 Grove Buildings, Back Bradford Road, Huddersfield. Educated at Hillhouse Council School. Employed as a clerk by Messrs T. and H. Blamires Limited, Leeds Road, Huddersfield. Single. Enlisted 28.12.1917. Reported missing, presumed killed, at Cambrai on 30.9.1918, aged 18. Buried **FLESQUIERES HILL BRITISH CEMETERY.** Grave location:- Plot 5, Row B, Grave 8. ROH:- Fartown and Birkby War Memorial.

CALVERT, JOHN WILLIAM. Private. No 240820. 2/5th Battalion Duke of Wellington's Regiment. Born Marsden's Buildings, Rashcliffe, 12.12.1881. Son of William and Eliza Jane Calvert, 12 Northgate, Huddersfield. Educated at Huddersfield Parish Church School and

Thomas Street Council School. Employed by Messrs Jarmaine and Sons, of Kirkheaton, as a wool extractor. Single. Enlisted 21.11.1914. Reported missing, presumed killed, at the Battle of Bullecourt, 3.5.1917. Has no known grave. Commemorated on the **ARRAS MEMORIAL TO THE MISSING**. ROH:- Huddersfield Drill Hall.

CALVERT, LEWIS. Private. No 4349. 1/5th Battalion Duke of Wellington's Regiment. Born 6 Sheepridge Road, Huddersfield, 1.8.1879. Educated at Deighton Council School. Employed as a moulder. Enlisted 3.7.1915. Reported missing, presumed killed, in the attack on the Schwaben Redoubt on 3.9.1916. Has no known grave. Commemorated on the **THIEPVAL MEMORIAL TO THE MISSING**. ROH:- Huddersfield Drill Hall.

CAMPNETT, ARNOLD. Acting Bombardier. No 117571. 256th Siege Battery Royal Garrison Artillery. Born Linthwaite, Huddersfield. Married. Lived Royds End, Linthwaite. Employed by Messrs George Mallinson and Sons Limited, Linthwaite. Was secretary of the Hoyle Ing Working Men's Club and served for a time on the committee of the Linthwaite Cooperative Society. Killed in action, 4.10.1917, aged 32 years. Buried in **BUFFS ROAD CEMETERY, St. JEAN-LES-YPRES, BELGIUM.** Grave location:- Row E, Grave 9. ROH:- Linthwaite War Memorial.

CANDLER, FRANK. Private. No 42236. Hertfordshire Regiment. Formerly No 93553 Sherwood Foresters. Born Upper Quarry Road, Bradley, Huddersfield, 19.10.1898. Son of Cant and Sarah Candler, 60 Bradley Road, Bradley. Educated at Bradley Church of England School. Employed as a junior clerk at Kirkheaton Station by the London and North Western Railway Company. Enlisted 23.3.1917. Wounded, 27.10.1918, and died of his wounds at St. Dunstan's Hospital, Northampton, on 5.11.1918, aged 20 years. Buried in **St. THOMAS'S CHURCHYARD, BRADLEY, HUDDERSFIELD.** Grave location:- in the South part. ROH:- St. Thomas's Church, Bradley; London and North Western Railway Company Roll.

CARBERT, THOMAS. Private. No 89671. 16th Company Machine Gun Corps. Born Escrick, York. Son of the late Thomas and Ellen Carbert. Husband of Mary E. Carbert, 19 Sandhurst, Marsden. Reported missing, presumed killed, 21.3.1918, aged 31 years. Has no known grave. Commemorated **POZIERES MEMORIAL TO THE MISSING**. ROH:- Marsden War Memorial.

CARGILL, HARRY. Rifleman. No C/7999. 18th Battalion King's Royal Rifle Corps. Born Nottingham. Lived Longwood prior to enlistment. Employed as a fettler at Messrs Crosland's Mill at Crosland Moor. Married. His wife and daughter lived at 10 North Street, Smallbridge, Rochdale. Enlisted 1915. Invalided home after 18 months service. Returned to France in March, 1918. Killed in action, 3.10.1918. Buried **PERTH CEMETERY (CHINA WALL), YPRES.** Grave location:- Plot 5, Row A, Grave 9.

CARLTON, HERBERT. Private. No 31709. 12th Battalion Durham Light Infantry. Born Horsforth, Leeds. Son of William and Ann Carlton of Lascelles Hall, Kirkheaton, Huddersfield. Employed by Messrs Hodkinsons, printers, New Street, Huddersfield, as a compositor. Was a Sunday School teacher at Cowmes Wesleyan Chapel and a member of the Lascelles Hall Cricket Club. Was also a member of the Almondbury Society of the Sons of Temperance. Enlisted April, 1916, and embarked for France in July, 1916. Killed in action, 7.10.1916, aged 29 years. Has no known grave. Commemorated on the **THIEPVAL MEMORIAL TO THE MISSING**. ROH:- St. John's Church, Kirkheaton; Lepton Parish Church; commemorated on headstone in Kirkheaton Cemetery.

CARR, JAMES. Private. No 242940. 1/5th Battalion Duke of Wellington's Regiment. Born Leeds. Son of Mr and Mrs Peter Carr, 53 Craven Road, Woodhouse Street, Leeds. Educated at Meanwood Road Council School, Leeds. Employed as a scourer and miller by Messrs T. Calverley and Sons, Milnsbridge. Husband of Elsie May Carter, 40 Cobden Row, Marsden Road, Huddersfield. At the time of enlistment, was living 119 Cottage Retreat, Marsden Road, Huddersfield. Enlisted 4.8.1914. Came home on leave a few days before his death. Had been in hospital previously suffering from the effects of an accident. Killed in action near Ypres, 23.3.1917, aged 21. Buried **BELGIAN BATTERY CORNER CEMETERY, YPRES.** Grave location:- Plot 2, Row G, Grave 4. ROH:- Huddersfield Drill Hall.

CARTER, ALBERT EDWARD. Private. No 19796. 10th Battalion Duke of Wellington's Regiment. Born West Derby, Lancashire Lived Meltham. Killed in action, 23.5.1917. Buried **RAILWAY DUGOUTS BURIAL GROUND (TRANSPORT FARM)**. Grave location:- Plot 4, Row F, Grave 12. ROH:- St. Bartholomew's Church, Meltham.

CARTER, ALFRED. Private. No 2832. 1/7th Battalion Duke of Wellington's Regiment. Second son of Mr Samuel Carter, 2 Industrial Terrace, Greenside, Dalton. Attended St. Paul's Wesleyan Church, Dalton and the Moldgreen Adult School. Employed as a polisher by Mr Harry Roebuck, furnisher, of Moldgreen. A keen cross country runner. Enlisted January 1915. Killed in action, 20.12.1915, aged 22 years. Has no known grave. Commemorated on the **MENIN GATE MEMORIAL TO THE MISSING.** ROH:- St. Paul's Wesleyan Church, Dalton; Huddersfield Drill Hall.

CARTER, ALFRED ERNEST. Private. No 23692. 8th Battalion Royal Fusiliers. Born Meltham. Son of Mr William Carter (clerk to the Meltham Urban District Council) and Eliza Carter. Employed as a cashier at the Market Place branch of the London, City and Midland Bank Limited. Attended Meltham Parish Church. Killed in action at the Battle of Arras, 3.5.1917, aged 34. Has no known grave. Commemorated on the **ARRAS MEMORIAL TO THE MISSING.** ROH:- St. Bartholomew's Church, Meltham.

CARTER, ARTHUR WILLIAM. Sergeant. No 1713. 1/5th Battalion Duke of Wellington's Regiment. Born Kirkburton. Son of Albert F. and Sarah Ann Carter, Prospect Cottages, Highburton, Kirkburton. Assisted his father in the family business of Messrs Henry Carter and Sons, edge toolmakers. Was secretary of the Kirkburton Conservative Club. Enlisted in August, 1914, and embarked for France in April, 1915. On completing his period of service he was given a months leave and returned to France on 30.6.1916. Killed in action at the Battle of the Somme, 12.7.1916, aged 28 years. Buried in **CONNAUGHT CEMETERY, THIEPVAL.** Grave location:- Plot 3, Row J, Grave 4. ROH:- All Hallows Church, Kirkburton; Huddersfield Drill Hall.

CARTER, DYSON. Sapper. No WR/342959. Inland Waterways and Docks, Royal Engineers. Born Bradley, Huddersfield. Husband of Sarah Carter, Bank Road, Colne Bridge, Bradley. Died at home, 6.12.1918, aged 29 years. Buried **St. THOMAS'S CHURCHYARD, BRADLEY.** Grave location:- in the South part. ROH:- St. Thomas's Church, Bradley.

CARTER, ERNEST ARTHUR. Private. No 24167. 10th Battalion Duke of Wellington's Regiment. Born Kirkburton. Fifth son of Robert and Harriet Carter of Kirkburton; husband of Eva Carter, Slantgate, Kirkburton. Employed by Messrs Robert Carter and Sons, spade and shovel makers, Kirkburton. Embarked for France in October, 1916. Killed in action, 7.6.1917, aged 25 years. Buried **LA BRIQUE MILITARY CEMETERY No 2, St. JEAN, BELGIUM.** Grave location:- Plot 2, Row C, Grave 2. ROH:- All Hallows Parish Church, Kirkburton.

CARTER, FRANK. Private. No 2045. Household Battalion. Son of John Edward and Lois Carter, 26 Ingfield Terrace, Linthwaite. Assisted his father in the family butchery business at Britannia Road, Slaithwaite. Attended Slaithwaite Wesleyan Church. Enlisted November 1916. Embarked for France in February, 1917. Killed in action, 3.5.1917, aged 21 years. Buried **WANCOURT BRITISH CEMETERY.** Grave location:- Plot 8, Row E, Grave 16.

CARTER, FRED. Corporal. No 201898. 4th Battalion Seaforth Highlanders. Born Slaithwaite. Married. At the time of enlistment, was living at 4 Warrington Terrace, Marsden. Employed as a weaver by Messrs Crowther, Bruce and Company Limited. Killed in action, 12.10.1918, aged 26 years. Has no known grave. Commemorated on the **VIS-en-ARTOIS MEMORIAL TO THE MISSING.** ROH:- Slaithwaite War Memorial.

CARTER, GEORGE. Private. No 28956. 9th Battalion The Yorkshire Regiment. Born Huddersfield. Son of Mr and Mrs R. Carter, 33 Malvern Road, Primrose Hill, Huddersfield. Attended Hall Bower Sunday School and was a member of the Primrose Hill Liberal Club and cricket club. Reported missing, presumed killed, 20.9.1917, aged 33 years. Buried in **HOOGE CRATER CEMETERY.** Grave location:- Plot 7, Row D, Grave 12. ROH:- Lowerhouses War Memorial.

CARTER, HERBERT. Private. No 42411. 9th Battalion North Staffordshire Regiment. Formerly No 6/24155 Leicestershire Regiment. Born 11 Duke Street, Huddersfield. Son of Henry and Kate Carter, 11 Duke Street, Huddersfield. Educated at Spring Grove Council School. Employed as a woollen piecer at Priestroyd Mills. Enlisted 15.3.1917. Killed in action near Bapaume, 12.9.1918, aged 19 years. Buried in **BERTINCOURT CHATEAU BRITISH CEMETERY.** Grave location:- Row A, Grave 8. ROH:- High Street United Methodist Church.

CARTER, JAMES FRANCIS. Gunner. No 140928. Royal Field Artillery. Born Kirkburton. Son of Frank and Elizabeth Carter, of Smith's Croft, Highburton, Kirkburton. Employed as a weaver by Messrs W. and E. Armitage, of Shepley. Had served in Mesopotamia for two years. Died of pneumonia in the Connaught Hospital, Aldershot, 26.10.1918, aged 28 years. Buried **ALL HALLOWS CHURCHYARD, KIRKBURTON.** Grave location:- 19, 1488. ROH:- All Hallows Parish Church, Kirkburton.

CARTER, JOHN WILFRED. 2nd Lieutenant. 8th Battalion Duke of Wellington's Regiment. Born 9.2.1891 in Kirkburton. Son of Councillor Wilfred Carter, shovel and shaft importer, and Selina (nee Jackson) Carter of Rose Cottage, Kirkburton. He gained a scholarship at King James' Grammar School, Almondbury, where he remained for five years. At the age of 16 he matriculated and, gaining other scholarships, went to Leeds University. At the age of 19 he earned his BA and was subsequently awarded a Gilchrist scholarship, with which he studied in Germany at Bonn and Leipzig Universities. On his return to England, in 1911, he was appointed German and French master at Leeds Central High School. On 26.8.1914, he was gazetted 2nd Lieutenant in the 8th Battalion Duke of Wellington's Regiment. Killed in action in the Dardenelles, 7.8.1915. He was 23 years of age. *He was originally buried in the vicinity of Salt Lake, however, following the reoccupation of the Gallipoli peninsula in 1919, his grave was unable to be located by the Imperial (later Commonweath) War Graves Commission, and so today he is commemorated on the* **HELLES MEMORIAL TO THE MISSING.** ROH:- All Hallows Parish Church, Kirkburton.

CARTER, NORMAN. Private. No CH/20284. Royal Marine Light Infantry. *HMS Laurentic.* Born Kirkburton. Son of Lewis and Eliza Carter, of Slant Gate, Kirkburton. Killed by a mine explosion off the Irish coast on 25.1.1917, aged 18 years. Has no known grave. Commemorated on the **CHATHAM NAVAL MEMORIAL TO THE MISSING.** ROH:- All Hallows Parish Church, Kirkburton; commemorated on headstone in Kirkburton Churchyard.

CARTER, SAM. Private. No A/24119. 5th Battalion Canadian Infantry. (Saskatchewan Regiment). Son of Mrs Law Carter of Dogley Bar, Kirkburton. Enlisted December, 1914, and was attached to 'B' Company, 5th Canadian Battalion, 2nd Infantry Brigade, 1st Canadian Division. Arrived in England in July, 1915. After being in the trenches for ten months, he came home on leave not having seen his mother and sisters and brothers for five years. On returning to the front he was attached to a different platoon and was killed in action on 6.6.1916, aged 33 years, during a heavy bombardment. Buried **LARCH WOOD (RAILWAY CUTTING) CEMETERY, ZILLEBEKE, BELGIUM.** Grave location:- Plot 5, Row C, Grave 3. ROH:- All Hallows Parish Church, Kirkburton.

CARTWRIGHT, BEN. Private. No 202166. 1/4th Battalion Northumberland Fusiliers. Born Wooldale, Holmfirth. Son of Walker and Grace Cartwright, of Cliffe, Holmfirth. Educated at Holmfirth National School and was also connected with Cliffe Sunday School. Employed by Messrs John Woodhead, of Thongsbridge. Enlisted May 1916. Trained at Hornsea for ten weeks. Embarked for France July, 1916. Reported missing, presumed killed, 15.11.1916, aged 27 years. Buried **WARLENCOURT BRITISH CEMETERY.** Grave location:- Plot 8, Row C, Grave 30. ROH:- Wooldale War Memorial. (Brother of Private **JAMES WILLIAM CARTWRIGHT**, reported missing, 23.9.1917, q.v.).

CARTWRIGHT, CHARLES. Lance Corporal. No 175305. 1/1st Queen's Own Yorkshire Dragoons. Born 281 Church Lane, Moldgreen, 20.7.1888. Son of Charles and Mary Ellen Cartwright. Educated at Moldgreen Church of England School. Employed by Messrs Rippon Brothers as a motor car builder. Single. Enlisted

1.9.1914. Embarked for France in July, 1915. Killed by the bursting of a shell at Brandhoek, Belgium, 2.5.1918, aged 29 years. Buried **BRANDHOEK NEW MILITARY CEMETERY No 3**. Grave location:- Plot 3, Row A, Grave 15. (Brother of Private **GORDON CARTWRIGHT**, who died of wounds, 9.7.1915, q.v.). ROH:- Christ Church, Moldgreen; commemorated on headstone in Kirkheaton Cemetery.

CARTWRIGHT, DYSON. Private. No M/272121. V1 Corps Mechanical Transport Company, Army Service Corps. Born Jacob's Row, Lockwood, 17.11.1889. Son of the late William Henry and Hannah Cartwright; husband of Edith Cartwright, 202 Whitehead Road, Primrose Hill. Educated at Mount Pleasant Board School, Huddersfield. Employed as a motor driver. Enlisted 27.11.1916. Accidentally drowned in France, 11.8.1918, aged 28. Buried **HUBY-St. LEU BRITISH CEMETERY**. Grave location:- Row D, Grave 2. ROH:- Lockwood Baptist Church.

CARTWRIGHT, ERNEST. 2nd Lieutenant. 5th Battalion Duke of Wellington's Regiment. Son of Herbert and Minnie Cartwright, Cooperative Terrace, Wooldale. Educated at Holmfirth Day School. Attended Wooldale Wesleyan Church and Sunday School, being a member of the Church choir. Employed by Mr W E Goldthorpe, mill furnisher, of Thongsbridge. Married. Enlisted at the outbreak of the war in the 9th Battalion Duke of Wellington's Regiment as a signaller. Killed in action near Famars, 1.11.1918, aged 26. Buried **MAING COMMUNAL CEMETERY EXTENSION**. Grave location:- Row C, Grave 5. ROH:- Wooldale War Memorial.

CARTWRIGHT, FRED. Private. No 202823. 1/4th Battalion King's Own Yorkshire Light Infantry. Son of Mr and Mrs James Cartwright, Dogley Farm, Kirkburton. Assisted his father on the farm. Married, with two children. Enlisted September, 1916, and embarked for France in January, 1917. Killed in action at Nieuport, 23.7.1917, aged 29 years. Buried **RAMSCAPELLE ROAD MILITARY CEMETERY**. Grave location:- Plot 4, Row D, Grave 5. ROH:- All Hallows Parish Church, Kirkburton.

CARTWRIGHT, FREDERICK. Private. No 240023. 1/6th Battalion Duke of Wellington's Regiment. Born 42 Micklegate, York. Worked as a wool extractor at Armitage Bridge Mills. Husband of Lucy Cartwright, 28 Waingate, Berry Brow. Enlisted at the outbreak of the war. Killed in action in Nieppe Forest, north west of Armentieres, 11.4.1918, aged 29 years. Has no known grave. Commemorated on the **TYNE COT MEMORIAL TO THE MISSING** ROH:- Armitage Bridge War Memorial; Armitage Bridge Mills.

CARTWRIGHT, GORDON. Private. No 2082. 1/7th Battalion Duke of Wellington's Regiment. Born 291 Wakefield Road, Moldgreen, Huddersfield. Son of Charles and Marion Cartwright. Educated at Moldgreen Church of England School. Was a member of Moldgreen Church Boy Scouts. Employed in his father's grocery business as a grocer's assistant. Enlisted 8.9.1914. Wounded in the head, 9.7.1915, near Ypres. Died of wounds at No 10 Casualty Clearing Station on 12.7.1915, aged 17 years. Buried **LIJSSENTHOEK MILITARY CEMETERY**. Grave location:- Plot 3, Row C, Grave 3. Brother of Private **CHARLES CARTWRIGHT**, killed in action, 2.5.1918, q.v.). ROH:- Christ Church, Moldgreen; Huddersfield Drill Hall; commemorated on headstone in Kirkheaton Cemetery.

CARTWRIGHT, HERBERT. Private. No M/375345. 'C' Battery Siege Park Army Service Corps. Born Kirkburton. Son of Mr and Mrs Henry Cartwright of Westfield Farm, Flockton, and formerly of Kirkburton. Died of pneumonia at the 2nd Australian Casualty Clearing Station, 25.2.1919, aged 30 years. Buried **ATH COMMUNAL CEMETERY**. Grave location:- Row A, Grave 8. ROH:- All Hallows Parish Church, Kirkburton.

CARTWRIGHT, JAMES WILLIAM. Private. No 40761. 2/5th Battalion South Staffordshire Regiment. Son of Walker and Grace Cartwright of Cliffe, Holmfirth. Husband of Annie Cartwright, Sude Hill, New Mill. Employed by Messrs Beaumonts, dyers, of Honley. Killed in action, 23.9.1917, aged 33 years. Has no known grave. Commemorated on the **TYNE COT MEMORIAL TO THE MISSING.** (Brother of Private **BENJAMIN CARTWRIGHT**, killed in action, 15.11.1916, q.v.). ROH:- New Mill Working Men's Club.

CARTWRIGHT, THOMAS EDWARD. Private. No 22072. 1st Battalion Lancashire Fusiliers. Born 5 Castle Lane, Carlisle, 9.7.1896. Son of Walter and Mary Cartwright, 67 Manchester Road, Huddersfield. Educated at St. Patrick's Roman Catholic Schools in Carlisle and Huddersfield. Employed as a mill hand by Messrs Arthur Dawson and Sons, cotton spinners, of Aspley. Enlisted 1915. Died of wounds, 26.8.1916, aged 19 years. Buried **BRANDHOEK MILITARY CEMETERY.** Grave location:- Plot 2, Row K, Grave 16.

CARTWRIGHT, WILLIE. Acting Company Quarter Master Sergeant. No S/2982. 11th Battalion Argyll and Sutherland Highlanders. Born New Mill 19.12.1890. Son of the late Novello and Ann Cartwright, 43 Crosland Street, Crosland Moor, Huddersfield. Educated at Stile Common Council School. Was a member of the choir at St. Matthew's Church, Primrose Hill, and a member of Lockwood Liberal Club. Employed as a warehouseman by Messrs Joseph Taylor and Sons, iron merchants, of Kirkgate, Huddersfield. At the time of enlistment, was living at 6 Burbeary Road, Lockwood. Enlisted 31.8.1914. Killed in action on the Somme, 15.9.1916, aged 26 years. Buried **ADANAC MILITARY CEMETERY.** Grave location:- Plot 6, Row J, Grave 28. ROH:- St. Barnabas Church, Crosland Moor; St. Matthew's Church, Primrose Hill.

CARTY, JAMES. Private. No 49701. 9th Battalion The King's Liverpool Regiment. Formerly Duke of Wellington's Regiment. Born County Mayo, Ireland. Enlisted Halifax. Lived Huddersfield. Killed in action, 31.7.1917. Has no known grave. Commemorated **MENIN GATE MEMORIAL TO THE MISSING.**

CASEY, STEPHEN. Private. No 15333. 8th Battalion Duke of Wellington's Regiment. Born Lockwood. Adopted son of Mrs Holland, 22 Victoria Street, Lockwood. Employed as a feeder by Messrs J. Lumb and Sons Limited, Folly Hall, Huddersfield. Enlisted February, 1915, and had served in Egypt and the Dardenelles. Killed in action on the Somme, 29.9.1916, aged 21 years. Has no known grave. Commemorated on the **THIEPVAL MEMORIAL TO THE MISSING.** ROH:- St. Stephen's Church, Rashcliffe.

CASSELLS, JOHN. Corporal. No 3925. 53rd Company Machine Gun Corps. Formerly No 17319 Duke of Wellington's Regiment. Born Royston, Yorkshire. Son of Mr and Mrs Cassells of Golcar Brow, Meltham. Reported missing, presumed killed, 21.10.1916, aged 19 years. Has no known grave. Commemorated on the **THIEPVAL MEMORIAL TO THE MISSING.** ROH:- St. Bartholomew's Church, Meltham.

CASTLE, HENRY. Private. No 2835. 1/5th Battalion Duke of Wellington's Regiment. Born 9 Newsome Cross Road, Almondbury, 3.2.1893. Son of Mary Castle. Educated at Newsome Church of England School. Employed as a blacksmith's striker by Messrs Whiteley's, of Lockwood. Single. Enlisted 17.9.1914. Wounded 14.12.1915. His mother received a telegram on the 31.12.1915, stating that her son was dangerously ill from gunshot wounds at No 14 General Hospital at Wimereux. A second telegram stated that he had died from his wounds on 8.1.1916, aged 23 years. Buried **WIMEREUX COMMUNAL CEMETERY.** Grave location:- Plot 1, Row L, Grave 11a. ROH:- St. John's Church, Newsome; Huddersfield Drill Hall.

CASTLE, HENRY WILMOTT. Private. Deal/4211(S) Royal Marine Medical Unit, Royal Naval Division. Born Glasgow 27.11.1895. Son of the Rev Thomas Brain and Letitia B. Castle. Educated at Kingswood School (for sons of Wesleyan Ministers, Bath). Left Huddersfield as a child. At the time of enlistment, was living in Oldham. Employed in the cotton industry in Manchester. Enlisted 14.11.1914. Killed in action, 4.1.1917 by a German shell while trying to save a wounded German Officer. Buried **St. JULIEN DRESSING STATION CEMETERY.** Grave location:- Plot 3, Row B, Grave 28. ROH:- Mount Pleasant Chapel, Lockwood.

CASTLE, JAMES ARTHUR. Sapper. No 58257. 139th A.T. Company Royal Engineers. Born Grasscroft, Almondbury, 30.4.1882. Educated at St. Paul's School, Huddersfield. Husband of Caroline Castle, 12 Lockwood's Yard, Upperhead Row, Huddersfield. Employed as an organ builder. Enlisted 1.12.1914. Died of Blackwater Fever in Salonica on 22.4.1918, aged 36 years. Buried in **MIKRA BRITISH CEMETERY, SALONIKA, GREECE.** Grave location:- No 246. ROH:- St. Paul's Church, Southgate, Huddersfield.

CASTLE, JOHN ARTHUR. Private. No 12336. 2/7th Battalion Duke of Wellington's Regiment. Born Golcar. Son of the late Firth and of Mrs Castle, 316 Fairfield, Manchester Road, Milnsbridge. Employed as a beamer by Messrs John Crowther and Sons Limited, Union Mills, Milnsbridge. Enlisted September, 1914, and had been twice wounded. Reported missing, presumed killed, at the Battle of Cambrai, 28.11.1917, aged 28 years. Has no known grave. Commemorated on the **CAMBRAI MEMORIAL TO THE MISSING.** ROH:- Milnsbridge War Memorial; Huddersfield Drill Hall.

CATER, GEORGE EDWARD. Lance Corporal. No 305484. 1/7th Battalion Duke of Wellington's Regiment. Born Marsden. Second son of Mr and Mrs W E Cater, Side Ing, Marsden, Huddersfield. Employed as a spinner at Bank Bottom Mills, Marsden. Was an able student at the Marsden Evening School, where he was awarded a gold medal in the session before he joined the army, in August 1914. Was a member of the Order of Rechabites. Embarked for France in April, 1915. Killed in action, 13.4.1918, aged 23 years. Buried **LE GRAND BEAUMART BRITISH CEMETERY, STEENWERCK.** Grave location:- Special Memorial A 7. ROH:- Huddersfield Drill Hall; Marsden War Memorial.

CATON, RICHARD. Private. No 241376. 1/5th Battalion Duke of Wellington's Regiment. Married, with four children. Lived 111, Wakefield Road, Huddersfield. Employed by Messrs M. Bedforth and Sons of Aspley. Killed at Nieuport, 7.8.1917, aged 42 years. Buried **RAMSCAPELLE ROAD MILITARY CEMETERY.** Grave location:- Plot 2, Row A, Grave 7.

CAWTHRA, WALTER EDWIN (TEDDY). Private. No 241295. 2/5th Battalion Duke of Wellington's Regiment. Born 12 Orchard Terrace, Newsome Road, Huddersfield, 7.9.1897 Son of Edwin and Mary Elizabeth Cawthra, 5 Bell Street, Newsome Road, Huddersfield. Educated at Stile Common Church of England School, Hillhouse Higher Elementary School and Huddersfield Technical College. Employed as a clerk at the Huddersfield Corporation Gasworks, Leeds Road, Huddersfield. Single. Enlisted 7.8.1915. Killed in action at Marfaux, near Rheims, 20.7.1918, aged 20 years. Buried **COURMAS BRITISH CEMETERY.** Grave location:- Plot 2, Row D, Grave 10. ROH:- St. Stephen's Church, Rashcliffe; Huddersfield Drill Hall; Huddersfield Corporation Roll; Almondbury War Memorial.

CHADWICK, JOHN WILLIAM. Private. No 57347. 14th Battalion (Pioneers) Northumberland Fusiliers. Formerly No 205881 Royal Engineers. Born Huddersfield 25.3.1888. Only son of Mrs Emily Chadwick, 100 Church Street, Paddock. Employed as a joiner. Killed in action near Ypres, 14.11.1917. Buried **THE HUTS CEMETERY, DICKEBUSCH, BELGIUM.** Grave location:- Plot 14, Row C, Grave 17. ROH:- All Saints Church, Paddock; St. Philip's Church, Birchencliffe.

CHALONER, ARTHUR. Private. No 36708. 10th Battalion Duke of Cornwall's Light Infantry. Formerly No 213364 Royal Engineers. Born 169 Rashcliffe Hill, Huddersfield, 31.3.1888. Educated at Mount Pleasant Council School. Employed as a moulder by Messrs Jere Kaye and Company. At the time of enlistment was living at 12 Manor Street, Kings Mill Lane, Huddersfield. Married. Was a member of St. Andrew's Cricket Club and also a member of the Ramsden Street Men's Own Class. Killed in action, 1.12.1917, aged 29 years. Buried **HERMIES HILL BRITISH CEMETERY.** Grave location:- Plot 1, Row C, Grave 13. ROH:- Almondbury War Memorial; Christ Church, Moldgreen.

CHAMBERS, ABRAHAM. Lance Corporal. No C/7245. 'A' Company King's Royal Rifle Corps, posted to 12th Battalion London Regiment (The Rangers). Born Brook Fold, Honley, 29.3.1896. Son of Seth and Clara Chambers, 18 Schofield's Yard, Longroyd Lane, Huddersfield. Educated at St. Paul's Church School, Huddersfield. Employed as a finisher by Messrs Crowther Brothers, Union Mills, Milnsbridge. Single. Enlisted 12.10.1915. Died of wounds at No 55 Casualty Clearing Station, 24.8.1918, aged 22 years. Buried **DAOURS COMMUNAL CEMETERY EXTENSION.** Grave location:- Plot 6, Row A, Grave 23. ROH:- Honley War Memorial.

CHAMBERS, ERNEST, ALWYN. Sergeant. No 79994. 6th Armoured Car Company, Machine Gun Corps (Motors), attached Dunster Force. Born White Stones, Stocksmoor, 7.2.1889.

Educated at Thurstonland Endowed Schools. Employed as a motor driver by Messrs Taylor and Littlewood Limited, Newsome Mills, Huddersfield. Married, with three children, living at Bankfoot, Almondbury. Enlisted 11.3.1918. Died of typhus in Mesopotamia, 19.9.1918. Has no known grave. Commemorated on the **BASRA MEMORIAL, IRAQ. ROH:-** Almondbury War Memorial; Messrs. Taylor and Littlewood, Newsome Mills.

CHAMBERS, CHARLES EDWARD. Sergeant. No 240111. 1/5th Battalion Duke of Wellington's Regiment. Born Kirkburton. Son of Henry and Emma Chambers, Park View, Kirkburton. Attended Dogley Lane Congregational Church. Employed by Messrs B. H. Moxon and Sons, of Kirkburton. Was in the local Territorials before the outbreak of war. Embarked for France in April, 1915. Killed in action at Nieuport, 7.8.1917, aged 25 years. Buried **RAMSCAPELLE ROAD CEMETERY.** Grave location:- Plot 2, Row A, Grave 4. ROH:- All Hallows Parish Church, Kirkburton; Huddersfield Drill Hall.

CHAMBERS, REGINALD HAROLD. Private. No 3/10663. 2nd Battalion Duke of Wellington's Regiment. Born 42 Stafford Street, Crewe, 31.12.1894. Son of Harold C. and Harriet Chambers, 55 Thomas Street, Northgate, Huddersfield. Educated at St. Paul's Church School, Crewe. Employed as a labourer by Messrs W. C Holmes and Company Limited, engineers, of Turnbridge. Enlisted 4.8.1914. Gassed at Hill 60 in May, 1915. Reported missing, presumed killed, at Le Transloy on 12.10.1916, aged 21 years. Has no known grave. Commemorated on the **THIEPVAL MEMORIAL TO THE MISSING.** ROH:- Huddersfield Parish Church; commemorated on headstone in Kirkheaton Cemetery.

CHAMBERS, WILLIAM EDMUND. Private. No 12016. 8th Battalion Duke of Wellington's Regiment. Born Boston, Lincolnshire. Came to Huddersfield in 1910. Son of Mr and Mrs G. E. Chambers, 14 Lindley Street, Longwood. Had also resided at Kirkburton and Ramsden Mill Lane, Linthwaite. Was an apprentice in the tool-room of Messrs J. Hopkinson and Company, Birkby. Was a member of the St. John Ambulance Association. Attended Milnsbridge Baptist Sunday School. Enlisted August, 1914, and sailed for the Dardenelles on 2.7.1915. Died from Enteric Fever and pneumonia at Alexandria, 12.11.1915, aged 17 years. Buried **CHATBY WAR MEMORIAL CEMETERY, ALEXANDRIA, EGYPT.** Grave location:- Row A, Grave 7. ROH:- Longwood War Memorial.

CHAPLIN, ALFRED. Able Seaman. No J/40505. Royal Navy. *HMS Saumarez*. Born Hinchliffe Mill, Holmbridge, Holmfirth. Son of Mary Chaplin, Glen Royd, Hinchliffe Mill, Holmbridge. Educated at Field End School and Hall Sunday School. Played with Hinchliffe Mill Brass Band and later with Holme Brass Band. Employed in the twisting department of Messrs J. Greenwood and Sons, Digley Mills. Enlisted in August, 1914, into the Duke of Wellington's Regiment and underwent training in Dorset. He was discharged due to rheumatism and went to work at Yew Tree Mills. On the formation of the Holme Valley Battery, Royal Field Artillery, tried to re-enlist but was turned down on medical grounds. Was finally accepted into the Royal Navy in June, 1915. Was accidentally drowned through the capsizing of the whaler *HMS Saumarez* on 29.6.1918, aged 26 years. Has no known grave. Commemorated on the **PLYMOUTH NAVAL MEMORIAL TO THE MISSING.** His mother received a letter from the Captain of *HMS Saumarez* who wrote, *'I am very sorry indeed to have to inform you that it is true that your son lost his life through the capsizing of our whaler at about 4pm on the 29th June. The whaler was struck by a sudden squall which took her aback and before the sails could be eased off she capsized and sank. It is believed that your son got entangled in the sails or the gear and was taken down with the boat but we were unable to recover either the boat or his body so I have no certain information on that point. Divers were at work endeavouring to recover the bodies and the boat for five days but after that it was felt it was useless going on searching. His loss is very severely felt in the ship by all his shipmates and I wish to express my most sincere sympathy with you in your loss.'* ROH:- Holme and Holmbridge War Memorial.

CHAPLIN, HERBERT. Private. No 22014. 'B' Company 17th Battalion Lancashire Fusiliers. Born Holmfirth. Son of Harry and Mary Ann Chaplin, 131 Woodhead Road, Hinchliffe Mill, Holmfirth. Employed by Messrs W.H. and

J. Barber at Clarence Mills, Holmbridge. Was a member of Holmbridge Rugby Football club and a keen athlete. Being just five foot three inches in height he enlisted in a bantam battalion of the Lancashire Fusiliers at Bolton. Suffered a severe compound fractures to the skull and knee and died in No 5 Casualty Clearing Station, at 2.30pm, on 27.8.1916, aged 27 years. Buried **CORBIE COMMUNAL CEMETERY EXTENSION**. Grave location:- Plot 2, Row B, Grave 57. ROH:- Holme and Holmbridge War Memorial. (Brother of Private **JOHN HENRY CHAPLIN**, killed in action, 8.10.1916, q.v.).

CHAPLIN, JOHN HENRY. Private. No 153151. 43rd Battalion Canadian Infantry (Manitoba Regiment). Born Hinchliffe Mill in 1883. Son of Harry and Mary Ann Chaplin, 131 Woodhead Road, Hinchliffe Mill, Holmfirth. Before emigrating to Canada, in 1908, was a firer at Messrs W. H. and J. Barbers at Clarence Mill, Holmbridge. Married. Enlisted at the outbreak of the war. Was wounded in the head in April, 1915, near Ypres. Returned to the trenches six weeks later. Reported missing, presumed killed, 8.10.1916, aged 33 years. Buried **REGINA TRENCH CEMETERY**. Grave location:- Plot 1, Row D, Grave 23. ROH:- Holme and Holmbridge War Memorial. (Brother of Private **HERBERT CHAPLIN**, who died of wounds, 27.8.1916, q.v.).

CHAPMAN, ERNEST. Private. No 38308. 16th Battalion (1st Bradford Pals) West Yorkshire Regiment. Born Bradley, Huddersfield. Husband of Mrs E. Chapman, 14 Wood Terrace, Primrose Hill, Huddersfield. Killed in action, 27.2.1917, aged 24 years. Buried **OWL TRENCH CEMETERY**. Grave location:- Row A. ROH:- St. Stephen's Church, Rashcliffe; Fartown and Birkby War Memorial.

CHAPMAN, FRED. Private. No 202261. 'A' Company 2/4th Battalion Leicestershire Regiment. Born Holywell, North Wales, 31.3.1897. Son of Mr and Mrs Fred Chapman, 'Glan-y-Morfa', 63 Luck Lane, Marsh, Huddersfield. Educated at Paddock Council School. Employed as a cloth finisher by Messrs Liddell and Brierley Limited, Stanley Mills, Marsh. Was a member of the Young Men's Class at Gledholt Wesleyan Church where he was assistant organist. Enlisted 11.11.1915. Embarked for France Feburary, 1917. Wounded, 18.4.1917, near Hesbecourt and died of wounds, 19.4.1917, aged 20 years. Buried **PERONNE COMMUNAL CEMETERY AND EXTENSION**. Grave location:- Plot 1, Row B, Grave 11 ROH:- Gledholt Wesleyan Church; All Saint's Church, Paddock

CHAPMAN, JOHN WILLIAM. Private. No 152793. 6th Dragoons (Inniskilling). Formerly No 6190 Scottish Horse. Son of Mr and Mrs T. J. Chapman, Woodhouse, Holmbridge. Employed as a teamer by Messrs Henry Mitchell and Sons, provision merchants, of Holmfirth. Enlisted November 1915. Died of wounds, 9.8.1918. Has no known grave. Commemorated on **VIS-en-ARTOIS MEMORIAL TO THE MISSING**. ROH:- Holme and Holmbridge War Memorial.

CHAPPELL, ARTHUR. Rifleman. No R/19790. 16th Battalion King's Royal Rifle Corps. Born Milnsbridge. Son of Harry and Mary Chappell, 93 Luck Lane, Marsh. Educated Paddock Council School. Employed as a twister-in. Enlisted 28.2.1916. Killed in action at Croissilles, 25.6.1917, aged 26. Buried **CROISSILLES BRITISH CEMETERY**. Grave location:- Plot 1, Row G, Grave 12. ROH:- All Saints Church, Paddock; Shared Church, Paddock.

CHAPPELL, ERNEST. Guardsman. No 21466. Coldstream Guards. Born Sunset Terrace, Birkby, 27.6.1891. Son of Eleanor Chappell, 49 Clement Street, Birkby. Educated at Thomas Street Council School. Employed as a grocer's traveller by the Cash Supplies Stores, New Street, Huddersfield. Enlisted 8.1.1917. Killed in action at the Battle of Cambrai, 27.11.1917. Has no known grave. Commemorated on the **CAMBRAI MEMORIAL TO THE MISSING**. ROH:- Great Northern Street Congregational Church; Fartown and Birkby War Memorial. (Brother of Private **STANLEY CHAPPELL**, killed in action, 13.8.1915, q.v.).

CHAPPELL, HARRY. Private. No 3815. 1/7th Battalion Duke of Wellington's Regiment. Son of Mr and Mrs Ben Chappell, Bank Top, Hill Top, Slaithwaite. Employed in the finishing room at Messrs W and E Crowther Limited, Brook Mills, Crimble, Slaithwaite. Attended Zion Baptist Church and Sunday School. Was also an active member of the Slaithwaite Liberal Club. Enlisted

March 1916. Killed in action on the Somme, 8.8.1916, aged 26 years. Buried **LONSDALE CEMETERY, AUTHUILLE.** Grave location:- Plot 8, Row E, Grave 1. ROH:- St James' Church, Slaithwaite; Slaithwaite War Memorial; Huddersfield Drill Hall. His parents received the following letter from Private H Carter who was a comrade of their son and also lived at Bank Top, Slaithwaite, *'I am very sorry to inform you that Harry was killed early this morning whilst we were out on a working party. He only lived about five minutes after he had been wounded. He was unconscious at the time of death so he would suffer no pain. I did not know he had been hit until half an hour later when we were coming back and then they told me that my pal had been killed. It was a great blow to me as we had been together all the time until last night when we got separated in the dark and could not find each other. I have lost my best friend for he was a good lad and respected by all who knew him out here. You have my deepest sympathy in your great and sad loss.'*

CHAPPELL, STANLEY. Private. No 3392. 1/5th Battalion Duke of Wellington's Regiment. Born 20 Thomas Street, Huddersfield, 14.5.1892. Son of Eleanor Chappell, 49 Clement Street, Birkby. Educated Thomas Street Council School. Employed as a grocer's assistant. Enlisted 4.11.1914. Killed in action near Ypres, 14.8.1915. Buried **TALANA FARM CEMETERY.** Grave location:- Plot 4, Row A, Grave 19. ROH:- Great Northern Street Congregational Church; Fartown and Birkby War Memorial; Huddersfield Drill Hall. (Brother of Private **ERNEST CHAPPELL**, killed in action, 27.1.1917, q.v.).

CHAPPELL, STANLEY. Private. No 27317. 1st Battalion Royal Warwickshire Regiment. Formerly No 3888 2/5th Battalion Duke of Wellington's Regiment. Born Nook, Newsome Road, 12.5.1890. Son of of Mr and Mrs Chappell, 160 Newsome Road, Huddersfield. Educated at Stile Common Board School. Employed as a warehouseman by Messrs Bairstows, wholesale clothiers, of Fitzwilliam Street, Huddersfield. Married in 1915. Wife living at 79 Baker Street, Oakes. Enlisted February 1915. Reported missing, presumed killed, near Hinges, north of Bethune, 15.4.1918. Has no known grave. Commemorated on the **PLOEGSTEERT MEMORIAL TO THE MISSING.**

CHARLESWORTH, ENOCH. Sergeant. No G/59440. Royal Fusiliers, posted to 4th Battalion London Regiment. Born Marsden. Son of Mr and Mrs David Charlesworth, Pinewood Grove Marsden. Married Susannah Whitham in the autumn of 1914. Lived at 1 Brook Terrace, Slaithwaite. Employed as a pattern weaver at New Mills, Marsden. Attended Marsden Parish Church. A keen footballer and boxer Enlisted 1.11.1915. Killed in action, 25.8.1918, aged 27 years. Buried **BRONFAY FARM MILITARY CEMETERY.** Grave location:- Plot 2, Row F, Grave 14. ROH:- St. James Church, Slaithwaite; Slaithwaite War Memorial; Marsden War Memorial.

CHARLESWORTH, FRED. Rifleman. No 260050. 1st Battalion Monmouthshire Regiment. Born Kirkburton. Son of John and Martha Charlesworth of Dene Road, Kirkheaton. Husband of Amy Hilda Charlesworth of Back Lane, Shelley. Employed as a painter by Messrs J. and W. Lodge of Kirkburton. Killed in action, 10.11.1917, aged 39 years. Has no known grave. Commemorated on the **LOOS MEMORIAL TO THE MISSING.** ROH:- All Hallows Parish Church, Kirkburton; Emmanuel Church, Shelley.

CHARLESWORTH, FRED. Lieutenant. 2nd Battalion Duke of Wellington's Regiment. Born Brockholes. Son of the late Mr and Mrs Ralph Charlesworth of Brockholes. Educated at St. Mary's College, Bangor, and had been a teacher in Sheffield for twenty years. Had served with the Colours both in Egypt and France and had been wounded twice and gassed in April, 1918. Returned to Sheffield for medical treatment but never recovered. Died 1.2.1919, aged 41 years. Buried **St. GEORGE'S CHURCHYARD, BROCKHOLES.** Grave location:- H. 31, South of Church. ROH:- Honley War Memorial; Brockholes War Memorial.

CHARLESWORTH, GEORGE ADAM. Gunner. No 74499. 122nd Heavy Battery Royal Garrison Artillery. Born Kirkburton. Son of Adam and Sarah Ann Charlesworth of Dean Brow, Kirkburton. Employed by his father as a tailor. Was a member of Kirkburton

Liberal Club. Attended Highburton Primitive Methodist Church. Enlisted April, 1915. Killed in action, 30.9.1917, aged 24 years. Buried **VLAMERTINGHE NEW MILITARY CEMETERY**. Grave location:- Plot 12, Row G, Grave 23. ROH:- All Hallows Parish Church, Kirkburton; commemorated on headstone in Kirkburton Churchyard.

CHARLESWORTH, GEORGE VERNON. 2nd Lieutenant. 6th Battalion Duke of Wellington's Regiment. Born Lockwood 3.3.1892. Son of John William and Elizabeth Ann Charlesworth, 2 Northfield, Lockwood. Educated at Huddersfield Higher Grade School. Employed as a clerk in the office of Messrs John Taylor Limited, Colne Road, Huddersfield. Single. Enlisted as a Private in the 1/5th Battalion Duke of Wellington's Regiment on 12.10.1914. Embarked for France in April, 1915. Wounded three times. Killed in action, 28.9.1918, aged 26 years. Buried **GRAND RAVINE CEMETERY, HAVRINCOURT**. Grave location:- Row A, Grave 3. ROH:- St. Stephen's Church, Rashcliffe; Huddersfield Drill Hall.

CHARLESWORTH, HAROLD. Private. No 28959. 2nd Battalion Durham Light Infantry. Born Scar End, Thurstonland 14.7.1897. Son of Mr and Mrs Joe Charlesworth, 24 Firth Street, Huddersfield. Educated at Brockholes National School and Stile Common Council School. Employed at the National Shell Factory, Fitzwilliam Street, Huddersfield. Single. Enlisted May 1916. Wounded, 11.2.1918, and died of his wounds at No 3 Casualty Clearing Station on 24.2.1918, aged 20 years. Buried **GREVILLERS BRITISH CEMETERY**. Grave location:- Plot 10, Row E, Grave 19. ROH:- Brockholes War Memorial.

CHARLESWORTH, HARRY. Gunner. No 151447. 87th Siege Battery Royal Garrison Artillery. Born Netherthong, Holmfirth, 10.6.1886. Son of the late James and of Millicent Charlesworth, 34 Whitehead Lane, Primrose Hill, Huddersfield. Educated at Netherthong National School. Employed as a cloth finisher by Messrs Shaw Brothers of Firth Street, Huddersfield. Single. Enlisted March 1917. Wounded at the Battle of Arras, 7.9.1917, but returned to duty. Died of wounds at No 23 Casualty Clearing Station, 7.9.1918, aged 32. Buried **DUISANS BRITISH CEMETERY**. Grave location:- Plot 5, Row H, Grave 40. ROH:- St. Matthew's Church, Primrose Hill; Netherthong and Thongsbridge; commemorated on his parents' headstone in All Saints Churchyard, Netherthong.

CHARLESWORTH, HENRY LEROY. Lance Corporal. No 42545. 1/5th Battalion South Staffordshire Regiment. Formerly No 41513 King's Own Yorkshire Light Infantry. Born Honley. Son of Wright and Constance M Charlesworth of Fisher Green, Honley. Was head confectioner for Mr A W Whiteley of Westgate, Huddersfield. Was treasurer of the Honley St. John Ambulance Brigade. Enlisted September 1916. Killed in action, 28.9.1918, aged 23 years. Has no known grave. Commemorated on the **VIS-en-ARTOIS MEMORIAL TO THE MISSING**. ROH:- Honley War Memorial.

CHARLESWORTH, HERBERT. 2nd Lieutenant. 91st Company Machine Gun Corps. Formerly Army Cyclist Corps. Son of the late Mr and Mrs Henry Charlesworth of Quarry Mount, Holmfirth. Educated at Holmfirth National School. Attended Holmfirth Parish Church Sunday School, where he played the organ and was a member of the bible class. On leaving school he was employed by Messrs Rushworths of Westgate, Huddersfield, but at the time of enlistment was employed by Messrs Graham, contractors, of Huddersfield. Enlisted in June 1915. Was wounded on 3.9.1916 and returned to England. Returned to France in December, 1916. Was commissioned in February, 1917. Was married in August, 1917, to Miss E A Hirst of Cirencester at St. John's Church, Bognor. A fortnight after his wedding he returned to France. Killed in action, 26.10.1917, aged 26 years. Buried **HOOGE CRATER CEMETERY**. Grave location:- Plot 10, Row F, Grave 1. ROH:- Holmfirth War Memorial.

CHARLESWORTH, JOHN EDWARD. Private. No 7199. 1/9th Battalion Durham Light Infantry. Son of the late William Charlesworth of Liphill and Mrs Alfred Woodhead (formerly Charlesworth) of Towngate, Holmfirth. Educated at St. John's School, Holmfirth. Attended St. John's Parish Church and Sunday School and was a member of the choir. After leaving school was employed by Messrs Henry Mitchell and Sons for two years and then for Messrs Wallaces branch shop at Lockwood, at which branch he became manager, and was later transferred to the New Mill branch as manager.

In partnership with a friend he commenced business at Horwich in the grocery and provision trade. Enlisted, 1916, and embarked for France in October, 1916 The family received a postcard from him, dated 5.11.1916, saying the following, *'I promised in my last letter to send you the nature of the next move. Well it will give you a shock as I am a German prisoner of war. We went over the top on November 5th and got cut off. I am not yet at a permanent place so that you will no be able to write. I hope you have not been too much alarmed at my letters ceasing. I did not get wounded at all and am at present living in barracks in France and am being treated alright.'* The next time the family received any news from him was a postcard which arrived in Holmfirth on 19.3.1916, dated 31.12.1916. He wrote, *'I have been in hospital eleven days with my leg. It started swelling, blood poisoning I think. The doctor cut it slightly and it is going on alright. I've started knocking about in camp but have not started working outside yet.'* On 1.4.1917, after enquiries through the British Red Cross, the family were told that he had died on 7.1.1917, aged 32 years. Buried **ACHIET-LE- GRAND COMMUNAL CEMETERY EXTENSION.** Grave location:- Plot 4, Row N, Grave 1. ROH:- Holmfirth War Memorial.

CHARLESWORTH, JOHN SHEPHERD. Private. No 3/10732. 2nd Battalion Duke of Wellington's Regiment. Born 111 Castlegate, Huddersfield, 21.3.1895. Son of Mr and Mrs John Charlesworth. Educated at St. Paul's Church of England School. Employed as a mechanic's labourer by Messrs Cliffe and Company, of Longroyd Bridge. Single. Enlisted 14.8.1914. Was wounded and gassed at Hill 60 in May, 1915. Wounded on the first day of the Battle of the Somme, on 1.7.1916, and died of wounds on 2.7.1916, aged 21 years. Buried **COUIN BRITISH CEMETERY.** Grave location:- Plot 2, Row A, Grave 4. ROH:- Huddersfield Parish Church.

CHARLESWORTH, WILFRED. Private. No 242836. 1/6th Battalion Duke of Wellington's Regiment. Born Holmfirth. Son of Mr and Mrs C. W. Charlesworth, 33 Cinderhills Road, Holmfirth. Attended Holmfirth Parish Church Sunday School and was a member of Holmfirth Conservative Club. Had worked at both at Dover Mills and Rock Mills, Holmfirth. Was a keen football player, playing with the Underbank rugby team, the Hinchliffe Mill Temperance team and the Netherthong association team. Enlisted September 1916. Killed in action, 14.4.1918, aged 29 years. Has no known grave. Commemorated on the **TYNE COT MEMORIAL TO THE MISSING.** ROH:- Underbank War Memorial.

CHARLESWORTH, WRIGHT. Corporal. No TR/023604. Army Service Corps. Born 32a Deighton Road, Deighton. Educated at Deighton Council School. Employed as a cloth presser. Husband of Edith Charlesworth. Enlisted 8.11.1914. Discharged from the army, 22.4.1919. Died of the effects of malaria at 32a Deighton Road, Deighton on 10.10.1922. ROH:- Deighton War Memorial.

CHEETHAM, GEORGE CLIFFORD. Air Mechanic 2nd Class. No 29343. 45th Squadron Royal Air Force. Son of Edwin and Annie Cheetham of Brockholes. Employed by Messrs Mitchell and Sons of Brockholes. Was well known as a vocalist and was a member of the Brockholes church choir. Died of bronchial pneumonia, 8.10.1918, aged 21. Buried **CHARMES MILITARY CEMETERY. (VOSGES).** Grave location:- Plot 1, Row C, Grave 10. ROH:- Honley War Memorial; Brockholes War Memorial.

CHEETHAM, HERBERT. Rifleman. No C/7622. 18th Battalion King's Royal Rifle Corps. Born Marsden. Moved to Milnsbridge in 1912. Son of Mr and Mrs Sam Cheetham, 11 Casson Street, Milnsbridge. Employed by Mr Richardson, hairdresser of Bradford Road, Huddersfield, and formerly by Mr H Crowther, hairdresser, of Peel Street, Marsden. Had also been employed by Messrs John Crowther and Sons of Milnsbridge. Played football with Marsden Villa team and Holme City. Attended Milnsbridge Christadelphian Society. Enlisted 15.11.1915. Embarked for France 2.5.1916. Killed in action, 15.9.1916, aged 21 years. Has no known grave. Commemorated on the **THIEPVAL MEMORIAL TO THE MISSING.**

CHILD, GEORGE. Corporal. No 17554. 10th Battalion The Cameronians (Scottish Rifles). Son of James and Ellen Child of Cliffe, Wooldale, Holmfirth; husband of Harriet Maria Child, 4 Spring Row, Keighley Road, Colne. On leaving school was employed in the shop of Mrs Brook, Victoria Street, Holmfirth. Was then employed by the Netherthong Cooperative Society, until he left to take up a position with the Colne Cooperative Society. At the time of enlistment, was employed as a tram conductor on the Colne tramways. Enlisted 1.1.1915. Trained in Scotland and embarked for France on 10.10.1916. Killed in action, 1.8.1917, aged 30 years. Has no known grave. Commemorated on the **MENIN GATE MEMORIAL TO THE MISSING.**

CHINN, EDWARD WILLIAM. No 39571. Signal Depot (Fenny Stratford) Royal Engineers. Formerly Lance Corporal No 6938, King's Own Yorkshire Light Infantry. Born High Royd, Moldgreen. Educated at Spring Grove Board School. Married. At the time of enlistment was living at Luck Lane, Paddock. Before enlistment was in the employ of Huddersfield Corporation Tramways Department as a driver. Enlisted 26.11.1901. Was on leave at home when he was involved in an accident; (the following report was in the Huddersfield Daily Examiner for 16.8.1917, *'Between 12 and 1pm this afternoon a collision took place at Aspley, where St. Andrew's Road and Firth Street enter at right angles into the main thoroughfare from Huddersfield, between a taxi cab, owned and driven by Mr Arthur Brook of Packhorse Yard, and a motor waggon converted from a motor car owned and driven by Mr Willie Whiteley, dyer of Aspley Dyeworks (St. Andrew's Road). As a result Lance Corporal EDWARD WILLIAM CHINN of the Royal Engineers (signal department), Bletchley Camp, whose wife and children live at Luck Lane, Paddock, who was a passenger in the taxi, is lying in the Huddersfield Royal Infirmary suffering from a fractured pelvis and other injuries and his condition is stated to be serious.'* Died in Huddersfield Royal Infirmary, 16.8.1917, aged 33 years. Buried with full military honours in **EDGERTON CEMETERY, HUDDERSFIELD** on 20.8.1917. Grave location:- 11B, 175. ROH:- New North Road Baptist Church.

CHIPPINDALE, NORMAN R. Private. No 4396. 1/5th Battalion Duke of Wellington's Regiment. Born Linthwaite. Son of Walter and Emily Chippindale, 10 Wood Street, Longwood. Husband of Agnes Chippindale, 10 Causeway Side, Linthwaite. Educated Crow Lane Board School, Milnsbridge. Employed as a night piecer at the Colne Valley Spinning Company. Attended Linthwaite Wesleyan Church and formerly the Milnsbridge Wesleyan Sunday School. A keen rugby player. Had served for four years with the local Territorials before the outbreak of war but, not having received his discharge papers, was called up with the remainder of the Battalion. After a few days he was granted his discharge and allowed to return home. In June, 1915, he voluntarily re-enlisted and, after training at Clipstone Camp where he was in the bomb throwing section, he embarked for France in May, 1916. His death occurred on the morning of Wednesday, 25.10.1916, whilst on guard-duty behind the lines, a piece of shrapnel hitting him on the head and killing him instantly. Buried **FONQUEVILLERS MILITARY CEMETERY.** Grave location:- Plot 1, Row K, Grave 23. ROH:- Linthwaite; St. Mark's Parish Church, Longwood; Huddersfield Mission, Milnsbridge; Crow Lane Board School, Milnsbridge; Huddersfield Drill Hall; commemorated in Salendine Nook Chapel yard, 443E.

CHORLTON, JAMES EDWARD. Private. No 38230. The Yorkshire Regiment. Born Golcar. Married. Lived 13 New North Road, Crimble, Slaithwaite. Employed as a firer by Messrs Joseph Thomas junior. Attended Zion Baptist Chapel, Slaithwaite. Enlisted 26.9.1916. Embarked for France the week before Christmas. Came home on sick leave in March, 1917, and returned to France during the latter part of July, 1917. Killed in action at the Battle of Passchendaele, 19.10.1917, aged 35 years. Has no known grave. Commemorated on the **TYNE COT MEMORIAL TO THE MISSING.** ROH:- St. James Church, Slaithwaite; Slaithwaite War Memorial.

CHURCHILL, THOMAS. Sergeant. No 5768. 6th Battalion Northamptonshire Regiment. Born Dartford, Kent. Married, with one child. Employed by Messrs Read, Holliday and Sons Limited and previously as a warehouseman by Messrs R. Cuthbert Limited, Chemists, of Westgate, Huddersfield. Enlisted August 1914. Wounded at the Battle of Neuve Chapelle on 10.3.1915. Killed in action, 26.10.1916, aged 38 years. Buried **REGINA TRENCH CEMETERY.** Grave location:- Plot 1, Row B, Grave 4.

CLARK, ARCHIBALD GRASSAM. Private. No 204566. 2/5th Battalion Duke of Wellington's

Regiment. Born Falkirk, Scotland, 6.2.1885. Son of John Clark, 8 Millflat Street, Carron Road, Falkirk. Educated at Falkirk Schools. Husband of Mrs L Clark, 5 Brunswick Yard, Albert Street, Lockwood. Employed as a moulder by the Hygienic Stove Company. Enlisted July 1915. Reported missing, presumed killed, at Bourlon Wood during the Battle of Cambrai, 27.11.1917. Has no known grave. Commemorated on the **CAMBRAI MEMORIAL TO THE MISSING.** ROH:- St. Stephen's Church, Rashcliffe; Huddersfield Drill Hall.

CLARK, JAMES. Lance Sergeant. No 12650. 9th Battalion Duke of Wellington's Regiment. Born Glasgow. Lived Hill Top, Holmfirth. Employed at Hepworth Ironworks. Died of wounds at No 36 Casualty Clearing Station, 6.7.1916, aged 24 years. Buried **HEILLY STATION CEMETERY.** Grave location:- Plot 1, Row F, Grave 32. ROH:- Hepworth and Scholes War Memorial.

CLARK, JOEL LEE. Private. No 36652. 12th Battalion King's Own Yorkshire Light Infantry. Formerly No 56363 Cheshire Regiment. Born Huddersfield. Youngest son of Mr and Mrs James A. Clark, 6 School Street, Moldgreen. Before leaving the area for Stockport was employed by Messrs Wheatley, Dyson and Sons. Husband of Violet Clark, 85 Manchester Road, Heaton Norris, Stockport. Killed in action, 13.4.1918, aged 27 years. Has no known grave. Commemorated **PLOEGSTEERT MEMORIAL TO THE MISSING.**

CLARK, REGINALD. Rifleman. No C/7765. 18th Battalion King's Royal Rifle Corps. Born Upthorpe, Gloucestershire. Son of Mrs Clark, 41 Norman Road, Birkby, Huddersfield. Employed by Mr George Mell, Wholesale Market, Huddersfield. Enlisted November 1915. Embarked for France in May, 1916. Reported wounded and missing, 15.9.1916, aged 23 years. Has no known grave. Commemorated on the **THIEPVAL MEMORIAL TO THE MISSING.** ROH:- Fartown and Birkby War Memorial.

CLARK, TOM. Rifleman. No A/3226. 2nd Battalion King's Royal Rifle Corps. Born Halifax. Lived 28 The Rock, Linthwaite. Lived previously at Pickle Top, Slaithwaite, and had worked at the Colne Valley Tweed Mill. Prior to enlistment, was employed as a fettler for Messrs George Mallinson and Sons Limited at Spring Grove Mills, Linthwaite. Was a member of the Hoyle Ing Working Men's Club. Married, with an eight month old child. Enlisted August 1914. Killed in action, 10.1.1915. Has no known grave. Commemorated on the **LE TOURET MEMORIAL TO THE MISSING.** ROH:- Linthwaite War Memorial.

CLARK, WALTER TOM RICHARD. Private. No 82786. 15th Battalion Durham Light Infantry. Formerly No 38834 East Yorkshire Regiment. Born Sidmouth, Devon. Son of Mr and Mrs Clark, Britannia Road, Slaithwaite. Employed as a teaser by Messrs Pogson and Company. Had only been in France for 14 days when he was killed by a shell on 9.9.1918, aged 18 years. Buried **GOUZEAUCOURT NEW BRITISH CEMETERY.** Grave location:- Plot 6, Row C, Grave 16. ROH:- St. James Church, Slaithwaite; Slaithwaite War Memorial.

CLARKE, GEORGE A. Private. No 6115. 1st Battalion Connaught Rangers. Born Grimsby 8.11.1886. Educated at Grimsby Schools. Employed as a house furnisher's shop assistant. Husband of Mary E. Clarke, 167 Yews Hill Road, Lockwood. Enlisted 12.12.1916. Reported missing, 9.7.1917, in Mesopotamia. Has no known grave. Commemorated on the **BASRA MEMORIAL TO THE MISSING, IRAQ.** ROH:- St. Stephen's Church, Rashcliffe; Crosland Moor Wesleyan Church.

CLARKSON, HARRY. Private. No 291575. 12/13th Battalion Northumberland Fusiliers. Son of Frank and Elizabeth Clarkson of Town End, Lepton, Huddersfield. Employed in his father's greengrocery business. Killed in action, 4.10.1917, aged 33 years. Has no known grave. Commemorated on the **TYNE COT MEMORIAL TO THE MISSING.** ROH:- Lepton Parish Church.

CLARKSON. JOSEPH. Rifleman. No C/7629. 13th Battalion King's Royal Rifle Corps. Born Kirkheaton. Son of Ben and Emma Clarkson, 5 Tandem, Kirkheaton. Was employed by Messrs Rhodes and Brierley, Vale Mills, Kirkheaton. Enlisted 15.11.1915. Embarked for France in July, 1916. Killed in action, 15.11.1916, aged 20 years. Has no known grave. Commemorated on the **THIEPVAL MEMORIAL TO THE**

MISSING. ROH:- St. John's Church, Kirkheaton; Lepton Parish Church.

CLAY, ALFRED. Gunner. No 118313. 261st Siege Battery Royal Garrison Artillery. Born Slaithwaite. Son of Mr and Mrs Tom Clay, 64 New North Road, Crimble, Slaithwaite. Employed as head warehouseman by Messrs W. and E. Crowther Limited, Crimble Mills, Slaithwaite. Was a member Slaithwaite Conservative Club. Enlisted September 1916. Embarked for France June, 1917. Killed in action, 27.7.1917, aged 38 years. Buried **HAGLE DUMP CEMETERY**. Grave location:- Plot 3, Row C, Grave 4. ROH:- St. James Church, Slaithwaite; Slaithwaite War Memorial.

CLAY, EDMUND WILKINSON. Lance Corporal. No 19693. 'C' Company, 9th Battalion Duke of Wellington's Regiment. Born Slaithwaite. Son of Susannah and the late W F Clay of Causeway Foot, Slaithwaite. Employed as a spinner at Colne Mill, Slaithwaite. Attended Holthead Sunday School. Wounded in the arm and leg and died of his wounds at No 3 General Hospital, Le Treport, 26.11.1918, aged 22. Buried **MONT HUON MILITARY CEMETERY**. Grave location:- Plot 10, Row B, Grave 10a. ROH:- St. James Church, Slaithwaite; Slaithwaite War Memorial.

CLAY, ELTON. Sergeant Signaller. No 12469. 8th Battalion Duke of Wellington's Regiment. Born Sheepridge, Huddersfield, 4.5.1890. Son of Mr and Mrs G. Clay, 35 Dewhurst Road, Fartown, Huddersfield. Educated at St. Thomas's Church of England School, Huddersfield. Employed as a brass finisher by Messrs J. Hopkinson and Company Limited of Birkby. Was a teacher at Sheepridge Wesleyan Sunday School, where he was also the secretary. Single. Enlisted 27.8.1914. Took part in the landing at Suvla Bay, Gallipoli, in August, 1915, and served throughout the campaign until the withdrawal in December, 1915, when he was transferred to Egypt and then to France. Killed in action, 29.4.1917, aged 26 years. Buried **HERMIES BRITISH CEMETERY**. Grave location:- Row A, Grave 15, ROH:- Christ Church, Woodhouse Hill; Fartown and Birkby War Memorial.

CLAY, HARRY. Private. No 24516. 9th Battalion Duke of Wellington's Regiment. Born Thongsbridge 8.4.1897. Son of Arthur and Mary Hannah Clay, 86 Kirkgate, Huddersfield. Educated at St. John's School, Hillhouse, Huddersfield. Employed as an under-percher by Messrs Middlemost Brothers, of Birkby. Enlisted 17.6.1916. Killed in action near Martinpuich, south west of Bapaume, 26.8.1918, aged 21 years. Buried **ADANAC MILITARY CEMETERY**. Grave location:- Plot 6, Row J, Grave 13. ROH:- Netherthong and Thongsbridge War Memorial.

CLAY, JOHN WILLIAM. Private. No 50739. 10th Battalion Cheshire Regiment. Formerly No 32532 King's Shropshire Light Infantry. Born Cleckheaton. Son of Samuel and Emma Clay of Huddersfield. Husband of Gertrude Clay, 22a, Honoria Street, Fartown. Killed in action, 23.7.1917, aged 37 years. Has no known grave. Commemorated on the **MENIN GATE MEMORIAL TO THE MISSING**.

CLAY, LOUIS. Private. No 4905. 2/5th Battalion Duke of Wellington's Regiment. Born Golcar. Husband of Sarah Clay, 2 Slades, Linthwaite. Employed as a weaver by Messrs Charles Lockwood and Sons. Attended Golcar Baptist Church and was a member of Golcar Liberal Club. Enlisted 4.3.1916. Embarked for France January, 1917. Wounded by shrapnel in both thighs during his first time in the trenches. Died at No 4 Casualty Clearing Station, 23.2.1917, aged 31 years. Buried **VARENNES MILITARY CEMETERY**. Grave location:- Plot 1, Row I, Grave 47. ROH:- Linthwaite War Memorial; St. John's Church, Golcar; Golcar Baptist Church; Huddersfield Drill Hall.

CLAYTON, FRANK. Lance Corporal. No 40455. 16th Battalion Northumberland Fusiliers. Born Victoria Street, Moldgreen, 10.7.1893. Son of Henry and Grace Clayton, 5 Riley Street, Newsome Road, Huddersfield. Employed as a warehouseman in the costume department of Messrs Bairstow, Sons and Company Limited, wholesale clothiers, Fitzwilliam Street, Huddersfield. Attended Milton Church Sunday School and was a member of the Church Brotherhood. Played the violin with the Huddersfield Orchestral Society and played in the orchestra at services held at Ramsden Street Church. Single. Enlisted May 1916. Wounded at Beaumont Hamel, 10.2.1917. Died at No 20 General Hospital, Camiers, 2.3.1917. His mother was with him when he died. Buried **ETAPLES MILIITARY CEMETERY.** Grave location:- Plot 21, Row K, Grave 5A. ROH:- Milton Independent Church.

CLAYTON, FREDERICK. Private. No 13095. 1st Battalion King's Own Yorkshire Light Infantry. Born Aston's Yard, Upperhead Row, Huddersfield, 25.8.1895. Son of the late William and Kate Clayton, 20 Ellis's Buildings, Fitzwilliam Street, Huddersfield. Educated at Huddersfield Parish Church Schools. Employed firstly at Messrs Broadbents, Central Ironworks and then by the London and North Western Railway Company as a goods porter. Single. Enlisted 1.9.1914. Killed in action at Ypres, 8.5.1915, aged 19. Has no known grave. Commemorated on the **MENIN GATE MEMORIAL TO THE MISSING.** ROH:- Huddersfield Parish Church; St. Andrew's Church, Leeds Road, Huddersfield. London and North Western Railway Company Roll. (Brother of Private **NORMAN CLAYTON,** killed in action, 5.7.1916, q.v.).

CLAYTON, KENNETH ANDERSON. Private. No 9464. 1st Battalion East Yorkshire Regiment. Born Deighton, Huddersfield, 17.2.1892. Son of Mr and Mrs A E Clayton, 3 Grizedale Avenue, Birkby. Educated at Heywood School, Lancashire. Formerly articled to an accountant in London. Enlisted in the army in 1911. Had served in India before the war and came over with the Indian contingent at Christmas, 1914. Wounded in the legs, 6.5.1915. Returned to France in February, 1916. Killed in action at Guedecourt, 25.9.1916. Has no known grave. Commemorated on the **THIEPVAL MEMORIAL TO THE MISSING.** ROH:- St. Cuthbert's Church, Birkby; Fartown and Birkby War Memorial.

CLAYTON, NORMAN. Private. 5th Reserve Battalion Sherwood Foresters. Born Huddersfield 10.2.1899. Son of John Herbert and Ann Smith Clayton, 40 Cobcroft Road, Fartown. Educated at Almondbury Grammar School. A keen cricketer. Employed as a clerk. Enlisted 17.3.1917. Gassed 15.8.1918. Died at home, 40 Cobcroft Road, Fartown, from pneumonia and the effects of gas poisoning, 13.4.1919, aged 20 years. Buried **EDGERTON CEMETERY, HUDDERSFIELD.** ROH:- Christ Church, Woodhouse Hill; Fartown and Birkby War Memorial.

CLAYTON, NORMAN. Lance Corporal. No 36. 1/5th Battalion Duke of Wellington's Regiment. Born Huddersfield. Son of William and Kate Clayton, 20 Ellis Buildings, Fitzwilliam Street, Huddersfield. Educated at Spring Grove Council and Huddersfield Parish Church Schools. Employed as a steel driller by Messrs James Hopkinson's engineering works at Birkby, Huddersfield. Husband of Kate Clayton, 13 Kirkmoor Place, off Northgate, Huddersfield. Had served with the local Territorials since 1908. Enlisted August 1914. Embarked for France April, 1915. Killed in action at Thiepval Wood 5.7.1916 age 26 years. Has no known grave. Commemorated on the **THIEPVAL MEMORIAL TO THE MISSING.** ROH:- Huddersfield Parish Church; Huddersfield Drill Hall. (Brother of Private **FREDERICK CLAYTON,** killed in action, 8.5.1915, q.v.).

CLAYTON, THOMAS. Private. No 30851. 90th Company Machine Gun Corps. Formerly No 17936 Duke of Wellington's Regiment. Born Castleford. Son of Thomas and Annie Elizabeth Clayton, 15 Lingards lane, Slaithwaite. Employed as a fettler at Bank Bottom Mills, Marsden, and formerly had worked for many years at the Globe Worsted Spinning Company at Slaithwaite. Attended Crimble Congregational Mission and Sunday School and was associated with the Slaithwaite Sons of Temperance. Had served in the local Territorials for four years before the outbreak of war and had been awarded medals for his proficiency in shooting. Enlisted January, 1916, and embarked for France in June, 1916. Killed in action, 23.4.1917. aged 23 years. Has no known grave. Commemorated on the **ARRAS MEMORIAL TO THE MISSING.** ROH:- St. James Church, Slaithwaite; Slaithwaite War Memorial.

CLEARY, JOHN. Driver. Royal Field Artillery. Born Westport, County Mayo, Ireland. Educated at Huddersfield schools. Husband of Sarah Cleary, 2 Kayes Square, Quay Street, Huddersfield. Employed as a hawker. Enlisted 22.8.1914. Discharged as physically unfit, 21.2.1918. Died of pneumonia at 2 Kayes Square, Quay Street, Huddersfield, on 9.7.1918.

CLEGG, BEN. Company Sergeant Major. No. 12658. 9th Battalion Duke of Wellington's Regiment. Born Emley. Son of Mrs Sam Clegg,

Church Street, Emley. Employed at Emley Moor Collieries. A keen footballer. Enlisted 1.9.1914. Embarked for France July, 1915. Killed in action, 22.3.1918. aged 25 years. Has no known grave. Commemorated on **ARRAS MEMORIAL TO THE MISSING**. ROH:- Emley War Memorial.

CLEGG, FRANK. Private. No 5561. 1/5th Battalion Duke of Wellington's Regiment. Born Milnsbridge. Son of Edwin and Grace Clegg, 1 Folly, Milnsbridge. Employed as a night piecer by Messrs John Lockwood and Sons Limited, Milnsbridge. A member of the Smith Ryding Working Men's Club and was a well known poultry fancier. Enlisted 30.3.1916. Embarked for France August, 1916. Reported missing in the attack on the Schwaben Redoubt, 3.9.1916. aged 19. Has no known grave. Commemorated on the **THIEPVAL MEMORIAL TO THE MISSING**. ROH:- Huddersfield Drill Hall.

CLEGG, HERBERT. Private. No 29388. 9th Battalion Duke of Wellington's Regiment. Born 11 Hillhouse Lane, Huddersfield, 20.4.1892. Son of Mrs Annie Saville (formerly Clegg), 14 Grayson's Yard, Chapel Hill, Huddersfield. Educated at Lockwood Church School. Employed as a woollen piecer at Bridge Street Mills, Lockwood. Single. At the time of enlistment was living at 10a Stoney Battery, Crosland Moor. Enlisted 5.9.1916. Killed in action, 26.5.1918, aged 26. Buried **AUCHONVILLERS MILITARY CEMETERY**. Grave location:- Plot 2, Row M, Grave 33.

CLEGG, THOMAS H. Lance Corporal. No 267788. 2nd Battalion West Yorkshire Regiment. Formerly No 2032 1/5th Battalion Duke of Wellington's Regiment. Born Huddersfield. Lived 197 Casson's Buildings, Milnsbridge. Employed by Messrs L. Halstead and Company Limited as a printer. Reported missing, presumed killed, 26.3.1918. Has no known grave. Commemorated on the **POZIERES MEMORIAL TO THE MISSING**.

CLIFFE, ALLAN. Private. No 11983. 8th Battalion Duke of Wellington's Regiment. Born Upper Edge, Elland. Son of Mr and Mrs Alfred Cliffe, 17 Union Street, Lindley. Educated at Oakes Council School. Employed as an apprentice fitter at Messrs James Hopkinson and Company Limited of Birkby. Attended Lindley Wesleyan Church. Single. Enlisted August 1914. Took part in the Suvla Bay landing at Gallipoli and subsequent fighting during which he was wounded and suffered frostbite. Killed by shellfire, 28.9.1916. aged 21 years. Has no known grave. Commemorated on the **THIEPVAL MEMORIAL TO THE MISSING**. ROH:- St. Stephen's Church, Lindley.

CLIFFE, EDGAR. Private. No M2/129874. 610 Motor Transport Coy, Army Service Corps. Born Longwood. Son of Mr and Mrs Alfred J. Cliffe, 122 Longwood Road, Huddersfield. A member of the choir at Paddock Wesleyan Church. Employed as a joiner by Messrs Hollingworths of Moldgreen. Prior to his enlistment in October, 1915, was engaged in the erection of the Royds Hall Military Hospital. Died very suddenly at Bath of a haemorrhage, 24.1.1916. aged 24. Buried **SALENDINE NOOK BAPTIST CHAPEL YARD**. Grave location:- in South-East part (298E). ROH:- Shared Church, Paddock.

CLIFFE, GEORGE EDWARD. Private. No 3330. 1/5th Battalion Duke of Wellington's Regiment. Born 45 Manchester Road, Huddersfield. Son of Whitehead and Bessie Cliffe, 45 Manchester Road, Huddersfield. Educated at St. Paul's Church of England School. Employed as an apprentice with Messrs J. Preston and Sons, painters and decorators, of Albion Street, Huddersfield. Single. Enlisted 10.11.1914. Embarked for France April, 1915. Was accidentally hurt by a pickaxe while in the rear of the trenches and was invalided home. Returned to France three weeks before he was killed in action near Ypres, 11.11.1915. aged 18 years. Buried **TALANA FARM CEMETERY**. Grave location:- Plot 4, Row D, Grave 1. ROH:- Huddersfield Drill Hall.

CLIFFE, HAROLD. Private. No 29473. 1/4th Battalion East Yorkshire Regiment. Born Longwood, Huddersfield, 21.9.1897. Son of Major and Elizabeth Cliffe, 11 Church Street, Longwood. Educated at Longwood and Crow Lane Board School, Milnsbridge. Attended Paddock United Methodist Church. Employed by his father at Bridgecroft Mills, Milnsbridge, as a woollen machine dealer. Engaged to Annie. Enlisted 18.2.1915. Taken prisoner by the Germans, 27.5.1915. Died of dysentery and starvation as a Prisoner of War on 18.10.1918.

aged 21 years. Buried **GLAGEON COMMUNAL CEMETERY EXTENSION.** Grave location:- Plot 2, Row A, Grave 10. ROH:- St. Mark's Parish Church, Longwood; Shared Church, Paddock; Crow Lane Board School, Milnsbridge.

CLIFFE, JAMES WILLIE. Private. No 24970. 2nd Battalion Duke of Wellington's Regiment. Born Crossley Hall, near Bradford, 20.3.1897. Son of Mr and Mrs Willie Cliffe, 7 Industrial Terrace, Dalton, Huddersfield. Educated at Moldgreen Board School. Was employed as a printer's apprentice by Preston Brothers, Fox Street, Huddersfield. Enlisted October 1914. Wounded four times on the Somme. Killed in action, 24.10.1918. aged 21 years. Buried **VERCHAIN BRITISH CEMETERY.** Grave location:- Row C, Grave 12, ROH:- St. John's Church, Kirkheaton; Almondbury War Memorial.

CLIFFORD, ARTHUR. Private. No 32526. 18th Battalion Manchester Regiment. Born Back Beech Terrace, Bradford Road, Huddersfield, 12.3.1893. Son of Fred and Rose Hannah Clifford, 198 Bradford Road, Huddersfield. Educated at Hillhouse Council School, Huddersfield. Attended Hillhouse Congregational Sunday School. Employed as a tailor's cutter by Messrs A. and G. Firth, of Huddersfield and, for some eighteen months before his enlistment, by Messrs Coe, Wilks and Company, of Cheetham, Manchester. Single. Enlisted February 1916. Reported wounded and missing at Guillemont on the Somme, 30.7.1916, aged 23. Buried **DELVILLE WOOD CEMETERY.** Grave location:- Plot 5, Row L, Grave 9. ROH:- Fartown and Birkby War Memorial. (Brother of Private **REGINALD CLIFFORD,** killed in action, 10.4.1918, q.v.).

CLIFFORD, REGINALD. Lance Corporal. No 34168 9th Battalion Loyal North Lancashire Regiment. Formerly No 26366 Manchester Regiment. Born Back Beech Terrace, Bradford Road, Huddersfield. Son of Fred and Rose Hannah Clifford, 198 Bradford Road, Huddersfield. Educated at Hillhouse Council School and the Municipal Secondary College, Huddersfield. Employed as a woollen warehouse clerk by Messrs J. Wilkinson and Son, St. George's Square, Huddersfield. Married. Enlisted July 1915. Missing, presumed killed, 10.4.1918. Has no known grave. Commemorated on the **PLOEGSTEERT MEMORIAL TO THE MISSING.** ROH:- Fartown and Birkby War Memorial. (Brother of Private **ARTHUR CLIFFORD,** killed in action, 30.7.1916 q.v.).

CLOUGH, ARTHUR HODGSON. Corporal. Duke of Wellington's Regiment. Lived Brierley's Buildings, Commercial Street, Huddersfield. Died 14.2.1919. aged 36 years. Buried **EDGERTON CEMETERY, HUDDERSFIELD.**

CLOUGH, ERNEST. Private. No 241509. 2/5th Battalion Duke of Wellington's Regiment. Born Hall Bottom Farm, Clifton, Brighouse, 21.4.1885. Son of Mr and Mrs William Clough, 3 Thorncliffe Street, Lindley. Educated at schools in Brighouse and Baliffe Bridge. Employed as a painter and decorator. Was a member of the Young Men's Class at Lindley Zion Sunday School. Married. Enlisted 2.3.1917. Wounded in the abdomen, 1.12.1917 and died of wounds at No 49 Casualty Clearing Station, 2.12.1917. aged 32. Buried **ACHIET-LE-GRAND COMMUNAL CEMETERY EXTENSION.** Grave Location:- Plot 1, Row Q, Grave 31. ROH:- St. James's Presbyterian Church; Lindley Zion Methodist Church; St. Stephen's Church, Lindley; Huddersfield Drill Hall.

CLOUGH, FRED. Private. No 7/1913. 1/7th Battalion Duke of Wellington's Regiment. Born Lindley September 1890. Son of Mr and Mrs Harry Clough, 3 East Street, Lindley. Educated Lindley National Schools. Employed as a wire drawer by Messrs Joseph Sykes, Acre Mills, Lindley. Single. Enlisted September 1914. Killed in action near Ypres, 12.7.1915. Buried **COLNE VALLEY CEMETERY.** Grave location:- Row D, Grave 13. ROH:- Lindley Zion Methodist Church; St. Stephen's Church, Lindley; Huddersfield Drill Hall; War Memorial outside St. Philip's Church, Birchencliffe.

COCK, FRANK LOCKWOOD. Air Mechanic 2nd Class. No 24218. 102nd Squadron Royal Air Force. Born Linthwaite. Son of of Joe Edwin and Elizabeth Alice Cock, of West View, Linthwaite. Lived with his sister, Mrs B Tomlinson of North Grove, Linthwaite. Attended Linthwaite Wesleyan Church and Reading Room. Was a member of Linthwaite Cricket Club and the All Blacks football club. Employed by Messrs George Cock Limited, dyers, of Linthwaite.

Died of pneumonia at the 1st Australian General Hospital, Rouen, 12.11.1918, aged 20 years. Buried **St. SEVER CEMETERY EXTENSION, ROUEN.** Grave location:- Block S, Plot 2, Row LL, Grave 24. ROH:- Linthwaite War Memorial.

COCK, JOSHUA HAROLD BLACKBURN. Private. No 28915. 13th Battalion Northumberland Fusiliers. Born Golcar. Son of the late Joe and Elizabeth Mary Cock, of Bank Top, Golcar. Brother of Mrs Ed Sykes, 131 Radcliffe Road, Golcar. Employed as a stonemason on his own account. Enlisted 28.8.1916. Reported missing, presumed killed, 16.6.1917, aged 35 years. Has no known grave. Commemorated on the **ARRAS MEMORIAL TO THE MISSING.** ROH:- St. John's Church, Golcar.

COCKER, CHARLES HENRY. Rifleman. No A/200533. 11th Battalion King's Royal Rifle Corps. Formerly No 5587 3rd Battalion London Regiment. Born Almondbury 29.4.1895. Son of Mr and Mrs H Cocker, 121 Armitage Road, Milnsbridge. Educated at Almondbury Council School. Employed as a postman at Huddersfield G.P.O. and was a member of the Messengers Band. Enlisted 16.3.1915. Killed in action, 20.9.1917. aged 23. Has no known grave. Commemorated on the **TYNE COT MEMORIAL TO THE MISSING.** ROH:- Huddersfield GPO; Almondbury War Memorial.

COCKER, FRIEND. Driver. No L/25671. 'B' Battery, 168th (Huddersfield) Brigade Royal Field Artillery. Born 57 Kings Mill Lane, Huddersfield. Son of Mr and Mrs E. Cocker, 53 Armitage Street, Primrose Hill, Huddersfield. Employed as a woollen twister-in by Messrs John Kaye and Son, Kings Mill. Single. Enlisted 13.5.1915. Killed in action at La Vallee Mulatre, 23.10.1918. aged 23. Buried **LA VALLEE MULATRE COMMUNAL CEMETERY EXTENSION.** Grave location:- Row A, Grave 13. ROH:- St. Paul's Church, Southgate, Huddersfield; Almondbury War Memorial.

COCKERILL, HARRY. Private. No 40505. 9th Battalion King's Own Yorkshire Light Infantry. Killed in action, 4.10.1917. Has no known grave. Commemorated **TYNE COT MEMORIAL TO THE MISSING.** ROH:- St. Thomas's Church, Bradley.

COCKHILL, ARTHUR. Private. No 32332. 'A' Company 2/4th Battalion Duke of Wellington's Regiment. Born Netherton. Son of Harry and Frances Cockhill, of Bank End, Netherton. Attended Netherton Wesleyan Sunday School. Employed by Messrs James Hopkinson and Company Limited, of Birkby. Enlisted August, 1917, and embarked for France in December, 1917. Killed in action, 9.4.1918. aged 19 years. Buried **BIENVILLERS MILITARY CEMETERY.** Grave location:- Plot 9, Row B, Grave 3. ROH:- South Crosland and Netherton War Memorial.

COCKHILL, PERCY. Guardsman. No 30045. 3rd Battalion Grenadier Guards. Born Shepley. Son of Willie and Mary E. Cockhill of Shepley; husband of Florence E. Cockhill of Abbey Road, Shepley. Employed by Messrs Moxon of Kirkburton. Was secretary and an active worker at the Shepley Cricket Club. Died of pneumonia whilst on active service in Germany, 18.2.1919. aged 32 years. Buried **COLOGNE SOUTHERN CEMETERY.** Grave location:- Plot 2, Row E, Grave 15. ROH:- Shepley War Memorial.

COCKING, ALBERT HENRY. Private. No DM2/155488. 976th Motor Transport Company Army Service Corps. Born Saddleworth. Lived 26 Royds Terrace, Marsden. Son of Walter and Alice Ann Cocking. Married. Employed as a cloth finisher at Bank Bottom Mills, Marsden. Died of pneumonia in Persia, 30.9.1918. aged 29. Buried **TEHRAN WAR CEMETERY, IRAN.** Grave location:- Plot 5, Row D, Grave 14. ROH:- Marsden War Memorial; commemorated on memorial in Marsden Churchyard.

COCKING, WILLIE. Private. No 35724. 9th Battalion King's Own Yorkshire Light Infantry. Formerly No 3/22808 Duke of Wellington's Regiment. Born 52 Dale Street, Huddersfield, 26.3.1892. Son of Mr and Mrs Cocking, 52 Dale Street, Huddersfield. Educated at Spring Grove Council School. Employed as a bottle washer by Messrs J. Bray and Company Limited, ale and porter bottlers, Rook Street, Huddersfield. Attended St. Joseph's Church, Huddersfield. Single. Enlisted 1.7.1916. Embarked for France, 5.11.1916. Killed in action at the Battle of Arras, 9.4.1917. aged 24 years. Buried **COJEUL BRITISH CEMETERY.** Grave location:- Row D, Grave 15.

COCKROFT, ALBERT. Private. No 52993. 15th Battalion Durham Light Infantry. Formerly No 32804 Northumberland Fusiliers. Born Sowerby Bridge. Son of Sam and Maria Cockroft, 1260 Pleasant View, Linthwaite. Employed as a weaver by Messrs Thomas, Bates and Son, Platt Mill, Slaithwaite. Enlisted July 1916. Underwent training at Newcastle-on-Tyne and South Shields with the Northumberland Fusiliers but on arrival in France was transferred to the Durham Light Infantry. He came home on sick leave in 1917, after having been in hospital with trench feet, but returned to the front line at Whitsuntide, 1917. Killed in action, 18.4.1918. aged 20 years. Has no known grave. Commemorated on the **TYNE COT MEMORIAL TO THE MISSING.** ROH:- Linthwaite War Memorial; St. James Church, Slaithwaite.

CODD, WILLIAM. Private. No 203067. 1/5th Battalion West Yorkshire Regiment. Formerly No 3/22808 Duke of Wellington's Regiment. Born Wakefield 4.7.1884. Son of Mr and Mrs George Codd, 2 Well Street, Longroyd Bridge. Educated at St. Thomas's school, Longroyd Bridge. Employed as a mason by Mr Baldwin, of Paddock. Married, with two children. Killed in action, 10.7.1917, aged 34. Buried **LAVENTIE MILITARY CEMETERY.** Grave location:- Plot 1, Row B, Grave 5. ROH:- St. Thomas's Church, Longroyd Bridge.

COE, HARRY. Private. No 30652. 8th Battalion North Staffordshire Regiment. Born Crosland Moor, Huddersfield. Son of Henry and Annie Elizabeth Coe, of Heymoor House, Abbey Road, Shepley. Employed by Messrs Firth Brothers, New Mills, Shepley. Died of wounds in Whitechapel Hospital, London, 15.4.1918, aged 21 years. Buried **EMMANUEL CHURCHYARD, SHELLEY.** Grave location:- 350. ROH:- Shepley War Memorial.

COFFEY, RICHARD. Private. No 4746. 23rd Battalion Royal Fusiliers. Born Dublin. Had lived in Linthwaite for 14 years. Lodged with Mrs Walker of Linthwaite Hall. Engaged to Miss Mitchel, of The Star Hotel, Slaithwaite. Employed in the tailoring department of the Slaithwaite Cooperative Society. Enlisted February 1916. Wounded in September, 1916, and was treated at the Corps Operating Station, France. A sister at the hospital wrote the following letter to his fiancé, *'I am so sorry to have to tell you that Private Coffey of the Royal Fusiliers has been wounded and is at present in this hospital. He is very seriously wounded and had to have an operation. Everything that is possible is being done for him and he is not suffering much pain. He is seriously ill and it is difficult to say much about his condition but we must hope for the best. I will write to you again as soon as I can and let you know how he is getting on.'* Miss Mitchell received word from the Infantry Records Office at Hounslow that he had died of his wounds on 13.9.1916, age 28 years. Buried **COUIN BRITISH CEMETERY.** Grave location:- Plot 3, Row A, Grave 8. ROH:- Linthwaite War Memorial; St. James Church, Slaithwaite.

COKER, JOSIAH. Private. No 21/804. 10th Battalion West Yorkshire Regiment. Born Boston, Lincolnshire. Son of Mr and Mrs A. Coker, Upperthong, Holmfirth. Educated Holmfirth Wesleyan Day School. Employed by Messrs H. and S. Butterworth, Lower Mills, Holmfirth. Was successful in enlisting, on his seventh attempt, in 1915. Killed in action, 20.9.1918. Buried **VILLERS HILL BRITISH CEMETERY.** Grave location:- Plot 7, Row C, Grave 7. ROH:- Upperthong War Memorial.

COLBRIDGE, GEORGE WILLIAM JACKSON. Corporal. No 23180. 8th Battalion The Yorkshire Regiment. Born Birstall, Leeds. Son of John and Elizabeth Colbridge, 6 Midland Street, Huddersfield. Employed as labourer by the London and North Western Railway Company at the Hillhouse engine shed. Attended Christ Church, Woodhouse Hill and the Salvation Army at Lockwood. Killed in action, 10.10.1917, aged 21 years. Buried **YPRES RESERVOIR CEMETERY.** Grave location:- Plot 1, Row H, Grave 27. ROH:- Christ Church, Woodhouse Hill; St. Andrew's Church, Leeds Road, Huddersfield; Fartown and Birkby War Memorial; London and North Western Railway Roll

COLDWELL, ARTHUR. Private. No 29/701. 20th (Tyneside Scottish) Battalion Northumberland Fusiliers. Born Meltham. Son of Mrs Coldwell, Mill Moor Meltham. Employed by the Meltham Urban District Council. Killed in action, 9.11.1917. Buried **WANCOURT BRITISH CEMETERY.** Grave location:- Plot 1,

Row E, Grave 7. ROH:- St. Bartholomew's Church, Meltham.

COLDWELL, HUBERT. Corporal. No 203618. 2/5th Battalion Duke of Wellington's Regiment. Son of Mr and Mrs A. B. Coldwell, Hill, Holmfirth. Attended Wooldale Free Church Sunday School. Played the flute with the Underbank Philharmonic Band. Mobilised with the Holmfirth Territorials on 4.8.1914 and embarked for France, 14.4.1915. He came home as a time expired soldier in 1916 and vowed he would never take off khaki until the war was over. He re-enlisted and embarked for France again on 3.5.1917. Was wounded in six places and spent some time in hospital in Boulogne. When fully recovered he was sent back to the trenches and was reported missing on 21.3.1918. However he wrote home stating that he had been captured on 28.3.1918 and was wounded in the left shoulder. Letters were regularly received from him until September when, in his last letter, he wrote that all the time he had been a prisoner he had never received either a letter or parcel from home. Died 7.10.1918, aged 26 years. Buried **MONS COMMUNAL CEMETERY.** Grave location:- Plot 8, Row B, Grave 3. ROH:- Holmfirth War Memorial; Huddersfield Drill Hall; commemorated on his parents' headstone in St. George's Churchyard, Brockholes.

COLDWELL, LEWIS. Private. No 20191. 2nd Battalion Duke of Wellington's Regiment. Born Holmfirth. Lived Underbank, Holmfirth. Employed by Messrs Wallaces and then became manager of the Cooperative Stores at Thurstonland. Enlisted, 12.4.16, and trained in Staffordshire. Embarked for France August, 1916. Died of wounds at 5.45pm, 9.11.1916, at No 5 General Hospital, Rouen, aged 25 years. His father was with him when he died. Buried **St. SEVER CEMETERY EXTENSION, ROUEN.** Grave location:- Block O, Plot 1, Row J, Grave 6. ROH:- Underbank War Memorial.

COLDWELL, SETH. Private. No 241435. 1/5th Battalion Duke of Wellington's Regiment. Born Holmfirth. Lived with his grandfather Mr James Brooke at Towngate, Wooldale. Educated at Wooldale Board School. Attended Wooldale Wesleyan Sunday School. Employed by Crowther Brothers, woollen manufacturers, of Stanley Mills, Milnsbridge. Enlisted 16.2.1916. Reported missing, 3.9.1916, presumed killed on that date, aged 21 years. Buried **MILL ROAD CEMETERY.** Grave location:- Plot 1, Row H, Grave 8. ROH:- Wooldale War Memorial; Huddersfield Drill Hall.

COLDWELL, WILLIAM BERTRAM. Private. No 53387. 'A' Company, 15th/17th Battalion West Yorkshire Regiment. Born Holmfirth. Son of Joe William and Sarah Margaret Coldwell, of Quarry Mount, Holmfirth. Educated Holmfirth Secondary School. Enlisted May 1917. Killed in action, 28.6.1918, aged 19 years. Buried **CINQ RUES BRITISH CEMETERY.** Grave location:- Row H, Grave 11. ROH:- Holmfirth War Memorial; Holmfirth Secondary School.

COLE, HARRY. Private. No 241340. 1/5th Battalion Duke of Wellington's Regiment. Lived Kirkheaton. Killed in action, 3.9.1916. Buried **MILL ROAD CEMETERY.** Grave location:- Plot 1, Row D, Grave 18. ROH:- Huddersfield Drill Hall.

COLEMAN, THOMAS. Private. No 18595. 2nd Battalion Duke of Wellington's Regiment. Born Huddersfield. Son of James Coleman, 37 Denton Lane, Huddersfield. Reported missing, presumed killed, 3.5.1917, aged 21 years. Has no known grave. Commemorated on the **ARRAS MEMORIAL TO THE MISSING.**

COLLIER, GEORGE. Private. No 2705. 1/7th Battalion Duke of Wellington's Regiment. Born 13 Mitchell Street, Nursery Lane, Ovenden, Halifax. Educated at a school in Ovenden. Employed as a wire temperer at Messrs Joseph Sykes Brothers Limited, Acre Mills, Lindley. Husband of Agnes Collier, 43 Baker Street, Oakes, Huddersfield. Enlisted October 1914. Killed in action on the Somme, 3.7.1916, aged 29 years. Has no known grave. Commemorated on the **THIEPVAL MEMORIAL TO THE MISSING.** ROH:-. St. Stephen's Church, Lindley; Huddersfield Drill Hall.

COLLIER, LEONARD. Rifleman. No R/19767. 16th Battalion King's Royal Rifle Corps. Born Milnsbridge. Son of Mrs Mary Maria Collier, 1 Bamford's Yard, Milnsbridge. Attended Milnsbridge Church and Sunday School. Employed by Messrs Ben Hall and Sons, of Milnsbridge, as a weaver. Was a member of Milnsbridge Socialist Club. Enlisted 1.3.1916.

Embarked for France in July, 1916. Was wounded on 5.11.1916 but remained in France and returned to the trenches on Christmas Day. Killed in action, 27.1.1917, aged 22 years. Has no known grave. Commemorated on the **THIEPVAL MEMORIAL TO THE MISSING.** ROH:- Milnsbridge War Memorial.

COLLINGS, JAMES. Corporal. No 15189. 10th Battalion Duke of Wellington's Regiment. Born Horsforth, Leeds. Son of Henry and Mary Collings, Town Street, Horsforth, Leeds. Educated at Horsforth Schools. Employed as a labourer by Messrs J. Kenworthy and Sons, railway wagon builders, of Lockwood. Husband of Mary Collings, 3 Lee and Burley's Yard, Lowerhead Row, Huddersfield. Enlisted 12.6.1915. Reported missing, presumed killed, at the Battle of Passchendaele, 20.9.1917. Has no known grave. Commemorated on the **TYNE COT MEMORIAL TO THE MISSING.**

COLLINS, FRANK. Private. No S/25158. 2nd Battalion Seaforth Highlanders. Formerly TR/1/15109 Territorial Reserve Battalion. Born Huddersfield 1.6.1899. Youngest son of the late Mr and Mrs Tom Collins of St. Andrew's Road, Huddersfield. Brother of Edwin Collins, 56 West Street, Lindley. Educated at Spring Grove Council School. Employed as an audit clerk by Messrs Armitage and Norton, Chartered Accountants, Huddersfield. At the time of enlistment, was living at 9 Spring Grove Street, Huddersfield. Enlisted 4.10.1917. Was first attached to the 41st T.R.Battalion Argyll and Sutherland Highlanders in training at Cambusbarron, Scotland. He was subsequently transferred to the 2nd Battalion Seaforth Highlanders and embarked for France on 12.5.1918. Was seriously wounded at La Bassee, 23.5.1918. Admitted to No 6 Casualty Clearing Station, where he died of his wounds on 5.6.1918. Buried **PERNES BRITISH CEMETERY.** Grave location:- Plot 2, Row F, Grave 20. ROH:- New North Road Baptist Church.

COLLINS, FRANK. Private. No 301953. 5/6th Battalion The Royal Scots (Lothian Regiment). Born Brighouse. Lived 49 Handel Street, Golcar. Employed by Messrs Pearson Brothers, Victoria Mills, Golcar. Died of wounds, 19.8.1918, aged 20 years. Buried **VILLERS-BRETONNEUX MILITARY CEMETERY.**

Grave location:- Plot 8, Row BB, Grave 2. ROH:- St. John's Church, Golcar.

COLLINS, J. Private. No 1797. 5th Battalion Duke of Wellington's Regiment. Died at home, 19.5.1915. Buried **ALMONDBURY CEMETERY.** Grave location:- 3, 'U', 30.

COLLINSON, GEORGE HENRY. Private. No 12171. 10th Battalion Duke of Wellington's Regiment. Born Huddersfield. Lived 16 Corporation Tenements, Kirkgate, Huddersfield. Employed in the Borough Engineer's Department of Huddersfield Corporation. Enlisted at the outbreak of war. Wounded, 1.9.16, and died of his wounds at No 8 Casualty Clearing Station, 6.9.1916. Buried **BAILLEUL COMMUNAL CEMETERY EXTENSION.** Grave location:- Plot 2, Row F, Grave 205. ROH:- Huddersfield Corporation Roll.

COMERSKEY, JOHN. Private. No 22219. 7th Battalion King's Own Yorkshire Light Infantry. Born Emley. Married, with two children. Employed as a miner at Emley Moor Collieries. Enlisted in 1915. Was wounded in the Somme offensive. Reported missing, presumed killed, at Passchendaele, 16.8.1917, aged 32 years. Has no known grave. Commemorated on the **TYNE COT MEMORIAL TO THE MISSING.** ROH:- Emley War Memorial.

COMYN, ALEXANDER. Private. No 25247. 266th Protection Company, Royal Defence Corps. Died at home 7.3.1919. Buried **EDGERTON CEMETERY, HUDDERSFIELD.** Grave location:- 66, 121G.

CONNELL, CHARLES JOSEPH. Private. No 11883. 1/6th Battalion Duke of Wellington's Regiment. Born West Ham, Middlesex. Lived 74 Bradford Road, Huddersfield. Killed in action, 13.4.1918. Has no known grave. Commemorated **TYNE COT MEMORIAL TO THE MISSING.** ROH:- St. Andrew's Church, Leeds Road, Huddersfield.

CONRY, WILLIAM. No 64785. 69th Protection Company, Royal Defence Corps. Husband of Agnes Conry, 43a Back Northgate, Huddersfield. Enlisted in the Duke of Wellington's Regiment at the outbreak of war. Wounded three times. Died from pneumonia in Colchester Hospital, 24.11.1918, aged 41 years. Buried **EDGERTON CEMETERY, HUDDERSFIELD.** Grave location:- 23, 26.

COOK, FRANK EADEN, MC. Lieutenant. 1/10th Battalion Manchester Regiment. Formerly Private 20th Battalion Royal Fusiliers. Born Huddersfield 22.5.1890. Son of Fred Lilley and Eleanor Beatrice Cook, 'Middle House,' High Flatts, Denby Dale. Educated New College, Harrogate. Employed as a wool merchant with Messrs Cook, Sons and Company Limited, of Huddersfield and Dewsbury. Married January, 1918, Nora, the younger daughter of Mr J. H. Richardson of Richmond Avenue, Fartown. Enlisted, 1.9.1914, as a Private in the Public Schools Battalion (20th) Royal Fusiliers. Promoted to Lance Corporal in October, 1914, and Corporal in October, 1915. Promoted Sergeant July, 1916. Obtained his commission in November, 1916, in the 1/10th Battalion Manchester Regiment. Made full Lieutenant April, 1918. Wounded at La Bassee, 11.3.1916, and on the Somme, 16.8.1917. He suffered a bullet wound through the calf of the left leg and was treated in hospital in Manchester. Was awarded the Military Cross, in connection with the capture of a village on 30.8.1918. The citation reads, *'This officer, minding that the platoon on his left was held up, after reconnoitring the hostile position, successfully pushed on with his platoon, with great gallantry and skill drove the enemy from his position, thus enabling the platoon on his left to gain its objective. Twice he led his platoon forward at critical moments. This iniative and determination greatly assisted towards the success of the operation'.* (London Gazette 11th January 1919). The medal was bestowed on him on 7.10.1918, in France, and after his death forwarded home to his widow. Killed in action, 20.10.1918, aged 28 years. Buried **BELLE VUE BRITISH CEMETERY, BRIASTRE.** Grave location:- Plot A, Grave 13. ROH:- New North Road Baptist Church. (Brother of Private **JOHN (JACK) EADON COOK,** reported missing, presumed killed, 20.7.1916, q.v.).

COOK, JOHN (JACK) EADON. Private. No 4671. 20th Battalion Royal Fusiliers. Born Lindley, Huddersfield, 22.9.1891. Son of Fred Lilley and Eleanor Beatrice Cook, 'Middle House', High Flatts, Denby Dale. Educated at New College, Harrogate. Employed as assistant designer with Mr F H McGrath of Birdsedge Mills. Was a member of the Thornhill Amateur Football Club. Single. Enlisted 1.9.1914. Embarked for France November, 1915. On the morning of 20.7.1916 took part in the capture of High Wood and was noticed by his Officer to be wounded and on his way to the field dressing station. He was also seen by a fellow Private further down the line but was never seen again. Killed in action, 20.7.1916, aged 24. Has no known grave. Commemorated on the **THIEPVAL MEMORIAL TO THE MISSING.** ROH:- New North Road Baptist Church. (Brother of Lieutenant **FRANK EADEN COOK,** killed in action, 20.10.1918, q.v.).

COOK, LAWRENCE. Private. Driver. Army Service Corps. Born Dalton 2.5.1891. Son of Stephen Edward and Mary Hannah Cook, 77 Woodhead Road, Lockwood. Husband of Florence Cook, 74 West End, Newsome. Educated at Lockwood Church of England School. Employed as a motor driver. Enlisted 11.12.1915. Died of malaria at 74 West End, Newsome 6.4.1920. ROH:- St. John's Church, Newsome; Emmanuel Church, Lockwood.

COOKE, FREDERICK CHARLES. Sergeant. No L/25421. 'C' Battery. 161st Brigade Royal Field Artillery. Born 1880 but place of birth not known. Raised in the Doctor Barnado's Home, Stepney, East London. Employed as a boot and shoemaker before coming to Huddersfield to join the police, aged 24 years. He was accepted on 15.1.1912 and sworn in as a constable on 4.3.1912. Husband of Eliza Cooke, 84 Lightcliffe Road, Crosland Moor, Huddersfield. Enlisted March 1915. Wounded, 19.10.1917, and died of his wounds at a dressing station a few hours later. Buried **MINTY FARM CEMETERY, St. JAN. BELGIUM.** Grave location:- Plot 1, Row D, Grave 12. ROH:- St. Barnabas Church, Crosland Moor; Huddersfield Corporation Roll; Huddersfield Police Headquarters.

COOKE, HARRY. Private. No 13244. 1st Battalion King's Own Yorkshire Light Infantry. Born Birchencliffe, Huddersfield. Lived Bradford Road North. Killed in action, 24.4.1915. Has no known grave. Commemorated on the **MENIN GATE MEMORIAL TO THE MISSING.** ROH:- Fartown and Birkby War Memorial.

COOP, ALFRED. Private. No 50847. 10th Battalion Cheshire Regiment. Born Carlton Terrace, Bradford Road, Huddersfield, 29.10.1893. Son of Alfred and Louisa Coop, 33 Moorbottom Road, Huddersfield. Husband of Kathleen Amelia Coop, 99 Laund Road, Salendine Nook, Huddersfield. Was employed in the butchering department of the Marsh Cooperative Stores and later went as manager to the Salendine Nook branch. Enlisted 22.2.1917. Killed in action at Messines, 10.6.1917, aged 23. Has no known grave. Commemorated on the **MENIN GATE MEMORIAL TO THE MISSING.**

COOPER, ARTHUR VERNON. Lance Corporal. No CMT/2436. 74th Anti-Aircraft Section Army Service Corps (Motor Transport). Born 47 Whitestone Road, Fartown, 17.3.1894. Son of Frederick Ogden and Theresa Cooper, Prospect House, Outcote Bank, Huddersfield. Educated at Fartown Board School. Employed as a motor driver, and fitter for Messrs Thomas A. Nicol and Sons Limited, dyers, Providence Works, of Huddersfield. Single. Signed on 3.3.1914 at Recruiting Office, Fitzwilliam Street West and Northgate, Huddersfield. Received mobilisation papers, 5.8.1914. Left Huddersfield for Seaforth Camp, Liverpool, 5.8.1914. Left Huddersfield for Salonika on 19.7.1918. Sailed from Avonmouth Docks, Bristol. Died of dysentery at Lahone, Salonika, 28.10.1918, aged 24 years. Buried **MIKRA BRITISH CEMETERY, SALONIKA.** Grave location:- No 1798.

COOPER, LEONARD. Private. No 9939. 1st Battalion King's Own Yorkshire Light Infantry. Born Chesterfield. Son of Mrs Doughty, 8 Bradley Street, Huddersfield. Enlisted when he was 15 years and 8 months old. He was in China at the outbreak of the war. and came over to England in November, 1914. Killed in action at Hill 60, 25.4.1915, aged 22 years. Has no known grave. Commemorated on the **MENIN GATE MEMORIAL TO THE MISSING.** ROH:- St. Paul's Church, Southgate, Huddersfield; St. Thomas's Church, Bradley.

COOPER, STANLEY. Private. No 62295. 2nd Battalion West Yorkshire Regiment. Born May Street, Crosland Moor. Son of Albert E. and Lucy Ellen Cooper, 76 College Street, Crosland Moor, Huddersfield. Educated at Crosland Moor Church of England School. Attended St. Barnabas Church and Sunday School. Employed as a joinery apprentice for his father at Crosland Moor and then for Messrs Cooper and Rushworth of Greenhead Row, Huddersfield. Single. Enlisted 20.8.1917. Killed in action, 6.6.1918, aged 18 years Has no known grave. Commemorated on the **SOISSONS MEMORIAL TO THE MISSING.** ROH:- St. Barnabas Church, Crosland Moor.

COOPER, THOMAS. Private. No 12999. 9th Battalion Duke of Wellington's Regiment. Born Luddendenfoot, Halifax. Had lived in Marsden since 1911. Native of Littleborough. Lodged with Mrs Parkin at 3 Warehouse Hill, Marsden. Employed as a weaver by Mr J E Crowther, Bank Bottom Mills. Prior to enlistment, was employed on the London and North Western Railway at Marsden. Killed in action, 11.9.1915, aged 28 years. Has no known grave. Commemorated on the **MENIN GATE MEMORIAL TO THE MISSING.** ROH:- Marsden War Memorial.

COOPER, WILLIE, OBE VD. Lieutenant-Colonel. 5th Battalion Duke of Wellington's Regiment. Son of James Cooper of Huddersfield. Husband of the late Amy Louisa Cooper, 107 Spring Bank Road, Huddersfield. Died at home, 18.12.1920, aged 58 years. Buried **EDGERTON CEMETERY, HUDDERSFIELD.** Grave location:- 53, 'C', 7.

COPLEY, ALLAN. 2nd Lieutenant. 19th Battalion Manchester Regiment. Formerly Private. Honourable Artillery Company. Born 22.4.1893. Son of Joseph and Hannah Copley, 9 Station Lane, Berry Brow. Educated at Berry Brow Council School and the evening continuation classes in connection with Huddersfield Technical College. As a boy he sang in the choir at Armitage Bridge Church. After leaving school assisted his father in his business as a hairdresser in Berry's Yard, off New Street, Huddersfield. Then for two years was a member of the staff of the Western Australian Insurance Company Limited, of Queen Victoria Street, London, learning the business of underwriter in the shipping losses department. Enlisted November, 1915, in the Honourable Artillery Company. Gazetted as 2nd Lieutenant in January, 1917, in the 19th Battalion Manchester Regiment. Embarked for France, 13.2.1917.

Killed in action near Arras, 2.4.1917, aged 23 years. Buried **HENIN CRUCIFIX CEMETERY**. Grave location:- Row A, Grave 4. ROH:- Armitage Bridge National School; Armitage Bridge War Memorial.

COPSEY, CHRISTOPHER SIMEON. Private. No 44960. 1/5th Battalion York and Lancaster Regiment. Born Glemsford, Suffolk. Son of Mr and Mrs Copsey, 21 Crimble Bank, Slaithwaite. Was a member of the Slaithwaite Conservative Club. Employed as a twister at the Colne Valley Tweed Company's mill at Crimble. Enlisted in 1915. Killed in action, 20.10.1917, aged 30 years. Has no known grave. Commemorated on the **TYNE COT MEMORIAL TO THE MISSING.** ROH:- St. James Church, Slaithwaite; Slaithwaite War Memorial.

CORDEN, JOSEPH. Private. No 2276. 1/7th Battalion Duke of Wellington's Regiment. Lived Binn House, Marsden. Married, with three children all under eight years of age. Enlisted August 1914. Embarked for France April, 1915. Was killed instantenously by being hit on the head by shrapnel, 3.7.1916, aged 28 years. Has no known grave. Commemorated on the **THIEPVAL MEMORIAL TO THE MISSING.** ROH:- Huddersfield Drill Hall; Marsden War Memorial.

COSTELLO, JOHN. Private. 3rd Battaliion Duke of Wellington's Regiment. Born Maitland Street, Glasgow, 6.7.1864. Educated at schools in Glasgow. Husband of Jane Costello, 85 Fenton Road, Lockwood. Employed as a moulder. Enlisted 20.9.1914. Died three months after discharge from the army, from pneumonia, on 19.10.1916, aged 52, at 183 Lockwood Road, Huddersfield. Buried **LOCKWOOD CEMETERY**. (Father of Private **WILLIAM J. COSTELLO**, who died 16.10.1920 q.v.).

COSTELLO, WILLIAM J. Gunner. 168th (Huddersfield) Brigade Royal Field Artillery. Born St. Peter's Lane, Leicester, 30.4.1894. Son of John and Jane Costello, 85 Fenton Road, Lockwood. Educated at Mount Pleasant Council School, Lockwood. Employed as a grocer's assistant. Single. Enlisted 2.5.1915. Died, 16.10.1920, at 183 Lockwood Road, of the effects of gas, aged 26. Buried **LOCKWOOD CEMETERY**. (Son of Private **JOHN COSTELLO**, who died, 19.10.1916, q.v.).

COTTON, ALBERT WILLIAM. Private. No 32973, 22nd Battalion Durham Light Infantry. Born Lindley, Huddersfield. Son of Jane Cotton and the late Richard Cotton, 13 Dean Street, Oakes. Died, 14.12.1918, aged 41. Buried **CRONENBOURG FRENCH NATIONAL CEMETERY**. Grave location:- Allied Plot 1. Grave 18. ROH:- St. Stephen's Church, Lindley; memorial in St. Stephen's Churchyard.

COTTON, SAMUEL (SAUL). Stoker Petty Officer. No 291887. Royal Navy. *HMS Lance*. Born Leeds Road, Huddersfield, 23.11.1878. Son of Robert Cotton, 117 Leeds Road North, Huddersfield and later of 11 Church Stairs Street, Long Westgate, Scarborough. Educated at St. Andrew's Church of England Schools, Leeds Road, Huddersfield. Prior to enlistment, was employed as a textile worker. Enlisted in the Navy 1898. On, 5.7.1915, he was married at Fairlie Parish Church, Ayrshire, Scotland, his wife residing at Railway Buildings, Fairlie, Ayrshire. On the morning of 18.7.1915, in very heavy weather, Cotton fell overboard from *HMS Lance* and, although the spot was searched for more than an hour, no trace could be found of him and the search had to be abandoned. Commemorated on the **CHATHAM NAVAL MEMORIAL TO THE MISSING.**

COTTRELL, LEONARD. Private. No 306350. 'C' Company, 1/7th Battalion Duke of Wellington's Regiment. Born Dobcross. Son of Dyson and Mary Hannah Cottrell, 21 Royds Terrace, Marsden. Employed as a weaver at Clough Lea Mills, Marsden. Was a member of the Marsden Liberal Club. Enlisted, 22.11.1915, and crossed over to France in February, 1916. Killed by a shell on the morning of 12.3.1918, aged 23 years. Buried **DUHALLOW A.D.S. CEMETERY, YPRES**. Grave location:- Plot 9, Row C, Grave 16. His parents received the following letter from Sergeant Smith, of the same Company, *'I am sorry to have to tell you that your son was killed by a shell dropping on his dugout on the morning of the 12th inst. He had just come off sentry duty in the trenches and had fallen asleep when he was killed and I can assure you he suffered no pain whatsover. He was not wounded but I think it must have been the shock of the explosion that did it. He has been in my Lewis gun section sometime and was one of the best and steadiest soldiers I have met. He was always cheerful under the* *most trying circumstances and was a favourite with all his comrades. His Corporal was badly crushed at the same time and I can assure you that it has made a mess of one of the best teams in the battalion.'* ROH:- Marsden Liberal Club; Huddersfield Drill Hall; Marsden War Memorial.

COULTER, HENRY. Corporal. No 17/1570. 17th Battalion West Yorkshire Regiment. Born Ardwick, Manchester 2.11.1891. Son of Henry Coulter, 39 Lister Street, Chorlton-upon-Medlock, Manchester. Educated at Spring Grove Council School. Lived with his Aunt, Mrs A. Schofield at 12 Westbourne Road, Marsh. Employed as a clerk in Huddersfield Tramway Offices. Was a member of Gledholt Wesleyan Chapel Bible Class. Enlisted 31.5.1915. Embarked for France in April, 1916. Suffered serious injuries on 10.10.1916, when part of a trench fell on him. Admitted to No 37 Casualty Clearing Station but he died of his injuries on 19.10.1916, aged 24 years. Buried **AVESNES-LE-COMTE COMMUNAL CEMETERY EXTENSION.** Grave location:- Plot 2, Row B, Grave 7. ROH:- Marsh War Memorial; Gledholt Wesleyan Church; Huddersfield Corporation Roll.

COUPLAND, ROBERT ROBINSON. Private. No 241649. 2/5th Battalion Duke of Wellington's Regiment. Born Dumfries 6.3.1897. Educated at St Michael's State School, Dumfries. Prior to enlistment, lived 64 Bradford Road, Huddersfield. Employed as a dental mechanic. Enlisted February 1916. Reported missing, presumed killed, at the Battle of Bullecourt, 3.5.1917, aged 22. Has no known grave. Commemorated on the **ARRAS MEMORIAL TO THE MISSING.** ROH:- Huddersfield Drill Hall.

COVERLEY, JOHN WILLIAM. Private. No 305115. 1/7th Battalion Duke of Wellington's Regiment. Born Moldgreen 28.2.1893. Son of John William and Mary Coverley, 13 Back Garden Street, Lockwood. Educated at Rashcliffe Church of England School. Employed as a teamer by Mr John Cooke, concreter, of Folly Hall, Huddersfield. Enlisted 6.8.1914. Demobilised, 13.2.1919, after serving in France since April, 1915. Died of pneumonia following upon influenza, 22.2.1919, at Royds Hall War Hospital, aged 24 years. Buried **LOCKWOOD CEMETERY.** Grave location:- C, 642. ROH:- St. Stephen's Church, Rashcliffe; Huddersfield Drill Hall.

COWGILL, ALLEN. Private. No 4723. 1/5th Battalion Duke of Wellington's Regiment. Born Honley. Son of Mrs Cowgill of Dyson Hill, Honley. Educated at the Primitive Methodist School. Was a member of Honley Working Men's Club and was a bowler with the Honley Cricket Club. Employed by Messrs France, Littlewood and Company. Enlisted February 1916. Was wounded and taken prisoner by the Germans in the attack on the Schwaben Redoubt, 17.9.1916. His mother received a postcard from him dated,14.9.1916, from the War Prisoner's Camp at Lager Grasenwohr, Germany:- *'I am doing well at present. Will you send me a parcel as soon as you can. You must keep your spirits up and let me have a letter with all the news from home'.* On 17.10.1918 his mother received a letter from Herr Pastor Fl. Hayler, the Military Chaplain at the camp, telling her that her son had died of his wounds on 24.9.1916, aged 23 years. Buried **NIEDERZWEHREN CEMETERY, CASSEL, GERMANY.** Grave location:- Plot 4, Row H, Grave 11. ROH:- Huddersfield Drill Hall; Honley War Memorial.

COWGILL, ERNEST. Private. No 240781. 1/5th Battalion Duke of Wellington's Regiment. Born Huddersfield. Reported missing, presumed killed, in the attack on the Schwaben Redoubt, 3.9.1916. Has no known grave. Commemorated on the **THIEPVAL MEMORIAL TO THE MISSING.** ROH:- Huddersfield Drill Hall.

COWGILL, HERBERT. Private. No 205207. 1/5th Battalion Duke of Wellington's Regiment. Son of Mr and Mrs J T Cowgill, Golf House, Lingards, Slaithwaite. Husband of Isabel Cowgill, 16 Old Hardend Cottages, Marsden. Attended the Lingards Church Sunday School, Slaithwaite. Was a member of the Marsden branch of the Sons of Temperance. Employed as a warper by Mr J E Crowther at Bank Bottom Mills. Enlisted 11.4.1917. Embarked for France in July, 1917. Sustained a severe compound fracture to the right leg, 11.10.1917, and died of his injuries at No 44 Casualty Clearing Station near Poperinghe, Belgium, on the same day. He was 28 years of age. Buried **NINE ELMS BRITISH CEMETERY.** Grave location:- Plot 4, Row D, Grave 12. ROH:- Huddersfield Drill Hall; Marsden War Memorial.

COWGILL, WILLIE. Rifleman. King's Royal Rifle Corps. Born Huddersfield. Lived Dalton,

Huddersfield. Died as a result of wounds on 14.11.1919, age 31 years.

COWLING, OLIVER. Private. No 3/2341. 2nd Battalion King's Own Yorkshire Light Infantry. Born Wakefield. Son of Hannah and the late John Cowling of Wakefield. Employed as a shunter by the Lancashire and Yorkshire Railway Company at Shepley Railway Station. Single. Lodged with Mrs Woods of Railway Cottages, Shepley. As a naval reservist he was called up in August, 1914, being transferred to the army later on. Died of wounds at No 46 Casualty Clearing Station, 13.1.1918, aged 30 years. Buried **MENDINGHEM MILITARY CEMETERY.** Grave location:- Plot 9, Row C, Grave 11. ROH:- Shepley War Memorial; Lancashire and Yorkshire Railway Roll.

COX, CHARLES, MM. Company Sergeant Major. No 5/2678. 1/5th Battalion Duke of Wellington's Regiment. Formerly East Yorkshire Regiment. Born Harston, Cambridge. Lived 313, Knowl, Crimble, Slaithwaite. Employed by Messrs J. Hopkinson and Sons Limited, Birkby. Before the outbreak of war had served for twelve years with the East Yorkshire Regiment. Enlisted August 1914. Embarked for France April, 1915. Awarded the Military Medal a few days before his death. He went out into No Man's land about seven times for the purpose of looking for and bringing back the wounded. Was wounded on August 4th, 1916, but the wound was only slight. Returned to the trenches and he was killed instantenously by a splinter from a shell on 5.8.1916. Buried **CONNAUGHT CEMETERY.** Grave location:- Plot 3, Row M, Grave 6. ROH:- St. James Church, Slaithwaite; Slaithwaite War Memorial.

COX, FRED. Private. No 42014. 2/5th Battalion West Yorkshire Regiment. Born Manchester 1.3.1893. Both parents deceased. Brother of Albert Cox, 18 Church Lane, Moldgreen. Educated at Moldgreen Council School. Lived 5 Church Lane, Moldgreen, Huddersfield. Employed as a tailor by Mr Wilkinson of Cloth Hall Street. Single. Enlisted 24.1.1917. Reported missing, presumed killed, at the Battle of Cambrai, 22.11.1917, aged 24 years. Has no known grave. Commemorated on the **CAMBRAI MEMORIAL TO THE MISSING.** ROH:- Christ Church, Moldgreen.

COX, GERALD. Private. No 71490. 17th Battalion Sherwood Foresters. Formerly No 32250 North Staffordshire Regiment. Born Acre Street, Lindley, 23.12.1888. Son of Mary Cox, 8 Croft House Lane, Marsh, Huddersfield. Educated at Oakes Council Schools and Huddersfield Technical College. Employed as a book keeper in the office of Messrs Riley and Hinchliffe, wool merchants, of Cambridge Buildings, Huddersfield. Was a tenor singer and a member of St. Stephen's Church choir, and of the Huddersfield Amateur Operatic and Huddersfield Light Opera Societies. His sister, Miss Emily Cox, was also a well known soprano singer. Enlisted 15.11.1916. Killed in action near Ypres, 31.7.1917, aged 28 years. Has no known grave. Commorated on the **MENIN GATE MEMORIAL TO THE MISSING.** ROH:- Marsh; St. Stephen's Church, Lindley.

CRABTREE, ARTHUR. Private. No 31697. 13th Battalion York and Lancaster Regiment. Formerly No 4783 Duke of Wellington's Regiment. Born Meltham. Son of John and Mary Crabtree. Killed in action 10.1.1917 age 25 years. Buried **SAILLY-AU-BOIS MILITARY CEMETERY.** Grave location:- Plot 2, Row H, Grave 10. ROH:- St. Bartholomew's Church, Meltham.

CRABTREE, EDGAR. Private. No 36748. 12th Battalion East Yorkshire Regiment. Born Linthwaite. Son of Mrs M. E. Crabtree, of Bath Cottages, Linthwaite. Reported missing, presumed killed, at the Battle of Arras, 3.5.1917, aged 34 years. Has no known grave. Commemorated on the **ARRAS MEMORIAL TO THE MISSING.**

CRABTREE, FRANK. Private. No 5619. 1/5th Battalion Duke of Wellington's Regiment. Born Marsden. Son of Mr and Mrs William Crabtree, 20 Sandhurst Cottages, Marsden. Employed as a teaser at Bank Bottom Mills, Marsden. Enlisted March, 1916, and embarked for France, 30.6.1916. Killed in action, 25.9.1916, aged 19 years. Has no known grave. Commemorated on the **THIEPVAL MEMORIAL TO THE MISSING.** ROH:- Huddersfield Drill Hall; Marsden War Memorial.

CRABTREE, FRED. Private. No 241553. 2/5th Battalion Duke of Wellington's Regiment. Born Slaithwaite. Third son of Mr and Mrs Edwin

Crabtree of Colne View, Slaithwaite. Employed as a dyer's labourer by Messrs William Brook and Sons, of Slaithwaite. Attended Carr Lane United Methodist Church. Enlisted March, 1916, and embarked for France in January, 1917. Reported missing at the Battle of Bullecourt, 3.5.1917, aged 21 years. Has no known grave. Commemorated on the **ARRAS MEMORIAL TO THE MISSING**. ROH:- St. James Church, Slaithwaite; Slaithwaite War Memorial; Huddersfield Drill Hall.

CRABTREE, JOSEPH. Private. No 3/2186. 2nd Battalion King's Own Yorkshire Light Infantry. Born Hull. Lived Shady Row, Meltham. Married. Father of Joseph Crabtree, 2 Spa Yard, Batley Carr, Batley. Was a reservist and re-enlisted in August, 1914. Had served in the Tirah campaign (North West Frontier province, India) and the South African War. Took part in the fighting at Neuve Chapelle and at Hill 60. Met his death whilst bearing a stretcher, a shell bursting near him and killing him instantly, 7.5.1915, aged 40 years. Has no known grave. Commemorated on the **MENIN GATE MEMORIAL TO THE MISSING**. ROH:- St. Bartholomew's Church, Meltham.

CRABTREE, LAWRENCE C. 2nd Lieutenant. 2nd Battalion West Yorkshire Regiment. Born Lower Brow, Paddock, 4.1.1896. Son of Robert and Sarah Crabtree, The Lodge, Edgerton House, Huddersfield. Educated at Thomas Street and Berry Brow Council Schools. Employed as an engineer. At the time of enlistment, was living at Castlehouses, Castle Hill. Husband of Minne Crabtree. Killed in action, 24.4.1918, at Villers-Bretonneux. Buried **CRUCIFIX CORNER CEMETERY, VILLERS-BRETONNEUX**. Grave location:- Plot 7, Row E, Grave 19.

CRAGG, ARTHUR HARRY. Private. No 2794. 1/5th Battalion Duke of Wellington's Regiment. Born Newton Moor, Cheshire, 28.6.1894. Son of Captain Arthur Robinson and Annie Cragg of Rio de Janeiro, Brazil. Educated at Eaton Lodge School and Almondbury Grammar School. Employed as an apprentice at Huddersfield Corporation Electricity Works. At the time of enlistment, was living at 'Wyngarth,' Park Drive, Huddersfield. Single. Enlisted September 1914. Embarked for France April, 1915. His father had spent a number of years in Brazil and arrived in England just one hour after his son's troopship had sailed for France. Killed in action, 15.5.1915, aged 20 years. Buried **RUE-DAVID MILITARY CEMETERY, FLEURBAIX**. Grave location:- Plot 1, Row B, Grave 19. His parents received a letter from Major Gilbert P. Norton of the 6th Battalion Duke of Wellington's Regiment, who wrote, *'You will have heard from his Platoon Commander that your son was killed in action on the 15th inst. by a high explosive shell whilst the Germans were bombarding our trenches. He lived for a short time after receiving his wound but the injuries were of such a nature that he could not have suffered any pain and he never regained consciousness. I know that nothing one can say will help to make your loss any lighter but you will like to know that he was very highly thought of by his Officers and his comrades and is a great loss to us all. During the time we were raising 250 recruits in Huddersfield he worked like a slave, filling in forms for recruits and the work could never have been got through without him. It was the same all the time he was a soldier, always willing and always cheerful. I trust you will find some consolation in remembering that he answered the call of his country at a time when she was fighting for her existence and that he died in helping to save Britain from the frightfulness of the German barbarian. He is buried not far behind the trenches and his grave is marked with a neat white cross. His comrades made a wreath of wild flowers and placed it on the grave.'* ROH:- Holy Trinity Church, Huddersfield; Almondbury Grammar School; Huddersfield Drill Hall; Huddersfield Corporation Roll.

CRAMPTON, MORRIS, MM. Private. No 306012. 1/7th Battalion Duke of Wellington's Regiment. Born Golcar. Son of David and Jane Crampton, 115 Swallow Lane, Golcar. Attended the Scapegoat Hill Baptist Chapel. Employed as a weaver by Messrs Hirst and Mallinson Limited, Cliffe End Mills, Longwood. Enlisted March 1915. Embarked for France, 29.6.1915. Awarded the Military Medal a fortnight before his death. Died of the effects of gas poisoning, 26.11.1917, at No 14 General Hospital, Wimereux, aged 22. Buried in **WIMEREUX COMMUNAL CEMETERY**. Grave location:- Plot 8, Row A, Grave 1A. ROH:- St. John's Church, Golcar.

CRAMPTON, RUFUS. Private. No 38589. 8th Battalion York and Lancaster Regiment. Born Meltham. Lived 28 Mitre Street, Marsh.

Killed in action, 7.6.1917. Has no known grave. Commemorated on the **MENIN GATE MEMORIAL TO THE MISSING.** ROH:- St. Bartholomew's Church, Meltham; Marsh War Memorial; Wilshaw Church.

CRAVEN, ALFRED. Private. No 45467. 16th Battalion The Cameronians (Scottish Rifles). Son of Joseph and Clara Craven of Scissett. Died of accidental injuries, 5.12.1918, aged 20 years. Buried **St. AUGUSTINE'S CHURCHYARD, SCISSETT.** Grave location:- in South-East part. ROH:- Scissett War Memorial; Clayton West and High Hoyland War Memorial.

CRAVEN, FRED. Private. No 204383. 2/4th Battalion Duke of Wellington's Regiment. Born Moldgreen 25.3.1888. Son of Robert Henry and Fenetta Craven, 55 Fitzwilliam Street, Huddersfield. Educated at Huddersfield Parish Church Schools. Employed as a chemical labourer. Married. Living at 83 Dock Street, off Castlegate, Huddersfield. Enlisted 6.3.1917. Reported missing, presumed killed, at the Battle of Cambrai, 20.11.1917. Has no known grave. Commemorated on the **CAMBRAI MEMORIAL TO THE MISSING.**

CRAWFORD, JAMES. Private. No 35278. 2nd Battalion Duke of Wellington's Regiment. Born Huddersfield. Lived 6 Croft Lane, Bradford Road, Huddersfield. Educated at St. John's School, Hillhouse. Employed by Mr W. T. Johnson, cloth finisher, Bankfield Mills, Moldgreen. Killed in action, 9.4.1917, aged 29 years. Has no known grave. Commemorated on the **ARRAS MEMORIAL TO THE MISSING.** ROH:- St. John the Evangelist Church, Birkby; St. Andrews' Church, Leeds Road; Fartown and Birkby War Memorial.

CRAWSHAW, WILLIAM. Private. No 41515. 2nd Battalion Lincolnshire Regiment. Formerly No 34301 Leicestershire Regiment. Born Lockwood. Lived Meltham. Killed in action, 21.3.1918. Has no known grave. Commemorated on the **POZIERES MEMORIAL TO THE MISSING.** ROH:- St. Bartholomew's Church, Meltham; Huddersfield GPO Roll.

CREATON, HARRY EDWARD. Lance Corporal. No 1570. 2/5th Battalion Duke of Wellington's Regiment. Born Violet Street, Turnbridge, Huddersfield, 18.7.1894. Son of Edward A. and Minnie Creaton. Educated at Huddersfield Parish Church Schools. Attended Northumberland Street Primitive Methodist Church and Sunday School. Employed by Messrs Walter Sykes Limited as a cloth finisher. Single. Enlisted 11.3.1916. Killed in action at Bullecourt, 3.5.1917, aged 22 years. Has no known grave. Commemorated on the **ARRAS MEMORIAL TO THE MISSING.** ROH:- Northumberland Street Primitive Methodist Church; Huddersfield Drill Hall.

CRINES, H. Private. No 4604481. 5th Battalion Duke of Wellington's Regiment. Died at home, 31.7.1921. Buried **EDGERTON CEMETERY, HUDDERSFIELD.** Grave location:- 11B, 177.

CRITCHLEY, PETER. Private. No 4124. 1/5th Battalion Duke of Wellington's Regiment. Son of Mrs Henry of Lockwood's Yard, Duke Street, Huddersfield. Attended St. Patrick's Roman Catholic Church, New North Road, Huddersfield. Worked at Turnbridge coalpit. Single. Enlisted May, 1915, and after 12 months training embarked for France. Had been there about seven weeks when he was killed on 3.7.1916, aged 19 years. Has no known grave. Commemorated on the **THIEPVAL MEMORIAL TO THE MISSING.** ROH:- Huddersfield Drill Hall.

CROMACK, CHARLES WILLIE. Gunner. No 108082. 253rd Siege Battery Royal Garrison Artillery. Born Lockwood Road, Lockwood, 26.7.1880. Educated at Stile Common Council School. Employed as a finisher by Messrs Taylor and Littlewood of Newsome Mill. Husband of Beatrice Ellen Cromack, 87 Barcroft Road, Close Hill, Newsome. Enlisted 18.7.1916. Killed in action near Ypres, 12.11.1917, aged 37 years. Buried **MENIN ROAD SOUTH MILITARY CEMETERY, YPRES.** Grave location:- Plot 3, Row M, Grave 13. ROH:- St. John's Church, Newsome; Messrs. Taylor and Littlewood, Newsome Mills.

CROOKS, ARTHUR. Private. No 29952. 3rd Battalion Duke of Wellington's Regiment. Born Golcar. Son of George and Alice Crooks, 25 Clay Well, Golcar. On Sunday, 23.12.1917, his body was found on the rocks of the shore at Tynemouth. An inquest was held on Monday 24.12.1917, at Tynemouth, when the evidence showed that Crooks was awaiting his discharge from the army, being unfit for active service. On Saturday night when the roll call was made he was found to be missing and on Sunday he was found dead on the sands with a cut in his throat. Doctor Wilkinson said Crooks had cut his throat from ear to ear with the blade of a safety razor but the cut was not deep and was not sufficient to cause death. The fall over the cliffs on to the sands had caused a fatal injury. The jury's verdict was that Crooks died from injuries caused by falling over the cliff whilst attempting to commit suicide by cutting his throat and that he was in an unsound state of mind. Crooks had previously been under treatment at the hospital. Buried **GOLCAR BAPTIST CHAPEL YARD.** Grave location:- SE, N, 16. ROH:- St. John's Church, Golcar; Golcar Baptist Church.

CROSLAND, ARTHUR. Private. No 32495. 1st Battalion North Staffordshire Regiment. Born Wasp Nest Road, Hillhouse. Son of Fred and Jane Crosland, of Berry Brow. Educated at Berry Brow Council School. Attended Berry Brow Wesleyan Church. Employed as a pattern weaver. Single. Enlisted November 1916. Was under treatment in No 35 General Hospital at Calais for bronchial pneumonia, following gas poisoning, when he was killed by enemy aircraft during an air raid on the hospital, 31.5.1918, aged 29 years. Buried **LES BARAQUES MILITARY CEMETERY, SANGATTE.** Grave location:- Plot 4, Row A, Grave 13a. ROH:- Armitage Bridge War Memorial.

CROSLAND, ERNEST. Private. No 64756. 25th Battalion Durham Light Infantry. Formerly No 33779 West Yorkshire Regiment. Born Holmfirth. Son of Sam and Mary Hannah Crosland, of Woodhead Road, Hinchliffe Mill. Attended St. David's Church, Holmbridge. Husband of Zillah Crosland of Harehills, Leeds. Had three children - Arthur, Alice and Herbert. Formerly employed as manager of the Holmfirth branch of the Hinchliffe Mill Cooperative Society. He then took up a post as a commercial traveller in Leeds. Enlisted under the Derby scheme. Came home on leave in January, 1917, when he appeared to be in good health. Died of heart failure, 30.3.1917, aged 32 years. Was buried, but grave destroyed in later actions. Has no known grave. Commemorated on the **THIEPVAL MEMORIAL TO THE MISSING.** ROH:- Wooldale War Memorial.

CROSLAND, ERNEST. Private. No 18053. 2nd Battalion Duke of Wellington's Regiment. Born Victoria Street, Lindley, 2.7.1892. Son of Charles Harry and Betsy Crosland, 12 Savile Road, Lindley. Educated at Lindley Council School. Employed as a lithographic artist. Single. Enlisted Feburary 1916. Killed on the first day of the Battle of the Somme at Beaumont Hamel, 1.7.1916, aged 24 years. Buried **SERRE ROAD CEMETERY No 2.** Grave location:- Plot 1, Row E, Grave 23. ROH:- St. Stephen's Church, Lindley.

CROSLAND, GEORGE WILLIAM. Corporal. No 12634. 9th Battalion Duke of Wellington's Regiment. Born Honley. Lived Thirstin Road, Honley. Employed at Armitage Bridge Mills. Killed whilst leading a bombing party, 2.3.1916. Has no known grave. Commemorated on the **MENIN GATE MEMORIAL TO THE MISSING.** ROH:- Honley War Memorial; Armitage Bridge Mills.

CROSLAND, GILBERT. Private. No 4757. 1/5th Battalion Duke of Wellington's Regiment. Born 7 Sparks Road, Oakes, Huddersfield. Son of Jane Crosland, Oakfield House, Oakes. Employed as a tailor's trimmer by Mr George Crosland, of Chancery Lane, Huddersfield. Attended Oakes Baptist Sunday School. Single. Killed in action, 20.11.1916, aged 25 years. Buried **FONCQUEVILLERS MILITARY CEMETERY.** Grave location:- Plot 1, Row J, Grave 33. ROH:- Oakes Baptist Church; St. Stephen's Church, Lindley; Huddersfield Drill Hall.

CROSLAND, G.W. KILNER, DSO. Major. Duke of Wellington's Regiment. Eldest son of the late Mr George William Crosland and grandson of the late Mr T. P. Crosland, M.P. Major Crosland was one of the Honorary Surgeons of Huddersfield Royal Infirmary; was made Honorary Surgeon at the Infirmary in February, 1905, and for some years before that had been House Surgeon at the Infirmary. During the Boer War Dr Crosland was a civilian surgeon in the South African field force. He was associated with the formation of the local Territorial battalion and with them he embarked for France. For services with the troops he was awarded the DSO in June, 1916, and he relinquished his commission in the Duke of Wellington's Regiment in August, 1917, and was then granted the honorary rank of Major, Upon returning to Huddersfield he recommenced work at the Infirmary, where he was in charge of the X-ray department and took over additional work at the Milton Church and the Drill Hall Auxiliary Military Hospital. He married Miss Anne Frances Crookstan of Pangbourne in February, 1918, at Pangbourne Parish Church. Died at his home, 18 New North Road, 31.12.1919, aged 50 years. Buried **EDGERTON CEMETERY, HUDDERSFIELD.** Grave location:- 41, 130C.

CROSLAND, TOM. Corporal. No 240118. 1/5th Battalion Duke of Wellington's Regiment. Born Holmfirth. Son of Mr and Mrs John Crosland, of Underbank Old Road, Holmfirth. Attended Underbank Wesleyan School. Employed by Messrs Thornton, cloth finishers of Honley. Joined the Territorials at 17 years of age. Invalided home at Christmas, 1916, with trench feet. Hit by shrapnel whilst going into the trenches, 4.8.1917, aged 21 years. Has no known grave. Commemorated on the **NIEUPORT MEMORIAL TO THE MISSING.** ROH:- Underbank War Memorial; Huddersfield Drill Hall; memorial in Holy Trinity Churchyard, Holmfirth.

CROSLAND, TREVOR ALLINGTON. 2nd Lieutenant. 2nd Battalion Royal Welsh Fusiliers. Born Birkby Grange 30.12.1896. Son of Thomas Pearson, woollen manufacturer, J.P. for the West Riding of Yorkshire and Borough of Huddersfield and Charlotte Elizabeth Crosland, New House Hall, Sheepridge, Huddersfield. Educated at Harrow Public School and Sandhurst Military Academy. Was twice medically rejected for Sandhurst, the first time in August, 1914, and then at Christmas, 1914. After an operation he was accepted and went straight from Sandhurst to the Royal Welsh Fusiliers in August, 1915. Embarked for France on 12.5.1916. Was killed on the occasion of the explosion of a large German mine at Givenchy on 22.6.1916, aged 19. (The resulting crater, measuring 120 yards long by 70 feet wide and 30 feet deep was the largest crater on the Western Front at the time. Its name, 'Red Dragon', from the design of the regiment's cap badge, became the Army name for the crater). 2nd Lieutenant Crosland's body was not found until 1st July, 1925, during ploughing. Buried **CABARET ROUGE BRITISH CEMETERY, SOUCHEZ.** Grave location:- Plot 31, Row A, Grave 27. His parents received the following letter from Lieut. Colonel Crawshay, Commanding Officer of the 2nd Battalion Royal Welsh Fusiliers, '*He was a splendid boy and one of the sort we can ill afford to spare. On the night of the 22nd June at midnight the enemy exploded an enormous mine and I regret that the trench in which your son was, was blown up. They then attacked us after a very intense barrage but got badly defeated leaving a certain number of dead in our hands. It is really too sad, we all miss him and everyone was very fond of him. It will be some satisfaction to you to know that he was a real soldier and a leader of men.*' ROH:- Christ Church, Woodhouse Hill; Fartown and Birkby War Memorial.

CROSLAND, WILLIE. Lance Corporal. No 19/146. 17th Battalion West Yorkshire Regiment. Born 27.7.1897. Educated at Spring Grove Council School. Employed as a tailor. Single. Enlisted 4.11.1915. Killed in action near Peronne, 14.7.1917, aged 19. Buried **TEMPLEUX-LE-GUERARD BRITISH CEMETERY.** Grave location:- Plot 2, Row G, Grave 33.

CROSLAND, WRIGHT. Corporal. No 61459 1st Infantry Labour Company, Durham Light Infantry, transferred to No 18716 32nd Company Labour Corps. Born Holmfirth. Son of Mr Willie Crosland, Catch Bar Farm, Hade Edge, Holmfirth. Husband of Elizabeth Crosland, of Hade Edge, Holmfirth. Educated at Hade Edge Council School. Attended Magnum Mission Church. Assisted his father on the family farm and was a good horse breaker. Enlisted 28.8.1914. Served in the Gallipoli campaign and was invalided home with dysentery. He was also invalided home from the fighting in France. Died of wounds, 14.12.1917, aged 31 years. Buried **DUHALLOW A.D.S. CEMETERY, YPRES.** Grave location:- Plot 3, Row D, Grave 8. ROH:- Hade Edge War Memorial.

CROSLEY, WILLIAM BERTRAM. Private. No 235132. 2/7th Battalion Worcestershire Regiment. Formerly No 205216 Duke of Wellington's Regiment. Born Newsome, Huddersfield, 30.10.1880. Son of Jonathan W. and Elizabeth Crosley, 202 Birkby Hall Road, Huddersfield. Husband of Amy Crosley (later of 'Thomas', 44, St. James Road, Bridlington). Educated Spring Grove Council School. Was Scoutmaster for the Lockwood Baptist Church troop and was a member of the Lockwood Philharmonic Society. Before moving to Bradford, was in the employ of Messrs George Crosland and Sons, Crosland Moor. Prior to enlistment was a clerk in the merchantile department of Messrs Mitchell Brothers, Bradford. Married. Enlisted April 1917. Killed in action near Cambrai, 4.12.1917, aged 37 years. Has no known grave. Commemorated on the **CAMBRAI MEMORIAL TO THE MISSING.** ROH:- Lockwood Baptist Church; Fartown and Birkby War Memorial.

CROSSLAND, KENNETH ELY. Private. No 62498. 5th Battalion King's Own Yorkshire Light Infantry. Born Moldgreen 29.9.1899. Son of Mrs Amy Crossland, 257 New Hey Road, Salendine Nook, Huddersfield. Educated at Oake Council School. Employed as a card machine tenter by Messrs Joseph Sykes, Acre Mills, Lindley. Single. Enlisted October 1917. Killed in action, 20.6.1918, aged 18 years. Buried **BIENVILLERS MILITARY CEMETERY.** Grave location:- Plot 20, Row D, Grave 15. ROH:- Salendine Nook Baptist Church.

CROSSLAND, THOMAS. Private. No 18058. 2nd Battalion Duke of Wellington's Regiment. Born Southowram, Halifax, 28.9.1895. Educated at Southowram Council School. Employed as a cloth finisher by Messrs C. and J. Hirst Limited. At the time of enlistment, was living at 27 Ivy Street, Crosland Moor. Single. Enlisted 24.1.1916. Killed in action on the first day of the Battle of the Somme, 1.7.1916, aged 20 years. Has no known grave. Commemorated on the **THIEPVAL MEMORIAL TO THE MISSING.** ROH:- St. Barnabas's Church, Crosland Moor.

CROSSLEY, JOHN HAIGH. Private. No 203450. 11th Battalion Northumberland Fusiliers. Son of Haigh and Elixabeth Crossley, 146 Manchester Road, Milnsbridge. Attended Milnsbridge Wesleyan Sunday School. Employed as a night piecer by Messrs Ben Hall and Sons of Milnsbridge. Enlisted July 1916. Embarked for France April, 1917. Killed in action, 20.9.1917, aged 20 years. Has no known grave. Commemorated on the **TYNE COT MEMORIAL TO THE MISSING.**

CROSSLEY, NORRIS H. Sergeant. No 305856. 2/7th Battalion Duke of Wellington's Regiment. Born Slaithwaite. Son of Hinchliffe and Elizabeth Crossley, 46 Royd Street, Hill Top, Slaithwaite. Attended Carr Lane United Methodist Church, Slaithwaite, and was secretary of the Sunday School. Employed by the Globe Worsted Company as a colour mixer. Enlisted November 1914. Killed in action at the Battle of Bullecourt, 3.5.1917, aged 24 years. Has no known grave. Commemorated on the **ARRAS MEMORIAL TO THE MISSING.** His parents received the following letter from the Commanding Officer of his Company, *'As Platoon Sergeant he had under his care some fifty or sixty men who looked to him for training and instruction in military matters. He fell in an attack on a German position having first assumed command of his platoon on his Officer being hit a few moments earlier. He was a brave soldier and popular with the Officers and men and his loss will be felt in the Regiment.'* ROH:- Carr Lane United Methodist Church; St. James Church, Slaithwaite; Slaithwaite War Memorial; Huddersfield Drill Hall

CROSSLEY, ROBERT CLIFFORD. Sergeant. No 105869. Royal Engineers. Lived Deighton. Died at home, 12.5.1916. Buried **KIRKHEATON CEMETERY.** Grave location:- 'C', 2330. ROH:- Deighton War Memorial.

CROSSLEY, STANLEY. Gunner. No 111178. 'A' Battery 59th Brigade Royal Field Artillery. Born 2.6.1897. Son of Herbert and Ellen Crossley, 34 Abbot Street, Marsh, Huddersfield. Educated at Stile Common Board School. Employed as a woollen warehouseman. Enlisted 17.4.1916. Wounded, 24.12.1916, and died on the same day at No 49 Casualty Clearing Station on Christmas Eve, 1916, during the singing of the carol 'While Shepherds Watched.' Buried **CONTAY BRITISH CEMETERY.** Grave location:- Plot 7, Row B, Grave 4. ROH:- Holy Trinity Church, Huddersfield.

CROUGHAN, PAUL. Private. No 44699. 2nd Battalion Lincolnshire Regiment. Born 42 Dock Street, Huddersfield. Son of James and Sarah Croughan, 43 Dock Street, Huddersfield. Educated at St. Patrick's Roman Catholic School, Huddersfield. Worked as a labourer. Enlisted 10.2.1916. Died of wounds, 12.8.1918. Buried **BAGNEUX BRITISH CEMETERY.** Grave location:- Plot 4, Row A, Grave 26.

CROWE, FRED THEWLIS. Private. No 268353. 2/5th Battalion Duke of Wellington's Regiment. Born Taylor Hill 3.5.1882. Son of Mr and Mrs Anthony Crowe, 6 Stocks Buildings, Taylor Hill, Huddersfield. Attended Berry Brow Wesleyan Church. Employed as a clerk at Deanhouse Institution. Husband of Lucy Crowe, Bank Terrace, Armitage Bridge, Huddersfield. Enlisted 18.10.1916. Wounded at Bullecourt, 3.5.1917. Killed in action, 29.8.1918, at Vaulx north east of Bapaume, aged 36 years. Buried **VAULX HILL CEMETERY**. Grave location:- Plot 1, Row H, Grave 9. ROH:- Huddersfield Drill Hall; Armitage Bridge War Memorial.

CROWTHER, ARNOLD. Private. No 24665. 'C' Company 6th Battalion East Yorkshire Regiment. Born 24 Green Hill, Longwood, Huddersfield, 8.11.1892. Son of John Richard and Rachel Ann Crowther. Educated at Goitfield Council School. Employed as a woollen spinner by Messrs J. I. Swallow and Company, commission spinners, Parkwood Mills. Attended Longwood Wesleyan Chapel. Single. Enlisted 2.6.1916. Killed in action near Yser Canal, Ypres, 3.7.1917, aged 24 years. Buried **BRANDHOEK MILITARY CEMETERY**. Grave location:- Plot 1, Row K, Grave 1. ROH:- Longwood Wesleyan Chapel; Longwood War Memorial.

CROWTHER, BEAUMONT. Private. No S/23791 1st Battalion Cameron Highlanders. Born 10 Church Street, Paddock, 7.2.1894. Son of Mr and Mrs John Edward Crowther, 71 Bradford Road, Huddersfield. Educated at Almondbury Grammar School. Employed as an agent of the Royal Insurance Company. Single. Enlisted 10.1.1916. Reported missing on the Somme, 3.9.1916, aged 22 years. Buried **CATERPILLAR VALLEY CEMETERY**. Grave location:- Plot 9, Row H, Grave 17.

CROWTHER, CHARLES EDWARD. Gunner. No 154235. Royal Garrison Artillery. Born 14 Laund Road, Salendine Nook, Huddersfield, 25.3.1886. Son of Thomas and Elizabeth Crowther, Chapel House, Salendine Nook. Educated Oakes Council School. Employed as a hydraulic presser. Single. Enlisted 10.4.1917. Died in Northumberland War Hospital of shell shock, 12.8.1918, aged 32 years. Buried **SALENDINE NOOK BAPTIST CHAPEL YARD**. Grave location:- in East part. ROH:- Salendine Nook Baptist Chapel, 379E.

CROWTHER, EDGAR. Private. No 4095. 2/4th Battalion Royal Scots Fusiliers, transferred to No 449631 822nd Employment Company, Labour Corps. Son of James and Rebecca Crowther, 75 Fenton Road, Lockwood. Employed as a weaver by Messrs Armitage Brothers of Milnsbridge. Killed in action, 20.4.1918, aged 28 years. Buried **CHOCQUES MILITARY CEMETERY**. Grave location:- Plot 6, Row A, Grave 30. ROH:- St. Stephen's Church, Rashcliffe.

CROWTHER, ERNEST. 2nd Lieutenant. 92nd Field Company Royal Engineers. Son of George Rowland Crowther and Mary Crowther, 66 East View, Chapel Fold, Staincliffe, Batley. His father was Minister in Charge of the Boothroyd Lane Congregational Mission, Dewsbury, and formerly Pastor of the Crimble Congregational Mission at Slaithwaite. Enlisted as Private in May, 1915, and after eighteen months service in France was granted a commission. Killed in action, 25.10.1918, aged 25 years. Buried **LE CATEAU MILITARY CEMETERY**. Grave location:- Plot 2, Row A, Grave 9. ROH:- St. James Church, Slaithwaite; Slaithwaite War Memorial.

CROWTHER, FRANK. Private. No 24733. 9th Battalion Duke of Wellington's Regiment. Born Huddersfield. Son of Mrs Crowther, 2 Sand Street, Aspley and formerly of Kilner Bank, Huddersfield. Employed by the Hygienic Stove Company, St. Thomas's Road, Huddersfield. Killed in action, 21.3.1918, aged 20 years. Has no known grave. Commemorated on the **ARRAS MEMORIAL TO THE MISSING**.

CROWTHER, FREDERICK WILLIAM. Private. No 31726. 2/4th Battalion Duke of Wellington's Regiment. Born South Street, Huddersfield, 5.2.1891. Employed as a woollen scourer by Messrs J. Hoyle and Sons, Quarmby Clough Mills, Longwood. Was a member of the Crosland Moor Conservative Club and of the United Methodist Church, Crosland Moor. Husband of Elsie Crowther, 45 Hawthorne Terrace, Crosland Moor. Enlisted 25.5.1917. Embarked for France, 3.10.1917. Killed in action at the Battle of Cambrai, 21.11.1917, aged 26 years. Has no known grave. Commemorated **CAMBRAI MEMORIAL TO THE MISSING**. ROH:- St. Barnabas Church, Crosland Moor; United Methodist Church, Crosland Moor.

CROWTHER, HAROLD. Private. No 306169. 9th Battalion Duke of Wellington's Regiment. Born Mytholmroyd, Halifax. Son of Mr and Mrs David Crowther, 22 Quarmby Road, Longwood, and formerly of 62 George Street, Milnsbridge. Employed as a finisher at Messrs John Lockwood and Sons Limited, Milnsbridge. Enlisted in the army at the outbreak of the war. Killed in action, 1.9.1918, aged 21 years. Has no known grave. Commemorated **VIS-en-ARTOIS MEMORIAL TO THE MISSING.** ROH:- Longwood War Memorial.

CROWTHER, HERBERT. Private. No 32704. 16th Battalion Northumberland Fusiliers. Born Golcar. Husband of Mrs Crowther, 97 James Street, Golcar. Employed as a weaver by Messrs Pearson Brothers, Victoria Mills, Golcar. Attended Golcar Baptist Chapel and Sunday School and was a member of the Young Men's Reading Room. Was one of the founders of the Golcar Lily subdivision of the Order of Temperance. Enlisted July, 1916, and embarked for France, 7.11.1916. Had been in France 10 weeks when he died of kidney disease at No 3 Casualty Clearing Station, 20.1.1917, aged 24 years. Buried **PUCHEVILLERS BRITISH CEMETERY.** Grave location:- Plot 5, Row A, Grave 21. ROH:- St. John's Church, Golcar; Golcar Baptist Church.

CROWTHER, HUBERT. Corporal. No 241797. 2/5th Battalion Duke of Wellington's Regiment. Born 59 East Street, Lindley, 30.11.1891. Son of Florence E. Crowther and the late Joe William Crowther. Educated at Lindley Church of England School, Huddersfield Higher Grade School and Huddersfield Technical College. Worked in the family business as a painter and decorator. Single. Enlisted 20.3.1916. Wounded at the Battle of Bullecourt, 3.5.1917, aged died of his wounds on, 3.5.1917, aged 25 years. Has no known grave. Commemorated **ARRAS MEMORIAL TO THE MISSING.** ROH:- St. Stephen's Church, Lindley; St. Philip's Church, Birchencliffe; Huddersfield Drill Hall.

CROWTHER, IRVING. Private. No 41625. 15th/17th Battalion West Yorkshire Regiment. Born Bradley Mills, Huddersfield, 6.8.1887. Educated at St. Andrew's School, Huddersfield. Employed as a woollen spinner by Messrs T. and H. Blamires Limited. Husband of Sarah Crowther, 24 Hawk Street, Huddersfield. Killed in action, 27.3.1918, aged 31 years. Buried **TWO TREE CEMETERY, MOYENVILLE.** Grave location:- Row B, Grave 21. *(The 15th Battalion West Yorkshire Regiment held the front of the 31st Division at Moyenville on March 26th–27th 1918 for 36 hours averting disaster at the cost of 700 casualties).*

CROWTHER, LESLIE TAYLOR. 2nd Lieutenant. 'D' Company, 1/5th Battalion Duke of Wellington's Regiment. Born Huddersfield. Son of Mr and Mrs Norman Crowther, 'Viso House', Edgerton, Huddersfield. Educated at Huddersfield College School. Employed by Messrs Read, Holliday and Sons Limited as an assistant in one of the laboratories. Played hockey with the Huddersfield club at Armitage Bridge and also played cricket. Single. Enlisted in the local Territorials in 1911. When war was declared held the rank of Sergeant. Was gazetted Second Lieutenant, 21.10.1914. Embarked for France April, 1915. Killed in action at Croix Marechal near Fleurbaix, 16.6.1915, aged 23 years. Buried **RUE-DAVID MILITARY CEMETERY.** Grave location:- Plot 1, Row B, Grave 11. ROH:- Holy Trinity Church, Huddersfield; St. Stephen's Church, Lindley; Huddersfield College School; Huddersfield Drill Hall. The following letter was written by Private **FREDDIE SMITH**, of No 16 Platoon, 'D' Company, 1/5th Battalion, writing home to his parents who lived at 22 Stoney Cross Street, Lockwood, on the 19.6.1915, *'Lieutenant Crowther was especially popular with his men. On Tuesday 15.6.1915 he was out on patrol accompanied by Captain Stott, Lieutenant Liddel and Corporal Convoy when they went straight into a German patrol of six men and a bomb thrower. One of them instantly hurled a highly explosive detonator, which killed Lieutenant Crowther instantly. Lieutenant Liddel who was nearest to Lieutenant Crowther immediately emptied his revolver on the Germans who took to their heels making for the trenches. The remainder of the patrol acting with great gallantry returned for assistance taking back stretcher-bearers and carried back the dead Lieutenant under heavy rifle fire. Lieutenant Crowther was buried opposite the battalion headquarters, the service being conducted by the Colonel.'*

CROWTHER, PERCY. Wireless Operator. SS 'Clan Alpine'. Born Longwood 6.9.1890.

Son of Mrs O. Crowther, 63 Prospect Row, Longwood, Huddersfield. Educated at Goitfield Council School, Longwood, and Hillhouse Higher Elementary School. Employed as a clerk in the office of Messrs John Broadbent and Sons, Parkwood Mills. Attended Longwood Wesleyan Chapel. Joined a wireless school in Leeds in March, 1916, and was successful in passing his examinations. On 16.4.1917, he joined the Marconi Company in London and went afloat the following month. On 9.6.1917, the *SS Clan Alpine* was struck by a torpedo in the North Sea. Has no known grave. Commemorated on the **TOWER HILL MEMORIAL TO THE MISSING OF THE MERCHANTILE MARINE.** ROH:- St. Mark's Parish Church, Longwood; Longwood Wesleyan Chapel.

CROWTHER, PHILIP TOWNSEND. Lieutenant. 211th Field Company, Royal Engineers. Formerly 12th Battalion King's Own Yorkshire Light Infantry. Born 'The Wood', Fixby, 22.11.1883. Son of the late John Herbert Crowther and Hannah Elizabeth Crowther of Rose Cottage, Woodhouse, Huddersfield. Educated at Alconham School and Leeds University where he graduated with a BSc. in engineering. Prior to the outbreak of the war was an engineer on the Canadian Northern and Intercolonial railways. He returned to England in 1914 and joined the Leeds University OTC. and was afterwards awarded a commission in the K.O.Y.L.I,. with whom he served in Egypt and France. He afterwards transferred to the Royal Engineers. Killed in action at Bailleul-sur-Bertholt, 5.5.1917, aged 33 years. Buried **ALBUERA CEMETERY.** Grave location:- North, Row A, Grave 2. ROH:- Christ Church, Woodhouse Hill; War Memorial outside St. Philip's Church, Birchencliffe.

CROWTHER, STANLEY. Private. No 18633. 2nd Battalion Duke of Wellington's Regiment. Born Lowerhouses, Almondbury, 14.1.1897. Son of Mrs Crowther, 7 Haigh Square, Dalton, Huddersfield. Educated at Moldgreen Board School. Employed by Messrs Godfrey Sykes and Sons of Moldgreen as a beamer and twister-in. Attended Moldgreen United Methodist Church and was a member of the U.M.C. Harriers. Enlisted, 14.1.1916, and embarked for France in April, 1916. Died, 12.10.1916, whilst trying to save one of his comrades, aged 19 years. Has no known grave. Commemorated on **THIEPVAL MEMORIAL TO THE MISSING.** ROH:- St. Andrew's Church, Huddersfield; Christ Church, Moldgreen.

CRUIKSHANK, NELSON. Private. No 12649. 9th Battalion Duke of Wellington's Regiment, attached 175th Company, Royal Engineers. Born Camberwell. Adopted son of Mrs Anne Rhodes, of Commercial Road, Skelmanthorpe, and formerly of Church Street, Emley. Employed by Messrs Stringer and Jagger. Was the first man from Emley to enlist, in August 1914. Killed in action, 14.11.1915, aged 22 years. Buried **MAPLE COPSE CEMETERY, ZILLEBEKE, BELGIUM.** Grave location:- Special Memorial J 19. ROH:- Emley War Memorial. His mother received the following letter from Private **BEN CLEGG**, q.v. (who was later killed in action on 22.3.1918), *'Nelson was a favourite with the whole Company and his death has cast a gloom over them all. I want to convey to you the heartfelt sympathy of all his comrades and in adding my own I can honestly assure you that he died as he had lived – a good lad, a clean soldier and a above all a man.'*

CRUICKSHANK, WILLIAM. Private. No 24650. 9th Battalion Duke of Wellington's Regiment. Born Staincliffe, near Batley, 17.12.1894. Son of Mr and Mrs Joe Cruickshank, 89 Hillhouse Lane, Huddersfield. Educated at St. John's School. Worked with his father as a metal refiner. Enlisted 11.9.1916. Killed in action, 26.6.1917, aged 23 years. Has no known grave. Commemorated **ARRAS MEMORIAL TO THE MISSING.**

CRYER, JAMES. Private. No 28962. 8th Battalion King's Own Royal Lancaster Regiment. Formerly No 5567 East Surrey Regiment. Lived 34 Silver Street West, Moldgreen, Huddersfield. Employed at Huddersfield Goods Station and previously at the Wholesale fruit market. Married, with one daughter. Enlisted 1916. Killed in action, 27.9.1918. Buried **LOWRIE CEMETERY, HAVRINCOURT.** Grave location:- Row J, Grave 16.

CUMMINGS, ALBERT G.T. Private. No 15224. 9th Battalion Royal Berkshire Regiment. Died at home, 1.12.1918. Buried **CHRIST CHURCH CHURCHYARD EXTENSION, NEW MILL.** Grave location:- G, 401. ROH:- New Mill Working Men's Club; Fulstone War Memorial.

CUNNINGHAM, CLIFFORD THOMAS SYDNEY. Private. No 240267. 1/5th Battalion Duke of Wellington's Regiment. Born Hoyland Common. Lived Denby Dale. Son of Police Constable William Cunningham and Elizabeth Cunningham of Denby Dale. Employed by Messrs G. H. Norton. Embarked for France April, 1915. Reported missing, 3.9.1916. Has no known grave. Commemorated **THIEPVAL MEMORIAL TO THE MISSING.** ROH:- Denby Dale and Cumberworth War Memoral; G. H. Norton Roll of Employees; Huddersfield Drill Hall.

CUNNINGHAM, THOMAS. Private. No 113911. 2nd Battalion Duke of Wellington's Regiment. Born Linthwaite. Killed in action at Hill 60, 18.4.1915. Has no known grave. Commemorated on the **MENIN GATE MEMORIAL TO THE MISSING.** ROH:- Linthwaite War Memorial.

CURRAN, JOHN. Private. No 22751. 2/6th Battalion Duke of Wellington's Regiment. Born Northumberland Street, Huddersfield, 10.8.1896. Educated at St. Patrick's Roman Catholic School. Employed as a brick maker by the Huddersfield Brick and Tile Company. Living at 84 Alder Street, Bradford Road, Huddersfield. Single. Enlisted 26.6.1916. Killed in action at the Battle of Cambrai, 27.11.1917, aged 21 years. Has no known grave. Commemorated on the **CAMBRAI MEMORIAL TO THE MISSING.**

CUTTELL, HENRY. Private. No 40798. 7th Battalion Bedfordshire Regiment. Formerly No 37373 Leicestershire Regiment. Born Netherton. Husband of Ellen Thomas, Thomas Street, Netherton. Attended Netherton Wesleyan Church and was a teacher in the Sunday School. Employed by Messrs F. J. Hickson of Healey House as a warper. Died of gas poisoning and shell wounds at No 64 Casualty Clearing Station, 18.7.1917, aged 39 years. Buried **MENDINGHEM MILITARY CEMETERY.** Grave location:- Plot 1, Row F, Grave 57. ROH:- South Crosland and Netherton War Memorial.

CUTTS, KELVIN EWART. Private. No 3162. 1/5th Battalion Duke of Wellington's Regiment. Son of William Henry and Elizabeth Cutts, of Thomas Street, Crosland Moor, Huddersfield. Worked as a clerk for Mr Law Dyson, Registrar of Births and Deaths, at Crosland Moor. Enlisted at the outbreak of war. Died of wounds at No 23 General Hospital, Etaples, 4.10.1916, aged 20 years. Buried **ETAPLES MILITARY CEMETERY.** Grave location:- Plot 11, Row F, Grave 15a. ROH:- Huddersfield Drill Hall.

DAGG, HEWSON. Gunner. No 891023. 'B' Battery 286th Brigade Royal Field Artillery. Born Kirkheaton. Son of Edward and Sarah Dagg, Peace Hall, Wakefield Road, Lepton. Employed by Mr George Thomas, finishers of Rowley Hill, Fenay Bridge. Reported missing, presumed killed, 9.4.1918, aged 19 years. Has no known grave. Commemorated on the **PLOEGSTEERT MEMORIAL TO THE MISSING.** ROH:- Lepton Parish Church; St. John's Church, Kirkheaton.

DAKIN, EDWIN. Private. No 250760. 1/6th Battalion Durham Light Infantry. Formerly No 3849 2nd Battalion Duke of Wellington's Regiment. Born The Heys, Thongsbridge, 20.10.1895. Son of George and Sarah Jane Dakin, Cold Hill, Berry Brow. Educated at Berry Brow Council School. Attended Berry Brow Wesleyan Church. Employed as an engine man at Armitage Bridge Mills. Married. Enlisted October 1914. Reported missing, 29.9.1918, and afterwards presumed died on that date. Buried **GRAND SERAUCOURT BRITISH CEMETERY.** Grave location:- Plot 8, Row D, Grave 8. ROH:- Armitage Bridge War Memorial; Armitage Bridge Mills; Honley War Memorial.

DALBY, CHARLES. Regimental Quarter Master Sergeant. No 107736. 51st (Graduated) Battalion West Yorkshire Regiment. Married. Wife and family living at 18 Lindrick Street, Longwood. Had seen 23 years service in the Army and went through the South African War, for which he received the Queen's Medal with 6 clasps. At the outbreak of the war was employed by Messrs Hirst and Mallinson, of Longwood, as time-keeper. Was a Primo in the Order of Buffaloes. Re-enlisted in August, 1914, and had served at Gallipoli. Died suddenly at Thoresby Camp, 20.6.1918, aged 48 years. Buried with full military honours in **St. JOHN'S CHURCHYARD, GOLCAR.** Grave location:- A, North-West, 92. ROH:- St. John's Church, Golcar.

DALEY, WILLIAM. Private. No 3914. 1st Battalion Northumberland Fusiliers. Born Huddersfield. Son of Mrs Elizabeth Daley, 63

Upperhead Row, Huddersfield. Killed in action, 16.6.1915, aged 20 years. Has no known grave. Commemorated **MENIN GATE MEMORIAL TO THE MISSING.**

DALGLEISH, ANDREW. Private. No S4/094962. 17th Field Bakery, Army Service Corps. Born Galashiels, Scotland. Son of Andrew and Jane Dalgleish, 2 Rutland Road, Royd Street, Longwood. Was a baker by trade and, before his family came to Huddersfield from Galashiels, was employed by Messrs McVitie and Price of Edinburgh. Died of bronchial pneumonia, 14.5.1918, aged 32 years. Buried **BOULOGNE EASTERN CEMETERY.** Grave location:- Plot 9, Row B, Grave 84. ROH:- Longwood War Memorial.

DALLAGHER, GEORGE WILLIAM. Private. No 25555. 2nd Battalion The Yorkshire Regiment. Born Huddersfield. Son of Mr and Mrs J. W. Dallagher, 29 Watergate, Castlegate, Huddersfield. Employed as a cord cutter by Messrs Lockwood and Keighley, of Upperhead Mills. Attended St. Patrick's Roman Catholic Church, Huddersfield. Died of wounds at No 10 Casualty Clearing Station, 4.8.1917, aged 26 years. Buried **LIJSSENTHOEK MILITARY CEMETERY.** Grave location:- Plot 17, Row E, Grave 12a.

DALY, P. Driver. No 100409. 20th Reserve Battery, Royal Field Artillery. Died at home, 25.3.1916. Buried **EDGERTON CEMETERY, HUDDERSFIELD.** Grave location:- 11B, 115.

DANIEL, FRANK. Rifleman. No C/7364. 16th Battalion King's Royal Rifle Corps. Born Lowergate, Longwood, 8.5.1892. Son of Mr and Mrs William Daniel, 45 New Street, Paddock. Educated at Paddock Council School. Employed by Messrs C. and J. Hirst of Longwood as a woollen weaver. Attended Queens Street Mission, Huddersfield. Reported missing, presumed killed, 23.4.1917, aged 25 years. Has no known grave. Commemorated on the **ARRAS MEMORIAL TO THE MISSING.** ROH:- All Saints Church, Paddock.

DANIEL, GERALD. Private. No 250761. 1/6th Battalion Durham Light Infantry. Formerly No 3416 Duke of Wellington's Regiment. Born Holmfirth. Son of Laura Anne Schofield (formerly Daniel) and Sam Schofield, (stepfather), 47 Park Street, Sowerby Bridge, Halifax. Lived Holme, Holmfirth. Killed in action, 21.5.1918. Has no known grave. Commemorated **SOISSONS MEMORIAL TO THE MISSING.** ROH:- Holme War Memorial.

DARBY, JOSEPH CHARLES. Private. No 41974. 12th Battalion Manchester Regiment. Formerly No 32672 North Staffordshire Regiment. Born Upperthong, Holmfirth. Son of Mr and Mrs Edward Darby of Bank Top, Dewsbury. Educated Holmfirth Wesleyan Day School and the United Methodist Church Sunday School. Employed at Albert Mills, Holmfirth. Husband of Sarah Darby, Spring Buildings, Holmfirth. Enlisted November 1916. Reported missing, presumed killed, 25.4.1917, aged 26 years. Has no known grave. Commemorated **ARRAS MEMORIAL TO THE MISSING.** ROH:- Holmfirth War Memorial.

DARLINGTON, WILLIAM. Private. No 32619. 8th Battalion York and Lancaster Regiment. Born Rastrick 1883. Educated Longroyd Council School, Rastrick. Employed as a chemical worker by Messrs Robert McAlpine and Sons. Husband of Alice Darlington, 44 Bradley Mills, Leeds Road, Huddersfield. Enlisted 10.2.1917. Killed in action near Ypres, Belgium, 13.7.1917. Buried **RAILWAY DUGOUTS (TRANSPORT FARM) BURIAL GROUND.** Grave location:- Special Memorial C 4. ROH:- St. Andrew's Church, Leeds Road, Huddersfield; commemorated on his parents' headstone in Edgerton Cemetery, Huddersfield.

DAVIS, ALFRED. Sapper. No 290620. 96th Light Railway Operating Company, Royal Engineers. Born Windinom, Leicestershire. Son of Annie Sadler (formerly Davis) and stepson of John Sadler, of Owler Ing, Binn. Marsden. Husband of Florence Davis, Binn House, Marsden. Employed as a cloth scourer at Bank Bottom Mills, Marsden. Enlisted 1.8.1917 Reported drowned when the transport 'Aragon' was torpedoed by a U boat and sunk in the Eastern Mediterrean, 30.12.1917, aged 23 years. Has no known grave. Commemorated on **CHATBY MEMORIAL, ALEXANDRIA, EGYPT.** (Brother of Private **WILLIAM DAVIS MM**, killed in action, 26.3.1918, q.v.). *The ship was a luxuriously fitted liner of the Royal*

Mail Steam Packet Company and was formerly engaged in the South American passenger service. She was bound from Marseilles to Egypt with destroyers as escort. At 10.30am on the day of the disaster she was within sight of land and fifteen minutes later she had disappeared. One of the destroyers whilst picking up survivors from the 'Aragon' was itself torpedoed and sunk. A lot of the soldiers were picked up from rafts and taken on board a number of boats and trawlers which happened to be at hand. Hundreds got on board a destroyer which almost immediately was torpedoed midships cutting her clean in half. ROH:- Marsden War Memorial.

DAVIES, WALTER OWEN. 2nd Lieutenant. 1/5th Battalion Duke of Wellington's Regiment. Born Huddersfield 8.3.1895. Son of the late Mr R O Davies and Mrs Davies, 163 Wakefield Road, Moldgreen. Educated Almondbury Grammar School. Employed as a bank clerk at the Market Place branch of the Lancashire and Yorkshire Bank, Huddersfield. Joined the local Territorial battalion a few months before the outbreak of the war and embarked for France with them in April, 1915. Was recommended for commissioned rank and, after serving with an Officer's Cadet battalion at Galea in Ayrshire, was gazetted to his old Regiment. Killed in action at Bourlon Wood, 27.11.1917. Has no known grave. Commemorated on the **CAMBRAI MEMORIAL TO THE MISSING.** ROH:- Christ Church, Moldgreen; Almondbury Grammar School; Huddersfield Drill Hall.

DAVIES, WILLIAM. Corporal. No 203977. 1/4th Battalion Duke of Wellington's Regiment. Born Stalybridge, Cheshire. Son of Mr and Mrs Thomas Davies, 91 Calderbrook Road, Littleborough. Married. Living at 48 New Street, Paddock. Employed by the Westfield Cotton Company as a dyer. Enlisted 4.8.1914. Killed in action near Cambrai, 11.10.1918, aged 29 years. Buried **IWUY COMMUNAL CEMETERY.** Grave location:- Row B, Grave 41. ROH:- All Saints Church, Paddock.

DAVIS, WILLIAM, MM. Sergeant. No 240661. 2/5th Battalion Duke of Wellington's Regiment. Born Marsden. Son of Mrs Annie Sadler, Old House End Farm, Binn, Marsden. Enlisted November 1914. After 14 months service in France was severely wounded and returned to England, spending seven months in hospital. He returned to France in June, 1917. He was awarded the Military Medal for gallant conduct during the Battle of Cambrai. Was hit by a sniper's bullet on 26.3.1918, aged 23 years. Has no known grave. Commemorated **ARRAS MEMORIAL TO THE MISSING.** (Brother of Private **ALFRED DAVIES**, drowned at sea, 30.12.1917, q.v.). ROH:- Huddersfield Drill Hall; Marsden War Memorial.

DAWSON, ARTHUR. Lance Corporal. No 10687. 1st Battalion Royal Fusiliers. Born Milnsbridge 25.9.1883. Son of Walter and Ann Dawson, Cowlersley House, Milnsbridge. Educated at Milnsbridge National School and was a day student at Huddersfield Technical College for three years. Later he attended the evening classes for eight years for chemistry and dyeing. Was a member of the firm of Messrs Emerson and Dawson, chemical manufacturers, Longroyd Bridge, Huddersfield. Was a member of the Crosland Heath Golf Club, played cricket with the Milnsbridge club and football with the Milnsbridge Church and Meltham clubs. Was also a member of the St. George's Society, the Society of Dyers and Colourists and of the Commercial Travellers Association. Single. Enlisted 11.4.1916. Embarked for France in July, 1916. Killed in action at Messines, 7.6.1917, aged 33. Has no known grave. Commemorated **MENIN GATE MEMORIAL TO THE MISSING.** ROH:- Milnsbridge War Memorial.

DAWSON, ARTHUR HOWARD. Private. No 14232. 9th Battalion Duke of Wellington's Regiment. Born Holmfirth. Son of Mrs Firth Dawson of Hinchliffe Mill, Holmfirth. Employed as a tailor by his elder brother, Mr Walter Dawson. Attended Hinchliffe Mill Liberal Club. Played football for the Holmbridge football club. Killed in action, 7.7.1916, aged age 26 years. Has no known grave. Commemorated **THIEPVAL MEMORIAL TO THE MISSING.** (Brother of Private **GEORGE WILLIE DAWSON**, killed in action, 1.7.1916, q.v.). ROH:- Holme and Holmbridge War Memorial.

DAWSON, FRANK. Private. No 5292. 'A' Company, 2/5th Battalion Duke of Wellington's Regiment. Born 51 Yews Mount, Lockwood. Son of Mrs Edith Dawson, 24 Crosland Road, Thornton Lodge, Huddersfield. Educated Mount

Pleasant Council School. Employed as a twister-in by Messrs Shaw Brothers, Larchfield Mills, Firth Street, Huddersfield. Enlisted 22.3.1916. Killed at Miraumont on the Somme, 27.2.1917, aged 23 years. Has no known grave. Commemorated **THIEPVAL MEMORIAL TO THE MISSING.** ROH:- St. Stephen's Church, Rashcliffe; Huddersfield Drill Hall.

DAWSON, GEORGE WILLIE. Private. No 14907. 2nd Battalion Duke of Wellington's Regiment. Born Holmfirth. Son of Mrs Firth Dawson of Hinchliffe Mill, Holmfirth. Attended Hinchliffe Mill Liberal Club and played football with the Holmbridge football club. Was an old scholar of Hinchliffe Mill Wesleyan School. Employed by Messrs Whiteley and Green Limited as a weaver. Enlisted January 1916. Killed in action on the first day of the Battle of the Somme, 1.7.1916, aged 23 years. Has no known grave. Commemorated on the **THIEPVAL MEMORIAL TO THE MISSING.** (Brother of Private **ARTHUR HOWARD DAWSON**, killed in action, 7.7.1916, q.v.). ROH:- Holme and Holmebridge War Memorial.

DAWSON, HAROLD. Private. No 31974. 12th Battalion York and Lancaster Regiment. Formerly No 34957 West Yorkshire Regiment. Born Milnsbridge. Son of the late Mr and Mrs Thomas Harry Dawson, of the firm of Messrs S. Dawson, dyers, of Milnsbridge. Died of wounds, 26.11.1916, aged 38 years. Buried **COUIN BRITISH CEMETERY.** Grave location:- Plot 6, Row B, Grave 17.

DAWSON, JAMES. Sergeant. No 203641. 'A' Company, 1/5th Battalion Duke of Wellington's Regiment. Born Huddersfield 3.1.1889. Educated at Huddersfield Parish Church Schools. Employed as a tram conductor by Huddersfield Corporation Tramways Department. Married. Living at Longley Farm, Longley, Huddersfield. Enlisted 4.8.1914. Killed in action at Passchendaele, 27.11.1917. Has no known grave. Commemorated **TYNE COT MEMORIAL TO THE MISSING.** ROH:- Huddersfield Parish Church; Huddersfield Drill Hall; Almondbury War Memorial; Huddersfield Corporation Roll.

DAWSON, JOE. Private. No 52525. 1st Battalion West Yorkshire Regiment. Born Linthwaite 1886. Son of Squire and Charlotte Dawson of Linthwaite. Married Edna Thornton on 5th January, 1917. Lived 3 Chapel Hill, Linthwaite. Reported missing, presumed killed, 21.3.1918, aged 39 years. Has no known grave. Commemorated **ARRAS MEMORIAL TO THE MISSING.** ROH:- Linthwaite War Memorial.

DAWSON, JOHN IRVIN WILLIE. Private. No 35698. 2nd Battalion King's Own Yorkshire Light Infantry. Formerly No 6088 1/5th Battalion Duke of Wellington's Regiment. Born 84 Upper Mount Street, Lockwood, 21.11.1894. Son of John and Sarah Margaret Dawson, 96 Upper Mount Street, Lockwood. Educated at Mount Pleasant and Spring Grove Council Schools and also at Mr Jenning's Academy. Employed by Mr A. E. Spivey as an auctioneer's clerk. Attended St. Stephen's Church, Rashcliffe. Single. Enlisted 4.8.1914. Had twice been invalided home through illness. On the first occasion he came home, he was drafted to Clipstone Camp where he acted as Orderly Room Sergeant before being sent back to France. Had only been back at the front five weeks after hospital leave when he was killed near Cambrai, 20.11.1917. Buried **HERMIES HILL BRITISH CEMETERY.** Grave location:- Plot 2, Row F, Grave 39. ROH:- St. Stephen's Church, Rashcliffe; Emmanuel Church, Lockwood.

DAWSON, VINCENT. Private. No 32152. 2/7th Battalion West Yorkshire Regiment. Born Townend, Almondbury. Son of George Dawson, 67 Northgate, Almondbury. Educated at Almondbury Council School. Employed as a carpenter and joiner. Enlisted 18.8.1916. Died at No 24 General Hospital, Etaples, of pneumonia following a gunshot wound, 1.7.1918. Buried **ETAPLES MILITARY CEMETERY.** Grave location:- Plot 68, Row F, Grave 7. ROH:- Almondbury War Memorial.

DAY, ALBERT. Company Sergeant Major. No 235317. 6th Battalion Duke of Wellington's Regiment. Born New Mill, Holmfirth, 20.11.1877. Son of Mr and Mrs William Day, 38 Blacker Road, Birkby. Husband of Florence M. Day, 48 Armitage Road, Birkby. Educated at New Mill National School. Employed as a commercial traveller. Attended St. John's Church, Birkby, where he held the office of sidesman and churchwarden. Enlisted in the 2nd Volunteer Battalion Duke of Wellington's Regiment in 1894. Volunteered for the Boer War and served from 1900–1901. Mobilised with the local Territorial battalion on 4.8.1914 as Colour Sergeant. Wounded and gassed on Passchendaele Ridge, 20.11.1917. On recovering, he trained recruits of a Reserve battalion at Ipswich. At the beginning of September, 1918, he was troubled with a carbuncle and was admitted into hospital. He developed septicaemia and died in Ipswich Military Hospital, 19.9.1918. Buried with full military honours in **EDGERTON CEMETERY, HUDDERSFIELD.** Grave location:- 36, 'C', 9. ROH:- St. John's Church, Birkby; Fartown and Birkby War Memorial.

DAY, NORMAN. Private. No 201856. 1/4th Battalion Seaforth Highlanders. Born Blue Bell Hill, Taylor Hill, Huddersfield, 5.1.1891. Son of James and Annie Eliza Day (nee Marsden), 51 Taylor Hill Road, Lockwood. Educated Berry Brow Council School. Employed as a scourer by Messrs C. and J. Hirst Limited. Single. Attended Taylor Hill Primitive Methodist Church. Played football with the Netherton football club and was connected with the physical training class at Huddersfield Technical College. Enlisted 19.2.1916. Killed in action near Ypres, 2.8.1917, aged 25 years. Has no known grave. Commemorated **MENIN GATE MEMORIAL TO THE MISSING.** ROH:- Emmanuel Church, Lockwood; Taylor Hill Primitive Methodist Church.

DEAKIN, THOMAS. Sergeant. No 25420. 'A' Battery, 28th Brigade Royal Field Artillery. Born Cadeby, Doncaster. Lived 16 Moss Street, Newsome, Huddersfield. Had served as a constable in the Metropolitan Police force before joining Huddersfield Borough Police Force on 10.11.1911. Husband of Nora Deakin. Enlisted 1915. Died of wounds 21.9.1917, aged 32 years. Buried **BUS HOUSE CEMETERY, VOORMEZEELE.** Grave location:- Row H, Grave 30. ROH:- Almondbury War Memorial; Huddersfield Corporation Roll; Huddersfield Police Headquarters.

DEAN, FRANK. Private. No 3412. 1/5th Battalion Duke of Wellington's Regiment. Born Newsome 28.11.1892. Son of Mr and Mrs William Dean, 61 Barcroft Road, Newsome, Huddersfield. Educated Newsome Church of England School. Employed as a metal plate worker by Messrs Fred Shaw, tinners and coppersmiths of Huddersfield. Attended Newsome Church Sunday School and the Newsome Working Men's Club. Prior to the war was secretary at the Newsome Adult School. Enlisted 13.11.1914. Was awarded a 'Distinguished Conduct Certificate' for bomb throwing in a damaged sap on 26.9.1915. On Saturday, 13.11.1915, he died of wounds received by the accidental explosion of a box of bombs he was carrying. Sapper G. Winterbottom, of the 10th Entrenching Battalion of the Royal Engineers, in a letter to Mrs Dean says:- *'He was carrying a box with another chap when one of them slipped and caused the bombs to explode. His mate was killed outright. We were working about 50 yards away and saw the flash. At first we thought it was a German shell exploding as they had been shelling us that morning. We could not get to him very quickly because of the state of the roads. We did all we could to help him. One of us got a stretcher and then we took him to a first aid dressing shed and got a doctor to him. He was then taken in the ambulance to the hospital.'* He died shortly after admission to hospital, 13.11.1915, aged 22 years. Buried **HOSPITAL FARM CEMETERY, ELVERDINGHE, BELGIUM.** Grave location:- Row C, Grave 14. ROH:- St. John's Church, Newsome; Huddersfield Drill Hall.

DEAN, HANDEL OLIVER. Private. No 3205. 1/5th Battalion Duke of Wellington's Regiment. Born Lindley 18.3.1893. Son of Mr and Mrs J. Dean, 49 West Street, Lindley. Educated Lindley National School. Employed as a woollen weaver by Messrs Ben Crosland of Oakes, Huddersfield. Attended Lindley Zion United Methodist Sunday School and the Lindley Adult School. Enlisted October 1914. Died of severe wounds to the abdomen at No 10 Casualty Clearing Station, 22.11.1915, aged 23 years. Buried **LIJSSENTHOEK MILITARY CEMETERY.** Grave location:- Plot 2, Row D, Grave 2a. ROH:- Lindley Zion United Methodist Church; St. Stephen's Church, Lindley; Huddersfield Drill Hall.

DEAN, JOHN. Private. No 13059. 11th Battalion West Yorkshire Regiment. Married. Wife living at 'The Boy and Barrel Inn', Beast Market, Huddersfield. Employed by Messrs Proctor's wireworks, Leeds. Reported missing, presumed killed, 10.6.1917, aged 24 years. Has no known grave. Commemorated **MENIN GATE MEMORIAL TO THE MISSING.**

DEARNALY, ALBERT. Corporal. No 116318. Royal Army Medical Corps. Born Occupation Road, Sheepridge, Huddersfield. Son of William and Emma Dearnley, 22 Norman Road, Birkby. Educated at St. John's Church Schools, Birkby. Employed as a woollen weaver. Single. Enlisted 8.5.1917. Died of pneumonia, 24.10.1919, aged 29 years, at Cannock Chase Hospital, Rugeley, Staffordshire. Buried **St. MARY'S CHURCHYARD, MIRFIELD.** Grave location:- 9, U13. ROH:- Fartown and Birkby War Memorial.

DEARNLEY, ARNOLD. Private. No 75548. 10th Battalion West Yorkshire Regiment. Born 46 Brian Street, Lindley, Huddersfield, 1.9.1897. Son of Allen and Fanny Dearnley. Educated Lindley National School. Employed as an engineer. Enlisted 20.5.1918. Killed in action, 21.10.1918, aged 21 years. Buried **MONTAY-NEUVILLY ROAD CEMETERY.** Grave location:- Plot 1, Row C. Grave 22. ROH:- St. Stephen's Church, Lindley.

DEARNLEY, ERNEST. Private. No 3074. 1/5th Battalion Duke of Wellington's Regiment. Born Almondbury 19.1.1898. Son of John William Dearnley, 33 Cadogan Avenue, Lindley. Educated at Almondbury National School. Employed as a finisher. Single. Enlisted 21.9.1914. Killed in action, 21.12.1915. Has no known grave. Commemorated on the **MENIN GATE MEMORIAL TO THE MISSING.** ROH:- St. Stephen's Church, Lindley; Huddersfield Drill Hall; Almondbury War Memorial.

DEARNLEY, GEORGE. Wheeler. No 35676, 'C' Battery, 106th Brigade Royal Field Artillery. Born Shelley. Killed in action, 24.7.1917. Buried **PERTH CEMETERY (CHINA WALL), ZILLEBEKE, BELGIUM.** Grave location:- Plot 1, Row J, Grave 24. ROH:- Emmanuel Church, Shelley.

DEARNLEY, GEORGE FREDERICK. Private. No 240340. 2/5th Battalion Duke of Wellington's Regiment. Born Rosebery Street, Birkby, 10.4.1897. Son of Mr John H. Dearnley, Thornton Lodge Hall, Crosland Moor. Educated at Almondbury Grammar School. Attended Crosland Moor Wesleyan Church. Employed as an engineer's apprentice. Single. Enlisted August 1914. Killed in action near Bullecourt, 4.7.1917. Buried **QUEANT ROAD CEMETERY, BUISSY.** Grave location:- Plot 2, Row H, Grave 30. ROH:- Almondbury Grammar School; Crosland Moor Wesleyan Church; St. Stephen's Church, Rashcliffe; St. Barnabas Church, Crosland Moor; Huddersfield Drill Hall; memorial in Lockwood Cemetery.

DEARNLEY, JAMES ARNOLD. Private. No 7693. 1/4th Battalion Duke of Wellington's Regiment. Living 3 Bank Nook, Slaithwaite. Married Mary Shaw in December, 1914. One child. Employed as a teaser by Mr John Edward Crowther, Bank Bottom Mills, Marsden. Attended Slaithwaite Wesleyan Chapel. Enlisted 4.8.1916. Embarked for France a fortnight before Christmas, 1916. Was admitted to the No 20 Casualty Clearing Station on 16.2.1917, with severe wounds in the shoulder and the head. He never regained consciousness and died, 18.2.1917, aged 31 years. Buried **WARLINCOURT HALTE BRITISH CEMETERY.** Grave location:- Plot 6, Row A, Grave 1. ROH:- St. James Church, Slaithwaite; Slaithwaite War Memorial.

DEIGHTON, WILLIAM HENRY. Private. No 10361. 6th Battalion Leicestershire Regiment. Born Thurlastone, Yorkshire. Son of Charles Henry and Lucy Deighton, 4 Lower Haigh House, Lindley Moor, Huddersfield. Died of wounds, 10.5.1917, aged 25 years. Buried **BUCQUOY ROAD CEMETERY.** Grave location:- Plot 1, Row F, Grave 18.

DEMETRIADI, LOUIS P. Lieutenant Colonel. Royal Army Medical Corps. Born Manchester 1862. Educated at Manchester Grammar School and at Kings College, London. Attended Leeds University, taking the degrees of M.D. (Durham), F.R.C.S. (Edinburgh) and a Diploma in Public Health. He commenced medical work in Huddersfield as an assistant to the late Doctor Macaskie. In 1886 to 1887 he was one of the house surgeons at the Huddersfield Royal Infirmary. He commemced in practice on his own account at 30 New North Road, Huddersfield and removed to Lindley in 1891. He continued in General Practice until 1912. In 1897, Doctor Demetriadi joined the 2nd Volunteer Battalion Duke of Wellington's Regiment with the rank of Lieutenant and served as Medical Officer for

18 years. He took a keen interest in training and organising the stretcher-bearers in ambulance work. When war was declared he went out with the local battalion to their training ground and, in April 1915, he was given command of the West Riding (49th) Casualty Clearing Station and took that unit to the front. He remained with this unit for nearly two years until his health gave way and, in November 1917, he was compelled to relinquish his commission. He was a church warden at Lindley Church for 4 years. He was founder-president and the first Captain of the Outlane Golf Club. He died at Southport on 26.10.1918, aged 56 years. Buried with full milllitary honours in **St. STEPHEN'S CHURCHYARD, LINDLEY.** Grave location:- 5, J, ROH:- St. Stephen's Church, Lindley, there is also a chair in the church dedicated to his memory.

DENHAM, AUBREY CRAWSHAW. Lieutenant. 6th Battalion Bedfordshire Regiment. Born Hartford House, Gledholt, Huddersfield, 14.6.1881. Son of John William and Annie Denham, 3 Woodland Mount, Trinity Street Huddersfield. Educated at Huddersfield College School and Mill Hill School, London, from 1896 to 1897. Enlisted November 1914. Died at home, Woodland Mount, Trinity Street, Huddersfield, on 1.4.1915 of pleurisy and pneumonia contracted during training. He was 34 years of age. Buried **EDGERTON CEMETERY, HUDDERSFIELD.** Grave location:- 37, 135. ROH:- Huddersfield College School; Mill Hill School, London.

DENHAM, CHARLES. Rifleman. No B/203506. 1st Battalion The Rifle Brigade. Born Congleton. Son of Mary Ann Denham, 2 Cross Street, Congleton. Lived with his sister at Moldgreen. Employed by Messrs Hilton Limited, at their King Street boot shop. Killed in action, 3.10.1917, aged 21. Buried **BARD COTTAGE CEMETERY.** Grave location:- Plot 3, Row I, Grave 2.

DENNIS, ILLINGWORTH. Private. No 29469. 1/4th Battalion Duke of Wellington's Regiment. Born Huddersfield 31.3.1886. Son of Lucy Dennis, 12 Spring Grove Street, Huddersfield. Educated at Thomas Street Board School. Employed as a permanent wayman on the London and North Western Railway. Attended Queen Street Mission Church. Husband of Margaret Oakes Dennis, 45 Well Green, Lockwood. Enlisted September 1916. Died of gunshot wounds and gas gangrene at No 24 General Hospital, 13.10.1917, aged 32 years. Buried **ETAPLES MILITARY CEMETERY.** Grave location:- Plot 30, Row C, Grave 14. ROH:-. Emmanuel Church, Lockwood.

DENNIS, HERBERT. Private. No 307764. 9th Battalion Duke of Wellington's Regiment. Born Chapel Hill, Huddersfield, 1.6.1891. Son of Mrs E. Dennis, 82 Manchester Road, Huddersfield. Educated at St. Paul's School. Employed as a mill hand by Messrs Hirst and Mallinson, of Longwood. Was a well known local swimmer and had won many swimming prizes. Husband of Sarah Dennis, 21 Varley's Yard, Chapel Hill. Killed in action, 26.8.1918, aged 27 years. Has no known grave. Commemorated on the **VIS-en-ARTOIS MEMORIAL TO THE MISSING.** ROH:- St. Paul's Church, Southgate, Huddersfield.

DENTON, CHARLES SINGLETON. Lance Corporal. No 17394. 1/5th Battalion Duke of Wellington's Regiment. Born 19.6.1895. Son of Mr and Mrs Alfred Denton. Educated Stile Common Council School and St. Thomas's Church of England School. At the time of enlistment, was living at 53 Longroyd Lane, Huddersfield. Single. Employed at Bay Hall Mills, Birkby. Enlisted at the outbreak of the war. Had served in Gallipoli and Egypt and took part in the evacuation of Suvla Bay. Wounded in the thigh, 14.9.1916, and was treated at Gosforth Hospital, Newcastle-on-Tyne. Reported missing, presumed killed, 29.3.1918, aged 21 years. Buried **GOMMECOURT BRITISH CEMETERY No 2.** Grave location:- Plot 5, Row A, Grave 2. ROH:- St. Thomas's Church, Longroyd Lane; Huddersfield Drill Hall.

DENTON, FRED. Private. No 4506. 1/5th Battalion Duke of Wellington's Regiment. Born Lepton. Son of Sam and Mary Jane Denton of Highgate Lane, Lepton. Killed in action, 3.9.1916, aged 19 years. Has no known grave. Commemorated **THIEPVAL MEMORIAL TO THE MISSING.** ROH:- Lepton Parish Church; Huddersfield Drill Hall.

DENTON, JOHN WHITTELL. Sergeant. No 9887. 2nd Battalion West Yorkshire Regiment. Born Kirkheaton. Enlisted Bradford. Died

9.6.1918. Buried **SETE (LE PY) CEMETERY. (GULF of LYONS)**. Grave location:- Grave 341.

DEPLEDGE, HARVEY. Private. No 28095. 9th Battalion Loyal North Lancashire Regiment. Formerly No 81355 Training Reserve Battalion. Born Denby. Son of Mr and Mrs John Depledge, Birks Terrace, Millhouse, Penistone. Enlisted Halifax. Lived Huddersfield. Killed in action, 28.4.1918. Has no known grave. Commemorated **TYNE COT MEMORIAL TO THE MISSING.**

DEWHIRST, GEORGE DYSON. Private. No 240678. 2/5th Battalion Duke of Wellington's Regiment. Born Lockwood 25.12.1893. Son of John William and Jane Dewhirst, 57 Manchester Street, Huddersfield. Educated Rashcliffe Church of England School. Employed as a concreter's labourer by Mr John Cooke of Folly Hall. Enlisted October 1914. Reported missing, presumed killed, at the Battle of Bullecourt, 3.5.1917, aged 24 years. Has no known grave. Commemorated **ARRAS MEMORIAL TO THE MISSING.** ROH:- Huddersfield Drill Hall.

DICKINSON, FRANK. Private. No G/52463. 2nd Battalion Middlesex Regiment. Formerly No 41904 York and Lancaster Regiment. Born New Mill. Married. Lived 43 Mearhouse Bank, Jackson Bridge, Huddersfield. Killed in action, 1.8.1917. Has no known grave. Commemorated **MENIN GATE MEMORIAL TO THE MISSING.** ROH:- New Mill Working Men's Club; Fulstone War Memorial.

DIGMAN, WILLIAM JOHN. Gunner. No 4/25843. Royal Field Artillery. Married, with three children. Lived 20 Grange Avenue, Marsden. Employed as a teamer by the Marsden Equitable Industrial Society Limited. Attended Marsden Wesleyan Church and was a teacher in the Sunday School. Closely associated with the local branch of the Sons of Temperance. Enlisted May 1915. Embarked for France in December, 1915. At the time of his death was employed as a Groom with the General Staff. Killed in action, 9.4.1918, aged 32 years. Buried. **HAVERSKERQUE BRITISH CEMETERY.** Grave location:- Special Memorial No 2. ROH:- Marsden War Memorial. His wife received the following letter from the offices of the British Red Cross Society, 18 Carlton House Terrace, London, dated 9.5.1918. The letter read as follows:- *'With reference to your enquiry for details of your husband's death - we have just received the following information from the Chaplain at the 33rd Casualty Clearing Station. He says that Driver Dignam was admitted to the hospital severely wounded in the head and back and although he had every possible care and attention he died before any operation could be performed. He was quite unconscious and therefore could not speak or have any messages. I do trust it will be some small consolation for you to know that he did not suffer. He was buried in the British Military Cemetery at Haverskerque near St. Venant (about 5 miles west of Merville). A wooden cross marks his grave with his name, number and regiment enscribed upon it. I feel for you so deeply in your sorrow but you must indeed be proud of your husband who gave his life so bravely for his country. With sincere sympathy, Miss G. de Stein, for the Earl of Lucan.'*

DISKIN, JOHN. Private. No 10945. 8th Battalion Duke of Wellington's Regiment. Born Longwood 4.7.1884. Son of the late Michael and Annie Diskin of Outlane and brother of Mr W. Diskin, of Tram Terminus, Outlane. Educated at Longwood Church School and Outlane Council School. Employed as a woollen spinner. Was a well known cornet player and played with the Slaithwaite Brass Band. Enlisted August 1914. Killed in action in the attack on Tekke Tepe Ridge, Suvla, Gallipoli, 9.8.1915, aged 30. Has no known grave. Commemorated **HELLES MEMORIAL TO THE MISSING, GALLIPOLLI.** ROH:- Bethel United Methodist Chapel, Outlane.

DITCHBURN, JAMES BENJAMIN. Private. No 2631. 'A' Company, 1/5th Battalion Duke of Wellington's Regiment. Only son of Mr and Mrs James Ditchburn of 'Overdale', Park Drive, Huddersfield who was one of the directors of Joseph Lumb and Son, worsted spinners, Centre Mills, Folly Hall, Huddersfield. Educated at Almondbury Grammar School and Huddersfield College School. Employed by Messrs Lumbs to learn the textile business. Spent two years in Australia acquiring a knowledge of wool growing and spinning. Had served for five years with the local Territorials and re-enlisted at the outbreak of the war. Was wounded in the head, 10.7.1915. He was admitted to No 23 Canadian General Hospital at Etaples. A telegram was sent to his parents in Huddersfield, informing them of the seriousness of his condition and Mr G. D. Moxon embarked for France to visit Private Ditchburn and arrived there before he died, on 24.7.1915, aged 22 years. His body was brought home to Huddersfield and he was buried with full military honours in **EDGERTON CEMETERY, HUDDERSFIELD.** Grave location:- 30. 'C', 199. ROH:- Almondbury Grammar School; Huddersfield College School; All Saints Church, Paddock; Huddersfield Drill Hall.

DOBSON, SYKES, Private. No 31905. North Staffordshire Regiment. Born Kirkheaton 14.3.1898. Son of Martha Ann Dobson, 113 May Street, Crosland Moor. Educated at Milnsbridge and Crosland Moor Church Schools. Employed as a woollen spinner. Enlisted 6.11.1916. Reported wounded and taken prisoner by the Germans, 25.3.1918. Reported died between 25.3.1918 and 25.6.1918, aged 20. **COMMEMORATED ON ARRAS MEMORIAL TO THE MISSING.** ROH:- St. Barnabas Church, Crosland Moor.

DOBSON, WILLIAM VICTOR. Private. No 23396. 8th Battalion Duke of Wellington's Regiment. Born Thirsk 7.8.1887. Educated at Thirsk Board School. Employed as a coach painter by Messrs Rippon Brothers. Husband of Beatrice Dobson, 15 Scholes Road, Birkby. Enlisted 3.8.1916. Killed in action, 11.8.1917, aged 30 years. Has no known grave. Commemorated **MENIN GATE MEMORIAL TO THE MISSING.** ROH:- Fartown and Birkby War Memorial.

DODSON, ALFRED. Private. No 40969. 8th Battalion Lincolnshire Regiment. Formerly No 20546 Duke of Wellington's Regiment. Born 20 Rose Cottage, Hall Bower, Huddersfield, 22.4.1883. Son of Phillis Ann Dodson, 4 Waingate, Berry Brow. Educated at Berry Brow Council School. Employed as a healder and twister-in at Crosland Factory. Single. Attended Hall Bower Sunday School. Enlisted 23.5.1916. Wounded 22.6.1917 near Arras. Killed in action near Ypres, 23.12.1917, aged 34 years. Buried **HOOGE CRATER CEMETERY.** Grave location:- Plot 9a, Row C, Grave 8. ROH:- Armitage Bridge War Memorial.

DODSON, BEN. Private. No 57800. 1/5th Battalion York and Lancaster Regiment. Born Cross Lane, Marsh, 10.4.1886. Son of Ann Dodson, 4 Cross Cottages, Marsh. Attended Holy Trinity Church of England School, Huddersfield. Employed as a firer. Husband of Beatrice Dodson, 162 New Hey Road, Oakes. Enlisted 28.1.1917. Wounded 13.10.1918. Died of wounds, 14.10.1918, aged 32. Buried **QUEANT COMMUNAL CEMETERY BRITISH EXTENSION.** Grave location:- Row E, Grave 3. ROH:- St. Stephen's Church, Lindley.

DODSON, PERCIVAL. Private. No 3388. 1/5th Battalion Duke of Wellington's Regiment. Born Farnley Tyas 27.7.1895. Son of Shaw and Clara Dodson, 107 Thornton Lodge Road, Huddersfield. Educated at Mount Pleasant Council School. Employed as a piecer by Messrs Allen Priest and Sons, of Lockwood. Was a scholar at Mount Pleasant Sunday School, Lockwood. Single. Enlisted at the outbreak of the war. Embarked for France in Apri, 1915. Was shot by a sniper on 18.11.1915, aged 20 years. Buried **TALANA FARM CEMETERY.** Grave location:- Plot 4, Row F, Grave 13. ROH:- St. Stephen's Church, Rashcliffe; Mount Pleasant Chapel, Lockwood; Huddersfield Drill Hall.

DODSON, TEDDY. Private. No 267417. 9th Battalion Duke of Wellington's Regiment. Born Longroyd Bridge 2.10.1893. Son of Sam and Mary Elizabeth Dodson, 31 Quaker Row, Luck Lane, Marsh. Attended Holy Trinity Church of England School, Huddersfield. Employed as a general dealer by his father. Single. Attended the Marsh United Methodist Church and the Queen Street Mission. Enlisted 24.1.1916. Embarked for France in June, 1916, and was admitted to hospital in September, 1916, suffering from trench fever. Killed in action near Arras, 18.5.1917, aged 23 years. Has no known grave. Commemorated **ARRAS MEMORIAL TO THE MISSING.** ROH:- Marsh War Memorial.

DOLLIVE, JOHN EDWARD. Private. No 42373. 20th Battalion (Tyneside Scottish) Northumberland Fusiliers. Born Upperthong, Holmfirth. Son of Mr and Mrs John Dollive, 18 Upperthong, Holmfirth. Employed as a carding engineer by Messrs Allen Priest of Lockwood. Was an active member of the Holmfirth Harriers Athletic Club and won five medals. Attended Upperthong Church and Institute. Enlisted June 1916. Embarked for France October, 1916.

Wounded in December, 1916, which required several months treatment in hospital in England. Returned to France in July, 1917, and was severely wounded in the back and buttock on 30.8.1917. Admitted to No 13 Casualty Clearing Station, where he died of his wounds on 31.8.1917, aged 26 years. Buried **TINCOURT NEW BRITISH CEMETERY**. Grave location:- Plot 1, Row F, Grave 21. ROH:- Upperthong War Memorial.

DONKERSLEY, REYNOLD, MC. 2nd Lieutenant. 2/5th Battalion West Yorkshire Regiment. Formerly Boy Bugler and Drummer, 1/5th Battalion Duke of Wellington's Regiment. Born 39 Bradford Road, Huddersfield, 1.9.1894. Second son of John W. and Mary Louise Donkersley, 144 Northgate, Almondbury. Educated Almondbury Council School. Employed as a tailor by Mr Ephraim Dyson of Northgate, Huddersfield. Enlisted, 31.9.1914, as a Private and attained the rank of Sergeant during 1915. He was gazetted Second Lieutenant in November, 1917, and posted to the West Yorkshire Regiment. Was wounded, 20.5.1918, in the right arm and for his gallantry on this occasion was awarded the Military Cross. The offical citation in the London Gazette of 16.9.1918 reads, *'for conspicuous gallantry and devotion to duty in command of a fighting patrol sent out to obtain an identification. Two hostile sentries were found to be on the alert. He disposed of one of them himself but the other escaped. A large enemy party then rushed forward to reinforce the post and hand to hand fighting ensued in which he was wounded. He held to his ground and persisted in his endeavour to obtain an identification until forced by superior numbers to retire which he succeeded in doing after having inflicted heavy casualties on the enemy. By his fine tenacity of purpose and cool leadership he set a fine example to his men.'* Killed in action near Rheims, 20.7.1918, aged 23. Buried **MARFAUX BRITISH CEMETERY**. Grave location:- Plot 1, Row F, Grave 11. ROH:- Almondbury War Memorial; memorial in Almondbury Cemetery.

DONKERSLEY, WILLIAM. Private. No 240003. 1/5th Battalion Duke of Wellington's Regiment. Born Lockwood. Son of Frank and Mary Donkersley, 36 Yew Green, Lockwood. Employed as a weaver. Enlisted 4.8.1914. Wounded in both legs, 26.12.1917, and died of his wounds at No 10 Casualty Clearing Station, 27.12.1917, aged 29. Buried **LIJSSENTHOEK MILITARY CEMETERY**. Grave location:- Plot 27, Row CC, Grave 1a. ROH:- Rehoboth Baptist Chapel; 'Rising Sun' Public House, Crosland Hill; St. Barnabas Church, Crosland Moor; Huddersfield Drill Hall.

DONNELLAN, WILLIAM. Private. No 240649. 2/5th Battalion Duke of Wellington's Regiment. Born Castlegate, Huddersfield, 19.10.1898. Educated St. Patrick's Roman Catholic School. Employed as a mill hand by Mr T. A. Cocking, Waterloo Mills. Lived 27 Gelder Terrace, Moldgreen. Married. Enlisted October 1914. Reported missing, presumed killed, at the Battle of Bullecourt, 3.5.1917, aged 19 years. Has no known grave. Commemorated **ARRAS MEMORIAL TO THE MISSING**. ROH:- Moldgreen; Huddersfield Drill Hall.

DOOSEY, JOHN HENRY. Private. No 241358. 1/7th Battalion Duke of Wellington's Regiment. Born Kirkgate, Huddersfield, 11.11.1896. Educated St. Patrick's Roman Catholic School. Employed as a cloth presser by Messrs T. A.Nicholl and Sons, dyers, of Folly Hall. Husband of Edith Doosey, 5 Knight Street, Northgate, Huddersfield. Enlisted 11.10.1914. Killed in action near Cambrai, 11.10.1918, aged 33 years. Buried **WELLINGTON CEMETERY**. Grave location:- Plot 2, Row C, Grave 7. ROH:- Huddersfield Drill Hall.

DOUGHERTY, JOHN EDWARD (JACK). Private. No 4/25843. 6th Battalion Royal Irish Regiment. Formerly 1/5th Battalion Duke of Wellington's Regiment. Born Military Barracks, Kilkenny, Ireland. Son of Company Sergeant Major Edward Dougherty (also of the Royal Irish Regiment) and Mrs Dougherty, 113 Bradford Road, Huddersfield. Educated Moldgreen Council School and St. Paul's School, Huddersfield. Employed as a brass finisher by Messrs Hopkinsons of Birkby. Enlisted in the Huddersfield Territorials at the outbreak of the war, 4.8.1914. Transferred to the Royal Irish Regiment to serve alongside his father in December, 1914. Killed in action at Ginchy, 9.9.1916, aged 22 years. Has no known grave. Commemorated **THIEPVAL MEMORIAL TO THE MISSING**. ROH:- Fartown and Birkby War Memorial.

DOUGHTY, LAWRENCE. Private. No 203406. 2/4th Battalion Duke of Wellington's Regiment. Born 3 Ramsden's Yard, Charles Street, Huddersfield, 29.10.1894. Educated at St. Patrick's Roman Catholic School. Employed as a ring cropper by Messrs Alfred Sykes and Company, rug manufacturers, of Viaduct Street, Huddersfield. Single. Lived with his sister Miss M. Dougherty at 3 Ramsden's Yard. Enlisted 4.8.1914. Killed in action at the Battle of Cambrai, 25.11.1917, aged 23 years. Has no known grave. Commemorated **CAMBRAI MEMORIAL TO THE MISSING.**

DOUGLAS, ARCHIE. Rifleman. No R/19149. 13th Battalion King's Royal Rifle Corps. Born Stalybridge, Cheshire. Lived Colne Terrace, Manchester Road, Linthwaite. Employed as a piecer by the Colne Valley Tweed Company. Played cricket with the Linthwaite Hall cricket team. Enlisted 1915. Killed in action, 21.8.1918, aged 22 years. Buried **DOUCHY-LES-AYETTE BRITISH CEMETERY.** Grave location:- Plot 4, Row G, Grave 22. ROH:- Linthwaite War Memorial.

DOWNS, WILSON. Private. No 32121. 2nd Battalion West Yorkshire Regiment. Educated at Rashcliffe Church School. Employed as a brewer's labourer by Messrs Bentley and Shaw Limited, Lockwood Brewery. Husband of Florence Downs, 108 Rashcliffe Hill, Folly Hall, Lockwood, Huddersfield. Played cricket with the Primrose Hill Cricket Club. Enlisted 13.5.1916. Died of wounds at No 2/2nd London Casualty Clearing Station, 1.1.1917, aged 29 years. Buried **GROVE TOWN CEMETERY.** Grave Location:- Plot 2, Row J, Grave 25. ROH:- St. Stephen's Church, Rashcliffe.

DOWNSBOROUGH, SMITH. Private. No 33664. 1/8th Battalion Royal Warwickshire Regiment. Formerly No 22227 Army Service Corps. Born Manor Street, Halifax, 27.12.1884. Son of Rosina Downsborough, 131 Wellington Street, Oakes, Huddersfield. Educated Oakes Council School. Employed as a steam roller driver by the Huddersfield Corporation. Single. Enlisted 6.8.1914. Suffered serious abdominal wounds at Beaurevoir, 6.10.1918, and died of his wounds at No 58 (West Riding) Casualty Clearing Station on 17.10.1918, aged 33 years. Buried **TINCOURT NEW BRITISH CEMETERY.** Grave location:- Plot 6, Row F, Grave 43.

ROH:- Oakes Baptist Church; St. Stephen's Church, Lindley; Huddersfield Corporation Roll; commemorated in Salendine Nook Baptist Chapel yard, F214.

DRAKE, HARRY. Private. No 235327. 4th Battalion Lincolnshire Regiment. Formerly No 205246 West Yorkshire Regiment. Born Golcar. Son of Joshua and Jane Drake, 3 Stanley Place, Golcar. Employed by Messrs Drake and Company, waste dealers, of Manor Mills, Golcar. Attended St. John's Church, Golcar and was a member of the Golcar Conservative Club. Enlisted April 1917 and embarked for France in July 1917. Wounded in the left arm and shoulder on 14.4.1918 and was admitted to Liverpool Hospital where he died on 1.6.1918, aged 31 years. Buried **St. JOHN'S CHURCHYARD, GOLCAR.** Grave location:- A, North-West, 70. ROH:- St. John's Church, Golcar.

DRAKE, PERCY. Sapper. No 126287. Inland Water Transport Royal Engineers. Born Kirkheaton 4.1.1880. Son of William Medley Drake and Sarah Ann Drake, Finley House, 34 Springdale Avenue, Huddersfield. Employed as an insurance agent for the Pearl Assurance Company. Attended the Paddock Wesleyan Church and was a member of the choir. For some years he was secretary of the Sunday School and was an ardent worker for the Band of Hope. Husband of Lily Drake, 34 Lowergate, Longwood, Huddersfield. Enlisted 4.9.1916. Died in the Minster Hospital, Ramsgate of a cerebral haemorrhage, 4.5.1917, aged 37 years. Buried **LINDLEY WESLEYAN METHODIST CHAPEL YARD.** Grave location:- J, 46. ROH:- Longwood War Memorial; Shared Church Paddock.

DRANSFIELD, ERNEST. Private. No 241302. 1/5th Battalion Duke of Wellington's Regiment. Born Crosland Hill, 11.10.1885. Son of Mr and Mrs Tom Dransfield, 8 Quarry Road, Crosland Hill. Educated Milnsbridge National School. Employed as a teaser by Messrs J. Wimpenny and Company, Linthwaite. Enlisted 1.8.1915. Died of wounds at No 10 Casualty Clearing Station, 18.11.1917, aged 32 years. Buried **LIJSSENTHOEK MILITARY CEMETERY.** Grave location:- Plot 27, Row AA, Grave 6a. (Brother of Private **NORMAN DRANSFIELD**, killed in action, 18.4.1915, q.v.). ROH:- 'Rising Sun' Public House, Crosland Hill; Huddersfield Drill Hall.

DRANSFIELD, ERNEST. Private. No 30710. 1st Battalion Lancashire Fusiliers. Born Thurlestone, Yorkshire. Son of John and Sarah Dransfield of The Green, Shepley. Employed by Messrs Firth Brothers, Shepley New Mills. Single. Killed in action, 10.6.1918, aged 35 years. Has no known grave. Commemorated **PLOEGSTEERT MEMORIAL TO THE MISSING.** ROH:- Shepley War Memorial.

DRANSFIELD, FRED. Ordinary Seaman. No J/61410. Royal Navy. *HMS Partridge*. Only son of Mr and Mrs James Dransfield, 47 Southern Road, Milnsbridge. Employed by Mr Sam Hirst, cloth finisher, of Milnsbridge. Attended Milnsbridge Baptist Sunday School. Taught to swim by his father who was the instructor at New Street Council School. Enlisted in the Navy, 6.11.1916, and went on board *HMS Partridge* after six week's training. Lost at sea when the destroyer was sunk in a convoy disaster in the North Sea, 12.12.1917, aged 19 years. Originally buried in **GULEN CHURCHYARD, NORWAY** but in 1961 was reinterred in **FREDRIKSTAD MILITARY CEMETERY, NORWAY** (80 Kilometres south of Oslo). Grave Location:- 3, A, Col. 1–16. (Three other men from Huddersfield were aboard *HMS Partridge* and were drowned when the ship was sunk, they were Able Seaman **DONALD HAIGH, WALKER BAMFORTH** and Ordinary Seaman **SHEARD WINDLE,** q.v.).

DRANSFIELD, GEORGE EDWARD, DCM MM. Sergeant. No 202990. 9th Battalion Duke of Wellington's Regiment. Son of Sydney and Mary Jane Dransfield, 19 Whitestone Lane, Hillhouse, Huddersfield. Employed as a finisher by Messrs James Haigh Limited, Colne Road. Was a keen cricketer and footballer and played in the Buxton Road Sunday School team. Killed in action, 12.10.1918, aged 22 years. Awarded the DCM. posthumously in June, 1919, for the following act, *'During the operations on the 18th September 1918, in the attack on Cavalry Trench he went ahead of his Company into our own barrage in order to locate two enemy machine guns which were causing a lot of trouble to his Company. He located and silenced them by killing the two gunners working them and had held up the remainder of the crew who had come up out of a dugout until the remainder of his Company arrived. After his objective was gained he went forward under very heavy machine gun fire and ascertained the dispositions of the enemy bringing back most important information. His courage and daring behaviour greatly inspired the men of his Company.'* Buried **MONTAY-NEUVILLY ROAD CEMETERY.** Grave location:- Plot 1, Row E. Grave 20. ROH:- Fartown and Birkby War Memorial; St. Andrew's Church, Leeds Road, Huddersfield.

DRANSFIELD, NORMAN. Private. No 10682. 2nd Battalion Duke of Wellington's Regiment. Born Crosland Hill. Son of Mr and Mrs Tom Dransfield, 8 Quarry Road, Crosland Hill. Educated Milnsbridge National School. Employed as a spinner. Husband of Harriet Dransfield, 54 Handel Street, Golcar. Enlisted 20.8.1913. Killed in action at Hill 60, 18.4.1915, aged 23 years. Has no known grave. Commemorated **MENIN GATE MEMORIAL TO THE MISSING.** (Brother of Private **ERNEST DRANSFIELD,** who died of wounds 18.11.1917 q.v.). ROH:- 'Rising Sun' Public House, Crosland Hill; St. John's Church, Golcar.

DRINKWATER, ISAAC WALTER. Private. No 6711. 1/5th Battalion Duke of Wellington's Regiment. Born Milnsbridge. Son of Mr and Mrs Harry Drinkwater of Wingate Avenue, Cowlersley Lane, Milnsbridge. Employed as a plumber by Messrs T. Allinson Limited, of Milnsbridge. Lived in Morecambe for five years and was a choirboy at Morecambe Parish Church. Returned to Milnsbridge in 1911. Enlisted 27.1.1916. Embarked for France 23.8.1916. Died from gunshot wounds to the head at No 2 Stationary Hospital, Abbeville, 24.9.1916, aged 19 years. Buried **ABBEVILLE COMMUNAL CEMETERY EXTENSION.** Grave location:- Plot 1, Row C, Grave 9. ROH:- Huddersfield Drill Hall.

DRIVER, FRED. Private. No S/40348. 1st Battalion Queen's Own Cameron Highlanders. Born Kilner Bank, Moldgreen, 3.10.1892. Son of Mr George Harry Driver, 35 High Royd, Moldgreen. Employed as a bookbinder by Messrs Preston Brothers and Company, Fox Street, Huddersfield. Single. Enlisted January 1916. Embarked for France July 1916. Killed in action, 1.12.1916, aged 24 years. Buried **OVILLERS MILITARY CEMETERY.** Grave location:- Plot 14, Row Q, Grave 9. ROH:- Moldgreen; Christ Church, Moldgreen.

DRURY, JOHN. Air Mechanic 1st Class. No 21960. No 6 Stores Depot, Royal Air Force. Formerly Duke of Wellington's Regiment. Born Stocks Buildings, Northgate, Huddersfield, 26.6.1892. Educated St. Patrick's Roman Catholic School. Employed as a brass turner. Husband of Laura Drury, 84 Luck Lane, Marsh, Huddersfield. Enlisted 20.6.1912 in the local Territorial battalion. Died at Connaught Hospital, Aldershot, 28.10.1918. Buried **ALDERSHOT MILITARY CEMETERY.** Grave location:- R, 352.

DUCE, ERNEST. Private. No 20410. 1st West Riding Divisonal Cyclist Company, Army Cyclist Corps. Formerly No 133 West Riding Divisional Cyclist Corps. Born Stoney Lane, Taylor Hill, Huddersfield, 22.8.1895. Son of the late Herbert and Mrs Duce. Educated at Lockwood Church of England School. Employed by Messrs B. Vickerman and Sons Limited of Taylor Hill as an apprentice loom tuner. Single. Enlisted 6.11.1915. Killed in action at the Canal du Nord near Cambrai, 4.9.1918, aged 23 years. Buried **ONTARIO CEMETERY, SAINS-LES-MARQUION.** Grave location:- Plot 1, Row B, Grave 14. ROH:- Emmanuel Church, Lockwood; Taylor Hill Primitive Methodist Church.

DUFFY, CLIFFORD. Private. No 21147. 9th Battalion West Yorkshire Regiment. Born Moss Street, Newsome Road, Huddersfield, 12.8.1893. Son of Alice Duffy, 44 Thomas Street, Thornton Lodge, Huddersfield. Educated at Rashcliffe Church School. Employed as a goods porter by the London and North Western Railway at Huddersfield railway station. Single. Enlisted 22.5.1915. Killed in action during the Battle of the Somme, 8.9.1916, aged 23 years. Buried **BLIGHTY VALLEY CEMETERY.** Grave location:- Plot 1, Row E, Grave 6. ROH:- London and North Western Railway Roll.

DUNKERLEY, JOHN RICHARD. Private. No 200743. 5th Battalion Durham Light Infantry. Born Swan Lane, Lockwood, 28.8.1888. Educated Lockwood Church School. Employed as a road sweeper. Husband of Mabel Dunkerley, 268 Whitehead Road, Primrose Hill, Huddersfield. Enlisted 28.7.1916. Taken prisoner, 26.3.1918, and returned to England on 25.11.1918. Died of pneumonia in St. George's Hospital, London, 2.12.1918, aged 30. Buried **LOCKWOOD CEMETERY, HUDDERSFIELD.** Grave location:- A, 207. ROH:- Lockwood Baptist Church.

DUNN, JOHN. Private. No 15545. 10th Battalion The Yorkshire Regiment. Lived Jackson Bridge, Holmfirth. Served with the Briitsh Expeditionary Force. Was at the Retreat from Mons and the Battle of Loos. Discharged in February, 1916, with gas poisoning, from which he died at home, 1.10.1916, aged 40 years. Buried **CHRIST CHURCH CHURCHYARD EXTENSION, NEW MILL.** Grave location:- G, 387.

DUNSTAN, ALBERT. Lance Corporal. No 22676. 20th Battalion The King's (Liverpool Regiment). Born Rotherham. Lived Meltham. Killed in action, 20.10.1916. Has no known grave. Commemorated **THIEPVAL MEMORIAL TO THE MISSING.** ROH:- St. Bartholomew's Church, Meltham; Christ Church, Helme.

DURHAM, JOHN ALFRED. Private. No 40811. 23rd Battalion (Tyneside Scottish) Northumberland Fusiliers. Born Cliffe, near Selby, 11.8.1891. Son of Frank and Sarah Durham, 62 Meltham Road, Lockwood. Educated Mount Pleasant Board School, Lockwood. Employed by Mr W .H. Charlesworth, greengrocer and fruiterer, of Lockwood. Single. Enlisted 29.4.1916. Killed in action at Arras, 26.2.1917, aged 25 years. Buried **FAUBOURG D'AMIENS CEMETERY, ARRAS.** Grave location:- Plot 2, Row D, Grave 31. ROH:- Emmanuel Church, Lockwood; memorial in Lockwood Cemetery.

DURKIN, JOHN. Corporal. No 240216. 2/5th Battalion Duke of Wellington's Regiment. Born 56 Northumberland Street, Huddersfield. Nephew of Miss Margaret Connolly, 11 Hawk Street, Huddersfield. Educated St. Patrick's Roman Catholic School. Employed as a weaver at Messrs T. and H. Blamires Limited, Leeds Road, Huddersfield. Single. Enlisted in the local Territorial battalion before the outbreak of war, on 13.6.1912. Reported missing at the Battle of Bullecourt, 3.5.1917, and afterwards presumed killed on that date. Has no known grave. Commemorated **ARRAS MEMORIAL TO THE MISSING.** ROH:- Huddersfield Drill Hall; Commemorated on his parents' headstone in Edgerton Cemetery, Huddersfield.

DURRANS, FRED. Lance Sergeant. No 2845. 1/5th Battalion Duke of Wellington's Regiment. Born Hartshead 29.11.1883. Son of Arthur and Elizabeth Durrans, 16 Wellington Street, Oakes, Huddersfield. Educated at Oakes Board School. Employed as a card maker by Messrs Joseph Sykes Brothers, Acre Mills, Lindley. Married. Enlisted 4.9.1914. Wounded in the thigh on 3.9.1916. Died of wounds, 14.9.1916, at No 14 General Hospital, Wimereux. Buried **WIMEREUX COMMUNAL CEMETERY.** Grave location:- Plot 1, Row Q, Grave 9a. ROH:- St. Stephen's Church, Lindley; Huddersfield Drill Hall; memorial in Lindley Churchyard.

DURRANS, GEORGE. Private. No 29/287. 9th Battalion Northumberland Fusiliers. Born Cleckheaton. Son of William and Alice Durrans, 7 King Street, Lindley. Before the outbreak of war worked as a compositor at the 'Worker' office, Market Street, Huddersfield. Attended the Lindley Church Young Men's Bible Class. Single. Enlisted April, 1916. Killed in action, 9.11.1916, aged 32 years. Has no known grave. Commemorated **THIEPVAL MEMORIAL TO THE MISSING.** ROH:- St. Stephen's Church, Lindley.

DURRANT, GEORGE FREDRICK. Corporal. No 8728. 2nd Battalion Manchester Regiment. Born Guildford, Surrey. Son of John and Elizabeth Durrant of Magnolia Villa, Manor Road, Guildford. Husband of Olive Annie Durrant. Employed by the Huddersfield Board of Guardians as a bookkeeper at Deanhouse Institution; (His wife was also on the staff at Deanhouse). As a reservist he was called to the colours on 4.8.1914. Reported missing at the Battle of Mons, 26.8.1914, aged 26 years. Has no known grave. Commemorated **LA FERTE-SOUS-JOUARRE MEMORIAL TO THE MISSING.** ROH:- Netherthong War Memorial.

DYCHE, WILFRED HAROLD. Private. No 24119. 2/5th Battalion Duke of Wellington's Regiment. Son of Mr and Mrs A. G. Dyche, 'The Butcher's Arms', Netherton. Attended Netherton Wesleyan Sunday School. Employed by Messrs J. Thomas and Sons of Longwood. Enlisted April 1915. Killed in action at the Battle of Cambrai, 20.11.1917, aged 24 years. Has no known grave. Commemorated **CAMBRAI MEMORIAL TO THE MISSING.** ROH:- South Crosland and Netherton; Huddersfield Drill Hall.

DYER, FRANK MORGAN. Corporal. No 5/2602. 1/5th Battalion Duke of Wellington's Regiment. Born Abergavenny, Monmouth. Lived Huddersfield. Employed as a locomotive cleaner by the London and North Western Railway Company at Huddersfield Station. Killed in action, 23.8.1915. Buried **ARTILLERY WOOD CEMETERY.** Grave location: Plot 2, Row A, Grave 14. ROH:- London and North Western Railway Company Roll.

DYSON, ARNOLD. Private. No 41985. 6th Battalion Lincolnshire Regiment. Born 554 South View, New Hey Road, Mount, Outlane. Son of Fred and Ada Dyson. Educated Crosland Moor Council School. Employed as a piecer by Messrs Liddle and Brearley, Stanley Mills, Marsh. Single. Enlisted 17.5.1916. Killed in action, 6.11.1918, aged 20 years. Buried **ROISIN COMMUNAL CEMETERY.** Grave location:- Row A, Grave 13. ROH:- Longwood War Memorial.

DYSON, ARNOLD GARSIDE. Private. No 2844. 1/5th Battalion Duke of Wellington's Regiment. Born Lindley 5.3.1895. Son of Mr and Mrs Joe Dyson, 11 Norman Terrace, Lidget Street, Lindley, Huddersfield. Educated Oakes Council School. Employed as a wire drawer by Messrs Joseph Sykes, Acre Mills, Lindley. Single. Enlisted 3.9.1914. Wounded near Ypres, 8.11.1915. Died of his wounds at No 17 Casualty Clearing Station, 10.11.1915, aged 20 years. Buried **LIJSSENTHOEK MILITARY CEMETERY.** Grave location:- Plot 4, Row B, Grave 7a. His parents received the following letter from Nurse N. Wharton, Sister in charge at the C.C.S., which reads as follows, *'It is with much regret and the deepest sympathy that I send you very sad news. Your son passed quietly away yesterday afternoon. He never rallied after admission but got gradually worse. He was too ill to speak or send any message. He will be laid to rest in our soldiers' cemetery and a cross bearing his name, number and regiment will mark his grave. He will have a military funeral and every respect will be shown him. He bore his sufferings very patiently and never made a murmur.'*
The Rev. J. Henry Martin, Wesleyan Chaplain attached to the 44th Field Ambulance also wrote, *'You will be sorry to hear of the death of your brave laddie, Private A. G. Dyson. I was sent for yesterday but it was too late. He was badly wounded in the chest and there was very little*

hope from the first. He very bravely bore his pain. I was in the Field Ambulance on duty when he died at the Casualty Clearing Station some miles away. He had no pain I gather and my friend, the Rev. J. H. Preston was with him when he died. I buried him yesterday in a beautiful place beside a wayside road with a hedge around.' ROH:-. St. Stephen's Church, Lindley; Lindley Zion Wesleyan Methodist Chapel; Huddersfield Drill Hall.

DYSON, ARTHUR, MM. Lance Corporal. No 22793. 10th Battalion Duke of Wellington's Regiment. Son of William and Emma Elizabeth Dyson, of Hey Lane Farm, Scammonden. Embarked for France at Christmas, 1916. Was awarded the Military Medal for *'taking command of his platoon and reorganising it during heavy shellfire.'* He was reported missing, presumed killed, 17.10.1917, aged 23 years. Has no known grave. Commemorated **TYNE COT MEMORIAL TO THE MISSING.**

DYSON, ARTHUR. Private. No 24467. 2nd Battalion Duke of Wellington's Regiment. Born Hope Street, Deadwaters, Huddersfield, 7.2.1897. Son of John William and Eliza Dyson, 94 East View, Springdale Street, Huddersfield. Educated Rashcliffe Church of England School. Employed by Messrs George Mallinson and Sons Limited, Spring Grove Mills, Linthwaite. Attended Buxton Road Wesleyan Sunday School all his life. Was also a member of the Buxton Road Wesleyan Cricket Club. Single. Enlisted 29.3.1916. Killed in action near Ypres, 10.10.1917, aged 20 years. Buried **POELCAPELLE BRITISH CEMETERY.** Grave location:- Plot 42, Row C, Grave 13. ROH:- St. Stephen's Church, Rashcliffe.

DYSON, CHARLES. Captain. 8th Battalion (Leeds Rifles) West Yorkshire Regiment. Son of Hiram and Ruth Dyson, of Salendine Nook, Huddersfield. Husband of Gwendoline Dyson of Park Ryding, Honley. Educated at Huddersfield College School and Charterhouse Public School. He then went to Hertford College, Oxford, which he left in 1899. He then joined the firm of Messrs Joseph Dyson and Sons, of Milnsbridge, and became a director. He had been a member of the Oxford University Volunteers and enlisted October, 1914, in the West Yorkshire Regiment. Embarked for France, 11.1.1917, and was killed by a high explosive shell whilst acting as second in command of his Battalion on Good Friday, 6.4.1917, aged 36 years, at Ecoust-St.-Mein. Buried **H.A.C. CEMETERY, ECOUST-St.-MEIN.** Grave location:- Plot 4, Row B, Grave 1. ROH:- Honley War Memorial.

DYSON, EDWARD. Private. No 43509. 4th Battalion Bedfordshire Regiment. Formerly No 242115 East Surrey Regiment. Born Honley. Son of Law and Hannah Dyson, 'Shoulder of Mutton Inn', Slaithwaite. Educated Longwood Grammar School. Was a member of the Slaithwaite Conservative Club and the Cricket Club. Employed in the office of Messrs Pearson Brothers, Commercial Mills, Slaithwaite. Enlisted February 1917. After serving in France for twelve months he came home on leave for seven weeks, before he was killed in action on 9.11.1918, aged 20. Buried **BOUGNIES COMMUNAL CEMETERY.** Grave location:- North Corner. His parents received the following letter of sympathy from his Captain, *'Your son had served with my Company for many months and I had grown to look upon him as one of my old hands. He met his death so gallantly too, advancing on a beaten enemy on November 9th and was killed by a shell. He was buried at Quievy le Petit about six miles south of Mons. Your son held a responsible position of No 1 of the Lewis gun section and he carried his gun to the last.'* ROH:- St. James Church, Slaithwaite; Slaithwaite War Memorial.

DYSON, EDWARD. Private. No 41567. 24th Battalion (Tyneside Irish) Northumberland Fusiliers. Formerly No 10587 2nd Battalion Duke of Wellington's Regiment. Born Upperhead Row 29.4.1896. Son of Willie and Betsy Dyson, 37 St. Andrew's Road, Turnbridge, Huddersfield. Educated Moldgreen Board School. Employed as a core-maker. Enlisted 19.6.1913. Embarked for France in September, 1914. Had been invalided home on two occasions suffering from trench fever. Killed in action near Arras, 28.4.1917, aged 21 years. Buried **SUNKEN ROAD CEMETERY, FAMPOUX.** Grave location:- Plot 1, Row A, Grave 4

DYSON, EDWIN. Private. No 7818. 2nd Battalion The Royal Scots (Lothian Regiment). Born Elgin, Scotland. Lived Huddersfield. Killed in action, 14.9.1914. Has no known grave. Commemorated **LA FERTE-SOUS-JOUARRE MEMORIAL TO THE MISSING.**

DYSON, E. Private. No 142003. 8th Company Royal Army Medical Corps. Died at home, 16.3.1919. Buried **HOLY TRINITY BURIAL GROUND, HOLMFIRTH.** Grave location:- South, 5, 100.

DYSON, FRANK. Private. No 351039. 22nd Battalion Durham Light Infantry. Born Meltham. Son of Tom and Dinah Dyson of Bank View, Blackmoorfoot, Linthwaite. Killed in action, 26.3.1918, aged 22 years. Has no known grave. Commemorated **POZIERES MEMORIAL TO THE MISSING.** ROH:- Linthwaite War Memorial.

DYSON, FRANK CROSSLEY. Private. No 240948. 2/5th Battalion Duke of Wellington's Regiment. Born Pogwell Farm, Dalton Green, Huddersfield, 27.2.1896. Son of Tom Edward and Martha Dyson, 3 Dalton Green Lane, Huddersfield. Educated Kirkheaton Church of England School. Employed by Mr Sam Leeson of Moldgreen as a butcher. Killed in action near Havrincourt, 12.9.1918, aged 22 years. Has no known grave. Commemorated **VIS-en-ARTOIS MEMORIAL TO THE MISSING.** (Brother of Private **JOHN ROLAND DYSON**, died of wounds, 11.8.1917, q.v). ROH:- St. John's Church, Kirkheaton; Huddersfield Drill Hall; commemorated on headstone in Kirkheaton Cemetery.

DYSON, FRANKLIN. Private. No 203734. 9th Battalion West Yorkshire Regiment. Born Lindley, Huddersfield. Son of Fred and Clara Dyson, of 37 Birchencliffe Hill, Lindley; husband of Ethel Dyson, 41 Birchencliffe Hill, Lindley. Employed as a warper by Messrs Martin, Sons and Company Limite, of Lindley. Killed in action, 9.10.1917, aged 30 years. Has no known grave. Commemorated **TYNE COT MEMORIAL TO THE MISSING.** ROH:- Memorial in Salendine Nook Churchyard; War Memorial outside St. Philips' Church, Birchencliffe.

DYSON, GEORGE. Private. No 37593. 10th Battalion King's Own Yorkshire Light Infantry. Formerly No 4788 Duke of Wellington's Regiment. Born Bradley, Huddersfield. Son of Henry and Mary Dyson, 13 Wood Top, Marsden. Before moving to Marsden, in 1914, he attended the Upper Heaton Wesleyan Chapel at Kirkheaton. Employed in the tentering department at Bank Bottom Mills, Marsden. Enlisted February 1916. Reported missing, presumed killed, 25.9.1916. The parents received official intimation that he had been killed on that date one year later. Has no known grave. Commemorated **THIEPVAL MEMORIAL TO THE MISSING.** ROH:- Marsden War Memorial.

DYSON, GEORGE DONALD. Private. No 18054. 2nd Battalion Duke of Wellington's Regiment. Born Lindley, Huddersfield. Son of Mr Charles Dyson, greengrocer, and Mrs Dyson of Acre Street, Lindley. Employed as a compositor at the 'Advertiser' Press. Was a member of the Lindley Church Young Men's Class. Killed in action, 11.7.1917, aged 23 years. Buried **BROWN'S COPSE CEMETERY, ROEUX.** Grave location:- Plot 3, Row D, Grave 19. ROH:- St. Stephen's Church, Lindley.

DYSON, GEORGE EARNSHAW. Driver. No 199445 87th Field Company Royal Engineers. Born Lindley 3.12.1884. Son of Ginnethan and Mary Jane Dyson, 12 Meg Lane, Longwood. Educated Oakes Board School, Lindley. Formerly employed as a pattern weaver by Messrs Learoyd Brothers, Trafalgar Mills, Huddersfield. At the time of enlistment, was working at British Dyes Limited. Married, with four children, and living at 60 Croft End Hill, Longwood. Was a founder member of the Milnsbridge Socalist Brass Band. Enlisted 22.9.1916. Embarked for France in March, 1917. Died of wounds, 4.4.1917, aged 32 years. Buried **St. CATHERINE BRITISH CEMETERY, ARRAS.** Grave location:- Row A, Grave 1. His widow, Gladys Earnshaw, received the following letter from a Major of her husband's Regiment, *'I very much regret to have to inform you that your husband Driver G. E. Dyson died of wounds on the 4th April. He was hit by a piece of shell as he was riding the leading pair of horses of a four horse team drawing a store wagon on the night of the 31st inst. All the horses were wounded, also the driver and the N.C.O in charge as a shell burst right on the road. He was taken to the nearest dressing station where he received every attention. He was buried two days later.'*

DYSON, GEORGE HENRY. Private. No 2003. 1/7th Battalion Duke of Wellington's Regiment. Born Slaithwaite. Son of George and Eliza Dyson, 11 Booth Banks, Slaithwaite. Employed by Mr Joseph Thomas, woollen manufacturer. Single. Enlisted 31.8.1914 and embarked for France in April, 1915. On the night of the 24.6.1915, he was out with a working party, constructing trenches, when he was shot in the head and never regained consciousness. He was 28 years old. Buried **RUE-DAVID MILITARY CEMETERY, FLEURBAIX.** Grave location:- Plot 1, Row B, Grave 9. ROH:- St. James Church, Slaithwaite; Slaithwaite War Memorial; Huddersfield Drill Hall.

DYSON, GEORGE HENRY. Private. No 300109. 2/4th Battalion Duke of Wellington's Regiment. Born Linthwaite. Son of Mr and Mrs D. Dyson, 3 Lees Mill, Golcar. Employed in the warehouse at the Globe Worsted Company Limited, Slaithwaite. Enlisted at the outbreak of the war. Embarked for France in April, 1915. Killed in action, 12.9.1918, aged 24 years. Buried **HERMIES HILL BRITISH CEMETERY.** Grave location:- Plot 2, Row B, Grave 29. ROH:- Linthwaite War Memorial.

DYSON, HAROLD. Private. No 24447. 1/6th Battalion Duke of Wellington's Regiment. Born Golcar. Son of Mrs Fred Dyson, 79 Scarborough Terrace, Townend, Golcar. Attended Golcar Providence United Methodist Church and Sunday School and was a member of the Reading Room. Employed by Mr John Ed Crowther at Bank Bottom Mills, Marsden. Embarked for France 17.10.1916. Invalided home during December, 1916, suffering from trench feet and returned to France on 2.6.1917. Killed in action, 8.10.1917. Has no known grave. Commemorated **TYNE COT MEMORIAL TO THE MISSING.** His mother received the following letter from a chum of her son, in the same Company, who wrote, *'I am sure no one feels the loss of him more than we do as he was our best chum, both in England and out here and he was next to me when he was killed during a bombardment of our trenches. He suffered no pain being killed instantly by a shell and we buried him as well as the circumstances permitted.'* ROH:- St. John's Church, Golcar.

DYSON, HAROLD FREEMAN. Company Sergeant Major. No 240039. 1/5th Battalion Duke of Wellington's Regiment. Born Little Carr Green, Dalton, 10.6.1892. Son of John Freeman and Emily Dyson, 10 Manor Street, Kings Mill Lane, Huddersfield. Educated at Huddersfield College and Technical College. Attended St. Matthew's Church, Primrose Hill. Employed as a cloth designer by Messrs Kaye and Stewart Limited of Lockwood. Single. Enlisted as a Private in the local Territorials, 14.6.1909. Killed in action, 3.9.1916, aged 24 years. Buried **MILL ROAD CEMETERY.** Grave location:- Plot 1, Row B, Grave 19. ROH:- Huddersfield Parish Church; Huddersfield Drill Hall; Almondbury War Memorial.

DYSON, HERBERT. Private. No 241800. 2/5th Battalion Duke of Wellington's Regiment. Born Marsden. Son of John and Martha Ann Dyson, The Grove, Marsden. Attended Marsden Adult School. Employed by Messrs Crowther, Bruce and Company as a pattern weaver. He was taken prisoner at Bullecourt on 3.5.1917 but not wounded. After some weeks he wrote home from Dulmen Camp, Germany. His parents received several letters or cards from him. He died of pneumonia on 17.6.1917, at the Prisoner's Internment Camp at Munster, Westphalia, Germany, aged 23. His parents received the following letter from Mr Oswald Frost, Durham Light Infantry, Acting Pastor, Gefangenen Lager, Hans Spital, bearing the date 21.6.1917. He says, *'Your son Herbert was transferred to this camp from Dulmen. After a few days here he fell ill on the night of the 7.6.1917. On the 9th he was taken into the Lazarette suffering from pneumonia. He struggled bravely until the afternoon of Sunday 17.6.1917 when he died at 3.30pm. We did everything that we possibly could for him but without avail. He was buried yesterday, June 30th.'* Buried **COLOGNE SOUTHERN CEMETERY, GERMANY.** Grave location:- Plot 18, Row A, Grave 19. ROH:- Huddersfield Drill Hall; Marsden War Memorial.

DYSON, HILTON. Private. No 42643. 8th Battalion The Yorkshire Regiment. Formerly No 29/148 Northumberland Fusiliers. Born Slaithwaite. Only son of Mr J. Dyson, 31 Bridge Street, Slaithwaite. Employed in the grocery department at the Junction House Cooperative Society. Was a member of the Slaithwaite Conservative Club. Enlisted June 1916. Embarked for France 8.1.1917. Killed in action, 19.10.1917, aged 28 years. Has no known grave. Commemorated **TYNE COT MEMORIAL TO THE MISSING.** ROH:- St. James Church, Slaithwaite; Slaithwaite War Memorial.

DYSON, HINCHLIFFE. Private. No 54345. 9th Battalion Manchester Regiment. Formerly No 50695 North Staffordshire Regiment. Was born in Slaithwaite in 1897. Son of David and Alice Dyson, Broadfields, Lingards, Slaithwaite. His father was a farmer and cattle dealer. Killed in action, 21.3.1918. Has no known grave. Commemorated **POZIERES MEMORIAL TO THE MISSING.** ROH:- St. James Church, Slaithwaite; Slaithwaite War Memorial.

DYSON, HUBERT. Private. No 29/438. 1/7th Battalion Northumberland Fusiliers. Born Huddersfield. Killed in action, 19.4.1918. Buried **FONCQUEVILLERS MILITARY CEMETERY.** Grave location:- Plot 2, Row B, Grave 2. ROH:- St. Stephen's Church, Lindley.

DYSON, JOE. Private. No 24520. 10th Battalion Duke of Wellington's Regiment. Born Huddersfield. Married. Lived 9 Batley Street, Moldgreen, Huddersfield. Employed as a butcher by the Huddersfield Industrial Society Limited. Was a member of the Deighton Peace Lodge. Killed in action, 23.5.1917, aged 21 years. Buried **RAILWAY DUGOUTS (TRANSPORT FARM) BURIAL GROUND.** Grave location:- Plot 4, Row F, Grave 9. ROH:- Moldgreen War Memorial; Christ Church, Moldgreen.

DYSON, JOHN ROLAND. Private. No 267722. 1/5th Battalion Duke of Wellington's Regiment. Born Pogwell Farm, Dalton Green, Huddersfield, 20.1.1893. Son of Tom Edward and Sarah Dyson. Educated Kirkheaton National School. Worked as a farm labourer on his father's farm. Enlisted August 1916. Invalided home on one occasion with trench feet. Wounded at Langemarck, 9.8.1917. Had his wounds dressed at the dressing station but died before arriving at the Casualty Clearing Station. Died of wounds, 11.8.1917. Buried **NEW IRISH FARM CEMETERY.** Grave location:- Plot 13, Row F, Grave 7. (Brother of Private **FRANK CROSSLEY DYSON**, killed in action, 12.9.1918, q.v). ROH:- St. John's Church, Kirkheaton; Huddersfield Drill Hall; commemorated on headstone in Kirkheaton Cemetery.

DYSON, JOHN WOODHOUSE. Private. No 23774. 2nd Battalion Duke of Wellington's Regiment. Born Leymoor, Golcar, 1.1.1880. Brother of Mrs Amy Hirst, 18 Ballroyd, Longwood. Educated Goitfield Board School, Longwood. Employed as a yardman for Messrs William Shaw, coal merchants. Was a member of the Milnsbridge County Working Men's Club and Institute. Single. Enlisted 26.5.1916. Embarked for France 13.9.1916. Died of acute bronchitis, 17.2.1917, aged 37 years. Buried **BRAY MILITARY CEMETERY.** Grave location:- Plot 2, Row A, Grave 20. ROH:- St. Mark's Parish Church, Longwood; Salendine Nook Baptist Churchyard D370.

DYSON, JOSEPH. Private. No 32261. 1st Battalion Northumberland Fusiliers. Born Paddock 5.7.1893. Son of Tom and Naomi Dyson, 144 Albion Terrace, Manchester Road, Longroyd Bridge. Educated Paddock Church of England School. Employed as a woollen fettler by Mr B. Armistead, spinner, Longroyd Bridge. Single. Enlisted 20.6.1916. Killed in action near Poperinghe, 27.9.1917, aged 24 years. Has no known grave. Commemorated **TYNE COT MEMORIAL TO THE MISSING.** ROH:- All Saints Church, Paddock.

DYSON, NORMAN. Corporal. No 780088. 'B' Battery, 246th Brigade Royal Field Artillery. Born Lindley 16.4.1892. Educated Oakes Council School. Employed as a tram conductor by the Huddersfield Corporation Tramways Department. Lived 8 Back Victoria Street, Lindley. Single when he enlisted on 20.5.1912. Wounded by shrapnel on Passchendaele Ridge in 1917. Returned to duty. Whilst on leave from France was married on 4.12.1918. Died of pneumonia and septic poisoning, caused by gas and shrapnel, at Royds Hall Military Hospital Huddersfield on 9.12.1918. Buried **EDGERTON CEMETERY HUDDERSFIELD.** ROH:- Commemorated on screen wall, St. Stephen's Church, Lindley; Huddersfield Corporation Roll.

DYSON, PERCY. Private. No 32146. 9th Battalion Border Regiment. Formerly No 828 29th Battalion Northumberland Fusiliers. Born Lindley, Huddersfield. Son of the late William and Henry Dyson of Lindley. Lived with his brother at Stonefield Terrace, Milnsbridge. Employed by the Ramsden Mill Company, Linthwaite. Died of malaria in Salonica, 31.10.1917, aged 39 years. Buried **KIRECHKOI-HORTAKOI MILIITARY CEMETERY, GREECE.** Grave location:- No 28. ROH:- Milnsbridge War Memorial.

DYSON, SAMUEL. Private. No 33819. 2nd Garrison Battalion East Yorkshire Regiment. Formerly No 34463 King's Own Yorkshire Light Infantry. Born Marsden. Son of Mr and Mrs David Dyson, Thorpe Cottages, Marsden. Married, with one child. Lived Bowsers, Pule Side, Marsden. Employed as a weaver at Bank Bottom Mills, Marsden. Before enlistment he had worked for Messrs J. and J. Bottomley, painters and plasterers, of Marsden. Enlisted August 1916. Had been in training in various camps in England. Died in Hull Miltary Hospital, 17.4.1917, aged 29 years. Buried with full military honours **St. BARTHOLOMEW'S CHURCHYARD, MARSDEN.** Grave location:- Southm 24, 12. ROH:- Marsden War Memorial.

DYSON, SYKES. Private. No 42376. 24th (Tyneside Irish) Battalion Northumberland Fusiliers. Born Slaithwaite. Employed by Messrs Edwin Shaw and Son, Clough House Mills, as a scourer. Attended the Shred Mission Church. Married. Enlisted 1915. Trained at Hornsea and embarked for France in October, 1915. Killed in action on Easter Monday, 9.4.1917. Buried **ROCLINCOURT VALLEY CEMETERY.** Grave location:- Plot 2, Row B, Grave 15. ROH:- St. James Church, Slaithwaite; Slaithwaite War Memorial.

DYSON, THOMAS HOLMES. Private. No G/14739. 6th Battalion East Kent Regiment (The Buffs). Born 56 Commercial Street, Huddersfield. Son of the late Cook- Sergeant George Dyson and Mrs Dyson. Educated St. Paul's Church of England School. Employed as a motor driver. Single. Enlisted September 1916. Was killed 29.9.1918, aged 20. He was attempting to clear a grenade in order to save his comrades in the trench with him when the grenade exploded. Buried **UNICORN CEMETERY.** Grave location:- Plot 2, Row B, Grave 14. ROH:- St. Paul's Church, Southgate, Huddersfield.

DYSON, TOM. Private. No 241896. 2/5th Battalion Duke of Wellington's Regiment. Born Milnsbridge. Son of Fred and Clara Jane Dyson, 22 Scar Lane, Milnsbridge. Educated Crow Lane Board School, Milnsbridge. Employed by Messrs B. and J. Whitwam and Sons Limited of Golcar. Attended Milnsbridge Wesleyan Sunday School. Embarked for France January, 1917. Reported missing, presumed killed, at the Battle of Bullecourt, 3.5.1917, aged 23 years. Has no known grave. Commemorated **ARRAS MEMORIAL TO THE MISSING.** ROH:- Huddersfield Mission, Milnsbridge; St. John's Church, Golcar; Crow Lane Board School, Milnsbridge; Huddersfield Drill Hall.

DYSON, WALTER. Private. No 45155. 2nd Battalion Durham Light Infantry. Formerly No 31688 Duke of Wellington's Regiment. Born Huddersfield. Killed in action, 21.3.1918. Has no known grave. Commemorated **ARRAS MEMORIAL TO THE MISSING.**

DYSON, WILLIAM HENRY. Private. No 201735. 2/4th Battalion King's Own Yorkshire Light Infantry. Son of Mr and Mrs J. Dyson, 33 Stanhope Street, Scissett. Died of wounds, 3.5.1917, aged 26 years. Buried **ACHIET-LE-GRAND COMMUNAL CEMETERY EXTENSION.** Grave location:- Plot 1, Row E, Grave 13.

DYSON, WILLIE. Private. No 132709. 42nd Battalion Canadian Infantry (Quebec Regiment). Born Marsden. Son of the late Jonathan Dyson, Rock House, Brougham Road, Marsden. Employed as a scribbling engineeer by Messrs Robinson Brothers of Marsden. Left Marsden for Canada in 1910. Killed in action, 28.8.1918. Buried **VIS-en-ARTOIS BRITISH CEMETERY.** Grave location:- Plot 9, Row A, Grave 12. The news of his death was conveyed in a letter to Miss Annie Mellor from his chum, Private A Jackman who wrote, *'Willie was killed in an attack on the enemy's lines. He received the full burst of bullets from a German machine gun that was only ten feet away as he was passing from one shell hole to another. Death was instantenous.'*

EAGLAND, HARRY. Private. No 45333. 13th (1st Barnsley) Battalion York and Lancaster Regiment. Born Slaithwaite. Son of David and Emma Eagland, Byrne Place, Slaithwaite. Employed by Messrs Pogson and Company, Bridge Street Mills, Slaithwaite. Was a member of the Old Slaithwaite Church gymnasium. Died of wounds, 12.4.1918, aged 33 years. Buried **LA KREULE MILITARY CEMETERY.** Grave location:- Plot 1, Row A, Grave 20. ROH:- St. James Church, Slaithwaite; Slaithwaite War Memorial.

EAGLETON, FREDERICK W. Petty Officer Stoker. No 285839. Royal Navy. *HMS Undaunted*. Married, with two sons. Lived 6 Allen Row, Paddock. Prior to enlistment in the Royal Navy, he was employed in the Tramways Department of Huddersfield Corporation. Returned to his ship the week prior to his death and died of heart failure on board ship, 1.2.1918. Buried **EDGERTON CEMETERY, HUDDERSFIELD**. Grave location:- 2, 92G. ROH:- St. Mark's Church, Paddock; Huddersfield Corporation Roll.

EARNSHAW, ALBERT. Sergeant. No 60746. The King's Liverpool Regiment, transferred to 171047 308th Company, Labour Corps. Born Bradley. Had been employed as Head Boots at the Cherry Tree Hotel, Huddersfield, prior to enlistment. Lived Batley. Died from influenza at Bramshott Hospital, Aldershot, 19.10.1918. The week previous to his death he had visited his brother, who was in hospital at Nottingham suffering from wounds. Buried with full military honours **St. THOMAS'S CHURCHYARD, BRADLEY**. Grave location:- in the South part. ROH:- St. Thomas's Church, Bradley.

EARNSHAW, ALBERT. Private. No 240462. 1/5th Battalion Duke of Wellington's Regiment. Born Kirkheaton. Son of Mr and Mrs E. Earnshaw, of Shawcross. Employed by Messrs Broadhead and Graves, of Kirkheaton. Killed in action, 3.9.1916. Buried **MILL ROAD CEMETERY**. Grave location:- Plot 1, Row F, Grave 11. ROH:- St. John's Church, Kirkheaton; Huddersfield Drill Hall.

EARNSHAW, ALBERT. Gunner. No L/29256. 'A' Battery, 93rd Brigade (Holme Valley Battery) Royal Field Artillery. Son of Mr and Mrs Ben Earnshaw of Hogley Green. Prior to enlistment, was a weaver at Digley Mills. Was a member of the Holmbridge Northern Union football team. Killed in action on Easter Monday, 9.4.1917, aged 21 years. Buried **LA TARGETTE BRITISH CEMETERY (AUX RIETZ)**. Grave location:- Plot 3, Row D, Grave 22. ROH:- Holme and Holmbridge War Memorial.

EARNSHAW, BOWER. Private. No 45835. 1/6th Battalion Northumberland Fusiliers. Born Meltham. Enlisted Halifax. Died 24.4.1918. Has no known grave. Commemorated **POZIERES MEMORIAL TO THE MISSING**. ROH:- St. Bartholomew's Church, Meltham.

EARNSHAW, FRED. Private. No 27793. 12th Battalion East Yorkshire Regiment. Formerly No 41425 Durham Light Infantry. Born Holmfirth. Son of John and Sarah Earnshaw of Magnum, Hade Edge, Holmfirth. Attended Magnum Mission Church, where he was a member of the choir. Worked in the quarries of Mr J. Hinchliffe of Dunford Bridge. Enlisted September 1916. Embarked for France February, 1917. Died from gunshot wounds to the abdomen at No 8 Casualty Clearing Station, 6.7.1917, aged 37 years. Buried **DUISANS BRITISH CEMETERY**. Grave location:- Plot 4, Row O, Grave 9. The Matron of the Casualty Clearing Station wrote to his parents, telling them that from the first the staff feared that his condition was hopeless,. *'He did not suffer much after he came here but he was hardly conscious of what was going on around him. He was too ill to speak much.'* ROH:- Hade Edge War Memorial.

EARNSHAW, FRED, MM. Lance Corporal. No 43452. 1/5th Battalion Royal Scots Fusiliers. Born Meltham. Son of Arthur and Charlotte Earnshaw of Wentworth Farm, Meltham. Prior to enlistment was employed as a joiner. Awarded the Military Medal posthumously. Killed in action, 1.10.1918, aged 20 years. Buried **CANTAING BRITISH CEMETERY**. Grave location:- Row B, Grave 4.

EARNSHAW, GEORGE. Private. No 241557. 5/6th Battalion The Cameronians (Scottish Rifles). Born South Crosland. Third son of Mr Sam Earnshaw of Magdale, Honley. Employed by Messrs Eastwood Brothers, of Thirstin Mills. Enlisted September 1916. Killed in action, 14.4.1917, aged 19 years. His father received a letter from a pal of his son, Sergeant Norman Long, also from Huddersfield, saying that the two of them had been together all through the day's fighting and were digging for shelter in the evening when Private Earnshaw was shot through the neck by a sniper. Has no known grave. Commemorated **ARRAS MEMORIAL TO THE MISSING**. ROH:- Honley War Memorial.

EARNSHAW, HAROLD. Private. No 241542. 2/5th Battalion Duke of Wellington's Regiment. Born Huddersfield. Lived with his sister, Miss Amelia Earnshaw, at 44 Upper Brow Road,

Paddock. Attended All Saints Church, Paddock. Employed as a teaser by Messrs C. and J. Hirst Limited, Longwood. Reported missing at the Battle of Bullecourt, 3.5.1917, and afterwards presumed to have died on that date, aged 27 years. Has no known grave. Commemorated **ARRAS MEMORIAL TO THE MISSING.** ROH:- All Saints Church, Paddock; Huddersfield Drill Hall.

EARNSHAW, HERBERT ADAM. Rifleman. No A/7919. 8th Battalion King's Royal Rifle Corps. Born 28 Leeds Road, Huddersfield, 4.1.1893. Son of Lewis and Edith Earnshaw, Primrose Lane, Far Dene, Kirkburton. Educated at St. Andrew's School, Leeds Road, Huddersfield. Was a teacher at Kirkburton National School. Single. Enlisted 30.11.1915. Reported missing, presumed killed, 4.4.1918, aged 25 years. Has no known grave. Commemorated **POZIERES MEMORIAL TO THE MISSING.** ROH:- All Hallows Parish Church, Kirkburton; Fartown and Birkby War Memorial.

EARNSHAW, HILTON, DCM. Sergeant. No 3/11416. 9th Battalion Duke of Wellington's Regiment. Born Meltham. Son of Vandeleur and Sarah Hannah Earnshaw, of Lower Mill, Meltham. Was an employee of Messrs Quarmby and Sykes Limited of Meltham Mills. Was a member of the Meltham Mills Church choir. Enlisted September, 1914, and after ten months training went over to France in June, 1915. Awarded the DCM in April, 1916, for leading a party of the 1st Battalion Gordon Highlanders, whose Officers had been wounded, up to a German trench which was captured and taking 20 prisoners. (Was the first Meltham man to be awarded the DCM). He was an instructor in a bombing school and on 31.8.1916 met his death through the explosion of a defective bomb. Buried **St. AMAND BRITISH CEMETERY.** Grave location:- Plot 1, Row B, Grave 7. ROH:- St. Bartholomew's Church, Meltham.

EARNSHAW, IRVIN. Private. No 28609. 13th Battalion Northumberland Fusiliers. Born Holmfirth. Son of Mr and Mrs G. H. Earnshaw of Paris Road, Scholes, Thongsbridge. Educated Lane Bottom Board School, Wooldale and attended the Primitive Methodist Sunday School at Scholes. Prior to enlistment was employed at Messrs Farrar's dyeworks at Thirstin, Honley.

Enlisted May 1916. Had been out in France about ten months when he was killed in action, 2.6.1917, aged 27 years. Has no known grave. Commemorated **ARRAS MEMORIAL TO THE MISSING.** His parents received the following letter from an Officer of their son's Regiment, *'He was in the Lewis gun team and was in the trench near the gun during a bombardment of our lines when he was struck by a piece of shell which burst over the trench and he died instantly. I know how much it must harm you to read this letter but I thought that you would prefer to know what I can tell you rather than be left in uncertainty. Earnshaw was a good soldier and most reliable and both myself and my comrades feel for you the very deepest sympathy. I hate to lose any of these lads for their pluck and cheerfulness in all dangers and discomforts is splendid beyond all words. Much as I feel the loss though, I know how much more it must be to you his parents and I can only pray that God in his mercy will comfort you for a life given in this service is a life used in the service of God and taken by him for his own purpose.'* ROH:- Hepworth and Scholes War Memorial.

EARNSHAW, JOHN ARTHUR. Lance Corporal. No 305635. 2/7th Battalion Duke of Wellington's Regiment. Born Thornton Lodge, Huddersfield, 8.4.1896. Son of Benjamin and Mary E. Earnshaw, 3 Crosland Street, Crosland Moor. Educated Spring Grove Council School. Attended Bentley Street (Lockwood United Methodist Church). Employed as a printer's apprentice by Messrs Wheatley, Dyson and Sons, of New Street, Huddersfield. Enlisted 11.9.1914. Killed in action, 29.3.1918, aged 23 years. Buried **St. AMAND BRITISH CEMETERY.** Grave location:- Plot 1, Row C, Grave 4. ROH:- St. Barnabas Church, Crosland Moor; Huddersfield Drill Hall; Memorial in Lockwood Cemetery.

EARNSHAW, JOHN THOMAS. Private. The Welsh Regiment. Born Paddock 4.4.1876. Husband of Mrs M. E. Earnshaw, 83 May Street, Crosland Moor, Huddersfield. Educated Paddock Council School. Employed as a cloth finisher. Enlisted 4.6.1915. Died at home, 83 May Street, Crosland Moor, on 3.1.1917 after being discharged through illness. Buried **LOCKWOOD CEMETERY.** ROH:- St. Barnabas Church, Crosland Moor.

EARNSHAW, LEWIS. Lance Corporal. No 11972. 10th Battalion West Yorkshire Regiment. Born 19a Oak Road, Bradley, 22.12.1888. Son of Mrs Earnshaw, 19a Oak Road, Bradley. Educated Bradley Church of England School. Employed as a locomotive cleaner by the London and North Western Railway Company at the Hillhouse Railway Sheds. Single. Enlisted 31.8.1914. Killed in action on the first day of the Battle of the Somme, 1.7.1916, aged 23 years. Buried **DANTZIG ALLEY BRITISH CEMETERY.** Grave location:- Plot 5, Row L, Grave 7. ROH:- St. Thomas's Church, Bradley; London and North Western Railway Company Roll.

EARNSHAW, LEWIS. Private. No 38540. 1st Battalion Lancashire Fusiliers. Formerly No 273141 Army Service Corps (Motor Transport). Born Hanley, Staffordshire. Lived Golcar Brow, Meltham. Son of Mrs Hannah Steet of Little Dene, Meltham. Attended Christ Church, Helme. Employed as a millwright at Messrs Eastwood Brothers Limited, of Honley. Killed in action, 7.8.1917, aged 32 years. Has no known grave. Commemorated **MENIN GATE MEMORIAL TO THE MISSING.** ROH:- St. Bartholomew's Church, Meltham; Christ Church, Helme.

EARNSHAW, NORMAN. Ordinary Seaman. No J/82270. (Dev). Royal Navy. *HM Drifter Vanguard*. Born Honley. Son of the late Sam Earnshaw of Magdale, Honley. Lived with his brother, Harry Earnshaw, at Lockwood Scar, Huddersfield. Enlisted in the Royal Navy in November, 1917. Drowned at sea, 10.9.1918, aged 18 years. Buried **St. FINIAN'S CEMETERY, CASTLETOWN BEREHAVEN, COUNTY CORK, EIRE.** Grave location; - in North-East part. ROH:- Honley War Memorial.

EARNSHAW, SAMUEL. Corporal. No 25473. 'C' Battery (Holme Valley), 168th Brigade Royal Field Artillery. Born Holmfirth. Son of Mr and Mrs Herbert Earnshaw, 70 Dunford Road, Holmfirth. Educated Holmfirth National School and a member of Mr Fletcher's bible class. Employed as a percher by Messrs T. and J. Tinker of Bottoms Mill. Enlisted 11.4.1915. Killed in action, 11.11.1917, aged 21 years. Buried **MINTY FARM CEMETERY.** Grave location:- Plot 2, Row B, Grave 3. His parents received the following letter from a comrade of their son, who wrote, '*I hardly know how to start this letter, but I feel that I must write and express to you the regrets and sympathy not only of myself but of the whole Battery in your sad bereavement. I know quite well how you will miss Sammy for I know how we miss him out here. In fact it is very difficult to realise that we shall not see him again. I thought I should like to write to you tonight not only to express my sympathy but also to tell you as much as possible how Sammy met his death. Unfortunately no one can tell you how or where he was killed as he was alone at the time but as I was one of the search party who found him perhaps I can tell you as much as anyone can. The last time I saw Sammy was on the afternoon of the 11th November when he was leaving the Battery for Signal Headquarters. As usual he stopped and had a few cheery words with me and then went on his way. From what I can gather he left the Signal Headquarters some hours later and returned to the Battery which however he never reached.*' His comrade goes on to relate how the lad's non appearance before midnight caused uneasiness and it was decided to organise a search party as soon as daylight came, '*This we did,*' he writes further, '*and we found him about a mile away from the Battery. Evidently he had decided to overhaul one of the telephone wires on his way back to the Battery for we found him laid beside the wire which was some distance from his usual way back. You will be glad to know as we were that he must have died instantenously as he was wounded through the head and heart. Poor lad - he died as he would have wished to have died, doing his duty and working to the last. He will be missed by all of us for I can safely say that there isn't a man in the Battery whom he had not helped sometime or other even it has only been by his cheery smile.*' ROH:- Underbank War Memorial.

EARNSHAW, WILLIE. Private. No 240891. 2/5th Battalion Duke of Wellington's Regiment. Son of Mr and Mrs John Willie Earnshaw, Cinderhills, Holmfirth. Educated at Mr J. D. Brown's school and was connected with the Parish Church Sunday School. Employed as a weaver by Messrs H. and S. Butterworth, Lower Mills, Holmfirth. He was a keen football player and he played for both the Holmbridge and Underbank teams. Enlisted January 1915. Embarked for France the following January. Killed in action, 27.3.1918. Has no known grave. Commemorated **ARRAS MEMORIAL**

TO THE MISSING. ROH:- Underbank War Memorial; Huddersfield Drill Hall.

EASTWOOD, ALBERT EDWARD. Private. No 41940. 2/9th Battalion Manchester Regiment. Formerly No 31745 North Staffordshire Regiment. Son of Wellington and Emma Eastwood, 137 Northgate, Almondbury. Employed by Messrs Lockwood and Keighley, Upperhead Row, Huddersfield. Was a well known campanologist and a member of the Huddersfield Parish Church Society of Service Ringers. Reported missing, presumed killed, 21.3.1918, aged 39 years. Has no known grave. Commemorated **POZIERES MEMORIAL TO THE MISSING.** ROH:- Almondbury War Memorial; memorial in Almondbury Cemetery.

EASTWOOD, ALBION. Rifleman. No S/28217. 10th Battalion The Rifle Brigade. Formerly No R/19534 King's Royal Rifle Corps. Born Primrose Hill, Huddersfield. Son of Robert Cunnliffe and Maggie Eastwood, 135 Whitehead Road, Primrose Hill. Educated Stile Common Council School, Huddersfield. Employed by Mr Haigh, skep maker of Bankfield Road, Huddersfield. Single. Enlisted 22.1.1916. Was taken prisoner in 1917. Died of pleurisy following influenza, 18.10.1918, aged 23 years. Buried **COLOGNE SOUTHERN CEMETERY, GERMANY.** Grave location:- Plot 5, Row E, Grave 4. (Brother of Private **HUBERT EASTWOOD**, killed in action, 9.8.1918, q.v.). ROH:- Memorial in Lockwood Cemetery.

EASTWOOD, FRED. Private. No 2434. 1/7th Battalion Duke of Wellington's Regiment. Son of the late Mr and Mrs George Eastwood of Smith Ryding, Linthwaite. His parents died when he was quite young and he had lived with his cousin, Mrs Mary Hannah Gledhill, 9, Slantgate, Linthwaite, since he was seven years old. Educated at Linthwaite Church Day School. Employed as a twister-in by Messrs John Lockwood and Sons Limited, Scarbottom Mills, Golcar. Died from a compound fracture of the skull at No 1 Canadian General Hospital, Etaples, on Tuesday, 8.6.1915, aged 19 years. Buried **ETAPLES MILITARY CEMETERY.** Grave location:- Plot 2, Row B, Grave 5a. ROH:- Linthwaite; Huddersfield Drill Hall. (Brother of Private **RICHARD EASTWOOD**, who died of wounds, 21.9.1915, q.v.).

EASTWOOD, GEORGE HENRY. Corporal. No 2852. 1/5th Battalion Duke of Wellington's Regiment. Born Huddersfield 5.7.1890. Brother of Mr W. Eastwood, 29 Primrose Street, Huddersfield. Educated Stile Common Council School. Employed as a warehouseman by Messrs Brook, Sugden and Company, wholesale clothiers, Paige Street, Huddersfield. Single. Living at 11 Jackroyd, Newsome, Huddersfield. Enlisted September 1914. On the night of September 17th/18th, Corporal Eastwood was in command of his platoon. A shell burst and severed one of his legs from his body and, notwithstanding his agony, he called to his men to proceed. Before he could be properly attended to he passed away with a bright smile on his face. Died 17.9.1916, aged 26 years. Has no known grave. Commemorated **THIEPVAL MEMORIAL TO THE MISSING.** ROH:- Marsh War Memorial; Huddersfield Drill Hall; memorial in Almondbury Cemetery; Almondbury War Memorial.

EASTWOOD, HUBERT. Private. No 36280. 9th Battalion Northumberland Fusiliers. Born Primrose Hill, Huddersfield 8.11.1892. Son of Robert Cunliffe and Maggie Eastwood, 135 Whitehead Road, Primrose Hill. Educated Stile Common Council School. Was in business with his father at Engine Bridge Works, Chapel Hill, as a doffin plate maker. Was a member of the Primrose Hill Cricket Club. Single. Enlisted 5.1.1917. Killed in action, 9.8.1918, aged 25 years. Buried **MERVILLE COMMUNAL CEMETERY EXTENSION.** Grave location:- Plot 2, Row D, Grave 3. (Brother of Private **ALBION EASTWOOD**, who died as a Prisoner of War in Germany, 18.10.1918, q.v.). ROH:- Memorial in Lockwood Cemetery.

EASTWOOD, JOE. Rifleman. No R/20080. 12th Battalion King's Royal Rifle Corps. Born Standiforth, Dalton, 16.12.1886. Son of Mr and Mrs Arthur Haigh, 45 Victoria Street, Dalton. Educated Moldgreen Council School and Huddersfield Higher Grade School. Employed as a tailor's cutter at Stewart's tailors of Middlesbrough. Husband of Clara Eastwood, Rutland Mount, Dalton. Enlisted 1.3.1916. Reported missing, presumed killed, 2.4.1918, aged 32 years. Has no known grave. Commemorated **POZIERES MEMORIAL TO THE MISSING.** ROH:- Christ Church, Moldgreen; commemorated on his parents' headstone in Edgerton Cemetery.

EASTWOOD, RICHARD. Private. No 3/1985. 7th Battalion King's Own Yorkshire Light Infantry. Born Linthwaite. Eldest son of the late Mr and Mrs George Eastwood, of Smith Ryding, Linthwaite. Cousin of Mrs Mary Hannah Gledhill, 9 Slantgate, Linthwaite. Since the death of his parents he had lived for about seven years with Mr Joseph Williams, of 10 Slantgate, Linthwaite, with whom he was engaged in a general hawker's business. Enlisted soon after the outbreak of the war. Came home on leave in June, 1915. Was severely wounded in the chest and abdomen on 20.9.1915. Died of his wounds at the 2nd London Casualty Clearing Station, 21.9.1915, aged 22 years. Buried **MERVILLE COMMUNAL CEMETERY**. Grave location:- Plot 4, Row D, Grave 4. (His cousin, Mrs Gledhill, received the following letter from the Rev. F. G. Goddard, Chaplain to the 2nd London C.C.S., dated 22.9.1915, *'I am the Church of England Chaplain at the 2nd London C.C.S., 1st Army. I regret to have to write sad news about Private R. Eastwood, No 1985, 7th Battalion K.O.Y.L.I. He was brought in here yesterday severely wounded in the chest and died shortly after admission. Your name and address was found on him so perhaps you would kindly let his relatives know. Of course probably you are related yourself and must at least be a friend. Will you tell all concerned and assure them of our real and sincere sympathy. I cannot very well write more at present as you can realise. I officiated at his funeral this morning. I hope all of you will feel if he died away from his people yet he did so among those who did their best for him. May God comfort you and bless all those bereaved.'* (Brother of Private **FRED EASTWOOD**, who died of wounds, 8.6.1915, q.v.). ROH:- Linthwaite War Memorial.

EASTWOOD, TOM. Private. No 3509. 1st Battalion King's Own Yorkshire Light Infantry. Born Holmfirth. Enlisted Pontefract. Died of wounds, 14.6.1915. Buried **HAZEBROUCK COMMUNAL CEMETERY**. Grave location:- Plot 2, Row F, Grave 13. ROH:- Holmfirth War Memorial.

ECCLES, JAMES. Private. No 203657. Depot Battalion Duke of Wellington's Regiment. Born Darwen, Lancashire, 6.10.1896. Son of Richard and Anne Eccles, Molewarp Hall, Huddersfield. Educated at Honley National School. Employed as a labourer. Enlisted May 1916. Died, 14.3.1918, whilst working on munitions at Huddersfield Central Ironworks. Buried **EDGERTON CEMETERY, HUDDERSFIELD**. Grave location:- 3, 'C', 137. ROH:- St. Hilda's Church, Cowcliffe; Fartown and Birkby War Memorial.

ECCLESBY, JOE. Private. No 242449. 2nd Battalion West Yorkshire Regiment. Born Well Head, Almondbury, 4.12.1886. Educated Almondbury Church of England School. Employed as a mechanic's labourer. Married. At the time of enlistment, was living at 32 Back Ivy Street, Moldgreen. Enlisted 16.10.1916. Reported missing, presumed killed, 29.5.1918, aged 31. Has no known grave. Commemorated **SOISSONS MEMORIAL TO THE MISSING**. ROH:- Christ Church, Moldgreen.

EDINBURGH, FRED. Private. No G/13965. 7th Battalion East Kent Regiment. Born Shepley 12.10.1888. Son of the late Alfred and Sarah Jane Edinburgh. Brother of Mrs Joe Wood, 30 Stoney Lane, Taylor Hill, Lockwood. Educated at Shepley School. Employed as a weaver by Messrs John Taylor, Colne Road Mills. Was a member of the Milton Church cricket club. Single. Enlisted November 1916. Reported missing, presumed killed, 12.10.1917, aged 29 years. Has no known grave. Commemorated **TYNE COT MEMORIAL TO THE MISSING**.

EDMONDSON, FRANK. No 5742. 20th (County of London) Battalion (Blackheath and Woolwich). Formerly No 78297 Royal Army Medical Corps. Son of Charlotte and the late John Edmondson, of Ashton-in-Makerfield, Wigan. Was assistant master at the Linthwaite Central Council School from 7.12.1912 until 19.3.1914. Lodged with Mr G. H.Rawcliffe of Fern Lea, Hoylehouse. Attended Linthwaite Wesleyan Church and Sunday School. Was a member of the choir, the Young Men's Class, the Reading Room and the cricket and billiard teams. Died of wounds at No 42 Casualty Clearing Station, 28.7.1916, aged 26 years. Buried **AUBIGNY COMMUNAL CEMETERY EXTENSION**. Grave location:- Plot 1, Row D, Grave 51.

EDWARDS, WALTER. Private. No 14491. 10th Battalion Duke of Wellington's Regiment. Born 15 Stocks Buildings, Huddersfield in January,

1874. Son of Harry Edwards, 16 Stocks Buildings, Fitzwilliam Street, Huddersfield. Educated Thomas Street Board School. Employed as a brass moulder. Married. Enlisted September 1914. Killed in action at Delville Wood, 10.7.1916. Has no known grave. Commemorated **THIEPVAL MEMORIAL TO THE MISSING.** ROH:- St. Andrew's Church, Leeds Road, Huddersfield.

EGLINGTON, CLAUDE, MM. Corporal. No240981. 2/5th Battalion Duke of Wellington's Regiment. Born Newsome Cross, Huddersfield, 21.4.1897. Son of Alice Eglinton, 78 West End, Newsome. Educated Newsome Church of England Mixed School. Attended Newsome United Methodist Church. Employed as an iron turner and mechanic's labourer by Messrs W. Whiteley and Sons Limited, of Lockwood. Single. Enlisted 6.1.1915. Killed in action at the Battle of Cambrai, 27.11.1917, aged 20. Has no known grave. Commemorated **CAMBRAI MEMORIAL TO THE MISSING.** ROH:- Newsome United Methodist Church; St. John's Church, Newsome; Huddersfield Drill Hall.

ELLAM, LEWIS. Private. No 268692. 1/7th Battalion West Yorkshire Regiment. Born 7 St. John's Square, Newtown, Huddersfield, 12.10.1887. Educated Thomas Street Board School. Employed as a hoist man. At the time of enlistment, was living at 19 William Street, Huddersfield. Widower. Wounded, 2.5.1917, at Beaumont Hamel. Died of influenza whilst a Prisoner of War, 24.10.1918, aged 29. Buried **ERQUELINNES COMMUNAL CEMETERY.** Grave location:- Grave 103. ROH:- Great Northern Street Congregational Chapel; St. Andrew's Church, Leeds Road, Huddersfield.

ELLINGWORTH, THOMAS. Private. No 36253. 13th (1st Barnsley) Battalion York and Lancaster Regiment. Born Aylesbury, Buckinghamshire. Enlisted Huddersfield. Son of the late Henry and Mary Ellingworth. Husband of Emily Etty Ellingworth, of Intake Head, Marsden. Killed in action, 13.4.1918, aged 38 years. Has no known grave. Commemorated **PLOEGSTEERT MEMORIAL TO THE MISSING.** ROH:- Marsden War Memorial.

ELLIOTT, ARTHUR. Private. No 42362. 2nd Battalion King's Own Yorkshire Light Infantry. Formerly No 29/704 Northumberland Fusiliers. Born Halifax. Lived with his Aunt, Mrs Mary A Lockwood, at Middle Carr House, Deighton, Huddersfield. Prior to enlistment, was employed as a butcher. Killed in action at Nieuport, Belgium, 10.7.1917. Buried **RAMSCAPELLE ROAD MILITARY CEMETERY.** Grave location:- Plot 5, Row A, Grave 13. ROH:- Christ Church, Woodhouse Hill.

ELLIOTT, JOHN FRANCIS. Stoker 1st Class. No 288465. Royal Navy. *HMS Amethyst*. Son of Mrs E. Strong (formerly Elliott) and John Frederick Elliott, of Barrowden, Rutland; husband of Annie Elliott, of Chapel Hill, Clayton West. Had been in the Navy before the outbreak of war and re-enlisted in January, 1915. Died of wounds received in attack on the Dardenelles, 16.3.1915, aged 37 years. Has no known grave. Commemorated **PORTSMOUTH NAVAL MEMORIAL TO THE MISSING.** ROH:- Clayton West and High Hoyland War Memorial.

ELLIOTT, THOMAS ROLLO. Private. No 204551. 2/4th Battalion Duke of Wellington's Regiment. Born Birkby Lodge Road, Huddersfield. Son of Thomas William and Gertrude Anna Elliott, 57 Eldon Road, Marsh. Educated Holy Trinity Church of England School, Portland Street, Marsh. Employed as a butler. At the time of enlistment, was living at 9 Waverley Terrace, Marsh. Single. Enlisted 20.4.1915. Killed in action at the Battle of Cambrai, 26.11.1917. Has no known grave. Commemorated **CAMBRAI MEMORIAL TO THE MISSING.**

ELLIS, CHARLES. Private. No 203662. 1/4th Battalion Duke of Wellington's Regiment. Born Brighouse. Parents lived at 16 Thornhill Bridge Lane, Brighouse. Husband of E. B. Ellis, 271 Marsden Road, Brierley Wood, Huddersfield; with one daughter. Employed as a twiner by Mr Charles Haigh, cotton spinner, of Colne Bridge. Was a member of the Bradley Working Men's Club, St Andrew's bible class and St James' Church, Brighouse. Enlisted July 1916. Wounded on three occasions and gassed once. Died at No 36 Casualty Clearing Station, 15.4.1918, the day after being wounded in the abdomen. He was 37 years of age. Buried **BANDAGHEM MILITARY CEMETERY.** Grave location:- Plot 1, Row E, Grave 11. ROH:- Brighouse War Memorial.

ELLIS, CHARLES, DCM. Battery Sergeant Major. No 16457. 'A' Battery, 110th Brigade, Royal Field Artillery. Born Huddersfield. Son of Tom and Hannah Ellis, 57 Chapel Street, Blackpool. Awarded the DCM 3.6.1918. Killed in enemy raid, 4.10.1918, aged 35 years. Buried **BELLICOURT BRITISH CEMETERY.** Grave location:- Plot 2, Row N, Grave 5.

ELLIS, ERNEST. Private. No 31907. 1/5th Battalion North Staffordshire Regiment. Born Meltham. Lived Meltham. Killed in action, 1.7.1917. Has no known grave. Commemorated **ARRAS MEMORIAL TO THE MISSING.** ROH:- St. Bartholomew's Church, Meltham.

ELLIS, FRED. Private. No 6146. 1st Battalion The Yorkshire Regiment. Born Meltham. Son of Mary Ellis, 32 Huddersfield Road, Meltham, and the late Sam Ellis. Died in India, 1.8.15, aged 37 years. Buried **RAWALPINDI CEMETERY, INDIA.** Also commemorated **DELHI MEMORIAL, INDIA.** ROH:- St. Bartholomew's Church, Meltham.

ELLIS, HARRY. Private. No 5558. 1/6th Battalion Duke of Wellington's Regiment. Born 1 St. John's Road, Huddersfield, 15.5.1896. Son of Mr and Mrs Fred Ellis, 62 Fitzwilliam Street, Huddersfield. Educated Spring Grove Council School. Assisted his father in the family restaurant at the corner of St. John's Road and Fitzwilliam Street, Huddersfield. Attended the United Methodist Church in Brunswick Street. Single. Enlisted 27.1.1916. Went over to France in Whit week, 1916. Killed in action by the bursting in the trench of a high explosive shell which buried him and others at Authuile, about three miles from Albert, France, on 16.9.1916, aged 20 years. Buried **BLIGHTY VALLEY CEMETERY.** Grave location:- Plot 1, Row G, Grave 7.

ELLIS, HARRY. Private. No 241547. 2/5th Battalion Duke of Wellington's Regiment. Born Primrose Hill, Huddersfield. Son of Mr and Mrs W. Ellis, 306 Saville Place, Milnsbridge. Employed as a night weaver by Messrs Ben Hall and Sons, Milnsbridge. Reported missing at the Battle of Bullecourt, 3.5.1917, and afterwards presumed to have been killed on that date. Has no known grave. Commemorated **ARRAS MEMORIAL TO THE MISSING.** ROH:- Huddersfield Drill Hall.

ELLIS, HARRY. Rifleman. No 51911. 2/8th Battalion West Yorkshire Regiment. Born Cumberworth. Son of Allan Ellis of Birdsedge, Denby Dale. Reported missing, presumed killed, at the Battle of Cambrai, 22.11.1917, aged 19 years. Has no known grave. Commemorated **CAMBRAI MEMORIAL TO THE MISSING.** ROH:- Denby Dale and Cumberworth War Memorial.

ELLIS, HERBERT. Private. No 242072. 1/5th Battalion Duke of Wellington's Regiment. Born Longroyd Bridge 21.8.1894. Son of Walter and Mary Ellis, 85 Thorne Road, Thornton Lodge, Crosland Moor. Educated at Paddock Church Schools. Employed as a worsted and woollen weaver. At the time of enlistment, was living at 19 Queen Street, Paddock. Single. Enlisted 7.4.1916. Reported missing, presumed killed, in the attack on the Schwaben Redoubt, 3.9.1916, aged 22 years. Has no known grave. Commemorated **THIEPVAL MEMORIAL TO THE MISSING.** ROH:- Shared Church, Paddock; Huddersfield Drill Hall.

ELLIS, HUBERT. Private. No CH/1452 (S) Royal Marine Light Infantry. 1st Royal Marine Battalion Royal Naval Division. Born Flatts 7.4.1887. Fourth son of Charles Ewart and Hannah Ellis, 13 Lower Park, Berry Brow. Educated Farnley Tyas School. Attended the Spiritualist Church in St. Peter's Street, Huddersfield. Employed as a spinner at Priestroyd Mills. Enlisted 1915. Reported wounded and missing, 28.4.1917. Has no known grave. Commemorated **ARRAS MEMORIAL TO THE MISSING.** (Brother of Private **WESTON ELLIS**, who died of wounds, 15.2.1916, q.v.). ROH:- St. Stephen's Church, Rashcliffe.

ELLIS, LEVI. Private. No 17648. 2nd Battalion Duke of Wellington's Regiment. Born Hepworth's Yard, Bradford Road, Huddersfield. Son of Mr A. Ellis, 11 Field Street, Marsh. Employed as a tailor's presser by Mr George Crosland, of Chancery Lane. Single. Enlisted November 1915. Reported missing, 3.5.1917, since presumed died on that date. Has no known grave. Commemorated **ARRAS MEMORIAL TO THE MISSING.** ROH:- Holy Trinity Church, Huddersfield.

ELLIS, LUTHER. Private. No 75356. 1/6th Battalion Northumberland Fusiliers. Born Huddersfield 16.4.1899. Son of Martha

Ellis, 3 Spring Street, Huddersfield. Educated Spring Grove Counil School. Employed as a warehouseman by Messrs Firth and Company, St. Peter's Street, Huddersfield. Enlisted 3.5.1917. Wounded and taken prisoner, 27.5.1918. Died of septic poisoning, the result of gunshot wounds received in action, in the hospital at Saarlouis, Saarbrucken, Germany, 14.6.1918, aged 19. Buried **NIEDERZWEHREN CEMETERY, CASSEL, GERMANY.** Grave location:- Plot 2, Row D, Grave 8. ROH:- High Street United Methodist Church.

ELLIS, SAM. Private. No 25398. 6th Battalion York and Lancaster Regiment. Born Denby. Lodged with Mr Joe Field, Commercial Road, Skelmanthorpe. Worked as a mason, employed by Messrs Cook and Heywood, contractors, Cumberworth. Enlisted April 1916. Killed in action, 22.8.1916. Buried **LONDON RIFLE BRIGADE CEMETERY, PLOEGSTEERT.** Grave location:- Plot 2, Row D, Grave 29. ROH:- St. Aidan's Church, Skelmanthorpe.

ELLIS, WESTON. Private. No 5109. 2nd Battalion Sherwood Foresters. Born Wood Royd 22.3.1882. Son of Charles Ewart and Hannah Ellis, 13 Lower Park, Berry Brow. Educated Farnley Tyas School. Employed as a motor driver at the Commercial Mills, Firth Street, Huddersfield. Widower. Enlisted August 1914. Wounded whilst leaving his billet in France on 13.2.1916. Died of wounds to stomach at No 2 Casualty Clearing Station, 15.2.1916, aged 33 years. Buried **BAILLEUL COMMUNAL CEMETERY EXTENSION.** Grave location:- Plot 2, Row C, Grave 144. (Brother of Private **HUBERT ELLIS**, reported missing, 28.4.1917, q.v.). ROH:- St. Stephen's Church, Rashcliffe.

ELLIS, WILFRED. Private. No 50754. 1st Battalion Lancashire Fusiliers. Born Hawthorne Terrace, Crosland Moor 5.1.1885. Son of Fred and Ann Ellis, 3 College Street, Crosland Moor. Educated Crosland Moor Council School. Employed as a printer by Messrs B. Brown and Sons, of Westgate, Huddersfield. Attended Crosland Moor Wesleyan Church and school, where he held the office of steward, secretary and teacher. Husband of Emily Ellis, 44 College Street, Crosland Moor. Enlisted 14.8.1917. Reported missing near Estaires, 12.4.1918, and was officially reported to have been killed on that date one year later, aged 33. Has no known grave. Commemorated **PLOEGSTEERT MEMORIAL TO THE MISSING.** ROH:- Crosland Moor Wesleyan Church; St. Barnabas Church, Crosland Moor.

EMSLEY, JOSEPH E. Private. No 32161. 21st Battalion West Yorkshire Regiment. Born Pudsey. Son of Mr J. Emsley, 8 Albion Street, Crimbles, Pudsey, Leeds. Lived Huddersfield. Killed in action, 2.7.1917. Buried **LEVEL CROSSING CEMETERY, FAMPOUX.** Grave location:- Plot 1, Row E, Grave 37.

ENGLAND, ARTHUR. Private. No 4741. 2/5th Battalion York and Lancaster Regiment. Born Penistone. Lived Cumberworth. Son of Ben and Janet England. Prior to enlistment he worked as a carrier between Huddersfield and Cumberworth. Single. Was a member of the Cumberworth Wesleyan Reform Choir. Enlisted March 1917. Died of wounds at No 4 Casualty Clearing Station, 7.3.1917, aged 36. Buried **VARENNES MILITARY CEMETERY.** Grave location:- Plot 1, Row I, Grave 83. ROH:- Denby Dale and Cumberworth War Memorial.

ENGLAND, FRED. Lance Bombardier. No 35516 'A' Battery, 38th Brigade Royal Field Artillery. Born New Mill, Holmfirth. Son of Ben and Emily England of Sycamore Cottage, New Mill. Educated at New Mill National School and also attended the Sunday School. Employed as a dyer by Messrs Beaumonts, of Honley. Enlisted, 9.11.1914, with his brother, Percy, the two joining the R.F.A. Crossed the Channel together in September, 1915. Percy was wounded on 17.7.1916 and spent a long time in hospital, eventually being discharged from the Army. Fred was wounded in the head on 27.4.1918. Admitted into No 14 General Hospital, Boulogne, the following day and died of his wounds on 9.5.1918, aged 27 years. Buried **BOULOGNE EASTERN CEMETERY.** Grave location:- Plot 9, Row B, Grave 61. ROH:- New Mill Working Men's Club; Fulstone War Memorial.

ENGLAND, FRED WATSON. Private. No 29041. 2nd Battalion Duke of Wellington's Regiment. Born Hepworth. Son of Councillor George England of Hepworth. Brother of Mrs C. Kenworthy of Totties, Thongsbridge. Employed by the Prudential Insurance Company. Killed in action, 15.4.1918, aged 33 years. Buried **POINT-du-HEM MILITARY CEMETERY.** Grave location:- Plot 5, Row B, Grave 8. ROH:- Hepworth and Scholes.

ENGLAND, JONATHAN. Private. No 38232. 15th Battalion (1st Leeds Pals) West Yorkshire Regiment. Born Fulstone, Yorkshire. Lived Denby Dale. Husband of Bertha England, of 'Church View', Upper Cumberworth. Killed in action at Gavrelle during the Battle of Arras, 3.5.1917, aged 33 years. Has no known grave. Commemorated **ARRAS MEMORIAL TO THE MISSING.** ROH:- Denby Dale and Cumberworth War Memorial.

ETTENFIELD, JOSEPH WILLIAM. Sergeant. No 13538. 9th Battalion Duke of Wellington's Regiment. Born Lockwood 28.9.1893. Son of William and Hannah Ettenfield, 223 Yews Hill Road, Lockwood. Educated Crosland Moor Church of England School. Employed as a millhand by Messrs Kaye and Stewart, Broadfield Mills, Lockwood. Single. Enlisted 4.9.1914. He was gassed at Hill 60 on 5.5.1915 and invalided home. Returned to France in February, 1916, and was slightly wounded on Easter Monday, 24.4.1916, when a piece of shrapnel pierced his cigarette case. Killed in action, 3.8.1916, aged 22 years. Buried **A.I.F. BURIAL GROUND.** Grave location:- Plot 16, Row A, Grave 4. ROH:- Rehoboth Baptist Chapel; St. Barnabas Church, Crosland Moor.

EVANS, DAVID FERDINAND. Private. No 24971. 2nd Battalion Duke of Wellington's Regiment. Born Linthwaite. Son of David and Elizabeth Evans, 566 Manchester Road, Linthwaite. Employed as a butcher by Mr Joe Greaves of Honley. Enlisted 23.10.1914. Had been wounded and returned to France in January, 1917. Killed in action, 11.4.1917, aged 22 years. Has no known grave. Commemorated **ARRAS MEMORIAL TO THE MISSING.** ROH:- Linthwaite War Memorial.

EVANS, PERCY LEWIS. Lieutenant. Royal Air Force. Born Sowerby, near Halifax, 10.8.1891. Son of William Cumnor and Evangeline Hermans Evans, Moorville, 46 Waspnest Road, Fartown. (His father was pastor of the Great Northern Street Congregational Church, Huddersfield). Educated at Sowerby National School, Heath Grammar School and Edinburgh University. Prior to enlistment was a senior theological student at the United College, Bradford, where he was studying for the Congregational Ministry. Single. Served with the Friends Ambulance Brigade for eighteen months until enlisting as a Private in the Artist's Rifles in April, 1916. Was later transferred to the R.A.F, in which he received his commission in August, 1917. Killed in a flying accident on Friday, 22.11.1918, aged 27 years, at Stockbridge, near Andover, Hampshire, whilst testing a machine prior to flying to another camp. Buried **EDGERTON CEMETERY, HUDDERSFIELD.** Grave location:- 51, 150. ROH:- Great Northern Street Congregational Church; Fartown and Birkby War Memorial; Heath Grammar School, Halifax.

EVENNETT, KEBLE THOMAS. Private. No 204359. 2/4th Battalion Duke of Wellington's Regiment. Born Denby Dale. Husband of Rosetta Evenett, of Lower Denby. Died of pneumonia at No 42 Casualty Clearing Station, 25.2.1918, aged 33 years. Buried **AUBIGNY COMMUNAL CEMETERY EXTENSION.** Grave location:- Plot 3, Row C, Grave 25. ROH:- Denby Dale and Cumberworth War Memorial.

EVENSON, GEORGE. Private. No 57525. 2/5th Battalion West Yorkshire Regiment. Born Union Street, Lindley, 24.10.1885. Educated Oakes Council School and Higher Grade School, Huddersfield. Employed as a millhand. Husband of Mabel Evenson, 9, Occupation Road, Lindley. Enlisted 16.7.1917. Died, 17.2.1918, at No 42 Casualty Clearing Station of septic poisoning. Buried **AUBIGNY COMMUNAL CEMETERY EXTENSION.** Grave location:- Plot 3, Row C, Grave 22. ROH:- St. Stephen's Church, Lindley.

EVERETT, WILFRED. Driver. No 72320. 'C' Battery, 283rd Brigade Royal Field Artillery. Born Scissett. Son of Walter and Annie E. Everett of Spital Hill, Thirsk. Lived Scissett. Killed in action, 21.10.1916, aged 24 years. Buried **GUARDS' CEMETERY, (LESBOEUFS).** Grave location:- Plot 10, Row P, Grave 10. ROH:- Scissett War Memorial.

EVERITT, ALBERT EDWARD. Private. No 24521. 10th Battalion Duke of Wellington's Regiment. Born Huddersfield. Son of Mr and Mrs Henry Everitt, 44 Rufford Road, Scar

Lane, Milnsbridge. Educated Crow Lane Board School, Milnsbridge. Employed in the butchering department at the Milnsbridge Perseverance Cooperative Society Limited. Attended Parkwood United Methodist Church and Sunday School, Longwood. Enlisted June, 1916, and embarked for France on 24.10.1916. Reported missing, presumed killed, 20.9.1917, aged 24 years. Has no known grave. Commemorated **TYNE COT MEMORIAL TO THE MISSING**. (Brother of Private **HUBERT EVERITT**, reported missing, 21.3.1918, q.v.). ROH:- St. John's Church, Golcar; Longwood War Memorial; Crow Lane Board School, Milnsbridge.

EVERITT, HUBERT. Rifleman. No R/19514. 8th Battalion King's Royal Rifle Corps. Born Huddersfield. Son of Mr and Mrs Henry Everitt, 44 Rufford Road, Scar Lane, Milnsbridge. Educated Crow Lane Board School, Milnsbridge. Employed as a clerk by Messrs Greenhalgh of John William Street, Huddersfield. Attended Parkwood United Methodist Church and was secretary of the Band of Hope. Reported missing, 21.3.1918, and afterwards presumed to have been killed on that date. Has no known grave. Commemorated **POZIERES MEMORIAL TO THE MISSING**. (Brother of Private **ALBERT EDWARD EVERITT**, killed in action, 20.9.1917, q.v.). ROH:- St. John's Church, Golcar; Parkwood Methodist Chapel; Longwood War Memorial; Crow Lane Board School, Milnsbridge.

EWART, CHARLES FREDERICK. Private. No 45033. 2nd Battalion York and Lancaster Regiment. Born Huddersfield. Married. Lived 41 Blackhouse Road, Fartown. Employed by Messrs D. Broadbent and Sons Limited, Central Ironworks, as a motor driver. Reported missing, presumed killed, 21.3.1918. Has no known grave. Commemorated **ARRAS MEMORIAL TO THE MISSING**. ROH:- Fartown and Birkby War Memorial.

EWART, NORMAN. Private. No 44725. 10th Battalion Essex Regiment. Born Engine Bridge. Son of Mrs Ewart, 204 Albert Street, Lockwood. Educated Mount Pleasant Board School. Employed as a mule piecer. Reported missing, 23.8.1918. Has no known grave. Commemorated **VIS-en-ARTOIS MEMORIAL TO THE MISSING**. ROH:- Emmanuel Church, Lockwood.

EWING, GEORGE. Private. No 26323. 2nd Battalion Loyal North Lancashire Regiment. Formerly No 3/19406 Duke of Wellington's Regiment. Born Liverpool 10.12.1887. Husband of Ellen Ewing, 6 Hampshire Street, Moldgreen. Employed as a boot repairer by Messrs A. and D. Hoyle of Aspley. Enlisted 1.3.1916. Killed in action, 1.8.1918, aged 30 years. Buried **RAPERIE BRITISH CEMETERY VILLE-MONTOIRE**. Grave location:- Plot 9, Row C, Grave 5. ROH:- Christ Church, Moldgreen.

EWING, JOE WILLIE. Private. No 24817. 9th Battalion Duke of Wellington's Regiment. Born Berry Brow 14.6.1889. Educated Rashcliffe Church of England School. Employed as a dyer's labourer by Mr Whiteley of St. Andrew's Road. Husband of May Southwell Ewing, 4 Smithy Lane, Moldgreen. Enlisted 8.8.1916. Wounded 26.4.1917. Died of his wounds at No 8 Casualty Clearing Station, 29.4.1917, aged 27 years. Buried **DUISANS BRITISH CEMETERY**. Grave location:- Plot 3, Row H, Grave 46. ROH:- St. Paul's Church, Southgate, Huddersfield; Christ Church, Moldgreen; St. Stephen's Church, Rashcliffe; Almondbury War Memorial.

EXLEY, ERNEST. Private. No 31702. 'A' Company, 13th Battalion York and Lancaster Regiment. Formerly No 5556 Duke of Wellington's Regiment. Born Scissett. Son of Samuel and Mary Exley, of Water Street, Scissett. Died of wounds at No 2 Casualty Clearing Station, 15.5.1918, aged 30 years. Buried **EBBLINGHEM MILITARY CEMETERY**. Grave location:- Plot 2, Row B, Grave 18. ROH:- Scissett War Memorial; Clayton West and High Hoyland War Memorial.

EXLEY, PERCY. Signaller. No 28028. 'A' Battery, 256th Brigade Royal Field Artillery. Born Scissett. Killed in action, 24.10.1918. Buried **THIANT COMMUNAL CEMETERY**. Grave location:- Row B, Grave 10. ROH:- Scissett War Memorial.

EXLEY, SAM. Private. No 36909. 8th Battalion Duke of Cornwall's Light Infantry. Lived Station House, Clayton West. Employed as a roller-coverer by Messrs R. Beanland and Company, Clayton West. Enlisted May 1916. Died of pneumonia in Bulgaria, 5.12.1918, aged 21 years. Buried **SOFIA WAR CEMETERY**. Grave location:- Plot 3, Row A, Grave 13. ROH:- Clayton West and High Hoyland War Memorial.

EXLEY, WILLIAM HENRY. Private. No 1559. 12th Battalion West Yorkshire Regiment. Born Dewsbury. Son of Mr and Mrs Ledgard Exley, 55 St. Andrew's Road, Huddersfield. Employed as a presser by Messrs J. Holroyd and Company, Seed Hill. Attended the Huddersfield Mission Sunday School and the Band of Hope. Died of wounds at No 8 Casualty Clearing Station, 9.4.1917, aged 20 years. Buried **DUISANS BRITISH CEMETERY.** Grave location:- Plot 3, Row A, Grave 1. ROH:- Christ Church, Moldgreen.

FAHEY, THOMAS. Private. 8th Battalion South Staffordshire Regiment. Lived 28 Lowerhead Road, Huddersfield.

FAHY, MICHAEL. Private. No 4114. 1/5th Battalion Duke of Wellington's Regiment. Adopted son of Mr and Mrs J. W. Dwyer, 7 Freehold Street, Primrose Hill, Huddersfield. Educated at St. Patrick's Roman Catholic School and Spring Grove Council School. Attended the Huddersfield Technical College evening classes. Was employed as an apprentice chemist by British Dyes Limited and assistant to Mr Alfred Dixon. Was a member of the St. Joseph's Catholic Church and the Young Men's Catholic Association. Enlisted June 1915. Reported missing, 3.9.1916, aged 19 years. Buried **MILL ROAD CEMETERY.** Grave location:- Plot 3, Row F, Grave 6. ROH:- Huddersfield Drill Hall.

FAIRBANK, WILLIAM HAROLD. Private. No 306338. 2/7th Battalion Duke of Wellington's Regiment. Born Wellhouse, Golcar. Son of Mr and Mrs Sam Henry Fairbank, 26 Grange Avenue, Marsden. Employed as a weaver by Messrs Robinson Brothers at Clough Lea Mill, Marsden. Was a keen cyclist and a member of the Clarion Cycling Club. Enlisted November 1915. Embarked for France in January, 1916. Killed in action, 3.5.1917, aged 23 years. Has no known grave. Commemorated **ARRAS MEMORIAL TO THE MISSING.** ROH:- Huddersfield Drill Hall; Marsden War Memorial.

FALCONER, WILLIAM ALEXANDER. Private. No 66825. 12/13th Battalion Northumberland Fusiliers. Born Slaithwaite. Educated Crow Lane Board School, Milnsbridge. Employed as a junior clerk by the London and North Western Railway Company. Enlisted Halifax. Died 14.4.1918. Has no known grave. Commemorated **TYNE COT MEMORIAL TO THE MISSING.** ROH:- St. James Church, Slaithwaite; Slaithwaite War Memorial; Crow Lane Board School, Milnsbridge; London and North Western Railway Company Roll.

FARNHILL, NORMAN. Private. No 12125. 8th Battalion York and Lancaster Regiment. Born Milnsbridge. Son of Mr and Mrs Jacob Farnhill, 30 Casson Street, Milnsbridge. Husband of Mrs Farnhill, of Whiteley Street, Milnsbridge. Assisted his father in the business of joiner and undertaker at 3 Pickford Street, Milnsbridge. Formerly attended the Milnsbridge Wesleyan Sunday School and later was an active member of the Salvation Army. Reported missing on the first day of the Battle of the Somme, 1.7.1916, aged 28 years. Has no known grave. Commemorated **THIEPVAL MEMORIAL TO THE MISSING.** ROH:- Milnsbridge War Memorial; Huddersfield Mission, Milnsbridge; St. Mark's Parish Church, Longwood.

FARRAR, GEORGE W. Private. No 59781. West Yorkshire Regiment, transferred to No 650654 302nd Prisoner of War Company, Labour Corps. Lived New North Road, Crimble, Golcar. Died in Becketts Park Hospital, Leeds, 13.8.1921, aged 35. Buried **SLAITHWAITE CEMETERY.** Grave location:- A, 3, 57.

FARRAR, HAROLD. Rifleman. No C/7226. 18th Battalion King's Royal Rifle Corps. Born Holmfirth. Son of Mr and Mrs J. Sydney Farrar of Underbank Holmfirth. Husband of Irene Farrar, of Church Terrace, Holmfirth. Educated at Hade Edge Council School. Employed at Washpit Mills, Holmfirth. Enlisted 1915. Came home on leave shortly before his death and had only been back in France four weeks when he was wounded and died of his wounds on 24.8.1918, aged 23 years. Buried **LIJSSENTHOEK MILITARY CEMETERY.** Grave location:- Plot 25, Row G, Grave 27. ROH:- Holmfirth War Memorial.

FARRAR, JAMES ERNEST. Private. No 203680. 1/5th Battalion Duke of Wellington's Regiment. Born 45 Albert Street, Lockwood, 26.4.1896. Son of Mr and Mrs W H Farrar, 6 Blamires Yard, Swan Lane, Lockwood. Educated Mount

Pleasant Council School, Lockwood. Employed as a labourer by Messrs John Quarmby and Sons, paper bag manufacturers, East Parade, Huddersfield. Enlisted 1.3.1916. Reported missing, presumed killed, 20.3.1917, aged 21 years. Has no known grave. Commemorated **LOOS MEMORIAL TO THE MISSING.** ROH:- Lockwood Baptist Church; Emmanuel Church, Lockwood; Huddersfield Drill Hall.

FARRELL, PETER, DCM. Sergeant. No 353034. 2/9th Battalion Manchester Regiment. Lived 29 Rosemary Lane, Huddersfield. Married, with three children. Employed at British Dyes Limited. Enlisted December 1916. Reported missing, presumed killed, 9.10.1917, aged 31 years. Has no known grave. Commemorated **TYNE COT MEMORIAL TO THE MISSING.**

FARRON, ALBERT. Private. No 5764. 1st Battalion King's Own (Royal Lancaster Regiment). Born Christchurch, Ashton-under-Lyne. Enlisted Lancaster. Husband of Beatrice Mary Farron, West End, Golcar. Employed as a weaver by Mr J. E. Crowther, Bank Bottom Mills, Marsden. Enlisted in the army at the age of 16 years, saw service in India and went through the whole of the South African campaign. Re-enlisted at the outbreak of the war. His wife received the following letter from him telling her that they had landed at Boulogne on 23.8.1914, *'We got stuck into the Germans somewhere in the Mons district on the 26th August and a ripping do it was too I can tell you. We had to retire nearly to Paris, the Germans were about 3 to our 1, at least so the papers say and judging by the iron that came over I should say too. So never worry I dodged them that day and I am dodging them yet. The General has complimented our regiment and two Privates of our Company have been mentioned in despatches for bringing in a wounded comrade out of the firing line. They deserve it too. I suppose you will think I am telling you old news but we are only allowed to tell you what happened a month back. I have written this to let you know that I am in France alright. Fine country too, grand farms, tons of fruit and the people, well they would give you anything nearly. We sleep mostly in barns amongst the straw. We are in a barn now and there is about two ton of tobacco leaf behind our heads. Just at present we have lots of smoking stuff but don't forget the writing paper I told you about. I don't know how long the war will last but I think that shortage of money will beat Germany in the end. The fighting in South Africa was soft up to this lot but South Africa could beat it hollow for hardships. Outposts, grub and weather were all worst in South Africa but the scrapping here is mustard. We shall have a Merry Christmas this time you see if we don't.'* Reported missing, presumed killed, 20.10.1914, aged 31 years. Has no known grave. Commemorated **PLOEGSTEERT MEMORIAL TO THE MISSING.** ROH:- St. John's Church, Golcar.

FAULDER, HAROLD. Captain. 3rd, attached 1/4th, Battalion York and Lancaster Regiment. Born Huddersfield 15.2.1885. Son of the late Joseph T. Faulder (of the firm of Messrs Stothart and Faulder, formerly merchants, of Huddersfield), and of Mrs Faulder, 2 Wellfield Road, Marsh. Educated Mr Wild's School, Huddersfield, and Marlborough Public School. Employed by Mr John Edward Crowther, of Bank Bottom Mills, Marsden, for about six years as manager of the weaving department. Subsequently he was in business as a woollen manufacturer in Colne Road, Huddersfield. Went over to the U.S.A., where he held a position at the Peacedale Woollen Mills, Rhode Island. Left the U.S.A. to enlist in April, 1915, in the Inns of Court Officers' Training Corps. Husband of Marjorie Faulder, 65 Broadhurst Gardens, Hampstead, London. N.W.3. Embarked for France in June, 1916. Mentioned in despatches in January, 1918. Killed in action, 26.4.1918, aged 33. Has no known grave. Commemorated **TYNE COT MEMORIAL TO THE MISSING.** ROH:- Holy Trinity Church, Huddersfield; Huddersfield College School.

FAWCETT, ARNOLD. Rifleman. No 372239. 8th (City of London) Battalion (Post Office Rifles). Born Albert Street, Lindley, 9.1.1893. Son of William and Ellinor Fawcett, 33 George Street, Lindley. Educated Lindley National Day School. Attended St. Stephen's Church, Lindley and was secretary of the Lindley Adult School. Employed as a sorting clerk and telegraphist at the Huddersfield Post Office. Enlisted 22.11.1915. Killed instantenously on 7.10.1916, aged 23, by a machine gun bullet striking him in the neck whilst making for a shell hole and already wounded in the right shoulder. Has no known grave. Commemorated **THIEPVAL MEMORIAL**

TO THE MISSING. ROH:- St. Stephen's Church, Lindley; Huddersfield General Post Office.

FAWCETT, JAMES ALBERT. Private. No 1871. 1/7th Battalion Duke of Wellington's Regiment. Born Marsden. Son of Mr and Mrs William Fawcett of Netherleigh, Marsden. Attended Marsden Congregational Sunday School. Employed as a dyer's labourer by Mr John Ed Crowther at Bank Bottom Mills. Was a keen cricketer and won a medal in Marsden Cricket Club's championships in 1913. Enlisted at the outbreak of war. Died of wounds to the head, 21.11.1915, aged 22 years. Buried **ETAPLES MILITARY CEMETERY.** Grave location:- Plot 3, Row G, Grave 7a. ROH:- Huddersfield Drill Hall; Marsden War Memorial.

FAWLEY, WALTER LEONARD. Private. No 24741. 9th Battalion Duke of Wellington's Regiment. Born 9 Calton Street, Bradford Road, Huddersfield. Son of Fred and Edith Annie Fawley, 18 Row Street, Crosland Moor. Educated at Huddersfield Parish Church School. Employed as a tailor's cutter by Messrs H. Booth and Son Limited, wholesale clothiers, St. John's Road, Huddersfield. Enlisted 4.8.1914. Was killed in action near Cambrai in No Man's Land, 27.2.1918, aged 24 years, a fortnight after his return from leave at home. Buried **HERMIES HILL BRITISH CEMETERY.** Grave location:- Plot 1, Row G, Grave 19. ROH:- Huddersfield Parish Church; St. Barnabas's Church, Crosland Moor.

FEARNES, SAM ILLINGWORTH. Corporal. No 33381. Transferred to No 24017, 41st Company, Labour Corps. Son of Mrs Emily Fearnes. Husband of Amy Fearnes of New Town, Holmfirth. Employed as an engine tenter at Underbank Mill. Enlisted 1917. Died in Germany, 28.3.1919, aged 28 years. Buried **COLOGNE SOUTHERN CEMETERY, GERMANY.** Grave location:- Plot 3, Row E, Grave 8. ROH:- Holmfirth War Memorial.

FEARNLEY, ANTHONY. Private. No 203043. 1/4th Battalion King's Own Yorkshire Light Infantry. Formerly No 5737 Duke of Wellington's Regiment. Born Lepton. Son of Charles Fearnley, Spa Bottom, Lepton. Employed as a piecer by Messrs John Kaye and Son, Kings Mill Lane. Enlisted 1915. Died of wounds (gas), 25.7., aged 28 years. Buried **COXYDE MILITARY CEMETERY.** Grave location:- Plot 1, Row K, Grave 41. ROH:- Lepton Parish Church.

FEARNLEY, ARTHUR. Private. No 39480. 2/4th Battalion King's Own Yorkshire Light Infantry. Formerly No 32299 Duke of Wellington's Regiment. Son of Willie and Annie Fearnley, of Moor Top, Kirkheaton. Died 26.6.1918, aged 18 years. Buried **BAGNEUX BRITISH CEMETERY.** Grave location:- Plot 3, Row C, Grave 3. ROH:- St. John's Church, Kirkheaton.

FELL, C. Private. No 305018. 1/7th Battalion Duke of Wellington's Regiment. Born Marsden. Son of William and Ellen Fell. Husband of Margaret Ann Fell, 36 Woods Avenue, Marsden. Died at home, 29.8.1919, aged 39 years. Buried **St. BARTHOLOMEW'S CHURCHYARD, MARSDEN.** Grave location:- South, 32, 11. ROH:- Marsden War Memorial.

FENTON, HENRY PERCIVAL. Private. No 46743, 12th/13th Battalion Northumberland Fusiliers. Born Willoughton, Lincolnshire. Enlisted Halifax. Lived with his sister, Mrs Herman Shaw, at Commercial Road, Skelmanthorpe. Was a shoe-maker prior to enlisting on 13.5.1916. Embarked for France in December, 1916. Killed in action, 7.11.1917, aged 30 years. Has no known grave. Commemorated **TYNE COT MEMORIAL TO THE MISSING.** ROH:- St. Aidan's Church, Skelmanthorpe.

FETHNEY, LOUIE. Assistant Inspector Munitions for the Government. Born Bradford 23.6.1898. Son of Peter and Clara Fethney, 246 Halifax Old Road, Grimscar, Huddersfield. Educated Oaklea Academy, Galashiels, Scotland. Single. Employed at the Naval Munition Works, Crosland Moor. Killed at Crosland Moor in an explosion, 6.5.1918, aged 20 years. Buried **EDGERTON CEMETERY, HUDDERSFIELD.** ROH:- St. Cuthbert's Church, Birkby.

FIDLER, CLIFFORD. Private. No 5/2266 'A' Company, 1/5th Battalion Duke of Wellington's Regiment. Born Leeds 14.4.1897. Son of Fred and Lily Fidler, 7a Hebble Street, Bradford Road, Huddersfield. Educated Richmond Hill School, Leeds. Employed as an engineer. Single. Enlisted in the local Territorials in April, 1913.

Killed in action near Ypres, 18.9.1915, aged 18 years. Buried **NEW IRISH FARM CEMETERY.** Grave location:- Plot 17, Row E, Grave 3. ROH:- Milton Independent Church; Fartown and Birkby War Memorial; St. Andrew's Church, Leeds Road; Huddersfield Drill Hall; also commemorated on his parents' headstone in Edgerton Cemetery.

FIELD, ALBERT EDWARD SMITH. Sergeant. No 306157. 2/7th Battalion Duke of Wellington's Regiment. Married, with two children. Lived 20 Hardend Cottages, Marsden. Employed in the warehouse at Bank Bottom Mills, Marsden. Enlisted July 1915. Embarked for France in January, 1917. Died of wounds at No 49 (West Riding) Casualty Clearing Station, 3.12.1917, aged 28 years. Buried **ACHIET-LE-GRAND COMMUNAL CEMETERY EXTENSION.** Grave location:- Plot 2, Row A, Grave 11. ROH:- Huddersfield Drill Hall; Marsden War Memorial.

FIELD, ARTHUR. Private. No 62554. 2/4th Battalion King's Own Yorkshire Light Infantry. Formerly No 5/93748 Territorial Reserve Battalion. Born Skelmanthorpe. Son of Clifton and Annie Field, of Station Road, Skelmanthorpe. Killed in action, 20.7.1918, aged 18 years. Buried **CHAMBRECY BRITISH CEMETERY.** Grave location:- Plot 1, Row B, Grave 8. (Brother of Private **JOSEPH WILSON FIELD**, reported missing, 27.5.1918, q.v.). ROH:- St. Aidan's Church, Skelmanthorpe.

FIELD, HARLAND. Gunner. No 141005. 'B' Battery, 97th Brigade Royal Field Artillery. Born Knottingley, near Pontefract, 3.6.1894. Son of John William and Edith Ellen Field, 14 Portland Street, Huddersfield. Educated at the Wesleyan School, Knottingley. Employed as a railway fireman by the North Eastern Railway Company. Single. At the time of enlistment, was living at 28 Alder Street, Huddersfield. Enlisted 16.5.1916. Wounded 16.4.1918 and died of his wounds on 17.4.1918, aged 23 years. Buried **ETAPLES MILITARY CEMETERY.** Grave location:- Plot 29, Row F, Grave 2a. ROH:- North Eastern Railway Roll.

FIELD, HARRY, MM. Lance Corporal. 2nd Battalion Duke of Wellington's Regiment. No 204573. Born Earls Eaton 16.4.1898. Son of Mr and Mrs Ernest Field, 8 Sufton Street, Birkby.

Educated at St. John's School, Birkby and Oakes Council School. Attended New North Road Baptist Sunday School. Employed as a book salesman by Messrs Tyler, of King Street, Huddersfield. Enlisted 1.9.1915. Awarded the Military Medal on 25.10.1917 for, *'distinguished conduct and gallantry in the field. In the attack on 9.10.1917 near Poelcappelle when several members of his Lewis gun team including Numbers 1 and 2 had been knocked out he picked up his gun and carried on with it in the face of heavy machine gun and rifle fire. He then forced his way to a very forward position and by keeping up an effective fire on the enemy was largely responsible for beating off a counter attack. He showed great spirit and determination throughout.'* (The medal was sent to his parents on 28.11.1918) Killed in action near La Bassee, 15.4.1918. (The day before his 20th birthday). Has no known grave. Commemorated **PLOEGSTEERT MEMORIAL TO THE MISSING.** ROH:- New North Road Baptist Church; Fartown and Birkby War Memorial.

FIELD, JOSEPH WILSON. Lance Corporal. No 250766. 1/6th Battalion Durham Light Infantry. Formerly No 5386 Duke of Wellington's Regiment. Born Skelmanthorpe. Son of Clifton and Annie Field, Station Road, Skelmanthorpe. Prior to enlistment, was employed by Messrs Field and Botterill. Was commended by the General commanding his Division on his gallant conduct at the Battle of the Somme. Reported missing, 27.5.1918, aged 21 years. Has no known grave. Commemorated **SOISSONS MEMORIAL TO THE MISSING.** (Brother of Private **ARTHUR FIELD**, killed in action, 20.7.1918, q.v.). ROH:- St. Aidan's Church, Skelmanthorpe.

FIELD, LAWRENCE WILLIAM. Private. No 53206. 10th Battalion West Yorkshire Regiment. Born Skelmanthorpe. Son of Willie and Elizabeth Field, of Commercial Road Road, Skelmanthorpe. Assisted his father in the grocery and corn business. Killed in action, 24.8.1918, aged 19 years. Buried **POZIERES BRITISH CEMETERY.** Grave location:- 4, T, 39. ROH:- St. Aidan's Church, Skelmanthorpe.

FIELD, NORMAN. Private. No 45390. 1st Battalion East Yorkshire Regiment. Born 15 Fern Lea Road, Lindley, 11.10.1892. Son of James S. and Mary Elizabeth Field, Chatham

Cottage, Outlane, and formerly of 37 Trinity Street, Huddersfield. Educated Christ Church Schools, Huddersfield. Single. Enlisted 7.8.1914. Killed in action, 16.4.1918, aged 25 years. Has no known grave. Commemorated **TYNE COT MEMORIAL TO THE MISSING.** ROH:- Holy Trinity Church, Huddersfield.

FIELD, NORMAN. Lieutenant. 5th Battalion Manchester Regiment, attached 25th Squadron Royal Flying Corps. Son of the late Edgar Field and Eliza Field, of Box Cottage, Skelmanthorpe. Educated New College, Harrogate. Employed by Messrs Edwin Field and Sons, of Skelmanthorpe, and later with his Uncle, Mr J. T. Field. He then joined the Bingley Weaving Company Limited and was appointed Managing Director, which position he held at the time he volunteered for service. Received his commission in November, 1915, and was promoted Lieutenant in October, 1916. Embarked for France again in December, 1916, and transferred to the Royal Flying Corps in April, 1917. Reported missing, presumed killed, 14.8.1917, aged 24 years. Buried **CABARET ROUGE BRITISH CEMETERY.** Grave location:- Plot 7, Row H, Grave 10. ROH:- St. Aidan's Church, Skelmanthorpe.

FIELD, SAMUEL. 1st Class Stoker. No SS/101225 (RFR/B/3546). Royal Navy. *HMS Broke*. Born Huddersfield 27.9.1880. Husband of Florence S. Field, 120 Netheroyd Hill Road, Cowcliffe, Huddersfield. Employed as a whitesmith by Messrs T. A. Heaps and Company, ironmongers, of Westgate, Huddersfield. Was a teacher at the Cowcliffe Wesleyan Sunday School. Had served nearly twelve years in the Navy and, at the outbreak of the war, was in the Royal Fleet Reserve. Re-enlisted 4.8.1914. Took part in the Battle of Jutland and came home on leave in March, 1917. On Friday, 20.4.1917, six German destroyers raided the Dover Straits but failed to cause serious military or civil damage. They were encountered by two flotilla leaders of the Dover Patrol, 'Swift' and 'Broke.' Killed on board *HMS Broke*, 21.4.1917, aged 36 years. Buried with full military honours in **EDGERTON CEMETERY, HUDDERSFIELD.** Grave location:- 3B, 164. ROH:- St. Hilda's Church, Cowcliffe; Cowcliffe Wesleyan Church; Fartown and Birkby War Memorial.

FIELD, THOMAS. Private. No 10368. Durham Light Infantry, transferred to No 47921 Labour Corps. Died at home 6.2.1920. Buried **SALENDINE NOOK BAPTIST CHAPEL YARD.** Grave location:- in East part, 357E.

FIELDING, ELI. Gunner. No 68405. 109th Siege Battery, Royal Garrison Artillery, attached 13th Battalion Tank Corps. Son of J. W. Fielding of 'North View', Golcar. Husband of F. M. Fielding, 111 Townend, Golcar. Was a member of Golcar Conservative Club. Employed as a tailor. Enlisted, 21.2.1916, and spent three years in France. On 10.6.1919 he was one of the crew of a tank which got of control and in trying to jump clear he was accidentally killed. He was 26 years of age. Buried **THEUX COMMUNAL CEMETERY.** Grave location:- Grave No 1. ROH:- St. John's Church, Golcar.

FIELDING, FRANK. Private. No 27115. 16th Battalion (1st Manchester Pals) Manchester Regiment. Born Marsden. Lived at 'The Swan Inn', Marsden. Employed as an assistant in the shop of Mr S. T. Shaw, chemist, Peel Street, Marsden. Enlisted 7.5.1915. Embarked for France 24.12.1915. Killed in action, 1.7.1916, aged 18 years. Buried **DANTZIG ALLEY BRITISH CEMETERY.** Grave location:- Vernon Street Cemetery Memorial 25. His brother, Gilbert Fielding, received the following letter from Captain Wilfrith Elstub (who won the Victoria Cross in March 1918). After expressing his sorrow the Captain goes on to say that Private Fielding was killed in the great battle of July 1st and 2nd, whilst carrying up material for the purpose of consolidating the village of Montauban that they had captured, *'He died instantenously whilst we were going forward. I personally regret his loss immensely as his young and cheerful face often caught my notice as I used to go round the Company. He was a good brave young soldier and he nobly died doing his duty for the old country. Please accept my deepest sympathy.'*. ROH:- Marsden War Memorial.

FIELDSEND, ROBERT CHARLES. Gunner. No 98331. 231st Siege Battery, Royal Garrison Artillery. Born Huddersfield. Son of the late R. C. Fieldsend. Husband of the late Sarah Fieldsend. Died of wounds, 29.3.1917, aged 36 years. Buried **EUSTON ROAD CEMETERY.** Grave location:- Plot 5, Row F, Grave 9.

FINLAYSON, HENRY ARCHIBALD NEWTON (ARCHIE). Lance Corporal. No 252185. 2/6th Battalion Manchester Regiment. Born Salford, Lancashire. Lived Meltham, Huddersfield. Killed in action, 10.5.1917, aged 36. Buried **CAMBRIN MILITARY CEMETERY.** Grave location:- Row J, Grave 4. ROH:- St. Bartholomew's Church, Meltham; Helme Parish Church.

FINNIGAN, MICHAEL. Private. No 58940. 3rd Garrison Battalion Royal Welsh Fusiliers. Formerly No 8912 South Wales Borderers. Born Owston Ferry, Doncaster. Lived Huddersfield. Son of John and Bridget Finnigan. Died at home, 28.7.1917, aged 43. Buried **OSWESTRY GENERAL CEMETERY, SHROPSHIRE.** Grave location:- T.N.C., 242.

FIRTH, ARNOLD. Second Lieutenant. 7th London Brigade Royal Field Artillery. Son of Wilson and Mary Firth of Gowan Lea, Park Drive, Huddersfield. Left Huddersfield in 1912 for London where he took up a business appointment. Killed in action, 15.4.1917, aged 35 years. Buried **H.A.C. CEMETERY.** Grave location:- Plot 3, Row G, Grave 23.

FIRTH, ARTHUR. Private. No 81306. 18th Battalion Machine Gun Corps. Born Marsden. Only son of Samuel and Louisa Firth, Field House, Marsden. Employed by his father as a painter and decorator. Was a member of the Wesleyan Adult Bible Class and had been assistant secretary to the Sunday School. Was also a member of the Marsden Liberal Club. Enlisted in the R.A.O.C. on 26.10.1915 and embarked for France on Good Friday, 1916. In October, 1916, he returned home and trained for the Infantry, becoming a member of the Machine Gun Corps. He returned to France and was gassed on two occasions. He died from the effects of gas poisoning at No 11 Stationary Hospital, Rouen, 7.9.1918, aged 22 years. Buried **St. SEVER CEMETERY EXTENSION, ROUEN.** Grave location:- Block R, Plot 2, Row M. Grave 6. ROH:- Marsden Liberal Club; Marsden War Memorial.

FIRTH, ARTHUR. Private. No 19932. 6th Battalion King's Own Scottish Borderers. Born Cumberworth. Son of George Thomas and Emma Firth of Upper Cumberworth. Educated at Leeds College and was a teacher at Garforth Council School. Enlisted May 1915. Killed in action, 3.5.1917, aged 24 years. Has no known grave. Commemorated **ARRAS MEMORIAL TO THE MISSING.** ROH:- Denby Dale and Cumberworth War Memorial.

FIRTH, FRED. Private. No 13240. 7th Battalion King's Own Yorkshire Light Infantry. Born Denby 4.10.1894. Youngest son of Benjamin and Eliza Firth of The Lodge, Bagden Hall, Scissett, Huddersfield. Attended Scissett Church and sang in the choir. Played in the Denby Dale Brass Band. Employed at Skelmanthorpe Cooperative Society Limited as a teamer. Enlisted at the outbreak of the war. Killed in action, 8.10.1915, aged 21 years. Buried **RUE-du-BOIS MILITARY CEMETERY, FLEURBIX.** Grave location:- Plot 1, Row A, Grave 1. ROH:- Denby Dale and Cumberworth War Memorial.

FIRTH, HORACE, MM. (Served as **DEPLEDGE**). Sergeant. No 842282. 24th Battalion Canadian Infantry. Born Denby Dale. Son of Amos and Louisa Firth. Emigrated to the United States in 1907. At the outbreak of war he travelled from California to British Columbia to enlist. He joined the Canadian Navy and served for a time as an Able Seaman on board the *Niobe* but was apparently dissatisfied by finding no fighting and transferred to the Infantry. He was awarded the Military Medal in December, 1917. Died of wounds, 25.2.1918, aged 30 years. Buried **BARLIN COMMUNAL CEMETERY EXTENSION.** Grave location:- Plot 3, Row E, Grave 41.

FIRTH, LEONARD. Private. No 5549. 1/5th Battalion Duke of Wellington's Regiment. Born Nettleton, Dalton, 27.9.1880. Son of Tom and Catherine Firth, 24 Lane End, Dalton. Educated Kirkheaton National School. Employed as a pattern weaver by Messrs R. Mitchell and Company, Spa Mills, Lepton. Enlisted 4.4.1916. Wounded in the chest and arm at Thiepval Wood, 3.9.1916. Died of his wounds at Warloy Operating Centre, 13.9.1916, aged 21 years. Buried **WARLOY-BAILLON COMMUNAL CEMETERY.** Grave location:- Plot 2, Row H, Grave 8. ROH:- St. John's Church, Kirkheaton; Huddersfield Drill Hall; also commemorated on headstone in Kirkheaton Cemetery.

FIRTH, PERCY. Private. No 303705. 10th Company, Labour Corps. Formerly No 4798 3/5th Battalion Seaforth Highlanders. Born Huddersfield. Married. Lived 2 Sheepridge Road, Huddersfield. Employed as a twister by Messrs Learoyd Brothers and Company, of Trafalgar Mills. Accidentally killed by a fall of masonry in France, 31.10.1918, aged 29 years. Buried **'Y' FARM MILITARY CEMETERY, BOIS-GRENIER.** Grave location:- Row C, Grave 89. ROH:- Christ Church, Woodhouse Hill.

FIRTH, THOMAS RHODES. Rifleman. No 43729. 16th Battalion, The County of London Regiment, attached to King's Royal Rifle Corps. Formerly TR/5/19003 5th Territorial Reserve Battalion and No 58234 Northumberland Fusiliers. Born 72 Sheepridge Road, Huddersfield, 3.4.1899. Son of Mrs Eva Firth, 49 Sheepridge Road, Huddersfield. Educated Deighton Council School. Employed as a tailor's cutter by Messrs Bairstow and Company, of Fitzwilliam Street, Huddersfield. Single. Enlisted 11.5.1917. Killed in action at Sauchy-Cauchy, north north-west of Cambrai, on 27.9.1918, aged 19 years. Buried **SAUCHY-CAUCHY COMMUNAL CEMETERY EXTENSION.** Grave location:- Row A, Grave 27. ROH:- Sheepridge Providence United Methodist Sunday School; Christ Church, Woodhouse Hill.

FIRTH, WILLIAM. Private. No 41605. 2nd Battalion Lincolnshire Regiment. Formerly No 34334 Leicestershire Regiment. Born Diggle 27.5.1884. Educated St. Andrew's School, Leeds Road, Huddersfield. Employed as a compositor by Messrs Netherwood, Dalton and Company, Folly Hall. Attended St. Philip's Church, Birchencliffe. Husband of Mary Ellen Firth, 9 Burn Road, Birchencliffe. Enlisted 24.2.1917. Killed in action, 31.7.1917, aged 33 years. Has no known grave. Commemorated **MENIN GATE MEMORIAL TO THE MISSING.** ROH:- St. Philip's Church, Birchencliffe.

FISHER, DYSON ARMSWORTH. Private. No 1813. 1/5th Battalion Duke of Wellington's Regiment. Born Luddenden, Halifax. Son of Mr and Mrs Harry Fisher, 21 Riley Avenue, Dean, Bolton and formerly of Springdale Avenue, Longroyd Bridge. After his parents left Huddersfield for Bolton he lodged in Scholes Road, Birkby. Employed as a machinist by Messrs Hopkinsons of Birkby. Played with the Grimscar Rugby football club. He was a trombone player and for some time was in the Almondbury and Fire Brigade Bands. Enlisted at the outbreak of war and embarked for France in April, 1915. Killed in action at Fleurbaix, 24.6.1915, aged 21 years. Buried **RUE-DAVID MILITARY CEMETERY, FLEURBAIX.** Grave location:- Plot 1, Row B, Grave 10. ROH:- Huddersfield Drill Hall. His parents received the following letter from Major G. P. Norton (Officer commanding 'A' Company, 1/5th Battalion D.W.R.), '*I regret to have to inform you that your son No 1813 Private D. A. Fisher was mortally wounded this morning and died almost immediately. He was working in front of the trenches, digging a new listening post when he must have been hit from a shot fired from a flank some distance away but it was still dark and it was impossible to say exactly what happened. I feel this will be a great blow to you and that little I can say will help to make your loss easier to bear but I should like you to know that he had made himself highly proficient as a bomb-thrower for which section he volunteered some time ago. He was highly thought of by his Officers and his comrades as was always so cheerful which means a lot out here. I trust in time to come you will find some consolation in remembering he was one of those who died to save England and English women and children from the frightfulness of German militarism.*' PS.' *Your son was doing six days in the trenches in order to make way for some others to be trained as bomb throwers. I attended his funeral this morning. He was placed in a separate grave which will be marked with a neat white cross with his name, number and regiment posted on it. A wreath of wild flowers was placed on the grave.*'

FISHER, HERBERT. Private. No 47920. 12th Battalion Durham Light Infantry. Born Skelmanthorpe. Son of George Henry and Johanna Fisher of 10 Sunnyside Cottages, Skelmanthorpe. Employed as a stoker by Messrs Field and Botterill of Skelmanthorpe. Enlisted October 1916. Died of wounds, 2.6.1917, aged 23 years. Buried **HOP STORE CEMETERY, VLAMERTINGHE, BELGIUM.** Grave location:- Plot 1, Row A, Grave 29. ROH:- St. Aidan's Church, Skelmanthorpe.

FISHER, LOCKBURN. Private. No 3/10818. 2nd Battalion Duke of Wellington's Regiment. Born Hillhouse, Huddersfield. Son of Samuel and Emily Fisher, late of 53 Wellington Street, Lindley. In 1914 the family removed to Blackpool. Prior to enlistment, employed by Messrs Martin, Sons and Company. Enlisted August 1914. Killed in action, 1.4.1915, aged 23 years. Buried **TUILERIES BRITISH CEMETERY.** Grave location:- Special Memorial D 1. ROH:- Oakes Baptist Church; St. Stephen's Church, Lindley.

FISHER, OSWALD. Private. No PLY/585(S). Royal Marine Light Infantry. 2nd R.M. Battalion Royal Naval Division. Born Paddock 4.2.1895. Son of Thomas D. and Edith Fisher, 11 Mark Street, Paddock. Educated Paddock Council School and Huddersfield Technical College. Employed by Messrs James Shires and Sons of Milnsbridge as a pattern weaver and student designer. Attended the Brunswick Street United Methodist Chapel and was a member of the Young Men's Bible Class. Enlisted 5.11.1914. After 3 months training he was sent with the first contingent to the Dardenelles and was amongst the last to leave on evacuation in January, 1916. Killed in action at Beaumont Hamel, 30.10.1916, aged 21 years. Buried **HAMEL MILITARY CEMETERY.** Grave location:- Plot 2, Row C, Grave 20. ROH:- All Saints Church, Paddock.

FITTON, BENJAMIN ARTHUR. Air Mechanic 2nd Class. No 17729. 'C' Squadron, Royal Flying Corps. 2nd Training Centre. Son of Mr and Mrs Fitton of Meadow House, Shepley. Educated Spring Grove Council School. Employed by Messrs John Robinsons Limited, of Leeds Road. He left Huddersfield to take up newspaper work and at the time of his enlistment he was engaged by a London agency for the supply of photographs for the illustrated papers. He attempted to enlist in the Royal Flying Corps on several occasions but was rejected on the grounds of poor eyesight. Died from fever whilst in training, 17.2.1916, aged 24 years. Buried **CURRAGH MILITARY CEMETERY, COUNTY KILDARE, IRELAND.** Grave location:- Grave No 1222.

FLAGG, ARTHUR ERNEST. Private. No G/52469. 2nd Battalion Middlesex Regiment. Formerly No 41894 York and Lancaster Regiment. Born West Plumstead 15.2.1887. Son of the late Arthur Henry and Charlotte Flagg, 'The Homestead', Cucketfield Grove, Leigh-on-Sea, Essex. Educated at schools in Woolwich and Greenwich. Husband of Violet Gertrude Flagg, 28 Imperial Road, Edgerton, Huddersfield. Employed as a mechanical dentist. Enlisted 11.4.1917. Killed in action, 1.8.1917, aged 30 years. Has no known grave. Commemorated **MENIN GATE MEMORIAL TO THE MISSING.** ROH:- Holy Trinity Church, Huddersfield.

FLATLEY, JAMES. Corporal. No 9193. 3rd Dragoon Guards (Prince of Wales' Own). Born County Galway, Ireland. (Both parents deceased). Nephew of Mr and Mrs C. Reid, 154 Lea Head, Blacker Road, Birkby. Educated in County Galway Catholic Schools. Employed as a mason's labourer. Lodged with Mrs Davis in Rosemary Lane, Huddersfield. Enlisted 4.8.1914. Wounded at Hooge, near Ypres, 4.6.1915. Died of a haemorrhage from the lungs at St. Thomas's Hospital, London, 8.7.1915. Buried **St. MARY'S ROMAN CATHOLIC CEMETERY, KENSALL GREEN, HAMMERSMITH, LONDON.** Grave location *'Mr and Mrs Reid went to London and were present at his burial at Kensall Green Cemetery, London, on 13.7.1915.'* ROH:- Commemorated on screen wall.'

FLEMMING, WILLIAM. Private. No 6977. 2nd Battalion Yorkshire Regiment. Born Sheffield. Husband of Mrs Fleming of Bryan Road, Birchencliffe. Prior to enlistment, was employed by Messrs Read, Holliday and Sons Limited. Called up at the outbreak of the war as a Reservist, he had served in India. Killed at Ypres 30.10.1914. Has no known grave. Commemorated **MENIN GATE MEMORIAL TO THE MISSING.** ROH:- St. Philip's Church, Birchencliffe.

FLETCHER, JOSEPH EDWIN, MM. Private. No 202892. 9th Battalion Duke of Wellington's Regiment. Born Huddersfield. Husband of Alice Fletcher, 100 Church Lane, Moldgreen, Huddersfield. Prior to enlistment was employed by Messrs Haigh and Brierley, of Turnbridge, Huddersfield. Died of wounds, 20.9.1918, aged 31 years. Buried **Ste. MARIE CEMETERY, LE HAVRE.** Grave location:- Plot 5. Row E. Grave 6. ROH:- Christ Church, Moldgreen.

FLETCHER, NORMAN FREDERICK. Private. No 268074. 1/6th Battalion Duke of Wellington's

Regiment. Born Elland. Enlisted Marsden. Son of Mr and Mrs Sam Fletcher, 42 Varley Road, Slaithwaite. Husband of Agnes Fletcher, 34 Grange Avenue, Marsden. Employed as a warper at Bank Bottom Mills, Marsden. Was a keen cricketer, having at one time or another being associated with the Linthwaite Hall and Marsden cricket teams and Haslingden, where he assisted his father who was then a professional. Enlisted August, 1916, and embarked for France in July, 1917. Was killed on 12.4.1918, along with three other soldiers, by the bursting of a shell in a forward position. Has no known grave. Comemorated **TYNE COT MEMORIAL TO THE MISSING.** ROH:- Marsden War Memorial.

FLETCHER, SAMUEL. Private. No 47055. 15th Battalion Durham Light Infantry. Formerly No 75546 West Yorkshire Regiment. Born 12 Croft House Lane, Marsh 1.11.1898. Son of Mr and Mrs S. Fletcher, 6 Forrest Avenue, Marsh. Educated Holy Trinity Church of England School and Huddersfield College. Employed as an apprentice with Messrs Sykes and Sugden, electrical engineers, George Street, Marsh. Enlisted May 1918. Killed in action near Maubege, 7.11.1918. Buried **DOURLERS COMMUNAL CEMETERY EXTENSION.** Grave location:- Plot 2, Row A, Grave 7. ROH:-. Holy Trinity Church, Huddersfield.

FLINTON, FREDERICK WILLIAM. Private. No 11584. 2nd Battalion Duke of Wellington's Regiment. Born Wormsgate Lodge 11.9.1885. Son of Thomas and Rachel Flinton, 2 Long Croft, Almondbury. Educated Almondbury National School. Employed as a plush cutter by Messrs Dyson and Hall of Dalton, Huddersfield. Enlisted 4.9.1914. Embarked for France in January, 1915. Killed in action at Hill 60, 5.5.1915, aged 31 years. Has no known grave. Commemorated **MENIN GATE MEMORIAL TO THE MISSING.** (Brother of Private **THOMAS FLINTON**, reported missing, 27.1.1917, q.v.). ROH:- Almondbury War Memorial.

FLINTON, THOMAS. Private. No 240174. 'C' Company 2/5th Battalion Duke of Wellington's Regiment. Born Birks Mill, Almondbury, 19.9.1892. Son of Thomas and Rachel Flinton, 2 Long Croft, Almondbury. Educated Almondbury National School. Employed as a weaver by Messrs T. and H. Blamires Limited, Leeds Road, Huddersfield. Attended Almondbury Parish Church and was a member of the church football team. Enlisted 4.8.1914. Killed in action at Bourlon Wood, 27.11.1917, aged 23 years. Has no known grave. Commemorated **CAMBRAI MEMORIAL TO THE MISSING.** (Brother of Private **FREDERICK WILLIAM FLINTON**, killed in action, 5.5.1915, q.v.). ROH:- Huddersfield Drill Hall; Almondbury War Memorial.

FLYNN, JOHN. No 91896. Royal Defence Corps. Formerly No 1971. 10th Battalion King's Own Yorkshire Light Infantry. Born Watergate, Huddersfield, 12.5.1877. Educated St. Patrick's Roman Catholic School, Huddersfield. Husband of Margaret Flynn, 9 Love's Yard, High Street, Huddersfield. Employed as a wool packer. Had served in the Boer War. Enlisted 10.8.1914. Wounded three times whilst serving in France. Died at 9 Love's Yard, High Street, Huddersfield, on 16.12.1920, of tuberculosis and the effects of war. Buried **EDGERTON CEMETERY, HUDDERSFIELD.** Grave location:- 66, 63G.

FORD, JOE. Private. No 77928. 1/6th Battalion Durham Light Infantry. Born Newtown. Son of Private William Ford, 8 Dyson Hill, Honley. (His father served in the army for the duration of the war). Attended Honley Primitive Methodist Chapel. Employed at Rock Mills. Enlisted 1917. Embarked for France in January, 1918. Killed in action, 9.4.1918, aged 19 years. Has no known grave. Commemorated **PLOEGSTEERT MEMORIAL TO THE MISSING.** ROH:- Honley War Memorial.

FORSHAW, EDWARD HORACE. Corporal. No 305235. 2/7th Battalion Duke of Wellington's Regiment. Born Golcar. Son of William Richard and Mary Emma Forshaw, 85 Swallow Lane, Golcar. Employed at Dale Street Mills, Longwood. Attended St. John's Church, Golcar. Embarked for France in December, 1916. Killed in action, 14.5.1917. Has no known grave. Commemorated **ARRAS MEMORIAL TO THE MISSING.** (Brother of Private **TOM HAMER FORSHAW**, reported missing, 3.5.1917, q.v.). ROH:-St. John's Church, Golcar; Huddersfield Drill Hall.

FORSHAW, TOM HAMER. Private. No 306364. 'A' Company, 2/7th Battalion Duke of Wellington's Regiment. Born Golcar. Son of William Richard and Mary Emma Forshaw, 85

Swallow Lane, Golcar. Employed by Messrs B. and J. Whitwam, Stanley Mills, Golcar. Attended St. John's Church, Golcar. Reported missing, presumed killed, at the Battle of Bullecourt, 3.5.1917, aged 22. Has no known grave. Commemorated **ARRAS MEMORIAL TO THE MISSING**. (Brother of Private **EDWARD HORACE FORSHAW**, killed in action, 14.5.1917, q.v.). ROH:- Huddersfield Drill Hall.

FOSTER, ALAN EDWARD. Corporal. No 11124. 8th Battalion Duke of Wellington's Regiment. Born Sheffield 4.5.1889. Son of William Henry and Ann Eliza (nee Wragg) Foster, 6 Norman Avenue, Birkby. Educated at Western Road and Broomhill Board Schools, Sheffield. Employed as a draughtsman by Hopkinsons of Birkby. Single. Enlisted 26.8.1914. Reported wounded and missing in the assault on Ismail Oglu Tepe, Suvla, Gallipoli, 21.8.1915, and afterwards presumed to have been killed on that date. He was 26 years of age. Has no known grave. Commemorated **HELLES MEMORIAL TO THE MISSING, GALLIPOLI**. ROH:- Fartown and Birkby War Memorial.

FOSTER, CLARENCE. Private. No 23/392. 19th Battalion Durham Light Infantry. Born Huddersfield. Enlisted Huddersfield. Killed in action, 6.5.1917. Buried **MARTEVILLE COMMUNAL CEMETERY, ATTILLY**. Grave location:- Row A, Grave 29.

FOSTER, FRED. Private. No 19449. 2nd Battalion Duke of Wellington's Regiment. Born Lee and Burley's Yard, Leeds Road, Huddersfield, 6.6.1886. Son of Isaac and Elizabeth Foster, 61 Northumberland Street, Huddersfield. Educated Thomas Street Council School, Huddersfield. Attended Queen Street Mission Young Men's Class. Employed as a painter and decorator by the London and North Western Railway Company. Single. Enlisted March 1916. Died of exhaustion during action on 10.12.1916, near Combles, aged 30 years. Has no known grave. Commemorated **THIEPVAL MEMORIAL TO THE MISSING**. ROH:- Commemorated on his parents' headstone in Edgerton Cemetery, Huddersfield; London and North Western Railway Company Roll.

FOSTER, JACK HERMAN. Private. No 96097. Royal Army Medical Corps, attached 2nd Base Hospital. Born Huddersfield 18.3.1890. Nephew of Mrs Sam Scholes of Rothwell Street, Moldgreen. Lived 17 Cross Grove Street, Huddersfield. Married, with four children. Was a music teacher. Enlisted in the R.A.M.C. in November 1915. Went out to Mesopotamia in January, 1916. Died, 13.7.1916, in Mesopotamia of heat stroke. Buried **AMARA WAR CEMETERY, IRAQ**. Grave location:- Plot 13, Row J, Grave 5.

FOSTER, JAMES. Private. No 21486. 9th Battalion West Yorkshire Regiment. Born Glossop 21.7.1898. Son of Emma Foster, 47 Dock Street, Huddersfield. Educated St. Patrick's Roman Catholic School, Huddersfield. Employed as a tailor's presser by Messrs Brook and Sugden and Company. Single. Enlisted June 1915. Served 10 months in Egypt and then was transferred to France in July, 1916. Killed in action, 28.9.1916, aged 18 years. Has no known grave. Commemorated **THIEPVAL MEMORIAL TO THE MISSING**. (Son of Private **JAMES THOMAS FOSTER**, killed, 15.10.1915, in France. q.v.).

FOSTER, JAMES THOMAS. Private. No 11007. 2nd Battalion Duke of Wellington's Regiment. Born Glossop 11.1.1877. Educated St. Mary's School, Glossop. Husband of Emma Foster, 47 Dock Street, Huddersfield. Employed as a labourer. Attended St. Patrick's Roman Catholic Church. Served in the South African War. Volunteered for service in August, 1915. Was accidentally killed in the trenches, 15.10.1915, aged 37. The news of his death reached Huddersfield on the day that his son sailed for Egypt. Buried **CARNOY MILITARY CEMETERY**. Grave location:- Row O, Grave 4. (Father of Private **JAMES FOSTER**, killed in action, 28.9.1916, q.v.).

FOSTER, ROBERT. Private. No 21122. 9th Battalion West Yorkshire Regiment. Formerly East Yorkshire Regiment. Born Burley-in-Wharfedale. Son of Mr Foster, 51 St. Andrew's Road, Huddersfield. Enlisted in the East Yorkshire Regiment a few months before the outbreak of the war but in August, 1914, he was discharged on account of deafness. He went to work at Messrs Holmes, Turnbridge Ironworks, but at the end of September he applied to join the forces and was successful and enlisted in the

West Yorkshire Regiment. Was killed in action at Jephson's Post, Suvla, Gallipoli on 21.11.1915, aged 18 years. Buried **HILL 10 CEMETERY, SUVLA, GALLIPOLI.** Grave location:- Plot 2, Row G, Grave 3.

FOWLE, CHARLES ALFRED. Private. No 247. 2nd Battalion Lancashire Fusiliers. Born Norwich 2.3.1884. Son of the late John Bark Fowle and Georgina Fowle, 21 Row, Lakenham, Norwich. Husband of Alice Selina Fowle, 2 Cuthbert's Buildings, Northgate, Huddersfield. Was a native of Norwich and had lived for five years in Huddersfield. Employed as a labourer. Had served in South Africa during the Boer War. Enlisted 2.5.1904. Killed in action, 13.10.1914, aged 33 years. Has no known grave. Commemorated **PLOEGSTEERT MEMORIAL TO THE MISSING.** (Brother of Private **WALTER ERNEST FOWLE**, died, 5.3.1919, q.v.).

FOWLE, WALTER ERNEST. Private. No 8035. 3rd Battalion Norfolk Regiment; transferred to No 67350 Labour Corps. Born Lakenham, Norwich, in August 1878. Son of the late John Bark and Georgina Fowle. Husband of Eva Fowle, 58 Essex Street, Norwich and 2 Cuthbert's Buildings, Northgate, Huddersfield. Employed as a caretaker at Norwich Catholic Church. Served in the South African War. Was making his home in Huddersfield when the war commenced. Died in Huddersfield Royal Infirmary of pneumonia, 5.3.1919, aged 41 years. Buried **EDGERTON CEMETERY, HUDDERSFIELD.** Grave location:- 11B, 116. (Brother of Private **CHARLES ALFRED FOWLE**, killed in action, 13.10.1914, q.v.).

FOWLER, WILLIAM OSCAR. Private. 1/5th Duke of Wellington's Regiment. Born 20, Ravensknowle Road, Dalton, 14.6.1890. Son of Joe Hirst and Clara Fowler, 100, Birkhouse Lane, Dalton. Educated Moldgreen Council School and The College Secondary School, Huddersfield. Employed as a tailor's cutter. Married after enlisting on 3.9.1914. Discharged from the forces on medical grounds, 16.12.1914. Died on 4.8.1917 from a haemorrhage of the lungs at 33 Belton Street, Dalton.

FOWLES, WILLIE. Private. No 2170. 1/7th Battalion Duke of Wellington's Regiment. Son of John Fowles, Chain, Marsden. Attended Marsden Wesleyan Sunday School and Chapel. Employed as a healder by Messrs Crowther, Bruce and Company of Marsden. Enlisted September 1914. Spent his 21st birthday in the trenches. Was engaged in fetching water for use in the trenches when he was shot by a sniper on 24.8.1915, aged 21 years. Buried **BARD COTTAGE CEMETERY.** Grave location:- Plot 1, Row F, Grave 27. ROH:- Huddersfield Drill Hall; Marsden War Memorial.

FOX, JOHN. Private. No 241331. 1/5th Battalion Duke of Wellington's Regiment. Husband of Nellie Fox, 178 Albert Street, Lockwood, Huddersfield. Was employed by Messrs Taylor and Lodge of Rashcliffe. Was a member of the Dyers Club. Killed in action, 3.9.1916, aged 34 years. Has no known grave. Commemorated **THIEPVAL MEMORIAL TO THE MISSING.** ROH:- Emmanuel Church, Lockwood; Huddersfield Drill Hall.

FOX, NORMAN. Private. No 14622. 2nd Battalion Duke of Wellington's Regiment. Born South Crosland, Huddersfield, 3.8.1894. Son of Robert and Sarah Fox, 75 Lowerhouses, Almondbury, Huddersfield. Educated at Lowerhouses schools. Employed by Messrs E. Brook Limited as an electrical engineer. Single. Enlisted 16.11.1914. Reported missing at Hill 60, 5.5.1915, aged 17 years. Has no known grave. Commemorated **MENIN GATE MEMORIAL TO THE MISSING.** ROH:- Milton Independent Church; Lowerhouses War Memorial; Almondbury War Memorial.

FRANCE, ARCHER. Private. No 17/1037. 17th Battalion West Yorkshire Regiment. Born Kirkheaton. Husband of Mrs France, Bog Hall, Colne Bridge, Bradley. Employed as a coal miner. Killed in action, 24.7.1916, aged 31 years. Has no known grave. Commemorated **THIEPVAL MEMORIAL TO THE MISSING.** ROH:- St. John's Church, Kirkheaton; St. Thomas's Church, Bradley.

FRANCE, FRANK LEEMING. Private. No 36352. 'D' Company, 10th Battalion The Yorkshire Regiment. Born Liverpool 23.6.1891. Son of Joe and Ann France, 28 Cross Lane, Primrose Hill, Huddersfield. Educated Stile Common Council School, Primrose Hill. Employed as a warehouseman by Messrs. Taylor and Littlewood, Newsome Mills where he worked for twelve years.

Husband of Evelyn France, 19 New Laithe Hill, Newsome, Huddersfield. Enlisted February 1915. Died of wounds at No 21 Casualty Clearing Station, 7.5.1917, aged 26 years. Buried **WARLINCOURT HALTE BRITISH CEMETERY.** Grave location:- Plot 9, Row G, Grave 16. ROH:- Messrs. Taylor and Littlewood, Newsome Mills

FRANCE, FRED. Rifleman. No C/7548. 18th Battalion King's Royal Rifle Corps. Born Almondbury. Only son of Mr and Mrs James France, 13 Fairhill, Berry Brow. Was secretary of Salem Sunday School, a member of the church choir and keenly interested in church work. Employed by Messrs Revell and Revell, accountants. Killed in action, 15.9.1916, aged 19 years. Buried **BRONFAY FARM MILITARY CEMETERY.** Grave location:- Plot 1, Row A, Grave 21. His parents received the following letter from his friend, Private H. ROBSON. He wrote on the 19th September that they had then just come out of action in the front line, *'They went into action on the 15th September and Fred was in a very hot place. A shell exploded a very short distance in front of him and Fred lost consciousness immediately and never recovered. Those nearest to him did all they could for him but the case was hopeless from the first. Fred has walked straight ever since he joined the Army. He has always stood up for the weak against the strong and lived a life such as no man need be ashamed of.'* ROH:- Armitage Bridge War Memorial.

FRANCE, JOHN ARTHUR. Private. No 24400. 8th Battalion The King's Own (Royal Lancaster Regiment). Born Lockwood 16.6.1888. Son of Allan and Emily France, 19 May Street, Crosland Moor, Huddersfield. Educated Crosland Moor Board School. Prior to moving to Barrow-in Furness, was employed as an organ builder by Messrs P. Conacher and Company of Huddersfield. Husband of Ida France, 25 Moor End Road, Lockwood. Enlisted 17.7.1916. Wounded at Ypres, 29.4.1917. Died of wounds at Etaples Base Hospital, 5.5.1917, aged 28 years. Buried **ETAPLES MILITARY CEMETERY.** Grave location:- Plot 18, Row J, Grave 8. ROH:- Lockwood Baptist Church; Emmanuel Church, Lockwood; St. Barnabas Church, Crosland Moor; Memorial in Lockwood Cemetery.

FRANCE, JOSEPH WILLIAM. Private. No 55011. 15th/17th Battalion West Yorkshire Regiment. Born Paddock 2.4.1890. Educated Paddock National School. Husband of Lucy France, 3 Lees Yard, Lockwood. (Re-married – Gallagher – 4 Scar, Lockwood). Employed by Messrs J. Hopkinson and Sons Limited, of Birkby, as a moulder's labourer. Enlisted January 1918. Killed in action, 24.8.1917, aged 28 years. Buried **METEREN MILITARY CEMETERY.** Grave location:- Plot 5, Row A, Grave 566.

FRANCE, NORMAN. Driver. No L/18933. 'B' Battery, 82nd Brigade Royal Field Artillery. Born 99 Lockwood Road, Huddersfield. Fourth son of Mr and Mrs Tom France. Educated Mount Pleasant Board School. Employed as an iron moulder by Messrs Calvert Limited, Folly Hall. Attended Milton Congregational Church. He had been secretary of the Sunday School, secretary of the Band of Hope and a member of the church choir. Single. Enlisted 7.4.1915. Killed in action near Dickebusch, Belgium, 21.8.1917, aged 33 years. Buried **THE HUTS CEMETERY, DICKEBUSCH.** Grave location:- Plot 3, Row D, Grave 9. ROH:- St. Stephen's Church, Rashcliffe; Milton Independent Church.

FRANCE, NORMAN. Private. No 34262. 6th Battalion Leicestershire Regiment. Born Primrose Hill 21.6.1898. Son of Albert and Ada France, 97 Birch Road, Berry Brow, Huddersfield. Educated Stile Common and Berry Brow Council Schools and Huddersfield Technical College. Attended Berry Brow Wesleyan Church. Employed in the design department at Zetland Mills. Attended Berry Brow Wesleyan School. Was a member of the local cricket and football clubs. Single. Enlisted 17.2.1917. Killed in action at Epehy, 22.3.1918, aged 19 years. Has no known grave. Commemorated **POZIERES MEMORIAL TO THE MISSING.** ROH:- Armitage Bridge War Memorial.

FRANCE, TOM. Corporal. No 27716. 2nd Battalion West Yorkshire Regiment. Born Slaithwaite. Son of the late Fred and of Sarah France, Bank Bottom Farm, Marsden. Attended Lingards Wood Bottom Sunday School and a member of Marsden Liberal Club. Employed in the warehouse of Messrs Fisher, Firth and Company, Cellars Clough Mills. Enlisted 5.8.1914. For some time acted as bombing instructor in an English training camp. He embarked for France on Easter Monday, 1917. Killed in action, 24.4.1918. Has no known grave. Commemorated **POZIERES MEMORIAL TO THE MISSING.** ROH:- Marsden Liberal Club; Marsden War Memorial; St. James Church, Slaithwaite.

FRANCE, WILFRED LAWSON. Private. No 2794. 1/7th Battalion Duke of Wellington's Regiment, attached 147th Brigade Machine Gun Company. Born Linthwaite. Son of Henry and Ellen France, 53 Wood Top, Slaithwaite. Employed by Messrs J. and J. Sykes and Sons, coal merchants. Enlisted Christmas 1914. Embarked for France April, 1915, when he was transferred into the transport section and the Machine Gun Company. His work in the transport section kept him in touch with horses and he won 100 francs in a competition for the best groomed horse. Came home on leave a fortnight before his death. Killed in action, 2.7.1916, aged 37 years. Buried **CONNAUGHT CEMETERY, THIEPVAL.** Grave location:- Plot 12, Row M, Grave 1. The first intimation of his death was contained in a letter from Captain W. H. Sproule of the same Company. He wrote, '*It is with deep regret that I have to inform you that Private France was killed in action on the night of the 2nd inst. His loss is a great blow to me as he had always been a most bright and cheerful worker in the transport section. I trust that the knowledge that he died whilst doing his duty will be some consolation to you. He was bringing up ammunition for the machine guns on pack mules at the time and was hit by a fragment of high explosive shell, killing him instantly.*' ROH:- Carr Lane Methodist Church, Slaithwaite; St. James Church, Slaithwaite; Slaithwaite War Memorial; Huddersfield Drill Hall.

FRASER, WILLIAM DAVID, MM. Sergeant. No 2667. 1/5th Battalion Duke of Wellington's Regiment. Born Talybont, Brecon, Wales. Lived 28 Wooler's Yard, Chapel Hill, Huddersfield. Employed as a chemical worker at Messrs J. W. Leach of Milnsbridge. Married. Had served throughout the South African War Enlisted 8.8.1914. Embarked for France, 15.4.1915. Was known to his friends as 'Taffy'. Died of wounds to the skull as a Prisoner of War, 8.9.1916, aged 35 years. Buried **MORCHIES COMMUNAL CEMETERY.** Grave location:- Grave 2. ROH:- Huddersfield Drill Hall.

FREEBOROUGH, MALLINSON. Private. No 86036. 4th Battalion The Middlesex Regiment. Born Primrose Hill 27.6.1898. Son of Mrs Emma Hartley, 3 Prince Street, Primrose Hill, Huddersfield. Educated Stile Common Council School. Employed as a wire heald maker by Messrs Barlow and Hocknell. Single. Enlisted 18.2.1917. Died from shrapnel wounds to the chest at No 56 Casualty Clearing Station, Gezaincourt, 26.8.1918, aged 20 years. Buried **BAGNEUX BRITISH CEMETERY.** Grave location:- Plot 4, Row E, Grave 3. ROH:- St. Matthew's Church, Primrose Hill; Almondbury War Memorial.

FREEDMAN, MYER, MM. Private. No 13105. 10th Battalion Duke of Wellington's Regiment. Born Huddersfield 13.10.1892. Son of Mr and Mrs Freedman, 132 Fitzwilliam Street, Huddersfield. Educated at Huddersfield College. He was the only Jewish man born in Huddersfield who was of military age. Before enlistment assisted his father in the tailoring business. He then helped his father in the management of the Olympian Cinema at Longroyd Bridge. He then left Huddersfield to manage a cinema in Yeadon, Leeds, but gave it up when he enlisted in September, 1914. Single. Was awarded the Military Medal on 17.9.1916 for '*attending to a trench mortar battery No 69/2 single-handed for four days under trying circumstances with great skill between 16.5.1916 and 21.5.1916.*' He was killed in action near Contalmaison on 19.9.1916, aged 23 years. Buried **GORDON DUMP CEMETERY.** Grave location:- Plot 4, Row A, Grave 7. His parents received the following letter from Captain G F Sulman, '*I am sorry to say that I have some bad news about your son Private M. Freedman. We were suddenly shelled and I regret to say that among other casualties your son was killed. I enclose herewith a letter which I found in his paybook addressed to you. I am also sending you his Military Medal ribbon which was presented to him the day before for good work in this battery some months ago. I am sure you will prize the decoration he won.*'

FRENCH, EDWARD. Private. No 12619. 9th Battalion Duke of Wellington's Regiment. Born Huddersfield. Son of the late Martin French (an old Huddersfield Veteran) and Mrs French, 8 Old Post Office Yard, Castlegate, Huddersfield. Employed by the Huddersfield Corporation

Cleansing Department. Enlisted at the outbreak of the war. Had served nine months at the front when he was killed on 28.2.1916, by a shell exploding on his dugout. He was 25 years of age. Buried **SPOILBANK CEMETERY, ZILLEBEKE, BELGIUM.** Grave location:- Plot 1, Row L, Grave 3. (Brother of Private **JAMES FRENCH**, reported missing, 29.7.1916, q.v.).

FRENCH, JAMES. Private. No 14927. 10th Battalion Duke of Wellington's Regiment. Born Huddersfield. Son of the late Martin French (an old Huddersfield Veteran) and Mrs French, 8 Old Post Office Yard, Castlegate, Huddersfield. Employed by Bentley's Yorkshire Brewery Limited. Reported missing, presumed killed, 1.10.1916, aged 23 years. Has no known grave. Commemorated **THIEPVAL MEMORIAL TO THE MISSING.** (Brother of Private **EDWARD FRENCH**, killed in action, 28.2.1916. q.v.).

FRETWELL, FRANK. Private. No 36552. 1/6th Battalion Northumberland Fusiliers. Born Penistone. Husband of Charlotte Fretwell of Friezland House, Sovereign, Shepley. Employed by British Dyes Limited, of Huddersfield. Enlisted January 1916. Reported missing, presumed killed, 11.4.1918, aged 30 years. Has no known grave. Commemorated **PLOEGSTEERT MEMORIAL TO THE MISSING.** ROH:- Shepley War Memorial.

FRETWELL, FRANK FOSTER. Trooper. No 8664. 5th Dragoon Guards (Princess Charlotte's Own). Born 5 William Terrace, Alexandra Street, Hull, 27.1.1895. Son of Sam and Harriet Ann Fretwell, 1 Back Spring Street, Huddersfield. Employed as a labourer. Enlisted 10.9.1911. Died of wounds to the head in No 12 Casualty Clearing Station, Proven, Belgium, 30.10.1917. Buried **MENDINGHEM MILITARY CEMETERY.** Grave location:- Plot 6, Row A, Grave 33.

FRISBY, EDWIN HERBERT (TED). Trooper. No L/12834. 9th Lancers (Queen's Royal). Born St. Helens, Lancashire, 24.12.1882. Son of Tom and the late Sarah Frisby, 25 Arpley Street, Warrington. Educated Spring Grove Board School, Huddersfield. Husband of Helen Gertrude Frisby, 49 Blackhouse Road, Fartown. Employed as a carter on the London and North Western Railway. Had served in the South African War and in India. Called up as a Reservist, 5.8.1914, in the 9th Lancers in which he had served for 22 years. Died of gunshot wounds to the buttock and pelvis in No 2 Stationary Hospital, Abbeville, 24.3.1918, aged 36 years. Buried **ABBEVILLE COMMUNAL CEMETERY EXTENSION.** Grave location:- Plot 1, Row A, Grave 29. ROH:- Christ Church, Woodhouse Hill; Fartown and Birkby War Memorial; London and North Western Railway Company Roll.

FROGGATT, ARTHUR. Sapper. No 1496. 2/1st West Riding Field Company, Royal Engineers. Son of Joseph and Margaret Froggatt of Netherton. Was a cabinet maker and had been employed in Sheffield prior to enlistment but previously by Messrs J. Blakeley and Sons of Netherton. Was a member of the Netherton Wesleyan Choir. Single. Enlisted at the outbreak of war. Killed in action, 7.7.1916, aged 27 years. Buried **BOUZINCOURT COMMUNAL CEMETERY EXTENSION.** Grave location:- Plot 2, Row E, Grave 9. ROH:- South Crosland and Netherton War Memorial.

FROGGATT, GEORGE. Private. No 241855. 2/5th Battalion Duke of Wellington's Regiment. Born Wakefield. Son of Mr and Mrs Matthew Froggatt, of Rowley Hill, Lepton. Attended Rowley Hill Wesleyan Sunday School and a member of the Rowley Hill cricket club. Employed by Messrs George Thomas and Sons Limited, Fenay Bridge. Enlisted March, 1916, and had been in France nearly twelve months when he was killed on 26.11.1917, at the Battle of Cambrai, aged 21 years. He has no known grave. Commemorated **CAMBRAI MEMORIAL TO THE MISSING.** ROH:- Lepton Parish Church; Huddersfield Drill Hall; memorial in Emley Churchyard.

FROMENT, HAROLD. Rifleman. No R/19788. 9th Battalion King's Royal Rifle Corps. Born 73 Woodfield Road, Lockwood. Son of Sam and Martha Froment, 2 Meltham Road, Lockwood. Educated Mount Pleasant Council School. Employed as a cotton warehouseman by Messrs William Hirst and Sons of Turnbridge. Attended Lockwood Baptist Chapel. Single. Enlisted February 1916. Had only been in France for three weeks when he was killed on 15.9.1916, aged 23 years. Has no known grave. Commemorated **THIEPVAL MEMORIAL TO THE MISSING.** ROH:-

Lockwood Baptist Chapel; Emmanuel Church, Lockwood; Mount Pleasant Chapel, Lockwood.

FULLER, JOHN. Sapper. No 131603. 236th A.T. Company, Royal Engineers. Born 3 Leeches Yard, Chapel Hill, Huddersfield. Son of the late John Fuller and Jane Fuller. Educated St. Paul's Church of England School, Southgate, Huddersfield. Employed as a plumber by Messrs J. H. Taylor and Company, Macauley Street, Huddersfield. Attended St. Paul's Church. Husband of Laura Fuller, Woodbine Cottage, Fitzwilliam Street, Huddersfield. Enlisted 4.12.1915. Died of wounds, 30.11.1917, aged 27. Buried **YPRES RESERVOIR CEMETERY.** Grave location:- Plot 3, Row B, Grave 22. ROH:- St. Paul's Church, Southgate, Huddersfield; St. Andrew's Church, Leeds Road.

FULLER, JOHN HENRY. Private. No 11341. 8th Battalion Duke of Wellington's Regiment. Born Barrow Buildings, Moldgreen, Huddersfield. Son of Susannah Whittaker, 154 Wakefield Road, Moldgreen. Educated Moldgreen Council School. Employed as a woollen piecer by Messrs Middlemost Brothers of Birkby. Attended Moldgreen United Methodist Sunday School. Single. Enlisted 26.8.1914. Killed in action at Jephson's Post, Suvla, Gallipoli, 28.8.1915, aged 21 years. Has no known grave. Commemorated **HELLES MEMORIAL TO THE MISSING, GALLIPOLI.** His mother received a letter from a comrade of her son, Corporal **R. L. BRADSHAW.** In the letter he states, *'that Private Fuller was killed by a sniper. He had been at his post all day and had just got out of his dug-out in order to have a drink of tea when a bullet struck him in the chest and killed him instantly. Fuller was in Corporal Bradshaw's squad of stretcher-bearers and the Corporal adds that he had done very good work in bringing in the wounded under heavy fire'*. ROH:- St. Andrew's Church; Moldgreen; Christ Church, Moldgreen.

FULLER, WALTER. Corporal. No 3/1924. 7th Battalion King's Own Yorkshire Light Infantry. Born Halifax 13.9.1893. Son of Walter and Hannah Fuller, 10 Broomfield Road, Marsh. Educated Oakes Council School. Employed as a tailor's cutter by Messrs Bairstow of Fitzwilliam Street, Huddersfield. Enlisted, 27.8.1914, with his elder brother **LAWRENCE FULLER** who also served in the 7th Battalion K.O.Y.L.I. Married, on 10.7.1915, Ethel G. L. Fuller at Nap Hill, Surrey. Left for France on 29.7.1915. Killed in action, 13.9.1915 (his 22nd birthday), one and a quarter miles east of Croix Blanche, near Laventie. Buried **RUE-PETILLION MILITARY CEMETERY, FLEURBAIX.** Grave location:- Plot 1, Row B, Grave 36. His brother, Lawrence, wrote home to his parents on the 13.9.1915 which reached them on the morning of 18.9.1915. He wrote, *'You remember perhaps better than I do it was Walter's birthday today. It seems so hard he should be hit on this day. He was a Corporal in charge of a party working just behind the parapet. He was in his shirtsleeves at the time and I expect was joking as usual when a shell burst a good distance away. He immediately signalled a washout (or miss) at which those round about of course were compelled to laugh. Another shell burst ten foot away as he was going out of the danger zone and he went down on to his face. He never spoke and passed away without regaining consciousness. There is little condolence in the fact perhaps but he was a soldier always even then. My Officer (Lieutenant Barnaby) has asked me to say he was an esteemed N.C.O. and a fine fellow, one of whom he always admired.'*

FULTON, JAMES. Private. No 24559. 1/6th Battalion Duke of Wellington's Regiment. Born Stockport, Cheshire. Son of William and Euphemia Fulton, 1 Spring Terrace, Binn Road, Marsden. Employed as a woollen piecer at Spring Grove Mills, Linthwaite. Enlisted 4.8.1914. Discharged on 5.1.1915 on medical grounds but twice later sought re-enlistment, eventually succeeding in June, 1916. Embarked for France in October, 1916. Was killed in action on the eve of his 21st birthday, 3.5.1918, by the bursting of a shell. Has no known grave. Commemorated **TYNE COT MEMORIAL TO THE MISSING.** ROH:- Marsden War Memorial.

GALLAGHER, JAMES. Private. No 11265. 'Y' Company, 8th Battalion Duke of Wellington's Regiment. Born Huddersfield. Lived 2a Folly Hall, Huddersfield. Killed in action in the assaault on Tekke Tepe, Suvla, Gallipoli, 9.8.1915, aged 38 years. Has no known grave. Commemorated **HELLES MEMORIAL TO THE MISSING, GALLIPOLI.** ROH:- St. Stephen's Church, Rashcliffe.

GALLAGHER, JAMES. Private. No 10951. 2/4th Battalion Duke of Wellington's Regiment. Born Leeds. Son of Patrick Gallagher, 5 Mill Street, Meadow Road, Leeds. Lived with his aunt, Mrs Ryan, at 17 River View, Aspley, Huddersfield. Enlisted August 1914. Served in Gallipoli, Egypt and France. Died of influenza on leave on 29.10.1918, aged 27 years. Buried **LODGE HILL CEMETERY, BIRMINGHAM.** Grave location:- B.10, 8, 597D.

GALLAGHER, JAMES WILLIAM. Private. No 240815. 2/5th Battalion Duke of Wellington's Regiment. Born Spivey's Yard, Castlegate, Huddersfield. Educated St. Patrick's Roman Catholic School. Employed as a labourer by Messrs G. H. Day and Sons, of Milnsbridge. Married, with four children, and lived at 28 Duke Street, Huddersfield. Had served in the South African War. Enlisted January 1915. Killed in action near Cambrai, 28.9.1918, aged 36 years. Buried **GRAND RAVINE BRITISH CEMETERY, HAVRINCOURT.** Grave location:- Row A, Grave 5. ROH:- Huddersfield Drill Hall.

GALLAGHER, JOHN. Private. No 15727. 8th Battalion Duke of Wellington's Regiment. Born 11 Windsor Court, Castlegate, Huddersfield, 29.9.1896. Son of Thomas and Fanny Gallagher. Educated St. Patrick's Roman Catholic School. Employed as a foundry labourer by Messrs Hopkinson's, of Birkby. Single. Enlisted 7.3.1915. Sailed from Liverpool in *SS Aquitania* 3.7.1915 at 3am for Gallipoli. On November 2nd he was operated on for gunshot wounds in the head and left thigh at No 54 Casualty Clearing Station, east of Suvla Point. He died of his wounds the following day on 3.11.1915. He was 19 years of age. Has no known grave. Commemorated **HELLES MEMORIAL TO THE MISSING, GALLIPOLI.** (Brother of Private **PATRICK GALLAGHER,** reported missing, presumed killed, 26.4.1915, q.v.).

GALLAGHER, MICHAEL. Rifleman. No B/203508. 1st Battalion The Rifle Brigade. Formerly No C/7623 King's Royal Rifle Corps. Born 7 Swallow Street, Huddersfield. Brother of Margaret Ann Gannon, 4 Quay Street, Huddersfield. Educated St. Patrick's Roman Catholic School. Employed as a dyer's labourer by the Westfield Cotton Company. Single. Enlisted 13.11.1915. Embarked for France in June, 1916. Killed in action on the Somme, 19.10.1916, aged 25 years. Has no known grave. Commemorated **THIEPVAL MEMORIAL TO THE MISSING.**

GALLAGHER, PATRICK. Private. No 4345. 1st Battalion Connaught Rangers. Born Bradford. Son of Thomas and Fanny Gallagher, 11 Windsor Court, Castlegate, Huddersfield. Single. Killed in action, 26.4.1915, aged 35 years. Has no known grave. Commemorated **MENIN GATE MEMORIAL TO THE MISSING.** (Brother of Private **JOHN GALLAGHER,** killed in action at Gallipoli, 3.11.1915, q.v.).

GALLAGHER, PATRICK JAMES. Private. No 16053. 'D' Company, 8th Battalion Bedfordshire Regiment. Born Swineford, County Mayo, Ireland. Lived 17 Whitestone Lane, Fartown, Huddersfield. Killed in action, 16.10.1916, aged 22. Buried **BANCOURT BRITISH CEMETERY.** Grave location:- 3, K, 4.

GALLAGHER, TIMOTHY. Private. No 15128. 9th Battalion Duke of Wellington's Regiment. Born Castlegate, Huddersfield, 3.5.1890. Son of the late Timothy and Mary Gallagher, Fisher's Ford, Castlegate. Educated St. Patrick's Roman Catholic School. Employed as an iron fettler by Messrs David Brown and Sons Limited. Married, with one child, lived at 1 Haigh's Yard, Thomas Street, off Northgate, Huddersfield. Enlisted December 1914. His widow received a letter from Captain Benjamin, of 'B' Company, who wrote that on the morning of Sunday, December 19th, whilst they were passing through the streets of Ypres at daybreak, Private Gallagher was struck by a piece of shell in the leg and side and died instantenously. Killed in action, 19.12.1915, aged 26 years. Buried **YPRES RESERVOIR CEMETERY.** Grave location:- Plot 1, Row B, Grave 8. ROH:- St. Andrew's Church, Leeds Road, Huddersfield.

GALLOWAY, HENRY JOSEPH, DCM. Sergeant. No 4/8307. 2nd Battalion West Yorkshire Regiment. Son of Catherine Galloway and the late George Galloway, of 86 Whiteley Street, Milnsbridge. Employed by Messrs Joseph Dyson and Sons of Milnsbridge. Single. Enlisted at the outbreak of the war. Awarded the DCM in March, 1917, for *'long and gallant service with his battalion in France during the past twenty* *eight months.'* Died from wounds received during the German offensive, 12.4.1918, aged 25 years. Buried **WIMEREUX COMMUNAL CEMETERY.** Grave location:- Plot 10, Row A, Grave 2.

GALVIN, PETER. Private. No 14404. 8th Battalion Duke of Wellington's Regiment. Born 10 Swallow Street, Huddersfield. Educated St. Patrick's Roman Catholic School, Huddersfield. Employed as a chemical labourer by Messrs Read, Holliday and Sons. Married, with three children. Lived at 3 Holdroyd's Yard, Storths, Moldgreen. Had served in the Dardenelles. Died in Alexandria, Egypt, of pneumonia, 19.10.1915. Buried **CHATBY WAR MEMORIAL CEMETERY, ALEXANDRIA, EGYPT.** Grave location:- Plot F, Grave 26. ROH:- Almondbury War Memorial.

GARBUTT, JOSEPH. Private. No 3/8389. 2nd Battalion The Yorkshire Regiment. Born Eston near Middlesbrough. 6.11.1887. Son of Henry and Rachel Garbutt, 492 One Ash Terrace, Leeds Road, Huddersfield. Educated at Barnaby Moor near Middlesbrough. Employed as a weaver by Messrs Learoyd Brothers. Single. Enlisted 22.8.1914. Killed in action at Neuve Chapelle, 14.5.1915, aged 27 years. Has no known grave. Commemorated **LE TOURET MEMORIAL TO THE MISSING.** ROH:- Learoyd Brothers; Christ Church, Woodhouse Hill.

GARGRAVE, JOHN WILLIAM. Sapper. No 358445. 5th Field Company, Royal Engineers. Formerly No 15426 Duke of Wellington's Regiment. Born Kirby Malzeard near Ripon, Yorkshire, 24.5.1879. Husband of Hannah Gargrave, 71 Dewhurst Road, Fartown, and father of five children. Employed as a tram driver by Huddersfield Corporation Tramways. Enlisted 15.2.1915. Went to the Dardenelles. Had also served in Egypt and later in France. Had been wounded twice. Killed in action, 29.3.1918, aged 38 years. Has no known grave. Commemorated **POZIERES MEMORIAL TO THE MISSING** ROH:- Fartown and Birkby War Memorial.

GARNER, ALBERT. Rifleman. No 2256. 1st Battalion King's Royal Rifle Corps. Born Leicester. Son of Mr and Mrs Aaron Gardiner. Lived Huddersfield. Had served in the South African Campaign. Killed in action, 10.3.1915. Has no known grave. Commemorated **LE TOURET MEMORIAL TO THE MISSING.** ROH:-. St. John's Church, Kirkheaton; Lepton Parish Church.

GARRINGTON, GEORGE WILLIAM. Private. No 19617. 12th Battalion West Yorkshire Regiment. Born West Hartlepool. Enlisted Huddersfield. Lived Lindley, Huddersfield. Died in Germany, 15.12.1918. Buried **HAMBURG CEMETERY, OHLSDORF, GERMANY.** Grave location:- Plot 6, Row B, Grave 15. ROH:- St. Stephen's Church, Lindley.

GARSIDE, ADDIN. Gunner. No 127356. 128th Battery, 29th Brigade Royal Field Artillery. Fourth son of Mr and Mrs Garside, Oak Terrace, 683 Manchester Road, Linthwaite, Huddersfield. Attended Linthwaite Church and Sunday School and was a member of the Church bible class. Employed as a weaver by Messrs Charles Lockwood and Sons Limited, Black Rock Mills, Linthwaite. Was a playing member of the Broad Oak Cricket Club. Enlisted 1.1.1916. Embarked for France 10.4.1916. Killed in action, 18.10.1916, aged 25 years. Has no known grave. Commemorated **THIEPVAL MEMORIAL TO THE MISSING.** ROH:- Linthwaite War Memorial.

GARSIDE, ARTHUR, MM. Private. No 11010. 8th Battalion Duke of Wellington's Regiment. Born Lowergate, Huddersfield, 1892. Parents lived at Wilson's Buildings, Great Northern Street, Huddersfield. Educated at Paddock Church School. Employed as a fettler by Messrs Middlemost Brothers, Clough House. Husband of Mrs L. Garside, 49 Northumberland Street, Huddersfield. Three children. Enlisted 10.8.1914. Awarded the Military Medal in 1916 for *'gallantry and bravery on the field of battle'*. Wounded in the Dardenelles, 5.9.1915. Killed in action, 26.4.1917, aged 25, in France. Buried **HERMIES BRITISH CEMETERY.** Grave location:- Row D, Grave 3. ROH:- New North Road Baptist Church.

GARSIDE, FRED. Private. No 72044. 11th Battalion Sherwood Foresters. Formerly No 23041 North Staffordshire Regiment. Born Linthwaite. Son of Daniel and Jane Garside. Husband of Bessie Garside, 172 Wag Lane, Atherton, near Manchester. Killed in action, 22.10.1918. Buried **HONNECHY BRITISH**

CEMETERY. Grave location:- Plot 1, Row B, Grave 61. ROH:- Linthwaite War Memorial.

GARSIDE, HARRY. Private. No DM2/231791. 738th Motor Transport Company, Army Service Corps. Born Slaithwaite. Husband of Lucy H. Garside, 20 Waverley Street, Hill Top, Slaithwaite. Died in the Colne and Holme Joint Hospital at Meltham Moor from Enteric Fever on 14.8.1919, aged 39 years, a few days after returning from Constantinople. Buried **SLAITHWAITE CEMETERY.** Grave location:- B, 1, 110. ROH:- St. James Church, Slaithwaite; Slaithwaite War Memorial.

GARSIDE, JOE. Private. No 39664. 8th Battalion King's Own Yorkshire Light Infantry. Born Longwood. Son of Mrs Tom Garside, 12 Ray Gate, Mount, Longwood. Husband of Sarah Jane Garside of 19 High Street, Scapegoat Hill, Golcar. Employed by Messrs Peckett and Sons, Portland Mills, Lindley as a weaver. Was a member of the Golcar Cricket and Bowling Club. Attended the Scapegoat Hill Baptist Chapel and was a member of the Liberal Club. Killed in action, 7.6.1917, aged 34 years. Has no known grave. Commemorated **MENIN GATE MEMORIAL TO THE MISSING.** ROH:- St. John's Church, Golcar; Bethel United Methodist Chapel; Outlane.

GARSIDE, JOSEPH. Private. No 16434. 2/5th Battalion Duke of Wellington's Regiment. Born New Mill, Holmfirth. Enlisted Earsdon, Northumberland. Reported missing, presumed killed, 26.3.1918. Has no known grave. Commemorated **ARRAS MEMORIAL TO THE MISSING.** ROH:- New Mill Working Men's Club; Fulstone War Memorial; Huddersfield Drill Hall.

GARSIDE, JOSEPH. Private. No 41924. 1/5th Battalion York and Lancaster Regiment. Born Slaithwaite. Lived 127 Royd Street, Hill Top, Slaithwaite. Employed as a fettler by Messrs Pogson and Company, Bridge Street Mills, Slaithwaite. Was a member of the Slaithwaite Socialist Institute and a playing member of the Slaithwaite juniors football club. Enlisted April 1916. Embarked for France after three months training. Reported missing, presumed killed, 9.10.1917, aged 37 years. Buried **TYNE COT CEMETERY.** Grave location:- Plot 28, Row H, Grave 22. ROH:- St. James Church, Slaithwaite; Slaithwaite War Memorial.

GARSIDE, THOMAS HENRY. Private. No 241814. 2/5th Battalion Duke of Wellington's Regiment. Born Longwood. Son of Richard and Elizabeth Garside, 10 Kew Hill, Lindley. Reported missing, presumed killed, at the Battle of Bullecourt, 3.5.1917, aged 25 years. Has no known grave. Commemorated **ARRAS MEMORIAL TO THE MISSING.** ROH:- Huddersfield Drill Hall.

GARSIDE, THOMAS OUGHTIBRIDGE. 2nd Lieutenant. 4th Battalion Royal Berkshire Regiment. Born Lindley 24.1.1886. Son of Frank Oughtibridge Garside and Annie Frances Garside, Netherfield, South Crosland, Huddersfield. Educated at Wakefield Grammar School and Queens College, Oxford, which he left in 1905. Before enlisting, in August 1915, was a schoolmaster at Dulwich College, London. Single. Joined the Inns of Court Officers' Training Corps in April, 1915. Wounded during an attack on Thiepval in August, 1916, and invalided home. Went out again in February, 1917. Killed in action, 5.4.1917, during the attack and capture of the village of Ronnsoy during the German retreat from the Somme. Buried **TEMPLEUX-LE-GUERARD BRITISH CEMETERY.** Grave location:- Plot 1, Row D, Grave 29. ROH:- South Crosland and Netherton War Memorial; Fartown and Birkby War Memorial.

GARTHWAITE, EDGAR. Private. No 241966. 2/6th Battalion West Yorkshire Regiment. Born Kirkheaton. Worked at Fields Cooperative Store, Kirkheaton, as a shop assistant. Was a member of the choir at Fields Congregational Church. Enlisted March 1916. Reported missing, presumed killed, at the Battle of Bullecourt, 3.5.1917, aged 31 years. Has no known grave. Commemorated **ARRAS MEMORIAL TO THE MISSING.** ROH:- St. John's Church, Kirkheaton.

GARTHWAITE, JACK. Private. No 95157. Royal Fusiliers, posted to 2nd/2nd Battalion (London Regiment) Royal Fusiliers. Born Bradley Mills 23.12.1898. Son of James and Florence Garthwaite, of 24 Lane End, Dalton, Huddersfield. Educated at Kirkheaton Schools. Employed as an under-spinner by Messrs J. Fenton and Sons Limited, Bradley Mills. Single. Enlisted 2.4.1917. Wounded 20.9.1918. Died of his wounds at No 2 Stationary Hospital, Abbeville, 23.10.1918, aged 19 years. Buried

ABBEVILLE COMMUNAL CEMETERY EXTENSION. Grave location:- Plot 4, Row J, Grave 1. ROH:- St. John's Church, Kirkheaton; commemorated on headstone in Kirkheaton Cemetery.

GARTSIDE, JOHN WILLIAM. Private. No 31708. 13th (1st Barnsley Pals) Battalion York and Lancaster Regiment. Formerly No 4170 Duke of Wellington's Regiment. Eldest son of Fred and Sarah Mary Lawson Gartside, 3 Birchencliffe Hill, Huddersfield. Employed by Mr Sam Wilkinson at Blackley Brick Works, Elland. Killed in action, 29.6.1917, aged 25 years. Buried **ALBUERA CEMETERY.** Grave location:- Row D, Grave 13. ROH:- St. Philip's Church, Birchencliffe.

GARTSIDE, WILLIAM. Corporal. No 10761. 2nd Battalion Duke of Wellington's Regiment. Born Huddersfield. Husband of Edith Gartside, 138 Springdale Street, Longroyd Bridge, Huddersfield. Three children. Employed in the dyehouse of Messrs Cock Brothers of Linthwaite. Enlisted August 1914. Shortly before he met his death he received a Distinguished Service Certificate for bringing in two wounded men after a raid. Killed in action, 2.9.1917, aged 35. Buried **St. NICOLAS BRITISH CEMETERY, ARRAS.** Grave location:- Plot 2, Row C, Grave 7. ROH:- St. Stephen's Church, Rashcliffe.

GATEHOUSE, FRED. Private. No 16/1577. 16th Battalion (1st Bradford Pals) West Yorkshire Regiment. Born Bramley, near Leeds, 5.8.1896. Son of Ben and Emma Gatehouse, 603 Woodlands Terrace, Leeds Road, Huddersfield. Employed as a textile engineer. Single. Enlisted 16.1.1915. Killed in action on the Somme, 3.7.1916, aged 19 years. Buried **COUIN BRITISH CEMETERY.** Grave location:- Plot 1, Row C, Grave 19. ROH:- Christ Church, Woodhouse Hill.

GAULTON, JAMES HUMPHREY. Private. No 77088. 7th Battalion Durham Light Infantry. Born Tunstall, Staffordshire, 6.1.1880. Son of Humphrey and Mary Gaulton of Tunstall. Educated at Tunstall school. Husband of Sarah Ann Gaulton, 23 St. Paul's Street, Huddersfield. Employed as a bricklayer. Enlisted 9.9.1916. Killed in action, 11.11.1917, aged 37 years. Buried **BARD COTTAGE CEMETERY,**

BOESINGHE, BELGIUM. Grave location:- Plot 6, Row B, Grave 33. ROH:- Northumberland Street Primitive Methodist Church.

GAUNT, CHARLES HENRY. Private. No 23347. 9th Battalion Duke of Wellington's Regiment. Born Merthyr Tydvil, South Wales. Son of Mr and Mrs Gaunt, Laurel Lea, Cowlersley Lane, Milnsbridge. Husband of Mrs Gaunt, 3 Lodge, Linthwaite. Employed as a weaver by Messrs John Crowther and Sons of Milnsbridge. Was a member of Linthwaite Church choir. Enlisted 1.8.1916. Embarked for France December, 1916. Was taken prisoner at Monchy-le-Preux, 25.4.1917. Died of wounds in Germany, 25.6.1917. Buried **COLOGNE SOUTHERN CEMETERY, GERMANY.** Grave location:- Plot 17, Row B, Grave 29. His wife received the following letter from the Chief Medical Officer at Reserve Lazarett, Berkkaserne, Munster; '*I regret to inform you that your husband, Private CHARLES HENRY GAUNT of the Duke of Wellington's Regiment died in this hospital in consequence of a wound in the right thigh sustained in the battle near Monchy in April. Accompanied by a priest and his comrades he has been buried at the cemetery of the prisoners of war not far from this city.*' Mrs Gaunt also received a letter from a Private in the King's Liverpool Regiment who was an orderly in the camp. He wrote, '*Your husband came with a transport of his comrades wounded from the front and as far as his wounds were concerned made excellent progress. Unfortunately his very weak state and the condition of his heart could not enable him to recover and in spite of all efforts he passed peacefully away this morning. I who write this letter are the English Prisoner Orderly in charge of English patients here and I can assure you that everything that could be done was done for your husband.*' ROH:- Linthwaite War Memorial.

GERMAIN, HAROLD. Private. No 57358. 17th Battalion Lancashire Fusiliers. Formerly No 38067 Leicestershire Regiment. Born 61 Beech Street, Paddock. Son of Mr and Mrs Robert Germain, 154 Longwood Road, Longwood. Educated Paddock Council School. Attended Paddock Wesleyan Church. Employed as a cloth finisher by Messrs Martin, Sons and Company Limited. Enlisted 20.12.1917. Died, 18.7.1918, aged 18 years. Buried **GODEWAERSVELDE**

GIBSON, ALFRED. Private. No 21216. 10th Battalion King's Own Yorkshire Light Infantry. Born Huddersfield 6.2.1893. Educated St. Andrew's School, Huddersfield. Employed as a labourer at Central Ironworks, Huddersfield. Married. Prior to enlistment, lived at 22a York Street, Huddersfield. Enlisted January 1915. Reported missing, presumed killed, on the first day of the Battle of the Somme, 1.7.1916. Has no known grave. Commemorated **THIEPVAL MEMORIAL TO THE MISSING.** ROH:- St. Andrew's Church, Leeds Road, Huddersfield.

GIBSON, ARTHUR. Private. No 29706. 2nd Battalion Dublin Fusiliers. Formerly No 369 Durham Light Infantry. Born Kilner Bank, Moldgreen 30.7.1890. Educated Moldgreen Council School. Employed as a hoist tenter by Messrs Joshua Lumb and Sons of Folly Hall, Huddersfield. Married, with two children. Prior to enlistment lived at 1 Kaye's Yard, Thomas Street, Huddersfield. Died of pneumonia at No 21 Casualty Clearing Station, Gezaincourt, 30.9.1918, aged 28 years. Buried **BAGNEUX BRITISH CEMETERY.** Grave location:- Plot 5, Row G, Grave 7. ROH:- Huddersfield Parish Church.

GIBSON, ERNEST ALFRED. Lance Corporal. No 305494. 1/7th Battalion Duke of Wellington's Regiment. Son of Mr and Mrs A. J. Gibson of Irthlingboro', Northamptonshire. Employed at Ready Carr Mill, Marsden. Single. Lived with his cousin, Sergeant Gibson, at Hard End, Marsden. Had served four years as a Territorial in the Northamptonshire Regiment. Enlisted August 1914. Wounded, 25.7.1917, at Nieuport, Belgium, and died the following day, 26.7.1917, aged 24 years. Buried **COXYDE MILITARY CEMETERY.** Grave location:- Plot 1, Row L, Grave 7. ROH:- Huddersfield Drill Hall; Marsden War Memorial.

GIBSON, FRED BAMFORTH. Private. No 1929. 1/7th Battalion Duke of Wellington's Regiment. Born Slaithwaite. Son of John William and Jane Gibson, 7 Linfit Hall, Linthwaite. Attended Slaithwaite Wesleyan Church and was a member of the Linthwaite Hall Cricket Club. Had worked as a weaver before the war but ill health had forced him out of work. Enlisted September 1914. In October, 1915, he was severely wounded in the thigh and was in hospital in England for some time. Killed in action, 21.2.1917, aged 24 years. Buried **LA FERMONT MILITARY CEMETERY.** Grave location:- Plot 2, Row E, Grave 8. His parents received the following letter from Lieutenant Doggett of their son's Company. He wrote, *'Private Gibson was in a dugout in the front line trenches while the enemy were shelling and one shell blew in the dugout he was in. We all feel his loss very much as he was a good soldier and had been recommended for promotion.'* ROH:- Linthwaite War Memorial; Huddersfield Drill Hall.

GIBSON. GEORGE. Private. No 3/9637. 2nd Battalion Duke of Wellington's Regiment. Born Huddersfield. Killed in action at Hill 60, 5.5.1915. Has no known grave. Commemorated **MENIN GATE MEMORIAL TO THE MISSING.**

GIBSON, GEORGE EDWARD. Private. No 64010. 11th Battalion The Welsh Regiment. Born Denby Dale. Son of George Edward and Fanny Gibson of Birdsedge, Denby Dale. Killed in action in Salonika, Greece, 18.9.1918, aged 22 years. Buried **DOIRAN MILITARY CEMETERY, GREECE.** Grave location:- Plot 1, Row E, Grave 19. ROH:- Denby Dale and Cumberworth War Memorial.

GIBSON, GLADSTONE. Lance Corporal. No 2865. 1/5th Battalion Duke of Wellington's Regiment. Born High Hoyland. Son of Alma and Elizabeth Gibson, of Clayton West. A shell fell on his dugout on 3.7.1916 and he was killed instantly, he was 26 years old. Buried **CONNAUGHT CEMETERY, THIEPVAL.** Grave location:- Plot 7, Row J, Grave 4. ROH:- Clayton West and High Hoyland War Memorial; Huddersfield Drill Hall.

GIBSON, JOHN WILLIAM. Corporal. No 1791. 1/7th Battalion Duke of Wellington's Regiment. Born Primrose Hill, Huddersfield. Lived 12 Clough Lane, Paddock. Employed as a teamer by the London and North Western Railway Company. Killed in action, 3.7.1916, aged 27 years. Has no known grave. Commemorated **THIEPVAL MEMORIAL TO THE MISSING.** ROH:- All Saint's Church, Paddock; Huddersfield Drill Hall; London and North Western Railway Company Roll.

GIBSON, MANSFIELD. Private. No 242183. 12th Battalion East Surrey Regiment. Born Huddersfield. Son of Mr and Mrs William Gibson, 18 Midland Street, Hillhouse, Huddersfield, and nephew of Mr Albert Townend of Crosland Moor. Employed as a fitter at British Dyes Limited. Killed in action, 5.8.1917, aged 19 years. Has no known grave. Commemorated **MENIN GATE MEMORIAL TO THE MISSING.** ROH:- St. Andrew's Church, Leeds Road; Fartown and Birkby War Memorial.

GIBSON, MILNER. Private. No S/40361. 1st Battalion The Queen's Own (Cameron Highlanders). Born Dalton. Son of Fred and Christine Gibson, 13 Dalton Fold, Dalton. Killed in action, 17.11.1917, aged 28 years. Has no known grave. Commemorated **TYNE COT MEMORIAL TO THE MISSING.** ROH:- Christ Church, Moldgreen.

GIBSON, STANLEY. Private. No 59009. 2nd Battalion King's Own Yorkshire Light Infantry. Son of Alfred and Sarah Ann Gibson, 2 Hawthorne Terrace, Crosland Moor. Employed as a warehouse clerk by Messrs Crowther Brothers of Milnsbridge. Enlisted 4.3.1916. Wounded in March, 1918. Died of pneumonia following upon influenza in Germany on 13.2.1919, aged 25 years. Buried **COLOGNE SOUTHERN CEMETERY, GERMANY.** Grave location:- Plot 12, Row A, Grave 12. ROH:- Milton Independent Church; St. Barnabas Church, Crosland Moor.

GIFFORD, WALTER. Private. No 23893. 2/5th Battalion Duke of Wellington's Regiment. Born Huddersfield 24.11.1893. Son of Mrs A. Gifford, 64 South Street, Huddersfield. Educated Spring Grove Council School. Employed as an upholsterer by Messrs Hobson and Taylor, furnishers, New Street, Huddersfield. Single. Enlisted January 1915. Reported missing, presumed killed, at the Battle of Cambrai, 21.11.1917. Has no known grave. Commemorated **CAMBRAI MEMORIAL TO THE MISSING.** ROH:- Huddersfield Parish Church; Huddersfield Drill Hall.

GIGGLE, ALBERT. Private. No 2205. 1/7th Battalion Duke of Wellington's Regiment. Son of Mr and Mrs R. Giggle, 44 Scar Lane, Milnsbridge. Employed as a cutter by Messrs Bairstows, Sons and Company, wholesale clothiers, of Huddersfield. Attended St. Michael's Mission Church and Sunday School, Golcar. Enlisted at the outbreak of war and embarked for France in April, 1915. When home on leave in May, 1916, he married Miss Walker, of Lindley Street, Longwood. Killed in action, 17.9.1916, (the day following his 23rd birthday). Has no known grave. Commemorated **THIEPVAL MEMORIAL TO THE MISSING.** ROH:- St. Mark's Parish Church, Longwood; St. John's Church, Golcar; Huddersfield Drill Hall.

GILBY, WILLIE. Private. No 18634. 9th Battalion Duke of Wellington's Regiment. Born Hay Green, Marsden 23.5.1893. Educated Spring Grove Council School. Employed as a warehouseman. Single. At the time of enlistment, was living at 5 Kirk Place, Trinity Street, Huddersfield. Enlisted 28.1.1916. Killed in action on the Somme, 7.7.1916, aged 23 years. Buried **GORDON DUMP CEMETERY.** Grave location:- Plot 3, Row E, Grave 4.

GILDEA, DANIEL, DCM. Corporal. No 3/7822. 6th Battalion The Yorkshire Regiment. Born Huddersfield 27.9.1894. Nephew of Miss M. Gildea, 7 Tindall's Buildings, Leeds Road, Huddersfield. Educated St. Patrick's Roman Catholic School. Employed as a mason on the new Post Office Buildings in Northumberland Street, Huddersfield. Single. Was called up on 4.8.1914 as a Reservist. Was wounded in the battle of Neuve Chapelle and had served in Gallipoli and Egypt. Was awarded the DCM. for *'conspicuous gallantry in going out sniping night after night.'* (London Gazette 21st June 1916). Was also mentioned in despatches. Reported missing and later presumed to have been killed on 27.9.1916, aged 25 years. Has no known grave. Commemorated **THIEPVAL MEMORIAL TO THE MISSING.**

GILLING, GEORGE FREDERIC. Private. No 3396. 1/5th Battalion Duke of Wellington's Regiment. Born 55 Merton Street, Huddersfield, 9.12.1894. Son of George and Mary Ellen Gilling, 15 Thornton Lodge Road, Huddersfield. Educated Spring Grove Council School. Employed as a cloth finisher by Messrs Lockwood and Keighley Limited, Upperhead Mills, Huddersfield. Single. A keen sportsman. Was in the local Territorials prior to the war.

Enlisted October 1914. Killed by shrapnel, 4.8.1916, aged 21 years. Buried **CONNAUGHT CEMETERY, THIEPVAL.** Grave location:- Plot 3, Row M, Grave 1. ROH:- Huddersfield Parish Church; Huddersfield Drill Hall.

GILL, ARCHIBALD. Rifleman. No R/19777. 16th Battalion King's Royal Rifle Corps. Born Honley. Son of Mr and Mrs Fred Gill, 29 Yew Street, Honley. Attended Honley Wesleyan Sunday School. Was a member of Honley Wesleyan Cricket Club and a former member of the Honley Day School football team. Employed at Messrs Oldham's dyeworks at Moll Spring. Enlisted March 1916. Embarked for France in July, 1916. Reported missing, presumed killed, 5.11.1916, aged 21 years. Has no known grave. Commemorated **THIEPVAL MEMORIAL TO THE MISSING.** ROH:- Honley War Memorial.

GILL, EDMUND. Corporal. No 40436. Royal Air Force. Born Thurstonland. Elder son of the late Henry Gill of East View, Thurstonland. Was a trustee of the Wesleyan Chapel and a member of the choir. Was also a member of the Church Institute and an officer of the Order of Druids. Played cricket for the Thurstonland club. Employed on the works staff at Storths Hall Asylum. Married. Was accidentally killed, 5.11.1918, at an aerodrome in England. Major Denniston, of the R.A.F, wrote to the widow telling her how the accident happened, '*A machine belonging to the other squadron on this aerodrome had crashed in the field next to the men's mess and your husband along with several others rushed to the scene with fire extinguishers as the machine had by this time caught fire. While they were giving all the assistance they possibly could the bombs the machine was carrying exploded and I am sorry to say fatally injured your husband. The squadron mourns his loss with you as he was one of our finest men and I on behalf of all the Officers, N.C.O.'s and men offer you my most sincere sympathy at this trying time.*' Buried in **St. THOMAS'S CHURCHYARD, THURSTONLAND.** Grave Location:- 204, South-West. ROH:- Thurstonland War Memorial.

GILL, HAROLD. Private. No 23565. 2nd Battalion Royal Warwickshire Regiment. Formerly No 173767 Royal Engineers. Born Hepworth. Son of Councillor and Mrs Edric Gill of Newfield House, Cumberworth. Employed as a farmer. Enlisted Aldershot.. Killed in action, 2.4.1917. Buried **CROISILLES BRITISH CEMETERY.** Grave location:- Plot 3, Row A, Grave 6. ROH:- New Mill Working Men's Club; Fulstone War Memorial.

GILL, JACK EASTWOOD. Sergeant. No 2455. 1/7th Battalion Duke of Wellington's Regiment, attached 147th Machine Gun Corps. Born Windhill, Shipley, Yorkshire. Adopted son of Walter and Eliza Ann Gill, 27 Station Road, Golcar. Employed as a weaver at Messrs Pearson Brothers, Victoria Mills. Single. Enlisted October 1914. Embarked for France April, 1915. He wrote home frequently and one of the characteristics of his letters to his relatives and friends was a cheerful and optimistic spirit that always pervaded them. He never complained about anything and always counselled those at home to keep smiling. Killed in action during the Battle of the Somme, 16.7.1916, aged 22 years. Buried **CONNAUGHT CEMETERY, THIEPVAL.** Grave location:- Plot 12, Row J, Grave 6. His mother received a letter from his Captain in which he wrote, '*It is with deep regret that I have to send you the sad news of Sergeant Gill's death. He was killed while building a machine gun emplacement last night (the 15th inst). His loss is a very great blow to me and to all who were in any way connected with him. He was one of the very best Sergeants and was the most willing, keen and hard worker it has ever been my lot to meet. He never regained consciousness after being hit and died about twelve hours later. I sincerely trust that the knowledge that he died nobly, was doing his duty for King and Country will be of some comfort to you in your great bereavement.*' ROH:- St. John's Church, Golcar; Huddersfield Drill Hall.

GILL, STANLEY. Private. No 29049. 1st Battalion East Yorkshire Regiment. Born Netherthong, Holmfirth. Son of Mr and Mrs B. Gill, Stoney Croft, Netherthong. Educated Netherthong Day School where Mr James Jackson was the headmaster. Attended Netherthong Church Sunday School and was a member of the boy scouts. He became a student at the Holmfirth Day School, where he studied chemistry, drawing and building construction. He became an apprentice with Messrs John Ratcliffe and Sons, builders and contractors, St.

John's Road, Huddersfield. Enlisted February 1917. Killed in action at Passchendaele, 26.10.1917, aged 19 years. Has no known grave. Commemorated **TYNE COT MEMORIAL TO THE MISSING.** ROH:- Netherthong and Thongsbridge War Memorial; Netherthong Working Men's Club.

GIRLING, THEODORE AUGUSTUS. Captain. Canadian Army Veterinary Corps, attached 2nd Canadian Div. H.Q. Born Huddersfield. Son of the late Rev. William Henry Girling, of Wilshaw, Meltham, and of Lockwood and of Mrs Mary Lucy Girling, 38 Stanley Street, Lindley. Husband of Dora Simcox Girling, 121 Beechwood Avenue, Victoria, British Colombia, Canada. Went to Canada in 1902. Was a veterinary surgeon in Canada. Enlisted in 1915. Died of bronchial pneumonia at Namur, Belgium, 1.3.1919, aged 43 years. Buried **BELGRADE CEMETERY, NAMUR.** Grave location:- Plot 2, Row A, Grave 15. Captain Girling wrote the following poem entitled 'DUMB HEROES':

There's a DSO for the Colonel,
A Military Cross for the Sub.,
A medal or two when we all get through,
And a bottle of wine with our grub.
There's a stripe of gold for the wounded,
A rest by the bright seashore.
And a service is read when we bury our dead,
When our country has one hero more.

But what of our poor dumb heroes,
That we send without choice to the fight?
That strain at the load on the shell swept road,
As they take up the rations at night.
They are shelling at Hellfire Corner
There's shrapnel bursting fast o'er the square;
And the bullets drum as the transports come
With food for the soldiers there.

The halt till the shelling is over,
The rush through the line of fire,
The glaring light in the dead of night
And the terrible sights in the mire.
It's the daily work of the horses
And they answer the spur and the rein
With quickened breath, mid the toll of death
In the mud and the holes and the rain.

There's a fresh healed wound on the chestnut,
The black mare's neck has a mark;
The brown mule's new mate won't keep the same gait
As the one killed last night in the dark.
But they walk with the spirit of heroes
They dare, not for medal or cross;
But for duty alone, into peril unknown
They go, never counting their loss.

There's a swift painless death for the hopeless,
With a grave in a shell hole or field;
There's a hospital base for the casualty case,
And a vet for those easily healed.
But there's never a shadow of glory,
A cheer or speech in their praise,
As patient and true they carry us through
With limbers on shot riven ways.

So here's to dumb heroes of Britain,
Who serve her as nobly and true
As the best of her sons, mid the roar of the guns
And the best of her boys on the blue.
They are shocked, they are bruised and they're broken,
They are wounded and torn as they fall,
But they're strong and they're brave,
To the verge of the grave, and of heroes they're truest of all.

GLEDHILL, AGUR. Private. No 40870. 2/6th Battalion North Staffordshire Regiment. Born Spring Mill, Milnsbridge. Son of Joe and Martha Gledhill, 274 Blackmoorfoot Road, Crosland Moor. Husband of Sarah H. Gledhill, 272 Blackmoorfoot Road, Crosland Moor. Educated Crosland Moor Council School. Employed as a tailor. Reported missing at the Battle of Cambrai, 29.11.1917, aged 34 years. Has no known grave. Commemorated **CAMBRAI MEMORIAL TO THE MISSING.** ROH:- Crosland Moor Wesleyan Church; St. Barnabas Church, Crosland Moor.

GLEDHILL, ALBERT. Sergeant. No 23891. 8th Battalion Duke of Wellington's Regiment. Born New Hey Road, Oakes, Huddersfield, 18.2.1882. Son of Mr J. Gledhill, Dalton Bank Road, Colne Bridge, Bradley. Educated at Oakes Council School, Lindley. Employed as a night piecer by Messrs T. and H. Blamires Limited, Leeds Road, Huddersfield. Was a member of the Cliffe End Working Men's Club. Played in the Linthwaite and Milnsbridge Socalist Brass Bands. Married, with five children. Lived 64 Cliffe End Hill, Longwood. Enlisted July 1915. Embarked for France in October, 1916. Severely wounded in the jaw and shoulder on 10.12.1916. Died of his wounds at No 9 Casualty Clearing Station on 13.12.1916, aged 34 years. Buried **CONTAY BRITISH CEMETERY.** Grave location:- Plot 8, Row E, Grave 14. ROH:- St. Mark's Parish Church, Longwood.

GLEDHILL, ALBERT. (Served under the assumed name of **ALBERT SYKES**). Private. No 9481. Depot Battalion Worcestershire Regiment. Born Golcar. Son of Thomas and Mary Gledhill of Golcar; husband of Jennie Gledhill, 36 West Hill Road, Wandsworth, London. Died at home, 5.7.1917, aged 51 years. Buried **St. JAMES CHURCHYARD, NORTON-JUXTA-KEMPSEY, WORCS.**

GLEDHILL, CHARLES. Private. No 41588. 17th Battalion (2nd Leeds Pals) West Yorkshire Regiment. Born Leeches, Outlane, 12.3.1886. Son of Thomas and Alicia Gledhill, Lea Farm, Outlane. Educated Outlane Board School. Attended Bethel United Methodist Sunday School, Outlane. Employed as a weaver by Messrs Gee and Whiteley Limited, Parkwood Mills, Longwood. Married, with three children, living at 3 St. George's Square, Outlane. Enlisted 22.8.1916. Reported missing, presumed killed, 31.8.1917, aged 31 years. Has no known grave. Commemorated **THIEPVAL MEMORIAL TO THE MISSING.** ROH:- Bethel United Methodist Chapel, Outlane.

GLEDHILL, FRANCIS (FRANK) AINLEY. Gunner. No 151438. 342nd Siege Battery, Royal Garrison Artillery. Born Marsh, Huddersfield. Son of the late John and Harriet Gledhill, 863 North Grove, Manchester Road, Linthwaite. Was a partner in the firm of Messrs Gledhill Brothers, of Lockwood. Attended Golcar Baptist Chapel. Was a member of the Craft Mark and Royal Arch Masonic Lodges of Slaithwaite. Was also a member of the Slaithwaite and District Golf Club. Prior to enlistment was an enthuastic member of the Motor Volunteers. Embarked for France in May, 1917, after training at Lydd, Kent. Died from gunshot wounds to the right side and thigh, 20.9.1918, aged 35 years. Buried **TERLINCTHUN BRITISH CEMETERY.** Grave location:- Plot 5, Row A, Grave 5. ROH:- Linthwaite War Memorial; Golcar Baptist Church.

GLEDHILL, GEORGE RICHARD. 2nd Lieutenant. 1/5th Battalion Duke of Wellington's Regiment. Born Manchester Road, Huddersfield 24.11.1896. Son of Walter and Hannah Mary Gledhill, Wellhouse, Thongsbridge. Spent his childhood in Petrograd, Russia. Educated at Mr Wild's College School, Huddersfield, Ackworth School, Pontefract, and Institut Dr Schmidt, St. Gallen, Switzerland. Was a member of the firm of Walter Gledhill and Sons Limited, woollen manufacturers, Bridge Mills, Holmfirth. At the time of enlistment was living at Neva Bank, 86 New North Road, Huddersfield. Single. Enlisted 3.9.1914. Killed in action in the attack on the Schwaben Redoubt, 3.9.1916, aged 20 years. Has no known grave. Commemorated **THIEPVAL MEMORIAL TO THE MISSING.** ROH:- Huddersfield College School; Huddersfield Drill Hall.

GLEDHILL, HARRY. Private. No 350342. 12th Battalion Highland Light Infantry. Formerly No 11381 Royal Scots Fusiliers. Born Snowlee, Longwood, 6.12.1898. Son of Mark and Sarah Jane Gledhill, 160 South Street, The Moor, Sheffield (late of 1 Colwyn Street, Marsh). Educated Outlane Council School. Employed as a pawnbroker's assistant by Mr Claude Hill of King Street, Huddersfield. Single. Enlisted 6.11.1916. Killed in action, 16.7.1918, aged 20 years. Buried **KLEIN-VIERSTRAAT BRITISH CEMETERY.** Grave location:- Plot 6, Row A, Grave 6. ROH:- High Street United Methodist Church; memorial in Salendine Nook Churchyard.

GLEDHILL, JACK GUDGER. Private. No 2206. 1/7th Battalion Duke of Wellington's Regiment, attached 147th Company, Machine Gun Corps. Born Golcar 9.3.1895. Son of Mrs Lena Gledhill, 5 Thornhill Avenue, Lindley. Educated at Oakes Council School. Was a member of Oakes Baptist Sunday School. Employed as an electrician's apprentice by Messrs J. A. Taylor and Company, Macaulay Street, Huddersfield. Single. Enlisted 10.9.1914. Embarked for France in April, 1915. Had been twice wounded and once in hospital suffering from trench fever. Killed in action at Thiepval as he advanced with his gun to the German lines, 3.9.1916, aged 21 years. Buried **CONNAUGHT CEMETERY, THIEPVAL.** Grave location:- Plot 12, Row M, Grave 10. (Brother of Private **STANLEY GLEDHILL**, killed in action, 22.3.1918, q.v.). ROH:- Oakes Baptist Church; St. Stephen's Church, Lindley; Huddersfield Drill Hall.

GLEDHILL, JOE. Sergeant. No 305068. 2/7th Battalion Duke of Wellington's Regiment. Born Golcar. Son of Charles and Amelia Gledhill, of Southport, and formerly of Golcar. Husband of Mary A. Gledhill 160 Leymoor Road, Golcar. Attended St. John's Church, Golcar. Prior to enlistment, had worked for Mr S. T. Shaw, chemist, of Golcar and then for Messrs Hirst and Mallinson of Longwood as a weaver. Had served eight years in the local Territorials. Enlisted at the outbreak of the war. During the Battle of Bullecourt, on 3.5.1917, Sergeant Gledhill was reported missing but it was later ascertained that he and a few of his men were imprisoned in a shellhole for five days and were utterly exhausted when eventually discovered at the end of that time. Killed in action, 17.9.1917, aged 26 years. Buried **FAVREUIL BRITISH CEMETERY.** Grave location:- Plot 1, Row F, Grave 20. His widow received letters from four of his chums and one the letters said, *'Your husband was in charge of a working party when he was hit in the back of the head by a shell and he never regained consciousness, death being instantaneous. Sergeant Gledhill was very highly thought of by all, his cheery disposition and true heartedness endearing him to Officers and men alike.'* ROH:- St. John's Church, Golcar; Huddersfield Drill Hall.

GLEDHILL, JOHN MILTON. Private. 8th Training Reserve Battalion. Born Oakes, Lindley, 4.10.1899. Educated Paddock Council School. Employed as a labourer. Single. Enlisted 5.11.1917. Died on 6.9.1918 at Storths Hall Asylum.

GLEDIIILL, JOHN TAYLOR. Private. No 40858. 16th Battalion (1st Bradford Pals) West Yorkshire Regiment. Formerly No 29/706 Northumberland Fusiliers. Eldest son of Mr and Mrs Joe Gledhill, 33 Knowle Bank, Golcar. Attended St. John's Church, Golcar. Employed as a weaver by Messrs George Mallinson and Sons of Linthwaite. Was a member of Golcar Conservative Club. Enlisted May 1916. Embarked for France in September 1916. Reported missing after an engagement on 27.2.1917. Twenty two weeks later he wrote home to say that he was a Prisoner of War and in good health. Died as a Prisoner of War, 24.7.1917, aged 33 years. Buried **VALENCIENNES COMMUNAL CEMETERY.** Grave location:- Plot 4, Row D, Grave 27. ROH:- St. John's Church, Golcar; memorial in St. John's Churchyard.

GLEDHILL, PERCY. Private. No 205238. 1/6th Battalion Duke of Wellington's Regiment. Born Skelmanthorpe. Husband of Ellen Gledhill, Queen Street, Skelmanthorpe. Employed as a weaver by Messrs Field and Botterill of Skelmanthorpe. Enlisted May 1917. Died of gunshot wounds to the jaw, 15.5.1918, aged 29 years. Buried **BOULOGNE EASTERN CEMETERY.** Grave location:- Plot 9, Row B, Grave 84. ROH:- St. Aidan's Church, Skelmanthorpe.

GLEDHILL, PHILIP COULSON. Private. No 130269. 'C' Company, 45th Battalion Royal Fusiliers. Formerly 52nd Battalion West Yorkshire Regiment. Born 82 Birkby Hall Road, Huddersfield, 13.6.1900. Son of the late Harry Coulson Gledhill and of Florence Augusta Gledhill. Educated at St. John's Church of England School, Birkby and Almondbury Grammar School. Employed as a metallurgical chemist at Messrs Hopkinsons, of Birkby. Enlisted, 20.6.1918, in the West Yorkshire Regiment. Demobilized after the Armistice. Re-enlisted in General Ironside's relief force to Russia on 14.4.1919. Killed in action, 10.8.1919, as 2nd Lewis gunner, at Seltso near Lipovets on the Dvina river, about 173 miles south east of Archangel, North Russia. Has no known grave. Commemorated **ARCHANGEL MEMORIAL TO THE MISSING, RUSSIA.** Is also commemorated on **BROOKWOOD RUSSIA MEMORIAL** in Brookwood Military Cemetery, Surrey. ROH:- Almondbury Grammar School; Fartown and Birkby War Memorial; St. Cuthbert's Church, Birkby.

GLEDHILL, ROBERT RANDOLPH. Lance Corporal. No 41894. 2/5th Battalion Duke of Wellington's Regiment. Born Golcar. Son of James and Sarah Gledhill, The Rock, Golcar. Attended St. John's Church, Golcar and was secretary of the sick and funeral society at the school. Employed as a clerk in the warehouse of Messrs Fisher and Company, Upperhead Row, Huddersfield. Enlisted March 1916. Embarked for France 10.1.1917. Reported missing, presumed killed, at the Battle of Bullecourt, 3.5.1917, aged 29 years. Has no known grave. Commemorated **ARRAS MEMORIAL TO THE MISSING.** ROH:- St. John's Church, Golcar; Huddersfield Drill Hall.

GLEDHILL, STANLEY. Sergeant. No 12621. 9th Battalion Duke of Wellington's Regiment. Born Golcar 31.5.1893. Educated Oakes Council School. Attended Oakes Baptist Sunday School and was a member of the Lindley Liberal Club. Employed as a pattern weaver by Messrs Martin, Sons and Company of Oakes. Single. Enlisted 1.9.1914. Shortly before his death had been recommended for a commission and had been awarded the French Croix-de-Guerre. Had also received a Divisional Certificate for Gallantry, *'Presented to No 12621 Corporal Stanley Gledhill of the Duke of Wellington's (West Riding Regiment). In recognition of conspicuous gallantry and devotion to duty under heavy fire at Arras on the night of 6th and 7th September 1917.'* Killed in action at Havrincourt, 22.3.1918, aged 24 years. Buried **LOWRIE CEMETERY, HAVRINCOURT.** Grave location:- Row A, Grave 14. (Brother of Private **JACK GUDGER GLEDHILL,** killed in action, 3.9.1916, q.v.). ROH:- Oakes Baptist Church; St. Stephen's Church, Lindley.

GLEDHILL, WALTER. Private. No 32040. 8th Battalion North Staffordshire Regiment. Born Kew Hill, Longwood. Son of Maria Gledhill, 509 New Hey Road, Mount, Outlane. Educated Oakes Council School. Employed as a woollen piecer by Messrs F. Peckett and Sons Limited, Portland Mills, Lindley. Single. Enlisted 7.11.1916. Killed in action south west of Armentieres, 7.9.1918, aged 20. Has no known grave. Commemorated **LOOS MEMORIAL TO THE MISSING.** ROH:- Longwood War Memorial; Bethel United Methodist Church, Outlane.

GOLDSBROUGH, HORACE. Private. No 241905. 2/5th Battalion Duke of Wellington's Regiment. Born Mirfield 23.8.1895. Son of Walter Goldsborough, 22 South Parade, Huddersfield. Educated at Spring Grove Council School. Worked for his father in the tailoring and costume business at 22 South Parade, Huddersfield. Enlisted 16.3.1916. Reported missing, 3.5.1917, and afterwards presumed to have died on that date, aged 21. Has no known grave. Commemorated **ARRAS MEMORIAL TO THE MISSING.** ROH:- St. Mark's Parish Church, Longwood; Huddersfield Drill Hall.

GOLDTHORPE, FRANK. Lance Corporal. No 4/3585. 4th Battalion Duke of Wellington's Regiment. Husband of Mrs Goldthorpe, 'Portlands', Marsh, Huddersfield. Killed in action, 16.8.1916, aged 25. Buried **CONNAUGHT CEMETERY, THIEPVAL.** Grave location:- Plot 4, Row M, Grave 10.

GOLDTHORPE, JOHN WILLIAM. Gunner. No 151078. Royal Garrison Artillery. Son of Albert and Sarah Goldthorpe, of New Hagg Farm, Oldfield, Honley. Died at home 19.2.1919. Buried **HONLEY CHURCH BURIAL GROUND.** Grave location:- 61, 3639. ROH:- Honley War Memorial.

GOLDTHORPE, LEWIS. Private. No 38129. 17th Battalion (2nd Leeds Pals) West Yorkshire Regiment. Born Kirkburton. Son of Mr Mr Albert Goldthorpe of North Road, Kirkburton. Reported missing, 17.4.1917, and afterwards presumed to have been killed on that date. He has no known grave. Commemorated **THIEPVAL MEMORIAL TO THE MISSING.** ROH:- All Hallows Parish Church, Kirkburton.

GOMERSAL, JOHN CHARLES. Private. No 40242. 9th Battalion West Yorkshire Regiment. Born 12 Colne Bridge, Bradley, 8.4.1889. Son of Albert Gomersall, 12 Colne Bridge, Bradley. Educated at Bradley Church of England School. Employed as a cloth finisher by Messrs H. Walker and Sons of Mirfield. Single. Enlisted in 1916. Reported wounded and missing, 1.10.1918. Has no known grave. Commemorated **VIS-en-ARTOIS MEMORIAL TO THE MISSING.** ROH:- St. Thomas's Church, Bradley.

GOODRICK, HERBERT. Private. No 2872. 1/5th Battalion Duke of Wellington's Regiment. Born Hillhouse, Huddersfield, 22.7.1889. Son of Ashley and Annie Goodrick, 1 Colne Terrace, Aspley, Huddersfield. Educated St. John's School, Hillhouse. Employed as a tailor's presser by Messrs Brook and Sugden, Paige Street, Huddersfield. Married. Living at 15 Robinson Street, Aspley. Enlisted 3.9.1914. Reported missing, presumed killed, 17.9.1916, aged 27 years. Has no known grave. Commemorated **THIEPVAL MEMORIAL TO THE MISSING.** ROH:- St. Paul's Church, Southgate, Huddersfield; Christ Church, Moldgreen; Huddersfield Drill Hall.

GOODWIN, HARRY. Private. No 32963. 6th Battalion York and Lancaster Regiment. Born Hillhouse, Huddersfield. Son of Peter T. and Zillah Goodwin, 47 Clement Street, Birkby. Educated Hillhouse Council School. Employed as a clerk in the Huddersfield Corporation rate office. Single. Enlisted January 1917. Wounded at Armentieres 20.3.1918. Died of wounds at Queen's Hospital, Frognal, Sidcup, Kent, 10.6.1918, aged 21 years. Buried **EDGERTON CEMETERY, HUDDERSFIELD.** Grave location:- 5B, 1. ROH:- Huddersfield Corporation Roll; Fartown and Birkby War Memorial.

GOODWORTH, HARRY. Private. No 235144. 2/7th Battalion Worcestershire Regiment. Formerly 205196 Duke of Wellington's Regiment. Born Clayton West 31.3.1884. Educated at Clayton West Schools and Kayes Board School. Employed as a credit draper and also by Messrs Hirst, Kettlewell and Company, Dundas Street, Huddersfield, as a tailor's cutter. Husband of Elsie Taylor Goodworth, 4 Spring Grove Street, Huddersfield. Enlisted 10.4.1917. Was in training for twelve weeks and then embarked for France on 3.7.1917. Was transferred to the Worcestershire Regiment on arriving in France. Wounded at the Battle of Cambrai, 4.12.1917. Died of his wounds at Le Treport, 13.12.1917, aged 33 years. Buried **MONT HUON MILITARY CEMETERY.** Grave location:- Plot 5, Row C, Grave 6B. ROH:- Clayton West and High Hoyland War Memorial.

GOODYEAR, THOMAS. Sapper. No 282721. 66th Wagon Erecting Company Royal Engineers. Born Slaithwaite 26.2.1899. Educated Mount Pleasant Council School. Married, with two children. Prior to enlistment, lived at 26 Crosland Road, Thornton Lodge, Huddersfield. Employed as an iron moulder by Messrs France and Brook, of Slaithwaite. Enlisted 24.2.1917. Died of a cerebral haemorrhage at No 35 General Hospital, Calais, 7.5.1918, aged 31 years. Buried **LES BARAQUES MILITARY CEMETERY, SANGATTE.** Grave location:- Plot 3, Row B, Grave 4. ROH:- St. Stephen's Church, Rashcliffe.

GOODYEAR, WILLIAM. Bombardier. No 110237. 219th Siege Battery, Royal Garrison Artillery. Born Jim Lane, Marsh, 21.9.1879. Son of the late Joseph and Sarah Goodyear. Husband of Elizabeth Goodyear. Educated Paddock Council School. Employed as a gardener. At the time of enlistment, was living at Arden Cottage, Shirley Road, Acocks Green, Birmingham. Enlisted July 1916. Killed in action, 7.10.1917, aged 38 years. Buried **VOORMEZELE ENCLOSURE No 1 & 2.** Grave location:- Plot 1, Row K, Grave 42. ROH:- Shared Church, Paddock.

GORDGE, JAMES. Lance Corporal. No 17419. 10th Battalion Duke of Wellington's Regiment. Born Bury 9.8.1878. Educated at St. Thomas's School, Huddersfield. Employed as a boiler firer. Husband of Elizabeth Ann Gordge, 58 Thomas Street, off Northgate, Huddersfield. Enlisted 16.8.1915. Killed during the Battle of the Somme, 10.7.1916, aged 37 years. Has no known grave. Commemorated **THIEPVAL MEMORIAL TO THE MISSING.** ROH:- Huddersfield Parish Church.

GOULDER, GEORGE THOMAS. Gunner. No 103844. 115th Heavy Battery, Royal Garrison Artillery. Born Carlton, Nottinghamshire. Married, with two children. Lived 12 Booth Banks, Slaithwaite. Employed as a weaver by Messrs Pearson Brothers, Commercial Mills, Slaithwaite. Played in the first team for Slaithwaite Cricket Club. Was a member of the Slaithwaite Socalist Club. Died as a result of a fractured skull at No 46 Casualty Clearing Station on 20.11.1917, aged 28 years. Buried **MENDINGHEM MILITARY CEMETERY.** Grave location:- Plot 1, Row G, Grave 13. (Brother of Privates **SYDNEY** and **WILLIAM HENRY GOULDER,** both of whom died of wounds, q.v.). ROH:- St. James Church, Slaithwaite; Slaithwaite War Memorial.

GOULDER, SYDNEY. Private. No 306335. 2/7th Battalion Duke of Wellington's Regiment. Son of George Goulder, 5 Gladstone Buildings, Marsden. Employed as a piecer by Messrs Robinson Brothers, Clough Lee Mills, Marsden. Played cricket for the Marsden second eleven. Enlisted in 1916 and embarked for France at Christmas, 1916. Died of gunshot wounds at No 49 Casualty Clearing Station, 18.4.1917, aged 30 years. Buried **ACHIET-LE-GRAND COMMUNAL CEMETERY EXTENSION.** Grave location:- Plot 1, Row C, Grave 9. (Brother of Privates **GEORGE THOMAS GOULDER** and **WILLIAM HENRY GOULDER,** both of whom died of wounds, q.v.). ROH:- Huddersfield Drill Hall; Marsden War Memorial.

GOULDER, WILLIAM HENRY. Private. No 306020. 9th Battalion Duke of Wellington's Regiment. Son of George Goulder, 5 Gladstone Buildings, Marsden. Husband of Rachel Goulder, 12 Plains Terrace, Marsden. Employed in the dyehouse at Fall Lane Mills. Died of wounds, 27.8.1918, aged 23 years. Buried **FIENVILLERS BRITISH CEMETERY.** Grave location:- Row C, Grave 14. (Brother of Privates **GEORGE THOMAS** and **SYDNEY GOULDER** both of whom died of wounds q.v.).

GOULDSTONE, EDWARD. Private. No 6/51608. 52nd Battalion Sherwood Foresters. Son of the late Mr and Mrs Gouldstone, 49 Crosland Buildings, Longroyd Bridge. Lived with his sister at 3 Ramsden Mill Lane, Linthwaite. Employed by Messrs France and Brook, Slaithwaite. Died of illness at Clipstone Camp on Monday, 18.11.1918, aged 18. Buried **St. ALBAN CHURCHYARD, FOREST TOWN, NOTTINGHAMSHIRE.** ROH:- Linthwaite.

GOULDSTONE, REGINALD. Private. No 204519. 1/4th Battalion Duke of Wellington's Regiment. Born King Cross, Halifax, 31.1.1900. Son of the late William and Annie Gouldstone. Educated Spring Grove Council School. Employed as an apprentice baker. Single. At the time of enlistment, was living at 106 Lowergate, Longwood. Single. Enlisted October 1914. Killed in action, 14.4.1918, aged 19 years. Has no known grave. Commemorated **TYNE COT MEMORIAL TO THE MISSING.** ROH:- Longwood War Memorial.

GRACE, ERNEST EDWIN. Private. No 2650. 1/5th Battalion Duke of Wellington's Regiment. Son of Frederick and Louie Grace of Crewe. Husband of May Grace, 96 Bradford Road North, Huddersfield. Employed as a crane driver at Messrs Holmes's iron foundry at Turnbridge. Killed in action, 10.7.1915, aged 29 years. Buried **BARD COTTAGE CEMETERY, BOESINGHE, BELGIUM.** Grave location:- Plot 1, Row A, Grave 41. His widow received a letter from Lieutenant Stott, of 'C' Company, 1/5th Battalion, who wrote that, *'Private Grace was a very faithful and most trustworthy servant to me for a long time. I shall never get one to equal him. He was buried last night in a little military cemetery just behind the trenches. His grave will be carefully cared for while we are in this sector.'* ROH:- St. Andrew's Church, Leeds Road; Salvation Army Citadel; Huddersfield Drill Hall.

GRAHAM, BEN. Sapper. No 231948. 224th Field Company Royal Engineers. Born Huddersfield 10.10.1889. Son of Ben and Emma J. Graham, 16 Prospect Street, Huddersfield. Educated Spring Grove Council School and Higher Grade College. Was in business with his father as a builder and contractor. Husband of Mrs Graham, 74 Branch Street, Paddock. Enlisted January 1917. Was wounded and taken prisoner, 9.4.1918. His wife received a postcard from him on 21.6.1918, which was written on 21.4.1918. He said he was suffering from a wound in the thigh and a broken leg but was 'alright.' Died of wounds in the Reserve Hospital Camp at Aachen, Germany, 23.9.1918, aged 29. Buried **COLOGNE SOUTHERN CEMETERY, GERMANY.** Grave location:- Plot 13, Row E, Grave 13.

GRAHAM, GEORGE HENRY. Private. No 205090. 2/4th Battalion Hampshire Regiment. Born Moldgreen. Son of Thomas and Mary Ann Graham; husband of Emily Graham, 9 New Street, Paddock. Employed by Messrs W. E. Cotton and Sons, of Slaithwaite. Served four years in the army. Had served in Egypt for three years and three months and was demobilised three days before his death, on 10.4.1919, from pneumonia, age 41 years. Buried **EDGERTON CEMETERY.** Grave location:- 54, 113. ROH:- All Saints Church, Paddock.

GRAHAM, HARRY. Private. No 266939. 2/6th Battalion Duke of Wellington's Regiment. Born Halifax Old Road, Hillhouse, 4.5.1896. Son of Oliver Graham, 34 Hawthorn Terrace, Calton Street, Huddersfield. Educated Huddersfield Parish Church School. Was a member of the Huddersfield Parish Church football team, which won the school challenge cup, and he was also a member of the Otley Cricket Club. Employed as a cloth scourer and miller by Messrs Duncan Barraclough and Company, Otley Mills, Otley. Single. Enlisted 15.11.1915. Killed in action at the Battle of Bullecourt, 3.5.1917, aged 21 years. Has no known grave. Commemorated **ARRAS MEMORIAL TO THE MISSING.** ROH:- St. John the Evangelist, Birkby; St. Andrew's Church, Leeds Road; Fartown and Birkby War Memorial.

GRAHAM, HIRST, MM. Private. No 240310. 2/5th Battalion Duke of Wellington's Regiment. Born Huddersfield 16.9.1893. Son of Kossuth and Lavinia Graham, 81 Victoria Road, Lockwood. Educated at Huddersfield Parish Church School and Rashcliffe Church of England School. Employed as a labourer. Single. Enlisted in the local Territorials in June, 1914. Awarded the Military Medal for *'bravery on the field and carrying wounded during a heavy bombardment, shell and sniping fire on 9.10.1917.'* Died on 16.3.1918 at Marcoing, aged 24 years. Buried **MAROEIL BRITISH CEMETERY**. Grave location:- Plot 4, Row H, Grave 10. ROH:- St. Stephen's Church, Rashcliffe; Huddersfield Drill Hall; memorial in Lockwood Cemetery.

GRAHAM, MALCOLM HEWLEY. Lieutenant. 3rd, attached 2nd, Battalion The Yorkshire Regiment. Born 22.11.1894, at New Mill. Only son of Mr and Mrs H. S. Graham, of Oxley Woodhouse, Sheepridge, Huddersfield. His father was principal of the firm of Messrs Graham and Barnfather, worsted spinners, of New Mill. Educated at Huddersfield College School and Repton School. Was studying at Pembroke College, Cambridge, with a view to entering the medical profession but, on the outbreak of the war, he joined the Army. Was a fine athlete and oarsman and was a member of the Leander Club. Killed in action at Givenchy, 15.6.1915, aged 20 years. Has no known grave. Commemorated **LE TOURET MEMORIAL TO THE MISSING**. His parents received a letter from Captain F. W. Stansfield, informing them that their son had been shot in the neck and died instantly, *'The men charged like heroes and out of eleven Officers and three hundred and sixty men who took part in the attack only one Officer and about eighty men got back untouched. All the rest are killed, wounded or missing. Your son was a most gallant officer, very keen and hard working and he will be a great loss to the battalion. Please accept the deepest sympathy of all ranks in your great loss.'* ROH:- Huddersfield College School; Christ Church, Woodhouse Hill, (a chancel screen was dedicated to his memory in the church on Sunday, 21.4.1917. It bears the inscription, *'He died as few men get the chance to die; fighting to save a world's morality. He died the noblest death a man may die, fighting for God and right and liberty and such a death's immortality.'*

GRAHAM, WALTER HUDDLESTON. Sergeant. No 240113. 1/5th Battalion Duke of Wellington's Regiment. Born Lockwood. Lived 234 Lockwood Road, Mount Pleasant, Lockwood. Killed in action, 3.9.1916. Has no known grave. Commemorated **THIEPVAL MEMORIAL TO THE MISSING**. ROH:- St. Stephen's Church, Rashcliffe; Huddersfield Drill Hall.

GRANGE, C. SAMUEL. Driver. No T/325247. Army Service Corps. Son of Elizabeth Hannah Grange. Died 31.5.1918. Buried **KIRKHEATON CEMETERY**. Grave location:- 'C', 365.

GRANGE, JOE. Private. No 6164. 9th Battalion Highland Light Infantry. Formerly No 31317 Northumberland Fusiliers. Born Huddersfield. Son of Mr and Mrs Ben Grange, Winget Avenue, Cowlersley, Milnsbridge. Employed as a piecer by Messrs Joseph Dyson and Sons, Elm Ing Mills, Milnsbridge. Was a member of the South Ryding Working Men's Club. Attended the Linthwaite Church and Sunday School. Enlisted 4.4.1916. Embarked for France 25.11.1916. Reported missing, 27.12.1916, aged 21 years. Has no known grave. Commemorated **THIEPVAL MEMORIAL TO THE MISSING**. ROH:- Linthwaite War Memorial.

GRANGE, NORRIS. Rifleman. No 38231. 2/8th Battalion West Yorkshire Regiment. Born Golcar. Son of Joseph and Mary Jane Grange, 83 Spring Terrace, Radcliffe Road, Golcar. Attended the Crimble Congregational Mission. Employed as a twister-in by Messrs Shaw, Sons and Company, Lees Mill, Slaithwaite. Enlisted October 1916. Embarked for France in June, 1917. Wounded in the legs, shoulder and head on 10.10.1917. Died of his wounds at No 3 Canadian Casualty Clearing Station on 12.10.1917, aged 19 years. Buried **GREVILLERS BRITISH CEMETERY**. Grave location:- Plot 7, Row C, Grave 9. ROH:- St. John's Church, Golcar.

GRAVES, CEDRIC CHARLES. Driver. No T/35991. Army Service Corps, attached to Fife and Forfar Yeomanry. Born Lockwood, Huddersfield, in 1891. Son of George and Clara Graves. Educated Rastrick Common Council School. Attended Mount Pleasant Chapel, Lockwood. Employed as a painter and decorator by Hirst and Barraclough, of Brighouse. At the time of enlistment, in September 1914, was living at

3A Hill Crest, Woodhouse, Brighouse. Died of pneumonia on 5.9.1916 in Egypt. He was 25 years of age. Buried **CAIRO WAR MEMORIAL CEMETERY, EGYPT.** Grave Location:- H, 49. ROH:- Mount Pleasant Chapel, Lockwood; Brighouse War Memorial; Rastrick War Memorial.

GRAYSON, JOHN Private. No M/323465. Army Service Corps. Formerly No 25541 13th Battalion The Yorkshire Regiment. Born Huddersfield. Youngest son of Mr and Mrs Robert Grayson, 164 Bradford Road North, Huddersfield. Employed as an apprentice motor-body builder by Messrs Rippon Brothers, coach and motor builders. Enlisted 1915. Reported missing, believed drowned. 30.12.1917. Has no known grave. Commemorated **CHATBY MEMORIAL TO THE MISSING, EGYPT.** ROH:- St. John's Church, Birkby; Fartown and Birkby War Memorial.

GREAVES, ARNOLD. Private. No 367115. Labour Corps. Born Sheffield. Enlisted Huddersfield. Lived Meltham. Died at home 20.1.1918. Buried **St. MARY'S CHURCHYARD, BOLSTERSTONE.** ROH:- St. Bartholomew's Church, Meltham.

GREAVES, JOHN. Private. No 241577. 2/5th Battalion Duke of Wellington's Regiment. Born Honley. Son of Mr and Mrs Friend Greaves, Thirstin Road, Honley. Employed by Messrs Shaw Brothers, Larchfield Mills, Firth Street, Huddersfield. Enlisted March 1916. Reported missing on 3.5.1917 and later presumed to have died on that date. He was 20 of age. Has no known grave. Commemorated **ARRAS MEMORIAL TO THE MISSING.** ROH:- Huddersfield Drill Hall; Honley War Memorial.

GREAVES, WILLIAM. Corporal. No 11449. 2/5th Battalion Duke of Wellington's Regiment. Born Ipswich. Enlisted Huddersfield. Son of Mrs Adelaide Sheard, 4 Fountain Street, Northgate, Huddersfield. Reported missing, presumed killed, at the Battle of Cambrai, 27.11.1917, aged 24 years. Has no known grave. Commemorated **CAMBRAI MEMORIAL TO THE MISSING.** ROH:- St. Andrew's Church, Leeds Road, Huddersfield; Huddersfield Drill Hall.

GREEN, FRED. Private. No 242029. 1/5th Battalion Duke of Wellington's Regiment. Born Holmbridge. Son of Mr and Mrs F. W. Green, Bank Top, Holmbridge. Educated Dobb Council School. Attended Hinchliffe Mill Sunday School. Employed as a weaver at Clarence Mills, Holmbridge. Single. Was a member of Holmbridge football club. Suffered serious gunshot wounds to the leg on 23.7.1918. Died of his wounds at No 12 General Hospital, Rouen, 25.7.1918, aged 24 years. Buried **St. SEVER CEMETERY EXTENSION, ROUEN.** Grave location:- Block Q, Plot 3, Row J, Grave 7. ROH:- Holme and Holmebridge; Huddersfield Drill Hall.

GREEN, GEORGE STANLEY. Private. No 10718. 2nd Battalion Duke of Wellington's Regiment. Born Shelley, Huddersfield. Son of John Albert and Harriet Green, 20 New Grange, Marsden. Prior to enlistment, had worked in the finishing department of Messrs C. and J. Hirst Limited, Milnsbridge, and previous to that had worked for Messrs Crowther, Bruce and Company at Marsden. Enlisted October 1914. On 30.6.1916, he was seriously wounded in the chest and the leg. He was taken to the VIII Corps Collection Station at Acheux, which had been prepared in readiness for the Battle of Somme. He died of his injuries on 2.7.1916, aged 20. He was the first man to be buried in **ACHEUX BRITISH CEMETERY.** Grave location:- Plot 1, Row 1, Grave 1. ROH:- Marsden War Memorial.

GREEN, NORMAN. Private. No 24122. 8th Battalion Duke of Wellington's Regiment. Born Paddock 14.9.1893. Son of George C. Green, 'Brown Cow Inn', Millgate, Paddock. Educated Spring Grove Council School. Attended Paddock United Methodist Church. Employed as a woollen piecer by Messrs E.H. Sellars Limited, yarn spinners. Single. Enlisted 4.8.1914. Killed in action near Langemarck, Belgium, 11.8.1917, aged 22 years. Has no known grave. Commemorated **MENIN GATE MEMORIAL TO THE MISSING.** (Stepbrother of Private **FRANK LITTLEWOOD**, killed in action at Bullecourt, 3.5.1917, q.v.). ROH:- All Saints Church, Paddock; Shared Church, Paddock.

GREEN, NORRIS. Private. No 19939. 10th Battalion West Yorkshire Regiment. Born Church Lane, Moldgreen, 5.1.1891. Son of Martha A.

Green, 34 Church Street, Moldgreen. Educated Moldgreen Church of England School. Employed as a fireman by the London and North Western Railway Company. Single. Enlisted 10.5.1915. Killed in action in the attack on Fricourt, 1.7.1916, aged 25 years. Buried **FRICOURT NEW MILITARY CEMETERY.** Grave location:- Row D, Grave 2. ROH:- Christ Church, Moldgreen; London and North Western Railway Company Roll.

GREEN, THOMAS EWART. Private. No 42253. 10th Battalion Worcestershire Regiment. Formerly No 32033 1/7th Battalion Duke of Wellington's Regiment. Born Kingscliffe, Peterborough. Son of John W. and Elizabeth Green of Peterborough. Educated at Kingscliffe Church of England School. Employed by the London and North Western Railway Company in the goods yard as a caller-off at Huddersfield railway station. Husband of Eleanor Green, 3, Horseshoe Yard, Blacker Road, Birkby. Enlisted July 1917. Died from influenza whilst a Prisoner of War, 27.10.1918, aged 27 years. Buried **TOURNAI COMMUNAL CEMETERY ALLIED EXTENSION.** Grave location:- Plot 4, Row N, Grave 32. ROH:- Fartown and Birkby War Memorial; London and North Western Railway Company Roll.

GREEN, WALTER. Private. No 32178. 18th Battalion West Yorkshire Regiment. Born Moldgreen, Huddersfield, 14.4.1887. Educated Moldgreen and St. Paul's Church of England Schools. Employed as a teamer. At the time of enlistment, was living at 22 Gelder Terrace, Moldgreen. Enlisted 23.5.1916. Killed in action on the Somme, 13.11.1916. buried **SAILLY-AU-BOIS MILITARY CEMETERY.** Grave location:- Plot 2, Row E, Grave 3.

GREENFIELD, WILFRED. Private. No 20009. 2nd Battalion Duke of Wellington's Regiment. Born Marsh 9.8.1896. Son of Walter and Kate Greenfield, 28 Filbert Street, Birkby. Educated Hillhouse Council School. Employed as a shop assistant at the Hillhouse Cooperative Society. On the roll of honour of Birkby Baptist Church where he had been a Sunday School scholar for seventeen years. Single. Enlisted 7.4.1916. Had only been in France for two months when he was killed at Le Transloy, near Combles, on 12.10.1916, aged 20 years. Buried **GUARDS' CEMETERY, LESBOEUFS.** Grave location:- Plot 5, Row W, Grave 10. ROH:- Fartown and Birkby War Memorial; Birkby Baptist Church.

GREENHOW, HERBERT. Private. No 241386. 5/6th Battalion The Cameronians (Scottish Rifles). Born Newsome, Huddersfield. Attended Newsome Church. Husband of Ruth Greenhow, 9 Chapel Street, Scapegoat Hill, Golcar, and father of six children. Prior to enlistment, was employed as a weaver by Messrs Ben Hall and Sons, of Milnbridge. Enlisted 11.9.1916. Embarked for France in January, 1917. Killed in action, 14.4.1917, aged 32 years. Buried **HENINEL CROISILLES ROAD CEMETERY.** Grave location:- Plot 1, Row C, Grave 3.

GREENSMITH, HUBERT HENRY (BERTIE). Private. No 24172. 10th Battalion Duke of Wellington's Regiment. Son of William and Francis Greensmith, Ford Gate, Hinchliffe Mill. Educated Dobb School. Employed as a shop assistant at the Hinchliffe Mill Cooperative Society and at Milnsbridge Cooperative Stores. Attended Hinchliffe Wesleyan Sunday School. Enlisted firstly in the Royal Field Artillery and was later transferred into the Duke of Wellington's Regiment. Embarked for France on his thirtieth birthday, 2.10.1916. Killed in action, 24.1.1917. Buried **RAILWAY DUGOUTS BURIAL GROUND (TRANSPORT FARM).** Grave location:- Plot 7, Row F, Grave 16. ROH:- Holme and Holmbridge War Memorial.

GREENWOOD, ANDREW. Ordinary Seaman. No 2/13436. R.N.R. Royal Navy Depot (Crystal Palace) Tyneside. Born Holmfirth. Son of Arthur and Annie Maud Greenwood, Glenfield Bottoms, Holmfirth. Educated Upperthong National School. Attended St. John's Sunday School and Church and was a member of the choir. Employed in the finishing department (with his father) by Messrs T. and J. Tinker at Bottoms Mill, Holmfirth. Had only been in the R.N.R. for five weeks when he died of pneumonia at Croydon General Hospital, 24.10.1918, aged 18 years. Buried **HOLY TRINITY BURIAL GROUND, HOLMFIRTH.** Grave location:- South, S, 42–52. ROH:- Holmfirth War Memorial; commemorated on his parents' headstone in Holy Trinity Churchyard.

GREENWOOD, FREDERICK. Private. No 20122. 2nd Battalion Duke of Wellington's Regiment. Born North Street, Lockwood, 16.2.1886. Son of Sarah Hannah Greenwood, 25 Blagden Lane, Close Hill, Huddersfield. Educated Stile Common Council School and the Higher Grade School. Was a member of Primrose Hill Baptist Church and had been a member of the choir. Was formerly a salesman employed by Mr J.W. Hobson, tobacconist, of Buxton Road, Huddersfield and, prior to enlistment, was a partner in the firm of Messrs W. and H. Heaton, tobacconists and confectioners, 8 Kirkgate, Huddersfield. Single. Enlisted 11.4.1916. Killed in action at Le Transloy, 12.10.1916, aged 31. Buried **LONDON CEMETERY EXTENSION; NOMINAL ROLL.** Grave location:- Plot 9, Row D, Grave 16. ROH:- St. John's Church, Newsome.

GREENWOOD, GEORGE ALFRED. Private. No 2163. 1/5th Battalion Duke of Wellington's Regiment. Born Lindley 26.3.1894. Son of Emma Greenwood, 15 Longroyd Lane, Longroyd Bridge, Huddersfield. Educated St. John's Church of England School. Employed as a labourer by David Brown and Son Limited. Had served with the local Territorials before the war. Enlisted 4.8.1914. Embarked for France April 1915. Killed by the explosion of a shell during the battle of the Somme, 2.7.1916, aged 22 years. Has no known grave. Commemorated **THIEPVAL MEMORIAL TO THE MISSING.** ROH:- St. Thomas's Church, Longroyd Bridge.

GREENWOOD, HARRY. Private. No G/66913. 23rd Battalion Royal Fusiliers. Born Thornhill Briggs, Brighouse, 10.1.1883. Employed as a cotton twiner at the Tandem Mills, Waterloo. At the time of enlistment, was living at 3 Parkin's Yard, Spring Grove Street, Huddersfield. Married. Enlisted 18.3.1917. Reported missing, presumed killed, 25.3.1918. Has no known grave. Commemorated **ARRAS MEMORIAL TO THE MISSING.**

GREENWOOD, HARRY. Private. No 43139. 9th Battalion King's Own Yorkshire Light Infantry. Born Somerset Crescent, Huddersfield, 17.2.1882. Brother of Edith Short, 6 Somerset Place, Mulberry Street, Moldgreen. Employed as a dyer's labourer. Single. Enlisted 12.11.1916. Killed in action, 2.9.1918, aged 36 years. Buried **VAULX HILL CEMETERY, VAULX-VRAUCOURT.** Grave location:- Plot 1, Row K, Grave 8. ROH:- Christ Church, Moldgreen.

GREENWOOD, TOM. 2nd Lieutenant. 1/5th Battalion The King's (Liverpool Regiment). Born Aspley, Huddersfield, 14.8.1881. Son of the late Thomas Alfred and Lavinia Greenwood, 10 Dalton Green Lane, Huddersfield. Educated at Mr Ed. Mellor's Academy, Spring Street, Huddersfield and Kirkheaton National Schools. Employed as a stockbroker's clerk in the office of Mr T. K. Mellor, stock and share broker. Single. Enlisted as a Private in the 1/8th (Irish) Battalion King's (Liverpool Regiment) on 11.11.1914. Embarked for France in April, 1915. In October, 1917, was recommended for a commission and went through the course with a Cadet Battalion at Newmarket. Was gazetted to his old regiment and returned to France on 13.8.1918. He had only been with his Battalion a few days when he was killed in action, 31.8.1918, aged 37 years. Buried **ECOUST-St.-MEIN BRITISH CEMETERY.** Grave location:- Row D, Grave 26. ROH:- St. John's Church, Kirkheaton.

GREENWOOD, WILFRED. Private. No 150017. 743rd Area Employment Company Labour Battalion. Formerly No 3968 Duke of Wellington's Regiment. Born Linthwaite. Son of John Henry and Emma Greenwood, North View Terrace, Linthwaite. Employed as a weaver at Holme Mills, Marsden. Was a member of the Young Men's Class at Slaithwaite Zion Baptist Church. Died from pneumonia following influenza at No 1 General Hospital, Etretat, France, 8.11.1918, aged 24 years. Buried with full military honours **ETRETAT CHURCHYARD EXTENSION.** Grave location:- Plot 3, Row D, Grave 8. ROH:- Linthwaite War Memorial.

GREGSON, WILLIAM PILKINGTON. 2nd Lieutenant. Tank Corps. Born Huddersfield. Son of the late Mr W. P. Gregson of Preston and formerly of Springwood Avenue, Huddersfield. Employed at the Karrier Car Works, Huddersfield. Enlisted in the Duke of Wellington's Regiment in August, 1914. Was gazetted to the Tank Corps in January, 1918, after two and a half years service in France. Died of wounds, 18.10.1918, aged 27 years, Buried **VADENCOURT BRITISH CEMETERY.** Grave location:- Plot 3, Row A, Grave 24.

GRIFFIN, HERBERT HENRY. Private. No M2/222698. 648th Motor Transport Company, Army Service Corps. Born Liverpool. Employed as a chauffeur for Colonel Beadon, of Longley Hall. Married, with two children, and lived at Longley Hall Cottage. Died from dysentery at Dar-es-Salaam, East Africa, 4.4.1918. Buried **PEMBA CEMETERY, MOZAMBIQUE.** Grave location:- Row A, Grave 12.

GRIFFITHS, HERBERT HAROLD. Driver. No 141315. Royal Field Artillery. Born Hammersmith, London 12.5.1897. Son of Herbert and Sarah Ann Griffiths, 24 South Street, Huddersfield. Educated Christ Church School, Bow Lane, Preston. Employed as a pattern maker. Enlisted 6.5.1916. Wounded in the left ankle with shrapnel, 3.12.1917. Discharged from the artillery 3.9.1918. Died from osteomyelitis of the ankle following the shrapnel wound on 5.5.1920, aged 22 at 24 South Street, Huddersfield. Buried **EDGERTON CEMETERY, HUDDERSFIELD.**

GRIMES, ROBERT. Private. No G/17283. 11th Battalion Royal Sussex Regiment. Born Horsham. Son of Albert and Sarah Ann Grimes of Whitley Hall, Lepton. Employed by Messrs Kilner Brothers, woollen manufacturers, of Lepton. Reported wounded and missing, 25.4.1918, aged 19 years. Buried **HOOGSTADE BELGIAN MILITARY CEMETERY.** Grave No 947. ROH:- Lepton Parish Church; St. John's Church, Kirkheaton.

GRINES, JOHN. Lance Sergeant. No 24446. North Staffordshire Regiment. Lived 9 Kirkmoor Place, Northgate, Huddersfield. Discharged from the army due to illness on 31.7.1917. Died of tuberculosis 29.12.1921.

GRUNDY, HARRY. Private. No 2084. 'A' Company, 1/7th Battalion Duke of Wellington's Regiment. Born 91 South Street, Huddersfield, 24.9.1895. Son of Albert Edward and Mary Hannah Grundy, 100 South Street, Huddersfield. Educated Spring Grove Board School. Employed as an iron turner by Mr John Haigh of Firth Street, Huddersfield. Enlisted 5.9.1914. Shot by a sniper whilst in the trenches on the morning of 16.12.1915, aged 20 years. Buried **BARD COTTAGE CEMETERY, BOESINGHE, BELGIUM.** Grave location:- Plot 1, Row J, Grave 13. ROH:- South Street Methodist Church; St. Thomas's Church, Longroyd Bridge; Huddersfield Drill Hall.

GUEST, HERBERT. Lance Corporal. No 2124. 2nd Battalion The Black Watch. Formerly No 10078 Duke of Wellington's Regiment. Born Douglas, Isle of Man, 26.11.1892. Son of Arthur Henry and Sarah Ann Guest, 12 South Parade, Huddersfield. Educated Spring Grove Board School. Employed as a grocer's assistant. Single. Enlisted in May 1911. When war broke out he had been stationed in India for nine months. He came over to France with the 1st Indian Expeditionary Force in September, 1914. The last letter his parents received from him was on 22.9.1915, when he asked them *'not to send him any further parcels or letters as he expected to be home on leave in the course of a few days'*. Killed in action at the Battle of Loos, 25.9.1915, aged 23 years. Has no known grave. Commemorated **LOOS MEMORIAL TO THE MISSING.** His parents received a letter from Captain M. E. Raylin, of the 2nd Battalion Black Watch who wrote, *'I am very sorry indeed to tell you that your son, No 2124 Lance Corporal Herbert Guest, was killed in action on the morning of the 25th September during an exceedingly successful charge in which the Regiment completely broke the German line. Your son had only just received the lance stripe but I had every reason to be more than pleased having recommended him for it. He was an N.C.O. of quite unusual promise and had already shown himself a most useful and fearless soldier. He is a very great loss to the Company.'*

GUNN, HAROLD. Private. No 241601. 2/5th Battalion Duke of Wellington's Regiment. Born Victoria Street, Chesterton, near Newcastle-on-Tyne, 14.11.1885. Son of Josiah James and Elizabeth Gunn, 24 Back Fair Street, Lockwood. Educated Spring Grove Board School. Married. Employed as a dyer's labourer by Messrs E. Priest and Sons Limited. Was a member of the Queen Street Mission Brass Band and the St. John Ambulance Brigade. At the time of enlistment, was living at 50 Albert Street, Lockwood. Enlisted 10.3.1916. Reported missing at the Battle of Bullecourt, 3.5.1917, aged 31 years. Has no known grave. Commemorated **ARRAS MEMORIAL TO THE MISSING.** ROH:- Huddersfield Drill Hall.

GUNSON, LESLIE. Private. No 28642. Northumberland Fusiliers. Born Huddersfield. Lived 2 Primrose Street, Primrose Hill, Huddersfield. Killed in action 16.9.1916.

GUTTERIDGE, HERBERT JAMES (HENRY). Private No 150430. 'A' Company, 52nd Canadian Infantry (Manitoba Regiment). Son of Mr and Mrs George R. Gutteridge, 471 Columbia Street East, New Westminster, British Columbia. (His father was born in Holmfirth and he left for Canada in 1897). He had been eighteen months in the Army and ten months in France. Admitted to Royds Hall War Hospital, Huddersfield, on 11.5.1917 suffering from wounds. Died of wounds, 13.5.1917, aged 20 years. Buried **HOLY TRINITY CHURCHYARD, HOYLAKE, CHESHIRE,** where his uncle resided. Grave location D, 517. ROH:- Holmfirth War Memorial.

GUY, GEORGE. *See* **SUTCLIFFE, GEORGE GUY.**

HAGGAS, WALTER. Able Seaman. No Z/7874. R.N.R. 'Hood' Battalion Royal Naval Division. Son of Harold and Martha Haggas, 103 Occupation Road, Lindley. Killed in action, 3.6.1918, aged 21. Buried **ENGLEBELMER COMMUNAL CEMETERY EXTENSION.** Grave location:- Row D, Grave 18.

HAGUE, WILLIE. Private. No 241005. 2/5th Battalion Duke of Wellington's Regiment. Born Shelley. Son of Mrs Hague, of Royd House, Shelley. Prior to enlistment worked for Messrs Stringer and Jagger at Emley Moor Colliery. Reported missing at the Battle of Bullecourt, 3.5.1917, and afterwards presumed to have died on that date. He was 21 years of age. Has no known grave. Commemorated **ARRAS MEMORIAL TO THE MISSING.** ROH:- Emmanuel Church, Shelley.

HAIGH, ALBERT. Private. No 72045. Sherwood Foresters. Formerly No 31748 North Staffordshire Regiment. Born Holme, Holmfirth. Only son of Abraham and Alice Haigh, Burnlee, Holmfirth. Attended Holme Day and Sunday School. Employed by Messrs W. H. and J. Barber, Clarence Mills, Holmbridge. Enlisted November 1916. Killed in action, 23.8.1917, aged 19. Has no known grave. Commemorated **TYNE COT MEMORIAL TO THE MISSING.** His parents received a letter from a comrade of their son telling them how he died. The soldier writes that Albert was killed as he was getting behind a corner, '*Just as Albert as about to go round the corner he was hit in the stomach. He did not suffer any pain as he was killed instantly. The last words Albert was heard to say were 'We are alright, I have a parcel on the way and we will have a good 'do' when we get out.*' ROH:- Upperthong War Memorial.

HAIGH, ALBERT. Gunner. No 128036. Royal Field Artillery. Born 16 Allen Row, Paddock. Son of G. H. Haigh, 16 Allen Row, Paddock. Educated Paddock Council School. Employed as a tram driver by Huddersfield Corporation Tramways Department. Married. Enlisted 9.1.1915. Died in the Huddersfield Royal Infirmary of tuberculosis, 16.1.1920, aged 26 years. Buried **EDGERTON CEMETERY, HUDDERSFIELD.**

HAIGH, ALBERT EDWARD. Rifleman. No 71044. Royal Fusiliers, posted to 2nd/2nd London Regiment (Royal Fusiliers). Formerly No 33954 Res. Cavalry Regiment. Born Milnsbridge. Son of Charles Henry and Alice Matilda Haigh, 7 Scar Lane, Milnsbridge. Killed in action at Passchendaele, 26.10.1917, aged 19 years. Has no known grave. Commemorated **TYNE COT MEMORIAL TO THE MISSING.** ROH:- Longwood War Memorial.

HAIGH, ALFRED. Private. No 41928. 1/5th Battalion York and Lancaster Regiment. Born Mexborough 10.12.1885. Educated at Mexborough schools. Husband of Clara Haigh, 1 Robinson's Yard, Bradford Road, Huddersfield. Employed as an agent for the Pearl Assurance Company, Huddersfield. Enlisted 12.4.1917. Killed in action in Belgium, 17.11.1917, aged 32 years. Buried **HOOGE CRATER CEMETERY.** Grave location:- Plot 14, Row C, Grave 16.

HAIGH, ALLEN. Gunner. No 80650. 244th Siege Battery, Royal Garrison Artillery. Born 8 Bank End, Nettleton Hill, Golcar, 19.7.1887. Eldest son of the late Sutcliffe and Ellen Haigh, 8 Bank End, Nettleton Hill, Golcar. Educated Scapegoat Hill Council School. Employed as a weaver by Messrs John Crowther and Sons, Milnsbridge. Single. Enlisted

15.5.1916. Killed in action, 4.10.1918, aged 31 years. Buried **FIFTEEN RAVINE BRITISH CEMETERY, VILLERS-PLOUICH.** Grave location:- Plot 2, Row G, Grave 15. (Brother of Private **SUTCLIFFE HAIGH,** died of wounds, 12.4.1918, q.v.).

HAIGH, ALLEN MORTIMER. 2nd Lieutenant. The King's Own (Royal Lancaster Regiment), attached 1/4th Battalion King's Own Yorkshire Light Infantry. Born 'The Holly', Marsh, 3.8.1898. Son of the late Edward and Kate Haigh, 'The Holly', Marsh, Huddersfield. Educated at Sedbergh Public School from 1912 until 1915. Employed at Messrs Haigh's stores, Huddersfield merchants. Single. Enlisted August 1916. Was a cadet in the Officers' Training Corps at Bristol University. Killed in action, 13.4.1918, at Neuve Eglise, aged 19 years. Has no known grave. Commemorated **TYNE COT MEMORIAL TO THE MISSING.** ROH:- Marsh War Memorial; St. Stephen's Church, Lindley; commemorated in Salendine Nook Baptist Chapel yard D388.

HAIGH, ANDREW. Private. No 31707. 12th Battalion Durham Light Infantry. Born Golcar. Son of John and Elizabeth Haigh of Lowergate, Wellhouse, Golcar. Was wounded in the neck whilst serving in the trenches in France. Sent to England with a convoy of wounded. Was treated in hospital in Warrington, where attempts were made to remove the shrapnel, which proved unsuccessful and he died on 31.12.1917, aged 36 years. Buried **GOLCAR UNITED METHODIST CHAPEL YARD, WELLHOUSE.** Grave location:- North, G, 7. ROH:- St. John's Church, Golcar; memorial in Wellhouse Churchyard.

HAIGH, ARTHUR. Private. No 41978. 12th Battalion Manchester Regiment. Formerly No 32557 North Staffordshire Regiment. Born Primrose Hill, Huddersfield. Son of George Haigh, 'The White Lion' Inn, Lepton. Killed in action, 25.4.1917, aged 30 years. Has no known grave. Commemorated **ARRAS MEMORIAL TO THE MISSING.** ROH:- Lepton Parish Church; St. John's Church, Kirkheaton.

HAIGH, ARTHUR. Sergeant. No 99729. 110th Squadron Royal Air Force. Born Sowerby Bridge, Halifax 17.9.1900. Parents lived at 191 Bradford Road, Huddersfield. Educated Hillhouse Council School. Employed as a motor engineer. Single. Enlisted September 1917. Reported missing and afterwards known to be a Prisoner of War in Germany. Died, 16.9.1918, aged 20 years. Buried **NIEDERZWEHREN CEMETERY, CASSEL, GERMANY.** Grave location:- Plot 4, Row L, Grave 18. (Brother of Private **CHARLEY HAIGH,** reported missing, 3.10.1918, q.v.). ROH:- Fartown and Birkby War Memorial.

HAIGH, AUGUSTUS DANIEL. Rifleman. No 43556. 16th Battalion, The County of London Regiment, attached to King's Royal Rifle Corps. Born 18 St George's Square, Huddersfield, 1.2. 1899. Son of Daniel and Edith Eliza Haigh, Longfield House, 236 Lockwood Road, Huddersfield. Educated Spring Grove Board School, Huddersfield, Secondary School and Hillhouse Higher Elementary School. Employed as a clerk. Single. Enlisted in the week before Easter, 1917. Wounded at Bullecourt, 27.8.1918. Died of his wounds at the University War Hospital, Southampton, 23.9.1918, aged 19 years. Buried **EDGERTON CEMETERY, HUDDERSFIELD.** Grave location:- 46, 120. ROH:- Huddersfield Parish Church; Mount Pleasant Chapel, Lockwood.

HAIGH, BEAUMONT. Private. No 3/10837. 8th Battalion Duke of Wellington's Regiment. Born Meltham, Huddersfield. Lived Meltham. Brother of Mr Dan. Haigh, of Station Street, Meltham. Employed as a cotton piecer. Served at Gallipoli. Died 8.12.1915, aged 27 years. Buried **PORTIANOS MILITARY CEMETERY, WEST MUDROS, LEMNOS, GREECE.** Grave location:- Plot 5, Row D, Grave 160. ROH:- St. Bartholomew's Church, Meltham; Helme Parish Church.

HAIGH, BEN. Private. No 38511. 17th Battalion West Yorkshire Regiment. Born 13 Coal Pit Lane, Outlane, 6.5.1895. Educated at Outlane School. Employed as a fettler. Married. Prior to enlistment, lived at 61 James Street, Golcar. Enlisted 28.10.1916. Killed in action, 14.9.1917. Buried **VILLERS-FAUCON COMMUNAL CEMETERY EXTENSION.** Grave location:- Plot 1, Row F, Grave 18. ROH:- Bethel United Methodist Church, Outlane; Longwood War Memorial.

HAIGH, CHARLEY. Private. No 32042. 1/6th Battalion North Staffordshire Regiment.

Born Sowerby Bridge in October 1898. Son of Fred and Ada Haigh, 191 Bradford Road, Huddersfield. Educated Hillhouse Council School. Employed as a piano tuner. Single. Enlisted October 1916. Reported missing, 3.10.1918, aged 20. Buried **RAMICOURT BRITISH CEMETERY**. Grave location:- Row B, Grave 10. (Brother of Private **ARTHUR HAIGH**, who died as a Prisoner of War, 16.9.1918, q.v.). ROH:- Fartown and Birkby War Memorial.

HAIGH, DONALD. Able Seaman. No J/50850. Royal Navy. *HMS Partridge*. Son of William and Ann Haigh, 22 Union Street, Slaithwaite. Employed as a weaver by Messrs W. and E. Crowther at Crimble Mills, Slaithwaite. Was a member of Slaithwaite Liberal Club and the Slaithwaite Swimming Club. Enlisted in the Royal Navy in March, 1916. 'The destroyer *Partridge* was a unit of the force based on Lerwick, Shetland Isles for the purpose of escorting convoys to and from Scandinavia. On December 11th, 1917, the destroyer left the port in company with the destroyer *Pellew* and the armed trawlers *Livingstone, Commander Fullerton, Lord Alverstone* and *Tokio*, escorting a convoy of six ships. At 11.45am on the 12th the convoy was S.W. of Bjorne Fjord when enemy ships were sighted to northward. After signalling the merchant ships to scatter, Lt. Commander J. R. C. Cavendish, of *Pellew,* commanding the convoy, went into action followed by *Partridge,* and a wireless signal was sent to the Commander-in-Chief. The enemy raiders, consisting of four destroyers, commanded by Captain Hans Kolbe, formed in one line of three ships with a fourth detached for the purpose of sinking the merchantmen. In a very few minutes *Partridge* was hit by a shell which severed her main steam-pipe and left her helpless. Her after gun was knocked out and she was struck forward by a torpedo. Under these conditions her Captain, Lt. Commander R.H. Ransome, gave orders to abandon ship. She was hit by two more torpedoes and sank. The losses were heavy, *Partridge* going down with five officers and 92 ratings, while three officers and 21 ratings became prisoners.' (Extract taken from Dictionary of Disasters at Sea during the Age of Steam'). Reported missing at sea, 12.12.1917, aged 24 years. On the 1.2.1918 his parents received official information from the Accounts Department of the Royal Navy in London to the effect that Able Seaman Donald Haigh must now be presumed to be dead, '*With reference to the communication from this department on the 17.12.1917 respecting Donald Haigh, Able Seaman of HMS Partridge I deeply regret to inform you that his name does not appear in the list of prisoners of war captured from the vessel received from the German authorities through the International Red Cross Committee of Geneva. The list is believed to be complete and in these circumstances it is my painful duty to state that no doubt is now entertained that your son lost his life when his ship was sunk.*' Commemorated on **PORTSMOUTH NAVAL MEMORIAL TO THE MISSING.** (Three other men from Huddersfield were aboard *HMS Partridge* and were drowned when the ship was sunk on 12.12.1917. They were Ordinary Seaman **FRED DRANSFIELD**, Able Seaman **WALKER BAMFORTH** and Ordinary Seaman **SHEARD WINDLE**, q.v.). ROH:- St. James Church, Slaithwaite; Slaithwaite War Memorial.

HAIGH, ERNEST. Private. No 3603. 'A' Company, 1st Battalion Honourable Artillery Company. Born Stile Common, Huddersfield, 4.5.1893. Son of Fred and Florrie Haigh, Rosedene, Dark Lane, St. Helens, Almondbury. Educated Stile Common Council School and Almondbury Grammar School. Employed as a picture frame maker. Single. Enlisted 30.5.1915. Wounded at Thiepval 27.10.1916. Suffered from shell shock and neurasthenia. Died at Dark Lane, Almondbury, 29.12.1918, after discharge from the army. Buried **ALMONDBURY CEMETERY.** Grave location:- 10, 'C', 13. ROH:- Almondbury Grammar School; Almondbury War Memorial; Fitzwilliam Street Unitarian Church, Huddersfield.

HAIGH, FRANCIS EDWARD. Trooper. No 10510. 3rd Dragoon Guards (Prince of Wales' Own). Born Crofton. Foster son of Charles and Frances Haigh, Netherton Square, Netherton. Employed as a clerk by the Lancashire and Yorkshire Railway Company at the goods department at Huddersfield Station. Was a forward in the second team of the Huddersfield Northern Union football club. Enlisted 29.8.1914. Killed in action by a high explosive shell on 1.6.1915, aged 20 years. Has no known grave. Commemorated. **MENIN GATE MEMORIAL TO THE MISSING.** ROH:-

South Crosland and Netherton War Memorial; Lancashire and Yorkshire Railway Roll.

HAIGH, FRED. Private. No 40973. 10th Battalion Lincolnshire Regiment. Formerly No 20282 Duke of Wellington's Regiment. Born Slaithwaite. Son of George and Jane Haigh of Moorside, Slaithwaite. Employed as a spinner by Mr Joseph Thomas, Colne Mills, Slaithwaite. Killed in action, 28.4.1917, aged 25. Has no known grave. Commemorated **ARRAS MEMORIAL TO THE MISSING.** ROH:- St. James Church, Slaithwaite; Slaithwaite War Memorial.

HAIGH, FRED. Gunner. No 158873. 'A' Battery, 255th Brigade Royal Field Artillery. Born Golcar. Second son of Mr and Mrs George Haigh, 3 Junction House, Slades Road, Golcar. Employed by Mr Henry Garside, farmer, of Golcar. Attended Westwood Mission Church. Killed in action, 3.8.1917. Buried **ARTILLERY WOOD CEMETERY, BOESINGHE, BELGIUM.** Grave location:- Plot 3, Row A, Grave 20. (Brother of Private **GEORGE HAIGH,** killed in action, 7.8.1917, q.v.). ROH:- St. John's Church, Golcar; Pole Moor Baptist Church.

HAIGH, GEORGE. Private. No 203744. 1/5th Battalion Duke of Wellington's Regiment. Born Golcar. Third son of Mr and Mrs George Haigh, 3 Junction House, Slades Road, Golcar. Employed as a weaver by Messrs W. and E. Crowther, Crimble Mills, Slaithwaite. Attended Westwood Mission Church. Killed in action at Nieuport, 7.8.1917, aged 22 years. Buried **RAMSCAPELLE ROAD MILITARY CEMETERY.** Grave location:- Plot 2, Row A, Grave 30. (Brother of Private **FRED HAIGH,** killed in action, 3.8.1917, q.v.). ROH:- St. John's Church, Golcar; Huddersfield Drill Hall.

HAIGH, GEORGE. Private. No 54873. 1/5th Battalion West Yorkshire Regiment. Born Golcar. Enlisted Huddersfield. Killed in action, 25.4.1918. Has no known grave. Commemorated **TYNE COT MEMORIAL TO THE MISSING.**

HAIGH, GEORGE. Private. No 41827. 10th Battalion The Cameronians (Scottish Rifles). Formerly No 4622 Highland Light Infantry. Born Kirkburton. Son of Alfred and Ann Haigh, of Storthes Hall, Kirkburton. Brother of Miss Haigh, St John's Terrace, Dogley Bar, Kirkburton.

Employed by Messrs Liversedge and Company of Dogley Mills. Embarked for France in August, 1917. Killed in action, 28.3.1918, aged 23 years. Has no known grave. Commemorated **ARRAS MEMORIAL TO THE MISSING.** ROH:- All Hallows Parish Church, Kirkburton.

HAIGH, GEORGE HENRY. Private. No 36555. 1/5th Battalion Northumberland Fusiliers. Born Berry Brow, Huddersfield. Son of Mrs Haigh, 25 Bentley Street, Lockwood. Employed by Messrs E. H. Sellars and Sons Limited of Lockwood. Enlisted Huddersfield. Reported missing on 10.4.1918 and afterwards presumed to have died on that date. He was 20 years of age. Has no known grave. Commemorated **PLOEGSTEERT MEMORIAL TO THE MISSING.** ROH:- Emmanuel Church, Lockwood; Armitage Bridge National School.

HAIGH, HAROLD. Corporal. No 25732. 7th Battalion The Yorkshire Regiment. Born Horbury, Wakefield, 24.6.1897. Lived 5 Albert Street, Lockwood. Employed as a woollen piecer. Single. Reported missing, presumed killed, 8.2.1917. Has no known grave. Commemorated **THIEPVAL MEMORIAL TO THE MISSING.** ROH:- St. Stephen's Church, Rashcliffe.

HAIGH, HAROLD. Private. No 33961. 10th Battalion West Yorkshire Regiment. Born Barton Road, Crosland Moor, Huddersfield. Son of George Albert and Ellen Haigh, 43 Matlock Street, Crosland Moor. Educated Crosland Moor Board School. Employed as a lithographic printer. At the time of enlistment, was living at 13 Nowells Walk, Harehills Lane, Leeds. Husband of Lily Haigh, 5 Church Street, Crosland Moor. Enlisted on Whit Monday, 1916. Wounded twice. Was taken prisoner by the Germans in March, 1918. He was interned at the Langensalza Camp, Germany. On 17.11.1918 there was a riot at the camp, when 16 prisoners were killed and 50 injured. Private Haigh was severely wounded in the leg and back. He was transported to Leith General Hospital, Scotland, where he died from his wounds and partly from exhaustion and starvation, on Monday 30.12.1918, aged 35. Buried **EMMANUEL CHURCHYARD, LOCKWOOD.** Grave location:- 6, S.W., 34. ROH:- Emmanuel Church, Lockwood; 'Rising Sun' Public House, Crosland Moor.

HAIGH, HAROLD. Corporal. No 376948. 1/8th Battalion Manchester Regiment. Formerly No 13192 King's Own Yorkshire Light Infantry. Born Crosland Moor. Husband of M. E. Haigh, 17 Bath Street, Lockwood. Died of wounds, 29.9.1918, aged 24 years. Buried **GREVILLERS BRITISH CEMETERY.** Grave location:- Plot 14, Row E, Grave 14. ROH:- St. Barnabas Church, Crosland Moor.

HAIGH, HARRY. Private. No 241919. 1/5th Battalion Northumberland Fusiliers. Born Rochdale 5.3.1883. Son of Mr and Mrs George Haigh, 1 Portland Street, Reinwood Road, Lindley. Educated Oakes Board School. Employed as a clip cutter. Single. Enlisted 20.5.1916. Killed in action, 14.11.1916, aged 34 years. Has no known grave. Commemorated **THIEPVAL MEMORIAL TO THE MISSING.** ROH:- Oakes Baptist Church; St. Stephen's Church, Lindley.

HAIGH, HARRY. Private. No 25507. 'D' Company, 2nd Battalion The Yorkshire Regiment. Born Green Mount Street, Moldgreen, 9.10.1892. Son of the late Joe and Margaret Haigh, 15 Rawthorpe Lane, Dalton. Employed as a cotton and woollen goods packer. Single. Enlisted 14.11.1915. Died in Mill Hill Sanatorium, Huddersfield, of tuberculosis of the lung following bronchial pneumonia on 27.6.1919. Buried **St. JOHN'S CHURCHYARD NEWSOME, HUDDERSFIELD.** Grave location:- I, 75. (Brother of Private **HERBERT HAIGH,** killed in action, 9.10.1917, q.v.).

HAIGH, HERBERT. Private. No 24887. 'X' Company, 8th Battalion Duke of Wellington's Regiment. Born Green Mount Street, Moldgreen, 9.10.1892. Son of the late Joe and Margaret Haigh, 15 Rawthorpe Lane, Dalton. Employed as a dyer's labourer. Single. Enlisted 6.10.1916. Killed in action at Passchendaele, 9.10.1917, aged 25 years. Has no known grave. Commemorated **TYNE COT MEMORIAL TO THE MISSING.** (Brother of Private **HARRY HAIGH,** died at home, 27.6.1919, q.v.). ROH:- Huddersfield Parish Church.

HAIGH, HERBERT. Lance Corporal. 2/5th Battalion Duke of Wellington's Regiment. Born Crosland Moor 29.6.1898. Son of Mr and Mrs James William Haigh, 16 St Peter's Street, Huddersfield. Educated St. Barnabas School, Crosland Moor. Employed as a labourer and millhand. Enlisted in the local Territorials prior to the outbreak of the war. Died in Mill Hill Sanatorium, Huddersfield, of tuberculosis after being gassed on 14.11.1918.

HAIGH, HERBERT. Private. No 35388. 1st Battalion Leicestershire Regiment. Formerly No 2038 Duke of Wellington's Regiment. Born Joanroyd, Cubley, Penistone, 29.6.1893. Son of Emily Haigh, Brooks Fold, Colnebridge, Bradley, Huddersfield. Educated at schools in Penistone, Cubley, Longsett and Burbage. Employed by Messrs Learoyd Brothers and Company Limited. Attended St. Thomas's Church, Bradley. Single. Enlisted September 1914. Wounded 4.12.1917. Died of wounds at No 21 Casualty Clearing Station, Ytres, 5.12.1917, aged 25 years. Buried **ROCQUIGNY-EQUANCOURT ROAD BRITISH CEMETERY.** Grave location:- Plot 5, Row E, Grave 6. (Brother of Private **JOE HAIGH,** died of wounds, 5.9.1918, q.v.). ROH:- St. Thomas's Church, Bradley; Learoyd Brothers.

HAIGH, HERBERT. Private. No 81125. 1/5th Battalion Durham Light Infantry. Born Huddersfield. Son of Mr and Mrs David Haigh, 28 Ash Street, Hillhouse, Huddersfield. Employed by William Greenhalgh and Sons, wholesale drapers. Killed in action, 11.4.1918, aged 19 years. Has no known grave. Commemorated **PLOEGSTEERT MEMORIAL TO THE MISSING.** ROH:- Fartown and Birkby War Memorial; memorial in Almondbury Cemetery.

HAIGH, HERBERT. Private. No 63603. 'C' Company, 2/4th Battalion King's Own Yorkshire Light Infantry. Born Scammonden. Enlisted Halifax. Son of Amos and Clara Haigh, 97 Swallow Lane, Golcar. Killed in action, 27.9.1918, aged 18 years. Buried **RIBECOURT ROAD CEMETERY, TRESCAULT.** Grave location:- Plot 2, Row B, Grave 10. ROH:- St. John's Church, Golcar.

HAIGH, HERBERT. Gunner. No L/29317. 'C' Battery, 160th Brigade, Royal Field Artillery. Second son of Mr and Mrs Edward Haigh, 2 Mould Hill, Nettleton Hill, Longwood. Prior to enlistment, had been employed at various times by Messrs C. and J. Hirst and Sons Limited, Messrs Hirst and Mallinson Limited and Mr A.

Illingworth, of Longwood. Attended Scapegoat Hill Baptist Church and Sunday School. Was a member of the Scapegoat Hill Brass Band. Single. Enlisted 1.6.1915. Killed in action, 7.6.1917, aged 22 years. Buried **St. NICOLAS BRITISH CEMETERY, ARRAS.** Grave location:- Plot 2, Row A, Grave 3.

HAIGH, HERBERT LESLIE. Gunner. No 270645. 'B' Battery, 156th Brigade Royal Field Artillery. Born Newsome, Huddersfield, 1.2.1899. Son of Ben and Alice Haigh, 77 Barcroft Road, Newsome. Educated Newsome National School. Employed as an iron moulder by Messrs Edwin Mills and Son of Aspley. Single. Enlisted 1.5.1918. Killed in action near Le Cateau, 23.10.1918, aged 19 years. Has no known grave. Commemorated **VIS-en-ARTOIS MEMORIAL TO THE MISSING.** ROH:- St. John's Church, Newsome; memorial in Newsome Churchyard.

HAIGH, JAMES. Private. No 29310. 10th Battalion West Yorkshire Regiment. Born Holmfirth. Third son of Mr and Mrs Henry Haigh, New Town, Holmfirth. Educated Holmfirth National School and the Wesleyan Sunday School. Was in business with his brothers as a plasterer. Enlisted Easter 1915. Killed in action, 27.8.1918, aged 22 years. Buried **BULLS ROAD CEMETERY, FLERS.** Grave location:- Plot 3, Row H, Grave 2. ROH:- Holmfirth War Memorial.

HAIGH, JAMES ASPINALL. Lieutenant. 2/5th Battalion Duke of Wellington's Regiment. Born Huddersfield 9.9.1894. Only son of the late Allen Haigh and grandson of the late James Haigh, of the firm of Messrs James Haigh Limited, dyers, of Globe Works, Colne Road, Aspenhurst, Huddersfield. Lived with his mother at Greenbank, 5 Elmfield Road, Birkby. Was a member of the choir at St. John's Church, Birkby, and was formerly a member of the Amateur Operatic Society. Prior to the outbreak of the war had been learning the art of dyeing in Germany at the firm of Badische and Bayer. He continued his studies when he joined the family firm in Colne Road. Joined the local Territorials in Spring, 1911. Received his commission in the Duke of Wellington's Regiment on 21.2.1915 and was promoted Lieutenant on 16.6.1916. Wounded at Bourlon Wood, near Cambrai, 20.11.1917. Died of wounds at No 21 Casualty Clearing Station at Ytres, 22.11.1917, aged 23 years. Buried **ROCQUIGNY-EQUANCOURT ROAD BRITISH CEMETERY.** Grave location:- Plot 3, Row B, Grave 10. ROH:- Huddersfield Drill Hall; Fartown and Birkby War Memorial.

HAIGH, JAMES WILLIAM. Private. No 307531. 1/6th Battalion West Yorkshire Regiment. Born Meltham. Lived Town Bottom, Meltham. Enlisted Halifax. Reported missing, presumed killed, 25.4.1918. Has no known grave. Commemorated **TYNE COT MEMORIAL TO THE MISSING.** ROH:- St. Bartholomew's Church, Meltham.

HAIGH, JOE. Private. No 46343. 2nd Battalion King's Own Yorkshire Light Infantry. Born Midhope, near Penistone, 31.10.1898. Son of the late Frederick C. Haigh and Emily Haigh, of Brooks Fold, Colnebridge, Bradley. Educated at Langsett, Burbage, High Lane and Bradley Schools. Employed as a scourer by Messrs Jarmaine and Sons, of Kirkheaton. Single. Enlisted November 1916. Died of wounds, 5.9.1918, aged 19 years. Buried **HEATH CEMETERY, HARBONNIERES.** Grave location:- Plot 9, Row A, Grave 5. (Brother of Private **HERBERT HAIGH**, died of wounds, 5.12.1917, q.v.). ROH:- St. Thomas's Church, Bradley.

HAIGH, JOE. Private. No 240133. 2/5th Battalion Duke of Wellington's Regiment. Born Crosland Moor 12.1.1893. Son of James William and Emma Haigh, 16 Peters Street, Huddersfield. Educated Crosland Moor Council Church of England School. Employed in a card room. Single. Enlisted 4.8.1914. Reported missing, presumed killed, at the Battle of Bullecourt, 3.5.1917, aged 24 years. Has no known grave. Commemorated **ARRAS MEMORIAL TO THE MISSING.** ROH:- Huddersfield Parish Church; Huddersfield Drill Hall.

HAIGH, JOE WILLIE. Private. No 36155. 10th Battalion York and Lancaster Regiment. Born Helme. Son of the late Allen and Sarah Haigh of Meltham. Husband of Mary Hannah Haigh, of Half Roads, Meltham. Employed as a joiner by Mr George Pogson of Meltham. Killed in action, 28.4.1917, aged 33 years. Buried **CHILI TRENCH CEMETERY, GAVRELLE.** Grave location:- Special Memorial C 5. ROH:- St. Bartholomew's Church, Meltham.

HAIGH, JOEL. Private. No 3995. 2/5th Battalion Duke of Wellington's Regiment. Born Huddersfield. Son of Joseph and Sarah Ann Haigh, 7 Riley Street, Damside, Huddersfield. Employed as a tram conductor by the Huddersfield Corporation tramways department. Single. Killed in action, 14.2.1917, aged 33 years. Buried **AUCHONVILLERS MILITARY CEMETERY.** Grave location:- Plot 2, Row K, Grave 11. ROH:- Huddersfield Drill Hall; Huddersfield Corporation Roll.

HAIGH, JOHN SCOT. 2nd Lieutenant. 24th Squadron Royal Air Force. Born Quaker Lane, Paddock, 23.1.1899. Son of Schofield and Lilian Haigh, 174 Taylor Hill Road, Lockwood. Educated Huddersfield College. Employed as a junior clerk by Messrs Thomas Hirst and Son, wool merchants, of Huddersfield. Played cricket with the Armitage Bridge Club and was also a member of the cricket and football teams of the Y.M.C.A. Single. Enlisted as a Private in the R.A.F. 3.4.1917. Accidentally killed at Bertangles, France, 15.8.1918, aged 19. Buried **VIGNACOURT BRITISH CEMETERY.** Grave location:- Plot 5, Row C, Grave 3. ROH:- Huddersfield College School; Armitage Bridge War Memorial.

HAIGH, JOSEPH ARTHUR. Private. No 25511. 1/6th Battalion Duke of Wellington's Regiment. Husband of Annie Haigh, 10 Armitage Road, Milnsbridge. Employed as a woollen teaser by Messrs C. and J. Hirst and Sons Limited, of Longwood. Enlisted March 1917. Embarked for France in April 1917. Killed in action, 16.4.1918, aged 36 years. Has no known grave. Commemorated **TYNE COT MEMORIAL TO THE MISSING.** ROH:- St. Mark's Parish Church, Longwood.

HAIGH, L. Private. No 82216. Royal Air Force. Died at home 14.3.1919. Buried **LINDLEY WESLEYAN METHODIST CHAPEL YARD.** Grave location:- J, 72.

HAIGH, NORMAN. Sergeant. No 240338. 2/5th Battalion Duke of Wellington's Regiment. Born Quarmby Road, Huddersfield, 27.3.1897. Son of Walter and Sarah Jane Haigh, 23 Arnold Street, Birkby. Educated Hillhouse Council School. Attended King Cliffe United Methodist Sunday School, Hillhouse. Employed as an auctioneer's clerk by Messrs Edison, Taylor and Booth, auctioneers, of High Street, Huddersfield. Was a promising vocalist. Enlisted at the outbreak of the war. Mentioned in a despatch from Sir Douglas Haigh, dated 7.11.1917, '*for gallant and distinguished service in the field. One evening he crawled out without any orders to reconnoitre an enemy post and managed to get quite close to the enemy wire. He was most anxious to do more than his duty and had he lived he would have most certainly have received a decoration for the gallant part he played in the attack on the Hindenburg Line on November 20th. That was a glorious day for the battalion,*' Wounded in the thigh, 20.11.1917. Died in a dressing station of his wounds, 21.11.1917, aged 20 years. Buried **HERMIES HILL BRITISH CEMETERY.** Grave location:- Plot 3, Row E, Grave 28. ROH:- St. Andrew's Church, Leeds Road, Huddersfield; Huddersfield Drill Hall; Fartown and Birkby War Memorial.

HAIGH, OLIVER. Able Seaman. No J/52167. Royal Navy. *HMS Lady Cory Wright.* Born Milnsbridge. Son of Wilfred and Elizabeth Ann Haigh, 34, Rufford Road, Milnsbridge. Attended Milnsbridge Wesleyan Sunday School and Ramsden Street Chapel, Huddersfield. Was a member of the Milnsbridge Church Institute. Employed as an under-engineer by Messrs C. and J. Hirst and Sons Limited, Commercial Mills, Milnsbridge. Enlisted in the Navy in 1916. Was married on 27.2.1918 to Nellie H. Haigh, 105 Spring Place, Manchester Road, Milnsbridge. Killed in action involving a submarine in the English Channel, 26.3.1918, aged 25 years. Has no known grave. Commemorated **PLYMOUTH NAVAL MEMORIAL TO THE MISSING.** ROH:- Milnsbridge War Memorial; Huddersfield Mission, Milnsbridge.

HAIGH, PERCY. Private. No 65594. 203rd Company, 66th Battalion Machine Gun Corps. Formerly No 17721 Duke of Wellington's Regiment. Born Skelmanthorpe. Enlisted Halifax. Lived Skelmanthorpe. Died of wounds, 14.4.1918. Buried **St. SEVER CEMETERY EXTENSION, ROUEN.** Grave location:- Block P, Plot 7, Row P, Grave 18. ROH:- St. Aidan's Church, Skelmanthorpe.

HAIGH, ROBERT FIRTH. Private. No 21/709. 1/6th Battalion West Yorkshire Regiment. Born

Lindley 6.12.1891. Youngest son of Mrs E. Haigh, 39 George Street, Lindley. Educated at Lindley Church of England School. Employed as a brush maker by Messrs C. Buckley and Company, of Longroyd Bridge. Single. Reported missing, presumed killed, 25.4.1918, aged 26 years. Has no known grave. Commemorated **TYNE COT MEMORIAL TO THE MISSING.** ROH:- St. Stephen's Church, Lindley.

HAIGH, ROBERT HUGH. Company Sergeant Major. No 241260. 1/6th Battalion Duke of Wellington's Regiment. Born Lockwood 26.11.1882. Son of John and Elizabeth Haigh, 20 Queen Street, Paddock. Educated Paddock Church of England School. Employed as a cloth presser in the finishing department of Messrs Hirst and Mallinson, of Milnsbridge. Married, with two children. At the time of enlistment, was living at 19 Clough Lane, Paddock. Enlisted June 1915. Was twice mentioned in despatches and received a certificate from the General commanding his division for distinguished conduct in the field. Was killed by a bomb from hostile aircraft whilst carrying in wounded to the Etaples Base Hospital on 19.5.1918, aged 36 years. Buried **ETAPLES MILITARY CEMETERY.** Grave location:- Plot 67, Row C, Grave 23. ROH:- All Saints Church, Paddock.

HAIGH, ROWLAND NORCLIFFE. Private. No 202522. 1st Battalion The Royal Scots Fusiliers. Born Stainland, Halifax. Son of Mr and Mrs Joe Haigh, 14 Francis Street, Milnsbridge. Employed as a night feeder by Messrs Job Thomas and Son Limited, Woodland Mills, Longwood. Enlisted 6.10.16. Served in France until March, 1918, when he was invalided home with trench fever. Returned to France on 2.5.1918. Killed in action, 5.6.1918. Has no known grave. Commemorated **LOOS MEMORIAL TO THE MISSING.** ROH:- Beestonley Lane Providence Chapel, Stainland; St. Andrew's Church Stainland.

HAIGH, SAM. Private. No 41151. 11th Battalion Suffolk Regiment. Formerly No 11/20671 Duke of Wellington's Regiment. Born Halifax. Son of Luke Haigh. Husband of Adeline Haigh, 27 Albion Street, Huddersfield. Enlisted Huddersfield. Reported missing, presumed killed, 9.4.1918, aged 38 years. Has no known grave. Commemorated **PLOEGSTEERT MEMORIAL TO THE MISSING.** ROH:- St. Paul's Church, Southgate, Huddersfield; Stainland Wesleyan Church.

HAIGH, SUTCLIFFE. Private. No 42012. 3rd Battalion Worcestershire Regiment. Born 9 Bank End, Nettleton Hill, Golcar. Son of the late Sutcliffe and Sarah Haigh. Educated Scapegoat Hill Council School. Employed as a cloth finisher by Messrs Joseph Hoyle and Son. Attended the Scapegoat Hill Baptist Church and was a worker in the Sunday School. Enlisted 17.5.1917. Died of wounds, 12.4.1918, aged 19 years. Buried **LA KREULE MILITARY CEMETERY, HAZEBROUCK.** Grave location:- Plot 1, Row C, Grave 23. (Brother of Private **ALLEN HAIGH** and Private **WILFRED HAIGH**, both killed in action, q.v.).

HAIGH, WHITWAM. Private. No 20392. 9th Battalion Duke of Wellington's Regiment. Born Golcar. Son of Mr and Mrs Ben Haigh, 162 Leymoor Road, Golcar. Employed by Messrs F. Calverley and Company Limited, of Milnsbridge. Attended Scapegoat Hill Baptist Sunday School. Was a playing member of the Leymoor Cricket Club. Enlisted May 1916. Embarked for France in August 1916. Killed in action, 25.4.1917, aged 28 years. Has no known grave. Commemorated **ARRAS MEMORIAL TO THE MISSING.** ROH:- St. John's Church, Golcar.

HAIGH, WILFRID. Guardsman. No 26396. 1st Battalion Grenadier Guards. Born 8 Bank End, Nettleton Hill, Golcar. Son of the late Sutcliffe and Ellen Haigh. Educated Scapegoat Hill Council School. Attended Scapegoat Hill Baptist Church. Employed by Messrs Hirst and Mallinson of Longwood. Single. Enlisted 16.8.1916. Killed in action, 13.10.1918, aged 23 years. Buried **St. VAAST COMMUNAL CEMETERY EXTENSION.** Grave location:- Row C, Grave 4. (Brother of Private **ALLEN HAIGH**, and Private **SUTCLIFFE HAIGH** both killed in action q.v.).

HAIGH, WILFRED. Lance Corporal. No 13444. 2nd Battalion Duke of Wellington's Regiment. Born Halifax. Son of Mr and Mrs Tom Haigh of Shoe Broads, Meltham. Husband of Amy L. Haigh, 86 Manchester Road, Huddersfield. Employed at Meltham Station. Attended Meltham Wesleyan Church. Enlisted September 1916. Was wounded at Suvla Bay, Gallipoli.

Killed in action, 27.3.1918, aged 25 years. Buried **FEUCHY CHAPEL BRITISH CEMETERY.** Grave location:- Plot 2, Row G, Grave 3. ROH:- St. Bartholomew's Church, Meltham.

HAIGH, WILFRED. Ordinary Seaman. No SS/6447. Royal Navy. *HMS Indefatigable*. Son of Alfred and Harriet Hannah Haigh, of Skelmanthorpe. Killed in action at the Battle of Jutland, 31.5.1916. Has no known grave. Commemorated **PLYMOUTH NAVAL MEMORIAL TO THE MISSING.**

HAIGH, WILLIAM DEANHOUSE. Gunner. No 326692. 33rd Siege Battery Royal Garrison Artillery. Born Honley. Son of the late Walter and Ann Haigh. Husband of Beatrice Alice Haigh, 57 Ivy Cottages, Deanhouse, Thongsbridge. Attended the Netherthong Parish Church and Sunday School. Was a member of the Working Men's Club, an official of the Netherthong Gardener's Friendly Society and was keen on cricket and football. Employed by Messrs Vickermans of Thongsbridge. Killed in action, 18.7.1917, aged 30 years. Buried **DICKEBUSCH NEW MILITARY CEMETERY EXTENSION.** Grave location:- Plot 2, Row C, Grave 12. ROH:- Netherthong and Thongsbridge War Memorial; Netherthong Working Men's Club.

HAIGH, WILLIE. Private. No 241833. 2/5th Battalion Duke of Wellington's Regiment. Born Kirkburton. Son of Mary Haigh, of Smith's Croft, Highburton. Employed by Messrs Thomas and Sons Limited, Rowley Mills. Attended Highburton Primitive Methodist Chapel bible class. Enlisted March 1916. Embarked for France in January, 1917. Reported missing at the Battle of Bullecourt, 3.5.1917, aged 21 years. Has no known grave. Commemorated **ARRAS MEMORIAL TO THE MISSING.** ROH:- All Hallows Parish Church, Kirkburton; Huddersfield Drill Hall.

HAIGH, WOODHEAD. Private. No 242189. 1/5th Battalion Northumberland Fusiliers. Born Wooldale, Holmfirth. Husband of Alice May Haigh, 16 Uppergate, Hepworth. Employed at Stoney Bank Mills. Was a member of the Netherthong football club. Killed in action, 26.10.1917, aged 29 years. Has no known grave. Commemorated **TYNE COT MEMORIAL TO THE MISSING.** ROH:- Hepworth and Scholes War Memorial; Hepworth Parish Church.

HALE, JOHN FRANCIS. Private. No 45252. 20th Battalion Durham Light Infantry. Formerly No 11438 Duke of Wellington's Regiment. Born Ranby, Nottinghamshire. Enlisted Huddersfield. Lived Meltham. Died of wounds at No 29 Casualty Clearing Station, 23.3.1918. Buried **GREVILLERS BRITISH CEMETERY.** Grave location:- Plot 12, Row E, Grave 6. ROH:- St. Bartholomew's Church, Meltham; Helme Parish Church.

HALL, CLARENCE TRIGG. No J/6309. Telegraphist. Royal Navy. *HM Submarine E6*. Born Huddersfield. Son of James and Isabelle Hall, 4 Commercial Square, Commercial Street, Huddersfield. Accidentally drowned from *Submarine E6* on 22.9.1915, aged 21 years. Has no known grave. Commemorated **CHATHAM NAVAL MEMORIAL TO THE MISSING.** ROH:- St. Paul's Church, Southgate, Huddersfield.

HALL, GEORGE. Private. No 18172. 9th Battalion Duke of Wellington's Regiment. Born Moldgreen, Huddersfield. Only son of Annie Hall, 5 Dalton Fold Road, Dalton. Prior to enlistment, was employed as a baker by Miss Hardy of Moldgreen. Enlisted 25.1.1916. Reported missing at the Battle of the Somme on 7.7.1916 and afterwards presumed to have been killed on that date, aged 19. Has no known grave. Commemorated **THIEPVAL MEMORIAL TO THE MISSING.** ROH:- Christ Church, Moldgreen.

HALL, HENRY. Sapper. No 361986. 364th Forestry Company, Royal Engineers. Born Reinwood Road, Quarmby Cliffe in April 1892. Son of Mr and Mrs J. W. Hall, 151 Roydhouse Lodge, Reinwood Road, Quarmby, Lindley. Educated Oakes Council School. Employed as a healder. Married. Enlisted in January 1916. Died of bronchial pneumonia in No 2 Stationary Hospital, Abbeville, 29.10.1918, aged 24 years. Buried **ABBEVILLE COMMUNAL CEMETERY EXTENSION.** Grave location:- Plot 4, Row K, Grave 13. ROH:- Lindley Zion Methodist Church; St. Stephen's Church, Lindley.

HALL, HERBERT. Private. No 30447. 2/5th Battalion Royal Warwickshire Regiment.

Formerly No 3/32362 North Staffordshire Regiment. Born Paddock 18.11.1888. Third son of Mr and Mrs Alfred Hall, Market Street, Paddock. Educated Paddock Council School. Attended Paddock United Methodist Church. Married. Employed as an organ pipe maker by Messrs Peter Conacher and Company. At the time of enlistment, was living with his wife's parents at 'The Woodman Inn', Marsden Road, Crosland Moor. Enlisted 16.11.1916. Reported missing at the Battle of Cambrai, 3.12.1917, and later presumed to have been killed on that date. Has no known grave. Commemorated **CAMBRAI MEMORIAL TO THE MISSING.** ROH:- St. Barnabas Church, Crosland Moor; Shared Church, Paddock.

HALL, HORACE. Private. No 31300. 6th Battalion The King's Own Scottish Borderers. Born Huddersfield. Son of the late George Henry Thomas Hall (who was Headmaster of Wilshaw Church School for thirty years) and Mary H. Hall, 34 Inglewood Terrace, Slaithwaite. Moved to Slaithwaite in 1909. Prior to enlistment, was employed as a groom at Lilburn Towers, Northumberland, the home of Mr Collingwood, a descendant of Admiral Collingwood. Enlisted St. Boswells. Killed in action, 17.7.1918, aged 34. Buried **LA KREULE MILITARY CEMETERY.** Grave location:- Plot 2, Row D, Grave 9. ROH:- St. James Church, Slaithwaite; Slaithwaite War Memorial.

HALL, JOHN. Private. No TR5/209748. 52nd Battalion West Yorkshire Regiment. Born Shelley. Son of Annie Hall, of Town End, Shelley. Prior to enlistment, was employed by Mr Percy Hopwood, grocer, of Bank Bottom, Shelley. Enlisted June 1918. Died in hospital, 14.7.1918, aged 18 years. Buried **EMMANUEL CHURCHYARD, SHELLEY.** Grave location:- 200. ROH:- Emmanuel Church, Shelley.

HALL, JOHN WILLIAM. Private. No 24662. 9th Battalion Duke of Wellington's Regiment. Lived 6 Armitage Street, Primrose Hill. Employed as a painter by Mr H. Booth of Marsh, Huddersfield. Was a member of the Newsome Working Men's Club. Enlisted October 1916. Killed in action, 1.2.1917, aged 34 years. Has no known grave. Commemorated **THIEPVAL MEMORIAL TO THE MISSING.**

HALL, SAMUEL. Pioneer. No WR/286846. R.T.D. Royal Engineers. Son of Benjamin and Sarah Hall of Marsden. Died of apoplexy, 30.4.1919, aged 37 years. Buried **JERUSALEM WAR CEMETERY.** Grave location:- Row U, Grave 24.

HALL, STANLEY. Private. No 34255. 12th/13th Battalion Northumberland Fusiliers. Formerly No 21201 The Hussars. Born Quarmby 14.10.1894. Son of Benjamin and Emily Jane Hall, 5 Hall Avenue, Springdale, Longroyd Bridge. Educated Oakes Council School. Employed as a woollen warehouseman by Messrs Fisher and Company, Upperhead Row, Huddersfield. Single. Enlisted March 1916. Wounded in February, 1917, and returned to France in October, 1917. Killed in action, 28.3.1918, aged 23 years. Has no known grave. Commemorated **POZIERES MEMORIAL TO THE MISSING.** ROH:- Oakes Baptist Church; St. Stephen's Church, Rashcliffe.

HALL, WALTER. Private. No 52536. 1st Battalion West Yorkshire Regiment. Born Lockwood 15.11.1896. Son of Joe Walter and Amelia Hall, Fair Street, Lockwood. Educated at Mount Pleasant Council School. Employed as a motor driver. Single. Enlisted June 1917. Reported missing at Lagnicourt on 21.3.1918 and afterwards presumed to have been killed on that date. Has no known grave. Commemorated **ARRAS MEMORIAL TO THE MISSING.** ROH:- St. Stephen's Church, Rashcliffe; Mount Pleasant Chapel, Lockwood; memorial in Lockwood Cemetery.

HALLAS, CHARLES. Private. No 24940. 2nd Battalion Duke of Wellington's Regiment. Born Huddersfield. Enlisted Halifax. Lived 30 Brian Street, Lindley, Huddersfield. Reported missing at the Battle of Arras, 3.5.1917. Has no known grave. Commemorated **ARRAS MEMORIAL TO THE MISSING.**

HALLAS, FRED. Guardsman. No 14045. Coldstream Guards. Born Shelley. Son of Charles Hallas, of Gatefoot, Shepley. He had been employed as an attendant at Storths Hall Asylum at the time of enlisting, in November 1914, but prior to then had worked for Messrs Kaye and Stewart, Huddersfield. Played football with the Lower Cumberworth club. Trained at Windsor and Caterham and embarked for France in July, 1915. Killed in action at Vermelles, 20.10.1915, aged 24 years. Has no known grave. Commemorated **LOOS MEMORIAL TO THE MISSING.** His brother, Company Sergeant Major Hallas, who fought in the Boer War and was on the staff of the Huddersfield Recruiting Staff, received the following letter from Lieutenant Ferguson, '*Your brother Private Fred Hallas was in my platoon and was killed by a shell on the evening of October 19th. Two German shells exploded right in the bit of a trench which my platoon was holding, killing six and wounding three men. Your brother Fred Hallas was killed instantenously. He was buried the same night and a cross with his name and the date he was killed marks his grave. Next morning our Chaplain read the service beside the grave and those of the other men who had been killed at the same time. May I say how much I sympathise with you all in your loss. Your brother had not been out here long poor fellow but at any rate you must all have the consolation of knowing that he died in action, a soldier's death. I am glad to hear of the spirit shown amongst many young men when the news of his death became known.*' ROH:- New Mill Working Men's Club; Fulstone War Memorial; Shepley War Memorial.

HALLAS, GEORGE WILLIAM STANLEY. Private. No 33240 6th Battalion York and Lancaster Regiment. Formerly No 31369 Duke of Wellington's Regiment. Born Mirfield 14.9.1891. Son of Mrs M. Hallas, 7 Dudley Avenue, Marsh. Educated Mirfield National School. Employed as a clerk. Single. Enlisted 23.3.1917. Reported missing, presumed dead, 19.10.1917, aged 27, near Poelcapelle at the Battle of Passchendaele. Has no known grave. Commemorated **TYNE COT MEMORIAL TO THE MISSING.** ROH:- Marsh War Memorial.

HALLAS, JOE. Private. No 241993. 2/5th Battalion Duke of Wellington's Regiment. Born Lepton. Son of Mrs E. Hallas of Highgate Lane, Lepton. Prior to enlistment, was employed by Messrs Brierley and Wall Limited, Spa Mills, Lepton. Died of wounds at No 56 Casualty Clearing Station on 5.10.1918. Buried **GREVILLERS BRITISH CEMETERY.** Grave location:- Plot 15, Row D, Grave 17. ROH:- Lepton Parish Church; Huddersfield Drill Hall.

HALLAS, PERCY. Private. No 250769. 1/6th Battalion Durham Light Infantry, Son of Watson and Louisa Hallas, 34 Parkgate, Berry Brow, Huddersfield. Prior to enlistment had worked at Stanley Mills, Milnsbridge. Enlisted April 1916. Was wounded in April 1917. Died of wounds, 30.10.1917, aged 23 years. Buried **WIMEREUX COMMUNAL CEMETERY.** Grave location:- Plot 6, Row F, Grave 11. ROH:- Armitage Bridge War Memorial.

HALLAS, STANLEY ISAAC. Private. No 36252. 6th Battalion King's Own Yorkshire Light Infantry. Formerly No 5/86652 91st Territorial Reserve Battalion. Born Shepley. Son of Joe and Susannah Hallas, Yew Tree Terrace, Shepley. Prior to enlistment, was employed by Messrs S. Drake and Sons Limited, of Honley. Enlisted February 1917. Killed in action, 24.9.1917, aged 19 years. Has no known grave. Commemorated **TYNE COT MEMORIAL TO THE MISSING.** ROH:- Shepley War Memorial.

HALSTEAD, ARTHUR. Private. No 30445 2/5th Battalion Royal Warwickshire Regiment. Formerly No 3/32043 North Staffordshire Regiment. Born 'Royal Oak Hotel', 14.5.1893. Son of Emma Halstead, 2 Garden Street, Lockwood. Educated Spring Grove Board School. Employed as a packing case maker by Messrs Wilson, Travis and Company. Was a member of the Buxton Road Young Men's Bible Class. Single. Enlisted 9.11.1916. Killed in action whilst helping to carry a wounded man to the dressing station on 6.9.1917, aged 24 years. Buried **AEROPLANE CEMETERY, YPRES.** Grave location:- Plot 1, Row C, Grave 22. (Brother of Private **FRANK HALSTEAD,** died of wounds 3.7.1916, q.v.). ROH:- St. Stephen's Church, Rashcliffe.

HALSTEAD, ARTHUR. Private. No 80380 13th Battalion Durham Light Infantry. Born Wren Street, Paddock 5.3.1899. Son of Herbert and Emma Halstead, 4 Branch Street, Paddock. Educated All Saints School, Paddock. Employed as a finisher by Messrs John Lockwood and Sons Limited. Single. Enlisted April 1917. Killed in action, 23.10.1918, aged 19 years. Buried **CROSS ROADS CEMETERY, FONTAINE-AU-BOIS.** Grave location:- Plot 2, Row H, Grave 28. ROH:- All Saints Church, Paddock; Shared Church, Paddock; Salendine Nook Churchyard; Milnsbridge War Memorial.

HALSTEAD, FRANK. Private. No 154. 12th Battalion King's Own Yorkshire Light Infantry. Born 'Royal Oak Hotel' 5.3.1886. Eldest son of Emma Halstead, 2 Garden Street, Lockwood. Educated Spring Grove Board School. Prior to enlisting, was employed as a miner at Parkdale Colliery, Clayton West. Was a member of the Young Men's Bible Class at Buxton Road Wesleyan Chapel. Was married in September, 1915. Lived Bradford Road, Huddersfield. Enlisted at the outbreak of the war. Served in Egypt and had been in France for eight months. Wounded at Bertrancourt, 1.7.1916. Died of wounds, 3.7.1916, aged 31 years. Buried **BERTRANCOURT MILITARY CEMETERY.** Grave location:- Plot 1, Row A, Grave 16. (Brother of Private **ARTHUR HALSTEAD,** killed in action, 4.9.1917, q.v.). ROH:- St. Stephen's Church, Rashcliffe; Clayton West and High Hoyland War Memorial.

HALSTEAD, FRANK. Private. No 28889 13th Battalion York and Lancaster Regiment. Born Marsh, Huddersfield 17.9.1885. Son of Sarah Jane Halstead, 48 Wellington Street, Mexborough. Educated at Portland Street School and Huddersfield Higher Grade School. Employed as a joiner. Enlisted 31.7.1916. Wounded 4.4.1918. Died in a field dressing station, 12.4.1918, aged 32 years. Has no known grave. Commemorated **PLOEGSTEERT MEMORIAL TO THE MISSING.** ROH:- Holy Trinity Church, Huddersfield.

HALSTEAD, GEORGE. Private. No 38454. 15th (1st Leeds Pals) Battalion West Yorkshire Regiment. Born 65 South View, Paddock. Educated Paddock Church of England School. Attended Paddock United Methodist Church. Apprenticed at the Huddersfield Examiner office and remained on the staff as a linotype operator until he enlisted on 24.10.1916. Husband of Amy Halstead, Stoney Croft, Stoney Lane, Longwood. Reported missing at the Battle of Arras on 3.5.1917 and afterwards presumed to have died on that date. Has no known grave. Commemorated **ARRAS MEMORIAL TO THE MISSING.** ROH:- Shared Church, Paddock.

HALSTEAD, GILBERT ARTHUR. Private. No 301967. 2nd Battalion The Royal Scots (Lothian Regiment). Born Huddersfield 11.6.1891. Son of Frank and Lamona Halstead, 159 Thornton Road, Crosland Moor. Educated at Thomas Street Council School. Employed as a cashier and book-keeper. Single. Enlisted 2.10.1916. Killed in action near Ypres, 26.9.1917, aged 26 years. Has no known grave. Commemorated **TYNE COT MEMORIAL TO THE MISSING.** ROH:- St. Barnabas Church, Crosland Moor.

HALSTEAD, PERCY. Private. No 40106 10th Battalion West Yorkshire Regiment. Born Armitage Road, Milnsbridge. Son of Albert Halstead, 1 Armitage Road, Milnsbridge. Educated at Milnsbridge Council School and Longwood Grammar School. Employed as a painter and decorator by Messrs Bottomley and Fisher. Was a member of the Milnsbridge Liberal Club billiard team. Single. Enlisted May 1916. Died of trench feet and shell shock in Etaples Base Hospital, 19.11.1916, aged 29 years. Buried **ETAPLES MILITARY CEMETERY.** Grave location:- Plot 20, Row A, Grave 6a. ROH:- St. Mark's Parish Church, Longwood; Huddersfield Mission, Milnsbridge.

HAMER, CHARLIE. Private. No 3310 1/5th Battalion Duke of Wellington's Regiment. Born Dalton Fold, Dalton, 20.10.1895. Son of the late Jacob Hamer. Lived with his aunt, Mrs Hartley, at 46 Chapel Street, Berry Brow. Educated Moldgreen Church of England School and Kirkheaton Parish Church School. Employed by Messrs Jarmaine and Sons of Kirkheaton as a woollen feeder. Single Enlisted 7.1.1914. Embarked for France in April, 1915. Was one of a party of four local Territorials who went out in daytime to capture a German flag and one of the party succeeded in bringing it in to the Territorial's trenches. Was shot through the head by a sniper on the morning of 9.11.1915, aged 20. Buried **TALANA FARM CEMETERY.** Grave location:- Plot 4, Row F, Grave 7. ROH:- Huddersfield Drill Hall; Armitage Bridge War Memorial.

HAMER, HAROLD. Acting Bombardier No 1185. 2nd West Lancashire Brigade Royal Field Artillery. Born 57 Scarr Wood Terrace, Lockwood, 23.10.1895. Youngest son of Joseph Hamer, of Scarr Wood Terrace, Lockwood. Educated Mount Pleasant Board School. Attended the Young Men's class at Mount Pleasant Wesleyan Chapel. Was formerly employed in the National Telephone Company's office in Huddersfield but, when the Government took over the telephone system, he was sent to Preston. Had served with the local Territorials in Huddersfield and transferred to the battalion in Preston. On the outbreak of war the Preston Territorials were mobilised and were sent to Edinburgh Barracks for training. At 7pm on 29.9.1914, his parents received a telegram from Craigleith Military Hospital, Edinburgh, informing them that he was seriously ill and that an operation was necessary. Two hours later they received a second message telling them that he had died. The cause of death was found to be a ruptured intestine, which had occurred during training. Buried **LOCKWOOD CEMETERY.** Grave Location A, 'U', 466. ROH:- Mount Pleasant Chapel, Lockwood.

HAMER, THOMAS. Private. No 240673. 2/5th Battalion Duke of Wellington's Regiment. Born Albert Street, Lockwood, 10.5.1893. Both parents deceased. Lived with his Uncle and Aunt, Mr and Mrs Henry Sunderland Hodgson, at 14 Henry Street, off South Street, Huddersfield. Educated Rashcliffe Church of England School. Employed as a window cleaner by the Royal Crown Window Cleaning Company, of Henry Street. Single. Enlisted November 1914. Reported missing at the Battle of Bullecourt, 3.5.1917, and afterwards presumed to have died on that date. Has no known grave. Commemorated **ARRAS MEMORIAL TO THE MISSING.** ROH:- Huddersfield Drill Hall.

HAMPSHIRE, HAROLD. Private. No 38748. 7th Battalion York and Lancaster Regiment. Born New Mill, Holmfirth. Son of Aaron and Sarah Hampshire, Greenhill Bank Road, New Mill. Educated New Mill National School. Attended the Sunday School, being a member of the Rev. R. Warburton's bible class. Was a playing member of New Mill A.F.C. and also a member of the Holmfirth Harriers. Employed by Messrs Graham and Pott Limited, Kirkbridge Mills, as a pattern weaver. Wounded in the chest by a shell in June, 1917. After treatment at a hospital in Reading returned to France. Killed in action on 19.7.1918, when a shell burst in the trench where he was working, killing him instantly. He was 20 years of age. Buried **HARPONVILLE COMMUNAL EXTENSION.** Grave location:- Row E, Grave 21. ROH:- New Mill Working Men's Club; Fulstone War Memorial; memorial in Christ Church Churchyard, New Mill.

HAMPSHIRE, HARRISON. Private. No 40018. 6th Battalion King's Own Yorkshire Light Infantry. Born Emley Moor. Son of William Hampshire, Factory Farm, Emley Moor. Killed in action, 9.5.1917, aged 23. Has no known grave. Commemorated **ARRAS MEMORIAL TO THE MISSING.** ROH:- Emley War Memorial.

HAMPSHIRE, LEWIS. Private. No 241893. 2/5th Battalion Duke of Wellington's Regiment. Born Huddersfield. Son of Mr and Mrs Hampshire, 4 Benson Square, Northumberland Street, Huddersfield. Attended St. Mark's Church. Employed by British Dyes as a laboratory assistant. Reported missing, presumed killed, at the Battle of Bullecourt, 3.5.1917. Has no known grave. Commemorated **ARRAS MEMORIAL TO THE MISSING.** ROH:- Huddersfield Drill Hall.

HAMPSHIRE, STANLEY. Lieutenant. 2nd/4th Battalion East Lancashire Regiment. Son of Samuel and Eliza Hampshire. Born Castleford, Yorkshire, in 1890. On the 1911 census he was listed as employed as a Photographic artist, living in Baildon. Was married to Annie Moores on June 28th,1916, at St. Giles Parish Church, Colchester, Essex. Killed in action, 9.10.1917. Buried **TYNE COT CEMETERY.** Grave location:- Plot 35, Row F, Grave 12. ROH:- Brockholes War Memorial.

HAMPSHIRE, TOM. Private. No CH/1298(S). 1st Royal Marine Battalion R.M.L.I., Royal Naval Division. Born Holmfirth 28.11.1887. Son of the late Jonas Hampshire, Lane End, Holmfirth. Lived with his brother Herbert Hampshire, at Chapel Street, Netherton, and then at Mearhouse, New Mill. Attended the Netherton Wesleyan Chapel and Sunday School and was a member of the Sons of Temperance. Employed as a labourer in the dyehouse at Turnbridge Mills. Enlisted 29.11.1915. Embarked for France in September, 1916. Reported missing 28.4.1917. Has no known grave. *(During the research for this book I discovered that the Commonwealth War Graves Commission had no record of Private Tom Hampshire. Due to the efforts of Esther Barrett Page of the CWGC, Kyle D. Tallett, of Ashford, Kent, and myself, Tom Hampshire's name is now engraved on the* **ARRAS MEMORIAL TO THE MISSING**). ROH:- Fulstone War Memorial; South Crosland and Netherton War Memorial.

HANDLEY, ARTHUR. Guardsman. No 4991. Scots Guards. Born Middlesbrough in August 1882. Educated at a council school in Middlesbrough. Husband of Edith Handley, 122 Kilner Bank, Moldgreen, Huddersfield. Employed as a banksman at Messrs Read Holliday's coal pit. Enlisted 4.8.1914. Was taken prisoner, 28.10.1914. Died of typhus fever at Schneidemuehl Prison Camp, Germany, 14.3.1915. In his last letter to his wife, dated 28.2.1915, he told her that he was quite well; but the Sergeant who informed her of his death stated that he had been ill for some time and wrote the letter saying he was quite well so that she should not worry about him. Buried **BERLIN SOUTH-WESTERN CEMETERY, STAHNSDORF, GERMANY.** Grave location:- Plot 2, Row C, Grave 9. His widow received the following letter from an Officer of the Scots Guards who wrote, *'It is my painful duty to inform you that a letter received this morning from the Secretary of the War Office states that your husband, No 4991 Private A. Handley, 1st Battalion Scots Guards, died whilst a prisoner of war at Schneidemuehl, Germany, on the 14.3.1915. His death was probably due to typhus fever. May I express my deep sympathy with you in your bereavement.'* ROH:- Moldgreen War Memorial.

HANNAH, JOHN OGILVIE. Sergeant. No 204088. 1/7th Battalion Duke of Wellington's Regiment. Born 'The Glen', Innerleithlen, Peebleshire, Scotland, 13.10.1888. Son of Mr Hannah, 'Braemar', 1 Fort Terrace, Bridlington. Educated at 'The Glen', (a Private School). Married. At the time of enlistment, was living at Longley, Huddersfield. Employed as a forester. Enlisted December 1914. Killed in action at Kemmel Hill, 29.4.1918. Has no known grave. Commemorated **TYNE COT MEMORIAL TO THE MISSING.** ROH:- Huddersfield Drill Hall; Almondbury War Memorial.

HANSOM, GEORGE THOMAS. Private. No 30546. 1/7th Battalion Duke of Wellington's Regiment. Son of Amanda Maria Hansom, 21 Gatehead, Marsden. Attended Holthead General Sunday School. Prior to enlistment, was employed for some time at Bank Bottom Mills, Marsden and later at Slaithwaite Railway Station. Enlisted in August, 1914, when he was only 16 years of age. Embarked for France in April 1915. Was wounded twice, once during 1915 and the second time in July, 1916, during the Somme campaign. Returned to France in September, 1917. Killed in action, 13.4.1918, aged 20 years. Has no known grave. Commemorated **TYNE COT MEMORIAL TO THE MISSING.** ROH:- Huddersfield Drill Hall; Marsden War Memorial.

HANSON, ALBERT HAROLD. Corporal. No 13152. 10th Battalion Duke of Wellington's Regiment. Born Westgate, Almondbury, 8.1.1897. Son of Fred and Mary H. Hanson, 61 Cross Lane, Primrose Hill, Huddersfield. Educated Stile Common Council School. Attended Queen Street Mission Young Men's Bible Class. Employed as a spinner. Single. Enlisted 10.9.1914. Killed in action at Inverness Copse on 20.9.1917. Has no known grave. Commemorated **TYNE COT MEMORIAL TO THE MISSING.** (Brother of Private **ERNEST HANSON**, reported missing at the Battle of Bullecourt, 3.5.1917 q.v.).

HANSON, BEN. Lance Corporal. No 2042 1/5th Battalion Duke of Wellington's Regiment. Born Barnsley. Son of George Henry and Lucy Hanson, of Ebor House, Honley. Enlisted at the outbreak of the war and embarked for France in April, 1915. Killed in action, 7.3.1916, aged 20 years. Has no known grave. Commemorated **THIEPVAL MEMORIAL TO THE MISSING.** (Brother of Private **COLIN HANSON**, reported missing at the Battle of Bullecourt, 3.5.1917, q.v.). ROH:- Honley War Memorial.

HANSON, BENJAMIN. Lance Corporal. No 39597. 9th Battalion King's Own Yorkshire Light Infantry. Formerly No 5/86657 Territorial Reserve Battalion. Born Spark Hall, Longwood, 17.5.1889. Son of the late Benjamin and Emma Hanson. Educated at Goitfield Council School, Longwood. Attended Parkwood Methodist Church and was a member of the choir. He was a well known tenor vocalist and was a member of the Gledholt Vocal Union. Employed as a dyer's labourer at Leymoor Dyeworks. Husband of Beatrice Hanson, Church Street, Longwood. Enlisted September 1916. Received severe shrapnel wounds to the abdomen on 4.10.1917. Died of wounds at No 17 Casualty Clearing Station (Remy Siding) on 6.10.1917, aged 28 years. Buried **LIJSSENTHOEK MILITARY CEMETERY.** Grave location:- Plot 20, Row E, Grave 16. ROH:- Parkwood Methodist Church; St. Mark's Parish Church, Longwood.

HANSON, COLIN. Private. No 241556. 2/5th Battalion Duke of Wellington's Regiment. Born Monk Bretton near Barnsley. Son of George and Lucy Hanson, of Ebor House, Honley. Employed in the office at Mr Brook's dyeworks, Wood Royd, Honley. Reported missing at the Battle of Bullecourt, 3.5.1917, and afterwards presumed to have been killed on that date, aged 20. Has no known grave. Commemorated **ARRAS MEMORIAL TO THE MISSING.** (Brother of Private **BEN HANSON**, killed in action, 7.3.1916, q.v.). ROH:- Huddersfield Drill Hall; Honley War Memorial.

HANSON, EDGAR. Private. No 267791. 1/7th Battalion West Yorkshire Regiment. Born 30 Poplar Street, Birkby, Huddersfield. Son of John E. Hanson, 51 Tanfield Terrace, Birkby, Huddersfield. Employed at the telephone exchange. Enlisted October 1914. Died of gunshot wounds, 2.5.1918, aged 20 years. Buried **BOULOGNE EASTERN CEMETERY.** Grave location:- Plot 9, Row B, Grave 22. ROH:- Fartown and Birkby War memorial.

HANSON, ERNEST. Private. No 240565. 2/5th Battalion Duke of Wellington's Regiment. Born 12 Industrial Street, Primrose Hill, Huddersfield, 28.4.1895. Son of Fred and Mary H. Hanson, 61 Cross Lane, Primrose Hill. Educated Stile Common Council School. Employed as a coach and motor trimmer. Single. Was a member of the Young Men's class at Queen Street Mission. Enlisted 30.10.1914. Reported missing, presumed killed, at the Battle of Bullecourt, 3.5.1917, aged 22 years. Has no known grave. Commemorated **ARRAS MEMORIAL TO THE MISSING.** (Brother of Private **ALBERT HAROLD HANSON**, killed in action, 20.9.1917, q.v.). ROH:- Huddersfield Drill Hall; memorial in Almondbury Cemetery.

HANSON, HAROLD. Private. No 143173. 17th Battalion Machine Gun Corps. Formerly No 5545 Duke of Wellington's Regiment. Born Armitage Bridge 9.9.1896. Son of George and Frances Ada Hanson, 21 Park Terrace, Yews Green, Lockwood. Educated Armitage Bridge Church of England School. Employed as a weaver by Messrs George Mallinson and Sons Limited, Spring Mill, Hoylehouse, Huddersfield. Single. Enlisted 30.3.1916. Died of wounds, 19.9.1918, aged 22 years. Buried **FIVE POINTS CEMETERY, LECHELLE.** Grave location:- Row C, Grave 7. ROH:- Emmanuel Church, Lockwood.

HANSON, HAROLD. Captain. 5th Battalion Duke of Wellington's Regiment. Elder son of John Henry Hanson (of the firm of Messrs Abbey and Hanson, surveyors, Cloth Hall Street, Huddersfield) and Annie Hanson, Daisy Lea, Lindley, Huddersfield. Attended Leeds University. Had served in the Territorials before the war and was re-commissioned on 21.9.1914, with the rank of Captain. Died of wounds at No 44 Casualty Clearing Station, 1.12.1917, aged 36 years. Buried **NINE ELMS CEMETERY, POPERINGHE, BELGIUM.** Grave location:- Plot 13, Row A, Grave 1. ROH:- St. Stephen's Church, Lindley; Huddersfield Drill Hall; Leeds University Roll.

HANSON, HAROLD SCHOFIELD. Private. No 19321. 10th Battalion Duke of Wellington's Regiment. Born Milnsbridge. Youngest son of Joe and Mary Hannah Hanson, 106 Scar Lane, Milnsbridge. Attended Golcar Parish Church and Sunday School. Was a member of Golcar Conservative Club and the Golcar Lily Cycling Club. Employed by Messrs John Lockwood and Sons Limited, Milnsbridge. Enlisted February, 1916, and embarked for France 13 weeks later. On 14.11.1916, he was wounded by shrapnel in the right arm. He underwent an operation at Bolton Infirmary but died on Sunday, 24.12.1916, aged 23 years. Buried with full military honours in **St. JOHN'S CHURCHYARD, GOLCAR.** Grave location:- G, south of Church, 22.

HANSON, HARRY. Private. No 41900. 2/4th Battalion York and Lancaster Regiment. Born Almondbury. Husband of Florence Hanson, 57 Cross Lane, Primrose Hill, Huddersfield. Enlisted 11.4.1917. Killed in action near Rheims, 20.7.1918, aged 29 years. Buried **COURMAS BRITISH CEMETERY.** Grave location:- Plot 2, Row A, Grave 5. ROH:- Almondbury War Memorial.

HANSON, JOHN HENRY. Private. No 37531. 14 Platoon, 'D' Company, 9th Battalion King's Own Yorkshire Light Infantry. Formerly No 5/86657 Territorial Reserve Battalion. Son of John William and Maria Hanson of Lea Head, Shepley. Employed at Shepley Cooperative Society. Killed in action, 26.4.1918, aged 19 years. Has no known grave. Commemorated

TYNE COT MEMORIAL TO THE MISSING. ROH:- Shepley War Memorial.

HANSON, SUTCLIFFE. Private. No 97979. 2nd Battalion Machine Gun Corps. Formerly No 16248 West Yorkshire Regiment. Born Gasworks Street, Huddersfield, 27.8.1889. Both parents deceased. Lived with his sisters and brothers at 57 Union Street, Huddersfield. Educated Thomas Street Council School. Employed as a warehouseman by Messrs T. and H. Blamires Limited, Leeds Road, Huddersfield. Single. Enlisted 13.1.1917. Killed in action, 23.10.1918. Buried **QUIETISTE BRITISH CEMETERY,** two and half miles south west of Le Cateau. Grave location:- Row C, Grave 5. ROH:- St. Andrew's Church, Leeds Road, Huddersfield.

HANSON, VINCENT. Private. No 228889. 1st Battalion Monmouthshire Regiment. Born Huddersfield. Died of wounds, 15.4.1918. Buried **WIMEREUX COMMUNAL CEMETERY.** Grave location:- Plot 10, Row D, Grave 5.

HANSON, WILLIAM. Private. No 2861. 2/7th Battalion Duke of Wellington's Regiment. Born Manor House Farm, Crosland Hill, 8.3.1884. Son of William and Eliza Hanson, Starling End Farm, Hanson Lane, Lockwood. Educated Crosland Moor Church of England School. Assisted his father on the family farm. Single. Enlisted 27.8.1914. He was with his Regiment at Thoresby Park when, on 1.6.1915, he was severely kicked by a mule. He was transferred to Becketts Park Hospital, where he underwent an operation and died on 9.6.1915, aged 31 years. Buried with full military honours at **HOLY TRINITY CHURCHYARD, SOUTH CROSLAND.** Grave location:- South of Church. His parents received the following letter from Lieutenant Colonel R. R. Mellor, the Officer commanding the 2/7th Battalion Duke of Wellington's Regiment, *'I regret to inform you in reference to the wire received by you that your son No 2861 Private W. Hanson died at the Becketts Park Hospital, Leeds on Wednesday 9.6.1915 as the result of an accident sustained whilst in the execution of his duties. It appears that one of the mules broke loose and your son along with some other men of the transport section tried to catch it. He succeeded in catching it around the neck when the mule twisted round. This made him release his grip of the animal which then kicked him in the stomach. Private Hanson did not report to the Doctor till about noon on the following day when he was immediately removed to the Field Ambulance and from there to Becketts Park Hospital, Leeds, where he was unfortunately taken worse and died. Any communication with reference to his effects must be addressed to the War Office direct. I wish to convey to you and his relatives my deepest sympathy. He was a man respected by his comrades and I at all times found him ready and willing to do his duty as a good soldier in a pleasant manner.'* ROH:- Emmanuel Church, Lockwood; Mount Pleasant Chapel, Lockwood.

HARDCASTLE, ALBERT EDMUND. Private. No 10958. 1st Battalion The Cameronians (Scottish Rifles). Born 19 Croft House, Lindley, 18.12.1892. Son of Mrs F. Hardcastle, 2 Smithfield Terrace, South Lane, Elland. Educated Lindley National School. Employed as a warehouseman at Plover Mills, Lindley. Enlisted 1.1.1912. He came from an old soldiering family. His grandfather fought in the Indian Mutiny and his father and three Uncles all served their King and Country. Re-enlisted 4.8.1914. Wounded by shrapnel in the shoulder and leg on 26.8.1914 in France. He was invalided home and died in The University Hospital, Edgbaston, Birmingham, on 27.9.1914, aged 20. Buried with full military honours at **St. STEPHEN'S CHURCH, LINDLEY.** Grave location:- 21, S. ROH:- Elland War Memorial.

HARDCASTLE, GILBERT. Private. No 32508. 1/4th Battalion. The King's Own (Royal Lancaster Regiment). Formerly No 16357 Lancashire Fusiliers. Born Deighton, Huddersfield 29.4.1883. Parents lived at 34 Ashgrove Road, Leeds Road North, Huddersfield. Educated Deighton Council School. Employed as a painter by Lunn and Cardno, High Street, Huddersfield. Married. Lived at 18 Shaw's Yard, St. Peter's Street, Huddersfield. Enlisted 18.1.1915. Wounded in the arm in 1916. Killed in action near Ypres, 20.9.1917, aged 35. Buried **BEDFORD HOUSE CEMETERY ENCLOSURE No 4.** Grave location:- Plot 11, Row E, Grave 22. ROH:- Huddersfield Parish Church.

HARDCASTLE, WILLIAM. Private. No 38753. 2nd Battalion York and Lancaster Regiment. Born Underbank, Holmfirth, 1.11.1897. Son of John and Ellen Hardcastle, 21 Burnroyd, Newsome, Huddersfield. Educated Newsome Church of England School. Employed as a piecer by Messrs E.H. Sellars and Sons Limited, of Scar Mills. Single. Enlisted in 1916. Wounded and taken prisoner near Cambrai, 21.3.1918. Died in Germany after an operation to amputate his right leg on 12.4.1918, aged 20 years. Buried **BERLIN SOUTH-WESTERN CEMETERY, STAHNSDORF, GERMANY.** Grave location:- Plot 5, Row H, Grave 2. ROH:- St. John's Church, Newsome.

HARDCASTLE, HAYDN. Private. No 14294. 'Y' Company, 8th Battalion Duke of Wellington's Regiment. Born Thurstonland. Son of Matt and Mary Hannah Hardcastle of Northgate, Shepley. Killed in action in the assault on Tekke Tepe Ridge, Suvla, Gallipoli, 9.8.1915, aged 20 years. Has no known grave. Commemorated **HELLES MEMORIAL TO THE MISSING, GALLIPOLI.** ROH:- Thurstonland War Memorial; Shepley War Memorial.

HARDY, FRED. Lance Corporal. No 240386. 1/5th Battalion Duke of Wellington's Regiment. Born Meltham. Son of James Hardy, 149 Longwood Road, Longwood. Husband of Mary Hardy, 9 Learoyd's Yard, Leeds Road, Huddersfield. Father of five children. Employed as a teaser and fettler at Messrs Middlemost Brothers. Enlisted 8.8.1914. Was the Company Cook. Killed in action at Nieuport, Belgium, 7.8.1917, aged 34 years. Buried **RAMSCAPELLE ROAD MILITARY CEMETERY.** Grave location:- Plot 2, Row A, Grave 6. ROH:- St. Mark's Parish Church, Longwood; Huddersfield Drill Hall.

HARDY, FRED. Private. No 38236. 5th Battalion The Yorkshire Regiment. Born Holmfirth. Son of Mr and Mrs J. Hardy, 25 Brownhill Lane, Holmbridge. Educated at Holmbridge Day and Sunday School. Employed firstly at Yew Tree Mill and then at Hinchliffe Mill Mill. Prior to enlistment, was employed by Messrs Whiteley and Green. Enlisted September 1916. Embarked for France in January, 1917. Came home on sick leave in March, 1918, but returned to France in April, 1918. Reported missing 27.5.1918. Died as a Prisoner of War in Germany, 18.9.1918, aged 22 years. Buried **NIEDERZWEHREN CEMETERY, CASSEL, GERMANY.** Grave location:- Plot 4, Row C, Grave 14. His parents received the following letter from a comrade of their son, who wrote, '*I must say Mrs Hardy he got the best attention that could be given to him by either his comrades or the camp staff but owing to him being far through with dysentery and weakness it was impossible for him to come through it. As I was his bedmate and a little stronger than he I gladly gave him every best attention which was appreciated very much. I must say he was a dear chum of mine. Before I close on behalf of all the lads in the ward I offer their greatest sympathy.*' ROH:- Holme and Holmbridge War Memorial.

HARDY, GEORGE RIPPON, MM. Private. No 40016. 1st Battalion Northumberland Fusiliers. Son of Thomas Robert and Isabella Catherine Hardy. (One of a family of ten children). Born Wheatly Grange Farm, near Tow Law, County Durham. Educated at Satley School, where both his father and grandfather had received their education. Sang in the choir at Satley Parish Church. Moved to the 'Ford Inn', Holmfirth in 1912. Was a good judge of cattle and, in his early teens, was able to go up to County Durham to purchase cattle and bring them home himself. Soon after moving to this district he was employed in the finishing department of Messrs J. Greenwood and Sons, Digley Mills. Enlisted January, 1917, when he became eighteen years old. Embarked for France 11.10.1917. Was wounded on one occasion but returned to France in July, 1918. Seriously wounded in the back and arm and died of his wounds at No 2/1st Northumbrian Casualty Clearing Station, 21.9.1918, aged 20 years. Buried **SUNKEN ROAD CEMETERY, BOISLEUX-St. MARC.** Grave location:- Plot 2, Row D, Grave 23. Was awarded the Military Medal, posthumously, in February, 1919. ROH:- Holmfirth War Memorial; St. Bartholomew's Church, Meltham.

HARDY, HAROLD. Private. No 242026. 2/5th Battalion Duke of Wellington's Regiment. Born 62 Beech Street, Paddock 19.3.1897. Son of Mr and Mrs Charles Edward Hardy, 62 Beech Street, Paddock. Educated at Paddock Church of England School. Employed as a tailor's cutter by Messrs Chilton, Wrigley and Company, wholesale clothiers. Attended All Saints Church, Paddock. Single. Enlisted 29.3.1915. Killed in action, 4.2.1918, aged 20 years. Buried **ROCLINCOURT**

MILITARY CEMETERY. Grave location:- Plot 4, Row A, Grave 4. ROH:- All Saints Church, Paddock; Huddersfield Drill Hall.

HARDY, HERBERT. Corporal. No 240288. 2/5th Battalion Duke of Wellington's Regiment. Born 16 Spring Grove Street, Huddersfield, 23.4.1896. Educated Crosland Moor Church of England School. Employed as a tinsmith. At the time of enlistment, was living at 17 Thorn Road, Thornton Lodge, Huddersfield. Enlisted in the local Territorial battalion in May, 1914. Reported missing, presumed killed, 3.5.1917, at the Battle of Bullecourt. Has no known grave. Commemorated **ARRAS MEMORIAL TO THE MISSING.** ROH:- St. Barnabas Church, Crosland Moor; Huddersfield Drill Hall.

HARDY, JOE. Private. No 10/1834. Wellington Regiment, New Zealand Expeditionary Force. Born 10 New House, Bradley Lane, Huddersfield, 7.12.1878. Fourth son of Harry and Eva Cliff Hardy, Westwood Conservative Club, 12 Springwood Street, Huddersfield. Was trained as an electrical engineer. Went out to New Zealand in 1907. In October, 1913, he was married in New Zealand. Enlisted 14.12.1914. Reported missing at Gallipoli, 8.8.1915, at the Battle of Sari Bair and afterwards was presumed to have been killed during the assault on Chunuk Bair.. Has no known grave. Commemorated **CHUNUK BAIR MEMORIAL TO THE MISSING OF THE N.Z.E.F.**

HARDY, VICTOR. Rifleman. No B/203511. 5th Battalion The Rifle Brigade. Born Somerset Road, Huddersfield. Son of Walter and Hannah Hardy, 37 Senior Street, Moldgreen. Educated Moldgreen Church of England School. Employed as a plush weaver. Enlisted 15.11.1915. Wounded and gassed 25.8.1918. Admitted to Sheerness Military Hospital, Kent. His parents received the following letter from the Matron, Miss F. M.Tosh, on 18.3.1919, *'I regret to say your son is not so well. He has gone back these last few days. The Medical Officer does not think he is in immediate danger but in order that you may come and see him and get a warrant he will be put on the 'dangerously ill list' again and you will receive a wire telling you so. He does not complain and does not have any pain. Hoping you can come.'* He died of his wounds on 2.4.1919, aged 25 years. Buried **ALMONDBURY CEMETERY.** Grave location:- 6, 'C', 69. ROH:- St. Paul's Church, Southgate, Huddersfield; Christ Church, Moldgreen. Almondbury War Memorial.

HARDY, WILFRED FAIRBURN. Private. No 240195. 1/5th Battalion Duke of Wellington's Regiment. Born Bank Top Farm, Almondbury, 20.11.1893. Son of Arthur and Annie E. Hardy, 95 Almondbury Bank, Moldgreen. Educated Moldgreen Council School. Employed as a millhand. Single. Enlisted 16.5.1913 in the local Territorials at the outbreak of war. Reported missing in the attack on the Schwaben Redoubt, 3.9.1916, and afterwards presumed to have been killed on that date, aged 22. Has no known grave. Commemorated **THIEPVAL MEMORIAL TO THE MISSING.** ROH:- Almondbury War Memorial; Christ Church, Moldgreen; Huddersfield Drill Hall.

HARESNAPE, THOMAS EDWARD. Pioneer. No 172339. 20th Company, Royal Engineers. Born Huddersfield. Lived 10 Spinkfield Road, Birkby. Employed at the Huddersfield GPO as a sorting clerk and telegraphist. Died of heat stroke on Thursday, 10.7.1919. Buried **RAWALPINDI WAR CEMETERY, INDIA (now Pakistan).** Grave location:- 2, B. 2. ROH:- Fartown and Birkby War Memorial; Huddersfield GPO.

HARGREAVES, FRED. Private. No 31499. 11 Platoon, 'C' Company, 2/4th Battalion Duke of Wellington's Regiment. Born Armley, Leeds, 2.4.1878. Employed as a painter by the London and North Western Railway Company. Husband of Emma J. Hargreaves, 15 Hall Bower, Newsome, Huddersfield. Enlisted 18.3.1917. Killed in action at Bourlon Wood, 27.11.1917. Buried **ORIVAL WOOD CEMETERY.** Grave location:- Plot 2, Row B, Grave 14. ROH:- Almondbury War Memorial; London and North Western Railway Company Roll.

HARGREAVES, HERBERT. Private. No 240834. 2/5th Battalion Duke of Wellington's Regiment. Born Huddersfield. Reported missing, presumed killed, 27.11.1917. Has no known grave. Commemorated **CAMBRAI MEMORIAL TO THE MISSING.** ROH:- Huddersfield Drill Hall.

HARGREAVES, HOLMES. Private. No 19685. 10th Battalion Canadian Infantry (Alberta Regiment). Born Armitage Bridge, Huddersfield,

26.2.1890. Son of Mr and Mrs G. H. Hargreaves, 14 Water Street, Springwood, Huddersfield. Educated Spring Grove Board School. In 1907 he joined the local Territorials. He emigrated to Canada in July, 1910, where he was employed as a head pastry cook in a cafe. Single. Enlisted 14.8.1914. He served under an assumed name as **ERNEST BATES**. Embarked for France in February, 1915. Was seriously wounded in the chest, 21.5.1915, near Richebourg-l'Avoue, France. Was taken to the No 6 Casualty Clearing Station, where he died of wounds on 30.5.1915, aged 24 years. Buried **MERVILLE COMMUNAL CEMETERY.** Grave location:- Plot 3, Row H, Grave 7. His sister received the following letter from Nurse Grayson at the C.C.S, '*Your brother was much worse when I came on duty. He was so glad to have your letter. It has been God's will to take him to himself at 3.30am. The poor lad had such difficulty in breathing and yet he struggled so hard to get better. He was longing to see you all again. All the orderlies were fond of him, he was so anxious not to give any trouble. He will be laid to rest in the large cemetery quite close to this hospital. Just his name and the date will put on a simple wooden cross above his head.*' ROH:- Huddersfield Parish Church; Armitage Bridge War Memorial.

HARKER, LEWIS. 2nd Lieutenant. 2nd Battalion King's Own Yorkshire Light Infantry. Born Ford Cottage, Holmfirth. Son of Mr and Mrs William Harker, Cliffe Wood Terrace, Neiley, Honley. Educated Wooldale Council School and at New Mill National School. Attended Mount Tabor United Methodist Sunday School and was a member of the choir. Employed by Messrs Moorhouse and Brooks at Moorbottom Mill. Enlisted as a Private in the Duke of Wellington's Regiment at Whitsuntide, 1915. Served in Egypt and Gallipoli, where he took part in the Suvla bay landings. Left Egypt for France and was then recommended for a commission, in January 1918. He came home for training at Lichfield and was gazetted to the East Lancashire Regiment and then to the King's Own Yorkshire Light Infantry. Visited Holmfirth at the beginning of August, 1918, and left for France on 13.8.1918. Killed in action, 1.10.1918. Buried **BELLICOURT BRITISH CEMETERY.** Grave location:- Plot 7, Row A, Grave 10. ROH:- Fulstone War Memorial; Honley War Memorial; Brockholes War Memorial.

HARLING, HAROLD ZETLAND. Private. No 38697. 'C' Company, 9th Battalion King's Own Yorkshire Light Infantry. Born Golcar. Enlisted Huddersfield. Grandson of the late Richard Whitwam, 78 Church Street, Golcar. Reported missing, presumed killed, 27.5.1918, aged 19 years. Has no known grave. Commemorated **SOISSONS MEMORIAL TO THE MISSING.** ROH:- St. John's Church, Golcar.

HARPER, HERBERT. Private. No 11140. 4th Battalion (1st Central Ontario Regiment) Canadian Forces. Born Huddersfield 4.6.1891. Son of the late Richard and Elizabeth Harper. Sister of Florence Harper, 2 Wilkinson's Buildings, Bradford Road, Huddersfield. Educated Spring Grove Council and Huddersfield Parish Church Schools. Before going out to Canada in 1906, was employed at Messrs. Jackson's hat shop in John William Street, Huddersfield. In Canada he became an electrical engineer. Enlisted September 1914. Seriously wounded at the beginning of 1915. Was invalided home and, after a period of convalescence, returned to Belgium in August, 1915. Killed in action, 6.5.1916, aged 25 years. Has no known grave. Commemorated **MENIN GATE MEMORIAL TO THE MISSING.**

HARPIN, FRED. Private. No 36761. 1/4th Battalion East Yorkshire Regiment. Formerly No 33322 Northumberland Fusiliers. Born Newsome 11.12.1879. Son of Joseph Harpin, 250 Newsome Road, Newsome. Educated Newsome Church of England School. Employed as a cloth finisher at Broadfield Mills, Lockwood. Single. Enlisted July 1916. Reported missing near Rheims, 27.5.1918. Has no known grave. Commemorated **SOISSONS MEMORIAL TO THE MISSING.** ROH:- St. John's Church, Newsome.

HARPIN, HENRI ROGERS. Private. No 240317. 2/5th Battalion Duke of Wellington's Regiment. Born Cowcliffe, Huddersfield, 19.10.1888. Son of Thomas Kilner Harpin, 3 Bow Street, Huddersfield. Educated Thomas Street Council School and Warwick Road Board School. Employed as an engineer. Married. Lived Springwood Avenue, Huddersfield. Enlisted 4.8.1914. Reported missing, presumed killed, at the Battle of Bullecourt, 3.5.1917, aged 29. Has no known grave. Commemorated **ARRAS MEMORIAL TO THE MISSING.** ROH:- St.

Andrew's Church, Leeds Road, Huddersfield; Huddersfield Drill Hall.

HARRIS, FRANK. Private. No 36367. 8th Battalion Northumberland Fusiliers. Born Slad, Gloucestershire. Husband of Ellen Ann Harris, Chapel Terrace, Honley. Attended Honley Parish Church. Employed by Messrs Spencer and Company, painters and decorators. Enlisted January 1917. Killed in action, 1.2.1918, aged 29 years. Buried **PHILOSOPHE BRITISH CEMETERY, MAZINGARBE.** Grave location:- Plot 3, Row B, Grave 17. ROH:- Honley War Memorial.

HARRIS, STANLEY. Lance Corporal. No 1746. 'B' Company, 1/5th Battalion Duke of Wellington's Regiment. Born Rashcliffe Hill, Huddersfield, 16.12.1894. Son of the late Alfred and Caroline Harris, 10 Spring Grove Street, Huddersfield. Educated Spring Grove Council School. Employed as a labourer. Enlisted 4.8.1914. Embarked for France April, 1915. Killed in action, 14.6.1915, aged 21 years. Buried **RUE-DAVID MILITARY CEMETERY, FLEURBAIX.** Grave location:- Plot 1, Row B, Grave 14. ROH:- Huddersfield Drill Hall.

HARRIS, WILLIAM. Private. No 11511. 2nd Battalion Duke of Wellington's Regiment. Born Salford, Manchester. Enlisted Huddersfield. Employed in the Sanitary Department of Huddersfield Corporation. Killed in action at Hill 60 on 5.5.1915. Has no known grave. Commemorated **MENIN GATE MEMORIAL TO THE MISSING.** ROH:- Huddersfield Corporation Roll.

HARRISON, FRANK HOLLAND. Private. No 241068. 'C' Company, 2/5th Battalion Duke of Wellington's Regiment. Born Wakefield 10.1.1897. Son of Police Constable Henry Bailey Harrison and Mary Eleanor Harrison, 65 Merton Street, Huddersfield. Employed as an assistant waiter at the Huddersfield Club. Enlisted 2.3.1915. Reported missing, presumed killed, at the Battle of Bullecourt, 3.5.1917, aged years. Has no known grave. Commemorated **ARRAS MEMORIAL TO THE MISSING.** ROH:- New North Road Baptist Church; Huddersfield Drill Hall.

HARRISON, JOHN IRVINE. Private. No 307772. 1/7th Battalion Duke of Wellington's Regiment. Born Outlane. 5.4.1890. Son of John and Martha Harrison, 1 Back Green, Outlane. Educated Outlane Council School. Employed as a pattern weaver by Messrs Edward Sykes and Sons, Gosport Mills, Outlane. Attended Pole Moor Baptist Chapel. Single. Enlisted 20.3.1916. Wounded in the chest at Kemmel Hill, 5.5.1918. Died in No 13 General Hospital, Boulogne, 11.5.1918, aged 29 years. Buried **BOULOGNE EASTERN CEMETERY.** Grave location:- Plot 9, Row B, Grave 69. ROH:- Outlane Trinity Methodist Church; Pole Moor Baptist Church; Bethel United Methodist Church, Outlane; Huddersfield Drill Hall.

HARRISON, LEWIS HAYWOOD. Private. No 4/8306. 1st Battalion West Yorkshire Regiment. Born 15 Greenhow Grove, Burley, Leeds, 12.11.1893. Son of Thompson and Sarah Elizabeth Harrison, 8 Barton Road, Crosland Moor, Huddersfield. Educated Crosland Moor Board School and Higher Grade School, Huddersfield. Employed as a cloth finisher by Messrs Joseph Dyson and Son Limited. Attended the Queen Street Mission and an active worker in connection with the Wesleyan Church, Crosland Moor. Was a skilled violinist. Single. Enlisted 5.8.1914. Killed in action, 18.9.1916, aged 22 years. Has no known grave. Commemorated **THIEPVAL MEMORIAL TO THE MISSING.** ROH:- Crosland Moor Wesleyan Church; St. Barnabas Church, Crosland Moor.

HARRISON, SAM. Private. No 4261. 1/5th Battalion Duke of Wellington's Regiment. Born Huddersfield. Married. Lived 17 Lane Top, Linthwaite. Prior to going to France, in April 1915, was employed as a mason. His wife received a field postcard from him, dated 2.9.1916, stating that he was then 'alright' but that was the last communication she received from him. Reported missing, 3.9.1916, in the attack on the Schwaben Redoubt and afterwards presumed to have been killed on that date. Has no known grave. Commemorated **THIEPVAL MEMORIAL TO THE MISSING.** ROH:- Linthwaite War Memorial; Huddersfield Drill Hall.

HARRISON, THOMAS. Private. Royal Army Medical Corps. Born Woodhouse, near Sheffield, 18.5.1895. Educated at Woodhouse. Employed as a labourer. Married. Lived 27 Iredale's Buildings, Longroyd Bridge, Huddersfield. Wounded twice in France. Died in the Huddersfield Royal

Infirmary on 12.10.1919. Buried **EDGERTON CEMETERY, HUDDERSFIELD.** ROH:- St. Thomas's Church, Longroyd Bridge.

HARRISON, WILFRED. Sapper. No WR/251629. 46th Broad Gauge Company, Railway Operating Division Royal Engineers. Born Huddersfield. Son of Henry and Sarah Jane Harrison, 10 Cross Lane, Primrose Hill, Huddersfield. Employed as a porter at Lockwood station. Single. Enlisted February 1915. Died of pneumonia following influenza, 25.11.1918, aged 21 years. Buried **LES BARAQUES MILITARY CEMETERY, SANGATTE.** Grave location:- Plot 6, Row H, Grave 9.

HARROLD, WILLIAM ALFRED. Corporal. No 131125. 232nd Company, Royal Engineers. Born Bramley, near Leeds, 8.9.1892. Son of Company Sergeant Major Alfred and Adelaide Harrold, Thornhill Road, Longwood. Educated Belle Vue Higher Grade School, Bradford. Attended Longwood Wesleyan Church and Sunday School. Employed as a power loom tuner at Prospect Mills. Had served for five years as a bugler with the Bradford Rifles and was a Sergeant in the Milnsbridge Company when he enlisted on 24.10.1915. Was married at Huddersfield Parish Church, on 22.10.1917, to Miss Doris Ibbetson of Yeadon. Killed in action at Loos 30.10.1917, aged 25. Buried firstly in **CORKSCREW CEMETERY, LOOS.** His grave was then removed to **LOOS BRITISH CEMETERY.** Grave location:- Plot 20, Row C, Grave 8. ROH:- Longwood Wesleyan Church; St. Mark's Parish Church, Longwood.

HARTLEY, ARTHUR LEE. Private. 1/5th Battalion Duke of Wellington's Regiment. Born Norman Road, Birkby 19.5.1896. Son of Fred and Annie Hartley, 27 Thorn Road, Thornton Lodge, Huddersfield. Employed as a clerk. Single. Enlisted March 1915. Died at home, 27 Thorn Road, Thornton Lodge of 'consumption of throat.' ROH:- St. Stephen's Church, Rashcliffe; Mount Pleasant Chapel, Lockwood; Huddersfield Drill Hall.

HARTLEY, FRANK. Private. No 17926. 2nd Battalion Duke of Wellington's Regiment. Born Bradford 5.1.1895. Second son of Mr and Mrs W. Hartley, 34 Woodside Road, Lockwood. Educated Idle Council School. Attended the Rashcliffe Church and Sunday School. Employed as a butcher by Mr Alfred Dyson, The Shambles, Huddersfield. Killed in action at the Battle of Arras, 3.5.1917, aged 22 years. Buried **BROWN'S COPSE CEMETERY, ROEUX.** Grave location:- Plot 2, Row G, Grave 1. ROH:- Emmanuel Church, Lockwood; St. Stephen's Church, Rashcliffe.

HARTLEY, GEORGE FREDERICK WILLIAM. Rifleman. No C/7214. 12th Battalion King's Royal Rifle Corps. Born 86a Manchester Road, Huddersfield, 14.5.1898. Son of Mr and Mrs George Hartley, 25 Milford Street, Chapel Hill, Huddersfield. Educated St. Paul's School. Employed as a printer's assistant at the Huddersfield Examiner office. Single. Enlisted 11.10.1915. Reported missing, 2.4.1918 and afterwards presumed to have died on that date. Has no known grave. Commemorated **POZIERES MEMORIAL TO THE MISSING.** ROH:- St. Paul's Church, Southgate, Huddersfield.

HARTLEY, HARRY. Lance Corporal. No 11766. 8th Battalion York and Lancaster Regiment. Born Briggate, Dalton 4.7.1894. Son of Hervey and Annie E. Hartley, 32 Lane End, Kirkheaton. Educated Kirkheaton National School. Employed as a twister by Messrs Broadhead and Graves Limited, Kirkheaton. Attended Kirkheaton Parish Church. Single. Enlisted 25.8.1914. Served in Gallipoli. Killed in action at Zillebeke near Ypres, 9.4.1917. Buried **RAILWAY DUGOUTS BURIAL GROUND (TRANSPORT FARM).** Grave location:- Plot 7, Row L, Grave 24. His parents received the following letter from their son's platoon commander, *'Your son was a splendid soldier and stuck to his post, displaying the greatest courage and coolness despite the almost superhuman nerve strain through which we were all passing.'* ROH:- St. John's Church, Kirkheaton.

HARTLEY, JOHN VINCENT. Private. No 201978. 4th Battalion Seaforth Highlanders. Born St. Andrew's Road, Huddersfield, 11.4.1885. Son of Robert and Mary G. Hartley, 1 Buckrose Terrace, Hillhouse, Huddersfield. Educated at Huddersfield Parish Church Schools. Employed as a manager of the Rashcliffe butchering branch of the Huddersfield Industrial Society Limited. Single when he enlisted on 4.5.1916. Was wounded twice – once in September 1916 and the second time in 1917. Was married on 22.4.1918 to Miss Violet Brooke. Killed in action, 20.7.1918, aged 32 years. Buried **MARFAUX BRITISH CEMETERY.** Grave location:- Plot 1, Row J, Grave 13. (His wife died on 31.10.1918). ROH:- Fartown and Birkby War Memorial.

HARTLEY, LUTHER. Lance Corporal. No 267866. 1/6th Battalion Duke of Wellington's Regiment. Son of Sydney and Mary Jane Hartley, Sude Mill, New Mill. Husband of Alice Hartley, Cooper Lane, Holmfirth. Attended New Mill National School. Attended Christ Church and Sunday School where he was sidesman, teacher and Sunday School treasurer. Employed as a weaver by Messrs Graham and Pott. Enlisted June 1915. After training at Clipstone Camp, he embarked for France at Christmas, 1916. Killed in action near Cambrai, 11.10.1918, aged 28 years. Buried **WELLINGTON CEMETERY.** Grave location:- Plot 2, Row D, Grave 3. His widow received the following letter from a Huddersfield officer who wrote, *'He was killed by a shell as we went over the top and he suffered no pain. I know no word of mine can lessen the blow for you but it may be some consolation to know that he was very popular both with Officers and men. I myself am a Huddersfield man and knew your husband before the war and knew his true worth. He was one of my best N.C.O's, a good soldier and always cheerful under the worst conditions which after all is most important to our N.C.O. duty. So please accept my very deep sympathy in your great sorrow.'* ROH:- New Mill Working Men's Club; Fulstone War Memorial.

HARTLEY, WALTER. Driver. No 36121. 60th Howitzer Battery, Royal Field Artillery. Born Lane Bottom, Walsden, Todmorden. Educated Todmorden National and Secondary School. Married, with one child. Lived Clegg's Row, Shepley. Employed as a postman. Enlisted August 1914. Served with the Persian Gulf Expedition. Died in Mesopotamia, 25.7.1916, aged 30 years. Buried **AMARA WAR CEMETERY.** Grave location:- Plot 7, Row C,. Grave 2. ROH:- Todmorden War Memorial; Shepley War Memorial; Huddersfield GPO.

HARVATT, HENRY. Sergeant. No 5953. 'A' Battery, 155th Brigade Royal Field Artillery. Born Beverley 1894. Employed as an Asylum attendant before joining the Huddersfield police on 9.1.1914. Killed in action, 4.8.1917, aged 23 years. Buried **DUHALLOW A.D.S. CEMETERY.** Grave location:- Plot 1, Row A, Grave 26. ROH:- Huddersfield Police Headquarters.

HAWES, RADFORD. Sapper. No 198329. Railway Operating Division Royal Engineers. Formerly No 390 York and Lancaster Regiment. Born Penistone. Brother of Jim Hawes, 20 Castle Green, Penistone. Lived Gatefoot, Shepley. Died of wounds, 31.5.1918, aged 26. Buried **LONGUENESSE (St. OMER) SOUVENIR CEMETERY.** Grave Location:- Plot 5, Row B, Grave 50. ROH:- Shepley War Memorial.

HAWKSWORTH, HARRY. Corporal. No 240599. 2/5th Battalion Duke of Wellington's Regiment. Born Lockwood 6.12.1886. Educated Mount Pleasant Council School, Lockwood. Employed as a warehouse man. Married. Lived 2 Mark's Square, Market Street, Paddock. Enlisted 8.8.1917. Killed in action near Bapaume, 26.3.1918, aged 31 years. Has no known grave. Commemorated **ARRAS MEMORIAL TO THE MISSING.** ROH:- St. Stephen's Church, Rashcliffe; All Saints Church, Paddock; Huddersfield Drill Hall.

HAWKYARD, FRED. Private. No 22451. 6th Battalion East Lancashire Regiment. Formerly No 153 King's Own Yorkshire Light Infantry. Born Huddersfield. Son of Walter and Rosetta Hawkyard. Enlisted Wakefield. Lived Elland. Died in Mesopotamia, 14.7.1916. Buried **AMARA WAR CEMETERY.** Grave location Plot 11, Grave E, Row 8. ROH:- Shared Church, Paddock.

HAW, HERBERT EDWARD. Lance Corporal. No 29588. 1/6th Battalion Duke of Wellington's Regiment. Born Kirkheaton. Husband of Sarah Ann Haw, 4 Wellhouse Lane, Kirkheaton. Killed in action near Cambrai, 11.10.1918, aged 31. Buried **WELLINGTON CEMETERY.** Grave Location:- Plot 2, Row D, Grave 10. ROH:- All Hallows Parish Church, Kirkburton.

HAYDEN, JOSEPH. Rifleman. No C/6670. 18th Battalion King's Royal Rifle Corps. Born Huddersfield 20.7.1898. Son of Joseph and Ann Hayden, 5 Bradley Street North, Huddersfield. Attended St. Joseph's Church, Commercial Street,

Huddersfield. Employed as a bottle washer at the Watergate Breweries. Single. Enlisted 10.8.1916. Killed in action, 31.7.1917, aged 19 years. Has no known grave. Commemorated **MENIN GATE MEMORIAL TO THE MISSING.**

HAYES, EDWARD DYSON. Sergeant. No 628. 1/7th Battalion Duke of Wellington's Regiment. Born Slaithwaite. Son of John and Emily Hayes, 13 Waterside, Slaithwaite. Employed as a cotton spinner at the Slaithwaite Spinning Company Limited. Was an able amateur electrician. Was a member of the Slaithwaite United Methodist choir, a member of the Slaithwaite Glee and Madrigal Society, where at one time he was treasurer and choirmaster. Attended the Crimble Primitive Methodist Chapel. Was also a member of the Slaithwaite Liberal Club. Enlisted at the outbreak of the war. Killed in action, 22.10.1915, aged 27 years. Buried. **TALANA FARM CEMETERY.** Grave location:- Plot 4, Row C, Grave 16. His father received the following letter from Lieutenant Cyril Bain, *'I am writing to say how sorry I am about the death of your son. Words fail one utterly on an occasion like this for it only happened this morning and the section and I are still a bit stunned by it all. If you could see them this evening as I can, absolutely lost you might realise what it means to us. They all feel they have lost a really good friend. Sergeant E. D. Hayes was one of the best and his loss to the machine gun section is one that we can never hope to replace. He was killed by a shell bursting on his dugout which also killed two more and wounded three. He was unconscious from the first and died within half an hour. He is going to be buried tomorrow by our Padre at Talana Farm Cemetery about three quarters of a mile from the firing line. I have collected his things to give to his brother when he comes back.'* (Brother of 1st Air Mechanic **EWART HAYES**, killed in an aeroplane accident, 23.10.1918, q.v.). ROH:- Carr Lane Methodist Church; St. James Church, Slaithwaite; Slaithwaite War Memorial; Huddersfield Drill Hall.

HAYES, EWART. Air Mechanic 1st Class. No 22782. Royal Air Force. Born Slaithwaite. Son of John and Emily Hayes, 13 Waterside, Slaithwaite. Attended Carr Lane United Methodist Church, Slaithwaite. Was a member of Slaithwaite Conservative Club. Employed by Messrs Bamforth Brothers, engineers, of Slaithwaite.

Enlisted February 1916. Stationed in Orfordness, Suffolk. Died as a result of an aeroplane accident at the Accoustical Experimental Station at Butley, Suffolk, on 23.10.1918, aged 32 years. Buried **SLAITHWAITE CEMETERY.** Grave location:- C, 4, 82. (Brother of Private **EDWARD DYSON HAYES**, killed in action, 22.10.1915, q.v.). ROH:- St. James Church, Slaithwaite; Slaithwaite War Memorial.

HAYWOOD, PHILIP. 2nd Lieutenant. 2/6th Battalion West Yorkshire Regiment. Born Huddersfield 18.6.1891. Son of Joseph and Lydia Haywood, 3 Park Drive, Huddersfield. Educated Ashville College, Harrogate. Was in business as a printer and stationer at the Huddersfield Exchange. Single. Served for about eighteen months with Lieutenant Colonel Demetriadi (q.v.) at the 2nd West Riding Casualty Clearing Station. Was commissioned in February, 1917. Killed in action at the Battle of Cambrai, 22.11.1917, aged 26 years. Has no known grave. Commemorated. **CAMBRAI MEMORIAL TO THE MISSING.**

HAYWOOD, WALTER. Private. No 14409. 8th Battalion Duke of Wellington's Regiment. Born Burnlee, Holmfirth. Son of Mr and Mrs William Kippax. Reported missing at Suvla Bay, Gallipoli, 7.8.1915. Has no known grave. Commemorated **HELLES MEMORIAL TO THE MISSING.** His parents appealed for information in the 'Holmfirth Express' and received the following letter from one of Walter's chums, *'I have noticed your letter in the 'Express' two or three times asking for information about Walter. You see we trained together in Halifax and went to Grantham together. There were not many of us from Holmfirth way so we used to stick together as much as possible. I am now going to tell you the story about him as far as I know it. We landed here on the Friday night (August 6th) and had to start fighting as soon as we landed and if ever a lad won distinction Walter did that night. He carried a wounded Captain of our regiment right out of the Turk's trenches to a place of safety and the bullets were simply raining all around him. He then dashed back to his regiment but it appears he got lost and got in with some other regiment in the 10th Division. He was with that regiment when he received his wound. Lance Corporal Wood was with him and it was from him that I got to hear of him. This* was on Monday August 9th. He said they both got lost and found themselves with the Dublin Fusiliers so not knowing where they were they decided to stay with them for the time being. That very night they had a bayonet charge in which Walter got wounded and Lance Corporal Wood stayed with him as they had got lost again. It is easy to get lost in a charge for you can't see ten yards in front of you for bushes and ravines all over the hillsides. Well not being able to carry him himself he went for assistance but he never found him again and he got killed himself on the Wednesday, else I would have asked him to write to you. I sincerely hope that someone did find him and carry him down but I have asked about him scores of times and he is regarded as wounded and missing in our regiment.' On Saturday 18.11.1916 more information was published in the 'Holmfirth Express' regarding Private Haywood. His mother received an official certificate which read, *'Certified that it appears that an unofficial report received in this office that No 14409 Private Walter Haywood, 8th Battalion Duke of Wellington's Regiment who was officially reported missing at Suvla Bay on 7.8.1915 was killed in action on or about that date.'* A Corporal Bloomer, of the 4th Battalion West Yorkshire Regiment, who was in hospital in York was able to give the following information, *'On the night of the 22nd September we were going down the communication trench of Jephson's Post to dig the trench a little deeper. It was a moonlight night and about 2am one of my chums just managed to see a body laid under a bush. The exact words he used were 'Look at that body lying there, let us have some fun' but I being the section commander replied 'No he has done his duty, let's bury him in a decent way'. So on going up to the body we found it was a British tommy. He was laid on his stomach and on turning him over his face was not recognisable. He must have been shot by a sniper as there were no bayonet wounds on his body and what I could gather of his face one could see there had been a bullet wound there. In his right hand he had a canteen full of bully beef and biscuits and his hand was bent in carrying it. Round his body was what we call a bandolier full of ammunition and his helmet was a few yards away. All I can say is this that I am positively sure that the lad whom I buried was the same one (Private Walter Haywood) and I shall stick to my words that he was not wounded by a bayonet but I am almost* sure that he was killed by a sniper. I am very sorry for his mother, Mrs Kippax, but that is my story.' ROH:- Holmfirth War Memorial.

HAYWOOD, WILLIE. Private. No 12474. 8th Battalion Duke of Wellington's Regiment. Born Golcar. Son of Mr and Mrs Whittaker Haywood, 39 Cowcliffe Hill, Birkby. Employed by Messrs Hopkinsons of Birkby. Enlisted at the outbreak of the war. Went out to the Dardenelles in August, 1915. Killed in action in the assault on Lala Baba, Suvla, when he went to the assistance of a wounded officer and was killed by a sniper on 7.8.1915, aged 30 years. Has no known grave. Commemorated **HELLES MEMORIAL TO THE MISSING.** ROH:- Fartown and Birkby War Memorial; Golcar Baptist Church.

HEAD, CHARLES A. Private. No 3/6622. 2nd Battalion East Yorkshire Regiment. Born East Lexham, Norfolk. Lived 2 Silver Street, Moldgreen, Huddersfield. Married. Killed in action, 17.2.1915, aged 42. Has no known grave. Commemorated **MENIN GATE MEMORIAL TO THE MISSING.**

HEADEY, PERCY. Lance Corporal. No 240512. 1/5th Battalion Duke of Wellington's Regiment. Born 22 Grove Street, Huddersfield, 6.10.1882. Son of William Henry and Elizabeth Headey, 30a, South Street, Huddersfield. Employed as a weaver by Messrs Lockwood and Keighley, Upperhead Mills, Huddersfield. Married to Annie Headey and father of three children. Enlisted 5.9.1914. Killed in action at Nieuport, 7.8.1917, aged 34 years. Buried **RAMSCAPELLE ROAD MILITARY CEMETERY.** Grave location:- Plot 2, Row A, Grave 27. ROH:- St. James's Presbyterian Church, Huddersfield; Huddersfield Drill Hall.

HEALD, ALBERT. Private. No 3591. 1/7th Battalion Duke of Wellington's Regiment. Youngest son of Mrs Heald, 9 Pymroyd, Milnsbridge. Employed at Messrs J. W. Leech and Company's chemical works. Attended the Huddersfield Mission. Single. Enlisted October 1915. Embarked for France in April, 1916. Killed in action at the Battle of the Somme, 3.7.1916, aged 25 years. Has no known grave. Commemorated **THIEPVAL MEMORIAL TO THE MISSING.** ROH:- Huddersfield Drill Hall.

HEALEY, ALBERT. Private. No 15364. 2nd Battalion Duke of Wellington's Regiment. Born Huddersfield. Married. Lived 133 Leeds Road, Huddersfield. Employed by the Standard Fireworks Company, Crosland Hill. Killed in action at the Battle of Arras, 3.5.1917, aged 37 years. Has no known grave. Commemorated **ARRAS MEMORIAL TO THE MISSING.** (Brother of Private **ALLEN HEALEY,** killed in action, 14.9.1916, q.v.). ROH:- Fartown and Birkby War Memorial.

HEALEY, ALLEN. No not known. 9th Battalion West Yorkshire Regiment. Born Lockwood. Lived Leeds. Killed in action, 14.9.1916. (Brother of Private **ALBERT HEALEY,** killed in action, 3.5.1917, q.v.). ROH:- Fartown and Birkby War Memorial.

HEALEY, WILFRED DOMINIC. Private. No 129331. 21st Company, Machine Gun Corps. Formerly No S/23584 Seaforth Highlanders. Born Manchester. Enlisted Huddersfield. Son of the late Mr and Mrs John Healey. Husband of Beatrice H. Healey. Prior to enlistment, was a dentist in practice in South Street, Huddersfield. Killed in action, 26.4.1918, aged 33 years. Has no known grave. Commemorated **TYNE COT MEMORIAL TO THE MISSING.**

HEAP, ARTHUR. Private. No 43036. 9th Battalion King's Own Yorkshire Light Infantry. Born Arrunden, Holmfirth. Son of the late John Heap, 'The Tollemarche Hotel', Woodhead, Holmfirth. Lived with his sister and brother-in-law, Mr and Mrs Littlewood, at Yateholme. Employed as cattle dealer. Went out to New Zealand with his brother, Henry Heap, and worked on a sheep farm. Unfortunately Henry's health deteriorated and they returned to Holmfirth just before the outbreak of the war. Enlisted in 1916 and, after a period of training in the North Riding of Yorkshire, embarked for France in December, 1916. Killed in action, 21.2.1917, aged 38 years. Buried **CAMBRIN MILITARY CEMETERY.** Grave location:- Row G, Grave 52. ROH:- Holme and Holmbridge War Memorial.

HEALEY, DYSON. Private. No 34309. 8th Battalion Leicestershire Regiment. Born Flockton. Son of Mr and Mrs Healey of 'The Thomas's Arms Inn', Netherton. Prior to enlistment, was a farmer on his father's farm at Netherton. Acted as a groundsman for the Netherton Tennis Club. Killed in action, 9.10.1917, aged 23 years. Has no known grave. Commemorated **TYNE COT MEMORIAL TO THE MISSING.** ROH:- South Crosland and Netherton War Memorial.

HEAP, EDWIN. Private. No DM2/171335. Army Service Corps, attached 196th Siege Battery Ammunition Column. Born Ripponden near Halifax. Lived Bank View, Blackmoorfoot, Linthwaite. Died at No 36 Casualty Clearing Station, 24.1.1918. Buried **BANDAGHEM MILITARY CEMETERY.** Grave location:- Plot 1, Row C, Grave 4. (Brother of Private **WALKER HEAP,** killed in action, 9.10.1917, q.v.). ROH:- St. Bartholomew's Church, Meltham; Helme Parish Church.

HEAP, FRED. Private. No 29294. 10th Battalion Duke of Wellington's Regiment. Born Holmfirth. Enlisted Halifax. Killed in action in Italy, 27.10.1918. Buried **TEZZE BRITISH CEMETERY, VAZZOLA, ITALY.** Grave location:- Plot 2, Row A, Grave 11.

HEAP, HAROLD. Private. No 205047. 1/4th Battalion Duke of Wellington's Regiment. Born Far End Lane, Honley 7.9.1888. Son of Albert Heap. Educated Honley National School. Employed as a twister-in by Messrs Brook and Woodhouse Limited, Queens Mill, Huddersfield. Husband of Lily Heap, 16 Berry Row, Berry Brow. Enlisted 26.3.1917. Wounded at Nieuport 9.10.1917. Had only just returned to France after recovering from his wounds when he was killed at Kemmel Hill on 29.4.1918, aged 30 years. Has no known grave. Commemorated **TYNE COT MEMORIAL TO THE MISSING.** ROH:- Armitage Bridge War Memorial; Honley War Memorial.

HEAP, JAMES ARTHUR. Private. No 241715. 9th Battalion Duke of Wellington's Regiment. Born Holmfirth. Son of Sam and Mary Alice Heap of Ward Place, Holmfirth. Educated at Dobb Day School. Attended Cartworth Moor Wesleyan School. Was a playing member of the Cartworth Moor Cricket Club. Employed at Lower Mills, Holmfirth. Enlisted, 17.4.1916, on his 19th birthday. Embarked for France at the beginning of 1917. Died of wounds, 24.3.1918, aged 21 years. Buried **DOULLENS COMMUNAL CEMETERY EXTENSION No 1.** Grave location:- Plot 5, Row B, Grave 65.

ROH:- Cartworth War Memorial; memorial in Holmfirth Cemetery.

HEAP, LUTHER. Private. No 10971. 8th Battalion Duke of Wellington's Regiment. Born Armitage Bridge, Huddersfield, 28.4.1881. Son of Grace Heap, 149 Lockwood Road, Huddersfield. Educated at South Crosland National School. Employed as a labourer by Mr Stead Harrison, contractor, of Milnsbridge. Single. Enlisted 18.8.1914. Served in the Dardenelles and took part in the evacuation of Suvla Bay. He then went to Egypt and had been in France for about eight weeks when he was wounded on the Somme, 17.9.1916. Died of a haemorrhage at Frensham Hill Military Hospital, Surrey, on 30.9.1916. Buried **SOUTH CROSLAND CHURCH BURIAL GROUND.** Grave location:- N.E., 314. ROH:- Gospel Mission, Huddersfield; Emmanuel Church, Lockwood.

HEAP, WALKER. Private. No 203741. 1/4th Battalion Duke of Wellington's Regiment. Lived with his sister at Bank View, Blackmoorfoot, Linthwaite. Employed in the dyeing department of Messrs Joseph Dyson and Sons, Milnsbridge. Was a member of the Slaithwaite Socalist Club. Killed in action, 9.10.1917, aged 20 years. Has no known grave. Commemorated **TYNE COT MEMORIAL TO THE MISSING.** (Brother of Private **EDWIN HEAP,** died of wounds, 24.1.1918, q.v.). ROH:- St. Bartholomew's Church, Meltham; Helme Parish Church.

HEAP, WILFRED. Gunner. No 162132. 279th Siege Battery Royal Garrison Artillery. Born Shepley. Son of Henry and Sarah Alberta Heap, of Stocks Hill, Shepley. Single. Enlisted Huddersfield. Invalided home with trench fever. Rejoined his unit and was again taken ill. Sent to Brighton where he underwent an operation for appendicitis, which was unsuccessful. Died on 22.9.1918, aged 24 years. Buried **St. PAUL'S CHURCHYARD, SHEPLEY.** Grave location:- in North part. ROH:- Shepley War Memorial.

HEATH, REGINALD STUART. Sapper. No 91697. 216th Army Transport Company, Royal Engineers. Born Emley. Son of Mr F. C. Heath, Woodside, Emley. Husband of Hilda A. Heath, of Woodville, Emley. Enlisted Cambridge. Killed by a shell, 7.2.1916, aged 22years. Buried **BETHUNE TOWN CEMETERY.** Grave location:- Plot 5, Row A, Grave 2. ROH:- Emley War Memorial.

HEATON, ARTHUR. Ordinary Seaman. No J/50817. Royal Navy. *HMS Pilorus*. Son of Philemon and Sarah Heaton, 1 Upper Mount, Meltham. Was a member of the choir at St. James's Church, Meltham Mills, a former secretary of the Meltham Mills bible class and a secretary of the Meltham Mills Adult School. Employed in the warehouse at the Bent Ley Silk Mills. Enlisted in the Navy on 8.3.1916. Was drowned by falling overboard from *HMS Pilorus* on 1.8.1916, aged 21 years. Has no known grave. Commemorated **PLYMOUTH NAVAL MEMORIAL TO THE MISSING.** ROH:- St. Bartholomew's Church, Meltham.

HEATON, HARRY. Private. No 90810. 75th Company Machine Gun Corps. Formerly No DM2/209998 Army Service Corps. Born Manchester. Married. Lived 38 Arnold Street, Birkby. Was a partner in a local firm of tobacconists. Enlisted Huddersfield. Reported missing, 5.8.1917, and afterwards presumed to have been killed on that date. Has no known grave. Commemorated **MENIN GATE MEMORIAL TO THE MISSING.** ROH:- Fartown and Birkby War Memorial.

HEATON, NORMAN. Private. No 37746. 10th Battalion King's Own Yorkshire Light Infantry. Formerly No 19314 Duke of Wellington's Regiment. Born Stile Common, Primrose Hill, 20.9.1891. Son of William and Eliza Heaton, 75 Cottage Retreat, Manchester Road, Huddersfield. Educated Stile Common Council School. Attended the Baptist Church, Primrose Hill, and was an active worker in the Sunday School and a member of the choir. When the family moved to Milnsbridge he attended the Milnsbridge Baptist Church. Employed as a scourer. Single. Enlisted 2.3.1916. Killed in action, 25.9.1916. Has no known grave. Commemorated **THIEPVAL MEMORIAL TO THE MISSING.**

HEBBLETHWAITE, HENRY. Private. No 235108. 1/4th Battalion Duke of Wellington's Regiment. Son of Mr and Mrs Wilson Hebblethwaite of Wooldale. Husband of E. A. Hebblethwaite, 187 Sunny Bank, Holmbridge. Employed at Digley Mills. Enlisted October 1915. Embarked for France March, 1916. Killed in action, 25.11.1917, aged 27 years. Buried **OXFORD ROAD CEMETERY.** Grave location:- Plot 3, Row A, Grave 20. (His widow received the following letter from her husband's Officer who wrote, *'By now you will probably have heard the dreadful news of the death of your husband. I know I cannot realise your terrible grief for I know how devoted you were to each other. It has been my painful duty to return some of your letters to him. He was in my Company and was one of my very best men. It is nearly always the best who seem to be hit. The next time there was an opening for a commission I was going to put his name forward. He was killed by a shell and died almost instantly. He is buried by the side of one of his Company Officers. At this time please accept my deepest and most heartfelt sympathy and may you be given the strength to bear your terrible loss.'* ROH:- Holme and Holmbridge War Memorial.

HEBBLETHWAITE, WALTER. Private. No 105825. 177th Company, Labour Corps. Formerly No R/27584. 23rd Battalion King's Royal Rifle Corps. Born 77 Cliffe End Road 8.3.1896. Son of Herbert and Caroline Hebblethwaite. Educated Longwood National School. Was a chorister at Longwood Parish Church. Employed as a yarn warehouseman. Enlisted 27.2.1916. Wounded at Delville Wood, 20.8.1916. Accidentally killed in a railway accident at Mariolles, Northern France, on 11.12.1918, aged 22 years. Buried **St. SOUPLET BRITISH CEMETERY.** Grave location:- Maroilles Communal Cemetery German Extension Memorial No 1. ROH:- St. Mark's Parish Church, Longwood.

HEELEY, ALBERT. Private. No 71775. 11th Battalion Sherwood Foresters. Born Netherton. Son of John William and Laura Heeley, 10 Church Street, Honley. Killed in action, 16.9.1917, aged 19 years. Has no known grave. Commemorated **TYNE COT MEMORIAL TO THE MISSING.** ROH:- South Crosland and Netherton War Memorial; Honley War Memorial.

HEELEY, ARTHUR. Private. No 29323. 10th Battalion Duke of Wellington's Regiment. Born Thongsbridge. Son of Elliot and Sarah Jane Heeley, 24 Albert Place, Thongsbridge. Educated Wooldale Council School. Was a member of Thongsbridge Cricket Club. Attended Thongsbridge Mission Church. Enlisted 4.9.1916. Embarked for France in January, 1917. Died of wounds at No 7 Stationary Hospital, Boulogne, on 12.6.1917, aged 25 years. Buried **BOULOGNE EASTERN CEMETERY.** Grave location:- Plot 4, Row A, Grave 1. (Brother of Private **HAROLD HEELEY**, killed in action, 25.8.1916). His parents had received a message on 10.6.1917 from the Sister in charge of the hospital informing them of his serious condition and adding, *'He wished me to write you and send you his love.'* ROH:- Netherthong and Thongsbridge War Memorial.

HEELEY, FRED. Private. No 76881. 12th Battalion Manchester Regiment. Formerly No 367798 Labour Corps. Born Hade Edge, Holmfirth, 7.12.1899. Son of Jonathan and Elizabeth Heeley, 63 Laund Road, Salendine Nook. Educated Fenay Bridge and Hillhouse Council Schools. Employed as a spinner by Messrs Hirst and Mallinson of Longwood. Single. At the time of enlistment, was living at Gibson Street, Oakes. Enlisted 7.12.1917. Killed in action near Cambrai, 12.10.1918, aged 18 years. Has no known grave. Commemorated **VIS-en-ARTOIS MEMORIAL TO THE MISSING.**

HEELEY, HAROLD. Private. No 19329. 10th Battalion Duke of Wellington's Regiment. Born Wooldale. Son of Eliot and Sarah Jane Heeley, 24 Albert Place, Thongsbridge. Educated Wooldale Council School. Was a member of Thongsbridge Cricket Club. Attended Huddersfield Technical College evening classes for six years, learning chemistry and dyeing. Employed as foreman dyer at Messrs Vickermans of Thongsbridge. Enlisted at the outbreak of the war. Went into training at North Shields but, on going to France, was attached to the King's Own Yorkshire Light Infantry. Killed in action, 25.8.1916, aged 21 years. Has no known grave. Commemorated **THIEPVAL MEMORIAL TO THE MISSING.** (Brother of Private **ARTHUR HEELEY**, died of wounds, 12.6.1917, q.v.). His parents received the news of his death in a letter from Bugler F. Brown, 6 Platoon, 'B' Company, 10th Battalion K.O.Y.L.I. who wrote, *'just a line in answer to your parcel and letters which you wrote to your son Harold. I am sorry to have to tell you that your son got killed on the 25th. I am sorry to have put it so bluntly but I find it is not much good telling you he is missing when* *we know for sure that he has got killed because it only puts you about and makes you wonder where he is. I know he has got killed. I would like them to tell my dear father and mother when I had got killed.'*. ROH:- Netherthong and Thongsbridge War Memorial.

HEELEY, WILLIE. Private. No 48332. 20th (Tyneside Scottish) Battalion Northumberland Fusiliers. Formerly No 117659 Royal Garrison Artillery. Born Denby. Son of Mr and Mrs Tom Heeley, Sunny Bank, Denby Dale. Married, with one child. Employed in the finishing department at Messrs J. Kenyon and Sons Limited, of Denby Dale. Died of wounds, 8.5.1917, aged 25 years. Buried **ETAPLES MILITARY CEMETERY.** Grave location:- Plot 19, Row R, Grave 1a. ROH:- Denby Dale and Cumberworth War Memorial.

HEELEY, WILLIE. Private. No. 38654. 1/5th Battalion York and Lancaster Regiment. Born Denby. Enlisted Penistone. Killed in action, 15.4.1918. Buried **CABARET ROUGE BRITISH CEMETERY.** Grave location:- Plot 20, Row B, Grave 15. ROH:- Denby Dale and Cumberworth War Memorial.

HELLAWELL, ERNEST. Private. No 241930. 2/5th Battalion Duke of Wellington's Regiment. Born Kirkheaton. Lived New Mill. Second son of Mr and Mrs W. Helliwell. Employed as a spinner at Stoney Bank Mills. Enlisted March 1916. Embarked for France in January, 1917. Reported missing at the Battle of Bullecourt, 3.5.1917 and afterwards presumed to have been killed on that date. Has no known grave. Commemorated **ARRAS MEMORIAL TO THE MISSING.** ROH:- New Mill Working Men's Club; Fulstone War Memorial Huddersfield Drill Hall.

HELLAWELL, HARRY. Private. No 42321. 2nd Battalion King's Own Yorkshire Light Infantry. Born Huddersfield. Son of Emma Hellawell, 6 Station Terrace, Golcar. Lived Cowlersley Lane, Milnsbridge. Employed as a clerk by Messrs David Brown and Sons, Park Gear Works, Crosland Moor. Was a member of the Golcar Central Liberal Club. Attended St. John's Church, Golcar. Enlisted in 1915 and embarked for France in October, 1916. Killed in action, 11.2.1917, aged 23 years. Has no known grave. Commemorated **THIEPVAL MEMORIAL TO THE MISSING.** ROH:- St. John's Church, Golcar.

HELLAWELL, JACK. Private. No 52609. 1st Battalion West Yorkshire Regiment. Born Swan Lane, Lockwood, 3.10.1896. Son of Joseph and Annie Hellawell, 39 Hope Street, Folly Hall, Huddersfield. Educated Mount Pleasant Board School. Employed as a warehouseman by Messrs Gledhill Brothers of Lockwood. Attended Primrose Hill United Methodist Church. Single. Enlisted 29.3.1916. Reported missing on 21.3.1918 and afterwards presumed to have been killed on that date. Has no known grave. Commemorated **ARRAS MEMORIAL TO THE MISSING.** ROH:- St. Stephen's Church, Rashcliffe.

HELLAWELL, JOHN. Private. No 58848. 11th Battalion The Welsh Regiment. Born Marsden. Son of Mr and Mrs Tom Hellawell. Enlisted Bradford. Killed in action in Salonika, 18.9.1918, aged 28. Buried **DOIRAN MEMORIAL TO THE MISSING, GREECE.**

HELLAWELL, LUTHER. Private. No 14981. 2/5th Battalion Duke of Wellington's Regiment. Born Holmfirth. Son of Mr and Mrs Charles Hellawell of Gully, Holmfirth. Educated Holmfirth National Day School. Attended Underbank Wesleyan Sunday School. Employed by Messrs James Robinson and Sons of Smithy Place, Holmfirth. Married, with two children. Enlisted Christmas 1914. Embarked for France in July, 1915. Wounded in the left foot and right thigh in July, 1916. Returned to France at Whitsuntide, 1917. On the 16.11.1917 his wife received a letter from him stating that, *'It is very cold out here now but I am in the best of health and hope this letter will find you the same.'* Eight days later he was wounded in the chest. He was removed to No 21 Casualty Clearing Station, where he died of his wounds on 21.11.1917, aged 34 years. Buried **ROCQUIGNY-EQUANCOURT ROAD BRITISH CEMETERY.** Grave location:- Plot 2, Row D, Grave 25. His wife received a message from the Matron of the C.C.S informing her that her husband had died, *'It is with much regret I have to tell you of the death of your husband on the 21st inst. in this hospital from wounds sustained in battle. He was brought to us badly wounded in the chest and in spite of all we could do for him he succumbed to his injuries. He passed away very peacefully without any pain in the end. He was laid to rest in the Military Cemetery near here.'* ROH:- Netherthong and

Thongsbridge War Memorial; St. Bartholomew's Church, Meltham; Huddersfield Drill Hall.

HELLAWELL, WILFRED. Private. No 241428. 1/5th Battalion Duke of Wellington's Regiment. Born Golcar. Enlisted Huddersfield. Reported missing, 3.9.1916, and afterwards presumed to have been killed on that date. Has no known grave. Commemorated **THIEPVAL MEMORIAL TO THE MISSING.** ROH:- St. John's Church, Golcar; Pole Moor Baptist Church; Huddersfield Drill Hall.

HELLAWELL, WILLIE. Private. No 28926. 9th Battalion The Yorkshire Regiment. Born Golcar. Enlisted Halifax. Lived Golcar. Killed in action, 5.10.1918. Has no known grave. Commemorated **VIS-en-ARTOIS MEMORIAL TO THE MISSING.** ROH:- St. John's Church, Golcar; Golcar Baptist Church.

HELLAWELL, JOHN ARTHUR. Private. No 15518. 8th Battalion The King's Own (Royal Lancaster Regiment). Born Longwood, Huddersfield. Son of Mrs Broadbent, 'Wellington Inn', Ripponden Road, Oldham. His father was the late Mr Arthur Helliwell, of Brockholes, who was formerly in business in the corn trade at Longwood. The family then lived at Ingfield View, Longwood Gate, and later resided at Marsden. Employed by his uncles, Messrs J. and J. Bottomley, contractors, of Marsden. Enlisted November 1914. Had been wounded on one occasion. Killed in action, 26.4.1917, aged 24 years. Has no known grave. Commemorated **ARRAS MEMORIAL TO THE MISSING.**

HELLAWELL, SELWYN. Private. No 204384. 8th Battalion Duke of Wellington's Regiment. Born Lightridge Farm, Fixby, 8.4.1890. Son of John William and Elizabeth Helliwell, Lightridge Farm, Fixby, Huddersfield. Employed as a farmer. Single. Enlisted 3.3.1917. Reported missing, 9.10.1917 and afterwards presumed to have been killed on that date, aged 27. Has no known grave. Commemorated **TYNE COT MEMORIAL TO THE MISSING.** ROH:- St. Hilda's Church, Cowcliffe; Fartown and Birkby War Memorial.

HELM, ALBERT. Private. No 12592. 'A' Company 9th Battalion Duke of Wellington's Regiment. Born Holmfirth. Son of Wilson and Harriet E. Helm of Hade Edge, Holmfirth. Attended Hade Edge Wesleyan Chapel. Employed as a clerk by Messrs Revill and Revill, accountants, of Huddersfield. Enlisted September 1914. Underwent training at Bovington Camp, Dorset, and later at Wimbourne. Embarked for France in July, 1915. Wounded in the legs on 25.4.1916. Taken to the No 4 Casualty Clearing Station, where he died of his wounds on 26.4.1916, aged 19 years. Buried **BAILLEUL COMMUNAL CEMETERY EXTENSION.** Grave location:- Plot 2, Row D, Grave 157. His parents received the following letter from Nurse Jollie, Sister-in-charge at the hospital where he died, *'I am sorry to tell you Private Albert Helm was brought to No 4 Casualty Clearing Station last Tuesday night soon after midnight, very very severely wounded in both legs and quite unconscious. Everything was done for him but he passed peacefully away at ten minutes to one on Wednesday morning living less than an hour after admission. He will be buried in a part of the cemetery here reserved specially for our brave troops and there will be a little wooden cross bearing his name and the date marking his resting place.'* ROH:- Hade Edge War Memorial.

HEMINGWAY, ARTHUR. Rifleman. No R/18179. 2nd Battalion King's Royal Rifle Corps. Born Forrest Road, Huddersfield, 5.9.1893. Son of Mr and Mrs O. Hemingway, 28 Dale Street, Chapel Hill, Huddersfield. Educated at Hillhouse Council School. Employed as a leather worker by Messrs B. Crook and Sons, Fitzwilliam Street, Huddersfield. Was a member of the choir at St. Paul's Church, Southgate, Huddersfield. Single. Enlisted 27.1.1916. Killed in action at Nieuport on 10.7.1917, aged 23. Has no known grave. Commemorated **NIEUPORT MEMORIAL TO THE MISSING.** ROH:- St. Paul's Church, Southgate, Huddersfield.

HEMSWORTH, JOHN BERNARD. Sapper. No 223179. Royal Engineers. Born New Hey Road, Marsh. Son of William Hemsworth, 6 Mount Street, Marsh. Educated Holy Trinity Church of England School. Employed as a wheelwright. Single. Enlisted 31.12.1916. Died at Chatham of pneumonia on 21.1.1917, aged 19 years. Buried **St. STEPHEN'S CHURCHYARD, LINDLEY.** Grave location:- 7, T. ROH:- Holy Trinity Church, Huddersfield; memorial in St. Stephen's Churchyard, Lindley.

HENRY, BERNARD. Driver. No 92839. Royal Field Artillery. Formerly No S/2/SR04325 Army Service Corps. Born 1 Hebble Street, Bradford Road, Huddersfield. Son of Mrs S. E. Ackroyd, Daisy Cottage, Calton Street, Huddersfield, and the late Colour Sergeant B. Henry, 1st Battalion Lincolnshire Regiment, and stepson of the late Mr Samuel Ackroyd, yarn manufacturer, of Huddersfield. Educated at Huddersfield Higher Grade School. Prior to enlistment was living at 11 Clifton Grove, Harehills, Leeds. Employed by the Leeds Corporation Gas Department as a costing clerk. Married, with one child. Enlisted June 1915. Killed in action near Cambrai, 20.11.1917, aged 30 years. Buried **HERMIES BRITISH CEMETERY.** Grave location:- Row E, Grave 1. ROH:- St. Andrew's Church, Leeds Road, Huddersfield; Fartown and Birkby War Memorial.

HEPPENSTALL, GEORGE FREDERICK. Private. No 60817 2nd/1st Yorkshire Hussars. Born Holmfirth. Son of Mr J.W. Heppenstall. Employed as a piecer at Dover Mills, Holmfirth. Enlisted in 1916. Was stationed in County Cork, Ireland and was expecting to be demobilised shortly. Was severely injured in an explosion and died within 24 hours. Buried with full military honours. He was 24 years of age. ROH:- Hade Edge War Memorial.

HEPWORTH, FRANK. Private. No 204083. 2/4th Battalion Duke of Wellington's Regiment. Son of Thomas and Mary Hepworth of Wakefield. Husband of Ellen Hepworth, 84 Alder Street, Bradford Road, Huddersfield. Employed by Messrs Thewlis, Jagger and Company, of Folly Hall, Huddersfield. Killed in action, 12.4.1918, aged 24 years. Buried **BIENVILLERS MILITARY CEMETERY.** Grave location:- Plot 9, Row C, Grave 6. ROH:- St. Andrew's Church, Leeds Road, Huddersfield.

HEPWORTH, FRED. Rifleman. No C/6135. 18th Battalion King's Royal Rifle Corps. Died at home 22.12.1916. Buried **EDGERTON CEMETERY, HUDDERSFIELD.** Grave location:- 3B, 57. ROH:- St. Paul's Church, Southgate, Huddersfield.

HEPWORTH, JOE WILLIAM. Rifleman. No 57681. 1/7th Battalion West Yorkshire Regiment. Born 15.11.1884. Son of Richard and Ellen Hepworth. Educated Spring Grove Council School. Husband of Violet Hepworth, 6 Highroyd Terrace, Moldgreen. Employed as a cloth finisher by Messrs Joseph Wrigley and Sons, Littleroyd Mills. Was a member of the Rashcliffe Liberal Club and of the Milton Church P.S.A. Enlisted 24.7.1917. Wounded 24.3.1918. Died of his wounds at No 64 Casualty Clearing Station on 13.4.1918, aged 33 years. Buried **MENDINGHEM MILITARY CEMETERY.** Grave location:- Plot 9, Row E, Grave 18. ROH:- Christ Church, Moldgreen.

HEPWORTH, JOSEPH ALBERT. Private. No 62109. 15th/17th Battalion West Yorkshire Regiment. Born Fremont, West Derby, Liverpool, 18.4.1899. Son of Albert and Annie Hepworth, Cliffe Gardens, Stubbins Vale, Ramsbottom, near Manchester, and formerly of 44 Clement Street, Birkby. Educated Liverpool Council School. Employed as an apprentice dyer by Messrs Brown and Company, Bay Hall, Birkby. Single. Enlisted 18.5.1917. Reported missing, presumed killed, 12.4.1918, aged 19. Has no known grave. Commemorated **PLOEGSTEERT MEMORIAL TO THE MISSING.** ROH:- Fartown and Birkby War Memorial.

HEPWORTH, LESLIE. Private. No 17566. 2nd Battalion Duke of Wellington's Regiment. Born Spring Street, Huddersfield, 15.2.1889. Son of Mr and Mrs Fred Hepworth, 6 The Avenue, Moldgreen. Employed as a butcher. Single. Enlisted 15.8.1914. Killed at Hill 60, 18.4.1915, aged 27. Has no known grave. Commemorated **MENIN GATE MEMORIAL TO THE MISSING.** The deceased's brother, who was serving with the same Regiment, sent the news home in a letter, He said that, '*Leslie was shot through the head and died instantly with a smile on his face. He urges his mother and sisters to bear up, saying he died a soldier's death for King and Country.*' ROH:- Moldgreen War Memorial; Christ Church, Moldgreen.

HEPWORTH, SAM. Private. No 267982. 18th Battalion Northumberland Fusiliers. Born Sun Green, Thorpe, Almondbury. Son of Ephraim Hepworth, 196 Sun Green, Thorpe, Almondbury. Educated Almondbury National School. Employed as a woollen piecer by Messrs Jarmaines, of Kirkheaton. Single. Enlisted 3.4.1917. Taken prisoner at Armentieres, 10.4.1918. Died in the hospital attached to Quedlinburg Camp, Germany, on 25.10.1918. Buried **NIEDERZWEHREN**

CEMETERY, CASSEL, GERMANY. Grave location:- Plot 8, Row D, Grave 14. ROH:- Almondbury War Memorial.

HEPWORTH, WILFRED. Private. No 38148. 1st Battalion Lancashire Fusiliers. Formerly No 32214 South Staffordshire Regiment. Born Huddersfield 11.1.1889. Educated Moldgreen Council School. Employed as a tailor's presser by Messrs Wrigley and Tinker, wholesale clothiers, of Alfred Street, Huddersfield. Married. Lived 39 Cowcliffe Hill, Birkby. Enlisted August 1917. Reported missing on 13.4.1918 and afterwards presumed to have been killed on that date. Has no known grave. Commemorated **PLOEGSTEERT MEMORIAL TO THE MISSING.** ROH:- St. Andrew's Church; Fartown and Birkby War Memorial.

HERBERT, FRED. Private. No 241120. 2/5th Battalion Duke of Wellington's Regiment. Born Hey Laithe Farm, Marsden, 25.12.1897. Son of Robert and Elizabeth Herbert, West Street, Lindley. Educated Moldgreen Church of England School. Employed as a teaser by Messrs John Lockwood and Sons Limited, of Milnsbridge. Single. Enlisted May 1915. Embarked for France in January, 1917. Reported missing at the Battle of Bullecourt, 3.5.1917, and afterwards presumed to have been killed on that date. Has no known grave. Commemorated **ARRAS MEMORIAL TO THE MISSING.** (Brother of Private **ROBERT HERBERT,** died of wounds, 15.9.1916, q.v.). ROH:- Huddersfield Drill Hall; Marsden War Memorial.

HERBERT, ROBERT. Private. No 5618. 1/5th Battalion Duke of Wellington's Regiment. Born Grimsby. Fourth son of Robert and Elizabeth Herbert, Hey Laithe Farm, Marsden. Employed as a fettler by the Colne Valley Spinning Company Limited, Linthwaite. Enlisted 4.4.1916. Wounded in the right thigh on 3.9.1916. On 13.9.1916, he wrote home stating that his right leg had been amputated. Died of wounds at No 9 General Hospital, Rouen, 15.9.1916, aged 22 years. Buried **St. SEVER CEMETERY, ROUEN.** Grave location:- Plot B, Row 21, Grave 46. (Brother of Private **FRED HERBERT,** reported missing, 3.5.1917, q.v.). ROH:- Huddersfield Drill Hall; Marsden War Memorial.

HEWITT, F. Private. No 29923. 10th Battalion Duke of Wellington's Regiment. Son of Thomas Wilson Hewitt and Lily Hewitt, 5 North View, Marsden. Died at home, 18.1.1921, aged 25 years. Buried **St. BARTHOLOMEW'S CHURCHYARD, MARSDEN.** Grave location:- South, 29, 24. ROH:- Marsden War Memorial.

HEY, HERBERT. Private. No 7/1912. 'B' Company, 1/7th Battalion Duke of Wellington's Regiment. Born Thomas Street, Lindley, 2.11.1887. Son of Joseph and Alice Ann Hey, 51 Thomas Street, Lindley. Educated Lindley Church of England School. Employed as a card grinder by Messrs Joseph Sykes Brothers, Acre Mills, Lindley. Single. Enlisted 4.9.1914. Was wounded in the head on 20.8.1915. Was taken to the 15th Casualty Clearing Station, where he died of his wounds on 20.8.1915. Buried **HAZEBROUCK COMMUNAL CEMETERY.** Grave location:- Plot 2, Row G, Grave 13. Nurse G. M. Allen, the sister-in-charge of the hospital, wrote to his parents, stating that, Private Hey was so badly wounded that he had little chance from the first but she thought he had not suffered much. ROH:- St. Stephen's Church, Lindley; Lindley Zion Wesleyan Church; Huddersfield Drill Hall.

HEYWOOD, JOHN. Private. No 19658 2nd Battalion Duke of Wellington's Regiment. Born Top of Bank, Thurstonland, 6.6.1887. Son of Eliza Heywood, 388 Blackmoorfoot Road, Crosland Moor. Employed as a stone dresser by Messrs Joe Shaw and Sons, Crosland Hill. Single. Enlisted December 1915. Reported missing at the Battle of Arras, 3.5.1917 and afterwards presumed to have been killed on that date. Has no known grave. Commemorated **ARRAS MEMORIAL TO THE MISSING.** (Brother of Private **JOSEPH HEYWOOD,** killed in action, 27.3.1918, q.v.). ROH:- 'Rising Sun' Public House, Crosland Hill; St. Barnabas Church, Crosland Moor.

HEYWOOD, JOSEPH. Private. No 241513. 2/5th Battalion Duke of Wellington's Regiment. Born Top of Bank, Thurstonland, 23.4.1885. Son of Eliza Heywood, 388 Blackmoorfoot Road, Crosland Moor. Employed as a stone planer by Messrs Joe Shaw and Sons, Crosland Hill. Was a member of the Crosland Moor Working Men's Club. Single. Enlisted December 1915. Embarked for France in January, 1917. Killed in action, 27.3.1918, aged 33 years. Has no known grave. Commemorated **ARRAS MEMORIAL TO THE MISSING.** (Brother of Private **JOHN HEYWOOD,** reported missing, 3.5.1917, q.v.). ROH:-. 'Rising Sun' Public House, Crosland Hill; St, Barnabas Church, Crosland Moor; Huddersfield Drill Hall.

HIBBERD, GEORGE. Private. No 3389. 1/5th Battalion Duke of Wellington's Regiment. Born Colne Bridge, Kirkheaton, 4.2.1891. Son of Mrs Lumb, 29 Dalton Fold Road, Dalton. Educated St. Thomas's Church of England School, Bradley. Attended Moldgreen Congregational Church and the Ramsden Street Men's Own class. Played football with the Moldgreen Congregational Church, Huddersfield Wednesday and Cowlersley teams. Prior to enlistment, had worked at Lepton Edge Colliery and then for Messrs Read, Holliday as a banksman. Single. Enlisted 9.11.1914. Embarked for France in April, 1915. Was wounded and returned to the front in April, 1916. Died of cerebro-spinal meningitis at No 12 Stationary Hospital on 25.12.1916, aged 25 years. Buried **St. POL COMMUNAL CEMETERY EXTENSION.** Grave location:- Row C, Grave 12. ROH:- Christ Church, Moldgreen; Huddersfield Drill Hall.

HICKS, GEORGE HAROLD. Rifleman. No S/28939. 3rd Battalion The Rifle Brigade. Born Leeds. Lived with his brother-in-law and sister, Mr and Mrs B. Kenworthy, at 111 Longwood Gate, Longwood. Prior to enlistment was a weaver employed by Messrs John Crowther and Sons, of Milnsbridge. Was a member of the Milnsbridge Liberal Club and attended the Milnsbridge Baptist Sunday School. Enlisted February, 1916, and embarked for France on 14.12.1916. Died of wounds, 10.6.1917, aged 24 years. Has no known grave. Commemorated **MENIN GATE MEMORIAL TO THE MISSING.** ROH:- St. Mark's Parish Church, Longwood.

HICKMAN, HERBERT. Private. No 34750. Royal Field Artillery. Born Huddersfield. Lived 57 Upper Brow Road, Paddock. Married. Died in the Huddersfield Royal Infirmary, of nephritis, on 28.4.1922.

HIGGINSON, BERTRAM. Private. No 201251. 1st Battalion The Royal Scots Fusiliers. Born Elland, West Yorkshire. Son of Mr and Mrs James Higginson, Burnlee, Holmfirth. Prior to enlistment, was employed in the finishing department at Digley Mills, Holmfirth. Enlisted February 1916. Trained at Chelmsford and then was sent to Ireland. Embarked for France in December, 1917. Reported missing, 28.3.1918 and afterwards presumed to have been killed on that date. Has no known grave. Commemorated **ARRAS MEMORIAL TO THE MISSING.** ROH:- Upperthong War Memorial.

HILES, SAM. Private. No 24821. 9th Battalion Duke of Wellington's Regiment. Born Cowcliffe, Huddersfield. Son of Mr and Mrs Henry Hiles, 103 Cottage Retreat, Marsden Road, Huddersfield. Prior to enlistment, was employed as a cloth finisher by Messrs George Crosland and Sons, Crosland Moor. Enlisted September 1914. Killed in action, 4.11.1918, aged 29 years. Buried **ROMERIES COMMUNAL CEMETERY EXTENSION.** Grave location:- Plot 7, Row A, Grave 15.

HILL, BEN. Private. No 24757. 8th Battalion Duke of Wellington's Regiment. Born Kirkburton. Lived Lowgate, Kirkburton. Married, with six children. Had served in the old Militia. Died of wounds, 20.12.1917, aged 36 years. Buried **LONGUENESSE (St. OMER) SOUVENIR CEMETERY.** Grave location:- Plot 4, Row F, Grave 29. ROH:- All Hallows Parish Church, Kirkburton.

HILL, CHARLES ALBERT WILMOTTE. Private. No 9824. 1st Battalion West Yorkshire Regiment. Born Shaw, Oldham, Lancashire, 2.2.1892. Son of Mr W. H. Willmotte Hill, Moss Hey, Shaw, Lancashire. Educated at Shaw schools. Employed as a labourer in the Huddersfield Corporation Tramways Department. Husband of Emily Hill, 41 St. Andrews Road, Huddersfield. Was in the army before the war and was stationed at Malta. Had served on the Western Front since September, 1914, except for a short period when he was invalided home with frostbite and rheumatism. Killed in action at Montauban, 15.9.1916, aged 24 years. Buried **FLATIRON COPSE CEMETERY.** Grave location:- Plot 10, Row D, Grave 6. ROH:- Almondbury War Memorial.

HILL, EDWARD. Private. No 27358. 10th Battalion Royal Warwickshire Regiment. Formerly No 6235 Duke of Wellington's Regiment. Eldest son of Mr and Mrs John Hill, 28a, Lowerhead Row, Huddersfield. Educated Crow Lane Board School, Milnsbridge. Prior to enlistment, was employed in the goods yard at Longwood Station. Was mobilised with the local Territorial battalion at the outbreak of war and had served in Ireland. Died of wounds at No 49 Casualty Clearing Station, 21.11.1916, aged 18 years. Buried **CONTAY BRITISH CEMETERY.** Grave location:- Plot 4, Row E, Grave 11. ROH:. Crow Lane Board School, Milnsbridge.

HILL, ERNEST. Private. No 35279. 15th Battalion (1st Leeds Pals) West Yorkshire Regiment. Born 7 Woodside Road, Lockwood, 22.5.1890. Son of William and Mary Ann Hills. Educated Mount Pleasant Council School. Employed as a porter by the Lancashire and Yorkshire Railway at Brockholes Station. Married. Lived Lower Hagg, Brockholes. Enlisted 9.6.1916. Reported missing in the attack at Gavrelle, 3.5.1917. Has no known grave. Commemorated **ARRAS MEMORIAL TO THE MISSING.** ROH:- St. Barnabas Church, Crosland Moor; Mount Pleasant Chapel, Lockwood.

HILL, FRANK. Private. No 43153. 9th Battalion King's Own Yorkshire Light Infantry. Formerly No 33320 Northumberland Fusiliers. Born Huddersfield. Son of the late Joseph and Ann Ellen Hill, 80 Wood Terrace, Primrose Hill, Huddersfield. Prior to enlistment, was employed as a healder and twister by Messrs Henry Roebuck and Company, Springdale Mills. Enlisted July 1916. Killed in action, 4.10.1917, aged 37 years. Has no known grave. Commemorated **TYNE COT MEMORIAL TO THE MISSING.**

HILL, FRANK. Private. No 238021. 2/4th Battalion Duke of Wellington's Regiment. Born Kirkheaton. Enlisted Huddersfield. Killed in action at the Battle of Bullecourt, 3.5.1917. Has no known grave. Commemorated **ARRAS MEMORIAL TO THE MISSING.** ROH:- St. John's Church, Kirkheaton.

HILL, FRANK. Private. No 6657. 1/7th Battalion Duke of Wellington's Regiment. Elder son of the late Mr and Mrs James Henry Hill, 62 Woodhead Road, Holmfirth. (Brother of Ethel Hill, of the same address). Employed as a teaser by Messrs Whiteley and Green, Hinchliffe Mill Mill. Played the double bass with the Holme Brass Band. Attended the St. John's Institute. Enlisted 5.10.1914. Embarked for France in April, 1915. In July, 1915, he returned to England suffering from a hernia and returned to the front in August, 1915. In 1916 he was boiling water in a bully beef tin when it exploded in his face. Septic poisoning set in and again he was invalided home, returning to France in December, 1916. Was seriously wounded in the head and chest on 15.3.1917. He was taken to No 7 Casualty Clearing Station at Merville but he died of his wounds on 15.3.1917, aged 24 years. Buried **MERVILLE COMMUNAL CEMETERY EXTENSION.** Grave location:- Plot 1, Row B, Grave 21. His sister, Miss Ethel Hill, received the following letter from the Sister-in-charge at the C.C.S, dated 15.3.1917, *'I am very sorry to say that your dear brother died yesterday. He passed away most peacefully suffering no pain at all. He received every possible care and attention here and the best of surgical skill but God had need of him. I cannot tell you how sorry I feel for you but you will find solace in the thought that your dear brother is now safe and free from all earthly cares and sorrows of the world. For him we need not grieve but it is for those left to mourn. We must pray for resignation until they are reunited in God's good care. He was visited frequently by the Padre. Accept my heartfelt sympathy.'* ROH:- Upperthong War Memorial; Huddersfield Drill Hall.

HILL, HARRY. Private. No 78298. 71st Field Ambulance, Royal Army Medical Corps. Born Kirkburton. Son of Nathaniel and Ellen Hall of Causeway Side, Linthwaite. Prior to enlistment, was employed as a tuner by Messrs Marshall and Kaye and Marshall, Ravensthorpe, Dewsbury. Was wounded whilst serving in Italy and taken to the 11th General Hospital at Genoa, where he died of his wounds on 30.8.1918, aged 29 years. Buried **STAGLIENO CEMETERY, GENOA, ITALY.** Grave Location:- Plot 1, Row B, Grave 33. ROH:- Linthwaite War Memorial; Golcar Baptist Church.

HILL, HERBERT HENRY. Private. No 42398. 24th (Tyneside Irish) Battalion Northumberland Fusiliers. Born Leeds 11.4.1877. Both parents deceased. Brother of John Hill, 5 Chapman Street, Beckett Street, Leeds. Educated St. John's National Schools, Leeds. Employed as an insurance agent. At the time of enlistment was living at 205 Wakefield Road, Dalton, Huddersfield. Single. Reported missing 28.4.1917 and afterwards presumed to have been killed on that date, aged 40. Has no known grave. Commemorated **ARRAS MEMORIAL TO THE MISSING.** ROH:- Memorial in Almondbury Cemetery.

HILL, IRVIN. Private. No 31725. 8th Battalion North Staffordshire Regiment. Born Kirkburton. Son of Isaac and Mary Hill of Hallas, Kirkburton. Prior to enlistment, was employed by Mr Giessler, manufacturer, of Kirkburton. Died of wounds at No 44 Casualty Clearing Station, 30.4.1918, aged 20 years. Buried **ARNEKE BRITISH CEMETERY.** Grave location:- Plot 2, Row D, Grave 1. ROH:- All Hallows Parish Church, Kirkburton.

HILL, JAMES. Private. No 3/9474. 1st Battalion West Yorkshire Regiment. Born Huddersfield. Married. Lived 44 Perseverance Street, Primrose Hill, Huddersfield. Was employed at the ironworks of Messrs Broadbent and Company, Queens Street South, Huddersfield. Enlisted shortly after the outbreak of the war. Killed by a shell near High Wood during the Battle of the Somme, 17.9.1916, aged 29 years. Buried **LONDON CEMETERY AND EXTENSION.** Grave location:- Plot 4, Row B, Grave 14.

HILL, JAMES BRACEWELL. Private. No 71. 51st Battalion Australian Imperial Forces. Born Marsden. Son of Joseph and Jane Ann Hill of Fern Lea, Marsden. Before leaving Marsden for Australia, he was a member of the firm of Messrs Joseph Hill and Sons, tailors, Peel Street, Marsden. Was a member of Marsden Liberal Club and continued to pay his subscriptions when he went abroad. Went out to Australia for health reasons in 1908 and worked on a sheep station near Adelaide. Enlisted, 12.4.1916, and arrived in France in September, 1916. Killed in action, 1.4.1918, aged 38 years. Buried **RIBEMONT COMMUNAL CEMETERY EXTENSION.** Grave location:- Plot 2, Row D, Grave 2. ROH:- Marsden Liberal Club; memorial in Marsden Churchyard.

HILL, PHILIP J. Sergeant. No 64374. 135th Siege Battery Royal Garrison Artillery. Born Huddersfield. Elder son of Mr J. J. Hill, 175 Bradford Road, Huddersfield. Prior to enlistment, was employed by Messrs Crowther Brothers, of Stanley Mills, Milnsbridge. Enlisted 19.8.1916. Died of illness, 3.7.1917, aged 21 years. Buried **FAUBOURG D'AMIENS CEMETERY, ARRAS.** Grave location:- Plot 4, Row J, Grave 19. ROH:- Fartown and Birkby War Memorial.

HILTON, HARRY. Private. No 201767. 8th Battalion Northumberland Fusiliers. Born New Mill, Holmfirth. Son of George and Sarah Hilton, Sude Hill, New Mill. Educated New Mill National School. Attended the Parish Church Sunday School and was a member of the Young Men's Class. Was also a member of the New Mill Working Men's Club and was a keen billiard player. Employed by Messrs Mitchel, cloth finishers, of Folly Hall, Huddersfield. Embarked for France 16.6.1917. Killed in action, 16.8.1917, aged 22 years. Buried **LA BRIQUE MILITARY CEMETERY No 2.** Grave location:- Plot 1, Row D, Grave 9. ROH:- New Mill Working Men's Club; Fulston War Memorial.

HINCHCLIFFE, ALLAN. Private. No 235069. 2/4th Battalion Duke of Wellington's Regiment. Born Holmfirth 12.12.1893. Son of the late Joseph Hinchcliffe, of Holmbridge, and of Mrs Dickinson of 'The Victoria Hotel', Meltham. Educated Field End School and was also a scholar at the Holmbridge Church Sunday School. Was a member of the Holmbridge Cricket Club. Employed by Messrs T. and J. Tinker at Bottoms Mill. Embarked for France in April, 1915. Was wounded during the fighting on the Somme in September, 1916. Was treated in England and returned to France in February, 1917. Reported missing at the Battle of Bullecourt, 3.5.1917 and afterwards presumed to have been killed on that date. Has no known grave. Commemorated **ARRAS MEMORIAL TO THE MISSING.** ROH:- Holme and Holmbridge War Memorial; St. Bartholomew's Church, Meltham.

HINCHCLIFFE, G. W. Gunner. No 108957. 138th Heavy Battery, Royal Garrison Artillery. Born Marsden Lived Spring Street, Marsden. Died from bronchial pneumonia following upon influenza, 27.11.1918. Buried **LE CATEAU COMMUNAL CEMETERY.** Grave location:- Plot 1, Grave 22. ROH:- Marsden War Memorial.

HINCHCLIFFE, HERBERT. Corporal. No 241570. 2/5th Battalion Duke of Wellington's Regiment. Born Henry Street, Huddersfield, 2.1.1897. Youngest son of the late Mr James Hinchliffe. Lived with his sister, Mrs Shaw, at 26 Grasscroft Road, Marsh. Employed as a postman at Golcar Post Office. Attended St. Aidan's Mission Church. Single. Enlisted 8.3.1916. Embarked for France in January, 1917. Killed in action at the Battle of Cambrai, 20.11.1917, aged 20 years. Has no known grave. Commemorated **CAMBRAI MEMORIAL TO THE MISSING.** ROH:- Huddersfield Parish Church; Huddersfield GPO; Huddersfield Drill Hall.

HINCHCLIFFE, SAM. Private. No 305638. 1/7th Battalion Duke of Wellington's Regiment. Lived Holmbridge. Killed in action, 18.9.1916. Has no known grave. Commemorated **THIEPVAL MEMORIAL TO THE MISSING.** ROH:- Holme and Holmbridge War Memorial; Huddersfield Drill Hall; memorial in Hade Edge Burial Ground.

HINCHLIFF, IRVIN. Private. No DM2/134734. 913th Motor Transport Company, Army Service Corps. Born Cowcliffe, Huddersfield, 15.7.1893. Son of Albert and Louisa Hinchliff, 75 Netheroyd Hill Road, Huddersfield. Educated at Cowcliffe Schools. Employed as a textile worker. Single. Enlisted October 1915. Died in Salonica of malaria and influenza at No 49 Casualty Clearing Station, 17.7.1919, aged 25 years. Buried **BRALO BRITISH CEMETERY.** Grave No 97. (Brother of Private **JOE HINCHLIFF**, died in East Africa, 7.12.1918, q.v.). ROH:- St. Hilda's Church, Cowcliffe; Fartown and Birkby War Memorial.

HINCHLIFF, JOE. Private. No DM2/171355. Army Service Corps. Born Cowcliffe, Huddersfield, 23.6.1889. Son of Albert and Louisa Hinchliff, 75 Netheroyd Hill Road, Huddersfield. Educated at Cowcliffe and Hillhouse schools. Employed as a textile worker. Enlisted 6.5.1916. Died at Port Amelia, East Africa, of malaria, 7.12.1918, aged 29. Buried **PEMBA CEMETERY, MOZAMBIQUE.** Grave location:- C, 1. (Brother of Private **IRVIN HINCHLIFF**, died in Salonica, 17.1.1919, q.v.). ROH:- Fartown and Birkby War Memorial; St, Hilda's Church, Cowcliffe, Huddersfield.

HINCHLIFFE, CHARLES ERNEST, MM. 2nd Lieutenant. 4th Battalion King's Own Yorkshire Light Infantry. Born Sunset Terrace, Birkby, 22.1.1894. Son of Charles and Mary E. Hinchliffe, 13 Alexandra Road, Lindley. Husband of Hildred Hinchliffe, 4 King's Road, Guildford. Educated Spring Grove Council School and Huddersfield Technical College. Employed as an assistant woollen designer. Enlisted as a Private in the 8th Battalion Duke of Wellington's Regiment. Served in Egypt and Gallipoli. Killed in action near Rheims, 20.7.1918, aged 24 years. Has no known grave. Commemorated on the **SOISSONS MEMORIAL TO THE MISSING.**

HINCHLIFFE, CHARLES GODFREY. Guardsman. No 13956. Coldstream Guards. Born Gunthwaite, near Penistone. Son of the late Wright Hinchcliffe and Elizabeth Town (formerly Hinchcliffe), of Upper Denby. Killed in action, 19.6.1917, aged 23. Buried **ARTILLERY WOOD CEMETERY.** Grave location:- Plot 7, Row C, Grave 14. ROH:- Denby Dale and Cumberworth War Memorial.

HINCHLIFFE, FRANK. Private. No 5403. 2/5th Battalion Duke of Wellington's Regiment. Born Holmbridge, Holmfirth, 22.8.1891. Son of Ben and Mary Hinchcliffe, 4 Dewhurst Road, Fartown, Huddersfield. Educated Holmbridge Parish Church Schools. Employed by Mr Boothroyd, baker and confectioner, of Fartown Bar as a van driver. Enlisted January 1916. Killed in action at Beaumont Hamel, 14.2.1917, aged 25 years. Buried **AUCHONVILLERS MILITARY CEMETERY.** Grave location:- Plot 2, Row K, Grave 8. ROH:- Christ Church, Woodhouse Hill; Huddersfield Drill Hall; Fartown and Birkby War Memorial.

HINCHLIFFE, HAROLD. Private. No 241910. 2/5th Battalion Duke of Wellington's Regiment. Born Honley. Son of Alfred and Annie Hinchliffe, 5 Cross Street, Honley. Attended the Honley Primitive Methodist Sunday School and Church. Was secretary for Honley Musical Festival, the Adult bible class, Grey's orchestral band and the Rechabite Sick Club. Employed by Thornton's of Honley. He was fatally wounded in the same battle as his younger brother, Drummer **LEWIS HINCHLIFFE**, was wounded. They each tended the other's injuries and the Drummer was conveyed to hospital unaware of Harold's death. Died of wounds, 4.5.1917, aged 28 years.

Buried **ACHIET-LE-GRAND COMMUNAL CEMETERY EXTENSION**. Grave location:- Plot 1, Row E, Grave 24; ROH:- Huddersfield Drill Hall; Honley War Memorial.

HINCHLIFFE, HENRY (HARRY). Private. No 95059. Posted 2/4th Battalion London Regiment Royal Fusiliers. Formerly No 37323 Durham Light Infantry. Born Golcar. Youngest son of Mrs Martha Hinchliffe, 44 Spring Mill, Milnsbridge. Prior to enlistment, was employed as a teaser by Messrs George Thomas and Sons, Dale Street Mills, Longwood. Enlisted 1916. Killed in action, 9.8.1918, aged 25 years. Has no known grave. Commemorated **VIS-en-ARTOIS MEMORIAL TO THE MISSING**. ROH:- Milnsbridge War Memorial.

HINCHLIFFE, IRVINE. Private. No CH/1481(S). Royal Marine Light Infantry, 1st Royal Marine Battalion Royal Naval Division. Son of Joe and Annie Hinchliffe, Greenfield Road, Holmfirth. Employed as a shop assistant at the Holmfirth branch of Messrs Wallaces Limited. Enlisted February 1916. Went over to France in September, 1916. Killed in action at Beaumont Hamel, 16.2.1917, aged 20 years. Buried **ANCRE BRITISH CEMETERY**. Grave location:- Plot 7, Row C, Grave 19. The Rev. J. F. Beamish, of Upperthong, made enquiries and received a letter from the Rev. W. Whitehead, Chaplain to the forces, who wrote, *'I have seen the Sergeant of his company and I am informed that as he was going to the trenches on the night of February 14th the path was shelled and he was hit on the head by a piece of explosive shell. He was taken to the dressing station where he passed away. His comrades thought at the time that he was killed outright so I think his mother may rest assured that though he lingered several hours he was unconscious and could not feel any pain or suffering. He has been buried in the soldier's cemetery near the dressing station. The church service was said and his grave marked and on it there will be placed a wooden cross with his name and regiment so that when the war is over there should be no difficulty in finding the place.'* ROH:- Holmfirth War Memorial.

HINCHLIFFE, J. Private. No 29/838. 33rd Battalion Northumberland Fusiliers. Son of Mrs Clara Hinchliffe, of Lane Head Hill, Honley. Died of sickness, 15.8.1916, aged 38 years. Buried **HONLEY CHURCH BURIAL GROUND**. Grave location:- 61, 3711. ROH:- Honley War Memorial.

HINCHLIFFE, JACK. Gunner. No L/25686. 'D' Battery, 84th Brigade Royal Field Artillery. Born Allen Row, Paddock, 30.7.1895. Son of Mr and Mrs Job Hinchliffe, 211 Marsden Road, Brierley Wood, Huddersfield. Educated Crosland Moor Council School. Employed as a woollen weaver. Single. Enlisted April 1915. Wounded in the head, 9.9.1917. Died of his wounds, 15.9.1917, aged 22 years. Buried **DOZINGHEM MILITARY CEMETERY**. Grave location:- Plot 8, Row B, Grave 17. ROH:- Crosland Moor Wesleyan Church.

HINCHLIFFE, JAMES ALFRED. Acting Sergeant. No 67000. 92nd Battery, Royal Field Artillery. Born 9 Birkby Hall Road, Birkby, 11.3.1891. Lived with his Aunt, Mrs Thorpe, at 11 Birkby Hall Road, Birkby. Educated Hillhouse Board School. Employed as a porter at Huddersfield Railway Station. Enlisted in the army in August, 1911. Served in the Dardenelles. Killed in action, 12.4.1917, aged 26. Buried **TILLOY BRITISH CEMETERY**. Grave location:- Plot 4, Row B, Grave 9. ROH:- Fartown and Birkby War Memorial; commemorated on his parents' headstone in Edgerton Cemetery.

HINCHLIFFE, JOHN. Private. No 235191. 2/7th Battalion West Yorkshire Regiment. Born Highroyd, Honley, 6.10.1878. Son of the late William and Sarah Ann Hinchliffe. Lived 229 Rose Cottages, Yews Hill Road, Lockwood. Educated at Newsome Church School and Armitage Bridge Church of England School. Employed as a cloth finisher by Messrs Crowther and Vickerman at Crosland Moor Bottom. Played cricket with the Hall Bower team. Was a member of the Newsome Adult School. Married. Enlisted November 1916. Wounded at Bullecourt, 3.5.1917. Killed in action, 16.3.1918, aged 39 years. Buried **ROCLINCOURT MILITARY CEMETERY**. Grave location:- Plot 6, Row A, Grave 13. ROH:- St. John's Church, Newsome; St. Stephen's Church, Rashcliffe.

HINCHLIFFE, KENNETH. Private. No 29318. 8th Battalion King's Own (Royal Lancaster Regiment). Born Holmfirth. Son of Walter and Lucy Hinchliffe, of West Gorton, Manchester. Was the grandson of the late Mr Joah Swallow of New

Mill. Attended Cliffe Sunday School, Holmfirth, and was a member of the gymnasium class. Employed by Messrs John Woodhead, Albion Mills, Thongsbridge. Killed in action, 23.8.1918, aged 18. Buried **DOUCHY-LES-AYETTE BRITISH CEMETERY.** Grave location:- Plot 1, Row B, Grave 4. ROH:- Memorial in Christ Church Churchyard, New Mill.

HINCHLIFFE, LOUIS. Private. No 41529. 1/5th Battalion West Yorkshire Regiment. Born Huddersfield. Youngest son of Mr and Mrs George Hinchliffe, 10 Barlboro Place, Scar Lane, Milnsbridge. Was a cornet player in the Milnsbridge Socalist Brass Band. Attended St. Michael's Mission Church. Employed by Messrs Joseph Dyson and Sons, Milnsbridge. Enlisted September 1916. Embarked for France on New Years Day, 1917. In March, 1917, he was brought to Bradford wounded and suffering from trench feet. He returned to France on 7.6.1917. Was reported missing, presumed killed, 9.10.1917. Buried **DOCHY FARM NEW BRITISH CEMETERY, LANGEMARCK, BELGIUM.** Grave location:- Plot 1, Row E, Grave 28. ROH:- Longwood War Memorial; St. John's Church, Golcar.

HINCHLIFFE, NORMAN. Private. No 99533. 6th Battalion The King's (Liverpool Regiment). Born Holmfirth. Son of Harry and Emma Hinchliffe, 29 Upperthong, Holmfirth. Educated Upperthong National School. Was a member of the choir at Lane Congregational Church and was an old scholar of Upperthong Sunday School. Was employed as an apprentice in the bakehouse of Messrs Dawson and Birch. Enlisted July 1917. Embarked for France in April, 1918. Died of wounds at No 6 Casualty Clearing Station, 8.9.1918, aged 19 years. Buried **PERNES BRITISH CEMETERY.** Grave location:- Plot 6, Row B, Grave 3. ROH:- Upperthong War Memorial.

HINCHLIFFE, RANDEL. Lance Corporal. No 22975. 8th Battalion Duke of Wellington's Regiment. Born Holmbridge. Son of John and Sarah Hinchliffe, of Stubbin, Holmbridge. Prior to enlistment, had served in the Wakefield police force and had also been an attendant at Storths Hall Asylum. He had also worked for Messrs J. Watkinson and Sons Limited, Washpit Mills. Married. Arrived in France 19.12.1916.

Killed in action, 29.12.1916, aged 23 years. Has no known grave. Commemorated **THIEPVAL MEMORIAL TO THE MISSING.** ROH:- Holme and Holmbridge War Memorial; memorial in St. David's Churchyard.

HINCHLIFFE, WILLIE. Gunner. No 152570. 'C' Battery, 223rd Brigade Royal Field Artillery. Born Holmfirth. Educated Hade Edge Council School and also attended Choppards Sunday School. Employed by Messrs J. Watkinson and Sons Limited, Washpit Mills. Lived Arrunden Wood Nook. Was a member of Cartworth Moor Cricket Club. Married in 1913. Enlisted 7.8.1916. Embarked for France on 24.4.1917. Was wounded in the back, 31.10.1917. Died of wounds at No 4 Casualty Clearing Station, 1.11.1917, aged 29 years. Buried **DOZINGHEM MILITARY CEMETERY.** Grave location:- Plot 12, Row D, Grave 15. A member of the hospital staff wrote to Gunner Hinchliffe's wife, *'I have regret in writing to confirm the death of No 152570 Gunner W. Hinchliffe of the R.F.A. in this hospital on the 1st inst. He was admitted on October 31st so badly wounded in the back that there was no chance of his recovery. Everything possible was done for him during the short time he was under our care but he gradually became weaker and passed away at 7am on 1.11.1917. He didn't appear to suffer at all and was conscious almost to the end. With sincerest sympathy - C.M. Roy.'* ROH:- Cartworth War Memorial.

HINDLE, SAM. Guardsman. No 27640. No 1 Company, 4th Battalion Grenadier Guards. Born Kirkburton. Eldest son of Lydia Ann Hindle, of Lee Lane, Kirkburton, and the late Albert Hindle. Prior to enlistment, was employed as a spinning overlooker by Messrs A. Crabtree and Company, Springfield Mills, Kirkburton. Was a member of the Kirkburton Liberal Club. Enlisted November 1916. Embarked for France in June, 1917. Killed in action, 2.8.1917, aged 19 years. Buried **ARTILLERY WOOD CEMETERY, BOESINGHE, BELGIUM.** Grave location:- Plot 11, Row A, Grave 13. ROH:- All Hallows Parish Church, Kirkburton; commemorated on headstone in Kirkburton Churchyard.

HIRST, ADAM ALFRED. Private. No 22458. 2nd Battalion East Lancashire Regiment. Formerly No 2051 King's Own Yorkshire

Light Infantry. Born Sharlston, Yorkshire. Son of Enos and Martha Hirst of 'Ladcar', Emley Moor, Huddersfield. Lived Shelley, Huddersfield. Reported missing, presumed killed, 31.7.1917, aged 31 years. Has no known grave. Commemorated **MENIN GATE MEMORIAL TO THE MISSING.** ROH:- Emley War Memorial; commemorated in Emley Churchyard.

HIRST, ALBERT. Private. No 64593. 25th (Tyneside Irish) Battalion Northumberland Fusiliers. Formerly No 43936 The Yorkshire Regiment. Born 86 Back Whitehead Lane, Huddersfield, 1.3.1899. Son of John William and Emma Hirst, 2 Hopkinson's Yard, Lockwood Road, Huddersfield. Educated Rashcliffe Church of England Elementary School. Attended Buxton Road Sunday School. Employed by Mrs T. H. Smith, pork butcher, of Folly Hall, Huddersfield. Single. Enlisted 10.4.1917. Embarked for France three weeks before he died. Died of gas poisoning at 5th General Hospital, Leicester, 13.4.1918, aged 19 years. Buried **LOCKWOOD CEMETERY, HUDDERSFIELD.** Grave location:- C, 'C', 672. ROH:- St. Stephen's Church, Rashcliffe.

HIRST, AMOS. Private. No 31711. 13th (1st Barnsley Pals) Battalion York and Lancaster Regiment. Born Slaithwaite. Son of the late Mr and Mrs James Hirst, Potters, Slaithwaite. Was well known in Slaithwaite amongst the local farmers and cattle dealers, being for many years a right hand man for Mr Levi Tweed, of Scammonden, in the cattle trade. He had also worked as a weaver for Messrs. Crowther, Bruce and Company, of Marsden. Single. Had been in France for two months when he died from shell wounds on 14.11.1916, aged 39 years. Has no known grave. Commemorated **THIEPVAL MEMORIAL TO THE MISSING.** ROH:- St. James Church, Slaithwaite; Slaithwaite War Memorial; Pole Moor Baptist Church.

HIRST, ARNOLD. Private. No 12500. 9th Battalion Duke of Wellington's Regiment. Born Milnsbridge. Son of Mr and Mrs H. Hirst, 15 Dowker Street, Milnsbridge. Lived with his sister at 99 Whitehead Lane, Primrose Hill, Huddersfield. Prior to enlistment, was employed as a chain maker by Messrs. Learoyd Brothers and Company at Trafalgar Mills, Leeds Road, Huddersfield. Attended the Young Men's Class at St. Thomas's Church, Longroyd Bridge. Enlisted September, 1914, and embarked for France in June, 1915. Came home on leave at Christmas, 1915. Died of wounds, 12.11.1916, aged 20 years. Buried **St. SEVER CEMETERY EXTENSION, ROUEN.** Grave Location:- Block O, Plot 1, Row P, Grave 6. ROH:- Huddersfield Parish Church; Learoyd Brothers; Longwood War Memorial.

HIRST, ARTHUR BOOTHROYD. Private. No 4255. 1/5th Battalion Duke of Wellington's Regiment. Born Deighton, Huddersfield, 1883. Son of Harry Boothroyd Hirst, Brick Bank, Northgate, Huddersfield. Educated Deighton Council School. Employed as a labourer. Married. Lived 4 Stott's Buildings, Upperhead Row, Huddersfield. Enlisted 1915. Killed in action, 12.7.1916. Has no known grave. Commemorated **THIEPVAL MEMORIAL TO THE MISSING.**

HIRST, BEN ALLEN. Private. No 0505. 'D' Company, 1st Battalion Hampshire Regiment. Son of Thomas and Mary Ethel Hirst, of Owen's Terrace, Honley. Died of sickness at home, 17.3.1920, aged 20 years. Buried **HONLEY CHURCH BURIAL GROUND.** Grave location;- 37, 1442. ROH:- Honley War Memorial.

HIRST, EDGAR BRAMLEY. Sapper. No 312424. Fifth Army H.Q. Signal Company, Royal Engineers. Born Delph Terrace, Linthwaite, 26.9.1892. Son of Arthur Edward and Frances Mary Hirst, 2 Oakes Road, Lindley. Educated Linthwaite Church of England School and Huddersfield Technical College. Employed as a twist frame overlooker. Single. Enlisted 17.3.1916. Killed in action near Ypres, 17.11.1917, aged 25. Buried **BARD COTTAGE CEMETERY, BOESINGHE.** Grave location:- Plot 5, Row C, Grave 3. ROH:- St. Stephen's Church, Lindley.

HIRST, FRANK. Air Mechanic 1st Class. No 38401. H.Q. (France) Royal Air Force. Born Taylor Hill, Huddersfield, 21.5.1897. Son of Edith and the late Willie Hirst, 2 Mellor's Buildings, Stoney Lane, Taylor Hill. Educated Mount Pleasant Council School. Employed as a motor driver by Messrs Kaye and Stewart. Single. Enlisted 20.7.1916. Came home on leave from France and contracted pneumonia on the journey. Died in Royds Hall Military Hospital,

17.2.1919, aged 21 years. Buried **LOCKWOOD CEMETERY.** Grave location:- A, 462. ROH:- Emmanuel Church, Lockwood; Taylor Hill Primitive Methodist Church.

HIRST, FRANK. Private. No 4810. 56th Battalion Australian Imperial Forces. Born Huddersfield 8.6.1886. Son of J. W. and M. J. Hirst, Yorke House, 18 Norman Avenue, Birkby, Huddersfield. Educated at Spring Grove Council and Hillhouse Schools. Was living in Sydney, New South Wales, Australia, at the time of enlistment. Was employed as an electrician. Killed in action, 1.9.1918, aged 32 years. Buried **PERONNE COMMUNAL CEMETERY AND EXTENSION.** Grave location:- Plot 4, Row E, Grave 9. (Brother of Private **HARRY HIRST,** killed in action, 10.11.1918, q.v.). ROH:- Fartown and Birkby War Memorial.

HIRST, FRED. Private. No 3/20320. 2nd Battalion Duke of Wellington's Regiment. Born Kirkburton. Lived Cinder Hill, Kirkburton. Died of wounds, 10.4.1917, aged 26 years. Buried **St. NICOLAS BRITISH CEMETERY, ARRAS.** Grave location:- Plot 1, Row D, Grave 11. ROH:- All Hallows Parish Church, Kirkburton.

HIRST, FRED. Private. No 32736. 8th Battalion York and Lancaster Regiment. Formerly No 22824 Duke of Wellington's Regiment. Born Meltham. Son of George and Mary Hirst, Woodbine Terrace, Spark Green, Meltham. Reported missing, presumed killed, 11.10.1917, aged 27 years. Has no known grave. Commemorated **TYNE COT MEMORIAL TO THE MISSING.** ROH:- St. Bartholomew's Church, Meltham; Helme Parish Church.

HIRST, FRED. Private. No 5/241361. 1/5th Battalion Duke of Wellington's Regiment. Son of Sarah Ann Hirst, 55 Station Road, Brockholes, Huddersfield. Attended Brockholes Wesleyan Chapel. Employed by Messrs Robinson, Smithy Place, Brockholes. Enlisted at the beginning of 1916. Killed in action, 3.9.1916, aged 19 years. Buried **CONNAUGHT CEMETERY, THIEPVAL.** Grave location; Plot 1, Row C. Grave 26. ROH:- Huddersfield Drill Hall; Honley War Memorial.

HIRST, FRED. Private. No 41932. 2 Platoon, 'A' Company, 7th Battalion Leicestershire Regiment. Born Skelmanthorpe, Huddersfield. Son of Jere and Clara Hirst, 16 Parkside, Scholes. Prior to enlistment, was employed by Messrs Vickerman Limited, Thongsbridge. Enlisted Easter, 1917, and embarked for France at Easter 1918. Reported missing near Rheims, 27.5.1918, aged 19 years. Has no known grave. Commemorated **SOISSONS MEMORIAL TO THE MISSING.** ROH:- Fulstone War Memorial.

HIRST, FREDERICK GEORGE. Private. No 31245. 2nd Battalion Duke of Wellington's Regiment. Born Fieldhouse, Huddersfield, 18.6.1893. Son of Seth and Margaret Hirst, 9 Ashbrow Road, Fartown. Educated Deighton Council School. Employed as a packing case maker by Mr. T.A. Cockin, Waterloo Mills, Huddersfield. Single. Enlisted 18.3.1917. Killed in action near Arras, 31.8.1918, aged 25 years. Buried **VIS-en-ARTOIS BRITISH CEMETERY.** Grave location:- Plot 1, Row A, Grave 39. ROH:- Sheepridge Providence United Methodist Sunday School; Christ Church, Woodhouse Hill; Fartown and Birkby War Memorial.

HIRST, GEORGE. Private. No 47514. 26th (Tyneside Irish) Battalion Northumberland Fusiliers. Born Thurstonland. Son of Frank Hirst of Thurstonland. Husband of E. A. M. Hirst, 2 The Avenue, Moldgreen. A keen cricket player. Had been a professional for Meltham, Skelmanthorpe and other clubs and had also played for Almondbury. Prior to enlistment, was employed as a french polisher by Messrs Taylor and Hobson of Huddersfield. Died of wounds at No 24 Casualty Clearing Station on 9.4.1917, aged 38 years. Buried **AUBIGNY COMMUNAL CEMETERY EXTENSION.** Grave location:- Plot 1, Row L, Grave 5. ROH:- Thurstonland War Memorial; Moldgreen War Memorial.

HIRST, GEORGE. Rifleman. No S/28212. 10th Battalion The Rifle Brigade. Born Holmfirth. Son of Tom and Annie Hirst, of Longley, Holmfirth. Killed in action at the Battle of Cambrai, 27.11.1917, aged 21 years. Has no known grave. Commemorated **CAMBRAI MEMORIAL TO THE MISSING.** ROH:- Hade Edge War Memorial.

HIRST, HAROLD. Private. No 6655. 1/7th Battalion Duke of Wellington's Regiment. Born Meltham. Son of Charles Richard and Annie Hirst, of School Hill, Meltham. Killed in action

19.1.1917, aged 23 years. Buried **BERLES NEW MILITARY CEMETERY.** Grave location:- Plot 1, Row C, Grave 3. ROH:- St. Bartholomew's Church, Meltham.

HIRST, HAROLD. Private. No 241784. 2/5th Battalion Duke of Wellington's Regiment. Born South Crosland, Huddersfield. Son of Edward and Hannah Hirst, 3 Manse Side, Marsden. Prior to enlistment was employed by Messrs Crowther, Bruce and Company Limited as a weaver. Was a member of the Marsden Conservative Club and attended St. Bartholomew's Church. Enlisted March 1916. Embarked for France in January, 1917. Reported missing at the Battle of Bullecourt, 3.5.1917. Has no known grave. Commemorated **ARRAS MEMORIAL TO THE MISSING.** ROH:- Huddersfield Drill Hall; Marsden War Memorial; memorial in Marsden Churchyard.

HIRST, HARRY. Guardsman. No 24348. 2nd Battalion Coldstream Guards. Born Springwood Street, Huddersfield, 3.1.1883. Son of J. W. and M. J. Hirst, Yorke House, Norman Avenue, Birkby. Educated Spring Grove Council School. Employed as a licensed victualler in Leeds. Husband of A. M. Hirst of 'Blooming Rose Inn', Leeds. Enlisted 1917. Killed in action, 10.11.1918. Buried **VILLERS-POL COMMUNAL CEMETERY EXTENSION.** Grave location:- Row I, Grave 5. (Brother of Private **FRANK HIRST,** killed in action 1.9.1918, q.v.). ROH:- Fartown and Birkby War Memorial.

HIRST, HARRY. Private. No 242671. 1/5th Battalion King's Own Yorkshire Light Infantry. Formerly No 3880 3/7th Battalion Duke of Wellington's Regiment. Born 85 Back Morecambe Terrace, Huddersfield 12.8.1896. Son of John and Ann Hirst, 5 Cowcliffe Hill Road, Birkby. Educated at Lowerhouses National School, Huddersfield Parish Church School and St. Andrew's School. Was a member of Woodhouse Church Young Men's Bible Class. Employed as a motor driver by Messrs Shaws Limited of Moldgreen. Single Enlisted 19.2.1916. Was gassed on one occasion. Killed in action at Passchendaele, 21.10.1917, aged 21 years. Has no known grave. Commemorated **TYNE COT MEMORIAL TO THE MISSING.** ROH:- Christ Church, Woodhouse Hill; Fartown and Birkby War Memorial.

HIRST, HARRY. Private. No 24893. 8th Battalion Duke of Wellington's Regiment. Born 57 Dale Street, Huddersfield, 20.1.1897. Son of Arthur and Amelia Hirst, 47 Manchester Road, Huddersfield. Educated St. Paul's Church of England School, Huddersfield. Employed as an upholsterer by Mr Harry Roebuck of Aspley. Attended Buxton Road Wesleyan Sunday School. Enlisted 9.10.1916. Was killed in action exactly one year later, on 9.10.1917, aged 19. Buried **NEW IRISH FARM CEMETERY, BELGIUM.** Grave location:- Plot 21, Row A, Grave 9. ROH:- High Street United Methodist Church.

HIRST, HARRY. Private. No 37962. 2nd Battalion York and Lancaster Regiment. Youngest son of Mr Wyndham Hirst, 2 Barlboro Place, Scar Lane, Milnsbridge. Educated Crow Lane Board School, Milnsbridge. Had attended the Milnsbridge Baptist Church and Sunday School and also Scapegoat Hill Baptist Chapel. Employed as a beamer by Messrs Whitwam and Company, Ramsden Mill, Linthwaite. Enlisted June 1916. Embarked for France in September, 1916. Killed in action, 21.3.1918, aged 25 years. Has no known grave. Commemorated **ARRAS MEMORIAL TO THE MISSING.** ROH:- St. John's Church, Golcar; Crow Lane Board School, Milnsbridge; Milnsbridge War Memorial.

HIRST, HARRY. Private. No 33513. 185th Company, Machine Gun Corps. Formerly No 4606 Duke of Wellington's Regiment. Born Holmfirth. Son of Mr and Mrs Wright Hirst, Lane End, Holmfirth. Educated Hade Edge Council School. Attended Cartworth Moor Wesleyan Sunday School. Played cricket for the Cartworth Moor Cricket Club. Employed as a motor driver at the Victoria Mill, Lockwood. Had been in hospital with dysentery at Secundurabad, India, where his doctor was from Holmfirth, the ward orderly was a Lindley soldier and the nurse was from Oughtibridge. Died on board *HM Hospital Ship Kalyon* during the evening of Sunday, 28.4.1918. Buried **PIETA MILITARY CEMETERY, MALTA.** Grave location:- Plot C, Row 17, Grave 1. His parents received the following letter from the Rev. Arthur Outram, Chaplain to the Forces, giving details of Harry's last hours, *'Your son Harry was brought on board with very little chance of getting through but still there was a chance that he might get home in time to see you all which he was very* *anxious to do. However this was not to be and in spite of all the doctors, Sister and Orderlies did he passed peacefully away on the evening of the 28th April. He was just as well off for comfort on board as on land and he did not suffer you will be glad to know. He simply was tired out and wearying to go. He sent his love to you all and asked me to tell you he was quite ready to go 'home'. He was buried with full military honours at Malta as we happened to call there.'* ROH:- Holmfirth War Memorial.

HIRST, HARRY ATKINSON. Private. No 3/15217. Lincolnshire Regiment. Born Huddersfield 1879. Lived 5 Benson's Square, Northumberland Street, Huddersfield. Discharged from the army due to illness on 15.5.1916. Died of valvular disease of the heart on 8.10.1921.

HIRST, HARRY LAWRENCE. Private. No 32645. 10th Battalion Durham Light Infantry. Born Meltham, Huddersfield. Son of Mrs Hirst, Upper Mount, Meltham, and the late Mr Joe Hirst who was a well known local cricketer. Played cricket with the Meltham and Meltham Mills teams. Killed in action, 27.9.1917, aged 36 years. Buried **MESSINES RIDGE CEMETERY.** Grave location:- Plot 5, Row A, Grave 33. ROH:- St. Bartholomew's Church, Meltham.

HIRST, HENRY (HARRY). Private. No 4495. 3/5th Battalion Duke of Wellington's Regiment. Born Marsden. Lived 5 Gladstone Buildings, Marsden. Employed as a dyer's labourer by Mr J. E. Crowther at Ready Carr Mills. Was a member of the Marsden Socalist Club and of the Marsden Cricket Club. Married, with one child. Was home on leave at Christmas, 1915. Died of pneumonia at Clipstone Camp, 3.1.1916, aged 41 years. Buried with full military honours at **ST. BARTHOLOMEW'S PARISH CHURCHYARD, MARSDEN.** Grave location:- South, 29, 5. ROH:- Marsden War Memorial.

HIRST, HENRY, MM MSM. Sergeant. No 307747. 1/7th Battalion Duke of Wellington's Regiment. Son of Mary Hannah Hirst, 158 Woodbridge Road, Holmbridge. Attended Holmbridge Church and Sunday School, where he was a sidesman and a teacher. Played both cricket and football for the local teams. Employed as a weaver at Clarence Mills, Holmbridge. Enlisted August 1914. Embarked for France in April, 1915. Awarded the MM. Killed in action, 28.4.1918, aged 28 years. Has no known grave. Commemorated **TYNE COT MEMORIAL TO THE MISSING.** His cousin, Private Hirst Naylor wrote, *'It is hard for me to write these few lines. It is to tell you that Henry got killed and I did not want to be the first to break the news to you but I think it is my duty to let you know because we have been like brothers out here. I can tell you I shall miss him and only God knows how I feel it but we never know whose turn it is next. He has given his life fighting for the right and I can tell you he was one of the best N.C.O's in the battalion and everyone liked him. I was with him the night before he went into the line and he was as happy as ever.'* ROH:- Holme and Holmbridge War Memorial; Huddersfield Drill Hall.

HIRST, HERBERT. Private. No 25208. 10th Battalion Duke of Wellington's Regiment. Born Colne Bridge, Huddersfield. Son of Mr and Mrs Fred Hirst, 6 Whittaker Street, Deighton. Employed by Messrs John Lee Walker and Sons Limited, Woodhouse Mills. Single. Killed in action at Passchendaele, 20.9.1917, aged 19 years. Has no known grave. Commemorated **TYNE COT MEMORIAL TO THE MISSING.** ROH:- Deighton War Memorial.

HIRST, HILDRED. Private. No 64097. 1st Battalion West Yorkshire Regiment. Son of Arthur and Mary Hirst, Eastwood Mount, Marsden. Employed in the weft department at Bank Bottom Mills, Marsden. Attended Marsden Wesleyan Church and Adult School. Enlisted February 1918. Embarked for France 15.8.1918. Reported missing, 17.9.1918, aged 18. Buried **CHAPELLE BRITISH CEMETERY, HOLNON** Grave location:- Plot 2, Row E, Grave 14. *On December 20th, 1918, his parents received their son's pocket book from a fellow soldier, who was in hospital in Leeds, with the news that Private Hirst was killed in action by a machine gun bullet at St. Quentin on 17.9.1918. Mr and Mrs Hirst went to see the wounded soldier in hospital and learned from him that the pocket book was found on the battlefield near to Private Hirst whose body was lying in a shellhole. His name and address were written inside and he had no doubt as to the identity of the deceased as he was a personal friend of his.* ROH:- Marsden War Memorial.

HIRST, HUBERT IRVIN. Private. No 5360. 2/5th Battalion Duke of Wellington's Regiment. Born Golcar. Son of Mitchell Hirst, 13 West End Road, Golcar. Employed by Messrs Pearson Brothers at Victoria Mills, Golcar. Was a member of Golcar Conservative Club. Enlisted 27.3.1916. Embarked for France at the beginning of January 1917. Killed in action, 14.2.1917, aged 21 years. Buried **AUCHONVILLERS MILITARY CEMETERY.** Grave location:- Plot 2, Row K, Grave 7. ROH:- St. John's Church, Golcar; Huddersfield Drill Hall.

HIRST, HUMPHREY. Private. No 43084. 200th Area Employment Company, Labour Corps. Formerly 9th Battalion King's Own Yorkshire Light Infantry. Born Linthwaite, Huddersfield. Son of Seth Hirst, 105 Albert Terrace, Linthwaite. Employed as a weaver at Platt Mill, Slaithwaite. Was a member of Linthwaite Hall Cricket Club and attended Slaithwaite Church. Enlisted May 1916. Died of a cerebral haemorrhage at Rouen Base Hospital, 7.8.1918, aged 28 years. Buried **St. SEVER CEMETERY EXTENSION.** Grave location:- Block Q, Plot 3, Row M, Grave 2. ROH:- Linthwaite War Memorial; St. James Church, Slaithwaite.

HIRST, JOE. Private. No 13004. 2nd Battalion Duke of Wellington's Regiment. Born Paddock 13.2.1883. Educated All Saints Church of England School, Paddock. Employed as a spinner by Messrs J. Rayner and Company Limited, Turnbridge, Huddersfield. At the time of enlistment, was living at 56 Lower Brow Road, Paddock. Married, with three children. Enlisted 8.8.1914. Killed in action, 28.3.1915. Has no known grave. Commemorated **MENIN GATE MEMORIAL TO THE MISSING.** ROH:- All Saints Church, Paddock.

HIRST, JOHN. Private. No 14908. 2nd Battalion Duke of Wellington's Regiment. Lived Round Close, Hade Edge, Holmfirth. Married, with three children. Known locally as 'Jack O' Dodds'. Employed in the teasing department at Washpit Mills. Killed in action at Flers, 9.10.1916, aged 32 years. Has no known grave. Commemorated **THIEPVAL MEMORIAL TO THE MISSING.** ROH:- Hade Edge War Memorial.

HIRST, JOHN. Private. No 41457. 26th (Tyneside Irish) Battalion Northumberland Fusiliers. Formerly No 19621 Duke of Wellington's Regiment. Son of the late Eli Hirst of Upperthong. Brother of Lucy Hirst, 26 Upperthong, Holmfirth. Employed at Spring Lane Mills. Enlisted in the Spring of 1916 and went into training at North Shields. Three months later he crossed to France. Killed in action, 23.4.1917, aged 29 years. Has no known grave. Commemorated **ARRAS MEMORIAL TO THE MISSING.** ROH:- Upperthong War Memorial.

HIRST, JOSEPH ALLEN. Private. No 32341. 7th Battalion North Staffordshire Regiment. Born Schofield's Buildings, Quarmby Road, Lindley, 17.3.1885. Son of George Hirst, 3 Park Road West, Crosland Moor. His mother died when he was seven years old. Educated Longwood Church of England School. Attended All Saints Church, Paddock and sang in the choir. Employed as a painter and decorator by Mr John Littlewood of Berry Brow. Husband of Edith Ann Hirst, (Later Ramsden), 3 Park Road West, Crosland Moor. Enlisted November 1916. Died of heat stroke in Mesopotamia, 20.7.1917, aged 32 years. Buried **BAGHDAD (NORTH GATE) WAR CEMETERY.** Grave location:- 19, J, 11. ROH:-. St. Mark's Parish Church, Longwood; All Saints Church, Paddock; St. Barnabas Church, Crosland Moor; United Methodist Church, Crosland Moor.

HIRST, LEONARD. Private. No 39590. 9th Battalion King's Own Yorkshire Light Infantry. Born Lindley, Huddersfield. Son of Alfred Hirst, Vicarage Road, Longwood. Husband of Emma Hirst, 336 Scar Lane, Golcar. Employed by Messrs Smiths, Plover Mills, Lindley. Was a member of the Longwood Church choir. Played cricket for Golcar Cricket Club. Reported missing, presumed killed, 4.10.1917, aged 25 years. Has no known grave. Commemorated **TYNE COT MEMORIAL TO THE MISSING.** ROH:- St. Mark's Parish Church, Longwood.

HIRST, LEWIS. Private. No 24667. 9th Battalion Duke of Wellington's Regiment. Lived Upperthong, Holmfirth. Worked as a plasterer on his own account. Married, with three children. Had been in France for five weeks when he was killed in action on 1.2.1917, aged 35 years. Has no known grave. Commemorated **THIEPVAL MEMORIAL TO THE MISSING.** ROH:- Upperthong War Memorial; St. Bartholomew's Church, Meltham; Marsden Conservative Club.

HIRST, LEWIS. Private. No 41842. 8th Battalion The Cameronians (Scottish Rifles). Formerly No 4331 Highland Light Infantry. Born New Mill, Holmfirth. Son of Mr and Mrs Aaron Hirst, Scholes Moor. Attended Hepworth Church Sunday School. Was a member of Hepworth Silver Prize Band. A keen cyclist. Employed by Messrs Wagstaffe and Turner, builders and contractors. Enlisted on the Thursday of Easter week, 1916. Trained in London. Served for a time in Ireland and crossed to France in August, 1917. Suffered from trench feet and came back to England for treatment. Returned to France on 10.9.1918. Killed in action, 14.10.1918, aged 22 years. Buried **HOOGE CRATER CEMETERY.** Grave location:- Plot 20, Row D, Grave 14. ROH:- Hepworth and Scholes War Memorial; Hepworth Church.

HIRST, NORMAN. Engineer Sub-Lieutenant. Royal Naval Reserve. Royal Garrison Artillery. *HMS Reliance*. Born Huddersfield 29.4.1879. Son of Joseph and Lucy Ann Hirst, 'The Hawthornes', Thornhill Road, Marsh. Educated Longwood Grammar School and Huddersfield College School. He was apprenticed to Messrs Schofield and Taylor, engineers of Turnbridge, Huddersfield. He became a seagoing engineer with a firm of Glasgow shipowners in whose vessels he sailed for 12 years as Chief Engineer. On 23.8.1915 the ship on which he was serving, *SS Trafalgar*, was torpedoed and sunk by the Germans. On reaching England he enlisted in October, 1915, in the Royal Garrison Artillery, serving for two years in France with a Trench Mortar Battery and was twice wounded. On being recommended for a commission he was transferred to the Royal Naval Reserve on 11.7.1917. He died on board *RFA Reliance*, 9.10.1918, aged 39, at Mudros in the Aegean Sea. Buried **EAST MUDROS CEMETERY, LEMNOS.** Grave location:- Plot 3, Row I, Grave 250. ROH:- St. Stephen's Church, Lindley; Huddersfield College School; commemorated in Salendine Nook Baptist Chapel yard, D434.

HIRST, NORMAN. Ordinary Seaman. No J/55990 (PO). Royal Navy. *HMS Victory*. Son of the late Mr and Mrs Henry Hirst, 30 Ingfield Terrace, Manchester Road, Linthwaite. Attended Slaithwaite Wesleyan Sunday School. Was a member of Slaithwaite Socialist Club. Employed in the warehouse by Messrs W. E. Cotton and Sons Limited, of Slaithwaite. Called up from the Naval Reserve in July, 1916. Died in hospital at Plymouth, 4.12.1916, aged 22 years, after an illness lasting over ten weeks. Buried **SLAITHWAITE CEMETERY.** Grave location:- B, 1, 89. ROH:- Linthwaite War Memorial.

HIRST, NORMAN. Private. No 43130. 8th Battalion King's Own Yorkshire Light Infantry. Formerly No 29114 Northumberland Fusiliers. Born Gosport Bridge, Outlane, 13.4.1891. Son of Eliza Ann Hirst, Prospect Place, Outlane. Employed as a loom tuner by Messrs T. and H. Blamires Limited, Leeds Road, Huddersfield. Attended the Wesleyan Young Men's Institute. Single. Enlisted 2.6.1916. Killed in action in Italy, 14.12.1917, aged 26. Buried **GIAVERA BRITISH CEMETERY, ITALY.** Grave location:- Plot 1, Row C, Grave 3. ROH:- Salendine Nook Baptist Church; Bethel United Methodist Church, Outlane.

HIRST, THOMAS TEMPLE. Private. No 50168. 1/7th Battalion The King's (Liverpool Regiment). Formerly No 29359 Duke of Wellington's Regiment. Born Well Hill, Honley, Huddersfield, 8.12.1881. Son of Elizabeth and the late John Hirst, 6 Marsh, Honley. Educated Honley National School. Employed as a warehouseman by Mr James Sykes of Milnsbridge. Husband of Julia Hirst, 76 Blackmoorfoot Road, Crosland Moor. Enlisted 3.9.1916. Died of wounds at No 23 Casualty Clearing Station, 11.4.1918, aged 36. Buried **LAPUGNOY MILITARY CEMETERY.** Grave location:- Plot 6, Row C, Grave 12. ROH:- St. Barnabas Church, Crosland Moor; Honley War Memorial.

HIRST, WILFRED. Private. No 28992. 'C' Company, 1st Battalion East Yorkshire Regiment. Born Storthes, Moldgreen, Huddersfield, 1.6.1898. Son of Emma Hirst, 29 Highroyd Lane, Moldgreen. Educated Moldgreen Council School. Employed as a pattern man in the woollen and worsted trade. Single. Enlisted 31.1.1917. Reported missing, 22.3.1918 and afterwards presumed to have been killed on that date. Has no known grave. Commemorated **POZIERES MEMORIAL TO THE MISSING.** ROH:- Christ Church, Moldgreen; Almondbury War Memorial.

HIRST, WILFRED HEAP. Private. No 39089. 9th Battalion King's Own Yorkshire Light

Infantry. Formerly No 86676 Territorial Reserve Battalion. Born Berry Brow 1898. Son of Mr and Mrs Flinton, 4 Back Albert Street, Lockwood. Educated Mount Pleasant Council School. Employed as a teaser by Mr F. Lawton, Lockwood Mills. Single. Enlisted February 1917. Reported missing, presumed killed, 22.3.1918, aged 20 years. Buried **PERONNE COMMUNAL CEMETERY AND EXTENSION.** Grave location:- Plot 4, Row F, Grave 12. ROH:- Milton Independent Church; Emmanuel Church, Lockwood.

HIRST, WILLIE. Private. No 53429. 15th/17th Battalion West Yorkshire Regiment. Born Meltham. Son of William and Ruth Elizabeth Hirst, Clarke Lane, Meltham. Reported missing, presumed killed, 12.4.1918, aged 19 years, Buried **LE GRAND BEAUMART BRITISH CEMETERY, STEENWERCK.** Grave location:- Steenwerck Germany Cemetery, Memorial 7. ROH:- St. Bartholomew's Church, Meltham.

HIRST, WILLIE. Private. No 38609. 2nd Battalion York and Lancaster Regiment. Born Warley, Halifax. Son of the late William Hirst. Husband of Clara Hirst, 79 Swallow Lane, Golcar. Was a partner in the firm of Messrs Milnes and Hirst, painters and decorators, Leymoor Road, Golcar. Attended Scapegoat Hill Baptist Chapel. Enlisted November 1916. Killed in action, 22.4.1917, aged 39 years. Has no known grave. Commemorated **LOOS MEMORIAL TO THE MISSING.** ROH:- St. John's Church, Golcar.

HOBSON, BENJAMIN. Private. No DM2/135357. 648th Motor Transport Company, Army Service Corps. Born Farnley, Leeds. Eldest son of Mrs Hobson, The Grove, Binn Lane, Marsden. Attended Marsden Adult School. Employed as a fettler by Mr J. E. Crowther, Bank Bottom Mills, Marsden. Enlisted in August, 1914, and was discharged in January 1915. Re-enlisted in October, 1915, and went to East Africa in March, 1916. Died of Blackwater Fever, 6.9.1917, aged 28 years. Buried **MOROGORO CEMETERY** (90 miles west of Dar-es-Salaam). Grave location:- Plot 3, Row B, Grave 10. ROH:- Marsden War Memorial.

HOBSON, DAVID WILLIAM. Private. No 240189. 1/5th Battalion Duke of Wellington's Regiment. Born 27 Birkby Crescent, Hillhouse, Huddersfield, 2.3.1895. Son of the late Charles Edward and Emily Hobson, 19 Yew Street, Fartown. Educated Hillhouse Council School. Employed as a clerk. Single. Enlisted in the local Territorials in 1913. Embarked for France April 1915. Killed in action in the attack on the Schwaben Redoubt, 3.9.1916, aged 19 years. Has no known grave. Commemorated **THIEPVAL MEMORIAL TO THE MISSING.** ROH:- Huddersfield Drill Hall; Fartown and Birkby War Memorial.

HOBSON, EDWARD. Private. No 28786. 2nd Battalion Duke of Wellington's Regiment. Born Armitage Bridge, Huddersfield. Son of Henry and Hannah Hobson. Husband of Mary Elizabeth Hobson, 20 Rock, Linthwaite. Employed by Messrs George Cock Limited, Longfield Dyeworks, Linthwaite. Killed in action, 3.5.1917, aged 29 years. Buried **POINT-du-JOUR MILITARY CEMETERY.** Grave location:- Plot 3, Row H, Grave 1. ROH:- Linthwaite War Memorial; Armitage Bridge War Memorial.

HOBSON, FRANK. Private. No 366747. 2nd/1st Northern Cyclist Battalion, Army Cyclist Corps. Son of Fred and Alice Hobson, 12a West Parade, Huddersfield. Employed as a junior clerk in a clothier's office. Enlisted 12.9.1916. Died at home, 12a West Parade, Huddersfield, of heart strain and influenza 29.6.1918 age 19 years. Buried **ALMONDBURY CEMETERY.** Grave location:- 6, 'C', 30. ROH:- Huddersfield Parish Church.

HOBSON, GEORGE. Private. No 2901. 1/5th Battalion Duke of Wellington's Regiment. Born Upperthong, Holmfirth. Son of Mr and Mrs Joseph E. Hobson, 90 Blacker Road, Birkby. Educated Wilshaw School, near Meltham, Huddersfield. Employed as a cloth shrinker by Messrs Jennens, Welch and Company, of Huddersfield. Enlisted September 1914. Was married April 13th, 1915. Left for France April 15th, 1915. Was killed instantly by a shell at 8pm on Thursday, 1.10.1915, whilst ration carrying. He was 28 years of age. Has no known grave. Commemorated **MENIN GATE MEMORIAL TO THE MISSING.** (Brother of Private **NORMAN HOBSON,** died of wounds, 9.10.1917, q v). *On the day of his death Private Hobson wrote a letter to his wife informing her that he was in good health and that he was* *keeping his spirits up.* ROH:- Huddersfield Drill Hall; Fartown and Birkby War Memorial.

HOBSON, HUBERT. Lance Corporal. No 14235. 2nd Battalion Duke of Wellington's Regiment. Born Netherthong, Holmfirth. Son of Jonas and Alice Hobson of Outlane, Netherthong, Thongsbridge, near Huddersfield. Attended Netherthong Wesleyan Church, where he was the Sunday School Secretary. He played the clarinet in the Sunday School orchestra and was a member of the choir. Was a playing member of the Netherthong Association football team and was also a member of the Working Men's Club. Was employed at Deanhouse Mills. Killed in action during the Battle of the Somme on 2.7.1916, aged 25 years. Buried **BERTRANCOURT MILITARY CEMETERY.** Grave location:- Plot 1, Row G, Grave 25. ROH:- Netherthong and Thongsbridge War Memorial; Netherthong Working Men's Club.

HOBSON, JOHN ROBERT. Private. No 19349. 12th Battalion West Yorkshire Regiment. Born Newcastle-on-Tyne. Lived Moldgreen. Killed in action, 12.10.1916. Buried **BERTRANCOURT MILITARY CEMETERY.** Grave Location:- Plot 1, Row F, Grave 16.. ROH:- Moldgreen War Memorial.

HOBSON, LEWIS. Private. No 44691. 5th Provisional Company, 1st Battalion Royal Scots Fusiliers. Son of Woodhouse and Leah Hobson, 10 Cooperative Terrace, Honley. Died at home, 7.7.1921, aged 29 years. Buried **HONLEY CHURCH BURIAL GROUND.** Grave location:- 32,1909. ROH:- Honley War Memorial.

HOBSON, NORMAN. Private. No 49943. 6th Battalion The King's (Liverpool Regiment). Formerly No 36988 4th Battalion North Staffordshire Regiment. Born Upperthong. Son of Mr and Mrs Joseph Hobson, 90 Blacker Road, Birkby. Educated Wilshaw Council and Mount Pleasant School, Lockwood. Employed as a plumber and sanitary engineer. Husband of Janie Hobson, 46 Woodhouse Avenue, Fartown. Enlisted 1.3.1917. Died of wounds at No 46 Casualty Clearing Station, 9.10.1917. Buried **MENDINGHEM MILITARY CEMETERY.** Grave location:- Plot 7, Row E, Grave 47. ROH:- Lockwood Baptist Church; Fartown and Birkby War Memorial.

HOBSON, ROBERT. Lance Corporal.. No 24244. 1/5th Battalion Northumberland Fusiliers. Born Mossley. Husband of Ann Charlesworth Hobson, 2, Ing Head, Marsden. Employed as a mule minder by Messrs Robinson Brothers, Clough Lea Mills, Marsden. Was a well known local football player. Enlisted July 1916. Embarked for France in November, 1916. Was taken prisoner on 27.5.1918, after being seriously wounded. Died as a Prisoner of War in Germany, 14.8.1918, aged 29 years. Buried **NIEDERZWEHREN CEMETERY, CASSEL, GERMANY.** Grave location:- Plot 1, Row G, Grave 16. ROH:- Marsden War Memorial.

HOBSON, TOM. Private. No TR/5/64839. 31st Battalion Northumberland Fusiliers. Born Newsome, Huddersfield. Died at home, 31.1.1917, aged 38. Buried **EDGERTON CEMETERY, HUDDERSFIELD.**

HODGSON, EDWARD. Lance Corporal. No 20412. 2nd Battalion Essex Regiment. Formerly No 74041 Royal Field Artillery. Born Holmfirth. Adopted son of Mr John Crosland, Underbank, Holmfirth. Employed by Messrs Watkinson of Washpit Mills, Holmfirth. Prior to the war was a soldier in the Royal Field Artillery. Embarked for France at the beginning of the war and was invalided home after nine months service. He was the only survivor of his Battery and it was thought unlikely he would be fit for foreign service again. But he recovered and was posted to the machine gun section of the Essex Regiment. Died of wounds, 2.7.1916, aged 21 years. Buried **COUIN BRITISH CEMETERY.** Grave location:- Plot 2, Row A, Grave 2. ROH:- Underbank War Memorial.

HODGSON, FRED. Private. No 41944. 12th Battalion Manchester Regiment. Formerly 3/31833 North Staffordshire Regiment. Born Lepton. Son of Mr and Mrs Hodgson, Botany, Lepton. Employed by Messrs Kilner Brothers, Whitley Willow Mills. Killed in action, 4.9.1918, aged 20 years. Buried **LEBUCQUIERE COMMUNAL CEMETERY EXTENSION.** Grave location:- Plot 2, Row E, Grave 6. ROH:- Lepton Parish Church; St. John's Church, Kirkheaton.

HODGSON, HARRY. Private. No 12555. 8th Battalion Duke of Wellington's Regiment. Born

Huddersfield. Son of the late John and Mary Midd Hodgson. Killed in action in the assault on Lala Baba, Suvla, Gallipoli on 7.8.1915, aged 18. Has no known grave. Commemorated **HELLES MEMORIAL TO THE MISSING**.

HODGSON, HORACE CHARLES. Lance Corporal. No 13225. Coldstream Guards. Born York. Enlisted Huddersfield. Employed as a clerk at the Huddersfield Labour Exchange. Was for some time head chorister at York Minster. Enlisted October 1914. Killed in action, 15.9.1916, aged 22 years. Has no known grave. Commemorated **THIEPVAL MEMORIAL TO THE MISSING**. ROH:- Huddersfield Parish Church.

HODGSON, VICTOR. Private. No 62721. 9th Battalion King's Own Yorkshire Light Infantry. Born Salford Road, Birks, Lockwood, 20.11.1899. Son of George Herbert and Isabella Hodgson, 67 Perseverance Street, Primrose Hill, Huddersfield. Educated Stile Common Council School. Employed as a woollen piecer by Messrs Gledhill Brothers. Single. Enlisted 1.8.1917. He was guarding the flank of his platoon when a shell struck him and killed him instantly on 15.8.1918, aged 18 years. Has no known grave. Commemorated **VIS-en-ARTOIS MEMORIAL TO THE MISSING**. ROH:- St. Paul's Church, Southgate, Huddersfield.

HODGSON, WILFRED ALMA. Private. No 142568. Machine Gun Corps. Formerly No 32333 Duke of Wellington's Regiment. Born Barmby, near Howden, Yorkshire, 18.9.1896. Son of Mrs Eliza Jane Hodgeson, 42 Spring Grove Street, Huddersfield. Educated at Barmby School. Employed as a railway porter at Berry Brow Station by the Lancashire and Yorkshire Railway. At the time of enlistment, was living at 26 Bankfield Terrace, Outcote Bank, Huddersfield. Enlisted 4.9.1917. Wounded in France, 31.3.1918. Died of wounds in Cambridge Hospital, Aldershot, 15.4.1918, aged 21 years. Buried **EDGERTON CEMETERY, HUDDERSFIELD**. Grave location:- 47, 99. ROH:- Almondbury War Memorial; Lancashire and Yorkshire Railway Roll.

HOGAN, JOHN Lance Corporal. No 42081. Labour Corps. Formerly No 11611 7th Battalion The Yorkshire Regiment. Born Edinburgh. Son of James and Christina Hogan, 31 Castlegate, Huddersfield. Died at home, 9.3.1919, aged 27 years. Buried **EDGERTON CEMETERY, HUDDERSFIELD**. Grave location:- 13, RC, 137.

HOGGARTH, THOMAS EDWARD. Private. No 76238. 22nd Battalion Durham Light Infantry. Born Scarborough. Son of Thomas Hoggarth, 137 Hillhouse Lane, Huddersfield. Killed in action, 26.4.1918, aged 18 years. Has no known grave. Commemorated **POZIERES MEMORIAL TO THE MISSING**.

HOGLEY, HERBERT FARRAND. Private. No 29304. 2nd Battalion Duke of Wellington's Regiment. Born Holmfirth. Son of Stephen Enoch and Mary Jane Hogley of Spring Grove, Thongsbridge; husband of Florence Hogley of 'Rock View', Liphill Bank, Holmfirth. Educated Holmfirth Wesleyan Day School and at the Higher Grade School, Huddersfield. Was employed in his father's business of Messrs Lawson and Hogley, painters and decorators, of Holmfirth. Enlisted September 1916. Embarked for France in January, 1917. Twice wounded. Killed in action, 23.6.1918, aged 34 years. Buried **LE VERTANNOY BRITISH CEMETERY, HINGES**. Grave location:- Row C, Grave 27. His wife received the following letter from a Second Lieutenant, commanding her husband's platoon, which read, '*It is with deep regret that I must inform you that your husband has paid the supreme sacrifice. He had only been with my platoon a few days and even in so short a time I have seen in him a thoroughly sound man. It was during 'stand-to' on the morning of the 23rd I had just visited that post where your husband was sentry when a shell burst just in front forming shrapnel, a piece of which killed Private Hogley instantenously. Perhaps it will be a little consolation to know that he was taken to a cemetery behind the lines and there received a proper burial service. The N.C.O.'s and men of his platoon wish me to convey to you their deepest sympathy in your sad bereavement and I also Madam wish to convey to you my deepest sympathy.*' ROH:- Holmfirth War Memorial.

HOGTON, FREDERICK WILLIAM. Rifleman. No 3694. 1st Battalion King's Royal Rifle Corps. Born Rotherham. Lived 4 Garforth Street, Aspley, Huddersfield. Married, with four children. Had already served eight years in the Army and spent five years on the Reserve.

Employed as a switchgear maker by Messrs Brook, electricians, of Colne Road and at night time worked as a checker at the Palace Theatre. Embarked for France 8.9.1914. Killed in action, 26.10.1914, aged 33 years. Has no known grave. Commemorated **MENIN GATE MEMORIAL TO THE MISSING.**

HOLDEN, JOHN WILLIAM. Rifleman. No C/7845. 18th Battalion King's Royal Rifle Corps. Born Kilner Bank, Moldgreen, 18.2.1887. Educated Moldgreen Board School. Attended Moldgreen United Methodist Church and Sunday School. Employed by Messrs Middlemost Brothers, of Birkby, as a dyer's labourer. Husband of Mrs. L. Holden, 4 Robert's Yard, Brook Street, Moldgreen. Enlisted 10.10.1915. Died at No 10 Casualty Clearing Station of the effects of gas on 9.8.1916, aged 31 years. Buried **LIJSSENTHOEK MILITARY CEMETERY.** Grave location; Plot 8, Row D, Grave 13a. His widow received a letter from a Chaplain to the Forces, who wrote, *'He was brought in after a gas attack, was practically unconscious and died very shortly afterwards.'* ROH:- Moldgreen War Memorial; St. Andrew's Church, Leeds Road, Huddersfield.

HOLROYD, GEORGE LINFORD. Private. No 3811. 10th/11th Battalion Highland Light Infantry. Born Huddersfield. Younger son of Mrs Holdroyd, 27 Green Lane, Dalton, Huddersfield. Attended Kirkheaton Church Sunday School. Employed by Mr W. H. Murgatroyd, cloth finisher, of Leeds Road, Huddersfield. Enlisted February 1915. Was wounded at Christmas, 1915. Died of gunshot wounds at No 36 Casualty Clearing Station, 18.9.1916, aged 20 years. Buried **HEILLY STATION CEMETERY.** Grave location:- Special Memorial 16. ROH:- St. John's Church, Kirkheaton.

HOLDROYD, TOM. Lance Corporal. No 19657. 8th Battalion Duke of Wellington's Regiment. Born 39 Shirley Hill, Berry Brow, 9.11.1887. Son of Mrs H. Holdroyd, 15 Orchard Terrace, off Malvern Road, Primrose Hill, Huddersfield. Educated at Berry Brow School. Employed as a stone mason by Mr I. Timmins, Firth Street, Huddersfield. Attended Hall Bower Sunday School. Was a member of the Primrose Hill Liberal Club and also of the Longwood Harriers. Single. Enlisted 2.3.1915. Wounded near Ypres, 12.8.1917. Died of wounds at the 7th Canadian General Hospital, 22.8.1917, aged 29 years. Buried **ETAPLES MILITARY CEMETERY.** Grave location:- Plot 22, Row Q, Grave 15.

HOLDSWORTH, JOE WILLIE. Rifleman. No C/6237. 18th Battalion King's Royal Rifle Corps. Born Huddersfield. Son of Sarah E. Holdsworth, 16, Victoria Street, Lockwood, and the late Fred Holdsworth; husband of Rebecca Holdsworth, 55 Whitestone Lane, Hillhouse, Huddersfield. Employed by British Dyes Limited. Killed instantly by a sniper on 20.9.1917, aged 33 years. Has no known grave. Commemorated **TYNE COT MEMORIAL TO THE MISSING.** ROH:- South Crosland and Netherton War Memorial; St. Stephen's Church, Rashcliffe.

HOLDSWORTH, PHILIP EDWARD. Private. No 601. 2nd Battalion Machine Gun Corps, Australian Infantry, Australian Imperial Force. Born 'Austerfield', 102 Somerset Road, Huddersfield, 8.5.1891. Son of Tom and Harriet Holdsworth. Educated Moldgreen Council School. Emigrated to Australia in 1912. Employed as a farmer. Lived St. Edmund's Farm, Cecil Street, Gordon, Sydney, New South Wales, Australia. Reported missing, presumed killed, at Passchendaele, 10.10.1917. Has no known grave. Commemorated **MENIN GATE MEMORIAL TO THE MISSING.** ROH:- St. Paul's Methodist Church, Dalton; Almondbury War Memorial; memorial in Almondbury Cemetery.

HOLLAND, HERBERT. Private. No 203742. 1/4th Battalion Duke of Wellington's Regiment. Born 9.9.1889. Son of Mrs Holland, 202 Dod Lee Green, Longwood. Educated Knowl Bank Council School, Golcar. Employed in the milling department at Messrs John Broadbent and Sons Limited, Parkwood Mills. Attended Salendine Nook Baptist Church. Played cricket for Lidget Green in the Bradford league. Single. Enlisted 7.8.1916. Embarked for France in December, 1916. Died of wounds 9.8.1917, aged 27 years. Buried **COXYDE MILITARY CEMETERY.** Grave location:- Plot 2, Row F, Grave 14. ROH:-. Salendine Nook Baptist Church; St. Mark's Parish Church, Longwood; Longwood War Memorial; commemorated in Salendine Nook Baptist Chapel yard, 120E.

HOLLAND, JOHN EDWARD. Private. No 22409. 6th Battalion King's Own Yorkshire Light

Infantry. Born Longwood, Huddersfield. Killed in action, 15.9.1916. Buried **GUARDS' CEMETERY, (LESBOEUFS)**. Grave location:- Plot 6, Row R, Grave 5. ROH:- Longwood War Memorial.

HOLLAND, ROBERT SINCLAIR. Private. No 4729. 'A' Company, 1/5th Battalion Seaforth Highlanders. Born 1 Peel's Yard, Kirkgate, Huddersfield. 23.2.1882. Son of the late Arthur and Anne Holland. Lived Whitestone Lane, Hillhouse. Educated Huddersfield Parish Church School and St. John's Church of England School. Employed at Hillhouse Sidings and later in a torpedo factory in Gourock, Scotland. Single. Enlisted, 28.12.1915, after special permission was granted from the Admiralty. Died of gunshot wounds to the abdomen at No 4 Casualty Clearing Station, 15.11.1916, aged 24 years. Buried **VARENNES MILITARY CEMETERY**. Grave location:- Plot 1, Row E, Grave 62. ROH:- Huddersfield Parish Church.

HOLLAND, STANLEY. Private. No 39017. 2/8th Battalion Lancashire Fusiliers. Born Huddersfield 6.3.1898. Son of Mr and Mrs S. H. Holland, 8 Bank Top, Lowerhouses, Huddersfield. Educated Lowerhouses National School and the Higher Elementary School, Huddersfield. Employed as a clerk at Bate and Company, yarn spinners, of Colne Road. Attended St. Mary's Church, Longley and was a member of Lowerhouses Working Men's Club. Single. Enlisted January 1917. Wounded 9.10.1917. Died of wounds at Rouen Base Hospital, 17.10.1917, aged 19 years. Buried **St. SEVER CEMETERY EXTENSION, ROUEN**. Grave location:- Block P, Plot 3, Row J, Grave 11b. ROH:- Lowerhouses War Memorial; Almondbury War Memorial.

HOLLAS, EDWIN. Pioneer No 131102. 47th Base Park Company, Royal Engineers. Born Paddock in December 1887. Son of Henry Hollas, 65 Thorn Road, Thornton Lodge. Educated Paddock Board School. Employed on the Huddersfield Tramways. Married, with five children. Lived 38 Storths, Moldgreen. Enlisted September 1914. Died of heatstroke in Mesopotamia on 13.7.1917, aged 29 years. Buried **BASRA WAR CEMETERY, IRAQ**. Grave location:- Plot 4, Row H, Grave 17. ROH:- Moldgreen War Memorial; Christ Church, Moldgreen.

HOLLIDAY, FRIEND. Private. No 2214. Duke of Wellington's Regiment. Son of Tom and Mary Hannah Holliday, 34 Thomas Street, Northgate, Huddersfield. Died at home, 18.11.1916, aged 20 years. Buried **EDGERTON CEMETERY, HUDDERSFIELD**. Grave location:- 18B, 'C', 133.

HOLLINGS, ARTHUR. Private. No 11929. 9th Battalion Duke of Wellington's Regiment. Born 201 Cowcliffe Hill Road, Huddersfield, 14.7.1890. Son of Samuel and Eliza Hollings. Educated Cowcliffe National School. Employed as a driller by Messrs Hopkinsons of Birkby. Attended Netheroyd Hill Congregational Sunday School. Single. Enlisted, 11.8.1914, in the 8th Battalion Duke of Wellington's Regiment. Was wounded at Gallipoli in August, 1915, and was at home at Christmas, 1915, before going out to France with the 9th Battalion Duke of Wellington's Regiment. Killed in action, 2.3.1916, aged 25 years. Has no known grave. Commemorated **MENIN GATE MEMORIAL TO THE MISSING**. ROH:- Netheroyd Hill Methodist Chapel; Fartown and Birkby War Memorial.

HOLLINGWORTH, EDGAR ALLEN. Private. No 235498. 9th Battalion York and Lancaster Regiment. Born Wakefield Road, Moldgreen 14.9.1893. Son of Henry and Mary Hollingworth, Lyn Dene, Dalton. Educated Almondbury Grammar School. Employed as a manufacturer's apprentice. Single. Enlisted Easter Saturday, 1917. Killed in action, 1.10.1917, aged 24. Has no known grave. Commemorated **TYNE COT MEMORIAL TO THE MISSING**. ROH:- St. Andrew's Church; Christ Church, Moldgreen; Almondbury Grammar School.

HOLLINGWORTH, JOHN HENRY. Private. No 240837. 2/5th Battalion Duke of Wellington's Regiment. Born Holmfirth. Lived Burnlee, Holmfirth. Enlisted October 1914. Embarked for France November, 1915. Reported missing, presumed killed, at the Battle of Bullecourt, 3.5.1917, aged 29 years. Has no known grave. Commemorated **ARRAS MEMORIAL TO THE MISSING**. ROH:- Upperthong War Memorial; Huddersfield Drill Hall.

HOLMES, ARTHUR. Private. No 41537. 23rd (Tyneside Scottish) Battalion Northumberland Fusiliers. Formerly No 19939 Duke of Wellington's

Regiment. Born Linthwaite. Son of Mr and Mrs J.E. Holmes, 10 Barber Row, Linthwaite. Employed by Messrs George Mallinson and Sons Limited as a pattern weaver. Enlisted 10.4.1916. Embarked for France in the summer of 1916. Reported missing, presumed killed, 20.3.1918, aged 24 years. Has no known grave. Commemorated **ARRAS MEMORIAL TO THE MISSING.** ROH:- Linthwaite War Memorial.

HOLMES, CHARLES E. Sergeant. No 204495. 2/5th Battalion Duke of Wellington's Regiment. Born King Street, Huddersfield. Son of Mrs M. A. Senior, 492 Spuy Street, Pretoria, Transvaal, South Africa. Educated St. Paul's Church of England School. Had lived for sometime in South Africa, where he was employed with his brother at the Premier Diamond Mine near Pretoria. Had also been employed as a bookbinder. At the time of enlistment was living at Ashbrow Road, Sheepridge, Huddersfield. Enlisted September 1914. Wounded in the stomach near Rheims. Died of wounds, 20.7.1918. Buried **MARFAUX BRITISH CEMETERY.** Grave location:- Plot 3, Row BB, Grave 3. ROH:- Christ Church, Woodhouse Hill; Huddersfield Drill Hall.

HOLMES, FRANK. Private. No 35937. 21st (Tyneside Scottish) Battalion Northumberland Fusiliers. Formerly No 50637 Durham Light Infantry. Born Honley. Married. Lived 418 Almondbury Road, Moldgreen. Employed at Rock Mills, Brockholes. Reported missing, presumed killed, 5.6.1917, aged 27 years. Has no known grave. Commemorated **ARRAS MEMORIAL TO THE MISSING.** ROH:- Honley War Memorial.

HOLMES, FRANCIS RICHARD. Petty Officer. No J/16086. Royal Navy. *HMS Victory.* Born Huddersfield 1895. Lived 'The Ferns', Grimscar, Huddersfield. Married. Killed in an accidental fall at Culver Cliffe, near Sandown on 4.6.1921.

HOLMES, FRANK. Corporal. No 42810. 12th Battalion Royal Irish Rifles. Formerly No C/7900 King's Royal Rifle Corps. Born 8 Back Thornhill, Longwood, Huddersfield. Fourth son of Friend and Emma Jane Holmes, 11 Siggott Street, Longwood. Educated Longwood Grammar School. Employed as a clerk in the office at Messrs Armitage Brothers, Burdett Mill, Milnsbridge. Attended Parkwood United Methodist Church where he was a Sunday School teacher as well as joint secretary of the school. Single. Enlisted, 23.11.1915, at the age of 17. Embarked for France in June, 1917. Reported missing, presumed killed, 16.8.1917, aged 19 years. Has no known grave. Commemorated **TYNE COT MEMORIAL TO THE MISSING.** ROH:- Parkwood Methodist Church; St. Mark's Parish Church, Longwood.

HOLMES, GEORGE FREDERICK. Private. No 241976. 2/5th Battalion Duke of Wellington's Regiment. Born Northumberland Street, Huddersfield, 14.7.1881. Son of Mr and Mrs Frederic Holmes, 28 Eldon Road, Marsh. Educated Thomas Street Board School. Employed as a plasterer's labourer by Mr Robinson of Marsh. Single. Enlisted 28.3.1916. Reported missing, presumed killed, at the Battle of Bullecourt, 3.5.1917. Has no known grave. Commemorated **ARRAS MEMORIAL TO THE MISSING.** (Brother of Private **NORMAN GLEDHILL HOLMES**, died 28.1.1919, q.v.). ROH:- Holy Trinity Church, Huddersfield; Huddersfield Drill Hall.

HOLMES, HARRY. Drummer. No 241538. 2/5th Battalion Duke of Wellington's Regiment. Born Holmfirth 1886. Son of Mr and Mrs Amor Holmes, Dunford Road, Holmfirth. Educated Holmfirth National School and Underbank Wesleyan School. Employed by Messrs J. Bower and Sons, Dover Mills. Was a keen musician, playing for a time with the Underbank Philharmonic Band and later he played the first tenor horn with the Hepworth Silver Prize Band. He enlisted in March, 1916, with his friend Private **FRED SANDFORD**, (q.v.). They left Holmfirth by train together and were both reported missing, presumed killed, at the Battle of Bullecourt on 3.5.1917. Has no known grave. Commemorated **ARRAS MEMORIAL TO THE MISSING.** ROH:- Underbank War Memorial; Huddersfield Drill Hall.

HOLMES, HARRY. Corporal. 3/5th Battalion Duke of Wellington's Regiment. Born Wakefield 15.1.1873. Lived 77 Cross Lane, Primrose Hill, Huddersfield. Employed as a cloth presser. Married. Enlisted 4.8.1915. Died at home, 15.11.1918.

HOLMES, HARRY ACKROYD. Private. No 91010. 70th Company, Machine Gun Corps.

Born Lockwood 24.8.1889. Son of Timothy and Hannah Holmes, 39 North Street, Lockwood. Educated Mount Pleasant Council School and Higher Grade School, Huddersfield. Employed as a saddler and harness maker. Single. At the time of enlistment, was living at 215 Lockwood Road, Huddersfield. Enlisted 5.1.1917. Killed in action near Ypres, 3.7.1917, aged 27 years. Has no known grave. Commemorated **MENIN GATE MEMORIAL TO THE MISSING.** ROH:- Lockwood Baptist Church.

HOLMES, JAMES. Driver. No 27047. 15th Divisional Ammunition Column, Royal Field Artillery. Born Huddersfield. Son of Arthur Holmes (who was also serving in France). Lived with his aunt, Mrs Knott, 7 Jowett's Court, off Manchester Street, Huddersfield. Educated Paddock Church of England School. Employed by Messrs C. and J. Hirst of Longwood. Killed in action, 17.7.1917, aged 22 years. Buried **BRANDHOEK MILITARY CEMETERY.** Grave location:- Plot 1, Row M, Grave 25.

HOLMES, NORMAN. Private. No 29720. 10th Battalion Duke of Wellington's Regiment. Born Scales, Cumberland. Son of Willie and Alice Ann Holmes of Sandy Gate, Holmfirth. Husband of Hannah Holmes of Far Lane, Holmfirth. Educated Hepworth Town School. Attended Scholes United Primitive Methodist Church. He was also a member of the P.S.A. at Holmfirth United Methodist Church. Employed as a teamer by Messrs Dawson and Birch, confectioners, of Holmfirth. Enlisted 16.6.1916. Embarked for France 12.1.1917. Killed in action, 18.10.1917, aged 26 years. Has no known grave. Commemorated **TYNE COT MEMORIAL TO THE MISSING.** His widow received the following letter from Lieutenant Waite of her husband's Company, *'It is with sincere regret that I have to inform you of the death of your husband who was killed in action a few days ago. He was a good man and his death is a severe loss to us. A shell fell near him and killed him instantenously. He was buried in a shellhole and the position of the grave has been notified to the authorities. I offer you the sympathies of the whole platoon and of myself in your sad bereavement.'* ROH:- Hepworth and Scholes War Memorial; Hepworth Church.

HOLMES, NORMAN GLEDHILL. Sergeant. No 252594. 9th Transport Company, Royal Engineers. Born 28 Eldon Road, Marsh. 13.5.1895. Son of Frederic and Martha Ann Holmes. Educated Spring Grove Council School. Employed as a telegraph clerk at the Huddersfield Railway Station. Single. Enlisted 20.6.1915. Died of bronchial pneumonia at 8th Canadian Stationary Hospital, 28.1.1919, aged 23 years. Buried **DUNKIRK TOWN CEMETERY.** Grave location:- Plot 4, Row E, Grave 13. (Brother of Private **GEORGE FREDERICK HOLMES**, reported missing, 3.5.1917, q.v.).

HOLMES, SIDNEY. Driver. No L/29271. 'B' Battery, 16th Brigade Royal Field Artillery. Son of Joseph and Florence Holmes of Battye Mill, Colne Bridge. Employed as a coal-getter at Battye Mill Colliery. Enlisted at Whitsuntide, 1915. Died from pneumonia at No 39 Casualty Clearing Station, 3.3.1917, aged 27 years. Buried **CERISY-GAILLY MILITARY CEMETERY.** Grave location:- Plot 1, Row D, Grave 4. ROH:- St. John's Church, Kirkheaton.

HOLROYD, ALBERT. Gunner. No L/25383. 223rd Brigade Royal Field Artillery. Born Rashcliffe Hill, Huddersfield, 15.1.1889. Educated Mount Pleasant Council School. Employed as a motorman on the Huddersfield Corporation Tramways. Husband of Rebecca Holroyd, 96 St. Thomas's Road, Huddersfield. Enlisted April 1915. Died at home, 1.3.1919, of pneumonia. He came home on leave the week before he died. Buried **EDGERTON CEMETERY, HUDDERSFIELD.** Grave location:- 36, 140C. ROH:- St. Stephen's Church, Rashcliffe.

HOLROYD, FREDERICK FEARNLEY. Gunner. No 117721. 256th Siege Battery Royal Garrison Artillery. Born Penistone. Son of Suttliffe and Annie Holroyd of Abbey Road, Shepley. Husband of Eliza Ellen Holroyd of Lea Side Cafe, Shepley. Employed by Messrs Firth Brothers of Shepley. Killed in action, 24.9.1918, aged 34 years. Buried **VIS-en-ARTOIS BRITISH CEMETERY.** Grave location:- Plot 6, Row G, Grave 1. ROH:- Shepley War Memorial.

HOLROYD, GEORGE LINDFORD. Private. No 3811. 10th/11th Highland Light Infantry. Born Huddersfield. Only son of Mrs Holroyd, 27 Green Lane, Dalton, Huddersfield. Attended Kirkheaton Church Sunday School. Employed by Mr. W. H. Murgatroyd, cloth finisher, Leeds Road, Huddersfield. Enlisted February 1915. Wounded Christmas 1915. Returned to France. Died of gunshot wounds in No 36 Casualty Clearing Station, 18.9.1916, aged 20 years. Buried **HEILLY STATION CEMETERY**. Grave location:- Special Memorial 16. ROH:- St. John's Church, Kirkheaton.

HOLROYD, GEORGE WILLIE. Private. No 75550. 2nd Battalion Durham Light Infantry. Born Linthwaite. Lived Linthwaite. Killed in action, 21.3.1918. Has no known grave. Commemorated **ARRAS MEMORIAL TO THE MISSING.** ROH:- Linthwaite War Memorial.

HOLROYD, HAROLD SYKES. Probationery Flight Officer. Royal Naval Air Service. Born Longwood 5.8.1894. Only son of Sam Holroyd, 30 Rufford Road, Scar Lane, Milnsbridge. Educated Crow Lane Board School, Milnsbridge, and the Huddersfield Secondary School for boys. Attended Milnsbridge Wesleyan Church and Sunday School and was a member of the choir and had been secretary of the Sunday School for sometime. He entered the teaching profession but had to relinquish his post due to health reasons. He then worked at the National Health Insurance Office at Huddersfield and later took the Civil Service examinations and went to the Admiralty, London, in August, 1914. Enlisted in the Duke of Wellington's Regiment in October, 1914, and embarked for France in September, 1916, serving there until December, 1916. He then volunteered for the Royal Naval Air Service and returned to England for training. He came home on leave the week before he was killed. Was killed whilst flying at Sleaford, Lincolnshire, on 21.8.1917, aged 23 years. Buried **BETHEL UNITED METHODIST CHURCHYARD, OUTLANE.** ROH:- Fitzwilliam Street Unitarian Church; St. Mark's Parish Church, Longwood; Huddersfield Mission, Milnsbridge; Crow Lane Board School, Milnsbridge.

HOLROYD, HARRY. Private. No 204501. 2nd Battalion Duke of Wellington's Regiment. Husband of Agnes Holroyd, 92 Lidget Street, Lindley. Died at home, 25.10.1919, aged 27 years. Buried **LINDLEY WESLEYAN METHODIST CHAPEL YARD.** Grave location:- J, 63. ROH:- St. Stephen's Church, Lindley.

HOLROYD, HARRY. Private. No 241655. 2/5th Battalion Duke of Wellington's Regiment. Born Linthwaite. Lived Clifton Terrace, Linthwaite. Killed in action at the Battle of Bullecourt, 3.5.1917. Has no known grave. Commemorated **ARRAS MEMORIAL TO THE MISSING.** ROH:- Linthwaite War Memorial; Huddersfield Drill Hall.

HOLROYD, HERMAN AINLEY. Private. No 119748. 47th Battalion Machine Gun Corps. Formerly No DM2/230618 Army Service Corps. Born Kirkburton 28.2.1885. Son of George and Sarah Ann Holroyd, Clifton House, Mount, Longwood. Educated Outlane Council School. Attended Outlane Methodist New Connection Church. Since 1907 had managed the woollen manufacturing business carried on by his father at Knighton, Wales. Husband of Mrs E. Holroyd, 11 West Street, Knighton, Radnorshire. Enlisted August 1916. Embarked for France in November, 1917. Wounded at Cambrai 26.3.1918. Died of wounds at St. Sever Base Hospital, 28.3.1918, aged 33 years. Buried **St SEVER CEMETERY EXTENSION.** Grave location:- Block P, Plot 7, Row J, Grave 10b. ROH:- Bethel United Methodist Church, Outlane.

HOLDROYD, HUBERT WILSON. Lance Corporal. No 10374. 1st Battalion King's Own Yorkshire Light Infantry. Born Huddersfield 4.6.1896. Son of Levi and Jane E. Holroyd, 17 Longroyd Place, Longroyd Bridge, Huddersfield. Educated St. Thomas's Church of England School, Longroyd Bridge. Enlisted at the outbreak of the war. Reported missing, presumed killed, 8.5.1915, aged 18 years. Has no known grave. Commemorated **MENIN GATE MEMORIAL TO THE MISSING.** ROH:- St. Thomas's Church, Longroyd Bridge. The following extract is taken from 'British Battalions on the Western Front January to June 1915' by Ray Westlake. Pages 173: *'May–June. Withdrew from front line 3rd May and to camp west of Ypres. Moved forward to reserve dugouts near Friezenberg on 5th and took over front line trenches 7th. Enemy attacked 8th. War diary records 'C' and 'D' Companies forced out of their trenches, 'A' and 'B' drove off three German attacks. Casualties for 8th May – 418 killed, wounded or missing.'*

HOLROYD, JAMES WILLIAM. Sergeant. No 22522. 12th Battalion Manchester Regiment.

Born Salford, Manchester. Son of George Benjamin and Margaret Holroyd of Clough Lea, Marsden. Married. Lived Higher Broughton, Manchester. Employed as an engraver on copper for calico printers in Manchester. Enlisted November, 1914, and embarked for France at Christmas, 1915. Was wounded in August, 1917, and came home for treatment. After recovery and some time on home service, he was married on 6.4.1918 and returned to France on 27.4.1918. Killed in action, 24.8.1918, aged 28 years. Buried **COURCELETTE BRITISH CEMETERY**. Grave location:- Plot 3, Row F, Grave 3. ROH:- Marsden War Memorial.

HOLROYD, NORRIS. Private. No DM2/163027. 596th Mechanical Transport Company, Army Service Corps. Born Linthwaite. Youngest son of the late John Holroyd and of Alice Ann Holroyd, 13 Slant Gate, Linthwaite. Employed as a pattern weaver by Messrs George Mallinson and Sons Limited, Spring Grove Mills, Linthwaite. Enlisted February 1916. Died of Enteric Fever at Basra on the Persian Gulf, 10.7.1916, aged 21. Buried **BASRA WAR CEMETERY**. Grave location:- Plot 6, Row P, Grave 6. ROH:- Linthwaite War Memorial.

HOLROYD, WALTER. Private. No 240121. Duke of Wellington's Regiment. Born Huddersfield. Lived 67 Castlegate, Huddersfield. Died at home of tuberculosis on 20.7.1921.

HOLROYD, WILLIAM. Private. No 202071. 2/4th Battalion Duke of Wellington's Regiment. Born Halifax. Son of the late John and Mary Ann Holroyd, 14 Ainley Top, Lindley, Huddersfield. Employed as a weaver at Plover Mills, Lindley. Killed in action at the Battle of Bullecourt, 3.5.1917, aged 32 years. Has no known grave. Commemorated **ARRAS MEMORIAL TO THE MISSING**. ROH:- Blackley Baptist Chapel; Elland War Memorial.

HOLSEY, WILLIAM. Private. No 148434. 78th Battalion Canadian Infantry (Manitoba Regiment). Born Shelley. Son of William Holsey, of Shelley Woodhouse, Huddersfield. Killed in action, 2.9.1918, aged 41 years. Buried **DURY MILL BRITISH CEMETERY**. Grave location:- Plot 1, Row B, Grave 38. ROH:- Emmanuel Church, Shelley.

HOLT, ADDISON BOOTHROYD. Gunner. No 47. Royal Garrison Artillery. Born Huddersfield. Enlisted Hull. Lived Huddersfield. Died at home, 8.6.1915, aged 38. Buried **GREENWICH CEMETERY**. Grave Location:- 3, 'C', A, 106.

HOLT, ARTHUR. Private. No 29007. 8th Battalion The Yorkshire Regiment. Born Almondbury 29.1.1891. Educated Almondbury Board School. Employed as a warehouseman by Messrs Sykes and Tunnacliffe, Northfield Mills, Almondbury. Attended Zion Methodist Church, Almondbury, and was a member of the mixed choir. At the time of enlistment, was living at 77 Hill Top Road, Paddock. Single. Enlisted 20.3.1916. Wounded 18.10.1917. Died of wounds at No 2 Canadian Casualty Clearing Station, 22.10.1917, aged 26 years. Buried **LIJSSENTHOEK MILITARY CEMETERY**. Grave location:- Plot 25, Row G, Grave 12a. ROH:- Almondbury War Memorial.

HOLT, BENJAMIN. Able Seaman. No J/50716 (DEV). Royal Navy. *HMS Crescent*. Son of Thomas Henry and Eleanor Holt of Upperheaton, Kirkheaton. Died at home, 8.12.1918, aged 25 years. Buried **KIRKHEATON CEMETERY**. Grave location:- 'U', 613. ROH:- St. John's Church, Kirkheaton.

HOLT, JOHN WILLIAM. Captain. 8th Battalion Duke of Wellington's Regiment (formerly 4th Battalion). Son of the late James Holt of Halifax and of Mrs Holt of Hipperholme, Halifax. Husband of Annie Holt, Mayroyd, Lea Street, Lindley, Huddersfield. Employed as a cashier at the West Yorkshire Bank, Huddersfield. Was Superintendent of the Lindley Zion Wesleyan Sunday School. Enlisted November, 1914, with the local Territorial battalion. Embarked for France as a Private in April, 1915. Gazetted Second Lieutenant in June, 1915. Returned to England for training at Clipstone Camp, appointed to a temporary Captaincy whilst he was at Clipstone. Gazetted Captain, 25.6.1917. Returned to France and was killed in action on 27.8.1917, aged 37 years. Buried **POELCAPELLE BRITISH CEMETERY**. Grave location:- Plot 35, Row B, Grave 17. ROH:- St. Stephen's Church, Lindley; Lloyds Bank Roll.

HOLT, WALTER. Private. No 2754. 1/5th Battalion Duke of Wellington's Regiment. Born

Halifax. Lived 25 Back Freehold Street, Primrose Hill. Married, with five children. Employed as a relief porter by the London and North Western Railway Company at Huddersfield station. Attended St. Matthew's Church, Primrose Hill. Was an old Volunteer and a member of the National Reserve. He enlisted at the outbreak of the war. Died of wounds, 7.7.1916, aged 30 years. Buried **PUCHEVILLERS BRITISH CEMETERY.** Grave location:- Plot 1, Row D, Grave 43. ROH:- St. Matthew's Church, Primrose Hill; Huddersfield Drill Hall; London and North Western Railway Company Roll.

HOLTOM, CHARLES CECIL. Lieutenant. 181st Company, Machine Gun Corps. Son of Doctor and Mrs C. J. Holtom of London. Husband of H. K. Holtom, of Victoria Cottage, Lindley. Was honorary secretary of the Huddersfield Playgoers Society. Killed in action in Israel, 31.10.1917, aged 32 years. Buried **BEERSHEBA WAR CEMETERY, ISRAEL.** Grave location:- Row P, Grave 69. ROH:- St. Stephen's Church, Lindley.

HOOPER, RONALD M. Lieutenant. 3rd Field Survey Company, Royal Garrison Artillery. Born Dumbarton 4.3.1878. Son of the Rev. J. H. Hooper, who was a Wesleyan Minister in the Buxton Road circuit, stationed at Lockwood. Educated Kingswood School, Bath. Employed as a college teacher at Bushey Park, London. Single. Enlisted January 1916. Killed in action, 21.3.1918, aged 40 years. Buried **LEBUCQUIERE COMMUNAL CEMETERY EXTENSION.** Grave location:- Plot 2, Row A, Grave 24. ROH:- Mount Pleasant Chapel, Lockwood.

HOPKINS, THOMAS G. G. Guardsman. No 20500. 3rd Battalion Grenadier Guards. Born Shelley. Son of Mr and Mrs George Henry Hopkin, Prospect Terrace, Shelley. Employed at Messrs Stringer and Jagger's Emley Moor colliery. Was a member of the Shelley Liberal Club. Enlisted at the outbreak of the war. Had been wounded on two occasions. Died of wounds, 16.9.1917, aged 21 years. Buried **BLEUET FARM CEMETERY, ELVERDINGHE, BELGIUM.** Grave location:- Plot 1, Row A, Grave 1. ROH:- Emmanuel Church, Shelley.

HOPKINSON, JAMES. Private. No 2290. 1/7th Battalion Duke of Wellington's Regiment. Son of Mrs Buckley, 39 St. Paul's Street, Huddersfield. Died of wounds, 20.12.1915, aged 21 years. Buried **LIJSSENTHOEK MILITARY CEMETERY.** Grave location:- Plot 2, Row D, Grave 23a. ROH:- Huddersfield Drill Hall. His mother received a letter from the Rev. Sidney Hobson, dated Sunday, 19.12.1915, *'I promised your son, Private Hopkinson of the 7th Battalion West Riding Regiment, that I would let you know that he was seriously wounded this morning in a German attack on our lines. He asked me to tell you not to worry but I am told by the Doctor that his case must be regarded as a very serious one. Both his legs were very badly fractured by the explosion of an enemy shell and the Doctor holds out very little hope of recovery. Your son is a brave lad, never have I seen one bear his sufferings more bravely. He is a hero in every sense of the word. When he left here (the 3rd Field Ambulance Dressing Station) he was quite conscious and he was only anxious about you. His one and only concern seemed to be that you should not fret. I pray that God may comfort you in these sad days.'*

HOPKINSON, JOHN. Private. No 19718. 9th Battalion West Yorkshire Regiment. Born Huddersfield 12.7.1893. Son of Mary Hopkinson, 13 Castlegate, Huddersfield. Educated St. Patrick's Roman Catholic School. Employed at the Central Liberal Club for five years as a billiard marker and later as hall assistant. Married. Lived at 6a Bradford Road, Huddersfield (After his enlistment his wife, Amy, lived with her parents at 13 Garden Street, Masborough, Rotherham). Enlisted at the outbreak of the war and went out to the Dardenelles. Died of wounds, 10.11.1915, aged 22 years. Buried **HILL 10 CEMETERY, SUVLA.** Grave location:- Plot 1, Row F, Grave 2. A letter was received from Sergeant A. Maclean of the 35th Field Ambulance R.A.M.C., 11th Division, British Expeditionary Mediterrean Force, who wrote from Suvla Bay, saying that, *'Private Hopkinson was carried into the hospital on the morning of the 10th November and although everything was done for him it was impossible to save his life. He was buried the same afternoon.'*

HORNCASTLE, NORMAN. Private. No 41484. 26th (Tyneside Irish) Battalion Northumberland Fusiliers. Formerly No 19664 Duke of Wellington's Regiment. Born Emley. Son of Joe and Sarah H. Horncastle, 20 Royds Street,

Marsden. Employed as a spinner at Bank Bottom Mills, Marsden. Was a member of the Wesleyan Adult Bible Class and the Marsden Liberal Club. Enlisted March 1916. Embarked for France in July, 1916. Killed in action, 15.10.1917, whilst acting as a stretcher-bearer. He was 23 years of age. Buried **CEMENT HOUSE CEMETERY, LANGEMARCK, BELGIUM**. Grave location:- Plot 1, Row K, Grave 3. ROH:- Marsden Liberal Club; Marsden War Memorial.

HORNE, EDGAR PERCIVAL. Private. No 34432. 1st Battalion King's Own Yorkshire Light Infantry. Born Golcar. Husband of Lizzie Horne, 46 Mary Brow, Golcar. Employed as a pattern weaver by Messrs Ben Hall and Son, of Milnsbridge. Served in Salonica for two years. Had only been in France for a few weeks when he was severely wounded in the chest on 18.10.1918. He was taken to the 41st Casualty Clearing Station where he died of his wounds six days later, on 24.10.1918, aged 36 years. Buried **ROISEL COMMUNAL CEMETERY EXTENSION**. Grave location:- Plot 2, Row D, Grave 24. ROH:- St. John's Church, Golcar.

HORNE, WALTER. Private. No 91839. 5th Battalion The Tank Corps. Formerly No 41167 King's Own Yorkshire Light Infantry. Born Huddersfield. Enlisted Sheffield. Reported missing, presumed killed, 22.3.1918. Has no known grave. Commemorated **POZIERES MEMORIAL TO THE MISSING**.

HORN, CHARLES. Private. No 77662. 23rd Battalion Cheshire Regiment. Formerly No 28381 Northumberland Fusiliers. Born Delph. Enlisted Halifax. Lived Marsden. Killed in action, 31.8.1918. Buried **NIEPPE-BOIS (RUE-DU-BOIS) BRITISH CEMETERY, VIEUX-BERQUIN**. Grave location:- Row D, Grave 15. ROH:- Marsden War Memorial.

HORNER, FRANK. Private. No 18148. 10th Battalion Duke of Wellington's Regiment. Born Spring Street, Huddersfield, 6.7.1895. Son of Mr and Mrs Robert Horner, 427 Woodlands Terrace, Leeds Road, Huddersfield. Educated Spring Grove Board School. Employed as a motor driver by Mr Harry Tomlinson, removal contractor, of Crosland Moor. Attended Brunswick Street Sunday School and the Band of Hope. Single. Enlisted December, 1915, and joined his Regiment on January 24th, 1916. Killed by a sniper on 21.8.1916, aged 21 years. Buried **BERKSHIRE CEMETERY EXTENSION, PLOEGSTEERT, BELGIUM**. Grave location:- Plot D, Row 18.

HORSFALL, ERNEST ARTHUR. Private. No 3707. 1/5th Battalion Duke of Wellington's Regiment. Born 1 Bradley Lane, New North Road, Huddersfield. Son of Arthur and Lily Horsfall, 190 Halifax Old Road, Birkby. Educated Holy Trinity Church of England School, Portland Street, Huddersfield. Employed as a heald maker by Messrs Barlow and Hucknall, Colne Road, Huddersfield. Single. Enlisted 27.12.1914. Suffered a severe wound to the groin near Thiepval Wood, 3.9.1916. Died of wounds on 27.9.1916 at King George's Hospital, London, aged 21 years. Buried **EDGERTON CEMETERY, HUDDERSFIELD**. Grave location:- 10B, 174. ROH:- Huddersfield Drill Hall; Fartown and Birkby War Memorial.

HORSFALL, FRANK. Private. No 241651. 2/5th Battalion Duke of Wellington's Regiment. Born Marsden. Son of Edwin and Rebecca Horsfall, 5 Wood Top, Marsden. Employed as a weaver at Bank Bottom Mills, Marsden. Attended Marsden Parish Church and was a member of the Socalist Institute. Enlisted March, 1916, and embarked for France in January, 1917. Reported missing, presumed killed, at the Battle of Bullecourt, 3.5.1917, aged 28 years. Has no known grave. Commemorated **ARRAS MEMORIAL TO THE MISSING**. ROH:- Huddersfield Drill Hall; Marsden War Memorial.

HORSFALL, FRED. Private. No 305042. 1/7th Battalion Duke of Wellington's Regiment. Son of Mr and Mrs Horsfall, 178 Albert Street, Lockwood. Employed at Parkwood Mills, Lockwood. Married, with three children. Enlisted 1915. Killed in action, 29.4.1918. Has no known grave. Commemorated **ARRAS MEMORIAL TO THE MISSING**. ROH:- Emmanuel Church, Lockwood; Huddersfield Drill Hall.

HORSFALL, HARRY. Private. No 24895. 2nd Battalion Duke of Wellington's Regiment. Born 106 Rashcliffe Hill Road, Lockwood, Huddersfield, 12.12.1894. Son of Tom and Polly Horsfall, 89 Rashcliffe Hill Road, Lockwood. Educated Mount Pleasant Board School. Employed as a baker by Mr E. A. Sykes, confectioner, of Folly Hall. Single. Enlisted 6.10.1916. Killed in action at Pacaut Wood, near Merville and the La Bassee Canal, 15.4.1918, aged 23 years. Has no known grave. Commemorated **PLOEGSTEERT MEMORIAL TO THE MISSING.** ROH:- St. Stephen's Church, Rashcliffe.

HORSFALL, RICHARD SENIOR. Private. No 42350. 11th Battalion Leicestershire Regiment. Born 17.8.1899. Son of John and Elizabeth Horsfall, 29 Kew Hill, Longwood. Educated at Birchencliffe and Lindley Church of England Schools. At the time of enlistment, was living at Branch Farm, Birchencliffe. Enlisted 26.9.1917. Died of wounds at No 7 General Hospital, Boulogne, 4.5.1918, aged 18 years. Buried **BOULOGNE EASTERN CEMETERY.** Grave location:- Plot 9, Row B, Grave 38. ROH:- St. Philip's Church, Birchencliffe.

HORSFALL, TOM. Private. No 15159. 9th Battalion Duke of Wellington's Regiment. Born Holmfirth. Son of Anthony and Matilda Horsfall, Well Hill, Underbank, Holmfirth. Killed in action, 7.8.1915, aged 27 years. Buried **RIDGE WOOD MILITARY CEMETERY, VOORMEZEELE, BELGIUM.** Grave location:- Plot 2, Row G, Grave 6. Private Horsfall's brother, Harry, received a letter from Private Thorpe Brook. In the letter he tells how his brother died, *'Your brother has given his life fighting as a true and brave British soldier. The wounds in both his legs were so severe that he lost a great quantity of blood and he passed away soon afterwards. He was quite conscious at the end and he died with his head in my hands knowing that he had done his duty well. He is to be buried quite close to a number of his brave comrades who died giving their lives in the brave manner he has done. I can realise how sad the news will come to you and it is consolation to know that yours is a home to which grief has entered like it has to many thousands more. There is no doubt whatever that your brother is now in the land where nothing but peace reigns and I pray that God will strengthen you all so that you are able to bear the trouble as well as it is possible to do.'* ROH:- Underbank War Memorial.

HORSFIELD, STANLEY. Corporal. No 241536. 2/5th Battalion Duke of Wellington's Regiment. Born 25 Paddock Foot, Huddersfield, 19.5.1884. Son of Mr and Mrs John Horsfield. Educated St. Thomas's School. Employed as a cotton spinner by the Britannia Mills Company Limited, Crosland Moor. Attended St. Thomas's Church. Single. Reported missing, presumed killed, at the Battle of Bullecourt, 3.5.1917, aged 24 years. Has no known grave. Commemorated **ARRAS MEMORIAL TO THE MISSING.** ROH:- New North Road Baptist Church; All Saints Church, Paddock; Huddersfield Drill Hall.

HORTON, HERBERT. Able Seaman. No R/6038. R.N.R. 'Howe' Battalion, Royal Naval Division. Born Lower Brow, Paddock. Son of Mary Ann Collins, 3 St. Paul's Street, Huddersfield. Educated at St. Paul's Church of England School. Employed as a comber by Messrs. J. Hopkinson and Company Limited, Birkby. Single. Enlisted August 1917. Had only been in France for five weeks when he was killed on 13.1.1918, aged 19 years. Buried **FIFTEEN RAVINE BRITISH CEMETERY, VILLERS-PLOUICH.** Grave location:- Plot 1, Row D, Grave 4/5.

HOSKIN, TOM. Sergeant. No 240419. 2/5th Battalion Duke of Wellington's Regiment. Born Rashcliffe, Huddersfield. Son of Hannah Hoskin, 15 Park Road, Lockwood. Husband of Mary Alice Hoskin of Mexborough. Before the outbreak of the war he had done fourteen years service in the Volunteers and the Territorials. Went to live in Mexborough in 1913 to carry on a grocery business. Killed in action, 14.4.1918, aged 35 years. Buried **BIENVILLERS MILITARY CEMETERY.** Grave location:- Plot 9, Row C, Grave 18. ROH:- Huddersfield Drill Hall.

HOUGHLAND, THOMAS. Corporal. No 241201. 2/5th Battalion Duke of Wellington's Regiment. Born Kirkheaton. Enlisted Huddersfield. Lived Poulton-le-Fylde. Reported missing, presumed killed, at the Battle of Bullecourt, 3.5.1917. Has no known grave. Commemorated **ARRAS MEMORIAL TO THE MISSING.** ROH:- St. John's Church, Kirkheaton; Lepton Parish Church; Huddersfield Drill Hall.

HOWARD, BEN. Private. No 270584. 2nd Battalion The Royal Scots. Formerly No 270584 York and Lancaster Regiment; No 240986 Scottish Rifles. Born Denby Dale. Son of Walter and Sarah Howard. Lived Denby Dale. Died of wounds, 22.3.1918, aged 22 years. Buried **BAC-**

du-SUD BRITISH CEMETERY. Grave location:- Plot 1, Row A, Grave 6. ROH:- Denby Dale and Cumberworth War Memorial.

HOWARD, OLIVER. Rifleman. No C/7893. 18th Battalion King's Royal Rifle Corps. Born Holmfirth. Lived The Holt, Holmfirth. Attended Hinchliffe Mill Wesleyan School. After leaving school was employed as a newsboy by Mr S. Collins, Victoria Street, Holmfirth. He then became a telegraph messenger and, prior to enlistment, a postman in the Holmfirth district. Enlisted, 23.11.1915, and underwent training at Andover, Banbury and Wimbledon before leaving for France in June, 1916. Killed in action, 15.9.1916, aged 22 years. Has no known grave. Commemorated **THIEPVAL MEMORIAL TO THE MISSING.** ROH:- Holmfirth War Memorial; Huddersfield GPO Roll.

HOWARD, THOMAS. Corporal. No 203745. 1/6th Battalion Duke of Wellington's Regiment. Born Holmfirth. Son of Mr and Mrs George Henry Howard, Liphill Farm, Holmfirth. Husband of Hilda Howard of Dam Head, Hinchliffe Mill, Holmbridge. Educated at Field End School and attended St David's Sunday School, Holmbridge. Employed as a weaver by Messrs Greenwood of Digley Mills. Enlisted at the outbreak of the war and embarked for France in September, 1916. Killed in action, 14.4.1918, aged 24 years. Has no known grave. Commemorated **TYNE COT MEMORIAL TO THE MISSING.** His widow received a letter from a chum of her son who wrote, *'I am very sorry to be the bearer of bad news to you and very much regret to tell you that Thomas lost his life about five days ago. From enquiries I have made, it appears that he was in the market place of a certain town when an enemy shell exploded near him, killing two and wounding two. Lads from his section tell me that he had been slightly wounded previously in the hand but did not go away with it and they speak very highly of his conduct. Later on I may be able to give you more particulars. I know what a terrible blow this will be to you. I pray that God may be with you in this terrible hour of trial. As a friend I mourn his loss very deeply. We were always good pals. My deepest sympathy is with you.'* ROH:- Holme and Holmbridge War Memorial.

HOWARTH, FRED. Sapper. No 251954. 33rd Light Railway Operating Company, Royal Engineers. Formerly No 3/29296 Duke of Wellington's Regiment. Born Holmfirth. Son of Isaac and Lydia Howard, of Holmfirth. Educated at St. John's School, Holmfirth. Husband of Lucy Howarth, 28 Holt Lane, Holmfirth. Employed as a weaver, firstly at Ribbleden Mills and then at Messrs Kaye and Stewarts of Lockwood. Enlisted 4.9.1916. Embarked for France 9.1.1917. Came home on leave, returning to France on 30.1.1918. Died of wounds at No 44 Casualty Clearing Station, Poperinghe, Belgium, 25.4.1918, aged 35 years. Buried **NINE ELMS BRITISH CEMETERY, POPERINGHE.** Grave location:- Plot 14, Grave C, Row 3. ROH:- Holmfirth War Memorial.

HOWARTH, JOHN. Private. No 301782. 1/8th Battalion Durham Light Infantry. Formerly No 29509 Northumberland Fusiliers. Born Primrose Hill, Huddersfield. Son of Joe and Sarah Anne Howarth, 264 Wakefield Road, Dalton. Prior to enlistment, was employed by a Warrington firm as a plumber and electrician. Reported missing, presumed killed, 5.11.1916, aged 25 years. Has no known grave. Commemorated **THIEPVAL MEMORIAL TO THE MISSING.** ROH:- St. John's Church, Kirkheaton.

HOWARTH, RICHARD. Bombardier. No L/25530. 'A' Battery, 168th Brigade Royal Field Artillery. Married. Living at Primrose Hill, Huddersfield. Killed in action, 1.7.1916. Has no known grave. Commemorated **THIEPVAL MEMORIAL TO THE MISSING.** ROH:- Milton Independent Church.

HOWARTH, WALTER. Private. No 5311. 2/5th Battalion Duke of Wellington's Regiment. Born Back Hill, Marsh, 13.7.1896. Son of Mr and Mrs Friend Howarth, 47 Eldon Road, Marsh. Educated Holy Trinity Church of England School, Marsh. Employed as a coachman by the Standard Fireworks Company. Single. Enlisted 15.3.1916. Embarked for France in January, 1917. Killed at the Wonder-Werk near Thiepval, 28.2.1917, aged 20 years. Has no known grave. Commemorated **THIEPVAL MEMORIAL TO THE MISSING.** ROH:- Holy Trinity Church, Huddersfield; Marsh War Memorial; Huddersfield Drill Hall.

HOWELL, ERNEST. Private. No 40979. 10th Battalion Lincolnshire Regiment. Formerly No

32363 North Staffordshire Regiment. Born Linthwaite. Son of Mr and Mrs William Howell, 22 Lowestwood Lane, Golcar. Was a member of the committee of the Wellhouse Liberal Club and also the Golcar Floral and Horticultural Society. Attended the Wellhouse United Methodist Chapel. Enlisted September 1916. Embarked for France in December, 1916. Reported missing, 28.4.1917, aged 31 years. Buried **ROEUX BRITISH CEMETERY.** Grave location:- Special Memorial D 11. ROH:- St. John's Church, Golcar.

HOWE, JOE. Private. No 8318. 2nd Battalion King's Own Yorkshire Light Infantry. Born St. Thomas, Huddersfield. Lived Back Union Street, Huddersfield. Reported missing, 1.11.1914 and afterwards presumed to have been killed on that date. Has no known grave. Commemorated **LE TOURET MEMORIAL TO THE MISSING.**

HOWITT, CECIL JOHN. Corporal. No 265962. 2/7th Battalion West Yorkshire Regiment, attached 185th Trench Mortar Battery. Son of John Thomas and Charlotte Eleanor Emma Howitt of Stoke, Lincolnshire. Husband of Hetty Howitt, of Elm Street, Skelmanthorpe. Employed by Messrs Edwin Field and Sons, Tentercroft Mills. Enlisted November 1914. Killed in action, 24.4.1918, aged 23 years. Buried **GOMMECOURT BRITISH CEMETERY No 2.** Grave location:- Plot 4, Row H, Grave 21/22. ROH:- St. Aidan's Church, Skelmanthorpe.

HOYLAND, GEORGE NEAVERSON. Trooper. No 2392. Royal Horse Guards. Born Cumberworth. Son of Elizabeth Sharpe Hoyland, of High Street, Denby Dale and the late Albert Edward Hoyland. Died of wounds, 8.11.1917, at No 10 Casualty Clearing Station, 8.11.1917, aged 24 years. Buried **LIJSSENTHOEK MILITARY CEMETERY.** Grave location:- Plot 22, Row AA, Grave 1. ROH:- Denby Dale and Cumberworth War Memorial.

HOYLE, ALBERT. Private. No 53433. 15th/17th Battalion West Yorkshire Regiment. Born Slaithwaite. Son of Nellie and the late Anthony Hoyle, 27 Nabbs Lane, Slaithwaite. Employed as a piecer by Messrs James Holroyd and Son of Uppermill. Enlisted 1.5.1917. Embarked for France on 3.4.1918. Killed in action, 23.5.1918, aged 19 years. Buried **CAESTRE MILITARY CEMETERY.** Grave location:- Plot 1, Row B, Grave 26. ROH:- St. James Church, Slaithwaite; Slaithwaite War Memorial.

HOYLE, ARCHIBALD CYRIL (ARCHIE). Private. No 31738. 7th Battalion North Staffordshire Regiment. Born Halifax. Son of Mr and Mrs John Hoyle, 3 Chapel Lane, Milnsbridge. Attended the Milnsbridge Wesleyan Sunday School. Employed as a cotton spinner by Messrs Shaw and Shaw, Britannia Mills, Milnsbridge. Enlisted 6.11.1916. Sailed for India 5.1.1917. Died from Enteric Fever in India, 19.4.1917, aged 25 years. Buried **BELGAUM GOVERNMENT CEMETERY, INDIA.** (Now Commemorated on the **KIRKEE 1914-1918 MEMORIAL, INDIA**). (Brother of Private **JOE HARRY HOYLE**, killed in action, October, 1914, q.v.). ROH:- Milnsbridge War Memorial.

HOYLE, EDWIN HAROLD. Private. No 91366. 1/6th Battalion Sherwood Foresters. Born Milnsbridge, Huddersfield. Enlisted Ilkeston, Derbyshire. Husband of Alice Hoyle, 6 East Street, Ilkeston, Derbyshire. Killed in action, 31.8.1918. Buried **FOUQUIERES CHURCHYARD EXTENSION.** Grave location:- Plot 4, Row F, Grave 1. ROH:- Milnsbridge War Memorial.

HOYLE, ERNEST ALBERT. Lance Sergeant. No 203711. 1/7th Battalion Duke of Wellington's Regiment. Born Intake Farm, Stainland, Halifax, 28.8.1896. Son of John T. and Clara Hoyle, 64 Holly Bank Road, Lindley. Educated Outlane Council School. Employed by Messrs Smith and Calverley of Lindley. Single. Enlisted 16.2.1916. Wounded at Cambrai. Died of wounds, 18.11.1918, at the 7th General Hospital, Boulogne, aged 22 years. Buried **TERLINCTHUN BRITISH CEMETERY.** Grave location:- Plot 11, Row B, Grave 34. ROH:- St. Stephen's Church, Lindley; Bethel United Methodist Church, Outlane; Huddersfield Drill Hall.

HOYLE, FRED. Private. No 202936. 1/4th Battalion King's Own Yorkshire Light Infantry. Born Linthwaite. Lived Jovil, Linthwaite. Married. Attended Linthwaite Parish Church. Was a member of the Smith Ryding Working Men's Club. Employed by Messrs Charles Lockwood and Sons, Black Rock Mills. Enlisted 22.9.1916. Embarked for France in the second week of January, 1917. Killed in action, 10.4.1917, aged 36 years. Buried **RUE-du-**

BACQUEROT No 1 MILITARY CEMETERY, LAVENTIE. Grave location:- Plot 3, Row A, Grave 4. ROH:- Linthwaite War Memorial; St. John's Church, Golcar.

HOYLE, GEORGE EWART. Private. No 276279. 1/9th Battalion Durham Light Infantry. Born Linthwaite. Son of Edwin and Phoebe Hoyle, of One Ash, Linthwaite. Attended Carr Lane United Methodist Church, Slaithwaite, where he was a member of the Young Men's Class, the Band of Hope and the Pierrot troupe. He was also a member of the Slaithwaite Y.M.C.A. Employed as a weaver at Spring Grove Mills, Linthwaite. Prior to enlistment, he worked for twelve months as a volunteer for the Y.M.C.A at Thoresby Park and, later, at Doncaster. Enlisted at Doncaster February, 1916. Reported missing near Rheims, 21.7.1918 and afterwards was presumed to have been killed on that date. He was 27 years of age. Has no known grave. Commemorated **SOISSONS MEMORIAL TO THE MISSING.** ROH:- Carr Lane Methodist Church, Slaithwaite; Linthwaite War Memorial.

HOYLE, GEORGE WILLIAM. Private. No 34769. 15th (1st Leeds Pals) Battalion West Yorkshire Regiment. Born Cliff End, Longwood, 13.10.1878. Son of the late Mr and Mrs Dan Hoyle, Ballroyd, Longwood. Educated Longwood National School. Attended Longwood Parish Church and also the Milnsbridge Baptist Chapel. Married, with three children. Employed as a sterilizer at the Leeds General Infirmary. At the time of enlistment, was living at 35 Thornhill Road, Longwood. Enlisted 17.6.1916. Died of wounds at No 41st Casualty Clearing Station, 18.6.1917, aged 39 years. Buried **DUISANS BRITISH CEMETERY.** Grave location:- Plot 3, Row L, Grave 14. ROH:- St. Mark's Parish Church, Longwood; Longwood War Memorial.

HOYLE, HAROLD. Gunner. No 77631. 47th Siege Battery Royal Garrison Artillery. Born Slaithwaite. Lived with his sister, Mrs John W. Hirst, 14 Hill Top, Lingards, Slaithwaite. Employed as a weaver by Messrs Ben Hall and Sons, Milnsbridge. Was a member of the Booth Banks Working Men's Club. Enlisted May 1916. Killed in action, 21.7.1917, aged 27 years. Buried **DICKIEBUSCH NEW MILITARY CEMETERY EXTENSION.** Grave location:- Plot 2, Row E, Grave 8. ROH:- St. James Church, Slaithwaite; Slaithwaite War Memorial.

HOYLE, HARRY. Private. No 41481. 26th (Tyneside Irish) Battalion Northumberland Fusiliers. Formerly No 19259 Duke of Wellington's Regiment. Born Snow Lea 25.11.1884. Son of William Hoyle, 497 Mount, Outlane. Educated Outlane National School. Employed as a weaver. Enlisted 26.2.1916. Killed in action, 28.4.1917. Buried **BROWN'S COPSE CEMETERY, ROEUX.** Grave location:- Plot 3, Row A, Grave 26. ROH:- Bethel United Methodist Church, Outlane.

HOYLE, HARRY. Lance Corporal. No 267790. 1/7th Battalion West Yorkshire Regiment. Formerly No 6064 3/5th Battalion Duke of Wellington's Regiment. Born Paddock 17.10.1896. Son of Walter and Agnes Hoyle, 49 Beech Street, Paddock. Educated Paddock Council School. Attended Paddock United Methodist Church. Employed as a weaver. Single. Enlisted 17.3.1916. Killed in action at Ypres, 21.3.1918, aged 22 years. Buried **MENIN ROAD SOUTH MILITARY CEMETERY, YPRES.** Grave location:- Plot 3, Row F, Grave 25. (Brother of Private **WILFRED HOYLE**, killed in action, 11.8.1917, q.v.). ROH:- All Saints Church, Paddock; Shared Church, Paddock.

HOYLE, HARRY. Private. No 23020. 8th Battalion Duke of Wellington's Regiment. Born Brighouse. Son of Robert Shaw Hoyle and Hannah Hoyle, 122 Northgate, Almondbury. Husband of Beatrice Hoyle, 33 Barrow Buildings, Moldgreen. Employed as a dyer's labourer by Messrs Isaac Robson and Sons, of Dalton. Was a member of the Dyer's Club. Killed in action at Passchendaele, 9.10.1917, aged 26 years. Has no known grave. Commemorated **TYNE COT MEMORIAL TO THE MISSING.** ROH:- Moldgreen War Memorial; Christ Church, Moldgreen; Almondbury War Memorial.

HOYLE, HERBERT STANLEY. Private. No 241539. 2/5th Battalion Duke of Wellington's Regiment. Born Huddersfield. Son of John and Emily Hoyle, 1 Perseverance Street, Primrose Hill, Huddersfield. Employed by Messrs F. Eastwood and Company, Colne Road. Was a member of Primrose Hill Liberal Club. Enlisted 1916. Died of wounds at No 48 Casualty Clearing Station, 27.11.1917, aged 30 years. Buried **ROCQUIGNY-EQUANCOURT ROAD BRITISH CEMETERY**. Grave location:- Plot 3, Row D, Grave 18. ROH:- Huddersfield Drill Hall.

HOYLE, JAMES FREDERICK. Gunner. No 162511. 301st Siege Battery, Royal Garrison Artillery. Born Halifax. Son of James Hoyle: Husband of Edith Hoyle, 7 Towngate, Marsden. Employed as a spinner by the Colne Valley Spinning Company Limited, Linthwaite. Enlisted May 1916. Embarked for France in August, 1916. On 14.11.1917, was admitted into No 49 Casualty Clearing Station suffering from severe burns accidentally received in the trenches. His wife was informed by the Sister-in-Charge that from the first his case was almost hopeless and he died of his wounds on 23.11.1917, aged 26 years. Buried **ACHIET-LE-GRAND COMMUNAL CEMETERY EXTENSION**. Grave location:- Plot 1, Row P, Grave 24. ROH:- Marsden War Memorial; Bethel United Methodist Church, Outlane.

HOYLE, JOE HARRY. Private. No 8262. 2nd Battalion The Yorkshire Regiment. Born Siddal, Halifax. Son of Mr and Mrs John Hoyle, 3 Chapel Lane, Milnsbridge. Prior to enlisting in the army, in 1905, was employed by Messrs B. and J. Whitwam and Sons Limited, Stanley Mills, Golcar. Had served nine years in the army and, under ordinary circumstances, would have been discharged in November, 1914. Had been stationed in York and Richmond and was in South Africa for two or three years after the war. Had occupied the position of waiter in the Officer's Mess. Killed in action, 30.10.1914, aged 31 years. Has no known grave. Commemorated **MENIN GATE MEMORIAL TO THE MISSING**. (Brother of Private **ARCHIBALD CYRIL HOYLE**, died in India, 19.4.1917, q.v.). ROH:- Milnsbridge War Memorial.

HOYLE, JOHN HENRY. Private. No PS/10120. 9th Battalion Royal Fusiliers. Born Wilson's Square, Netherthong. Youngest son of Ben Hoyle, of The Heys, Thongsbridge. Served as a pupil teacher under Mr J. T. Jackson at Netherthong Church School. Was afterwards a teacher at Clayton West Council School. Was organist at the Wesleyan Chapel, Deanhouse. Married to Miss Fanny Kaye, daughter of Mr Henry Kaye.

Was in business as a music dealer at Clayton West. Enlisted at Oxford in January, 1916, in the Public Schools Battalion of the Royal Fusiliers. Wounded on one occasion. Reported missing at Bayonet Trench, near Gueudecourt, during the Battle of the Transloy Ridges on 7.10.1916, aged 36 years. Has no known grave. Commemorated **THIEPVAL MEMORIAL TO THE MISSING**. ROH:- Clayton West and High Hoyland War Memorial; Netherthong Working Men's Club.

HOYLE, JOHN HENRY. Gunner. No 49313. Royal Garrison Artillery. Born Huddersfield. Lived 875 Leeds Road, Deighton, Huddersfield. Married. Discharged from the army, due to illness, on 18.6.1918. Died of chronic nephritis and bronchitis on 27.5.1922.

HOYLE, JOSEPH WILLIAM. Private. No 33543. 6th Battalion The Yorkshire Regiment. Born 4 Ivy Street, Crosland Moor, 5.4.1893. Son of George and Martha Hoyle, 2 Ivy Street, Crosland Moor. Educated Crosland Moor Council School. Employed as a healder and twister-in. Single. Enlisted 17.6.1916. Wounded at Poelcapelle, Belgium, 9.10.1917. Died of wounds at No 3 General Hospital, Le Treport, 16.10.1917, aged 24 years. Buried **MONT HUON MILITARY CEMETERY**. Grave location:- Plot 5, Row A, Grave 6a. ROH:- St. Barnabas Church, Crosland Moor: United Methodist Church; memorial in Lockwood Cemetery.

HOYLE, THOMAS HENRY. Sergeant. No 240578. 1/5th Battalion Duke of Wellington's Regiment. Born Outcote Bank, Huddersfield in May, 1892. Son of Joseph and Mary Hannah Hoyle, 29 Cross Grove Street, Huddersfield. Educated Spring Grove Council School. Employed as a bookbinder and lithographer by Messrs J. Broadbent and Company, printers and bookbinders, Albion Street, Huddersfield. Attended Buxton Road Chapel. Single. Enlisted December 1914. Died of wounds at No 3 General Hospital, Le Treport, 27.10.1917, aged 24 years. Buried **MONT HUON MILITARY CEMETERY**. Grave location:- Plot 6, Row A, Grave 12a. ROH:- Huddersfield Drill Hall.

HOYLE, WILFRED. Private. No 24754. 8th Battalion Duke of Wellington's Regiment. Born Paddock 28.2.1888. Son of Walter and Agnes Hoyle, 49 Beech Street, Paddock. Educated

Paddock Council School. Attended Paddock United Methodist Church. Employed as a dyer by Messrs Crowther Brothers, Stanley Mills, Milnsbridge. Attended Queen Street Chapel. Single. Enlisted July 1916. Killed in action, 11.8.1917, aged 31, at Steenbeek, Belgium. Has no known grave. Commemorated **MENIN GATE MEMORIAL TO THE MISSING**. (Brother of Private **HARRY HOYLE**, killed in action, 21.3.1918, q.v.). ROH:- All Saints Church, Paddock; Shared Church, Paddock.

HUDSON, ALBERT ALFRED. Corporal. No 306035. 2/5th Battalion Duke of Wellington's Regiment. Lived Milnsbridge. Enlisted Doncaster. Killed in action 15.9.1918. Buried **HERMIES HILL BRITISH CEMETERY**. Grave location:- Plot 2, Row E, Grave 24. ROH:- Huddersfield Drill Hall; Longwood War Memorial.

HUDSON, ERNEST. Private. No 203738. 1/4th Battalion Duke of Wellington's Regiment. Born Sheepridge, Huddersfield, 29.9.1891. Son of Harry and the late Harriet Hudson, 20 Mitre Street, Marsh. Educated Deighton Council School. Employed as a cloth finisher by Messrs Edwin Walker and Company, Leeds Road, Huddersfield. Single. Died of gas poisoning, 29.6.1917, aged 25 years. Buried **NOEUX-LES-MINES COMMUNAL CEMETERY**. Grave location:- Plot 2, Row C, Grave 28. ROH:- Marsh War Memorial.

HUDSON, FRED. Private. No 32803. 2/4th Battalion Duke of Wellington's Regiment. Born Bradley, Huddersfield. Son of Mr and Mrs Geoffrey Hudson, Lower Farm, Cockley Hill, Kirkheaton and late of Leeds Road, Bradley. Employed as a coal miner by Messrs Benjamin Elliot and Sons of Lepton. Had been in France for seven months when he was killed near Rheims on 20.7.1918, aged 21 years. Buried **MARFAUX BRITISH CEMETERY**. Grave location:- Plot 3, Row B, Grave 6. ROH:- St. John's Church, Kirkheaton.

HUDSON, JULIUS. Private. No 75586. Royal Army Medical Corps, attached 1st/3rd (West Riding) Field Ambulance. Born Delph. Son of J. H. and Edna Hudson of Mount Royd, Marsden. Husband of Ethel Hudson, of 'Broadbent', Golcar Brow, Meltham, Huddersfield. Employed as a weaver at Bank Bottom Mills, Marsden. Was a member and secretary of the St. John Ambulance Association. He was also a member of the Wesleyan Adult Bible Class. Enlisted October, 1915, and was drafted to India on 24.11.1915. In March, 1916, he embarked for France and came home on leave in January, 1917. Was taken ill whilst at home and received treatment at the Royds Hall Military Hospital, Huddersfield, and later at the Meltham Convalescent Home. He returned to France and was again invalided home, with trench fever, being for sometime in hospital in Eastbourne. He was transferred to Blackpool, and returned to France once more on 2.11.1917. Killed in action, 28.11.1917, aged 30 years. Has no known grave. Commemorated **TYNE COT MEMORIAL TO THE MISSING**. ROH:- St. Bartholomew's Church, Meltham: Marsden War Memorial.

HUDSON, ROBINSON. Private. No 3/9280. 2nd Battalion Duke of Wellington's Regiment. Born 10 Sheepridge Road, Huddersfield. Son of Sam and Matilda Burleigh Hudson, 3 Sunny View, Deighton. Educated Woodhouse Church School. Employed as a labourer. Single. Enlisted 30.11.1908. Killed in action at the First Battle of Ypres, 11.11.1914, aged 25. Has no known grave. Commemorated **MENIN GATE MEMORIAL TO THE MISSING**. ROH:- Christ Church, Woodhouse Hill.

HUGHES, JAMES. Private. No 241902. 2/5th Battalion Duke of Wellington's Regiment. Enlisted Halifax. Lived Moldgreen. Killed in action, 20.11.1917. Buried **HERMIES HILL BRITISH CEMETERY**. Grave location:- Special Memorial A 15. ROH:- Christ Church, Moldgreen; Huddersfield Drill Hall.

HUGHES, JOHN CHARLES. Private. No 38430. 7th Battalion The Yorkshire Regiment. Born Mexborough 15.8.1875. Son of Charles Edward and Emily Hughes, 98 Lockwood Road, Huddersfield. Educated Garden Street Board School, Mexborough. Employed as a tramcar cleaner by the Huddersfield Corporation Tramways Department at the Great Northern Street Depot. Single. Enlisted 23.3.1916. Died of bronchitis at Rouen Base Hospital, 31.1.1917, aged 41 years. Buried **St. SEVER CEMETERY EXTENSION**. Grave location:- Block O, Plot 4, Row H, Grave 1. ROH:- Rashcliffe United

Methodist Church; St. Stephen's Church, Rashcliffe; memorial in Lockwood Cemetery.

HULMES, ALBERT. Private. No 203314. 1/4th Battalion Duke of Wellington's Regiment. Born 34 High Street, Paddock, 11.1.1897. Son of the late William and Mary Hulmes. Lived with his brother, Frank Hulmes, at 34 High Street, Paddock. Educated Paddock Council School. Employed as a warehouseman by Messrs J. Fenton and Sons Limited, Bradley Mills. Single. Enlisted 30.3.1916. Was taken prisoner by the Germans in April, 1918, and put to work behind the German lines. Was killed at Fournes, Northern France, on 21.8.1918 by a bomb dropped from an aeroplane, aged 21. Buried **CABARET ROUGE BRITISH CEMETERY, SOUCHEZ.** Grave location:- Plot 7, Row F, Grave 3. ROH:- All Saints Church, Paddock.

HUMPHRIES, ARTHUR GEORGE. Private. No 36488. 1/7th Battalion Northumberland Fusiliers. Born Stroud, Gloucestershire, in 1881. Educated at Newtown, Montgomery, North Wales. Husband of Elizabeth Humphries, 4 Newhouse Place, Bradley Lane, Huddersfield. Employed as a tram driver by the Huddersfield Corporation Tramways Department. Enlisted 24.1.1917. Reported missing, presumed killed, at the Battle of Passchendaele, 26.10.1917, aged 36. Has no known grave. Commemorated **TYNE COT MEMORIAL TO THE MISSING.** ROH:- Holy Trinity Church, Huddersfield.

HUNNEYBELL, CLARENCE VICTOR. Private. No 49948. 6th Battalion The King's (Liverpool Regiment). Born Huddersfield. Fourth son of the late Colour Sergeant Hunneybell and Mrs Hunneybell, 9, Wood Terrace, Primrose Hill. Attended St. Matthew's Church, Primrose Hill. Employed as junior numbertaker by the London and North Western Railway Company. Killed in action at Passchendaele, 20.9.1917, aged 20 years. Has no known grave. Commemorated **TYNE COT MEMORIAL TO THE MISSING.** ROH:- St. Matthew's Church, Primrose Hill; London and North Western Railway Company Roll.

HUNSLEY, HERBERT. Driver. No 14901. 32nd Divisional Ammunition Column, Royal Field Artillery. Born Beverley. Lived 2 Scholes Road, Birkby. Died of wounds, 17.8.1916, aged 23 years. Buried **BOULOGNE EASTERN CEMETERY.** Grave location:- 8, B, 143.

HUNT, FREDERICK. Private. No 10425. 2nd Battalion Duke of Wellington's Regiment. Born Huddersfield. Son of John and Anne Hunt. Wounded at Mons in August, 1914. Died at home, 5.1.1917, aged 25 years. Buried **EDGERTON CEMETERY, HUDDERSFIELD.** Grave location:- 11B, 125. ROH:- St. Paul's Church, Southgate, Huddersfield.

HUNTER, JAMES. Private. No 44365. 8th Battalion Cheshire Regiment. Born Thatch House, Bramham Park near Wetherby. Son of James and Margaret Hunter, 36 Netheroyd Hill Road, Huddersfield. Educated Hillhouse Council School, Huddersfield. Employed as a mule minder. Single. Enlisted 19.6.1916. Killed in action near Baghdad, Mesopotamia, 30.4.1917, aged 24. Has no known grave. Commemorated **BASRA MEMORIAL, IRAQ.** ROH:- Netheroyd Hill Methodist Church; Fartown and Birkby War Memorial.

HUTCHINSON, JOHN. Private. No 24748. 'Y' Company, 8th Battalion Duke of Wellington's Regiment. Born Honley. Son of Granby and Emily Hutchinson, Chapel Terrace, Bradshaw Road, Honley. Attended Honley Wesleyan Chapel. Employed as a twister at Rock Mills. Enlisted, 1916, and embarked for France in January, 1917. Killed in action at Passchendaele, 9.10.1917, aged 20 years. Has no known grave. Commemorated **TYNE COT MEMORIAL TO THE MISSING.** ROH:- Honley War Memorial.

HUTTON, STANLEY ROEBUCK. Private. No 24525. 10th Battalion Duke of Wellington's Regiment. Born Huddersfield. Youngest son of Mr and Mrs Thomas Hutton, 31 Mulberry Street, Moldgreen. Married, with one child. Lived 2 Park Valley, Lockwood. Employed by Mr Tom Crossley, flock and waste dealer, Canal Bridge, Aspley, Huddersfield. Killed in action at Passchendaele, 20.9.1917, aged 27 years. Has no known grave. Commemorated **TYNE COT MEMORIAL TO THE MISSING.** ROH:- Emmanuel Church, Lockwood; Christ Church, Moldgreen.

HYDE, THOMAS. Private. No 2408. 1/5th Battalion Duke of Wellington's Regiment. Born Moldgreen. Son of Frank and Lena Hyde, 40 Newsome Cross, Huddersfield. Was a member of the Boys Brigade, connected with Queen Street Mission. Employed by Messrs Fox and Company, yarn spinners, Wells Mills, Huddersfield. Enlisted August 1914. Embarked for France in April, 1915. Killed in action, 11.7.1915, aged 19 years. Buried **BARD COTTAGE CEMETERY.** Grave location:- Plot 1, Row A, Grave 40. ROH:- Huddersfield Drill Hall; Almondbury War Memorial.

HYNES, FRANCIS. Private. No 32677. 1/4th Battalion Duke of Wellington's Regiment. Born Huddersfield. Killed in action, 11.10.1918. Buried **WELLINGTON CEMETERY.** Grave location:- Special Memorial B 1.

HYNES, JAMES HENRY. Private. No 97735. 236th Company, Machine Gun Corps. Formerly No 2141 Duke of Wellington's Regiment. Born John Street, Huddersfield in 1896. Grandson of Mrs C. Hynes, 12 Swallow Street, Huddersfield. Educated St. Patrick's Roman Catholic School. Employed as a millhand by Messrs Middlemost Brothers and Company Limited. Single. Enlisted in 1915. Wounded 5.12.1917. Died of wounds at No 4 Casualty Clearing Station, 6.12.1917, aged 20 years. Buried **DOZINGHEM MILITARY CEMETERY.** Grave location:- Plot 14, Row F, Grave 1.

IBBERSON, WILLIE. Private. No 35614. 26th (Tyneside Irish) Battalion Northumberland Fusiliers. Formerly No 37933 Durham Light Infantry. Born Penistone. Son of the late Mrs Anne Ibberson, Bunkers Hill, Holmfirth. Lived at Burnlee, Holmfirth with Mr Arthur Wells. Employed as a blacksmith by Messrs F. and J. Marsden at Newgate Quarries. Embarked for France in September 1916. Killed in action, 9.4.1917, aged 37 years. Buried **ROCLINCOURT VALLEY CEMETERY.** Grave location:- Plot 2, Row C, Grave 10. ROH:- Holmfirth War Memorial.

IDDON, GEORGE. Private. No 2783. 1/5th Battalion Duke of Wellington's Regiment. Born 20 Trafalgar Street, Rochdale, 21.1.1897. Son of Joseph and Anne Iddon, 17 Beech Terrace, Bradford Road North, Huddersfield. Educated Mount Pleasant Council School. Was a bandsman in the local Salvation Army. Employed as a tailor for Messrs Brook, Sugden and Company, Paige Street, Huddersfield. Single. Enlisted 2.9.1914. Wounded on 3.9.1916, whilst taking a message to Headquarters. He lay in a shell hole for three days before being brought in with a severely crushed leg. Died of wounds at No 6 General Hospital, Rouen, 11.9.1916, aged 19 years. Buried **St. SEVER CEMETERY, ROUEN.** Cemetery location:- Plot B. Row 25. Grave 20. ROH:- Salvation Army; St. Andrew's Church, Leeds Road; Huddersfield Drill Hall; Fartown and Birkby War Memorial.

ILLINGWORTH, DENNIS. Corporal. No 54548. 24th Battalion Machine Gun Corps. Formerly No 3231 Duke of Wellington's Regiment. Born Huddersfield. Eldest son of Mr and Mrs Alfred Illingworth, 5 Brackenhall Road, Sheepridge, Huddersfield. Employed as a butcher by the Argentine Meat Company, Buxton Road, Huddersfield. Enlisted at the outbreak of the war. Killed in action near Cambrai, 8.10.1918, aged 22 years. Buried **PROVILLE BRITISH CEMETERY.** Grave location:- Plot 1, Row C, Grave 33. ROH:- Christ Church, Woodhouse Hill.

ILLINGWORTH, GEORGE STANLEY. Private. No 301908. 1/8th Battalion Durham Light Infantry. Formerly No 29117 Northumberland Fusiliers. Born Honley. Son of George and Polly Illingworth, Rock Terrace, Brockholes. Attended Brockholes Church Sunday School and was a member of Honley Bowling Club and the Working Men's Club. Employed by Mr T. A. Thornton of Honley. Died of wounds at Sedgemoor Park Hospital, Old Trafford, Manchester, on 7.5.1917, aged 24 years. Buried **St. GEORGE'S CHURCHYARD, BROCKHOLES.** Grave location:- F, 42. East of Church. ROH:- Honley War Memorial; Brockholes War Memorial.

INESON, BEN. Private. No 4/8254. 1st Battalion West Yorkshire Regiment. Born Big Valley, Huddersfield, 19.7.1892. Son of Mr and Mrs Frank Ineson, 263 Thornton Road, Crosland Moor. Educated Mount Pleasant Board School, Lockwood. Employed as a mill mechanic by Messrs Joseph Dyson and Sons Limited, Milnsbridge. Single. Enlisted 6.8.1914. Embarked for France 26.12.1914. Killed in action, 28.3.1915, aged 23 years. Buried **HOUPLINES COMMUNAL CEMETERY EXTENSION.** Grave location:- Plot 2, Row E, Grave 25. His father received a letter written by his son's Platoon Commander, F. Bastow, 1st Battalion West

Yorkshire Regiment, 18th Brigade, 6th Division, on 30.3.1915, *'I regret to have to tell you that your son, Private Ineson, was killed in action on the evening of March 28th. A bomb from a trench mortar was flung into the trenches which were occupied by the men of my platoon. It burst, killing your son instantly and wounding four others, one of whom died two hours later. Your son Ben was buried in a churchyard behind the lines. Captain Armitage read the burial service. 15 of his comrades and I attended the burial service. Captain Armitage, comrades and I wish you to accept our sincere sympathy. This will be sad news to you but it is the fortune of war. He was killed whilst doing his duty as a soldier. His personal belongings will be forwarded to you through the usual channel.'* ROH:- Lockwood Baptist Church: Rehoboth Baptist Church; St. Barnabas Church, Crosland Moor.

INGHAM, LEWIS SAMUEL SUTCLIFFE. Private. No 38595. 8th Battalion York and Lancaster Regiment. Born Hawk Street, Huddersfield, 17.11.1880. Educated Huddersfield Parish Church School. Became a messenger at the Post Office when he was 14 years of age and was appointed a postman two years later. Husband of Ada M. Ingham, 29 Cross Lane, Primrose Hill, Huddersfield. Enlisted 31.10.1916. Killed in action, 9.4.1917, aged 36 years. Buried **RAILWAY DUGOUTS (TRANSPORT FARM) BURIAL GROUND.** Grave location:- Plot 7, Row L, Grave 27. ROH:- Huddersfield GPO Roll.

INGHAM, PERCY. Private. No 240079. 1/6th Battalion Duke of Wellington's Regiment. Born Huddersfield. Only son of Mr and Mrs A. Ingham, 'Thornlea', Birkhouse Lane, Moldgreen. Was a member of the Huddersfield Parish Church choir and later attended Christ Church, Moldgreen. A keen footballer. Employed as a clerk and traveller with Mr R. A. Bell, wholesale chemist, of Huddersfield. Joined the local Territorials in 1911. Enlisted at the outbreak of the war. Embarked for France in April, 1915. Killed in action, 11.4.1918, aged 23 years. Has no known grave. Commemorated **TYNE COT MEMORIAL TO THE MISSING.** ROH:- Christ Church, Moldgreen.

INGRAM, HERBERT WILLIAM. Guardsman. No 30053. 3rd Battalion Grenadier Guards. Born Butterknowle, Durham, 16.9.1890. Son of Thomas and Eliza Ingram, 2 Duke Street, Huddersfield. Employed as a relief signalman on the Lancashire and Yorkshire railway. Single. Enlisted 21.6.1917. Killed in action, 23.8.1918. Buried **BUCQUOY ROAD CEMETERY.** Grave location:- Plot 6, Row D, Grave 15. (Brother of Private **SIDNEY ROWLAND INGRAM,** killed in action, 26.10.1917, q.v.). ROH:- High Street United Methodist Church.

INGRAM, SIDNEY ROWLAND. Corporal. No PO/1397(S). Royal Marine Light Infantry, 1st Royal Marine Battalion, Royal Naval Division. Born Shildon, County Durham. Son of Thomas and Eliza Ingram, 2 Duke Street, Huddersfield. Educated Bradley Board School, Huddersfield. Attended the High Street Chapel. Employed as manager of Messrs Wallace's grocery shop in Bradford Road, Huddersfield. At the time of enlistment, was living at Fairfield House, Grange Avenue, Birkby. Single. Enlisted 8.2.1916. Killed in action on Passchendaele Ridge, 26.10.1917, aged 23 years. Has no known grave. Commemorated **TYNE COT MEMORIAL TO THE MISSING.** ROH:- High Street United Methodist Church. (Brother of Private **HERBERT WILLIAM INGRAM,** killed in action, 23.8.1918, q.v.).

INMAN, ARCHIBALD. Private. No 82039. 29th Infantry Labour Company, The King's Liverpool Regiment, transferred to No 193980 738th Employment Company, Labour Corps. Born Huddersfield 29.7.1888. Son of William and Emma Inman, 1 Moorside Avenue, Crosland Moor. Educated Spring Grove Council School. At the time of enlistment, was working in Manchester as a tailor's presser. Died of wounds, 17.6.1918, aged 30 years. Buried **LIJSSENTHOEK MILITARY CEMETERY.** Grave location:- Plot 28, Row F, Grave 11.

INMAN, GEORGE HAMILTON. (Served under the assumed name of **GEORGE MARSH**). Trooper. No 21038. 6th (Inniskilling) Dragoons, attached 1st Life Guards. Born Storths, Moldgreen, 10.7.1880. Son of Richard Henry and Sarah Inman, Colne Villa, Kings Mill Lane, Huddersfield. Educated Almondbury Grammar School. Employed as a motor engineer at the Karrier Car Works. Single. Embarked for France 5.10.1914. Landed at Zeebrugge 7.10.1914. Killed in action on Zandvoorde Ridge,

30.10.1914, aged 34. *During the research for this book I discovered that the Commonwealth War Graves Commission held no records for this man. Due to the efforts of Esther Barrett Page, of the CWGC, and myself we concluded that George Hamilton Inman had served under the assumed name of George Marsh. His name is now engraved on the* **MENIN GATE MEMORIAL TO THE MISSING.** ROH:- Almondbury War Memorial.

INNS, WALTER EDWARD. Private. No 7794. 1st Battalion King's Own Royal Lancaster Regiment. Born Uxbridge. Lived 35 Colne Road, Huddersfield. Employed by Messrs David Brown and Sons Limited, Park Works, Lockwood. Married, with two children. Was a Reservist and re-enlisted at the outbreak of the war. Killed in action, 26.8.1914. Buried **LIGNY-en-CAMBRESIS COMMUNAL CEMETERY.** Grave location:- Section 9. ROH:- Lockwood Baptist Church.

IREDALE, BERTRAND. Gunner. No 26377. 'B' Battery, 232nd Brigade Royal Field Artillery. Born Longwood 2.6.1897. Son of Thomas and Lily Iredale, 27 Cliffe End Road, Longwood. Educated Oakes Board School. Employed as a weft man by Messrs C. and J. Hirst of Longwood. Attended St. Mark's Parish Church, Longwood. Single. Enlisted 17.12.1914. Embarked for France in July 1915. Was wounded and in hospital in Aberdeen in October, 1916, and returned to France in January, 1917. Killed in action at Passchendaele, 12.10.1917, aged 20 years. Buried **PASSCHENDAELE NEW BRITISH CEMETERY.** Grave location:- Plot 11, Row D, Grave 8. ROH:- St. Mark's Parish Church, Longwood.

IREDALE, EDGAR. Private. No 4957. 4th Battalion Seaforth Highlanders. Born Linthwaite. Only son of Mr and Mrs George E. Iredale, 14 Lower Clough, Linthwaite. Married. Employed as a weaver by Messrs Charles Lockwood and Sons Limited, Blackrock Mills, Linthwaite. Was a member of the Hoyle Ing Working Men's Club. Enlisted March 1916. Embarked for France in July 1916. Killed in action, 12.10.1916, aged 23 years. Buried **COURCELLES-AU-BOIS COMMUNAL CEMETERY EXTENSION.** Grave location:- Row A, Grave 2. His wife received a letter from Lieutenant McLeod, who stated that, *'Private Iredale was one of 40 men whom the writer was in charge of in the firing line. They were engaged in constructing dugouts and in other fatigue duties. It was pure bad luck that Private Iredale was hit during very heavy shelling. He died instantly and was reverently buried behind the lines. He died instantenously and did not suffer any pain'.* ROH:- Linthwaite War Memorial.

IREDALE, FARRAR. Private. No 46046. 8th Battalion Northumberland Fusiliers. Born Ing Top, Longwood, 3.9.1886. Son of Thomas and Sarah Iredale, 100 Prospect Road, Longwood. Educated Goitfield and Longwood Grammar School. Attended Salendine Nook Baptist Church. Employed as a clerk in the Public Health Department, Huddersfield. Single. Enlisted 17.5.1916. Wounded at Wytschaete, Belgium, on 11.6.1917. Died of a haemorrhage, caused by a shrapnel wound in the jugular vein, at the 3rd Canadian General Hospital, Boulogne, 23.6.1917, aged 30 years. Buried. **BOULOGNE EASTERN CEMETERY.** Grave location:- Plot 4, Row A, Grave 14. ROH:- Salendine Nook Baptist Church; Huddersfield Corporation Roll; commemorated in Salendine Nook Baptist Chapel yard, D430.

IREDALE, HARRY. Private. No 91229. 18th Battalion Durham Light Infantry. Born Paddock, Huddersfield. Son of John W. and Mary Jane Iredale, 12 High Street, Scapegoat Hill, Golcar. Killed in action, 1.10.1918, aged 19 years. Buried **LANCASHIRE COTTAGE CEMETERY, BELGIUM.** Grave location:- Plot 3, Row E, Grave 1.

IREDALE, JOHN WILLIAM. Private. No 14973. 8th Battalion Duke of Wellington's Regiment. Born Primrose Hill, Huddersfield, 18.11.1896. Son of William and Clara Iredale, 14 Armitage Street, Primrose Hill. Educated Stile Common Board School. Employed as a joiner by Messrs Joseph Lumb and Sons, Folly Hall, Huddersfield. Single. Had served at the Dardenelles and in Egypt and was present at the evacuation of Suvla Bay. Wounded, 15.9.1916, during the Battle of the Somme. Died of wounds at No 44 Casualty Clearing Station, 17.9.1916, aged 19 years. Buried **PUCHEVILLERS BRITISH CEMETERY.** Grave location:- Plot 4, Row D, Grave 8. ROH;- St. Matthew's Church, Primrose Hill.

IREDALE, JOHN WILLIAM. Lance Corporal. No 1777. 1/7th Battalion Duke of Wellington's Regiment. Born Slaithwaite. Eldest son of Richard and Clara Iredale, 26 Grove Street, Hill Top, Slaithwaite. Was a teacher at St. James's Church Sunday School and was a member of the Slaithwaite United Harriers. Employed by Messrs J. E. Crowther, of Marsden. Had been a member of the local Territorials for four years. Embarked for France in April, 1915. Killed in action, 9.5.1915, aged 25 years. (He was the first Slaithwaite Territorial to be killed). Buried **RUE-DAVID MILITARY CEMETERY, FLEURBAIX.** Grave location:- Plot 1, Row H, Grave 7. His younger brother, Lance Corporal **GEORGE HENRY IREDALE,** who was also serving in the 1/7th Battalion, received the following message from Captain and Adjutant Burberry, *'I very much regret to have to inform you that your brother Corporal Iredale was killed this morning (Sunday) and is being buried this afternoon in the corner of the convent wall. The Commanding Officer directs me to add that he is extremely sorry that you cannot attend the funeral but he does not consider it advisable for you to do so whilst the shelling is going on.'* ROH:- St. James Church, Slaithwaite; Slaithwaite War Memorial; Huddersfield Drill Hall.

IREDALE, THOMAS ALBERT. York and Lancaster Regiment. Lived 183 Rashcliffe Hill Road, Huddersfield. Died after being discharged from the Army on 21.10.1920, from bronchitis and the effects of gas. ROH:- St. Stephen's Church, Rashcliffe.

IREDALE, THOMAS. Lance Corporal. No 28794. 7th Battalion The Yorkshire Regiment. Born Golcar. Son of Sam Iredale, 13 East Street, Golcar. Employed as a wheeler by Messrs G. N. Whiteley of Milnsbridge. Attended Golcar Baptist Chapel and was a member of the Outlane Harriers. Reported missing, presumed killed, at the Battle of Arras, 14.5.1917, aged 23 years. Has no known grave. Commemorated **ARRAS MEMORIAL TO THE MISSING.** ROH:- Golcar Baptist Church; St. John's Church, Golcar.

IRELAND, ALEXANDER FORSYTH. Private. No 88056. 1/6th Battalion Northumberland Fusiliers. Born Huddersfield 7.11.1899. Eldest son of Richard and Sarah Elizabeth Ireland, 25 Northgate, Huddersfield. Educated St. Thomas's School and Huddersfield Higher Grade School. Assisted his father in the family grocery business. Was a member of the Huddersfield Y.M.C.A. and the swimming club. Enlisted 7.11.1917. Died of pneumonia on Tuesday, 3.12.1918, aged 19, at Surrey House Hospital, Margate. Buried **EDGERTON CEMETERY, HUDDERSFIELD.** Grave location:- 48, 23C. ROH:- Huddersfield Parish Church.

IRVINE, DAVID. Private. No 267324. 1/8th Battalion Sherwood Foresters. Formerly No 3166 Duke of Wellington's Regiment. Born Midmill, Forfar, Scotland. Son of Mr and Mrs John Irvine of Hill Top, Shepley. Married. Lived Cliffe Side, Shepley. Enlisted October 1914. Died of wounds, 3.10.1918, aged 24 years. Buried **VADENCOURT BRITISH CEMETERY.** Grave location:- Plot 3, Row C, Grave 6. ROH:- Shepley War Memorial; Shelley War Memorial.

McIRVINE, HARRY (HENRY). Rifleman. No 81415. 1/8th Battalion West Yorkshire Regiment. Formerly No 52306 Duke of Wellington's Regiment. Born Dundee. Husband of Ethel Mc. Irvine, Bankside, Shelley. Killed in action, 20.10.1918. Buried **BELLE VUE BRITISH CEMETERY, BRIASTRE.** Grave location:- Row A, Grave 5. ROH:- Shepley War Memorial; Shelley War Memorial.

IVES, ROBERT HENRY. Private. No 3/10220. 9th Battalion Norfolk Regiment. Husband of Amy Ives, 58 Cowrakes Road, Lindley, Huddersfield. Demobilized from the army on 9.2.1919. Died of pneumonia in Huddersfield Royal Infirmary on 10.5.1921, aged 44 years. Buried **St. STEPHEN'S CHURCHYARD, LINDLEY.** Grave location:- 6, Z.

JACKSON, ALBERT EDWARD, MM. Private. No 57267. 1st Battalion West Yorkshire Regiment. Born Meltham. Lived 1 Brackenfield Terrace, Golcar Brow, Meltham. Employed as a spinner at a mill in Meltham. Awarded the MM, 13.3.1918. Killed in action, 17.9.1918, aged 21 years. Buried **CHAPELLE BRITISH CEMETERY.** Grave location:- Plot 1, Row D, Grave 13. ROH:- St. Bartholomew's Church, Meltham.

JACKSON, ARTHUR. Guardsman. No 26395. 2nd Battalion Grenadier Guards. Born Huddersfield 16.3.1888. Educated St. Andrews

Church of England School. Married. Lived 40 North Bank, Fartown. Employed as a stone mason by Messrs Harrison and Battye of Linthwaite. Attended Gledholt Wesleyan Sunday School and was a member of the Young Men's Class. Enlisted August 1916. Killed in action at Bourlon Wood, 1.12.1917. Has no known grave. Commemorated **CAMBRAI MEMORIAL TO THE MISSING.** ROH:- Christ Church, Woodhouse Hill; Gledholt Wesleyan Church; Fartown and Birkby War Memorial.

JACKSON, DONALD RICHARD FIELD. Lieutenant. 5th Battalion Duke of Wellington's Regiment. Son of Sir Percy and Lady Jackson of 'Woodlands', Scissett, Huddersfield. Educated at New College, Harrogate, and afterwards entered his father's business, Messrs Field and Botterill of Skelmanthorpe. Enlisted as a Private in the Duke of Wellington's Regiment on 4.9.1914. Was commissioned in March, 1915. Embarked for France in September, 1915. Killed in action, 27.8.1917, aged 24 years. Has no known grave. Commemorated **TYNE COT MEMORIAL TO THE MISSING.** ROH:- St. Aidan's Church, Skelmanthorpe; Huddersfield Drill Hall; Scissett War Memorial.

JACKSON, EDWIN. Private. No PO/1144(S). Royal Marine Light Infantry, 2nd Royal Marine Battalion, Royal Naval Division. Born Denby, near Huddersfield. Son of Allen and Martha Anne Jackson, Richmond Terrace, Denby. Killed in action, 28.4.1917, aged 19 years. Has no known grave. Commemorated **ARRAS MEMORIAL TO THE MISSING.** (Brother of Private **HERBERT NORTON JACKSON**, killed in action, 3.5.1917, q.v.). ROH:- Denby Dale and Cumberworth War Memorial.

JACKSON, FRED. Private. No 307804. 1/7th Battalion Duke of Wellington's Regiment. Born Jagger Green, near Elland. Lived Holme Villas, Marsden. Married. Employed as a weaver at Holme Mills. Killed in action, 28.3.1918, aged 28 years. Buried **BELGIAN BATTERY CORNER CEMETREY, YPRES.** Grave location:- Plot 2, Row I, Grave 15. ROH:- Huddersfield Drill Hall; Jagger Green Baptist Sunday School; Marsden War Memorial; commemorated in Salendine Nook Chapel yard, 23E.

JACKSON, GEORGE WILLIAM. Lance Corporal. No 305256. 2/7th Battalion Duke of Wellington's Regiment. Born Albion Street, Nottingham, 20.8.1897. Son of Inspector and Mrs Sarah Ann Jackson, 30 Hawthorne Terrace, Crosland Moor, Huddersfield. Educated St. Paul's School, Huddersfield. Employed as a colour blender by Messrs Kaye and Stewart Limited. Single. Enlisted 4.8.1914. Reported to have been killed by machine gun fire in Bourlon Wood whilst attending to wounded on 27.11.1917, aged 20 years. Has no known grave. Commemorated **CAMBRAI MEMORIAL TO THE MISSING.** (Brother of Private **JOHN JACKSON**, died of wounds, 10.6.1918, q.v.). ROH:- St. Barnabas Church, Crosland Moor; Huddersfield Drill Hall.

JACKSON, HARRY. Sergeant. No 240010. 1/5th Battalion Duke of Wellington's Regiment. Born Primrose Hill 21.9.1886. Eldest son of Ex Colour Sergeant Jackson, of the Duke of Wellington's Regiment, who retired after 30 years service and who, on the outbreak of the war, joined the Northumberland Fusiliers. Educated Stile Common Board School. Employed as a painter and decorator by Messrs W. and B. Holroyd, High Street, Huddersfield. Married, with one child. Lived 118 Whitehead Lane, Primrose Hill. Enlisted in the 2nd Volunteer Battalion in 1896. Mobilized 3.8.1914. Reported missing in the attack on the Schwaben Redoubt on 3.9.1916, aged 31 years. Has no known grave. Commemorated **THIEPVAL MEMORIAL TO THE MISSING.** ROH:- St. Matthew's Church, Primrose Hill; Huddersfield Drill Hall.

JACKSON, HERBERT NORTON. Private. No 241594. 'B' Company, 2/5th Battalion Duke of Wellington's Regiment. Born Denby. Son of Allen and Martha Ann Jackson, Richmond Terrace, Denby. Reported missing at the Battle of Bullecourt, 3.5.1917, aged 24 years. Has no known grave. Commemorated **ARRAS MEMORIAL TO THE MISSING.** (Brother of Private **EDWIN JACKSON**, killed in action, 28.4.1917, q.v.). ROH:- Huddersfield Drill Hall; Denby Dale and Cumberworth War Memorial.

JACKSON, JAMES. Private. No 3/6959. 7th Battalion East Yorkshire Regiment. Born Hull. Married, with five children. Lived 106 Church Lane, Moldgreen. Employed as a loader by the London and North Western Railway Company in the goods yard at Huddersfield Railway Station. Killed in action, 29.10.1915, aged 28 years. Has no known grave. Commemorated **MENIN GATE MEMORIAL TO THE MISSING.** His widow received a letter from Captain G. East King, Officer Commanding 'D' Company, who wrote, *'I feel that not only have I lost a good soldier and my own servant but a true friend as well, as he was one of the true and straightest men I have ever met. I shall miss him fearfully and could ill afford to lose him. What else can I say to help you to bear up in this sad time I do not know but in time both you and his children will be proud to remember that he died doing his duty like a hero to help in protecting you at home against the horrors of war in our own land. All my brother Officers who admired him and liked him join with me in assuring you of our deepest sympathy in your sad trouble.'* ROH:- Moldgreen War Memorial; London and North Western Railway Roll.

JACKSON, JOHN. Private. No 58961. 1/5th Battalion West Yorkshire Regiment. Born East Parade, Huddersfield 15.11.1898. Son of Inspector and Mrs Sarah Ann Jackson, 30 Hawthorne Terrace, Crosland Moor. Educated St. Paul's School, Huddersfield. Employed as a cloth finisher. Single. Enlisted 24.4.1917. Died of gunshot wounds to the thigh, 10.6.1918, aged 20 years. Buried **RETHEL FRENCH NATIONAL CEMETERY.** Grave location:- No 1713. (Brother of Private **GEORGE WILLIAM JACKSON**, killed in action, 27.11.1917, q.v.). ROH:- St. Barnabas Church, Crosland Moor.

JACKSON, WALTER. Stoker 1st Class. No 291824. (R.F.R./CH/B/7551 Royal Navy. 'D' Company, 'Hood' Battalion, Royal Naval Divison. Born Bradford. 10.7.1881. Husband of Mary Ellen Jackson, 199 Lockwood Road, Huddersfield. Employed as a stoker at Messrs Gledhill Brothers and Company Limited, Lockwood Road. On April 6th, 1899, he enlisted in the Royal Navy and on April 22nd, 1911, he enrolled in the Royal Fleet Reserve. On 3.8.1914, he was mobilised from the R.F.R. and in October, 1914, he served at the Siege of Antwerp. Killed in action at the Third Battle of Krithia, Gallipoli, on 4.6.1915, aged 33 years. Has no known grave. Commemorated **HELLES MEMORIAL TO THE MISSING.** At the beginning of July, 1916, Mrs Jackson received a letter from the Record Office, Royal Naval Divison, stating that her husband was now officially accepted as dead, *'It has been assumed that he was killed in action when serving with the Hood Battalion, Royal Naval Division, on the Gallipoli Peninsula upon the 4.6.1915. Previously he has only been officially reported as missing.'* ROH:- Emmanuel Church, Lockwood.

JACKSON, WILLIAM T. Private. No 241595. 2/5th Battalion Duke of Wellington's Regiment. Born Luddendenfoot, Halifax. Son of Mr and Mrs Thomas Jackson, 4 Upper Side, Linthwaite. Employed as a piecer by the Colne Valley Spinning Company Limited, Linthwaite. Attended Christ Church, Linthwaite. Enlisted March 1916. Killed in action, 16.3.1917, aged 20 years. Buried **QUEENS CEMETERY, BUCQUOY.** Grave location:- Plot 3, Row E, Grave 9. ROH:- Linthwaite War Memorial; Huddersfield Drill Hall.

JAGGER, JOHN HERBERT. Private. No 12391. 2nd Battalion Duke of Wellington's Regiment. Born Halifax. Lived Honley. Killed by a bomb in the German lines on the first day of the Battle of the Somme, 1.7.1916, aged 27 years. Has no known grave. Commemorated **THIEPVAL MEMORIAL TO THE MISSING.** ROH:- Honley War Memorial; Armitage Bridge War Memorial; Salendine Nook Baptist Chapel.

JAGGER, LUTHER. Private. No 43013. 15th (1st Leeds Pals) Battalion West Yorkshire Regiment. Born Emley. Son of George and Frances Hannah Jagger, of Emley Moor. Died of wounds, 14.4.1918, aged 25 years. Buried **ETAPLES MILITARY CEMETERY.** Grave location:- Plot 33, Row G, Grave 1a. ROH: Emley War Memorial; memorial in Emley Churchyard.

JAMES, HENRY IVOR. Sergeant. No 21816. 12th Battalion Royal Welsh Fusiliers. Born Stockton-on-Tees 16.11.1889. Son of the late Morris and Margaret James. Husband of Margaret James, 193, Cowcliffe Hill Road, Birkby. Employed as a steel blower. Enlisted 5.11.1914. Killed in action at Gouzeaucourt near Cambrai, 19.9.1918. Buried **GOUZEAUCOURT NEW BRITISH CEMETERY.** Grave location:- Plot 5, Row D, Grave 2. ROH:- St. Hilda's Church, Cowcliffe; Fartown and Birkby War Memorial.

JAMESON, WILLIAM, MM. Gunner. No 146239. 168th Siege Battery, Royal Garrison Artillery. Born 58 Wear Street, Sunderland 14.12.1885. Son of Robert Jameson, 35 Thompson Street, Hendon, Sunderland. Educated Gray School, Sunderland. Lived with his sister, Mrs Hardcastle, at 49 Tanfield Terrace, Birkby, Huddersfield. Employed as a painter by Messrs Lunn and Cardno. Single. Awarded the Military Medal on 16.10.1918, for *'bringing in messages through heavy shell fire.'* Died of the effects of gas poisoning at No 9 General Hospital, Rouen, on 18.10.1918, aged 31 years. Buried **St. SEVER CEMETERY EXTENSION.** Grave location:- Block S, Plot 2, Row J, Grave 7. ROH:- Fartown and Birkby War Memorial.

JARRELL, JOHN EDWARD. Private. No 241923. 1/4th Battalion Duke of Wellington's Regiment. Born Tindall's Yard, Hawk Street, Huddersfield, 28.2.1897. Son of Samuel Henry and Mary Blanche Jarrell, 13 Greenhead Road, Huddersfield. Educated Thomas Street Council School. Employed as a cloth tenterer by Messrs Middlemost Brothers and Company Limited, Birkby. Single. Enlisted January 1916. Died of wounds, 12.10.1918, aged 22. Buried **QUEANT COMMUNAL CEMETERY BRITISH EXTENSION.** Grave location:- Row D, Grave 53. ROH:- High Street United Methodist Church.

JEBSON, LAWRENCE. Gunner. No 127364. 189th Brigade Royal Field Artillery. Born Linthwaite. Son of the late Walter and of Elizabeth Jebson, Bankfield, Linthwaite. Attended Linthwaite Wesleyan Sunday School. Employed as a fettler at Priestroyd Mills, Huddersfield. A keen cricketer. Enlisted 1.1.1916. Embarked for France in April 1916. Died of wounds, 21.3.1918, aged 23 years. Buried **ROYE NEW BRITISH CEMETERY.** Grave location:- Marchelepot Memorial 46. ROH:- Linthwaite War Memorial; memorial in Linthwaite Methodist Chapel Cemetery.

JEFFERSON, DONALD PERCY. Private. No 2908. 1/5th Battalion Duke of Wellington's Regiment. Born Blacker Road North, Birkby, 28.9.1891. Son of Frederick Henry and Mary Jane Jefferson, Arnold Street, Birkby. Educated at Huddersfield Higher Grade School. Attended Birkby Baptist Church and Sunday School. Had been Sunday School Secretary for six years. Employed as an accountant's clerk. Single. Enlisted 2.9.1914. Embarked for France in April, 1915. Killed in action at Croix Marechal, near Fleurbaix, on 15.5.1915, aged 23 years. Buried **RUE-DAVID MILITARY CEMETERY, FLEURBAIX.** Grave location:- Plot 1, Row B, Grave 17. A letter from one his comrades describes what happened, *'Our last four days in the trenches was the most awful of our experience. The casualties in our Company alone were 4 killed and 6 injured but thank God the rest of the Birkby chaps came through injured. On Thursday night we received orders that we had to open rapid fire at 1am for three minutes, then two minutes silence, then two minutes more rapid fire. All the time our artillery were blazing away behind us. Then the Germans replied with their artillery. On Friday we again received orders to the same effect for five o' clock and nine o' clock Saturday morning. It was our first experience of anything like warfare. The noise was terrific but the worst time of all was at 9am when the German artillery replied to our fire with a vengence. It was at this time that poor Donald was struck, killed instantaneously.'* ROH:- Huddersfield Drill Hall; Fartown and Birkby War Memorial.

JEFFRIES, CHARLES. Private. No 41721. 7th Battalion King's Own Royal Lancaster Regiment. Born Padiham, Lancashire. Married. Lived 6 Brougham Road, Marsden. Employed as a cotton weaver near Skipton. Enlisted in 1916. Embarked for France in August, 1918. Killed in action, 27.9.1918, aged 19 years. Has no known grave. Commemorated **VIS-en-ARTOIS MEMORIAL TO THE MISSING.**

JEFFRIES, THOMAS CHARLES. Lance Corporal. No 585. 11th Battalion Royal Warwickshire Regiment. Born Winchcombe, Gloucestershire. Lived 12 Grayson's Yard, Chapel Hill, Huddersfield. Employed as a teamer by Messrs Smith Brothers, Viaduct Street, Huddersfield. Was a Reservist and called up at the outbreak of war. Twice wounded. Was killed in the trenches by a minnenwerfer on 1.10.1916, aged 23 years. Buried **TRANCHEE DE MECKNES CEMETERY, AIX-NOULETTE, FRANCE.** Grave location:- Row J, Grave 16.

JELFS, CHARLES EDWARDS. Private. No 21470. 1st Battalion Royal Fusiliers. Born

Denby. Son of Abel and Jessie Jelfs of Denby. Enlisted Hounslow. Killed in action, 13.7.1917, aged 20. Buried **ARTILLERY WOOD CEMETERY, BOESINGHE, BELGIUM.** Grave location:- Plot 3. Row C. Grave 4. ROH:- Denby Dale and Cumberworth War Memorial.

JENKINS, ARTHUR. Sergeant. No 35742. 9th Battalion King's Own Yorkshire Light Infantry. Formerly No 3/17899 Duke of Wellington's Regiment. Born Greenwich, London, 23.3.1893. Son of Tamar and J. W. Barden, 18 Syringa Street, Marsh. Educated New Cross School, London. Employed as a waiter at the Huddersfield Liberal Club. Enlisted January 1915. Killed in action near Arras on 12.5.1917, aged 24 years. Buried **BUCQUOY ROAD CEMETERY.** Grave location:- Plot 1, Row G, Grave 4. ROH:- Marsh War Memorial; Holy Trinity Church, Huddersfield.

JENKINS, EDWARD. Private. No 11937. 8th Battalion Duke of Wellington's Regiment. Born Netherroyd Hill, Huddersfield, 27.4.1891. Eldest son of the late Thomas Jenkins, weaver, and Lavinia (nee Cooper) Jenkins, 16 Netheroyd Hill. Educated at Cowcliffe Church of England School. Employed as a warehouseman at Messrs Hopkinsons of Birkby. Enlisted, 26.8.1914, in Huddersfield on 26.8.1914. He came home on leave in June, 1915, and was married on June 3rd, 1915, at Halifax, Yorkshire, to Lily. Sailed from Liverpool in *SS Aquitania* on 3.7.1915 for the Dardenelles. Died of wounds on 23.8.1915, aged 24. Buried **LALA BABA CEMETERY, SUVLA, GALLIPOLI.** Grave location:- Plot 2, Row B, Grave 7. ROH:- St. Hilda's Church, Cowcliffe; Fartown and Birkby War Memorial.

JENKINSON, CLEMENT. Corporal. No 6380. 2nd Regiment South African Infantry. Born Town Top, Kirkheaton, 22.3.1892. Son of John W. and the late Mary Elizabeth Jenkinson, 158 Taylor Hill Road, Huddersfield. Educated Christ Church, Moldgreen. Employed in the grocery department of the Huddersfield Industrial Society. Emigrated to South Africa in March, 1912. Employed as a traveller in wine and spirits. Lived Dundee, Natal. Enlisted at the outbreak of the war. Joined General Botha's forces and went through the German South West African campaign and then volunteered for service in France. Came to England with the first detachment of South African troops. Served in Egypt in 1916 and took part in the fighting against the Senussi Arabs. Sent to France in April, 1916. Wounded at Delville Wood, 15.7.1916. After being wounded, he was on his way to the dressing station and stopped to help a wounded Sergeant when another shell burst, which killed them both. Killed in action, 15.7.1916, aged 24 years. Has no known grave. Commemorated **THIEPVAL MEMORIAL TO THE MISSING.** ROH:- Emmanuel Church, Lockwood; Armitage Bridge War Memorial.

JENNINGS, GEORGE HENRY. Private. No 10403. 1st Battalion King's Own Yorkshire Light Infantry. Born Sowerby Bridge. Son of the late John Jennings and of Mrs Roebuck, 56 Quarmby Fold, Quarmby. Had been in the army for several years. He was in India at the outbreak of the war and was home on leave at Christmas, 1914. Embarked for France in January, 1915. Killed in action, 13.2.1915, aged 23 years. Has no known grave. Commemorated **MENIN GATE MEMORIAL TO THE MISSING.** His mother received a letter from Lieutenant-Colonel C. E. Ingham-Brooke. who wrote, '*I must regret to inform you that Number 10403 Private H. Jennings was killed in action on the morning of the 13th February. It will I hope be some comfort to you to know that he died a most noble death having dashed out of the trenches to the assistance of a wounded comrade. It was whilst he was helping this wounded man that he was unfortunately shot dead by the enemy. He gave his life to help his comrade. It is impossible to do anything more noble. Offering you my deepest sympathy believe me.*' ROH:- St. Stephen's Church, Lindley.

JENNINGS, THOMAS. Private. 18th Battalion West Yorkshire Regiment. Born Huddersfield. Son of Mrs Norah Jennings, 33 Rosemary Lane, Huddersfield. Educated St. Patrick's Roman Catholic School, Huddersfield. Employed as a slater's labourer. Married. At the time of enlistment, was living at 44 Manchester Street, Huddersfield. Enlisted 22.1.1916. Died at home, 33 Rosemary Lane, Huddersfield, of bronchitis and pneumonia on 29.1.1921.

JEPSON, HAROLD WILKINSON. Private. No TR5/61940. 30th Battalion Northumberland Fusiliers. Formerly 85th Training Reserve

Battalion. Born Kirkburton. Son of Jane Jepson, of Garden View, Upper Cumberworth, and the late James Jepson. Died at Hull City Hospital whilst in training on 26.3.1917, aged 20 years. Buried **ALL HALLOWS CHURCHYARD, KIRKBURTON**. Grave location:- 24, 1821. ROH:- All Hallows Parish Church, Kirkburton.

JEPSON, JOSEPH. Private. No 41541. 24th/27th (Tyneside Irish) Battalion Northumberland Fusiliers. Born Battyeford, Mirfield, 27.4.1880. Son of Mrs Louisa Jepson, 33 Victoria Road, Lockwood, Huddersfield. Educated at Rashcliffe Church of England School, Lockwood. Employed as a woollen teaser by Messrs Brierley Brothers Limited, Albert Mills, Lockwood. Single. Enlisted 10.4.1916. Embarked for France in July, 1916. Invalided home to England with trench feet in January, 1917. Returned to France in September, 1917. Killed in action, 13.10.1917, aged 38. Buried **SOLFERINO FARM CEMETERY, BRIELAN, BELGIUM**. Grave location:- Plot 1, Row B, Grave 17. ROH:- St. Stephen's Church, Rashcliffe.

JESSOP, ARTHUR WILLIAM. Private. No 5062. 2/5th Battalion Duke of Wellington's Regiment. Born Fenay Bridge. Employed in his father's business as a yeast merchant. Attended Rowley Hill Wesleyan Church. Enlisted March 1916. Died of acute bronchitis and pneumonia at No 4 Casualty Clearing Station on 6.3.1917, aged 25 years. Buried **VARENNES MILITARY CEMETERY**. Grave location:- Plot 1, Row I, Grave 78. ROH:- Lepton Parish Church; Huddersfield Drill Hall.

JESSOP, ERNEST. Private. No 240797. 2/5th Battalion Duke of Wellington's Regiment. Born Slaithwaite 30.1.1897. Son of Richard and Emma Jessop. Educated Lockwood Church of England School. Lived Dykes Side, Lockwood. Employed as a cloth finisher. Enlisted November 1914. Killed in action near Cambrai on 20.11.1917, aged 20 years. Has no known grave. Commemorated **CAMBRAI MEMORIAL TO THE MISSING**. ROH:- Mount Pleasant Chapel, Lockwood; Huddersfield Drill Hall.

JESSOP, FRANK. Private. No 21002. 10th Battalion West Yorkshire Regiment. Born Bradley Mills, Huddersfield. Married. Lived 45 Leeds Road North, Huddersfield. Employed as a motor steerer by Messrs Tomlinsons, carriers, Crosland Moor. Enlisted May 1915. Killed in action, 21.2.1916, aged 33 years. Buried **SPOILBANK CEMETERY, ZILLEBEKE, BELGIUM**. Grave location:- Plot 1, Row A, Grave 2.

JESSOP, LEWIS HALLAS. Private. No 4262. 1/5th Battalion Duke of Wellington's Regiment. Born Lascelles Hall, Lepton, in 1892. Adopted son of Mrs Isabella Armitage, 30a Victoria Road, Lockwood. Educated Lepton National School. Employed as a greengrocer by Mr O. Littlewood, fruiterer, of Victoria Lane. Enlisted October 1915. Wounded in the left shoulder during the Battle of the Somme. Died on board the hospital ship 'Asturias', 8.7.1916, during the voyage to England. He was 23 years of age. Death was due to shell wounds in the left shoulder and gangrene. Buried **NETLEY MILITARY CEMETERY, HAMPSHIRE**. Grave location:- CE, 1802. ROH:- St. Stephen's Church, Rashcliffe; St. Paul's Church, Southgate, Huddersfield; Huddersfield Drill Hall.

JOHNSEY, HERBERT. Private. No 241991. 2/5th Battalion Duke of Wellington's Regiment. Born Dogley, Kirkheaton, Huddersfield. Son of Mrs Johnsey, Rose Terrace, Moorside, Kirkheaton. Employed in the finishing department of Messrs Broadhead and Graves, Kirkheaton. Killed in action near Rheims, 22.7.1918, aged 28 years. Has no known grave. Commemorated **SOISSONS MEMORIAL TO THE MISSING**. ROH:- St. John's Church, Kirkheaton; Huddersfield Drill Hall.

JOHNSEY, WALTER. Private. No 14341. 8th Battalion Duke of Wellington's Regiment. Born Lindley, Huddersfield. Adopted son of Mr and Mrs Gray, Ivy Cottage, Farnley Tyas. Employed by Messrs J. Hoyle and Son, Longwood. Enlisted 14.10.1914. Had served in Gallipoli. Embarked for France in June, 1916. Killed in action, 14.9.1916, aged 26 years. Has no known grave. Commemorated **THIEPVAL MEMORIAL TO THE MISSING**. ROH:- Farnley Tyas War Memorial, Thurstonland War Memorial.

JOHNSON, ARNOLD. Sergeant. No 175027. 1/1st Battalion Queen's Own Yorkshire Dragoons. Born Huddersfield. Died, 21.5.1918, at No 10 Stationary Hospital, St. Omer. Buried **LONGUENESSE (ST OMER) SOUVENIR CEMETERY**. Grave Location:- Plot 5, Row B, Grave 23.

JOHNSON, BERNARD COPESTAKE.
Lieutenant. 2/7th Battalion Duke of Wellington's Regiment. Lived Holmfirth. Had been Headmaster of Holmfirth National School for seven years prior to enlistment. Trained at St. John's College, Battersea and commenced as a teacher in London in 1900, remaining there for six years. He then took up a post at Kirkham, Lancashire before starting as Headmaster at Holmfirth National School. Married, with two children. Enlisted, 2.10.1914, and received his commission in the 7th Battalion Duke of Wellington's Regiment in September, 1915. Was wounded during the Battle of the Somme, in July 1916, and returned to France a fortnight before he was killed, during the Battle of Arras, on 14.5.1917, aged 37 years. Buried **ECOUST MILITARY CEMETERY**. Grave location:- Plot 2, Row A, Grave 38. ROH:- Holmfirth War Memorial; Huddersfield Drill Hall.

JOHNSON, FREDDY. Private. No 202779. 'D' Company, 1/6th Battalion Northumberland Fusiliers. Formerly No 144998 Royal Field Artillery. Born Holmfirth. Son of Mrs S. E. Johnson, 3 Upperthong Road, Holmfirth and the late Edward Johnson. Attended Holmfirth Wesleyan Church. Employed in the dyehouse at Thirstin Mills, Honley. Was a member of Holmfirth Liberal Club. Enlisted May 1916. Embarked for France during the last week in September, 1916. Killed in action, 17.5.1917, aged 28 years. Has no known grave. Commemorated **ARRAS MEMORIAL TO THE MISSING.** ROH:- Holmfirth War Memorial.

JOHNSON, JOHN WILFRED. Private. No 39517. 1/4th Battalion Duke of Wellington's Regiment. Born Keighley. Youngest son of Mr and Mrs John Johnson of Totties, Holmfirth. His parents moved to Holmfirth from Keighley in 1911. Educated Wooldale Council School. Attended Lane Bottom Wesleyan Church and Sunday School. Employed at Ford Mill and later at Lee Mill. Enlisted, 29.10.1917, and embarked for France in July, 1918. Died of wounds, 14.10.1918, aged 19 years. Buried **QUEANT COMMUNAL CEMETERY BRITISH EXTENSION**. Grave location:- Row E, Grave 9. ROH:- Wooldale War Memorial; memorial in Christ Church Churchyard, New Mill.

JOHNSON, JOSEPH. Private. No 22719. 8th Battalion East Lancashire Regiment. Born Huddersfield. Lived Moorbottom Road, Thornton Lodge, Huddersfield. Prior to enlistment lived 3 Huntingdon Bank, West Street, Rochdale. Employed as a plate-layer on the Lancashire and Yorkshire railway. Was married in April 1915. Reported missing, presumed killed, during the Battle of the Somme on 15.7.1916. He was 23 years of age. Has no known grave. Commemorated **THIEPVAL MEMORIAL TO THE MISSING.**

JOHNSON, WILLIAM. Private. No 138796. 18th Battalion Machine Gun Corps. Formerly No 6299 Duke of Wellington's Regiment. Born Huddersfield. Son of Mr and Mrs Johnson, 21 Whitestone Lane, Hillhouse, Huddersfield. Employed at the Huddersfield Corporation Electrical Department. Enlisted in 1914 at the age of 15. Killed in action, 20.9.1918, aged 19. Buried **SAULCOURT CHURCHYARD EXTENSION**. Grave location:- Row B, Grave 13. ROH:- St. Andrew's Church, Leeds Road; Fartown and Birkby War Memorial.

JONES, ALFRED. Rifleman. No C/12696. 21st Battalion King's Royal Rifle Corps. Born Lower Brow, Paddock. 26.6.1893. Son of Mrs Collins, 3 St. Paul's Street, Huddersfield. Educated Paddock Council School. Employed as a cloth finisher by Messrs J. L. Walker and Sons Limited, Woodhouse, Huddersfield. Single. Killed in action at Flers, 17.9.1916, aged 24 years. Has no known grave. Commemorated **THIEPVAL MEMORIAL TO THE MISSING.**

JONES, ARTHUR BARRON. Private. No 240574. 'C' Company, 2/5th Battalion Duke of Wellington's Regiment. Born Moldgreen, Huddersfield, 3.1.1889. Employed as a moulder by the Hygienic Stove Company Limited. Married. At the time of enlistment, was living at 2 Grafton Place, Huddersfield. Enlisted 7.10.1914. Killed in action, 9.4.1918, aged 29 years. Buried **BIENVILLERS MILITARY CEMETERY**. Grave location:- Plot 9, Row B, Grave 9. ROH:- St. Paul's Church, Southgate, Huddersfield; Huddersfield Drill Hall.

JONES, ARTHUR THOMAS. Private. No 242450. 1/6th Battalion West Yorkshire Regiment. Born Huddersfield. Husband of A. T.

Jones, 19 Kilner Bank, Moldgreen, Huddersfield. Died at home, 2.4.1919. Buried **KIRKHEATON CEMETERY**. Grave location:- 'C', 2018.

JONES, CHARLES. Corporal. No 11246. 8th Battalion Duke of Wellington's Regiment. Born Rhyl, North Wales, 7.5.1895. Son of William Thomas and Florence Jones, 6 Broomfield Road, Marsh. Educated Brownlow Fold Council School, Bolton, Lancashire. Employed as an apprentice motor trimmer. Played for three seasons with the Great Northern Street Sunday School team. At the time of enlistment, was living at 21 Sufton Street, Birkby. Enlisted 23.8.1914. Killed in action at Suvla Bay, Gallipoli, 21.8.1915, aged 21 years. Has no known grave. Commemorated **HELLES MEMORIAL TO THE MISSING**. ROH:- Great Northern Street Congregational Chapel; Marsh War Memorial.

JONES, CHARLES ERNEST. Ordinary Seaman. No J/79340. Royal Navy. *HMS Lady Cory Wright*. Born Shelley. Son of Florence Edith Jones, Bank Side, Shelley. Killed during an attack by a submarine in the English Channel, 26.3.1918, aged 18. Has no known grave. Commemorated **PLYMOUTH NAVAL MEMORIAL TO THE MISSING**. ROH:- Emmanuel Church, Shelley.

JONES, CYRIL. Private. No 8032. 7th Battalion The Yorkshire Regiment. Born Newtown. Enlisted Halifax. Lived 19 Ivy Street, Crosland Moor, Huddersfield. Killed in action, 7.10.1916. Has no known grave. Commemorated **THIEPVAL MEMORIAL TO THE MISSING**.

JONES, GEORGE VICTOR, DCM. DSM. Company Sergeant Major. No 240222. 2/5th Battalion Duke of Wellington's Regiment. Born The Tower, Middlesex. Married. Lived 27 Garforth Street, Aspley, Huddersfield. After serving twelve years with the Gordon Highlanders he joined the Huddersfield Territorials. Employed by Messrs Read Holliday and Sons. Was mobilised on 4.8.1914. Embarked for France in April, 1915. Killed in action near Rheims, 23.7.1918, aged 32 years. Awarded the DCM on 3.9.1918. The official citation in the London Gazette reads, *'for conspicuous gallantry and devotion to duty. When strong enemy attacks were being made at night against his Company, and there was some confusion,* *he rallied the men and successfully drove out the enemy under intense machine gun and rifle fire.'* Buried **MARFAUX BRITISH CEMETERY**. Grave location:- Plot 10, Row I, Grave 4. ROH:- Huddersfield Drill Hall.

JONES, HENRY. Private. No 59615. Machine Gun Corps. Formerly No 37040 Durham Light Infantry. Born Llanelly Hill, Brecon, South Wales. Enlisted Halifax. Lived Paddock, Huddersfield. Drowned at sea when the Cunard Steamship 'Ivernia' was sunk by a U- boat.in the Mediterranean on 1.1.1917. Has no known grave. Commemorated **MIKRA MEMORIAL TO THE MISSING, SALONICA**.

JONES, JACK. Signaller. No 3/22841. 2nd Battalion Duke of Wellington's Regiment. Born Dale Street, Huddersfield, 2.4.1897. Son of Edgar and Frances Jones, 2 South Terrace, South Street, Huddersfield. Educated Moldgreen Council School. Prior to enlistment, was working in London as a joiner. Enlisted June 1916. Died of wounds at No 8 Casualty Clearing Station, Etrun, on 26.3.1918, aged 20. Buried **DUISANS BRITISH CEMETERY**. Grave location:- Plot 5, Row F, Grave 58.

JONES, JOSEPH. Private. No 241393. 1/5th Battalion Duke of Wellington's Regiment. Born Huddersfield. Lived 168 Kilner Bank, Moldgreen, Huddersfield. Employed by Mr H. Williams, wool merchant of Upperhead Row, Huddersfield. Killed in action at Nieuport, 7.8.1917. Buried **RAMSCAPELLE ROAD MILITARY CEMETERY**. Grave location:- Plot 2, Row A, Grave 11. ROH:- Moldgreen War Memorial; Huddersfield Drill Hall.

JONES, PERCIVAL MARTIN. Guardsman. No 14497. 2nd Battalion Grenadier Guards. Born Aslockton, Nottinghamshire. Lived Chapel House Farm, Emley. Killed by a shell on 19.10.1915. Age 23 years. Buried **VERMELLES BRITISH CEMETERY**. Grave location:- Plot 1, Row B, Grave 11. ROH:- St. John's Church, Kirkheaton; Emley War Memorial; commemorated on headstone in Kirkheaton Cemetery.

JONES, RICHARD CYRIL. Private. No 8032. 7th Battalion The Yorkshire Regiment. Born Newtown, Montgomery, North Wales, 27.10.1897. Son of Mr and Mrs William

2nd Battalion Duke of Wellington's Regiment leaving Dublin. They sailed for France on 14th August 1914.

Courtesy of the Trustees of the Duke of Wellington's Regiment Museum and Archives.

Officers of the 2nd Battalion Duke of Wellington's Regiment, Dublin, August 1914.

Courtesy of the Trustees of the Duke of Wellington's Regiment Museum and Archives.

Soldiers from 9th Duke of Wellington's Regiment in camp before mobilisation November 1914 before receiving their uniforms.

Soldiers of the Duke of Wellington's Regiment prior to mobilisation in 1914.

Courtesy of the Trustees of the Duke of Wellington's Regiment Museum and Archives.

GALLANTRY MEDALS

DISTINGUISHED SERVICE ORDER (DSO)
Instituted by Royal Warrant in the London Gazette of 9th November, 1886. Awarded for "rewarding individual instances of meritorious or distinguished services in war", to junior Officers, who were not eligible for the CB, and Brevet rank was not appropriate. On 1st January, 1917, an order was issued to all commanders in the Field that the DSO should, as far as possible, be restricted to the 'fighting services'.

MILITARY CROSS (MC)
Instituted by Royal Warrant on 28th December, 1914, announced in the London Gazette of 1st January, 1915. To be awarded to Officers whose distinguished and meritorious service had been brought to the attention of the King. "No person shall be eligible.... unless he is a Captain, Commissioned Officer of lower grade, or a Warrant Officer."

DISTINGUISHED CONDUCT MEDAL (DCM)
Inaugurated 4th December, 1854, to reward Other Ranks with a medal and gratuity for "distinguished or gallant conduct in the Field". Originally limited to one Sergeant, four Corporals and 10 Privates per Battalion sized unit.

DISTINGUISHED SERVICE MEDAL (DSM)
Instituted 14th October, 1914. Awarded to petty officers and ratings of the Royal Navy, NCOs and other ranks of the Royal Marines....for acts of bravery not sufficiently meritorious to make them eligible for the Conspicuous Gallantry Medal. Later extended to cover the Merchant Navy and Army.

MILITARY MEDAL (MM)
Instituted by Royal Warrant on 25th March, 1916, for "the appreciation of acts of gallantry and devotion to duty performed by non-commissioned officers and men for individual and associated acts of bravery on the recommendation of a Commander-in-Chief in the Field."

MERITORIOUS SERVICE MEDAL (MSM)
The MSM for the Army was introduced on 19 December, 1845, to recognise Meritorious Service by Sergeants and other Senior NCOs. As an annuity was also paid, the number of medals issued each year was limited. The ribbon design was altered in 1916, with white edges to the crimson ribbon being authorised, and again in 1917, when a centre stripe was introduced.

HUDDERSFIELD'S ROLL OF HONOUR 1914–1922

CAMPAIGN MEDALS

1914 STAR

This bronze star was authorised in April, 1917, by King George V, to be awarded to those who had served in France or Belgium on the strength of a unit, or service in either of those two countries between 5th August to midnight on 22nd November 1914 inclusive.

In October, 1919, the King sanctioned the award of a clasp sewn onto the ribbon, bearing the dates '5th AUG. – 22nd NOV. 1914', to this Star to all who had been under fire in France or Belgium during, or between, the above dates. Recipients who received the medal with the clasp were also entitled to wear a small silver rose in the centre of the ribbon when the medal was not worn.

An estimated 380,000 'Mons Stars' were issued.

1914–15 STAR

This bronze medal was authorised in December, 1918. It is very similar to the 1914 Star but was issued to a much wider range of recipients. It was awarded to all who served in any theatre of war against the Central Powers between 5th August 1914 and 31st December 1915 (apart from those who had been awarded the 1914 Star).

An estimated 2.4 million of these medals were issued.

THE BRITISH WAR MEDAL, 1914–18

The medal (in silver or bronze) was authorised on 26th July, 1919, and awarded to officers and men of the British and Imperial Forces who either entered a theatre of war or entered service overseas between 5th August 1914 and 11th November 1918 inclusive. This was later extended to services in Russia, Siberia and some other areas in 1919 and 1920.

Approximately 6.5 million British War Medals were issued.

ALLIED VICTORY MEDAL, 1914–18

This bronze medal was awarded to all who received the 1914 or 1914–15 Star and, with certain exceptions, to those who received the British War Medal. Those who were mentioned in Despatches were allowed to wear an oak leaf on the ribbon.

Approximately 5.7 million Victory Medals were issued.

2/4th Battalion Duke of Wellington's Regiment Machine Gun Section 1916.

Courtesy of the Trustees of the Duke of Wellington's Regiment Museum and Archives.

Basilica in Albert, The Somme 1916.

Medals and Death Plaque of Private Stafford Pogson (image supplied by Alan Stansfield).

Courtesy of the Trustees of the Duke of Wellington's Regiment Museum and Archives.

Trench map of Bullecourt in 1918.

Courtesy of the Trustees of the Duke of Wellington's Regiment Museum and Archives.

Henry Jones, 19 Ivy Street, Crosland Moor, Huddersfield. Educated at Penygllodfa Council School, Newtown. Employed as a woollen piecer. Enlisted 11.8.1914. Killed in action during the Battle of the Somme, 7.10.1916. Has no known grave. Commemorated **THIEPVAL MEMORIAL TO THE MISSING.** ROH:- St. Barnabas Church, Crosland Moor.

JOWITT, VINCENT. Private. No 24355. 1st Battalion York and Lancaster Regiment. Born Wortley, Sheffield. Son of Titus and Rosina Caroline Jowitt of Storrs Farm, Wortley, Sheffield. Was an assistant on the staff of the Emley Council School. Lodged with Mrs S. Clegg at Church Street, Emley. Enlisted January 1916. Had been serving in Salonica for seven weeks when he was killed on 11.10.1916, aged 20 years. Has no known grave. Commemorated **DOIRAN MEMORIAL TO THE MISSING, GREECE.** ROH:- Emley War Memorial.

JUBB, MATTHEW HENRY. Private. No 29633. 1/4th Battalion Duke of Wellington's Regiment. Born Linthwaite. Lived Linthwaite. Died of wounds, 12.4.1918. Buried **RUE-DAVID MILITARY CEMETERY, FLEURBAIX.** Grave location:- Plot 3, Row G, Grave 8. ROH:- Linthwaite War Memorial.

JURY, REGINALD. 2nd Lieutenant. 4th Battalion Duke of Wellington's Regiment. Born Marsh 4.11.1893. Son of Francis and Emma Jury, 16 Elmfield Road, Birkby. Educated Fartown Grammar School. Was a member of the firm of Messrs F. Jury and Company, woollen merchants. Single. Joined the local Territorial battalion in 1910. Enlisted August, 1914, and embarked for France as a Private in April, 1915. Was invalided home in October, 1915, and, after a period of convalescence, went to a Reserve Battalion at Clipstone Camp, where he was promoted to the rank of Sergeant-Instructor in signalling. He was gazetted as Second Lieutenant in the Duke of Wellington's Regiment on 28th March, 1917, and returned to France in May, 1917. Was attending a course at the Signal School, Dunkirk, when that town was subjected to an enemy air raid on September 29th, 1917. Was severely wounded on that day and taken to the Queen Alexandra's Hospital at Malo-les-Bains, where he died of wounds on 6.10.1917, aged 23 years. Buried **MALO-LES-BAINS COMMUNAL CEMETERY.**

Grave location:- Row A, Grave 16. ROH:- Christ Church, Woodhouse Hill; Fartown and Birkby War Memorial.

KATHRO, HARRY. Private. No 29301. 9th Battalion Duke of Wellington's Regiment. Born Huddersfield. Lived 8 Back Colne Terrace, Aspley, Huddersfield. Married, with one child. Killed in action, 7.1.1918, aged 35 years. Has no known grave. Commemorated **ARRAS MEMORIAL TO THE MISSING.**

KAY, HAROLD HARRISON. Private. No 18998. 9th Battalion King's Own Yorkshire Light Infantry. Born 7 East Parade, Huddersfield 24.4.1885. Son of Harold H. and Esther Emma Kay, 4 Back Clifton Street, Marsh, Huddersfield. Educated St. Thomas's Church of England School. Employed as a scourer by Messrs George Crosland and Sons Limited. Single. Enlisted 3.11.1914. Was killed instantly in the trenches on 2.6.1916, aged 31 years. Buried **DARTMOOR CEMETERY.** Grave location:- Plot 1, Row B, Grave 29.

KAYE, ALFRED. Private. No 22459. 1st Battalion West Yorkshire Regiment. Born Crosland Moor. Educated Crosland Moor Council School. Employed as a teamer by the butchering department of the Huddersfield Industrial Society Limited. Married. Lived 5 Providence Place, Lockwood. Enlisted 25.10.1915. Wounded on two occasions. Killed in action near Havrincourt, 22.3.1918. Buried **FLESQUIERES HILL BRITISH CEMETERY.** Grave location:- Plot 4, Row D, Grave 13. ROH:- Emmanuel Church, Lockwood.

KAYE, ARTHUR. Private. No 39396. 5th Platoon, 'D' Company, 2/4th Battalion King's Own Yorkshire Light Infantry. Formerly No 6520 Duke of Wellington's Regiment. Born Hepworth, Holmfirth. Son of Mr and Mrs William Kaye, of Jackson Bridge. Husband of Mary E. Kaye, 24 Underbank Old Road, Holmfirth. Educated Hepworth Council School. Employed at Stoney Bank Mill and later at Lower Mill, Holmfirth. Enlisted 6.7.1916. Was in training with the Duke of Wellington's Regiment at Clipstone Camp and at Rugeley. Embarked for France in October, 1916. In June, 1917, he came home and was in hospital for some months. After recovering he went into training and proceeded to France a second time on 29.3.1918. Reported missing near Rheims on 20.7.1918 and afterwards presumed to have been killed on that date. Buried **BOUILLY CROSSROADS MILITARY CEMETERY.** Grave location:- Plot 1, Row D, Grave 6. ROH:- Hepworth and Scholes War Memorial

KAYE, ARTHUR. Private. No G/36117. 25th Battalion Royal Fusiliers. (Frontiersmen). Born 47 Prospect Street, Huddersfield. Son of the late Joseph and Mary Anne Kaye. Educated Spring Grove Board School. Employed as an organ builder in Leeds. Husband of Florence Kaye, Dial House, Halton, Leeds. Enlisted 8.5.1916. Killed in action in British East Africa, 3.8.1917, aged 37 years. Has no known grave. Commemorated **DAR-ES-SALAAM MEMORIAL TO THE MISSING.** ROH:- Huddersfield Parish Church.

KAYE, ARTHUR. Private. No 5165. 2/6th Battalion West Yorkshire Regiment. Born Huddersfield. Son of John and Fanny Kaye, Block Row, Lepton. Employed by Messrs Rhodes and Brierley Limited, Kirkheaton. Killed in action, 20.2.1917, aged 25 years. Has no known grave. Commemorated **THIEPVAL MEMORIAL TO THE MISSING.** ROH:- Lepton Parish Church; St John's Church, Kirkheaton.

KAYE, ARTHUR. Private. No 32850. 2nd Battalion Lincolnshire Regiment. Formerly No 27974 West Yorkshire Regiment. Born Cumberworth. Son of Mrs Maria Kaye of Butterley, New Mill, Holmfirth. Had worked as a collier but, prior to enlistment, had been working on the Broadstones Reservoir. Enlisted in April 1916. Embarked for France just before Christmas, 1916. Invalided home in 1917 due to a sprained ankle. Returned to France in the autumn of 1917. Killed in action, 2.1.1918, aged 38 years. Has no known grave. Commemorated **TYNE COT MEMORIAL TO THE MISSING.** ROH:- New Mill Working Men's Club; Fulstone War Memorial.

KAYE, ARTHUR PERCY. Private. No 266685. 'B' Company, 6th Battalion Gordon Highlanders. Born Huddersfield. Son of Mr and Mrs Sam Kaye, 235 Quarmby Road, Lindley. Employed as a warehouseman by Messrs Martin Sons and Company Limited of Lindley. Attended Oakes Baptist Sunday School and was a member of the Young Men's Class. Died of wounds at No 26 General Hospital, 25.4.1917, aged 23 years. Buried **ETAPLES MILITARY CEMETERY.** Grave location:- Plot 29, Row J, Grave 9a. ROH:- St. Stephen's Church, Lindley.

KAYE, CHARLES WILLIAM DONALDSON. Engine Room Artificer. No M/17439. Royal Navy. *HMS Juno*. Born Bradford 15.7.1888. Son of Mrs Jane Anne Keighley, Greenhead Hall, Dalton. Educated Ripon Grammar School. For some time he was an engineer onboard one of the mail boats of the Union Castle Line and later became a director of Messrs Lockwood and Keighley Limited, Upperhead Mills, Huddersfield. Married in 1915. (His wife died in July 1918). Held a commission with the 2/5th Battalion Duke of Wellington's Regiment but had to retire on account of ill health. Enlisted in the Royal Navy in October, 1915. Died, 10.2.1917, on board *HMS Juno* from pneumonia. Buried **MUSCAT NEW NAVAL CEMETERY, OMAN, PERSIAN GULF.** Grave location:- 3, 4. ROH:- St. John's Church, Kirkheaton.

KAYE, DAVID. Private. No 23797. 2nd Battalion Duke of Wellington's Regiment. Formerly No 29006 Northumberland Fusiliers. Born Leeds. Son of the late Matthew and Sarah Kaye. Lived Netherton, Huddersfield. Employed at British Dyes Limited as a dry stone waller. Was a member of the Honley Prize Band. Single. Embarked for France in September, 1916. Reported missing, 12.10.1916, and afterwards presumed to have been killed on that date. He was 36 years of age. Has no known grave. Commemorated **THIEPVAL MEMORIAL TO THE MISSING.** ROH:- South Crosland and Netherton War Memorial.

KAYE, DYSON. Private. No 41947. 12th Battalion Manchester Regiment. Formerly No 3/32330 North Staffordshire Regiment. Born Huddersfield. Elder son of Mrs Jane Kaye, 15 Spring Mill, Milnsbridge. Employed as a cloth finisher by Messrs John Crowther and Sons Limited, Spring Mills, Milnsbridge. Attended Milnsbridge Church and played football with the school team. Enlisted October, 1916, and embarked for France in February, 1917. Came home on 14 days leave in February, 1918. Died of gas poisoning three days after returning to France on 14.3.1918, aged 20, at No 48 Casualty Clearing Station. Buried **ROCQUIGNY-EQUANCOURT ROAD BRITISH CEMETERY.**

Grave location:- Plot 10, Row C, Grave 26. ROH:- Milnsbridge War Memorial.

KAYE, EDGAR. Private. No 5068. 1/4th Battalion Northumberland Fusiliers. Born Kirkheaton. Son of Mr and Mrs Sidney Kaye, Spring Gate, Kirkburton. Employed by Messrs Learoyd Brothers. Killed in the trenches near Butte de Warlencourt, 28.10.1916, aged 37 years. Has no known grave. Commemorated **THIEPVAL MEMORIAL TO THE MISSING.** ROH:- All Hallows Parish Church, Kirkburton; Learoyd Brothers.

KAYE, EDWARD. Private. No 23988. 8th Battalion Duke of Wellington's Regiment. Born New Mill, Holmfirth. Son of Mrs Frank Kaye, Butterley Lane, New Mill. Educated New Mill National School. Enlisted March 1915. Embarked for France in March 1916. Killed in action, 17.12.1916, aged 20 years. Has no known grave. Commemorated **THIEPVAL MEMORIAL TO THE MISSING.** His mother received a letter from Private A. E. Hutchison of the same platoon as her son. He wrote a description of Private Kaye's movements, 'He was coming from the trenches with Private Fletcher of Cheadle, Staffordshire, who gave me the information as he belonged to 'Y' Company and mine is 'X'. They had been detailed off to stay behind and give the relieving men knowledge of the positions and how it worked. They came to a dugout lower down and stayed there until four in the afternoon. They set off to join the Company and had not gone far when Neddy, as they called him, fell forward on his face. Private Fletcher at once attended to him but he only breathed once. He died a painless death. At the same time it was most unlucky as it was a stray bullet and according to some Northumberland Fusiliers stretcher-bearers who were passing it was through his heart. He is buried close by and will have a cross with name and number to mark his grave. Private Fletcher says he handed his pay-book, etc, to the Officer. It was most unlucky as the place is scarcely ever free from shell fire but rifle fire is very rare. I have also gone for water myself during the day over the same ground when bad for a drink. I should not risk snipers if I risk shells.' ROH:- New Mill Working Men's Club; Fulstone War Memorial.

KAYE, ERNEST. Private. No 35114. 25th (Tyneside Irish) Battalion Northumberland Fusiliers. Born Moldgreen, Huddersfield, in December 1889. Son of Arthur and Mary Kaye, 34 Mount Pleasant Street, Hill Top Road, Jolly Lane, Dalton. Educated Moldgreen Council School. Husband of Beatrice Kaye, 55 Ravensknowle Road, Moldgreen. Employed as a picture framer. Killed in action, 26.4.1917, aged 28. Buried **ATHIES COMMUNAL CEMETERY EXTENSION.** Grave location:- Row E, Grave 25. ROH:- Christ Church, Moldgreen.

KAYE, ERNEST. Private. No 42912. 7th/8th Battalion Royal Inniskilling Fusiliers. Born 16.3.1887. Son of Maria Kaye, Northgate, Almondbury. Educated Almondbury Council School. Employed as a cloth scourer by Messrs Walter Sykes Limited, Zetland Mills, Huddersfield. Husband of Lily Kaye, 14 Hudroyd, Almondbury. Was a member of Almondbury Liberal Club. Reported missing, 21.3.1918 and afterwards presumed to have been killed on that date. Has no known grave. Commemorated **POZIERES MEMORIAL TO THE MISSING.** Almondbury War Memorial.

KAYE, FRED. Private. No 241925. 1/5th Battalion Northumberland Fusiliers. Born Camberwell, London. Son of William Henry Kaye, Butterley, New Mill, Holmfirth. Educated Hepworth Church School. Employed by Messrs J. Sykes and Company Limited, Rock Mills. Enlisted in 1916. Wounded 26.10.1917. Died of wounds at No 4 Casualty Clearing Station, 11.11.1917, aged 21 years. Buried **DOZINGHEM MILITARY CEMETERY.** Grave location:- Plot 13, Row F, Grave 17. ROH:- New Mill Working Men's Club; Fulstone War Memorial.

KAYE, FRED. Private. No 240247. 1/5th Battalion Duke of Wellington's Regiment. Born 24 Swallow Street 10.5.1896. Son of Mary Ellen Kaye, 39 Blackhouse Road, Fartown. Educated Spring Grove Council School. Employed as a wire drawer by Messrs Joseph Sykes Brothers, Acre Mills, Lindley. Attended High Street Sunday School. Mobilised 4.8.1914. Died of meningitis at the Welsh Metropolitan War Hospital, Whitchurch, Cardiff, on 23.4.1917, aged 21 years. Buried with full military honours in **EDGERTON CEMETERY, HUDDERSFIELD.** Grave location:- 10B, 41.

(Son of Private **OLIVER KAYE**, reported missing, 3.9.1916, q.v.). ROH:- High Street United Methodist Church: Christ Church, Woodhouse Hill; Huddersfield Drill Hall; Fartown and Birkby War Memorial.

KAYE, FRED. Private. No 242869. 1/5th Battalion Duke of Wellington's Regiment. Born Lockwood, Huddersfield. Married. Lived 19 Damside, Huddersfield. Employed at the Hillhouse depot of the Huddersfield Brick, Tile and Stone Company Limited. Killed in action, 12.4.1917, aged 34 years. Buried **LE TOURET MILITARY CEMETERY**. Grave location:- Plot 4, Row C, Grave 18. ROH:- Huddersfield Drill Hall.

KAYE, GEORGE. Private. No 156627. 56th Battalion Machine Gun Corps. Formerly No 6043 Duke of Wellington's Regiment. Born Moldgreen, Huddersfield. Married. Lived 8a Chapel Hill, Huddersfield. Employed by Messrs M. Bedforth and Sons, Aspley. Killed in action, 20.9.1918, aged 29 years. Buried **VIS-en-ARTOIS BRITISH CEMETERY**. Grave location:- Plot 1, Row D, Grave 49.

KAYE, GEORGE. Private. No 40786. 2/5th Battalion South Staffordshire Regiment. Formerly No 31489 Duke of Wellington's Regiment. Born Thongsbridge. Son of Mr Job Kaye, Vickerman's Buildings, Thongsbridge. Married, with two children. Lived Crodingley, Thongsbridge. Attended St. Andrew's Church, Thongsbridge. Employed by Messrs John Woodhead of Thongsbridge. Joined up under the Derby scheme. Died of wounds at No 44 Casualty Clearing Station, 23.9.1917, aged 31 years. Buried **NINE ELMS BRITISH CEMETERY, POPERINGHE**. Grave location:- Plot 1, Row F, Grave 4. ROH:- Netherthong and Thongsbridge War Memorial.

KAYE, GEORGE EDGAR. Private. No 260074. 2/6th Battalion North Staffordshire Regiment. Born Lepton. Lived Lepton. Killed in action at the Battle of Cambrai, 30.11.1917. Has no known grave. Commemorated **CAMBRAI MEMORIAL TO THE MISSING**. ROH:- Lepton Parish Church.

KAYE, HAROLD, MM. Private. No 301793. 1/8th Battalion Durham Light Infantry. Formerly No 29505 Northumberland Fusiliers. Born New Mill, Holmfirth. Son of Mr and Mrs Frank Kaye. Educated New Mill National School. Employed as a spinner by Messrs Rayner of New Mill. Attended New Mill Parish Church and Sunday School. Married, with one daughter. Lived New Street, Honley. Enlisted 8.6.1916. Reported missing and afterwards presumed killed on 5.11.1916, aged 23 years. Has no known grave. Commemorated **THIEPVAL MEMORIAL TO THE MISSING**. ROH:- New Mill Working Men's Club; Fulstone War Memorial; Honley War Memorial.

KAYE, HAROLD SYKES. Private. No 241069. 2/5th Battalion Duke of Wellington's Regiment. Born 68 Storths, Moldgreen. Educated Moldgreen Council School. Employed as a newsagent's assistant by Mr C. H. Pickles, Station Street, Huddersfield. Married. Lived 28 Wakefield Road, Moldgreen. Enlisted December 1914. Taken prisoner at the Battle of Bullecourt, 3.5.1917. Died of wounds and pneumonia as a Prisoner of War at Soltau, near Munster, Germany, 15.10.18, aged 25 years. Buried **HAMBURG CEMETERY, OHLSDORF, GERMANY**. Grave location:- Plot 2, Row G, Grave 11. ROH:- St. Andrew's Church; Christ Church, Moldgreen; Huddersfield Parish Church; Huddersfield Drill Hall.

KAYE, HARRY. Private. No 40555. 16th Battalion Northumberland Fusiliers. Born Mount Street, Lockwood 22.9.1882. Educated Mount Pleasant Council School. Employed as a weaver by Messrs Smith and Calverley at Plover Mills, Lindley. Single. At the time of enlistment, was living at 92 Rashcliffe Hill, Lockwood. Enlisted 24.5.1916. Embarked for France in September, 1916. Killed in action during the Battle of the Somme, 23.11.1916, aged 33 years. Buried **MUNICH TRENCH CEMETERY**. Grave location:- Row B, Grave 22. ROH:- St. Stephen's Church, Rashcliffe.

KAYE, HARRY. Corporal. No 240266. 2/5th Battalion Duke of Wellington's Regiment. Lived Holmfirth. Killed in action at the Battle of Bullecourt, 3.5.1917. Has no known grave. Commemorated **ARRAS MEMORIAL TO THE MISSING**. ROH:- Huddersfield Drill Hall.

KAYE, HERBERT. Private. No 241370. 1/4th Battalion Duke of Wellington's Regiment. Born

Hade Edge, Holmfirth. Son of Mr and Mrs H. Kaye, Folly Farm, Hade Edge. Educated Hade Edge Council School. Employed at Washpit Mills, Holmfirth. Enlisted during the latter part of 1915 and trained at Clipstone Camp. Embarked for France in May, 1916. Suffered from trench feet but returned to his Regiment after seven weeks. Was gassed in September, 1916. Invalided to England with Enteric Fever in January, 1918. Returned to France in April, 1918. Suffered a serious gunshot wound to the neck a fortnight later. Died of wounds at No 8 British Red Cross Hospital, 1.5.1918. Buried **BOULOGNE EASTERN CEMETERY.** Grave location:- Plot 9, Row B, Grave 11. ROH:- Hade Edge War Memorial.

KAYE, HERBERT. Corporal. No 70089. 5th Battery, 45th Brigade, Royal Field Artillery. Born Hepworth, Holmfirth. Adopted son and nephew of Mr and Mrs Henry Kaye, 41 Towngate, Hepworth. Educated Hepworth Endowed School. Attended Hepworth Church Sunday School. Employed firstly in the local coal pits and then as a teamer for Messrs Henry Mitchell and Sons, grocers, of Holmfirth. Engaged to Miss Florrie Turner, of Royd House, Holmfirth. Enlisted in the local Territorials in 1911. Wounded in the shoulder and abdomen on 14.11.1917. Died of wounds at No 17 Casualty Clearing Station, 19.11.1917, aged 23 years, Buried **LIJSSENTHOEK MILITARY CEMETERY.** Grave location:- Plot 27, Row B, Grave 5a. Mrs Kaye received a letter from a young lady whose brother and Herbert were close friends. The letter reads, *'You will be rather surprised to receive this letter from me. I have no doubt you have heard the sad news of your son. Yesterday (November 27) I received a letter from my brother who is in the same Battery. He and Herbert were very big pals and he asked me to come and see you and explain things to you but I did not like breaking the news if you had not heard. My brother and Herbert were together the same night it happened and were joking as to what they would leave each other in their will. He said Herbert was bringing up ammunition to the lines when he was wounded in the stomach and shoulder with shrapnel and was removed to hospital and died of his wounds. My brother is very much upset as he said he was his best pal and it came as a shock.'* ROH:- Hepworth and Scholes War Memorial; Hepworth Church.

KAYE, HERBERT HOLMES. Gunner. No 176840. Royal Garrison Artillery. Born Holmfirth. Son of the late Mr Benjamin Kaye and Mrs Kaye of Fartown, Huddersfield and formerly of Lansdowne Terrace, Holmfirth. Educated Almondbury Grammar School. Employed in the counting house of Messrs A. and S. Henry of Huddersfield. Married, with one child who was born just before his father enlisted. Lived Glenthorpe, Holmfirth. Enlisted September 1917. Embarked for France in May, 1918. Died of gunshot wounds, 30.9.1918. Buried **TINCOURT NEW BRITISH CEMETERY.** Grave location:- Plot 5, Row G, Grave 4. ROH:- Almondbury Grammar School; Cartworth War Memorial.

KAYE, JAMES EDWARD. Corporal. No 15180. 10th Battalion Duke of Wellington's Regiment. Born Skircoat Moor, Halifax, 31.5.1893. Only son of the late Jonas Kaye and of Eliza Kaye, 99 Ravensknowle Road, Moldgreen, Huddersfield. Educated Moldgreen Council School. Employed as a scourer and finisher by Messrs Godfrey Sykes and Sons, Moldgreen. Played cricket for the Dalton second eleven cricket team. Single. Enlisted February 1915. Wounded 7.6.1917. Died of wounds, 9.6.1917, aged 23, at No 17 Casualty Clearing Station. Buried **LIJSSENTHOEK MILITARY CEMETERY.** Grave location:- Plot 15, Row H, Grave 5. ROH:- Christ Church, Moldgreen; commemorated on headstone in Kirkheaton Cemetery.

KAYE, JOE. Private. No 29145. 10th Battalion Duke of Wellington's Regiment. Born Lowergate, Paddock 30.3.1886. Son of the late John and of Mary Ann Kaye, 129 Church Street, Paddock. Educated Paddock Council School. Attended Paddock United Methodist Church. Employed as an accountant's clerk by Messrs Netherwood and Lee, New Street, Huddersfield. Single. Enlisted 1.9.1916. Killed in action near Ypres, 7.6.1917, aged 31. Has no known grave. Commemorated **MENIN GATE MEMORIAL TO THE MISSING.** ROH:- All Saints Church, Paddock; Shared Church, Paddock.

KAYE, JOE WILLIE. Lance Corporal. No 38146. 17th Battalion West Yorkshire Regiment. Born Primrose Hill, Huddersfield, 9.11.1888. Son of Mary Ann Kaye, 20 Low Road, Berry Brow, Huddersfield. Educated Mount Pleasant Council School, Lockwood. Employed as a dyer's labourer. Husband of Mary Kaye, 29 Robin Hood Hill, Berry Brow. Enlisted 21.10.1914. Killed in action, 17.4.1917, aged 29 years. Has no known grave. Commemorated **THIEPVAL MEMORIAL TO THE MISSING.** ROH:- Armitage Bridge War Memorial.

KAYE, JOHN. Private. No 6/5729. 1/6th Battalion Duke of Wellington's Regiment. Born Milnsbridge. Son of Emily Shaw, 70 Scar Lane, Milnsbridge. Educated Crow Lane Board School, Milnsbridge. Attended Milnsbridge Wesleyan Sunday School and later St. Michael's Mission Church in Scar Lane, Milnsbridge. Employed as a teamer by Messrs John Crowther and Sons, Union Mills, Milnsbridge. Enlisted 16.1.1916. Embarked for France from Clipstone Camp on the Thursday of Whit week. Killed in action during the Battle of the Somme, 25.7.1916, aged 22 years. Buried **LONSDALE CEMETERY.** Grave location:- Plot 7, Row E, Grave 7. ROH:- Crow Lane Board School, Milnsbridge. His mother received a letter from Captain Sam H. Cliffe containing news of her son's death. He stated that *'Private Kaye during afternoon of July 25th was returned as missing but early on Thursday morning his body was found in a shell hole. Evidently a shell had burst underneath him.* ROH:- Huddersfield Mission, Milnsbridge; St. Mark's Parish Church, Longwood; St. John's Church, Golcar.

KAYE, JOHN Sergeant. No S/312587. Army Service Corps, attached GHQ. Only surviving son of Mr Joah Kaye, 47 Colne Road, Huddersfield. Died of bronchial-pneumonia following upon influenza at a Casualty Clearing Station, in Italy. on 6.12.1918, aged 29 years. Buried **MONTECCHIO-PRECALCINO COMMUNAL CEMETERY EXTENSION.** Grave location:- Plot 9, Row C, Grave 4.

KAYE, LEWIS. Private. Army Service Corps. (Motor Transport). Born 8 Armitage Buildings, Crosland Moor. Son of William Henry and Ann Megson Kaye, 32 Crosland Street, Crosland Moor. Educated St. Barnabas Church of England School, Crosland Moor. Employed as a textile machine fitter. Married. Died at home on 8.8.1921, at 32 Crosland Street, Crosland Moor, of chronic nephritis and uraemia after discharge on medical grounds. Buried **LOCKWOOD CEMETERY.**

KAYE, LEWIS B. Gunner. No 123352. Royal Garrison Artillery. Born Huddersfield. Lived 34 Firth Street, Huddersfield. Died of heart disease due to war service on 19.11.1921.

KAYE, LEWIS HERBERT. Private. No 270125. 16th Battalion The Royal Scots (Lothian Regiment). Born 21 West Place, Dalton, 25.3.1895. Son of Mrs C. Kaye. Educated Christ Church School, Moldgreen. Employed as a tailor by Messrs J. Sykes and Sons, tailors, Chapel Hill, Huddersfield. Single. Enlisted 11.4.1916. Killed in action, 26.8.1917, aged 23 years. Buried **HARGICOURT BRITISH CEMETERY.** Grave location:- Plot 1, Row C, Grave 14.

KAYE, MATTHEW. Lance Corporal. No 21729. 1st Battalion King's Own Yorkshire Light Infantry. Born Berry Brow, Huddersfield, 12.7.1889. Educated at Berry Brow Schools. Employed as a coal miner at Haigh near Barnsley. Single. Enlisted 22.2.1915. Served in France with the B.E.F. from 2.6.1915 until 24.10.1915. Sailed from Marseilles on 25.10.1915 for Salonika via Alexandria. In Salinika until 21.12.1916. Died at the home of his sister, Mrs Ada Searle, 65 Ravensknowle Road, Moldgreen, of Malaria on 18.11.1918.

KAYE, OLIVER. Private. No 240912. 1/5th Battalion Duke of Wellington's Regiment. Born Huddersfield 15.9.1875. Educated Thomas Street Board School. Employed as stoker. Husband of Mary Ellen Kaye, 24 Swallow Street, Huddersfield. Enlisted 31.12.1914. Reported missing, presumed killed, in the attack on the Schwaben Redoubt, 3.9.1916, aged 41 years, Has no known grave. Commemorated **THIEPVAL MEMORIAL TO THE MISSING.** (Father of Private **FRED KAYE,** who died, 23.4.1917, q.v.). ROH:- Huddersfield Drill Hall; Christ Church, Woodhouse Hill; Fartown and Birkby War Memorial.

KAYE, PERCY. Rifleman. No C/7649. 21st Battalion King's Royal Rifle Corps. Born Lepton 17.9.1891. Educated Lepton Council School and Highburton National School. Employed as a gardener. At the time of enlistment, was living at Green Grove, Kirkburton. Married. (Single when he enlisted). Enlisted 15.11.1915. Wounded at Flers in September, 1916. Reported missing, presumed killed, near Ypres, 20.9.1917. Has no known grave. Commemorated **TYNE**

COT MEMORIAL TO THE MISSING. ROH:- All Hallows Church, Kirkburton; Thurstonland War Memorial.

KAYE, PERCY PENNINGTON. Private. No 241326. 1/4th Battalion Duke of Wellington's Regiment. Lodged with Mrs Crow, 9 Hope Street, Folly Hall, Huddersfield. Employed as a wool comber by Messrs J. Lumb and Sons. Embarked for France in the early part of 1916. Killed in action, 25.2.1918. Buried **AEROPLANE CEMETERY, YPRES.** Grave location:- Plot 7, Row C, Grave 3. ROH:- St. Stephen's Church, Rashcliffe.

KAYE, REGINALD CROMBY. Private. No 26982. 20th Battalion Durham Light Infantry. Formerly No 29134 Northumberland Fusiliers. Born Fartown 24.7.1892. Son of Mary Alice Kaye, 213 Leeds Road, Huddersfield. Educated Hillhouse Board School. Employed as a scourer by Messrs T. and H. Blamires Limited, Leeds Road, Huddersfield. Single. Enlisted 1.6.1916. Killed in action, 3.6.1917. Buried **DICKIEBUSCH NEW MILITARY CEMETERY EXTENSION.** Grave location:- Plot 3, Row B, Grave 8. ROH:- St. Andrew's Church, Leeds Road; Fartown and Birkby War Memorial.

KEIGHLEY, HAROLD. Private. No 240845. 2/5th Battalion Duke of Wellington's Regiment. Born Manchester 29.9.1895. Son of Samuel and Louisa Keighley, 9 Newsome Road, Huddersfield. Educated Stile Common Council School. Attended St. Paul's Sunday School Employed as an organ builder by Messrs Peter Conacher and Company. Single. Enlisted 11.12.1914. Killed in action at the Battle of Arras, 3.5.1917, aged 21 years. Buried **BAILLEUL ROAD EAST CEMETERY.** Grave location:- Plot 2, Row B, Grave 29. ROH:- St. Paul's Church, Southgate, Huddersfield; Huddersfield Drill Hall; Almondbury War Memorial.

KEIR, EDWARD HUGH. Lieutenant. 3rd Battalion King's Own Royal Lancaster Regiment, attached 16th Squadron Royal Flying Corps. Born Huddersfield. Son of Samuel and Anne Keir of 'Rossmore', Scotforth Road, Lancaster. Educated at the Lancaster Royal Grammar School. Was commissioned into the King's Own Royal Lancaster Regiment in December, 1914, whilst serving in the Officers' Training Corps at the Lancaster Royal Grammar School. Served for some time on the Staff of the Southern Command School of Instruction at Tidworth. He transferred to the Royal Flying Corps in March, 1917, and embarked for France in August, 1917. Killed in action, in an air combat in the area Souchez - Carency on 28.10.1917, aged 20 years. Buried **AUBIGNY COMMUNAL CEMETERY EXTENSION.** Grave location:- Plot 6, Row J, Grave 2. ROH:- Brighouse War Memorial.

KELAVEY, LAWRENCE. Guardsman. No 22573. Coldstream Guards. Formerly No 2465 Household Battalion. Born Huddersfield. Lived with his parents at 28 Baker Street, Oakes and, formerly, at 200 Old Black Road, Dalton. Employed by Messrs Maplestone and Wilkinson Limited, dyers, Long Lane, Huddersfield. Enlisted 1916. Killed in action, 4.11.1918, aged 27 years. Buried **VILLERS-POL COMMUNAL CEMETERY EXTENSION.** Grave location: Row G, Grave 9.

KELLY, DANIEL. Private. No 11967. 2nd Battalion Duke of Wellington's Regiment. Born Castlegate, Huddersfield, 10.7.1878. Educated St. Patrick's Roman Catholic School, Huddersfield. Lived with his married sister, Mrs Mary Ellen Pinnance, 1 Hawk Street, Huddersfield. Had worked for ten years as out porter at the Huddersfield Railway Station. Had served for three years with the Royal Garrison Artillery and, during part of that time, was in India. Single. Enlisted 21.8.1914. Died of wounds (gas) received at Hill 60 on 5.5.1915, aged 33 years. Buried **LARCH WOOD (RAILWAY CUTTING) CEMETERY, ZILLEBEKE, BELGIUM.** Grave location:- Plot 2, Row C, Grave 4.

KELLY, FRANK. Private. No 36377. 8th Battalion Northumberland Fusiliers. Born Ireland 12.1.1882. Son of John and Janet Kelly. Educated St. Patrick's Roman Catholic School. Employed as a wire operator by Messrs Joseph Sykes Brothers Limited, Acre Mills, Lindley. Was a member of Lindley Working Men's Club. Attended St. Patrick's Church. Husband of Janet Kelly, 11 Back Thomas Street, Lindley. Enlisted 16.1.1917. Killed in action, 19.6.1917, aged 34 years. Has no known grave. Commemorated **MENIN GATE MEMORIAL TO THE MISSING.** ROH:- St. Stephen's Church, Lindley.

KELLY, JAMES EDWARD. Private. No 31745. 2/4th Battalion Duke of Wellington's Regiment. Born Huddersfield 12.9.1889. Educated St. Patrick's Roman Catholic School. Employed as a tram driver by the Huddersfield Corporation Tramways Department. Married, with two children. At the time of enlistment was living at 124 Bradford Road, Huddersfield. Enlisted 28.5.1917. Embarked for France on 3.10.1917. Killed in action at the Battle of Cambrai, 21.11.1917, aged 28 years. Has no known grave. Commemorated **CAMBRAI MEMORIAL TO THE MISSING.** ROH:- Huddersfield Corporation.

KELLY, JAMES HENRY. Driver. No L/5956. 'A' Battery, 155th Brigade Royal Field Artillery. Born Huddersfield. Husband of Mary Ellen (Nellie) Kelly, 32 Upperhead Row, Huddersfield. Employed in the street cleansing department of Huddersfield Corporation. Enlisted April 1915. Died of pneumonia and pleurisy at No 3 Casualty Clearing Station on 26.5.1918, aged 32 years. Buried **BAGNEUX BRITISH CEMETERY.** Grave location:- Plot 2, Row D, Grave 30. (Brother of Able Seaman **JAMES WILLIAM KELLY**, killed accidentally, 2.10.1917). ROH:- Huddersfield Corporation Roll.

KELLY, JAMES WILLIAM. Private. No 241358. 10th Battalion The Cameronians (Scottish Rifles). Born Huddersfield. Married. Lived 40 Cowcliffe Hill, Huddersfield. Employed by the Huddersfield Corporation Tramways Department. Died of wounds, 25.7.1918, aged 33 years. Buried **ROYALLIEU FRENCH NATIONAL CEMETERY,COMPIEGNE.** Grave location:- Plot G, Row I, Grave 17.

KELLY, WILLIAM. Private. No 1977. 6th Battalion King's Own Yorkshire Light Infantry. Born Barnsley. Son of James and Margaret Kelly. Educated at Barnsley Schools. Employed as a labourer by Messrs A. Helm and Sons, timber merchants. Married, with six children. Lived 37 Back Dock Street, Huddersfield. Had served 12 years in the 2nd Battalion K.O.Y.L.I. and re-enlisted in September, 1914. As the 2nd Battalion had suffered great losses during the retreat from Mons he was attached to the 6th Battalion. Died of epilepsy at No 17 Casualty Clearing Station, 1.2.1916. Buried **LIJSSENTHOEK MILITARY CEMETERY.** Grave location:- Plot 4, Row B, Grave 38. Private S. Vallance, 6th Battalion K.O.Y.L.I., the dead soldier's chum, in the course of a letter to Mrs Kelly said that *'Private Kelly had a stroke in the trenches and died two hours later.'*

KELSALL, ERIC. Private. No 5/4468. 1/5th Battalion Duke of Wellington's Regiment. Born Nelson, Lancashire, 18.4.1899. Son of Thomas and Grace Kelsall, 91 Wellington Street, Oakes, Huddersfield. Educated at Ashbourne, Manchester and Huddersfield schools. Employed as a beamer in a woollen mill. Single. Enlisted, 13.8.1915, at the age of 16 years. Embarked for France in April, 1916. Killed in action at Thiepval Wood on 28.7.1916, aged 17 years. Buried **CONNAUGHT CEMETERY, THIEPVAL.** Grave location:- Plot 3, Row M, Grave 8. ROH:- St. Stephen's Church, Lindley; Huddersfield Drill Hall.

KENDALL, HERBERT REEVES. Private. No GS/18254. East Riding Yeomanry. Born Hull. Son of Mr and Mrs Arthur Kendall, 54 Tanfield Road, Birkby, Huddersfield. Enlisted November. Was drowned on 15.4.1917, when the *Transport Arcadian* was sunk by a torpedo. Buried **SYRA NEW BRITISH CEMETERY, GREECE.** Grave location:- Plot 2, Row A, Grave 9.

KENNEALLY, LUKE LACKY. Private. No 1765, Royal Army Medical Corps. Born Swallow Street, Huddersfield, 2.1.1884. Son of Martin and Elizabeth Kenneally, 12 Henry Street, Huddersfield. Employed as a labourer. Single. Enlisted September 1914. Died of bronchitis and the effects of being gassed at Royds Hall Military Hospital on 2.3.1919, aged 36 years. Buried **EDGERTON CEMETERY, HUDDERSFIELD.** Grave location:- 17R, 44G.

KENNEDY, GEORGE PERCIVAL. Private. No 30176. 8th Battalion Northumberland Fusiliers. Born New Laithe Hill, Almondbury, 6.5.1897. Son of Percival and Sarah Kennedy, 36 Back Ivy Street, Moldgreen. Educated Christ Church School, Moldgreen. Employed as a picture frame polisher. Enlisted 19.6.1916. Killed in action, 6.12.1916, aged 19 years. Has no known grave. Commemorated **THIEPVAL MEMORIAL TO THE MISSING.** ROH:- Christ Church, Moldgreen.

KENNEDY, NORMAN. Private. No 366836. 1/6th Battalion Northumberland Fusiliers. Born

Halifax Old Road, Huddersfield, 11.5.1899. Son of Lea and Alice Kennedy, 34 St Paul's Street, Huddersfield. Educated Thomas Street Council School. Employed as a cloth finisher. Single. Enlisted March 1917. Killed in action, 2.4.1918. Has no known grave. Commemorated **POZIERES MEMORIAL TO THE MISSING**. ROH:- Huddersfield Parish Church.

KENNEDY, PATRICK. Corporal. No 22882. 15th/17th West Yorkshire Regiment. Formerly No 6025 Duke of Wellington's Regiment. Born Huddersfield. Enlisted Halifax. Killed in action, 23.3.1918. Buried **CABARET ROUGE CEMETERY**. Grave location:- Plot 8, Row R, Grave 23. ROH:- Almondbury War Memorial.

KENNEDY, WILLIAM. Driver. No 81973. 'B' Battery, 124th Brigade Royal Field Artillery. Born 45 Whitestone Road, Huddersfield, 5.3.1889. Son of George William and Edith Kennedy, 35 Clement Street, Birkby. Educated Hillhouse Council School. Employed as a weaver. Husband of Miriam Kennedy, 17 Manchester Road, Huddersfield. Enlisted January 1915. Served in France and Belgium for one year and ten months. Killed in action at Mount Kemmel, 11.8.1917, aged 28 years. Buried **KEMMEL CHATEAU MILITARY CEMETERY**. Grave location:- Row D, Grave 35. ROH:- St. John's Church, Birkby; Fartown and Birkby War Memorial.

KENNERDALE, TOM. Private. No 11294. 8th Battalion Duke of Wellington's Regiment. Born Huddersfield. Son of Mrs E. Kennerdale, 18 Hawk Street, Huddersfield. Attended the Huddersfield Parish Church Sunday School. Employed by Messrs J. Brown and Company Limited, Bay Hall Works. Reported missing, believed killed, on 27.8.1917. Buried **CEMENT HOUSE CEMETERY**. Grave location:- Plot 4, Row C, Grave 9. ROH:- Huddersfield Parish Church.

KENNY, ARTHUR. (Real Name - **KILKELLY**). Private. No 11939. 'Y Company, 8th Battalion Duke of Wellington's Regiment. Born Marsh. Only son of Mrs Kilkelly, Prospect Street, Huddersfield, and the late Sergeant Kilkelly, who had served for 21 years in the Army and went through the Egyptian war. Employed for four and a half years for Messrs James Haigh and Sons Limited, dyers and finishers, Globe Works, Colne Road, Huddersfield. Enlisted at the outbreak of the war. Was wounded on 24.11.1915, in Gallipoli, by a bullet which passed in at the back and lodged just above the heart. Evacuated to England where he died of his wounds at Birmingham War Hospital on 13.12.1915, aged 24 years. Buried **EDGERTON CEMETERY, HUDDERSFIELD**. Grave location:- 11B, 115.

KENNY, THOMAS. Private. No 41286. 7/8th Battalion The Royal Inniskilling Fusiliers. Son of Joseph Kenny, of Huddersfield, and the late Mary Ann Kenny. Killed in action, 21.3.1918, aged 28 years. Buried **TEMPLEUX-LE-GUERARD BRITISH CEMETERY**. Grave location:- Plot 2, Row D, Grave 8.

KENT, CHARLES. Sergeant. No 2884. 1/7th Battalion Duke of Wellington's Regiment. Born Brightside, Yorkshire. Enlisted Slaithwaite. Lived Binn, Slaithwaite. Husband of Ethel Kent. Before enlistment the family removed to 6 Uppertown, Oxenhope, Keighley. Killed in action during the Battle of the Somme on 17.9.1916. Has no known grave. Commemorated **THIEPVAL MEMORIAL TO THE MISSING**. ROH:- Linthwaite; St. James Church, Slaithwaite; Slaithwaite War Memorial; Huddersfield Drill Hall.

KENWORTHY, F. Private. 8th Battalion Duke of Wellington's Regiment. Born Moldgreen, Huddersfield. Lived Green Mount Street, Moldgreen. Invalided home from the National Reserves Training in Northumberland. Died, 22.10.1914, aged 33. ROH:- Moldgreen War Memorial.

KENWORTHY, HARRY. Sergeant. No S4/157127. 13th Field Bakery, Army Service Corps. Born Holmfirth. Son of Henry and Mary A. Kenworthy of Holmfirth, husband of Edith R.H. Kenworthy, 47 Bayswater Crescent, Harehills Road, Leeds. Died of pneumonia, 28.1.1918, aged 43 years. Buried **BOULOGNE EASTERN CEMETERY**. Grave location:- Plot 8, Row I, Grave 154.

KENWORTHY, HERMAN. Private. No 32478. 8th Battalion York and Lancaster Regiment. Born New Mill, Holmfirth. Son of Ann Elizabeth Kenworthy, Kemp's House, Jackson Bridge, New Mill. Killed in action, 7.6.1917, aged 19 years. Has no known grave. Commemorated **MENIN GATE MEMORIAL TO THE MISSING**. ROH:-

Hepworth and Scholes War Memorial; Hepworth Church.

KENWORTHY, HAROLD. Private. No S/11853 'A' Company, 8th Battalion Seaforth Highlanders. Born Glasgow. Enlisted Huddersfield. Lived 18 Annisfield Avenue, Greenfield. Brother of Mr H. Kenworthy, 3 Berry Street, Greenfield, Oldham. Employed as a tram driver by Huddersfield Corporation Tramways Department. Killed in action, 22.8.1917, aged 27 years. Has no known grave. Commemorated **TYNE COT MEMORIAL TO THE MISSING.** ROH:- Huddersfield Corporation Roll.

KENWORTHY, WILFRED. Private. No 35591. 26th (Tyneside Irish) Battalion Northumberland Fusiliers. Formerly No 37534 Durham Light Infantry. Born Halifax. Son of Hugh and Alice Kenworthy, 7 Glen Royd, Marsden. Employed as a weaver at Bank Bottom Mills, Marsden. Enlisted July 1916. Embarked for France in October, 1916. Reported missing, 28.4.1917 and afterwards presumed to have died on that date, aged 28. Buried **BROWN'S COPSE CEMETERY, ROEUX.** Grave location:- Plot 3, Row E, Grave 18. His mother received a letter from a comrade, written on 26.5.1917, *'I am sorry to say that Wilfred was seriously wounded by a sniper. The bullet entered his left eye and passed through his head. He was unconscious whilst I was with him. I reported his case to the Officer. I am anxious to know whether he is recovering but have not heard of him since. It must be a terrible blow to you but I hope it may be lessened if possible by the fact that he fought for liberty, home and country. He was esteemed very highly here by all who knew him and his dearest chums miss him sadly.'* ROH:- Marsden War Memorial.

KENYON, HAROLD. Private. No 3490. 2nd Battalion Monmouthshire Regiment. Born Barnsley. Son of Tom Cooper Kenyon. Lived Huddersfield. Died of wounds, 23.7.1916, aged 33. Buried **COUIN BRITISH CEMETERY.** Grave location:- Plot 2, Row B, Grave 2.

KENYON, HERBERT. Private. No 122275. 9th Company Machine Gun Corps. Formerly No 8043 West Yorkshire Regiment. Born Huddersfield. Married. Lived 24 Back Colne Street, Aspley. Employed by Messrs Jarmaine and Sons of Kirkheaton. Invalided home suffering from trench fever. Killed in action, 21.3.1918, aged 24 years. Has no known grave. Commemorated **POZIERES MEMORIAL TO THE MISSING.** ROH:- St. Andrew's Church, Leeds Road.

KENYON, WILLIE. Private. No 24363. 2/6th Battalion Duke of Wellington's Regiment. Born South Street, Huddersfield, 2.12.1890. Son of Mr and Mrs J. B. Taylor, 8 Marsh Terrace, Marsh. Educated Portland Street Church School. Employed as a cloth finisher by Messrs Jennens, Welch and Company, of Springwood Street, Huddersfield. Husband of Elsie Kenyon, 21 Bankfield Road, off Manchester Road, Huddersfield. Attended Holy Trinity Church and was a member of the choir for eight years. Enlisted 2.12.1915. Was killed by a sniper whilst acting as battalion runner somewhere in the lines near Cambrai on 27.11.1917, aged 26 years. Has no known grave. Commemorated **CAMBRAI MEMORIAL TO THE MISSING.** ROH:- Holy Trinity Church, Huddersfield.

KENYON, WILLIE. Private. No 242868. 1/5th Battalion York and Lancaster Regiment. Born Meltham. Husband of Annie Kenyon of Greenend, Meltham. Died of wounds, 22.12.1917, aged 38 years. Buried **LIJSSENTHOEK MILITARY CEMETERY.** Grave location:- Plot 27, Row C, Grave 12. ROH:- St. Bartholomew's Church, Meltham.

KERFOOT, JOHN EDWARD. Private. No 2918. 1/5th Battalion Duke of Wellington's Regiment. Born Holywell, North Wales. Son of John Edward and Mrs Kerfoot, Flint, North Wales. Educated Holywell schools. Employed as a worsted weaver. Husband of Emily Kerfoot, Woodland Vale, Big Valley, Berry Brow. Enlisted 4.9.1914. Wounded near Ypres on 13.11.1915. Died at St. John Ambulance Brigade Hospital, Etaples, on 18.11.1915, aged 28. Buried **ETAPLES MILITARY CEMETERY.** Grave location:- Plot 3, Row G, Grave 1. ROH:- St. John's Church, Newsome; Huddersfield Drill Hall; Armitage Bridge War Memorial.

KERGON, HENRY. Private. No 204087. 1/4th Battalion Duke of Wellington's Regiment. Born Northumberland Street, Huddersfiel 17.12.1899. Son of John Oliver and Mary Ann Kergon, 19 Halifax Old Road, Hillhouse, Huddersfield.

Educated St. John's School. Employed as an apprentice fitter by Messrs J. Hopkinson and Company, of Birkby. Single. Enlisted 2.11.1914. Killed in action near Cambrai, 11.10.1918, aged 19 years. Buried **WELLINGTON CEMETERY**. Grave location:- Plot 2, Row E, Grave 1/10. ROH:- St. John's Church, Birkby; Fartown and Birkby War Memorial.

KEWLEY, DYSON. Private. No 37192. 10th Battalion King's Own Yorkshire Light Infantry. Formerly No 85555 Territorial Reserve Battalion. Born Slaithwaite. Son of John James and Grace Annie Kewley, 4 Bank Bottom Terrace, Marsden. Employed as a weaver at Bank Bottom Mills, Marsden. Attended West Slaithwaite Sunday School. Was one of the most promising students at Marsden Evening School, winning several special prizes. Enlisted February 1917. Embarked for France in November, 1917. Died of wounds near Ypres, Belgium, on 8.3.1918, aged 19 years. Buried **CANADA FARM CEMETERY, ELVERDINGHE, BELGIUM.** Grave location:- Plot 3, Row G, Grave 11. ROH:- Marsden War Memorial; St. James Church, Slaithwaite.

KEWLEY, FRED. Private. No 235292. 2nd Battalion Duke of Wellington's Regiment. Eldest son of Thomas Arthur and Frances Kewley, Holme Mill Cottages, Marsden. Attended Lingards Wood Bottom Sunday School. Employed as a woollen piecer by Messrs Charles Lockwood and Sons Limited, Black Rock Mills, Linthwaite. Enlisted November 1916. Embarked for France 1.3.1917. Was wounded and taken prisoner during the Battle of Arras on 3.5.1917. Taken to Cassel, Germany. He wrote home in June, 1917, stating that he was wounded in the leg and was a prisoner in Germany. Died of wounds as a Prisoner of War at Cassel, Germany, on 10.10.1917, aged 20 years. Buried **NIEDERZWEHREN CEMETERY, CASSEL, GERMANY.** Grave location:- Plot 9, Row C, Grave 9. (Brother of Private **NORMAN KEWLEY** who died as a Prisoner of War in Germany, 1.12.1918, q.v.). ROH:- Marsden War Memorial; St. James Church, Slaithwaite.

KEWLEY, NORMAN. Private. No 35474. 2nd Battalion The Yorkshire Regiment. Formerly No 5/108007 8th Territorial Reserve Battalion. Born Marsden. Son of Thomas Arthur and Frances Kewley, Holme Mill Cottages, Marsden.

Employed by Messrs S. and C. Firth, Holme Mill, Marsden. Was taken prisoner on 8.5.1918. Died of cerebro-spinal meningitis at Limburg Camp, Germany, on 1.12.1918, aged 19 years. Buried **NIEDERZWEHREN CEMETERY, CASSEL, GERMANY.** Grave location:- Plot 3, Row L, Grave 11. (Brother of Private **FRED KEWLEY**, who died of wounds as a Prisoner of War on 10.10.1917, q.v.). ROH:- Marsden War Memorial; St. James Church, Slaithwaite

KILBURN, EDWARD. Private. No 15176. 10th Battalion Duke of Wellington's Regiment. Born Dalton 13.12.1886. Son of William and Jane Kilburn, 23 Dalton Fold Road, Dalton. Educated Moldgreen Board School. Employed as a cobbler by Messrs Freeman, Hardy and Willis, of Elland. Husband of Ethel Kilburn, 14a West Parade, Huddersfield. Enlisted 12.1.1915. Embarked for France 23.10.1915. Killed in action, 4.10.1916, aged 29 years. Buried **ADANAC MILITARY CEMETERY.** Grave location:- Plot 2, Row D, Grave 33. ROH:- Holy Trinity Church, Huddersfield; Christ Church, Moldgreen.

KILBURN, WILFRED. Private. No 241586. 'D' Company, 1/5th Battalion Duke of Wellington's Regiment. Born Aspley 18.4.1885. Son of Councillor Henry and Margaret Kilburn, Ireby House, 93 Bradford Road, Huddersfield. Was employed in his father's fish business in the wholesale market. Reported missing at the Battle of Bullecourt, 3.5.1917, aged 32 years. Has no known grave. Commemorated **ARRAS MEMORIAL TO THE MISSING.** ROH:- Huddersfield Drill Hall.

KILLARNEY, JOHN. Private. No 2913. 'D' Company, 1/5th Battalion Duke of Wellington's Regiment. Born 20 Cross Grove Street, Huddersfield, 28.8.1892. Son of John Henry and Annie Killarney, 8 Dobson's Yard, Cross Church Street, Huddersfield. Educated St. Thomas's Church of England School and Spring Grove Council School. Employed as a dyer's finisher and scourer by Messrs James Haigh, dyers and finishers, of Colne Road. Single. Had served four years with the local Territorials and on the outbreak of the war he re-enlisted in September, 1914. Embarked for France in April, 1915. Wounded in the chest and head on 23.8.1915 at St. Julien, near Ypres, Belgium. Died of wounds on 23.8.1915, aged 22 years.

Has no known grave. Commemorated **MENIN GATE MEMORIAL TO THE MISSING.** His parents received a letter from their younger son, Private **GEORGE KILLARNEY**, who wrote on 24.8.1915, '*I am sorry to tell you, in fact I don't know how to put it, but our John died from wounds yesterday. He was asleep in a dugout when a shell hit it and it fell in. His pal Jack and two more comrades began digging him out and another shell burst and wounded the two comrades. They telephoned up to me about 3 o'clock in the afternoon and told me my brother was wounded. I went down to the place straight away but when I got there he was unconscious. I stopped there up to the last. I saw him put away in a decent grave. There was one blessing Mother, that he did not know anything about it. He got his parcel alright yesterday morning, I got the photos out of his pocket. They are sending the rest of his things, such as his purse, pouch, etc. I have his cigarette case and watch. I think this is all Mother. I hope God will help you all to bear up. Just break it gently to my Father. I cannot write anymore now. With best love to you all, I am your broken hearted son, George.*' ROH:- Huddersfield Parish Church; Huddersfield Drill Hall.

KILNER, FRANK GILBERT. Bombardier. No 79128. 1st/1st (Wessex) Heavy Battery, Royal Garrison Artillery. Born Skelmanthorpe 31.7.1887. Son of Police Constable George Kilner, 30 Fenton Square, Longroyd Bridge, Huddersfield. Educated Spring Grove Council School. Employed as a french polisher by Mr Marshall Haley, West End, Halifax. Attended Rashcliffe United Methodist Church and Sunday School, where he had held the positions of Sunday School teacher, Superintendent and lay preacher. Husband of Alice Kilner, 47 Morley's Yard, Folly Hall, Huddersfield. Enlisted 4.5.1916. Killed in action, 14.6.1917, aged 29, near Ypres. Buried **VLAMERTINGHE NEW MILITARY CEMETERY.** Grave location:- Plot 3, Row A, Grave 14. ROH:- Rashcliffe United Methodist Church.

KILNER, WILLIAM. Corporal. No 24767 49th Battalion Machine Gun Corps. Formerly No 473 Duke of Wellington's Regiment. Born Greinton, Somerset. Son of Mr and Mrs A. Reid, 284 Manchester Road, Milnsbridge. Employed by Messrs Fred Calverley and Company Limited, Milnsbridge. Had served four years with the Colne Valley Territorials and was mobilised at the outbreak of the war. Killed in action near Cambrai, 11.10.1918, aged 25 years. Buried **WELLINGTON CEMETERY.** Grave location:- Plot 2, Row B, Grave 1. ROH:- Milnsbridge War Memorial.

KINDER, FRED. Lance Corporal. No C/7328. 2nd Battalion King's Royal Rifle Corps. Born Honley. Son of Mr and Mrs Nathan Kinder, Victoria Place, Honley. Educated Honley Church School. Played cricket with the Honley second eleven. Employed by Messrs Brook and Sons of Armitage Bridge. Died of wounds, 10.9.1916, aged 25 years. Buried **FLATIRON COPSE CEMETERY, MAMETZ.** Grave location:- Special Memorial 12. ROH:- Honley War Memorial; Armitage Bridge Mills.

KINDER, REGINALD MARSDEN. Private. No 44510. 8th Battalion Lincolnshire Regiment. Born New Mill, Holmfirth. Son of Mr and Mrs W. Kinder, Mount Pleasant, Hade Edge. Attended Townhead Sunday School, Dunford Bridge. Employed at Washpit Mills. Enlisted February 1918. Embarked for France in March, 1918. Reported missing, presumed killed, 5.4.1918, aged 19 years. Buried **GOMMECOURT BRITISH CEMETERY No 2.** Grave location:- Plot 2, Row D, Grave 9. ROH:- Hade Edge War Memorial.

KINDER, SAMUEL. Private. No 11299. 2nd Battalion Duke of Wellington's Regiment. Born Huddersfield. Son of Joe and Mary Kinder, of Moldgreen: husband of Mary Kinder, 44 Northumberland Street, Huddersfield. Died of wounds, 26.4.1915, aged 35 years. Buried **POPERINGHE OLD MILITARY CEMETERY.** Grave location:- Special Memorial 3. ROH:- Christ Church, Moldgreen.

KINDER, STUART WHITEHEAD. Sergeant. No 151. 1/7th Battalion Duke of Wellington's Regiment. Born Marsden. Son of Mr and Mrs Samuel Kinder, The Grove, Marsden. Husband of Elsie Kinder, Rough Lee, Marsden. Educated Marsden National School and also attended Huddersfield Technical College. He was then a teacher at Thurnscoe, near Barnsley, for about two months after which he became assistant master at Kirkheaton National School for about 18 months. He then went to Bradford as manager of a coal business for Mr Harrop Moseley, formerly Headmaster at Kirkheaton, but returned to the teaching profession at Slaithwaite National School for twelve months. He then became assistant master at Marsden National School and had been there for six months when the Territorials were mobilised. He was a member of the choir at St. Bartholomew's Church, Marsden. He was a keen footballer and cricketer, being a playing member of Marsden Cricket Club and also a member of the Marsden Liberal Club. Enlisted in the local Territorials in 1908. Was mobilised at the outbreak of the war. Embarked for France in April, 1915. Wounded in the left leg on 26.10.1915. Died of wounds at No 17 Casualty Clearing Station on 27.10.1915, aged 27 years. Buried **LIJSSENTHOEK MILITARY CEMETERY**. Grave location:- Plot 1. Row B. Grave 36a. His wife received the following letter from the Church of England Chaplain, the Rev. D. Tait-Patterson, who wrote, *'I am sorry to send the sad news of your husband's death. He came here on the 26th with his leg severely shattered. He was in a very weak condition when he wrote to you having lost a considerable amount of blood. We did our best for him, amputating the leg in the hope of saving his life. But he gradually sank until he died last night. I saw a good deal of him and learned to like him. He will be buried this afternoon by the Church of England Chaplain, the Rev. McKea, in a military cemetery one and half miles south of Poperinghe, Belgium. May God strengthen you in the sad loss you have met and may the memory of a brave man ,who died with you in his thoughts, cheer the weary hours that await you.'* ROH:- Huddersfield Drill Hall; Marsden War Memorial.

KING, ALBERT. Private. No 11559. 2nd Battalion Duke of Wellington's Regiment. Born Keighley. Son of James King. Husband of Emily King, 2 Colin's Yard, Duke Street, Huddersfield. Was a Reservist and re-enlisted in September, 1914. Killed in action, 3.3.1915, aged 35 years. Has no known grave. Commemorated **PLOEGSTEERT MEMORIAL TO THE MISSING.**

KINGSTON, THOMAS. Private. No 53065. 78th Company, Machine Gun Corps (Infantry). Transferred to (487155) 968th Employment Company, Labour Corps. Born Preston-on-Stour. Son of Henry Kingston. Husband of Amy Eliza Kingston, 7 First Avenue, Long Lane, Dalton. Died, 28.11.1918, in Salonika, aged 38 years. Buried **MIKRA BRITISH CEMETERY, SALONIKA.** Grave location:- No 944. ROH:- St. John's Church, Kirkheaton.

KIRK, JOE. Guardsman. No 23285. Coldstream Guards. Born Shelley. Adopted son of John Henry and Hannah Thomas, Big Valley, Armitage Bridge. Employed in the commercial department at Messrs Whiteley's works at Lockwood. Enlisted in 1917. Killed in action, 4.11.1918, aged 20 years. Buried **CROSSROADS CEMETERY, FONTAINE-AU-BOIS.** Grave location:- Plot 3, Row D, Grave 3. ROH:- Emmanuel Church, Shelley.

KITCHEN, GIDEON SHAW. Private. No 67273. 171st Company, Machine Gun Corps. Formerly No 36173 York and Lancaster Regiment. Born Birchencliffe 10.12.1897. Son of Mary Hannah Kitchen, 6 Brier Lane, Birchencliffe, Huddersfield. Educated Lindley Church of England School. Employed as a textile worker by Messrs Martin, Sons and Company, Wellington Mills, Oakes. Was a member of the Lindley Wesleyan Sunday School. Enlisted August 1916. Wounded in France, 21.4.1917. Died of wounds, 24.4.1917, aged 20 years. Buried **ESTAIRES COMMUNAL CEMETERY EXTENSION.** Grave location:- Plot 4, Row F, Grave 2. (Brother of Private **WALTER KITCHEN,** who died of wounds, 30.5.1918, q.v.). ROH:- St. Philip's Church, Birchencliffe.

KITCHEN, WALTER. Private. No 65134. 61st Company, Machine Gun Corps. Formerly No 23549 Duke of Wellington's Regiment. Son of Mary Hannah Kitchen, 6 Brier Lane, Birchencliffe, Huddersfield. Educated Oakes Board School. Employed as a stone mason by Messrs Bentley and Swift of Kirkheaton. Husband of Nellie Kitchen, 11 Burn Road, Birchencliffe. Enlisted July 1916. Died of wounds at No 54 Casualty Clearing Station on 30.5.1918, aged 35 years. Buried **AIRE COMMUNAL CEMETERY.** Grave location:- Plot 2, Row K, Grave 47. (Brother of Private **GIDEON SHAW KITCHEN,** who died of wounds, 24.4.1917, q.v.). ROH:- St. Philip's Church, Birchencliffe.

KITSON, CHARLES HENRY. Private. No 32412. 2nd Battalion South Staffordshire Regiment. Born Gosport, Stainland, Halifax 24.12.1894. Educated Sowood Green Board School, Stainland. Married. Lived Brooks

Terrace, Lindley Moor. Employed as a woollen spinner by Messrs Frederick Peckett and Sons Limited, Oakes, Huddersfield. Was a member of the Outlane Brass Band. Attended Outlane United Methodist Sunday School. Enlisted 14.11.1916. Played cornet in the band of the South Staffordshire Regiment. Died of wounds at No 56 Casualty Clearing Station on 23.3.1918, aged 24 years. Buried **DERNANCOURT COMMUNAL CEMETERY EXTENSION**. Grave location:- Plot 3, Row J, Grave 58. ROH:- Bethel United Methodist Church, Outlane; Brighouse War Memorial.

KITSON, PERCY. Private. No 31740. 1/4th Battalion Duke of Wellington's Regiment. Born Lepton. Son of William Henry and Eliza Kitson of Rowley Hill, Lepton. Was a teacher at the Rowley Hill Wesleyan Sunday School. Played cricket for the Rowley Hill Cricket Club. Employed by Messrs George Thomas and Sons, Rowley Mills, Fenay Bridge. Killed in action, 17.4.1918, aged 19 years. Has no known grave. Commemorated **TYNE COT MEMORIAL TO THE MISSING**. ROH:- Lepton Parish Church.

KNAPTEN, ERNEST ROBERT. Private. No 2916. 1/5th Battalion Duke of Wellington's Regiment. Born Huddersfield. Son of Albert and Agnes Knapton, 3 Bank Terrace, Armitage Bridge. Employed by Messrs Calvert, of Folly Hall. Enlisted at the outbreak of the war. Embarked for France in April, 1915. Killed in action, 15.5.1915, aged 20 years. Buried **RUE-DAVID MILITARY CEMETERY, FLEURBAIX**. Grave location:- Plot 1, Row B, Grave 23. ROH:- Huddersfield Drill Hall; Armitage Bridge War Memorial.

KNIGHT, FRED. Lance Corporal. No 34666. 12th Battalion Durham Light Infantry. Born Almondbury. Son of George and Emma Knight, 5 Westgate, Almondbury. Employed by his father in the family greengrocery business. Enlisted May 1916. Embarked for France on 26.10.1916. He was leaving the trenches for home leave when he was killed by a sniper on 19.10.1917, aged 23 years. Buried **RAILWAY DUGOUTS (TRANSPORT FARM) BURIAL GROUND**. Grave location:- Plot 7, Row F, Grave 25. ROH:- Almondbury War Memorial; memorial in Almondbury Cemetery.

KNIGHT, HERBERT. Lance Corporal. 1/5th Battalion Duke of Wellington's Regiment. Born Huddersfield. Lived 150 Long Ashes Lane, Almondbury, Huddersfield. Died from the effects of shell shock, 26.12.1918,

KNIGHT, TOM. Private. No 44352. 2nd Battalion Northumberland Fusiliers. Born Victoria Street, Lindley, 24.7.1889. Educated Oakes Council School. Employed as a card grinder by Messrs Joseph Sykes, Acre Mills, Lindley. Single. Enlisted 12.5.1916. Killed in action, 5.10.1918. Has no known grave. Commemorated **VIS-en-ARTOIS MEMORIAL TO THE MISSING**. ROH:- Lindley Zion Methodist Chapel; St. Stephen's Church, Lindley.

KNOWLES, HARRY WILFRED, MC. Lieutenant. 1st, attached 11th, Battalion West Yorkshire Regiment. Born 4.8.1877. Son of Richard and Margaret Knowles, of Kirkburton. Lived 61 Ashbrow Road, Fartown, Huddersfield. Served in China, South Africa and India. Was serving with the 1st Indian Cavalry Division and, when war broke out in August 1914, immediately sailed for France. Wounded twice. Awarded the Military Cross for *'conspicuous gallantry in action. With a party of men he cut eight lanes through the barbed wire in order to assist the infantry advance. Later he carried out several daring patrols, and obtained most valuable information.'* (London Gazette, 25th November, 1916). Killed in action, 8.6.1917, aged 39 years. Buried **RAILWAY DUGOUTS (TRANSPORT FARM) BURIAL GROUND**. Grave location:- Plot 7, Row N, Grave 5. ROH:- Christ Church, Woodhouse Hill.

KRAMER, ARTHUR. Private. No 241582. 2/5th Battalion Duke of Wellington's Regiment. Born Bingley Street, Bradford, 15.3.1896. Son of John and Annie Kramer, 10 Eastwood Street, Moldgreen. Educated at Bradford and Moldgreen Council Schools. Employed as a fishmonger's assistant by Messrs J. E. Wood and Sons and Company, fishmongers, of Victoria Street, Huddersfield. Single. Enlisted March 1916. Reported missing, presumed killed, at the Battle of Bullecourt, 3.5.1917, aged 21 years. Has no known grave. Commemorated **ARRAS MEMORIAL TO THE MISSING**. ROH:- St. Paul's Methodist Church, Dalton; Christ Church, Moldgreen; Huddersfield Drill Hall.

LACK, WILLIAM. Private. No 49668. 7th Battalion Leicestershire Regiment. Born Staveley, Derbyshire. Lived 1 William Street South, Huddersfield. Son of Harry and Maria Lack. Killed in action, 8.10.1918, aged 22 years. Commemorated **VIS-en-ARTOIS MEMORIAL TO THE MISSING.**

LACY, ALFRED HARRY. Private. No 2046. 1/5th Battalion Duke of Wellington's Regiment. Born Kingston-upon Thames. Enlisted Kirkburton. Lived 47 Stanhope Street, Scissett. Killed in action, 9.11.1915. Has no known grave. Commemorated **MENIN GATE MEMORIAL TO THE MISSING.** ROH:- Scissett War Memorial; All Hallows Parish Church, Kirkburton; Emmanuel Church, Shelley; Huddersfield Drill Hall.

LACY, WILLIAM BRAITHWAITE. 2nd Lieutenant. 15th (County of London) Battalion The London Regiment (Prince of Wales's Own, Civil Service Rifles). Born Goole. Son of George Hudson Lacy and Jane Lacy, 157 Old Road, Birkby. Died of wounds, 14.12.1917, aged 28 years. Buried **ROCQUIGNY-EQUANCOURT ROAD BRITISH CEMETERY.** Grave location:- Plot 8, Row A, Grave 27. ROH:- Fartown and Birkby War Memorial; commemorated on his parents' headstone in Edgerton Cemetery, Huddersfield.

LAMB, JOHN WILLIAM. Private. No 19257. 2nd Battalion Duke of Wellington's Regiment. Born Horsforth near Leeds. Son of Michael and Rebecca Lamb, 4 Kew Hill, Lindley. Educated at Leeds and Elland schools. Employed as a woollen piecer by Messrs T. Calverley and Company Limited, woollen spinners, of Milnsbridge. Single. Enlisted 20.2.1916. Embarked for France on 20.7.1916. Reported missing and afterwards presumed to have been killed on 12.10.1916. Buried **GUARDS' CEMETERY, LESBOEUFS.** Grave location:- Plot 10, Row AA, Grave 4. ROH:- Blackley Baptist Chapel.

LANCASTER, HENRY. Private. No 240211. 1/4th Battalion Duke of Wellington's Regiment. Born Melsonby, Durham. Son of Henry Lancaster: husband of Mary Lancaster, 3 Brunswick Yard, Albert Street, Lockwood, Huddersfield. Employed by Messrs David Brown and Son Limited. Enlisted at the outbreak of the war. Died of wounds, 30.4.1918, aged 24 years. Buried. **ARNEKE BRITISH CEMETERY.** Grave location:- Plot 2, Row D, Grave 23. ROH:- St. Stephen's Church, Rashcliffe; Christ Church, Woodhouse Hill.

LANCASTER, JOHN. Private. No 29789. 12th Battalion Northumberland Fusiliers. Born Thongsbridge 16.12.1890. Son of C. A. Lancaster, 62 Grove Street, Huddersfield. Educated at Oakworth School, near Keighley. Assisted in the management of the Spread Eagle Hotel, Manchester Street, Huddersfield. Was Superintendent of the High Street United Methodist Sunday School Primary Department. Married, with one child. Enlisted June 1916. Killed in action, 31.3.1917, aged 26 years. Buried **BUCQUOY ROAD CEMETERY.** Grave location:- Plot 6, Row E, Grave 22. ROH:- High Street United Methodist Church.

LAND, LAWRENCE. Private. No 47408. 7th Battalion King's Own Yorkshire Light Infantry. Born Huddersfield 25.3.1884. Son of John Land, 1 Ibbotson Yard, Thomas Street, Huddersfield. Educated Huddersfield Parish Church School. Employed as a fruit salesman by Mr William Fish, fruit merchant, of Huddersfield wholesale market. Married. Enlisted 21.6.1917. Was wounded and taken prisoner on 25.3.1918. Underwent an amputation of his right leg below the knee at the Royal Fortress Hospital, Cologne, Germany. Died of wounds, 11.4.1918, aged 33 years. Buried **COLOGNE SOUTHERN CEMETERY, GERMANY.** Grave location:- Plot 8, Row C, Grave 26. ROH:- Huddersfield Parish Church.

LANGRICK, CHARLES LINDLEY. Private. No 1939. 1/5th Battalion Duke of Wellington's Regiment. Born Barrow-in-Furness. Son of Benjamin and Marion Thirza Langrick, 55 Birch Road, Berry Brow. Educated Almondbury Grammar School. Employed at the Huddersfield office of the London, Liverpool and Globe Insurance Company. Was a sidesman at Armitage Bridge Church. Played tennis with the Armitage Bridge Tennis Club. Had served three years with the local Territorials before the war. Was mobilised on the outbreak of war. Embarked for France in April, 1915. Was wounded by a sniper in the neck, 22.8.1915, as he was walking along one of the advanced trenches, where he lay until dark when he was brought out at great risk by volunteers from his Battalion. The wound was not considered likely to prove fatal at the time. He was removed to No 17 Casualty Clearing Station, where he died of his wounds on 23.8.1915, aged 20. Buried **LIJSSENTHOEK MILITARY CEMETERY.** Grave location:- Plot 3, Row C, Grave 25. ROH:- Huddersfield Drill Hall; Armitage Bridge War Memorial.

LAVENDER, ERNEST. Private. No 24767. 8th Battalion Duke of Wellington's Regiment. Born Huddersfield. Son of John and Mary Lavender, 9 Stocks Buildings, Fountain Street, Huddersfield. Killed in action, 10.8.1917, aged 20. Has no known grave. Commemorated **MENIN GATE MEMORIAL TO THE MISSING.** ROH:- St. Andrew's Church, Leeds Road, Huddersfield.

LAW, HERBERT. Private. No 52779. 8th Battalion North Staffordshire Regiment. Born Ramsden Wood Road, Todmorden. Son of Edgar and Esther Law, 17 Bradford Road, Huddersfield. Educated Thomas Street Council School. Employed as a tailor by Mr Thomas Wilson of Station Street, Huddersfield. Single. Enlisted March 1917. Wounded at Epernay, on 30.5.1918. Treated at the Aubon Moet Hospital, Epernay. Died of wounds, 31.5.1918, aged 19 years. Buried **TERLINCTHUN BRITISH CEMETERY.** Grave location:- Plot 7, Row AC, Grave 17.

LAWLEY, JOSEPH. Private. No 46424. 17th Battalion Lancashire Fusiliers. Formerly No 2601 Duke of Wellington's Regiment. Born St. Barnabas, Cheshire. Son of Ernest and Emma Lawley, 24 Peel Street, Crewe. Lived Clara Street, Fartown, Huddersfield. Employed as a fireman at Hillhouse Locomotive Sheds by the London and North Western Railway Company. Enlisted at the outbreak of war. Died of wounds at Fairfield Court Hospital, Eastbourne, 14.11.1918, aged 26 years. Buried **COPPENHALL CEMETERY, CREWE, CHESHIRE.** Grave location:- Grave No. 2315. ROH:- London and North Western Railway Company Roll.

LAWRENCE, MARSHALL. Able Seaman. No 155822. Royal Navy. *HMS Revenge.* Born Huddersfield. Lived 13 Milford Street, Huddersfield. Single. Died whilst serving, 4.12.1918.

LAWRENCE, MATTHEW. Private. No 2399. 1/5th Battalion Duke of Wellington's Regiment. Born Tadcaster 15.2.1892. Son of Mr and Mrs Matthew Lawrence, 21 South Parade, Huddersfield. Educated Spring Grove Council School. Employed as an overlooker by Messrs J. Lumb and Sons Limited, Folly Hall. Single. Was a member of the local Territorials prior to the outbreak of the war. Enlisted August 1914. Embarked for France April 1915. Killed by a sniper at La Bassee, 23.8.1915, aged 22 years. Has no known grave. Commemorated **MENIN GATE MEMORIAL TO THE MISSING.** His parents received a letter from the Captain of their son's Company, dated August 24th, 1915. It reads as follows, *'It is my sad duty to inform you of the death in action of your son, Private Matthew Lawrence, No 2399, who was killed last evening. He was standing talking to Sergeant Grayson in a part of the trench which is considered practically safe from rifle fire when both were instantaneously killed by what must have been a stray long distance bullet. Sergeant Grayson was hit first, the bullet passing through his neck and into your son's head. It is particularly distressing to lose two such men in so unfortunate a way. A double grave was dug by comrades a few yards in the rear of the trenches and they were buried side by side after dark, the funeral being attended by several of their friends and Officers. I trust you will accept my deepest sympathy with you in your loss.'* (The grave must have been destroyed in later fighting.). ROH:- St. Thomas's Church, Longroyd Bridge.

LAWTON, CYRIL. Private. No 3305. 1/5th Battalion Duke of Wellington's Regiment. Born Springdale Avenue, Huddersfield. Son of Thomas Henry and Mary Anne Lawton, 'Rookholme', Gledholt, Huddersfield. Educated Almondbury Grammar School and New College, Harrogate. In 1912 he joined his father in the family business of Messrs William Lawton Limited, spinners, Paddock. Single. Enlisted October 1914. Was shot through the head by a German sniper on 17.8.1915. Died of wounds at a Field Ambulance Dressing Station on 17.8.1915, aged 20 years, Buried **FERME-OLIVER CEMETERY, ELVERDINGHE, BELGIUM.** Grave location:- Plot 1, Row H, Grave 11. ROH:- All Saints Church, Paddock; Huddersfield Drill Hall; commemorated on his parents' headstone in Edgerton Cemetery, Huddersfield.

LAWTON, HAROLD. Signaller. No 241545. 9th Battalion The Cameronians (Scottish Rifles). Born Primrose Hill, Huddersfield, 9.1.1897. Son of Alderman Fred and Elizabeth Lawton, 71 Perseverance Street, Primrose Hill. Educated Stile Common Council School. Employed in his father's business as a yarn spinner at Lockwood Mills. Attended Primrose Hill United Methodist Church and was a member of the Young Men's Class. Single. Enlisted September 1915. Wounded 27.4.1918. Died of wounds at No 7 General Hospital, Boulogne, on 4.5.1918, aged 20 years. Buried **BOULOGNE EASTERN CEMETERY.** Grave location:- Plot 9, Row B, Grave 41.

LAWTON, WILLIAM. Private. No 241369. 1/5th Battalion Duke of Wellington's Regiment. Son of Mr and Mrs Sam Lawton, Woodland View, Brockholes. Assisted his father as scribbling engineer at Rock Mills, Brockholes. Was a member of the bible class at Brockholes Church. Enlisted October 1915. Embarked for France in the New Year, 1916. Reported missing in the attack on the Schwaben Redoubt on 3.9.1916 and afterwards presumed to have been killed on that date. Has no known grave. Commemorated **THIEPVAL MEMORIAL TO THE MISSING.** A letter was received by William's brother from Corporal Brierley who had been in the attack on 3.9.1916 and was in hospital in England who wrote, *'Well Willie was in my section and he went over with me on the 3rd September on the Sunday morning at 5.5.am. We reached the German first and second lines in quick time and we were there for some time when they started to shell us very heavily and I lost my men nearby. Your brother was in the second line when he was killed with two other men. They all died together I am sorry to say. Willie was a great pal of mine, we had spent some time in the trenches together. You will see where I am and I should like to see you.'* ROH:- Huddersfield Drill Hall; Honley War Memorial; Brockholes War Memorial.

LEAKE, FRED. Private. No 28383. 9th Battalion Northumberland Fusiliers. Born Holme, Holmfirth. Son of Alfred Leake, Hogley Green Farm, Holmfirth. Educated Holme National School. Assisted his father on the family farm and was also a weaver at Digley Mills. Enlisted April 1916. Killed in action during the Battle of Arras on 13.4.1917, aged 23 years. Has no known grave. Commemorated **ARRAS MEMORIAL TO THE MISSING.** His father received the following letter from Captain Griffin, of the R.A.M.C., who wrote, *'It will be some consolation to you in your great loss to know that since he belonged to my section he has always behaved himself in the most gallant manner and only a fortnight ago his conduct was brought before the notice of the General.'* He then describes the particular movement in which Private Leake met his death. *'The Battalion had broken through the German lines and the men were resting in a newly won trench when we were subjected to very heavy shelling. Four men were badly wounded and, despite the fact that it was almost certain death to go into that part of the trench, Private Leake immediately ran up and started to dress the wounds of the fallen. Another large shell then burst quite near him and he was struck through the heart and died before I could reach him.'* ROH:- Holme and Holmbridge War Memorial.

LEATHAM, FRED. Gunner. No 29177. Royal Field Artillery. Born Huddersfield. Lived 2 Crosland Court, Brow Road, Paddock, Huddersfield. Died at Storths Hall Asylum, of double pneumonia, on 2.1.1922.

LEE, ARNOLD THOMAS. 2nd Lieutenant. 87th Siege Battery, Royal Garrison Artillery. Son of Mr and Mrs Job Lee, Ashfield House, Thongsbridge. Educated Wooldale Council School. Attended the Lydgate Unitarian Church and was organist there up to the time of his enlistment. Employed firstly in the office of Messrs Kidd, Mellor and Fletcher of Holmfirth and then by Mr F. Sheard, accountant and auditor, Kirkgate, Huddersfield. Enlisted November 1915. Was gazetted as an Officer in October 1917. Was married in October, 1917, to Miss Charlotte Sarah Evans, daughter of the Rev. M. Evans, pastor at Lydgate Unitarian Church. Killed in action near Arras on 1.9.1918 aged 26 years. Buried **ACHICOURT ROAD CEMETERY.** Grave location:- Row D, Grave 1. His widow received the following letter from Major White, the Officer commanding her late husband's siege battery, *'It is with great grief that we record the fact that Second Lieutenant Arnold Thomas Lee was killed in action this morning, September 1st, at about 4.15am. Lieutenant Lee was on duty at the time in the Battery, which was exposed to very severe artillery fire when he was killed instantaneously. Lieutenant Lee was an excellent Officer and was always one of the first* *to do a dangerous piece of work and was greatly admired by all his brother Officers. The Battery was taking part in one of the greatest battles of the war at the time.'* ROH:- Wooldale War Memorial.

LEE, FREDERICK. Private. No 201852. No 4 Company, 1/4th Battalion Seaforth Highlanders. Born Lockwood, Huddersfield, 11.5.1893. Youngest son of John and Ellen Lee, 6 Shoulder of Mutton Yard, Lockwood. Educated Mount Street Church School, Lockwood. Employed as a grocer's assistant at the Thornton Lodge branch of the Huddersfield Industrial Society. Single. Enlisted 15.2.1916. Reported missing on 1.8.1917 and afterwards presumed to have been killed on that date, aged 24. Has no known grave. Commemorated **MENIN GATE MEMORIAL TO THE MISSING.** ROH:- Emmanuel Church, Lockwood.

LEE, GEORGE. Private. No 1985. 1/5th Battalion Duke of Wellington's Regiment. Born Batley. Husband of Agnes Lee, 53 Station Road, Holywell Green, Halifax, and later of 3 Shady Row, Meltham. Killed in action, 4.11.1915, aged 21 years. Buried **BARD COTTAGE CEMETERY.** Grave location:- Plot 1, Row D, Grave 22. (His father and two brothers were also serving in the Army at the time of his death). ROH:- St. Bartholomew's Church, Meltham; St. Andrew's Church, Stainsland; Huddersfield Drill Hall.

LEE, GEORGE HENRY. Private. No 15815. 2/6th Battalion Duke of Wellington's Regiment. Eldest son of Mr and Mrs Tom Lee. Husband of Nancy Lee, Highwood Lane, Kirkburton. Employed as a miner by Messrs Stringer and Jagger, Emley Collieries. Enlisted Feburary 1915. Went to the Dardenelles in August, 1915. Saw service in Egypt and then in France. Reported missing at the Battle of Cambrai on 20.11.1917 and afterwards was presumed to have been killed on that date. He was 21 years of age. Has no known grave. Commemorated **CAMBRAI MEMORIAL TO THE MISSING.** ROH:- All Hallows Parish Church, Kirkburton.

LEE, HENRY. Private. No 5193. 18th Battalion Army Cyclist Corps. Born Marsh 19.3.1892. Fourth son of Henry and Ada E. Lee, 6 Springfield Place, Marsh. Educated Holy Trinity School, Huddersfield. Employed as a presser by Mr Powney, tailor, John Street, Huddersfield. Attended Holy Trinity Church. Single. Enlisted 14.8.1914. Died of wounds at No 4 Casualty Clearing Station on 22.10.1917, aged 25 years. Buried **DOZINGHEM MILITARY CEMETERY.** Grave location:- Plot 10, Row E, Grave 19. (Brother of Private **JOHN (JACK) LEE,** died of wounds, 29.5.1915, and Sergeant **STEPHEN HARGILL LEE, DCM and Bar,** killed in action, 7.11.1918, q.v.). ROH:- Holy Trinity Church, Huddersfield.

LEE, HERBERT. Private. No 235502. 9th Battalion York and Lancaster Regiment. Formerly No 205141 Duke of Wellington's Regiment. Lived 10 Mount Pleasant, Wellhouse, Golcar. Married. Employed by Messrs C. and J. Hirst and Sons Limited, of Longwood. Attended Oakes Baptist Church and was a member of the Oakes Working Men's Club. Enlisted 4.4.1917. Embarked for France on 25.6.1917 after ten weeks training. Was killed by a shell on 23.9.1917, aged 24 years. Has no known grave. Commemorated **TYNE COT MEMORIAL TO THE MISSING.** ROH:- St. John's Church, Golcar; Oakes Baptist Church.

LEE, HERBERT BRADLEY. Air Mechanic 2nd Class. No 44112. Royal Air Force. Son of James and Ruth Lee, 208 Rashcliffe Hill Road, Huddersfield. Employed by Messrs Mills and Garside, plumbers, Upperhead Row, Huddersfield. Died at a local auxiliary hospital on 23.6.1918, aged 23 years. Buried with full military honours in **EMMANUEL CHURCHYARD, LOCKWOOD.** Grave location:- G, 4. ROH:- St. Stephen's Church, Rashcliffe.

LEE, JOHN (JACK). Private. No 25607. 14th Battalion, 1st Royal Montreal Regiment, 1st Canadian Contingent. Born Huddersfield 21.6.1885. Son of Henry and Ada E. Lee, 6 Springfield Place, Marsh. Educated Spring Grove Council School. Was a member of the Longwood and Huddersfield Harriers and also of the Lockwood Cycling Club. Emigrated to Canada in 1912. Enlisted at the outbreak of the war. Married. Was wounded near Bethune on 28.5.1915. He was shot by a sniper whilst bringing in a wounded German prisoner. Died of wounds on 29.5.1915, aged 29 years. Buried **HINGES MILITARY CEMETERY.** Grave location:- Row A, Grave 27. (Brother of Private **HENRY LEE,** killed in action, 22.10.1917, and Sergeant **STEPHEN HARGILL**

LEE, DCM and Bar, died of wounds, 7.11.1918, q.v.). ROH:- Marsh War Memorial; Holy Trinity Church, Huddersfield.

LEE, LEONARD. Corporal. No 240220. 'A' Company, 1/5th Battalion Duke of Wellington's Regiment. Born Huddersfield 21.9.1895. Son of John William and Emma Lee, 46a Upper Spring Street, Huddersfield. Educated Spring Grove Council School. For five years he was an apprentice in the textile department at the Huddersfield Technical College. He then became an assistant designer, employed by Messrs Lockwood and Keighley, Upperhead Mills. Attended Brunswick Street Church and Sunday School. Enlisted in the local Territorials in 1913. Embarked for France in Apri,l 1915. Reported missing, presumed killed, in the attack on the Schwaben Redoubt on 3.9.1916, aged 21. Has no known grave. Commemorated **THIEPVAL MEMORIAL TO THE MISSING.** ROH:- Huddersfield Drill Hall.

LEE, LEWIS. Corporal. No 10326. 6th Battalion Leicestershire Regiment. Born Kirkheaton. Died 2.5.1918. Buried **LE QUESNOY COMMUNAL CEMETERY.** Grave location:- Plot 3, Row C, Grave 1.

LEE, PERCY RICHARD. Private. No 40787. 2/5th Battalion South Staffordshire Regiment. Born Spring Street, Huddersfield, 3.3. 1882. Son of Mrs Walter Lee, 5 Back Thornhill, Longwood. Educated Holy Trinity School, Huddersfield. Employed as a beamer by Messrs John Crowther and Sons, Stanley Mills, Milnsbridge. Single. Reported wounded and missing on 26.9.1917 and afterwards presumed to have been killed on that date. Has no known grave. Commemorated **TYNE COT MEMORIAL TO THE MISSING.** (Brother of Private **TOM WALKER LEE,** died of wounds, 19.11.1916, q.v.). ROH:- St. Mark's Parish Church, Longwood; Salendine Nook Baptist Church.

LEE, STEPHEN HARGILL, DCM and BAR. 2/5th Battalion Duke of Wellington's Regiment. Sergeant. No 240076. Born Marsh 25.5.1894. Son of Henry and Ada E. Lee, 6 Springfield Place, Marsh. Educated Holy Trinity School, Huddersfield. Employed as a presser by Messrs W. P. Willis and Company. Single. Enlisted 4.8.1914. Awarded the DCM in January, 1918, '*for conpicuous gallantry and devotion to duty. Always cheerful and absolutely fearless he was ever ready to undertake any dangerous duty, going out on four occasions and bringing in missing men. His courage and resource when in charge of an advanced Lewis gun post, under trying circumstances were magnificent.* (London Gazette 17.4.1918). Awarded a bar to the DCM in December 1918 for, '*magnificent courage and good leadership during the attack on St. Python on 20.10.1918. Throughout the action he showed the greatest dash and when his platoon was held up by machine gun fire from a post containing two guns and at a barricade at a crossroad he crawled forward, covered by the fire of the platoon, and with only one other man rushed the barricade, himself killing two of the enemy, while his men completed the capture of the post and guns. Later he again encountered strong opposition from a post containing two trench mortars and a machine gun held by 20 of the enemy, killing and capturing the whole post. He at once led a bayonet charge on the postion, killing and capturing the whole post. This NCO's fearless determination swept down the enemy's resistance at a time when the fortunes of the attack were in the balance and his fine example was a great factor in the complete success of the attack.*' (London Gazette 12.3.1919). Killed in action at Mecquignies, near Maubeuge, on 7.11.1918, aged 24 years. Was buried originally in **MECQUIGNIES CHURCHYARD** but he was re-interred in **MAUBEUGE CENTRE CEMETERY.** Grave location:- Row B, Grave 17. (Brother of Private **HENRY LEE,** died of wounds, 22.10.1917, and Private **JOHN (JACK) LEE,** who died of wounds, 29.5.1915, q.v.). ROH:- Holy Trinity Church, Huddersfield; Huddersfield Drill Hall.

LEE, TOM WALKER. Private. No 40561. 16th Battalion Northumberland Fusiliers. Born Mission Street, Marsh, 9.9.1888. Son of Mrs Walker Lee, 5 Back Thornhill, Longwood. Educated Holy Trinity School, Huddersfield. Employed as a mechanic at the Karrier Car Works, Huddersfield. Attended Salendine Nook Baptist Church and Sunday School. Was a playing member of the Salendine Nook Cricket Club and a member of Longwood Conservative Club. Single. Enlisted at Whitsuntide 1916. Died of wounds at No 4 Casualty Clearing Station on 19.11.1916, aged 25 years. Buried **VARENNES**

MILITARY CEMETERY. Grave location:- Plot 1, Row G, Grave 28. ROH:- Salendine Nook Baptist Church.

LEESE, HARRY. Gunner. No 154366. 297th Siege Battery, Royal Garrison Artillery. Born Kidsgrove, Staffordshire. Was a Police Constable in the Holmfirth district. Married Miss Annie Armitage, of Towngate, Holmfirth, on Whit Tuesday, June 1917, at Holmfirth United Methodist Church. Enlisted April 1917. Embarked for France in July, 1917. Died of wounds at No 8 Casualty Clearing Station on 26.3.1918, aged 28 years. Buried **DUISANS BRITISH CEMETERY.** Grave location:- Plot 5, Row F, Grave 11. ROH:- Holmfirth War Memorial.

LEES, FRED. Private. No 35202. 5th Battalion The Yorkshire Regiment. Born Marsden. Son of Harry and Martha Hannah Lees, 7 Grange Avenue, Marsden. Killed in action, 11.4.1918, aged 18 years. Has no known grave. Commemorated **PLOEGSTEERT MEMORIAL TO THE MISSING.** ROH:- Marsden War Memorial.

LEIGH, WILLIAM HENRY. Private. Malay States Volunteer Rifles. Born Almondbury, Huddersfield 6.10.1889. Son of Joseph and Ellen Leigh, 38 Wormald Street, Almondbury. Educated Almondbury Church of England School and Huddersfield Technical College. After leaving school was employed as a barrister's clerk by Mr J. H. Dransfield. At the age of 21 he secured a position with Messrs Guthrie and Sons, foreign and colonial rubber merchants, of London. After nine months he went out to Singapore to work on one of the Singapore and Penang rubber plantations. At the outbreak of war in Europe he wanted to return home to Huddersfield as he had been a member of the local Territorials but was persuaded to stay in Singapore and join the Malay States Volunteer Rifles. Was killed during the Singapore Mutiny on 15.2.1915, aged 25 years. Buried **KRANJI WAR CEMETERY, SINGAPORE.** Grave location:- Plot 37, Row G, Grave 1. ROH:- Almondbury War Memorial.

LEMON, HUBERT. Private. No 240699. 2/5th Battalion Duke of Wellington's Regiment. Born Castlegate, Huddersfield, 16.11.1898. Third son of Peter and Mary E. Lemon, 3 Commercial Square, Huddersfield. Educated St. Joseph's and St. Patrick's Roman Catholic Schools. Employed as a labourer by the Ramsden Estate. Attended St. Joseph's Church. Single. Enlisted November 1914. Died 5.5.1917. Buried **SAUCHY-LESTREE COMMUNAL CEMETERY.** Grave location:- 1A. ROH:- Huddersfield Drill Hall.

LEONARD, HARRY. Private. No 38358. 16th (Bradford Pals) Battalion West Yorkshire Regiment. Born Leeds Road, (bottom of Thomas Street, Huddersfield), 9.4.1884. Son of the late William and Elizabeth Leonard, 13 Great Northern Street, Huddersfield. Educated Huddersfield Parish Church Schools. Employed in the finishing department of Messrs T. and H. Blamires Limited, Leeds Road, Huddersfield. Single. Enlisted 25.10.1916. Reported missing, presumed killed, at Oppy Wood during the Battle of Arras on 3.5.1917, aged 30 years. Has no known grave. Commemorated **ARRAS MEMORIAL TO THE MISSING.** ROH:- Great Northern Street Congregational Chapel; St. Andrew's Church, Leeds Road, Huddersfield.

LEONARD, THOMAS. Private. No 50803. 1st Battalion East Yorkshire Regiment. Formerly No 6333 Duke of Wellington's Regiment. Born William Street, Huddersfield. 11.9.1892. Son of the late Brook and Emma Leonard, 88 Dewhurst Road, Fartown. Educated St. Andrew's School, Leeds Road, Huddersfield. Employed as a tailor's cutter by Messrs W. Pickup and Company, Queen Street South, Huddersfield. Single. Enlisted September 1916. Killed in action, 24.8.1918, aged 25 years. Buried **REGINA TRENCH CEMETERY.** Grave location:- Special Memorial B 4. ROH:- St. Andrew's Church, Leeds Road; Christ Church, Woodhouse Hill; Fartown and Birkby War Memorial.

LEVELL, FRANK. Ordinary Seaman. Tyneside Z/13068. R.N.R. R.N. Depot (Crystal Palace). Born Slaithwaite. Son of John and Alice Levell, 62 Varley Road, Slaithwaite. Employed as a millwright's assistant by Mr Edgar Proctor. Enlisted in the Navy in July, 1918. Died of natural causes at Croydon Hospital on 16.10.1918, aged 18 years. Buried **SLAITHWAITE CEMETERY.** Grave location:- B, 4, 44. ROH:- St. James Church, Slaithwaite; Slaithwaite War Memorial.

LEVER, JOHN EDWARD. Sergeant. No 27535. Machine Gun Corps. Born Huddersfield. Lived

21 Mitre Street, Marsh, Huddersfield. Discharged from the army due to the effects of war service, 14.11.1917. Died from heart disease on 22.4.1922.

LEVETT, FREDERICK WALTER. Drummer. No 8277. 2nd Battalion East Yorkshire Regiment. Born Cumberland Street, London, in January, 1883. Son of Alfred William and Caroline Levett, 9 Commercial Square, Huddersfield. Educated St. Paul's Church School, Huddersfield. Employed as a woollen minder. Single. Enlisted in January, 1905. Killed in action at St. Julien, Belgium, on 23.4.1915, aged 32 years. Has no known grave. Commemorated **MENIN GATE MEMORIAL TO THE MISSING.** His parents received the following letter from Private George Brummett who was in hospital in Leicester, '*I was drafted out to the 2nd Battalion East Yorkshire Regiment on February 17th and joined them in Belgium. Your son was in the same Company as I was and I soon got to know him as he was so highly respected and well known to everybody. I told him my parents had removed and now lived in South Street, Huddersfield and we used to talk about what we would do when we got home. He said he would show me round. He was known as Dusty in the Company, he was such a jolly lad. I was quite close to him, about 4.30pm on April 23rd, when we advanced to certain death with the Canadians and other Regiments. Fred and I were right in the front of it all. As you know he was Major Berthon's (our Company Officer's) servant and I had to help with him as the Major was severely wounded. As I was jumping over the parapet of a trench we had captured, Fred yelled out 'Good lad Brian' to me and I laughed back and that was the last I saw of him. I think he was hit with a bullet near that spot and killed instantly. That afternoon we had 600 casualties in our Battalion and I lost some good pals that day.*' ROH:- St. Paul's Church, Southgate, Huddersfield; Almondbury War Memorial.

LEWIS, ARTHUR FREDERICK. Corporal. No 1592. 1/5th Battalion Duke of Wellington's Regiment. Born King Cross, Halifax. Husband of Harriet Lewis, Linfit Lane, Kirkburton. Embarked for France in August, 1915. Wounded on 17.9.1916. Died of wounds at Etaples Base Hospital on 24.9.1916, aged 31 years. Buried **ETAPLES MILITARY CEMETERY.** Grave location:- Plot 11, Row A, Grave 12a.

ROH:- All Hallows Parish Church, Kirkburton; Huddersfield Drill Hall.

LEWIS, RICHARD ASHTON. Private. No 290096. 7th Battalion Royal Welsh Fusiliers. Born Newtown, Montgomery, Wales. Lived 177 Upper Brow Road, Paddock, Huddersfield. Died Monday, 26.3.1917. Commemorated **JERUSALEM MEMORIAL, ISRAEL.**

LEWIS, WILLIE. Private. No 241519. 2/5th Battalion Duke of Wellington's Regiment. Born Grove Street, Huddersfield, 7.8.1885. Son of George Lewis, 510 Carlton Terrace, Leeds Road, Huddersfield. Educated Deighton Council School. Employed as a sewerage worker. by Huddersfield Corporation. Husband of Edith Lewis, 32 Ashgrove Road, Leeds Road, Huddersfield. Enlisted February 1916. Reported missing, presumed killed, at the Battle of Bullecourt, 3.5.1917. Has no known grave. Commemorated **ARRAS MEMORIAL TO THE MISSING.** ROH:- Deighton United Methodist Chapel; Huddersfield Drill Hall; Huddersfield Corporation Roll.

LIDDELL, PERCY. Private. No 5663. 1/7th Battalion Northumberland Fusiliers. Born Marsh 9.9.1889. Son of Charles and Eliza Liddell, 85 Syringa Street, Marsh, Huddersfield. Educated Holy Trinity School. Employed as a tailor by the Huddersfield Industrial Society. Married. Lived 33a Grove Street, Huddersfield. Enlisted 3.6.1916. Killed in action, 15.1.1917, aged 27 years. Buried **WARLENCOURT BRITISH CEMETERY.** Grave location:- Plot 3, Row G, Grave 17. ROH:- Gledholt Wesleyan Church.

LIGHTFOOT, THOMAS LAWSON. Private. No 29113. 1/7th Battalion Duke of Wellington's Regiment. Born Dalston, Carlisle. Son of Thomas and Elizabeth Lightfoot, Healey House, Netherton. Employed as a clerk in the office of Messrs Armitage, Sykes and Hinchiffe, solicitors, of Huddersfield. Enlisted August 1916. Killed in action, 13.4.1918, aged 19 years. Has no known grave. Commemorated **TYNE COT MEMORIAL TO THE MISSING.** ROH:- Huddersfield Drill Hall; South Crosland and Netherton War Memorial.

LILLEY, FRED. Lance Corporal. No 20253. 2nd Battalion Duke of Wellington's Regiment.

Born Paddock 30.10.1894. Son of John William and Annie Lilley, 46 Westbourne Road, Marsh. Educated Paddock Elementary School. Was in business with his father as a gardener. Single. Attended Paddock Congregrational Church and was a member of the choir. Enlisted 8.4.1916. Killed in action at Passchendaele, 10.10.1917. Buried **CEMENT HOUSE CEMETERY.** Grave location:- Plot 10, Row F, Grave 47. ROH:- Marsh War Memorial; Shared Church, Paddock.

LILLEY, THOMAS EDWARD. Private. No 34007. The Yorkshire Regiment. Born Huddersfield 1889. Lived 1 Spring Grove Street, Huddersfield. Married. Died of tuberculosis, 14.5.1921.

LINDLEY, ARTHUR. Private. No 5763. 1/4th Battalion King's Own Yorkshire Light Infantry. Born Honley. Lived Armitage Bridge. Attended Armitage Bridge Church and served on the committee of the Armitage Bridge Conservative Club. Employed by Messrs J. Brook and Sons Limited at Armitage Bridge Mills. A keen sportsman and a good billiards player. Was a playing member of the Armitage Bridge Cricket Club and was formerly half-back for the Berry Brow and Honley Association football teams. Single. Died of wounds at the 1/1st South Midland Casualty Clearing Station on 12.2.1917, aged 35 years. Buried **WARLINCOURT HALTE BRITISH CEMETERY.** Grave location:- Plot 4, Row J, Grave 6. ROH:- Armitage Bridge Mills; Armitage Bridge War Memorial.

LINDLEY, HIRST. Sergeant. No 20845. 63rd Squadron Royal Air Force. Born Shepley. Son of Mr H. Lindley of The Marsh, Shepley. Attended Shepley Wesleyan Church and was a local preacher in the Holmfirth Wesleyan circuit. Employed by Mr George Lindley at Sovereign Quarries. Had served over two years in Mesopotamia and had just received his demobilisation papers when he was accidentally killed at Basra on 15.6.1919, aged 31 years. Buried **BAGHDAD (NORTH GATE) WAR CEMETERY.** Grave location:- Plot 20, Row D, Grave 7. ROH:- Shepley War Memorial.

LINDLEY, JOHN. Lance Corporal. No 306314. 1/7th Battalion Duke of Wellington's Regiment. Born Marsden. Son of Sam and Mary Ann Lindley, 26 Grange Cottages, Marsden. Employed as a pattern weaver at a local mill. Attended Lingards Wood Bottom Sunday School. Enlisted October 1915. Embarked for France in February, 1916. Reported missing, presumed killed, at Passchendaele on 10.10.1917, aged 23 years. Has no known grave. Commemorated **TYNE COT MEMORIAL TO THE MISSING.** ROH:- Huddersfield Drill Hall; Marsden War Memorial.

LINDLEY, WILLIE. Rifleman. No C/7667. 10th Battalion King's Royal Rifle Corps. Born Honley, Huddersfield. Son of Joe Lindley, Bright's Buildings, Neiley, Honley. Employed by Messrs Gledhill and Roberts, bobbin makers, Honley. Enlisted November 1915. Reported missing at the Battle of Cambrai, 30.11.1917, aged 20 years, and afterwards presumed to have been killed on that date. Has no known grave. Commmemorated **CAMBRAI MEMORIAL TO THE MISSING.** ROH:- Honley War Memorial.

LINGARD, TOM. Private. No 203783. 1/4th Battalion Duke of Wellington's Regiment. Son of Mr and Mrs Lingard, Holt Farm, Slaithwaite. Employed as a teamer by Messrs Joseph Sykes and Sons, coal merchants of Slaithwaite. Attended Holthead General Sunday School. Enlisted 2.8.1916. Embarked for France in December, 1916. Killed whilst on sentry duty by a trench mortar shell on 22.4.1917, aged 21 years. Buried **LE TOURET MILITARY CEMETERY.** Grave location:- Plot 4, Row C, Grave 23. ROH:- St. James Church, Slaithwaite; Slaithwaite War Memorial.

LINTON, JOHN. Private. No 17987. 8th Battalion Northumberland Fusiliers. Born Northumberland Street, Huddersfield. Educated St. Paul's Church School, Huddersfield. Employed as a drysalter's labourer by Messrs Lewis S. Cocking and Company, drysalters, of Folly Hall. Husband of Mary Linton, 9 Victoria Road, Lockwood. Enlisted early in the war and had served in Egypt. Suffered severe wounds on 30.9.1916. Died of wounds at No 14 General Hospital, Wimereaux, on 1.10.1916, aged 28 years. Buried **WIMEREUX COMMUNAL CEMETERY.** Grave location:- Plot 1, Row Q, Grave 29. ROH:- St. Stephen's Church, Rashcliffe.

LINTON, RICHARD HENRY. Private. No 31817. 2/6th Battalion North Staffordshire Regiment. Born Thomas Street, Huddersfield,

16.12.1897. Son of Mr and Mrs Joseph William Linton, 35 Union Street, off Northgate, Huddersfield. Employed as a glazier by Messrs W. H. Heywood and Company, Bay Hall, Birkby. Single. Enlisted 4.11.1916. Killed in action, 22.4.1917, aged 19 years. Buried **JEANCOURT COMMUNAL CEMETERY EXTENSION.** Grave location:- Plot 1, Row F, Grave 6. ROH:- St. Andrew's Church, Leeds Road, Huddersfield.

LISLE, JOHN THOMAS. Private. No 31783. 1/4th Battalion Duke of Wellington's Regiment. Born Longroyd Bridge 23.1.1891. Son of Mrs Bairstow, Chapel Street, Taylor Hill, Lockwood. Educated Rashcliffe Church School. Husband of Laura A. Lisle, 131 Whitehead Road, Primrose Hill, Huddersfield. Employed as a cloth shrinker by Messrs Kaye and Stewart. Enlisted May 1917. Reported missing, presumed killed, 10.4.1918, aged 27 years. Has no known grave. Commemorated **TYNE COT MEMORIAL TO THE MISSING.**

LISTER, ARTHUR. Private. No 71051. Posted 2/2nd London Regiment Royal Fusiliers. Formerly No 33767 3rd Cavalry Reserve. Born Farsley. Lived Huddersfield. Killed in action, 26.10.1917. Has no known grave. Commemorated **TYNE COT MEMORIAL TO THE MISSING.**

LISTER, FRANK JESSOP. Private. No 2761. 1/5th Battalion Duke of Wellington's Regiment. Born 8 King's Mill Lane, Huddersfield, 13.4.1894. Son of Captain Albert Edward Lister (also of the 5th Battalion Duke of Wellington's Regiment) and Jane Elizabeth Lister, Brier Edge, 8 King's Mill Lane, Huddersfield. Educated at Huddersfield College. Employed as a mechanical engineer. Played cricket with the Almondbury Club. Single. Enlisted August 1914. Embarked for France in April, 1915. Came home on leave in June, 1916. Suffered serious gunshot wounds to both thighs on 2.7.1916. Died of wounds at No 2 Stationary Hospital, Abbeville, on 6.7.1916, aged 22 years. Buried **ABBEVILLE COMMUNAL CEMETERY.** Grave location:- Plot 4, Row F, Grave 16. ROH:- Huddersfield Drill Hall; Almondbury War Memorial.

LISTER, HERBERT. Private. No 34338. 8th Battalion North Staffordshire Regiment. Formerly No 13039 Duke of Wellington's Regiment.

Born Shaws Row, Berry Brow, Huddersfield, 5.12.1888. Son of James Lister, 33a, Chapel Street, Berry Brow. Educated Berry Brow Council School. Employed as a teamer by Mr Tom Taylor. Single. Enlisted 14.11.1914. Reported missing, presumed killed, 24.3.1918, aged 29 years. Buried **DELSAUX FARM CEMETERY.** Grave location:- Plot 2, Row A, Grave 12. ROH:- Armitage Bridge War Memorial.

LISTER, TOM. Private. No 202166. 1/4th Battalion York and Lancaster Regiment. Born Shelley, near Huddersfield. Married, with two children. Lived Hill Top, Shelley. Prior to enlistment, had worked at White Lee Colliery. Killed in action, 14.4.1918. Has no known grave. Commemorated **TYNE COT MEMORIAL TO THE MISSING.** ROH:- Emmanuel Church, Shelley.

LITTLE, GEORGE ERNEST. Private. No 5202. 2/5th Battalion Duke of Wellington's Regiment. Born Huddersfield. Lived 3 Spivey's Yard, Castlegate, Huddersfield. Employed as a labourer. Single. Died from tuberculosis, 28.3. 1921.

LITTLEWOOD, BEN. Private. No 23189. 1/7th Battalion Duke of Wellington's Regiment. Born Honley. Son of Mrs Littlewood, of Moorbottom, Honley. Employed by Messrs B. Vickerman and Sons Limited, Thongsbridge Mills. Enlisted in the Holme Valley Battery of the Royal Field Artillery in June, 1916, but was discharged. He was afterwards recalled to the Colours and joined the Duke of Wellington's Regiment. Reported missing, presumed killed, on 12.4.1918, aged 30 years. Buried **CABARET ROUGE BRITISH CEMETERY.** Grave location:- Plot 20, Row C, Grave 11. ROH:- Huddersfield Drill Hall; Honley War Memorial.

LITTLEWOOD, BENJAMIN. Lance Corporal. No 9222. 3rd Battalion (1st Central Ontario Regiment). Born Underbank, Holmfirth. Prior to emigrating to Canada, in 1906, was an engine tenter at Messrs Vickerman and Sons, Thongsbridge. Married. Killed in action, 9.6.1916, aged 39 years. Has no known grave. Commemorated **MENIN GATE MEMORIAL TO THE MISSING.** ROH:- Underbank War Memorial.

LITTLEWOOD, ERNEST. Corporal. No 2179. 1/7th Battalion Duke of Wellington's Regiment.

Lived 126 Woodhead Road, Hinchliffe Mill. Attended Holmbridge Wesleyan Chapel and was a member the Holmbridge football club. Employed as a weaver at Digley Mill. Enlisted at the outbreak of the war. Reported missing, presumed killed, on 18.9.1916, aged 22 years. Has no known grave. Commemorated **THIEPVAL MEMORIAL TO THE MISSING.** ROH:- Holme and Holmbridge War Memorial; Huddersfield Drill Hall.

LITTLEWOOD, FRANK. Private. No 241936. 2/5th Battalion Duke of Wellington's Regiment. Son of Mrs Green, The Brown Cow Inn, Millgate, Paddock. Employed by Messrs D. Brown and Sons, Crosland Moor. Reported missing, presumed killed, at the Battle of Bullecourt on 3.5.1917. Has no known grave. Commemorated **ARRAS MEMORIAL TO THE MISSING.** (Stepbrother of Private **NORMAN GREEN**, killed in action, 11.8.1917, q.v.). ROH:- Huddersfield Drill Hall.

LITTLEWOOD, FRED. Private. No 64613. 25th (Tyneside Irish) Battalion Northumberland Fusiliers. Born Rashcliffe Hill, Huddersfield, 6.3.1899. Son of William Marsden and Emily Littlewood, 98 Springdale Street, Longroyd Bridge. Educated Mount Pleasant Board School. Employed by Mr Oliver Littlewood, fruiterer, Victoria Lane, Huddersfield. Attended Buxton Road Wesleyan Church. Single. Enlisted 20.3.1917. Wounded by a gas shell at Poperinghe on 9.4.1918. Died of wounds at No 7 Stationary Hospital, 14.4.1918, aged 19 years. Buried **BOULOGNE EASTERN CEMETERY.** Grave location:- Plot 8, Row I, Grave 191. ROH:- St. Stephen's Church, Rashcliffe; memorial in Lockwood Cemetery.

LITTLEWOOD, STANLEY. Private. No 65718. 1/5th Battalion Northumberland Fusiliers. Born Kirkburton. Son of Ernest and Elizabeth A. Littlewood of Paddock Farm, Kirkburton. Died, 10.4.1918, aged 19 years. Buried **LAVENTIE COMMUNAL CEMETERY.** Grave location:- Special Memorial No 3. ROH:- All Hallows Parish Church, Kirkburton.

LITTLEWOOD, TOM CROWTHER. Private. No 28457. 18th Battalion West Yorkshire Regiment. Born Skelmanthorpe, near Huddersfield. Son of the late Walter Morley Littlewood and Clara Littlewood of Skelmanthorpe. Husband of Norah Littlewood, of Birdsedge, Huddersfield. Embarked for France in September, 1916, and was gassed the following month. Died of wounds, 30.4.1917, aged 22 years. Buried **AUBIGNY COMMUNAL CEMETERY EXTENSION.** Grave location:- Plot 2, Row J, Grave 38. ROH:- St. Aidan's Church, Skelmanthorpe; Denby Dale and Cumberworth War Memorial.

LITTLEWOOD, WILLIAM. Private. No 19220. 10th Battalion York and Lancaster Regiment. Formerly No 16687 King's Own Yorkshire Light Infantry. Born Emley. Son of George and Anne Littlewood of Butt's Farm, Emley Moor. Husband of Margaret Littlewood, of Beaufort, County Kerry, Ireland. Killed in action, 9.2.1916, aged 33 years. Buried **RUE-DAVID MILITARY CEMETERY.** Grave location:- Plot 1, Row H, Grave 32. ROH:- Emley War Memorial.

LIVERSEDGE, ERNEST. Sapper. No 166754. 22nd Field Company, Royal Engineers. Born Lepton. Son of Richard and Martha Liversedge, Rowley Hill, Lepton. Employed by Messrs Hollingworths, joiners and contractors, of Huddersfield. Attended the Rowley Hill Wesleyan Chapel and Sunday School. Was treasurer to the Rowley Hill Cricket Club. Enlisted April 1916. Embarked for France in November, 1916. Killed in action, 3.3.1917, aged 25 years. Buried **COURCELLES-AU-BOIS COMMUNAL CEMETERY EXTENSION.** Grave location:- Row F, Grave 4. ROH:- Lepton Parish Church.

LIVERSIDGE, HARRY ARTHUR. Sergeant. No 12657. 9th Battalion Duke of Wellington's Regiment. Born Meltham. Lived Meltham Mills. Killed in action, 2.3.1916, aged 27 years. Has no known grave. Commemorated **MENIN GATE MEMORIAL TO THE MISSING.** ROH:- St. Bartholomew's Church, Meltham.

LIVERSEDGE, TOM. Private. No 205256. 1/5th Battalion York and Lancaster Regiment. Born 31 Fitzwilliam Street, Huddersfield, 2.10.1884. Son of Hannah Liversedge, 189 Bradford Road, Huddersfield. Attended St. John's Church of England School, Birkby, and Thomas Street Council School. Employed as a checker by the London and North Western Railway Company at the goods yard, Huddersfield Station. Single.

Enlisted 9.8.1917. Reported wounded and missing on 12.4.1918 and afterwards presumed to have been killed on that date. Buried **CABARET ROUGE BRITISH CEMETERY.** Grave location:- Plot 20, Row D, Grave 25. ROH:- Fartown and Birkby War Memorial; St. John's Church, Birkby; memorial in Almondbury Cemetery; London and North Western Railway Company Roll.

LIVERSIDGE, JOHN T. M. Private. No 4526. 10th Battalion Royal Fusiliers (City of London Regiment). Born Huddersfield. Son of Samuel and Hannah Maria Liversidge of Lockwood, Huddersfield. Died in hospital at Brentwood, Essex, on 23.12.1916, aged 40 years. Buried **CHRIST CHURCH CEMETERY, GREAT WARLEY, ESSEX.** Grave Location:- K, 58.

LIVESEY, JOHN. Private. No 6951. 2nd Battalion Duke of Wellington's Regiment. Born Lockwood, Huddersfield. Educated at Lockwood schools. Employed as a teamer. Married. Enlisted 4.8.1914. Reported missing, presumed killed, at Ypres on 8.11.1914. Has no known grave. Commemorated **MENIN GATE MEMORIAL TO THE MISSING.** ROH:- Christ Church, Woodhouse Hill; Fartown and Birkby War Memorial.

LLOYD, ROBERT. Gunner. No 184275. Royal Field Artillery. Formerly Horsekeeper, Royal Army Veterinary Corps. Born Henllan, Denbigh, North Wales. Lived 1 Rock Cottages, Brockholes. Employed as a gardener for Mr E. Crowther, Rock Lea, Brockholes. Married, with three children. Killed in action, 30.8.1918, aged 35 years. Buried **VAULX HILL CEMETERY.** Grave location:- Plot 1, Row D, Grave 15. ROH:- Brockholes War Memorial.

LLOYD, THOMAS (JACK). Corporal. No 17393. 1/7th Battalion Duke of Wellington's Regiment. Born Derby. Adopted son of Mrs Bottomley, 21 Nabbs Lane, Slaithwaite. Employed by Messrs John Haigh and Company, oil merchants, of Slaithwaite. Was a member of No 2 Working Men's Club, Slaithwaite. Enlisted at the outbreak of the war. Embarked for France on 9.8.1915. Had been twice wounded. Killed in action near Cambrai on 11.10.1918, aged 37 years. Buried **WELLINGTON CEMETERY.** Grave location:- Plot 2, Row C, Grave 12. ROH:- St. James Church, Slaithwaite; Slaithwaite War Memorial; Huddersfield Drill Hall.

LOCKWOOD, ARTHUR. Ordinary Seaman. No J/64621. (Dev). Royal Navy. *HMS Vivid 1* Born Holme. Son of Mr and Mrs Lockwood, Pinfold, Holme. Educated Holmfirth Secondary School. Was organist at Holme Sunday School. Employed as a weaver at Digley Mills. Enlisted in January 1917. Died of illness at Devonport Naval Hospital, 18.2.1917, aged 18 years. Buried **ST. DAVID'S PARISH CHURCH, HOLMBRIDGE.** Grave location:- in South part. ROH:- Holme and Holmbridge War Memorial; Holmfirth Secondary School.

LOCKWOOD, ERNEST. Rifleman. No C/7646. 18th Battalion King's Royal Rifle Corps. Born Huddersfield. Son of Mr Sam Lockwood, 5 Garforth Street, Aspley. Employed by Messrs Dyson and Hall, Greenside, Dalton. Enlisted November 1915. Killed in action, 10.10.1916, aged 23 years. Has no known grave. Commemorated **THIEPVAL MEMORIAL TO THE MISSING.**

LOCKWOOD, FRANK. 2nd Lieutenant. 15 Training Squadron. Royal Flying Corps. Second son of Mr and Mrs Wilkinson Lockwood, Cragside, Milnsbridge. Educated at Crow Lane Board School, Milnsbridge, and at Doctor Haslem's School in Harrogate. Prior to enlistment, had been at the works of Messrs John Lockwood and Sons Limited, Scar Bottom Mills, Milnsbridge, of which firm his father was a Director. Enlisted in the R.F.C. as a Private on 27.3.1917. He went through the Cadet course and obtained his commission in July, 1917. Was killed in a flying accident at Grantham, Lincolnshire, on 4.11.1917, aged 18 years. Buried with full military honours **SALENDINE NOOK BAPTIST CHAPEL YARD.** Grave location:- South-East of Chapel. ROH:- Salendine Nook Baptist Chapel; St. John's Church, Golcar; St. Mark's Parish Church, Longwood; Crow Lane Board School, Milnsbridge; commemorated in Salendine Nook Baptist Chapel yard, 125E.

LOCKWOOD, FRANK. Private. No 235056. 10th Battalion West Yorkshire Regiment. Born Kirkheaton. Son of Joah and Sarah Lockwood of Cowmes, Kirkheaton. Killed in action, 14.10.1917, aged 36 years. Has no known grave. Commemorated **TYNE COT MEMORIAL TO THE MISSING.** ROH:- St. John's Church, Kirkheaton.

LOCKWOOD, FRED. Sergeant. No 1645. 1/7th Battalion Duke of Wellington's Regiment. Born Meltham. Formerly lived at Binns, Slaithwaite. His wife and four children moved to Oxenhope, near Keighley, in 1915. Enlisted at the outbreak of the war. Died of wounds 23.7.1916. Buried **WARLOY-BAILLON COMMUNAL CEMETERY EXTENSION.** Grave location:- Plot 5, Row C, Grave 22. ROH:- St. James Church, Slaithwaite; Slaithwaite War Memorial; Huddersfield Drill Hall.

LOCKWOOD, HAROLD. Rifleman. No S/28944. 1st Battalion The Rifle Brigade. Formerly No R/19962. King's Royal Rifle Corps. Born Moldgreen 8.11.1891. Son of Ben and Emma Lockwood, 49 Victoria Street, Moldgreen. Educated Moldgreen National School. Employed as a clerk by Messrs Godfrey Sykes and Sons, Moldgreen. Enlisted 1.3.1916. Killed in action near Lillers on 17.5.1918, aged 26 years. Buried **LE VERTANNOY BRITISH CEMETERY, HINGES.** Grave location:- Row B, Grave 10. ROH:- Christ Church, Moldgreen.

LOCKWOOD, HAROLD. Sergeant. No 8432. 2nd Battalion Duke of Wellington's Regiment. Born Holmbridge, Holmfirth. Killed in the attack at Lesboeufs on 12.10.1916. Has no known grave. Commemorated **THIEPVAL MEMORIAL TO THE MISSING.** ROH:- Holme and Holmbridge War Memorial.

LOCKWOOD, HARRY. Private. No 10570. 2nd Battalion Duke of Wellington's Regiment. Born Meltham. Son of Thomas and Violet Annie Bates. Killed in action, 24.8.1914, aged 24 years. Buried **HAUTRAGE MILITARY CEMETERY.** Grave location:- Plot 2, Row C, Grave 17. ROH:- St. Bartholomew's Church, Meltham.

LOCKWOOD, JOE. Rifleman. No 242342. 2/7th Battalion West Yorkshire Regiment, attached 185th Trench Mortar Battery. Born Austonley, Holmfirth. Son of Mr J. T. Lockwood, 169 Woodhead Road, Holmbridge. Educated Field End School. Employed at Bridge Foundry, Holmfirth. Played cricket for the Holmbridge Cricket Club. Enlisted October 1916. Killed in action, 24.5.1918, aged 26 years. Buried **GOMMECOURT BRITISH CEMETERY No 2.** Grave location:- Plot 4, Row H, Grave 21/22. ROH:- Holme and Holmbridge War Memorial.

LOCKWOOD, JOHN EDWARD. Lance Corporal. No 241381. 2/5th Battalion Duke of Wellington's Regiment. Lived 18 Daisy Street, off St. Andrew's Road, Huddersfield. Married, with two children. Employed at the Huddersfield Corporation Destructor works. Was a keen sportsman and played both cricket and football. He was at one time Captain and professional for the Paddock Cricket Club and he also played with the Bradley Mills and Denby Dale cricket clubs and the Denby Dale and Meltham football teams. Enlisted November 1915. Reported missing, 3.5.1917, at the Battle of Bullecourt and afterwards presumed to have been killed on that date. Has no known grave. Commemorated **ARRAS MEMORIAL TO THE MISSING.** ROH:- Huddersfield Drill Hall.

LOCKWOOD, JOHN LEWIS. Lance Corporal. No C/7695. 12th Battalion King's Royal Rifle Corps. Born Holmfirth. Son of the late Mr John Lockwood and Mrs Lockwood, 68 Dunford Road, Holmfirth. Educated Holmfirth National School and the Technical Institute. Employed by Mr Arthur Quarmby, butcher. Attended St. John's Church, Upperthong and a member of the Young Men's Class. Enlisted in 1915 and embarked for France in the Spring of 1916. Wounded on one occasion but after treatment in England returned to France. Killed in action in the attack on the German lines beyond Langemarck, 16.8.1917, aged 21 years. Has no known grave. Commemorated **TYNE COT MEMORIAL TO THE MISSING.** ROH:- Underbank War Memorial.

LOCKWOOD, NORMAN. Private. No 118697. 53rd Field Ambulance Royal Army Medical Corps. Born Deighton 16.7.1891. Educated Fartown Grammar School. Employed as a woollen salesman. Lived 29 Clara Street, Fartown. Single. Enlisted May 1917. Wounded at Albert, France on 18.8.1918. Died of wounds at No 2 British Red Cross Hospital, Rouen 21.8.1918 age 27 years. Buried **ST. SEVER CEMETERY EXTENSION, ROUEN.** Grave location:- Block Q, Plot 4, Row I. Grave 9. ROH:- Fartown and Birkby War Memorial.

LOCKWOOD, NORMAN. Private. No 14324. 2nd Battalion Duke of Wellington's Regiment. Born Shepley. Lived Pit House Farm, Shepley. Married, with two children. Employed by Mr Harris Wood, quarry owner. Killed in action, 15.4.1918. Has no known grave. Commemorated **PLOEGSTEERT MEMORIAL TO THE MISSING.** ROH:- Shepley War Memorial.

LOCKWOOD, REGINALD UGHTRED. Lieutenant Indian Army Reserve of Officers, attached 14th Labour Company. Son of Robert Walker Lockwood and Christiana Lockwood of Belmont, Meltham. Died of heatstroke in India, 10.1.1919, aged 23 years. Buried **TRIMULGHERRY CANTONMENT CEMETERY.** Commemorated **MADRAS 1914-1918 WAR MEMORIAL, CHENNAI, INDIA.** ROH:- St. Bartholomew's Church, Meltham.

LOCKWOOD, ROBERT. Ordinary Seaman. No J/87974. Royal Navy. *HM Motor Launch No 247.* Son of Benjamin B. and Ada L. Lockwood, Whitewalls, Austenley, Holmfirth. Attended Holmbridge Church Sunday School. Employed at Digley Mills and on his father's farm. Enlisted May 1918. 'On the evening of the 29.9.1918 the launch upon which Robert was engaged was observed making for shelter near St. Ives, Cornwall. Owing to a sudden change in the wind she was driven off course. Every effort was made and continued until after darkness had set in to help those on board but owing to the heavy seas and the rocky character of the coast these efforts were not of much assistance and apart from 1 Officer all the crew were drowned.' Has no known grave. Commemorated **PLYMOUTH NAVAL MEMORIAL TO THE MISSING.** ROH:- Holme and Holmbridge War Memorial.

LOCKWOOD, THOMAS. Private. No 240734. 1/5th Battalion Duke of Wellington's Regiment. Born Brockholes. Lived Rock Terrace, Brockholes. Educated Brockholes National School. Was a member of the staff of the Holme Valley Theatre. Enlisted November 1914. Embarked for France in April, 1915. Killed in action in the attack on the Schwaben Redoubt on 3.9.1916. Buried **MILL ROAD CEMETERY.** Grave location:- Plot 9, Row C, Grave 7. ROH:- Brockholes War Memorial; Thurstonland War Memorial; Huddersfield Drill Hall.

LOCKWOOD, THOMPSON. Private. No 14192. 9th Battalion Duke of Wellington's Regiment. Born Denby Dale. Son of Henrietta Lockwood and the late Charles Lockwood, High Street, Denby Dale. Employed as a collier at Messrs Naylor's colliery, Lower Denby. Was a keen athlete and a member of the Denby Dale Cricket Club. Reported missing in a bayonet charge on 2.3.1916, aged 28 years. Has no known grave. Commemorated **MENIN GATE MEMORIAL TO THE MISSING.** ROH:- Denby Dale and Cumberworth War Memorial.

LOCKWOOD, VICTOR. Private. No 29/508. 1st Battalion Northumberland Fusiliers. Born Kirkburton. Son of Fred and Caroline Lockwood, Duck Nest, Kirkburton. Prior to enlistment, was employed by his father as a blacksmith. Killed in action, 3.5.1917, aged 22 years. Buried **DURY CRUCIFIX CEMETERY.** Grave location:- Plot 3, Row A, Grave 41. ROH:- All Hallows Parish Church, Kirkburton.

LOCKWOOD, WILLIAM. Private. No 11447. 9th Battalion Duke of Wellington's Regiment. Born Haigh Head, Hoylandswaine. 31.3.1894. Educated Hoylandswaine Church of England School. Employed as a farm labourer. Husband of Ethel May Lockwood, 101 Sharpe Lane, Almondbury. Enlisted 4.9.1914. Died of wounds at No 17 Casualty Clearing Station on 14.3.1918, aged 23 years. Buried **LIJSSENTHOEK MILITARY CEMETERY.** Grave location:- Plot 27, Row EE, Grave 14a. ROH:- Almondbury War Memorial.

LOCKWOOD, WILLIAM. Private. No 92380. 15th Battalion Sherwood Foresters. Born Huddersfield 20.6.1898. Son of William and Sarah Ann Lockwood, 5 Thomas Street, Northgate, Huddersfield. Educated Huddersfield Parish Church School. Employed as a cooper's apprentice at British Dyes Limited. Single. Enlisted 20.1.1917. Killed in action, 14.7.1918, aged 20 years. Has no known grave. Commemorated **TYNE COT MEMORIAL TO THE MISSING.** ROH:- Huddersfield Parish Church.

LOCKWOOD, WILLIAM. Private. No 71408. 15th Battalion Durham Light Infantry. Formerly No 11952 Duke of Wellington's Regiment. Born Folly Hall, Huddersfield. Son of Mrs Mary Elizabeth Lockwood, 75 Hope Street, Folly Hall.

Employed by Messrs J. Hopkinson and Company Limited, Birkby. Enlisted at the outbreak of the war. Killed in action at Passchendaele, 22.10.1917, aged 25 years. Buried **TYNE COT CEMETERY**. Grave location:- Plot 44, Row H, Grave 2. ROH:- St. Stephen's Church, Rashcliffe.

LOCKWOOD, WILLIAM EDWARD. Private. No G/22897. 7th Battalion The Queens (Royal West Surrey Regiment). Formerly No 43320 King's Own Yorkshire Light Infantry. Born Huddersfield. Son of Albert and Mary Eliza Lockwood, 2 Upper Brow Road, Paddock. Reported missing 21.3.1918 and afterwards presumed to have been killed on that date, aged 21. Has no known grave. Commemorated **POZIERES MEMORIAL TO THE MISSING**. ROH:- All Saints Church, Paddock.

LOCKWOOD, WILLIE. Private. No 24769. 1st Company, Machine Gun Corps. Formerly No 1525 Duke of Wellington's Regiment. Second son of Mr and Mrs John William Lockwood, 13 Spring Street, Marsden. Attended Marsden Wesleyan Sunday School. Employed in the finishing department by Messrs Crowther, Bruce and Company. Was a member of the local Territorial battalion before the outbreak of the war. Killed in action at Passchendaele, 9.10.1917, aged 23 years. Buried **TYNE COT CEMETERY**. Grave location:- Plot 55, Row D, Grave 12. ROH:- Marsden War Memorial.

LODGE. FRED. Rifleman. No R/16561. 10th Battalion King's Royal Rifle Corps. Born Kirkburton. Son of Ben Lodge, of Slantgate, Kirkburton. Employed by Mr Taylor, of Darton, as head gardener. Killed in the trenches near Guillemont during the Battle of the Somme on 29.8.1916, aged 28 years. Has no known grave. Commemorated on the **THIEPVAL MEMORIAL TO THE MISSING**. ROH:- All Hallows Parish Church, Kirkburton.

LODGE, HAROLD. Lance Corporal. No 241083. 2/5th Battalion Duke of Wellington's Regiment. Born Holmfirth. Son of Mr John Lodge, Waterloo, Holmfirth. Employed at Washpit Mills, Holmfirth. Attended both the Choppards and Magnum Sunday Schools and was a member of the choir at both places. Was a member of the Holme Valley Male Voice Choir. Single. Enlisted March 1915. Embarked for France in June, 1916. Reported missing, presumed killed, at the Battle of Bullecourt, 3.5.1917, aged 33 years. Has no known grave. Commemorated **ARRAS MEMORIAL TO THE MISSING**. ROH:- Underbank War Memorial; Huddersfield Drill Hall.

LODGE, HARRY A. Bombardier. No 710677. 'C' Battery, 298th Brigade, Royal Field Artillery. Born Bolton. Son of the late Joe and Emma Lodge of Shepley. Lived Old Hall, Shepley. Employed as a motor driver for Messrs J. Barden and Sons, Shelley. Was a member of Shepley Liberal Club where he was a keen billiard player, being a member of the Shepley team when they won the league championship. He was also a member of the Shepley White Rose and the Shepley Corinthian football clubs. Single. Enlisted May, 1915, and was wounded the same year. Rejoined the colours in April, 1916. Killed in action, 16.6.1917, aged 34 years. Buried **RENINGHELST NEW MILITARY CEMETERY**. Grave location:- Plot 2, Row D, Grave 27. ROH:- Shepley War Memorial.

LODGE, HERBERT. Private. No 52616. 1st Battalion West Yorkshire Regiment. Formerly No 308189 Duke of Wellington's Regiment. Born Thurstonland. Lived Scar End, Brockholes. Married, with two children. Employed by Messrs James Lancaster and Son, Mytholm Bridge. Killed in action, 17.9.1918, aged 31 years. Has no known grave. Commemorated **VIS-en-ARTOIS MEMORIAL TO THE MISSING**. ROH:- Brockholes War Memorial; Thurstonland War Memorial; memorial in St. Thomas's Churchyard, Thurstonland.

LODGE, HIRAM. Gunner. No 117972. 306th Siege Battery Royal Garrison Artillery. Born Huddersfield. Father of Willie Lodge, Station Road, Skelmanthorpe. Killed in action, 13.11.1917, aged 40 years. Buried **BARD COTTAGE CEMETERY**. Grave location:- Plot 6, Row B, Grave 26.

LODGE, IRVIN. Able Seaman. No J/54715. *HMS Bittern*. Born Skelmanthorpe. Son of Thomas and Annie Lodge of Skelmanthorpe. Husband of Edith Lodge of Wood Street, Skelmanthorpe. Was Sunday School teacher at the Reformed Chapel and secretary for the Liberal

Club, Skelmanthorpe. Employed by Messrs E. Field, Tentercroft Mills, Skelmanthorpe. Joined the Navy on 4.6.1916. After twelve months service he was transferred to a destroyer. He married whilst on leave at the end of 1917. Drowned through collision in the English Channel on 4.4.1918, aged 25 years. Has no known grave. Commemorated **PLYMOUTH NAVAL MEMORIAL TO THE MISSING.** ROH:- St. Aidan's Church, Skelmanthorpe.

LODGE, JOHN ALLEN. Private. No 47400. 19th Battalion Durham Light Infantry. Formerly No 40069 Duke of Wellington's Regiment. Born Kirkburton, Huddersfield. Husband of Ellen Lodge, 19 Lister Street, Moldgreen. Died of wounds at No 46 Stationary Hospital, Etaples, 17.10.1918, aged 35 years. Buried **ETAPLES MILITARY CEMETERY.** Grave location:- Plot 66, Row J, Grave 9. ROH:- Christ Church, Moldgreen.

LODGE, NORMAN PERCY. Private. No 42044. 1 Platoon, 'A' Company, 6th Battalion York and Lancaster Regiment. Born Deighton Road, Huddersfield, December 1886. Son of Joe and Emma Lodge, 'Roslyn', Abingdon Street, Fartown. Educated Deighton Board School. Employed as a warehouseman by Messrs William Thomson and Sons Limited. Husband of Olive Maude Lodge, 181 Dives House, Wakefield Road, Dalton. Enlisted Easter 1917. Wounded at Poelcapelle, Belgium. Died of wounds at No 4 Casualty Clearing Station, 28.9.1917, aged 31 years. Buried **DOZINGHEM MILITARY CEMETERY.** Grave location:- Plot 6, Row F, Grave 3. ROH:- St. John's Church, Kirkheaton.

LODGE, WILLIAM. Private. No 240233. 2/5th Battalion Duke of Wellington's Regiment. Born Farnley Tyas, near Huddersfield. Son of Mr and Mrs Fred Lodge, 110 Northgate, Almondbury. Employed by Messrs Charles Midgley and Company, Seed Hill Dyeworks. Attended Almondbury Wesleyan Church. Killed in action at the Battle of Bullecourt, 3.5.1917, aged 20 years. Has no known grave. Commemorated **ARRAS MEMORIAL TO THE MISSING.** ROH:- Huddersfield Drill Hall; Almondbury War Memorial, Farnley Tyas War Memorial.

LODGE, WILLIAM. Private. No 38169. 6th Battalion The Yorkshire Regiment. Born Huddersfield. Son of Mr and Mrs Sam Lodge, 7 Learoyd Street, Leeds Road, Huddersfield. Husband of Hannah Lodge, 287 Leeds Road, Huddersfield. Killed in action at Passchendaele, 10.10.1917, aged 34 years. Has no known grave. Commemorated **TYNE COT MEMORIAL TO THE MISSING.** ROH:- St. Andrew's Church, Leeds Road; Fartown and Birkby War Memorial.

LONG, J. W. Private. No 13828. West Yorkshire Regiment, transferred to (2641033) Labour Corps. Died at home 14.8.1919. Buried **ST. LUKE'S CHURCHYARD, MILNSBRIDGE.** Grave location:- New ground. D, 31.

LONGBOTTOM, ALBERT. Private. No 36496. 1/6th Battalion Northumberland Fusiliers. Born 31 Queen Street, Paddock. Son of Hellawell and Henrietta Longbottom, 76 New Street, Paddock. Educated Paddock Council School. Employed as a cloth finisher. Enlisted 20.1.1917. Died of pneumonia as a Prisoner of War, 16.7.1918. Buried **LILLE SOUTHERN CEMETERY.** Grave location:- Plot 3, Row B, Grave 3. ROH:- All Saint's Church, Paddock; Shared Church, Paddock.

LONGBOTTOM. DONALD HAIGH. 2nd Lieutenant. 5th Battalion The King's (Liverpool) Regiment. Born Beech Street, Paddock, 20.8.1891. Son of Fred and Lucy Longbottom. Dingleside, Gledholt, Huddersfield. Educated Huddersfield College School and Silcoates School, Wakefield. Assisted his father in the family timber business of Messrs Jere Kaye and Company, Huddersfield. Was a keen footballer and was a member of the Y.M.C.A. tennis club. Was Captain of the first Huddersfield Boys Brigade Company at Paddock Congregational Church. Enlisted in 1910 as a Trooper in the Queens Own Yorkshire Dragoons. Completed his five years service in November, 1915. Returned from France to take up a commission in the 5th Battalion King's Liverpool Regiment. Was made bombing instructor of his Battalion and returned to France in March, 1916. Was shot through the head at Trones Wood on the Somme in a bombing attack on one of the German trenches on 8.8.1916, aged 25 years. Buried **PERONNE ROAD CEMETERY.** Grave location:- Plot 4, Row F, Grave 28. ROH:- Huddersfield College School; All Saints Church, Paddock; Shared Church, Paddock. *'The light extinguished, future killed, his day's work scarce begun.'*

LONGBOTTOM, JOHN WILLIAM TOULCHER. Private. No 30671. 2nd Battalion The Yorkshire Regiment. Born Scholes Square, Northgate, Huddersfield, 20.11.1890. Son of Mr and Mrs Longbottom, 88 Lockwood Road, Lockwood. Educated Rashcliffe Church of England School. Employed as an engineer's labourer by Messrs Clayton and Sons, Karrier Works, St. Thomas's Road, Huddersfield. Attended St. Stephen's Church, Rashcliffe, Lockwood. Single. Enlisted 16.6.1916. Embarked for France on 3.10.1916. Killed in action at the Battle of Arras on 9.4.1917, aged 19 years. Buried **NEUVILLE VITASSE ROAD CEMETERY.** Grave location:- Row B, Grave 8. ROH:- St. Stephen's Church, Rashcliffe; memorial in Almondbury Cemetery.

LONGDEN, ARTHUR OSBORNE. Company Sergeant Major. No 5625. 1st Battalion Northumberland Fusiliers. Born Shepley 14.9.1879. Son of John I. Longden. Educated Deighton Council School and St. Paul's Church of England School. Lived Commercial Street, Huddersfield. Employed as a stonemason. Served in the Boer War. Had also served in Mauritius for three years and in India. Returned to England in 1913. Embarked for France on 5.8.1914. Killed in action on the Aisne, 14.9.1914, whilst leading his Company. Buried **VAILLY BRITISH CEMETERY.** Grave location:- Plot 2, Row H, Grave 12.

LONGLEY, ARTHUR. Private. No 57383. 17th Battalion Lancashire Fusiliers. Formerly No 38033 Leicestershire Regiment. Born Holbeck, Leeds, 20.11.1899. Son of John Willie and Lottie Longley, 3 Charles Street, Crosland Moor, Huddersfield. Educated Crosland Moor Council School. Employed as a labourer by British Dyes Limited. Single. Killed in action near Ypres, Belgium, 10.9.1918, aged 18 years. Buried **PERTH CEMETERY (CHINA WALL).** Grave location:- Plot 1, Row K, Grave 5. ROH:- Crosland Moor Wesleyan Church; St. Barnabas Church, Crosland Moor; memorial in Lockwood Cemetery.

LORD, CHARLIE. Private. No 1790. 1/7th Battalion Duke of Wellington's Regiment. Born Longwood 13.9.1893. Son of the late Edgar and Elizabeth Lord. Educated Newsome School and New Street Council School. Lived with his sister, Amelia Firth, 52 Dewhurst Road, Fartown. Was a member of the Woodhouse Young Men's bible class. Employed as a cloth shrinker by Messrs J. Holt and Company. Single. Was a member of the local Territorials before the outbreak of the war. Enlisted 9.8.1914. Embarked for France in April, 1915. Killed in action during the Battle of the Somme, 17.9.1916, aged 23 years. Has no known grave. Commemorated **THIEPVAL MEMORIAL TO THE MISSING.** ROH:- Christ Church, Woodhouse Hill; Huddersfield Drill Hall; Fartown and Birkby War Memorial.

LORD, ERNEST OWEN. Lieutenant. 7th Squadron. Royal Air Force. Born Cleckheaton 4.4.1894. Son of Edward and Bertha Lord. Educated Bradford Grammar School. Lived Parkgate House, Berry Brow. Prior to enlistment, was a student in textile design. Husband of Doris C. Lord (later of 33 Audley Road, Hendon, London). Enlisted in September, 1913, in the local Territorial battalion. Served for two years in France with the 1/5th Battalion Duke of Wellington's Regiment. Commissioned into the Royal Flying Corps at the end of 1916. Killed in action on 18.9.1918, whilst flying over Poperinghe, chasing German aeroplanes. Buried **MENDINGHEM MILITARY CEMETERY.** Grave location:- Plot 10, Row E, Grave 15.

LORD, NORMAN. Private. No 11948. 8th Battalion Duke of Wellington's Regiment. Born Westbourne Road, Marsh. Son of John William and Carrie Lord, 2 Regent Road, Edgerton, Huddersfield. Educated Holy Trinity School. Single. Enlisted August 1914. Killed in action at Gallipoli on 21.8.1915, aged 21 years. Has no known grave. Commemorated **HELLES MEMORIAL TO THE MISSING.** ROH:- Holy Trinity Church, Huddersfield.

LORRIMAN, WILLIAM BRUCE. Private. No 13113. 5th Battalion (Saskatchewan) Canadian Infantry. Eldest son of Mr and Mrs John Lorriman, 26 Portland Street, Huddersfield. Before emigrating to Canada, in 1912, was employed by Messrs Firth and Miller, St. John's Road, Huddersfield. Had served for four years in the local Territorials. Took an active part in the formation of the boy Scout movement in Huddersfield. Enlisted at the outbreak of the war and came over to England with the first Canadian contingent. Was wounded at the Battle of Festubert in May, 1915. Returned to France in the New Year 1918. Killed in action, 9.8.1918.

Has no known grave. Commemorated **VIMY RIDGE MEMORIAL TO THE MISSING.**

LOVELL, GEORGE WILLIAM. Private. No 15035. 9th Battalion Duke of Wellington's Regiment. Born Leeds 10.11.1894. Educated Hillhouse Board School. Employed as a tailor's cutter. Lived 6 Clara Street, Fartown. Single. Enlisted December 1914. Killed in action near Ypres, Belgium, 19.12.1915, aged 22 years. Buried **MENIN ROAD SOUTH MILITARY CEMETERY.** Grave location:- Plot 3, Row E, Grave 7. ROH:- Great Northern Street Congregational Chapel; Fartown and Birkby War Memorial.

LOVELL, ARTHUR HEDLEY. Private. No 267672. 2/6th Battalion Duke of Wellington's Regiment. Born Newton Longville, Buckinghamshire, in 1888. Son of William and Elizabeth Lovell. In the 1911 census he was lodging with James and Esther Rayner, of 12 Townend, Thongsbridge, and was working as a teamer. Enlisted Holmfirth. Killed in action at the Battle of Bullecourt, 3.5.1917. Has no known grave. Commemorated **ARRAS MEMORIAL TO THE MISSING.** ROH:- Brockholes War Memorial.

LOVICK, EDWARD. Private. No 40833. 8th Battalion The King's Own (Royal Lancaster Regiment). Born 9 Broadway, Lancaster, 29.5.1899. Son of John and Isabella Lovick, 112 Longwood Gate, Longwood. Educated Holywell Green Board School, Stainland, Halifax. Employed as a cloth finisher. Single. Enlisted 29.6.1917. Killed in action during the second battle of the Somme, near Gommecourt, on 21.8.1918, aged 19 years. Has no known grave. Commemorated **VIS-en-ARTOIS MEMORIAL TO THE MISSING.** ROH:- St. Mark's Parish Church, Longwood.

LOWNDES, SAM. Lance Coporal. No 713. 18th Battalion West Yorkshire Regiment. Born Holmfirth. Son of Charles and Ellen Lowndes of Keighley. Killed in action on the first day of the Battle of the Somme, 1.7.1916, aged 27 years. Buried **MESNIL COMMUNAL CEMETERY EXTENSION.** Grave location:- Plot 2, Row A, Grave 7A. ROH:- Holmfirth War Memorial.

LUCAS, HARRY. Private. No 4896. 4th Battalion Seaforth Highlanders. Born Howden Clough, Birstall, 29.8.1896. Son of Mr and Mrs Fred Lucas, 192 Lockwood Road, Lockwood. Educated Mount Pleasant Council School. Employed by Messrs Job Thomas and Sons Limited, of Longwood, as a chain maker. Single. Enlisted 15.2.1916. Was wounded on 6.8.1916 at Beaumont Hamel, France. He and others were proceeding to the firing line when a shell burst and pieces penetrated his right lung, chest and shoulder. Was in hospital in France for a month before being sent to a hospital at Neath, South Wales, where he died of his wounds on 9.9.1916, aged 20 years. Buried **EDGERTON CEMETERY, HUDDERSFIELD.** Grave location:- 12, 'C', 107. ROH:- St. Stephen's Church, Rashcliffe; Mount Pleasant Chapel, Lockwood.

LUCAS, JOSEPH. Lance Sergeant. No 2555. 1/5th Battalion Duke of Wellington's Regiment. Born Moldgreen 27.6.1892. Son of Frederick Arthur and the late Clara Lucas, 19 West Place, Dalton. Educated Moldgreen Board School. Employed as a plasterer by Messrs Broadbent and Sons, Moldgreen. Attended Moldgreen United Methodist Church. Single. Had served in the local Territorials for five years prior to the war. Enlisted 4.8.1914. Killed by a rifle bullet on 1.8.1915, aged 23 years. Buried **BARD COTTAGE CEMETERY.** Grave location:- Plot 1, Row B, Grave 22. ROH:- Christ Church, Moldgreen; St. Andrew's Church, Moldgreen; Huddersfield Drill Hall.

LUCY, JAMES. Private. No 2424. 1/5th Battalion Duke of Wellington's Regiment. Born Paddington, London. Lived Low Town, Kirkburton. Killed by a sniper on 9.11.1915. Has no known grave. Commemorated **MENIN GATE MEMORIAL TO THE MISSING.** ROH:- All Hallows Parish Church, Kirkburton; Huddersfield Drill Hall.

LUMB, ALBERT EDWARD. Private. No 235584. 13th Battalion The Yorkshire Regiment. Formerly No 3726 Queen's Own Yorkshire Dragoons. Born Longwood 19.4.1888. Son of Mary Ann Lumb, 93 Prospect Road, Longwood. Educated Goitfield Council School. Employed as a clerk. Single. Enlisted in the Dragoons on 14.8.1915. Transferred to the Yorkshire Regiment in 1917. Reported missing at Bourlon Wood during the Battle of Cambrai on 23.11.1917, aged 29 years. Has no known grave. Commemorated **CAMBRAI MEMORIAL**

TO THE MISSING. ROH:- Salendine Nook Baptist Church; Longwood War Memorial; commemorated in Salendine Nook Baptist Chapel yard, 126E.

LUMB, ARTHUR. Private. No 39596. 9th Battalion King's Own Yorkshire Light Infantry. Born Slaithwaite. Married, with one child. Lived 21 Mona Street, Hill Top, Slaithwaite. Employed as a weaver by Messrs Crowther, Bruce and Company Limited, Marsden. Embarked for France at the beginning of 1917. Wounded in the arm and leg on the opening day of the Battle of Arras. Died of wounds on the same day, 9.4.1917. Buried **HENIN COMMUNAL CEMETERY EXTENSION.** Grave location:- Plot 2, Row D, Grave 3. ROH:- St. James Church, Slaithwaite; Slaithwaite War Memorial.

LUMB, BRUCE BROOK. Private. No 3234. 2/5th Battalion Duke of Wellington's Regiment. Born Cleveland Road, Marsh, Huddersfield, 2.6.1897. Son of Robert R. Lumb, 5 Nabcroft Lane, Crosland Moor. Educated Spring Grove Council School. Employed as a motor engineer. Enlisted just before his 18th birthday. '*Was wounded in his right thigh in 2 places and discharged after being over 6 months in various hospitals and was then receiving 27/6 per week and having to visit Huddersfield Infirmary twice a week for his thigh to be dressed. Was sent for to be examined to Halifax Military Medicos who kept him two hours naked. Pneumonia set in following day.*' (written by his father in 1922). Died of pneumonia at 5 Nabcroft Lane, Crosland Moor, on 5.12.1918, aged 21. ROH:- New North Road Baptist Church; Huddersfield Drill Hall.

LUMB, JOHN EDWIN. Private. No L/11660. 6th Battalion Royal West Kent Regiment. Formerly No 17303 Duke of Wellington's Regiment. Born Stainland, Halifax. Son of Edwin and Sarah Ann Lumb, Fairview Cottages, 136 Slades Road, Golcar. Employed by Messrs Pearson Brothers, woollen manufacturers, of Golcar. Attended Sunnybank Chapel as a boy and then Westwood Church. Enlisted 21.6.1915. Served in both France and Italy. Invalided home on one occasion with pneumonia, and afterwards debility caused by his having been cut off from his regiment and lost in No Man's Land for a week without food. Returned to France and was killed in action 7.9.1918, aged 25 years. Buried **FINS NEW BRITISH CEMETERY.** Grave location:- Plot 8, Row B, Grave 13. ROH:- St. John's Church, Golcar.

LUNN, CHARLES HENRY. Private. No 40565. 'C' Company, 1/5th Battalion Northumberland Fusiliers. Born Primrose Hill, Huddersfield, 30.12.1895. Son of James Edward and Eliza Frances Lunn, 88 Orchard Street, Primrose Hill. Educated Stile Common Council School. Employed as a baker by Mr Fred Kilburn, of Milnsbridge. Killed in action, 22.3.1918, aged 22 years. Has no known grave. Commemorated **POZIERES MEMORIAL TO THE MISSING.** ROH:- Memorial in Lockwood Cemetery.

LUNN, GEOFFREY CYRIL. 2nd Lieutenant. 20th Battalion Canadian Infantry (British Columbia) Regiment. Son of James Edgar and Mary Lunn of Netherton. Obtained a foundation scholarship at Almondbury Grammar School. In March, 1915, went to Canada as an articled Civil Engineer and a Land Surveyor to Mr B. A. Moorhouse of Penticton, British Columbia. Enlisted in the Special Battalion of the Universities of Western Canada for work in Europe and was gazetted in May, 1917. Killed in action, 30.5.1918, aged 20 years. Buried **BELLACOURT MILITARY CEMETERY, RIVIERE.** Grave location:- Plot 2, Row M, Grave 3. ROH:- South Crosland and Netherton; Almondbury Grammar School; Armitage Bridge National School.

LUNN, GEORGE. Private. No 10573. 2nd Battalion Duke of Wellington's Regiment. Son of Frank Sykes and Emma Amelia Lunn, South Street, Huddersfield. Gassed at Hill 60 on 5.5.1915. Died of the effects of gas poisoning at No 3 General Hospital, Rouen, on 9.5.1915, aged 21 years. Buried **St. SEVER CEMETERY, ROUEN.** Grave location:- Plot A, Row 9, Grave 16.

LUNN, HERBERT. Private. No 307810. 1/7th Battalion Duke of Wellington's Regiment. Born Milnsbridge. Son of William Henry and Hannah Lunn of Milnsbridge. Husband of Clara Lunn, 132 Brierley Road, Manchester Road, Huddersfield. Employed as a scourer by Messrs Kaye and Stewart, Broadfield Mills, Lockwood. Killed in action, 14.8.1917, aged 29 years. Buried **COXYDE MILITARY CEMETERY.** Grave location:- Plot 2, Row H, Grave 21. ROH:- Huddersfield Drill Hall.

LUNN, JAMES ARTHUR. Lance Corporal. No 235233. 2nd Battalion Duke of Wellington's Regiment. Adopted son of Mrs N. M. Hirst, Mill Moor, Meltham. Employed as a chauffeur by Doctor Gellataly, of Meltham. Died of wounds at No 8 Casualty Clearing Station, 3.5.1917, aged 25 years. Buried **DUISANS BRITISH CEMETERY**. Grave location:- Plot 4, Row B, Grave 14. ROH:- St. Bartholomew's Church, Meltham.

LUNN, JAMES EDWIN. Private. No 5987. 2nd Battalion Duke of Wellington's Regiment. Born Huddersfield. Lived 199 Fenay Moor Lane, Longley, Huddersfield. Killed in action near Mons, 23.8.1914. Buried **HAUTRAGE MILITARY CEMETERY**. Grave location:- Special Memorial 1. ROH:- Lowerhouses War Memorial; Almondbury War Memorial.

LUNN, JOHN WILLIAM. Lance Corporal. No 306286. 2nd Battalion Duke of Wellington's Regiment. Son of James and Eliza Lunn of Sparth, Marsden. Employed as a weaver at Clough Lea Mills, Marsden. Died from influenza, 14.11.1918, aged 27 years. Buried **ETAPLES MILITARY CEMETERY**. Grave location:- Plot 50, Row C, Grave 8. ROH:- Marsden War Memorial.

LUNN, LEWIS, Private. No 29199. 10th Battalion Duke of Wellington's Regiment. Born Marsden. Husband of Gertrude Lunn, of High Fold Farm, Marsden. Employed as a weaver by Messrs Crowther, Bruce and Company, of Marsden. Died of wounds at No 10 Casualty Clearing Station on 23.9.1917, aged 33 years. Buried **LIJSSENTHOEK MILITARY CEMETERY**. Grave location:- Plot 25, Row K, Grave 7a. ROH:- Marsden War Memorial.

LUSTY, PERCY GEORGE. Private. No 16216. 1/4th Battalion Duke of Wellington's Regiment. Born Stroud, Gloucestershire. Son of Mr and Mrs Lusty, Lower Acre Head Farm, Binn, Marsden, and formerly of Royd Street, Marsden. Educated Crow Lane Board School, Milnsbridge. Employed as a cloth finisher at Bank Bottom Mills, Marsden. Attended St. Michael's Mission Church. Enlisted June 1915. Had served in Egypt, the Dardenelles and in France. Returned to France in January, 1918, after recovering from an attack of mustard gas poisoning. Killed in action, 14.4.1918, aged 21 years. Has no known grave. Commemorated **TYNE COT MEMORIAL TO THE MISSING.** ROH:- Marsden War Memorial; Crow Lane Board School, Milnsbridge.

MACEY, ALBERT EDWARD. Bombardier. No 755683. 251st Brigade HQ, Royal Field Artillery. Born Plymouth 9.10.1891. Adopted son of A. W. and L. A. Macey, 56 Blacker Road, Birkby. Educated Spring Grove Council School and Huddersfield Technical College. Had served an apprenticeship to the timber trade with Messrs Jere Kaye and Company but, at the beginning of 1914, he left to take up work in the service of the Yorkshire Union of the Y.M.C.A. Attended Birkby Baptist Church. Enlisted June 1915. Received gas shell wounds on 2.11.1917. Died of the effects of gas poisoning at No 26 General Hospital, Etaples, on 12.11.1917, aged 26 years. Buried **ETAPLES MILITARY CEMETERY**. Grave location:- Plot 30, Row L, Grave 6. ROH:- Fartown and Birkby War Memorial.

MacGREGOR, ANDREW HAMILTON. Captain. 6th Battalion Seaforth Highlanders. Second son of Marcus and Bessie MacGregor. Born Valparaiso, Chile. His father was engineer of the London and North Western Railway, who superintended the construction of the Marsden tunnel. Attended Huddersfield College School where for nearly two years he was head boy. Employed by the Union of London and Smith's Bank. Killed in action, 13.11.1916, aged 26 years.. Buried **MAILLY WOOD CEMETERY**. Grave location:- Plot 1, Row F, Grave 32. ROH:- Huddersfield College School.

MACKMAN, ARTHUR. Private. No 240929. 2/5th Battalion Duke of Wellington's Regiment. Born Pinchbeck, West Lincolnshire on 19.1.1896. Son of Samuel and Betsy Mackman, 88 St. John's Road, Birkby. Educated Hillhouse Council School. Employed as a warehouseman by Messrs Bairstow, Sons and Company Limited, Fitzwilliam Street, Huddersfield. Attended Fartown Primitive Methodist Church. Single. Enlisted January 1915. Killed in action at the Battle of Bullecourt, 3.5.1917, aged 21 years. Has no known grave. Commemorated **ARRAS MEMORIAL TO THE MISSING.** (Brother of Lance Corporal **MATTHEW ALFRED**

MACKMAN, reported missing, 4.10.1917, q.v.). ROH:- Huddersfield Drill Hall; Fartown and Birkby War Memorial.

MACKMAN, MATTHEW ALFRED. Lance Corporal. No 16248. 2nd Battalion King's Own Scottish Borderers. Born Pinchbeck, West Lincolnshire, 24.6.1893. Son of Samuel and Betsy Mackman, 88 St. John's Road, Birkby. Lived with his Uncle at 17 Fern Terrace, Birkby. Educated Hillhouse Council School. Was employed as a patent glazier by Mr J. A. Milward, stained glass artist, 15 Albion Street, Huddersfield. Attended the Trinity Wesleyan Chapel, Fartown. Enlisted September 1914. Was wounded in April, 1917. Returned to France in March, 1917. Reported missing, presumed killed, at Passchendaele, 4.10.1917, aged 24 years. Has no known grave. Commemorated **TYNE COT MEMORIAL TO THE MISSING.** (Brother of Private **ARTHUR MACKMAN**, reported missing, 3.5.1917, q.v.). ROH:- Fartown and Birkby War Memorial.

MACKNESS, NORMAN. 2nd Driver. No DM2/171283. Attached 111 Corps H.Q., 'C' Siege Park Army Service Corps. Born Kilner Bank, Moldgreen, Huddersfield, 6.6.1892. Son of William and Mary Ann Mackness, 38 School Street, Moldgreen. Educated Moldgreen Council School. Was secretary of St. Paul's Wesleyan Sunday School, Dalton. Employed as a tailor by Mr Scholes, of Moldgreen. Enlisted 2.5.1916. Killed in action at St. Emile on 27.9.1918, aged 26. Buried **TEMPLEUX-LE-GUERARD BRITISH CEMETERY.** Grave location:- Plot 1, Row B, Grave 55. ROH:- St. Paul's Methodist Church, Dalton.

MADDEN, JAMES. Private. No 18239. 12th (Service Battalion) Highland Light Infantry. Born Huddersfield. Son of John and Jane Madden, 79 Dock Street, Huddersfield. Employed as a plasterer. Died of wounds, 18.5.1916, aged 34 years. Buried **BETHUNE TOWN CEMETERY.** Grave location:- Plot 5, Row C, Grave 81.

MALLALIEU, ERNEST. Rifleman. No C/7451. 2nd Battalion King's Royal Rifle Corps. Born Huddersfield. Son of Mr and Mrs Frederick Mallalieu, 37 Freehold Street, Primrose Hill, Huddersfield. Attended Primrose Hill Baptist Chapel. Was a member of the Liberal Club. Employed as a tailor by Messrs Chambers, of Honley. Enlisted November 1915. Died of wounds, 9.9.1916, aged 28 years. Buried **FLATIRON COPSE CEMETERY, MAMETZ.** Grave location:- Plot 1, Row F, Grave 61.

MALLINSON, ERNEST, MM. Sergeant. No L/18892. 'A' Battery, 155th Brigade, Royal Field Artillery. Born Linthwaite, Huddersfield. Son of William Henry and Mary Ellen Mallinson, 2 Slades, Linthwaite. Attended Linthwaite Church and was a member of the choir. Employed as a spinner by the Ramsden Mill Company. Enlisted February 1915. Embarked for France in December 1915. Awarded the Military Medal for distinguished conduct in the field on 21.9.1917. Killed in action, 3.10.1918, aged 22 years. Buried **CHAPEL CORNER CEMETERY, SAUCHY-LESTREE.** Grave location:- Row A, Grave 23. ROH:- Linthwaite War Memorial.

MALLINSON, FRANK BAXTER. Private. No 19108. 2/6th Battalion West Yorkshire Regiment. Born Huddersfield. Son of Arthur and Mary Mallinson, Hill Side, Kirkheaton. Killed in action at the Battle of Cambrai, 22.11.1917, aged 23 years. Has no known grave. Commemorated **CAMBRAI MEMORIAL TO THE MISSING.** ROH:- St. John's Church, Kirkheaton; commemorated on headstone in Kirkheaton Cemetery.

MALLINSON, HARRY, Private. No 301915. 8th Battalion Durham Light Infantry. Formerly No 5710 Duke of Wellington's Regiment. Born Huddersfield. Lived Longwood. Killed in action, 10.4.1918. Buried **ASSEVILLERS NEW BRITISH CEMETERY.** Grave location:- Plot 6, Row F, Grave 6. ROH:- St. Mark's Parish Church, Longwood.

MALLINSON, HERBERT. Private. No 205298. 8th Battalion Duke of Wellington's Regiment. Born Huddersfield. Seventh son of George and Annie Mallinson, 51 Leeds Road North, Huddersfield. Husband of Ada Mallinson, 4 Fieldhouse Road, Leeds Road, Huddersfield. Employed as a warper by Messrs T. and H. Blamires Limited, Leeds Road. Was a playing member of the Bradley Mills Cricket Club. Killed in action at Passchendaele, 9.10.1917, aged 32 years. Has no known grave. Commemorated **TYNE COT MEMORIAL TO THE MISSING.** ROH:- St. Andrew's Church, Leeds Road; Fartown and Birkby War Memorial.

MALLINSON, NORRIS. Private. No 267931. 1/7th Battalion West Yorkshire Regiment. Born Lockwood, Huddersfield. Lived Huddersfield. Died of wounds at No 17 Casualty Clearing Station on 24.2.1918. Buried **LIJSSENTHOEK MILITARY CEMETERY.** Grave location:- Plot 27, Row E, Grave 10.

MALLINSON, VICTOR. Private. No 3/11053. 2nd Battalion Duke of Wellington's Regiment. Born Golcar. Husband of Carrie Mallinson, Rose Cottage, Handel Street, Golcar. Employed as a fettler by Messrs C. and J. Hirst and Sons Limited, of Longwood. Attended Golcar Church School. Enlisted August 1914. Embarked for France in November, 1914. Came home on leave in July, 1917. Killed in action, 15.4.1918, aged 26 years. Buried **CHOCQUES MILITARY CEMETERY.** Grave location:- Plot 4, Row D, Grave 27. ROH:- St. John's Church, Golcar; memorial in Golcar Churchyard.

MALLINSON, WILFRED. Private. No 51841. 9th Battalion Duke of Wellington's Regiment. Born Kirkheaton. Son of Willie L. and Frances Mallinson of Gawthorpe Green, Kirkheaton. Employed as a works chemist by Messrs George Mallinson and Sons, Gawthorpe Green. Killed in action, 4.11.1918, aged 22 years. Buried **ROMERIES COMMUNAL CEMETERY EXTENSION.** Grave location:- Plot 7, Row A, Grave 11. ROH:- St. John's Church, Kirkheaton; Lepton Parish Church; commemorated on headstone in Kirkheaton Cemetery.

MALLINSON, WILLIE. Rifleman. No 268688. 2/7th Battalion West Yorkshire Regiment. Born 20.8.1889. Educated Armitage Bridge Church of England Schools. Employed as a grocer's assistant at the Berry Brow Cooperative Stores. Married. Lived 186 Lowerhouses Road, Lowerhouses. Enlisted 14.10.1916. Killed in action at Bullecourt on 10.4.1917, aged 28 years. Has no known grave. Commemorated **ARRAS MEMORIAL TO THE MISSING** ROH:- Armitage Bridge National Schools; Armitage Bridge War Memorial.

MALLORY, WALTER. Private. No 29718. 10th Battalion Duke of Wellington's Regiment. Born Burley-in-Wharfedale. Son of Herbert and Alice Mallory of Thunderbridge, Kirkburton. Employed by Mr Hallas, butcher, Highburton. Killed in action at Passchendaele, 20.9.1917, aged 20 years. Has no known grave. Commemorated **TYNE COT MEMORIAL TO THE MISSING.** ROH:- All Hallows Parish Church, Kirkburton.

MALLYON, JAMES JOSEPH. Private. No 7511. 2nd Battalion Duke of Wellington's Regiment. Stepson of Alfred Lindley, 12 Ainley Junction, Huddersfield. Died of wounds, 10.11.1914, aged 39 years. Buried **BOULOGNE EASTERN CEMETERY.** Grave location:- Plot 3, Row C, Grave 9.

MALONE, PATRICK. Corporal. No 3031. 1/5th Battalion Duke of Wellington's Regiment. Born Garden Walk, St. Andrew's Road, Turnbridge, Huddersfield 19.5.1891. Educated St. Patrick's Roman Catholic School. Employed as a labourer at Messrs Hopkinsons, Britannia Works, Birkby. Husband of Mary Malone, 9 Brick Bank, Northgate, Huddersfield. Enlisted August 1914. On 21.3.1916, Corporal Malone was working on the trench parapet when the Germans fired a volley. A bullet passed through his wrist and entered his thigh. An Army Chaplain wrote to Mrs Malone on 22.3.1916 to tell her not to worry and her husband was well on the way to recovery. But he died of his wounds at No 29 Casualty Clearing Station on 26.3.1916, aged 26 years. Buried **GEZAINCOURT COMMUNAL CEMETERY EXTENSION.** Grave location:- Plot 1, Row A, Grave 9. ROH:- Huddersfield Drill Hall.

MANCHESTER, LEONARD. Private. No 32158. 2/5th Battalion Duke of Wellington's Regiment. Born Meltham. Son of the late James and Hannah Manchester. Husband of Hilda Manchester, of New Road, Meltham. Employed for five years at Wallace's grocery stores in Market Place, Slaithwaite. At the time of enlistment, was manager of a branch of Wallace's stores at Meltham. Enlisted in 1917. Embarked for France in the early part of 1918. Killed in action, 27.3.1918, aged 28 years. Has no known grave. Commemorated **ARRAS MEMORIAL TO THE MISSING.** ROH:- Wilshaw Church; St. Bartholomew's Church, Meltham; Huddersfield Drill Hall.

MANSFIELD, STEPHEN ARTHUR, MM. Company Sergeant Major. No 787173. 38th Battalion Canadian Infantry (Eastern Ontario Regiment). Husband of Elinor Mansfield,

15 Longlands Road, Slaithwaite. Died of wounds, 4.11.1918, aged 22 years. Buried **VALENCIENNES COMMUNAL CEMETERY**. Grave location:- Plot 1, Row A, Grave 6.

MARSDEN, ARTHUR ARNOLD. Private. No S/7706. Army Ordnance Corps, 29th Division. Born Marsden. Son of Mr and Mrs John William Marsden, 6 Warrington Terrace, Marsden. Attended Marsden Wesleyan Church and Sunday School from childhood and, for two years prior to the war, was secretary to the Young Men's Bible Class. Employed in the office of the Colne Valley Spinning Company. Enlisted at the outbreak of the war. Went to the Dardenelles, arriving there on 25.4.1915 and returning to England on 9.1.1916. After leave at home he rejoined his unit in France in April, 1916. Was accidentally wounded in the body, hands, neck, right arm and left foot on 25.5.1917. Died of wounds at No 19 Casualty Clearing Station on 27.5.1917, aged 24 years. Buried **DUISANS BRITISH CEMETERY**. Grave location:- Plot 4, Row M, Grave 2. ROH:- Marsden War Memorial; memorial in Marsden Churchyard.

MARSDEN, CHARLIE. Private. No 31751. 2/4th Battalion Duke of Wellington's Regiment. Born Gardner Street, Lockwood, in 1883. Educated at Lockwood Schools. Husband of Caroline Marsden, 92 Whitehead Lane, Primrose Hill, Huddersfield. Employed as a scourer by Messrs Crowther Brothers, Stanley Mills, Milnsbridge. Enlisted 28.5.1917. Reported missing, presumed killed, at the Battle of Cambrai, 25.11.1917, aged 32. Has no known grave. Commemorated **CAMBRAI MEMORIAL TO THE MISSING**.

MARSDEN, EDGAR. Private. No 37679. 9th Battalion South Lancashire Regiment. Born Close Hill, Huddersfield, 8.2.1897. Son of Haigh and Agnes Marsden, 7 Blagden Lane, Close Hill. Educated Newsome Church of England School. Employed as a farm labourer by Mr Paul Mellor, Blagden Lane, Close Hill. Enlisted 18.9.1916. Died of wounds in Salonica, Greece, on 19.9.1918, aged 21 years. Buried **SARIGOL MILITARY CEMETERY, SALONIKA**. Grave location:- Row C, Grave 477. ROH:- St. John's Church, Newsome.

MARSDEN, HARRY. Rifleman. No A/204216. 9th Battalion King's Royal Rifle Corps. Born Paddock 25.2.1888. Educated Cowcliffe Church of England School. Employed as a spinner by Messrs William Hall and Company, Longroyd Bridge. Lived 114 Wellington Place, Moldgreen. Single. Enlisted November 1914. Reported missing on 27.3.1918 and afterwards presumed to have been killed on that date. Has no known grave. Commemorated **POZIERES MEMORIAL TO THE MISSING**. ROH:- St. Paul's Methodist Church, Dalton; Cowcliffe Wesleyan Church.

MARSDEN, HERBERT. Gunner. No 232345. 'D' Battery, 190th Brigade, Royal Field Artillery. Born Huddersfield. Lived Lane Head, Shepley. Married, with one child. Employed as a saddler. Died of pneumonia at No 10 Casualty Clearing Station, 27.10.1918, aged 32 years. Buried **LIJSSENTHOEK MILITARY CEMETERY**. Grave location:- Plot 35, Row B, Grave 2. ROH:- All Hallows Parish Church, Kirkburton; Shepley War Memorial.

MARSDEN, JOHN. Private. No 83395. 63rd Battalion Machine Gun Corps. Formerly No 38800 York and Lancaster Regiment. Born Slaithwaite. Son of Mr and Mrs Marsden, 4 Lower Wood, Slaithwaite. Employed at Shaw Carr Mills. Was a member of the Slaithwaite Cricket Club and the Socalist Institute. Enlisted 13.11.1916. Embarked for France in May, 1917. Came home on leave just six weeks before he was killed in action, in France, on 24.3.1918, aged 35 years. Buried **OVILLERS MILITARY CEMETERY**. Grave location:- Plot 12, Row Z, Grave 1. ROH:- St. James Church, Slaithwaite; Slaithwaite War Memorial.

MARSDEN, JOHN. Private. No 19158. 11th Battalion Sherwood Foresters. Born Holme, Holmfirth. Son of the late Mr George Marsden of Flowery Field, Hade Edge. Had worked as a quarryman, both at Magnum and in Derbyshire. Prior to enlistment, lived in Birkby, Huddersfield. Attended Hade Edge Wesleyan School and Chapel. Had served in France for a year when he was killed in action during the Battle of the Somme on 30.7.1916, aged 34 years. Has no known grave. Commemorated **THIEPVAL MEMORIAL TO THE MISSING**. ROH:- Hade Edge War Memorial.

MARSDEN, THOMAS FREDERICK. Private. No 2277. 'A' Company, 1/6th Battalion Manchester Regiment. Born Austonley, Holmfirth. Son of Joshua Beardsell and Jane Marsden, Rock Cottages, New Gate, Holmfirth. Was a pupil and teacher at the Wesleyan Day School for nearly twenty years. In 1912 he moved to Glossop, where he went into the coal business with his Uncle, Mr Platt. Enlisted September 1914. After training at Littleborough he was sent to Egypt. At the beginning of May, 1915, he went with his Regiment to the Dardenelles. Killed in action, 4.6.1915, aged 26 years. (He was the first man from Holmfirth to be killed). Buried **TWELVE TREE COPSE CEMETERY, HELLES.** Grave location:- Special Memorial, C 287. ROH:- Underbank War Memorial; Holmfirth Seconday School.

MARSDEN, THORNTON. Private. No 305525. 1/5th Battalion West Yorkshire Regiment. Born Huddersfield. Eldest son of the late George Marsden, yarn spinner, Huddersfield. Husband of Beatrice Marsden. Died of wounds received in action on 1.5.1918. Has no known grave. Commemorated **TYNE COT MEMORIAL TO THE MISSING.**

MARSH, GEORGE. Trooper. No 4686. (See 'INMAN' – the actual family name).

MARSH, GEORGE. Private. No 15678. 1/6th Battalion Duke of Wellington's Regiment. Son of Joseph and Mary E. Marsh. Lived Dunford Road, Underbank, Holmfirth. Employed firstly at Washpit Mills, Holmfirth and then for Messrs Haigh, plasterers. Enlisted just before Easter 1915. Was wounded in October, 1916, and came home on sick leave. Killed on 5.8.1917, aged 35, by a shell falling on his dugout. Buried **COXYDE MILITARY CEMETERY.** Grave location:- Plot 2, Row D, Grave 10. His sister, Miss M. E. Marsh, received the following letter from the Second Lieutenant of her brother's platoon who wrote, 'As the Officer in charge of your brother's platoon I have a very sad duty to perform in telling you of his fate yesterday. I was with him and part of my Lewis gun section. Five of us were sheltering from heavy shell fire in a dugout when a shell hit it square. When I recovered my senses I found I was alive and untouched and also one of the men by a miracle. All the dugout had been burst in over your poor brother and the other two so when we crawled out we ran for some Engineers and shovels and worked like mad at clearing it up. Eventually, after three quarters of an hour we dragged out the top man, a Corporal, alive. After another ten minutes we reached your brother and his friend. The poor fellows must have been killed instantenously, that is a small consolation. They could not have felt any pain as it was all over at once. I am afraid you will think a letter like this is one of words only. It isn't and I want you to realise how keenly we feel his loss here. He was always a most trusty man, a good, obedient soldier and a true comrade to all the other boys in the platoon. Your brother and thousands of good men like him were fighting for you all in England and since he has made the biggest sacrifice possible please try and carry on the fight he put up.' ROH:- Underbank War Memorial.

MARSHALL, JOHN. Private. No 26942. 1st Battalion Oxford and Bucks. Light Infantry. Born Meltham. Son of Herbert and Alice Maria Marshall, Windy Bank, Meltham. Died of dysentery in Mesopotamia, 30.11.1918, aged 23 years. Buried **BAGHDAD (NORTH GATE) WAR CEMETERY.** Grave location:- Plot 5, Row A, Grave 2. ROH:- St. Bartholomew's Church, Meltham.

MARSHALL, JOSEPH. Private. No 240785 'C' Company, 2/5th Battalion Duke of Wellington's Regiment. Born Cowcliffe Hill, Birkby, 17.7.1897. Son of John H. and Clara Marshall, Rose Cottage, 224 Halifax Old Road, Grimescar, Huddersfield. Employed as a clerk in the warehouse of his Uncle's firm, Messrs Fred Marshall and Company, merchants, St. Peter's Street, Huddersfield. Attended Cowcliffe Wesleyan Chapel. Single. Enlisted November 1914. Reported missing, presumed killed, at the Battle of Bullecourt, 3.5.1917, aged 19 years. Has no known grave. Commemorated **ARRAS MEMORIAL TO THE MISSING.** ROH:- St. John's Church, Birkby; Huddersfield Parish Church; Cowcliffe Wesleyan Church; Huddersfield Drill Hall; Fartown and Birkby War Memorial.

MARSHALL, THOMAS CROSSLEY. Private. No 260058. 1/6th Battalion West Yorkshire Regiment. Formerly No 268332 Duke of

Wellington's Regiment. Born 10 Grant Street, Halifax. Son of Mr and Mrs A. Marshall, 7 Cherry Nook Road, Deighton. Educated at Pellon Lane Board School, Halifax and Deighton Council School. Employed as a cotton twiner by Mr James Ackroyd, cotton doubler, Woodhouse Mills, Deighton. Single. Enlisted 10.10.1916. Killed in action at Laventie, 3.7.1917, aged 29. Buried **LAVENTIE MILITARY CEMETERY.** Grave location:- Plot 1, Row A, Grave 28. ROH:- Christ Church, Woodhouse Hill; Deighton United Methodist Chapel; Deighton War Memorial.

MARSTON, F. Private. No 263011. 1/4th Battalion King's Own Yorkshire Light Infantry. Son of the late Mr S. and Mrs Marston of Holme, Holmfirth. Educated Holme Day School and was also a scholar at the Sunday School. Employed by Messrs Whiteley and Green, Hinchliffe Mill. Enlisted August 1916. Taken prisoner by the Germans on 14.8.1918. Died whilst a Prisoner of War on 21.10.1918, aged 24 years. Buried **GLAGEON COMMUNAL CEMETERY EXTENSION.** Grave location:- Plot 2, Row C, Grave 7. ROH:- Holme and Holmbridge War Memorial.

MARTIN, GEORGE. Private. No S/946. 1st Battalion Royal West Kent Regiment. Born Stone, near Dartford, Kent. Lived Huddersfield. Killed in action, 18.4.1915. Has no known grave. Commemorated **MENIN GATE MEMORIAL TO THE MISSING.**

MARTIN, GEORGE. Company Quartermaster Sergeant. Army Ordnance Corps. Born Bacup, Lancashire, 24.8.1883. Educated Central Higher Grade School, Leeds. Employed as a police sergeant. Married. Lived 3 College Street East, Crosland Moor, Huddersfield. Enlisted as a Private in the A.S.C. on 20.6.1915. Died at home, 3 College Street East, Crosland Moor, on 26.1.1920. ROH:- St. Barnabas Church, Crosland Moor.

MASTERS, ARTHUR. Private. No 11250. 8th Battalion Duke of Wellington's Regiment. Born Toxteth Park, Lancashire. Son of Maria Minnie Masters, 30 Victoria Street, Lockwood, Huddersfield. Died of wounds received at Gallipoli on 27.8.1915, at Malta, aged 29 years. Buried **MALTA NAVAL CEMETERY.** Grave location:- Protestant Plot 276. ROH:- St. Stephen's Church, Rashcliffe.

MATHERS, SYDNEY. Private. No 263025. 2/5th Battalion Duke of Wellington's Regiment. Born Skelmanthorpe. Son of David and Alice Mathers, West End, Skelmanthorpe. Killed in action at the Battle of Bullecourt, 3.5.1917, aged 21 years. Has no known grave. Commemorated **ARRAS MEMORIAL TO THE MISSING.** ROH:- St. Aidan's Church, Skelmanthorpe; Huddersfield Drill Hall.

MATLEY, WILLIE. Private. No 235038. 10th Battalion West Yorkshire Regiment. Born Marsden. Son of Mrs Elizabeth Matley, 2 Mount Royd, Binn Road, Marsden. Employed as a fettler by Messrs Crowther, Bruce and Company Limited. Enlisted November 1916. Embarked for France February, 1917. Killed in action, 23.4.1917, aged 24 years. Has no known grave. Commemorated **ARRAS MEMORIAL TO THE MISSING.** ROH:- Marsden War Memorial.

MATTHEWS, AQUILLA. Private. No 4517. 1/5th Battalion Duke of Wellington's Regiment. Lived Kirkburton. Reported missing, presumed killed, in the attack on the Schwaben Redoubt on 3.9.1916. Has no known grave. Commemorated **THIEPVAL MEMORIAL TO THE MISSING.** ROH:- All Hallows Parish Church, Kirkburton; Huddersfield Drill Hall.

MATTHEWS, ARTHUR. Private. No 205589. 1/6th Battalion Duke of Wellington's Regiment. Born Huddersfield. Lived Quarry Lane, Netherton. Married. Killed in action near Cambrai, 11.10.1918, aged 29 years. Buried **WELLINGTON CEMETERY.** Grave location:- Plot 1, Row F, Grave 2. ROH:- South Crosland and Netherton War Memorial.

MATTHEWS, FRED BURLAND, MM. Lance Sergeant. No 11353. 8th Battalion, transferred to 2nd Battalion, Duke of Wellington's Regiment. Born Bradford. Both parents deceased. Lived with his aunt at 20 Clara Street, Fartown, Huddersfield. Educated at Hillhouse Schools. Employed as a railway carriage cleaner by the Lancashire and Yorkshire Railway Company. Single. Enlisted August 1914. Wounded in the Suvla Bay landing at Gallipoli in August 1915. Awarded the Military Medal on 6.2.1918. The official citation reads, *'No 11353 Corporal Fred Burland Matthews, 2nd Battalion Duke of Wellington's Regiment, at 8.30am on February*

2nd, 1918, during a raid on the enemy trenches east of Monchy-le-Preux. He led his men with great gallantry. He found a German officer and tried to take him prisoner. The Officer resisted and the Corporal after a struggle killed the officer and brought back his pocket book.' Killed in action, 31.8.1918, aged 23 years. Buried **VIS-en-ARTOIS BRITISH CEMETERY.** Grave location:- Plot 1, Row A, Grave 29. ROH:- Fartown and Birkby War Memorial.

MATTHEWS, HAROLD. Private. No 32694. 9th Battalion York and Lancaster Regiment. Formerly No 32629 West Yorkshire Regiment. Born Shepley. Son of George and Harriet Matthews, of Croft Nook, Shepley. Employed as a collier prior to joining the forces. Reported missing, presumed killed, at Passchendaele, 10.10.1917, aged 22 years. Has no known grave. Commemorated **TYNE COT MEMORIAL TO THE MISSING.** ROH:- Shepley War Memorial.

MATTHEWS, JOHN. Private. No 4073. 1/5th Battalion Duke of Wellington's Regiment. Died of wounds at home on 7.8.1916. Buried **LOCKWOOD CEMETERY, HUDDERSFIELD.** Grave location:- C, 'C', 654. ROH:- Huddersfield Drill Hall.

MAUDE, BEN. Gunner. No 117739. 256th Siege Battery, Royal Garrison Artillery. Born Cumberworth. Son of Mrs Mary Maude. Lived Piper House, Cumberworth. Was a widower, with two children. Employed by Mr Harris Wood, quarry owner, of Shepley. Enlisted September 1916. Killed by a shell at the Battle of Arras on 25.4.1917, aged 30 years old. Buried **FEUCHY BRITISH CEMETERY.** Grave location:- Plot 1, Row B, Grave 27. ROH:- New Mill Working Men's Club; Fulstone War Memorial.

MAUDE, HARRY. Private. No 204100. 1/4th Battalion Duke of Wellington's Regiment. Born Hall Ing, Honley, 6.2.1893. Educated Berry Brow Council School. Employed as a dyer's labourer at the Leeds Road Dyeworks, Huddersfield. Husband of Alma Maude, 23 Robin Hood Hill, Berry Brow. Enlisted 6.8.1916. Died of wounds at No 4 Casualty Clearing Station, 10.10.1917, aged 24 years. Buried **DOZINGHEM MILITARY CEMETERY.** Grave location:- Plot 10, Row J, Grave 14. ROH:- Armitage Bridge War Memorial.

MAY, EPHRAIM. Private. No 3040. 1/5th Battalion Duke of Wellington's Regiment. Born Linthwaite. Husband of Eva May, Platt Lane Farm, Dobcross, and formerly of Roydhouse, Linthwaite. Enlisted at the outbreak of the war. Embarked for France in April, 1915. He was with a working party in the trenches when he was killed by shellfire on 23.8.1915, aged 43 years. Has no known grave. Commemorated **MENIN GATE MEMORIAL TO THE MISSING.** ROH:- Linthwaite War Memorial; Huddersfield Drill Hall.

McCABE, THOMAS. Private. No 5632. 2nd Battalion Lancashire Fusiliers. Son of Tom and Kate McCabe of Burnley: husband of Rose McCabe, 23 Albion Street, Huddersfield. Worked as a licensed hawker in Hudderfield. Enlisted 1.9.1914. Died of wounds in a Manchester hospital on 1.11.1916 of shell wounds to the forehead, received in France on 24.5.1915, aged 35 years. Buried **ST. JOSEPH'S ROMAN CATHOLIC CEMETERY, MOSTON, MANCHESTER.** Grave location:- Soldier's Plot 168 (Screen Wall).

McCLUSKY, J. Sergeant. No 241167. 5th Battalion Duke of Wellington's Regiment. Died at home, 6.7.1918. Buried **EDGERTON CEMETERY HUDDERSFIELD.** Grave location:- 60, 126G.

McDERMOTT, CHARLES EDWARD. Private. 11th Battalion Duke of Wellington's Regiment. Born Water Lane, Huddersfield. Educated St. Patrick's Roman Catholic School. Husband of Elizabeth McDermott, 27 Violet Street, Turnbridge, Huddersfield. Employed as a window cleaner. Enlisted 24.8.1914. Died in Huddersfield Royal Infirmary, of pneumonia aggravated by war service, on 1.9.1919.

McDONALD, TOM. Corporal. No 12667. 2/5th Battalion Duke of Wellington's Regiment. Born 10 York Street, Huddersfield, 14.11.1894. Son of John F. and Clara McDonald, 10 York Street, Huddersfield. Educated Huddersfield Parish Church School. Employed as a brass finisher by Messrs J. H. Hopkinson and Company Limited, Birkby. Enlisted September 1914. Killed in action at the Battle of Cambrai, 27.11.1917, aged 23 years. Has no known grave. Commemorated **CAMBRAI MEMORIAL TO THE MISSING.** ROH:- Huddersfield Drill Hall.

McGIFF, WILLIAM. Sapper. No 6429. No 1 Siege Company, Royal Anglesey Royal Engineers. Born Leeds. Son of William McGiff, of Stalybridge, Cheshire. Lodged with Mrs Causfield, 12 Primitive Street, Huddersfield. Enlisted at the outbreak of the war. He was with a working party mending a bridge when he was shot by a sniper on 20.5.1915. Buried **RUE-DAVID MILITARY CEMETERY, FLEURBAIX.** Grave location:- Plot 1, Row H, Grave 4.

McGRATH, MICHAEL. Private. No 45333. 1/5th Battalion Duke of Wellington's Regiment. Born Huddersfield. Husband of Mrs McGrath, 3 Sutcliffe's Yard, Machester Street, Huddersfield. Employed as a stoker at the Huddersfield Corporation Gasworks. Enlisted September 1915. Embarked for France May, 1916. Reported missing, presumed killed, 3.9.1916, in the attack on the Schwaben Redoubt. He was 35 years of age. Has no known grave. Commemorated **THIEPVAL MEMORIAL TO THE MISSING.** ROH:- Huddersfield Drill Hall; Huddersfield Corporation Roll.

McGUIRE, JOHN. Private. No 17078. 12th Battalion West Yorkshire Regiment. Born Louth, Ireland. Lived Huddersfield. Killed in action at the Battle of Loos on 27.9.1915. Has no known grave. Commemorated **LOOS MEMORIAL TO THE MISSING.**

McKEAN, JOHN. Corporal. No 25500. 13th Battalion The Yorkshire Regiment. Born Maxwelltown, Dumfries, Scotland, 2.6.1895. Son of John and Pauline McKean, 14 The Avenue, Moldgreen. Educated Huddersfield Parish Church School. Employed as a dyer's finisher by Messrs James Haigh and Sons, dyers and finishers, Colne Road, Huddersfield. Enlisted November 1915. Killed in action, 22.3.1918. Has no known grave. Commemorated **ARRAS MEMORIAL TO THE MISSING.**

McLINTOCK, ARNOLD. Captain. 1/5th Battalion Duke of Wellington's Regiment. Born Marsden 23.4.1885. Son of the late Doctor McLintock, who was in practice in Marsden, and Mrs M. E. McLintock, 44 Queensborough Terrace, Hyde Park, London. Educated Edinburgh Academy and Bedford Grammar School. Was a partner in the Ramsden Mill Company, Linthwaite. Lived 33 Edgerton Cottages, Huddersfield. Enlisted at the outbreak of the war and was commissioned in October 1914. Embarked for France in April, 1915. Mentioned in Despatches by Field Marshall Sir John French on 1.1.1916 and Sir Douglas Haig on 30.4.1916. Reported missing, presumed killed, in the attack on the Schwaben Redoubt on 3.9.1916, aged 31 years. Buried **MILL ROAD CEMETERY, THIEPVAL.** Grave location:- Plot 13, Row C, Grave 2. ROH:- Holy Trinity Church, Huddersfield; Huddersfield Drill Hall.

McMATH, JAMES. Private. No 14237. 2nd Battalion Duke of Wellington's Regiment. Born Glossop. Lived 60 Station Road, Holmfirth. Married, with two children. Employed by Messrs B. Mellor nad Son, Albert Mill, Holmfirth. A keen football player. Enlisted October 1914. Was wounded in the left hand on 8.10.1916, when his Regiment attacked the village of Le Sars. He was under treatment at Becketts Park Hospital, Leeds, for two months. Killed in action, 18.4.1918, aged 30 years. Has no known grave. Commemorated **LOOS MEMORIAL TO THE MISSING.** ROH:- Holmfirth War Memorial.

McMILLAN, GEORGE HENRY. Sapper. No 61894. 207th Field Company, Royal Engineers. Born 15.11.1892. Son of J. N. and Helen McMillan, 54 Blacker Road, Birkby. Educated St. John's School, Hillhouse. Married. Lived 40 Rose Terrace, Calton Street, Huddersfield. Employed as a joiner and organ builder by Mr John Clarke of Birkby. Enlisted 3.1.1915. Died in 3rd Canadian General Hospital, Boulogne, from influenza on 15.10.1918, aged 26 years. Buried **TERLINCTHUN BRITISH CEMETERY.** Grave location:- Plot 5, Row F, Grave 19. ROH:- Great Northern Street Congregational Chapel; St. John's Church, Birkby; Fartown and Birkby War Memorial.

McNAB, WILLIAM. Private. No S/5975. 11th Battalion Argyll and Sutherland Highlanders. Born Huddersfield 1.4.1885. Son of William McNab, 52 Blackhouse Road, Fartown. Educated Thomas Street Board School. Attended Great Northern Street Congregational Sunday School. Was a cornet player in the Fire Brigade Band. Employed as a brass finisher by Messrs Harland and Wolff in Liverpool. Was secretary of the Friendly and Trades Society's Annual Sing. Enlisted October 1914. Wounded during the

Battle of the Somme on 31.8.1916. Died of wounds at No 2 British Red Cross Hospital, Rouen, on 10.9.1916, aged 31 years. Buried **St. SEVER CEMETERY, ROUEN.** Grave location:- Plot B, Row 25, Grave 22. ROH:- Great Northern Street Congregational Chapel; Fartown and Birkby War Memorial.

McPARTLAND, FRANK. Private. No 1632. 6th Battalion Connaught Rangers. Born County Leitrim, Ireland. Lived Huddersfield. Died of wounds, 17.9.1916. Buried **CORBIE COMMUNAL CEMETERY EXTENSION.** Grave location:- Plot 2, Row D, Grave 25.

McQUILLEN, JOHN. Sergeant. No 3/10905. 2nd Battalion Duke of Wellington's Regiment. Born Halifax. Son of the late Edward and Mary Patience McQuillen. Married. Lived 23 Tenements, Kirkgate, Huddersfield. He had served in the South African War, in which he had been wounded, and was present at the Relief of Ladysmith. Had served for 12 years in the 3rd Battalion Manchester Regiment. Was then placed on the Reserve and during this time (about six years) had worked as a labourer for Mr Thomas, contractor, of Huddersfield. Was called up on the outbreak of war. Sustained a gunshot wound in the head, which required an operation. Died of wounds at No 8 General Hospital, Boisguillaume, on 13.6.1915, aged 34 years. Buried **BOISGUILLAUME COMMUNAL CEMETERY.** Grave location:- Plot 1, Row B, Grave 12a.

McSHANE, JAMES. Private. No 12519. 4th Battalion The King's (Liverpool Regiment). Born Stockton-on-Tees. Husband of Sarah Elizabeth McShane, 4 Love's Yard, High Street, Huddersfield. Killed in action, 27.4.1915, aged 33 years. Has no known grave. Commemorated **MENIN GATE MEMORIAL TO THE MISSING.**

McVEAGH, CHARLES C. Private. No 6525. 2nd Battalion Duke of Wellington's Regiment. Born Derby 8.9.1877. Educated Spring Grove Board School. Husband of Isabel McVeagh, 37 Clement Street, Birkby. Employed as a tram conductor by the Huddersfield Corporation Tramways Department. Was a Reservist and was called up at the outbreak of the war. Reported missing at the first battle of Ypres, 8.11.1914, and was presumed dead six months later. Has no known grave. Commemorated **MENIN GATE MEMORIAL TO THE MISSING.** ROH:- Fartown and Birkby War Memorial; Huddersfield Corporation Roll.

MEAD, ERNEST JOHN. Sergeant. No L/2061. 'A' Battery, 148th Brigade Royal Field Artillery. Born London. Son of J. W. Mead, Manor Park, London. Educated at London schools. Husband of Alice Mead, 34 Lea Street, Lindley, Huddersfield. Employed as a traveller. Died of wounds, 8.10.1916, aged 32 years. Buried **A.I.F. BURIAL GROUND, FLERS.** Grave location:- Plot 2, Row E, Grave 10.

MEAKIN, A. HERBERT. Gunner. No 26735. 75th Battery, Royal Field Artillery. Born Nottingham. Lived 1 Bankend, Heath House, Golcar. Married, with one child. Employed as a fettler by Messrs George Whiteley, of Linthwaite. Was a Reservist with only three months to serve when the war broke out. Killed in action, 24.4.1915, aged 32 years. Has no known grave. Commemorated **MENIN GATE MEMORIAL TO THE MISSING.** ROH:- St. John's Church, Golcar.

MEDLEY, BENJAMIN. Lance Corporal. No 16438. 2nd Battalion Duke of Wellington's Regiment. Son of Mr J. Medley, 128 Rashcliffe Hill Road, Huddersfield. Employed as an apprentice at Messrs Wheatley, Dyson Limited. Attended Buxton Road Sunday School. Enlisted 27.8.1914. Embarked for France on 29.4.1915. Died from the effects of gas received at Hill 60, a week later, on 5.5.1915. He was 19 years of age. Buried **DIVISIONAL CEMETERY, DICKEBUSCH ROAD, VLAMERTINGHE, BELGIUM.** Grave location:- Row B, Grave 4. ROH:- St. Stephen's Church, Rashcliffe.

MEDLEY, ERNEST. Rifleman. No R/19535. 2nd Battalion King's Royal Rifle Corps. Born Bay Hall, Huddersfield, 30.5.1884. Son of Joseph and Eliza Medley, 4 Hillside Avenue, Fartown. Educated Hillhouse Board School. Employed as a cloth finisher. Single. Enlisted 14.2.1916. Killed in action, 20.8.1916, aged 33 years. Has no known grave. Commemorated **THIEPVAL MEMORIAL TO THE MISSING.** ROH:- Christ Church, Woodhouse Hill; Fartown and Birkby War Memorial.

MEDLEY, GEORGE FREDERICK. Rifleman. No C/7655. 20th Battalion King's Royal Rifle Corps. Born Dalton 4.5.1893. Only son of Mr and Mrs Harry Medley, High Royd, Dalton. Educated Almondbury Grammar School and Huddersfield Technical College, where he was awarded the Silver Medal for textile design in the City and Guilds of London Institute examinations. Employed as a commercial traveller for Messrs Moorhouse and Brook Limited, woollen manufacturers. Enlisted 1915. Wounded, 19.8.1916, near Guillemont during the Battle of the Somme. Killed by shellfire when entering trenches at Locon near Bethune at 10.15pm on 30.5.1918, aged 25 years. Buried **CHOCQUES MILITARY CEMETERY.** Grave location:- Plot 3, Row A, Grave 23. ROH:- Almondbury Grammar School St. Andrew's Church; Christ Church, Moldgreen.

MELLOR, ALFRED. Private. No 242926. 2/5th Battalion Duke of Wellington's Regiment. Born South Crosland. Lived Netherton. Killed in action near Rheims, 22.7.1918. Has no known grave. Commemorated **SOISSONS MEMORIAL TO THE MISSING.** ROH:- South Crosland and Netherton; Huddersfield Drill Hall.

MELLOR, ARTHUR. Private. No 241610. 2/5th Battalion Duke of Wellington's Regiment. Born Hepworth. Son of Joshua and Annis Mellor of Dean Bridge Farm, Hepworth. Employed as a miner by Messrs Tinker Brothers, Wood Pit, Hepworth, and by Messrs J. and J. W. Longbottom, Bridge Foundry, Holmfirth. Was well known in the Holmfirth district as a gymnast. Enlisted 13.3.1916. Reported missing, presumed killed, at the Battle of Bullecourt, 3.5.1917, aged 23 years. Has no known grave. Commemorated **ARRAS MEMORIAL TO THE MISSING.** (Brother of Private **LINDLEY MELLOR**, died of wounds, 25.12.1916, q.v.). ROH:- Hepworth and Scholes War Memorial; Hepworth Parish Church; Huddersfield Drill Hall.

MELLOR, BENJAMIN. Private. No 42367. 3rd Battalion Worcestershire Regiment. Born Shepley. Son of Jonas and Frances Mellor, of Yew Tree Cottages, Shepley. Employed by Messrs Johnsons, of Moldgreen, Died of dysentery as a Prisoner of War, 15.10.1918, aged 20 years. Buried **WORMS (HOCHEIM HILL) CEMETERY, GERMANY.** (The names are carved on a screen wall in the Allied Plot). ROH:- Shepley War Memorial.

MELLOR, CLEMENT. Private. No 242101. 1/5th Battalion Duke of Wellington's Regiment. Born Honley, Huddersfield. Son of Mrs Mellor, Springwood Terrace, Netherton. Employed by Messrs Walter Sykes Limited, Zetland Mills, Huddersfield. Enlisted at Easter 1916. Reported missing, 3.9.1916, in the attack on the Schwaben Redoubt and afterwards presumed to have been killed on that date. Has no known grave. Commemorated **THIEPVAL MEMORIAL TO THE MISSING.** ROH:- South Crosland and Netherton War Memorial; Huddersfield Drill Hall.

MELLOR, CYRIL RHODES. Lance Corporal. No 307644. 1/7th Battalion Duke of Wellington's Regiment. Born Honley, Huddersfield. Son of Mr and Mrs Hallas Mellor, Far End, Honley. Was the first drummer in Honley Civilian Bugle Band. Whilst under age volunteered for active service. Had been twice gassed. Was one of 12 volunteers to rush an enemy's post in broad daylight but was shot down by a machine gun within four yards of the objective. Killed in action, 4.7.1918, aged 37 years. Has no known grave. Commemorated **TYNE COT MEMORIAL TO THE MISSING.** ROH:- Huddersfield Drill Hall; Honley War Memorial.

MELLOR, GEORGE. Private. No 20377. 2nd Battalion Duke of Wellington's Regiment. Born South Crosland. Eldest son of Mr and Mrs Benson Mellor, Bethel Buildings, Netherton. Employed by Messrs John Wrigley and Sons, Cockin Steps Mill. Killed in action, 30.8.1918, aged 29 years. Buried **DURY CRUCIFIX CEMETERY.** Grave location:- Plot 2, Row D, Grave 33.

MELLOR, GEORGE ALBERT. Private. No 29/631. 12/13th Battalion Northumberland Fusiliers. Born Upperthong, Holmfirth. Son of Sandy and Rose Emma Mellor, The Victoria Inn, Holmfirth. Educated at St. John's Day School and Sunday School and was a member of the bible class. Served his apprenticeship with Messrs Haigh Brothers, plasterers and concreters, of Holmfirth. Was a member of the Cartworth Moor Cricket Club and the St. John's football club. Enlisted May 1916. Embarked for France after fourteen weeks training. Wounded twice and gassed once. Killed in action, 8.10.1918, aged 31 years. Buried **PROSPECT HILL CEMETERY, GOUY.** Grave location:- Plot 4, Row F, Grave 7. ROH:- Upperthong War Memorial.

MELLOR, HERBERT. Private. No 242818. 'D' Company, 1/7th Battalion Duke of Wellington's Regiment. Born Linthwaite. Son of Henry Mellor of Slaithwaite. Husband of Eva Mellor, 11 Hollins Glen, Slaithwaite. Killed in action, 25.4.1918, aged 35 years. Buried **POPERINGHE NEW MILITARY CEMETERY.** Grave location:- Plot 2, Row K, Grave 5. ROH:- St. James Church, Slaithwaite; Slaithwaite War Memorial; Linthwaite War Memorial; Milnsbridge War Memorial; Huddersfield Drill Hall.

MELLOR, IRVING. Private. No 20125. 2nd Battalion Duke of Wellington's Regiment. Born Holmfirth. Son of Mr and Mrs Wilson Mellor, Carr Lane, Flush House, Holmfirth. Educated Hall School. Employed firstly at Dover Mills and then at Clarence Mills, Holmbridge. Engaged to Miss Mary Jane Hirst, Lower Netherhouse, Upperthong. Enlisted April 1916. After being in France for 12 weeks he died of illness at No 39 Casualty Clearing Station on 19.10.1916, aged 28 years. Buried **ALLONVILLE COMMUNAL CEMETERY.** Grave location:- Row A, Grave 21. ROH:- Holme and Holmbridge War Memorial.

MELLOR, JAMES EDWARD. Private. No 242024. 1/5th Battalion Duke of Wellington's Regiment. Born Holmfirth. Son of James Mellor, 8 Flush House, Holmfirth. Educated Hall School. Played the cornet in the Holme Brass Band. Employed as a piecer at Yew Tree Mills. Killed in action, aged 20, on 3.9.1916 in the attack on the Schwaben Redoubt. Has no known grave. Commemorated **THIEPVAL MEMORIAL TO THE MISSING.** ROH:- Holme and Holmbridge War Memorial; Huddersfield Drill Hall.

MELLOR, JOE. Private. No 143316. 17th Battalion Machine Gun Corps. Formerly No 4237 Duke of Wellington's Regiment. Son of Mr and Mrs J. R. Mellor, 13 North Street, Lockwood, Huddersfield. Employed by Messrs Hirst and Mallinson, Longwood. Attended Lockwood Church Sunday School. Enlisted July 1915. Was wounded on 3.9.1916 and again in November, 1917. Died of wounds, 3.4.1918, aged 21 years. Buried **DOULLENS COMMUNAL CEMETERY EXTENSION No 1.** Grave location:- Plot 6, Row E, Grave 4. ROH:- Emmanuel Church, Lockwood.

MELLOR, JOE. Private. No 29062. 1st Battalion East Yorkshire Regiment. Born Golcar. Son of Mr and Mrs Sam Mellor, New York Farm, Stainland and formerly of Paddock. Employed in the finishing department of Messrs Hirst and Mallinson Limited, Longwood. Died of wounds at No 11 Casualty Clearing Station on 10.10.1917, aged 19 years. Buried **GODEWAERSVELDE BRITISH CEMETERY.** Grave location:- Plot 1, Row H, Grave 16.

MELLOR, JOSEPH. Private. No 22237. 2/4th Battalion Duke of Wellington's Regiment. Born Holmfirth. Son of the late Mr and Mrs Friend Mellor, Hill Top, Underbank, Holmfirth. Educated Holmfirth National School. Attended the Underbank Wesleyan Sunday School. Employed as a millhand by Mr John Woodhead, Albion Mills, Thongsbridge. Lodged with Mrs P. Lee, Underbank Old Road. Enlisted April 1917. After nine months training embarked for France. Killed in action near Rheims on 20.7.1918, aged 19 years. Buried **MARFAUX BRITISH CEMETERY.** Grave location:- Plot 2, Row C, Grave 7. ROH:- Underbank War Memorial.

MELLOR, LEWIS. Private. No DM2/171315. Army Service Corps, (Motor Transport), attached 206th Siege Battery, Royal Garrison Artillery. Born Linthwaite. Lived Hazlegrove, Lowerhouses, Linthwaite. Attended Linthwaite Parish Church. Employed as a weaver by Messrs Crowther Brothers, Stanley Mills, Milnsbridge. Was a keen cricketer, having played cricket for both the Broad Oak and Linthwaite Cricket Clubs. For four seasons he was the Saturday professional for Birstall Cricket Club. Enlisted 3.5.1916. *He suffered severe burns on the night of 21.8.1917 as the result of an accidental explosion of a petrol tank of a motor lorry. The accident took place when Mellor and his mate were preparing to retire for the night. It was their custom to sleep on the lorry and were undressing when the tank exploded. They were immediately enveloped in flames and Mellor was severely burned on the arms, legs and one side. He was admitted to hospital at Boulogne but died two days later from shock.* Buried **WIMEREUX COMMUNAL CEMETERY.** Grave location:- Plot 2, Row R, Grave 5. ROH:- Linthwaite War Memorial.

MELLOR, LEWIS. Corporal. No 31268. 'A' Company, 2nd Battalion Duke of Wellington's Regiment. Born Castle Hill, Huddersfield. Son of Paul and Elizabeth Mellor, 'Blagden', Close Hill, Lockwood. Husband of Florence Alberta Mellor, of Martin Nest, Netherton. Prior to enlistment, was in business as a butcher in Lidget Street, Lindley. Died of wounds at Etaples Base Hospital, 31.3.1918, aged 26 years. Buried **ETAPLES MILITARY CEMETERY.** Grave location: Plot 33, Row B, Grave 15a. ROH:- South Crosland and Netherton War Memorial.

MELLOR, LINDLEY. Private. No 450. 17th Battalion West Yorkshire Regiment (2nd Leeds Pals). Born Holmfirth. Son of Joshua and Annis Mellor, of Deanbridge, Hepworth, Holmfirth. He had tried to enlist on two occasions but had been rejected on account of his height. He was successful at the third attempt and enlisted in the West Yorkshire Bantam battalion as soon as it was formed on 19.12.1914. Embarked for France 20.1.1916. Died of wounds at No 41 Casualty Clearing Station on 5.12.1916, aged 30 years. Buried **WANQUETIN COMMUNAL CEMETERY EXTENSION.** Grave location:- Plot 1, Row A, Grave 5. (Brother of Private **ARTHUR MELLOR,** reported missing. 3.5.1917. q.v.). ROH:- Hepworth and Scholes War Memorial; Hepworth Parish Church.

MELLOR, LUTHER. Private. No 46117. 23rd (Tyneside Scottish) Battalion Northumberland Fusiliers. Born Burnlee, Holmfirth. Son of the late Sam and Mrs Mellor, of Underbank. Husband of Ellen Mellor, of Sinking Wood, New Mill, Huddersfield. Educated Parkhead Day School. Attended Underbank Wesleyan Sunday School. Was a member of the Underbank football club and the Holmfirth Cricket and Athletic club. Employed by Messrs Kaye and Stewart, of Lockwood. Enlisted in the summer of 1916. Whilst in training he came home and married a local girl. Embarked for France 1.1.1917. Killed in action at Passchendaele, 18.10.1917, aged 33 years. Has no known grave. Commemorated **TYNE COT MEMORIAL TO THE MISSING.** ROH:- Underbank War Memorial.

MELLOR, NOBLE. Private. No S/8591. 7th Battalion Seaforth Highlanders. Born Lockwood, Huddersfield. Lived 37 Waterside, Lockwood. Employed as a grocer's assistant at the Primrose Hill branch of the Huddersfield Industrial Society. Attended Emmanuel Church, Lockwood and Sunday School. Was a member of the Lockwood Liberal Club, where he was a keen billiard player. Enlisted Whit Wednesday 1915. Trained at Cromarty, Scotland. Had been in France 14 days when he was killed in action, 12.10.1915, aged 24 years. Has no known grave. Commemorated **MENIN GATE MEMORIAL TO THE MISSING.** ROH:- Emmanuel Church, Lockwood.

MELLOR, NORMAN. Private. No 31720. 13th Battalion York and Lancaster Regiment (1st Barnsley Pals). Formerly No 7974 Duke of Wellington's Regiment. Son of Benson and Mary Jane Mellor, of Netherton. Husband of Emily Mellor, Stone Pit Hill, Netherton. Employed as a cloth finisher by Messrs J. Wrigley and Sons, of Netherton. Killed in action at Gavrelle during the Battle of Arras on 11.5.1917, aged 25 years. Buried **ORCHARD DUMP CEMETERY.** Grave location:- Plot 5, Row G, Grave 6. ROH:- South Crosland and Netherton War Memorial.

MELLOR, STANLEY. Private. No 242012. 2/7th Battalion Duke of Wellington's Regiment. Son of Willie and A. M. Mellor, 22 Hill Top, Salendine Nook, Huddersfield. Wounded at the Battle of Bullecourt, 3.5.1917. Killed in action, 15.4.1918, aged 21 years. Buried **GOMMECOURT BRITISH CEMETERY No 2.** Grave location:- Plot 5, Row J, Grave 1. ROH:- Huddersfield Drill Hall.

MELLOR, WILLIAM. Private. No 21504. 10th Battalion Duke of Wellington's Regiment. Born Linthwaite. Son of Mr and Mrs H. Mellor, 36 Whiteley Street, Milnsbridge. Employed as a weaver by Messrs T. Calverley and Sons, Milnsbridge. Died of bronchial-pneumonia, in Italy, on 26.10.1918, aged 23 years. Buried **CREMONA TOWN CEMETERY, ITALY.** Grave location:- Row C, Grave 13. ROH:- Linthwaite War Memorial.

MENZIES, JAMES VEITCH. Private. No 12049. 2nd Battalion Highland Light Infantry. Born Edinburgh. Son of Duncan Menzies, 55a Ravensknowle Road, Dalton, and the late Jane Menzies. Killed in action during the Battle of the Aisne on 17.9.1914, aged 19 years. Has no known grave. Commemorated **LA FERTE-SOUS-JOUARRE MEMORIAL TO THE MISSING.**

MESSENGER, HAROLD. Ordinary Seaman. No J/61859 (PO). HMS *Victory*. Born Honley. Son of Mr John Messenger, Cooperative Terrace, Honley. Employed by the Refuge Assurance Society at Huddersfield. Attended Moorbottom Congregational Church. Was a keen cricketer. Enlisted in the Navy in November, 1916 and was stationed at Portsmouth. Came home on leave on Friday, 16.12.1916. Died of meningitis on 20.12.1916, aged 21 years. Buried **HONLEY CHURCH BURIAL GROUND**. Grave location:- 62, 550. ROH:- Honley War Memorial.

METTRICK, ARTHUR. Private. No 270061. 2nd Battalion West Yorkshire Regiment. Born Holmbridge, Holmfirth. Son of the late Mr and Mrs Jonas Mettrick, Digley Royd, Holmbridge. Husband of Mrs Mettrick, 38 Brownhill Lane, Holmbridge. Educated Field End School, Holmbridge. Attended St David's Church and Sunday School and was a member of the choir for 16 years. Employed as a weaver by Messrs W. H. Barber, Clarence Mills, Holmbridge. Enlisted April 1917. Embarked for France in July, 1917. Died as a Prisoner of War on 27.5.1918, aged 31 years. Buried **SISSONNE BRITISH CEMETERY**. Grave location:- Row C, Grave 11. (Brother of Private **FRANK METTRICK**, died of wounds, 28.9.1817, q.v.). ROH:- Holme and Holmbridge War Memorial.

METTRICK, ERNEST. Private. No 235211. 2nd Battalion Duke of Wellington's Regiment. Born Oakes 19.5.1888. Son of Robert and Sarah H. Mettrick, 22 Oakes Road, Lindley. Educated Oakes Council School. Attended the Thorncliffe Street (Lindley) Wesleyan Church, where he was a member of the choir. Employed by Messrs B. Crosland and Sons of Oakes. Married, with one child. Enlisted 30.11.1916. Came home on leave at the beginning of March 1918. Returned to France and was reported missing, presumed killed, on 28.3.1918. Has no known grave. Commemorated **ARRAS MEMORIAL TO THE MISSING**. (Brother of Private **SYKES METTRICK**, reported missing, 10.4.1917, q.v.). ROH:- St. Stephen's Church, Lindley.

METTRICK, FRANK. Private. No 242019. 2/5th Battalion Leicestershire Regiment. Formerly No 2762 Duke of Wellington's Regiment. Born Holmbridge. Son of the late Mr and Mrs Jonas Mettrick, Digley Royd, Holmbridge. Employed by Messrs W. H. and J. Barber, Clarence Mills, Holmbridge. Enlisted 7.12.1916. Embarked for France in February, 1917. Died of wounds at No 46 Casualty Clearing Station, 28.9.1917, aged 20 years. Buried **MENDINGHEM BRITISH CEMETERY**. Grave location:- Plot 6, Row F, Grave 8. (Brother of Private **ARTHUR METTRICK**, who died as a Prisoner of War on 27.5.1918, q.v.). ROH:- Holme and Holmbridge War Memorial.

METTRICK, SYKES. Private. No 235206. 2/7th Battalion West Yorkshire Regiment. Born Quarmby, Huddersfield, 4.11.1883. Son of Robert and Sarah Hannah Mettrick, 22 Oakes Road, Lindley. Educated Oakes Council School. Employed as a weaver by Messrs Martin Sons and Company, of Lindley. Was a member of the Thorncliffe Street (Lindley) Wesleyan choir. Married. Lived 104 Rock View, Quarmby Road, Huddersfield. Enlisted 22.11.1916. Reported missing on Easter Tuesday, 10.4.1917, at the Battle of Arras and afterwards presumed to have been killed on that date. Has no known grave. Commemorated **ARRAS MEMORIAL TO THE MISSING**. (Brother of Private **ERNEST METTRICK**, killed in action, 28.3.1918, q.v.). ROH:- St. Stephen's Church, Lindley.

MICKLETHWAITE, ARTHUR. Private. No 2083. 1/5th Battalion Duke of Wellington's Regiment. Born Kirkheaton. Enlisted at the outbreak of the war. Embarked for France in April, 1915. Killed in action 9.5.1915. Buried **RUE-DAVID MILITARY CEMETERY**. Grave location:- Plot 1, Row H, Grave 30.

MICKELTHWAITE, CLEVELAND. Private. No 203142. 1/4th Battalion Duke of Wellington's Regiment. Born Milnsbridge. Lived Marsh. Died 26.10.1918. Buried **ETAPLES MILITARY CEMETERY**. Grave location:- Plot 67, Row M, Grave 1. (Brother of Private **RICHMOND MICKELTHWAITE**, killed in action, 31.7.1917, q.v.). ROH:- St. Mark's Parish Church, Longwood; All Saints Church, Paddock; Longwood War Memorial; Huddersfield Corporation Roll.

MICKLETHWAITE, FRANK. Rifleman. No C/7426. 18th Battalion King's Royal Rifle Corps. Born Kirkburton, Huddersfield. Son of Arthur and Ellen Micklethwaite, North Road, Kirkburton. Employed by Messrs John Kaye and

Sons, Kings Mill, Huddersfield. Killed in action, 28.7.1916, aged 23 years. Buried **BERKSHIRE CEMETERY EXTENSION, PLOEGSTREET, BELGIUM.** Grave location:- Row G, Grave 11. His father received a letter from Captain Lester who wrote that, *'Rifleman Micklethwaite was returning from a listening post when he was killed. He had nearly reached the parapet when he was struck by a stray bullet which entered the left side and reached the heart'.* ROH:- All Hallows Parish Church, Kirkburton.

MICKLETHWAITE, GEORGE WILLIAM. Gunner. No 122953. 19th Forth Fire Command Royal Garrison Artillery. Died at home, 20.11.1918, aged 37 years. Buried **HONLEY CHURCH BURIAL GROUND.** Grave location:- 122, 4622. ROH:- Honley War Memorial.

MICKLETHWAITE, RICHMOND. Private. No 260106. 2nd Battalion The Yorkshire Regiment. Born Huddersfield. Killed in action, 31.7.1917. Has no known grave. Commemorated **MENIN GATE MEMORIAL TO THE MISSING.** (Brother of Private **CLEVELAND MICKLETHWAITE**, died 26.10.1918, q.v.). ROH:- Longwood War Memorial; St. Mark's Parish Church.

MIDDLETON, ELVEY. Private. No 19034. 9th Battalion King's Own Yorkshire Light Infantry. Born Marsh, Huddersfield. Son of Mr and Mrs R. Middleton of Bowling, Bradford, and formerly of 6 Cecil Street, Springwood, Huddersfield. Employed by Mr Whitehead, butcher, of Birkby. Killed in action on the first day of the Battle of the Somme, 1.7.1916. Buried **GORDON DUMP CEMETERY.** Grave location:- Plot 3, Row R, Grave 7. ROH:- Marsh War Memorial.

MIDDLETON, FRANCIS MELLOR. Private. No 23913. 8th Battalion Duke of Wellington's Regiment. Born Mossley 28.9.1885. Educated Wyre Street School, Mossley. Married, with four children. Lived Back Firth Street, Lockwood. Enlisted 5.9.1914. Embarked for France in April, 1915. Killed in action at Passchendaele on 9.10.1917. Has no known grave. Commemorated **TYNE COT MEMORIAL TO THE MISSING.** ROH:- St. Stephen's Church, Rashcliffe.

MIDDLETON, TOM. Private. No PLY/4342 (RMR/A/778. Royal Marine Light Infantry. *HMS Goliath.* Son of Christopher and Betsy Middleton. Brother of Mr W. Middleton, 35 Midland Street, Huddersfield. Employed as a labourer by the London and North Western Railway Company. Killed in an action with a Turkish destroyer in the Dardenelles on 13.5.1915, aged 45 years. Has no known grave. Commemorated **PLYMOUTH NAVAL MEMORIAL TO THE MISSING.** ROH:- London and North Western Railway Company Roll.

MILAN, SPENCER WALTON. Gunner. No 146434. 1st Reserve Brigade Royal Field Artillery. Born Lockwood 31.12.1898. Son of Mr G. F. Milan, 173 Victoria Road, Lockwood. Educated Mount Street Board School. Attended Rashcliffe United Methodist Sunday School and was a member of the senior bible class. Employed as an apprentice electrician by Mr Guy Laycock, of Cloth Hall Street, Huddersfield. Single. Enlisted 13.5.1916. Was in training at Forest Row, Sussex, when he was kicked by a horse on 4.6.1916. Died of pneumonia in hospital at Brighton on 10.7.1916, aged 18 years. Buried with full miliitary honours in **EDGERTON CEMETERY, HUDDERSFIELD.** Grave location:- 54, 157. ROH:- Rashcliffe United Methodist Church; Emmanuel Church, Lockwood; Mount Pleasant Chapel, Lockwood.

MILLER, ROBERT. Sapper. No 104318. 227th Field Company Royal Engineers. Born Huddersfield 16.4.1879. Son of John and Anne Miller, 23 Lily Street, St. Andrew's Road, Huddersfield. Educated Thomas Street Board School. Employed as a plasterer. Married. Enlisted August 1915. Wounded at La Bassee on 13.5.1916. Died of wounds at No 13 Stationary Hospital, Boulogne, on 20.5.1916, aged 37 years. Buried **BOULOGNE EASTERN CEMETERY.** Grave location:- Plot 8, Row A, Grave 113.

MILLS, WILLIE. Private. No 816. 1/7th Battalion Royal Welsh Fusiliers. Born Newtown, Montgomery. Lived Huddersfield. Single. Wounded at Gallipoli 10.8.1915. Died of wounds on board ship, 16.8.1915. Buried **EAST MUDROS MILITARY CEMETERY, LEMNOS, GREECE.** Grave location:- Plot 2, Row E, Grave 82. ROH:- Huddersfield Salvation Army Citadel.

MILNER, GEORGE SPENCER. Private. No 53196. 1st Battalion Lincolnshire Regiment. Born Blackley, Elland. Son of Mr and Mrs F. Milner, 4 Weatherhill Road, Lindley, Huddersfield. Killed in action, 25.8.1918. Buried **ADANAC MILITARY CEMETERY**. Grave location:- Plot 1, Row H, Grave 4.

MILNES, FRANK. Private. No 211799. 21st Battalion West Yorkshire Regiment. Born Huddersfield. Lived 79 Hillhouse Lane, Huddersfield. Died of wounds 28.6.1917. Buried **DUNKIRK TOWN CEMETERY**. Grave location:- Plot 1, Row A. Grave 7. ROH:- St. Andrew's Church, Leeds Road; Fartown and Birkby War Memorial.

MILNES, FRANK. Private. No 203083. 2/4th Battalion Duke of Wellington's Regiment. Born Linthwaite. Son of Thomas and Sarah Jane Milnes, Varley Road, Slaithwaite. Husband of Beatrice Milnes. Attended Slaithwaite Wesleyan Church and was a member of the Young Men's Class. Was a member of the Slaithwaite Conservative Club and also of the Independent Order of Rechabites. Employed as a mason by Messrs Eglans Limited and, formerly, with Messrs John Milnes and Sons, builders and contractors. Enlisted 24.6.1916. Was in training at Clipstone Camp when he died in the Military hospital, following an operation for appendicitis, after a week's illness, on 13.4.1917, aged 26 years. A service was held at Slaithwaite Wesleyan Church, with modified military honours at the family's request, only a bearer party attended, followed by burial in **SLAITHWAITE CEMETERY**. Grave location:- A, 4, 3. ROH:- Linthwaite War Memorial; St. James Church, Slaithwaite; Slaithwaite War Memorial.

MILNES, HAROLD. Private. No 36118. 1/4th Battalion King's Own Yorkshire Light Infantry. Born Blacker Road, Birkby, 9.7.1898. Son of Herbert and Sarah Ann Milnes, 61 Blacker Road, Birkby. Educated Hillhouse Church of England School and Higher Elementary School. Employed in his father's business of Messrs Milnes and Garside, sanitary and chemical plumbers, of Upperhead Row, Huddersfield. Was a playing member of the Netheroyd Hill cricket and football teams and was a member of the Netheroyd Hill Church and Sunday School. Single. Enlisted March 1917. Killed in action at Neuve Eglise, 13.4.1918, aged 19 years. Has no known grave. Commemorated **TYNE COT MEMORIAL TO THE MISSING**. ROH:- Netheroyd Hill Methodist Church; Fartown and Birkby War Memorial.

MILNES, HARRY. Private. No 306997. 2/7th Battalion Duke of Wellington's Regiment. Born Lindley 15.7.1888. Educated Oakes Board School. Employed as a labourer. At the time of enlistment, was living at Lea Green, Holywell Green, Halifax. Single. Enlisted 28.3.1916. Wounded at Bullecourt on 17.4.1917. Died of wounds at No 74a Lidget Street, Lindley, on 12.9.1920. Buried **EDGERTON CEMETERY, HUDDERSFIELD**. Grave location:- Screen Wall. ROH:- St. Stephen's Church, Lindley; Huddersfield Drill Hall.

MILNES, HARRY. Gunner. No 77883. 253rd Siege Battery, Royal Garrison Artillery. Born Huddersfield. Son of Mr and Mrs Tom Milnes, 77 Britannia Road, Milnsbridge. Employed in the finishing department at Scar Bottom Mills, Milnsbridge. Attended Milnsbridge Wesleyan Church and Sunday School. Accidentally killed in France, 17.9.1918, aged 22. *He was sleeping in a tent on the night of the 16th/17th September during a very heavy thunderstorm when a tree nearby was struck by lightning and fell, hitting him in the neck and causing instantenous death.* Buried **ROCQUIGNY-EQUANCOURT ROAD BRITISH CEMETERY**. Grave location:- Plot 1, Row A, Grave 8. ROH:- Longwood War Memorial; Huddersfield Mission, Milnsbridge.

MILNES, HARRY. Lance Corporal. No 29/633. 12th/13th Battalion Northumberland Fusiliers. (Machine gun section). Born Huddersfield. Youngest son of the late Mr and Mrs George Milnes. Lived with his sister at 63 Leymoor Road, Golcar. Employed in the finishing department at Messrs C. and J. Hirst and Sons Limited, Longwood. Attended Golcar Baptist Church. Enlisted May 1916. Embarked for France in August, 1916. Killed in action at Passchendaele, 4.10.1917, aged 28 years. Has no known grave. Commemorated **TYNE COT MEMORIAL TO THE MISSING**. ROH:- St. John's Church, Golcar; Golcar Baptist Church.

MILNES, HARRY. Private. No 240401. 1/5th Battalion York and Lancaster Regiment. Son of

Charles Henry Milnes, 23 Lowergate, Paddock. Killed in action at Passchendaele, 9.10.1917, aged 20 years. Has no known grave. Commemorated **TYNE COT MEMORIAL TO THE MISSING.**

MILNES, HERBERT. Private. No 241825. 2/5th Battalion Duke of Wellington's Regiment. Born Almondbury. Son of J. and Edith Milnes, 113a Watercroft, Almondbury. Educated Almondbury Council School. Employed as a builder's labourer by British Dyes Limited. Single. Enlisted 24.3.1916. Reported missing, presumed killed, at the Battle of Bullecourt, 3.5.1917. Has no known grave. Commemorated **ARRAS MEMORIAL TO THE MISSING.** ROH:- Huddersfield Drill Hall; Almondbury War Memorial.

MILNES, HERBERT. Private. No 696169. 31st Battalion Canadian Infantry (Alberta Regiment). Son of William and Alice Milnes, of Denby, Huddersfield. Died of wounds at No 24 General Hospital, 2.12.1917, aged 39 years. Buried **ETAPLES MILITARY CEMETERY.** Grave location:- Plot 31, Row A, Grave 20.

MILNES, JOHN. Private. No 5576. 1/7th Battalion Duke of Wellington's Regiment. Born Gilead Road, Longwood. Lived with his married sister, Mrs Annie Elizabeth Worsley, at 15 Hill Top, Lindley. Educated Goitfield Board School, Longwood, and at Crow Lane Board School, Milnsbridge. Employed as a warper's overlooker by Messrs C. and J. Hirst of Longwood. Attended Salendine Nook Baptist Chapel and Sunday School. Single. Enlisted 16.2.1916. Embarked for France in August 1916. Killed in action in the attack on the Schwaben Redoubt, 3.9.1916, aged 21 years. Has no known grave. Commemorated **THIEPVAL MEMORIAL TO THE MISSING.** ROH:- Salendine Nook Baptist Church; Crow Lane Board School, Milnsbridge; Huddersfield Drill Hall.

MILNES, JOHN R. Private. No 241407. 'B' Company, 2/5th Battalion Duke of Wellington's Regiment. Born 31 Royds Hall, Longwood Road, Huddersfield. Son of James Henry and Annie Milnes. Educated Paddock Council School. Attended Paddock Wesleyan Church. Employed as a woollen weaver. Enlisted 12.12.1915. Killed in action on 5.11.1918 at Frasnoy near Mons. He was 23 years of age. Buried **FRASNOY COMMUNAL CEMETERY.** Grave location:- Row A, Grave 7, ROH:- St. Mark's Parish Church, Longwood; Huddersfield Drill Hall.

MILNES, JOSEPH. Private. No 29497. 9th Battalion Duke of Wellington's Regiment. Born Kirkburton 25.12.1883. Son of Mrs Milnes, 7 Wood Top, Primrose Hill, Huddersfield. Educated Almondbury Board School. Employed as a painter and decorator by Mr S. Kendall, Bryam Street, Huddersfield. Married, with one child. Lived 27 Manchester Road, Huddersfield. Enlisted September 1916. Wounded in the abdomen, 12.7.1918. Died of wounds at No 3 Casualty Clearing Station on 12.7.1918. Buried **GEZAINCOURT COMMUNAL CEMETERY EXTENSION.** Grave location:- Plot 2, Row N, Grave 15. ROH:- All Hallows Parish Church, Kirkburton.

MILNES, STANLEY. Lance Corporal. No 5/3407. 1/5th Battalion Duke of Wellington's Regiment. Born Milnes Fold, Almondbury Bank, Almondbury, 17.8.1896. Son of Mary Ormerod, Hebble Cottage, 44 Bradford Road, Huddersfield. Educated Moldgreen Board School. Employed as a grocer's assistant at Messrs Wallace's shop at Marsh, Huddersfield. Single. At the time of enlistment, was living at 176 Wasp Nest, Almondbury Bank, Almondbury. Enlisted December 1914. Embarked for France April 1915. Killed in action, 4.7.1916, during the Battle of the Somme, aged 19. Buried **CONNAUGHT CEMETERY.** Grave location:- Plot 4, Row M, Grave 8. ROH:- Almondbury War Memorial; commemorated on headstone in Kirkheaton Cemetery.

MILNES, THOMAS. Driver. No 240684. 'B' Battery, 232nd Brigade, Royal Field Artillery. Son of J. F. Milnes. Husband of Polly Milnes, 475 New Hey Road, Mount, Outlane. Died of wounds at No 53 Casualty Clearing Station on 3.10.1918, aged 34 years. Buried **TINCOURT NEW BRITISH CEMETERY.** Grave location:- Plot 8, Row H, Grave 5. ROH:- Parkwood Methodist Chapel.

MILNES, THOMAS. Private. No 10103. 2nd Battalion Auckland Regiment, New Zealand Expeditionary Force. Born Denby Dale. Son of Mr Milnes, Inkerman Farm, Denby Dale. Emigrated to New Zealand in 1912. Enlisted for service abroad and was sent to Egypt. He then came over to England where he spent a short period on Salisbury Plain. Embarked for France in July, 1916. Killed in action during the Battle of Flers-Courcelette on 14.9.1916. Has no known grave. Commemorated **CATERPILLAR VALLEY (N.Z.) MEMORIAL TO THE MISSING, LONGUEVAL.**

MITCHELL, ERNEST. Corporal. No 5/4513. 1/5th Battalion Duke of Wellington's Regiment. Born Holmfirth. Son of George William and Emily Mitchell, 5 Back Stanley Street, Lockwood. Employed by Messrs J. Lumb and Sons Limited, Folly Hall, Huddersfield. Enlisted August 1915. Embarked for France in May, 1916. Struck by shrapnel and killed instantly, 31.7.1916, aged 20 years. Buried **CONNAUGHT CEMETERY.** Grave location:- Plot 3, Row M, Grave 10. ROH:- South Crosland and Netherton War Memorial; Emmanuel Church, Lockwood; Huddersfield Drill Hall.

MITCHELL, ERNEST. Private. No 34287. 6th Battalion Leicestershire Regiment. Born Hepworth, Holmfirth. Son of Mr Arthur Mitchell, formerly of Foster Place Farm, Hepworth, and, at the time of his son's death, living at the Kings Arms Inn, South Crosland. Assisted his father on the family farm. Enlisted 22.2.1917. Embarked for France in August, 1917. Killed in action at Passchendaele, 7.10.1917, aged 22 years. Has no known grave. Commemorated **TYNE COT MEMORIAL TO THE MISSING.** (Brother of Private **JOHN MITCHELL**, killed in action, 13.5.1917, q.v.). His father received a letter from one of his son's comrades who wrote, '*We were heavily bombarded for about two hours in the afternoon and a shell burst just behind us. Ernest, who was in my section, was severely wounded in the right thigh. I went at once to see if I could help him but it was impossible to do anything for him except call for the stretcher-bearers. I am sorry to say that Ernest passed away just after he was placed on the stretcher. I stayed close by him until the end: he was quite cheerful and asked me to write and tell you. I don't think he had much pain as he did not know where he was hit. Almost his last words were 'Corporal - I have done my bit.' I have felt his loss very much as we came out together on the same draft and I always found him to do his work willingly and cheerfully.*'

MITCHELL, FRED. Lance Corporal. No 41393. 2nd Squadron, Machine Gun Corps (Cavalry). Formerly No 9493 18th Hussars. Born Huddersfield. Son of Mr and Mrs Wright Mitchell, 23 East Parade, Huddersfield. Had been in the army for ten years and had served in France since August, 1914. Reported missing and afterwards presumed killed in action on 21.8.1918, aged 28. Has no known grave. Commemorated **VIS-en-ARTOIS MEMORIAL TO THE MISSING.**

MITCHELL, GEORGE. Private. No 3/10587. 2nd Battalion Duke of Wellington's Regiment. Born Huddersfield. Only son of Fred Mitchell, 3 Fitton's Yard, Halifax Old Road, Huddersfield. Employed as a tin and coppersmith's apprentice at the Hygienic Stove Company. Embarked for France on 28.4.1918. Died from the effects of gas poisoning at No 2 Casualty Clearing Station on 6.5.1915. Buried **BAILLEUL COMMUNAL CEMETERY EXTENSION.** Grave location:- Plot 1, Row C, Grave 167. ROH:- Fartown and Birkby War Memorial.

MITCHELL, GEORGE HERBERT, MM. Corporal. No 240588. 1/5th Battalion Duke of Wellington's Regiment. Born Almondbury. Son of George and Ruth A. Mitchell, 23 St. Helen's Farm, Almondbury. Educated Almondbury Council School. Attended the Church Sunday School and had been a member of the choir of All Saints for over three years. Prior to enlistment, was in business on his own account as a hairdresser in Almondbury. Embarked for France in April, 1915. Was the first Almondbury soldier to be awarded the Military Medal, in October 1916, for clearing a German trench with a hand grenade. Killed in action at Passchendaele, 6.10.1917, aged 23 years. Has no known grave. Commemorated **TYNE COT MEMORIAL TO THE MISSING.** ROH:- Huddersfield Drill Hall; Almondbury War Memorial.

MITCHELL, JAMES. Private. No 267425. 1/6th Battalion Duke of Wellington's Regiment. Born 4 Sykes Yard, Lockwood, 4.11.1895. Son of Mary Ann Mitchell, 10 Albert Street, Lockwood. Educated Mount Pleasant Council School, Lockwood. Employed as a moulder's labourer at the Bridgecroft Dyeworks. Was a member of the Dyer's Club and was a keen football player. Single. Attended St. Patrick's Church. Enlisted

11.12.1915. Killed in action at Sailly-Labourse (4 miles south east of Bethune) on 24.6.1917, aged 33 years. Buried **SAILLY-LABOURSE COMMUNAL CEMETERY EXTENSION.** Grave location:- Row A, Grave 19, ROH:- St. Stephen's Church, Rashcliffe.

MITCHELL, JOHN. Private. No 38660. 7th Battalion York and Lancaster Regiment. Born Hepworth. Son of Arthur Mitchell, Foster Place, Hepworth. Married, with one child. Lived Jackson Bridge. Previously employed as a teamer at Bridge Foundry, Holmfirth, but, prior to enlistment, was employed at Bridge Dyeworks, Honley. Enlisted 1.10.1916. Embarked for France 22.3.1917. Killed by a shell on 13.5.1917 at the Battle of Arras. He was twenty eight years of age. Buried **POINT-du-JOUR MILITARY CEMETERY, ATHIES.** Grave location:- Plot 1, Row C, Grave 10. (Brother of Private **ERNEST MITCHELL**, killed in action, 7.10.1917, q.v.). ROH:- New Mill Working Men's Club; Fulstone; Hepworth and Scholes War Memorial; Hepworth Parish Church.

MITCHELL, JOHN WILLIAM. Private. No 6178. 1st Battalion West Yorkshire Regiment. Born Johnson Street, Stocksbridge, 26.2.1880. Son of John and Jane Mitchell, 2 Buckley's Buildings, Spring Grove Street, Huddersfield. Educated St. Patrick's Church School. Employed as a gardener at Messrs Platt's nurseries, Grimscar. Single. Enlisted 1.11.1901. Had served in the Boer War, as well as India, on the North West Frontier, in 1908. Reported missing after the attack on Lesboeufs on 18.9.1916 and afterwards presumed to have been killed on that date, aged 36. Buried **GUARDS' CEMETERY, (LESBOEUFS).** Grave location:- Plot 13, Row D, Grave 3. ROH:- Commemorated on his parents' headstone in Edgerton Cemetery, Huddersfield.

MITCHELL, SQUIRE. Private. No 41657. 17th Battalion West Yorkshire Regiment (2nd Leeds Pals). Lived Huddersfield. Married. Died of wounds, 30.8.1917. Buried **VILLERS-FAUCON COMMUNAL CEMETERY.** Grave location:- Row E, Grave 1.

MITCHELL, THOMAS. Private. No 7596. 2nd Battalion Duke of Wellington's Regiment. Born Lockwood. Son of Mrs Sarah Mitchell, 82 Lockwood Road, Huddersfield. Was a Reservist and went out with the British Expeditionary Force in August, 1914. Went through all the major engagements from Mons, the Marne the Aisne and First Ypres, to Hill 60, where he was reported missing, presumed killed, on 5.5.1915, aged 35. Has no known grave. Commemorated **MENIN GATE MEMORIAL TO THE MISSING.** ROH:- St. Stephen's Church, Rashcliffe.

MITTON, NORMAN. Rifleman. No C/6904. 18th Battalion King's Royal Rifle Corps. Born Kirkheaton 22.2.1896. Educated Bradley Church of England School. Lived 10 Colne Bridge, Bradley. Employed as a cloth finisher by Messrs Learoyd Brothers. Enlisted 16.8.1915. Killed in action during the Battle of the Somme, 15.9.1916. Has no known grave. Commemorated **THIEPVAL MEMORIAL TO THE MISSING.** ROH:- St. Thomas's Church, Bradley; Learoyd Brothers.

MOODYCLIFFE, HERBERT. Acting Corporal. No 9165. 2nd Battalion Duke of Wellington's Regiment. Born Holmfirth. Son of Mr and Mrs J. W. Moodycliffe, Victoria, Holmfirth. Had served nine years with the army. Enlisted in Halifax, when he was 18 years of age. Had been stationed at Lichfield, Manchester, Tidworth and Dublin. Married, with one child, and lived at 28 Great Albion Street, Halifax. Embarked for France in August, 1914, with the British Expeditionary Force and was in the retreat from Mons, the fighting on the Marne, the Aisne and at Hill 60 in May 1915. In December, 1914, he wrote home to his parents, thanking them for gifts received, *'I am quite well at present. I received the fags from the boys at Bottoms and have written back thanking them for the same. Things are not so hot this last day or two as we have gained a great amount of ground. The enemy's position gets nearer their own country every day. The weather here is awfully cold. It is just like being on the top of Holme Moss. We have plenty of good clothing, scarves, etc. The German wellington boots I have got keep my feet warm. They come up to my knees and keep the wet out so that I cannot grumble. All the lads thank the people of England for their gifts. I don't know how we could have stood it without them. We have had a good share. Most of them come from Huddersfield and Halifax. Gloves, knitted hats, scarves, socks, shirts, drawers and useful* *things like these.'* Killed in action on the first day of the Battle of the Somme, 1.7.1916, aged 27 years. Has no known grave. Commemorated **THIEPVAL MEMORIAL TO THE MISSING.** ROH:- Underbank War Memorial; Halifax Civic Book of Remembrance.

MOORE, ANDREW RICHARDSON. Corporal. No 53517. 13th (Service) Battalion (1st Barnsley) York and Lancaster Regiment. Formerly No 401 Hussars. Born Midgley, Halifax. Lived New Mill, Holmfirth. Married. (His wife, Annie M. Moore, later went to live in Kilcullen, County Kildare, Ireland). Killed in action, 30.9.1918, aged 33 years. Buried **STRAND MILITARY CEMETERY, PLOEGSTEERT, BELGIUM.** Grave location:- Plot 8, Row D, Grave 10. ROH:- New Mill Working Men's Club, Fulstone.

MOORE, FRANK. Guardsman. No 8943. Scots Guards. Born Brierley Wood, Huddersfield. Son of Wilkinson Moore, 12 Proud Row, Sheepridge. Had been employed as a number-taker at Low Moor Station, Bradford, but, prior to enlisting, worked at Messrs Hopkinsons of Birkby. Embarked for France on 18.12.1914. Killed in action at Givenchy, 2.6.1915, aged 20. Has no known grave. Commemorated **LE TOURET MEMORIAL TO THE MISSING.** His last letter from the trenches, which is dated May 24th, 1915, to his father, reads as follows, *'I was in the trenches not long ago when one night we were getting relieved. We had been putting the West Yorkshires through trench work a bit as they had not been in the trenches before and I happened to come across some of my old friends from Bradford, Leeds and Huddersfield. Well it happened that they were relieving us and I laughed my sides sore that night. To begin with there was the first platoon coming up the communication trench. At that time it was dry compared with what it had been. One of the men slipped off the board and went up to the knees in water. He started, 'Tha wants a pair of bathing drawers on here. It's more like water works.!' Of course I knew who it was. These were the Leeds Rifles (West Yorkshires). There were some Huddersfield fellows in the West Ridings. They were billeted in the next town to us. I had a walk as far and I came across several of my old friends there. It is about a fortnight since the Leeds Rifles were in their first engagement and our Battalion was the first to go over the top. They proved which were the best soldiers. They took the first line of trenches, smoking cigarettes and pipes. You could see them puffing away as they doubled from our trench to the enemy trench. They did not lose very heavily in taking the first trench but I am sorry to say they did afterwards. Well one of the West Yorkshires' Sergeants saw them going over and they stuck together and I heard him say 'If we are needed you must do it like the Scots Guards did it and we shall not be far out.' They were all anxious to have a pop at the Huns but I don't think they got a chance. They were willing and that was good enough. I think they will all be the same who come from Yorkshire.'* ROH:- Christ Church, Woodhouse Hill; Deighton War Memorial.

MOORE, GEORGE. Private. No DM2/162379. Army Service Corps (Motor Transport), attached 29th Motor Ambulance Corps. Born Tunnacliffe Hill, Almondbury, 14.2.1894. Son of Joseph Henry Moore, 17 Raw Street, Crosland Moor, Huddersfield. Educated Crosland Moor Council School. Employed as a clerk in the office of Messrs Jere Kaye and Company, timber merchants, Turnbridge. Attended Paddock Congregational Church. Enlisted 12.2.1916. Sailed for East Africa in June, 1916. Died of malaria and dysentery in East Africa on 30.4.1917, aged 23 years. Buried **MOROGORA CEMETERY, EAST AFRICA.** Grave location:- Plot 2, Row B, Grave 1. ROH:- St. Barnabas Church, Crosland Moor; Shared Church, Paddock.

MOORE, GEORGE HENRY. Private. No 6057. 3/4th Battalion Duke of Wellington's Regiment. Born Quarmby Fold 7.5.1898. Son of Mr and Mrs I. H. Moore, Quarmby Fold, Quarmby, Huddersfield. Educated Oakes Council School. Employed as a woollen piecer. Enlisted 27.6.1916. Died at Clipstone Camp on 28.6.1916, aged 18, from a hysteric seizure immediately after entering Clipstone Camp, Mansfield. Buried **EDGERTON CEMETERY, HUDDERSFIELD.** Grave location:- Screen Wall. ROH:- Lindley Zion Methodist Church; St. Stephen's Church, Lindley; Longwood War Memorial.

MOORE, JAMES. Private. No 2339. 1/8th Battalion Durham Light Infantry. Born Upper Denby, near Huddersfield. Son of the late Matthew and Hannah Moore. Enlisted with friends while living at St. Bede's College, Durham. Killed in action, 14.5.1915, aged 21 years. Has no known grave. Commemorated **MENIN GATE MEMORIAL TO THE MISSING**. ROH:- Denby Dale and Cumberworth War Memorial.

MOORE, JOHN WILLIAM. 2nd Yeoman of Signals. No 169094. (RFR/DEV/B/1836). Royal Navy. *HMS Goliath*. Lived 100 Ashbrow Road, Fartown, Huddersfield. Killed in an action with a Turkish destroyer in the Dardenelles on 13.5.1915, aged 39 years. Has no known grave. Commemorated **PLYMOUTH NAVAL MEMORIAL TO THE MISSING**. ROH:- Christ Church, Woodhouse Hill; Fartown and Birkby War Memorial.

MOORE, NORMAN. Royal Garrison Artillery. Born 10 Commercial Square, Huddersfield. Educated St. Patrick's School. Lived 4 Seed Hill, Huddersfield. Married. Enlisted 24.6.1916. Died at home, 4 Seed Hill, Huddersfield, 30.12.1921, of tuberculosis caused through being gassed.

MOORE, THOMAS EDWIN. Lance Corporal. No 23086. 9 Platoon, 'Y' Company, 8th Battalion Duke of Wellington's Regiment. Born 17 Victoria Street, Lindley. Son of John Edwin and Mary Moore, 69 Laund Road, Salendine Nook. Educated Oakes Council School. Employed as a spinner by Messrs Martin, Sons and Company, Wellington Mill, Oakes. Attended St. Stephen's Church, Lindley, and was a member of the Band of Hope. Married. Reported missing, presumed killed, 11.8.1917, aged 26 years. Has no known grave. Commemorated **MENIN GATE MEMORIAL TO THE MISSING**. ROH:- St. Stephen's Church, Lindley.

MOORE, WALTER. Private. No 204284. 2nd Battalion Duke of Wellington's Regiment. Born Temple Street, Lindley, 3.10.1885. Educated Lindley National Council School. Employed as a tram conductor by the Huddersfield Corporation Tramways Department, Lived Burnside, Fixby. Married. Enlisted January 1917. Killed in action near Bethune on 15.4.1918. Has no known grave. Commemorated **PLOEGSTEERT MEMORIAL TO THE MISSING**. ROH:- Lindley Baptist Church; Lindley Zion Methodist Church; St. Philip's Church, Birchencliffe; Huddersfield Corporation Roll.

MOORES, FRED. Private. No 110413. The Tank Corps. Formerly No 38234, 3rd Battalion The Yorkshire Regiment. Son of James Edward and Sarah Moores of Lindley. Lived with his sister at 136 Acre Street, Lindley. Employed as a machine tenter at Acre Mills, Lindley. Was a member of the cricket team at Holy Trinity Church. Died of pneumonia at Bovington Camp, Dorset, on 27.10.1918, aged 25 years. Buried **St. STEPHEN'S CHURCHYARD, LINDLEY.** Grave location:- 21, M. ROH:- St. Stephen's Church, Lindley.

MOORHOUSE, ALBERT, MM. Private. No 28011. 63rd Company, Machine Gun Corps. Formerly No 3/17906 Duke of Wellington's Regiment. Born Quarmby Fold, Quarmby, 10.12.1893. Son of John and Ellen Moorhouse. Educated Oakes Council School. Employed as a weaver by Messrs Smith and Calverley, Plover Mills, Lindley. Single. Enlisted 5.12.1915. Awarded the Military Medal in October 1917. Killed in action at Inchy-en-Artois on 4.9.1918, aged 25 years. Has no known grave. Commemorated **VIS-en-ARTOIS MEMORIAL TO THE MISSING**. ROH:- Lindley Zion Wesleyan Chapel; St. Stephen's Church, Lindley.

MOORHOUSE, ALLEN. Private. No 766258. 28th (County of London) Battalion (Artists Rifles). Born Lockwood 1.10.1898. Son of Edgar and Frances Moorhouse, 56 Yews Hill Road, Lockwood. Educated Hillhouse Elementary School. Was a chemistry student at Huddersfield Technical College. Single. Enlisted 6.7.1917. Killed in action near Cambrai on 24.3.1918, aged 19. Buried **LEBUCQUIERE COMMUNAL CEMETERY EXTENSION**. Grave location:- Plot 1, Row A, Grave 4. ROH:- St. Barnabas Church, Crosland Moor; Huddersfield Corporation Roll; memorial in Lockwood Cemetery.

MOORHOUSE, BEN. Private. No 203123. 13th Battalion York and Lancaster Regiment. (1st Barnsley Pals). Third son of Mr and Mrs Moorhouse, Hall Ing Farm, Honley. Attended the Woodroyd Chapel. Employed by Messrs Woodhouse and Rawlinson, Holmfirth. Enlisted March 1916. Was gassed in August, 1917. Died of trench fever in hospital in Birmingham on 30.4.1918, aged 23 years. Buried **HEPWORTH WESLEYAN CHAPEL YARD, HOLMFIRTH**. Grave Location, F, 26. ROH:- Honley War Memorial.

MOORHOUSE, ERNEST. Driver. Royal Field Artillery. Born 113 Swan Lane, Lockwood. Son of Allen and Mary Ann Moorhouse, 113 Swan Lane, Lockwood. Educated Mount Pleasant Board School. Employed as a tailor's cutter. Single. Enlisted 20.12.1915. Invalided home on 19.5.1917. Died from nephritis, at home, on 5.9.1919, aged 24 years. Buried **LOCKWOOD CEMETERY.** ROH:- Emmanuel Church, Lockwood.

MOORHOUSE, ERNEST BRUMMITT. Private. No 42371. 3rd Battalion Worcestershire Regiment. Born Kirkheaton. Son of Joseph and Sarah Moorhouse of Dam Head Farm, Lepton. Employed by the Cowmes Industrial Society. Reported missing, presumed killed, near Rheims 27.5.1918, aged 19 years. Has no known grave. Commemorated **SOISSONS MEMORIAL TO THE MISSING.** ROH:- Lepton Parish Church.

MOORHOUSE, FRANK. Private. No 45801. Private. 9th Battalion Northumberland Fusiliers. Formerly No 37334 Durham Light Infantry. Born Huddersfield. Son of Mrs Moorhouse, Big Valley, Netherton. Employed by Messrs Gledhill Brothers, Broadfield Mills, Lockwood. Killed in action at the Battle of Arras, 16.4.1917, aged 31 years. Has no known grave. Commemorated **ARRAS MEMORIAL TO THE MISSING.** ROH:- South Crosland and Netherton War Memorial.

MOORHOUSE, GEORGE. Private. No 3/9582. 2nd Battalion Duke of Wellington's Regiment. Born Blacker Road, Birkby, 23.1.1892. Educated at Huddersfield schools. Lived 5a Jepson's Yard, Lockwood. Employed as an engine tenter. Single. Enlisted at the outbreak of the war. Embarked for France in August, 1914. Reported missing, presumed killed, at Hill 60 on 18.4.1915. Has no known grave. Commemorated **MENIN GATE MEMORIAL TO THE MISSING.** ROH:- Emmanuel Church, Lockwood.

MOORHOUSE, HERBERT. Private. No 36047. 'B' Company, 1st Battalion Loyal North Lancashire Regiment. Formerly No 174493 Royal Field Artillery. Born Holmfirth. Husband of Mary H. Moorhouse of 'Holme', Holmbridge. Reported missing, presumed killed, 18.4.1918, aged 33 years. Has no known grave. Commemorated **LOOS MEMORIAL TO THE MISSING.** ROH:- Holme and Holmbridge War Memorial.

MOORHOUSE, WILFRID. Private. No S/40091. 2nd Battalion Seaforth Highlanders. Born Paddock 17.4.1881. Educated Paddock Board School. Employed as a tailor's cutter by Mr Alfred Willis. Husband of Edith Moorhouse, 116 Netheroyd Hill Road, Huddersfield. Enlisted 4.6.1916. Reported missing at Poelcapelle on 4.10.1917, aged 35, and afterwards presumed to have been killed on that date. Buried **CEMENT HOUSE CEMETERY, LANGEMARCK, BELGIUM.** Grave location:- Plot 15m Row B, Grave 13. ROH:- All Saints Church, Paddock.

MOORHOUSE, WILFRED. Private. No 307874. 1st Battalion Lancashire Fusiliers. Formerly No 55716 Liverpool Regiment. Born Holmfirth. Son of the late Joe Moorhouse of Cinderhills, Holmfirth. Prior to enlistment was in business in Liverpool. Single. Died of wounds at No 3 General Hospital, Le Treport, on 3.7.1917, aged 26 years. Buried **MONT HUON MILITARY CEMETERY.** Grave location:- Plot 4, Row A, Grave 6b. ROH:- Holmfirth War Memorial.

MORELAND, ERNEST. Gunner. No 54776. 104th Battery Royal Field Artillery. Born Lancaster. Son of Thomas and Eleanor Moreland of Holt, Holmfirth. Was a bellringer at Holmfirth Parish Church. After leaving school was employed by Messrs James Lancaster and Son, cloth finishers, Mytholm Bridge. At the age of 18 he joined the Regular Army. At the outbreak of the war he was stationed with his Battery in Pretoria, South Africa. His unit was transferred to France soon afterwards. Wounded by gunshot in the head and arm on 27.9.1915 On 3.10.1915, he was admitted to the base hospital at Abbeville. His father received the following letter from a member of the nursing staff, who wrote on Thursday morning of 27.10.1915, '*Gunner Moreland is not so well. He was brought to this hospital on the 3.10.1915 and the injury to his head necessitated an operation. He progressed favourably until yesterday morning.*' His father received another letter on 30.10.1915 with the news that his son had died on 22.10.1915, '*Your son died last night (Thursday). He was most anxious all day that I should write to you and once I found him with pencil and paper in his hand trying to do so. Everything was done for him and we had hopes of his recovery until three days ago*'. Died at No 2 Stationary Hospital,

22.10.1915, aged 25 years. Buried **ABBEVILLE COMMUNAL CEMETERY.** Grave location:- Plot 3, Row C, Grave 6. (Brother of Private **JOHN MORELAND,** reported missing at Gallipoli, 8.8.1915, q.v.). ROH:- Holmfirth War Memorial.

MORELAND, JOHN. Private. No 12/1721. Auckland Regiment, New Zealand Expeditionary Force. Born Holmfirth. Son of Thomas and Eleanor Moreland, Holt, Holmfirth. Employed as a dyer at Kirkbridge Dyeworks, New Mill. Had been a member of the local Territorials. Emigrated to New Zealand in November, 1912. Was working on a sheep farm at the outbreak of war. Single. At the time of enlistment, he gave his address as c/o Willoughby, Kaipaki, North Cambridge. Was sent to the Dardenelles. Killed in action at the Apex during the assault on Chunuk Bair, Galipolli, on 8.8.1915, aged 27 years. Has no known grave. Commemorated **CHUNUK BAIR MEMORIAL TO THE MISSING, GALLIPOLI.** (Brother of Private **ERNEST MORELAND,** died of wounds, 22.10.1915, q.v.). ROH:- Holmfirth War Memorial.

MORGAN, HARRY. Private. No 37066. 8th Battalion North Staffordshire Regiment. Born Mirfield 30.12.1896. Son of William and Hannah Morgan, 25 Spinkfield Road, Birkby. Educated at Mirfield schools. Employed as a number taker on the railway. Single. Enlisted 2.3.1917. Wounded at Albert, 10.4.1918. Died of wounds at No 54 General Hospital, Aubergue, on 20.4.1918, aged 21 years. Buried **WIMEREUX COMMUNAL CEMETERY.** Grave location:- Plot 11, Row E, Grave 5a. (Brother of Private **WILFRED MORGAN,** died on 28.11.1918, q.v.). ROH:- Fartown and Birkby War Memorial.

MORGAN, JAMES CORNELIUS. Lance Corporal. No 240572. 2/5th Battalion Duke of Wellington's Regiment. Born Burton-on-Trent, Staffordshire, 11.1.1893. Son of John A. and Bridget Morgan, 11 Loves Yard, High Street, Huddersfield. Educated St. Patrick's Roman Catholic School and attended the church. Employed as a fitter's labourer by Messrs T. Brook and Sons Limited. Single. Enlisted 4.9.1914. Reported missing, presumed killed at the Battle of Bullecourt, 3.5.1917, aged 24 years. Has no known grave. Commemorated **ARRAS MEMORIAL TO THE MISSING.** ROH:- Huddersfield Drill Hall.

MORGAN, JOHN HERBERT (BERTIE). Lieutenant. 20th Battalion Canadian Infantry (1st Central Ontario Regiment). Second son of Mrs A. Morgan, 5 East Street, Golcar. Was formerly an assistant teacher at Crow Lane Board School, Milnsbridge, for five years and, for a short time, at the Slaithwaite National School and the Knowle Bank Council School, Golcar, Was a member of the Golcar Baptist Choir. Went to Canada in 1903. Married, with two children. Was engaged in the musical profession. Prior to the outbreak of the war was a Lieutenant in the Canadian Militia and volunteered for active service in September 1914. Embarked for France in June 1915. Came to Golcar on leave six weeks before he was accidentally killed by a train in France on 21.2.1918, aged 35 years. Buried **AIX-NOULETTE COMMUNAL CEMETERY EXTENSION.** Grave location:- Plot 2, Row B, Grave 1. ROH:- St. John's Church, Golcar; Golcar Baptist Church; Crow Lane Board School, Milnsbridge.

MORGAN, WILFRED. Private. No 58605. 63rd Field Ambulance, Royal Army Medical Corps. Born Mirfield 31.5.1890. Son of William and Hannah Morgan, 25 Spinkfield Road, Birkby. Educated Knowle Council School, Mirfield. Employed as a parcels porter by the London and North Western Railway Company at Huddersfield Railway Station. Married. Enlisted 14.5.1915. Died of influenza at Caudry, France, on 28.11.1918. Buried **CAUDRY BRITISH CEMETERY.** Grave location:- Plot 2, Row B, Grave 8. (Brother of Private **HARRY MORGAN,** died of wounds, 20.4.1918, q.v.). ROH:- Christ Church, Woodhouse Hill; Gledholt Wesleyan Church; Fartown and Birkby War Memorial; London and North Western Railway Roll.

MORLEY, FRANK. Private. No 241761. 2nd Battalion Duke of Wellington's Regiment. Born Shelley. Husband of Elizabeth Morley, Abbey Road, Shepley. Employed as a motor driver by Messrs S. Senior and Sons, Highfield Brewery. Killed in action, 31.8.1918, aged 35 years. Buried **VIS-en-ARTOIS BRITISH CEMETERY.** Grave location:- Plot 1, Row C, Grave 34. ROH:- Shepley War Memorial.

MORLEY, HORACE. Private. No 15530. 2/4th Battalion King's Own Yorkshire Light Infantry. Born Cawthorne, Barnsley. Son of Emma Illingworth (formerly Morley), of Cliff Hill, Cawthorne, Barnsley, and the late John Morley. Lived Clayton West. Killed in action, 5.6.1918, aged 25 years. Buried **QUEENS CEMETERY, BUCQUOY.** Grave location:- Plot 2, Row B, Grave 7. ROH:- Clayton West and High Hoyland War Memorial.

MORRIS, JAMES WILLIAM. Private. No 12512. 2nd Battalion Duke of Wellington's Regiment. Born Kirkheaton. Lived Square Hill, Kirkheaton. Embarked for France in August, 1914. Died of wounds (gas) received at Hill 60 on 5.5.1915, aged 29 years. Buried **RENINGHELST CHURCHYARD EXTENSION.** Grave No 30. ROH:- St. John's Church, Kirkheaton.

MORRISON, HARRY. Private. No 5/3116. 1/5th Battalion Duke of Wellington's Regiment. Born Huddersfield 14.10.1895. Son of Ernest and Mary Morrison, 3 Clara Street, Fartown. Employed as a grocer's assistant by Mr C. Fitton, Market Place, Huddersfield. Enlisted on his 19th birthday on 19.10.1914. Embarked for France in April, 1915. Returned to France on 13.6.1916 after 10 days leave. Killed in action at Thiepval Wood, 3.7.1916, aged 20 years. Buried **CONNAUGHT CEMETERY.** Grave location:- Plot 13, Row B, Grave 3. ROH:- Christ Church, Woodhouse Hill; Huddersfield Drill Hall; Fartown and Birkby War Memorial.

MORRISON, ROBERT. Private. No 12204. 9th Battalion Duke of Wellington's Regiment. Born Huddersfield 9.8.1896. Son of William and Mary Morrison, 67 Back Lane, Berry Brow, Huddersfield. Educated Berry Brow Council School. Attended Salem United Methodist Sunday School. Employed by the Lancashire and Yorkshire Railway Company, at Berry Brow Station, as a porter. Enlisted September 1914. On 13.11.1917, his parents received word that he was suffering from septic poisoning and that he hoped to be home shortly. He was on board the *Hospital Ship Anglia* on 17.11.1915, which was sailing from Calais to Dover when, about noon, she struck a mine in the English Channel. Of the 388 patients on board, 130 were lost, among them Private Robert Morrison. Has no known grave. Commemorated **HOLLYBROOK MEMORIAL TO THE MISSING.** ROH:- Armitage Bridge War Memorial; memorial in Armitage Bridge Churchyard; Lancashire and Yorkshire Railway Roll.

MORTIMER, IVAN ARTHUR. Private. No 71529 16th Battalion Sherwood Foresters. Formerly No 31652 North Staffordshire Regiment. Born Meltham. Son of John and Clara Mortimer, Clarke Lane, Meltham. Employed by the Meltham Cooperative Society. Was assistant secretary of the Meltham Wesleyan Sunday School. Enlisted November 1916. Killed in action, 3.8.1917, aged 19 years. Buried **NEW IRISH FARM CEMETERY, St. JEAN-LES-YPRES.** Grave location:- Plot 9, Row B, Grave 14. ROH:- St. Bartholomew's Church, Meltham.

MORTON, HERBERT. Sergeant. No 305192. 1/7th Battalion Duke of Wellington's Regiment. Born Brighouse 5.1.1895. Son of Samuel and Edith Morton, 107 Market Street, Milnsbridge. Educated Greengates Council School near Bradford. Employed as a cloth finisher. At the time of enlistment, was living at 4 Wood Top, Marsden. Single. Enlisted in the local Territorial battalion on 6.2.1912. Was mobilised in August 1914. Had been wounded on two occasions, the first time on 15.5.1915, and the second time in March, 1918, at Neuve Chapelle. He had also been gassed on two occasions. Killed in action near Cambrai on 11.10.1918, aged 23. Buried **WELLINGTON CEMETERY** Grave location:- Plot 3, Row B, Grave 6. ROH:- Huddersfield Drill Hall; Marsden War Memorial.

MORTON, WILLIAM. Private. No 29171. 8th Battalion The Yorkshire Regiment. Born Huddersfield. Son of Dan and Jane Morton of Moorside, Old Lindley, Holywell Green. Killed in action at Passchendaele, 28.9.1917, aged 31 years. Buried **TYNE COT CEMETERY.** Grave location:- Plot 64, Row E, Grave 2. ROH:- Salendine Nook Baptist Church.

MORTON, WILLIE. Private. No 52540. 1st Battalion West Yorkshire Regiment. Son of Halstead and Sarah Ann Morton, Birkenshaw Row, Outlane. Employed by Messrs John Broadbent and Sons, Parkwood Mills, Longwood. Was secretary of the Sunday School and Band of Hope at Outlane Wesleyan Church and a member of the choir. Twice wounded. Died of bronchial-pneumonia, following influenza, at No 5 Casualty Clearing Station on 12.12.1918. Buried **MAUBEUGE (SOUS-LE-BOIS) CEMETERY.** Grave location:- Row C, Grave 30. ROH:- Outlane Trinity Methodist Chapel; memorial in Outlane Methodist Churchyard.

MOSBY, JOHN. Private. No 3/3505. 3rd Battalion King's Own Yorkshire Light Infantry. Born Huddersfield. Lived 151 Upper Brow Road, Paddock, Huddersfield. Died in Hull Royal Infirmary on 3.1.1916, from a self-inflicted gunshot wound. Age 55 years. Buried **EDGERTON CEMETERY, HUDDERSFIELD.** Grave location:- 14B, 150.

MOSLEY, ALFRED. Lance Corporal. No 201861. 4th Battalion Seaforth Highlanders. Born Huddersfield. Son of Clara and the late Joseph Mosley, Fern Lea, Hoylehouse, Linthwaite. Employed as a pattern weaver by Messrs George Mallinson and Sons, Linthwaite. Was a member of the Linthwaite cricket team and also a member of the Liberal Club. Enlisted February 1916. Embarked for France in October, 1916. Wounded in the face in November, 1917. Died in No 18 General Hospital, Camiers, on 8.12.1917, aged 26 years. Buried **ETAPLES MILITARY CEMETERY.** Grave location:- Plot 31, Row B, Grave 3. ROH:- Linthwaite War Memorial.

MOSLEY, ARNOLD. Private. No 241890. 2/5th Battalion Duke of Wellington's Regiment. Born Shepley. Son of Fred Mosley, Station Road, Shepley. Enlisted March 1916. Reported missing, presumed killed, at the Battle of Bullecourt, 3.5.1917. Has no known grave. Commemorated **ARRAS MEMORIAL TO THE MISSING.** ROH:- Huddersfield Drill Hall; Shepley War Memorial.

MOSLEY, BERTRAM CYRIL. Private. No 38652. 8th Battalion York and Lancaster Regiment. Born Shepley. Lived Thirstin Road, Honley. Husband of Jesstina Mosley. Employed by Mr C. H. Marshall, solicitor, of Holmfirth. Killed in action, 28.8.1917, aged 27 years. Has no known grave. Commemorated **TYNE COT MEMORIAL TO THE MISSING.** ROH:- Honley War Memorial.

MOSLEY, NELSON. Private. No 35714. 8th Battalion King's Own Yorkshire Light Infantry. Formerly No 7977 Duke of Wellington's Regiment. Born Glossop. Son of Ellen Mosley, 47 Cliffe Road, Holmfirth, and the late Herbert Mosley. Employed by Messrs J. Lancaster and Son, Mytholm Bridge. Attended Cliffe Sunday School. Enlisted 29.3.1916. Embarked for France 4.11.1916. Wounded 10.2.1917. After two months treatment in England he returned to France. On 1.10.1917 he wrote home to his mother, *'Cheer up, I hope to be with you at Christmas.'* Killed in action at Passchendaele, 16.10.1917, aged 21 years. Has no known grave. Commemorated **TYNE COT MEMORIAL TO THE MISSING.** ROH:- Wooldale War Memorial.

MOSLEY, PERCY. 2nd Lieutenant. 5th Battalion Duke of Wellington's Regiment. Born Shepley. Son of Mr and Mrs John Mosley, Yew Tree Villas, Shepley. Was a student of the textile department at the Huddersfield Technical College. Employed as an assistant designer by Messrs Benjamin Armitage and Sons Limited, Victoria Warehouse, Shepley. Was a member of the Shepley Tennis Club and the Huddersfield Technical College gymnasium. Played football with the Shepley Amateur football club. Was a member of the choir at the United Methodist Church, Shepley. Killed in action, 28.3.1918, aged 24 years. Has no known grave. Commemorated **ARRAS MEMORIAL TO THE MISSING.** ROH:- Huddersfield Drill Hall; Shepley War Memorial.

MOSS, RALPH SUNDERLAND. Private. No 1917. 'A' Company, 1/5th Battalion Duke of Wellington's Regiment. Born Hebden Bridge 7.10.1893. Son of Charles Walter and Elizabeth Moss, 18 Lister Street, Moldgreen. Educated Moldgreen Church of England School and Huddersfield College. Employed as an organ repairer by Messrs Peter Conacher. Attended Moldgreen Parish Church. Was a member of the local Territorials for two years prior to the war. Enlisted at the outbreak of the war. Embarked for France in April, 1915. Killed in action near Ypres, 16.8.1915, aged 21 years. Has no known grave. Commemorated **MENIN GATE MEMORIAL TO THE MISSING.** His parents received a letter from Private W. Davis, of Moldgreen, who was in the same Company and wrote, *'We are only about twenty five yards from the German trenches, so you can imagine that if anyone shows his head above the top of the trench he is pretty certain to be hit. Ralph must have done this accidentally whilst making a dugout for* *himself. He died without regaining conciousness so you must not think he suffered any pain. I am sure I could pay him no better tribute than to say he was the best type of British soldier and knew no fear. We shall all miss terribly one of the best of pals.'* ROH:- Christ Church, Moldgreen; Huddersfield Drill Hall.

MOSS, THOMAS EDWARD. Corporal. No 18819. 7/8th Battalion King's Own Scottish Borderers. Born Widnes. Lived Huddersfield. Employed as a fireman by the London and North Western Railway Company at Huddersfield station. Killed in action, 2.1.1917, aged 26 years. Buried **PEAKE WOOD CEMETERY, FRICOURT.** Grave location:- Row D, Grave 1. ROH: London and North Western Railway Company Roll.

MOXON, DAVID. Private. No 241863. 2/5th Battalion Duke of Wellington's Regiment. Born Moldgreen, Huddersfield. Son of David Moxon, of Lascelles Hall, Kirkheaton. Reported missing, presumed killed, at the Battle of Bullecourt, 3.5.1917, aged 21 years. Has no known grave. Commemorated **ARRAS MEMORIAL TO THE MISSING.** ROH:- St. John's Church, Kirkheaton; Huddersfield Drill Hall.

MUDD, GEORGE. Private. No 38140. 5th Battalion The Yorkshire Regiment. Born Leicester 20.6.1881. Educated Belgrave National School, Leicester. Worked on his own account as a greengrocer. Lived 8 Lee and Burley's Yard, Leeds Road, Huddersfield. Married, with four children. Enlisted 20.9.1916. Killed in action on the Chemin-de-Dames, 27.5.1918. Has no known grave. Commemorated **SOISSONS MEMORIAL TO THE MISSING.**

MUIRHEAD, R.A. Private. No 35929 Highland Light Infantry, transferred to (372953) Labour Corps. Died at home, 3.1.1919. Buried **EDGERTON CEMETERY, HUDDERSFIELD.** Grave location:- 11B, 116.

MULLARKEY, HARRY. Private. No 31790. 2nd Battalion Machine Gun Corps. Born North's Arms, Thomas Street, Huddersfield, 6.7.1896. Son of Thomas and Louisa Mullarkey, 27 Hawk Street, Huddersfield. Educated St. Patrick's Roman Catholic School. Employed as a woollen minder. Single. Enlisted 22.8.1915. Died at No 36 Casualty Clearing Station, of malaria and broncho-pneumonia, 12.2.1919, aged 22, in Cologne, Germany. Buried **COLOGNE SOUTHERN CEMETERY, GERMANY.** Grave location:- Plot 2, Row B, Grave 18.

MULLARKY, JAMES. Private. No 2296. 'D' Company, 1/7th Battalion Duke of Wellington's Regiment. Born 18 Castlegate, Huddersfield, 16.11.1895. Son of the late John and Mary Mullarkey. Educated St. Patrick's Roman Catholic School. Lived 71 Pine Street, Huddersfield. Single. Employed as a dyehouse labourer by Messrs Allen Priest and Sons, of Lockwood. Attended St. Patrick's Church, was a member of the Young Men's Catholic Assocation and played football with the association team. Enlisted 4.9.1914. Embarked for France in April, 1915. Killed in action in the trenches near Ypres on 20.11.1915, aged 20 years. Buried **BARD COTTAGE CEMETERY, BOESINGHE, BELGIUM.** Grave location:- Plot 1, Row H, Grave 16. ROH:- Huddersfield Drill Hall.

MUNRO, ARCHIE. Private. No 11595. 2nd Battalion Duke of Wellington's Regiment. Born Hawick, Roxburghshire, Scotland. Son of Daniel Munro, Steps Cottage, Magdale, Honley. Employed by Messrs Josiah France, Queens Square Mill, Honley. Enlisted with his brother in September, 1914, in the 9th Battalion Duke of Wellington's Regiment. Embarked for France in August, 1915. After suffering from shell shock on July 1st, 1916, was transferred to the 2nd Battalion Duke of Wellington's Regiment. Killed in action, 12.10.1916, aged 19 years. Has no known grave. Commemorated **THIEPVAL MEMORIAL TO THE MISSING.** (Brother of Private **WILLIAM MUNRO,** reported missing, presumed killed, 30.7.1916, q.v.). ROH:- Honley War Memorial.

MUNRO, WILLIAM. Private. No 11596. 10th Battalion Duke of Wellington's Regiment. Born Hawick, Roxburghshire, Scotland. Son of Daniel Munro, Steps Cottage, Magdale, Honley. Employed in the warehouse of Messrs Josiah France Limited. Enlisted with his brother in September, 1914. Embarked for France in August, 1915. Reported missing, 30.7.1916 and afterwards presumed to have been killed on that date. Has no known grave. Commemorated **THIEPVAL**

MEMORIAL TO THE MISSING. (Brother of Private **ARCHIE MUNRO**, killed in action, 12.10.1916, q.v.). ROH:- Honley War Memorial.

MURPHY, ERNEST. Private. No 5/4822. 1/5th Battalion Duke of Wellington's Regiment. Born Moldgreen, Huddersfield, 19.3.1890. Son of Dennis and Sarah Hannah Murphy, 101 Lowerhouses, Almondbury. Educated Moldgreen Board School. Employed as a bookbinder by Messrs Preston Brothers and Company. Enlisted February 1916. Embarked for France in June, 1916. Killed in action near Bapaume on 25.9.1916, aged 26. Buried **GUARDS' CEMETERY, (LESBOEUFS)**. Grave location:- Plot 3, Row L, Grave 7. ROH:- Huddersfield Drill Hall; Almondbury War Memorial; Lowerhouses War Memorial; memorial in Almondbury Cemetery.

MURPHY, JAMES. Private. No 13442. 8th Battalion Duke of Wellington's Regiment. Born Meltham. Son of Patrick W. and Margaret Ann Murphy, 25 Ashworth Street, Binns Road, Liverpool. Died at home, 21.6.1916, aged 23 years. Buried **St. JAMES CHURCHYARD, MELTHAM MILLS**. Grave location:- East, F, 35. ROH:- St. Bartholomew's Church, Meltham.

MURPHY, JOSEPH. Corporal. No B/3008. 7th Battalion The Rifle Brigade. Born Exeter. Lived Huddersfield. Ward of E. Brown, 126 Edward Street, New Cross, London. Served in the Sudan campaign, the Nile expedition of 1898 and in the South African War. Died of wounds, 5.1.1916, aged 38 years. Buried **BOULOGNE EASTERN CEMETERY**. Grave location:- Plot 8, Row C, Grave 77.

MURPHY, PETER. Private. No 36533. 1/6th Battalion Northumberland Fusiliers. Born Kilkenny, County Mayo, Ireland. Husband of Annie Murphy, 26 Towngate, Marsden. Had lived for twenty years in Marsden. Employed as a mason's labourer by Messrs Brook and Holroyd, contractors, of Marsden. Enlisted July 1916. Embarked for France at Easter, 1917. Killed in action, 11.4.1918, aged 32 years. Has no known grave. Commemorated **PLOEGSTEERT MEMORIAL TO THE MISSING**. ROH:- Marsden War Memorial.

MURPHY, RICHARD. Gunner. No 44661. 98th Battery, 1st Brigade, Royal Field Artillery. Born 15 Old Post Office Yard, Huddersfield, 20.6.1893. Son of John and Annie Murphy, 40 Castlegate, Huddersfield. Educated St. Patrick's Roman Catholic School. Employed as an iron moulder. Single. Had been in America for two years when the war broke out and came home to enlist on 29.11.1914. Killed in action in Salonika, whilst working his gun on the banks of the river Struma, on 2.10.1916, aged 23 years. Buried **STRUMA MILITARY CEMETERY, SALONIKA, GREECE**. Grave location:- Plot 4, Row F, Grave 13.

MURRELL, AMBROSE. Private. No 242550. 1/5th Battalion Duke of Wellington's Regiment. Born Huddersfield. Son of Mrs Murrell, 16 Water Street, Huddersfield. Employed in the office of Messrs Wallaces Limited, St. John's Road, Huddersfield. Reported missing, presumed killed, at Nieuport, 16.8.1917, aged 28 years. Has no known grave. Commemorated **NIEUPORT MEMORIAL TO THE MISSING**. ROH:- Huddersfield Drill Hall.

NADIN, ALBERT. Private. No 20/135. 12th Battalion West Yorkshire Regiment. Born Nottingham. Only son of Mrs Jordan, 37 South Street, Huddersfield. Was a keen musician and a composer of poems. Single. Prior to the outbreak of the war had been employed at the Bradford Conditioning House. After war was declared, served in the Army Record Office at York. Enlisted October 1915. Embarked for France at Easter 1916. Killed in action during the Battle of the Somme on 19.7.1916, aged 32 years. Has no known grave. Commemorated **THIEPVAL MEMORIAL TO THE MISSING**.

NAIRN, WILLIAM CRAWFORD. Corporal. No 21/796. 21st Battalion West Yorkshire Regiment. Born Carluke, Lanarkshire, Scotland. Fourth son of Robert and Christina Nairn, 'Stoney Croft', 5 Brougham Road, Marsden. Was a member of the Marsden Adult School Institute. Played football with the Marsden United Football Club. Employed as a finisher by Mr J. E. Crowther, Bank Bottom Mills. Enlisted 14.2.1916. Embarked for France in June, 1916. Killed in action, 6.5.1917, aged 25 years. Buried **CRUMP TRENCH BRITISH CEMETERY**. Grave location:- Plot 1, Row C, Grave 31. His parents received the following letter from Captain Brazier, *'I deeply regret to inform you that your* son, Corporal W.C. Nairn, was killed in action on the night of Saturday May 5th. We were working in a trench and encounterred hostile shelling, your son unfortunately being hit in the body. He was taken to a dressing station quite near but the doctor gave but little hope of his recovery. He passed away half an hour later being unconscious all the time. What a sad blow it will be to you. We are all very much pained at the loss of such a splendid fellow. Your son was one of my trusted N.C.O's. He was with me ever since he joined the army. We buried him in a British cemetery close to where he fell and placed a wooden cross thereon inscribed with his name.'* ROH:- Marsden War Memorial.

NALSON, FREDERICK ALFRED. Private. 8th (City of London) Battalion (Post Office Rifles). Born Huddersfield 9.5.1885. Son of Mrs Nalson, 25 Fitzwilliam Street, Huddersfield. Educated at Huddersfield schools. Employed as a postman and sorter at Huddersfield General Post Office. Husband of Margaret Nalson (Later of 37 Higson Avenue, Chorlton-cum-Hardy, Manchester). Enlisted August 1915. Taken Prisoner of War by the Germans on 21.5.1916. *During the two and half years of his imprisonment in Munster, Germany, he was forced to work in a coal mine for twelve hours every day, including Sundays, without food except that sent by the British Red Cross.* Was released from imprisonment and returned to work at the Post Office in Huddersfield. Died of mitral valvular heart disease, caused by overwork during imprisonment in Germany, on 17.3.1921 at 25 Fitzwilliam Street, Huddersfield, aged 35. Buried **EDGERTON CEMETERY, HUDDERSFIELD.** ROH:- Huddersfield General Post Office.

NAYLOR, ARTHUR DIXON. Private. No 30/351. 13th Battalion Northumberland Fusiliers. Born 21.1.1889. Son of Charles and Mary Naylor, 2 Commercial Crescent, Huddersfield. Educated South Shore Council School, Blackpool, and St. Thomas's Church of England School, Longroyd Bridge, Huddersfield. Employed by Messrs J. Bray and Company Limited, ale and porter bottlers, Rook Street, Huddersfield. Attended St. Thomas's Church, Longroyd Bridge, and was a member of the bible class. Single. Enlisted April 1916. Had been in France six months when he was killed near Croisilles during the Battle of Arras on 14.4.1917, aged 28 years. Has no known grave. Commemorated **ARRAS MEMORIAL TO THE MISSING.** (Brother of Private **HENRY NAYLOR,** died as a Prisoner of War, 31.7.1918, q.v.). ROH:- St. Thomas's Church, Longroyd Bridge.

NAYLOR, ARTHUR VICTOR. Private. No 30/304. 13th Battalion Northumberland Fusiliers. Born Almondbury 20.3.1886. Son of John William and Mary Gayton Naylor, 43 Grasmere Road, Marsh. Educated Holy Trinity Church School and Spring Grove Council School. Employed as a draper. Single. Enlisted 28.5.1916. Reported missing, presumed killed, 16.6.1917. Has no known grave. Commemorated **ARRAS MEMORIAL TO THE MISSING.**

NAYLOR, HAROLD. Private. No 3547. 1/5th Battalion Duke of Wellington's Regiment. Born Holmbridge. Son of Fred and Emily Naylor, Brown Hill Lane, Holmbridge. Attended St. David's Church, Holmbridge and Sunday School and was a member of the choir. Was on the staff of the 'Holmfirth Express'. Enlisted at the outbreak of the war. Embarked for France in April, 1915. Wounded in the head on 23.12.1915. Died of wounds at No 10 Casualty Clearing Station, 26.12.1915, aged 22 years. Buried **LIJSSENTHOEK MILITARY CEMETERY.** Grave location:- Plot 2, Row B, Grave 27. ROH:- Holme and Holmbridge War Memorial; Huddersfield Drill Hall.

NAYLOR, HENRY. Private. No 28833. 6th Battalion Leicestershire Regiment. Formerly No 32828 Northumberland Fusiliers. Born Leeds 7.10.1890. Son of Mary Naylor, 2 Commercial Crescent, Huddersfield. Educated South Shore Council School, Blackpool and St. Thomas's Church of England School, Longroyd Bridge, Huddersfield. Single. Died as a Prisoner of War in Germany on 31.7.1918, aged 27 years. Buried **BERLIN SOUTH-WESTERN CEMETERY, STAHNSDORF, GERMANY.** Grave location:- Plot 16, Row A, Grave 6. (Brother of Private **ARTHUR DIXON NAYLOR,** killed in action, 14.4.1917, q.v.). ROH:- St. Thomas's Church, Longroyd Bridge.

NAYLOR, HERBERT. Private. No TF. 235113. 1/7th Battalion Middlesex Regiment. Born Gildersome near Morley, Leeds, 30.8.1884.

Employed as a woollen weaver at Ashbrow Mills. Husband of Edith Naylor, 15 Netheroyd Hill, Huddersfield. Enlisted 25.8.1916. Died of wounds, 16.8.1917, aged 32. Buried **BRANDHOEK NEW MILITARY CEMETERY No 3**. Grave location:- Plot 1, Row A, Grave 10. ROH:- Netheroyd Hill Methodist Church; Fartown and Birkby War Memorial.

NAYLOR, HERBERT HIRST. Battery Sergeant Major. No 19705. 225th Siege Battery, Royal Garrison Artillery. Born Hinchliffe Mill, Holmfirth. Son of the late Lot and Mrs Naylor. Educated Field End School. Attended St. David's Church, Holmbridge, where he was a member of the choir. Prior to enlistment, was employed as an apprentice by Messrs Lawton and Hogley, painters and decorators, of Holmfirth. Enlisted on his 18th birthday in the Royal Garrison Artillery, Easter Tuesday, 1897. Over the next six years he served in Nova Scotia, Quebec, British Columbia, Hong Kong and Singapore. He then returned to England and was put on the staff of the Garrison Artillery at New Brighton. Whilst at New Brighton he married a Liverpool girl and they had three children. He remained there for five years and then was again sent on foreign service, this time to Jamaica. On the outbreak of war he applied to go to France but this was refused on the grounds of his indispensibility. But, in 1916, his application was successful and he arrived in France in December, 1916. Died from burns on 17.10.1917, aged 38 years. Buried **HAZEBROUCK COMMUNAL CEMETERY.** Grave location:- Plot 3, Row F, Grave 25. ROH:- Holme and Holmbridge War Memorial.

NAYLOR, WILFRED. Private. No 241106. 1/6th Battalion Duke of Wellington's Regiment. Born Moldgreen, Huddersfield, 9.10.1897. Son of Arthur and Hannah Frances Naylor, 8 Wakefield Road, Moldgreen. Educated Almondbury Grammar School. Employed as an apprentice engineer by Messrs J. Hopkinson and Company of Birkby. Attended Moldgreen Congregational Church and Sunday School. Single. Killed in action, 11.4.1918, aged 21 years. Has no known grave. Commemorated **TYNE COT MEMORIAL TO THE MISSING.** ROH:- Almondbury Grammar School; Huddersfield Parish Church; Christ Church, Moldgreen; memorial in Almondbury Cemetery.

NAYLOR, WILLIE. Rifleman. No R/39492. 2nd Battalion King's Royal Rifle Corps. Formerly No 31763 Garrison Battalion Northamptonshire Regiment. Born Atherton. Son of Albert and Sophia Naylor, 52 Carr Lane, Slaithwaite. Attended Wellhouse Chapel. Employed as a night spinner by Messrs Pearson Brothers, Victoria Mills, Golcar. Enlisted March 1916. Invalided home from the front in September, 1916, suffering from dysentery. Returned to France in March, 1917. Wounded in the right groin and abdomen on 8.11.1917. Died of wounds at No 12 Casualty Clearing Station, 8.11.1917, aged 28 years. Buried **LIJSSENTHOEK MILITARY CEMETERY.** Grave location:- Plot 22, Row AA, Grave 26. ROH:- St. James Church; Slaithwaite; Slaithwaite War Memorial; St. John's Church, Golcar.

NEAL, WILLIAM HENRY. Private. No SS/18735 Army Service Corps, transferred to No 301432 719th Company, Labour Corps. Husband of Edith Neal, of Town End, Shelley. Suffered from shell shock and died in Warrington Hospital, 23.9.1917, aged 44 years. Buried with full military honours in **ALL HALLOWS CHURCHYARD, KIRKBURTON.** Grave location:- 26, 1994. ROH:- All Hallows Parish Church, Kirkburton.

NELSON, FREDERICK. Lance Corporal. No 14880. 9th Battalion King's Own Yorkshire Light Infantry. Born 21 Tunnicliffe Hill, Huddersfield. Son of Benjamin and Elizabeth Nelson, 49 Hope Street, St. Andrew's Road, Huddersfield. Educated Thomas Street Board School. Employed as a machine fitter by Messrs J. Hopkinson and Company Limited, Birkby. Attended Northumberland Street Primitive Methodist Church. Single. Enlisted 26.8.1914. Killed in action during the Battle of Arras on 9.4.1917, aged 23 years. Buried **COJEUL BRITISH CEMETERY.** Grave location:- Row D, Grave 7. ROH:- Northumberland Street Primitive Methodist Church and School.

NESS, DOUGLAS. Private. No 241765. 'C' Company, 2/5th Battalion Duke of Wellington's Regiment. Born Belle View, Sheepridge. Son of the late Edward Ness, 34 Sanitary Lane, Huddersfield. Educated Great Northern Street School. Employed as a mason by Messrs

Dawson and Jones, contractors, of Moldgreen. Single. Enlisted 17.3.1916. Reported missing, presumed killed, at the Battle of Bullecourt on 3.5.1917, aged 24 years. Has no known grave. Commemorated **ARRAS MEMORIAL TO THE MISSING**. ROH:- St. Andrew's Church, Leeds Road, Huddersfield; Huddersfield Drill Hall.

NESTOR, JOHN. Private. No 38087. 39th Field Ambulance Royal Army Medical Corps. Born York. Son of Mr and Mrs Thomas Nestor, 1 Castle Street, Slaithwaite. Before leaving Slaithwaite, was employed as a weaver by Messrs Pearson Brothers Limited, Commercial Mills, Slaithwaite. Played second cornet in the Slaithwaite Brass Band. In 1912 he left Slaithwaite for Oldham where he joined the Oldham Police Force. In September, 1914, with other members of the force, he enlisted in the R.A.M.C., 13th Division, which went to the Dardenelles, where he acted as a stretcher-bearer. Killed in action, 7.8.1915, aged 24 years. Buried **No 2 OUTPOST CEMETERY, ANZAC, GALLIPOLI**. Grave location:- Special Memorial 29. ROH:- St. James Church, Slaithwaite; Slaithwaite War Memorial. His parents received a letter from one of their son's chums, Private Thomas Mulcrone, who had also served in the Oldham Police force, *'It is my extremely sad and painful duty to have to inform you of the death of your son Jack, which occurred on August 7th. We had just moved to a new position and were going to collect some wounded when Jack and another stretcher-bearer were struck by a piece of shell which killed them both instantly. I saw him buried and obtained permission from my Commanding Officer to retain his watch which I will let you have at the first opportunity. Before closing I wish to express the deepest sympathy of all the men of the 39th in this your great loss. I can assure you that there was not a more popular man in the Ambulance than poor old Jack.'*

NESTOR, PATRICK. Private. No 10566. 2nd Battalion Duke of Wellington's Regiment. Born Margaret Street, Widnes, Lancashire. Son of James and Cecilia Nestor, 16 Dock Street, Huddersfield. Educated St. Patrick's Roman Catholic School, Huddersfield. Employed as a labourer in the Longwood goods yard. Single. Enlisted 18.4.1913. Mobilised 4.8.1914. Reported missing, presumed killed, during heavy fighting near Veldhoek Chateau during the first battle of Ypres on 11.11.1914, aged 20 years. Has no known grave. Commemorated **MENIN GATE MEMORIAL TO THE MISSING**.

NETHERWOOD, GEORGE EDGAR. Corporal. No 34732. 7th Battalion Border Regiment. Born Leeds Road North, Huddersfield, 20.9.1891. Son of George and Mary Jane Netherwood, 17 St. Peter's Street, Huddersfield. Educated at Hillhouse and Spring Grove Council Schools. Employed as a book keeper by Messrs Moxon, coal merchants, Westgate, Huddersfield. Single. Enlisted 26.10.1915. Died of bronchial pneumonia, following upon influenza, at No 46 Stationary Hospital on 26.10.1918, aged 27 years. Buried **ETAPLES MILITARY CEMETERY**. Grave location:- Plot 67, Row L, Grave 25. ROH:- Fartown and Birkby War Memorial.

NETHERWOOD, THOMAS. Private. No 208731. 5th Battalion Middlesex Regiment. Formerly No 2707 Duke of Wellington's Regiment. Born Moldgreen, Huddersfield, 6.1.1895. Son of Walter and Emily Netherwood, 13 Newsome Road, Huddersfield. Educated Stile Common Council School. Employed at the Karrier Car Works, Huddersfield. Single. Enlisted 1914. Wounded in the hand 24.12.1916. Died in 3rd Northern General Hospital, Sheffield, of pneumonia following upon influenza, 9.11.1918, aged 23 years. Buried **ALMONDBURY CEMETERY, HUDDERSFIELD**. Grave location:- 8, 'C', 31. ROH:- St. Paul's Church, Southgate, Huddersfield; Almondbury War Memorial.

NEWELL, BRIAN COLTHURST. Private. No 52543. 1st Battalion West Yorkshire Regiment. Formerly No 31935 Duke of Wellington's Regiment. Born London. Son of the late James and Dorothy Newell. Husband of Florence Newell, 6 Marsh Platt, Honley. Employed by Messrs Cooper, Liversedge and Wood Limited, Neiley Dyeworks, Honley. Killed in action, 17.9.1918, aged 27 years. Buried **CHAPELLE BRITISH CEMETERY, HOLNON**. Grave location:- Plot 2, Row A, Grave 4. ROH:- Honley War Memorial.

NEWMAN, CYRIL BROWN. 2nd Lieutenant. 7th Battalion Duke of Wellington's Regiment. Born Marsden. Son of Mr and Mrs J. E. Newman, 'West Leigh', Marsden. Educated

Marsden National School and Huddersfield Higher Grade School. He then spent twelve months in Switzerland learning the French language. He returned to England and was employed by Messrs Mellish, Richardson and Company, of Wortley, Leeds, cloth manufacturers, to learn the business. Was a teacher in Marsden Church Sunday School and a member of the Church of England Men's Society. Was also a member of the Marsden Conservative Club. Was a gifted musician, the violin being his favourite instrument. Enrolled in the Leeds University Officers' Training Corps for six months military training. On 23.7.1915 he was granted a commission in the Duke of Wellington's Regiment. Embarked for France 14.6.1916. Killed in action in the attack on the Schwaben Redoubt on Sunday, 3.9.1916, aged 20 years. Buried **LONSDALE CEMETERY**. Grave location:- Plot 8, Row E, Grave 3. ROH:- Marsden War Memorial; Marsden Conservative Club Roll; Huddersfield Drill Hall.

NEWSOME, ARTHUR. Corporal. No 45975. 11th Battalion Northumberland Fusiliers. Formerly No 36642 The Yorkshire Regiment. Son of Charlie and Sarah Ann Newsome, Commonside, Kirkburton. Was a bootmaker, in business with his father, before enlisting. Killed in action in Italy, 15.6.1918, aged 23 years. Buried **MAGNABOSCHI BRITISH CEMETERY**. Grave location:- Plot 3, Row C, Grave 1. ROH:- All Hallows Parish Church, Kirkburton.

NEWSOME, FRED. Rifleman. No B/203225. 13th Battalion The Rifle Brigade. Born Batley Carr, Yorkshire. Son of George and Annie Newsome, 7 Lower Fold, Honley. Employed at Thirstin Mill. Attended the Wesleyan Sunday School. Had been a keen follower of the Honley Hunt and kept one of the hounds. Enlisted with his brother in November, 1915. Killed by a German rifle grenade on 12.10.1916, aged 23 years. Buried **MAROC BRITISH CEMETERY**. Grave location:- Plot 1, Row E, Grave 7. (Brother of Private **WILLIE NEWSOME**, died of wounds, 16.9.1916, q.v.). ROH:- Honley War Memorial.

NEWSOME, HAROLD. Private. No 805. 21st Battalion West Yorkshire Regiment. Born Netherton, Huddersfield. Son of Joseph and Martha Ann Newsome, Scotgate Bottom, Netherton. Enlisted February 1916. Killed by a shell on 30.3.1917, aged 25 years. Buried **FAUBOURG D' AMIENS CEMETERY, ARRAS.** Grave location:- Plot 2, Row M, Grave 3. ROH:- South Crosland and Netherton War Memorial.

NEWSOME, WILLIE. Rifleman. No C/7671. 18th Battalion King's Royal Rifle Corps. Born Ravensthorpe, Dewsbury. Third son of George and Annie Newsome, 7 Lower Fold, Honley. Employed at Messrs Wrigley's Mill at Netherton. Attended Honley Wesleyan School. Was a member of the Honley Conservative Club. Enlisted with his brother in November, 1915. Died from gunshot wounds to the head at No 36 Casualty Clearing Station on 16.9.1916, aged 21 years. Buried **HEILLY STATION CEMETERY**. Grave location:- Plot 4, Row D, Grave 52. (Brother of Private **FRED NEWSOME**, killed in action, 12.10.1916, q.v.). ROH:- Honley War Memorial.

NEWTON, BEN. Gunner. No 161705. 144th Siege Battery, Royal Garrison Artillery. Born Golcar. Husband of Hetty Newton, 1 Scarhouse Lane, Golcar. Prior to his marriage in 1913, had lived at Garden Terrace, Linthwaite. Employed by Messrs George Cock Limited, dyers, Linthwaite. Attended Linthwaite Wesleyan Chapel and was a member of the Linthwaite Cricket Club. Enlisted 9.5.1917. Embarked for France, 22.10.1917. Killed in action, 28.11.1917, aged 29 years. Buried **BARD COTTAGE CEMETERY, BOESINGHE, BELGIUM**. Grave location:- Plot 5, Row C, Grave 25. His widow received a letter from the Chaplain in which he told her that, *'Gunner Newton was killed in action on 28.11.1917. He had been on duty with his Battery the previous night and just before midnight a shell struck the shelter in which he was sleeping. Death was instantenous and he could have suffered no pain whatsoever'*. ROH:- St. John's Church, Golcar.

NEWTON, FRANCIS (FRANK) HARTLEY. Private. No TR/5/113149. 31st Battalion (86th Training reserve) Northumberland Fusiliers. Born Clapham, London. Son of Ernest Priestley Newton and Alice Hartley Newton, 8 Muirdown Avenue, East Sheen, London. Lived Huddersfield. Employed as a mechanical draughtsman by Messrs Tasker and Crossley, patent agents, John William Street, Huddersfield. Attended Huddersfield Technical College. Was a member of the Y.M.C.A. Attended Christ Church,

Woodhouse Hill. Enlisted September 1917. Died at Scotton Camp, 22.11.1917, aged 18 years. Buried **St. JOHN'S CHURCHYARD, HIPSWELL, CATTERICK, NORTH YORKSHIRE.** Grave Location:- Row 21, Grave 7. ROH:- Christ Church, Woodhouse Hill.

NEWTON, JOE. Private. No 241888. 'D' Company 2/5th Battalion Duke of Wellington's Regiment. Born Holmfirth. Son of John and Mary Ann Newton, Half Roods, Meltham. Employed by Messrs A. T. Woodhead and Sons, Sunnybank Mills, Meltham. Was a member of the Meltham Conservative Club. Enlisted March 1916. Embarked for France in January, 1917. Died of wounds at No 48 Casualty Clearing Station on 28.11.1917, aged 38 years. Buried **ROCQUIGNY-EQUANCOURT ROAD BRITISH CEMETERY.** Grave location:- Plot 4, Row A, Grave 16. ROH:- St. Bartholomew's Church, Meltham; Huddersfield Drill Hall.

NICHOLLS, GEORGE HERBERT. Private. No 27658. 92nd Company Machine Gun Corps. Formerly No 17904 Duke of Wellington's Regiment. Born Taylor Hill, Lockwood, Huddersfield. Son of Walter and Elizabeth Nicholls, 10 Stoney Lane, Taylor Hill. Educated Lockwood Church Schools. Employed as a twister-in by Messrs B. Vickerman and Sons, Taylor Hill Mills. Attended Lockwood Parish Church and was a member of the Young Men's Class. Enlisted 21.1.1916. Died of wounds, 28.6.1916, aged 21 years. Buried **BERTRANCOURT MILITARY CEMETERY.** Grave location:- Plot 1, Row D, Grave 20. ROH:- Emmanuel Church, Lockwood; Taylor Hill Primitive Methodist Church.

NICHOLSON, GEORGE HENRY. Driver. No L/29298 Royal Field Artillery. Born Spring Street, Huddersfield, 24.6.1891. Educated Paddock Church of England Boys School. Employed as a woollen minder by Mr James Sykes, Stafford Mills, Milnsbridge. Attended Milton Church P.S.A. Married. Lived at Lark Street, Paddock. Reported missing, presumed killed, 24.3.1918, aged 26. Has no known grave. Commemorated **ARRAS MEMORIAL TO THE MISSING.** ROH:- St. Mark's Parish Church, Longwood.

NIND, ALBERT. Private. No 7712. 4th Battalion Worcestershire Regiment. Born Worcestershire in 1886. Married. Lived 10 Mills Row, Castlegate. Employed as a labourer. Was serving in the army prior to the outbreak of the war. Mobilised 4.8.1914. Killed in action at the Battle of Krithia Vineyard, Gallipoli, on 6.8.1915, aged 29 years. Has no known grave. Commemorated **HELLES MEMORIAL TO THE MISSING.** ROH:- Huddersfield Parish Church.

NOBLE, ARTHUR. Private. No 42570. 2nd Battalion West Yorkshire Regiment. Son of Mr and Mrs Alfred Noble, Wood Nook, Meltham. Husband of Hannah Noble, 8 Park Terrace, Upperthong Lane, Holmfirth. Had worked on the London and Yorkshire permanent way (Brockholes section). Enlisted 10.2.1917. Embarked for France 20.5.1917. Killed in action, 22.6.1917, aged 29 years. Buried **MENIN ROAD SOUTH MILITARY CEMETERY.** Grave location:- Plot 1, Row S, Grave 18. ROH:- Upperthong War Memorial; Honley War Memorial.

NOBLE, CHARLES. Private. No 37611. 10th Battalion King's Own Yorkshire Light Infantry. Formerly No 4489 Duke of Wellington's Regiment. Enlisted Huddersfield. Lived Lockwood, Huddersfield. (late of Norman Road, Birkby). Mother lived at 24 Weatherhill Road, Birchencliffe. Killed in action during the Battle of the Somme, 25.9.1916. Has no known grave. Commemorated **THIEPVAL MEMORIAL TO THE MISSING.** ROH:- Fartown and Birkby War Memorial.

NOBLE, GEORGE DUNBAR. Rifleman. No 45178. 1/5th London Regiment, The Rifle Brigade. Formerly No 30/392 Northumberland Fusiliers. Born Hopkinson's Yard, Lockwood Road, Huddersfield, 12.12.1892. Youngest son of Mr and Mrs J. Noble, 60 Lockwood Road, Huddersfield. Educated Rashcliffe Church of England School. Married. Lived 60 Lockwood Road, Huddersfield. Employed as a butcher by the Huddersfield Industrial Society in the Central butchering department. Killed in action, 29.8.1918. Has no known grave. Commemorated **VIS-en-ARTOIS MEMORIAL TO THE MISSING.** ROH:- St. Stephen's Church, Rashcliffe.

NOBLE, JAMES WILLIAM. Private. No 9182. 1st Battalion Wiltshire Regiment. Born Crosland Road, Lindley, 4.6.1890. Lived Birchencliffe.

Employed as an apprentice by Messrs John Haigh and Sons Limited, engineers, Firth Street, Huddersfield. Enlisted July 1914. Killed in action,n 24.12.1914. Buried **RUE-DAVID MILITARY CEMETERY, FLEURBAIX**. Grave location:- Plot 1, Row H, Grave 43. ROH:- Holy Trinity Church, Huddersfield.

NOBLE, REGINALD. Private. No 46510. 12th/13th Battalion Northumberland Fusiliers. Born Cowcliffe, Huddersfield, 4.8.1897. Son of Alfred and Annie Noble, 195 Cowcliffe Hill Road, Huddersfield. Educated Cowcliffe and St. John's schools, Huddersfield. Employed as a cloth finisher by Messrs J. Heywood and Sons, Marsh Mills. Attended Cowcliffe Wesleyan Chapel. Single. Enlisted 22.7.1916. Reported wounded and missing at the Battle of Passchendaele on 4.10.1917 and afterwards presumed to have been killed on that date, aged 19. Has no known grave. Commemorated **TYNE COT MEMORIAL TO THE MISSING**. ROH:- Netheroyd Hill Methodist Church; Cowcliffe Wesleyan Church; Fartown and Birkby War Memorial.

NOBLE, WILFRED. Private. No 291836. 1/7th Battalion Northumberland Fusiliers. Born Midhope. Son of Hannah Noble, 14 Water Street, Stand Lane, Radcliffe, Manchester. Before moving to Manchester lived at Hillhouse Lane, Huddersfield. Was employed as a teamer by Messrs Wallaces Limited, St. John's Road, Huddersfield. Killed in action at Passchendaele, 26.10.1917, aged 23 years. Has no known grave. Commemorated **TYNE COT MEMORIAL TO THE MISSING**. ROH:- Shared Church, Paddock.

NOBLE, WILLIE. Private. No G/66079. 10th Battalion Royal Fusiliers. Formerly No 77198 89th T.R. Battalion. Born Golcar. Only son of Mr and Mrs Thomas Noble, 79 Britannia Road, Milnsbridge. Employed as a weaver by Messrs Ben Hall and Son, Milnsbridge. Attended St. Michael's Church, Milnsbridge and was a member of the choir. Enlisted 29.12.1916. Embarked for France in May 1917. Killed by a shell on 5.8.1917, aged 19 years. Has no known grave. Commemorated **MENIN GATE MEMORIAL TO THE MISSING**. ROH:- St. John's Church, Golcar.

NORCLIFFE, HAROLD. Private. No 45882. 25th (Tyneside Irish) Battalion Northumberland Fusiliers. Born Slaithwaite. Son of John Edward and Nancy Jane Norcliffe, White Lea Farm, Marsden. Employed at Stanley Mills, Milnsbridge. Had been a chorister at Linthwaite Parish Church. Enlisted July 1916. Embarked for France in December, 1916. Reported missing, presumed killed, at Passchendaele, 12.10.1917, aged 20 years. Has no known grave. Commemorated **TYNE COT MEMORIAL TO THE MISSING**. ROH:- Marsden War Memorial.

NORCLIFFE, TOM. Private. No 39649. 9th Battalion King's Own Yorkshire Light Infantry. Son of Mr and Mrs Sam Norcliffe, 88 Alder Street, Huddersfield. Employed in the finishing department of Messrs T. and H. Blamires Limited, Leeds Road, Huddersfield. Killed in action, 7.7.1917, aged 20 years. Buried **St. LEGER BRITISH CEMETERY**. Grave location:- Row F, Grave 10. ROH:- St. Andrew's Church, Leeds Road, Huddersfield.

NORMINGTON, CYRIL. Private. No 40019. 25th (Tyneside Irish) Battalion Northumberland Fusiliers. Born Kirkheaton. Enlisted Halifax. Killed in action, 23.3.1918. Has no known grave. Commemorated **ARRAS MEMORIAL TO THE MISSING**. ROH:- St. John's Church, Kirkheaton.

NORRIS, HARRY. Private. No 204735. 2/5th Battalion Duke of Wellington's Regiment. Born Victoria Place, Dalton 26.6.1889. Lived with his sister, Sarah E. Norris, at 107 Almondbury Bank, Huddersfield. Educated Moldgreen Board School. Employed as a bobbin carrier in the warehouse of Mr J. L. Brierley, Turnbridge Mills. Was a member of the Forest Road Working Men's Club. Enlisted 16.2.1916. Killed in action at the Battle of Cambrai, 27.11.1917, aged 27 years. Has no known grave. Commemorated **CAMBRAI MEMORIAL TO THE MISSING**. ROH:- Huddersfield Drill Hall.

NORRIS, JOHN MEEK. Lance Corporal. No 8837. 1st Battalion Lincolnshire Regiment. Born Holbeach, Lincolnshire. Son of John Edward and Sarah Jane Norris, 28 Brook Terrace, Slaithwaite. Enlisted in the Lincolnshire Regiment on 20.1.1910. Served with the 2nd Battalion. At the outbreak of the war the battalion was in Bermuda. Returned to England on the 3.11.1914. Sailed for France, 5.11.1914, and landed at Le

Havre 6.11.1914. Invalided home with shell shock on 14.1.1915. Was admitted to Netley Hospital. Returned to France on the 9.8.1916. Served with the 1st Battalion Lincolnshire Regiment. Wounded in the chest and abdomen on 30.1.1917. Was admitted to the 20th Casualty Clearing Station, where he died of his wounds on 3.4.1917. Buried **WARLINCOURT HALTE BRITISH CEMETERY.** Grave location:- Plot 6, Row G, Grave 12. ROH:- St. James Church, Slaithwaite; Slaithwaite War Memorial.

NORTCLIFFE, ALBERT. Private. No 77988. 15th Battalion Durham Light Infantry. Born 97 High Royd Lane, Moldgreen, Huddersfield. Son of Joe and Annis Nortcliffe. Educated Moldgreen Church of England School. Employed as a shop assistant at the Huddersfield Industrial Society's branch at Thornton Lodge. Single. Enlisted 13.10.1916. Reported missing, presumed killed, 21.3.1918, aged 19 years. Has no known grave. Commemorated **POZIERES MEMORIAL TO THE MISSING.** ROH:- Christ Church, Moldgreen.

NORTCLIFFE, GILBERT. Private. No 23165. 9th Battalion Duke of Wellington's Regiment. Born Kilner Bank, Moldgreen, 24.5.1880. Educated Moldgreen Board School. Employed as a grocer's assistant at the Northumberland Street branch of the Huddersfield Industrial Society for 26 years. Husband of Gertrude Nortcliffe, 29 Blackhouse Road, Fartown. Enlisted 15.6.1916. Twice wounded. Suffered severe gunshot wounds to the head on 15.10.1918, at Cambrai. Was under treatment at the Tooting Military Hospital on arrival from France. Died of wounds at Brooklands Hospital, Weybridge, Surrey, on 17.1.1919, aged 39 years. Buried **EDGERTON CEMETERY, HUDDERSFIELD.** Grave location:- 31, 13C. ROH:- Huddersfield Parish Church; Christ Church, Woodhouse Hill; Fartown and Birkby War Memorial.

NORTH, ELI. Private. No 302105. 2/7th Battalion The Royal Scots. Born Honley. Son of Joe and Alice North. Husband of Frances North, 33 New Street, Honley. Died at home, 29.8.1917, aged 41 years. Buried **HONLEY CHURCH BURIAL GROUND.** Grave location:- 61, 669. ROH:- Honley War Memorial.

NORTH, ERNEST. Private. No 155410. 5th Battalion Machine Gun Corps. Formerly No 39310 Duke of Wellington's Regiment. Born Honley. Son of Mr and Mrs William North, 18 Sunny Woodhouse, Honley. Was an apprentice with Mr Edgar S. Jessop, plasterer, of Honley. Killed in action, 27.9.1918, aged 19 years. Buried **SUNKEN ROAD CEMETERY, VILLERS-PLOUICH.** Grave location:- Row A, Grave 35. ROH:- Honley War Memorial.

NORTH, HUBERT. Driver. No 104209. 234th Field Company, Royal Engineers. Born 1 Thomas Street, Huddersfield, 22.3.1896. Son of Joe and Lucy Annie North, Elder Cottage, 66 Luck Lane, Marsh, Huddersfield. Educated Siddal Council School, Halifax. Employed as a commercial traveller for Messrs Radcliffe Brothers, grease extractors, West Vale, Halifax. At the time of enlistment, was living at 20 Cinderhills Lane, Siddal, Halifax. Single. Enlisted 3.8.1915. Wounded at St. Julien, Belgium, on 31.7.1917, during the Battle of Pilckem Ridge. Died of wounds on 31.7.1917, aged 21. Buried at **DUHALLOW A.D.S. CEMETERY, YPRES.** Grave location:- Plot 1, Row A, Grave 46. ROH:- Marsh War Memorial.

NORTH, JAMES. Private. No 242870. 2nd Battalion Duke of Wellington's Regiment. Born Hillhouse, Huddersfield, 29.10.1883. Educated Hillhouse Council School. Employed as a teamer at Longwood Gasworks. Husband of Eva Lilian North, 119 South Street, Huddersfield. Enlisted 8.9.1916. Severely wounded in August 1917. Killed in action, 28.3.1918, aged 34 years. Has no known grave. Commemorated **ARRAS MEMORIAL TO THE MISSING.**

NORTH, NEVILLE MARRIOTT, MC. Captain. 5th Battalion Northumberland Fusiliers. Son of Frances North, 5 Goldington Avenue, Bedford and the late Harry North. Nephew of the Misses North of Sunwood House. Educated Huddersfield College School. Lived in Huddersfield until he was 15 years old. Prior to enlistment, was employed as a civil engineer at Newcastle-on-Tyne. Was among the earliest of the old boys of Huddersfield College School to win the Military Cross. It was awarded for distinguished conduct in action on the Belgian front, when he was attached to the 3rd Battalion of the Northumberland Fusiliers. (London Gazette 14th January 1916). Wounded on two occasions. Reported wounded and missing near Rheims on 27.5.1918 and afterwards presumed to have been killed on that date. Has no known grave. He was 24 years of age. Commemorated **SOISSONS MEMORIAL TO THE MISSING.** ROH:- Huddersfield College School.

NORTH, TOM. Private. No 10680. 2nd Battalion Duke of Wellington's Regiment. Born Upper Cumberworth. Lived Meltham. Died of wounds (gas) received at Hill 60 on 5.5.1915. Buried **DIVISIONAL CEMETERY, DICKEBUSCH ROAD, VLAMERTINGHE, BELGIUM.** Grave location:- Row C, Grave 18. ROH:- St. Bartholomew's Church, Meltham.

NORTON, ARTHUR EDWIN. Private. No 5/2219. 1/5th Battalion Duke of Wellington's Regiment. Born Westminster, London. Son of Arthur Edwin and Alice Norton, 22 Murphy Street, Lambeth, London. Was employed as a hurrier by Messrs Lockwood and Elliott at Shuttle Eye Colliery, Grange Moor, near Huddersfield. Lodged at Flockton Moor. Served with the Kirkburton Company of the 1/5th Battalion Duke of Wellington's Regiment. Was killed by a shell whilst in a dugout on 3.7.1916, aged 21, during the Battle of the Somme. Buried **CONNAUGHT CEMETERY, THIEPVAL.** Grave location:- Plot 1, Row E, Grave 2. ROH:- All Hallows Church, Kirkburton; Huddersfield Drill Hall.

NOWELL, PERCY. Private. No 32035. 20th Battalion Durham Light Infantry. Born Shelley. Son of Mr Bob Nowell, Bankside, Shelley. Attended Shelley United Methodist Church. Employed by Messrs Firth Brothers. Enlisted July 1916. Wounded in December, 1916. On recovering from his wounds he returned to France, Whitsuntide, 1917. Killed in action, 31.7.1917, aged 26 years. Has no known grave. Commemorated **MENIN GATE MEMORIAL TO THE MISSING.** ROH:- Emmanuel Church, Shelley.

NUGENT, EDWARD WILLIAM. Private. No 1655. 1/7th Battalion Duke of Wellington's Regiment. Born Forfar, Scotland. Came to Huddersfield in 1913. Formerly employed by Messrs Read Holliday and Sons Limited and, just prior to enlistment, was employed by Messrs William Whiteley and Sons, Lockwood. Was a widower, with two children. Lodged with Mr and Mrs Bedford, Three Nuns, Cross Grove Street, Huddersfield. Killed by the explosion of a shell on 25.7.1915, aged 36 years. Buried **BARD COTTAGE CEMETERY.** Grave location:- Plot 1, Row E, Grave 16. ROH:- Huddersfield Drill Hall. Captain Alfred Bruzzard, the Medical Officer of the 7th Battalion writing to his friends in Huddersfield wrote, *'I am very sorry to tell you that I have lost one of my best Bearers in the death of Bandsman E. W. Nugent. He was killed by a shell bursting near him. His death was instantenous from concussion. He was not hit but the severe explosion near to him was sufficient to kill him. It was only the previous day he had excelled himself in helping a wounded comrade. At his duty of stretcher-bearer he was fearless. I mourn the loss of a good man.'*

NUTTALL, ALBERT ARMITAGE (BERT). 2nd Lieutenant. 7th Battalion Duke of Wellington's Regiment. Only surviving son of Mr and Mrs Robert H. Nuttall, Hollins House, Marsden. Educated Marsden National School and the High School for boys, Huddersfield. He then attended Huddersfield Technical College on a course of instruction in mechanics. He then enrolled as a student in the technical department of mechanical engineering at Manchester University, where he was awarded a BSc degree. Was a member of Marsden Liberal Club and a playing member of the Slaithwaite Golf Club. In October, 1914, he joined the Manchester University Officers' Training Corps. On 23.8.1915, he was gazetted Second Lieutenant in the Duke of Wellington's Regiment. He went through training courses at Scarborough, Ripon, Clipstone and Strensall, after which he embarked for France, in July 1916 – just seven weeks before he died of wounds at a field dressing station, on 15.8.1916, aged 20 years. Buried **FORCEVILLE COMMUNAL CEMETERY EXTENSION.** Grave location:- Plot 2, Row D, Grave 1. ROH:- Marsden War Memorial; Marsden Liberal Club; Huddersfield Drill Hall.

NUTTALL, FRANK. Gunner. No 114638. 'C' Battery, 62nd Brigade, Royal Field Artillery. Born Marsden. Son of Joshua Nuttall, Sand Hill, Marsden and the late Susannah Nuttall. Died of bronchial-pneumonia, following upon influenza, at No 56 General Hospital on 10.12.1918, aged 26 years. Buried **ETAPLES MILITARY CEMETERY.** Grave location:- Plot 47, Row C,

Grave 17. ROH:- Marsden War Memorial.

NUTTALL, JOSEPH. Private. No 241559. 2/5th Battalion Duke of Wellington's Regiment. Born Meltham. Son of George Thomas and Martha Hannah Nuttall, 11 East Street, Golcar. Educated Crow Lane Board School. Apprenticed to Mr S. Kendall, painter and decorator, Byrom Street, Huddersfield. Killed in action near Rheims, 20.7.1918, aged 21 years. Buried **COURMAS BRITISH CEMETERY.** Grave location:- Plot 2, Row D, Grave 8. ROH:- St. John's Church, Golcar; Crow Lane Board School, Milnsbridge; Huddersfield Drill Hall.

NUTTON, GEORGE HENRY. Corporal. No 40015. 15th Siege Battery, Royal Garrison Artillery. Born Lindley 26.5.1893. Son of Albert and Annie Nutton, Green Lea Lodge, Lindley. Educated Oakes Board School. Employed as an apprentice at Acre Mills. Attended St. Stephen's Church, Lindley. Was a keen football player. Enlisted November 1913. Had served for three years in France and was awaiting leave to return home to be married when he was accidentally burned. Died of burns at No 13 Casualty Clearing Station on 25.9.1917, aged 24 years. Buried **TINCOURT NEW BRITISH CEMETERY.** Grave location:- Plot 2, Row C, Grave 3. ROH:- St. Stephen's Church, Lindley.

NUTTON, WILFRED. Private. No 18301. 8th Battalion Duke of Wellington's Regiment. Died at the 1st Birmingham War Hospital, Rednell, Birmingham. Lived 9 Kew Hill, Lindley. Died 29.11.1918, aged 25 years. Buried **LINDLEY WESLEYAN METHODIST CHAPEL YARD.** Grave location:- J, 23.

O'BRIEN, JAMES L. HADCOCK. Private. No 40315. 18th Battalion West Yorkshire Regiment. Son of Mr J. O'Brien, 84 Birkby Hall Road, Huddersfield. Was a teacher at the Hillhouse United Methodist Church for several years. His fiance, Miss Stead was also a teacher at the school. Was well known in art circles and had been a student at the Huddersfield Technical College and, later, at the Royal College of Art. He gained the A.R.C.A. Diploma in June, 1915, and was awarded £10 for the best work of the year. Was a member of the Huddersfield Art Society and was an assistant at the Holmfirth Art School. Had been recommended for a commission. Killed in action, 13.11.1916, aged 25 years. Buried **SAILLY-AU-BOIS MILITARY CEMETERY.** Grave location:- Plot 2, Row E, Grave 1. ROH:- Fartown and Birkby War Memorial; Holmfirth Secondary School.

O'BRIEN, JOSEPH PATRICK. Sergeant. No 240944. 2/5th Battalion Duke of Wellington's Regiment. Born Huddersfield. Married, with two children. Lived 84 Bankfield Road, Moldgreen, Huddersfield. Employed as a tram conductor on the West Vale and Almondbury routes of the Huddersfield Corporation Tramways Department. Reported missing, presumed killed, at the Battle of Bullecourt on 3.5.1917, aged 28 years. Has no known grave. Commemorated **ARRAS MEMORIAL TO THE MISSING.** ROH:- Christ Church, Moldgreen; Huddersfield Drill Hall; Huddersfield Corporation Roll.

O'HARA, JOSEPH SYKES. Private. No 306345. 2/7th Battalion Duke of Wellington's Regiment. Son of Mr and Mrs Roger O'Hara, Delves, Lingards, Slaithwaite. Employed by the Colne Valley Spinning Company Limited, Linthwaite. Attended Slaithwaite Roman Catholic Church. Enlisted 16.11.1915. Embarked for France 10.1.1917. Killed in the attack on Bourlon village during the Battle of Cambrai on 27.11.1917, aged 23 years. Has no known grave. Commemorated **CAMBRAI MEMORIAL TO THE MISSING.** ROH:- St. James Church, Slaithwaite; Slaithwaite War Memorial; Huddersfield Drill Hall

O'HARA, WILLIAM. Private. No 52546. 1st Battalion West Yorkshire Regiment. Formerly No 31941 Duke of Wellington's Regiment. Born Huddersfield 11.11.1884. Educated St. Patrick's Roman Catholic School. Employed as a tailor's presser. Married. Lived 40 Ivy Street, Moldgreen. Enlisted 28.6.1917. Reported missing, presumed killed, 21.3.1918. Has no known grave. Commemorated **ARRAS MEMORIAL TO THE MISSING.** ROH:- Christ Church, Moldgreen.

O'KELLY, JAMES WILLIAM, MM. Able Seaman. ZP/1037. Royal Naval Volunteer Reserve. 'Hood' Battalion. Royal Naval Division. Lived 23 Upperhead Row, Huddersfield. He was at Headquarters mess canteen and was returning to a train after helping the Officers with dinner when the accident happened. Whilst he was attempting to board a train, which was already on the move, an engine coming in the other direction caught him on the shoulder, knocking him under the wheels of his own train and he was killed instantly on 2.10.1917. He had served in Gallipoli. Awarded the Military Medal on 26.3.1917. Buried **HAZEBROUCK COMMUNAL CEMETERY.** Grave location:- 3, F, 21. (Brother of Private **JAMES HENRY KELLY**, died 26.5.1918).

O'MELIA, FRED. Lance Corporal. No 2939. 1/5th Battalion Duke of Wellington's Regiment. Born Upperthong, Holmfirth. Husband of Mrs O'Melia, Crown Bottom, Holmfirth. Was a member of a well known Irish family who had lived in the Holmfirth area for over a generation. Educated Holmfirth Wesleyan Day School. Employed in the moulding shop of Messrs J. and J. W. Longbottom, Bridge Foundry, Holmfirth. Enlisted at the outbreak of the war. Went into training at Riby Camp and Doncaster. Wounded in the abdomen in the attack on the Schwaben Redoubt on 3.9.1916. Died of wounds at No 23 General Hospital, 9.9.1916, aged 27 years. Buried **ETAPLES MILITARY CEMETERY.** Grave location:- Plot 10, Row C, Grave 13. ROH:- Holmfirth War Memorial; Huddersfield Drill Hall.

O'MELIA, HARRY. Private. No 267884. 1/6th Battalion Duke of Wellington's Regiment. Born Holmfirth. Son of John W. and Margaret O'Melia of Norridge Bottom, Holmfirth. Educated Holmfirth Wesleyan Day School. Employed by Messrs B. Mellor and Son, Albert Mills, Holmfirth. Enlisted at the outbreak of the war. Wounded on one occasion. After treatment in England, returned to France. Wounded again, in the leg. Underwent amputation of the leg at No 26 General Hospital, but died on 23.4.1918, aged 21 years. Buried **ETAPLES MILITARY CEMETERY.** Grave location:- Plot 29, Row L, Grave 4a. (Cousin of Private **JAMES WILLIAM O' MELIA**, killed in action, 20.7.1918, q.v.). ROH:- Holmfirth War Memorial.

O'MELIA, JAMES WILLIAM. Private. No 203160. 2/5th Battalion West Yorkshire Regiment. Born Holmfirth. Son of Edward and Julia O'Melia, of Norridge Bottom, Holmfirth. Employed by Messrs Firth and Marsden, Bridge Foundry, Holmfirth. Killed in action near Rheims on 20.7.1918. Buried **MARFAUX BRITISH CEMETERY.** Grave location:- Plot 5, Row C, Grave 12. (Cousin of Private **HARRY O'MELIA**, died of wounds, 23.4.1918, q.v.). ROH:- Holmfirth War Memorial.

OATES, FREDERICK. Private. No 241822. 2/5th Battalion Duke of Wellington's Regiment. Born Hillhouse, Huddersfield, 28.5.1888. Son of Mrs Julietta Oates, 3 Holroyd's Buildings, Halifax Old Road, Huddersfield. Educated Hillhouse National Schools. Employed as a leather worker by Messrs T. and H. Blamires Limited, Leeds Road, Huddersfield. Single. Enlisted 21.3.1916. Reported missing, presumed killed, at the Battle of Bullecourt, 3.5.1917. Has no known grave. Commemorated **ARRAS MEMORIAL TO THE MISSING.** ROH:- St. John's Church, Birkby; Huddersfield Drill Hall; Fartown and Birkby War Memorial.

OATES, GILBERT. Private. No 38227. 15th Battalion West Yorkshire Regiment (1st Leeds Pals). Born Paddock, Huddersfield, 3.9.1898. Son of Oscar and Sarah Hannah Oates, 4 Royds Hall, Longwood Road, Paddock Head. Educated Paddock Church Schools. Employed as a workroom manager by Messrs Chilton, Wrigley and Company Limited, Viaduct Street, Huddersfield. Attended Paddock Congregational Church and as a member of the school club won a cup for playing billiards. Single. Enlisted October 1916. Embarked for France in January, 1917. Killed in action, 11.5.1917, aged 19, during the Battle of Arras. Buried **POINT-DU-JOUR MILITARY CEMETERY, ATHIES.** Grave location:- Plot 1, Row D, Grave 2. (Brother of Private **HAROLD OATES**, died of wounds, 29.7.1917, q.v.). ROH:-. St. Mark's Parish Church, Longwood; All Saints Church, Paddock; Shared Church, Paddock; memorial in Salendine Nook Baptist Chapel yard, 370E.

OATES, HAROLD. Bombardier. No L/25669. 168th (Huddersfield) Brigade, Royal Field Artillery. Born Paddock 19.2.1894. Son of Oscar and Sarah Hannah Oates, 4 Royds Hall, Longwood Road, Paddock Head. Educated Paddock Church of England School. Attended Paddock Church and was a member of Paddock Institute. Employed by the Standard Fireworks Company. Single. Enlisted in 1914. Wounded in the hip and thigh during the Battle of Arras on 8.7.1917. Died of wounds at Dudley Road

Hospital, Birmingham, on 20.7.1917, aged 23 years. Buried **SALENDINE NOOK BAPTIST CHAPEL YARD.** Grave location:- in East part, 370E. (Brother of Private **GILBERT OATES**, killed in action, 11.5.1917, q.v.). ROH:- St. Mark's Parish Church, Longwood; All Saints Church, Paddock.

ODDY, TOM. Private. No 33217. 7th Battalion King's Own Yorkshire Light Infantry. Born Birstall, Yorkshire, 28.10.1891. Son of Mr and Mrs Oddy, 6 Upper Quarry Road, Bradley. Educated Bradley Church of England School. Employed as a groom. Single. Killed in action at Passchendaele, 19.8.1917. Has no known grave. Commemorated **TYNE COT MEMORIAL TO THE MISSING.** ROH:- St. Thomas's Church, Bradley.

OLDFIELD, ALFRED EDWARD. Private. No M2/078203. 605th Motor Transport Company, Army Service Corps. Born 21.7.1893. Son of Mr and Mrs Oldfield, 65 Manchester Road, Huddersfield. Educated Rashcliffe Church of England School. Reported missing from the Italian Transport ship 'Citta di Palermo', which was sunk by a mine in the Adriatic Sea, ten miles from Brindisi, on 8.1.1916, with the loss of 57 British soldiers. Has no known grave. Commemorated **HOLLYBROOK MEMORIAL TO THE MISSING.** ROH:- St. Thomas's Church, Longroyd Bridge.

OLDFIELD, FRED. Rifleman. No C/7399. 18th Battalion King's Royal Rifle Corps. Born Berry Brow, Huddersfield, 22.4.1886. Educated Newsome Church of England School. Married, with two children. Lived 12 Ing Lane, Newsome. Employed as a cloth finisher. Enlisted 2.11.1915. Killed in action at the Battle of Flers-Courcelette on 15.9.1916. Has no known grave. Commemorated **THIEPVAL MEMORIAL TO THE MISSING.** ROH:- Newsome United Methodist Church; St. John's Church, Newsome.

OLDHAM, HARRY. Private. No 45181. 1/5th Battalion London Regiment, The Rifle Brigade. Formerly No 32529 Durham Light Infantry. Born Denton, Manchester 3.8.1878. Son of the late Edward and Amanda Oldham. Educated at Denton schools and British School, Cleckheaton. Lived 39 North Street, Lockwood. Employed as a greengrocer. Single. Enlisted May 1916. Killed in action, 28.8.1918, aged 40. Has no known grave. Commemorated **VIS-en-ARTOIS MEMORIAL TO THE MISSING.** ROH:- Emmanuel Church, Lockwood.

OLDHAM, HARRY. Private. No 41134. 8th Battalion The King's Own (Royal Lancaster Regiment). Born 14 Shaw Row, Berry Brow, Huddersfield, 10.4.1899. Son of Mr and Mrs Saville Oldham, 34 School Lane, Berry Brow. Educated Berry Brow Council School and Hillhouse Higher Elementary School. Attended Berry Brow Wesleyan Church. Employed as a clerk at the Huddersfield gasworks. Single. Enlisted 12.4.1917. Died of wounds at the 1st Canadian Casualty Clearing Station on 20.7.1918, aged 19 years. Buried **PERNES BRITISH CEMETERY.** Grave location:- Plot 5, Row F, Grave 8. ROH:- Armitage Bridge War Memorial; Huddersfield Corporation Roll.

OLDHAM, JAMES. Private. No 3/2094. 2nd Battalion King's Own Yorkshire Light Infantry. Born Hawick, Roxburghshire, Scotland. Lived Mary's Rest, Slaithwaite. Employed by Messrs John Crowther and Sons, Milnsbridge. Married, with two children. Was an old Volunteer and enlisted 1.9.1914. Embarked for France on 18.11.1914. Took part in the fighting around Ypres and Hill 60, where he was wounded in the stomach on 5.5.1915. Died of wounds at No 2 Casualty Clearing Station on 7.5.1915, aged 30 years. Buried **BAILLEUL COMMUNAL CEMETERY EXTENSION.** Grave location:- Plot 1, Row C, Grave 163. ROH:- St. James Church, Slaithwaite; Slaithwaite War Memorial.

OLDHAM, JOHN. Private. No 19203. 7th Battalion Suffolk Regiment. Formerly No 8670 Hussars. Born Hawick, Scotland. Son of Wilfred Oldham, 636 West Mount, Linthwaite. Killed in action during the Battle of Loos on 13.10.1915, aged 22 years. Has no known grave. Commemorated **LOOS MEMORIAL TO THE MISSING.** ROH:- Linthwaite War Memorial.

OLDHAM, NORMAN. Private. Machine Gun Corps. Born 32 Chapel Street, Berry Brow, Huddersfield, 25.11.1882. Son of Mr and Mrs James Oldham, 11 School Lane, Berry Brow. Educated Berry Brow Council School. Employed as a painter and decorator. Married. Lived 45 Haigh Street, Lockwood. Enlisted 4.12.1916. Wounded in the left thigh at Messines Ridge on 28.9.1918. Died at home, 45 Haigh Street, Lockwood, on 8.11.1921.

OLDROYD, ALBERT. Private. No 20374. 9th Battalion Duke of Wellington's Regiment. Born Kirkburton. Son of Alfred and S. M. Oldroyd of Slantgate, Kirkburton. Employed as a baker by his father. Attended Highburton Primitive Methodist Church. Embarked for France October, 1915. Died of wounds at No 14 General Hospital, 16.12.1917, aged 21 years. Buried **WIMEREUX COMMUNAL CEMETERY.** Grave location:- Plot 8, Row B, Grave 3a. The inscription on his grave reads, *'We'll read the meaning of our tears in the better land.'* ROH:- All Hallows Parish Church, Kirkburton; commemorated on his parents' headstone in Kirkburton Churchyard.

OLDROYD, ERNEST. Private. No B/21023. 12th Battalion Highland Light Infantry. Born 211 Yews Hill Road, Lockwood, 30.3.1895. Son of Mr and Mrs Oldroyd, 211 Yews Hill Road, Lockwood. Educated Mount Pleasant Council School, Lockwood. Employed as a spinner by Messrs James Shires and Sons, Milnsbridge. Enlisted 2.2.1915. Killed in action, 12.3.1916, aged 20 years. Has no known grave. Commemorated **LOOS MEMORIAL TO THE MISSING.** ROH:- St. Barnabas Church, Lockwood.

OLDROYD, HORACE. Private. No 235086. 2/5th Battalion Duke of Wellington's Regiment. Born 58 Bradley Mills, Huddersfield. Son of Charlie and Sarah Oldroyd, 105 Hillhouse Lane, Huddersfield. Educated St. Andrew's School, Leeds Road, Huddersfield. Employed as a stoker on a steam wagon by Messrs J. Crowther, Milnsbridge. Single. In September, 1915, he rescued two little girls from the canal and was awarded a certificate in recognition of his gallantry. Was a member of the Ramsden Street Men's Own Class. Enlisted 25.10.1915. Reported missing, presumed killed, at the Battle of Bullecourt, 3.5.1917, aged 20 years. Has no known grave. Commemorated **ARRAS MEMORIAL TO THE MISSING.** ROH:- St. Andrew's Church, Leeds Road, Huddersfield; Huddersfield Drill Hall; Fartown and Birkby War Memorial.

ORTON, LEWIS. Private. No 31835. 9th Battalion North Staffordshire Regiment. Born St. Thomas's Road, Huddersfield, 25.12.1897. Son of John William and Elizabeth Ann Orton, 81 Cottage Retreat, Marsden Road, Huddersfield. Employed as a woollen piecer by Messrs John Crowther and Sons, Milnsbridge. Single. Enlisted 6.11.1916. Killed in action at Monchy-le-Preux during the Battle of Arras on 27.5.1917, aged 19 years. Buried **FEUCHY CHAPEL BRITISH CEMETERY.** Grave location:- Plot 1, Row A, Grave 9.

OVERTON, ALFRED. Private. No 12452. 8th Battalion Duke of Wellington's Regiment. Born Thomas Street, Netherton, Huddersfield, 20.6.1888. Son of Benjamin Overton. Lived with his sister, Mrs Arthur Bennett, 62 Poplar Street, Birkby. Educated at the Wesleyan Chapel Day School, Netherton. Employed as a machine hand at Messrs J. Hopkinsons of Birkby. Single. Enlisted 7.8.1914. Was in training at Whitley Camp, Surrey, when he became ill. Died of pneumonia at the Connaught Hospital, Aldershot, on 5.7.1915, aged 27 years. Buried **SOUTH CROSLAND CHURCH BURIAL GROUND.** Grave location:- 182. ROH:- Fartown and Birkby War Memorial.

OWEN, ROBERT. Corporal. No 290108. 7th Battalion Royal Welsh Fusiliers. Born Llanymynech, Montgomery. Son of Paul M. Owen and Caroline F. Owen, 10 Upper Grange, Marsden. Employed as a teamer by Mr Albert Schofield of Marsden. Enlisted at the outbreak of the war. Went to the Dardenelles in August 1915. On the 10.8.1915 he received a bullet wound in the right arm and his right knee got torn by shrapnel. Invalided home to England, where he was treated at the Royal Southern Hospital, Liverpool. He was drafted out to Egypt in the first week of 1917. Killed in action during the Battle of Gaza, Palestine, 26.3.1917, aged 24 years. Buried **GAZA WAR CEMETERY, PALESTINE.** Grave location:- Plot 2, Row C, Grave 8. ROH:- Marsden War Memorial.

OWEN, ROWLAND HELY. Lieutenant. 2nd Battalion Duke of Wellington's Regiment. Born 'Portlands', Lindley, Huddersfield, 16.9.1892, Son of Hely and Julia Owen. 35 Dalton Street, Huddersfield. Educated Stancliffe Hall Preparatory School, Derbyshire, and Dover College where he was a scholar, prefect, head of house and in the first XV for two years. On leaving school, he matriculated at the London University. In February, 1911, he joined the 3rd Special Reserve Battalion of the Duke of Wellington's Regiment and completed his training with the 2nd Battalion at Tidworth and Dublin. In November, 1911, he was articled to his father, in the firm of Messrs Owen and Bailey, solicitors, New Street, Huddersfield. Was a playing member of the Huddersfield Old Boys Rugby Union football club and was Captain of the team. Was a sidesman at St. Thomas's Church, Longroyd Bridge, 1912–1914, and Hon. Secretary of the Communicants Guild for Men. Was gazetted a full Lieutenant on 2.12.1912. When war was declared he was taking a course of musketry at Hythe. Was mobilised with the 2nd Battalion Duke of Wellington's Regiment and sailed with them to France on 13.8.1914. He was present at the Battles of Mons, Le Cateau, the Aisne, and also at La Bassee and Ypres. Wounded in the left knee at Ypres on 7.11.1914 and, after treatment at Boulogne, was invalided home. Embarked for France again on 17.2.1915 and was present at the Battle of St. Eloi between March 14th and 17th. Killed in action at Hill 60 on 18.4.1915, aged 22 years. Has no known grave. Commemorated **MENIN GATE MEMORIAL TO THE MISSING.** ROH:- St. Thomas's Church, Longroyd Bridge; Waterloo Rugby Union Football Club. (A set of his letters home from the Western Front to his parents were deposited in the Imperial War Museum by his nephew, C. H. H. Owen on 1.10.1990 - pictured on p.250).

OXLEY, HERBERT. Private. No 5544. 23rd (County of London) Battalion. Formerly No 75419 Royal Army Medical Corps. Lived Kirkburton. Son of Samuel Vincent and Eliza Oxley, of Far Dean, Kirkburton. Killed in action, 15.7.1916, aged 23 years. Buried **LOUEZ MILITARY CEMETERY.** Grave location:- Plot 1, Row E, Grave 8. ROH:- All Hallows Parish Church, Kirkburton.

OXLEY, HUBERT. Corporal. No 3799. 2/5th Battalion Duke of Wellington's Regiment. Born 1.4.1893. Son of Mr and Mrs John Henry Oxley, of The Station Hotel, Ravensthorpe, Dewsbury, and formerly of Huddersfield. Educated Hillhouse Council School. Single. Had been in training with the 2/5th Battalion Duke of Wellington's Regiment for eight months. Died of ptomaine poisoning at the Sheffield Northern General Hospital on Monday 12.9.1915, aged 22 years. Buried **EDGERTON CEMETERY HUDDERSFIELD.** Grave location:- 6B, 50. ROH:- St. Thomas's Church, Longroyd Bridge, Huddersfield; Huddersfield Drill Hall.

PALMER, GEORGE. Private. No 32868. 'A' Company, 9th Battalion Duke of Wellington's Regiment. Born Scotland 1.3.1893. Educated in Scotland and Ireland. Husband of Martha Palmer, 24 Trinity Street, Huddersfield. Employed as a derrick crane driver by Sir Robert McAlpine and Sons. Enlisted 4.10.1917. Killed in action near Cambrai on 21.9.1918, aged 25 years. Buried **GOUZEAUCOURT NEW BRITISH CEMETERY.** Grave location:- Plot 3, Row E, Grave 3. ROH:- Holy Trinity Church, Huddersfield.

PARISH, REGINALD. Private. No 29297. 10th Battalion Duke of Wellington's Regiment. Born Primrose Hill, Huddersfield, 7.11.1897. Son of Mr and Mrs Parish, 34 Wood Terrace, Primrose Hill. Educated Stile Common Council School. Employed in the warehouse of Messrs William Preston and Company, woollen merchants, of Station Street, Huddersfield. Attended Primrose Hill United Methodist Church Young Men's Class and Guild. Enlisted September 1916. Died of wounds received near Zillebeke Lake, near Ypres, on 7.6.1917, aged 19 years. Buried **RAILWAY DUGOUTS BURIAL GROUND (TRANSPORT FARM).** Grave location:- Special Memorial D 4.

PARKER, FRANCIS. Private. No 4005. 1/5th Battalion Duke of Wellington's Regiment. Born Mount Street, Lockwood. Son of Henry and Elizabeth Parker, 8 Thomas Street, Lindley. Educated Oakes Council School. Employed as a wire drawer by Messrs J. Sykes Brothers Limited at Acre Mills, Lindley. Was a member of the choir of West Vale St Patrick's Church. Enlisted March 1915. Married Ellen Agnes Connolly in Halifax in June, 1916. Reported missing, presumed killed, in the attack on the Schwaben Redoubt on 3.9.1916, aged 28. Buried **MILL ROAD CEMETERY.** Grave location:- Plot 4, Row C, Grave 1. ROH:- St. Stephen's Church, Lindley; Huddersfield Drill Hall.

PARKIN, ALBERT. Gunner. No 202700. 'A' Battery, 307th Brigade, Royal Field Artillery. Formerly No R/ 19776 King's Royal Rifle Corps. Born Honley. Son of Mr and Mrs Joe Parkin of Magdale, Honley. Employed in the finishing department at Messrs Crowthers, Milnsbridge. Enlisted March 1916. Killed in action, 10.5.1918, aged 28 years. Buried **VIELLE-CHAPELLE NEW MILITARY CEMETERY, LACOUTRE.** Grave location:- Plot 8, Row E, Grave 3. (Brother of Gunner **HENRY PARKIN**, killed in action, 15.10.1916, q.v.). ROH:- Honley War Memorial.

PARKIN, BROOKE WHITELEY. Private. No 241937. 1/5th Battalion Northumberland Fusiliers. Born 3 Luck Lane, Marsh, 4.8.1896. Son of Ben and Mary Jane Parkin, 17 Luck Lane, Marsh. Educated Paddock Board School. Employed as a warper by Messrs Liddle and Brierley. Was a member of the Lindley Liberal Club. Attended Marsh United Methodist Church. Enlisted 17.6.1915. Reported missing, presumed killed, 14.11.1916, aged 20 years. Has no known grave. Commemorated **THIEPVAL MEMORIAL TO THE MISSING.** ROH:- All Saints Church, Paddock.

PARKIN, HARRY. Private. No 36360, 152nd Company, Labour Corps. Formerly 3rd Battalion North Staffordshire Regiment. Born Primrose Hill, Huddersfield, 14.2.1867. Son of John and Mary Parkin, Back Armitage Street, Primrose Hill. Educated Stile Common Council School. Husband of Ann Ellen Parkin, 8 Love's Yard, High Street, Huddersfield. Employed as a woollen weaver by Messrs Brook and Woodhouse Limited, Queens Mill, Huddersfield. Was a member of the Rashcliffe Liberal Club. Enlisted 28.6.1915. Died of natural causes at No 4 Casualty Clearing Station on 29.10.1917, aged 50 years. Buried **DOZINGHEM MILITARY CEMETERY.** Grave location:- Plot 11, Row A, Grave 11.

PARKIN, HENRY. Gunner. No 62457. 126th Siege Battery, Royal Garrison Artillery. Born Honley. Son of Joe and Helen Parkin, of Magdale, Honley. Educated Honley Church School. Employed by Messrs Eastwood Brothers, Thirstin Mill. Was a member of the Honley Conservative Club. Enlisted November 1915. Had gained his first class certificate for signalling and telegraphy. Had been in France for fifteen weeks when he was seriously wounded by shell fire on 15.10.1916, aged 24 years. He died within a few minutes on his way to the dressing station. Buried **LONGUEVAL ROAD CEMETERY.** Grave location:- Row F, Grave 3. (Brother of Gunner **ALBERT PARKIN**, killed in action, 10.5.1918, q.v.). ROH:- Honley War Memorial.

PARKIN, TOM. Private. No 203610. 1/4th Battalion Duke of Wellington's Regiment. Born Slaithwaite. Son of Joseph and Grace Parkin of Slaithwaite Hall, Slaithwaite. Husband of Nora Parkin, Green Bottom, Booth, Slaithwaite. Employed as a weaver by Messrs Crowther, Bruce and Company of Marsden. Attended Lingards Wood Bottom Sunday School where he was a member of the Young Men's bible class and the gymnasium. Was a gymnastic instructor at the Marsden Evening School. At the international Olympic games at London in 1908, he represented Yorkshire in the British team. Enlisted September 1916. Embarked for France in December 1916. Died of wounds at No 44 Casualty Clearing Station 10.10.1917, aged 32 years. Buried **NINE ELMS BRITISH CEMETERY.** Grave location:- Plot 3, Row E, Grave 1. ROH:- St. James Church, Slaithwaite; Slaithwaite War Memorial.

PARKINSON, FRANK. Lance Corporal. No 242407. 9th Battalion Duke of Wellington's Regiment. Born Thornhill, Longwood, Huddersfield. Son of Mr and Mrs Joe W. Parkinson, 8 Orchard Street, Longwood. Educated Goitfield Board School. Employed as a cloth finisher by Mr Sam Hirst, cloth finisher, Milnsbridge. Married in 1917. Attended Salendine Nook Chapel and was a member of the Longwood Liberal Club. Lived 43 Taylor Hill Road, Huddersfield. Enlisted 27.1.1916. Invalided home with trench fever in 1917. Killed in action at Inchy, near Le Cateau, on 13.10.1918, aged 24 years. Buried **INCHY COMMUNAL CEMETERY EXTENSION.** Grave location:- Row B, Grave 14. ROH:- Salendine Nook Baptist Chapel.

PARKINSON, F. Private. No 4379665. 1st Battalion The Yorkshire Regiment. Son of Edwin Parkinson of Huddersfield. Died, 14.3.1921, in India, aged 31 years. Buried **TRIMULGHERRY CANTONMENT CEMETERY, INDIA.** Commemorated **MADRAS 1914-1918 WAR MEMORIAL, CHENNAI.**

PARKINSON, F. Private. No 1572. Duke of Wellington's Regiment. Died at home, 15.5.1916. Buried **EDGERTON CEMETERY, HUDDERSFIELD.** Grave location:- 11B, 115.

PARKINSON, HERBERT. Private. No 31964. 3rd Battalion Duke of Wellington's Regiment. Son of Schofield and Annie Elizabeth Parkinson, of Northumberland Street, Huddersfield. Husband of Mary Ann Parkinson, 96 Northumberland Street, Huddersfield. Died at home on 27.3.1919, aged 33. Buried **EDGERTON CEMETERY, HUDDERSFIELD.** Grave location:- 66, 120G.

PARR, JOHN WILLIAM. Private. No 241074. 2/5th Battalion Duke of Wellington's Regiment. Born Almondbury in 1877. Educated at Milnsbridge schools. Employed as a concreter by Messrs J. and J. Bottomly, contractors, of Marsden. Married, with four children. Lived 1 Chorley Row, Marsden. Attended Milnsbridge Baptist Sunday School. Enlisted 15.3.1915. Reported missing, presumed killed, on 3.5.1917, at the Battle of Bullecourt. He was 39 years of age. Has no known grave. Commemorated **ARRAS MEMORIAL TO THE MISSING.** *(In September 1917 his body was found lying out on the battlefield by his brother-in-law, Corporal NELSON WINTERBOTTOM, of Crosland Moor, who identified it by photographs of Mrs Parr together with an unfinished letter and two envelopes addressed to her, which were found on the body).* ROH:- Huddersfield Drill Hall; Marsden War Memorial.

PARR, WILLIE. Private. No 8339. 7th Battalion East Yorkshire Regiment. Formerly No 23501 The Yorkshire Regiment. Born Huddersfield. Son of Mrs Clara Parr, 21 Hillhouse Road, Fartown, Huddersfield. Killed in action 9.7.1917, aged 22 years, during the Battle of Arras,. Buried **LEVEL CROSSING CEMETERY, FAMPOUX.** Grave location:- Plot 1, Row E, Grave 12. ROH:- Fartown and Birkby War Memorial.

PARSELL, JAMES HENRY. Private. No 13823. 7th Battalion King's Own Yorkshire Light Infantry. Born Hartlepool 28.11.1890. Educated Hartlepool Council School. Came to Huddersfield in 1913. Employed as assistant to Mr G. Craven, pawnbroker, High Street, Huddersfield. Lived 180 Wakefield Road, Dalton, Huddersfield. Played football with the second eleven teams of the local Shop Assistants and Warehousemen's Union. Attended New North Road Baptist Church where he was a member of the Young Men's Class and the Christian Endeavour. Enlisted 2.9.1914. Embarked for France in July, 1915. Took part in the fighting at the Battle of Loos in September, 1915. Killed by a sniper's bullet at Elverdinghe near Ypres on 13.3.1916. Has no known grave. Commemorated **MENIN GATE MEMORIAL TO THE MISSING.** ROH:- New North Road Baptist Church.

PATTERSON, GEORGE. Corporal. No 6894. 1/5th Battalion Duke of Wellington's Regiment. Born Western Place, Spring Street, Huddersfield, 17.8.1892. Son of George and Emily Ann Denton, 47 New Street, Paddock, Huddersfield. Educated Mount Pleasant Council School. Employed as a woollen spinner by Messrs William Lawton Limited, Paddock. Single. Enlisted at the outbreak of the war. Died of gangrene at No 3 General Hospital, Le Treport, on 12.3.1917. Buried **MONT HUON MILITARY CEMETERY.** Grave location:- Plot 3, Row C, Grave 9. ROH:- All Saints Church, Paddock; Huddersfield Drill Hall.

PATTERSON, JAMES WILLIAM. Private. No 203824. 2nd Battalion Duke of Wellington's Regiment. Born Slaithwaite. Son of William James Patterson. Husband of Ellen Patterson, Kitchen Fold, Slaithwaite. Killed in action, 1.9.1918, aged 36 years. Has no known grave. Commemorated **VIS-en-ARTOIS MEMORIAL TO THE MISSING.** ROH:- St. James Church, Slaithwaite; Slaithwaite War Memorial.

PAVER, JOSEPH WILLIAM. Private. No 71946. 27th Battalion (Manitoba Regiment) Canadian Infantry. Born Milnsbridge, Huddersfield. Killed in action, 6.4.1916, aged 39 years. Has no known grave. Commemorated **MENIN GATE MEMORIAL TO THE MISSING.**

PAVIOUR, HAROLD. Private. No 44351 47th Company Machine Gun Corps. Formerly No 29/339 Northumberland Fusiliers. Born 1.11.1893. Educated St. Thomas's Church of England School, Bradley. Employed as a tram conductor by the Huddersfield Corporation Tramways Department. Husband of Sarah Ann Paviour, 13 Filbert Street, Birkby. Enlisted 20.4.1916. Killed in action near Cambrai on 23.3.1918, aged 25. Has no known grave. Commemorated **ARRAS MEMORIAL TO THE MISSING.** ROH:- St. Thomas's Church, Bradley; Fartown and Birkby War Memorial.

PAWSON, ERNEST SYKES. Private. No 235150. 6th Battalion King's Own Yorkshire Light Infantry. Born Brooks Yard, Thomas Street, Huddersfield, in January 1885. Son of Mrs Pawson, 6 Hurst's Yard, Back Thomas Street, Huddersfield. Employed as a postman at the Huddersfield General Post Office. Attended Huddersfield Parish Church and was one of the secretaries of the Sunday School. Single. Enlisted May 1916. Killed in action at Passchendaele, 24.8.1917, aged 31 years. Has no known grave. Commemorated **TYNE COT MEMORIAL TO THE MISSING.** ROH:- Huddersfield Parish Church; Huddersfield General Post Office.

PAXMAN, BOYNTON. Corporal. No 96. 1/5th Battalion Duke of Wellington's Regiment. Born Huddersfield. Husband of Edith Paxman, 16 John Street, Huddersfield. Employed by Messrs Walter Sykes Limited, Zetland Mills, Huddersfield. Had been a member of the local Territorials for eight years. Enlisted at the outbreak of the war. Was married in April, 1915. Killed in action 18.8.1915, aged 23. Buried **WHITE HOUSE CEMETERY, ST. JEAN-LES-YPRES.** Grave location:- Plot 3, Row O, Grave 18. His widow received the following letter from Major G. P. Norton, *'You will already have been informed by his Platoon Commander that your husband was killed by a bullet in the head last Tuesday night. I wish I could think that any words of mine would help you in your great trouble and make your loss easier to bear. You have every reason to be proud of your husband who was a splendid N.C.O. and a fine man all round. Every Officer and man in the Company feels his loss as a personal one for he was one of the most popular men in the Company. On duty he worked cheerfully and his beautiful voice used to entertain us when we were resting. He has died for his King and County and in doing so has died for you. His end was sudden and painless. We managed to take him out of the trenches and he was given a Christian burial. In expressing to you deepest sympathy I do so on behalf of the whole Company.'* ROH:- Gospel Mission, Huddersfield; Huddersfield Drill Hall.

PAYNE, JAMES EDWARD. Private. No 64955 12th/13th Battalion Northumberland Fusiliers. Formerly No 205528 East Yorkshire Regiment. Born Huddersfield. Married. Lived 3 Spivey's Yard, Denton Lane, Huddersfield. Employed by Messrs J. Ashton, Riley and Company, Manchester Road, Huddersfield. Died of a fractured leg as a Prisoner of War in a field hospital at Courtrai, 17.4.1918. Buried **KORTRIJIK (St. JAN) COMMUNAL CEMETERY.** Grave location:- Row C, Grave 45.

PAYTON, TIMOTHY. Private. No 242189. Highland Light Infantry. Died at home, 5.1.1920. Buried **EDGERTON CEMETERY, HUDDERSFIELD.** Grave location:- 17R, 43.

PEACE, ARTHUR. Private. No 291685. 1st Battalion Gordon Highlanders. Born Longwood Road, Huddersfield, 14.4.1891. Son of John and Selina Peace, 199 Longwood Road, Huddersfield. Educated at Paddock Schools. Attended Paddock Wesleyan Church. Employed as a cloth finisher by Messrs Frederick Peckett and Sons Limited. Attended Paddock Wesleyan Church. Single. Enlisted 15.11.1915. Died of gunshot wounds to the back at No 6 Casualty Clearing Station on 30.4.1918, aged 27 years. Buried **PERNES BRITISH CEMETERY.** Grave location:- Plot 2, Row A, Grave 26. ROH:- St. Mark's Parish Church, Longwood; Shared Church, Paddock.

PEACE, ARTHUR. Gunner. No L/25513. 168th (Huddersfield) Brigade Royal Field Artillery. Born Cumberworth 25.4.1897. Son of Mr and Mrs Walter Peace, 122 Barton Road, Crosland Moor, Huddersfield. Educated Cumberworth Schools. Employed as a spinner by Messrs James Shires and Sons Limited, Lockwood. Single. Enlisted 10.5.1915. Died of pneumonia following upon influenza at Hazebrouck on 16.10.1918, aged 21 years. Buried **LA KREULE MILITARY CEMETERY, HAZEBROUCK.** Grave location:- Plot 5, Row B, Grave 1. ROH:- St. Barnabas Church, Crosland Moor.

PEACE, ARTHUR ROBERT. Private. No 307824. 1/7th Battalion Duke of Wellington's Regiment. Born Fartown, Huddersfield. Son of Harrison Kilner and Elizabeth Peace, 113 Woodhead Road, Hinchliffe Mill, Holmfirth. Educated Field End School. Attended Hinchliffe Mill Wesleyan Sunday School. Employed as a spinner by Messrs J. Bower and Sons, Dover Mills. Single. Enlisted July 1916. Embarked for France in December, 1916. Died of nephritis at a Field Ambulance station on 12.3.1917, aged 31 years. Buried **LA GORGUE COMMUNAL CEMETERY.** Grave location:- Plot 3, Row C,

Grave 5. ROH:- Holme and Holmbridge War Memorial; Huddersfield Drill Hall.

PEACE, JAMES WILLIE. Private. No 32424. 2nd Battalion York and Lancaster Regiment. Born Huddersfield. Enlisted Penistone. Killed in action 21.3.1918. Has no known grave. Comnmemorated **ARRAS MEMORIAL TO THE MISSING.** ROH:- Denby Dale and Cumberworth War Memorial.

PEACE, JOB. Private. No 32558. 8th Battalion North Staffordshire Regiment. Born Golcar. Lived Pike Law, Scapegoat Hill, Golcar. Employed by Messrs Drakes of Townend, Golcar. Reported missing, presumed killed, 10.4.1918. Has no known grave. Commemorated **TYNE COT MEMORIAL TO THE MISSING.** ROH:- St. John's Church, Golcar.

PEACE, SQUIRE. Private. No 8573. 2/6th Battalion Duke of Wellington's Regiment. Born Firs Cottages, Longwood Road, Huddersfield. Educated Paddock Church of England School. Employed in a fish and chip shop. Married. Lived 154 Leeds Road North, Huddersfield. Enjoyed crown green bowling and was a member of three clubs. Enlisted October 1916. Died in No 4 Casualty Clearing Station of gunshot wounds to the back on 3.3.1917, aged 38 years. Buried **VARENNES MILITARY CEMETERY.** Grave location:- Plot 1, Row I, Grave 62. ROH:- All Saints Church, Paddock; St. Andrew's Church, Leeds Road, Huddersfield.

PEACE, STANLEY. Private. No 14193. 10th Battalion Duke of Wellington's Regiment. Born Cumberworth. Son of Mr and Mrs Herbert Peace, Old Post Row, Cumberworth. Employed by Messrs W. Naylor Brothers, Denby Dale. Killed in action at Passchendaele, 20.9.1917, aged 25 years. Has no known grave. Commemorated **TYNE COT MEMORIAL TO THE MISSING** ROH:- Denby Dale and Cumberworth War Memorial.

PEACOCK, ALFRED. Gunner. No 891043. 'A' Battery, 102nd Brigade Royal Field Artillery. Born 1 Alfred Street, Castleford, 17.4.1899. Son of Mr and Mrs Fred Clayton Peacock, 18 Charles Street, off South Street, Huddersfield. Attended High Street United Methodist Church. Employed as a general labourer. Single. Enlisted January 1915. Died 27.9.1917, aged 18 years. Buried **THE HUTS CEMETERY, DICKEBUSCH, BELGIUM.** Grave location:- Plot 7, Row C, Grave 17. ROH:- High Street United Methodist Church.

PEACOCK, AUGUSTUS. Private. No 20140. 34th Company, Labour Corps. Formerly Private No 64528 25th Battalion Durham Light Infantry. Born Wensleydale. Son of Isaac and Hannah Emma Peacock, 21 Fern Terrace, Birkby. Died of disease on 23.10.1918, at No 3 General Hospital, aged 23 years. Buried **MONT HUON MILITARY CEMETERY, LE TREPORT.** Grave location:- Plot 8, Row M, Grave 7b. ROH:- Fartown and Birkby War Memorial.

PEAKE, GEORGE. Bandsman. No 7924. 1st Battalion West Yorkshire Regiment. Born Gomersall. Son of William and Martha Peake, 51 Armitage Road, Birkby. Killed in action, 25.9.1914, aged 24 years. Buried **MONTCORNET MILITARY CEMETERY.** Grave location:- Row J, Grave 2.

PEARSON, CHARLIE. Private. No 41989. 12th Battalion Manchester Regiment. Formerly No 32555 North Staffordshire Regiment. Born Golcar. Second son of Mr and Mrs James Pearson, James Street, Golcar, Married, with one child. Employed as a packer by Messrs John Lockwood and Sons, Milnsbridge. Attended Golcar Providence United Methodist Church. Enlisted November 1916. Embarked for France in February, 1917. Wounded 25.4.1917. Died of wounds at No 12 Casualty Clearing Station, 27.4.1917, aged 30 years. Buried **DUISANS BRITISH CEMETERY.** Grave location:- Plot 2, Row M, Grave 13. ROH:- St. John's Church, Golcar.

PEARSON, CYRIL. Private. No 23035. 13th Battalion The Yorkshire Regiment. Born 8 Norwich Road, Lowestoft, Suffolk, 9.10.1896. Son of Willie and Ellen Pearson, 38 Manchester Road, Huddersfield. Educated Rowan Hill School, Lowestoft. Employed as a woollen piecer by Messrs Edwin Walker and Company Limited, Field Mills. Was a member of the Young Men's Class at the Buxton Road Wesleyan Church. Single. Enlisted August 1914. Wounded, 28.4.1917, during the Battle of Arras. Died of wounds at 136th Field Ambulance, 30.4.1917. Buried **FINS NEW BRITISH CEMETERY.** Grave location:- Plot 4, Row J, Grave 12. ROH:- St. Andrew's Church.

PEARSON, DAN. Lance Corporal. No 2946. 1/5th Battalion Duke of Wellington's Regiment. Elder son of Mr and Mrs Fred Pearson, 7 Brook Lane, Golcar. Employed in the warehouse by Messrs Firth and Miller, cloth merchants, St. John's Road, Huddersfield. Attended Golcar Baptist Sunday School and was a member of the Young Men's Bible Class. Had been a drill instructor in the Boys Brigade. Had served four years with the local Territorials. Was assistant secretary of the Golcar Liberal Club. Enlisted at the outbreak of the war. On Sunday morning, 15.8.1915, he was shot through the head by a sniper whilst in the act of raising his rifle. He never regained consciousness and died in about an hour, aged 22. Has no known grave. Commemorated **MENIN GATE MEMORIAL TO THE MISSING.** ROH:- St. John's Church, Golcar; Golcar Baptist Church; Huddersfield Drill Hall.

PEARSON, DENNIS. Private. Royal Army Medical Corps. Lived South View, Slack, Outlane. Married, with five children. Employed as cottom spinner by Messrs Edwin Sykes and Sons, Gosport Mills, Outlane. Enlisted in the R.A.M.C but was discharged on medical grounds. Since his discharge had been a patient at Mill Hill Hospital, Huddersfield. Died at his home of pneumonia, following upon influenza, on 26.7.1918, aged 38 years. Buried with military honours at **BETHEL UNITED METHODIST CHAPEL YARD, OUTLANE.** ROH:- St. Mark's Parish Church, Longwood.

PEARSON, ERNEST MEAL. Private. No 36765. 11th Battalion East Yorkshire Regiment. Formerly No 29385 Northumberland Fusiliers. Born Huddersfield. Son of James Edward and Ada Pearson, 104 Leymoor Road, Golcar. Reported missing, presumed killed, 24.3.1918, aged 27 years. Has no known grave. Commemorated **ARRAS MEMORIAL TO THE MISSING.** ROH:- Golcar Baptist Church; Longwood War Memorial.

PEARSON, GEORGE. Private. No 4293. 1/5th Battalion Duke of Wellington's Regiment (attached 47th Trench Mortar Battery). Son of David Pearson. Husband of Elizabeth Ann Pearson, Lascelles Hall, Huddersfield. Employed as a collier by Mr Benjamin Elliott of Lepton. Killed in action in the attack on the Schwaben Redoubt on 3.9.1916, aged 24 years. Has no known grave. Commemorated **THIEPVAL MEMORIAL TO THE MISSING.** ROH:- St. John's Church, Kirkheaton; Lepton Parish Church; Huddersfield Drill Hall.

PEARSON, HAROLD. Private. No 28807. 7th Battalion The Yorkshire Regiment. Born Burtoncliffe Head. Son of Mr and Mrs W. Pearson, 48 West End Road, Golcar. Husband of Mary Eliza Pearson. At one time he assisted his father in his greengrocery business but, prior to enlistment, was employed as a weaver by Messrs G. Mallinson and Sons Limited, Linthwaite. Attended Golcar Baptist Chapel. Enlisted 1.3.1916. Embarked for France on 17.7.1916. Killed in action at the Battle of Arras, 17.7.1917, aged 29 years. Buried **St. NICOLAS BRITISH CEMETERY, ARRAS.** Grave Location:- Plot 2, Row A, Grave 17. ROH:- St. John's Church, Golcar.

PEARSON, HARRY. Lance Corporal. No 300050. 7th Battalion Sherwood Foresters. Born 16 Charles Street, Crosland Moor, 27.2.1898. Educated Crosland Moor Council School. Employed as an apprentice scribbling engineer. Single. Lived 12 Barton Road, Crosland Moor. Enlisted 26.10.1916. Reported missing, presumed killed, 16.4.1918, aged 20. Has no known grave. Commemorated **PLOEGSTEERT MEMORIAL TO THE MISSING.** ROH:- St. Barnabas Church, Crosland Moor; United Methodist Church, Crosland Moor; memorial in Lockwood Cemetery.

PEARSON, JAMES. Private. No 29882. 2nd Battalion Northumberland Fusiliers. Born Green Street, St. John's Road, Huddersfield, 31.10.1891. Son of Thomas and Martha Pearson, 10 Rose Street, Turnbridge, Huddersfield. Educated Thomas Street Council School. Married. Lived Parkhead, Holmfirth. Employed as a teamer by Messrs Alfred Crowther Limited, plumber and glazier, Northumberland Street, Huddersfield. Married. Enlisted 10.6.1916. Died of gunshot wounds to the abdomen, Salonika, 5.6.1917, aged 25 years. Buried **STRUMA MILITARY CEMETERY.** Grave location:- Plot 9, Row B, Grave 6. ROH:- Upperthong War Memorial.

PEARSON, JOHN ALFRED. Private. No 458763. Agricultural Labour Company. Formerly No 20652 Duke of Wellington's Regiment. Born Kirkheaton, Huddersfield. Son of Mr G. S. Pearson, 7 Bath Terrace, Lockwood. Died at home, 25.9.1918, aged 24 years. Buried **KIRKHEATON CEMETERY.** Grave location:- 'U', 667. ROH:- Emmanuel Church, Lockwood; St. Barnabas Church, Crosland Moor.

PEARSON, JOHN ALLEN. Private. No 312498. The Tank Corps. Formerly No 301432 Royal Engineers. Son of the late Joe and Susannah Pearson of Crosland Moor, Huddersfield. Died at home, 26.9.1918, aged 31 years. Buried **SOUTH CROSLAND CHURCH BURIAL GROUND.** Grave location:- Middle South 529. ROH:- Emmanuel Church, Shelley.

PEARSON, JOHN ARTHUR. Private. 1/5th Battalion Duke of Wellington's Regiment. Born New Street, Paddock 21.5.1893. Son of Ben Allen and Lizetta Pearson, 102 New Street, Paddock. Educated Paddock Church of England School. Employed as a carriage cleaner at Huddersfield railway station by the London and North Western Railway Company. Single. Enlisted 16.12.1914. Died, 7.4.1919, at Storths Hall Asylum, Kirkburton, Huddersfield of 'results of French leave and gas poisoning.' ROH:- All Saints Church, Paddock; London and North Western Railway Company Roll.

PEARSON, JOSEPH SYKES. Acting Captain. Army Service Corps (Motor Transport). Eldest son of the late Henry Edward and Mrs Clara Pearson, Cliffe Ash, Golcar. Was a member of the firm of Messrs Pearson Brothers Limited, Slaithwaite and Golcar. He was a member of the Colne Valley Territorials at the outbreak of the war and rose to the rank of Major and Adjutant. He transferred to the Army Service Corps and, whilst serving in France, was awarded the French Croix-de-Guerre for conspicuous gallantry. He was married at Huddersfield Parish Church on Thursday, 11.11.1917, to Miss Elsie Marion (Mingy) Woolven, youngest daughter of Alderman J. A. Woolven of West Parade, Huddersfield. Lived 19 Trinity Street, Huddersfield. Died, 7.11.1918, of pneumonia following upon influenza. Buried **LES BARAQUES MILITARY CEMETERY, SANGATTE.** Grave location:- Plot 6, Row D, Grave 4. ROH:- St. John's Church, Golcar; memorial in Golcar Churchyard.

PEARSON, LEONARD. Private. No 267830. 1/4th Battalion Duke of Wellington's Regiment. Born Golcar. Son of Mrs Pearson, 4 Scar Bottom, Milnsbridge. Employed as a mason's labourer. Enlisted in 1915. Killed in action, 26.4.1918, aged 36 years. Has no known grave. Commemorated **TYNE COT MEMORIAL TO THE MISSING.** ROH:- St. John's Church, Golcar.

PEARSON, LEWIS. Rifleman. No R/19775. 7th Battalion King's Royal Rifle Corps. Born Huddersfield. Son of Wilson and Ann Pearson, 25 Moorbottom Row, Honley. Employed by Messrs France Littlewoods. Was a member of Honley Cricket Club committee, Mr W. Brook's bible class and Honley Working Men's Club. Enlisted February 1916. Was wounded in January, 1917, and returned to France in April, 1917. Reported missing, presumed killed at Passchendaele, 12.10.1917, aged 30 years. Has no known grave. Commemorated **TYNE COT MEMORIAL TO THE MISSING.** ROH:- Honley War Memorial.

PEARSON, NORRIS. Private. No 29/634. 1st Battalion Northumberland Fusiliers. Born Birchencliffe 5.12.1883. Son of Alfred and Elizabeth Pearson. Educated Sowood Green Board School, Stainland. Employed as a stone dresser by Messrs Joseph Hoyle and Son. Lived with his sisters at 517 New Hey Road, Mount, Outlane. Attended of St. Mary's Parish Church, Outlane, and was a former chorister. Was a member of Outlane Liberal Club and Cricket Club. Single. Enlisted May 1916. Wounded 24.9.1917. Died of wounds at No 46 Casualty Clearing Station, 25.9.1917, aged 33 years. Buried **MENDINGHEM MILITARY CEMETERY.** Grave location:- Plot 7, Row D, Grave 30. ROH:- Bethel United Methodist Church, Outlane; St. Mark's Parish Church, Longwood; St Mary Magdalene's Church, Outlane.

PEARSON, ROBERT FRANCIS. Private. No 260047. 2nd Battalion York and Lancaster Regiment. Formerly No 1325 Duke of Wellington's Regiment. Born Newtown, Leeds. Youngest son of Mr and Mrs Thomas Pearson, Spring Grove Buildings, Linthwaite. Husband of H. Pearson, 19a Hoylehouse, Linthwaite. Employed by the Colne Valley Spinning Company, Linthwaite. Had served in the old Militia and joined the local Territorial battalion two years before the outbreak of the war. He embarked for France as a Lance Corporal in the Duke of Wellington's Regiment but was transferred to the York and Lancaster Regiment when he arrived in France at Easter, 1917. Killed in action, 28.6.1917, aged 34 years. Buried **PHILOSOPHE BRITISH CEMETERY**. Grave location:- Plot 1, Row S, Grave 17. ROH:- Linthwaite War Memorial.

PEARSON, SAM. Corporal. No S4/143815 485th Company, Army Service Corps. Born Burfits Road, Quarmby, Huddersfield. Son of Henry and Anne Pearson of Quarmby. Husband of Anne Pearson, of Leeds. Educated Oakes Council School. Employed as a managing clerk by Messrs Skinner and Gray, solicitors, Fountain Street, Halifax. Lived Vicarage Terrace, Kirkstall, Leeds and formerly of Coronation Road, Halifax. Enlisted October 1915. Died of malaria in Salonika on 18.11.1918, age 43 years. Buried **MIKRA BRITISH CEMETERY, SALONIKA, GREECE**. Grave location:- No 843. ROH:- Lindley Baptist Church; Lindley Zion Wesleyan Chapel; Halifax Civic Book of Remembrance.

PEARSON, WALTER ERNEST. Lance Corporal. No M2/270093. 403rd Company, Mechanical Transport, Army Service Corps, attached 293rd Siege Brigade Ammunition Column, Born Paddock 2.12.1883. Son of Walter Pearson 27 Clough Lane, Paddock. Educated Paddock Church schools and Huddersfield Technical College. Employed as a commission agent for Messrs Bairstow, Sons and Company, Fitzwilliam Street, Huddersfield for sixteen years. Husband of Eva Pearson, Old Hall, Shepley. Enlisted 15.11.1916. Was wounded in the abdomen and right arm when trying to free his motor lorry which had become stuck in the mud. Died of wounds at No 4 Casualty Clearing Station, Proven, Belgium, on 15.7.1917, aged 34 years. Buried **DOZINGHEM MILITARY CEMETERY**. Grave location:- Plot 1, Row C, Grave 13. ROH:- All Saints Church, Paddock.

PEARSON, WILSON. Private. Northumberland Fusiliers. Born Kirkheaton 6.4.1878. Educated Kirkheaton Church of England School. Employed as a mason. Prior to enlistment, was employed by Mr Greensmith, contractor, of Tandem, Kirkheaton. Later he worked for Mr E. Broscrombe, carrier, of Hillhouse Lane, Huddersfield. Lodged with Mrs Batty at 26 Union Street, Northgate, Huddersfield. Single. Enlisted 1916. Killed in action, 1917.

PECKETT, HENRY. Gunner. No 300405. 13th Battalion The Tank Corps. Formerly No 26857 Royal Artillery. Born 10 Lily Street, Turnbridge, Huddersfield. Son of Mr and Mrs Edgar Peckett, 123 Wellington Street, Oakes, Huddersfield. Educated Oakes Council School. Employed as a warehouseman at Wellington Mills, Lindley. Single. Enlisted December 1914. Wounded on two occasions. Wounded near Lamotte-en-Santerre on 8.8.1918. Died of wounds, 9.8.1918, aged 22 years. Buried **VILLERS-BRETONNEUX MILITARY CEMETERY**. Grave location:- Plot 19, Row A, Grave 4. ROH:- Oakes Baptist Church; St. Stephen's Church, Lindley.

PEDLEY, JOSEPH, MSM. Company Quarter-Master Sergeant. No 240431. 2/5th Battalion Duke of Wellington's Regiment. Born Leek, Staffordshire, 10.9.1889. Son of Amelia Pedley, The Parochial Hall, Huddersfield. Educated Spring Grove Council School. Employed as an insurance agent. Married. Lived 28 Spring Grove Street, Huddersfield. Enlisted September 1914. Awarded the Meritorious Service Medal for *'gallantry in the field between February 25th and September 17th 1918'*. Killed in action near Cambrai on 17.10.1918, aged 26. Buried **QUIEVY COMMUNAL CEMETERY EXTENSION**. Grave location:- Row D, Grave 29. ROH:- Huddersfield Parish Church; Huddersfield Drill Hall.

PEEL, FRANK. Private. No 18839. 'B' Company, 8th Battalion King's Own Yorkshire Light Infantry. Born Skelmanthorpe. Son of William and Mary Peel of Croft Head, Skelmanthorpe. Employed at Messrs E. Stringer and Son's colliery at Skelmanthorpe. Enlisted 21.10.1914 and embarked for France in September, 1915. In his last letter to his parents, written on 18.1.1916, he stated that he had been out of the trenches for four days rest and was going back on the 21.1.1916. Died of wounds on 20.1.1916, aged 34 years. Buried **SAILLY-sur-la-LYS CANADIAN CEMETERY**. Grave location:- Plot 1, Row C, Grave 54. ROH:- St Aidan's Church, Skelmanthorpe.

PEEL, HAROLD. Private. No 24531. 10th Battalion Duke of Wellington's Regiment. Born Scissett. Killed in action at Passchendaele, 20.9.1917. Has no known grave. Commemorated **TYNE COT MEMORIAL TO THE MISSING**.

ROH:- Scissett War Memorial; Clayton West and High Hoyland War Memorial.

PEEL, JOHN HENRY. Private. No 46630. 11th Battalion Northumberland Fusiliers. Born Thurstonland, Holmfirth. Son of James and Eliza Ann Peel of Millmoor, Meltham. Husband of Jane Peel, Sefton Lane, Meltham. Killed in action at Passchendaele, 20.9.1917, aged 30 years. Has no known grave. Commemorated **TYNE COT MEMORIAL TO THE MISSING.** (Brother of Private **NORMAN PEEL,** killed in action, 23.4.1917, q.v.). ROH:- St. Bartholomew's Church, Meltham.

PEEL, NORMAN. Rifleman. No R/21404. 16th Battalion King's Royal Rifle Corps. Born Thurstonland. Son of James and Eliza Peel of Natty Fold, Millmoor, Meltham. Husband of Caroline Peel, Store Cottages, New Road, Meltham. Killed in action, 23.4.1917, aged 26 years. Has no known grave. Commemorated **ARRAS MEMORIAL TO THE MISSING.** (Brother of Private **JOHN HENRY PEEL,** killed in action, 20.9.1917, q.v.). ROH:- St. Bartholomew's Church, Meltham.

PEEL, STANLEY. Acting Sergeant. No 202611. 5th Battalion The King's (Liverpool Regiment). Born Huddersfield. Employed as a pattern weaver by Messrs Martin, Sons and Company, Oakes, Lindley. Had lived at Albert Street, off Acre Street, Lindley. Was a well known Huddersfield cricketer and had played with the Fartown and Paddock teams. Moved to Blackpool in 1913. Died from influenza whilst on home leave, 4.11.1918, aged 29 years. Buried **BLACKPOOL CEMETERY.** Grave Location:- T, 223.

PELL, TED. Lance Corporal No 19772. 2nd Battalion York and Lancaster Regiment. Formerly No 18501 King's Own Yorkshire Light Infantry. Born Hemsworth, Wakefield, in 1893. Employed as a Bioscope Operator before joining the police force on 28.7.1913, aged 20. Died as a Prisoner of War on 8.5.1918. Buried **BRAINE-LE-COMTE COMMUNAL CEMETERY.** Grave location:- Plot 1, Row A, Grave 8. ROH:- Huddersfield Police Headquarters.

PENISTON, SAMUEL. Private. Army Service Corps. Born Hunslet Hall Road, Leeds, 17.10.1879. Son of Mrs Hoar, Rilton Street, Spittle Hill, Sheffield. Educated Leeds schools. Employed as a yardman. Married. Lived 4 Eastwood Lane, Newsome, Huddersfield. Enlisted 1.9.1917. Died at home, 4 Eastwood Lane, Newsome, of pneumonia and heart failure, on 13.10.1920, as a result of weakness contracted by serving during the war. ROH:- St. John's Church, Newsome.

PENNINGTON, JAMES DENNIS. Sergeant. No 29959. 5/6th Battalion The Royal Scots. Born Bollington, Cheshire. Son of George and Sarah Ann Pennington, Bethany Farm, Blackmoorfoot, Linthwaite. Lived Lewisham Road, Slaithwaite. Employed by the Slaithwaite Spinning Company Limited. Was a teacher at Slaithwaite Providence Baptist Sunday School. Embarked for France in September, 1918. Killed in action, 2.10.1918, aged 26 years. Buried **SEQUEHART BRITISH CEMETERY No 2.** Grave location:- Row A, Grave 45. ROH:- St. James Church, Slaithwaite; Slaithwaite War Memorial.

PENTELOW, FRANK ALBAN. Corporal. No 3/3051. 6th Battalion King's Own Yorkshire Light Infantry. Born Whitwell, Mansfield, Nottinghamshire. Son of Ernest Pentelow, 35 Welbeck Street, Whitwell, Mansfield, and the late Agnes Pentelow. Previously employed as a miner. Came to Huddersfield in 1913 and joined the Huddersfield Borough police force, as a Constable, on 9.6.1913. Enlisted September 1914. Killed in action, in an attack on Delville Wood during the Battle of the Somme, on 15.9.1916, aged 25 years. Has no known grave. Commemorated **THIEPVAL MEMORIAL TO THE MISSING.** ROH:- Huddersfield Corporation Roll; Huddersfield Police Headquarters.

PERRY, ALFRED DAVID. Private. No 305238. 1/4th Battalion Duke of Wellington's Regiment. Born Malta. Son of Colin Campbell Perry and Edith E. Perry, 30 Spring Street, Upper Clough, Linthwaite. Killed in action near Cambrai, 11.10.1918, aged 21 years. Buried **WELLINGTON CEMETERY.** Grave location:- Special Memorial A 7. ROH:- Linthwaite War Memorial.

PETERS, WILLIAM HENRY. Sapper. No 131724. 235th Army Corps Company, Royal Engineers. Born Kimberworth, near Rotherham, 27.7.1879. Son of John Henry and Ann Peters, 60 Thornton Road, Crosland Moor.

Educated Babworth Church of England School, Retford. Employed as a mason. Single. Enlisted 1.11.1915. Killed in action near Zillebeke, Belgium, 20.8.1917, aged 38 years. Buried **BEDFORD HOUSE ENCLOSURE No 2.** Grave location:- Plot 2, Row B, Grave 7. ROH:- St. Barnabas Church, Crosland Moor; memorial in Lockwood Cemetery.

PEXTON, GEORGE ERNEST. Pioneer. No 146718. 4th Special Brigade, Royal Engineers. Born Huddersfield. Eldest son of Mr Edward Pexton, registrar of births and deaths, and Mary Elizabeth Pexton, Shop Lane, Kirkheaton. Educated Almondbury Grammar School and Leeds University, where he was awarded a King's scholarship on 1.10.1915. Was a teacher at Kirkheaton Parish Church Sunday School. Enlisted March 1916. Wounded at Loos 7.7.1916. Died in Birmingham War Hospital on Monday, 21.8.1916, aged 20. Buried with full military honours in **KIRKHEATON CEMETERY.** Grave location:- 'C'. 88. ROH:- St. John's Church, Kirkheaton; Almondbury Grammar School.

PHIPPARD, FREDERICK GEORGE. Company Sergeant Major. No 240025. 1/5th Battalion Duke of Wellington's Regiment. Born Brixton. Husband of Winifred Phippard, Linfit Lane, Kirkburton. A member of the Royal Ancient Order of Buffaloes (Dartmouth Lodge). Was connected with the local Territorials for six years prior to the war. Embarked for France, as a Corporal, with the Battalion in April, 1915. Died in No 44 Casualty Clearing Station on 8.10.1917, after having received a compound fracture of the right thigh and left hand. He was 27 years of age. Buried **NINE ELMS BRITISH CEMETERY, POPERINGHE.** Grave location:- Plot 4. Row B. Grave 5. ROH:- All Hallows Parish Church, Kirkburton; Huddersfield Drill Hall.

PICKARD, GEORGE. Sergeant Pilot. No 23959. 11th Squadron Royal Flying Corps. Born Moldgreen. Son of George R. and Florence L. Pickard, 1 Silver Street, Moldgreen, Huddersfield. Educated Christ Church and Higher Grade Schools. Employed as a grocer and provision merchant at 56/58 South Street, Huddersfield. Sang in the Huddersfield Parish Church choir. Killed in action, 25.1.1918, aged 24 years. Buried **WARLINCOURT HALTE BRITISH CEMETERY.** Grave location:- Plot 11. Row B. Grave 14. ROH:- Huddersfield Parish Church; Christ Church, Moldgreen.

PICKARD, HENRY. Private. No 15408. 2nd Battalion Duke of Wellington's Regiment. Born Huddersfield. Son of James and Margaret Pickard. Died of wounds at No 41 Casualty Clearing Station, 2.7.1916, aged 22. Buried **DOULLENS COMMUNAL CEMETERY EXTENSION No 1.** Grave location:- Plot 1. Row B. Grave 17.

PICKERING, CECIL. Private. No 29871. 2nd Battalion Northumberland Fusiliers. Born Kirkburton 2.10.1891. Son of James and Elizabeth Pickering, 2 Lumb Lane, Almondbury. Educated Almondbury Church of England school. Employed as a worsted weaver by Messrs Martin, Sons and Company, Lindley. Was a well known local cricketer and had played for both the Almondbury and Hall Bower clubs. Husband of Clara Pickering, 46 Broken Cross, Kaye Lane, Almondbury. Enlisted 15.6.1916. Died of malaria and dysentery in No 43 General Hospital, Salonika, Greece, on 6.12.1917, aged 26 years. Buried **MIKRA BRITISH CEMETERY.** Grave location:- Grave No 171. (Brother of Private **JOSEPH HERBERT PICKERING,** killed in action, 21.9.1917, q.v.). ROH:- Almondbury War Memorial.

PICKERING, JOSEPH HERBERT. Private. No 23416. 20th Battalion Durham Light Infantry. Born Flockton, near Wakefield, 12.6.1894. Son of James and Elizabeth Pickering, 2 Lumb Lane, Almondbury. Educated Almondbury Church of England school. Employed as a firer by Messrs Sykes and Tunnicliffe, Northfield Mills, Almondbury. A member of the Almonbury Conservative Club. Was married in October, 1916, before he left for France. Lived 45 Watercroft, Almondbury. Killed in action at Passchendaele, 21.9.1917, aged 23 years. Has no known grave. Commemorated **TYNE COT MEMORIAL TO THE MISSING.** (Brother of Private **CECIL PICKERING,** died in Salonika, 6.12.1917, q.v.). ROH:- Almondbury War Memorial.

PECKITT, JAMES HENRY. Private. No 59925. 1/6th Battalion The Royal Welsh Fusiliers. Born Highburton near Huddersfield. Son of Thomas R. and Mary E. Pickett of Broomstile, Kirkburton.

Employed by Messrs Singleton and Company, Brookfield Mills, Kirkburton. Enlisted January 1917. Killed in action in Israel, 6.11.1917, aged 19 years. Buried **BEERSHEBA WAR CEMETERY, ISRAEL** Grave location:- Row F. Grave 6. ROH:- All Hallows Parish Church, Kirkburton.

PICKLES, NORMAN. Lance Corporal. No 14060. 9th Battalion Duke of Wellington's Regiment. Born Clifton, Brighouse. Lived 9 Smithy Place, Brockholes. Was the goalkeeper for the Netherthong Association football team. Employed as a plasterer by Mr A. Peaker of Meltham. Had also worked at Thongsbridge and Brockholes Railway Stations. Married, with three children. Reported missing, presumed killed, 7.7.1916, aged 27 years. Has no known grave. Commemorated **THIEPVAL MEMORIAL TO THE MISSING.** ROH:- Holmfirth War Memorial.

PIERCY, GEORGE RICHARD. Private. No 240270 'C' Company, 2/5th Battalion Duke of Wellington's Regiment. Born Ardsley Parish, near Barnsley, 26.7.1897. Son of Mr and Mrs R. Piercy, 9 Whitestone Lane, Huddersfield. Educated Worsborough schools, near Barnsley. Employed as an apprentice heating engineer by Messrs Calvert and Company, Rashcliffe Ironworks, Folly Hall. Single. Was in the local Territorials prior to the outbreak of the war. Killed in action, 21.7.1918, near Rheims, aged 21 years. Buried **MARFAUX BRITISH CEMETERY.** Grave location:- Plot 5. Row F. Grave 8. ROH:- St. Paul's Church, Southgate; Huddersfield Drill Hall.

PIERCY, WILFRED ASHTON. Lieutenant. 17th (County of London) Battalion The London Regiment (Poplar and Stepney Rifles). Son of the late Rev. George Piercy and Mrs Piercy of Leytonstone, London, and youngest brother of Mr John Piercy of Huddersfield. Prior to enlistment was a teacher in London. Killed in action, 26.9.1915, at the Battle of Loos. Has no known grave. Commemorated **LOOS MEMORIAL TO THE MISSING.** His brother received a letter from the Brigadier-General who wrote, *'He came to his end as a brave and gallant soldier should do, leading his men in the attack on Loos. I deplore the loss of a brave and promising Officer.'*

PILKINGTON, FRANK ARTHUR. Private. No 27014. 98th Company, Machine Gun Corps. Formerly No R/18728 King's Royal Rifle Corps. Born Sheepridge, Huddersfield, 5.2.1898. Son of Herbert and Sarah Jane Pilkington, 71 Deighton Road, Huddersfield. Educated Deighton Council School and Hillhouse Higher Elementary School. Employed as a scourer by Messrs Crowther and Nicholson, Ashbrow Mills. Single. Enlisted 8.2.1916. Wounded, 13.7.1916, during the Battle of the Somme. Wounded by shell fire at Vimy Ridge, 6.7.1917. Died at No 3 General Hospital, Le Treport, of shell wounds, followed by pneumonia on 16.7.1917, aged 19 years. Buried **MONT HUON MILITARY CEMETERY.** Grave location:- Plot 4. Row A. Grave 11a. ROH:- Sheepridge Providence United Methodist Sunday School; Christ Church, Woodhouse Hill.

PILKINGTON, WILLIAM ECCLES. Sergeant. No 15038. 9th Battalion Duke of Wellington's Regiment. Born Stockport 14.4.1894. Son of John F. and Gertrude Pilkington, Tan-y-Bryn, Deighton Road, Huddersfield. Educated Deighton Elementary School and Huddersfield Technical College. Was formerly in the office of the Superintendent of the London and North Western Railway Company at Manchester. He then went to Maine, U.S.A., and returned to enlist on 27.12.1914. Was captured by the Germans near Bourlon Wood and died as a Prisoner of War on 31.1.1918. Buried **CAMBRAI EAST MILITARY CEMETERY.** Grave location:- Plot 7. Row B. Grave 14. ROH:- Christ Church, Woodhouse Hill; Deighton United Methodist Chapel; Deighton War Memorial.

PILLING, ARTHUR. Private. No 32982. 10th Battalion York and Lancaster Regiment. Born Albion Street, Huddersfield, 5.5.1898. Son of Edward and Annie Pilling, 28 Mitre Street, Marsh, Huddersfield. Educated at St. Paul's Church of England School and Oakes Council School. Attended Queen Street Mission and was a member of the Young Men's Class. Employed as a pattern man in the woollen warehouse of Messrs John Wilkinson and Son, St. George's Square, Huddersfield. Enlisted 5.1.1917. Embarked for France on 22.5.1917. Killed in action at Wytschaete, near the Messines Ridge, on 1.8.1917, aged 19 years. Has no known grave. Commemorated **MENIN GATE MEMORIAL TO THE MISSING.** His Officer wrote to Private Pilling's parents saying, *'I think it would comfort you to know that previously on the same day* *he had nobly volunteered to help to carry a wounded officer over the top from our our trench to another and carried out the job successfully. I felt quite proud of this act.'*

PILLING, JOE. Rifleman. No 235192. 2/7th Battalion West Yorkshire Regiment. Born Outlane 27.4.1888. Son of Joseph and Emma Pilling, Lea Farm, Outlane. Educated Outlane Council Schools. Employed as a dyer's labourer. Single. Enlisted 21.11.1916. Went out on a bombing raid and never returned at Bullecourt on 12.5.1917, aged 29. Has no known grave. Commemorated **ARRAS MEMORIAL TO THE MISSING.** ROH:- Outlane Trinity Methodist Chapel; Bethel United Methodist Church.

PILLING, NORMAN. Driver. No 25840. 78th Battery, Royal Field Artillery. Eldest son of Mrs Mary Ann Pilling, 40 Brier Lane, Birchencliffe, Huddersfield. Attended Lindley Wesleyan Sunday School. Employed as under-gardener for Mr. G. P. Norton, Birkby Lodge, Huddersfield. Died in India from a cerebral haemorrhage on 13.9.1917, aged 37 years, after being kicked by a mule. Buried **CAMPBELLPORE CEMETERY, INDIA. (PUNJAB AND DELHI PROVINCE).** Commemorated **KARACHI 1914-1918 WAR MEMORIAL, PAKISTAN.** ROH:- St. Philip's Church, Birchencliffe.

PILLING, OLIVER. Lance Corporal. No 174661. 5th Battalion Canadian Infantry (Saskatchewan Regiment). Son of William and Sarah Ann Pilling of Birchencliffe. Killed in action, 17.8.1917, aged 39 years. Buried **DUD CORNER CEMETERY.** Grave location: Plot 2. Row K. Grave 16.

PINDER, HORACE JENKINSON. Private. No 4743. 1/5th Battalion Duke of Wellington's Regiment. Born Nettleton, Dalton, 17.10.1892. Son of Arthur and Mary Pinder, 42 Arnold Street, Birkby. Educated Kirkheaton Church of England School. Employed as a grocer's assistant at the Dogley Bar Cooperative Society. Was a member of the Ramsden Street Congregational Church. Enlisted 9.2.1916. Embarked for France 14.5.1916. Was wounded in action in July, 1916. Reported missing, presumed killed, in the attack on the Schwaben Redoubt, 3.9.1916, aged 24 years. Has no known grave. Commemorated **THIEPVAL MEMORIAL TO THE MISSING.** ROH:- Fartown and Birkby War Memorial; Huddersfield Drill Hall.

PITCHFORK, JOHN. Private. No 34978. 9th Battalion Duke of Wellington's Regiment. Formerly No 38958 East Yorkshire Regiment. Born Hooton Pagnell, Yorkshire. Son of Mrs Martha Ann Pitchfork, 3 Pickford Square, Milnsbridge. Killed in action, 4.11.1918, aged 19 years. Buried **POIX-du-NORD COMMUNAL CEMETERY.** Grave location:- Plot 1. Row B. Grave 4. ROH:- Denby Dale and Cumberworth War Memorial.

PLAITER, JAMES WILLIAM (WILLIE). Private. No 3/11052. 2nd Battalion Duke of Wellington's Regiment. Born Shepley. Son of George and Isabella Plaiter of Dobroyd, Shepley. Was a tailor by trade but, prior to enlistment, was employed at Messrs Stringer's colliery, Park Mill, Clayton West. Was formerly a member of the Shepley United Brass Band. Enlisted 8.8.1914. Died from gas poisoning at Hill 60 on 5.5.1915, aged 20 years. Has no known grave. Commemorated **MENIN GATE MEMORIAL TO THE MISSING.** (Brother of Private **THOMAS PLAITER**, killed in action, 31.7.1917, q.v.). ROH:- Shepley War Memorial.

PLAITER, THOMAS. Lance Corporal. No 30761. 2nd Battalion The Yorkshire Regiment. Born Shepley. Son of George and Isabella Plaiter of Dobroyd, Shepley. Employed as a plumber and painter. Reported missing, presumed killed, 31.7.1917, aged 20 years. Has no known grave. Commemorated **MENIN GATE MEMORIAL TO THE MISSING.** (Brother of Private **JAMES WILLIAM (WILLIE) PLAITER.** Killed in action, 5.5.1915, q.v.). ROH:- Shepley War Memorial.

PLATT, HARRY. Private. No 30/356. 13th Battalion Northumberland Fusiliers. Born Castle Houses, near Castle Hill, Huddersfield. Son of Joe and Elizabeth Broadbent, 32 Close Hill Lane, Newsome, Huddersfield. Educated Lockwood Board School. Employed as a teamer by Messrs North and Bowler, Wholesale Market, Huddersfield. Single. Enlisted 9.5.1916. Killed in action at High Wood during the Battle of the Somme on 22.9.1916, aged 27 years. Has no known grave. Commemorated **THIEPVAL MEMORIAL TO THE MISSING.** (Brother of Private **JOE PLATT**, killed in action, 3.10.1918, q.v.). ROH:- St. John's Church, Newsome; Emmanuel Church, Lockwood.

PLATT, JOE. Gunner. No 176193. Royal Garrison Artillery, attached 317th Brigade, Royal Field Artillery. Born Castle Houses, Castle Hill, 28.10.1885. Son of Joe and Elizabeth Broadbent, 32 Close Hill Lane, Newsome. Educated Lockwood Board School. Married, with five children. Lived 76 Barcroft Road, Close Hill, Huddersfield. Employed as a labourer by British Dyes Limited. Enlisted 16.8.1917. Killed in action near Cambrai, 3.10.1918, aged 32 years. Buried **RIBECOURT ROAD CEMETERY.** Grave location:- Plot 3. Row A. Grave 7. (Brother of Private **HARRY PLATT**, killed in action, 22.9.1916, q.v.). ROH:- St. John's Church, Newsome; Emmanuel Church, Lockwood.

PLURIGHT, GEORGE DYSON. Corporal. No 11547. 2nd Battalion Duke of Wellington's Regiment. Born 13 Outcote Bank, Manchester Road, Huddersfield, 11.5.1879. Educated Spring Grove Council School. Husband of Mabel Bertha Pluright, 38 Spring Grove Street, Huddersfield. Employed as the local agent for Messrs Fattorini and Sons, of Bradford, and at night was employed at the Hippodrome as a ticket checker in the stalls. Attended Milton Congregational Church. Had served in the local Volunteer battalion for some years prior to the war. Was a Reservist and was mobilised on 4.8.1914. Embarked for France on 5.12.1914. Wounded in head and shoulder on 11.3.1915, but returned to the front line. On 18.4.1915 he was holding a communication trench on Hill 60, when he suffered severe head wounds and died instantly, aged 35 years. Has no known grave. Commemorated **MENIN GATE MEMORIAL TO THE MISSING.** ROH:- Milton Independent Church; Huddersfield Parish Church; St. Thomas's Church, Longroyd Bridge.

PLURIGHT, JOE. Private. No 11376. 2nd Battalion Duke of Wellington's Regiment. Born 3.1.1871. Son of Sarah and the late Dyson Pluright. Educated Spring Grove Council School. Husband of Clara Pluright, 12 Kilner's Buildings, Longroyd Bridge. Huddersfield. Employed as a machine warper at Messrs Glendinning Brothers Limited, Tanfield Mills. Was a member of the Friendly and Trades Club and the Primrose Hill Working Men's Club. Attended St. Thomas's Church, Longroyd Bridge. Enlisted 4.8.1914. Gassed at Hill 60 on 5.5.1915. Died of sickness following wounds (gas) received at Hill 60 on 5.5.1915 at Newcastle-on-Tyne Military Hospital, 19.1.1917, aged 47 years. Buried **EDGERTON CEMETERY, HUDDERSFIELD.** Grave location:- 106, 106. ROH:- St. Thomas's Church, Longroyd Bridge.

POGSON, BENJAMIN. Private. No 3/10223. 2nd Battalion Duke of Wellington's Regiment. Born Hunslet, Leeds. Lived 69 Clement Street, Birkby. Killed in action during the First Battle of Ypres on 11.11.14 (his 20th birthday). Has no known grave. Commemorated **MENIN GATE MEMORIAL TO THE MISSING.** ROH:- Fartown and Birkby War Memorial.

POGSON, FRED. Private. No 268691. 2/7th Battalion West Yorkshire Regiment. Born Wooldale, Holmfirth. Son of Mrs J. F. Dawson, Rotcher Bottom, Holmfirth. Educated Lane Bottom School and Holmfirth National School. After leaving school was employed by Messrs H. and S. Butterworth, Lower Mills, Holmfirth, and then by Mr Fred Lawton, Bridge Mills, Holmfirth. A member of the Holmfirth Cricket and Athletic Club and also of the Holmfirth Conservative Club. Was a bass player in the Wooldale Brass Band. Enlisted 14.10.1916. Embarked for France on 7.1.1917. Reported missing, presumed killed, at the Battle of Cambrai on 28.11.1917. Has no known grave. Commemorated **CAMBRAI MEMORIAL TO THE MISSING.** ROH:- Holmfirth War Memorial.

POGSON, HARRY. Private. No 2191. 1/7th Battalion Duke of Wellington's Regiment. Born Rosemary Lane, Huddersfield. Son of Mr James Pogson, 57 Thomas Street, off Northgate, Huddersfield. Employed as a brickyard labourer at Messrs Brook's pottery works at Bradley. Single. Enlisted September 1914. Acted as Officer's servant to the Sergeant Major of the 1/7th Battalion. In a letter written the day before his death, he wrote that he was, *'in the best of health and looking forward to coming over on leave at Christmas. He added that they had been having a bad time in the trenches.'* Died from wounds, 19.12.1915, aged 19 years. Buried **BARD COTTAGE CEMETERY.** Grave location:- Plot 1, Row D, Grave 18. ROH:- Huddersfield Drill Hall.

POGSON, HARRY. Private. No 87379. 12th Battalion The King's (Liverpool Regiment). Son of Arthur and Ellen Pogson, 29 Cliffe End

Road, Longwood, Huddersfield. Educated Paddock Board School. Employed in the scouring department at Messrs John Crowther and Sons, Union Mills, Milnsbridge. Attended Salendine Nook Baptist Chapel. Single. Enlisted 4.5.1917. Died of wounds received at the Battle of Cambrai at No 5 Casualty Clearing Station on 22.11.1917. Buried **TINCOURT NEW BRITISH CEMETERY**. Grave location:-
Plot 2, Row G, Grave 2. (Brother of Private **JOHN WADSWORTH POGSON,** died of wounds, 13.7.1916, q.v.). ROH:- St. Stephen's Church, Lindley; Salendine Nook Baptist Church; commemorated in the Chapel yard, F20.

POGSON, JOHN WADSWORTH. Corporal. No 2774. 'A' Company, 1/7th Battalion Duke of Wellington's Regiment. Born Dingle Road, Marsh, 1.8.1893. Son of Arthur and Ellen Pogson, 29 Cliffe End Road, Longwood, Huddersfield. Educated Paddock Board School. Employed as a weaver by Messrs John Crowther and Sons, Spring Mills, Milnsbridge. Single. Enlisted 8.11.1914. Died from shrapnel wounds to the thigh at No 6 British Red Cross Hospital (the Liverpool Merchants Hospital) on 13.7.1916, aged 22 years. Buried **ETAPLES MILITARY CEMETERY**. Grave location:-
Plot 14, Row A, Grave 12a. (Brother of Private **HARRY POGSON,** who died of wounds, 22.11.1917, q.v.). ROH:- St. Mark's Parish Church, Longwood; St. Stephen's Church, Lindley; Salendine Nook Baptist Church; Huddersfield Drill Hall; commemorated in Salendine Nook Baptist Chapel yard, F20.

POGSON, RONALD. Lance Corporal. No 49664. 8th Battalion Lincolnshire Regiment. Born Slaithwaite. Lived 7 Lingards Road, Slaithwaite. Employed in the finishing department at Crimble Mills, Slaithwaite. Attended Holthead General Sunday School. Enlisted March 1916. Embarked for France in January, 1918. Killed in action 22.8.1918, aged 20 years. Buried **BUCQUOY ROAD CEMETERY**. Grave location:- Plot 6, Row M, Grave 29. ROH:- St. James Church, Slaithwaite; Slaithwaite War Memorial.

POGSON, STAFFORD. Private. No 42617. 8th Battalion The Yorkshire Regiment. Formerly No 29/732 Northumberland Fusiliers. Born Golcar. Brother of Mrs E. E. Dyson, 15 Slantgate, Linthwaite. Employed as a weaver by Messrs B. and J. Whitwam and Sons, Golcar. Attended Scapegoat Hill Baptist Chapel and was a member of the Smith Ryding Working Men's Club. Enlisted June 1916. Embarked for France in January, 1917. Wounded in June, 1917, and admitted to No 10 Casualty Clearing Station. He wrote home to his sister and told her, *'that a shrapnel bullet had entered his right breast and he had undergone an operation. He said she was not to worry because they had some very clever doctors out there.* Died of his wounds, 2.7.1917, aged 33 years. Buried **LIJSSENTHOEK MILITARY CEMETERY**. Grave location:- Plot 15, Row C, Grave 3. ROH:- Linthwaite War Memorial. See image of medals and memorial plaque on page 255.

POGSON, THOMAS ALLEN. Private. No 241827. 2/5th Battalion Duke of Wellington's Regiment. Born Slaithwaite. Lived with his widowed mother at 23 Carr Lane, Slaithwaite. Employed as a cotton twiner by the Slaithwaite Spinning Company. Attended Carr Lane United Methodist Church and was a member of Slaithwaite Liberal Club. Enlisted March 1916. Critically wounded on 29.10.1917. Died of wounds at No 21 Casualty Clearing Station, 29.11.1917, aged 23 years. Buried **ROCQUIGNY-EQUANCOURT ROAD BRITISH CEMETERY**. Grave location:-
Plot 4, Row A, Grave 20. ROH:- St. James Church, Slaithwaite; Slaithwaite War Memorial; Huddersfield Drill Hall.

POLLARD, CLIFFORD. Boy 1st Class. No J/23543. Royal Navy. *HMS Hawke.* Son of Mr William Pollard, Park Head, Holmfirth. Educated St. John's School, Park Head, Holmfirth and Holmfirth Secondary School. On leaving school he was employed by Messrs H. and S. Butterworth, Lower Mills, Holmfirth, but only stayed there a short time as did not like the work. He was then apprenticed to Mr Cockroft, chemist, 51 Northgate, Huddersfield. In 1913 he enlisted in the Royal Navy two days after his sixteenth birthday. He spent twelve months at the Shotley Naval training barracks, where he gained first class marks. After completing his training he was drafted on to *HMS Hawke* which was used as a training ship. On the declaration of war the *Hawke* was manned for war. Killed in an action involving a submarine in the North Sea, 15.10.1914, aged 17. 526 men went down with the ship. Has no known grave. Commemorated

PORTSMOUTH NAVAL MEMORIAL TO THE MISSING. ROH:- Upperthong War Memorial; Holmfirth Secondary School.

POLLARD, HARRY. Private. No 4225. 1/5th Battalion Duke of Wellington's Regiment. Son of Mrs A. Pollard of Berry Brow, Huddersfield. Husband of Edith Ida Pollard, 7a William Street, Huddersfield. Killed in action in the attack on the Schwaben Redoubt on 3.9.1916, aged 19 years. Buried **CONNAUGHT CEMETERY.** Grave location:- Divion Wood Cemetery No 2, Memorial 1. ROH:- Armitage Bridge War Memorial; St. Andrew's Church, Leeds Road, Huddersfield; Huddersfield Drill Hall.

POLLARD, JOHN THOMPSON. Lance Corporal. No 202557. 1/4th Battalion King's Own Yorkshire Light Infantry. Married, with one child. Lived 25 Rock Street, Longwood. Killed in action, 13.4.1918, aged 26 years. Has no known grave. Commemorated **TYNE COT MEMORIAL TO THE MISSING.** ROH:- Longwood War Memorial.

POLLARD, LAWRENCE. Private. No 4875. 7th Battalion Australian Imperial Force. Born Huddersfield. Son of William and Sarah Elizabeth Pollard. Husband of Mrs H. E. Pollard of West Mills, Ballygord, Mirfield. Died of wounds, 27.8.1918, aged 38 years. Buried **TERLINCTHUN BRITISH CEMETERY.** Grave location:- Plot 2, Row F, Grave 8. (Half brother of Private **PERCY SPIVEY,** killed in action, 4.1.1918, and Private **WALTER SPIVEY,** killed in action near Rheims on 31.7.1918, q.v.).

POOL, SAM. Private. No 35067. 12th Battalion East Yorkshire Regiment (Hull Sportsmen). Died at home 14.5.1919. Buried **HONLEY CHURCH BURIAL GROUND.** Grave location:- 62, 3397. ROH:- Honley War Memorial.

POOLEY, EDGAR. Private. 8th Battalion Duke of Wellington's Regiment. Born Dalton 7.10.1896. Son of Mrs K. M. Pooley, 89 Westgate, Almondbury. Educated Almondbury Board School. Employed as a wholesale clothier's stockroom assistant. Single. Enlisted 22.11.1915. Died, 11.5.1921, at 130 Northgate, Almondbury of the after effects of war. ROH:- Almondbury War Memorial.

POOLE, G. Private. No 60788. 1/8th Battalion Essex Regiment. Died at home, 24.11.1920. Buried **St. BARTHOLOMEW'S CHURCHYARD. MARSDEN.** Grave location:- South, 29, 22.

POOLE, TOM. Private. No 24624. 11th Battalion Manchester Regiment. Born Normanton. Son of John and Mary Poole, 6 High House, Linthwaite. Employed in the dyehouse by Colne Valley Spinning Company Limited. Attended Linthwaite Wesleyan Sunday School. Played football for the Linthwaite All Blacks Club. Enlisted May 1915. Served in the Dardenelles campaign. Reported missing, presumed killed, 16.8.1917, aged 23. Has no known grave. Commemorated **TYNE COT MEMORIAL TO THE MISSING.** ROH:- Linthwaite War Memorial.

POPPLETON. WILLIE. Private. No 7269. 2nd Battalion Duke of Wellington's Regiment. Born 1879. Son of John and Naomi Poppleton, of Almondbury. Joined the army in 1902 and served in India. Died of wounds at home, 3.11.1916, aged 37 years. Buried **ALMONDBURY CEMETERY.** Grave location:- X, 'C', 140. ROH:- Almondbury War Memorial.

POTTS, ROBERT HENRY. Private. No 12467. 3rd Battalion Duke of Wellington's Regiment. Born Bolton. Lived 9 Freeman's Square, Trinity Street, Huddersfield. Died of wounds in a Newcastle hospital on 6.4.1915, aged 33 years. Buried **St. JOHN'S CHURCHYARD, NEWSOME, HUDDERSFIELD.** Grave location:- A, 27.

POUCHER, JOSEPH. Private. No 29678. 9th Battalion Duke of Wellington's Regiment. Born Marsden. Lived Green Top, Marsden. Killed in action, 25.4.1917, aged 20 years. Buried **VIS-en-ARTOIS BRITISH CEMETERY.** Grave location:- Plot 3, Row A, Grave 2. ROH:- Marsden War Memorial.

POUNDER, GEORGE WILLIE. Private. No 32032. 14th Battalion Durham Light Infantry. Born Parkgate, Berry Brow, Huddersfield 30.11.1890. Son of Mr and Mrs Albert Pounder, 45 Parkgate, Berry Brow. Educated Berry Brow Board School. Employed as a warehouseman. Married. Enlisted 29.4.1916. Reported missing on 3.12.1917 at the Battle of Cambrai and afterwards presumed to have died on that date, aged 27. Has no known grave. Commemorated **CAMBRAI MEMORIAL TO THE MISSING**. ROH:- Armitage Bridge War Memorial.

POWNALL, GEORGE. Private. No 362. 1/7th Battalion Duke of Wellington's Regiment. Son of Mr Alfred Pownall, 127 Edgefield Terrace, Milnsbridge. Employed by Messrs John Crowther and Sons, Milnsbridge. Died of wounds sustained during the Battle of the Somme on 12.7.1916, aged 25 years. Buried **AVELUY WOOD (LANCASHIRE DUMP) CEMETERY**. Grave location:- Special Memorial A 3. ROH:- Milnsbridge War Memorial; Huddersfield Drill Hall.

PRENDERGAST, THOMAS. Private. No 15163. Royal Irish Fusiliers. Born Ireland. Educated at Galway schools. Husband of Mary Prendergast, 7 Ramsden's Yard, off Manchester Street, Huddersfield. Employed as a labourer. Enlisted 4.11.1914. Wounded in the shoulder. Died in Beckett's Park Hospital, Leeds, after amputation of his arm on 13.7.1922.

PRESTON, WILFRID. 2nd Lieutenant. 7th Battalion Duke of Wellington's Regiment. Born Jesmond, Newcastle-on-Tyne, 29.11.1890. Second son of Mr and Mrs William Preston, Hill Crest, 153 Halifax Old Road, Birkby, Huddersfield. Educated Bede College, Whitley Bay. Was a member of the firm of Messrs W. Preston and Company, woollen merchants, Station Street, Huddersfield, and of the Huddersfield Commercial Travellers Association. Was commissioned with his younger brother, Second Lieutenant **HARRY PRESTON**, in August 1914. Trained at Clipstone Camp. Died from wounds received in action during the Battle of the Somme on 4.7.1916. Buried **BOUZINCOURT COMMUNAL CEMETERY EXTENSION**. Grave location:- Plot 2, Row B, Grave 8. ROH:- Huddersfield Parish Church; Christ Church, Woodhouse Hill; Fartown and Birkby War Memorial; Huddersfield Drill Hall.

PRICE, ALLEN. Private. No 40797. 2/5th Battalion South Staffordshire Regiment. Born Hill Top, Paddock 5.12.1890. Educated St. Paul's Church of England School. Employed as a plush weaver. Married. Lived 45 Dalton Fold, Dalton. Enlisted 10.7.1916. Died of wounds, 30.11.1917. Buried **ORIVAL WOOD CEMETERY**. Grave location:- Plot 2, Row C, Grave 21. ROH:- Christ Church, Moldgreen.

PRICE, ERNEST. Gunner. No 152210. 'D' Battery, 187th Brigade Royal Field Artillery. Lived Farnley Tyas. Killed in action, 25.4.1917. Buried **DICKEBUSCH NEW MILITARY CEMETERY**. Grave location:- Row BB, Grave 11. ROH:- Farnley Tyas War Memorial, Thurstonland War Memorial.

PRICE, WILLIAM JAMES. No 740. Lance Corporal. 7th Battalion Royal Welsh Fusiliers. Born Cwmpark, Glamorgan. Son of Mr and Mrs James Price, 1 Lot, Park Street, Newtown, Montgomery. Was employed by the Colne Valley Spinning Company. Lodged with Mrs Godfrey, Upper Clough, Linthwaite. Had been a member of the local Territorials for four years prior to the war. Served in the Dardenelles. Died from Enteric Fever, 7.9.1915, aged 22 years. Buried **EAST MUDROS MILITARY CEMETERY, LEMNOS**. Grave location:- Plot 2, Row M, Grave 226.

PRIESTLEY, ALFRED. Private. No 19871. 'B' Company, 16th Battalion Royal Welsh Fusiliers. Born Marsden. Son of Herbert W. Priestley and Mrs S. E. Priestley, Station Road, Shepley. Was a student in the designing department at Huddersfield Technical College. Educated St. Paul's School and was a member of Shepley Liberal Club. Enlisted with some college friends in January, 1915. Embarked for France in December, 1915. Killed in the attack on Mametz Wood during the Battle of Somme on 11.7.1916, aged 20 years. Has no known grave. Commemorated **THIEPVAL MEMORIAL TO THE MISSING**. His pal, Lance Corporal Matthews, wrote to the family *'that a German high explosive shell burst over Alfred and his companions, killing four and wounding eight. Death in Alfred's case was instantenous.'* ROH:- Shepley War Memorial.

PRIESTLEY, EDGAR, MM. Sergeant. No 241414. 'D' Company, 5th Battalion Duke of Wellington's Regiment. Born 6 Haugh's Road, Quarmby, Huddersfield, 15.4.1891. Son of A. E. and Mary A. Priestley, 23 Clara Street, Fartown. Educated Oakes Board School and Huddersfield Higher Grade School. Employed as a textile designer and foreman. At the time of enlistment was living at Brimscombe near Stroud, Gloucestershire. Single. Enlisted November 1915. Embarked for France on 11.1.1917. Followed the German retreat from the Somme to the Hindenburg Line. Was in the battles of Bullecourt, Cambrai, Achiet-le-Petit, and the Rheims forest, practically fighting to the Armistice as a Lewis Gunner and was an instructor in the Army of Occupation until 1.4.1919. Was awarded the Military Medal on 12.1.1918 for '*bravery in the field. During the Battle of Cambrai, on 22.11.1917, was in charge of his Company when all the Officers were out of action. Held on for 48 hours against heavy odds till relieved and took a large amount of prisoners*'. After being demobilised he reached home on 7.4.1919. He must have caught a chill on the way home and died of pneumonia at 32 Clara Street, Fartown, on 14.4.1919, aged 27 years. Buried **SALENDINE NOOK BAPTIST CHURCH** 114E. ROH:- Oakes Baptist Church; Fartown and Birkby War Memorial; Huddersfield Drill Hall.

PRIESTLEY, EDMUND. Private. No 47374. 22nd (Tyneside Scottish) Battalion Northumberland Fusiliers. Born Milnsbridge. Son of Mr and Mrs S. D. Priestley, 36 Scar Lane, Milnsbridge. Educated Crow Lane Board School, Milnsbridge. Employed as a weaver by Messrs F. Calverley and Company Limited, Dale Street Mills, Longwood. Attended St. Michael's Mission Church where he was a Sunday School teacher and a member of the choir. Enlisted July 1916. Embarked for France on New Years Day 1917. Died, 5.6.1917, aged 21 years. Has no known grave. Commemorated **ARRAS MEMORIAL TO THE MISSING.** ROH:- St. Mark's Parish Church, Longwood; St. John's Church, Golcar; Crow Lane Board School, Milnsbridge.

PRIESTLEY, JOHN. Private. No 11980. 8th Battalion Duke of Wellington's Regiment. Born Lockwood 29.11.1891. Son of Mrs Priestley, 21 West Street, Lindley. Educated Lindley Church of England School. Employed as a teamer by Messrs Ben Bottomley and Sons, contractors of Lindley. Single. Enlisted October 1914. Served in the Dardenelles, where he was critically wounded on 11.11.1915. Died of his wounds on board a hospital ship, 12.11.1915, aged 23 years. Was buried at sea. Commemorated **HELLES MEMORIAL TO THE MISSING.** An Army Chaplain wrote to Mrs Priestley on 11.11.1915 as follows, '*Private Priestley, of the Duke of Wellington's Regiment, has been wounded today. Whilst going about his work he was hit by the bursting of shrapnel in the back. He was very brave whilst the wound was being dressed and I hope he will come through it alright.*' Another letter was received from the Rev. A. Parisotti, Army Chaplain, who wrote, '*No doubt when you receive this you will already have heard the sad news of his death. No doubt it will comfort you to hear how died. He was brought on board this ship (the Hospital Ship 'Kildonan Castle') from the Field Hospital with the wounded men. He was at once seen to be a serious case and the surgeons on board concentrated all their efforts upon him in the hope of saving him. It was however a hopeless task. They did all in their power, their efforts were to some extent successful in that they made him much more comfortable and he died quite peacefully. He was praying with me quietly until practically his last breath. He knew he was dying but he did not seem afraid. He just quietly made his peace with God. He asked me to write home for him – this I gladly do, feeling it to be no small honour to assist in the last moments of so fine a lad. He was shot through the lung and died from internal haemorrhage.*'

PRIESTLEY, LEWIS. Private. No 267594. 1/5th Battalion Duke of Wellington's Regiment. Born Deighton 15.10.1888. Son of George and Mary Ann Priestley, 9 Nettleton Terrace, Kirkheaton. Educated Kirkheaton National School. Employed as a painter by Mr Watts, painter and decorator, of Kirkheaton. Single. Enlisted 1.3.1916. Killed in action on Passchendaele Ridge, 7.10.1917, aged 28 years. Has no known grave. Commemorated **TYNE COT MEMORIAL TO THE MISSING.** ROH:- St. John's Church, Kirkheaton; Huddersfield Drill Hall.

PRIESTLEY, NORMAN. Guardsman. No 26349. 2nd Battalion Grenadier Guards. Born Golcar. Younger son Alice Ann Priestley, 3 Share Hill. Golcar. Employed by Messrs James Dyson and Sons, Hoyle Ing Dyeworks, Linthwaite. Attended Golcar Baptist Church and was Captain of the Golcar Boys Life Brigade. Killed in action, 20.8.1918, aged 24 years. Buried **BUCQUOY ROAD CEMETERY.** Grave location:- Plot 3, Row K, Grave 5. ROH:- St. John's Church, Golcar; Golcar Baptist Church.

PRIESTLEY, TOM. Lance Corporal. No 203822. 1/4th Battalion Duke of Wellington's Regiment. Born Golcar. Son of Mr and Mrs Dan Priestley, 74 Whitehead Lane, Primrose Lane and formerly of Townend, Golcar. Attended Providence United Methodist Church and Sunday School. Employed by Messrs Ben Hall and Sons of Milnsbridge. Died of wounds, 16.10.1918, aged 21 years. Buried **QUEANT COMMUNAL CEMETERY BRITISH EXTENSION.** Grave location:- Row E, Grave 15a.

PROBYN, JOHN WILLIAM. 2nd Lieutenant. 1/5th Battalion Duke of Wellington's Regiment. Formerly Trooper 2nd Dragoon Guards (Queen's Bays). Born Huddersfield 12.2.1893. Son of John and Harriet Probyn, 59 Tanfield Road, Birkby, Huddersfield. Educated Thomas Street Council School and Huddersfield Higher Grade School, New North Road. Employed as a plumber. Attended Queen Street Chapel. Single. Enlisted, 28.8.1914, as a Trooper in the Dragoon Guards. Later he served in the K.O.Y.L.I. and was wounded in the Battle of the Somme. Shortly after he returned to his battalion he was promoted to the rank of Sergeant. Was gazetted 2nd Lieutenant in August, 1917, into the Duke of Wellington's Regiment. Killed in action at Bailleul on 12.4.1918, aged 25 years. Has no known grave. Commemorated **TYNE COT MEMORIAL TO THE MISSING.** ROH:- Fartown and Birkby War Memorial.

PROCTER, ROBERT CECIL. Gunner. No L/28185. 'C' Battery, 121st Brigade, Royal Field Artillery. Born Chesterfield 5.8.1897. Son of Herbert Robert and Alice Maud Procter, 117 Fitzwilliam Street, Huddersfield. Educated Almondbury Grammar School where he was awarded the Champions prize for athletics. Employed as an apprentice by Mr George Field, draper, John William Street, Huddersfield. Attended Huddersfield Parish Church. Single. Enlisted, 31.5.1915, in the 168th (Huddersfield) Brigade, Royal Field Artillery, but after 20 month's service in France was transferred to another Brigade. Wounded 22.8.1917. Died of wounds at No 4 Casualty Clearing Station on 24.8.1917. Buried **DOZINGHEM MILITARY CEMETERY.** Grave location:- Plot 3, Row H, Row 1. ROH:- Huddersfield Parish Church.

PROCTOR, SAMUEL LAKE. Sergeant. No 13/783. 13th Battalion York and Lancaster Regiment (Barnsley Pals). Born Ryhill, Wakefield. Husband of Sarah E. Proctor, 29 King Street, Oakes, Huddersfield. Employed as an electrical engineer at Darton near Barnsley. Enlisted September 1914. Was married in November 1914. Served in Egypt before being transferred to the Western Front, in March 1916. Suffered serious gunshot wounds to the head and a broken thigh on 1.7.1916. Died of wounds at No 2 Stationary Hospital on 11.7.1916, aged 30 years. Buried **ABBEVILLE COMMUNAL CEMETERY.** Grave location:- Plot 5, Row E, Grave 8.

PULMAN, CUTHBERT. Sergeant. No 25768. 9th Battalion The Cameronians (Scottish Rifles). Lived 10 South Street, Huddersfield. Married, with one son. Employed at the Huddersfield GPO. Was presiously in business as a corn-factor in Halifax. Killed in action, 21.3. 1918, aged 39 years. Has no known grave. Commemorated **POZIERES MEMORIAL TO THE MISSING.** ROH:- Huddersfield GPO; Halifax Civic Book of Remembrance.

PYBUS, TOM. Gunner. No 47410. Depot, Royal Horse Artillery. Born Slaithwaite. Lived Lord Street, Hill Top, Slaithwaite. Had eleven year's service in the Army, seven of which were spent in India. As a Reservist, was called up at the outbreak of the war. Fought at Mons, Le Cateau, the Marne, the Aisne and the first Battle of Ypres. In 1915, he took part in the engagements at Neuve Chapelle, the second battle of Ypres. In 1916 he fought in the Somme campaign. He was discharged from the army due to shell shock in 1917. Died at home on 8.1.1918 from diabetes, a complaint that he contracted in the army, through shell shock. He was 32 years of age. Buried **SLAITHWAITE CEMETERY.** Grave location:- B, 1, 92. ROH:- St. James Church, Slaithwaite; Slaithwaite War Memorial.

QUARMBY, ALBERT RICHARD. Private. No 12603. 8th Battalion Duke of Wellington's Regiment. Born 31.12.1883. Son of Mrs Annie Barker, 4 Longroyd Lane, Huddersfield. Educated Linthwaite Church of England School. Employed by the Silver Car Company. Married, with five children. Lived 15 Graham's Yard, Thornton Road, Huddersfield. Enlisted in August 1914 with his chum, Private **HARRY WARD,** of Longroyd Bridge (who was killed in action, 29.8.1915, q.v.). Wounded at Gallipoli on 13.10.1915. Died on board a hospital ship, 14.10.1915. Was buried at sea. Commemorated **HELLES MEMORIAL TO THE MISSING.** ROH:- St. Thomas's Church, Longroyd Bridge, Huddersfield.

QUARMBY, ARTHUR. Private. No 241918. 2/5th Battalion Duke of Wellington's Regiment. Born Honley. Son of the late Mr and Mrs Charles Quarmby, of Honley. Lived with his sister, Mrs J. B. Fawcett, 21 Oldfield, Honley. Employed in the finishing department by Messrs Thomas Dyson and Sons, Deanhouse Mills. Attended Honley Church and Sunday School and was a member of the Honley Wesleyan Cricket Club. Enlisted April 1916. Embarked for France in January, 1917. Killed by a sniper during the Battle of Cambrai on 20.11.1917, aged 26 years. Buried **HERMIES HILL BRITISH CEMETERY.** Grave location:- Special Memorial A 12. ROH:- Honley War Memorial; Huddersfield Drill Hall.

QUARMBY, FREDERICK. 2nd Lieutenant. 7th Battalion Duke of Wellington's Regiment. Son of Mr and Mrs J. W. Quarmby, Spark Green, Meltham. Educated Almondbury Grammar School and Huddersfield Technical College. Was awarded a scholarship to Leeds University, where he obtained his BSc. degree with honours. Was retained on the staff of the University where he was engaged in research work. A member of the University Officers' Training Corps and was granted a commission in the Duke of Wellington's Regiment in July, 1915. Was married only a few months before he left for France in May 1916. Husband of Esther Ann Quarmby, Clarke Lane, Meltham. Attended Meltham Wesleyan Church and was a local preacher on the Holmfirth circuit. He was last seen in the trenches on the 17.9.1916. On the 18.9.1916 he was reported missing, presumed killed, aged 24. Buried **LONGEAU BRITISH CEMETERY.** Grave location:- Plot 4, Row B, Grave 14. ROH:- Almondbury Grammar School; St. Bartholomew's Church, Meltham; Huddersfield Drill Hall; Leeds University.

QUARMBY, GEORGE. Private. No 24256. 2nd Battalion Duke of Wellington's Regiment. Formerly No 36133 Durham Light Infantry. Born Meltham 26.12.1889. Son of Mr J. W. Quarmby, 1 Helme Lane, Meltham. Educated Meltham Church of England School. Employed as a carpenter and joiner. Married. Lived 79 Church Street, Paddock. Attended Paddock Wesleyan Church. Enlisted 14.6.1916. Reported missing at the Battle of Arras on 11.4.1917. Buried **BROWN'S COPSE CEMETERY, ROEUX.** Grave location:- Plot 2, Row E, Grave 4. ROH:- All Saints Church, Paddock; Shared Church, Paddock; St. Bartholomew's Church, Meltham.

QUARMBY, JAMES SCHOFIELD. 2nd Lieutenant. 7th Battalion Duke of Wellington's Regiment. Eldest son of John Sykes Quarmby and Laura Helen Quarmby, Green Lea, Meltham. Attended St. Bartholomew's Church, Meltham. Educated New College, Harrogate. After leaving college he attempted to enlist on three occasions and was finally accepted under Lord Derby's scheme in the Earl of Chester's Imperial Yeomanry, with whom he served in France. Was attached for some time to the Manchester Regiment as a machine gunner. Gazetted Second Lieutenant in the Duke of Wellington's Regiment in March, 1917. Killed in action during the Battle of Cambrai on 2.12.1917, aged 20 years. Buried **HERMIES HILL BRITISH CEMETERY.** Grave location:- Plot 1, Row B, Grave 11. ROH:- St. Bartholomew's Church, Meltham; Huddersfield Drill Hall.

QUARMBY, LEWIS. Private. No 235113. 2/5th Battalion Duke of Wellington's Regiment. Born 20 Armitage Road, Milnsbridge. Son of Sam and Ada Quarmby, 62 Armitage Road, Milnsbridge. Educated New Street Council School. Employed by his brother at Honley as a boot repairer and shoemaker and, before that, worked as a butcher for abour eight years for Messrs A. Dawson and Sons, Milnsbridge. Enlisted 3.4.1916. Killed in action near Rheims on 28.7.1918, aged 28. Buried **MARFAUX BRITISH CEMETERY.** Grave location:- Plot 3, Row B, Grave 7. ROH:- St. Mark's Parish Church, Longwood; Huddersfield Drill Hall.

QUARMBY, PEARSON. Private. No 32639. 8th Battalion York and Lancaster Regiment. Born Swan Lane, Lockwood, 5.5.1887. Educated Mount Pleasant and Crosland Moor Council Schools. Prior to enlistment, was employed by his father-in-law, Mr William Sykes, joiner and builder. But for many years was employed by Messrs Joshua Marshall and Company Limited as a piano tuner. Attended Crosland Moor United Methodist Church. Married, with one child. Lived 1 Tom Lane, Crosland Moor. Enlisted

10.2.1917. Embarked for France at Easter 1917. Killed in action, 25.5.1917, aged 29 years. Buried **RAILWAY DUGOUTS BURIAL GROUND (TRANSPORT FARM)**. Grave location:- Plot 4, Row F, Grave 19. ROH:- St. Barnabas Church, Crosland Moor; United Methodist Church, Crosland Moor; memorial in Lockwood Cemetery.

QUARMBY, THOMAS. Boy 1st Class. No J/37890. Royal Navy. *HMS Queen Mary*. Lived with his mother at 8 Pike Law, Golcar. His father was the late Elijah Quarmby, of Crosland Hill, where the family lived until 1914. Attended Crosland Hill Wesleyan Sunday School. Employed as a piecer by Messrs Joseph Hoyle and Sons, Longwood and, before that, by Messrs C. and J. Hirst. Enlisted in the Navy at Easter, 1915. Killed in action at the Battle of Jutland, 31.5.1916, aged 16 years. Has no known grave. Commemorated **PORTSMOUTH NAVAL MEMORIAL**.

QUINN, THOMAS HENRY. Private. No 3/10332. 2nd Battalion West Yorkshire Regiment. Born Kidsgrove, Staffordshire. Son of Patrick Quinn, who was employed for 32 years at the Corporation Gasworks. Lived in lodgings at Beast Market, Huddersfield. Employed as a chemical worker by Messrs Read, Holliday and Sons Limited. Embarked for France on 21.12.1914. Was wounded in the head on Sunday, 24.1.1915. Was removed to No 6 Casualty Clearing Station the following day and died on 31.1.1915. Buried **MERVILLE COMMUNAL CEMETERY**. Grave location:- Plot 1, Row K, Grave 54.

RADCLIFFE, JOE. Born Thornton Lodge 3.1.1874. Educated Oakes Council School. Employed as a plumber. Married. Enlisted at the outbreak of the war. Killed in action, 6.6.1917. ROH:- Lindley Baptist Church; Lindley Zion Wesleyan Chapel.

RACE, SPENCER. Private. No SPTS/869. 23rd (Sportsman's) Battalion Royal Fusiliers. Born Deepcar. Formerly lived at Scissett. Was a keen footballer and played with the Scissett Association football team. Fatally wounded on 13.11.1916. His Platoon Commander wrote to his sister, Mrs G. Tyas to tell her that her brother, *'was hit in the stomach by a machine gun bullet on 13.11.1916 and died a few hours after being carried into a dugout.'* Has no known grave. Commemorated **THIEPVAL MEMORIAL TO THE MISSING**. ROH:- Scissett War Memorial.

RADLEY, EDWIN. Private. No 25132. 2/6th Battalion Duke of Wellington's Regiment. Born Skelmanthorpe. Son of William and Martha Ann Radley, of Bath Buildings, Skelmanthorpe: Husband of Martha Ann Radley, of King Street, Skelmanthorpe. Employed as a weaver. Enlisted February 1917. Killed in action at the Battle of Cambrai, 27.11.1917, aged 26 years. Has no known grave. Commemorated **CAMBRAI MEMORIAL TO THE MISSING**. ROH:- St. Aidan's Church, Skelmanthorpe.

RADLEY, PEARSON. Private. No 45891. 12/13th Battalion Northumberland Fusiliers. Formerly No TR/5/56168. Born Skelmanthorpe. Son of Mr and Mrs Charlie Radley, Sunnyside Cottages, Skelmanthorpe. Employed by Messrs G. H. Norton and Company, Norton Thorpe Mills. Enlisted July 1916. Killed in action at Passchendaele on 28.10.1917, aged 20 years. Has no known grave. Commemorated **TYNE COT MEMORIAL TO THE MISSING**. ROH:- G.H. Norton and Company; St. Aidan's Church, Skelmanthorpe.

RAE, JAMES. 2nd Lieutenant. 2nd Battalion Seaforth Highlanders. Born Dublin 15.6.1887. Son of Mr and Mrs Adam Rae, Castle Douglas, Scotland. Educated Castle Douglas Academy. Was in business as a heraldic stationer and printer at 31 John William Street, Huddersfield. Lived 21 Wentworth Street, Huddersfield. Married. Enlisted, 1.12.1915, in the 2/28th Battalion The London Regiment. Commissioned into the Seaforth Highlanders on 27.3.1917. Embarked for France on 18.6.1917. Killed in action at Passchendaele on 4.10.1917. Has no known grave. Commemorated **TYNE COT MEMORIAL TO THE MISSING**.

RAINBIRD, NORMAN. Lance Corporal. No 2556. 1/5th Battalion Duke of Wellington's Regiment. Born Wetherby, Yorkshire 21.7.1892. Son of William and Mary Rainbird, 18 Carr Pit Road, Moldgreen. Educated Moldgreen Council School. Employed as a labourer by Messrs Needhams Limited, chemists, at their Healey House branch. Single. Enlisted 5.8.1914. Killed in action in the attack on the Schwaben Redoubt on 3.9.1916, aged 24 years. Has no known grave. Commemorated **THIEPVAL MEMORIAL**

TO THE MISSING. ROH:- Moldgreen: Christ Church, Moldgreen; Almondbury War Memorial; Huddersfield Drill Hall.

RAMM, FREDERICK W. Lance Corporal. No 3483. 1/5th Battalion Duke of Wellington's Regiment. Born Huddersfield. Son of Frederick and Caroline Ramm. Killed in action at the Battle of the Somme, 10.7.1916, aged 34. Buried **FORCEVILLE COMMUNAL CEMETERY EXTENSION.** Grave location:- Plot 2, Row C, Grave 8. ROH:- Huddersfield Drill Hall.

RADLEY, ALEXANDER RITCHIE BROWN. Private. No 21/797. 21st Battalion West Yorkshire Regiment. Born Glasgow. Son of Mrs Agnes Radley, 31 Market Street, St. Andrews, East Fife, Scotland. Enlisted Huddersfield. Killed in action, 9.10.1917, aged 27 years. Buried **CEMENT HOUSE CEMETERY.** Grave location:- Plot 15, Row B, Grave 3. ROH:- St. Mark's Parish Church, Longwood.

RAMSDEN, ALBERT. Gunner. No L/5957. 'B' Battery, 155th Brigade Royal Field Artillery. Born Stanley, Wakefield, in 1887. He joined the Huddersfield Police force on 11.5. 1911. Enlisted in the Royal Field Artillery. Died of wounds, 29.9.1918. Buried **BUCQUOY ROAD CEMETERY.** Grave location: Plot 4, Row B, Grave 38. ROH:- Huddersfield Police Headquarters.

RAMSDEN, ARCHIE. Private. No 39977. 7th Battalion Leicestershire Regiment. Born Huddersfield. Son of Tom Herbert and Eliza Ramsden, 13 South Street, Huddersfield. Employed by the London and North Western Railway Company as a junior numbertaker at Huddersfield Goods Station. Enlisted March 1917. Reported missing, presumed killed, 23.3.1918, aged 20 years. Has no known grave. Commemorated **POZIERES MEMORIAL TO THE MISSING.** ROH:- London and North Western Railway Company Roll.

RAMSDEN, ARTHUR. Private. No 204881. 1/7th Battalion Duke of Wellington's Regiment. Born Holmfirth. Son of John Thomas and Frances Ramsden, Bank Top, Holmbridge. Attended Hinchliffe Mill Wesleyan Sunday School. Employed as a mill hand by Messrs T. and J. Tinker. Mobilised with the local Territorials at the age of 15. Embarked for France in June, 1917. Killed in action at Nieuport, 29.7.1917, aged 18 years. Has no known grave. Commemorated **NIEUPORT MEMORIAL TO THE MISSING.** His parents received a letter from their son's Officer who wrote, *'Your son was one of a party under my command who raided the German trenches on Sunday night and I am afraid I can hold out but very little hope with his being alive. Your son had only been in my platoon about two weeks and even in that short time I was able to appreciate his worth.'* (Brother of Private **HUBERT RAMSDEN,** killed in action, 30.11.1917, q.v.). ROH:- Holme and Holmbridge War Memorial; Huddersfield Drill Hall.

RAMSDEN, BEN. Private. No 242010. 2/5th Battalion Duke of Wellington's Regiment. Born Holmfirth. Son of of Hugh and Alice Ramsden, Cinderhills Road, Holmfirth. Employed by the Huddersfield Cooperative Society at the Lockwood grocery branch. Attended Holmfirth United Methodist Church and was former Sunday School secretary. Enlisted under the Derby scheme at the beginning of 1917. Reported missing, presumed killed, at the Battle of Bullecourt, 3.5.1917, aged 31 years. Buried **CROISSILLES BRITISH CEMETERY.** Grave location:- Plot 5, Row G, Grave 2; ROH:- Huddersfield Drill Hall; Underbank War Memorial.

RAMSDEN, CHARLIE. Private. No 220497. 11th Battalion East Yorkshire Regiment. Formerly No 204545 2/5th Battalion Duke of Wellington's Regiment. Born Lane Bottom, Wooldale. Son of Elizabeth Cecily Dyson and stepson of Benjamin Dyson, 5 Fern Street, St. Andrew's Road, Huddersfield. Educated St. Paul's Church of England School, Huddersfield. Employed as a carrier by his stepfather. Single. Lived 17 Colne Road, Huddersfield. Enlisted 20.2.1915. Killed in action, 12.8.1918, aged 19 years. Buried **LE GRAND HASARD MILITARY CEMETERY, MORBECQUE.** Grave location:- Plot 2, Row D, Grave 5. ROH:- St. Paul's Church, Southgate, Huddersfield.

RAMSDEN, CHARLES RICHARD. Private. No 242944. 2/5th Battalion Duke of Wellington's Regiment. Born 25 St. Helen's Gate, Almondbury. Eldest son of Mr and Mrs Samuel Ramsden, 56 Kaye Lane, Almondbury. Educated Almondbury Council School. Employed as a warehouseman at the Albany Mills, Firth Street, Huddersfield.

Was a member of the Almondbury Cricket Club. Enlisted 2.11.1914. Twice wounded. Killed in action near Rheims, 22.7.1918. Has no known grave. Commemorated **SOISSONS MEMORIAL TO THE MISSING.** ROH:- Huddersfield Drill Hall; Almondbury War Memorial.

RAMSDEN, EDGAR. Ordinary Seaman. No J/64610. Royal Navy. *HMS Locust*. Born Taylor Hill, Huddersfield 11.9.1897. Son of William and Hannah Ramsden, 97 College Street, Crosland Moor, Huddersfield. Educated Berry Brow Council Schools. Employed as an apprentice slater by Mr Alfred Bower of Crosland Moor. Attended Crosland Moor Wesleyan Church and Sunday School. Single. Enlisted 1.1.1917. Died of scarlet fever in the Shetland Isles on 4.1.1918, aged 20 years. Buried **LERWICK NEW CEMETERY, SHETLAND ISLES.** Grave location:- 7th Terrace, upper side, 26. ROH:- Crosland Moor Wesleyan Church; St. Barnabas Church, Crosland Moor.

RAMSDEN, ERNEST. Private. No 241947. 1/5th Battalion Northumberland Fusiliers. Born South Street, Paddock 7.3.1897. Son of Mr and Mrs G. H. Ramsden, 5 Beech Street, Paddock, Huddersfield. Educated Paddock Council School. Attended Paddock Congregational Church and Sunday School. Employed as a gas fitter's mate by the Longwood Gas Company. Single. Enlisted 19.6.1916. Reported missing, presumed killed, 14.11.1916, aged 19. Has no known grave. Commemorated **THIEPVAL MEMORIAL TO THE MISSING.** ROH:- All Saints Church, Paddock; Shared Church, Paddock.

RAMSDEN, HUBERT. Guardsman. No 19818. Coldstream Guards. Born Holmbridge. Son of John Thomas and Frances Ramsden, Bank Top, Holmbridge. Attended Hinchliffe Mill Wesleyan Chapel. Employed at Yew Tree Mills. Enlisted October 1916. Killed in action at the Battle of Cambrai, 30.11.1917, aged 19 years. Has no known grave. Commemorated **CAMBRAI MEMORIAL TO THE MISSING.** (Brother of Private **ARTHUR RAMSDEN**, killed in action, 29.7.1917, q.v.). ROH:- Holme and Holmbridge War Memorial.

RAMSDEN, JAMES HENRY (HARRY). Private. No 98790. 237th Company, Machine Gun Corps. Born Linthwaite 11.11.1893. Son of Mrs Ann Ramsden, 51 Thornton Lodge Road, Huddersfield. Educated Linthwaite Board School. Employed as a tram-driver by the Huddersfield Corporation Tramways Department. Was a playing member of the Linthwaite United Amateur Football Club. Single. Enlisted 8.1.1917. Killed in action at Dickebusch, 4.10.1917, aged 33 years. Buried **TYNE COT CEMETERY.** Grave location:- Plot 59, Row D, Grave 22. ROH:- Huddersfield Corporation Roll.

RAMSDEN, JOE. Private. No 11912. 1/7th Battalion Duke of Wellington's Regiment. Born Charles Street, Crosland Moor, Huddersfield, 27.4.1895. Son of Mr and Mrs Jimmy Ramsden, 83 College Street, Crosland Moor. Educated Crosland Moor Council School. Employed by Messrs J. Hopkinson and Company as a mechanic. Single. Enlisted 14.8.1914. Served in the Dardenelles. Wounded on three occasions. Killed in action near Cambrai, 11.10.1918, aged 23 years. Buried **WELLINGTON CEMETERY.** Grave location:- Plot 1, Row E, Grave 2. ROH:- Crosland Moor Wesleyan Church; St. Barnabas Church, Crosland Moor; Huddersfield Drill Hall.

RAMSDEN, THOMAS. Private. No 6973. 10th Battalion King's Own Yorkshire Light Infantry. Born Clifton, Brighouse. Married, with three children. At the time of enlistment, in August 1914, was living at Knowle, Mirfield. Had lived previously at 3 Bath Street, Huddersfield. Employed by the London and North Western Railway Company as a shunter and relief goods guard. As a boy was a member of the Huddersfield Parish Church Sunday School and the Boys Brigade. Joined the army in 1901. As a Reservist he was mobilised at the outbreak of the war and fought at Mons, the Marne, the Aisne and at Ypres where, in December 1914, he was wounded and returned to England. After a period of convalescence he was attached to a signalling section and returned to France. He was reported missing on the first day of the Battle of the Somme, 1.7.1916. Buried **GORDON DUMP CEMETERY.** Grave location:- Plot 7, Row L, Grave 3.

RAMSDEN, WILLIE. Private. No 77916. 1/8th Battalion Durham Light Infantry. Born 98 Briggate, Brighouse, 26.1.1899. Son of Mr and Mrs Herbert Brook Ramsden, 16 Deighton Road, Deighton. Educated Deighton Council School. Employed in the finishing department at

Woodhouse Mills. Single. Enlisted 13.4.1917. Killed in action near Rheims, 20.7.1918, aged 19 years. Buried **MARFAUX BRITISH CEMETERY.** Grave location:- Plot 7, Row I, Grave 10. ROH:- Christ Church, Woodhouse Hill; Deighton United Methodist Chapel; Deighton War Memorial.

RAMSDEN, WILLIE. Sapper. No 41835. 61st Field Company, Royal Engineers. Born Huddersfield. Son of Mr and Mrs J. Ramsden, 12 Dowker Street, Milnsbridge. Employed by Messrs W. C. Holmes and Sons, of Huddersfield. Attended Milnsbridge Church and Sunday School. Embarked for France in June, 1915. Killed instantly by a piece of shell on 16.8.1916, aged 28 years. Has no known grave. Commemorated **THIEPVAL MEMORIAL TO THE MISSING.** ROH:- Longwood War Memorial; Huddersfield Mission, Milnsbridge.

RANGELEY, LEWIS. Private. No 50739. 1st Battalion East Yorkshire Regiment. Born Lockwood, Huddersfield. Son of Mr and Mrs Sewell Rangeley, 18 Upper Brow Road, Paddock. Employed by Messrs E. Armitage and Son, Milnsbridge. Died of wounds, 26.9.1918. Buried **BOIS-GUILLAUME COMMUNAL CEMETERY EXTENSION.** Grave location:- Row G, Grave 4b. ROH:- All Saints Church, Paddock.

RANGELEY, WILLIE. Rifleman. No R/31463. 9th Battalion King's Royal Rifle Corps. Born Huddersfield. Son of Mr and Mrs Joe Rangeley of Huddersfield. Died of influenza as a Prisoner of War in Germany 25.10.1918, aged 28. Buried **HAMBURG CEMETERY, OHLSDORF, GERMANY.** Grave location:- Plot 1, Row H, Grave 4.

RAPER, CHARLES HENRY. Corporal. No 15054. 9th Battalion Duke of Wellington's Regiment. Born Scammonden near Huddersfield. Son of Mr and Mrs J. H. Raper of Hullet Hall, Scammonden. Attended Pole Moor Baptist Sunday School. Employed in the dyehouse at Gosport Mills, Outlane. Enlisted December 1914. Died of wounds at No 2 Stationary Hospital on 15.11.1917, aged 21 years. Buried **ABBEVILLE COMMUNAL CEMETERY EXTENSION.** Grave location:- Plot 3, Row E, Grave 6. His parents received the following letter from a comrade of their son, who wrote *'I am writing the following on behalf of the 10th Platoon and myself. The death of your son Charles is a very big loss to us as he was loved by everyone in the Battalion, Officers, N.C.O's and men. Many are the times we have been together under severe shellfire but he was ever cool with the same pleasant smile on his face which put spirit into all around him. We were returning from the trenches when a shell burst not far from the platoon and poor Charles was the unfortunate one to be hit. He was wounded in the legs and he was well looked after by the boys who saw him down to the dressing station where they left him in the very best of spirits. It was a dreadful shock to us when we received the news of his death but there is still the consolation that we shall meet in a better land where wars are no more.'* ROH:- Clough Head Methodist Church; Pole Moor Baptist Church; St. James Church, Slaithwaite;

RASTALL, ARTHUR WILLIAM. Private. No 3123. 1/5th Battalion Duke of Wellington's Regiment. Born Huddersfield. Husband of Nellie Rastall, 22 Dorset Street, Birkby. Employed as a machinist for nine years by Messrs J. Hopkinson and Company Limited, of Birkby. At night he was a vendor of newspapers. Enlisted October, 1914, along with a number of employees of Messrs Hopkinsons. Embarked for France in April, 1915. Killed in action, 1.10.1915, aged 27 years. Has no known grave. Commemorated **MENIN GATE MEMORIAL TO THE MISSING.** His widow received a letter from Sergeant R. Dyson, Acting Commander of No 13 Platoon, 'C' Company, in which he told her that, *'whilst carrying stores to his comrades in the trenches her husband was killed by a shell, death being instantenous.'* ROH:- Huddersfield Drill Hall; Fartown and Birkby War Memorial.

RASTALL, WILBERT BARKER. Private. No 4427. 8th (City of London) Battalion (Post Office Rifles). Born Sheepridge, Huddersfield, 21.7.1885. Only son of Samuel and Miriam Rastall, Fernleigh, 109 North Street, Lockwood. Educated Hillhouse Council School. Employed as a postman at Huddersfield General Post Office. For about 18 months he had held the position of Secretary to the Huddersfield branch of the Postmen's Federation. Single. Enlisted September 1915. Embarked for France February, 1916. Wounded at High Wood during the Battle of the Somme on 9.10.1916. Died of wounds at No 2 British Red Cross Hospital, Rouen, on 10.10.1916, aged 31 years. Buried **St. SEVER**

CEMETERY, ROUEN. Grave location:- Plot B, Row 16, Grave 21. ROH:- St. Stephen's Church, Rashcliffe; Huddersfield GPO.

RATTIGAN, PATRICK. Private. No 13844. 2nd Battalion Duke of Wellington's Regiment. Born 19 Windsor Court, Huddersfield, 5.8.1885. Son of John and Ellen Rattigan. Educated St. Patrick's Roman Catholic School, Huddersfield. Employed as a chemical labourer by Messrs Read, Holliday and Sons. Husband of Annie Rattigan, 11 Watergate, off Castlegate, Huddersfield. Had seen previous service in the army. Enlisted 9.9.1914. Killed in the attack on Lesboeufs on 12.10.1916, aged 31 years. Has no known grave. Commemorated **THIEPVAL MEMORIAL TO THE MISSING.**

RATTIGAN, PETER. Private. No 20725. 9th Battalion Duke of Wellington's Regiment. Born Rosemary Lane, Huddersfield, 19.6.1890. Son of Mr and Mrs Rattigan, 102 Kirkgate, Huddersfield. Educated St. Patrick's Roman Catholic School. Huddersfield. Employed as a labourer at British Dyes Limited. Attended St. Patrick's Church and was a member of the Irish National League. Enlisted June 1916. Killed in action, 7.11.1916, aged 25 years. Buried **BANCOURT BRITISH CEMETERY.** Grave location:- Plot 5, Row L, Grave 1.

RAWCLIFFE, EDMUND. Lance Corporal. No 201679. 1/5th Battalion Seaforth Highlanders. Born Handel Street, Golcar, 21.12.1885. Son of James E. Rawcliffe, 26 Woodbottom, Netherton, Huddersfield. Educated Goitfield Schools. Was in business as a joiner and carpenter and had served his apprenticeship with Mr A. Astley, of Marsh. Husband of Sarah E. Rawcliffe, 137 Belmont Terrace, Leeds Road, Bradley. Enlisted in 1915. Killed in action near Cambrai on 15.10.1918, aged 32 years. Buried **IWUY COMMUNAL CEMETERY.** Grave location:- Row A, Grave 14. ROH:- St. Mark's Parish Church, Longwood.

RAWCLIFFE, HARRY LINGARD. Sergeant. No 11247. 8th Battalion Duke of Wellington's Regiment. Born Urmston, Manchester, 8.3.1894. Son of Ellen and the late Samuel Robert Rawcliffe, 255 New Hey Road, Salendine Nook, Huddersfield. Educated Urmston Higher Grade and Ickneild Street School, Birmingham. Employed as a warehouseman by Messrs Fisher and Company, of Upperhead Row, Huddersfield. Single. Enlisted 21.8.1914. Reported wounded and missing at Suvla Bay, Gallipoli, on 9.8.1915 and afterwards presumed to have been killed on that date. He was 21 years of age. Has no known grave. Commemorated **HELLES MEMORIAL TO THE MISSING, GALLIPOLI.** ROH:- St. Stephen's Church, Lindley; Salendine Nook Baptist Church.

RAWLINSON, FRANK. Private. No 242454. 'B' Company, 2/6th West Yorkshire Regiment. Born 35 Mulberry Street, Moldgreen, Huddersfield. Son of John William Rawlinson, 35 Mulberry Street, Moldgreen. Educated Moldgreen Council School. Husband of Mary Rawlinson, 35 Kilner Bank, Moldgreen. Employed as a fettler and teaser at Victoria Mills, Lockwood. Attended St. Paul's Wesleyan Sunday School, Moldgreen. Enlisted October 1916. Killed in action at the Battle of Bullecourt, 3.5.1917, aged 24 years. Has no known grave. Commemorated **ARRAS MEMORIAL TO THE MISSING.** ROH:- St. Paul's Methodist Church, Dalton; Christ Church, Moldgreen; Almondbury War Memorial.

RAYNER, FRED. Private. No 36876. 6th Battalion South Lancashire Regiment. Born Paddock 16.5.1895. Son of Mr and Mrs Sam Rayner, 7 New Street, Paddock. Educated Paddock Church of England School. Attended Milton Independent Church and Paddock United Methodist Church. Employed as a woollen spinner by Messrs J. Rayner and Company Limited, Turnbridge, Huddersfield. Enlisted November 1916. Died of heatstroke in Mesopotamia on 23.8.1917, aged 19 years. Buried **BAGHDAD (NORTH GATE) WAR CEMETERY.** Grave location:- Plot 20, Row A, Grave 12. (Brother of Private **SQUIRE VICTOR RAYNER**, died of wounds, 18.4.1915, q.v.). ROH:- Milton Independent Church; All Saints Church, Paddock; Shared Church, Paddock.

RAYNER, FRIEND. Drummer. No 240309. 2nd Battalion Duke of Wellington's Regiment. Born Lockwood Road, Huddersfield, 5.8.1898. Son of Frank and Ada Rayner, 188 Lowerhouses, Almondbury. Educated Lowerhouses National School. Employed as a railway fitter's apprentice by the London and North Western Railway Company in the locomotive sheds at Hillhouse, Huddersfield. Was a member of the local

Territorials prior to the outbreak of the war. Mobilised 4.8.1914. Died of wounds received in the attack on Pacaut Wood, near Bethune, on 18.7.1918. Buried **LAPUGNOY MILITARY CEMETERY.** Grave location:- Plot 10, Row B, Grave 13. ROH:- Almondbury and Lowerhouses War Memorials; Milton Independent Church; memorial in Almondbury Cemetery; London and North Western Railway Roll.

RAYNER, HARRY. Private. No 40595. 1/5th Battalion Northumberland Fusiliers. Born Marsh, Huddersfield. Son of Mr and Mrs Albert Rayner, 6 Clifton Road, Marsh. Employed as a gardener by Mr J. W. Lilley, of Marsh. Single. Enlisted 1916. Reported missing, presumed killed, at Passchendaele, 26.10.1917. Has no known grave. Commemorated **TYNE COT MEMORIAL TO THE MISSING.**

RAYNER, 'SQUIRE' VICTOR. Private. No 10613. 2nd Battalion Duke of Wellington's Regiment. Born Paddock 22.6.1897. Son of Mr and Mrs Sam Rayner, 17a Market Street, Paddock. Educated Paddock Church of England School. Attended Paddock United Methodist Church. Employed as a woollen spinner. Single. Enlisted in the army in November, 1913. Mobilised 4.8.1914. Took part in the fighting at Mons, where he was one of those who found themselves cut off from the main force. Although slightly wounded, he managed to evade capture by the Germans and made his way to the Belgian coast where he was sent back to England. After a short furlough at home he returned to France. Wounded near Ypres on 11.4.1915. Died of wounds on 18.4.1915. Buried **RAILWAY DUGOUTS BURIAL GROUND (TRANSPORT FARM).** Grave location:- Plot 5, Row B, Grave 5. (Brother of Private **FRED RAYNER**, died, 23.8.1917, q.v.). ROH:- All Saints Church, Paddock; Shared Church, Paddock.

RAYNER, WALTER. Private. No 2516. 1/5th Battalion Duke of Wellington's Regiment. Born Hopkinson's Yard, Lockwood Road, Huddersfield. Son of Fred and Emily Rayner, 19 Allen Row, Paddock. Educated Holy Trinity Church of England School. Employed as a woollen piecer by Messrs Job Thomas and Sons, of Longwood. Attended Milton Church Sunday School. Single. Enlisted 4.8.1914. Embarked for France April, 1915. Killed in action during the Battle of the Somme on 21.9.1916, aged 20 years. Has no known grave. Commemorated **THIEPVAL MEMORIAL TO THE MISSING.** ROH:- All Saints Church, Paddock; Huddersfield Drill Hall.

RAYNOR, ALBERT EDWARD. Sergeant. No 240276. 2/5th Battalion Duke of Wellington's Regiment. Born Victoria Road, Lockwood, 15.9.1896. Son of John Edward and Jane Raynor, 101 Thornton Lodge Road, Huddersfield. Educated Mount Pleasant Council School. Employed as assistant overlooker by Messrs J. Lumb and Sons Limited. Was a primary teacher at Mount Pleasant Wesleyan Sunday School. Was a member of the local Territorials prior to the outbreak of the war. Killed in action near Cambrai on 20.11.1917, aged 21 years. Buried **HERMIES HILL BRITISH CEMETERY.** Grave location:- Special Memorial B 2. ROH:- Mount Pleasant Chapel, Lockwood; Huddersfield Drill Hall.

RAYNOR, WILLIAM LUCAS. Private. No 410865. 38th Battalion Canadian Infantry (Eastern Ontario Regiment). Born 46 Water Street, Huddersfield, 8.9.1892. Son of Albert Ed. Raynor, 16a Barnsdale Avenue North, Hamilton, Ontario, Canada. Educated Spring Grove Council School. Emigrated to Ontario, Canada, in 1913. Employed as a clerk. Enlisted 21.5.1915. Had only been in the trenches for one week when he was seriously wounded in the spine in August, 1916, during the Battle of the Somme. After treatment in a London hospital he returned to France. Wounded for the second time at Dickebusch, Belgium. Died of his wounds at Huddersfield Royal Infirmary on 30.6.1917, aged 24 years. Buried **EDGERTON CEMETERY, HUDDERSFIELD.** Grave location:- 41, 50C.

READSHAW, JAMES ROBERT. Private. No 30178. 8th Battalion Northumberland Fusiliers. Born Greenhead Road, Huddersfield, 24.5.1897. Son of Mr and Mrs C. E. Readshaw, 105a Storths, Moldgreen, Huddersfield. Educated Paddock Church of England School. Employed as a piecer by Messrs Taylor, Livesey and Company, Paddock Mills. Was a member of the Huddersfield Mission Band. Single. Killed in action, 16.6.1917, aged 20 years. Has no known grave. Commemorated **MENIN GATE MEMORIAL TO THE MISSING.** ROH:- Moldgreen War Memorial; Christ Church, Moldgreen.

REAST, WILLIE. Private. No 42926. 'C' Company, 7/8th Battalion Royal Inniskilling Fusiliers. Formerly No 32953 Royal Fusiliers. Son of William and Martha Reast, of Huddersfield. Husband of Clara Reast, 89 Cowlersley Lane, Milnsbridge. Died, 31.3.1918, aged 38 years. Buried **FOUQUESCOURT BRITISH CEMETERY.** Grave location:- Plot 2, Row BB, Grave 6.

REDFEARN, FRANK. Rifleman. No 235209. 2/7th Battalion West Yorkshire Regiment. Born Mill Moor, Meltham, 19.4.1887. Educated at Meltham schools. Employed as a cloth scourer by Messrs John Lockwood and Sons, Milnsbridge. Husband of Maria Louise Redfearn, 28 Charles Street, Crosland Moor, Huddersfield. Enlisted 22.11.1916. Reported missing, presumed killed, at the Battle of Bullecourt, 3.5.1917, aged 30 years. Has no known grave. Commemorated **ARRAS MEMORIAL TO THE MISSING.** ROH:- Crosland Moor Wesleyan Church; St. Barnabas Church, Crosland Moor.

REDGWICK, GEORGE HERBERT. Private. No 15177. 10th Battalion Duke of Wellington's Regiment. Born Kirkburton. Son of Henry and Clara Redgewick, Thorncliffe Green, Kirkburton. Died of accidental injuries, 22.11.1915, aged 20 years. Buried **SAILLY-sur-la-LYS CANADIAN CEMETERY.** Grave location:- Plot 2, Row A, Grave 20. His parents received the following letter from Lieutenant G. R. C. Heale, who wrote, *'A man was showing another man how to use a periscopic rifle and a loaded rifle was handed to him to fit into the stand. Of course all rifles are kept loaded in the fire trenches but this one happened to have the safety catch unapplied. One of the men nearby noticed this and remarked upon it. Whereupon the man who was handling the rifle placed his hand on the safety catch to apply it. In doing so he seems to have jerked the rifle causing it to go off. The bullet struck your son who was sleeping nearby. This is the most unfortunate and distressing thing that has happened since we have been out here. The men who were handling the rifle when it went off were devoted friends of your son and on their request I had taken him as one of the battalion snipers. Private Redgewick was in my platoon and always earned my highest opinion as well as the respect and esteem of all the Officers of the Company. His loss is mostly deeply felt by everyone in the Company and I leave to your imagination the extent of the distress on the part of his chums who were responsible for the accident. Three of them went to his funeral today. He is buried at Sailly. Please accept my deepest sympathies on your great loss.'* ROH:- All Hallows Parish Church, Kirkburton.

REECE, RUSSELL. Private. No S/10872. 9th Battalion The Black Watch. Born Lockwood, Huddersfield. Lived 37, Springdale Street. Killed in action during the Battle of the Somme on 17.8.1916. Has no known grave. Commemorated **THIEPVAL MEMORIAL TO THE MISSING.** ROH:- St. Stephen's Church, Rashcliffe.

REID, WILLIAM JOHN. Private. No 6105. 2nd Battalion Border Regiment. Born Workington, Cumberland. Husband of Isabella Reid, 5 Poplar Street, Moldgreen. Killed in action, 18.12.1914, aged 36 years. Has no known grave. Commemorated **PLOEGSTEERT MEMORIAL TO THE MISSING.**

REVELL, JOSEPH. Private. No 44074. 7th Battalion Lincolnshire Regiment. Formerly No 9272 East Yorkshire Regiment. Born Stepney, London. Husband of Lilian Revell, 9 Newsome Cross Road, Huddersfield. Died at home, 12.6.1918, aged 27 years. Buried **EDGERTON CEMETERY, HUDDERSFIELD.** Grave location:- 11B, 116.

RHODES, ALBERT. Private. No 2429. 1/5th Battalion Duke of Wellington's Regiment. Born Thurstonland. Son of Oliver and Ada Rhodes. Lived Ash Tree Farm, Thurstonland. Employed as a twister by Messrs B Crosland and Company, Oakes, Lindley. Was a member of the Thurstonland Cricket Club. Enlisted at the outbreak of the war. Wounded in the head on 3.9.1916. Died of wounds at No 3 Casualty Clearing Station on 6.9.1916, aged 21 years. Buried **PUCHEVILLERS BRITISH CEMETERY.** Grave location:- Plot 4, Row A, Grave 43. Thurstonland War Memorial; memorial in St. Thomas's Churchyard, Thurstonland; Huddersfield Drill Hall.

RHODES, ARTHUR. Private. No 141480. 1/5th Battalion Duke of Wellington's Regiment. Born Oakes, Huddersfield, 2.1.1889. Son of William Harry and Ellen Rhodes, 9 Crosland

Road, Oakes. Educated Oakes Council School and Higher Grade School, New North Road, Huddersfield. Employed as a warehouseman. Single. Enlisted 16.2.1916. Reported wounded and missing in the attack on the Schwaben Redoubt, 3.9.1916 and afterwards presumed to have been killed on that date, aged 27. Has no known grave. Commemorated **THIEPVAL MEMORIAL TO THE MISSING.** ROH:- Oakes Baptist Church; St. Stephen's Church, Lindley; Huddersfield Drill Hall.

RHODES, FRANK. Private. No 301982. 1/5th Battalion Durham Light Infantry. Born Longwood 15.3.1894. Son of Mr and Mrs Harry Rhodes, 10 Edge Terrace, Longwood. Educated Goitfield Council School. Employed as a gasworker at the Longwood Gasworks. Single. Enlisted 27.6.1916. Reported missing, presumed dead, 27.5.1918. Has no known grave. Commemorated **SOISSONS MEMORIAL TO THE MISSING.** ROH:- Longwood Wesleyan Chapel; St. Mary's Parish Church, Longwood.

RHODES, HORACE. Lance Corporal. No 205454. 2/5th Battalion West Yorkshire Regiment. Born Thurlstone. Son of Mr and Mrs Tom Rhodes, Bilham Road, Clayton West. Died of wounds near Epernay, France, on 19.7.1918, aged 20 years. Buried **VERTUS COMMUNAL CEMETERY.** Grave location:- Grave 55. ROH:- Clayton West and High Hoyland War Memorial.

RHODES, JOHN WILLIAM. Private. No 32162. 2nd Battalion West Yorkshire Regiment. Born Huddersfield. Son of Mrs Thomas Rhodes, 96 Brier Lane, Birchencliffe, Huddersfield. Employed as a mason by Mr E. Fox, contractor, of Lindley. Attended Birchencliffe Parish Church. Died of bronchitis at No 5 Casualty Clearing Station, 5.3.1917, aged 32 years. Buried **BRAY MILITARY CEMETERY.** Grave location:- Plot 2, Row B, Grave 28. ROH:- St. Philip's Church, Birchencliffe.

RHODES, THOMAS GEORGE. Lieutenant. 3rd Battalion Duke of Wellington's Regiment, attached 57th Squadron, Royal Air Force. Born 8.8.1892. Son of George Henry and Ellen Rhodes, 10 Bankfield Road, Huddersfield. Educated Paddock Council School and Higher Grade School, New North Road, Huddersfield. Employed by Messrs David Brown and Sons, Crosland Moor. Single. Enlisted August, 1914, as a Corporal in the 1/5th Battalion Duke of Wellington's Regiment. Was commissioned in 1917 and transferred to the Royal Flying Corps. Killed whilst flying on 11.6.1918, aged 25 years. Buried **HUBY-St.-LEU BRITISH CEMETERY, HESDIN.** Grave location:- Row B, Grave 4. ROH:- St. Thomas's Church, Longroyd Bridge.

RICHARDSON, ERNEST. Private. No 12205. 'B' Company, 2nd Battalion Duke of Wellington's Regiment. Born Marsh, 7.3.1889. Son of George and Emma Richardson, Marsh House Inn, Marsh. Educated Holy Trinity Church of England School. Employed as a tramcar cleaner by the Huddersfield Corporation Tramways Department. He was a time-expired soldier who volunteered for service at the outbreak of the war. Killed at Hill 60 on 18.4.1915. Has no known grave. Commemorated **MENIN GATE MEMORIAL TO THE MISSING.** ROH:- Marsh War Memorial.

RICHARDSON, RODNEY FRANCIS. 2nd Lieutenant. 17th Battalion Manchester Regiment (2nd Manchester Pals). Born St. John's Vicarage, Birkby, Huddersfield. Son of Mark and Evelyn Richardson, St. John's Vicarage, Birkby, Huddersfield. Educated Fartown Grammar School and St. Cuthbert's School, Worksop. Whilst still at school (aged 17) he obtained a commission in the Manchester Regiment in December, 1915. Had been in France for only eight weeks when he was reported missing, presumed killed, at Sanctuary Wood on 31.7.1917, aged 18. (This was the first day of the 3rd Battle of Ypres - the Battle of Passchendaele). Has no known grave. Commemorated **MENIN GATE MEMORIAL TO THE MISSING.** ROH:- St. John's Church, Birkby; St. Andrew's Church; Fartown and Birkby War Memorial.

RICHARDSON, THOMAS. Private. No 302001. 13th Battalion The Royal Scots (Lothian Regiment). Born Huddersfield. Eldest son of Mr and Mrs Harry Richardson, 47 Rashcliffe Hill, Huddersfield. Employed by Messrs W. H. Heywood and Company, Birkby. Enlisted 1916. Killed in action, 6.10.1918, aged 20 years. Buried **St. MARY'S A.D.S. CEMETERY.** Grave location:- Plot 14, Row F, Grave 2.

RICHARDSON, THOMAS. Private. No 35344. 24th Brigade Machine Gun Corps. Formerly No 19332 Duke of Wellington's Regiment. Born 76 Norman Road, Birkby, Huddersfield. Son of Herbert and Mary Ann Richardson, 17 Main Road, Primrose Hill, Huddersfield. Educated Stile Common Council School. Employed as a sweet boiler by Messrs Wallaces Limited, St. John's Road, Huddersfield for over seven years. Single. Attended Primrose Hill Baptist Chapel, where he was a member of the choir and the bible class. Enlisted 2.3.1916. Killed by a shell on 25.8.1916, aged 22 years. Buried **VERMELLES BRITISH CEMETERY.** Grave location:-Plot 3, Row P, Grave 15. ROH:- St. Stephen's Church, Rashcliffe.

RICHARDSON, WILLIAM HENRY. Private. No 1781. 1/7th Battalion Duke of Wellington's Regiment. Born Golcar. Son of Mrs Richardson, 102 Handel Street, Golcar and formerly of Lowergate, Longwood. Employed as a cloth presser by Messrs Armitage Brothers, of Milnsbridge. Enlisted at the outbreak of the war. Was killed on Saturday, 29.10.1915. A piece of shell hit him at the back of the head rendering him unconscious and he died a few minutes later. Buried **TALANA FARM CEMETERY.** Grave location:- Plot 3, Row D, Grave 5. ROH:- St. John's Church, Golcar; Huddersfield Drill Hall.

RICKETTS, NORMAN PRESTON. Rifleman. No 60476. 7th Reserve Battalion West Yorkshire Regiment. Son of Mr and Mrs George Henry Ricketts, Outlane, Netherthong. Educated Netherthong National School. Employed by Messrs J. and J. Lancaster, Mytholm Bridge, and later at Albert Mills, Holmfirth. Attended Netherthong United Methodist Church. Was a member of the Working Men's Club and the Gardeners Friendly Society. Enlisted 10.5.1917. Was in training at the Cannock Chase Military Camp, Staffordshire. Died of meningitis at Cannock Chase Military Hospital on 2.1.1918, aged 18 years. Buried with full military honours at **ALL SAINTS CHURCHYARD, NETHERTHONG.** Grave location:- in South-West part, L, 73. His parents received a letter from a chum of their son, also in training at Cannock Chase, *'I feel I must write a line or two to assure you that I am almost heartbroken over the sudden death of your son Norman. He and myself have been together ever since we joined up on May 10th 1917. He has been the best of pals and the last time I saw him was last Tuesday night. 'D' Company was isolated on Wednesday morning and Norman was taken to hospital at dinnertime. I made enquiries the next morning and was told by his Captain that he had passed away the night before after a short period of consciousness. His loss will be seriously felt by all who had the pleasure of his acquaintance. I can assure you that you have my heartfelt sympathy in your terrible bereavement'*. ROH:- Netherthong and Thongsbridge War Memorial; Netherthong Working Men's Club.

RIGBY, CORNELIUS THOMAS WILLIAM. Private No 3/11375. 10th Battalion Duke of Wellington's Regiment. Born Birmingham. Son of the Rev. T. N. Rigby, Field House, Denby Dale. Enlisted at the outbreak of the war. Killed in action at Munster Alley, near Pozieres, during the Battle of the Somme on 29.7.1916, aged 42 years. Has no known grave. Commemorated **THIEPVAL MEMORIAL TO THE MISSING.** ROH:- Denby Dale and Cumberworth War Memorial.

RIGGS, HARRY. Private. No 305504. 1/7th Battalion Duke of Wellington's Regiment. Born 30.1.1889. Lived 158 Acre Street, Lindley. Discharged from the army on medical grounds, 7.7.1917. Died at home, 10.4.1920. Buried **St. STEPHEN'S CHURCH, LINDLEY.** Grave location:- 21, H. ROH:- St. Stephen's Church, Lindley; Huddersfield Drill Hall.

RILEY, ARTHUR. Private. No 2958. 1/5th Battalion Duke of Wellington's Regiment. Born Outcote Bank, Huddersfield. Educated St. Thomas's Church of England School. Employed as a road sweeper by the Huddersfield Corporation and at nights worked behind the curtain at the Theatre Royal, Huddersfield. Married, with four children. Lived 28 Victoria Road, Lockwood. Enlisted 4.9.1914. Embarked for France in April, 1915. Killed instantly by a shell on 9.5.1915. Buried **RUE-DAVID MILITARY CEMETERY, FLEURBAIX.** Grave location:- Plot 1, Row H, Grave 29. ROH:- Huddersfield Drill Hall; St. Stephen's Church, Rashcliffe; Huddersfield Corporation Roll.

RILEY, WILLIAM. Private. No 235215. 2nd Battalion Duke of Wellington's Regiment. Born Huddersfield. Lived 5 Hoffman Street, Milnsbridge. Employed by Messrs Smiths, Plover

Mills, Lindley. Was a member of the Longwood Harriers. Reported missing, presumed killed, at the Battle of Arras, 3.5.1917. Has no known grave. Commemorated **ARRAS MEMORIAL TO THE MISSING.** ROH:- Milnsbridge War Memorial.

RIPPON, NORRIS. 2nd Lieutenant. 'D' Company, 1/5th Battalion Duke of Wellington's Regiment. Born Huddersfield 28.9.1892. Son of Joseph and Elizabeth Rippon, 'Longueville', Park Drive, Huddersfield. Educated Fartown Grammar School and Giggleswick Public School. Was a member of the firm of Messrs Rippon Brothers, coach makers and automobile engineers, of Huddersfield, Bradford and Leeds. Single. Engaged to Miss Dawson, 'Thorndene', Bath Street, Huddersfield. Was commissioned in October, 1914, and embarked for France in April, 1915. Killed in action, 18.11.1915, aged 23 years. Buried **BARD COTTAGE CEMETERY, BOESINGHE, BELGIUM.** Grave location:- Plot 1, Row L, Grave 18. His parents received a letter from Major G. W. Kilner Crosland, who wrote, *'I regret to say I am the bearer of very bad news indeed that your son, Lieutenant N. Rippon was killed instantly this morning whilst doing his duty in the front line of trenches. He was walking along a trench amongst the men and a sniper's bullet passed through his head killing him immediately. This sad event has cast much gloom over the Officers and men of the Battalion with whom he was a great favourite. We have lost a good and capable Officer and one we can ill spare. We all join in expressing to you our deepest sympathy in your sad loss.'* ROH:- Fartown and Birkby War Memorial; Waterloo Rugby Union Football Club; Huddersfield Drill Hall.

ROBERTS, ALBERT. Sergeant. No 23090. 13th Battalion Royal Welsh Fusiliers. Born Milnsbridge. Son of Mr and Mrs Charlie Roberts, 12 Mount Street, Milnsbridge. Employed as a book-keeper by the late Mr Fred Sykes, butcher, Westgate, Huddersfield. Was a well known local vocalist and was formerly principal bass at Holy Trinity Church, Huddersfield, but at the time of enlisting was choirmaster at Christ Church, Linthwaite. During training he conducted a soldier's choir which won first prize at Winchester Eisteddford in 1915. Enlisted January 1915. Was twice recommended for a commission. Died of wounds at No 56 General Hospital on 31.5.1918, aged 28 years. Buried **ETAPLES MILITARY CEMETERY.** Grave location:- Plot 67, Row E, Grave 9. ROH:- Milnsbridge War Memorial; Linthwaite War Memorial.

ROBERTS, ALBERT. Private. No 3487. 2/5th Battalion Duke of Wellington's Regiment. Born Holmfirth. Lived Norridge Bottom, Holmfirth. Married, with four children. Employed as a mason's labourer. Enlisted at the outbreak of the war. Was in training at Doncaster. Came home on Friday, 23.4.1915, without leave. Was arrested by the police the next day and taken to Holmfirth Police Station, where he committed suicide by hanging himself from the cell window with one of his puttees on 24.4.1915. He was 35 years of age. Buried **HOLY TRINITY BURIAL GROUND, HOLMFIRTH.** Grave location:- North-East, I, 95. ROH:- Huddersfield Drill Hall.

ROBERTS, ARCHIE. Gunner. No L/28105. 'C' Battery, 312th Brigade Royal Field Artillery. Lived Huddersfield. Killed in action, 5.2.1918. Buried **ROCLINCOURT MILITARY CEMETERY.** Grave location:- Plot 4, Row A, Grave 7. ROH:- Denby Dale and Cumberworth War Memorial; Scissett War Memorial.

ROBERTS, ARTHUR. Gunner. No 82177. 'A' Battery, 94th Brigade Royal Field Artillery. Born Leeds. Son of Alfred and Mary Elizabeth Roberts, 112 Handel Street, Golcar (and later of Oak Cottage, Guildford Road, Guildford, Sydney, Australia). Employed as a piecer by Messrs Ben Hall and Sons, Milnsbridge. Had served in the local Territorials prior to the war. Was called up in July, 1914, and had served in France for nearly three years. Killed in action, 22.9.1917, aged 20 years. Buried **LARCH WOOD (RAILWAY CUTTING) CEMETERY.** Grave location:- Special Memorial A 18. His parents received a message of sympathy from the Major of his Battery, who said that, *Gunner Roberts was with him as a telephonist at the Observation Post in the trenches when a shell struck the dugout where he was stationed and killed him instantly. He said that Gunner Roberts was a very brave lad and most cheerful under trying circumstances'*. (Brother of Private **JOHN ROBERTS**, killed in action, 2.8.1916, q.v.). ROH:- St. John's Church, Golcar.

ROBERTS, CYRIL AINLEY. 2nd Lieutenant. 13th Battalion The Tank Corps. Born Woodlands

Place, Lindley Moor, Huddersfield, 5.9.1895. Son of Fred and Elizabeth Roberts, Maplin Lea, Lindley Moor, Outlane. Educated at Outlane National School and Longwood Grammar School. Was a member of the Huddersfield Hockey Club and the Moorlands Tennis Club. Employed as a clerk. Single. Enlisted, 19.5.1915, as a motor despatch rider in the Machine Gun Corps (motors branch). Was awarded a commission in the Tank Corps in September 1917. Killed in action at Kemmel, Belgium, on 25.4.1918 age 22 years. Has no known grave. Commemorated **TYNE COT MEMORIAL TO THE MISSING.** ROH:- Bethel United Methodist Church, Outlane; St. Andrew's Church, Stainland.

ROBERTS, DAVID HENRY. Private. No 301806. 1/7th Battalion Durham Light Infantry, attached 50th Battalion Machine Gun Corps. Formerly No 28431 Northumberland Fusiliers. Born Kirkburton. Died 22.9.1918. Buried **GLAGEON COMMUNAL CEMETERY EXTENSION.** Grave location:- Plot 1, Row J, Grave 6. ROH:- All Hallows Parish Church, Kirkburton.

ROBERTS, GEORGE WILLIAM. Air Mechanic 2nd Class. No 302122. Royal Air Force. Born 166 Albert Street, Lockwood, Huddersfield, 6.10.1898. Son of Benjamin and Betty Roberts, 65 Yews Hill Road, Lockwood. Educated Mount Pleasant Council School. Employed as an apprentice auctioneer and valuer. Single. Enlisted 14.4.1918. Died of pneumonia at Royds Hall War Hospital on 6.1.1919. Buried **SOUTH CROSLAND CHURCH BURIAL GROUND, HUDDERSFIELD.** Grave location:- N.W., 143. ROH:- St. Stephen's Church, Rashcliffe; Mount Pleasant Chapel, Lockwood.

ROBERTS, HARRY. Gunner. No 68411. 174th Siege Battery, Royal Garrison Artillery. Born Holmbridge, Holmfirth. Son of Joe and Mary Roberts, 17 Kilnhouse Bank, Holmbridge. Attended Holmbridge Parish Church Sunday School where he was a teacher. Employed as a weaver by Messrs W. H. and J. Barber at Clarence Mills, Holmbridge. Was well known as one of the best batsmen playing for the Holmbridge team. Enlisted February 1916. Embarked for France in October, 1916. Killed in action at the Battle of Arras, 2.5.1917, aged 27 years. Has no known grave. Commemorated **ARRAS MEMORIAL TO THE MISSING.** ROH:- Holme and Holmbridge War Memorial.

ROBERTS, HARVEY. Private. No 6269. 2/6th Battalion Duke of Wellington's Regiment. Born Milnsbridge. Lived 6 Balmforth's Yard, Milnsbridge. Found drowned in a pond near Clipstone Camp, 30.9.1916. An inquest was held at Mansfield, Nottinghamshire, on Monday October 2nd, 1916. *The body was found on Saturday 30.9.1916 in a pond in the parish of Clipstone by a farm labourer who also discovered on the bank a soldier's coat and cap. Lance Corporal Calvert said that he last saw the deceased alive on the morning of September 22nd when he reported sick and was admitted to hospital. He seemed very slow and witness could not get anything out of him. He appeared to be very depressed in mind. Medical evidence was given to the effect that Roberts had been in hospital for observation of his mental condition. He was dull witted and constantly talked about the growth of his eyebrows. A letter was found on the deceased, addressed to the deceased's mother, was produced and after reading it the Coroner said it stated that he would be out of hospital on Friday and ended, 'So keep on smiling Mother.' There was nothing in the letter about committing suicide. The jury returned a verdict of suicide while in a state of unsound mind.* Buried **St, MARK'S CHURCHYARD EXTENSION, LONGWOOD.** Grave location:- 322.

ROBERTS, JAMES. Private. No 29394. 8th Battalion Duke of Wellington's Regiment. Born Huddersfield. Married, with two children. Lived 28 Brier Fold, Birchencliffe, Huddersfield. Employed as a spinner at the Hollins Mill, Marsh. Embarked for France in January, 1917. Died of wounds at No 46 Casualty Clearing Station on 1.9.1917. Buried **MENDINGHEM BRITISH CEMETERY.** Grave location:- Plot 5, Row A, Grave 20. ROH:- St. Philip's Church, Birchencliffe.

ROBERTS, JOHN. Private. No 266475. 9th Battalion The Yorkshire Regiment. Formerly No 1667 Duke of Wellington's Regiment. Born Oldham. Son of Percy and Ada Roberts, of Marsden. Fell in raid near Caiga, between Asiago and Canove, Italy, on 20.7.1918, aged 23 years. Has no known grave. Commemorated **GIAVERA MEMORIAL TO THE MISSING, ITALY.** ROH:- Marsden War Memorial.

ROBERTS, JOHN. Private. No 17907. 9th Battalion Duke of Wellington's Regiment. Born Leeds. Son of Alfred and Mary Elizabeth Roberts, 7 Hope Terrace, Leymoor Road, Longwood. Came to Longwood from Honley in 1910. Attended Netherthong Wesleyan School. Employed at the Thirstin and Deanhouse Mills, Honley. Enlisted January 1916. Killed in action at Delville Wood during the Battle of the Somme on 2.8.1916, aged 23 years. Has no known grave. Commemorated **THIEPVAL MEMORIAL TO THE MISSING.** Mr and Mrs Roberts were shown a letter written by Private G. W. Senior of the same regiment who wrote to his home at Milnsbridge, saying, *'John Roberts, he who used to teaze at Ben Halls, was buried alive by a shell and when we dug him out he was dead.'* (Brother of Private **ARTHUR ROBERTS**, killed in action, 22.9.1917, q.v.). ROH:- St. John's Church, Golcar; Longwood War Memorial.

ROBERTS, NATHANIEL. Private. No 40922. 8th Battalion North Staffordshire Regiment. Formerly No 31846 Lincolnshire Regiment. Born Holyhead. Lived Huddersfield. Killed in action, 6.6.1918, aged 19 years. Has no known grave. Commemorated **SOISSONS MEMORIAL TO THE MISSING.**

ROBERTS, WILLIE. Private. No 240631. 'A' Company, 2/5th Battalion Duke of Wellington's Regiment. Born Primrose Hill, Huddersfield, 9.4.1894. Son of Joe and Clara Roberts, 52 Cross Lane, Primrose Hill. Educated Stile Common Council School. Employed as a tool grinder by Messrs William Whiteley and Sons Limited, Lockwood. Attended Primrose Hill United Methodist Church. Single. Enlisted 15.10.1914. Reported missing, presumed killed, at the Battle of Bullecourt on 3.5.1917, aged 23 years. Has no known grave. Commemorated **ARRAS MEMORIAL TO THE MISSING.** ROH:- Huddersfield Drill Hall.

ROBERTSHAW, JACK. Private. No 14868. 1/4th Battalion Duke of Wellington's Regiment. Born Dewsbury. For many years prior to the war had lived with Mr and Mrs Simeon Quarmby, Broad Oak Farm, Linthwaite and was well known to the milk customers in Linthwaite and Milnsbridge. Had been wounded on one occasion and spent his convalescence with Mr and Mrs Quarmby. Killed in action, 9.10.1917. Has no known grave. Commemorated **TYNE COT MEMORIAL TO THE MISSING.** ROH:- Linthwaite War Memorial.

ROBERTSHAW, ROLAND. Private. No 235301. 9th Battalion Duke of Wellington's Regiment. Born Marsh, Huddersfield. Enlisted Halifax. Killed in action at the Battle of Arras on 25.4.1917. Has no known grave. Commemorated **ARRAS MEMORIAL TO THE MISSING.**

ROBERTSON, DAVID. Sergeant. No 71455. 'D' Battery, 18th Army Brigade, Royal Field Artillery. Born 'Commercial Inn', Moldgreen, 28.5.1894. Son of Mr and Mrs William Thomas Robertson, 18 Victoria Street, Huddersfield. Educated Moldgreen Council School and Huddersfield Higher Grade School. Husband of Elsie Robertson, 28 Cheltenham Parade, Harrogate. Employed as a butcher in Harrogate. Enlisted January 1915. Died of wounds, 22.8.1918, aged 24 years. Buried **BELLACOURT MILITARY CEMETERY, RIVIERE.** Grave location:- Plot 3, Row E, Grave 11. ROH:- Lepton Parish Church.

ROBINSON, ALBERT ARTHUR. Private. No L/10552. 2nd Battalion East Kent Regiment (The Buffs). Born Ripon. Son of Tom and Mary Jane Robinson of Minton Cottage, Linthwaite. Killed in action at the Battle of Loos on 28.9.1915, aged 24 years. Has no known grave. Commemorated **LOOS MEMORIAL TO THE MISSING.** (Brother of Private **SAM BENSON ROBINSON,** killed in action, 29.3.1918, and Private **THOMAS WADE ROBINSON,** killed in action, 21.3.1918, q.v.). ROH:- Linthwaite War Memorial.

ROBINSON, ALBERT VICTOR. Lance Sergeant. No 18145. 2nd Battalion Duke of Wellington's Regiment. Born Honley. Son of Mr and Mrs Albert Robinson of Hillcrest, Honley. Educated Almondbury Grammar School and New College, Harrogate. Associated with his father's business at Smithy Place Mills, Brockholes. Enlisted 1916. *His father was very reluctant for his son to enlist and appealed to him to stay at home but Albert Victor said, 'No father, all my pals are going. If I stay at home what shall I have to say to them when they come back?'* Had been in France for eighteen months when he died of wounds at No 26 General Hospital on 30.3.1918, aged 21 years. Buried **ETAPLES MILITARY CEMETERY.** Grave location:- Plot

33, Row A, Grave 11. ROH:- Honley War Memorial; Brockholes War Memorial.

ROBINSON, ALFRED. Private. No 2679. 5th Battalion The Yorkshire Regiment. Born Huddersfield. Lived 23 Springdale Avenue, Lockwood, Huddersfield. Enlisted Malton. Killed in action, 26.4.1915. Has no known grave. Commemorated **MENIN GATE MEMORIAL TO THE MISSING.** ROH:- St. Stephen's Church, Rashcliffe.

ROBINSON, BERTIE C. Private. No 268519. 1/7th Battalion Duke of Wellington's Regiment. Born Cockermouth. Son of John Edward and Mrs Robinson, 28 Rufford Road, Scar Lane, Milnsbridge and formerly of Outlane. (His father had served 16 years in the army before the war and volunteered for service in the Royal Artillery at the outbreak of the war. He was twice wounded). Employed as a finisher at Plover Mills, Lindley. Was taken ill whilst on home leave in January, 1918, and was admitted to Royds Hall Military Hospital. He was subsequently treated at Rugeley Military Hospital and at Studley Royal Military Hospital, near Ripon, where he died on 20.5.1918, from complications following an operation. Buried **St. MARK'S CHURCHYARD EXTENSION, LONGWOOD.** Grave location:- 173. ROH:- St. Mark's Parish Church, Longwood; Bethel United Methodist Church, Outlane; Huddersfield Drill Hall.

ROBINSON, CHARLES HERBERT. Private. No 3/9677. 2nd Battalion Duke of Wellington's Regiment. Born 26 York Street, Huddersfield, 4.7.1893. Educated Huddersfield Parish Church School. Married, with one child. Lived 4 Dunlop Place, Sheffield. Employed as a labourer. Enlisted at the outbreak of the war. Killed in action near Ypres on 23.2.1915, aged 22 years. Has no known grave. Commemorated **MENIN GATE MEMORIAL TO THE MISSING.**

ROBINSON, ERNEST. Private. No 35343. 24th Company, Machine Gun Corps. Formerly No 19451 Duke of Wellington's Regiment. Born Shepley, Huddersfield. Son of Henry and Ruth H. Robinson, 3 Club Houses, Armitage Bridge. Employed at Armitage Bridge Mills. Enlisted March 1916. Reported missing, presumed killed, on 23.10.1916, during the Battle of the Somme. He was 28 years of age. Has no known grave.

Commemorated **THIEPVAL MEMORIAL TO THE MISSING.** (Brother of Private **REGINALD ROBINSON,** killed in action, 26.8.1918, q.v.). ROH:- Armitage Bridge Mills; Armitage Bridge War Memorial.

ROBINSON, GILBERT. Private. No 327208. 7th Battalion Duke of Wellington's Regiment. Born Heckmondwike, Yorkshire, in January 1893. Son of Mr and Mrs Edward Robinson, 25 York Street, Huddersfield. Educated Batty Street Board School, Heckmondwike. Employed as a tripe dresser by Mr J. Andrews, Thomas Street, Huddersfield. Single. Enlisted 1916. Suffered serious gunshot wounds to the neck and spine in June, 1917. Was a patient at St. George's Hospital, London, from June 1917 until 15.4.1918, when he died of his wounds. He was 24 years of age. Buried **EDGERTON CEMETERY, HUDDERSFIELD.** Grave location:- 2B, 193C. ROH:- Huddersfield Parish Church; Huddersfield Drill Hall.

ROBINSON, HARRY. Private. No 241241. 2/5th Battalion Duke of Wellington's Regiment. Son of Harry and Thirza Robinson, 54 Viaduct Street, Huddersfield. Employed by Messrs Cook, Sons and Company Limited, leather merchants, of Fitzwilliam Street, Huddersfield. Attended St. Andrew's Mission Church. Died 6.10.1918, aged 23, in hospital at Mons, Belgium, while he was a Prisoner of War in German hands. Buried **MONS COMMUNAL CEMETERY.** Grave location:- Plot 7, Row B, Grave 6. ROH:- St. Andrew's Church, Leeds Road, Huddersfield; Huddersfield Drill Hall.

ROBINSON, JOSEPH. Lance Corporal. No 19909. 21st Battalion Manchester Regiment, (6th Manchester Pals). Born Royton, Oldham. Lived Cowcliffe, Huddersfield. Married, with one child. Formerly employed by Messrs. J. Hopkinsons and Company Limited, Birkby, but at the time of enlistment was working in the laundry at the Manchester Royal Infirmary. Was a member of the Cowcliffe football club. Killed in action at Passchendaele, 4.10.1917, aged 25 years. Has no known grave. Commemorated **TYNE COT MEMORIAL TO THE MISSING.**

ROBINSON, MARK. Private. No 333545. 1/9th Battalion Highland Light Infantry. Born Lindley, Huddersfield, 30.8.1892. Son of Jesse and Annie Amelia Robinson, 47 Burbeary Road, Lockwood, Huddersfield. Educated Lockwood Council School. Employed as a hairdresser. Married. Enlisted 12.12.1915. Killed in action, 13.4.1918. Has no known grave. Commemorated **PLOEGSTEERT MEMORIAL TO THE MISSING.** ROH:- Emmanuel Church, Lockwood.

ROBINSON, REGINALD. Corporal. No 13142. 10th Battalion Duke of Wellington's Regiment. Born Shepley. Son of Henry and Ruth H. Robinson, 3 Club Houses, Armitage Bridge, Huddersfield. Killed in a raid near Canove Station, Asiago Plateau, Italy, on 26.8.1918, aged 27 years. Has no known grave. Commemorated **GIAVERA MEMORIAL TO THE MISSING, ITALY.** (Brother of Private **ERNEST ROBINSON,** killed in action, 23.10.1916, q.v.). ROH:- Armitage Bridge War Memorial.

ROBINSON, SAM BENSON. Sergeant. No 240240. 2/5th Battalion Duke of Wellington's Regiment. Born Ripon. Lived Minton Cottage, Manchester Road, Linthwaite. Employed at the Bent Ley Silk Mills, Meltham. Enlisted 1915. Killed in action, 29.3.1918, aged 23 years. Has no known grave. Commemorated **ARRAS MEMORIAL TO THE MISSING.** (Brother of Private **ALBERT ARTHUR ROBINSON,** killed in action, 28.9.1915, and Private **THOMAS WADE ROBINSON,** killed in action, 21.3.1918, q.v.). ROH:- Linthwaite War Memorial; Huddersfield Drill Hall.

ROBINSON, TOM. Private. No 38148. 2nd Battalion York and Lancaster Regiment. Formerly No 21/370 West Yorkshire Regiment. Born Finsthwaite, Lancashire. Son of John and Agnes Robinson of Gouldmire Cottage, Kendal, Westmorland. Was a native of Benson Hall, Kendal. Employed as a Police Constable at Scammonden. Single. Enlisted 1915. Died of wounds, 2.10.1917, aged 32 years. Buried **NOEUX-LES-MINES COMMUNAL CEMETERY EXTENSION.** Grave location:- Plot 1, Row C, Grave 6.

ROBINSON, THOMAS WADE. Private. No M2/082263. Army Service Corps (Motor Transport), attached 'Q' Anti-Aircraft Battery. Born North Stainley, Yorkshire. Married, with two children. Lived Rock Street, Linthwaite. Employed as a chauffeur by Mr Manks of Bent Ley Silk Mills, Meltham. Enlisted May 1915. Killed in action, 21.3.1918, aged 28 years. Has no known grave. Commemorated **ARRAS MEMORIAL TO THE MISSING.** (Brother of Private **ALBERT ARTHUR ROBINSON,** killed in action, 28.9.1915, and Private **SAM BENSON ROBINSON,** killed in action, 29.3.1918 q.v.). ROH:- Linthwaite War Memorial.

ROBSHAW, GEORGE. Private. No 110127. 10th Battalion The Tank Corps. Formerly No 219465 Royal Field Artillery. Born Castleford. Son of Mary Robshaw and the late George Henry Robshaw, 43 Robroyd, Wellhouse, Golcar. Attended Wellhouse Church and Sunday School. Killed in action, 9.8.1918, aged 22 years. Buried **CHIPILLY COMMUNAL CEMETERY EXTENSION.** Grave location:- Row A, Grave 1. ROH:- St. John's Church, Golcar; memorial in Wellhouse Churchyard.

ROBSON, JOHN. Private. No 22626. 9th Battalion Duke of Wellington's Regiment. Born 70 Leeds Road, Huddersfield, 15.4.1899. Son of Joseph N. and Ada Robson, 122 Nursery Terrace, Newsome Road, Huddersfield. Educated St. Andrew's Church of England School and Stile Common Council School. Employed as a clerk in the Town Clerk's office at Huddersfield Town Hall. Single. Enlisted 5.4.1917. Killed in action at Martinpuich on 26.8.1918, aged 19. Buried **WARLENCOURT BRITISH CEMETERY.** Grave location:- Plot 8, Row L, Grave 11. ROH:- St. John's Church, Newsome; Huddersfield Corporation Roll.

ROCHELL, THOMAS RICHARD. Private. No 301925. 1/7th Battalion Durham Light Infantry. Formerly No 4504 Duke of Wellington's Regiment. Born Snake Hill, Mirfield. Son of John Rochelle, Clough, Battyeford, Mirfield. Educated Battyeford School, Mirfield. Employed as a miner. Married. Enlisted 1915. Killed in action, 22.9.1917. Has no known grave. Commemorated **ARRAS MEMORIAL TO THE MISSING.**

RODDIS, CHARLES HARRY. Private. No 3071. 'A' Company, 1/5th Battalion Duke of Wellington's Regiment. Born 17 Bingley Street, Sheffield, 6.2.1897. Son of Charles and Ellen Roddis, 13 Fieldhouse Lane, Leeds Road, Huddersfield. Educated Parson Cross School, Wadsley Bridge, near Sheffield. Came to

Huddersfield from Sheffield in 1910. Employed as an apprentice in the tool-room of David Brown and Sons Limited, Park Works, Lockwood. Was a member of the Huddersfield Swimming Club. Attended St. Saviour's Mission, Leeds Road, Huddersfield. Single. Enlisted October 1914. Embarked for France in April, 1915. Killed in action at Fleurbaix, 25.6.1915, aged 18 years. Buried **RUE-DAVID MILITARY CEMETERY.** Grave location:- Plot 1, Row B, Grave 7. His father received the following letter from Major Norton, who wrote, *'I very much regret to have to inform you that your son, No 3071 Private C. Roddis was mortally wounded by a shell about 4.45pm yesterday afternoon and that he died in the first aid post the same evening. The enemy were shelling our trenches and your son was in a dugout. About the last shell they fired landed on the top of the dugout and burst inside. The Doctor tells me his wounds were of such a nature that he would have suffered no pain. I fear this will be a great blow to you and that nothing I can say will help to make your loss easier to bear. He was such a nice lad and a splendid soldier. His heart was in his work. He took up bombing and turned out one of the best bombers in the brigade. He was having a turn in the trenches to make room for others to be trained as bombers and it is very hard that he should have been killed before he could use the bombs on the Germans. He is a great loss to me personally and to all the officers and his comrades. I trust you will be able to find some consolation in remembering that he died for his country and that he was one of those who came forward to help save Britain at the most critical period of their history.'* ROH:- Christ Church, Woodhouse Hill; Huddersfield Drill Hall.

RODEN, ARTHUR. Gunner. No 127576. 199th Siege Battery, Royal Garrison Artillery. Born Sandiway, Cheshire. Son of Fanny Roden, of Sandiway, Cheshire, and the late John Roden: Husband of Ada Mary, aged 32 years. Buried **BUCUOY ROAD CEMETERY.** Grave location:- Plot 2, Row G, Grave 13. ROH:- Emmanuel Church, Shelley.

RODGERS, WALTER SHAW. Private. No 30394. 'A' Company, 11th Battalion East Yorkshire Regiment (Hull Tradesmen). Born Holmfirth. Son of Dyson and Mary Rodgers, 197 Woodhead Road, Holmbridge, Holmfirth. Educated Dobb School. Attended Hinchliffe Mill Wesleyan School. Employed as a motor man with Messrs Henry Mitchell and Sons, provision dealers. Enlisted May 1917. Trained at Brocton Camp, Rugeley, and North Shields. Embarked for France on 30.3.1918, three days before his 19th birthday. Reported missing at the Battle of Hazebrouck, 12.4.1918 and afterwards presumed to have been killed on that date, aged 19. Has no known grave. Commemorated **PLOEGSTEERT MEMORIAL TO THE MISSING.** ROH:- Holme and Holmbridge War Memorial.

ROEBUCK, BEN. Private. No 5178. 16th Battalion Australian Imperial Force. Born Wood Nook, Honley, Huddersfield. Son of Joseph Hirst Roebuck and Rachel Roebuck, Cliffe View, Thongsbridge. Educated St. Mary's Church of England School, Wilshaw. Attended Netherthong Parish Church. Was a member of the Working Men's Club. Employed as a teamer by Mr Joseph Batley. Emigrated to Australia in 1910. Worked on his farm and orchard. Killed in action at Mouquet Farm during the Battle of the Somme on 12.8.1916, aged 37 years. Has no known grave. Commemorated **VILLERS-BRETONNEUX MEMORIAL TO THE MISSING.** ROH:- Netherthong and Thongsbridge War Memorial; Netherthong Working Men's Club; commemorated on his parents' headstone in All Saints Churchyard, Netherthong.

ROEBUCK, FRANK. Private. No 241645. 'C' Company, 2/5th Battalion Duke of Wellington's Regiment. Born Carr Street, Marsh, Huddersfield. Son of Mr and Mrs Herbert Roebuck, 95 Longwood Road, Huddersfield. Educated Paddock Council School. Attended Paddock Congregational Church. Employed as an assistant in the Northumberland Street branch of the Huddersfield Industrial Society. Single. Enlisted 16.3.1916. Reported missing, presumed killed, at the Battle of Bullecourt on 3.5.1917, aged 31. Has no known grave. Commemorated **ARRAS MEMORIAL TO THE MISSING.** ROH:- St. Mark's Parish Church, Longwood; Shared Church, Paddock; Huddersfield Drill Hall.

ROEBUCK, FRED. Private. 2/5th Battalion Duke of Wellington's Regiment. Born Lower Oldfield, Thongsbridge, Holmfirth, 6.9.1894. Son of Harry Roeburck, 25 Taylor Hill Road, Huddersfield. Educated Berry Brow Board School. Employed as a tailor. Single. Enlisted 1916. Was a Prisoner of

War in Germany. Died at home, 26.1.1919, at 25 Taylor Hill Road, Huddersfield, from pneumonia contracted as the result of treatment during the time he was in Germany. ROH:- Emmanuel Church, Lockwood; Taylor Hill Primitive Methodist Church; Huddersfield Drill Hall.

ROEBUCK, HARRY. Private. No 235317. 23rd (Tyneside Scottish) Battalion Northumberland Fusiliers. Married. Lived 1 Upperhead Row, Huddersfield. Attended St. Patrick's Roman Catholic Church. Employed in the Post Office telephone service. Enlisted January 1915. Had been wounded on one occasion. Killed in action, 9.9.1917. Buried **HARGICOURT BRITISH CEMETERY.** Grave location:- Plot 1, Row B, Grave 29.

ROEBUCK, HARRY. Private. No 28433. 25th (Tyneside Irish) Battalion Northumberland Fusiliers. Born Cliff, Holmfirth. Son of Mr William Roebuck. Educated at the National Day School and Cliffe Sunday School. Played football with the Underbank team. Employed at Bank Bottom Mills, Marsden. Enlisted 18.4.1916. Embarked for France in July, 1916. Killed in action, 17.4.1918, aged 22 years. Buried **MONT NOIR MILITARY CEMETERY.** Grave location:- Plot 1, Row C, Grave 6. His father received a letter from his son's Officer, who wrote, *'I cannot tell you how much I regret to have to inform you that your son Private H. Roebuck, of 'C' Company, 25th Battalion Northumberland Fusiliers, was killed in action on the 17th inst. He was killed outright along with another four men of the Company by a heavy shell. He had acted as my servant since the beginning of January and I found in him such fine a character that I looked upon him more as a true friend than anything else and we were scarcely ever separate. He was one of the bravest fellows I have ever met and no matter how dangerous the patrol I at times had to do he always insisted on going with me. By his bravery and utter disregard of danger during the heavy fighting from the 21st to 23rd March he was responsible for saving over fifty men of his Company from being completely surrounded by the enemy. It was with more than usual pleasure I put his name forward asking for some recognition for the splendid work he had done during this time. I assure you that you have the deepest sympathy not only of myself but of every Officer and man in the Company in the loss of such a brave man.'* ROH:- Wooldale War Memorial.

ROEBUCK, LAWRENCE CYRIL. Private. No 241061. 2/5th Battalion Duke of Wellington's Regiment. Son of Councillor and Mrs B. Roebuck, 31 Lydgate, New Mill, Holmfirth. Educated Lane Bottom and New Mill National Schools. He then enrolled at the Holmfirth Technical School in the designing class. Employed by Messrs Graham and Barnfather, Kirkbridge, New Mill. Attended Lydgate Unitarian Chapel. Enlisted 1.3.1915. Reported missing, 5.5.1917 and afterwards presumed to have been killed on that date. He was nineteen years of age. Buried **SAUCHY-LESTREE COMMUNAL CEMETERY.** Grave location:- Grave 1. His parents received a letter from a comrade of their son in which he acknowledged a parcel which had been sent to Lawrence. He wrote, *'I inform you with deep regret that Lawrence is believed missing. We cannot tell you any particulars but we thought we would drop you a few lines in answer to his parcel. We thank you very much for the contents of the parcel and we are all very sorry that he is not here to enjoy it himself. With deepest sympathy on behalf of his friends in the Battalion.'* ROH:- New Mill Working Men's Club; Fulstone War Memorial; Huddersfield Drill Hall; Holmfirth Secondary School.

ROEBUCK, LEONARD. Lieutenant. 38th Squadron, Royal Air Force. Born Somerset Road, Huddersfield, 28.9.1893. Son of Harry and Jane Roebuck, Glen Royd, 19 Somerset Road, Huddersfield. Educated Huddersfield College School and Cranbrook College, Kent. Employed in the office at his father's business at Moldgreen, Huddersfield. Single. Was a member of the Huddersfield Wednesday football club and a keen motor cyclist. Enlisted in the motor transport section of the Army Service Corps in September, 1915. Was commissioned in the Royal Flying Corps in April, 1917. Killed whilst night flying at Leadenham, near Sleaford, Lincolnshire, on 4.4.1918, aged 24 years. (He had been expected home on leave the following Thursday). Buried **ALMONDBURY CEMETERY, HUDDERSFIELD.** Grave location:- 11, 'C', 41. ROH:- Huddersfield Parish Church; Christ Church, Moldgreen; Huddersfield College School; Almondbury War Memorial; Memorial in Almondbury Cemetery.

ROEBUCK, ROLAND WHITE. Private. No 4873. 7th Battalion Gordon Highlanders. Born

Shepley. Son of Allen and Isabella Roebuck, 65 Whitehead Lane, Primrose Hill, Huddersfield. Attended Shepley Parish Church. Was a member of the Shepley Oddfellows Club and the Shepley and New Mill football clubs. He was also a member of the Scholes Cricket Club. Employed as a pattern weaver by Messrs Wallace and Company, Bradford. Enlisted 7.12.1915. Embarked for France in July, 1916. Wounded 18.11.1916. Died of wounds at No 13 General Hospital on 24.11.1916, aged 27 years. Buried **BOULOGNE EASTERN CEMETERY**. Grave location:- Plot 8, Row D, Grave 198. ROH:- Shepley War Memorial.

ROEBUCK, SANDY. Private. No 31839. 7th Battalion North Staffordshire Regiment. Born Denby Dale, near Huddersfield, 25.9.1884. Son of George Roebuck. Husband of Edith Annie Roebuck, 204 Albert Street, Lockwood (later of 93 Luck Lane, Marsh). Educated Mount Pleasant Board School. Employed as a wood turner by Messrs John Haigh and Sons, Firth Street, Huddersfield. Died in Persia of malaria on 3.10.1918, aged 34 years. Originally Buried in **HAMADAN MILITARY CEMETERY, IRAN** but re-interred in **TEHRAN WAR CEMETERY, IRAN**. Grave location:- Plot 5, Row E, Grave 6. ROH:- Salvation Army Citadel; Emmanuel Church, Lockwood.

ROGERS, JOHN. Private. No M2/050675. 1st Base Depot (France), Army Service Corps (Motor Transport). Born Huddersfield. Son of William and Ellen Rogers, 35 Buckrose Street, Hillhouse, Huddersfield. Died in Dyke Bar Hospital, Paisley, Scotland, on 17.1.1918, aged 35 years. Buried with full military honours **EDGERTON CEMETERY, HUDDERSFIELD**. Grave location:- 65, RC, 105. (Brother of Private **MICHAEL ROGERS,** killed in action, 26.9.1918, q.v.). ROH:- Fartown and Birkby War Memorial.

ROGERS, MICHAEL. Lance Corporal. No 95011. No 1 Water Boring Section, Royal Engineers. Born Huddersfield. Son of William and Ellen Rogers, 35 Buckrose Street, Hillhouse, Huddersfield. Husband of Mary Ellen Rogers, 29 Freehold Street, Primrose Hill, Huddersfield. Employed by Messrs Graham and Jessop. Enlisted 1915. Killed whilst asleep in his billet on 26.9.1918, aged 31 years. Buried **FINS NEW BRITISH CEMETERY**. Grave location:- Plot 6, Row D, Grave 13. (Brother of Private **JOHN ROGERS,** died, 17.1.1918, q.v.). ROH:- Commemorated on his parents' headstone in Edgerton Cemetery, Huddersfield.

ROLLIN, HAROLD. Private. No 138785. 3rd Battalion Machine Gun Corps. Formerly No 59512 Durham Light Infantry. Born Otley. Son of Henry Emsley Rollin, Temperance Hotel, Honley. Employed by Messrs David France and Company, of Honley, where his father was foreman finisher. Died of meningitis at No 38 Casualty Clearing Station on 24.10.1918, aged 19 years. Buried **AWOINGT BRITISH CEMETERY**. Grave location:- Plot 1, Row E, Grave 23. (Brother of Private **WALTER ROLLIN,** killed in action, 3.2.1917, q.v.). ROH:- Honley War Memorial.

ROLLIN, HERBERT. Private. No PO/1332(S). Royal Marine Light Infantry. 1st Reserve Battalion, Royal Naval Division. Born Linthwaite. Lived with his sister, Mrs Willie Pogson, 529 Jovil, Linthwaite, whose husband was serving in Salonika. Employed at Black Rock Mills, Linthwaite. Enlisted January 1916. Was wounded on one occasion. He was at Aldershot on his way home from leave when he contracted a cold which turned into pneumonia. Died at Aldershot, 20.11.1918, aged 32 years. Buried with full military honours **ALDERSHOT MILITARY CEMETERY**. Grave location:- AF, 2135. ROH:- Linthwaite War Mmeorial.

ROLLIN, WALTER. Private. No 13468. 2nd Battalion Duke of Wellington's Regiment. Born Halifax. Lived Huddersfield. Son of Henry Emsley Rollin. Killed in action 3.2.1917. Buried **FINS NEW BRITISH CEMETERY**. Grave location:- Plot 7, Row F, Grave 24. (Brother of Private **HAROLD ROLLIN,** died, 24.10.1918, q.v.).

ROLLINSON, JAMES WILLIE. Gunner. No 113140. 262nd Siege Battery Royal Garrison Artillery. Born Shelley. Son of Mrs Ben Rollinson, Old Post Office Yard, Shelley. Employed by Messrs Firth Brothers, Bank Bottom Mills. Attended Shelley Parish Church and was a member of the Church Institute. Killed in action, 1.7.1917, aged 23 years. Buried **VLAMERTINGHE NEW MILITARYCEMETERY**. Grave location:- Plot 2, Row E, Grave 2. ROH:- Emmanuel Church, Shelley.

ROLLINSON, THOMAS (JOE). Private. No 307830. 1/7th Battalion Duke of Wellington's Regiment. Born Honley. Son of C. and S. E. Rollinson of Honley. Husband of Mary Rollinson , 11 Oldfield Buildings, Honley. Employed by Mr P. Fox, butcher. Attended Honley Parish Church. Enlisted August 1916. Killed in action, 24.2.1918, aged 30 years. Buried **MENIN ROAD SOUTH MILITARY CEMETERY, YPRES.** Grave location:- Plot 3, Row H, Grave 30. ROH:- Honley War Memorial; Huddersfield Drill Hall.

ROODHOUSE, ARTHUR. Deckhand. No 14802 D.A. Royal Naval Reserve. *HM Drifter Silvery Harvest*. Son of Mrs Roodhouse of Sudehill, New Mill, Holmfirth. Educated New Mill National School. Employed at Moorbrook Mills. An able pianist. Enlisted 11.10.1916. Drowned after a collision off Berry Head, 16.5.1918, aged 33 years. Has no known grave. Commemorated **PLYMOUTH NAVAL MEMORIAL TO THE MISSING.** ROH:- New Mill Working Men's Club; Fulstone War Memorial.

ROOKE, RICHARD JAMES. Sergeant. No 6002. 2nd Battalion Duke of Wellington's Regiment. Born Biggleswade, Sandy, Bedfordshire, 7.4.1882. Educated Biggleswade National School. Husband of Catherine Rose Rooke, 33 Commercial Street, Huddersfield. Enlisted in the Duke of Wellington's Regiment on 27.10.1899. Served in the South African War. Mobilised at the outbreak of the war. Wounded at Ypres, 11.11.1914. Died of wounds, 4.12.1916, at Huddersfield Royal Infirmary, aged 34 years. Buried **EDGERTON CEMETERY, HUDDERSFIELD.** Grave location:- 53, 63G.

ROSE, WILLIAM. Private. No 2416. 1/5th Battalion Duke of Wellington's Regiment. Born Lightcliffe, Halifax. Son of Police Constable Thomas Rose and Mrs Mary Ann Rose, 25 Paris Road, Scholes, Holmfirth. Attended Hepworth Parish Church where he was the organ blower. *When the 1/5th Battalion were going to camp at Marske in July 1914 he cut an artery in his arm through the breaking of a carriage window. He carried his arm in a sling during the week and on retiring home was treated by Doctor Ed Trotter who put some stitches into the arm and gave his certificate that Rose was medically unfit. Then came the order for mobilisation. Young Rose was in bed but in the absence of his parents he donned his khaki and fell in with his comrades at Holmfirth Drill Hall where his comrades gave him a hearty cheer. Police Constable Rose was that evening on duty at the station entrance and was quite unaware of the fact that the Territorials marching past him to the train included his son Willie.* Killed in action, 28.9.1915, aged 19 years. Has no known grave. Commemorated **MENIN GATE MEMORIAL TO THE MISSING.** Lieutenant J. W. Clapham wrote to his parents, *'It is with deep regret that I write to tell you that your son, Private W. Rose was killed yesterday morning about 9.30am by a trench mortar during a bombardment. I feel his death very much myself as he was one of the most obliging fellows in my platoon. I often went out with him mending the wires in front of our lines and nothing seemed to frighten him. I hope it will be a little consolation to you to think that he gave his life for a noble cause.'* ROH:- Hepworth and Scholes War Memorial; Hepworth Parish Church.

ROTHERFORTH, JOSEPH BOTTOMLEY. Corporal. No 14113. 'A' Company, 2nd Battalion Duke of Wellington's Regiment. Born Denby Dale. Son of G. and Mary E. Rotherforth of Upper Denby, Denby Dale. Killed in action in the attack on Pacaut Wood on 15.4.1918, aged 23 years. Buried **MONT BERNENCHON BRITISH CEMETERY, GONNEHEM.** Grave location:- Plot 1, Row D, Grave 3. ROH:- Denby Dale and Cumberworth War Memorial.

ROTHERY, ARTHUR WILLIAM. Sub Conductor. No 05350. 21st Company, Army Ordnance Corps. Born Huddersfield. Son of Edwin and Sophia Rothery, Wood Cottage, Farnley Tyas. Employed as head store-keeper at Storths Hall Asylum since the opening of the institution in 1903. Was a member of the Farnley Tyas Urban District Council. Held the position of secretary to the Farnley Tyas Bowling Club. Had served 11 years with the Royal Garrison Artillery. Saw active service with the B.E.F. in Crete in No 4 Mountain Battery, Royal Artillery. On the outbreak of the South African War he served with the same Battery but was later transferred to Vickers Maxim guns. In March, 1915, he rejoined the Colours from the Reserve. Had suffered from an internal complaint and died following an operation at Lahore Military Hospital, Calais, on 7.1.1916, aged 44 years. Buried **CALAIS SOUTHERN**

CEMETERY. Grave location:- Plot B, Row 2, Grave 5. ROH:- Farnley Tyas War Memorial; Thurstonland War Memorial.

ROTHERY, JOE. Private. No 51935. 1st Battalion East Yorkshire Regiment. Formerly No 75534 West Yorkshire Regiment. Born Knowle Place, Golcar, in January, 1883. Son of Mr and Mrs Alfred Rothery, 59 Clement Street, Birkby. Educated Golcar National School. Employed as a woollen spinner by Messrs Middlemost Brothers and Company, of Birkby. Husband of Alice Rothery, 31 Blacker Road, Birkby. Enlisted 18.5.1918. Wounded near Cambrai on 23.10.1918. Died of wounds 24.10.1918, aged 36 years. Buried **INCHY COMMUNAL CEMETERY EXTENSION.** Grave location:- Row B, Grave 36. (Brother of Private **JOHN EDWARD ROTHERY,** killed in action, 5.5.1915, q.v.). ROH:- St. Hilda's Church, Cowcliffe; Fartown and Birkby War Memorial.

ROTHERY, JOHN EDWARD. Private. No 10230. 2nd Battalion Duke of Wellington's Regiment. Born Golcar 18.12.1895. Son of Mr and Mrs Alfred Rothery, 59 Clement Street, Birkby. Educated St. John's School, Hillhouse, Huddersfield. Employed as a goods porter by the London and North Western Railway Company at the Huddersfield Goods station. Single. Enlisted 8.8.1914. Embarked for France 20.9.1914. Gassed at Hill 60 and died the same day, 5.5.1915, aged 20 years. Buried **DIVISIONAL CEMETERY, DICKEBUSCH ROAD, VLAMERTINGHE, BELGIUM.** Grave location:- Row C, Grave 18. (Brother of Private **JOE ROTHERY,** died of wounds, 24.10.1918, q.v.). ROH:- St. Hilda's Church, Cowcliffe; Fartown and Birkby War Memorial; London and North Western Railway Company Roll.

ROTHERY, WILFRED. Private. No 41990. 1st Battalion Essex Regiment. Formerly No 834 Northumberland Fusiliers. Born 20 Meg Lane, Longwood, 15.5.1880. Educated Paddock Board School. Employed as a plumber. Enlisted 27.5.1916. Killed in action, 29.7.1917, near Ypres. Has no known grave. Commemorated **MENIN GATE MEMORIAL TO THE MISSING.** ROH:- St. Mark's Parish Church, Longwood.

ROTHWELL, JOHN THOMAS. Private. No 241780. 2/5th Battalion Duke of Wellington's Regiment. Born Halifax. Lived Lindley. Son of the late William Henry and Ellen Rothwell. Reported missing, presumed killed, at the Battle of Bullecourt, 3.5.1917, aged 29 years. Has no known grave. Commemorated **ARRAS MEMORIAL TO THE MISSING.** ROH:- Huddersfield Drill Hall; Blackley Baptist Chapel.

ROTHWELL, RICHARD. Private. No 136033. 58th Battalion Machine Gun Corps. Formerly No 41315 East Yorkshire Regiment. Born Huddersfield 25.3.1899. Son of Ernest William and Harriet Rothwell, 48 Victoria Street, Moldgreen. Educated Moldgreen Church of England School. Employed as a heald and stay maker. Single. Enlisted April 1917. Killed in action, 24.4.1918. Has no known grave. Commemorated **POZIERES MEMORIAL TO THE MISSING.** ROH:- Christ Church, Moldgreen.

ROUTLEDGE, JOSEPH EDWARD CHRISTOPHER. Private. No 2366. 1/5th Battalion Duke of Wellington's Regiment. Born Bolton, Lancashire 23.2.1897. Son of Mr and Mrs Routledge, 9 Brook Street, Moldgreen. (Later of 4 Oak Avenue, Moldgreen). Educated Almondbury Church of England School. Employed as an apprentice cutter by Messrs Samuel Taylor and Company, wholesale clothiers, Prospect Street, Huddersfield. Was a member of the choir at Almondbury Parish Church and attended Almondbury Church Sunday School. Single. Enlisted August 1914. Wounded in the attack on the Schwaben Redoubt during the Battle of the Somme on 3.9.1916. Died of wounds at St. George's Hospital, London, on 9.9.1916, aged 19 years. Buried with full military honours in **ALMONDBURY CEMETERY, HUDDERSFIELD.** Grave location:- B, 'C', 62. ROH:- Christ Church, Moldgreen; Almondbury War Memorial; Huddersfield Drill Hall.

ROWBOTTOM, SAMUEL. Private. No 3/12186. 2nd Battalion Duke of Wellington's Regiment. Born Lindley, Huddersfield. Lived Paddock. Killed in action in the attack on Lesboeufs during the Battle of the Somme, 12.10.1916. Has no known grave. Commemorated **THIEPVAL MEMORIAL TO THE MISSING.** ROH:- All Saints Church, Paddock.

ROWE, FRANK LEONARD. Private. No 43598. 1/4th The Yorkshire Regiment. Formerly No

110492 87th Territorial Reserve Battalion. Born Brook Street, Moldgreen, 27.6.1899. Son of Mr and Mrs Stephen Rowe, 9 Wormald Street, Almondbury. Educated Almondbury Council School. Employed by Messrs T. and H. Blamires Limited, Leeds Road, Huddersfield. Single. Enlisted 8.10.1917. Killed in action near Estaires, 9.4.1918, aged 18 years. Buried **CROIX-DU-BAC BRITISH CEMETERY, STEENWERCK.** Grave location:- Plot 3, Row E, Grave 11.

ROWE, WALTER. Private. No 240684. 2/5th Battalion Duke of Wellington's Regiment. Born Huddersfield Workhouse 5.10.1885. Parents lived at 48 Victoria Crescent, Lockwood. Educated Mount Pleasant Council School, Lockwood. Husband of Polly Rowe, 33 Swan Lane, Lockwood. Employed as a labourer by Messrs W. H. Heywood and Company, Birkby. Was a member of the Men's Own Class at Ramsden Street Chapel. Enlisted 10.11.1914. Wounded and taken prisoner at Bullecourt, 3.5.1917. Died of wounds, 23.6.1917, aged 33 years. Buried **TOURNAI COMMUNAL CEMETERY ALLIED EXTENSION.** Grave location:- Plot 1, Row A, Grave 2. ROH:- Emmanuel Church, Lockwood; Huddersfield Drill Hall.

ROWLANDS, GEORGE OSWALD. Sergeant. No 33333. 170th Company, Machine Gun Corps. Formerly No 1743 Duke of Wellington's Regiment. Born Emley near Huddersfield. Husband of Mabel Sylvia Rowlands, of Shelley. Killed in action, 3.6.1917, aged 24 years. Buried **RUE-du-BOIS MILITARY CEMETERY.** Grave location:- Plot 3, Row A, Grave 10. ROH:- Emmanuel Church, Shelley; All Hallows Church, Kirkburton.

ROWLEY, REGINALD THOMPSON. Private. No 2425. 7th Regiment South African Infantry. Son of Robert Thomas Rowley and Elizabeth Annie Weston Rowley, of Stanley House, Lindley, Huddersfield. Killed in the German attack on Salaita Hill, Kenya, on 12.2.1916, aged 24 years. Buried **TAVETA MILITARY CEMETERY, KENYA, EAST AFRICA.** Grave location:- Plot 9, Row B, Grave 1.

ROYLE, CHARLES. Corporal. No 2956. 1/5th Battalion Duke of Wellington's Regiment. Born 8 Manchester Street, Salford, Manchester. Educated Trafford Road Board School, Salford. Employed as a wire drawer and mechanic by Messrs Joseph Sykes Brothers Limited, Acre Mills, Lindley, Huddersfield. Married. Lived 25 Victoria Street, Lindley. Enlisted 5.9.1914. Killed in No Man's Land whilst out on patrol near Foncquevillers on 14.11.1916, aged 33. Buried **FONCQUEVILLERS MILITARY CEMETERY.** Grave location:- Plot 1, Row J, Grave 32. The following extract is taken from the 1/5th Battalion's War Diary, '*14.11.1916. At 4am a patrol left our sap K.3.b.70.95. to reconnoitre enemy wire. After proceeding 50 yards patrol saw an enemy patrol which got between them and our lines, upon which our patrol began to retire so as to approach the hostile patrol. The Germans saw our men when they were within 15 yards and threw 2 bombs. Our patrol fired their rifles into them and a scuffle ensued. The officer and 3 of our patrol pursued the enemy and secured one prisoner. The rest succeeded in getting away. Of the remaining two of our patrol only one returned. A search party failed to find the missing man, a Corporal*'. ROH:- St. Stephen's Church, Lindley; Huddersfield Drill Hall.

ROYSTON, PETER BATTYE. Sergeant. No L/25406. 'A' Battery, 168th (Huddersfield) Brigade, Royal Field Artillery. Born 23 Bow Street, Huddersfield, 10.6.1889. Parents both deceased - mother (Adelaide) in 1889 and Father (Fred) in 1909. Lived with his Uncle, James Lockhead, at 39 Crosland Street, Crosland Moor, Huddersfield. Educated Stile Common Council School. Employed as a weaver. Single. Enlisted 27.4.1915. Wounded 29.11.1916. Died of wounds at No 4 General Hospital, Camiers, 20.12.1916, aged 27 years. Buried **ETAPLES MILITARY CEMETERY.** Grave location:- Plot 20, Row J, Grave F. ROH:- St. Barnabas Church, Crosland Moor.

RUMBLE, WILLIAM ARTHUR. Private. No 302015. 2nd Battalion The Royal Scots (Lothian Regiment). Born Keighley 15.1.1882. Educated at Longwood School. Husband of Annie Rumble, 48 Blackhouse Road, Fartown. Employed as a woollen weaver at Ashbrow Mills. Enlisted 10.10.1916. Died of wounds at No 46 Stationary Hospital on 1.10.1917, aged 35 years. Buried **ETAPLES MILITARY CEMETERY.** Grave location:- Plot 27, Row C, Grave 5a. ROH:- Christ Church, Woodhouse Hill; Longwood War Memorial; Fartown and Birkby War Memorial.

RUSHFIRTH, FRANK. Private. No 2951. 'A' Company, 1/5th Battalion Duke of Wellington's Regiment. Born Taylor Hill, Huddersfield, 3.12.1883. Son of Joseph and Martha Rushfirth. Lived with his Aunt, Mrs Oates, of Fenton Road, Lockwood. Educated Lockwood National School. Employed as a tailor's fitter by Messrs Denton and Lee, wholesale clothiers, Dundas Street, Huddersfield. Attended Lockwood Church, where he was a member of the choir. Was a well known bass singer and had been a member of the chorus of the Huddersfield Choral and Glee and Madrigal Societies. Had at one time been a member of the Huddersfield Amateur Operatic Society and had sung in the choir of Leeds Musical Society. Was very fond of rugby football. Single. Enlisted 9.9.1914. Killed in action in the trenches near Boesinghe, Belgium, on 19.11.1915, aged 33 years. Buried **TALANA FARM CEMETERY.** Grave location:- Plot 4, Row G, Grave 5. ROH:- Emmanuel Church, Lockwood; Huddersfield Drill Hall.

RUSHWORTH, ALFRED. Gunner. No 223325. 84th Battery Royal Field Artillery. Born Skelmanthorpe. Son of John William Rushworth, Greenhouse Farm, Fartown. Educated Hillhouse Council School. Employed as a dairyman's assistant. Single. Enlisted 5.4.1917. Died at Greenhouse Farm, Fartown, of wounds and the effects of gas poisoning, 4.4.1919. ROH:- Fartown and Birkby War Memorial.

RUSHWORTH, ARTHUR. Gunner. No 25653. 'A' Battery, 168th (Huddersfield) Brigade Royal Field Artillery. Younger son of Alfred and Mary Ann Rushworth, 244 Halifax Old Road, Grimscar, Huddersfield. Was an apprentice with Mr Ellis Brooke, printer, Market Place, Huddersfield. Enlisted June 1915. Died of wounds at No 11 Stationary Hospital, Rouen, 22.11.1917, aged 23 years. Buried **St. SEVER CEMETERY EXTENSION, ROUEN.** Grave location:- Block P, Plot 3. Row P. Grave 11a. (Brother of Private **TOM RUSHWORTH**, died of wounds, 25.7.1918, q.v.). ROH:- Fartown and Birkby War Memorial; commemorated on his parents' headstone in Edgerton Cemetery, Huddersfield.

RUSHWORTH, HARRY. Private. No 41518. 'C' Company, 8th Battalion King's Own Royal Lancaster Regiment. Formerly No 220090 King's Own Yorkshire Light Infantry. Born Huddersfield. Son of Alfred and Annie Rushworth, 106 Blackhouse Road, Fartown. Killed in action, 29.8.1918, aged 18 years. Buried **MORY STREET MILITARY CEMETERY, St. LEGER.** Grave location:- Row A, Grave 6. ROH:- Fartown and Birkby War Memorial; Christ Church, Woodhouse Hill.

RUSHWORTH, ROLAND. Lance Corporal. No C/12507. 21st Battalion King's Royal Rifle Corps. Born Bradford 21.8.1892. Son of Mrs A. Rushworth, 49 Imperial Road, Edgerton, Huddersfield. Educated Spring Grove Council School and Huddersfield College. Employed as a solicitor's clerk by Messrs Ramsden, Sykes and Ramsden, of Huddersfield. Had been with the firm for ten years. Attended New North Road Baptist Church and Sunday School. Single. Enlisted November 1915. Shot through the right lung on 6.6.1916 and died of his wounds. He was twenty two years of age. Buried **STEENWERCK COMMUNAL CEMETERY.** Grave location:- Row A, Grave 2. ROH:- New North Road Baptist Church.

RUSHWORTH, TOM. Private. No 39398. 2/4th Battalion King's Own Yorkshire Light Infantry. Born Huddersfield. Son of Alfred and Mary Ann Rushworth, 244 Halifax Old Road, Grimscar, Huddersfield. Employed by Mr H. Platt, gardener, of Grimscar. Died of wounds, 25.7.1918, aged 40 years. Buried **St. SEVER CEMETERY EXTENSION, ROUEN.** Grave location:- Block Q, Plot 3, Row J. Grave 6. (Brother of Gunner **ARTHUR RUSHWORTH**, died of wounds, 24.11.1917, q.v.). ROH:- Fartown and Birkby War Memorial; commemorated on his parents' headstone in Edgerton Cemetery, Huddersfield.

RUSHWORTH, WILLIAM. Private. No 267568. 1/6th Battalion Duke of Wellington's Regiment. Born Lockwood Road, Lockwood, Huddersfield, 6.10.1888. Educated Deighton Board School. Lived 3 Cowcliffe Hill Road, Huddersfield. Employed as a motor driver by Messrs Shaw Limited, Moldgreen. Single. Enlisted 1.3.1916. Killed in action, 11.4.1918, aged 29 years. Has no known grave. Commemorated **TYNE COT MEMORIAL TO THE MISSING.** ROH:- Fartown and Birkby War Memorial.

RUSSELL, JACK. Guardsman. No 26359. 4th Battalion Grenadier Guards. Born Golcar. Son of R. H. and Mary Russell, Rob Royd Cottage, Golcar. Assisted his father, who was a gardener for Mr Ramsden Crowther. Attended Wellhouse Sunday School. Enlisted 1916. Seriously wounded in the neck in July, 1917. Taken to No 4 Casualty Clearing Station. An Army Chaplain wrote to the parents telling them not to worry as their son would be able to write to them as soon as he was able. Died of his wounds on 1.8.1917, aged 20 years. Buried **DOZINGHEM MILITARY CEMETERY.** Grave location:- Plot 1, Row I, Grave 26. ROH:- St. John's Church, Golcar.

RYAN, HARRY. Private. No 90081. 29th Battalion Machine Gun Corps. Born Huddersfield. Son of Michael Ryan. Husband of Ruth Ryan, 8 Kirkmoor Place, Northgate, Huddersfield. Employed at British Dyes Limited. Reported missing, presumed killed, on 20.4.1918, aged 28 years. Has no known grave. Commemorated **TYNE COT MEMORIAL TO THE MISSING.**

RYAN, JAMES. Private. No 62409. 32nd General Hospital, Royal Army Medical Corps. Born Huddersfield. Son of James and Teresa Ryan, 17 River View, Aspley, Huddersfield. Employed as an apprentice by Messrs J. Holroyd and Company Limited, dyers and dry cleaners, Seed Hill, Huddersfield. Died from fever in Mesopotamia on 5.6.1916, aged 21 years. Buried **BASRA WAR CEMETERY, IRAQ.** Grave location:- Plot 5, Row S, Grave 10.

RYE, CHARLES JAMES. Private. No 291807. 'B' Company, 1/7th Battalion Northumberland Fusiliers. Born Meltham, Huddersfield. Son of William Jesse and Bertha Rye, 3 Blue Slates, Meltham. Killed in action at Passchendaele 26.10.1917, aged 20 years. Has no known grave. Commemorated **TYNE COT MEMORIAL TO THE MISSING.** ROH:- St. Bartholomew's Church, Meltham; Helme Parish Church.

RYLANCE, ERNEST. Private. No 240733. 2/5th Battalion Duke of Wellington's Regiment. Born Pemberton, Wigan, 25.10.1897. Son of John William and Ann Rylance, 80 Newsome Road, Huddersfield. Educated Hillhouse Council School. Employed as a cloth presser. Was a member of the Queen Street Mission Young Men's Class. Single. Enlisted 10.11.1914. Reported missing, presumed killed, at the Battle of Bullecourt on 3.5.1917, aged 19 years. Has no known grave. Commemorated **ARRAS MEMORIAL TO THE MISSING.** ROH:- St. John's Church, Newsome; Huddersfield Drill Hall.

SAILE, LESLIE WILLIAM. Private. No 17699. Depot Battalion Duke of Wellington's Regiment. Born 31 New North Road, Huddersfield 1891. Son of Margaret Emily Rachel Saile (nee Wilcox), and the late William Francis Saile, Artist, of Huddersfield. Educated Holy Trinity Church of England School, Huddersfield. Employed as a motor mechanic. At the time of enlistment, was living at 22 Clifton Road, Maida Vale, London W.9. Single. Enlisted 29.11.1915. Wounded on the first day of the Battle of the Somme, 1.7.1916. In 1917, as a result of frostbite, he had to have both feet amputated. Upon his discharge from the Army he was unable to obtain proper exercise. This caused a duodenal ulcer and internal haemorrhage, from which he died on 4.12.1920, at 22 Clifton Road, Maida Vale, London, aged 29 years. Buried **PADDINGTON CEMETERY, WILLESDEN LANE, MIDDLESEX.** Grave Location:- S,P, 14498.

SALLIS, JAMES. Private. No 17/850. 17th Battalion West Yorkshire Regiment (2nd Leeds Pals). Born London. Son of Bessie Sallis, and the late James Sallis, 16 Marsh, Honley. Employed by Messrs Eastwood Brothers, Honley. Killed whilst acting as a stretcher-bearer attending to wounded men near Carnoy, 25.8.1916, during the Battle of the Somme, aged 19 years. Has no known grave. Commemorated **THIEPVAL MEMORIAL TO THE MISSING.** ROH:- Honley War Memorial; Armitage Bridge War Memorial.

SANDERSON, ERNEST. Private. No 77893. 15th Battalion Durham Light Infantry. Born Holmfirth. Son of Fred Sanderson, 78 Far Cliffe, Holmfirth. Killed in action, 31.3.1918, aged 20 years. Has no known grave. Commemorated **POZIERES MEMORIAL TO THE MISSING.** ROH:- Wooldale War Memorial.

SANDERSON, HERMAN. Private. No 4826. 5th Battalion Seaforth Highlanders. Born Thongsbridge. Son of Joseph Sanderson, Back Lane, Berry Brow, Huddersfield. Married, with two children. Employed as a confectioner by Messrs Whiteleys of Westgate, Huddersfield. Was a member of the Berry Brow Liberal Club and a former scholar of Salem School. Was a well known local vocalist. Enlisted April 1916. Embarked for France in September, 1916. Died of wounds at No 49 Casualty Clearing Station on 16.11.1916, aged 25 years. Buried **CONTAY BRITISH CEMETERY.** Grave location:- Plot 8, Row B, Grave 6. ROH:- Armitage Bridge War Memorial.

SANDFORD, CLEMENT RICHARD FOLLIOT, MC. Captain. 5th Battalion King's Own Yorkshire Light Infantry. Younger son of the Archdeacon and Vicar of Doncaster, and former Vicar of Huddersfield, the Venerable G. Sandford and Mrs Sandford. Educated Huddersfield College School, Repton Public School and was at Corpus Christi College, Cambridge, when war broke out. Had held a commission in the Doncaster Territorials and went into training with his Battalion. Embarked for France 13.4.1915. Wounded in the arm in December, 1915. Invalided home, due to blood poisoning, and returned to active service at the beginning of 1917. Was promoted to Captain in October, 1916. Awarded the Military Cross in June 1916. Killed in action, 22.2.1917, aged 22 years. Buried **CAMBRIN MILITARY CEMETERY.** Grave location:- Row G, Grave 55. ROH:- Huddersfield College School.

SANDFORD, FRED. Private. No 241540. 2/5th Battalion Duke of Wellington's Regiment. Born Catworth, Huntingdon. Son of John and Martha Ann Sandford, Pog Ing, Holmfirth. Employed by Mr W. Hardy, dyer, Holmfirth. Was a member of the Holmfirth Cricket and Athletic Club and was groundsman for a period. A keen footballer, being a member of the Underbank football club. Formerly connected with the Holmfirth Conservative Club where he was secretary. Enlisted March, 1916, with his friend, Private **HARRY HOLMES**, (q.v.), they went off by train from Holmfirth together and were both reported missing, presumed killed, on the same day, 3.5.1917, at the Battle of Bullecourt; Fred was aged 29. Has no known grave. Commemorated **ARRAS MEMORIAL TO THE MISSING.** ROH:- Wooldale War Memorial; Huddersfield Drill Hall.

SANDFORD, LEONARD. Private. No 4741. 1/5th Battalion Duke of Wellington's Regiment. Born Huddersfield. Son of Jonathan and Mary Sandford, Ash House, Underbank, Holmfirth. Husband of Mavis Sandford. Educated Holmfirth Secondary School and Fartown Grammar School. After leaving school he joined the family business of Messrs W. Sandford and Son, woollen manufacturers, Underbank Mill, Holmfirth. Was a keen cricketer, being a member of the Holmfirth first eleven team. He was married in 1916 to Miss Mavis Birkhead, youngest daughter of Mr Thomas Birkhead, cloth finisher, Bridge Mills, Holmfirth. Enlisted in 1916 and underwent training at Clipstone Camp. He had been in France six weeks when he died of wounds at No 20 General Hospital, Camiers, on 18.9.1916, aged 23 years. Buried **ETAPLES MILITARY CEMETERY.** Grave location:- Plot 15, Row A, Grave 3a; ROH:- Holmfirth Secondary School; Holmfirth War Memorial; Huddersfield Drill Hall; memorial in Holmfirth Parish Churchyard.

SANDIFORTH, ARTHUR. Private. No 5/2967. 1/5th Battalion Duke of Wellington's Regiment. Born Leeds. Son of John and Mary Sandiforth, 6 Alma Cottages, Headingley, Leeds. Lived in lodgings with Mrs Carter, 32 South Street, Huddersfield. Employed at the Scotch Bakery in Westgate, Huddersfield. Was a member of the Primrose Hill Cricket Club and the Primrose Hill Liberal Club. Enlisted at the outbreak of the war. Was struck on the head by a piece of shell on 1.10.1915 and died instantly. He was 22 years of age. Buried **NEW IRISH FARM CEMETERY, St. JEAN-LES-YPRES.** Grave location:- Plot 2, Row B, Grave 20. ROH:- Huddersfield Drill Hall.

SANDLAND, JOHN. Bombardier. No 33. 4th Divisional Ammunition Column, attached 'Y' Trench Mortar Battery, Royal Field Artillery. Born Kirkheaton. Son of Mr and Mrs Thomas Brier Sandland, Fields Terrace, Kirkheaton. Accidentally killed in France on 29.10.1916, aged 21 years. Buried **EUSTON ROAD CEMETERY, COLINCAMPS.** Grave location:- Plot 2, Row N, Grave 2. ROH:- St. John's Church, Kirkheaton.

SANDS, MICHAEL FRANCIS. Private. No 210020. 2nd Battalion Canadian Infantry (Eastern Ontario Regiment). Husband of M. Sands, 7 Commercial Crescent, Huddersfield. Died, 31.8.1918, aged 38 years. Buried **AUBIGNY COMMUNAL CEMETERY EXTENSION.** Grave location:- Plot 4, Row G, Grave 36.

SAUNDERS, FREDERICK. Private. No 12825. 9th Battalion The Yorkshire Regiment.

Born Liverpool. Enlisted Huddersfield. Lived Meltham Mills. Killed in action, 7.6.1917. Has no known grave. Commemorated **MENIN GATE MEMORIAL TO THE MISSING.** ROH:- St. Bartholomew's Church, Meltham; Helme Parish Church.

SAVERY, ROGER DE LA GARDE. Captain. 10th Battalion South Staffordshire Regiment. Born 18.6.1886 in Huddersfield. Only son of Mr Robert James Savery, financial secretary to Messrs. George Salter and Sons, of West Bromwich, and Elizabeth de la Garde (nee Grissell) Savery of 5 Polperro Mansions, Lyncroft Gardens, London, N.W. The family lived in Imperial Road, Edgerton, Huddersfield, before going to South Africa in 1896. Educated Huddersfield College School and the Diocesan College, Cape Town, South Africa and at Berkhamsted College, Hertfordshire. Single. In civil life he was employed as manager of the Salter Typewriter Company in West Bromwich. In 1906 he was commissioned 2nd Lieutenant in the Cape Town Highlanders and, on November 20th 1914, he was gazetted Lieutenant in the South Staffordshire Regiment. He was promoted to Captain on March 18th, 1915. Reported wounded and missing at Suvla Bay, Gallipoli, 7.8.1915. He was 29 years of age. Has no known grave. Commemorated **HELLES MEMORIAL TO THE MISSING.** ROH:- Huddersfield College School.

SAYLES, FRANK. Private. No 2784. 'A' Company, 1/5th Battalion Duke of Wellington's Regiment. Born Huddersfield 28.2.1895. Son of Mrs Mary Sayles and the late Reuben Sayles, 1 Springdale Avenue, Longroyd Bridge, Huddersfield. Educated Spring Grove Council School, Municipal Secondary School and Huddersfield Technical College. Employed as a bank clerk by the Lancashire and Yorkshire Bank. Single. Enlisted 5.9.1914. Killed in action, 16.11.1915, aged 20 years. Buried **TALANA FARM CEMETERY.** Grave location:- Plot 4, Row F, Grave 12. His mother received a letter from Sergeant A. E. Milnes, who wrote, *'It is with deep regret that I have to inform you that your son Frank was killed yesterday afternoon. He was hit in the head by a bullet and died a few hours later without regaining consciousness. I can fully understand how deeply you will feel the loss and I offer you my most heartfelt sympathy in your bereavement. He was a good signaller, always cheerful and I shall miss him a great deal. I am sure the members of the signalling section will feel keenly the loss of their comrade. You have the satisfaction of knowing that he died nobly while serving the King and Country in the hour of need.'* ROH:- Huddersfield Drill Hall.

SAYLES, ROY. Private. No 17371. 10th Battalion Duke of Wellington's Regiment. Born Cowcliffe, Huddersfield 29.9.1898. Son of George Henry and Emily Sayles, 20 Corby Street, Birkby. Educated Hillhouse Council School. Employed as an apprentice tailor by Mr E. Drake, tailor, Moldgreen. Single. Enlisted 2.8.1915. Embarked for France March 1916. Killed in action at Munster Alley during the Battle of the Somme, 29.7.1916, aged 17 years. Has no known grave. Commemorated **THIEPVAL MEMORIAL TO THE MISSING.** ROH:- Fartown and Birkby War Memorial.

SCAIFE, JOSEPH. 2nd Lieutenant. 1st Battalion Duke of Wellington's Regiment, attached 2nd Battalion York and Lancaster Regiment. Son of Mr and Mrs E. Scaife, Thornes, Lepton. Prior to enlistment, was employed as a clerk by Messrs Kilner Brothers, Whitley Willow Mills. Reported wounded and missing, 21.3.1918 and afterwards presumed to have been killed on that date. Has no known grave. Commemorated **ARRAS MEMORIAL TO THE MISSING.** ROH:- Lepton Parish Church.

SCARAMUZZA, LAWRENCE. Private. Italian Army. Born Newcastle-on-Tyne 1891. Son of Clement and Mary G. Scaramuzza, 4 Denton Lane, Huddersfield. Educated Newcastle-on-Tyne schools. Lived 4 Denton Lane, Huddersfield. Employed as a labourer. Single. Enlisted 26.6.1915. Killed in a trench by the explosion of a bomb on the Italian frontier on 31.1.1916, aged 25 years.

SCHOFIELD, ABEL HELLIWELL. Private. No 14241. 8th Battalion Duke of Wellington's Regiment. Born Netherthong. Son of John Frederick and Jane Schofield of Outlane, Netherthong. Was a member of the Working Men's Club. Had been the organ blower at the Parish Church for several years and, as a boy, a regular attender at Sunday School. Employed in the scouring department of Messrs A. Thornton and Son at Honley. Enlisted October 1914. Sailed from Liverpool on *SS Aquitania* on 3.7.1915 for the Dardenelles. Landed at Suvla Bay, Gallipoli, on 6.8.1915. Killed by a sniper on 30.10.1915, aged 28 years. Buried **HILL 10 CEMETERY, SUVLA, GALLIPOLI.** Grave location:- Plot 1, Row G, Grave 6. His parents received a letter from Private Allen Brown, who was the first man to go to the aid of their son. He wrote, *'I am sorry to have to inform you of the death of Private Abel Schofield who was shot through the head this morning by a Turkish sniper. Abel had only come out of the hospital yesterday with a wound in the han,d caused accidentally by a pick, and was going on duty trench repairing when he was hit in a trench called by us Green Lane. As a personal friend and as a regimental stretcher-bearer I went out to find him unconscious in which state he remained until his death, though the Medical Officer did all in his power to save his life. It was useless and the only consolation left is that he did his duty. I handed his personal effects to the Commanding Officer who asked me to express his deepest sympathy with you on behalf of the men of the Battalion and as a friend I can only add mine.'* ROH:- Netherthong and Thongsbridge War Memorial; Netherthong Working Men's Club.

SCHOFIELD, ALBERT EDWARD. Private. No 268556. 2/5th Battalion Duke of Wellington's Regiment. Son of John and Edith Schofield, 10 East Street, Lindley. Employed as a wire drawer by Messrs Joseph Sykes Brothers, Acre Mills, Lindley. Enlisted September 1914. Wounded on one occasion. Killed in action near Rheims on 22.7.1918, aged 25 years. Buried **MARFAUX BRITISH CEMETERY.** Grave location:- Plot 6, Row I, Grave 8. ROH:- Huddersfield Drill Hall.

SCHOFIELD, FRANK. Private. No 202257. 2/4th Battalion Leicestershire Regiment. Formerly 1/5th Battalion Duke of Wellington's Regiment. Born Huddersfield 25.10.1891. Son of Mr and Mrs Arthur Schofield, 24 Ravensknowle Road, Dalton. Educated Huddersfield Higher Grade School and Huddersfield Technical College. Employed as a clerk in the Huddersfield office of the Sun Insurance Company. Attended Moldgreen United Methodist Church and Sunday School. Single. Enlisted 4.8.1914. Was taken prisoner on 24.3.1918 by the Germans, after 3 years and 7 months service. Shot in the bladder whilst a Prisoner of War and died of wounds on 1.4.1918, aged 26. Buried **RUMAUCOURT COMMUNAL CEMETERY.** Grave location:- Grave No. 65. ROH:- Christ Church, Moldgreen.

SCHOFIELD, FRANK. Private. No 242474. 'C' Company, 1/5th Battalion Northumberland Fusiliers. Born Deighton, Huddersfield, 25.9.1879. Educated Deighton Board School. Lived 54 Deighton Road, Deighton. Employed as a brickyard labourer. Single. Enlisted 31.7.1916. Killed in action, 22.3.1918, aged 38 years. Has no known grave. Commemorated **POZIERES MEMORIAL TO THE MISSING.** ROH:- Christ Church, Woodhouse Hill; Deighton United Methodist Chapel; Deighton War Memorial.

SCHOFIELD, FRANK. Company Sergeant Major. No 801. 18th Battalion Australian Imperial Force. Born Linthwaite. Prior to emigrating to Australia lived at the Ivy Hotel, Linthwaite, near to which place his father had a farm. Enlisted early in 1915. Had served for over two years in Egypt, the Dardenelles, Mesopotamia and France. Died at Fargo Hospital, Salisbury, 14.10.1917. Buried with full military honours in **CHRIST CHURCH CHURCHYARD, LINTHWAITE.** ROH:- Linthwaite War Memorial.

SCHOFIELD, FRANK METCALFE. Private. No 2268. 1/5th Battalion Duke of Wellington's Regiment. Born Huddersfield 3.10.1895. Son of Eleanor Rigg Schofield, 33 Springfield Terrace, Somerset Road, Huddersfield, and the late John Schofield. Educated Huddersfield College and Technical College. Employed as a cloth finisher. Single. Enlisted in 1912 in the local Territorials. Embarked for France April, 1915. Killed in action near Ypres, 17.11.1915, aged 20 years. Has no known grave. Commemorated **MENIN GATE MEMORIAL TO THE MISSING.** ROH:- Huddersfield Parish Church; Christ Church, Moldgreen; Huddersfield Drill Hall; Almondbury War Memorial.

SCHOFIELD, FRANKLIN. Corporal. No 240898. 2/5th Battalion Duke of Wellington's Regiment. Born Thomas Street, Moldgreen, Huddersfield, 20.9.1896. Son of Charlotte Schofield, 191 New Hey Road, Oakes, Huddersfield. Educated Moldgreen Council School. Employed as a french polisher by Messrs Taylor and Hobson. Single. Enlisted 4.1.1915. Reported missing, presumed killed at the Battle of Cambrai, 27.11.1917, aged 21 years. Has no known grave. Commemorated **CAMBRAI MEMORIAL TO THE MISSING.** ROH:- St. Stephen's Church, Lindley; Huddersfield Drill Hall.

SCHOFIELD, FRED. Private. No 79143. 11th Battalion Durham Light Infantry. Born 4 Western Place, Spring Street, Huddersfield, 12.2.1899. Son of George and Louisa Schofield, 30 Upperhead Row, Huddersfield. Employed as a cloth finisher. Single. Enlisted March 1917. Reported missing, presumed killed, 27.3.1918, aged 19 years. Has no known grave. Commemorated **POZIERES MEMORIAL TO THE MISSING.** ROH:- Huddersfield Parish Church.

SCHOFIELD, FRED. Private. No 18919. 10th Battalion East Yorkshire Regiment (Hull Commercials). Born Bradley, Huddersfield, 12.8.1887. Son of John and Mary Ann Schofield, 449 Leeds Road, Huddersfield. Employed as a mechanic's labourer by Messrs Sellars and Company. machinists, Manchester Road, Huddersfield. Single. Enlisted 1916. Reported missing, presumed killed, at Oppy Wood on 3.5.1917, aged 29 years. Has no known grave. Commemorated **ARRAS MEMORIAL TO THE MISSING.** The following extract is taken from East Yorkshires in the Great War 1914-1918, by Everard Wyrall, '2.5.1917. At 11.30pm the 10th Battalion East Yorkshires moved up to their assembly positions, a new trench which had been dug by the 2nd Division before the Battle of Arleux which had taken place on the 28/29th April. The northern bounday of the frontage of attack allotted to the Battalion was along the southern edge of Oppy Wood to Oppy Support Trench: the southern bounds were along Link Trench to Oppy Support Trench. The latter trench ran from north-west to south-east about 200 yards east of the village. The move forward was carried out in brilliant moonlight and apparently observed by the enemy who, however did not open fire immediately. The Battalion was in position before midnight. Zero hour had been fixed for 3.45am but twice before that hour the enemy very heavily barraged the front line. At 3.45am there was a roar as the British barrage opened: it was timed to advance at 100 yards per 4 minutes. Almost immediately the German guns replied and soon clouds of smoke and dust added their pall to the darkness and it was impossible to see when the barrage lifted from the German trenches. With shells bursting all around them, the air whistling with machine gun and rifle bullets and all the infernal din of the battlefield deafening their ears, into the clouds of dust and smoke the advancing troops disappeared. On the right the 10th East Yorkshires found the German front line strongly held. The assaulting companies had gone forward beyond their barrage but ere they reached the hostiles lines the curtain fire had lifted and they were at once subjected to heavy machine-gun and rifle fire. Hacking at the barbed wire entanglements where they had not been cut by the guns or rushing through gaps which had been made, a considerable number of men of the 10th Battalion undoubtedly got into and beyond the first German line: some even penetrated to the first objective and one gallant man brought back eight prisoners to his own credit. All four Company Commanders had become casualties and the smoke and dust, added to the darkness, made it impossible to see what was going on on the flanks and, indeed, blotted out the objectives. In the struggle for the German first line the barrage had been lost, and it was rolling on far ahead by the time that small parties of men had penetrated the front system. As it was impossible to get forward or consolidate the line, the survivors of the 10th Battalion withdrew to the assembly trench occupied before the attack began and to shell holes in the neighbourhood, where they remained until the night of 3/4th May, for all day long the whole area was swept by artillery and machine-gun fire, whilst the enemy's snipers in Oppy Wood were continually on the watch for anyone who incautiously exposed himself.' 10th East Yorkshires – Attacking strength: 16 Officers, 484 other ranks. Losses: 13 Officers, 223 other ranks.

SCHOFIELD, HAROLD. Private. No 301954. 2nd Battalion The Royal Scots (Lothian Regiment). Born Meltham. Son of Firth and Martha Schofield, Lane End Cottage, Meltham. Killed in action at Polygon Wood on 26.9.1917, aged 20 years. Has no known grave. Commemorated **TYNE COT MEMORIAL TO THE MISSING.** ROH:- Wilshaw Church; St. Bartholomew's Church, Meltham.

SCHOFIELD, HARRY. Private. No G/52501. 2nd Battalion Middlesex Regiment. Formerly

No 41902 York and Lancaster Regiment. Born Huddersfield. Married, with one child. Lived 5 Hope Street, Deadwaters, Huddersfield. Employed by Mr Class, fish merchant, Wholesale Market, Huddersfield. Was a member of the Men's Own Class at Ramsden Street Congregational Church. Killed in action, 28.11.1917, aged 28 years. Buried **PASSCHENDAELE NEW BRITISH CEMETERY.** Grave location:- Plot 11, Row A, Grave 10. ROH:- St. Stephen's Church, Rashcliffe.

SCHOFIELD, HENRY. Driver. No 140401. 'W' 8th Trench Mortar Battery, Royal Field Artillery. Born Holmfirth. Fourth son of Mr J. Schofield, Wells Brook Farm, Holmfirth. Enlisted March 1915. Died of wounds at No 34 Casualty Clearing Station, 8.5.1917, aged 27 years. Buried **LA CHAPELETTE BRITISH CEMETERY, PERONNE.** Grave location:- Plot 2, Row B, Grave 12.

SCHOFIELD, HERBERT. Private. No 6738. 1/5th Battalion Northumberland Fusiliers. Born 95 Acre Street, Lindley, Huddersfield, 16.10.1885. Son of William Henry and Phoebe Ann Schofield, 35 Eldon Road, Marsh, Huddersfield. Educated Lindley Church of England Schools. Employed as a cloth finisher by Messrs Crowther Brothers, Stanley Mills, Milnsbridge. Single. Enlisted 24.5.1916. Wounded in the arm and leg, 29.10.1916. Died of wounds at No 8 British Red Cross Hospital, 4.11.1916, aged 31 years. Buried **ETAPLES MILITARY CEMETERY.** Grave location:- Plot 12, Row C, Grave 10a. (Brother of Private **WILLIE SCHOFIELD**, killed in action, 24.11.1916, q.v.). ROH:- Holy Trinity Church, Huddersfield; Marsh War Memorial.

SCHOFIELD, HERBERT. Lance Corporal. No 64986. 12/13th Battalion Northumberland Fusiliers. Born Huddersfield. Son of William and Sarah Alice Schofield, of Beechwood, Ashenhurst, Huddersfield. Assisted his father in the family business at Queen Street, Huddersfield. Taken prisoner on 29.5.1918. Died of wounds as a Prisoner of War on 21.6.1918, aged 20 years. Was originally buried **CHARLEVILLE COMMUNAL CEMETERY** but he is now buried in **TERLINCTHUN BRITISH CEMETERY.** Grave location:- Plot 16, Row E, Grave 1.

SCHOFIELD, JAMES. Private. No 14424. 8th Battalion Duke of Wellington's Regiment. Born Greenfield, Lancashire. Lived Linthwaite. Died in Malta of wounds received at the Dardenelles on 10.11.1915. Buried **PIETA MILITARY CEMETERY.** Grave location:- Plot D, Row 4, Grave 3. ROH:- Linthwaite War Memorial.

SCHOFIELD, JAMES ALBERT. Private. No 307837. 1/7th Battalion Duke of Wellington's Regiment. Born Huddersfield 26.2.1887. Son of Walter and Mary Ann Schofield, Laurel Lea, 344 Leeds Road, Huddersfield. Educated St. Andrew's Church of England School, Higher Grade College, Huddersfield Technical College and Leeds Teacher Training College. Husband of Helena Schofield, 14 Second Avenue, Long Lane, Dalton. Employed as an elementary school teacher at Kirkheaton National School. Attended St. Andrew's Church. Enlisted 4.8.1916. Killed in action at St. Jans Capelle, near Bailleul, on 19.4.1918, aged 31 years. Buried **METEREN MILITARY CEMETERY.** Grave location:- Plot 4, Row N, Grave 970. ROH:- St. Andrew's Church, Leeds Road, Huddersfield; St. John's Church, Kirkheaton; Huddersfield Drill Hall.

SCHOFIELD, JOHN ARTHUR. Private. No 204204. 1/4th Battalion Duke of Wellington's Regiment. Born Bradley, Huddersfield. Lived Huddersfield. Killed in action, 10.4.1918. Has no known grave. Commemorated **TYNE COT MEMORIAL TO THE MISSING.**

SCHOFIELD, JOSEPH. Lance Corporal. No 15862. 12th Battalion The Royal Scots (Lothian Regiment). Born Huddersfield. Son of Mr and Mrs W. H. Schofield, 2 James Street, Golcar. Employed as a plasterer and painter by Mr John Sutcliffe, Carr Lane, Slaithwaite. Was a member of the Hillhouse football club. Attended Golcar Baptist Church. Enlisted November 1914. Embarked for France May, 1915. Killed in action at the Battle of Loos, 25.9.1915, aged 28 years. Has no known grave. Commemorated **LOOS MEMORIAL TO THE MISSING.** His Commanding Officer wrote to the parents as follows, *'I am very sorry indeed to have to tell you that Lance Corporal Schofield was killed in action at La Bassee in the great battle at the end of September. He was a fine chap and his loss is felt by my Company. He set a fine example and was a N.C.O. of great promise. I am sorry I can* *give you no particulars of his death but at least I know this, that he was a member of a Division, the 9th Division, that made for itself an undying reputation on the 25th September and therefore he died a death that was as full of glory as any soldier can hope for.*' ROH:- St. John's Church, Golcar; Golcar Baptist Church.

SCHOFIELD, LEWIS THORPE. Private. No 241541. 1/7th Battalion Duke of Wellington's Regiment. Born Marsden. Son of Sam Thorpe and Mary Schofield, 6 Wood Top, Marsden. Employed as a weaver at Bank Bottom Mills, Marsden. Attended Marsden Wesleyan Sunday School and was a member of the Conservative Club. Was in the local Territorials prior to the outbreak of the war. Called up on 4.8.1914 and served with the 1/7th Battalion Duke of Wellington's Regiment for two and a half years and was then discharged. He again volunteered for service under the Lord Derby's scheme, was accepted and embarked for France in January, 1917. Died of wounds (gas) on 29.4.1918, aged 25 years. Buried **BOULOGNE EASTERN CEMETERY.** Grave location:- Plot 9, Row B, Grave 19. ROH:- Marsden War Memorial; Marsden Conservative Club; Huddersfield Drill Hall.

SCHOFIELD, NORMAN. Private. No 240809. 2/5th Battalion Duke of Wellington's Regiment. Born Honley. Only son of Mr and Mrs J. A. Schofield, 41 Berry Croft, Honley. Employed by Messrs A. Thornton and Sons, Crossley Mills, Honley. Attended Honley Primitive Methodist Church. Enlisted November 1914. Embarked for France January, 1917. Killed in action at the Battle of Cambrai, 20.11.1917, aged 21 years. Buried **HERMIES HILL BRITISH CEMETERY.** Grave location:- Special Memorial A 11. ROH:- Honley War Memorial; Huddersfield Drill Hall.

SCHOFIELD, OLIVER. Private. No 2317. 1/7th Battalion Duke of Wellington's Regiment. Born Delph. Lived Blackmoorfoot, Linthwaite. Employed by the Slaithwaite Spinning Company in the gas winding department. Enlisted at the outbreak of the war. After training at Riby and Doncaster embarked for France in April, 1915. Was in his dugout when a shell exploded at his side, killing him instantly and wounding three others, on 23.9.1915, aged 33 years. Buried **BARD COTTAGE CEMETERY.** Grave location:- Plot 1, Row H, Grave 20. ROH:- Linthwaite War Memorial; St. Bartholomew's Church, Meltham; Helme Parish Church; Huddersfield Drill Hall

SCHOFIELD, WILFRED. Company Quarter Master Sergeant. No 13752. 'A' Company, 10th Battalion King's Own Yorkshire Light Infantry. Born Quarmby, Huddersfield, 22.7.1891. Son of John W. Schofield and the late Sarah Jane Schofield, 278 Reinwood Road, Quarmby. Educated Oakes Council School. Employed as a clerk in the office at Portland Mills, Lindley. Attended Holy Trinity Church. Enlisted 31.8.1914. Killed in action near Hooge, 4.10.1917, aged 26 years. Has no known grave. Commemorated **TYNE COT MEMORIAL TO THE MISSING.** ROH:- Holy Trinity Church; St. Mark's Parish Church, Longwood.

SCHOFIELD, WILLIE. Private. No 40846. 23rd (Tyneside Scottish) Battalion Northumberland Fusiliers. Born 95 Acre Street, Lindley 25.12.1889. Son of William Henry and Phoebe Ann Schofield, 35 Eldon Road, Marsh. Educated Lindley Church of England School and Holy Trinity Church School. Employed as a milkman by Mr Herbert Hardy, milkdealer, of Birkby. Attended Holy Trinity Church, Huddersfield. Enlisted 4.5.1916. Embarked for France November,1916. Killed in action near Armentieres, 24.11.1916, aged 26 years. Buried **RATION FARM MILITARY CEMETERY.** Grave location:- Plot 3, Row A, Grave 5. (Brother of Private **HERBERT SCHOFIELD,** died of wounds, 4.11.1916, q.v.). ROH:- Holy Trinity Church, Huddersfield.

SCHOFIELD, WILLIE. Private. No 202897. 4th Battalion South Staffordshire Regiment. Born Denby Dale. Son of Albert and Lucy Ellen Schofield, 12 Sunny Bank, Denby Dale. Killed in action near Rheims, 31.5.1918, aged 24 years. Has no known grave. Commemorated **SOISSONS MEMORIAL TO THE MISSING.** ROH:- Denby Dale and Cumberworth War Memorial.

SCHOLES, ALBERT VINCENT, MM. 2nd Lieutenant. W.T. Flight, 21st Wing, Royal Air Force. Younger son of Mrs Scholes, 130 Bradford Road North, Huddersfield. Educated Hillhouse Council School, Municipal Secondary School. Employed as a sorting clerk and telegraphist at the Huddersfield General Post Office. Single. Enlisted in the Royal Flying Corps in 1915 as a wireless operator and was awarded the Military Medal in September, 1916, for efficiency in keeping in communication with an aeroplane while under heavy shell fire. Was wounded in the chest during the Battle of Arras on April 4th, 1917. A shrapnel bullet struck the bar of his Military Medal and glanced off, entering his chest about an inch above the heart. Was treated at Birmingham War Hospital. Died of injuries as a result of an aeroplane accident at Oxford on 1.11.1918. Buried **EDGERTON CEMETERY, HUDDERSFIELD**. Grave location:- 12, 59C. ROH:- Christ Church, Woodhouse Hill; Huddersfield General Post Office Roll; Fartown and Birkby War Memorial.

SCHOLES, ERNEST. Private. No 40979. 23rd (Tyneside Scottish) Battalion Northumberland Fusiliers. Born Huddersfield. Died 8.4.1918. Buried **LE GRAND BEAUMART BRITISH CEMETERY, STEENWERCK**. Grave location:- Plot 1, Row H, Grave 2. ROH:- St. Philip's Church, Birchencliffe.

SCHOLES, HARRY. Rifleman. No C/7856. 18th Battalion The King's Royal Rifle Corps. Born Huddersfield. Son of Mrs Scholes, Shop Lane, Kirkheaton. Employed by Messrs Broadbent and Graves, Kirkheaton. Lived with his sister, Mrs Albert Liversedge, at Thomas Street, Moldgreen, Huddersfield. Enlisted 24.11.1915. Embarked for France at Whitsuntide, 1916. Killed in action, 8.8.1916. Buried **ESSEX FARM CEMETERY**. Grave location:- Plot 3, Row B, Grave 46. ROH:- St. John's Church, Kirkheaton.

SCOTT, ARCHIBALD McDONALD. 2nd Lieutenant. 8th Battalion Northumberland Fusiliers. Born Newtown, North Wales, 13.2.1889. Son of Mr and Mrs Edwin James Scott, 228 Springbank, Bradford Road North, Fartown, Huddersfield. Educated Spring Grove Council School and Huddersfield Technical College. Was on the editorial staff of 'The Times' newspaper in Paris. Enlisted as a Private in the Northumberland Fusiliers in Paris in November, 1915. After only seven weeks service he was promoted to the rank of Sergeant and later received his commission on the recommendation of his Commanding Officer and Brigadier General Wolfe Murray. Was wounded once. Killed in action at the Battle of Langemarck on 16.8.1917, aged 28 years. Buried **NEW IRISH FARM CEMETERY, St. JEAN-LES-YPRES, BELGIUM**. Grave location:- Plot 11, Row B, Grave 18. ROH:- Christ Church, Woodhouse Hill; St. Thomas's Church, Longroyd Bridge; Fartown and Birkby War Memorial.

SCOTT, ROWLAND. Private. No 205543. 2/4th Battalion Duke of Wellington's Regiment. Born Morley, Leeds. Son of James and Elizabeth Scott. Husband of Amy Scott, 7 Park Lane, Golcar. Employed by the Ramsden Mill Company. Attended Golcar Providence United Methodist Church. Enlisted 16.7.1917. Was wounded on 28.5.1918. Had been back in France for three weeks when he was killed by a bursting shell near Marcoing on 29.9.1918. He was 30 years of age. Buried **GRAND RAVINE BRITISH CEMETERY, HAVRINCOURT**. Grave location:- Row C, Grave 25. ROH:- St. John's Church, Golcar.

SCOTT, THOMAS C. Private. No CH/20282. Royal Marine Light Infantry. *HMS Glory*. Lived with his Uncle and Aunt at The Hallas, Kirkburton. Employed as a grocer's assistant by his Uncle, Mr H. Boot, of Kirkburton. Died of pneumonia in Russia on 1.10.1918, aged 20 years. Originally buried in **KEM CEMETERY, RUSSIA**. Now re-interred in **MURMANSK NEW BRITISH CEMETERY, RUSSIA**. Grave Location:- Special Memorial B 32. Is also commemorated on the **BROOKWOOD RUSSIA MEMORIAL** in Brookwood Military Cemetery, Surrey. ROH:- All Hallows Parish Church, Kirkburton; commemorated on headstone in Kirkburton Churchyard.

SECKER, FRIEND. Gunner. No 162197. 179th Siege Battery Royal Garrison Artillery. Born Block Row, Lepton, 15.8.1879. Son of Charles and Ann Secker. Educated Lepton Schools. Employed as a woollen fettler by Messrs Brierley and Wall, Spa Mill, Lepton. Was a member of the Waterloo Bowling Club and played with the first team. At the time of enlistment, was living with his sister, Mrs Ric, at 9 School Street, Moldgreen. Single. Killed in action near Arras on 28.3.1918, aged 36 years. Buried **WANQUETIN COMMUNAL CEMETERY EXTENSION**. Grave location:- Plot 1, Row E, Grave 5. ROH:- St. John's Church, Kirkheaton.

SELLENS, GEORGE E. Stoker 1st Class.. No SS/105406 (RFR/CH/B/9466). *HMS Cressy*,

Royal Navy. Son of James Walter Sellens, 8, Smithy Place, Brockholes, Huddersfield. Killed when his ship was sunk by U-9 on 22.9.1914, aged 28. Commemorated **CHATHAM NAVAL MEMORIAL TO THE MISSING,** Panel reference 5.

SENIOR, ALBERT. Private. No 15628. 2nd Battalion Duke of Wellington's Regiment. Born Bradford. Lived Skelmanthorpe. Killed in action at Spectrum Trench at Lesboeufs on 23.10.1916. Has no known grave. Commemorated **THIEPVAL MEMORIAL TO THE MISSING.** ROH:- St. Aidan's Church, Skelmanthorpe.

SENIOR, AMOS. Private. No 54899. 1/5th Battalion West Yorkshire Regiment. Born Shelley, Huddersfield. Son of Job and Anne Senior, 92 Kirkgate, Huddersfield. Died as a Prisoner of War in Germany on 14.12.1918, aged 28 years. Buried **BERLIN SOUTH WESTERN CEMETERY, STAHNSDORF, GERMANY.** Grave location:- Plot 8, Row G, Grave 2. ROH:- Emmanuel Church, Shelley.

SENIOR, BEN. Gunner. No 77454. 135th Siege Battery, Royal Garrison Artillery. Born Deanhouse near Huddersfield. Son of the late George and Jane Senior of 'The Queen's Arms', Netherthong. Employed as a weaver at Deanhouse Mills. Was a member of the committee of Netherthong Working Men's Club and attended the United Methodist Church. Played football with the Netherthong Association football club. Embarked for France in July 1916. Died of wounds, 8.10.1916, aged 24 years. Buried **LONGUEVAL ROAD CEMETERY.** Grave location:- Row B, Grave 12. ROH:- Netherthong and Thongsbridge War Memorial; Netherthong Working Men's Club.

SENIOR, CLEMENT. Private. No 8407. 25th Battalion Durham Light Infantry, transferred to No 169069 Base Depot, Labour Corps. Husband of Amy Senior, Square Hill, Kirkheaton. Died at hom, 29.8.1920, aged 36. Burie **KIRKHEATON CEMETERY.** Grave location:- 'U', 693.

SENIOR, FRED. Private. No 5/241506. 1/5th Battalion Duke of Wellington's Regiment. Born Netherton, Huddersfield, 22.6.1891. Son of Herbert and Mary Senior, 439 Blackmoorfoot Road, Crosland Moor, Huddersfield. Educated South Crosland National School. Employed as a millhand. Single. Enlisted February 1916. Killed in the attack on the Schwaben Redoubt on 3.9.1916. Buried **CONNAUGHT CEMETERY.** Grave location:- Plot 1, Row E, Grave 7. ROH:- St. Barnabas Church, Crosland Moor; 'Rising Sun' Public House, Crosland Hill; Huddersfield Drill Hall.

SENIOR, FREDERICK. Sergeant. No 39058 King's Own Yorkshire Light Infantry. Formerly No 8614 West Yorkshire Regiment. Born Cliffe End, Longwood 1.10.1885. Son of Mr and Mrs Jackson, 68 Longwood Gate, Longwood. Educated Goitfield School, Longwood. Employed as a woollen card cleaner. Married. Killed in action, 22.3.1918. Has no known grave. Commemorated **POZIERES MEMORIAL TO THE MISSING.** ROH:- St. Mark's Parish Church, Longwood.

SENIOR, GEORGE. Private. No 31814. 2/4th Battalion Duke of Wellington's Regiment. Born Almondbury. Son of Mr and Mrs W. H. Senior, Fountain Grove, Milnsbridge. Educated Almondbury and Upper Whitley Board Schools, Huddersfield, and Manor Board and Dyers Hill Church School, Sheffield. Married, with one child. Lived 104 Brierley Wood, Huddersfield. Employed as a woollen spinner by Messrs John Crowther and Sons, Milnsbridge. Attended Milnsbridge Parish Church and was secretary of the New Upper Lodge Temperance Club. Wounded in the leg on 12.1.1918. Admitted to No 30 Casualty Clearing Station. It was necessary to amputate the leg below the knee. A sister at the C.C.S wrote to the parents to inform them that their son had died of seventeen wounds on 16.1.1918, aged 26 years. Buried **ANZIN-ST-AUBIN BRITISH CEMETERY.** Grave location:- Plot 3, Row A, Grave 8. ROH:- Milnsbridge War Memorial.

SENIOR, GEORGE. Private. No 241975. 2/5th Battalion Duke of Wellington's Regiment. Born Lepton, Huddersfield. Son of Mrs Elizabeth H. Senior, Knotty Lane, Lepton. Along with his brother, Thomas Senior, was employed as a mason on the Whitley Bow Estate. Enlisted March 1916. Killed in action, 16.3.1917. Buried **QUEEN'S CEMETERY, BUCQUOY.** Grave location:- Plot 3, Row E, Grave 8. (Brother of Private **THOMAS SENIOR,** died of wounds, 11.9.1916, q.v.). ROH:- Lepton Parish Church; Huddersfield Drill Hall.

SENIOR, HARRY. Private. No 92555. 1st Battalion Northumberland Fusiliers. Born Skelmanthorpe, Huddersfield. Son of Bernal and Lily Senior, Queen Street, Skelmanthorpe. Died in Egypt, 17.10.1919, aged 20 years. Buried **KANTARA WAR MEMORIAL CEMETERY, EGYPT.** Grave location:- Plot A, Grave 111. ROH:- St. Aidan's Church, Skelmanthorpe.

SENIOR, HARRY. Private. No 127119. 19th Battalion Machine Gun Corps. Formerly No 57311 West Yorkshire Regiment. Born Bradford Road, Huddersfield, 10.12.1893. Younger son of Mrs Mary Jane Senior, 28 Bradford Road, Huddersfield. Educated Thomas Street Board School. Employed as a clerk by Messrs Dugdale Brothers and Company, Northumberland Street, Huddersfield. Single. Enlisted 10.7.1917. Taken prisoner by the Germans on 22.3.1918. Died, 12.7.1918, at Alexander Strasse Hospital, Berlin, aged 24 years. Was initially buried in Hasenheide Garrison Cemetery, Berlin, but later re-interred at **BERLIN SOUTH-WESTERN CEMETERY, STAHNSDORF, GERMANY.** Grave location:- Plot 6, Row C, Grave 3. ROH:- St. Andrew's Church, Leeds Road, Huddersfield; Fartown and Birkby War Memorial.

SENIOR, HERBERT. Private. No 201244. 'C' Company, 1/5th Battalion Royal Scots Fusiliers. Formerly Duke of Wellington's Regiment. Son of the late William Booth. Senior and Annie Senior, 55 School Street, Moldgreen. Employed by Messrs Law Dyson and Company, waterproof cover makers, of Aspley, Huddersfield. Was a member of the Huddersfield Salvation Army band. Single. Enlisted February 1916. Went to Egypt in February, 1917. Wounded in action in the attack on Junction Station, where the Jerusalem line left the main railway to Damascus. He died of wounds in Palestine on 13.11.1917, aged 28 years. Buried **RAMLEH WAR CEMETERY, PALESTINE.** Grave location:- Row O, Grave 36. ROH:- Salvation Army Citadel; Christ Church, Moldgreen.

SENIOR, HILBERT. Private. No 43736. 11th Battalion West Yorkshire Regiment. Formerly No 17315 Duke of Wellington's Regiment. Lived Shelley. Killed in action in the attack and capture of Le Sars, during the Battle of the Somme, on 7.10.1916. Buried **ADANAC MILITARY CEMETERY.** Grave location:- Plot 4, Row K, Grave 5. ROH:- Shelley War Memorial.

SENIOR, JAMES. Private. No 300101. 9th Battalion Duke of Wellington's Regiment. Husband of Amy Senior, 20 Chapel Gate, Scholes Moor, Holmfirth. Employed by Messrs Kaye and Stewart. Reported missing at the Battle of Arras on 25.4.1917 and afterwards presumed to have been killed on that date. He was 28 years of age. Has no known grave. Commemorated **ARRAS MEMORIAL TO THE MISSING.** ROH:- Hepworth and Scholes War Memorial; Hepworth Parish Church.

SENIOR, JAMES ALBERT. Private. No 44679. 2nd Platoon, 'A' Company, 12th/13th Battalion Northumberland Fusiliers. Born Holmfirth. Son of Mr and Mrs George W. Senior, Muslin Hall, Thongsbridge, near Huddersfield. Educated Wooldale Council School. Employed as a presser by Messrs John Crowther and Sons, Union Mills, Milnsbridge. Enlisted 1916. Reported wounded and missing 18.4.1918, aged 27 years. Has no known grave. Commemorated **TYNE COT MEMORIAL TO THE MISSING.** ROH:- St. Andrew's Church, Thongsbridge.

SENIOR, JOE WILLIE. Private. No G/22932. 11th Battalion Royal West Surrey Regiment (The Queen's). Born Shepley. Son of John Senior of Shepley. Married Miss Alice Lodge at Emley on 9.11.1914. Lived Clegg Terrace, Shepley and at Folly Hall Cottage, Kirkburton. Employed as a traveller and agent by the Calder Vale Agricultural Trading Society, Elland. Attended Shepley United Methodist Church and was a member of the choir. Enlisted January 1917. Died of wounds, 23.9.1917, aged 33 years. Buried **OUTTERSTEENE COMMUNAL CEMETERY EXTENSION.** Grave location:- Plot 1, Row B, Grave 28. ROH:- Shepley War Memorial; All Hallows Parish Church, Kirkburton.

SENIOR, JOHN HENRY. Private. No 53380. 9th Battalion The King's (Liverpool Regiment). Formerly No 242189 East Surrey Regiment. Born Denby Dale. Son of Albert Edward and Nellie Senior of Market Green, Skelmanthorpe. Assisted his father on the family farm and as a butcher. Attended St. Aidan's Church and Sunday School. Enlisted February 1917. Embarked for France in September, 1917. Killed in action, 26.12.1917, aged 23 years. Buried **BLEUET FARM CEMETERY, ELVERDINGHE, BELGIUM.** Grave location:- Plot 2, Row B, Grave 49. ROH:- St. Aidan's Church, Skelmanthorpe.

SENIOR, LINTON. Private. No 201857. 4th Battalion Seaforth Highlanders. Born Berry Brow, Huddersfield, 28.3.1896. Son of Mr and Mrs John Senior, 23 Trinity Street, Huddersfield. Educated Spring Grove Council School. Employed as an apprentice bootmaker and repairer by Mr Harold Brook, bootmaker, Thornton Road, Huddersfield. Attended New North Road Baptist Church. Single. Enlisted 19.2.1916. Killed in action at Roclincourt near Arras on 8.4.1917. Buried **NINE ELMS MILITARY CEMETERY, THELUS.** Grave location: Seaforth Grave Memorial 5. ROH:- New North Road Baptist Church.

SENIOR, NORMAN. Private. No 53341. 2nd Battalion West Yorkshire Regiment. Born Blamires Yard, Rashcliffe, Huddersfield, 18.12.1898. Son of Thomas and Susannah Oldfield, 7 Megson's Fold, Lockwood Scar, Huddersfield. Educated at Newsome Church of England Schools. Employed as a teamer in the bottling department at Lockwood Brewery. Single. Enlisted February 1917. Reported missing, presumed killed, on 27.3.1918, aged 19 years. Has no known grave. Commemorated **POZIERES MEMORIAL TO THE MISSING.** ROH:- St. John's Church, Newsome; Emmanuel Church, Lockwood.

SENIOR, SAM. Corporal. No 9755. 'A' Company, 2nd Battalion Duke of Wellington's Regiment. Born Totties Hall, Hepworth, Holmfirth, 10.6.1888. Educated Wooldale Council School amd Deepcar Church of England School. Lived with his aunt, Lucy Jane Keeble, 10 Lockwood Crescent, Lockwood. Employed as a pit hand. Single. Reported missing, presumed killed, 7.1.1915, aged 26. Has no known grave. Commemorated **MENIN GATE MEMORIAL TO THE MISSING.** ROH:- St. Stephen's Church, Rashcliffe.

SENIOR, THOMAS. Private. No 5513. 1/5th Battalion Duke of Wellington's Regiment. Born Lepton. Son of Elizabeth H. Senior, Knotty Lane, Lepton. Along with his brother, Private **GEORGE SENIOR**, was employed as a mason on the Whitley Bow Estate. Enlisted March 1916. Died of wounds at No 13 General Hospital on 11.9.1916, aged 23 years. Buried **BOULOGNE EASTERN CEMETERY.** Grave location:- Plot 8, Row C, Grave 133. (Brother of Private **GEORGE SENIOR**, killed in action, 16.3.1917, q.v.). ROH:- Lepton Parish Church; Huddersfield Drill Hall.

SENNETT, JAMES. Private. No 3992. 2/4th Battalion Duke of Wellington's Regiment. Lived Huddersfield. Husband of Annie Sennett. He was travelling on a special train from Leeds to Allerton when he fell from the train. The train was between Hemsworth and South Elmsall when the accident happened. No carriage door was found open when the train pulled up and it was presumed that he fell through the window whilst leaning out on Sunday, 12.9.1915, aged 38 years. Buried **STONEY ROYD CEMETERY, HALIFAX.** Grave location:- K, D, 1672.

SEVILLE, JOHN WILLIAM. Guardsman. No 6450. Coldstream Guards. Born Greenfield, Lancashire. Son of the late Mr and Mrs Frank Seville of Lad Hill, Greenfield. Lived with his sister, Mrs Floyd, 12 Derby Terrace, Marsden. Had lived in Marsden for seven years. Employed in the carbonising department at Carrs Road Mill. As a reservist he was mobilised in August, 1914. Killed in action, 21.9.1917, aged 32 years. Has no known grave. Commemorated **TYNE COT MEMORIAL TO THE MISSING.** His sister received the following letter from a Chaplain, *'It is with deep regret that I have to inform you of the death of Private J. W. Seville who was killed on September 21st in the front line by a shell. He was killed instantenously but not disfigured and was buried near where he fell as it was impossible owing to the shelling to bring his body back. The battalion intends, when opportunity offers, to place a wooden cross on the spot.'* ROH:- Marsden War Memorial.

SEWELL, ARNOLD. Private. No 241494. 2nd Battalion Duke of Wellington's Regiment. Lived Lockwood, Huddersfield. Reported missing, presumed killed, 31.8.1918. Has no known grave. Commemorated **VIS-en-ARTOIS MEMORIAL TO THE MISSING.** ROH:- St. Stephen's Church, Rashcliffe.

SEWELL, LEWIS. Private. East Yorkshire Regiment. Born Crosland Moor 9.3.1899. Son of Mr and Mrs George Sewell, 18 Upper Brow Road, Paddock. Educated Paddock Church of England Schools. Employed as a woollen minder. Enlisted 13.4.1917. Wounded 26.8.1918. Died of wounds at Rouen, 26.9.1918.

SEWELL, TOM. Private. No 235093. 2/5th Battalion Duke of Wellington's Regiment. Born Longwood, Huddersfield. Lived with his aunt, Mrs William Howarth, at 50 Longroyd Lane, Huddersfield. Employed as a spinner by Messrs Bates and Company, Colne Royd Mills. Died of wounds, 18.4.1917, aged 31 years. Buried **MORY ABBEY MILITARY CEMETERY.** Grave location:- Plot 1, Row A, Grave 7. ROH:- St. Stephen's Church, Rashcliffe; Huddersfield Drill Hall.

SEYMOUR, LEWIS. Private. No 57558. 2/5th Battalion West Yorkshire Regiment. Born Netherton, Huddersfield. Husband of Lily Seymour, Westgate, Meltham. Employed by Mr J. A. Liversedge, dyer, Lord's Mill, Netherton. Was a playing member of Meltham Cricket Club. Attended Meltham Parish Church. Killed in action near Rheims on 20.7.1918, aged 33 years. Buried **MARFAUX BRITISH CEMETERY.** Grave location:- Plot 3, Row D, Grave 9. ROH:- St. Bartholomew's Church, Meltham.

SHANN, WILLIAM. Private. No 9215. 2nd Battalion Manchester Regiment. Born Miles Platting, Manchester. Was a pipe-fitter by trade, having been apprenticed to the firm of Messrs Hetherington, engineers, of Manchester. In 1913 he and his wife moved to High Street, Scapegoat Hill, Golcar and was employed by Messrs J. W. Leech and Company, chemical manufacturers, of Milnsbridge. Had been a Reservist for 9 years, prior to which he served for three years in India and China. He was recalled to the Colours on 5.8.1914. Enlisted Ashton-under-Lyne. Died of wounds at No 33 Casualty Clearing Station on 19.10.1914, aged 31 years. Buried **BETHUNE TOWN CEMETERY.** Grave location:- Plot 1, Row C, Grave 24. ROH:- St. John's Church, Golcar.

SHARPE, ARTHUR NOEL. Lieutenant. 5th Battalion Duke of Wellington's Regiment. Born Huddersfield 30.12.1888. Son of Arthur Calvert, of the firm of Messrs Sharpe and Sharpe, Chartered Accountants, Market Place, Huddersfield, and Mary Sharpe, 'Lynton', Mountjoy Road, Edgerton, Huddersfield. Educated Huddersfield College School. Employed as a printer's manager. Was a playing member of the Huddersfield Cricket Club and Captain of the Y.M.C.A. football club. Single. Enlisted 9.8.1914. Commissioned in the 1/5th Battalion Duke of Wellington's Regiment in December, 1914. Embarked for France, 4.7.1915. Reported wounded and missing, 3.9.1916, in the attack on the Schwaben Redoubt and afterwards presumed to have been killed on that date. Buried **MILL ROAD CEMETERY.** Grave location:- Plot 1, Row H, Grave 17. ROH:- Huddersfield Parish Church: Holy Trinity Church; Huddersfield College School; Huddersfield Drill Hall.

SHARP, HERBERT WILLIAM. Private. No PO/1441 (S). Royal Marine Light Infantry, 2nd Royal Marine Battalion, Royal Naval Division. Son of Mr and Mrs William Sharpe, 45 Lees Lodge, Dalton Bank Road, Kirkheaton. Employed as a presser by Messrs T. and H. Blamires Limited, Leeds Road, Huddersfield. Enlisted February 1916. Embarked for France in November, 1916. Died of wounds at No 4 Casualty Clearing Station, 3.2.1917, aged 23. Buried **VARENNES MILITARY CEMETERY.** Grave location:- Plot 1, Row H, Grave 23. ROH:- St. John's Church, Kirkheaton.

SHARP, FRIEND. Private. No 33936. 1/6th Battalion Duke of Wellington's Regiment. Born Colne Bridge, Huddersfield. Second son of the late Mr and Mrs Joe Sharpe. Employed by Messrs John Lee Walker and Sons, Deighton. Enlisted 4.8.1917. Died of wounds, 13.10.1918, aged 19 years. Buried **BUCQUOY ROAD CEMETERY.** Grave location:- Plot 3, Row G, Grave 20. ROH:- St. Thomas's Church, Bradley.

SHARP, HARRY. Private. No 77506. 15th Battalion Durham Light Infantry. Born 15 Roydfield Street, Fartown Green, Huddersfield, 29.7.1899. Son of William and Ada Sharp, 32 Ballroyd Road, Fartown Green. Educated Hillhouse Council School, where he won a scholarship to Almondbury Grammar School, which he attended for four years. Employed as a junior porter at Golcar Railway Station. Single. Enlisted 17.9.1917. Reported missing, presumed killed, 26.8.1918, aged 19 years. Has no known grave. Commemorated **VIS-en-ARTOIS MEMORIAL TO THE MISSING.** ROH:- Christ Church, Woodhouse Hill; Fartown and Birkby

War Memorial; London and North Western Railway Roll.

SHARP, SAM. Corporal. No 241343. 1/5th Battalion Duke of Wellington's Regiment. Enlisted Huddersfield. Killed in action in the attack on the Schwaben Redoubt, 3.9.1916. Buried **MILL ROAD CEMETERY**. Grave location:- Plot 1, Row F, Grave 6. ROH:- Huddersfield Drill Hall; Longwood War Memorial.

SHARP, SAMUEL. Private. No 241620. 9th Battalion Highland Light Infantry. Born Lindley, Huddersfield. Lived 62 George Street, Milnsbridge. Died of wounds, 5.8.1918, aged 23 years. Buried **CROIX-ROUGE MILITARY CEMETERY, QUAEDYPRE**. Grave location:- Plot 2, Row A, Grave 14. ROH:- Milnsbridge War Memorial.

SHARPLES, HENRY. Private. No 1104. 10th Battalion Lincolnshire Regiment. Born Wigan. Enlisted Wakefield. Lived Meltham. Killed in action, 28.4.1917. Buried **ROEUX BRITISH CEMETERY**. Grave location:- Row B, Grave 48. ROH:- St. Bartholomew's Church, Meltham.

SHARRATT, MERLE. Private. No 242347. 2/5th Battalion West Yorkshire Regiment. Born Ramsden Mills, Milnsbridge. Son of Reuben Henry and Maria Sharratt, 84 Brierley Wood, Marsden Road, Huddersfield. Educated Milnsbridge Board School. Employed as a weaver by Messrs John Crowther and Sons, Milnsbridge. Was President of the Milnsbridge Socalist Club, a well known trade unionist and a member of the Milnsbridge Perseverance Cooperative Society Limited. Husband of Alice Sharratt, 2 Lipscombe Street, Milnsbridge. Enlisted 11.11.1916. Embarked for France, 5.1.1917. Died of wounds, 22.4.1918, aged 35 years. Buried **BIENVILLERS MILITARY CEMETERY**. Grave location:- Plot 13, Row C, Grave 2. ROH:- Linthwaite War Memorial; Milnsbridge War Memorial.

SHAW, ALFRED. Private. No 2023. 11th Battalion Australian Imperial Force. Born Croydon. Son of Mr John Shaw, 36 George Street, Milnsbridge. Educated St. Thomas's School, Huddersfield. Employed by Dempsters, boiler-makers, of Manchester. Was a member of the Milnsbridge County Working Men's Club. Single. Emigrated to Australia in 1909. Lived Worsley Bush, Perth, Western Australia. Embarked at Melbourne on *HMAT Thermistodes* on October 22nd, 1914. Enlisted 28.1.1915. Went to Egypt before going to the Dardenelles, where he was killed on 1.8.1915, aged 46 years. Buried **SHELL GREEN CEMETERY, GALLIPOLI**. Grave location:- Plot 2, Row G, Grave 28.

SHAW, ALLEN CHARLESWORTH. 3rd Engineer with the Kenmore Cork Steam Packet Company, Mercantile Marine. Born Leef Street, Moldgreen, 1.7.1897. Son of Karl Augustus Shaw and Evangeline Charlesworth, 36 Woodbine Road, Fartown. Educated Hillhouse Council School. Employed as an electrical engineer by Messrs E. Brook Limited, Empress Works. Enlisted 23.1.1918. He was Third engineer on board *SS Kenmare*, which sailed from Liverpool on Saturday, 2nd March, 1918, and was torpedoed 'six hours after leaving port.' The ship was sunk by a German submarine 25 miles N.W. of the Skerries. The torpedo caused such damage to the *SS Kenmare* that she sank in less than two minutes. 29 men, including the Captain, were killed. Has no known grave. Commemorated **TOWER HILL MEMORIAL TO THE MISSING**. ROH:- Fartown and Birkby War Memorial; commemorated on headstone in Kirkburton Cemetery.

SHAW, ARTHUR. Private. No 4457. Labour Corps. Base and Lines of Communication Area. Formerly No 4457 York and Lancaster Regiment. Born Longwood, Huddersfield. Son of William and Emma Shaw of Marsh, Huddersfield. Husband of Sarah Ann Shaw, 6 Dowker Street, Milnsbridge. Father of 9 children, two of whom also served in the war. Before the war had served in both the Navy and the Army and had re-enlisted on the outbreak of hostilities. Served in France, Belgium, Egypt and Salonika, where he contracted Malaria for which he was treated at Malta. Accidentally killed in Salonika on 19.3.1918, aged 47 years. Buried **SALONIKA ANGLO-FRENCH MILITARY CEMETERY, LEMBET ROAD**. Grave location:- No 1380. ROH:- Shared Church, Paddock; Longwood War Memorial.

SHAW, ARTHUR. Private. No DM2/164584. Army Service Corps (Motor Transport Section). Born Linthwaite. Fifth son of the late Mr Joseph Shaw and Mrs Shaw, Lees House, Linthwaite.

Was in business on his own account as a cloth merchant. Enlisted March 1916. Went into training at Austerley Park, near London. After a week was transferred to Lee in Kent. Whilst there he contracted a severe cold which developed into influenza. He was transferred to Woolwich Hospital, where he died of pneumonia on 12.4.1916, aged 34 years. Buried **St. JAMES'S CHURCHYARD, SLAITHWAITE.** Grave location:- in North-East part. ROH:- St. James Church, Slaithwaite; Linthwaite War Memorial.

SHAW, ARTHUR. Private. No 204170. 1/4th Battalion Duke of Wellington's Regiment. Born Golcar. Son of James Edward and Sarah Jane Shaw. Married, with four children. Lived 57 Townend, Golcar. Employed as a pattern weaver by Messrs Pearson Brothers, Victoria Mills, Golcar. Was a member of the Golcar Socalist Club and the Scapegoat Hill bandroom. He was also connected with the Golcar Cricket and Bowling Club. Enlisted 23.9.1916. Embarked for France in January, 1917. Killed in action at Nieuport, Belgium, on 9.8.1917, aged 34 years. Buried **COXYDE MILITARY CEMETERY.** Grave location:- Plot 2, Row F, Grave 11. ROH:- St. John's Church, Golcar; Golcar Baptist Church.

SHAW, CHARLES. Private. No TR5/22571. 6th Training Reserve Battalion West Yorkshire Regiment. Son of the late James Shaw of Newgate, Slaithwaite, who hanged his wife and then hanged himself on 30.11.1916. The evidence at the inquest showed that the father was much upset owing to his son's exemption for military service being withdrawn. Private Shaw previously assisted his father in the business of farmer and blacksmith at Newgate, Slaithwaite. Had been in the army just six weeks and a fortnight of that period had been spent in hospital. Was found dead in a hospital at Rugeley Camp, Staffordshire, on Friday, 29.3.1917, aged 27 years. At the inquest the jury returned a verdict of suicide whilst of unsound mind. It was thought that the recent tragedy 'had got on his nerves.' Buried **POLE MOOR BAPTIST CHAPEL YARD EXTENSION.** Grave location:- New ground, 6, 21.

SHAW, CHARLIE. Private. No 21524. 1st Battalion The King's Shropshire Light Infantry. Formerly No 24847. 9th Lancers. Born Huddersfield. Lived 20 School Road, Scapegoat Hill, Golcar. Employed as a spinner by Messrs Joseph Hoyle and Son, Quarmby Clough Mills, Longwood. Died of wounds, 24.3.1918, aged 20 years. Buried **ONTARIO CEMETERY, SAINS-LES-MARQUION.** Grave location:- Plot 1, Row E, Grave 6.

SHAW, DAN. Corporal. No 305612. 2/7th Battalion Duke of Wellington's Regiment. Lived with his grandmother at 32 Golcar Hill, Golcar. Employed by Messrs B. and J. Whitwam and Sons Limited, Stanley Mills, Golcar. Attended Golcar Parish Church. Was a member of the Cliff Ash Labour Club. Enlisted October 1914. Embarked for France in January, 1917. Critically wounded at the beginning of September, 1917. Was admitted to No 3 Casualty Clearing Station, where he died of wounds on 20.9.1917, aged 20 years. Buried **GREVILLERS BRITISH CEMETERY.** Grave location:- Plot 7, Row A, Grave 14. ROH:- St. John's Church, Golcar; Huddersfield Drill Hall.

SHAW, DAVID. Corporal. No 2066. 1/5th Battalion Duke of Wellington's Regiment. Born Huddersfield. Son of Tom and Emma Shaw, 66 Upperhead Row, Huddersfield. Employed by the Borough Engineers Department of Huddersfield Corporation. Enlisted in the local Territorial battalion in 1912. Embarked for France in April, 1915. Came home on a week's leave from the trenches when he became ill and was admitted to Royds Hall War Hospital, Huddersfield. Died of pneumonia at Royds Hall on 20.12.1915, aged 20 years. Buried with full military honours in **EDGERTON CEMETERY, HUDDERSFIELD.** Grave location:- 11B, 115. (Brother of Corporal **HARRY SHAW**, killed in action, 30.4.1918, q.v.). ROH:- Huddersfield Drill Hall; Huddersfield Corporation Roll.

SHAW, DOUGLAS. Driver. No L/25805. 'C' (Holme Valley) Battery, 168th Brigade Royal Field Artillery. Born Shepley. Son of Walter and Elizabeth Shaw, of 'Heymoor', Abbey Road, Shepley. Employed as a weaver by Messrs Firth Brothers, New Mills, Shepley, where his father was a foreman spinner. Attended the Shelley Primitive Methodist Chapel and School. Played both football and cricket with the Shelley Cricket and Football club. Enlisted 2.5.1915. Killed instantly on Sunday, 30.6.1916, aged 22. (Both his horses were shot from under him). Buried

BOUZINCOURT COMMUNAL CEMETERY EXTENSION. Grave location:- Plot 2, Row C, Grave 21. ROH:- Shepley War Memorial.

SHAW, ERNEST. Private. No 242016. 2/5th Battalion Duke of Wellington's Regiment. Born Berry Brow, Huddersfield, 7.8.1893. Eldest son of Mr and Mrs G. H. Shaw, 10 John Berry's Row, Berry Brow. Educated Berry Brow Council School. Attended Berry Brow Wesleyan Church. Employed as a weaver by Messrs Kaye and Stewart. Was a member of the Berry Brow Wesleyan Young Men's Class. Single. Enlisted 11.3.1916. Reported missing, presumed killed, at the Battle of Bullecourt on 3.5.1917, aged 23 years. Has no known grave. Commemorated **ARRAS MEMORIAL TO THE MISSING.** ROH:- Armitage Bridge War Memorial; Huddersfield Drill Hall.

SHAW, FRANK. Private. No TR/5/208540. 53rd Battalion (Young Soldiers) West Yorkshire Regiment. Born Kirkburton, Huddersfield. Second son of Wright and Frances E. Shaw of 'The Rose and Crown Inn', Kirkburton. Employed as a clerk by Mr W. T. Johnson, Bankfield Mills, Huddersfield. Was a member of the Highburton Primitive Methodist Church, secretary of the Young Men's Bible Class, joint secretary of the restoration scheme and associated with the choir and the Christian Endeavour Group. Enlisted in March 1918. Died of pneumonia at Cannock Chase Military Hospital, Rugeley, Staffordshire, on 10.4.1918, aged 18 years. Buried **ALL HALLOWS CHURCHYARD, KIRKBURTON.** Grave location:- 18, 1261. ROH:- All Hallows Parish Church, Kirkburton.

SHAW, FRANK. Private. No 3/3052. 'A' Company, 2nd Battalion King's Own Yorkshire Light Infantry. Son of Mr H. Shaw, Dodds Royd, Berry Brow. Attended Berry Brow Wesleyan Church. Lived Ravensknowle Road, Moldgreen. Employed by Messrs Jennens, Welch and Company Limited. Married. Mobilised at the outbreak of the war. Killed in action, 26.3.1915, aged 33 years. Buried **BEDFORD HOUSE CEMETERY ENCLOSURE No 3.** Grave location: Row C, Grave 8. His widow received a letter from Company Sergeant Major R. Martin, who wrote, dated March 26th, 1915, *'I am sorry to have to inform you that your husband died yesterday about 10.30am. At the time of his accident he was getting ready to shave. A report was heard and Frank fell to the ground. All that was possible was done for him but he passed peacefully away a few minutes after we got him to the hospital. Your husband was in the same Company as me, both in South Africa and Malta and joined my Company early in December at Lindenhoek, Belgium. He was very ready to do anything that duty called for and was a comrade in whom I had every faith. The N.C.O.'s and men of his company deeply sympathise with you in your loss. He was buried about 5.45pm last night in the grounds of the Chateau Rosenthal. Six Sergeants carried him to his grave and the service was read by Captain Yates, his Company Commander. His comrades have put evergreens around his grave and a cross has been put up.'* ROH:- Moldgreen War Memorial; Shepley War Memorial.

SHAW, FRANK. Private. No 241208. 2/5th Battalion Duke of Wellington's Regiment. Born Northgate, Almondbury, 26.12.1895. Son of Sam and Alice Shaw, 61 Northgate, Almondbury. Educated Almondbury Council School and Huddersfield College. Employed as a clerk by Messrs J. W. and H. Shaw, St. George's Square, Huddersfield. Single. Enlisted 17.5.1915. Killed in action, 20.7.1918, aged 22 years. Buried **COURMAS BRITISH CEMETERY.** Grave location:- Plot 2, Row C, Grave 4. ROH:- Huddersfield Drill Hall; Almondbury War Memorial.

SHAW, FRANK. Private. No 41355. 1st Battalion The Royal Scots Fusiliers. Born John Berry's Row, Berry Brow, Huddersfield, 14.3.1899. Son of Hugh and Mary Shaw, 38 Dods Royd, Berry Brow. Educated Berry Brow Council School and Hillhouse Elementary School. Employed by Messrs Kaye and Stewart, of Lockwood. Single. Enlisted 13.11.1915. Reported wounded and missing on 12.4.1918 and afterwards presumed to have been killed on that date. Has no known grave. Commemorated **PLOEGSTEERT MEMORIAL TO THE MISSING.** ROH:- Armitage Bridge War Memorial.

SHAW, FRED. Private. No 242354. 12th Battalion East Surrey Regiment. Born Honley, Huddersfield. Son of William and Sarah Ann Shaw, 43 Hope Bank, Honley. Employed as a fettler by Messrs Thomas Dyson and Sons, Deanhouse Mills. Attended Netherthong Free Church Sunday School. Reported missing, presumed killed, 2.8.1917, aged 19 years. Has no known grave. Commemorated **MENIN GATE MEMORIAL TO THE MISSING.** ROH:- Honley War Memorial.

SHAW, FRED. Private. No 32534. 18th Battalion West Yorkshire Regiment. (2nd Bradford Pals). Born Batley. Lived Armitage Row, Shepley. Employed as a mason by Mr H. Wood of Shepley. Single. Enlisted May 1916. Reported missing at the Battle of Arras on 3.5.1917. Has no known grave. Commemorated **ARRAS MEMORIAL TO THE MISSING.**

SHAW, FRED. Private. No 268364. 2/6th Battalion Duke of Wellington's Regiment. Born Meltham. Lived Meltham. Killed in action, 3.5.1917. Has no known grave. Commemorated **ARRAS MEMORIAL TO THE MISSING.** ROH:- St. Bartholomew's Church, Meltham.

SHAW, FRED. Private. No 32008. 2/6th Battalion South Staffordshire Regiment. Born Holmfirth. Son of Firth and Annie Shaw, 18 Causeway Side, Linthwaite. Employed at Blackrock Mills, Linthwaite. Was a member of the Liberal Club. Enlisted November 1916. Embarked for France in June 1917. Died of gas shell wounds at No 26 Base Hospital on 9.12.1917, aged 19 years. Buried **ETAPLES MILITARY CEMETERY.** Grave location:- Plot 31, Row C, Grave 19. ROH:- Linthwaite War Memorial; Slaithwaite War Memorial.

SHAW, FREDDY. Rifleman. No C/7934. 18th Battalion King's Royal Rifle Corps. Born 10 Fenay Bridge, Almondbury, Huddersfield, 18.5.1896. Son of Edward Ellis and Lucy Shaw, 44 St. Helen's Gate, Almondbury. Educated Lepton Council School. Employed as a cloth finisher. Single. At the time of enlistment, was living at 7 and 8 Fenay Bridge. Enlisted 28.11.1915. Killed in action, 28.3.1918, at Vaulx, near Bapaume. Has no known grave. Commemorated **ARRAS MEMORIAL TO THE MISSING.** ROH:- Almondbury War Memorial.

SHAW, GEORGE. Private. No 31729. 13th Battalion York and Lancaster Regiment (1st Barnsley Pals). Formerly No 8082 Duke of Wellington's Regiment. Born Walker's Buildings, Delph Hill, Pudsey, Leeds, 8.2.1898. Son of Annie Shaw, 5 Grafton Place, Ramsden Street, Huddersfield. Educated Gipton Board School, Leeds. Employed as a tailor by Messrs Haigh, Moulden and Company. Single. Enlisted 11.9.1915. Killed in action, 21.6.1918, aged 20 years. Buried **LE GRAND HASARD MILITARY CEMETERY, HAZEBROUCK.** Grave location:- Plot 4, Row C, Grave 7. ROH:- St. Paul's Church, Southgate, Huddersfield.

SHAW, GEORGE EDMOND. Private. No 5159 Duke of Wellington's Regiment, transferred to No 269888 Labour Corps. Born Farnley Tyas. Son of Frances Shaw, of Thistle Hill, Wakefield Road, Lepton, and the late William Henry Shaw. Died of pneumonia, 23.10.1918, aged 26 years. Buried **St. LUCIUS CHURCHYARD,** FARNLEY TYAS WAR MEMORIAL. Grave location:- in South part.

SHAW, HAROLD THOMAS. Private. No 65766. 1/5th Battalion Northumberland Fusiliers. Born Scapegoat Hill, Golcar. Son of Mr and Mrs Walter Shaw, High Street, Scapegoat Hill. Reported missing, presumed killed, 11.4.1918, aged 19 years. Has no known grave. Commemorated **PLOEGSTEERT MEMORIAL TO THE MISSING.** ROH:- St. John's Church, Golcar.

SHAW, HARRY. Corporal. No 203848. 1/6th Battalion Duke of Wellington's Regiment. Son of Tom and Emma Shaw, 66 Upperhead Row, Huddersfield. Employed by the Huddersfield Corporation Highways Department. Killed in action, 30.4.1918, aged 20 years. Has no known grave. Commemorated **TYNE COT MEMORIAL TO THE MISSING.** (Brother of Private **DAVID SHAW,** who died from pneumonia on 20.12.1915, q.v.).

SHAW, HARRY. Private. No 82675. 230th Company Machine Gun Corps. Formerly No 29638 Duke of Wellington's Regiment. Husband of Mrs Shaw, 23 Bridge Street, Slaithwaite. Employed as a motor wagon steerer by the Slaithwaite Spinning Company. Served in France for six weeks before being drafted out to Egypt in April, 1917. Was admitted to hospital in April, 1918, for the fifth time since going out to Egypt, suffering from dysentery. Died at the 27th General Hospital, Abbassia, Cairo, Egypt, on 23.7.1918, aged 27, of heart failure following upon dysentery. Buried **CAIRO WAR MEMORIAL CEMETERY, EGYPT.** Grave location:- Plot O, Grave 214. ROH:- St. James Church, Slaithwaite; Slaithwaite War Memorial.

SHAW, HARRY. Private. No 16215. 8th Battalion Duke of Wellington's Regiment. Born Holthead Bridge, Slaithwaite. Son of Sykes and Clara Shaw, 11 Hill Top Road, Slaithwaite. Employed as a finisher by Mr John Ed Crowther of Marsden. Was a member of the Y.M.C.A. Slaithwaite Cricket Club. Attended the Holthead General Sunday School. Enlisted in 1915. Killed in action at Passchendaele on 28.8.1917, aged 22 years. Has no known grave. Commemorated **TYNE COT MEMORIAL TO THE MISSING.** ROH:- Carr Lane Methodist Church, Slaithwaite; St. James Church, Slaithwaite; Slaithwaite War Memorial.

SHAW, HERBERT. Private. No 350389. 12th Battalion Highland Light Infantry. Born Slaithwaite. Husband of Mrs Shaw, Bush Grove Farm, Holthead, Slaithwaite. Employed as a cloth finisher by Messrs Pearson Brothers. Attended Holthead General Sunday School. Enlisted 12.10.1916. Embarked for France 2.9.1917. Reported missing, presumed killed, 25.3.1918. Has no known grave. Commemorated **POZIERES MEMORIAL TO THE MISSING.** ROH:- St. James Church, Slaithwaite; Slaithwaite War Memorial; Helme Parish Church.

SHAW, IRVIN. Private. No 24139. 2/7th Battalion Duke of Wellington's Regiment. Son of Mrs Shaw, 236 Lees Croft, Townend, Golcar: husband of Lucy Shaw, 52 Longcroft Street, Golcar. Was a member of the Golcar Lily Cycling Club. Employed by Messrs B. and J. Whitwam Limited, Stanley Mills, Golcar. Attended St. John's Parish Church, Golcar. Was a member of the Colne Valley Territorials before the war. Mobilised at the outbreak of the war. Reported wounded and missing on 28.8.1917 and afterwards presumed to have been killed on that date, aged 23. Has no known grave. Commemorated **TYNE COT MEMORIAL TO THE MISSING.** ROH:- St. John's Church, Golcar; Huddersfield Drill Hall.

SHAW, JOE. Private. No 41056. 19th Battalion Northumberland Fusiliers (2nd Tyneside Pioneers). Born Honley. Son of Mrs B. Shaw, Burhouse Terrace, Honley. Employed at Rock Mills, Brockholes. Enlisted in 1916. Killed in action, 28.3.1918, aged 23 years. Has no known grave. Commemorated **POZIERES MEMORIAL TO THE MISSING.**

SHAW, JOHN. Corporal. No 43243. 16th Heavy Battery, Royal Garrison Artillery. Born Sowood near Halifax. Lived Huddersfield. Killed in action, 6.6.1917. Buried **WESTHOF FARM CEMETERY, BELGIUM.** Grave location:- Plot 1, Row B, Grave 6.

SHAW, JOHN. Private. No 18475. 2nd Battalion South Wales Borderers. Born Longwood. Lived with his sister, Mrs Byram, at 10 Ballroyd, Longwood. Employed by Messrs Buckleys, brush manufacturers, of Longroyd Bridge. Enlisted at the outbreak of the war. Whilst serving in the Dardenelles was wounded four times and suffered from an attack of dysentery. Died of wounds, 28.6.1916, aged 32 years. Buried **ENGLEBELMER COMMUNAL CEMETERY.** Grave location:- Plot 1, Row A, Grave 7. ROH:- Longwood War Memorial.

SHAW, JOHN LESLIE ROBERT. Private. No 1749. 1/5th Battalion Duke of Wellington's Regiment. Born Huddersfield. Son of Mr Sam Shaw, 32 College Street, Crosland Moor, Huddersfield. Joined the local Territorials in 1908 and, for a period of six months, served with the Royal Field Artillery at Newcastle-on-Tyne. Was in business as a taxi-cab proprietor at Huddersfield Railway Station. Took an active interest in the boy scout movement. Enlisted at the outbreak of the war. Embarked for France in April, 1915. Killed in action, 22.9.1915, aged 22 years. Has no known grave. Commemorated **MENIN GATE MEMORIAL TO THE MISSING.** Major Norton wrote to his father on 22.9.1915, *'I deeply regret to have to inform you that your son, No. 1749 Private J. L. R. Shaw, was killed yesterday by a sniper, being shot through the chest. He died almost immediately. He was buried last night by our Chaplain in a cemetery a few hundred yards behind the firing line. I feel this will be a great blow to you but I trust you will find consolation in remembering that he died for his King and Country. Your son has always done his duty and done it well and you will always have reason to be proud of him. His death is a great loss to the Company and he will be sorely missed by all his comrades. In expressing to you my sincere sympathy I do so on* *behalf of all the Officers, N.C.O's and men of the Company.'* ROH:- Huddersfield Drill Hall.

SHAW, JOHN WILLIAM. Lance Sergeant. No 2331. 1/7th Battalion Duke of Wellington's Regiment. Son of Mr and Mrs William Shaw, Wharf House, Warehouse Hill, Marsden. Employed as a weaver by Messrs Crowther, Bruce and Company Limited, New Mills, Marsden. Was a member of Marsden Brass Band. He was a well known local pianist and an association football player. As a young boy he was a chorister at Marsden Parish Church. Received severe wounds during the Battle of the Somme on 3.7.1916. Died of wounds at Bradford War Hospital on 31.7.1916, aged 25 years. A letter was received from the military authorities that they were unable to arrange a full military funeral but a gun carriage was sent for the funeral at **St. BARTHOLOMEW'S CHURCHYARD, MARSDEN.** Grave location:- SW, 23, 4. ROH:- Huddersfield Drill Hall; Marsden War Memorial.

SHAW, JOHN WILLIAM. Private. No 40803. 2/5th Battalion South Staffordshire Regiment. Born Fartown Green, Huddersfield, in 1882. Educated St. John's School. Employed as a woollen teaser by Messrs T. and H. Blamires Limited, Leeds Road, Huddersfield. Attended St. John's Church, Birkby. Married, with one child. Lived 18 Hillhouse Road, Huddersfield. Enlisted in 1917. Killed in action, 30.11.1917. Buried **ORIVAL WOOD CEMETERY.** Grave location:- Plot 1, Row A, Grave 35. ROH:- Fartown and Birkby War Memorial.

SHAW, JOSEPH HENRY. Lance Coporal. No 911. 2nd Battalion Duke of Wellington's Regiment. Born Almondbury. Enlisted Huddersfield. Mobilised at the outbreak of the war. Killed in action at the First Battle of Ypres on 15.11.1914. Has no known grave. Commemorated **MENIN GATE MEMORIAL TO THE MISSING.** ROH:- Almondbury War Memorial.

SHAW, JOSEPH LEONARD. Lance Sergeant. No 235794. 9th Battalion King's Own Yorkshire Light Infantry. Formerly No 2030 Duke of Wellington's Regiment. Born Huddersfield. Married. His wife lived with her parents, Mr and Mrs G.H. Pears, at 42 Armitage Road, Birkby. Had served 18 months in France when he was killed in action on 22.3.1918. Buried **PERONNE COMMUNAL CEMETERY EXTENSION.** Grave location:- Plot 4, Row F, Grave 15. ROH:- St. John's Church, Birkby; Huddersfield General Post Office; Fartown and Birkby War Memorial.

SHAW, LAURENCE. Private. No 268694. 2/7th Battalion West Yorkshire Regiment. Born Berry Brow, Huddersfield. Lived Drawer's Row, Berry Brow. Married. Attended Berry Brow Wesleyan Church and was assistant secretary of the Sunday School. Enlisted October 1916. Embarked for France in January 1917. Died of wounds at No 26 General Hospital on 31.5.1917, aged 23 years. Buried **ETAPLES MILITARY CEMETERY** Grave location:- Plot 25, Row F, Grave 7A. ROH:- Armitage Bridge War Memorial.

SHAW, OLIVER. Private. No 202894. 2/5th Battalion South Staffordshire Regiment. Born Dalton, Huddersfield, 28.4.1892. Son of Lewis and Charlotte Shaw, 72 Barcroft Road, Lockwood, Huddersfield. Educated Moldgreen Council School. Employed by the London and North Western Railway Company as a van setter. Single. Enlisted 27.11.1916. Killed in action, 2.12.1917, aged 25 years. Buried **ORIVAL WOOD CEMETERY.** Grave location:- Plot 2, Row C, Grave 15. ROH:- St. John's Church, Newsome; London and North Western Railway Company Roll.

SHAW, PERCY. Private. No 49794. 5th Battalion The King's (Liverpool Regiment). Formerly No 30502 Duke of Wellington's Regiment. Born Stanley Street, Lockwood, Huddersfield, 11.11.1896. Son of Ann Shaw, 18 Lockwood Scar, Lockwood. Educated Mount Street School, Lockwood and Railway Servants Orphanage, Derby. From April, 1911, until July, 1915, was a railway parcels van boy at Huddersfield Station. Prior to enlistment, on 12.3.1917, was a porter at Fenay Bridge Station. Single. Reported wounded and missing, presumed killed, at the Battle of Passchendaele on 20.9.1917. Has no known grave. Commemorated **TYNE COT MEMORIAL TO THE MISSING.** ROH:- New North Road Baptist Church; Emmanuel Church, Lockwood; London and North Western Railway Roll.

SHAW, PERCY. Private. No 12022. 8th Battalion Duke of Wellington's Regiment. Born Lepton, Huddersfield. Son of Mr E. Shaw, Sunnybank, Lepton. Killed in action at the

Dardenelles on 12.8.1915. Has no known grave. Commemorated **HELLES MEMORIAL TO THE MISSING.** ROH:- Lepton Parish Church; St. John's Church, Kirkheaton.

SHAW, RAYMOND. Sapper. No 440433. 428th Field Company, Royal Engineers. Born Crosland Moor, Huddersfield, 10.5.1893. Son of John William and Lizzie Shaw, 23 Frederick Street, Crosland Moor. Educated Crosland Moor Council School and Longwood Grammar School. Employed as a clerk at the Yorkshire Penny Bank, Huddersfield which he joined in September 1913. Had previously worked at the Hunslet and Cleckheaton branches. Single. Enlisted 15.8.1915. Was drowned in the Mediterrean on 1.1.1917, when the troopship *SS Ivernia* was sunk by a U-boat, aged 23. Has no known grave. Commemorated **MIKRA MEMORIAL TO THE MISSING, SALONIKA.** ROH:- Crosland Moor Wesleyan Church; St. Barnabas Church, Crosland Moor.

SHAW, ROGER RYAN. Private. No 62882. 25th Battalion Machine Gun Corps. Formerly No 36288 York and Lancaster Regiment. Born Kirkburton. Son of Robert Beeley Shaw and Mary Elizabeth Shaw of Low Gate, Kirkburton. Employed by Mr Allen Battye, bootmaker, of Shepley. Died at a Casualty Clearing Station of compression of the skull on 20.9.1918, aged 21. Buried **St. VENANT COMMUNAL CEMETERY EXTENSION.** Grave location:- Plot 4, Row A, Grave 16. (Brother of Private **WILLIAM PERCY SHAW**, who died on 8.1.1919, q.v.). ROH:- All Hallows Parish Church, Kirkburton; commemorated on headstone in Kirkburton Cemetery.

SHAW, THOMAS. Private. No 242084. 2nd Battalion Duke of Wellington's Regiment. Son of James and Mary Shaw of Golcar Brow, Meltham. Died of wounds at No 41 Casualty Clearing Station on 4.4.1918, aged 32 years. Buried **DUISANS BRITISH CEMETERY.** Grave location:- Plot 6, Row F, Grave 32. ROH:- St. Bartholomew's Church, Meltham.

SHAW, THOMAS HAROLD. Lance Corporal. No 241615. 2/5th Battalion Duke of Wellington's Regiment. Born 37 Kings Mill Lane, Huddersfield, 25.1.1894. Both parents deceased: Thomas Shaw, died 18.4.1917; mother, Hannah Shaw, died 4.10.1917. Educated Stile Common Board School, Primrose Hill, Huddersfield. Employed as a shop assistant by Messrs Whitfield Brothers, drapers, Manchester Road, Huddersfield. Attended Buxton Road Sunday School. Single. Enlisted 17.3.1916. Killed in action at the Battle of Cambrai, 27.11.1917, just ten days after his return from home leave. Has no known grave. Commemorated **CAMBRAI MEMORIAL TO THE MISSING.** ROH:- Huddersfield Drill Hall; memorial in Almondbury Cemetery.

SHAW, WILLIAM. Private. No 269176. 1/7th Battalion Duke of Wellington's Regiment. Born Huddersfield. Reported missing, presumed killed, at the Battle of Passchendaele on 9.10.1917. Has no known grave. Commemorated **TYNE COT MEMORIAL TO THE MISSING.** ROH:- All Saints Church, Paddock; Huddersfield Drill Hall.

SHAW, WILLIAM. Sapper. No 45204. 3rd Field Company, Canadian Engineers. Son of Alfred and Jane Shaw, of Armitage Bridge. Killed in action, 24.3.1915, aged 42 years. Buried **SAILLY-sur-la-LYS CANADIAN CEMETERY.** Grave location:- Plot 2, Row B, Grave 33. ROH:- Armitage Bridge War Memorial.

SHAW, WILLIAM PERCY. Private. No 40852. 23rd (Tyneside Scottish) Battalion Northumberland Fusiliers. Son of Robert Beeley Shaw and Mary Elizabeth Shaw of Low Gate, Kirkburton. Employed by Messrs John Kaye and Son, Colne Road, Huddersfield. Enlisted in 1915. Was taken prisoner by the Germans in 1917. Died on board *SS Guildford Castle* whilst returning home to Netley hospital on 8.1.1919, after being a Prisoner of War in Germany. He sustained an accident whilst working with a crane over a ship's hold at Emden and was taken to Munster Hospital. He was 25 years of age. Buried **ALL HALLOWS CHURCHYARD, KIRKBURTON.** Grave location:- 11, 776. (Brother of Private **ROGER RYAN SHAW**, died of wounds, 20.9.1918, q.v.). ROH:- All Hallows Parish Church, Kirkburton.

SHAW, WILLIE. Private. No 12553. 1/4th Battalion The King's Own (Royal Lancaster Regiment). Born Huddersfield 17.8.1883. Lived with his sister at 1 Edgerton Lane, Edgerton, Huddersfield. Educated Huddersfield Parish

Church Schools. Employed as a warehouseman at Blackpool Single. Enlisted August 1914. Killed in action, 9.7.1918, aged 35 years. Buried **HOUCHIN BRITISH CEMETERY.** Grave location:- Plot 2, Row D, Grave 5. ROH:- Huddersfield Parish Church.

SHAW, WILLIE. Private. No 97979. 2nd Battalion Sherwood Foresters. Born Chesterfield. Son of the late Mary Elizabeth Shaw of Honley. Lived with his grandmother at 9 Swift Fold, Honley. Employed by Messrs A. Thornton and Sons. Was a member of Mr W. Brook's bible class at Honley Parish Church. Enlisted July 1917. Killed in action, 23.3.1918, aged 19 years. Has no known grave. Commemorated **ARRAS MEMORIAL TO THE MISSING.** ROH:- Honley War Memorial.

SHAW, W. Trooper. No 490. 2nd Dragoon Guards (Queen's Bays). Died at home, 6.12.1915. Buried **EDGERTON CEMETERY, HUDDERSFIELD.** Grave location:- 11B, 115.

SHEARD, FRANK. Private. No 26407. 2nd Battalion Loyal North Lancashire Regiment. Born 5 Brick Bank, Almondbury, Huddersfield, 10.3.1897. Son of Joe Lister Sheard and Sarah E. Sheard. Educated Stile Common and Almondbury Council School. Employed as a lithographic printer by Messrs W. H. Cook Limited, Market Place, Huddersfield. Single. Enlisted 1.4.1916. Had served in German East Africa, Egypt and France. Killed in action at Kemmel Hill on 28.8.1918, aged 21 years. Buried **RENINGHELST NEW MILITARY CEMETERY, BELGIUM.** Grave location:- Plot 5, Row B, Grave 9. ROH:- Almondbury War Memorial.

SHEARD, GEORGE WILLIAM. Private. No 31262. 1st Battalion East Yorkshire Regiment. Formerly No 25976 West Yorkshire Regiment. Born Rocktown, Queensland, Australia. Son of Mr and Mrs Sheard, 17 Spring Street, Marsden. Had lived in Marsden for six years. Employed as a weaver at Bank Bottom Mills, Marsden. Enlisted October 1915. Killed by shrapnel in the attack on Gueudecourt on 16.9.1916, aged 25 years. Has no known grave. Commemorated **THIEPVAL MEMORIAL TO THE MISSING.** ROH:- Marsden War Memorial.

SHEARD, HARRY. Lance Corporal. No 23927. 9th Battalion York and Lancaster Regiment. Born High Hoyland, Barnsley. Husband of Olive Sheard of Upper Denby, Denby Dale. Employed at Denby Dale collieries. Played with the Clayton West and Denby Dale brass bands. Enlisted November 1915. Killed in action in Italy on 15.6.1918, aged 34 years. Buried **GRANEZZA BRITISH CEMETERY.** Grave location:- Plot 1, Row D, Grave 9. ROH:- Denby Dale and Cumberworth War Memorial; Clayton West and High Hoyland War Memorial.

SHEARD, JOHN EDWARD. Private. No 3/12767. 9th Battalion Duke of Wellington's Regiment. Born Silk Street, Huddersfield 27.4.1888. Son of Mrs Mary Ann Catton, 6 Birkby Lodge Road, Birkby. Educated St. Patrick's Roman Catholic School, New North Road, Huddersfield. Employed as a yardman at Elland Station. Lived 4 Brunswick Yard, Upper Brunswick Street, Hopwood Lane, Halifax. Married. Enlisted November 1914. Had been in France for a year and had been wounded twice. Killed in action at Contalmaison during the Battle of the Somme on 7.7.1916, aged 28 years. Has no known grave. Commemorated **THIEPVAL MEMORIAL TO THE MISSING.** (Brother of Corporal **JOSEPH WILLIAM SHEARD,** killed in action, 9.10.1917, and **ROBERT HENRY SHEARD,** who died on 5.2.1920, q.v.). ROH: Fartown and Birkby War Memorial.

SHEARD, JOSEPH WILLIAM. Corporal. No 12990. 8th Battalion Duke of Wellington's Regiment. Born Blackley, near Elland, 7.5.1895. Son of Mrs Mary Ann Catton, 6 Birkby Lodge Road, Birkby, Huddersfield. Educated St. Patrick's Roman Catholic School, New North Road, Huddersfield. Employed as a gas engine teneter by Messrs Thewlis, Jagger and Company, Chapel Hill, Huddersfield. Single. Enlisted 16.8.1915. Killed in action at Passchendaele on 9.10.1917, aged 27 years. Has no known grave. Commemorated **TYNE COT MEMORIAL TO THE MISSING.** (Brother of Private **JOHN EDWARD SHEARD,** killed in action, 7.7.1916, and **ROBERT HENRY SHEARD,** who died on 5.2.1920, q.v.). ROH:- Fartown and Birkby War Memorial.

SHEARD, ROBERT HENRY. Able Seaman. Royal Navy. *HMS Tumult.* Born Martin Green, Stainland, Halifax. Son of Mary Ann Catton,

6 Birkby Lodge Road, Birkby, Huddersfield. Educated St. Patrick's Roman Catholic School, New North Road, Huddersfield. Prior to the war had served with the Mercantile Marine Service. Enlisted just before Easter, 1915, at Portsmouth. Was married in 1919, after being demobilised. Hung himself at 18 Gelder Terrace Tenements, Moldgreen, Huddersfield, on the 5.2.1920 *'through the horrors of the war and the effects of malaria'*. (Brother of Private **JOHN EDWARD SHEARD**, killed in action, 7.7.1916, and Corporal **JOSEPH WILLIAM SHEARD**, killed in action, 9.10.1917, q.v.).

SHEARD, STANLEY. Private. No 241555. 2/5th Battalion Duke of Wellington's Regiment. Born Battyeford October 1891. Educated at Battyeford Schools. Employed as a cloth finisher at Woodhouse Mills. Married. Lived 11 Deighton Road, Deighton. Enlisted March 1916. Died of wounds near Epernay on 22.7.1918, aged 27 years. Buried **St. IMOGE CHURCHYARD.** Grave location:- Row B, Grave 15. ROH:- Christ Church, Woodhouse Hill; Deighton United Methodist Chapel; Huddersfield Drill Hall; Deighton War Memorial.

SHEARD, WILFRED ROBERT. Private. No 39365. 2/4th Battalion King's Own Yorkshire Light Infantry. Formerly No 6356 Duke of Wellington's Regiment. Employed by Mr Charles Walton Ellis, of Stainland and late of Birkby. Married, with one child. Lived 99 Ravensknowle Road, Moldgreen, Huddersfield. Reported missing 20.7.1918 and afterward presumed to have been killed on that date. Has no known grave. Commemorated **SOISSONS MEMORIAL TO THE MISSING.** ROH:- Christ Church, Moldgreen.

SHEFFIELD, HARRY. Corporal. No 52392. 8th Battalion Royal Fusiliers. Formerly No 1748 Army Service Corps. Born Pickering, Yorkshire. Son of Mrs Mary Sheffield, 41 Scarborough Road, Norton, Malton: husband of the late Maud Sheffield, of Skelmanthorpe, Huddersfield. Lived Lepton. Killed in action, 23.4.1917, aged 37 years. Has no known grave. Commemorated **ARRAS MEMORIAL TO THE MISSING.** ROH:- Lepton Parish Church.

SHEFFIELD, THOMAS EDWARD. Gunner. No 219467. 1089th Battery, Royal Field Artillery. Born Honley. Son of Edward and Jane Sheffield, 39 Reins Terrace, Honley. Employed by Messrs Eastwood Brothers, of Honley. Enlisted February 1918. Died of heatstroke in India on 17.5.1918, aged 41 years. Buried **JUBBULPORE CANTONMENT CEMETERY.** Commemorated **KIRKEE 1914–1918 MEMORIAL.** ROH:- Honley War Memorial.

SHELLS, HERBERT. Private. No 24779. 2nd Battalion Duke of Wellington's Regiment. Son of Charles France and Elizabeth Shells, 2 Riverside, Armitage Bridge. Employed at Armitage Bridge Mills. Was mobilised at the outbreak of the war. Reported missing, presumed killed, 15.4.1918, aged 22 years. Has no known grave. Commemorated **PLOEGSTEERT MEMORIAL TO THE MISSING.** (Brother of Private **WILLIAM SHELLS**, died of wounds, 15.10.1918, q.v.). ROH:- Armitage Bridge Mills; Armitage Bridge War Memorial.

SHELLS, WILLIAM. Sergeant. No 200788. 1/5th Battalion Durham Light Infantry. Born Armitage Bridge. Son of William France and Elizabeth Shells, 2 Riverside, Armitage Bridge. Employed as a presser at Armitage Bridge Mills. Was mobilised with the 1/5th Battalion Duke of Wellington's Regiment at the outbreak of the war and served as a cook with the Battalion. Died of wounds at No 62 Casualty Clearing Station on 15.10.1918, aged 25 years. Buried **LIJSSENTHOEK MILITARY CEMETERY.** Grave location:- Plot 30, Row D, Grave 18. (Brother of Private **HERBERT SHELLS**, killed in action, 15.4.1918, q.v.). ROH:- Armitage Bridge Mills; Armitage Bridge War Memorial.

SHEPPARD, WALTER WILLIAM. Private. No 4281. 1/5th Battalion Duke of Wellington's Regiment. Born Mexborough 13.7.1895. Son of George William and Emily Sheppard, 50 Blackhouse Road, Fartown, Huddersfield. Educated Hillhouse Council School. Employed as a tailor's trimmer by Messrs Bairstow and Company Limited. Attended Christ Church, Woodhouse Hill and was a member of the Church Cricket and Athletic Club. Single. Enlisted 13.7.1915. Reported missing, presumed killed, in the attack on the Schwaben Redoubt on 3.9.1916. Has no known grave. Commemorated **THIEPVAL MEMORIAL TO THE MISSING.**

ROH:- Christ Church, Woodhouse Hill; Fartown and Birkby War Memorial.

SHERBON, CHARLES. Private. No 240334. 1/5th Battalion Duke of Wellington's Regiment. Born Huddersfield. Son of Mr and Mrs Sherbon, 10 Honoria Street, Hillhouse, Fartown, Huddersfield. Employed as an apprentice by Messrs Robert Airey and Sons, coopers and vat builders, East Parade, Huddersfield. Enlisted September 1914. Was twice wounded. Died of wounds at Becketts Park War Hospital, Leeds, on 26.9.1918. Buried with full military honours in **EDGERTON CEMETERY, HUDDERSFIELD.** Grave location:- 23, 179. ROH:- Huddersfield Drill Hall; Fartown and Birkby War Memorial.

SHERIDAN, JAMES. Private. No 235264. 11th Battalion Lancashire Fusiliers. Born Liverpool. Lived Huddersfield. Brother of Michael Sheridan of Hollingworth Green, Meltham. Killed in action near Rheims on 28.5.1918, aged 20 years. Has no known grave. Commemorated **SOISSONS MEMORIAL TO THE MISSING.**

SHERRATT, FRANK. Lance Corporal. No M2/176022. 701st Company, Army Service Corps. Born Honley, Huddersfield, 6.2.1899. Son of Frederick and Ada Sherratt, 92 Gledholt Bank, Huddersfield. Educated at Honley Schools. Employed as a traveller by the Bradford Motors Company. Single. Enlisted 16.6.1916. Died from accidental injuries at No 6 Casualty Clearing Station on 18.8.1916, aged 26 years. Buried **BARLIN COMMUNAL CEMETERY EXTENSION.** Grave location:- Plot 1, Row C, Grave 26. ROH:- All Saints Church, Paddock.

SHIRES, DODSON. Private. No 23585. 6th Battalion The Dorsetshire Regiment. Formerly No 38748 West Yorkshire Regiment. Born Lockwood, Huddersfield. Lived 12 Second Block, Kirkgate, Huddersfield. Employed at the Corporation Tramsheds. Reported wounded and missing on 27.8.1918 and afterwards presumed to have been killed on that date. Buried **ACHIET-LE-GRAND COMMUNAL CEMETERY EXTENSION.** Grave location:- Plot 4, Row Y, Grave 7.

SHIRTCLIFFE, HARRY. Rifleman. No B/203488 1st Battalion The Rifle Brigade. Formerly No C/7763 King's Royal Rifle Corps. Born Dalton 14.3.1889. Son of James and Elizabeth Shirtcliffe, 51 Fleming House Lane, Dalton, Huddersfield. Educated Lepton Board School. Employed as a teamer by Messrs Rhodes and Brierley, Kirkheaton. Attended St. John's Parish Church, Kirkheaton. Single. Enlisted 19.11.1915. Killed in action near Combles on 18.2.1917, aged 26 years. Has no known grave. Commemorated **THIEPVAL MEMORIAL TO THE MISSING.** ROH:- St. John's Church, Kirkheaton; Almondbury War Memorial.

SHOESMITH, ARTHUR THOMAS, DCM. Private. No SS/21505. 28th Lines of Communication Company, Army Service Corps. Born Bolton, Lancashire, 1876. Son of John and Mary Shoesmith of Huddersfield. Husband of Amy Shoesmith, 62 Commercial Street, Huddersfield. Educated Spring Grove Council School. Employed as a firer at the Destructor Works by Huddersfield Corporation. Had served in the South African War, where he was awarded the DCM. As a Reservist was called up at the outbreak of the war. Served on the Western Front before going to Salonica in 1917. Died from dysentery in Salonika on 30.8.1917, aged 41 years. Buried **SALONIKA ANGLO-FRENCH MILITARY CEMETERY, LEMBET ROAD.** Grave location:- No 1161. ROH:- Huddersfield Corporation Roll.

SHOESMITH, CHARLIE. Private. No 134817. Royal Army Medical Corps. Son of Mr and Mrs W. H. Shoesmith, 71 Lockwood Road, Huddersfield. Died at home, 14.12.1920, aged 21 years. Buried **LOCKWOOD CEMETERY, HUDDERSFIELD.** Grave location:- C, 'C', 428.

SHORE, ALBERT. Private. No 4622. 'A' Company, 2/5th Battalion Duke of Wellington's Regiment. Born Huddersfield. Son of Mr J. A. Shore, 46 Bankfield Road, Moldgreen, Huddersfield. Educated Moldgreen Council Schools. Employed in a sealskin factory. Single. Killed in action, 27.2.1917. Has no known grave. Commemorated **THIEPVAL MEMORIAL TO THE MISSING.** ROH:- Huddersfield Parish Church; Christ Church, Moldgreen; Huddersfield Drill Hall.

SHORE, LEWIS. Sergeant. No 238005. 9th Battalion West Yorkshire Regiment. Formerly No 198, 'F' Company, 1/5th Battalion Duke of Wellington's Regiment. Born Holmfirth. Son of ex Lance Sergeant Jesse and Mrs Ruth Shore, of Hey Gap, Holmfirth. Husband of Emily Shore, 81 Taylor Hill Road, Berry Brow, Huddersfield. Served in the Volunteer and Territorial forces from 1901. Was a member of the Yorkshire Rifle Association. Attended St. John's Church and, as a boy was a member of the choir. Prior to enlistment, married Miss Chaffer, of Binns Farm, Holmfirth. Had been in France 14 weeks when he was killed, of concussion, from a shell which burst close to him on 12.6.1917, aged 33 years. Has no known grave. Commemorated **MENIN GATE MEMORIAL TO THE MISSING.** ROH:- Holmfirth War Memorial; Armitage Bridge War Memorial.

SHARROCKS, JOHN CHARLES. Private. No 3551. 1/7th Battalion Duke of Wellington's Regiment. Born Hayfield, Derbyshire. Lived Spring Terrace, Binn Road, Marsden. Employed in the dyehouse at Bank Bottom Mills, Marsden. Moved to Marsden in 1913. Had been a member of the Sherwood Foresters Territorial Force for three years whilst living at Hayfield, Derbyshire. Enlisted 1916. Had been in France six months when he was killed, on 18.9.1916, during the Battle of the Somme. He was 26 years of age. Has no known grave. Commemorated **THIEPVAL MEMORIAL TO THE MISSING.** ROH:- Huddersfield Drill Hall; Marsden War Memorial.

SHORT, OLIVER CROMWELL. Corporal. No 14400. 8th Battalion Duke of Wellington's Regiment. Born Coventry 5.11.1884. Educated at Coventry Schools. Husband of Mrs Edith Short, 6 Somerset Place, Mulberry Street, Moldgreen. Employed as a painter and paper-hanger by Messrs Littlewood. Enlisted 3.10.1914. Killed in action in the Dardenelles on 21.8.1915, aged 30 years. Has no known grave. Commemorated **HELLES MEMORIAL TO THE MISSING.** ROH:- Christ Church, Moldgreen; Almondbury War Memorial.

SHRIGLEY, WILLIAM H. No 19066. Company Sergeant Major. 12th Battalion Highland Light Infantry. Born Slaithwaite. Enlisted Glasgow. As a boy was apprenticed to his Uncle, Mr William Shrigley, joiner, of Golcar. Attended St. John's Church and Sunday School, Golcar. Had served in the Regular Army for twenty six and a half years. Fought in the Boer War and retired from active service. When the war broke out he rejoined the forces. He married Jeanie McMillan of Rosevale, Kilwinning, Ayrshire and had four children. Killed in action at the Battle of Loos on 25.9.1915, aged 52 years. Has no known grave. Commemorated **LOOS MEMORIAL TO THE MISSING.** His widow received a letter from CQMS Harry Forsyth, who wrote the following, *'It is with feelings of heartfelt sorrow that I write to let you know that your noble husband was killed on September 25th whilst leading his Company, which had achieved great feats to still greater feats. By his cheerful encouragement and bravery on the field he was a wonderful example to the younger men of the Company. I pray that the knowledge that your husband died a hero may be some consolation in this hour of cloud and sorrow. The older men realise that they have lost a leader and the younger men a father. I have lost a true comrade. Please accept the heartfelt sympathy of the N.C.O's and men of his Regiment.'*

SHUTTLEWORTH, HEDLEY. Private. No 241097. 2/5th Battalion Duke of Wellington's Regiment. Born Abbeysteads, Lancashire. Son of William and Isabel Shuttleworth, Chapel Lane Farm, Galgate, Lancaster. Husband of Elsie Eliza Jane Shuttleworth, of Badger Hey, Marsden. Attended Marsden Parish Church. Employed by Messrs Mallinsons, Spring Grove Mills, Linthwaite. Enlisted 14.4.1915. Embarked for France in January, 1917. Killed in action, 27.3.1918, aged 32 years. He was a stretcher-bearer engaged in carrying in wounded when he was hit by a bullet, death being instantenous. Has no known grave. Commemorated **ARRAS MEMORIAL TO THE MISSING.** ROH:- Huddersfield Drill Hall; Marsden War Memorial.

SILVERWOOD, HUGH, MM. Guardsman. No 18668. Coldstream Guards. Born Shelley. Husband of Edith Silverwood, Far Bank, Shelley. Awarded the Military Medal, 10.4.1918. Died at home, 6.6.1921, aged 28 years. Buried **EMMANUEL CHURCHYARD, SHELLEY.** Grave location:- O, 641. ROH:- Emmanuel Church, Shelley.

SILVER, JAMES. Private. No 10118. 1st Battalion East Yorkshire Regiment. Born 26 Victoria Crescent, Lockwood, Huddersfield, 21.1.1899. Son of Harry and Mary Silver, Armitage Street, Primrose Hill, Huddersfield.

Husband of Ada Silver, 2 Crowther Street, Lockwood. Employed as a labourer by Messrs David Brown, of Lockwood. Enlisted in December 1913. Killed in action, 21.8.1915, aged 22 years. Has no known grave. Commemorated **MENIN GATE MEMORIAL TO THE MISSING.** His widow received a letter from Sergeant Smith, of 'D' Company, to which her husband belonged, who wrote that they were going out to dig a new trench when Silver was shot by a bullet just above the heart and passed away two or three minutes later. The Sergeant added, *'He was a hard working young fellow and I wish every man was like him.'* ROH:- Emmanuel Church, Lockwood.

SILVESTER, WILLIAM HENRY. Private. No 4637. 3/5th Battalion Duke of Wellington's Regiment. Lived Marsden. Husband of Mary Alice Silvester, 79 Trinity Street, Huddersfield. Died at home, 29.5.1916, aged 32 years. Buried **CHRIST CHURCH CHURCHYARD, FRIEZLAND.** Grave location:- in East part, 297.

SIMMONDS, CHRISTOPHER GEORGE. No 9686. Corporal. Depot Battalion, The Worcestershire Regiment. Born Cork, Ireland. Husband of Sarah E. Simmonds, 98 Woodhead Road, Holmbridge. Had served in the army for 21 years. Died as the result of an accident on 24.1.1916, aged 46 years. Buried with full military honours at **St. JAMES CHURCHYARD, NORTON-JUXTA-KEMPSEY, WORCESTERSHIRE.** Grave location:- B. ROH:- Holme and Holmbridge War Memorial.

SIMPSON, EDGAR. Private. No 65214. 1st Battalion Northumberland Fusiliers. Born 79 King Street, Huddersfield, 10.5.1887. Son of Thomas Cook and Emma Simpson, 2 Summer Street, Lockwood. Educated Rashcliffe Church of England School. Employed as a woollen spinner by Messrs Allen Priest, Bath Mills. Husband of Edith Ellen Simpson, 8 Moorbottom Road, Thornton Lodge, Crosland Moor. Enlisted 28.3.1917. Killed in action near Arras on 23.8.1918, aged 31 years. Buried **RAILWAY CUTTING CEMETERY, COURCELLES-LE-COMTE.** Grave location:- Row A, Grave 63. ROH:- St. Stephen's Church, Rashcliffe.

SIMPSON, NORMAN. Private. No 18659. 1st Battalion East Yorkshire Regiment. Formerly No 19769 Hussars. Born Springdale Street, Huddersfield, 27.4.1898. Son of Emanuel and Eliza Ann Simpson, 55 Burbeary Street, Lockwood. Educated Mount Pleasant Board School. Employed as an apprentice fitter by Messrs William Whiteley and Sons Limited, Lockwood. Single. Enlisted 10.9.1914. Reported missing, presumed killed, 28.5.1918, aged 20 years. Has no known grave. Commemorated **SOISSONS MEMORIAL TO THE MISSING.** ROH:- Emmanuel Church, Lockwood; Mount Pleasant Chapel, Lockwood.

SIMS, WILLIAM CHARLES. Lance Corporal. No 19673. 8th Battalion Bedfordshire Regiment. Born Islington, Middlesex. Adopted son of Mr and Mrs Ashton, Wildspur Bottom, New Mill, Holmfirth. Employed at Wood Pit. Was a member of New Mill Working Men's Club. Enlisted St Pancras, London, at the outbreak of the war. Embarked for France in September, 1915. Killed in action, 20.11.1917, aged 21 years. Buried **VILLERS-PLOUICH COMMUNAL CEMETERY.** Grave location:- Row A, Grave 18. ROH:- New Mill Working Men's Club; Fulstone War Memorial.

SIMS, MALLINSON. Private. No 51844. 12th Battalion The Royal Scots (Lothian Regiment). Formerly No 4320 Highland Light Infantry. Born Lockwood, Huddersfield. Married. Lived 6 Cable Street, St. Thomas's Road, Huddersfield. Employed as a finisher by Mr W. H. Murgatroyd. Killed in action, 25.4.1918. Buried **MESSINES RIDGE CEMETERY.** Grave location:- Plot 3, Row E, Grave 25. ROH:- St. Stephen's Church, Rashcliffe.

SINGLETON, CLARENCE. Private. No 306140. 2/7th Battalion Duke of Wellington's Regiment. Son of Mr and Mrs Joe Singleton, 55 Roydhouse, Linthwaite. Educated Linthwaite Church School. Employed at the Globe Worsted Company, Slaithwaite. Reported missing, presumed killed, at the Battle of Arras, 3.5.1917, aged 19 years. Has no known grave. Commemorated **ARRAS MEMORIAL TO THE MISSING.** ROH:- Linthwaite War Memorial; Huddersfield Drill Hall.

SINGLETON, FRED. Private. No 43740. 11th Battalion West Yorkshire Regiment. Formerly No 12066 Duke of Wellington's Regiment.

Born Holmfirth. Son of Mrs Singleton, 'Cart and Horses Inn', (better known as 'The Weathercock'). Employed, firstly, as a millhand and later worked on the railway at Dunford Bridge. Enlisted 1915. Killed in action, 4.10.1916, during the Battle of the Somme. Has no known grave. Commemorated **THIEPVAL MEMORIAL TO THE MISSING.** His mother received a letter from a chum of her son, Private Marsland, who wrote, *'You will known that Fred was killed about the 5th of this month. Fred and I were chums together all along. We were in the same Company in the 9th Battalion Duke of Wellington's Regiment and we were in the same hospital in England and we came out to France together. The shell that killed him dropped between him and me. We were taking rations to the front line. I could not write any sooner because we have been on the move. I know it will upset you very much, it hurts me to write such a letter but it has to be done.'* ROH:- Hade Edge War Memorial.

SINGLETON, FRED. Private. No 418515. 42nd Battalion Canadian Infantry (Quebec Regiment). Born Golcar. Son of William Singleton, 108 High Street, Scapegoat Hill, Golcar. Had served through the South African War in which he was taken prisoner by the Boers and interned. Subsequently he went out to Canada and in a letter home, dated 5.4.1915, he said, *'You will be surprised to learn that I am a soldier once more, having joined the Canadian Overseas Expeditionary force, and I expect to leave here for Europe with the next contingent.'* In his last letter, dated 16.3.1916, he said that, *'he was in the best of health and did not expect leave for a long time. He was glad that the winter was over but the Canadians had been well looked after as regards boots, underclothing, socks and tobacco. He did not think the war would last more than five months longer and it would certainly be over this year.'* Killed in action, 25.3.1916, during a heavy bombardment. He was 40 years of age. Buried **SANCTUARY WOOD CEMETERY, ZILLEBEKE, BELGIUM.** Grave Location:- Special Memorial.

SINGLETON, HARRY. Private. No 45028. 2nd Battalion York and Lancaster Regiment. Born Holmfirth. Son of Elizabeth and the late George Singleton. Educated Hade Edge Council School. Employed by Messrs J. Watkinson and Sons, Washpit Mills, Holmfirth. Married. Lived Flowery Field, Hade Edge. Reported missing on 22.3.1918. His wife received a postcard from him, dated 25.3.1918, which arrived in Holmfirth on 23.4.1918. He told her that he was a Prisoner of War in Germany and getting along satisfactorily after an operation to amputate his right arm. She had not to worry and that, *'I shall come home and we shall be re-united.'* At the beginning of July, 1918, she received an official communication to the effect that her husband had died of wounds in Germany on 20.4.1918. He was 29 years of age. Buried **COLOGNE SOUTHERN CEMETERY, GERMANY.** Grave location:- Plot 17, Row A, Grave 5. (Brother of the late Private **JOHN SINGLETON**, died of wounds, 30.6.1917, q.v.). ROH:- Cartworth War Memorial.

SINGLETON, JAMES. Private. No 11960. 8th Battalion Duke of Wellington's Regiment. Born Bradford. Married, with three children. Lived Back Union Street, Huddersfield. Employed as a french polisher by Mr Harry Roebuck of Moldgreen. Enlisted August 1914. Took part in the Dardenelles campaign and had served in Egypt. Killed in the attack on Hessian Trench and Stuff Redoubt on 30.9.1916 He was 28 years of age. Has no known grave. Commemorated **THIEPVAL MEMORIAL TO THE MISSING.**

SINGLETON, JOHN. Private. No 42441. 24th/27th (Tyneside Irish) Battalion Northumberland Fusiliers. Born Golcar. Son of Mr and Mrs B. Singleton, 352 Scar Lane, Golcar. Employed by Messrs T. W. Thorpe Limited, Heath House Mills, Golcar. Was a member of Golcar Conservative Club. Attended St. John's Parish Church, Golcar. Enlisted 6.6.1916. Embarked for France in November, 1916. Reported wounded and missing on 9.4.1917 and afterwards presumed to have been killed on that date, aged 30. Buried **ORCHARD DUMP CEMETERY.** Grave location:- Plot 8, Row K, Grave 36. ROH:- St. John's Church, Golcar; memorial in Golcar Churchyard.

SINGLETON, JOHN. Private. No 35755. 26th (Tyneside Irish) Battalion Northumberland Fusiliers. Son of Elizabeth and the late George Singleton, 'Arnden', 2 Wood Nook, Holmfirth. Educated Hade Edge Council School. Attended Hade Edge Wesleyan Sunday School. Employed as a spinner at Weshpit Mills, Holmfirth.

Seriously wounded in June, 1917. Admitted to No 14 General Hospital at Wimereux. His mother was given permission to visit him there, where she found him quite bright and cheerful. He was able to give her an account of how he was wounded. *He said a number of them were laid in a reserve trench waiting for daylight, he himself was asleep at the time when an enemy shell burst amongst them. Of the 20 lads who were there 10 were killed and five were wounded.* When Mrs Singleton returned home to Holmfirth she expected her son to be invalided home. But he died of his wounds on 30.6.1917, aged 31 years. Buried **WIMEREUX COMMUNAL CEMETERY.** Grave location:- Plot 2, Row N, Grave 8. (Brother of Private **HARRY SINGLETON,** who died as a Prisoner of War on 20.4.1918, q.v.). His mother received a letter, dated 29.6.1917, from the Matron of the hospital, who wrote, *'I regret very much to tell you the very sad news that your son, Private John Singleton, passed away last night. He had been gradually sinking and seemed quite happy. He spoke most affectionately of you. He will be buried here at Wimereux.'* ROH:- Cartworth War Memorial.

SINGLETON, JOHN HERBERT. Private. No 4872. 1/5th Battalion Duke of Wellington's Regiment. Born 21 Lowergate, Longwood, Huddersfield, 9.4.1889. Son of Henry and Mary Singleton, 21 Lowergate, Longwood. Educated Paddock Council School. Employed as a woollen piecer by Messrs C. and J. Hirst of Longwood. Single. Enlisted 14.2.1916. Killed in action by shellfire on 16.9.1916, aged 27 years. Has no known grave. Commemorated **THIEPVAL MEMORIAL TO THE MISSING.** ROH:- St. Mark's Parish Church, Longwood; Huddersfield Drill Hall.

SISWICK, BENJAMIN. Private. No 41547. 1/5th Battalion Northumberland Fusiliers. Born 27 Milford Street, Huddersfield 26.12.1880. Son of Joseph and Mercy Siswick, 5 Colne Road, Huddersfield. Educated Spring Grove Board School. Employed as shop assistant by Messrs George Mason and Son, King Street, Huddersfield. Lived 8a East Parade, Huddersfield. Single. Enlisted 8.4.1916. Killed in action near Estaires on 10.4.1918. Has no known grave. Commemorated **PLOEGSTEERT MEMORIAL TO THE MISSING.** ROH:- New North Road Baptist Church.

SISWICK, EVELYN. Private. No 202620. 2/5th Battalion King's Own Yorkshire Light Infantry. Born Cliff End, Longwood, Huddersfield. Married, with three children. Lived 100 High Street, Scapegoat Hill, Golcar. Employed by Messrs Hirst and Mallinson Limited, Longwood. Reported missing, presumed killed, at the Battle of Cambrai, 27.11.1917, aged 36 years. Has no known grave. Commemorated **CAMBRAI MEMORIAL TO THE MISSING.** ROH:- St. Mark's Parish Church, Longwood.

SKEEN, HARRY. Private. No 23257. 8th Battalion Duke of Wellington's Regiment. Born Fartown, Huddersfield, 23.3.1898. Educated Thomas Street Board School. Employed as a moulder. Single. Lived 38 Bradford Road, Huddersfield. Enlisted August 1916. Killed in action at Passchendaele on 27.8.1917. Has no known grave. Commemorated **TYNE COT MEMORIAL TO THE MISSING.** ROH:- St. James's Presbyterian Church; St. Andrew's Church, Leeds Road, Huddersfield.

SKINNER, WILLIAM TEDMAS. Private. No 52558. 'A' Company, 1st Battalion West Yorkshire Regiment. Born Dewsbury 2.9.1897. Son of Gertrude Skinner, 52 Marsden Road, Huddersfield and the late Walter Skinner. Educated St. Barnabas's School, Crosland Moor. Employed as a woollen piecer. Single. Reported missing 21.3.1918 and afterwards presumed to have been killed on that date, aged 19. Has no known grave. Commemorated **ARRAS MEMORIAL TO THE MISSING.** ROH:- Milnsbridge War Memorial.

SKIPSEY, HAROLD. Private. No 25364. 6th Battalion The King's Own (Royal Lancaster Regiment). Born Norman Road, Birkby 17.4.1890. Son of William and Helena Skipsey, 18 Trinity Street, Huddersfield. Educated Spring Grove Council School. Attended New North Road Baptist Church. Prior to enlistment, was a clothing salesman for Messrs Bradleys, clothiers, of Barrow. Lived Hanson Street, Barrow-in-Furness. Single. Enlisted 29.5.1916. Went to Mesopotamia in October, 1916. Wounded near Kut on 10.2.1917. Died of wounds 12.2.1917, aged 27. Has no known grave. Commemorated

BASRA MEMORIAL TO THE MISSING, IRAQ. ROH:- New North Road Baptist Church; Holy Trinity Church.

SLATER, JAMES ARTHUR. Lance Corporal. No 5805. 1st Battalion The King's Own (Royal Lancaster Regiment). Born Dewsbury 5.10.1879. Married, with four children. Lived 21 Victoria Street, Moldgreen, Huddersfield. Employed as a tramcar cleaner by the Huddersfield Corporation Tramways Department. Had served through the Boer War. Was called up on 4.8.1914 and embarked for France in November, 1914. Killed in action, 3.5.1915, aged 36 years. Buried **BAILLEUL COMMUNAL CEMETERY EXTENSION.** Grave location:- Plot 1, Row F, Grave 16. His last letter home was written at the end of April, 1915. After thanking them for a parcel he says, *'This is Friday, your birthday, so I wish you many happy returns of the day. I am hoping to be home for mine if I am lucky enough to get through. I and several more of my comrades had a very narrow escape this morning when the Germans were shelling this place. They dropped one through a house not five yards away from where we were but there was no one hurt, thank goodness. You say it seems a long time since you saw me, it seems a jolly sight longer to me but it is to be hoped it won't be much longer before we see each other again. We must hope for the best as it no use bothering, it only makes things worse. We must look at the bright side of things if there is a bright side to this war. Do not upset yourself about me, try and keep at your best and keep the children the same. Keep telling them that their Daddy will be coming home someday and bringing them something home as well. You keep on asking me if there is anything I want. Well there are plenty of things I want but I don't want to put you to any expense. I daresay I could write to plenty of places for different things but I don't want to humble myself to anyone. I keep managing with the things I get. I don't like to see things sent out here at the price they have to pay for sending them so don't bother about sending anything till I ask you. Don't think that I don't value anything you send but I don't want you to spend money on things for me.'* In the closing part of the letter he again asks his wife to keep bright and cheerful. ROH:- Moldgreen War Memorial; Christ Church, Moldgreen; Huddersfield Corporation.

SLEAFORD, JOHN PINION. Stoker 2nd Class. No K/39557 (PO). Royal Navy. *HMS Victory*. Son of Charles and Hephizibah Sleaford, of Walcot Fen, Billinghay, Lincoln: husband of Ellen Sleaford, of Clayton West, Huddersfield. Died of pneumonia, 7.2.1917, aged 26 years. Buried **St. OSWALD CHURCHYARD, WALCOT-NEAR-BILLINGHAY, LINCOLNSHIRE.** ROH:- Clayton West and High Hoyland War Memorial.

SMEETON, SAMUEL. Private. No 14579. 10th Battalion Duke of Wellington's Regiment. Born Marsh, Huddersfield. Married. Lived 36 Manchester Street, Huddersfield. Prior to enlisting, in November 1914, he was a barber. Killed by a sniper at Munster Alley during the Battle of the Somme on 29.7.1916. He was 36 years of age. Has no known grave. Commemorated **THIEPVAL MEMORIAL TO THE MISSING.**

SMITH, ABRAHAM. Driver. No 107720. 40th Brigade, Royal Field Artillery. Born Huddersfield. Son of Lot and Elizabeth Smith, Fields Head Farm, Upper Clough, Linthwaite. Was a member of the Linthwaite Wesleyan Young Men's Class. Enlisted in the army in 1916, after being refused entry into the Royal Navy. Embarked for France but was invalided home on account of ill health. Died at the Southern General Hospital, Oxford, on 18.2.1917, aged 19 years. Buried with full military honours at **LINTHWAITE WESLEYAN METHODIST BURIAL GROUND.** Grave location:- Grave No 538. ROH:- Linthwaite.

SMITH, ALBERT, MM. Sergeant. No 242567. 1/4th Battalion Duke of Wellington's Regiment. Born 5 Hey Lane, Lowerhouses, Huddersfield, 24.11.1889. Son of Mr and Mrs William Arthur Smith, 154 Alma Terrace, Lockwood, Huddersfield. Educated Lowerhouses National School. Employed as a tailor's presser by W. S. Thomas and Company, Market Street, Huddersfield. Single. Enlisted 16.2.1916. Awarded the Military Medal for *'bravery in the field'* on 13.9.1918. Twice wounded. Killed in action near Cambrai on 11.10.1918, aged 28 years. Buried **WELLINGTON CEMETERY.** Grave location:- Plot 1, Row G, Grave 1/10. ROH:- St. Stephen's Church, Rashcliffe; Lowerhouses War Memorial; Almondbury War Memorial.

SMITH, ALFRED RICHARD. Private. No 22184. 2nd Battalion Border Regiment. Formerly No 369058. 936th Area Employment Company (Artisan), Labour Corps. Born Hereford 25.9.1885. Educated Hillhouse Schools, Huddersfield. Was a widower, with one son. Lived with his sister, Mrs Phoebe Greenwood, 193 Marsden Road, Brierley Wood, Huddersfield. Enlisted 8.6.1915. Died of bronchial pneumonia following upon influenza, 29.11.1918, at No 56 General Hospital, Etaples, aged 33 years. Buried **ETAPLES MILITARY CEMETERY.** Grave location:- Plot 51, Row D, Grave 10. ROH:- Fartown and Birkby War Memorial.

SMITH, ARNOLD STOTT. Private. No 50970. 9th Battalion Cheshire Regiment. Born Mark Street, Paddock, 10.7.1895. Son of Lewis Stott and Susan Smith, 48a Lidget Street, Lindley, Huddersfield. Educated All Saints, Paddock, and Lindley Church of England School, Lindley. Employed by Messrs R. Dempster and Sons, Elland. Attended Zion Chapel, Lindley. Single. Enlisted 30.12.1916. Wounded near Bailleul on 23.9.1917. Died of wounds, 24.9.1917, aged 22, at No 53 Casualty Clearing Station. Buried **BAILLEUL COMMUNAL CEMETERY EXTENSION.** Grave location:- Plot 3, Row E, Grave 156. ROH:- St. Stephen's Church, Lindley; Lindley Zion Wesleyan Chapel.

SMITH, ARTHUR. Private. No 241293. 1/5th Battalion Duke of Wellington's Regiment. Son of George and Ellen Smith of Almondbury Bank, Moldgreen. Husband of Clarice Lois Smith, 89a Gledholt Bank, Huddersfield. Employed by Huddersfield Corporation. Reported missing, presumed killed, in the attack on the Schwaben Redoubt on 3.9.1916, aged 27 years. Buried **MILL ROAD CEMETERY.** Grave location:- Plot 1, Row F, Grave 9. ROH:- All Saints Church, Paddock; Huddersfield Drill Hall.

SMITH, ARTHUR LEWIS. Private. No 2464. 1/7th Battalion Duke of Wellington's Regiment. Lived Golcar. Brother of Mr F. K. Smith, 5 Wellhouse Fields, Golcar. Killed in action near Ypres, 8.12.1915, aged 20 years. Buried **BARD COTTAGE CEMETERY.** Grave location:- Plot 1, Row D, Grave 20. (Brother of Private **WILLIAM HENRY SMITH,** reported missing, presumed killed, 16.9.1917, q.v.). ROH:- St. John's Church, Golcar; Huddersfield Drill Hall.

SMITH, BEAUMONT. Private. No 32512. 9th Battalion West Yorkshire Regiment. Born Almondbury. Son of Joe and Emma Smith, 25 Railway Yard, Honley. Employed as a mason by Mr Allen Hirst. Single. Embarked for France at Whitsuntide 1916. Died of wounds at No 2 Stationary Hospital on 5.2.1917 age 36 years. Buried **ABBEVILLE COMMUNAL CEMETERY EXTENSION.** Grave location:- Plot 2, Row A, Grave 26. ROH:- Honley War Memorial.

SMITH, CHARLES. Gunner. No L/25437. 'C' Battery, 34th Brigade, Royal Field Artillery. Husband of Mary Smith, 94 Ravensknowle Road, Huddersfield. Died, 15.11.1918, aged 37 years. Buried **ETAPLES MILITARY CEMETERY.** Grave location:- Plot 50, Row B, Grave 3.

SMITH, DAN. Private. No 37557. 20th Battalion Durham Light Infantry. Born Linthwaite. Son of David and Harriet Smith, 61 Hoyle House Fold, Linthwaite. Husband of Jane Smith, 25 Causeway Side, Linthwaite Employed as a weaver by Messrs John Crowther and Sons, Milnsbridge. Was a member of the Linthwaite Cricket and Bowling Club. Enlisted 27.7.1916. Embarked for France 8.12.1916. Killed in action, 9.4.1917, aged 27 years. Buried **TIGRIS LANE CEMETERY, WANCOURT.** Grave location:- Plot 1, Row D, Grave 7. ROH:- Linthwaite War Memorial.

SMITH, DAVID. Private. No 43600. 15th/17th Battalion West Yorkshire Regiment (2nd Leeds Pals). Formerly No 28983 The Yorkshire Regiment. Born Linthwaite. Son of Mr and Mrs George Smith, 17 Roydhouse, Linthwaite. Employed as a feeder by Messrs Charles Lockwood and Sons, Blackrock Mills. Attended Linthwaite Church. Was a member of Hoyle Ing Working Men's Club. Enlisted March 1916. Embarked for France in July, 1916, after training at Rugeley Camp, Staffordshire. Killed in an attack on the German lines on 19.7.1918, aged 21 years. Has no known grave. Commemorated **PLOEGSTEERT MEMORIAL TO THE MISSING.** ROH:- Linthwaite War Memorial.

SMITH, EDGAR. Private. No 3/10301. 8th Battalion Duke of Wellington's Regiment. Born Huddersfield 19.5.1888. Son of Henry Smith, 46 Charles Street, Crosland Moor. Educated Holy Trinity Church of England School. Employed as a millhand. Enlisted at the outbreak of the war.

Wounded on one occasion and had also been invalided home suffering from fever. Killed in action during the Battle of Arras on 29.4.1917. Buried **HERMIES BRITISH CEMETERY.** Grave location:- Row A, Grave 14. (Brother of Private **GEORGE WILLIAM SMITH**, killed in action, 28.9.1915, q.v.). ROH:- St. Barnabas Church, Crosland Moor.

SMITH, EDWARD. Private. No 19870. 1st Battalion West Yorkshire Regiment. Born Underbank, Holmfirth. After leaving school was employed at the Post Office at Holmfirth. He then worked as a feeder at Albion Mills, Thongsbridge. Married, with one child. Lived Mount Pleasant, Thongsbridge. Enlisted May 1915. Underwent training at Harrogate and Stafford. Embarked for France 17.11.1915. Wounded on one occasion. Killed in action during an attack on Mild and Cloudy Trenches, near Le Transloy, during the Battle of the Somme on 12.10.1916. The Battalion War Diary records, *'assembly positions heavily bombarded by both British and German guns – 'D' Company advanced but under heavy machine gun fire immediately withdrew. Bombing attack on right by 'C' Company also failed. Relieved and to Trones Wood on the 13.10.1916'*. Has no known grave. Commemorated **THIEPVAL MEMORIAL TO THE MISSING.** ROH:- Netherthong and Thongsbridge War Memorial.

SMITH, ERNEST. Private. No 29167. 2/5th Battalion Duke of Wellington's Regiment. Born Huddersfield 28.8.1895. Youngest son of Mrs M. Smith, 16 Mellor's Buildings, Stoney Lane, Taylor Hill, Lockwood. Educated Lockwood Church of England Schools. Employed as a woollen piecer at Queen's Mill. Single. Wounded on one occasion. Killed in action, 17.4.1918, aged 22 years. Has no known grave. Commemorated **POZIERES MEMORIAL TO THE MISSING.** ROH:- Emmanuel Church, Lockwood; Huddersfield Drill Hall.

SMITH, FRANK. Private. No 879 Royal Army Medical Corp, attached 53rd Battery, 2nd Brigade, Royal Field Artillery. Born Lindley 17.10.1888. Son of Mr R. A. Smith, 63 West Street, Lindley. Husband of Hilda Smith, Weatherhill Road, Lindley. Educated Oakes Council School. Employed as a weaver by Messrs Smith and Calverley, Plover Mills, Lindley. Enlisted at the outbreak of the war. Had served in France for 18 months. Killed in action, 12.7.1916, aged 27 years. His wife received information from an Army Chaplain to the effect that, *'Private Smith was driving with the water carts to fetch the water several miles behind the front line when a long range shell burst near inflicting fatal injuries and wounding his comrade'*. Buried **POPERINGHE NEW MILITARY CEMETERY.** Grave location:- Plot 2, Row B, Grave 3. (Brother of Private **JOHN SMITH**, 9th Battalion Duke of Wellington's Regiment. Killed in action, 25.4.1917, q.v.). ROH:- St. Stephen's Church, Lindley; Lindley Zion Wesleyan Church.

SMITH, FRANK. Private. No 28810. 12th Battalion Northumberland Fusiliers. Born Lindley, Huddersfield. Son of William Smith of Lindley Moor, Lindley. Killed in action, 15.4.1917, aged 29 years. Buried **WARLINCOURT HALTE BRITISH CEMETERY.** Grave location:- Plot 7, Row H, Grave 11. ROH:- Blackley Baptist Chapel.

SMITH, FRANK. Pioneer. No 115171. No 3 Army Tramway Company, Royal Engineers. Born Workington. Married, with two children. Lived 27 Damside, Huddersfield. Employed by Messrs J. Wimpenny and Company, contractors, of Linthwaite. Killed in action, 10.12.1917, aged 43 years. Buried **ROISEL COMMUNAL CEMETERY EXTENSION.** Grave location:- Plot 3, Row B, Grave 4.

SMITH, FREDERICK ARTHUR. Corporal. No 3/2448. 10th Battalion King's Own Yorkshire Light Infantry. Born 41 York Street, Northgate, Huddersfield, 23.7.1873. Son of Jane and the late Thomas Smith, 41 York Street, Northgate, Huddersfield. Educated Thomas Street Board School. Employed as a moulder by Messrs W. C. Holmes and Company, of Turnbridge. Enlisted, 25.9.1914, after serving 16 years in the Northamptonshire Regiment. Served in the Tirah Campaign on the North West Frontier. Was in India for 12 years. Reported wounded and missing at the Battle of Loos on 27.9.1915 and afterwards presumed to have been killed on that date. Has no known grave. Commemorated **LOOS MEMORIAL TO THE MISSING.**

SMITH, FRED TINKER. Driver. No 202701. 'B' Battery, 102nd Brigade, Royal Field Artillery.

Formerly No R/19542 King's Royal Rifle Corps. Born Golcar. Son of Eli Smith, 1 Intake, Leymoor, Golcar. Educated Crow Lane Board School, Milnsbridge. Employed by Messrs C. and J. Hirst and Sons of Longwood. Attended Parkwood Methodist Church and was a member of the football team belonging to the Sunday School. Played cricket with the Leymoor United Cricket team. Died of wounds, 10.8.1917. Buried **AEROPLANE CEMETERY, YPRES.** Grave location:- Plot 3, Row C, Grave 15. ROH:- Golcar Baptist Church; St. John's Church, Golcar; Longwood War Memorial; Parkwood Methodist Church; Crow Lane Board School, Milnsbridge.

SMITH, FREDERICK ARTHUR. Corporal. No 3565. 'D' Company, 1/5th Battalion Duke of Wellington's Regiment. Born Greenwood Street, Primrose Hill, Huddersfield, 19.8.1896. Son of William and Martha Alice Smith, 22 Stoney Cross Street, Taylor Hill, Huddersfield. Educated Berry Brow Council School. Employed as a tailor's apprentice by Mr William Addy, tailor, of Lockwood. Enlisted, 2.12.1914, into the 2/5th Battalion. Six days after reaching Derby he was posted to the 1/5th Battalion at Doncaster. Embarked for France, 15.4.1915. He wrote home to his parents on the same day, *'Dear Mam and Dad, we arrived safe and sound and I am in the best of health. It is blazing hot and we are about 4 or 5 miles behind the firing line and expecting to be in tonight. We can hear the Jack Johnsons (shells) whistling and the machine guns crackling. Several aeroplanes have passed over us as we are sat in a field having our feet inspected. I don't know whether you will get this letter or not but I will keep up correspondence with you by field postcards. I can't tell you where we are but I am keeping a diary and if I come back I will show you it. Talk about nationalities:- Indian, Scotch, French, Belgium and us. It is quite nutty. Please send me some cigs and a little cake. I shall get them alright. Freddie. xxxxxx'* Died of wounds received on the Yser Canal near Ypres on 16.10.1915, aged 19 years. Buried **BARD COTTAGE CEMETERY.** Grave location:- Plot 1, Row B, Grave 30. ROH:- Emmanuel Church, Lockwood; St. Stephen's Church, Rashcliffe; Taylor Hill Primitive Methodist Church; Huddersfield Drill Hall.

SMITH, GEORGE WILLIAM. Private. No 5/1718. 1/5th Battalion Duke of Wellington's Regiment. Born Townend Row, Huddersfield, 18.3.1884. Son of Henry Smith, 46 Charles Street, Crosland Moor, Huddersfield. Educated Paddock Church of England School. Employed by the Huddersfield Corporation in the Electricity Department. Married, with two children. Had served in the Volunteers and the local Territorials for a period of 12 years. Enlisted at the outbreak of the war. Embarked for France in April, 1915. Killed by shellfire, 28.9.1915, aged 31 years. Buried **NEW IRISH FARM CEMETERY, St. JEAN-LES-YPRES.** Grave location:- Plot 2, Row B, Grave 19. (Brother of Private **EDGAR SMITH**, killed in action, 29.4.1917, q.v.). His wife received a letter from a comrade, Lance Corporal H. Foulkes, her husband's Section Commander, who wrote, *'He was killed almost instantly. I remained with him in the last moments and succoured him as a comrade should. You may take great consolation in the fact that his last thoughts and words were of his dear wife and little ones until God called to him. As his Section Commander I deeply regret the loss of your husband as he was a steady, reliable man whom everyone could get along with and I can assure you that the men both of the section and platoon will keenly feel the loss of such a good comrade. You may take consolation also in the fact that he died a soldier's death, facing the foe and bore himself splendidly throughout the great crisis.'* ROH:- St. Barnabas's Church, Crosland Moor; Huddersfield Drill Hall; Huddersfield Corporation Roll.

SMITH, HARRY. Private. No 260075. 1st Battalion South Wales Borderers Regiment. Born Shelley. Son of Mr Joe Smith, Bank End, Shelley. Married, with two children. Died of wounds, 19.10.1918, aged 29 years. Buried **VADENCOURT BRITISH CEMETERY.** Grave location:- Plot 2, Row C, Grave 8. (Brother of Private **NORMAN SMITH**, killed in action, 5.6.1917, q.v.). ROH:- Emmanuel Church, Shelley.

SMITH, HENRY. Private. No 38160. 15th Battalion Lancashire Fusiliers. Born Gainsborough, Lincolnshire, 26.2.1891. Husband of May Smith, 7 Dale Street, Chapel Hill, Huddersfield. Prior to enlistment, was manager of the Hebden Bridge branch of the Meadow Dairy Company and, previous to that, was in the Cross Church Street branch, Huddersfield. Was a member of St. Paul's Church choir. Enlisted 9.11.1916. Killed in action,

13.8.1917, aged 28 years. Buried **COXYDE MILITARY CEMETERY.** Grave location:- Plot 2, Row H, Grave 11.

SMITH, HERBERT. Private. No 20037. 1st Battalion King's Own Scottish Borderers. Born Huddersfield. Married, with three children. Lived Dobroyd, Shepley. Employed as a miner by Messrs Stringer and Jagger, Emley Moor Colliery. Reported missing, presumed killed, on the first day of the Battle of the Somme, 1.7.1916. Buried **ANCRE BRITISH CEMETERY, BEAUMONT HAMEL.** Grave location:- Plot 8, Row D, Grave 4. ROH:- Shepley War Memorial.

SMITH, HERBERT E. Private. No 31449. 10th Battalion Duke of Wellington's Regiment. Born Sheepridge, Huddersfield. Second son of Mrs Smith, 30 Fenay Row, Sheepridge. Employed by Messrs J. Hopkinson and Company Limited, Birkby. Killed in action, 20.9.1917, during the Battle of Passchendaele. He was 27 years of age. Has no known grave. Commemorated **TYNE COT MEMORIAL TO THE MISSING.** ROH:- Christ Church, Woodhouse Hill.

SMITH, JOHN. Private. No 50842. 10th Battalion Cheshire Regiment. Born 17 Islington Street, Altrincham, Cheshire, 3.7.1896. Educated St. John's School, Altrincham. Lived with his aunt, Mrs Alice Epplestone, 59 Kirkgate, Huddersfield. Single. Employed as an iron dresser. Enlisted February 1917. Killed in action near Ypres on 1.8.1917. Has no known grave. Commemorated **MENIN GATE MEMORIAL TO THE MISSING.** ROH:- Huddersfield Parish Church.

SMITH, JOHN. Private. No 20430. 9th Battalion Duke of Wellington's Regiment. Born Lindley 27.3.1897. Son of Richard Arthur and Alice Smith, 63 West Street, Lindley, Huddersfield. Employed as a cobbler. Single. Enlisted in 1916. Killed in action near Monchy-le-Preux on 25.4.1917, aged 20 years. Has no known grave. Commemorated **ARRAS MEMORIAL TO THE MISSING.** (Brother of Private **FRANK SMITH**, Royal Army Medical Corps, killed in action, 12.7.1916, q.v.). ROH:- Lindley Baptist Church; Lindley Zion Methodist Church.

SMITH, JOHN BENSON. Private. No 6768. 1/5th Battalion Duke of Wellington's Regiment. Born Bradford. Son of Benson and Polly Smith, 39 Dyson Street, Moldgreen, Huddersfield. Employed as an assistant in the shop of Mr Thomas Mellor, Market Walk, Huddersfield. Enlisted at the outbreak of the war. Embarked for France in 1916. Died of wounds, 21.9.1916, aged 20 years. Buried **PUCHEVILLERS BRITISH CEMETERY.** Grave location:- Plot 4, Row D, Grave 22. ROH:- Christ Church, Moldgreen; Huddersfield Drill Hall; Commemorated on headstone in Kirkheaton Cemetery.

SMITH, JOHN EDWARD, MM. Driver. No 120853. 'B' Battery, 95th Brigade, Royal Field Artillery. Born 21 Sheepridge Road, Huddersfield 24.11.1895. Son of Joe and Mary Ellen Smith, 33 Netheroyd Hill Road, Huddersfield. Educated Woodhouse National Schools, Sheepridge. Employed as a ragshaker by Messrs Charles Lockwood and Sons of Blackrock Mills, Linthwaite. Was a member of the Woodhouse Church choir and of the Young Men's Bible Class. Single. Enlisted 1.11.1915. Was the first Netheroyd Hill soldier to be awarded the Military Medal, which was gazetted on 2.4.1917, for '*distinguished service in the field*'. Died of wounds, 23.9.1917, aged 21 years. Has no known grave. Commemorated **TYNE COT MEMORIAL TO THE MISSING.** ROH:- St. Hilda's Church, Cowcliffe; Christ Church, Woodhouse Hill; Fartown and Birkby War Memorial.

SMITH, LEONARD. Private. No 242693. 1/5th Battalion King's Own Yorkshire Light Infantry. Formerly No 3509 Duke of Wellington's Regiment. Lived Purhill Clough, Marsden. Employed as a finisher at Bank Bottom Mills, Marsden. Enlisted at the age of 17 years in 1915. Embarked for France, 17.7.1916. Was wounded in the left leg by gunshot on 15.11.1916. After treatment at a base hospital for several weeks he returned to the front line at the beginning of March, 1917. Killed in action through the firing of an enemy trench mortar on 18.3.1917. Buried **RUE-du-BACQUEROT No 1 MILITARY CEMETERY.** Grave location:- Plot 3, Row A, Grave 3. His parents received a letter from a Corporal in the R.A.M.C. attached to their son's battalion who wrote the following, '*I hope you will pardon my writing to you but although I am a total stranger I would just like to tell you how sorry I am about poor Len. He and I had recently become chums and although we had known each other for many months we never became the pals we were until recently. We had planned many excursions* *during our time out of the trenches but alas it cannot be. We used to pretend to a great many of the chaps that we were brothers and we became known to each other as 'our kid'! I need not tell you what I felt when I received the news. I immediately went to see him but it was too late as he had been prepared for burial. He was well liked here and was one of the best chaps it has been my priviledge to know.'* ROH:- Marsden War Memorial.

SMITH, LEWIS. Guardsman. No 12247. 2nd Battalion Irish Guards. Born Kirkheaton, Huddersfield. Enlisted Huddersfield. Son of Reuben and Sarah Ann Smith, Heaton Lodge Road, Colne Bridge, Bradley, Huddersfield. Killed in action, 14.4.1918. He was 25 years of age. Has no known grave. Commemorated **PLOEGSTEERT MEMORIAL TO THE MISSING.** ROH:- St. Thomas's Church, Bradley.

SMITH, NORMAN. Private. No 46115. 22nd (Tyneside Scottish) Battalion Northumberland Fusiliers. Born Shelley, Huddersfield. Son of Joe and Charlotte Smith, Bank End, Shelley. Killed in action, 5.6.1917, aged 22 years. Has no known grave. Commemorated **ARRAS MEMORIAL TO THE MISSING.** ROH:- Emmanuel Church, Shelley.

SMITH, O. G. Private. No TR/3/44632. 74th Training Reserve Battalion. Died at home, 17.3.1917. Buried **SLAITHWAITE CEMETERY.** Grave location:- D, 2, 22.

SMITH. ROBERT H. Private. No 33059. 10th Battalion York and Lancaster Regiment. Born Huddersfield. Killed in action, 1.7.1917. Buried **SOMER FARM CEMETERY, WYTSCHAETE, BELGIUM.** Grave location:- Plot B, Grave 34. ROH:- All Saints Church, Paddock.

SMITH, SIDNEY REGINALD VICTOR. Lance Bombardier. No 805909. H.Q. 296th Brigade, Royal Field Artillery. Born Stoke-on-Trent. Son of Sidney and Catherine E. Smith, 15 Lindley Street, Longwood, Huddersfield. Killed in action, 25.3.1918, aged 22 years. Buried **GOMMECOURT WOOD NEW CEMETERY.** Grave location:- Plot 1, Row K, Grave 3.

SMITH, TOM. Lance Corporal. No 201862. 4th Battalion Seaforth Highlanders. Born Linthwaite. Son of Mr and Mrs Allen Smith, Rodney Place, Royds Avenue, Linthwaite. Was a playing member of the Linthwaite Cricket Club. Attended the Wesleyan Sunday School. Killed in action during the Battle of Passchendaele on 20.9.1917. Has no known grave. Commemorated **TYNE COT MEMORIAL TO THE MISSING.** ROH:- Linthwaite War Memorial.

SMITH, WILFRED. Private. No 300136. 1/6th Battalion Duke of Wellington's Regiment. Married, with 3 children. Lived 15 Church Street, Golcar. Employed as a weaver by Messrs Joseph Hoyle and Sons, Prospect Mills, Longwood. Was a member of the Golcar Socalist Club. Attended Parkwood United Methodist Church. Enlisted September 1916. After three months training embarked for France on New Years Day, 1917. Came home on leave at the beginning of 1918. Died of wounds, 18.3.1918, aged 39. Buried **POLYGON WOOD CEMETERY.** Grave location:- Row H, Grave 12. His wife received a letter from his Captain, who wrote, *'that about 3.15pm on the 18th inst. Private Smith was severely wounded and died shortly afterwards. He was quite conscious all the time and spoke continually of you and the kiddies. All the Company join in expressing their deep sympathy with you. Words cannot describe your husband's courage after he was wounded.'* ROH:- Parkwood Methodist Church.

SMITH, WILFRED GARFIELD. Private. No 267895. 'C' Company, 1/6th Battalion Duke of Wellington's Regiment. Born Shepley. Son of Arthur and Hannah Smith, 'Holly View', Shepley. Killed in action, 14.4.1918, aged 28 years. Has no known grave. Commemorated **TYNE COT MEMORIAL TO THE MISSING.** ROH:- Shepley War Memorial.

SMITH, WILLIAM. Private. No 242019. 2/7th Battalion Duke of Wellington's Regiment. Born Lindley 25.12.1894. Son of Herbert and Hannah Smith, 23 Lockwood Scar, Lockwood, Huddersfield. Educated at Lindley and Lockwood Church Schools. Employed as a cloth finisher by the Longwood Finishing Company. Attended Lockwood Church Sunday School. Single. Killed in action, 25.3.1918, aged 23 years. Has no known grave. Commemorated **ARRAS MEMORIAL TO THE MISSING.** ROH:- Emmanuel Church, Lockwood; Huddersfield Drill Hall.

SMITH, WILLIAM. Private. No 24985. 2nd Battalion Duke of Wellington's Regiment. Born Huddersfield. Only son of Mrs N. Smith, 38 Northumberland Street, Huddersfield. Employed as a mule minder by Mr John Fenton of Bradley Mills. Attended Queen Street Mission. Reported missing, presumed killed, at the Battle of Arras on 3.5.1917, aged 23 years. Has no known grave. Commemorated **ARRAS MEMORIAL TO THE MISSING.**

SMITH, WILLIAM HENRY. Private. No 268347. 2/6th Battalion Duke of Wellington's Regiment. Born Bradford. Married, with one child. Lived 5 Wellhouse Fields, Golcar. Employed as a weaver by Messrs John Crowther and Sons, Milnsbridge. Was secretary to the Wellhouse branch of the Sons of Temperance. Enlisted 18.10.1916. Embarked for France in February, 1917. Reported missing, presumed killed, 16.9.1917, aged 39 years. Has no known grave. Commemorated **ARRAS MEMORIAL TO THE MISSING.** (Brother of Private **ARTHUR LEWIS SMITH**, killed in action, 8.12.1915, q.v.). ROH:- St. John's Church, Golcar.

SMITH, WILLIAM PICTON. Private. No 49788. 5th Battalion The King's (Liverpool Regiment). Formerly No 30153 Duke of Wellington's Regiment. Born Manchester 14.11.1883. Educated Thomas Street Board School. Married, with two children. Lived 14 Keat Street, Crosland Moor. Employed as a bookkeeper by Messrs C. H. Pickles Limited. Enlisted in March, 1917, along with Rifleman Ulrich (q.v.) and was killed on the same day - at St. Julien, on 20.9.1917, during the Battle of Passchendaele. Has no known grave. Commemorated **TYNE COT MEMORIAL TO THE MISSING.** ROH:- St. Barnabas Church, Crosland Moor.

SMITH, WILLIAM THOMAS SIDNEY. Lance Corporal. No 14295. 8th Battalion Duke of Wellington's Regiment. Born Chelsea, London. Lived Hepworth, Holmfirth. Killed in action at the Dardenelles on 21.8.1915, aged 22. Has no known grave. Commemorated **HELLES MEMORIAL TO THE MISSING.** ROH:- Hepworth and Scholes War Memorial; Hepworth Church.

SMITHIES, ALBERT. Private. No 242602. 1/4th Battalion King's Own Yorkshire Light Infantry. Lived Round Ings, Outlane. Employed by Messrs Edward Sykes and Sons, Gosport Mills, Outlane. Killed in action, 14.4.1918. Has no known grave. Commemorated **TYNE COT MEMORIAL TO THE MISSING.** ROH:- Outlane Trinity Methodist Chapel; Pole Moor Baptist Church.

SMITHIES, JOE HENRY. Private. No 42657. 7th Battalion The Yorkshire Regiment. Formerly No 29/735 Northumberland Fusiliers. Born Huddersfield. Lived Huddersfield. Died 23.1.1917. Buried **RAILWAY DUGOUTS BURIAL GROUND (TRANSPORT FARM).** Grave location:- Plot 7, Row F, Grave 9. ROH:- Pole Moor Baptist Church.

SMYTHE, DENIS. Lance Corporal. No 8135. 'B' Company, 6th Battalion Royal Dublin Fusiliers. Born Dublin. Son of Peter and M. A. Smythe, 7 Spring Street, Huddersfield. Died of meningitis in Salonika on 2.9.1916, aged 21 years. Buried **SALONIKA (LEMBET ROAD) MILITARY CEMETERY.** Grave Location:- No 343.

SNEE, JOHN. Private. No 8101. 6th Battalion Lincolnshire Regiment. Born Spivey's Yard, Castlegate, Huddersfield in December, 1885. Educated St. Patrick's Roman Catholic School, Huddersfield. Employed as a millhand. Single. Enlisted 2.8.1907. Killed in action, 25.4.1918. Buried **PHILOSOPHE BRITISH CEMETERY.** Grave location:- Plot 3, Row C, Grave 42.

SNOWDEN, CLARENCE. Private. No 39245. 5th Battalion King's Own Yorkshire Light Infantry. Born Scarborough. Son of Jacob and Margaret Snowden, 23 Albert Street, Lockwood, Huddersfield. Killed in action, 20.7.1918, aged 19 years. Buried **COURMAS BRITISH CEMETERY.** Grave location:- Plot 1, Row C, Grave 7. ROH:- Emmanuel Church, Lockwood.

SOWDEN, HERBERT. Private. No 36823. 12th Battalion Durham Light Infantry. Son of Mrs Sowden, 81 Dewhurst Road, Fartown, Huddersfield. Employed by Mr T. H. Rayner, Whitesmith. Killed in action, 20.10.1917, during the Battle of Passchendaele. He was 19 years of age. Has no known grave. Commemorated **TYNE COT MEMORIAL TO THE MISSING.** ROH:- Christ Church, Woodhouse Hill; Fartown and Birkby War Memorial.

SOWDEN, LEONARD. Rifleman. No 43647. 16th Battalion County of London Regiment, attached to the King's Royal Rifle Corps. Formerly No 31498 Duke of Wellington's Regiment. Born Milnsbridge. Son of Mr and Mrs Arthur Sowden, 10 High Street, Scapegoat Hill, Golcar. Employed by Messrs Joseph Hoyle and Sons, Prospect Mills, Longwood. Attended Scapegoat Hill Baptist Chapel. Killed in action, 24.8.1918. Has no known grave. Commemorated **VIS-en-ARTOIS MEMORIAL TO THE MISSING.** ROH:- St. John's Church, Golcar.

SPEIGHT, GEORGE HENRY. Private. No 202556. 1/4th Battalion King's Own Yorkshire Light Infantry. Born Rainton Gate, near Houghton-le-Springs, Durham, 4.9.1888. Son of James Henry and Elizabeth Speight, 3 Brookes Yard, Thomas Street, Northgate, Huddersfield. Educated Park Road School, Barnsley. Husband of Mary Emma Speight, 1 Brookes Yard, Thomas Street, Northgate, Huddersfield. Employed as a warehouseman by Messrs Moore Brothers, wool merchants, Dundas Street, Huddersfield. Enlisted August 1916. Died of wounds at No 3 General Hospital, Le Treport, on 28.7.1917, aged 34 years. Buried **MONT HUON MILITARY CEMETERY.** Grave location:- Plot 2, Row J, Grave 14a.

SPEIGHT, WILLIE. Private. No 18163. 13th Battalion Royal Welsh Fusiliers. Born Dewsbury. Son of Walter and Clara Speight, 18 High Street, Hanging Heaton, Batley, Yorkshire. Was employed as an assistant master at Huddersfield School of Art, connected to Huddersfield Technical College. He came to Huddersfield in 1910 from the Batley Technical School, where he rose from student to Assistant Art Master. He was killed by a shell whilst standing at the entrance to the Regimental Aid post, where he was a stretcher-bearer, on 6.7.1916. He was 30 years of age. Has no known grave. Commemorated **THIEPVAL MEMORIAL TO THE MISSING.** ROH:- Huddersfield Corporation Roll.

SPENCE, FREDERICK. Private. No 2571. 1/5th Battalion Duke of Wellington's Regiment. Born 4.10.1888. Son of Mr and Mrs Frederick Spence, 54 Long Lane, Grove Place, Dalton, Huddersfield. Educated St. Thomas's Church of England School, Longroyd Bridge. Employed as a postman at Huddersfield General Post Office. Single. Enlisted 8.8.1914. Killed in action, 19.9.1916, aged 28. Has no known grave. Commemorated **THIEPVAL MEMORIAL TO THE MISSING.** (Brother of Private **NORMAN SPENCE**, killed in action, 9.9.1915, q.v.). ROH:- St. Thomas's Church, Longroyd Bridge; Huddersfield General Post Office; Christ Church, Moldgreen; Huddersfield Drill Hall.

SPENCE, NORMAN. Private. No 2271. 'D' Company, 1/5th Battalion Duke of Wellington's Regiment. Born 17.12.1897. Son of Mr and Mrs Frederick Spence, 54 Long Lane, Grove Place, Dalton, Huddersfield. Educated St. Thomas's Church of England School, Longroyd Bridge, Huddersfield. Single. Enlisted at the outbreak of the war. Killed within five minutes of the return of the Battalion to the trenches on 9.9.1915. He was shot through the body and died almost immediately, aged 18 years. Buried **BARD COTTAGE CEMETERY, BOESINGHE.** Grave location:- Plot 1, Row H, Grave 26. (Brother of Private **FREDERICK SPENCE**, killed in action. 19.9.1916, q.v.). ROH:- Christ Church, Moldgreen; St. Thomas's Church, Longroyd Bridge; Huddersfield Drill Hall. Holmfirth Express of Saturday, 30.9.1916, – *HUDDERSFIELD LADY'S DOUBLE BEREAVEMENT.* 'A pathetic coincidence in war tragedies came to light on Wednesday at Blackpool. A few days ago Mrs Spence of Mount Green, Huddersfield arrived for the benefit of her health and stayed at the company house of Mrs Larroway, Central Drive, Blackpool. A year ago her youngest son, Norman Spence was killed in action while Mrs Spence was at Blackpool and she was still suffering from the effects of the shock when she reached the resort recently. Another son, Fred, who for some considerable time had been a despatch rider on the Western Front, wrote home last Friday that he had gone for recuperation to a rest-camp and was feeling the need of a short time there but he promised to write to her at Blackpool in a few days. This was last Friday but the expected letter failed to arrive and Mrs Spence became very uneasy. The landlady described to a newspaper representative the unexpected visit of Mrs Spence's daughter from Huddersfield at the house. It was immediately apparent that something was the matter and though her daughter did her best to soften the blow by saying that her brother Fred* had only been wounded the mother's intuition that he had been killed proved correct. The anniversary of the death of her first son who was only 18 years old was within three days of the second son's death. Fred who was known in Huddersfield as Ted had been four years in the Territorials and would have attained his 29th birthday in a week or two.'

SPENCER, EDWIN. Private. No 13445. 'Y Company, 8th Battalion Duke of Wellington's Regiment. Born Leeds. Son of the late Thomas Fisher Spencer and Sarah Agnes Spencer, of Wilshaw near Meltham. Employed at the bobbin mill of Messrs Jonas Brooke and Brothers, Meltham Mills. Enlisted at the end of August, 1914. Went to the Dardenelles as part of the 32nd Brigade, 11th Division, Mediterrean Expeditionary Force. Died of wounds at sea, sustained in the Dardenelles fighting, on 23.8.1915, aged 22 years. Has no known grave. Commemorated **HELLES MEMORIAL TO THE MISSING**. ROH:- Wilshaw Church; St. Bartholomew's Church, Meltham.

SPENCER, FRED. Private. No 32432. 2nd Battalion South Staffordshire Regiment. Born Moldgreen, Huddersfield. Son of Rachel Spencer, 78 Kilner Bank, Moldgreen, Huddersfield. Employed by Messrs Taylor and Lodge. Attended Moldgreen United Methodist Sunday School. Died of wounds, 6.2.1918, aged 19 years. Buried **ROCQUIGNY-EQUANCOURT ROAD BRITISH CEMETERY**. Grave location:- Plot 10, Row A, Grave 1. ROH:- St. Andrew's Church, Moldgreen; Christ Church, Moldgreen.

SPENCER, JAMES. Lance Corporal. No 23/340. 3rd Battalion Durham Light Infantry. Born Little Carr Green, Dalton, Huddersfield, 31.8.1889. Son of Mr and Mrs William Spencer, 6 Hampshire Street, High Royd, Moldgreen. Employed as a tuner by Messrs Godfrey Sykes and Sons of Moldgreen. Played cricket for the Dalton Cricket Club. Single. Enlisted 9.6.1916. Died of pneumonia on 11.12.1916 at Mill Dam Hospital, South Shields, aged 27. Buried **ALMONDBURY CEMETERY**. Grave location:- 2, 'C', 74. ROH:- Moldgreen; Christ Church, Moldgreen.

SPENCER, WILLIE. Lance Corporal. No 38896. 2/4th Battalion Royal Berkshire Regiment. Formerly No 5/107116 Territorial Reserve Battalion. Born 18 South Street, Huddersfield, 30.1.1899. Son of Joseph Starkey Spencer and Ann Spencer, 176 Wakefield Road, Dalton, Huddersfield. Educated Moldgreen Council School. Employed as an apprentice pattern maker at the ironworks of Mr H. Vickerman, of Moldgreen. Single. Enlisted 2.4.1917. Wounded and taken prisoner at Avesnes on 21.3.1918. Died of wounds as a Prisoner of War on 6.4.1918, aged 19 years. Buried **AVESNES-sur-HELPE COMMUNAL CEMETERY**. Grave location:- Row C, Grave 17. ROH:-. St. Paul's Methodist Church, Dalton; Holy Trinity Church, Huddersfield.

SPIVEY, ERNEST EDWIN. Private. No 036234. Depot Battalion Army Ordnance Corps. Formerly 1/5th Battalion Duke of Wellington's Regiment. Born Fleming House Lane, Dalton, Huddersfield, 20.6.1893. Son of Mrs M. N. Spivey, 484 Wakefield Road, Dalton. Educated Moldgreen Council School. Husband of Emilie Spivey, of Lascelles Hall, Kirkheaton. Employed as a plush weaver by Messrs Dyson, Hall and Company Limited, Greenside Mills. Enlisted 4.8.1914. Wounded three times and gassed twice. Died suddenly following an operation at the Royal Herbert Hospital, Woolwich, London, on 31.12.1918. Buried **KIRKHEATON CEMETERY, HUDDERSFIELD**. Grave location:- 'C', 2061. (Brother of Private **HERBERT HENRY SPIVEY**, killed in action at Gallipoli, 19.8.1915, q.v.). ROH:- St. John's Church, Kirkheaton.

SPIVEY, FRANK, MM and Bar. Sergeant. No 268050. 2/5th Battalion Duke of Wellington's Regiment. Born Kirkburton. Fourth son of the late Mr G. H. and Mrs Spivey, Bath Buildings, Kirkburton. Employed by Messrs Singleton and Company, Brookfield Mills, Kirkburton. Awarded the Military Medal for leading his platoon against the enemy in an attack. On the day of his death he was awarded a bar to the medal for great personal gallantry and good leadership during operations, when his platoon was held up by an enemy nest of machine guns. Died of wounds, 15.9.1918, aged 27 years. Buried **RUYAULCOURT MILITARY CEMETERY**. Grave location:- Row J, Grave 7. ROH:- All Hallows Parish Church, Kirkburton; Huddersfield Drill Hall.

SPIVEY, HERBERT HENRY. Private. No 4405. 8th Battalion Northumberland Fusiliers. Born Fleming House Lane, Dalton, Huddersfield, 16.12.1888. Son of Mrs M. N. Spivey, 484 Wakefield Road, Dalton. Educated Moldgreen Council School. Employed as a finisher by Messrs Dyson, Hall and Company, Greenside Mills, Dalton. Enlisted 4.8.1914. Killed in action near Dead Man's House, Suvla, Gallipoli, on 19.8.1915. Has no known grave. Commemorated **HELLES MEMORIAL TO THE MISSING.** (Brother of Private **ERNEST EDWIN SPIVEY**, died, 31.12.1918, q.v.). ROH:- St. John's Church, Kirkheaton.

SPIVEY, PERCY. Driver. No L/28164. 'D' Battery, 89th Brigade, Royal Field Artillery. Lived Huddersfield. Killed in action, 4.1.1918. Buried **ROCQUIGNY-EQUANCOURT ROAD BRITISH CEMETERY.** Grave location:- Plot 9, Row D, Grave 7. (Brother of Private **WALTER SPIVEY**, killed in action, 31.7.1918, and half brother of Private **LAWRENCE POLLARD**, died of wounds, 27.8.1918, q.v.). ROH:- St. Andrew's Church, Leeds Road, Huddersfield.

SPIVEY, WALTER. Private. No 63851. 2/5th Battalion West Yorkshire Regiment. Born Huddersfield. Killed in action near Rheims, 31.7.1918. Has no known grave. Commemorated **SOISSONS MEMORIAL TO THE MISSING.** (Brother of Private **PERCY SPIVEY**, killed in action, 4.1.1918, and half brother of Private **LAWRENCE POLLARD**, died of wounds, 27.8.1918, q.v.).

SPIVEY, WILLIAM HENRY. Private. No 3/9836. 2nd Battalion Duke of Wellington's Regiment. Born Union Street, Huddersfield, 1.6.1895. Son of Mr and Mrs W. H. Spivey, 21 Bradford Road North, Huddersfield. Educated Thomas Street Council School. Employed as a painter. Single. Enlisted 8.8.1914. Died from gas poisoning at Hill 60 on 5.5.1915, aged 19 years. Has no known grave. Commemorated **MENIN GATE MEMORIAL TO THE MISSING.** His last letter home was written on 2.5.1915, in which he wrote, *'We are having a rather hot time, what with gas, loss of sleep etc. We are not in any fixed place, having to keep shifting anywhere where they think an attack will be attempted but of course it will calm down when the Germans find they have lost their positions. The papers at home say they are starving but I don't believe it, I know different. We captured some as fat as pigs, a very determined lot they were.'* Referring to Ypres he said it was *'badly battered in November,'* when they were there, *'but now it is an absolute ruin and all the people have left. They had returned and were carrying on business almost as usual when the second bombardment occurred. When the top part of the Cloth Hall fell in the people made for the cellars and got away if they could. Next day escape was impossible as the roads were all commanded by the German artillery.'* ROH:- Fitzwilliam Street United Methodist Church; Fartown and Birkby War Memorial.

SPIVEY, WILLIE. Private. No 204599. 1/4th Battalion Duke of Wellington's Regiment. Son of Henry K. and Emily Spivey of Lepton. Employed by his father, contractor, of Lepton. Enlisted April 1916. Wounded on one occasion. Died in No 39 Stationary Hospital from gunshot wounds on 12.4.1918, aged 36. Buried **AIRE COMMUNAL CEMETERY.** Grave location:- Plot 2, Row B, Grave 10. ROH:- Lepton Parish Church.

STAFFORD, J. Aircraftsman 1st Class. No 103224. Royal Air Force. Son of Jim and Jane Stafford, Moor View, Cockley Hill, Kirkheaton. Died at home, 19.2.1920, aged 21 years. Buried **KIRKHEATON CEMETERY.** Grave location:- 'C', 459.

STAINTON, WILLIAM. Corporal. No 301394. 13th Battalion, Heavy Branch, The Machine Gun Corps. Formerly No 12605 Duke of Wellington's Regiment. Born Huddersfield 4.2.1894. Son of Joe and Nellie Stainton, 12 William Street South, Huddersfield. Educated at Huddersfield schools. Employed as a tailor's presser. Single. Enlisted August 1914. Died of wounds (gas) on 26.4.1918 at No 41 Stationary Hospital. He was 25 years of age. Buried **LIJSSENTHOEK MILITARY CEMETERY.** Grave location:- Plot 27, Row H, Grave 10. ROH:- St. Andrew's Church, Leeds Road, Huddersfield.

STAMPER, JOHN. Private. No 40841. 23rd (Tyneside Scottish) Battalion Northumberland Fusiliers. Born Oldtown, Hebden Bridge, Halifax, 25.2.1896. Son of Thomas and Fanny Stamper, 3 Colne Street, Paddock. Educated at Rochdale schools. Employed as a labourer to the electricians at the works of Messrs David

Brown and Sons, Lockwood. Single. Enlisted 4.5.1916. Reported missing near Armentieres on 11.2.1917 and afterwards presumed to have been killed on that date, aged 20. Has no known grave. Commemorated **PLOEGSTEERT MEMORIAL TO THE MISSING.** ROH:- All Saints Church, Paddock.

STANCLIFFE, OLIVER. Private. No 23967. 10th Battalion Duke of Wellington's Regiment. Born 1.12.1897. Son of Charles Frederick and M. E. Stancliffe, 48 Grove Street, Huddersfield. Educated Spring Grove Council School. Employed in the warehouse of Messrs F. Eastwood and Company, Colne Road, Huddersfield. Attended South Street Primitive Methodist Chapel. Single. Enlisted in the local Territorials in February, 1914. Embarked for France in October, 1916. Killed in action near Ypres, 5.1.1917, aged 19 years. Buried **MENIN ROAD SOUTH MILITARY CEMETERY.** Grave location:- Plot 1, Row Q, Grave 9. ROH:- South Street Primitive Methodist Chapel; St. Thomas's Church, Longroyd Bridge.

STANDISH, ALFRED, MM and Bar. Lance Corporal. No 300077. 2/5th Battalion Duke of Wellington's Regiment. Born Milnsbridge. Adopted son of Mrs C. Crawshaw, 35 School Street, Moldgreen. Employed as a tailor by Mr W. Moorhouse, Ramsden Street, Huddersfield. Enlisted September 1914. Embarked for France in April, 1915. Mentioned in despatches in May 1917. Awarded the Military Medal for '*great courage and devotion to duty on November 20 and 21st, 1917*'. He acted as runner and was on duty continuously for two days and a night carrying messages under heavy machine gun fire. Awarded a Bar to his Military Medal on 13.3.1918. Reported missing, presumed killed, 29.3.1918, aged 24 years. Has no known grave. Commemorated **ARRAS MEMORIAL TO THE MISSING.** ROH:- St. Paul's Methodist Church, Dalton; Huddersfield Drill Hall.

STANLEY, ADA. Staff Nurse. Territorial Nursing Service. Born Moss, near Doncaster, 8.12.1871. Daughter of William and Harriet Stanley. Trained as a nurse at Huddersfield Royal Infirmary. At the time of enlistment, was living in Manchester. Enlisted in January, 1915, at the 3rd Northern General Hospital, Sheffield. Left for the Dardenelles in July, 1915, on a hospital ship. Contracted dysentery on board the hospital ship, *Mauretania*, on a return trip to England but she refused to leave her post until every sick soldier was conveyed ashore. She then collapsed and died on 22.12.1915 at the Royal Victoria Hospital, Netley, aged 46. Buried **St. PAUL'S CHURCHYARD, ARMITAGE BRIDGE, HUDDERSFIELD.** Grave location:- in North-West part.

STANLEY, THOMAS. Private. No 129768. Royal Army Medical Corps. Born Huddersfield. Son of Thomas and Charine Stanley, Castlegate, Huddersfield. Lived 24 Dock Street, Huddersfield. Died in hospital at Blackpool on 28.6.1918, aged 44 years. Buried **EDGERTON CEMETERY, HUDDERSFIELD.** Grave location:- 17, RC, 3.

STANSFIELD, WILLIE. Private. No 46637. 11th Battalion Northumberland Fusiliers. Born Milnsbridge, Huddersfield. Son of Arthur Stansfield of Yew Tree, Cowlersley, Milnsbridge. Husband of Sarah A Stansfield, 46 Lowerhouses, Linthwaite. Killed in action, 7.6.1917, aged 32 years. Has no known grave. Commemorated **MENIN GATE MEMORIAL TO THE MISSING.** ROH:- Linthwaite War Memorial.

STANYER, VICTOR. Private. No 268385. 2/4th Battalion Duke of Wellington's Regiment. Born Marsden. Second son of William and Gertrude Ellen Stanyer, New Delight, Marsden. Employed as a teaser at Bank Bottom Mills, Marsden. Was a member of the Adult School. Enlisted October 1916. Embarked for France in January, 1917. Killed in action near Rheims, 20.7.1918, aged 21 years. Buried **MARFAUX BRITISH CEMETERY.** Grave location:- Plot 2, Row E, Grave 7. ROH:- Marsden War Memorial.

STARKEY, BERNARD. Driver. No 284657. 13th Battery, 17th Brigade Royal Field Artillery. Son of Willie and Millie Starkey, 2 Woodland Vale, Armitage Bridge. Died of Enteric Fever in India on 30.7.1920, aged 19 years. Buried **MHOW NEW CEMETERY.** Commemorated **KIRKEE 1914–1918 MEMORIAL, INDIA.**

STARKEY, CHARLIE. Private. No 81429. 1/8th Battalion West Yorkshire Regiment. Formerly No 52448 Duke of Wellington's Regiment. Born Firth Street, Aspley, Huddersfield. Educated Berry Brow Council Schools. Husband of Mary Ellen

Starkey, 14 Clement Street, Birkby. Employed as a painter and decorator by Mr E Oates of Birkby. Enlisted 6.6.1918. Killed in action near Solesmes on 20.10.1918, aged 35 years. Buried **QUIEVY COMMUNAL CEMETERY EXTENSION.** Grave location:- Row A, Grave 18. ROH:- Fartown and Birkby War Memorial; memorial in Lockwood Cemetery; Taylor Hill Primitive Methodist Church.

STARKEY, JAMES. Pioneer. No 11222. Royal Engineers. Born Hull 29.1.1879. Educated St. Patrick's Roman Catholic School. Husband of Jane Starkey, 28 Beast Market, Huddersfield. Employed as a bricklayer's labourer. Enlisted 1.6.1915. Suffered a gunshot wound to 3rd finger on 28.11.1917. Died at home, 29 Beast Market, of bronchitis and gas poisoning on 29.1.1919.

STAVERT, ALEXANDER. Ordinary Seaman. No Z/9726. R.N. Depot (Crystal Palace). Royal Naval Volunteer Reserve. Born Hawick, Scotland, 4.6.1884. Educated at Hawick Schools. Employed as a worsted designer. Lived 322 Greenside, Dalton, Huddersfield. Married. Enlisted August 1918. Died of pneumonia, 6.10.1918, at King's College Hospital, London. Buried **WILTON CEMETERY, HAWICK, SCOTLAND.** Grave Location:- G, Parochial, 1396. ROH:- St. James Presbyterian Church; St. John's Church, Kirkheaton.

STAWMAN, HARMAN. Private. No 300196. 9th Battalion Duke of Wellington's Regiment. Born Siddal, Halifax, 22.9.1896. Son of Harry Stawman, 1 Leys, Longwood, Huddersfield. Educated Longwood Church of England School. Employed as a piecer. Single. Enlisted in the local Territorials in March, 1914. Killed in action, 17.4.1917, aged 20 years. Has no known grave. Commmemorated **ARRAS MEMORIAL TO THE MISSING.** ROH:- St. Mark's Parish Church, Longwood; Salendine Nook Baptist Chapel.

STEAD, EDWARD. Private. No 31823. 20th Battalion Durham Light Infantry. Born Meltham Mills, near Huddersfield. Lived Meltham Mills. Employed by Messrs. Taylor and Littlewood, Newsome Mills. Killed in action during the Battle of the Somme on 29.9.1916. Has no known grave. Commemorated **THIEPVAL MEMORIAL TO THE MISSING.** ROH:- St. Bartholomew's Church, Meltham; Messrs. Taylor and Littlewood, Newsome Mills.

STEAD, JAMES. Rifleman. No S/26067. 8th Battalion The Rifle Brigade. Born Meltham Mills. Son of Mr Richard Stead of Meltham Mills. Married. Lived 3 Lane End, Holmfirth. Employed by Messrs Mallinsons, woollen manufacturers, of Linthwaite. Was a member of the Meltham Brass Band and, later, the Hinchliffe Mill Brass Band. Attended Meltham Mills Church. Died of severe wounds to the head on 23.3.1918, aged 28 years. Buried **NOYON NEW BRITISH CEMETERY.** Grave location:- Plot 2, Row C, Grave 4. His wife received a letter from a Chaplain at the Dressing Station, who wrote, *'He was quite unconscious and although he was immediately attended to by very skilful surgeons and nurses he never rallied at all and passed away quite peacefully shortly afterwards.* ROH:- St. Bartholomew's Church, Meltham; Holmfirth War Memorial.

STEAD, JOSEPH WILLIAM. Signaller. No 95092. Royal Fusiliers, posted to 2/4th Battalion London Regiment (Royal Fusiliers). Formerly No 43076 6th Battalion King's Own Yorkshire Light Infantry. Born Leeds 16.2.1897. Son of the late Herbert and Alice Amelia Stead, 4 Barrow Buildings, Moldgreen, Huddersfield. Brother of Nellie and Gertie Stead. Educated Moldgreen Council School. Employed as a weaver. Single. Enlisted 3.6.1916. Reported wounded and missing on 10.8.1918 and afterwards presumed to have been killed on that date, aged 21. Has no known grave. Commemorated **VIS-en-ARTOIS MEMORIAL TO THE MISSING.** ROH:- Christ Church, Moldgreen.

STEAD, THOMAS HENRY. Private. No 23338. 8th Battalion Duke of Wellington's Regiment. Born Holmfirth. Lived Meltham. Killed in action, 28.8.1917. Has no known grave. Commemorated **TYNE COT MEMORIAL TO THE MISSING.** ROH:- St. Bartholomew's Church, Meltham.

STEADMAN, ALBERT VICTOR. Private. No 36388. 10th Battalion Yorkshire Regiment. Born Scarborough. Enlisted Huddersfield. Lived Aspley, Huddersfield. Killed in action, 22.10.1916. Buried **VERMELLES BRITISH CEMETERY.** Grave location:- 5, F, 16.

STEEL, LUTHER. Private. No 16/1596. 1/6th Battalion West Yorkshire Regiment. Born Huddersfield. Lived 26 Cable Street, St. Thomas's Road, Huddersfield. Employed as teamer by the Huddersfield Industrial Society Limited. Was married on 6.6.1908 at Huddersfield Parish Church to Miss Lilian Oddy Mellor. Killed in action, 20.7.1918. Buried **HAGLE DUMP CEMETERY.** Grave location:- Plot 2, Row E, Grave 2. His wife received the following letter from the Chaplain of her husband's regiment who wrote, 'It is with great regret that I am writing to inform you that I buried on Sunday morning the body of your husband Private L. Steele of the 1/6th Battalion West Yorkshire Regiment. He was killed by a shell on the Saturday instantenously, along with another boy of the same regiment. I did not know your husband as he had only just joined the Battalion but I trust you will accept my deepest sympathy. God grant you strength in your great sorrow as I know the news will come as a great blow to you.'

STEMBRIDGE, HARRY. Lance Corporal. No 8711. 1st Battalion West Yorkshire Regiment. Born Leeds Road, Huddersfield, 27.1.1895. Son of Sarah Ann and the late Jack Stembridge, 14 Wilson's Buildings, Great Northern Street, Huddersfield. Employed as a woollen minder. Enlisted 9.2.1914. Killed in action near Armentieres, 29.4.1915, aged 20 years. Buried **ERQUINGHEM-LYS CHURCHYARD EXTENSION.** Grave location:- Plot 1, Row A, Grave 10. ROH:- St. Andrew's Church, Leeds Road, Huddersfield.

STEPHENSON, ERNEST. Private. No 18298. 2nd Battalion Duke of Wellington's Regiment. Born Hope Street, Folly Hall, 20.1.1893. Son of Edward Stephenson, Perseverance Street, Primrose Hill. Lived with his aunt and uncle, Mr and Mrs Albert Kaye, 98 St. Thomas's Road, Longroyd Bridge. Educated Mount Pleasant Council School. Employed as a grocery assistant at the Rashcliffe branch of the Huddersfield Industrial Society Limited. Was a member of the Rashcliffe Church choir. Single. Enlisted 26.1.1916. Wounded 3.9.1916. Admitted to No 36 Casualty Clearing Station, where he died of wounds on 11.9.1916, aged 19 years. Buried **HEILLY STATION CEMETERY.** Grave location:- Plot 4, Row C, Grave 28. ROH:- St.Stephen's Church, Rashcliffe; commemorated on his parents' headstone in Edgerton Cemetery, Huddersfield.

STEPHENSON, HARRY. Private. No 49837. 5th Battalion The King's (Liverpool Regiment). Formerly No 30624 Duke of Wellington's Regiment. Born Myrtle Square, Harrogate. Son of Elizabeth Stafford, 7 Back Chapel Lane, Moldgreen, Huddersfield. Educated St. Andrew's Church of England School, Oldham. Lived West Street, Oldham. Employed as a general labourer. Married. Enlisted 6.6.1912. Killed in action near Cambrai on 30.11.1917. Buried **VILLERS-FAUCON COMMUNAL CEMETERY EXTENSION.** Grave location:- Plot 1, Row A, Grave 10.

STEPHENSON, J. Driver. No 6570. Royal Field Artillery. Died at home, 29.5.1921. Buried **EDGERTON CEMETERY, HUDDERSFIELD.** Grave location:- 11B, 117.

STEVENS, WILLIAM T. Air Mechanic 3rd Class. No 132655. 32nd Training Wing, Royal Air Force. Husband of A. T. Stevens. Lived Fern Lea, Longwood, Huddersfield. Was Managing Director of Messrs Pearson and Stevens, dyers and finishers, Longwood. Died from bronchial-pneumonia in hospital at Suez, Egypt, on 30.11.1918, aged 33 years. Buried **SUEZ WAR MEMORIAL CEMETERY.** Grave location:- Row A, Grave 28. ROH:- St. Mark's Parish Church, Longwood.

STEVENSON, CHARLES. Private. No 268874. 2/6th Battalion Duke of Wellington's Regiment. Born Marsh, Huddersfield 4.10.1877. Educated Portland Street School. Married, with three children. Lived 43 Broomfield Road, Marsh. Was in partnership with his brother as a plasterer. Attended Holy Trinity Church. Enlisted 11.6.1917. Reported missing, presumed killed, at the Battle of Cambrai on 20.11.1917. Has no known grave. Commemorated **CAMBRAI MEMORIAL TO THE MISSING.** ROH:- Holy Trinity Church, Huddersfield.

STEVENSON, STANLEY. Private. No 22169. 6th Battalion King's Own Scottish Borderers. Born 19.3.1883. Son of Priscilla Stevenson, 3 Mark Street, Paddock, Huddersfield. Educated St. Thomas's Church of England School. Employed as a finisher by Messrs Taylor and Lodge,

Folly Hall, Huddersfield. Was a member of Paddock Conservative Club. Enlisted 4.11.1915. Embarked for France in January, 1915. Died of wounds at XIV Main Dressing Station on 15.7.1916, aged 33 years. Buried **DIVE COPSE BRITISH CEMETERY**. Grave location:- Plot 1, Row B, Grave 1. ROH:- St. Thomas's Church, Longroyd Bridge.

STEWART, HARRY. Stoker 1st Class. No K/10894 (PO). Royal Navy *Victor* Torpedo boat. Born Huddersfield 6.5.1888. Son of Mrs Stewart, 5 Thomas Street, Huddersfield. Educated Thomas Street Board School. Before enlisting in the Navy, in 11.12.1907, was employed as a jam boiler. Had served in India, the Persian Gulf and Somaliland. Was married on 3.7.1915 to Miss Edith Walker. The following day he returned to his ship, berthed at Glasgow. On 27.7.1915, he fell off the gangway into the sea whilst trying to help a shipmate. Another seaman dived into the sea to try and help him but no trace of him could be found and his body was not recovered until the next day. Buried with full military honours in **EDGERTON CEMETERY, HUDDERSFIELD.** Grave location:- 6B, 120. ROH:- Huddersfield Parish Church.

STEWART, ROBERT COLIN. Captain. 8th Battalion York and Lancaster Regiment. Born Peebles, Scotland, in March 1892. Son of John and Mary Stewart of 'Thornleigh', Huddersfield. Educated at Mr Roscoe's school, Harrogate, and Uppingham Public School. Shot at Bisley for his school in 1908 and 1909. Left Uppingham in December 1910. At the outbreak of the war he enlisted in the ranks and, a few months later, was granted a commission in the York and Lancaster Regiment. Was gazetted Captain before going to France in August, 1915. Killed in the attack on Ovillers on the first day of the Battle of the Somme, 1.7.1916. (*The casualties for the 8th Battalion York and Lancaster Regiment for 1.7.1916 were 635 men.*) He was 24 years of age. Buried **BLIGHTY VALLEY CEMETERY.** Grave location:- Plot 5, Row A, Grave 17. ROH:- St. Stephen's Church, Lindley, Huddersfield.

STEWART, WILLIAM. Able Seaman. No J/23575. Royal Navy. *HMS Black Prince.* Born Huddersfield. Son of Mr and Mrs Stewart, 78 Bradford Road, Huddersfield. Educated Hilhouse Council School. Enlisted in the Royal Navy in 1913. Came home on leave in November, 1915. Killed in action at the Battle of Jutland, 31.5.1916, aged 19 years. Has no known grave. Commemorated **PORTSMOUTH NAVAL MEMORIAL TO THE MISSING.** ROH:- St. Andrew's Church, Leeds Road, Huddersfield; Fartown and Birkby War Memorial.

STINTON, ALEXANDER. Lance Corporal. No C/7337. 18th Battalion King's Royal Rifle Corps. Born Balsham, Cambridgeshire, 4.4.1895. Educated Balsham schools. Employed as a labourer. Lived 3 Low Road, Berry Brow, Huddersfield. Single. Enlisted 23.9.1915. Reported missing, presumed killed, 28.3.1918. Has no known grave. Commemorated **ARRAS MEMORIAL TO THE MISSING.** ROH:- Armitage Bridge War Memorial.

STOCKDALE, ARTHUR. Private. No 32229. Special Reserve Battalion South Staffordshire Regiment. Born 54 Northgate, Huddersfield. Educated Huddersfield Parish Church School. Husband of Clara Stockdale, 51 Fitzwilliam Street, Huddersfield. Employed as a leather currier. Enlisted 13.11.1916. Died from illness, contracted in France, on 3.11.1917 at Royds Hall War Hospital, Huddersfield. Buried **EDGERTON CEMETERY HUDDERSFIELD.** Grave location:- 35, 29G. ROH:- Huddersfield Parish Church.

STOCKS, ALBERT. Private. No 242238. 12th Battalion East Surrey Regiment. Born Linthwaite. Son of Samuel and Sarah Ann Stocks, 22 Spring Mill, Milnsbridge. Employed by Mr Sam Hirst, cloth finisher, Bridge Croft, Milnsbridge. Attended Milnsbridge Church School. Reported missing, presumed killed, 21.9.1917, at the Battle of Passchendaele. He was 19 years of age. Has no known grave. Commemorated **TYNE COT MEMORIAL TO THE MISSING.** ROH:- Milnsbridge War Memorial.

STOCKS, ERNEST. Rifleman. No 58807. 2/8th Battalion West Yorkshire Regiment. Born Moor End, Lockwood, Huddersfield. Adopted son of Mr and Mrs Senior, 20 Hillhouse Road, Huddersfield. Educated St. John's School, Hillhouse. Employed as a cloth finisher by Messrs J. Hayward and Sons, woollen manufacturers, Marsh, Huddersfield. Single. Enlisted 16.2.1917. Killed in action near Arras on 7.2.1918. Buried **ROCLINCOURT MILITARY CEMETERY.**

Grave location:- Plot 4, Row A, Grave 12. ROH:- Fartown and Birkby War Memorial.

STOCKS, ERNEST. Private. No 116148. 20th Company, Royal Army Medical Corps. Son of the late Tom Stocks and Christiana Stocks, 33 Waterside, Lockwood. Employed by British Dyes Limited. Was a member of the Lockwood Church Young Men's Bible Class. Enlisted May 1917. Was based at the 3rd Southern General Hospital, Oxford. Died at home, 9.11.1917, aged 24 years. Buried **LOCKWOOD CEMETERY, HUDDERSFIELD.** Grave location:- B, 97. ROH:- Emmanuel Church, Lockwood.

STOCKS, J. A. Private. No 77864. 1/9th Battalion Durham Light Infantry. Born Yews Hill, Lockwood 23.8.1898. Youngest son of Mr and Mrs Hamer Stocks, 52 Springdale Street, Longroyd Bridge, Huddersfield. Educated Mount Pleasant Council School. Employed as an apprentice mason by his father. Married, with one child. Enlisted March 1917. Killed in action near Rheims on 23.7.1918. Buried **MARFAUX BRITISH CEMETERY.** Grave location:- Plot 10, Row J, Grave 3. ROH:- St. Stephen's Church, Rashcliffe.

STOCKS, ROY THORNTON. Sergeant. No 12860. 10th Battalion York and Lancaster Regiment. Born Holmfirth. Son of Mr H. T. Stocks of the firm of Messrs Stocks and Mallinson, Upperhead Mills, Huddersfield. Lived Bradshaw Road, Honley. Employed as a cutter by Mr Samuel Taylor, clothier, of Huddersfield. Enlisted Huddersfield. Killed in action at the Battle of Loos on 26.9.1915, aged 21 years. Has no known grave. Commemorated **LOOS MEMORIAL TO THE MISSING.** ROH:- Almondbury War Memorial; Honley War Memorial.

STOCKWELL, ROBERT EWING. Lance Corporal. No 37961. 2nd Battalion York and Lancaster Regiment. Formerly No 29238 Northumberland Fusiliers. Born 17 Rashcliffe Hill Road, Lockwood, Huddersfield. Educated Rashcliffe Church of England School. Employed as a scourer's labourer by Messrs Kaye and Stewart. Enlisted 9.6.1916. Reported missing, presumed killed, on 21.3.1918, aged 24. Has no known grave. Commemorated **ARRAS MEMORIAL TO THE MISSING.** ROH:- St. Stephen's Church, Rashcliffe.

STOKES, JOHN HENRY. Private. No 240230. 1/5th Battalion Duke of Wellington's Regiment. Born Hull. Lived Meltham. Killed in the attack on the Schwaben Redoubt on 3.9.1916. Has no known grave. Commemorated **THIEPVAL MEMORIAL TO THE MISSING.** ROH:- St. Bartholomew's Church, Meltham; Helme Parish Church; Huddersfield Drill Hall.

STOKES, WILLIAM. Private. No 240892. 1/5th Battalion Duke of Wellington's Regiment. Son of Mr F W and Rosa Stokes, 11 Shady Row, Meltham. Killed in the attack on the Schwaben Redboubt on 3.9.1916, aged 21 years. Buried **MILL ROAD CEMETERY.** Grave location:- Plot 1, Row D, Grave 6. ROH:- St. Bartholomew's Church, Meltham; Helme Parish Church; Huddersfield Drill Hall.

STOKES, WILLIAM THOMAS. Private. No 41054. 27th (Tyneside Irish) Battalion Northumberland Fusiliers. Son of Mr Mark Stokes, Greenhill Bank, New Road, New Mill, Holmfirth. Employed as a millhand by Messrs Middlemost at Birkby, Huddersfield. Was a keen association football player. Enlisted at Easter 1916. Seriously wounded in the chest at the beginning of November, 1916. Admitted to No 2 Casualty Clearing Station, where he died of wounds on 3.11.1916, aged 23 years. Buried **BAILLEUL COMMUNAL CEMETERY EXTENSION.** Grave location:- Plot 3, Row A, Grave 239. His parents received a letter from the Rev. W W Gardener, Chaplain to the forces, who wrote, *'I am very sorry to be the bearer to you of exceedingly sad news that your son, No 31826 Private W. Stokes of the 3rd Battalion Durham Light Infantry, attached to the 27th Battalion Northumberland Fusiliers, died in the 2nd Casualty Clearing Station on the 3rd November of the wounds he received in action. The wounds being in the chest he was breathing with great difficulty and though everything was tried to relieve him he suffered a great deal of pain. On the night before he died when I saw him and had prayers with him I noticed that he was very weak and worn out. It will be a source of consolation to you to know how bravely the poor lad bore his wounds as also to remember how faithful he had been to all his duty on the field and finally laid* *down his life in his country's cause. I conducted the funeral service this morning when his remains were reverently laid to rest in the pretty miiltary cemetery here.'* ROH:- New Mill Working Men's Club; Fulstone War Memorial.

STONEY, HERBERT ARTHUR. Private. No 40609. 8th Battalion Northumberland Fusiliers. Born Sheepridge, Huddersfield. Son of Arthur and Sarah Stoney, 61 Kilner Bank, Moldgreen, Huddersfield. Employed at Messrs Robson's dyeworks at Dalton. Attended Moldgreen United Methodist Church. Was a member of Moldgreen Liberal Club. Enlisted under the Derby scheme and embarked for France on 30.9.1916. Killed in action, 3.1.1917, aged 21 years. Has no known grave. Commemorated **THIEPVAL MEMORIAL TO THE MISSING.** ROH:- St. Andrew's Church, Moldgreen; Christ Church, Moldgreen; Moldgreen War Memorial.

STORER, JOSEPH. Acting Bombardier. No 204514. 123rd Brigade, Royal Field Artillery. Born Heanor, Derbyshire, 19.7.1891. Son of M. A. Storer, Nottingham Road, Gilt Brook, Nottinghamshire. Educated Heanor Church of England School. Married, with one child. Lived 59 Storths, Moldgreen. Huddersfield. For three years he was a Constable in the Huddersfield Borough police force and afterwards was employed as a picric charge-hand by British Dyes Limited. Enlisted 20.1.1917. Killed in action at Kemmel Hill, Belgium, on 23.10.1917. Buried **KEMMEL CHATEAU MILITARY CEMETERY.** Grave location:- Row O, Grave 39. ROH:- St. Andrew's Church.

STOTT, HARRY. Private. No 64145. 1st Reserve Garrison Battalion Suffolk Regiment. Born Wellington Street, Oakes, Huddersfield, 8.11.1892. Only son of Joseph Crawshaw Stott and Eliza Stott, Oakleigh, 6 Oakes Road, Lindley. Educated Oakes Council School and Longwood Grammar School. Employed as a joiner. Was a well known local athlete. Single. Enlisted in February 1917. Died of bronchial pneumonia at Broadway Military Hospital, Sheerness, on 19.11.1918, aged 26 years. Buried **ST. STEPHEN'S CHURCHYARD, LINDLEY, HUDDERSFIELD.** Grave location:- 6, P. ROH:- St. Stephen's Church, Lindley; Oakes Baptist Church.

STOTT, JAMES HERBERT. Rifleman. No A/203846. 18th Battalion King's Royal Rifle Corps. Born Beech Street, Paddock, Huddersfield, 18.4.1886. Educated Spring Grove Council School. Husband of May Evelyn Stott, 33 Grove Street, Huddersfield. Employed as a woolsorter by Messrs C. and J. Hirst Limited. Attended South Street Primitive Methodist Church. Enlisted 28.10.1915. Reported missing, presumed killed, near Bapaume on 24.3.1918. Buried **BANCOURT BRITISH CEMETERY.** Grave location:- Plot 1, Row L, Grave 6.

STOTT, KENNETH. Private. No 98034. 'N' Company (Ripon) Royal Army Medical Corps. Born Huddersfield. 25.5.1891. Son of Walter Wood Stott and Lucie Alberta Stott, late of Halton, Leeds, and now of State College Station, Raleigh, North Carolina, U.S.A. Educated Leeds Modern School. At the time of enlistment, was living at Wallasey near Liverpool. Employed as a chemist. Husband of E. Fannie Pearson (who re-married) and lived at 16 Balling Road, Ben Rhydding, Ilkley. Enlisted November 1916. Died at Ripon of pneumonia on 25.12.1916, aged 25 years. Buried **RIPON CEMETERY.** Grave location:- F, 261.

STRINGER, NELSON. Private. No 29/678. 9th Battalion Northumberland Fusiliers. Born Huddersfield. Son of Mrs J. Stringer, 9 King Cliffe, Birkby, Huddersfield. Employed by Messrs Crowther and Nicholson, Ashbrow Mills. Killed in action near St. Quentin on 14.9.1917, aged 29 years. Buried **HARGICOURT BRITISH CEMETERY.** Grave location:- Plot 1, Row D, Grave 10. ROH:- Fartown and Birkby War Memorial.

STUBBINGS, EDGAR WILKINSON. Private. No 27818. 9th Battalion Lancashire Fusiliers. Formerly No 23720 King's Own Yorkshire Light Infantry. Born Huddersfield. Son of the late Jim Stubbings (formerly cricket professional at Fartown) and Mrs Stubbings. Husband of Mildred Alice Stubbings, 20 Blacker Road, Birkby. Employed by Messrs Alfred Jubb and Son Limited, St. John's Road, Huddersfield. Killed in action at Passchendaele on 19.8.1917, aged 24 years. Has no known grave. Commemorated **TYNE COT MEMORIAL TO THE MISSING.** ROH:- Fartown and Birkby War Memorial.

STUBBS, OLIVER. Private. No 204232. 9th Battalion Duke of Wellington's Regiment. Born Huddersfield. Enlisted Huddersfield. Killed in action at Langemarck on 19.10.1917. Buried **RUISSEAU FARM CEMETERY, LANGEMARCK, BELGIUM.** Grave location:- Row D, Grave 8.

STYRING, JOHN CROSLAND. Private. No 11510. 2nd Battalion Duke of Wellington's Regiment. Born 26.3.1884. Son of the late Mr and Mrs James Crosland Styring. Educated at Birkby School. Married, with three children. (His wife was expecting another child when he was killed). Lived 13 Clayton Fields, Birkby. Attended Highfield Church. Worked on his own account as a taxi-cab proprietor. Enlisted 10.9.1914. Served as an orderly despatch rider. Died from the effects of gas poisoning received at Hill 60 on 6.5.1915. He was 31 years of age. Has no known grave. Commemorated **MENIN GATE MEMORIAL TO THE MISSING.** ROH:- Fartown and Birkby War Memorial; commemorated on his parents' headstone in Paddock Churchyard

SUGDEN, ARTHUR. Private. No 242835. 1/5th Battalion Duke of Wellington's Regiment. Born 107 Leeds Road, Bradley, Huddersfield, 22.11.1897. Fourth son of Frank and Emma Sugden, 107 Leeds Road, Bradley. Educated Bradley Church of England School. Employed as cloth finisher by Messrs J. L. Walker and Sons Limited, of Deighton. Single. Enlisted 8.9.1916. Died of shell wounds to the head at No 62 Casualty Clearing Station on 15.4.1918. He was 20 years of age. Buried **BANDAGHEM MILITARY CEMETERY.** Grave location:- Plot 2, Row D, Grave 17. ROH:- St. Thomas's Church, Bradley; Deighton War Memorial.

SUGDEN, JOHN. 2nd Lieutenant. 5th Battalion Duke of Wellington's Regiment. Born Liverpool 17.7.1896. Son of Mr and Mrs William Harry Sugden, 9 Henry Street, Huddersfield. Educated Spring Grove Council School. Employed as a solicitor's clerk by Mr Edwin Sykes, solicitor. Single. Joined the local Territorials as a Lance Corporal in 1910. Embarked for France in April, 1915. Was recommended for a commission and was gazetted in July 1917. Returned to France in October, 1917. Killed instantly by a shell on 29.3.1918 whilst leading his men at Bucquoy, France. Buried **GOMMECOURT BRITISH CEMETERY No 2.** Grave location:- Plot 5, Row D, Grave 11. ROH:- Huddersfield Drill Hall.

SULCH, ARTHUR. Private. No 2963. 'C' Company, 1/5th Battalion Duke of Wellington's Regiment. Born 4 Honoria Street, Bradford Road, Huddersfield, 21.3.1894. Son of John and Alice Sulch, 107 Blackhouse Road, Fartown, Huddersfield. Educated at Hillhouse Council School, Huddersfield Boys College and the Higher Grade School. Employed as an electrical engineer by Messrs T. Broadbent and Sons Limited, Central Ironworks, Huddersfield. Single. Enlisted 5.9.1914. Embarked for France in April, 1915. Killed by shellfire on 18.9.1915, aged 20 years. Has no known grave. Commemorated **MENIN GATE MEMORIAL TO THE MISSING.** His parents received a letter from Private Frank Schofield (who later died as a Prisoner of War on 1.4.1918, q.v.), who wrote, *'It is with great regret that I write these few lines, but it is on behalf of myself and my fellow comrades that I do it. Last night Arthur and myself had just had tea when the Germans started shelling us very heavily and we went to take precautions. But hearing that two of our fellows were buried I made a dash to the spot and as I thought left Arthur in safety. But somehow he thought it was safer in the trench bottom. So he and two more fellows lay prone on the ground when all of a sudden a shot hit the dug-out front and I am sorry to say my dear old pal and schoolmate caught the whole concussion but I am glad to say he had no suffering as his very sad death took place instantenously. He died as he lived – a soldier and a gentleman.'* ROH:- Christ Church, Woodhouse Hill; Huddersfield Drill Hall; Fartown and Birkby War Memorial.

SUNDERLAND, ARTHUR. Private. No 49290. 15th Battalion Lancashire Fusiliers. Formerly No 29457 Yorkshire Dragoons. Born Linthwaite. Son of John and Leah Sunderland, 1 Lane Side, Linthwaite. Was a former chorister in the Linthwaite Parish Church choir. Attended Milnsbridge Baptist Chapel. Was a member of Hoyle Ing Working Men's Club. Employed as a piecer by Messrs George Mallinson and Sons Limited. Enlisted 24.4.1918. Killed in action, 10.9.1918, aged 20 years. Has no known grave. Commemorated **VIS-en-ARTOIS MEMORIAL TO THE MISSING.** ROH:- Linthwaite War Memorial.

SUNDERLAND, FRED. Private. No 41033. 9th Battalion Northumberland Fusiliers. Born Lindley, Huddersfield. Son of Joseph and Elizabeth Sunderland, 17 Dearnes Cottage, West Street, Lindley. Killed in action, 22.3.1918, aged 25 years. Has no known grave. Commemorated **ARRAS MEMORIAL TO THE MISSING.** ROH:- St. Stephen's Church, Lindley.

SUNDERLAND, JOHN LESLIE. Lance Corporal. No 30640. 2nd Battalion Duke of Wellington's Regiment. Son of Harry and Esther M. Sunderland, Yew Tree Terrace, Shepley. Employed as a plumber by Messrs J. Marsden and Sons, Market Place, Huddersfield. Killed in action at Passchendaele on 10.10.1917, aged 18 years. Has no known grave. Commemorated **TYNE COT MEMORIAL TO THE MISSING.** ROH:- Shepley War Memorial.

SUNDERLAND, WALTER. Private. No 27001. 97th Company, Machine Gun Corps. Formerly No 8009 King's Royal Rifle Corps. Born Armitage Bridge, Huddersfield. Son of Mr and Mrs Sam Sunderland, Big Valley, Berry Brow, Huddersfield. Attended Berry Brow Wesleyan Church. Employed at the Lane Dyehouse Cooperative Society. Reported missing, presumed killed, 2.12.1917, aged 25 years. Has no known grave. Commemorated **TYNE COT MEMORIAL TO THE MISSING.** ROH:- Armitage Bridge War Memorial.

SURTEES, HERBERT. Private. No 3527. 1/7th Battalion Duke of Wellington's Regiment. Lived Meltham. Formerly of Coldwell Street, Hoylehouse, Meltham. Employed as night fireman by Messrs George Mallinson and Sons Limited, of Linthwaite. Married, with two children. Killed in action, 3.7.1916, aged 30 years. Has no known grave. Commemorated **THIEPVAL MEMORIAL TO THE MISSING.** ROH:- St. Bartholomew's Church, Meltham; Huddersfield Drill Hall.

SUTCLIFFE, CHARLEY. Rifleman. No 45404. 1/5th London Regiment The Rifle Brigade. Formerly No 4445 Durham Light Infantry. Son of the late Joseph and Harriet Sutcliffe of Paddock. Lived Middlesborough. Killed in action, 27.8.1918, aged 34 years. Buried **BUCQUOY ROAD CEMETERY.** Grave location:- Plot 7, Row C, Grave 13. ROH:- Memorial in Salendine Nook Churchyard, 41E.

SUTCLIFFE, ERNEST HENRY. Private. No 39747. 14th Infantry Labour Company, Lincolnshire Regiment, transferred to No 31620 53rd Company, Labour Corps. Born Slaithwaite. Only son of Mr and Mrs Alfred Sutcliffe, Carr Lane, Slaithwaite. Was in business with his father as a painter and paper-hanger. Married, with one child. Enlisted 1.12.1916. Embarked for France in March, 1917. Killed instantly by a stray shell on Friday, 17.8.1917, aged 35 years. Buried **THE HUTS CEMETERY. DICKEBUSCH, BELGIUM.** Grave location:- Plot 4, Row A, Grave 8. ROH:- St. James Church, Slaithwaite; Slaithwaite War Memorial.

SUTCLIFFE, GEORGE GUY. Private. No 268360. 2/4th Battalion Duke of Wellington's Regiment. Born 6 Jagger's Buildings, Bradford Road, Huddersfield, 8.12.1894. Was the adopted son of the late Mr and Mrs Sutcliffe, 75 Hebble Terrace, Bradford Road, Huddersfield. His name was George Guy but he was better known as George Guy Sutcliffe. Educated Thomas Street Board School and Huddersfield Higher Grade School. Employed as a blacksmith's striker by Messrs J. Haywood and Company Limited, Bay Hall, Huddersfield. Single. Enlisted 21.10.1916. Killed in action near Rheims on 20.7.1918, aged 23 years. Buried **MARFAUX BRITISH CEMETERY.** Grave location:- Plot 1, Row E, Grave 7. ROH:- Great Northern Street Congregational Chapel.

SUTCLIFFE, MALCOLM. Private. No 3/2098. 1st Battalion King's Own Yorkshire Light Infantry. Born Sands Terrace, Leeds Road, North Deighton, 8.1.1891. Son of Major and Emily Sutcliffe, Rosnall Holme, Beech Street, Paddock. Educated Spring Grove Board School. Employed on his own account as a painter and decorator. Single. Enlisted 31.8.1914. Embarked for France at the beginning of January, 1915. Killed in action at the Battle of Loos on 4.10.1915, aged 24 years. Has no known grave. Commemorated **LOOS MEMORIAL TO THE MISSING.** His parents received a letter from a chum of their son, Lance Sergeant Jack Walsh, who wrote, *'The last time I was speaking to him he was talking about his Father and Mother. He passed away like a good British soldier and fell fighting. His Company made an attack on part of the German trenches and he was killed in the attack by a rifle shot. One of his own Company who saw him* fall told me he suffered no pain and he is buried in a true British soldier's grave. He did his bit with a good heart. God has called him home and he alone can help you to bear the great trouble. Hoping you will accept my deepest sympathy in your hour of trial.' ROH:- St. Mark's Parish Church, Longwood; All Saints Church, Paddock; commemorated in Salendine Nook Baptist Chapel yard, 283E.

SUTCLIFFE, ROBERT. Private. No 1731. 3/5th Battalion Duke of Wellington's Regiment. Lived Meltham. Died at home, 31.3.1916, aged 22 years. Buried **MELTHAM OLD CHURCH BURIAL GROUND**. Grave location:- East, M, 8. ROH:- St. Bartholomew's Church, Meltham.

SUTCLIFFE, WILLIE. Private. No 29536. 14th Battalion Highland Light Infantry. Formerly No 25744 The Yorkshire Regiment. Born 11.3.1887. Educated Mirfield Parish Church Schools. Was one of the principal alto singers in the Huddersfield Parish Church choir. Employed as a labourer in engineering. Married. Lived 21a, Lower Quarry Road, Bradley. Enlisted 18.12.1915. Killed in action, 29.9.1916. Has no known grave. Commemorated **ARRAS MEMORIAL TO THE MISSING**. ROH:- Huddersfield Parish Church; St. Thomas's Church, Bradley.

SWAINE, MELLIN. Private. No 21/715. 1/5th Battalion West Yorkshire Regiment. Born Huddersfield. Son of John and Rebecca Swaine of Wall Nook, Cumberworth. Employed by Messrs S. Senior and Sons Limited, brewers, of Shepley. Single. Enlisted 1916. Reported missing, presumed killed, 25.4.1918, aged 22 years. Buried **SANCTUARY WOOD CEMETERY, BELGIUM**. Grave location:- Plot 3, Row D, Grave 18. ROH:- New Mill Working Men's Club; Fulstone War Memorial.

SWALE, SOLOMON (ROLLY), MM and Bar. Private. No 241184. 2/5th Battalion Duke of Wellington's Regiment. Son of Jonas and Martha Elizabeth Swale, 'Nont Sarah's Hotel', Scammonden. Enlisted in the Transport Section of the Duke of Wellington's Regiment in May, 1915. Embarked for France on 2.12.1916. Was an expert rider and driver. Awarded the Military Medal for *'splendid courage and coolness on the night of September 28th and 29th, 1918. He was in charge of a limber with two mules containing rations and water for one of the Companies. He had to pass through ----- which was being intensely shelled at the time to deliver rations to one of the bridges on the canal. He successfully accomplished his difficult task and got his limber and animals safely away. Entirely by his grit and determination was it possible to get the rations close to the front Company and so prevent a weakening of the line for ration carrying.'* Died of wounds at No 29 Casualty Clearing Station on 21.10.1918, aged 21 years. Awarded a bar to the Military Medal posthumously on 14.5.1919. Buried **DELSAUX FARM CEMETERY, BEUGNY**. Grave location:- Plot 1, Row H, Grave 7. ROH:- Huddersfield Drill Hall.

SWALLOW, ARTHUR. Private. No 3220. 1/5th Battalion Duke of Wellington's Regiment. Born Huddersfield. Son of John William and Jane Swallow, Lower Hall, Kirkheaton. Employed as a finisher by Messrs John Lee Walker and Sons Limited, Woodhouse Mills. Was a member of Kirkheaton Parish Church choir and the Cooperative Choir. Was keenly interested in bell ringing. Enlisted at the outbreak of the war. Embarked for France in April 1915. Killed in action, 4.11.1916, aged 20 years. Buried **FONCQUEVILLERS MILITARY CEMETERY**. Grave location:- Plot 1, Row J, Grave 17. (Brother of Private **WILLIAM HENRY SWALLOW**, killed in action, 23.4.1918, q.v.). ROH:- St. John's Church, Kirkheaton; Lepton Parish Church; Huddersfield Drill Hall.

SWALLOW, FRANK. Private. No 33550. 6th Battalion The Yorkshire Regiment. Formerly No 31186 11th Reserve Hussars Regiment. Born Thongsbridge. Son of Mr and Mrs Hugh Swallow of Deanhouse, Thongsbridge. Attended Netherthong Wesleyan Church. Employed at Deanhouse Mills. Was a member of the Netherthong boy scouts. Enlisted soon after the outbreak of the war at the age of 17 years and was discharged on account of illness. He enlisted again early in 1915 and was transferred from the Hussars to the Yorkshire Regiment. Killed by a shell on 15.8.1917, aged 20 years. Has no known grave. Commemorated **MENIN GATE MEMORIAL TO THE MISSING**. ROH:- Netherthong and Thongsbridge War Memorial; Netherthong Working Men's Club.

SWALLOW, HAROLD. Lance Corporal. No 26393. 4th Battalion Grenadier Guards. Born Holmfirth. Son of Mrs Lydia Swallow of Longley, Holmfirth. Employed at Washpit Mills, Holmfirth. Attended Choppards Sunday School, where he was a member of the singing class. Was a member of the cricket club and gymnasium. Enlisted 15.8.1916. Killed in action, 13.4.1918, aged 22 years. Has no known grave. Commemorated **PLOEGSTEERT MEMORIAL TO THE MISSING.** ROH:- Hade Edge War Memorial.

SWALLOW, JOSEPH. Gunner. No 127577. 207th Siege Battery, Royal Garrison Artillery. Born Hepworth, Holmfirth. Attended Hepworth Parish Church. Lived with his Uncle, Mr William Senior, at Hilltop, Cumberworth. Brother of Mrs Emily Barker, 48 The Green, Penistone, Sheffield. Employed at Lane End Quarries, Shepley. Killed in action, 1.9.1917, aged 36. Buried **CANADA FARM CEMETERY, ELVERDINGHE, BELGIUM.** Grave location:- Plot 2, Row G, Grave 31. ROH:- Hepworth and Scholes War Memorial; Hepworth Church.

SWALLOW, JOHN REGINALD. 2nd Lieutenant. 1st Battalion The King's Liverpool Regiment. Born Hepworth, Holmfirth. Son of Mr Charles Swallow of Wolverhampton. Married. Prior to enlistment was employed as a language master at a London secondary school. Reported wounded and missing after the attack on Guillemont on 8.8.1918 during the Battle of the Somme. The authorities stated that Lieutenant Swallow was wounded and after he was attended to he went on fighting and was then fatally wounded. Was afterwards presumed to have been killed on that date. Has no known grave. Commemorated **THIEPVAL MEMORIAL TO THE MISSING.**

SWALLOW, LUTHER. Private. No 24478. 2/6th Battalion Duke of Wellington's Regiment. Born Holme, Holmbridge. Son of Mr and Mrs Jonas Swallow of Holme. Employed by Messrs W. H. and J. Barber, Clarence Mills, Holmbridge. Enlisted March 1916. Reported missing, presumed killed, at the Battle of Cambrai on 27.11.1917, aged 22 years. Has no known grave. Commemorated **CAMBRAI MEMORIAL TO THE MISSING.** ROH:- Holme and Holmbridge War Memorial.

SWALLOW, PERCY. Private. No 35537. 2nd Battalion The Yorkshire Regiment. Formerly No 5/108062 10th Territorial Reserve Battalion. Born Huddersfield. Son of Mr and Mrs S C Swallow of Butter Nab, Berry Brow, Huddersfield. Killed in action, 8.5.1918, aged 18 years. Has no known grave. Commemorated **TYNE COT MEMORIAL TO THE MISSING.** ROH:- South Crosland and Netherton War Memorial.

SWALLOW, PERCY. Rifleman. No C/7769. 18th Battalion King's Royal Rifle Corps. Born Netherton, Huddersfield. Son of the late Albert and of Jane Swallow, The Oddfellows Hall, Netherton. Employed as a weaver by Messrs John Brook at Armitage Bridge Mills. Attended South Crosland Church, where he was a member of the choir and a teacher in the Sunday School. He was also a member of the Netherton Tennis Club. Single. Was wounded on 15.9.1916 during the attack on Flers during the Battle of the Somme. It was thought that he was making his way to the dressing station when he received other wounds which proved fatal. He was found four days later by a section of the Irish Rifles who buried him in **BULLS ROAD CEMETERY, FLERS.** He was 25 years of age. Grave location:- Plot 2, Row G, Grave 26. ROH:- Armitage Bridge Mills; South Crosland and Netherton War Memorial.

SWALLOW, WILLIAM HENRY. Private. No 40999. 1/5th Battalion The King's Own (Royal Lancaster Regiment). Born Kirkheaton. Son of John William and Jane Swallow of Lower Hall, Kirkheaton. Attended Kirkheaton Parish Church and School. Employed as a weaver at Spa Mills. Had been in France just one week when he was killed in action on 23.4.1918, aged 19 years. Has no known grave. Commemorated **LOOS MEMORIAL TO THE MISSING.** (Brother of Private **ARTHUR SWALLOW**, killed in action, 4.11.1916, q.v.). ROH:- St. John's Church, Kirkheaton; Lepton Parish Church.

SWAN, JOHN FREDERICK. Private. No 22074. 17th Battalion Lancashire Fusiliers. Born Huddersfield 12.1.1893. Son of Mr and Mrs Harry Swann, 8 Outcote Bank, Huddersfield. Educated St. Paul's School, Huddersfield. Employed as a railwayman at the goods yard of Huddersfield Railway Station. Single. Enlisted July 1915. Killed in action at Bernafay Wood, 23.7.1916, during the Battle of the Somme.

He was 23 years of age. Has no known grave. Commemorated **THIEPVAL MEMORIAL TO THE MISSING.**

SWANN, WILLIE. Corporal. No 2959. Machine Gun Corps (Motors). Born Lindley, Huddersfield. Son of Albert William and Mary Hannah Swann, 18 Union Street, Lindley. Employed by Messrs Joseph Sykes Brothers Limited, Acre Mills, Lindley. Died of wounds, 2.7.1916, during the Battle of the Somme. He was 25 years of age. Buried **FORCEVILLE COMMUNAL CEMETERY EXTENSION.** Grave location:- Plot 2, Row B, Grave 12. ROH:- St. Stephen's Church, Lindley; Huddersfield Drill Hall.

SWIFT, BEN. Gunner. No 240767. 130th Battery, 40th Brigade, Royal Field Artillery. Born Kirkburton. Son of Charles H. and Harriet Swift of Church Green, Kirkburton. Killed in action, 2.11.1918, aged 28 years. Buried **POIX-du-NORD COMMUNAL CEMETERY EXTENSION.** Grave location:- Plot 2, Row B, Grave 5. ROH:- All Hallows Parish Church, Kirkburton.

SWIFT, FRED. Private. No 33270 6th Battalion York and Lancaster Regiment. Formerly No 30697 Duke of Wellington's Regiment. Born Kirkheaton. Son of Alfred and Eliza Swift of Lascelles Hall, Kirkheaton. Killed in action, 1.10.1918, aged 20 years. Has no known grave. Commemorated **VIS-en-ARTOIS MEMORIAL TO THE MISSING.** ROH:- St. John's Church, Kirkheaton; Lepton Parish Church.

SWIFT, FRED. Gunner. No 68450. 232nd Siege Battery, Royal Garrison Artillery. Born Honley, Huddersfield. Son of John Edward and Ellen Swift, 24 Westgate, Honley. Employed by Messrs Learoyd Brothers, Leeds Road, Huddersfield, and Messrs John France and Sons of Honley. Was a playing member of the Honley Cricket Club. Enlisted February 1916. Killed in action, 2.9.1918, aged 26 years. Buried **FOUCAUCOURT COMMUNAL CEMETERY.** Grave location:- in the south-west corner of the Communal Cemetery; ROH:- Honley War Memorial.

SWIFT, JOSEPH, MM. Private. No 30760. 1st Battalion East Yorkshire Regiment. Formerly No 38059 The Yorkshire Regiment. Born Golcar. Lived in Golcar. Awarded the MM, 28.1.1918. Died of wounds as a Prisoner of War on 3.9.1918. Buried **HAUTMONT COMMUNAL CEMETERY.** Grave location:- Plot 4, Row A, Grave 46. ROH:- St. John's Church, Golcar.

SYKES, ALBERT. Private. No 9481. Depot Battalion Worcestershire Regiment. (See **GLEDHILL, ALBERT,** the true family name).

SYKES, ALBERT. Rifleman. No C/12505. 21st Battalion King's Royal Rifle Corps. Born Kirkheaton. Son of Tom B. and Emily Sykes of Stafford House, Kirkheaton. Employed by the Halifax Permanent Building Society, Market Place, Huddersfield. Reported missing, presumed killed, in the attack on Flers during the Battle of the Somme on 15.9.1916, aged 24 years. Has no known grave. Commemorated **THIEPVAL MEMORIAL TO THE MISSING.** ROH:- St. John's Church, Kirkheaton.

SYKES, ARNOLD WALKER. Captain. 3rd Battalion York and Lancaster Regiment. Born Huddersfield 26.6.1875. Son of John Henry and Emmeline Sykes, Bryancliffe, Huddersfield. Educated at Uppingham Public School, which he left in August, 1894. Was a member of the firm of Messrs Edward Sykes and Sons, woollen manufacturers, Gosport Mills, Outlane. Was greatly interested in amateur theatricals. For production by the Huddersfield Operatic Society he wrote 'A Merry Monarch' and 'The Squire of Harlington'. Was a freemason. Married, with three children. Lived 'Netherleigh', Huddersfield. Had long service with the Volunteers, in which he attained the rank of Captain. He joined the National Reserve on its formation and, on the outbreak of war, he was detailed for duty at the Halifax Depot and later at the York and Lancaster's depot at Pontefract, where he was appointed Adjutant. He was passed for general service and joined his Regiment in July, 1917. Killed in action, near Ypres on 30.9.1917, aged 42 years. Buried **BEDFORD HOUSE ENCLOSURE No 2.** Grave location:- Plot 1, Row E, Grave 12. ROH:- Holy Trinity Church, Huddersfield; St. Mary Magdalene Church, Outlane; St. Andrew's Church, Stainland.

SYKES, ARTHUR. Private. No 49943. 1st Battalion King's Own Yorkshire Light Infantry. Formerly No 5/30140 8th Territorial Reserve Battalion. Born Almondbury. Son of Walter and Charlotte Ann Sykes, 9 Squirrel Ditch,

Huddersfield. Employed by Messrs A. W. Scarr and Sons Limited, Market Hall, Huddersfield. Reported missing on 17.10.1918 and afterwards presumed to have been killed on that date, aged 20. Buried **HIGHLAND CEMETERY, LE CATEAU.** Grave location:- Plot 3, Row C, Grave 20.

SYKES, ARTHUR. Sergeant. No 2449. 2/5th Battalion Duke of Wellington's Regiment. Born Upperthong, Holmfirth. Son of Company Sergeant Major H J Sykes DCM and Mrs Sykes, Market Street, Holmfirth. Educated Holmfirth Technical Institute. Employed as a clerk by Messrs S. and S. Butterworth, Lower Mills, Holmfirth and then by Messrs Armitage and Rhodes of Ravensthorpe. Attended Holmfirth Wesleyan Sunday School. Was a member of the local Territorials prior to the outbreak of the war. Mobilised in August, 1914. He underwent training in Lincolnshire, Doncaster and Bedford. He followed the example of his father, who gained the DCM in the trenches at Ypres and was granted his discharge in 1916, after 31 years with the Volunteers and the Territorials. Had been in France for five weeks when he was killed in action on 14.2.1917, aged 20 years. Buried **AUCHONVILLERS MILITARY CEMETERY.** Grave location:- Plot 2, Row K, Grave 9. ROH:- Upperthong War Memorial; Huddersfield Drill Hall.

SYKES, ARTHUR. Private. No 20028. 2nd Battalion Duke of Wellington's Regiment. Born Kirkheaton. Son of Fred and Ellen of Jagger Hill, Dalton. Killed in action, 8.12.1916. Has no known grave. Commemorated **THIEPVAL MEMORIAL TO THE MISSING.** ROH:- St. John's Church, Kirkheaton; commemorated on headstone in Kirkheaton Cemetery.

SYKES, ARTHUR. Corporal. No 39094. 3/5th Battalion Lancashire Fusiliers. Born Heckmondwike 19.8.1888. Son of Percy and Ada Sykes, 3 Brick Bank, Almondbury. Educated Stile Common Council School. Employed as a joiner by Messrs Tom Sykes, joiners and builders, East Parade, Huddersfield. Attended St. Mary's Church, Longley, Huddersfield. Was a well known local cricketer and, as a left hand bowler, had won the bowling prize (gold medal) given by the Primrose Hill Club for five years. Husband of Edith Annie Sykes. Enlisted November 1916. Embarked for France in June, 1917. Killed in action at Passchendaele on 17.11.1917, aged 27 years. Has no known grave. Commemorated **TYNE COT MEMORIAL TO THE MISSING.** ROH:- St. Andrew's Church; Almondbury War Memorial; Lowerhouses War Memorial; memorial in Almondbury Cemetery.

SYKES, CHRISTOPHER TINKER. Private. No 12639. 10th Battalion Duke of Wellington's Regiment. Born Armitage Bridge, Huddersfield. Son of Anthony Noble and Ellen Sykes, 38 Parkgate, Berry Brow, Huddersfield. Educated Armitage Bridge Church of England School. Employed as a baker by the Huddersfield Cooperative Stores. Was a member of Armitage Bridge Conservative Club. Single. Enlisted 29.8.1914. Wounded in the head near Ypres on 25.2.1916. Reported missing, presumed killed on 7.6.1917, aged 25 years. Has no known grave. Commemorated **MENIN GATE MEMORIAL TO THE MISSING.** (Brother of Private **ROBERT SYKES**, killed in action, 7.8.1917, q.v.). ROH:- Armitage Bridge War Memorial; memorial in Armitage Bridge Churchyard.

SYKES, CLARENCE. Private. No 31779. 2/4th Battalion Duke of Wellington's Regiment. Born Marsden. Son of Mrs W Sykes, North View, Marsden. Reported wounded in the left arm on 21.11.1917 during the Battle of Cambrai and afterwards presumed to have died on that date. Has no known grave. Commemorated **CAMBRAI MEMORIAL TO THE MISSING.** ROH:- Marsden War Memorial.

SYKES, DAVID. Private. No 2316. 1/7th Battalion Duke of Wellington's Regiment. Prior to enlistment, lived at Elms Hill, Slaithwaite. Married. His wife lived at 273 Brierley Wood, Huddersfield. Employed as a woollen fettler by Messrs Robinson Brothers, Clough Lea, Marsden. Seriously wounded in the head and leg at the beginning of September, 1915. Died of wounds at No 13 General Hospital on 29.9.1915, aged 29 years. Buried **BOULOGNE EASTERN CEMETERY.** Grave location:- Plot 8, Row B, Grave 87. ROH:- St. James Church, Slaithwaite; Slaithwaite War Memorial; Huddersfield Drill Hall.

SYKES, DAVID. Private. No 235098. 2/7th Battalion Duke of Wellington's Regiment. Born Lepton. Son of John and Mary Sykes, Green

Balk Lane, Lepton. Killed in action, 26.3.1918, aged 37 years, Buried **HANNESCAMPS NEW MILITARY CEMETERY**. Grave location:- Row C. Grave 17. ROH:- Lepton Parish Church; Huddersfield Drill Hall.

SYKES, EDGAR. Private. No 2746. 1/7th Battalion Duke of Wellington's Regiment. Born Slaithwaite. Son of Mr Allan Sykes of Holme, Slaithwaite. Lived with a friend, Norris Ellis and his mother at Hollins Glen, Slaithwaite. Employed at No 1 Mill of the Slaithwaite Spinning Company. Was a member of the local Territorials prior to the outbreak of the war. Embarked for France in April, 1915. On 19.12.1915, during a gas attack by the Germans, Private Sykes was seriously affected by the gas and whilst trying to escape from its effects he fell into the river near the lines and was drowned. Had he not been suffering from the effects of the gas he would have escaped his unfortunate death as he was a strong swimmer. He was 21 years of age. Buried **BARD COTTAGE CEMETERY**. Grave location:- Plot 1, Row A, Grave 28. ROH:- St. James Church, Slaithwaite; Slaithwaite War Memorial; Huddersfield Drill Hall.

SYKES, EDWARD (EDDIE). Lance Corporal. No 9115. 2nd Battalion Northumberland Fusiliers. Born Leeches, Outlane 7.1.1885. Son of Mrs George Haigh, 66 Quarmby Road, Lindley. Educated Outlane and Oakes Board Schools. Employed as a textile worker. At the time of enlistment, was living at 64 Garside Buildings, Cliffe End, Lindley. Was a well known local footballer, playing as a three-quarter back in the Fartown team. Single. Enlisted 8.1.1903. Killed in action near Kemmel on 19.9.1915, aged 30. Buried **KEMMEL CHATEAU MILITARY CEMETERY**. Grave location:- Row D, Grave 74. His mother received a letter from her younger son, Lance Sergeant Harry Sykes, of the same Battalion who wrote, *'Just a few lines hoping you will bear up as much as possible when I break the news to you but we have had a bit of a rough time of it and our Eddie got killed in it. He has been buried in a proper cemetery not far from the firing line. I went down and saw his grave just after he was buried but I could not go to his funeral as I was too ill owing to having heard of his death and being knocked over myself and could not remember anything. I am alright now. He was a favourite out here and all the Company and a lot of the Battalion regret losing him. Remember me to all and I will write again when I am more at ease and settled.'* ROH:- Bethel United Methodist Church, Outlane; St. Stephen's Church, Lindley.

SYKES, EDWARD. Corporal. No 20387. 2nd Battalion Duke of Wellington's Regiment. Born Stainland near Halifax. Son of Walter and the late Ruth Ann Sykes, 23 Nabbs Lane, Slaithwaite. Employed as a weaver at Bank Bottom Mills, Marsden. Enlisted May 1916. Wounded on one occasion. Killed in action, 30.8.1918, aged 27 years. Buried **VIS-en-ARTOIS BRITISH CEMETERY**. Grave location:- Plot 1, Row E, Grave 29. ROH:- Providence Congregational Church, Stainland; St. James Church, Slaithwaite; Slaithwaite War Memorial; Huddersfield Drill Hall.

SYKES, ERIC TURNER. Captain. 5th Battalion Duke of Wellington's Regiment. Son of James and Emma Amelia Sykes, 'Dungarth', Honley, Huddersfield. Educated at Almondbury Grammar School, The Leys School, Cambridge, and was an exhibitioner at Gonville and Caius College, Cambridge, when war broke out. He joined the University OTC and received his commission in November, 1914. Embarked for France in December, 1915. Was wounded, 3.9.1916, and sent home for convalescence. He returned to France in March, 1917. At 4am on 3.5.1917 he was wounded in the right arm and hip during the early stages of the Battle of Bullecourt. His injuries were attended to but, in organising a counter-attack at noon on the same day and endeavouring to bring a machine gun into action, an enemy machine gun was trained on him and a comrade who was at school with Captain Sykes. The comrade was wounded and taken prisoner and Captain Sykes was killed on 3.5.1917, aged 22 years. Buried **BAILLEUL ROAD EAST CEMETERY**. Grave location:- Plot 2, Row D, Grave 22. ROH:- Honley War Memorial; Almondbury Grammar School; Huddersfield Drill Hall.

SYKES, ERNEST. Private. No 240730. 2/5th Battalion Duke of Wellington's Regiment. Born Fenay Grange, Almondbury, 17.10.1896. Second son of Mr George Sykes, 3 Holme Place, Grasscroft Road, Marsh, Huddersfield. Educated Almondbury Church of England School and

Hillhouse Higher Elementary School. Employed as an apprentice pattern maker by Mr F. Ives of Folly Hall, Huddersfield. Attended Holy Trinity Church. Single. Enlisted October 1914. Reported missing, presumed killed, 3.5.1917, at the Battle of Bullecourt. Has no known grave. Commemorated **ARRAS MEMORIAL TO THE MISSING.** ROH:- Holy Trinity Church, Huddersfield; Huddersfield Drill Hall; Almondbury War Memorial.

SYKES, FRANCE. Corporal. No 305462. 2/7th Battalion Duke of Wellington's Regiment. Son of Mrs Dyson, 13 Northview Cottages, Marsden. Employed as a piecer by Messrs Crowther, Bruce and Company. Was a member of the Adult School. Enlisted 12.8.1914. Embarked for France in January, 1917. Killed in action, 3.5.1917, at the Battle of Bullecourt. He was 19 years of age. Has no known grave. Commemorated **ARRAS MEMORIAL TO THE MISSING.** ROH:- Huddersfield Drill Hall; Memorial in Marsden Churchyard.

SYKES, FRANK. Private. No 3457. 7th Battalion The Royal Welsh Fusiliers. Born Almondbury, Huddersfield. Son of Mrs Sykes of Northgate, Almondbury. Married, with two children. Lived Ladywell Street, Newtown, Montgomeryshire. On the outbreak of war he attempted to enlist in Kitchener's Army but was rejected. He went to Wales and joined the 2/7th Battalion Royal Welsh Fusiliers. He was transferred to the front line and took part in the Suvla Bay landing in August, 1915, which he survived without any injury. On December 1st, however, as he was leaving the trenches he was shot. Killed in action at Gallipoli on 1.12.1915, aged 24 years. Buried **LALA BABA CEMETERY, SUVLA.** Grave location:- Special Memorial B 6. ROH:- Almondbury War Memorial.

SYKES, FRANK EDWARD. Private. No 2279. 1st/3rd (East Anglian) Field Ambulance, Royal Army Medical Corps. Born Cheetham Hill, Manchester, 9.6.1878. Son of William James Elijah and Annie Sykes, Springwood Hall, Huddersfield. Educated Paddock Church of England School and Spring Grove Council School. Attended Paddock United Methodist Church. Employed as a bank clerk. Single. Enlisted January 1915. Died of acute dysentery on board a hospital ship after serving in the Dardenelles. Was buried at sea on 24.11.1915, aged 37 years. Commemorated **HELLES MEMORIAL TO THE MISSING.** ROH:- All Saints Church, Paddock; Shared Church, Paddock.

SYKES, FRED. Private. No 242697. 1/6th Battalion North Staffordshire Regiment. Born Stoney Lane, Taylor Hill, Lockwood, 5.12.1883. Third son of the late Mr James Sykes and Hannah Sykes, 112 Emmanuel Terrace, Lockwood. Educated Mount Pleasant Board School, Lockwood. Employed as a worsted and woollen twister-in by Messrs Kaye and Stewart, Broadfield Mills. Husband of Lucy Sykes, 112 Emmanuel Terrace, Lockwood. Enlisted 15.11.1916. Killed in action at Bethune on 22.7.1918, aged 34 years. Buried **FOUQUIERES CHURCHYARD EXTENSION.** Grave location:- Plot 3, Row J, Grave 2. ROH:- Emmanuel Church, Lockwood; Taylor Hill Primitive Methodist Church.

SYKES, FRED. Private. No 35706. Labour Company, Lincolnshire Regiment. Born Holmfirth. Son of Henry and Ellen Sykes of Underbank, Holmfirth. Prior to the war was a Corporal in the Holmfirth Territorials and was disappointed because he was refused for active service on health grounds. He was determined to serve his country and subsequently joined a Labour Battalion in the Lincolnshire Regiment. Died of pneumonia, 27.4.1917, at the New Zealand Stationary Hospital, Amiens. He was 35 years of age. Buried **St. PIERRE CEMETERY, AMIENS.** Grave location:- Plot 7, Row C, Grave 8. ROH:- Underbank War Memorial.

SYKES, FRED, MM and Bar. Private. No 242408. 1/5th Battalion Duke of Wellington's Regiment. Born South Street, Huddersfield, 16.2.1896. Son of Mr and Mrs J. Sykes, 93 Gledholt Bank, Paddock. Educated Paddock Council School. Attended Paddock United Methodist Church. Employed as a woollen piecer by Messrs Allen Priest and Sons Limited, Bath Mills, Lockwood. Single. Enlisted 27.1.1916. Awarded the Military Medal in August, 1917, for wiring operations under shell fire. Killed in action, 6.10.1917, during the Battle of Passchendaele. He was 23 years of age. Has no known grave. Commemorated **TYNE COT MEMORIAL TO THE MISSING.** ROH:- All Saints Church, Paddock; Shared Church, Paddock; Huddersfield Drill Hall.

SYKES, GEORGE. Private. No 61647. 206th Company, Machine Gun Corps. Formerly No 23004 Duke of Wellington's Regiment. Born South Crosland, Huddersfield. Son of Joe and Sarah Ann Sykes, Moor Lane, Netherton. Husband of Mary Ellen Sykes of North End Farm, Netherton. Employed by Messrs John Brooke and Sons Limited, Armitage Bridge Mills. Killed in action at the Battle of Arras on 13.5.1917, aged 31 years. Has no known grave. Commemorated **ARRAS MEMORIAL TO THE MISSING.** ROH:- South Crosland and Netherton War Memorial; Armitage Bridge Mills.

SYKES, GEORGE. Private. No 32603. 2nd Battalion West Yorkshire Regiment. Born Clough Top, Almondbury, 12.5.1880. Son of Frank and Mary Ann Sykes, 174 Almondbury Bank, Huddersfield. Educated Moldgreen Council School. Employed as a labourer. Single. Enlisted 6.5.1916. Wounded in October 1916. Died in Edinburgh War Hospital of wounds on 11.5.1917, aged 37 years. Buried **ALMONDBURY CEMETERY, HUDDERSFIELD.** Grave location:- K, 'C', 243. ROH:- Almondbury War Memorial.

SYKES, GEORGE. Sergeant. No 200585. 1/4th Battalion King's Own Yorkshire Light Infantry. Born Slaithwaite. Son of John Edward Swift Sykes and A M Sykes of Talbot Street, Batley. In business on his own account as an upholsterer in Church Street, Slaithwaite. Was a member of the local Territorials and was mobilised at the outbreak of the war. Wounded in 1917, which resulted in him having both legs amputated. He had also been severely gassed. Died in Leeds Military Hospital on 11.3.1918, aged 33 years. Buried **SLAITHWAITE CEMETERY.** Grave location:- B, 1, 159. ROH:- St. James Church, Slaithwaite; Slaithwaite War Memorial.

SYKES, GEORGE. Lance Bombardier. No L/18894. 'A' Battery, 186th Brigade Royal Field Artillery. Born Huddersfield. Eldest son of the late Mr Bradley Sykes and Mrs Sykes, 12 Coldwell Street, Linthwaite. Attended Linthwaite Wesleyan Church. Employed as a weaver by Messrs W. and E. Crowther, Crimble Mills. Had been in France for nearly three years when he was killed on 13.10.1918, aged 24 years. Buried **St. AUBERT BRITISH CEMETERY.** Grave location:- Plot 4, Row E, Grave 17. His mother received a letter from his Commander who told her that *her son was killed during a bombardment of unusual severity on the night of October 13th. The British guns, it appears from the letter of the Officer, had been brought close to the rear of the retreating Germans with the object of giving them an additional push at dawn when the counter battery work of the Huns fell upon them and Sykes and his friend were killed. Sykes was to have been promoted Corporal the following day for good work during the week.* ROH:- Linthwaite War Memorial.

SYKES, GEORGE HERBERT. Private. No 8671. 20th Hussars. Born Paddock, Huddersfield, 1894. Son of Percy and M A Sykes, 19 Armitage Road, Milnsbridge. Educated Milnsbridge Church of England School. Employed as a woollen piecer by Messrs James Shires and Sons, George Street, Milnsbridge. Attended Milnsbridge Wesleyan Church. Enlisted February 1913. Embarked for France in August, 1914. Killed in action near Gouzeaucourt on 31.5.1917, aged 23. Buried **UNICORN CEMETERY, VENDHUILE.** Grave location:- Plot 2, Row H, Grave 15. (Brother of Private **WILFRED SYKES**, died of wounds, 29.5.1918, q.v.). ROH:- St, Mark's Parish Church, Longwood; Milnsbridge War Memorial.

SYKES, HAROLD. Private. No 14296. 8th Battalion Duke of Wellington's Regiment. Born Huddersfield. Son of Albert Sykes, Cross Grove Street, Huddersfield. Husband of Catherine Sykes, (later O' Toole), 23 Castlegate, Huddersfield. Employed by Robert Dempster Limited, Elland. Killed in action in the assault on Tekke Tepe Ridge, Suvla, Gallipoli, on 9.8.1915, aged 28. Has no known grave. Commemorated **HELLES MEMORIAL TO THE MISSING.** ROH:- Robert Dempster Ltd.

SYKES, HAROLD. Private. No 3932. 1/5th Battalion Duke of Wellington's Regiment. Born Longwood, Huddersfield, on 8.5.1897. Son of Eli and Hannah Maria Sykes, 41 Hill Top, Paddock, Huddersfield. Was a member of the Huddersfield Territorials at the outbreak of the war. Formerly employed at the Daimler motorworks at Coventry. Killed by a sniper on 22.12.1915, aged 28 years. Buried **TALANA FARM CEMETERY.** Grave location:- Plot 3. Row I, Grave 1. (Twin brother of Private **HARRY SYKES**, who died of wounds, 19.3.1916, q.v.). ROH:- All Saints Church, Paddock; Huddersfield Drill Hall.

SYKES, HAROLD. Private. No 241581. 2/5th Battalion Duke of Wellington's Regiment. Son of Mr and Mrs Sykes, 15 Ingfield Terrace, Crimble, Slaithwaite. Attended Crimble Primitive Methodist Chapel and was a former choirboy there. Was a well known local bass vocalist and a skilled violinist. Was a member of the Sons of Temperance. Employed by the Slaithwaite Spinning Company. Enlisted in 1916 and embarked for France in January, 1917. Killed in action, 17.3.1917, aged 28 years. Has no known grave. Commemorated **THIEPVAL MEMORIAL TO THE MISSING.** ROH:- St. James Church, Slaithwaite; Slaithwaite War Memorial; Huddersfield Drill Hall.

SYKES, HAROLD. Private. No 25889. 1/5th Battalion West Yorkshire Regiment. Born Linthwaite. Killed in action, 25.4.1918. Has no known grave. Commemorated **TYNE COT MEMORIAL TO THE MISSING.** ROH:- Linthwaite; St. James Church, Slaithwaite.

SYKES, HAROLD. Ordinary Seaman. No J/62495. Royal Navy. *HMS Candytuft*. Born Huddersfield. Son of Mr and Mrs T H Sykes, Royd Mount, 36 Ballroyd Road, Fartown. Educated Almondbury Grammar School. Was in business with his father, as a textile manufacturer, at Victoria Mills, Honley. Was a member of Honley Wesleyan Church choir. Single. Enlisted 17.11.1916. Was accidentally lost overboard and drowned on 25.9.1917, aged 20 years. Has no known grave. Commemorated **PLYMOUTH NAVAL MEMORIAL TO THE MISSING.** ROH:- Fartown and Birkby War Memorial.

SYKES, HARRY. Private. No 22433. 6th Battalion King's Own Yorkshire Light Infantry. Born Longwood, Huddersfield, on 8.5.1887. Son of Eli and Hannah Maria Sykes, 41 Hill Top, Paddock. Employed as a woollen feeder by Messrs John Taylor and Sons, of Milnsbridge. Was a member of Paddock Liberal Club. Enlisted at the beginning of 1915. Embarked for France at Christmas, 1915. Was wounded under the right shoulder on 3.3.1916. Died of wounds at No 11 Stationary Hospital, Rouen, on 19.3.1916, aged 28 years. Buried **St. SEVER CEMETERY, ROUEN.** Grave location:- Plot A, Row 18, Grave 28. (Twin brother of Private **HAROLD SYKES,** killed in action, 22.12.1915, q.v.). ROH:- All Saints Church, Paddock; Shared Church, Paddock; Longwood War Memorial.

SYKES, HARRY. Lance Corporal. No 50204. 9th Battalion North Staffordshire Regiment. Formerly No 216699 Royal Engineers. Born School Street, Moldgreen 18.10.1889. Son of Alfred and E Sykes, 52 Long Lane, Dalton, Huddersfield. Employed as a stonemason by Messrs Graham and Jessop. Single. Enlisted 19.12.1916. Died of wounds, caused by a German shell which struck him as he was returning to his billet from work, on 17.3.1918, aged 28. Buried **BEDFORD HOUSE ENCLOSURE No 2.** Grave location:- Plot 3. Row E, Grave 5. ROH:- Christ Church, Moldgreen.

SYKES, HARRY. Private. No 242696. 8th Battalion North Staffordshire Regiment. Son of Walter and Charlotte Sykes. Husband of Mary Sykes, 66 Upper Brow Road, Paddock. Employed as a mason by Messrs T. E. Barlow and Son, contractors, of Viaduct Street, Huddersfield. Attended Milton Church P.S.A. Killed in action, 20.9.1917, at Passchendaele, aged 32. Has no known grave. Commemorated **TYNE COT MEMORIAL TO THE MISSING.** ROH:- All Saints Church, Paddock.

SYKES, HARRY. Private. No 31829. 13th Battalion Durham Light Infantry. Born Stockport 5.7.1893. Son of Arthur Henry and Lizzie Sykes, 113 Town End, Golcar. Educated at Stockport schools. Employed in the finishing department at the Dale Street Mill of Messrs G. N. Whiteley Limited. Was a member of the choir at Paddock Congregational Church. Single. Enlisted May 1916. Embarked for France in the first week of July, 1916. Wounded 4.9.1916. Died of wounds at No 36 Casualty Clearing Station on 5.9.1916, aged 23 years. Buried **HEILLY STATION CEMETERY.** Grave location:- Plot 4, Row A, Grave 20. ROH:- St. John's Church, Golcar.

SYKES, HARRY. Leading Seaman. Palace Z/3594. Royal Naval Volunteer Reserve. *SS Southborough*. Son of Leyland and Edith Sykes, 107 Swallow Lane, Golcar. Attended Parkwood United Methodist Church. Was a member of Thorpe Green Working Men's Club. Prior to enlistment, was employed as a weaver by Messrs Smith and Wood and formerly by Messrs

Titus Calverley and Sons, of Milnsbridge. Had been in the Merchant Service since 1916. He joined at Devonport and made his first voyage to Archangel after a few weeks training. This proved a very eventful journey because shortly after arriving at their destination a big explosion occurred, destroying a number of vessels, the crews of which had to leave the ships and seek safety ashore. For four days and nights Harry found shelter in a thick wood and at the end of that time was piloted back to his ship by a Russian Officer. Saw much active service, having visited West Africa, Norway, Russia and France and, on the return from his second visit to Archangel, his ship was torpedoed on 24.9.1917. Nothing was heard from him for 14 weeks until his parents received a wire from Aberdeen, stating that their son was one of the survivors. Lost his life at sea on 16.7.1918 when the *SS Southborough*, on which he was serving as a member of the gun crew, was sunk by an enemy submarine off Scarborough. He was 21 years of age. Has no known grave. Commemorated **PLYMOUTH NAVAL MEMORIAL TO THE MISSING.** ROH:- St. John's Church, Golcar; Parkwood Methodist Church.

SYKES, HARRY ASHLEY. 2nd Lieutenant. 16th Battalion The Rifle Brigade. Formerly 3rd Battalioin The Cameron Highlanders. Born Huddersfield 11.1.1898. Educated Thomas Street Board School, Huddersfield Higher Grade School and Huddersfield Technical College. Was organist at the Hillhouse P.S.A. and at the Great Northern Street Congregational Church. Was employed as an assistant pupil teacher at Thomas Street School. At the time of enlistment, was living at Chapel House, Great Northern Street, Huddersfield. Enlisted as a Private in the Cameron Highlanders on 9.10.1916. Was recommended for a commission in January, 1917. He went through a Cadet course at Kinmel Park near Rhyl. Wounded and taken prisoner on 21.3.1918. Died in Huddersfield Royal Infirmary, of Meningitis, on 14.11.1921. ROH:- Fartown and Birkby War Memorial.

SYKES, HENRY. Private. No 267894. 9th Battalion Duke of Wellington's Regiment. Born South Crosland, Huddersfield. Son of Joe and Sarah Ann Sykes, Moor Lane, Netherton, Huddersfield. Reported missing, presumed killed, 1.9.1918, aged 26 years. Has no known grave. Commemorated **VIS-en-ARTOIS MEMORIAL TO THE MISSING.**

SYKES, HERBERT. Private. No 3971. 1/7th Battalion Duke of Wellington's Regiment. Born Linthwaite. Son of the late Mr Bradley Sykes and Mrs Sykes, Coldwell Street, Linthwaite. Employed by the Colne Valley Spinning Company Limited. Enlisted March 1916. Killed in action at Thiepval Wood during the Battle of the Somme on 14.7.1916, aged 19 years. Has no known grave. Commemorated **THIEPVAL MEMORIAL TO THE MISSING.** ROH:- Linthwaite War Memorial; Huddersfield Drill Hall.

SYKES, HERBERT WADSWORTH. Private. No 20246. 2nd Battalion Duke of Wellington's Regiment. Born Holmfirth. Son of the late Mr Ben Sykes. Lived Austonley, Holmbridge, Holmfirth. Employed as a confectioner. Enlisted April 1916. Invalided home in November suffering from trench feet. Returned to France on 10.5.1917. Killed in action, 9.8.1917, aged 27 years. Has no known grave. Commemorated **ARRAS MEMORIAL TO THE MISSING.** ROH:- Holme and Holmbridge War Memorial.

SYKES, HILTON. Sapper. No 482237. 49th Signal Company, Royal Engineers. Formerly No 245 Duke of Wellington's Regiment. Born Stalybridge, Cheshire. Son of John Denison and H. A. Sykes, 116 Town End, Golcar. Had been in America for 12 months prior to the outbreak of the war. Had been previously employed in the designing department at Messrs C. and J. Hirst and Sons Limited. Attended St. John's Church, Golcar. Was a member of Golcar Conservative Club. Enlisted in the local Territorials at the outbreak of the war. Embarked for France in April, 1915. Wounded on one occasion. Died of wounds caused by a gas shell, 25.7.1917, at No 3 General Hospital, Le Treport. He was 27 years of age. Buried **MONT HUON MILITARY CEMETERY.** Grave location:- Plot 4, Row B, Grave 6b. ROH:- St. John's Church, Golcar; memorial in Golcar Churchyard; St. James Church, Slaithwaite.

SYKES, HILTON WHITEHEAD. Lance Corporal. No 40427. 16th Battalion Northumberland Fusiliers. Born Marsden. Youngest son of Mrs Edwin Sykes, Far New Close, Binn, Marsden. Prior to the war he lived with his widowed mother and his brother and assisted with the general work on the farm. Reported missing, presumed killed, 10.2.1917, aged 22 years. Buried **SERRE ROAD CEMETERY No 1.** Grave location:- Plot 3, Row E. Grave 27. ROH:- Marsden War Memorial.

SYKES, HUBERT WOOD. Private. No 26878. 11th Battalion Lancashire Fusiliers. Born Slaithwaite. Eldest son of Mrs A Sykes, 21 Longlands Road, Slaithwaite. Employed as a weaver by Messrs Pearson Brothers, Commercial Mills, Slaithwaite. He formerly attended Slaithwaite Parish Church but afterwards went to the Zion Baptist Church. Was a member of the Socalist Club. Enlisted 5.11.1915. After seven months training at Clipstone Camp he embarked for France in June, 1916. Killed in action, 22.8.1916, during the Battle of the Somme. He was 28 years of age. Buried **LONSDALE CEMETERY.** Grave location:- Special Memorial B 5. (Brother of Private **TOM ERIC SYKES**, killed in action, 3.5.1917, q.v.). ROH:- St. James Church, Slaithwaite; Slaithwaite War Memorial.

SYKES, H. Private. No 33361. 11th Battalion Northumberland Fusiliers. Died at home, 26.5.1918. Buried **POLE MOOR BAPTIST CHAPEL YARD EXTENSION.** Grave location:- 7, 32.

SYKES, JAMES. Private. No 29160. 7th Battalion The Yorkshire Regiment. Born Almondbury. Son of Mrs Mary Sykes of Penistone Road, Fenay Bridge, Huddersfield. Reported missing, presumed killed, 13.5.1917, aged 26 years. Has no known grave. Commemorated **ARRAS MEMORIAL TO THE MISSING.** ROH:- Lepton Parish Church; Almondbury War Memorial.

SYKES, JAMES ARTHUR. Private. No 23534. 1st Battalion Oxford and Bucks. Light Infantry. Formerly King's Royal Rifle Corps. Born Marsden. Son of William and Elizabeth Sykes, of Ellesmere, Marsden. Employed by Messrs Liptons of Huddersfield. Enlisted in the K.R.R.C. on 17.1.1916 for a period of twelve years. Was afterwards transferred into the Oxford and Bucks. Light Infantry and went abroad, first to India and then to Mesopotamia, where he contracted dysentery and was admitted to hospital in Alexandria, Egypt. Died of typhoid fever in Bangalore, India, on 28.9.1919, aged 21 years. Buried **HOSUR ROAD CEMETERY, BANGALORE, INDIA.** Commemorated **MADRAS 1914-1918 WAR MEMORIAL, CHENNAI, INDIA.**

SYKES, JAMES HENRY. Lance Corporal. No 240663. 1/5th Battalion Duke of Wellington's Regiment. Born Almondbury. Son of Mr and Mrs Joe Sykes, 21 Northgate, Almondbury. Employed by Messrs John Eccles and Company, cotton spinners, Firth Street, Huddersfield. Enlisted November 1914. Embarked for France in April, 1915. Along with three of his comrades he was killed instantly whilst asleep in his billet behind the firing line by a shell on 27.8.1917. He was 22 years of age. Buried **COXYDE MILITARY CEMETERY.** Grave location:- Plot 3, Row C, Grave 21. ROH:- Huddersfield Drill Hall; Almondbury War Memorial.

SYKES, JIM. Private. No 205563. 10th Battalion Royal West Kent Regiment. Formerly No 20702 Durham Light Infantry. Born Slaithwaite. Son of the late Geoffrey and Eva Sykes. Lived with his brother, Mr George Sykes, at 10 Clough House, Slaithwaite. Employed as a piecer by Messrs Edwin Shaw and Sons, Clough House Mills. Attended the Providence Baptist Sunday School. Enlisted in October 1916. Had served on the Italian front for six months. Killed in action in Italy on 7.12.1917, aged 19 years. Buried **GIAVERA BRITISH CEMETERY.** Grave location:- Plot 6, Row E, Grave 11. ROH:- St. James Church, Slaithwaite; Slaithwaite War Memorial.

SYKES, JOE. Private. No 45897. 12th Battalion Northumberland Fusiliers. Born Golcar, Huddersfield 6.11.1885. Son of William Albert and Lois Sykes, 3 Oddfellow's Buildings, Deighton. Educated at Scapegoat Hill and Deighton schools. Employed as a putter-up by Messrs Edwin Walker and Company Limited, Field Mills, worsted cloth manufacturers. Husband of Clara Sykes, 9 Blackhouse Road, Fartown. Enlisted 24.7.1916. Was wounded by gunshot in the face and left arm on 17.4.1917. Died of wounds in No 7 Canadian General Hospital, Etaples, on 21.4.1917, aged 31 years. Buried **ETAPLES MILITARY CEMETERY.** Grave location:- Plot 19, Row E, Grave 11. ROH:- Christ Church, Woodhouse Hill; Fartown and Birkby War Memorial.

SYKES, JOE. Private. No 63852. 2/5th Battalion West Yorkshire Regiment. Born Slaithwaite. Lived 11 Sugden's Buildings, Slaithwaite. Attended West Slaithwaite Church School. Was a member of the local branch of the Y.M.C.A. and the Liberal Club. Enlisted February 1918. Embarked for France in July, 1918. Killed in action near Rheims on 29.7.1918, aged 18 years. Has no known grave. Commemorated **SOISSONS MEMORIAL TO THE MISSING.** (Brother of Private **TOM SYKES**, killed in action, 19.5.1917, q.v.). His parents received a letter from his Sergeant informing them that, *'he was killed instantenously and suffered no pain. He died a soldier's death, remaining at his post to the last during a heavy bombardment. During the time he was with the platoon he was a quiet and willing lad. The Sergeant says that he personally assisted in burying him near the place where he met his death and his comrades made and erected a cross which, though only rough, proved how he was missed'*. (The grave must have been destroyed in later fighting). ROH:- St. James Church, Slaithwaite; Slaithwaite War Memorial.

SYKES, JOE. Gunner. No L/25781. 'A' Battery, 168th (Huddersfield) Brigade, Royal Field Artillery. Born Milnsbridge 12.10.1887. Son of George and Hannah Sykes, 123 Church Street, Paddock. Educated Paddock Council School. Attended Paddock United Methodist Church. Employed as a woollen spinner by Messrs C. and J. Hirst and Sons Limited, Longwood. Husband of Sarah Ellen (Nelly) Sykes, 24 Royds Hall, Longwood. Enlisted 4.5.1915. Killed in action at Nieuport, Belgium, on 11.7.1917, aged 29 years. Has no known grave. Commemorated **NIEUPORT MEMORIAL TO THE MISSING.** ROH:- St. Mark's Parish Church, Longwood: All Saints Church, Paddock; Shared Church, Paddock.

SYKES, JOE EDWIN. Private. No 81071. 1/7th Battalion Durham Light Infantry. Born Golcar. Lived 6 Scar Top, Golcar. Died at Frelon as a Prisoner of War on 15.9.1918, aged 19 years. Buried **GLAGEON COMMUNAL CEMETERY EXTENSION.** Grave location:- Plot 1, Row L, Grave 4. ROH:- St. John's Church, Golcar; Golcar Baptist Church.

SYKES, JOHN. Private. No 2966. 3/5th Battalion Duke of Wellington's Regiment. Born Saddleworth 5.4.1893. Son of the late Mr Percival Poynton Sykes and Mrs Emma T Sykes, Croft House, 25 Newsome Road, Almondbury. Educated at Crossley and Porter School, Halifax. Was formerly in the employ of Messrs Sharp, Crampton and Smith, Chartered Accountants, but at the time of enlistment, he was engaged in clerical work at the office of Messrs John Beever and Sons, Brook Street, Huddersfield. Enlisted in the local Territorials in September, 1914. Embarked for France in April, 1915. Was wounded in the right arm and leg by a sniper's bullet on 1.8.1915. Was treated at Birmingham War Hospital and then returned to Huddersfield where he was discharged from military duties on medical grounds. Died in Huddersfield Royal Infirmary, from consumption, on 11.5.1916, aged 23 years. Buried with full military honours in **ALMONDBURY CEMETERY, HUDDERSFIELD.** Grave location:- CA, 'C', 85. ROH:- Almondbury War Memorial.

SYKES, LESLIE GORDON. Second Lieutenant. 168th (Huddersfield) Brigade, Royal Field Artillery, attached 190th (Night) Training Squadron, Royal Flying Corps. Born June 1898. Son of Lieutenant Colonel Herbert H Sykes and Mrs Sykes, Briarcourt, Lindley, and grandson of the late Mr John Sykes, of Acre House, Lindley. Educated at Aldro School, Eastbourne, and Uppingham Public School, which he left in December, 1914. Enlisted in the Huddersfield Artillery Brigade on its formation in May, 1915, and went through training with them but, on account of his youth, he was unable to proceed with them to the front. He was transferred to another Battery and later served at the front from July, 1916, to November, 1917. He was then transferred to the R.F.C. and had been training with them at Upwood, Cambridgeshire. Died from a compound fracture of the skull and laceration of the brain caused by falling to the ground whilst flying his aeroplane on 22.3.1918, aged 19 years. Buried with full military honours in **St. STEPHEN'S CHURCHYARD, LINDLEY.** Grave location:- in North-East corner. ROH:- St. Stephen's Church, Lindley.

SYKES, LEWIS. Private. No 17344. 10th Battalion Duke of Wellington's Regiment. Born Spring Street, Huddersfield, 25.1.1887. Educated Spring Grove Council School. Married. Lived 2 Waterworth's Yard, Cross Grove Street, Huddersfield. Employed as a dyer's labourer by Messrs C. and J. Hirst and Sons Limited, Longwood. Enlisted 12.7.1915. Killed in action in Belgium on 7.6.1917, aged 30 years. Buried **WOODS CEMETERY, ZILLEBEKE, BELGIUM**. Grave location:- Plot 3, Row E, Grave 15.

SYKES, NORMAN. Sergeant. No 1044. 1/7th Battalion Duke of Wellington's Regiment. Born Marsden. Son of Mr and Mrs Hiram Sykes, Church Avenue, Linthwaite. Had worked with his father who was surveyor of the Slaithwaite Urban District Council. Prior to enlistment had been in business on his own account as a contractor. Had been in the local Territorials since 1908 and, for a couple of years previous to that, was a Private in the old Volunteers. Enlisted at the outbreak of the war with the rank of Lance Corporal. Married. Embarked for France in April, 1915, and was promoted to the rank of Sergeant in July, 1915. Died of wounds at a Field Dressing Station on 17.10.1915, aged 28 years. Buried **FERME-OLIVER CEMETERY, ELVERDINGHE, BELGIUM**. Grave location:- Plot 2, Row K, Grave 1. His wife received a letter from Major William U Rothery, who wrote, *'You will no doubt have been informed that your husband didn't survive his wounds. He was wonderfully brave after he had been hit and we all thought he would pull through. I had a long talk with him whilst he was lying on the stretcher waiting to be carried to hospital. I assure you that his loss is a great grief to me. He was a splendid Sergeant and his fine personal character caused him to be liked by everybody. On behalf on myself, my brother Officers, and every member of the Company I offer you my deepest sympathy.'* ROH:- Linthwaite War Memorial; Huddersfield Drill Hall.

SYKES, NORMAN. Private. No 242409. 1/5th Battalion Duke of Wellington's Regiment. Born Halifax Old Road 14.11.1889. Son of George W and Alice Sykes, 2 Cobcroft Road, Fartown, Huddersfield. Educated Hillhouse Council School and Huddersfield Technical College. Employed as a warehouse and pattern room man. Single. Enlisted January 1916. Along with three other comrades he was killed whilst asleep in his billet by a shell on 27.8.1917, aged 22 years. Buried **COXYDE MILITARY CEMETERY**. Grave location:- Plot 3, Row C, Grave 20. (Brother of Private **STANLEY SYKES**, killed in action, 3.5.1917, q.v.). ROH:- Huddersfield Drill Hall; Fartown and Birkby War Memorial.

SYKES, NORMAN. Private. No G/20128. 1st Battalion Royal West Kent Regiment. Born Huddersfield. Son of Howard and Lavinia Sykes, Field View, 251 Bradford Road, Fartown. Educated at Almondbury Grammar School. Employed as a mungo manufacturer. Single. Reported missing, presumed killed, at Passchendaele on 26.10.1917. Has no known grave. Commemorated **TYNE COT MEMORIAL TO THE MISSING**.

SYKES, NORMAN. Rifleman. No R/19961. 16th Battalion King's Royal Rifle Corps. Born Marsden. Son of Mr and Mrs James Sykes, 21 Spring Street, Marsden. Employed as a weaver by Messrs Crowther, Bruce and Company, of Marsden. Was a member of Marsden Brass Band and of Marsden Conservative Club. Enlisted 1.3.1916. Embarked for France on 14.7.1916. Died of wounds at No 38 Casualty Clearing Station on 26.8.1916, aged 25 years. Buried **HEILLY STATION CEMETERY**. Grave location:- Plot 3, Row G, Grave 36. ROH:- Marsden War Memorial; Marsden Conservative Club.

SYKES, RICHARD. Private. No 7510. 2nd Battalion Duke of Wellington's Regiment. Born Moldgreen, Huddersfield. Enlisted Huddersfield. Died of wounds at No 2 Casualty Clearing Station on 6.5.1915. Buried **BAILLEUL COMMUNAL CEMETERY EXTENSION**. Grave location:- Plot 2, Row A, Grave 139.

SYKES, ROBERT. Gunner. No 50519. 'S' Battery, Royal Horse Artillery. Born Lepton, Huddersfield. Son of Mr Edward Sykes, Field House, Lepton. Employed as a clerk at the Lancashire and Yorkshire Bank, Market Place, Huddersfield. Enlisted in the R.H.A. in 1908 and had been stationed in India for seven years. Was serving with the Indian Expeditionary Force in Mesopotamia, where he died of wounds on 23.11.1915, aged 30 years. Has no known grave. Commemorated **BASRA MEMORIAL TO THE MISSING, IRAQ**. ROH:- Lepton Parish Church; commemorated on headstone in Kirkheaton Cemetery.

SYKES, ROBERT. Private. No 65097. 32nd Battalion Royal Fusiliers. Formerly No S/4/040942 Army Service Corps. Born Armitage Bridge. Son of Anthony Noble and Ellen Sykes, 66 Parkgate, Berry Brow, Huddersfield.

Educated Armitage Bridge Church of England School. Attended Armitage Bridge Church. Was a member of Armitage Bridge Conservative Club. Employed as a butcher by the Berry Brow Cooperative Society. Husband of Henney Etta Sykes, 1 Scott Gate Road, Honley. Enlisted 13.1.1915. Served as a butcher in the A.S.C. for 19 months. He was then transferred to the Royal Fusiliers and embarked for France in June, 1917. Killed in action near Ypres on 7.8.1917, aged 27 years. Has no known grave. Commemorated **MENIN GATE MEMORIAL TO THE MISSING.** (Brother of Private **CHRISTOPHER TINKER SYKES,** killed in action, 7.6.1917, q.v.). Armitage Bridge War Memorial; memorial in Armitage Bridge Churchyard.

SYKES, RONALD. Private. No 202497. 2nd Battalion The Royal Scots Fusiliers. Born 2 Hood Royd, Almondbury, 6.7.1885. Son of Israel and Mary Sykes of Almondbury. Educated at Almondbury Elementary School. Employed as a warper by Messrs Walter Sykes Limited, Zetland Mills and later by Messrs Kaye and Stewart. Husband of Fanny Sykes, Thomas Street, Netherton. Enlisted 27.10.1916. Had been offered but had refused a commission. Killed in action at Dadizeele, Belgium, on 14.10.1918, aged 33 years. Buried **DADIZEELE NEW BRITISH CEMETERY.** Grave location:- Plot 5, Row B, Grave 10. ROH:- Almondbury War Memorial.

SYKES, RONALD. Private. No 5/2417. 1/5th Battalion Duke of Wellington's Regiment. Born Union Street, Lindley, Huddersfield 27.6.1896. Son of William Isaac and Ada Ann Sykes, 32 Union Street, Lindley. Educated Oakes Council School. Employed as an apprentice tailor by Mr Irvine Kaye of Marsh. Single. Attended Lindley Church Sunday School. Enlisted at the outbreak of the war. Embarked for France in April, 1915. Killed in action near Ypres on 9.12.1915, aged 19 years. Buried **ARTILLERY WOOD CEMETERY, BOESINGHE, BELGIUM.** Grave location:- Plot 2, Row C, Grave 9. His parents received a letter from Lieutenant E Bond who wrote, *'I am extremely sorry to have to perform the painful duty of writing to inform you of the death of your son Ronald at the hands of a sniper whilst on duty with his machine gun in the front line trench. He was a jolly good fellow and a splendid willing soldier. All of us in the Battalion are very much concerned at his loss. It seems to us specially hard that he should go just as we are finishing our last spell in the trenches for some time as we were expecting shortly to have a long rest. Doubtless you will be comforted in the knowledge that he died nobly the death of a soldier and a Briton. He did his duty to the last and I am sure he will receive his reward. He is buried in our little cemetery in a pleasant spot within sound of the guns and above his grave has been placed a neat wooden cross.'* ROH:- St. Stephen's Church, Lindley; Huddersfield Drill Hall.

SYKES, STANLEY. Sergeant. No 240672. 'B' Company, 2/5th Battalion Duke of Wellington's Regiment. Born Birkby 10.11.1889. Son of George W and Alice Sykes, 2 Cobcroft Road, Fartown, Huddersfield. Educated at Fartown Grammar School and the Municipal College, Huddersfield. Employed as an engineer by Messrs T. Broadbent and Sons Limited. Husband of Mrs Edna Sykes, 10 Palm Street, Newsome Road, Huddersfield. Enlisted October 1914. Killed in action at the Battle of Bullecourt on 3.5.1917, aged 27 years. Has no known grave. Commemorated **ARRAS MEMORIAL TO THE MISSING.** (Brother of Private **NORMAN SYKES,** killed, 27.8.1917, q.v.). ROH:- Huddersfield Drill Hall; Fartown and Birkby War Memorial.

SYKES, STANLEY. Private. No 301987. 2nd Battalion Durham Light Infantry. Formerly No 6022 Duke of Wellington's Regiment. Born Huddersfield. Lived Milnsbridge. Killed in action, 12.10.1918. Has no known grave. Commemorated **VIS-en-ARTOIS MEMORIAL TO THE MISSING.** ROH:- Longwood War Memorial.

SYKES, TOM. Private. No PW/4797. 18th Battalion Middlesex Regiment. Born Slaithwaite, Huddersfield 20.12.1896. Eldest son of Mr and Mrs John William Sykes, 11 Sugden's Buildings, Manchester Road, Slaithwaite. Employed by Messrs Fisher, Firth and Company, Cellars Clough Mill, Marsden. Attended West Slaithwaite Sunday School. Enlisted 14.2.1916. After nine weeks training he embarked for France. Critically wounded by shellfire on 19.5.1917 and died the same day, aged 20 years. Buried **HENIN COMMUNAL CEMETERY EXTENSION** Grave location:- Plot 1, Row C, Grave 9. ROH:- St. James Church, Slaithwaite; Slaithwaite War Memorial.

SYKES, TOM. Private. No 11342. 2nd Battalion Duke of Wellington's Regiment. Born Honley. Son of John William and Selina Sykes, Town Head, Honley. Employed as a teamer by Mr Theaker of Honley. Enlisted at the outbreak of the war. Had been wounded and in hospital on two occasions. Died of wounds at No 26 General Hospital on 22.4.1917, aged 30 years. Buried **ETAPLES MILITARY CEMETERY.** Grave location:- Plot 19. Row F. Grave 7. ROH:- Honley War Memorial.

SYKES, TOM ERIC. Trooper. No 2044. Household Battalion. Born Slaithwaite. Youngest son of Mrs Albert Sykes, 21 Longlands Road, Slaithwaite. Employed as a weaver by Messrs W. and E. Crowther Limited, Brook Mills, Slaithwaite. Killed in action, 3.5.1917, aged 20 years. Has no known grave. Commemorated **ARRAS MEMORIAL TO THE MISSING.** (Brother of Private **HUBERT WOOD SYKES**, killed in action, 22.8.1916, q.v.). ROH:- St. James Church, Slaithwaite; Slaithwaite War Memorial.

SYKES, WALTER. Gunner. No L/25553. 'D' Battery, 282nd Brigade, Royal Field Artillery. Born Huddersfield. Son of Joseph and Clara Lizzie Sykes, Warehouse Hill, Marsden. Employed on the clerical staff of Messrs Crowther, Bruce and Company, New Mill, Marsden. Attended Marsden Parish Church and at one time was a member of the choir. Was deeply interested in ambulance work, often accompanying the Marsden Villa football team in the capacity of amateur medical attendant. Enlisted in 1915. Embarked for France in May, 1917. Killed in action, 4.7.1917, aged 20 years. Buried **BRANDHOEK MILITARY CEMETERY.** Grave location:- Plot 2, Row L, Grave 16. ROH:- Marsden War Memorial.

SYKES, WALTER. Lance Corporal. No PO/1440 (S). Royal Marine Light Infantry. 2nd Royal Marine Battalion, Royal Naval Division. Born Kirkheaton. Son of the late Mr William and Mrs Sykes, Hillside, Kirkheaton. Employed by Messrs Broadhead and Graves Limited, Kirkheaton. Was a teacher at the Kirkheaton Church Sunday School. Killed in action, 10.7.1917, aged 24 years. Buried **ORCHARD DUMP CEMETERY.** Grave location:- Plot 6, Row B, Grave 50.

SYKES, WILFRED. Private. No DM2/163108. 'Y' Siege Park, Army Service Corps. Born Paddock, Huddersfield in 1891. Son of Percy and M A Sykes, 19 Armitage Road, Milnsbridge. Educated Milnsbridge Council School. Employed as a woollen weaver by Messrs Fred Calverley and Company Limited, Milnsbridge. Single. Enlisted March 1916. Wounded near Ypres on 27.5.1918. Died of wounds at Zuydcoote on 29.5.1918, aged 27 years. Buried **ZUDYCOOTE MILITARY CEMETERY.** Grave location:- Plot 2, Row E, Grave 2. (Brother of Private **GEORGE HERBERT SYKES**, killed in action, 31.5.1917, q.v.). ROH:- Milnsbridge War Memorial.

SYKES, WILLIE. Private. No 32194. 2nd Battalion West Yorkshire Regiment. Born Linthwaite. Son of Mrs Sykes, 38 New Street, Upper Clough, Linthwaite. Employed as a weaver at Bank Bottom Mills, Marsden. Was a member of the Hoyle Ing Working Men's Club. Enlisted 16.5.1916. Had been in France for two months when he was reported missing, presumed killed, during the Battle of the Somme on 26.10.1916, aged 33 years. Has no known grave. Commemorated **THIEPVAL MEMORIAL TO THE MISSING.** ROH:- Linthwaite War Memorial.

SYKES, WILLIE. Private. No 265338. 2/5th Battalion Duke of Wellington's Regiment. Born Linthwaite. Son of Mr and Mrs Ned Sykes, 24 The Rock, Linthwaite. Reported missing, presumed killed, near Rheims on 27.7.1918, aged 21 years. Has no known grave. Commemorated **SOISSONS MEMORIAL TO THE MISSING.** ROH:- Linthwaite War Memorial.

SYKES, WILLIE. Corporal. No 12088. 9th Battalion Duke of Wellington's Regiment. Born Holmfirth. Son of the late Mr and Mrs Benjamin Sykes of Holmfirth. Lived 6 Newgate, Holmfirth. Educated at Holmfirth National School. Employed at Queens Mill, Huddersfield. Enlisted 4.9.1914. After training he embarked for France in July, 1915. Killed in action at Contalmaison on 7.7.1916 during the Battle of the Somme. He was 26 years of age. Has no known grave. Commemorated **THIEPVAL MEMORIAL TO THE MISSING.** ROH:- Underbank War Memorial.

TANN, WILLIAM HENRY. Lance Corporal. No 68440. 7th Battalion Machine Gun Corps. Formerly No 29392 Duke of Wellington's Regiment. Born Shelley, Huddersfield. Son of Herbert and Ada Tann. Husband of Ada Tann, 11 John Street, Milnsbridge. Employed by the Colne Valley Dye and Chemical Company of Milnsbridge. Enlisted September 1916. Embarked for France in July, 1917. Killed in action, 17.11.1917, aged 23 years. Buried **GORRE BRITISH CEMETERY, BEUVRY.** Grave location:- Plot 5, Row A, Grave 7. ROH:- Emmanuel Church, Shelley; Milnsbridge War Memorial.

TARBATT, LEWIS. Private. No 31574. 1st Battalion East Yorkshire Regiment. Born Birchencliffe 9.12.1897. Son of John C Tarbatt, Oak Cottage, 2 Edgerton, Huddersfield. Educated Hillhouse Secondary School. Employed as an apprentice joiner. Enlisted 8.6.1917. Reported missing at Wytschaete on 25.4.1918 and afterwards presumed to have been killed on that date. Has no known grave. Commemorated **TYNE COT MEMORIAL TO THE MISSING.** ROH:- New North Road Baptist Church.

TATE, WILFRED. Private. No 241613. 2/5th Battalion Duke of Wellington's Regiment. Born Golcar. Son of John William and Sarah Tate, 131 Station Road, Golcar. Assisted his father in his duties as a rate collector and sanitary inspector. Was secretary of the Christian Endeavour Society and also a teacher and assistant secretary of the Golcar Baptist Sunday School. Enlisted March 1916. Embarked for France in January, 1917. Reported missing, presumed killed, at the Battle of Bullecourt on 3.5.1917. He was 22 years of age. Has no known grave. Commemorated **ARRAS MEMORIAL TO THE MISSING.** ROH:- St. John's Church, Golcar; Golcar Baptist Church; Huddersfield Drill Hall.

TATTERSALL, HARRY SHAW. Private. No PO/1223 (S). Royal Marine Light Infantry. Portsmouth Division, Born Linthwaite. Son of Thomas and Helena Tattersall, 1 Lowerhouses, Linthwaite. Employed as a spinner by Messrs Thomas, Bates and Son, Platt Mill, Slaithwaite and previously at Messrs J. Crowther and Sons of Milnsbridge. Attended Linthwaite Church, where he had been a choirboy, and was a member of the Young Men's Class. Played football for the Pymroyd (Milnsbridge) Association football club. Enlisted in December 1915. Was stationed at Gosport, near Portsmouth, and was drafted to Ireland to take part in the quelling of the rebellion. Was accidentally shot on Sunday, 14.5.1916, at Queenstown, Ireland, and died at about 8.30am, aged 20. It appears that a comrade was cleaning his rifle in a tent some distance away from that in which Private Tattersall was living when the gun, which was loaded, went off and the shot penetrated two tents and struck him on the side of his head killing him instantly. Buried with full military honours at **CHRIST CHURCH, LINTHWAITE, HUDDERSFIELD.** Grave location:- C, 68. ROH:- Linthwaite War Memorial.

TATTERSALL, JOSEPH BERRY. Private. No 20657. 7th Battalion The Royal West Kent Regiment. Formerly No 208029 Labour Corps. Born Huddersfield. Lived with his sister at 22 Dowker Street, Milnsbridge. Employed as a teaser by Messrs Charles Lockwood and Sons Limited, of Linthwaite. Attended Milnsbridge Wesleyan Church. Was taken prisoner by the Germans on 21.3.1918. Died from dysentery as a Prisoner of War on 1.6.1918. Buried **ANNOIS COMMUNAL CEMETERY, AISNE, FRANCE.** Grave location:- Plot 1, Row C, Grave 14. ROH:- Longwood War Memorial.

TAYLOR, ALBERT. Private. No 241987. 2/5th Battalion Duke of Wellington's Regiment. Son of Mr and Mrs T Taylor, Hogley Green, Holmfirth. Educated Field End Day School. Attended Hall Sunday School. Employed as a weaver at Yew Tree Mills, Hinchliffe Mill. Enlisted March 1916. Embarked for France in January, 1917. Reported missing, presumed killed, 3.5.1917, at the Battle of Bullecourt. Has no known grave. Commemorated **ARRAS MEMORIAL TO THE MISSING.** ROH:- Holme and Holmbridge War Memorial; Huddersfield Drill Hall.

TAYLOR, ALBERT EDWARD, DCM. 2nd Lieutenant. 2nd Battalion Duke of Wellington's Regiment. Born Paddock, Huddersfield, 24.2.1890. Son of Arthur and Frances Taylor, 11 Branch Street, Paddock. Educated Paddock Council School. Attended Paddock United Methodist Church. Employed as a cotton spinner. Enlisted 19.4.1909. Was mobilised as a Private at the outbreak of the war. Awarded the DCM in November, 1914, for, *'conspicuous gallantry* *and skill in commanding his Company after the Officers were killed or wounded on 8.11.1914 near Ypres, in retaking trenches and bringing men out of action.'* He was promoted Company Sergeant Major. Was wounded at St. Eloi in 1915 and, whilst convalescing in England, was married to Miss Mary E Lumb of Paddock. Whilst in Huddersfield he took part in many recruiting meetings. His devoted service when he rejoined the Battalion earned him a recommendation for a commission. He had only been back with his Battalion in France for a few weeks, after going through the necessary Officers' training, when he was killed in action on 9.4.1917 at Fampoux, near Arras. He was 26 years of age. Has no known grave. Commemorated **ARRAS MEMORIAL TO THE MISSING.** ROH:- All Saints Church, Paddock; Shared Church, Paddock.

TAYLOR, ALFRED CASTLE. Private. No 98842. 3rd Battalion Sherwood Foresters. Born 94a Deighton Road, Deighton, Huddersfield. Son of John and Jane Taylor, 96 Deighton Road, Deighton. Educated Deighton Council School and Huddersfield Municipal Secondary School. Assisted his father in the family grocery business. Attended Deighton United Methodist Church and was a member of the choir. Single. Enlisted 31.5.1917. Died at Cannock Chase Isolation Hospital of meningitis on 12.1.1918, aged 19. Buried **DEIGHTON UNITED METHODIST CHAPEL YARD, HUDDERSFIELD.** Grave location:- West of Chapel. ROH:- Christ Church, Woodhouse Hill; Deighton United Methodist Chapel; Deighton War Memorial.

TAYLOR, ARNOLD. Private. No 133744. 61st Battalion Machine Gun Corps. Formerly No 98011 Sherwood Foresters. Born Golcar. Son of Mary H. Taylor, 19 Mount View, Leymoor Road, Golcar. Employed as a woollen piecer at Parkwood Mills, Longwood. Attended Wellhouse United Methodist Church. Was a member of the Golcar Central Liberal Club. Enlisted in 1917 and embarked for France on Easter Monday, 1918. Died of wounds, 25.10.1918, aged 19 years. Buried **St. AUBERT BRITISH CEMETERY.** Grave location:- Plot 5, Row D, Grave 7. ROH:- St. John's Church, Golcar.

TAYLOR, ARTHUR. Guardsman. No 26464. 4th Battalion The Grenadier Guards. Born Golcar. Educated at Golcar Schools. Employed as a weaver. Married. Lived 352 Blackmoorfoot Road, Crosland Moor, Huddersfield. Enlisted August 1916. Reported missing, presumed killed, 13.5.1918. Has no known grave. Commemorated **PLOEGSTEERT MEMORIAL TO THE MISSING.** ROH:- 'Rising Sun' Public House, Crosland Moor; St. Barnabas Church, Crosland Moor.

TAYLOR, ARTHUR WILLIAM. Private. No 57474. 2/6th Battalion West Yorkshire Regiment. Born Golcar. Son of James and Helen Taylor, Hill Top, Slaithwaite: husband of Alice Taylor, 6 Vine Terrace, Crimble, Slaithwaite. Employed by the Colne Valley Tweed Company, of Slaithwaite. Attended Crimble Congregational Church. Enlisted at the outbreak of the war. Was taken prisoner in the early months of 1917. Died of dysentery whilst a Prisoner of War on 20.3.1918. Buried **TOURNAI COMMUNAL CEMETERY ALLIED EXTENSION.** Grave location:- Plot 1, Row G, Grave 5. ROH:- St. James Church, Slaithwaite; Slaithwaite War Memorial.

TAYLOR, CHARLES. Rifleman. No R/20893. 16th Battalion King's Royal Rifle Corps. Born Golcar. Lived with his sister, Mrs Bottomley at 6 Victoria Street, Marsden. Employed as a spinner at Bank Bottom Mills, Marsden. Attended Marsden Parish Church and was a member of Marsden Conservative Club. Reported missing, presumed killed, 26.9.1917, aged 25 years. Has no known grave. Commemorated **TYNE COT MEMORIAL TO THE MISSING.** ROH:- Marsden War Memorial; Marsden Conservative Club.

TAYLOR, EDGAR. Private. No 35620. 16th Battalion Northumberland Fusiliers. Formerly No 37051 Durham Light Infantry. Husband of Edith Taylor, 1 Longcroft Station, Golcar. Employed as a teaser by Messrs Pearson Brothers, Victoria Mills, Golcar. Enlisted July 1916. Invalided home from France with trench fever at the beginning of 1917. Returned to France in May, 1917. Dangerously wounded in the side on Saturday 1.12.1917. Died of wounds at No 61 Casualty Clearing Station on Monday, 11.12.1917, aged 31 years. Buried **DOZINGHEM MILITARY CEMETERY.** Grave location:- Plot 15, Row F, Grave 5. (Brother of Private **JOHN WILLIAM TAYLOR,** killed in action, 18.3.1917, q.v.). ROH:- St. John's Church, Golcar.

TAYLOR, EDGAR. Sergeant. No 5514. 10th Battalion King's Royal Rifle Corps. Born Halifax. Enlisted Huddersfield. Lived Netherthong, Holmfirth. Had served eight years in the ranks and four in the reserves. He had fought in the Boer War and afterwards was stationed in India. Had been a porter at Thongsbridge Station for five years when he rejoined the Colours in September, 1914. He lodged with Mrs Rusby at Deanhouse. Attended Netherthong Parish Church. Was a member of the Netherthong Working Men's Club. Killed by a shell on 19.2.1917. Buried **A.I.F. BURIAL GROUND, FLERS.** Grave location:- Plot 4, Row K, Grave 27. ROH:- Netherthong and Thongsbridge War Memorial; Netherthong Working Men's Club; Halifax Civic Book of Remembrance; Lancashire and Yorkshire Railway Roll.

TAYLOR, EDWARD. Sergeant. No 2546. 1/5th Battalion Duke of Wellington's Regiment. Born Holme Place, Marsh, 18.2.1892. Second son of the late Mr George Washington Taylor and Mrs Taylor, 25 Water Street, Huddersfield. Educated Spring Grove Church of England School and Longwood Grammar School. Employed as a woollen engineer by Messrs Glendinning Brothers, Tanfield Mills, Leeds Road, Huddersfield. Had served six years in the local Territorials. Single. Enlisted 6.8.1914. Wounded on the Somme battlefield on 3.7.1916. Admitted to No 35 Casualty Clearing Station, where his left leg was amputated just below the knee. Died of wounds, 8.7.1916, aged 24 years. Buried **DOULLENS COMMUNAL CEMETERY EXTENSION No 1.** Grave location:- Plot 3, Row C, Grave 15. ROH:- Huddersfield Parish Church; Huddersfield Drill Hall.

TAYLOR, ERNEST. Private. No 29168. 1/6th Battalion Duke of Wellington's Regiment. Born Teddington, Middlesex. Son of William and Mary Taylor of Mentmore, Leighton Buzzard. Husband of Elizabeth Taylor, 38 Clayton's Yard, Northumberland Street, Huddersfield, Employed as a carter at the London and North Western Railway Company's goods yard at Huddersfield. Died of wounds, 27.7.1918, aged 30 years. Buried **ESQUELBECQ MILITARY CEMETERY.** Grave location:- Plot 3, Row D, Grave 14. ROH:- London and North Western Railway Roll.

TAYLOR, FRANK. Private. No 62791. 9th Battalion King's Own Yorkshire Light Infantry. Formerly No 5/93666 Territorial Reserve Battalion. Born 43 Upper Mount Street, Lockwood, Huddersfield. Son of the late James William and Annie Elizabeth Taylor. Lived with his sister, Mrs Mary Wigglesworth, at 43 Upper Mount Street, Lockwood. Educated Mount Pleasant Council School, Lockwood. Employed as a teamer by Messrs R. S. Dyson and Company, wholesale grocers, Albert Yard, Huddersfield. Single. Enlisted 30.10.1917. Killed in action, 24.8.1918, aged 18 years. Buried **REGINA TRENCH CEMETERY, GRANDCOURT.** Grave location:- Plot 7, Row B, Grave 20. ROH:- 'Rising Sun' Public House, Crosland Hill; St. Stephen's Church, Rashcliffe; St. Barnabas Church, Crosland Moor.

TAYLOR, FRANK. Private. No 44994. 2nd Battalion York and Lancaster Regiment. Born Birkby, Huddersfield, 14.6.1887. Son of James and Ellen Taylor, 5 Chadwick's Yard, Blacker Road, Birkby. Educated Hillhouse Board School. Employed as a pattern weaver. Husband of Elsie May Taylor, 40 Birkby Hall Road, Huddersfield. Enlisted 18.8.1917. Killed in action near St. Quentin on 18.9.1918, aged 31 years. Buried **TREFCON BRITISH CEMETERY.** Grave location:- Row D, Grave 17. ROH:- Fartown and Birkby War Memorial.

TAYLOR, FRANK WILLIAM. Private. No M2/046049. Army Service Corps (Motor Transport Section). Born Wedmore, Somerset. Husband of Jane Taylor, 42 Knowle Terrace, Slaithwaite. Attended Slaithwaite Wesleyan Chapel. Employed as a chauffeur by Mr William Crowther, J.P., Field House, Slaithwaite. Enlisted January 1915. Embarked for France in September, 1915, where he was employed on motor repair work. In June, 1916, he was crushed by a car reversing into him. His injuries were not regarded as serious and he was sent home to England. He was admitted to Lakenham Miltary Hospital, Norwich, where it was thought he would recover. But he suffered a relapse and died of his injuries on 10.7.1916, aged 33 years. Buried **SLAITHWAITE CEMETERY.** Grave location:- B, 4, 8. ROH:- St. James Church, Slaithwaite; Slaithwaite War Memorial.

TAYLOR, FRED. Corporal. No 24986. 2nd Battalion Duke of Wellington's Regiment. Born Huddersfield 25.6.1888. Educated Moldgreen Council School. Married. Lived 3 Standiforth Place, Dalton, Huddersfield. Employed as a woollen fettler and teaser at Commercial Mills, Firth Street, Huddersfield. Enlisted 10.8.1915. Killed during the Battle of Arras on 3.5.1917. Has no known grave. Commemorated **ARRAS MEMORIAL TO THE MISSING.** ROH:- Christ Church, Moldgreen.

TAYLOR, FRED. Rifleman. No 267798. 1/7th Battalion West Yorkshire Regiment. Born Milnsbridge 6.4.1895. Educated Crosland Moor Church of England School. Employed as a cloth finisher by Messrs Walker, Dyson and Sons of Milnsbridge. Lived 105 Cottage Retreat, Marsden Road, Huddersfield. Single. Enlisted November 1914. Killed in action at Passchendaele on 9.10.1917, aged 22 years. Has no known grave. Commemorated **TYNE COT MEMORIAL TO THE MISSING.**

TAYLOR, FRED. Private. No 29/601. 11th Battalion Northumberland Fusiliers. Born Golcar. Son of the late James Taylor and Leviah Atkinson (formerly Taylor). Married. Lived 7 Hanging Royd, Wellhouse, Golcar. Employed as a fettler on the night shift by the Colne Valley Spinning Company Limited. Was a member of the Wellhouse Liberal Club. Enlisted 16.5.1916. Embarked for France during the summer of 1916 and was invalided home with trench feet. Returned to the front in April, 1917. Died of wounds at No 44 Casualty Clearing Station on 7.6.1917, aged 23 years. Buried **BRANDHOEK MILITARY CEMETERY.** Grave location:- Plot 1, Row D, Grave 8. (Brother of Private **PERCY TAYLOR**, killed in action, 7.8.1917, q.v.). ROH:- St. John's Church, Golcar.

TAYLOR, GEORGE. Rifleman. No 268693. 1/7th Battalion West Yorkshire Regiment. Born Huddersfield. Married, with two children. Lived 27 Stile Common Road, Primrose Hill, Huddersfield. Employed by Mr Thomas, hairdresser, of Market Street, Huddersfield. Enlisted November 1915. Killed in action near Cambrai on 11.10.1918, aged 33 years. Buried **WELLINGTON CEMETERY.** Grave location:- Plot 1, Row H, Grave 7/10.

TAYLOR, GEORGE. Guardsman. No 22655. 1st Battalion Grenadier Guards. Born Marsden. Only son of Mr Joe Taylor of Nab Lane, Mirfield. Had worked in the Colne Valley for many years. At the time of enlisting was employed as a weaver by Mr J E Crowther of Marsden. Single. Enlisted February 1915. Embarked for France in November, 1915. Killed in action at the Battle of the Somme on 10.9.1916, aged 35 years. Has no known grave. Commemorated **THIEPVAL MEMORIAL TO THE MISSING.** ROH:- Marsden War Memorial.

TAYLOR, HAROLD. Ordinary Seaman. No J/74720. Royal Navy. *HMS Cornwall*. Born South Parade, Stainland, 26.7.1899. Son of Joe and Emily Taylor, 44 Crosland Road, Thornton Lodge, Huddersfield. Educated Bowling Green Council School, Stainland. Employed as a warehouseman. Single. Enlisted 28.7.1917. Died of pneumonia on 30.6.1918, following upon influenza, at Belmont Auxiliary Hospital, Liverpool. He was 18 years of age. Buried **PROVIDENCE CONGREGATIONAL CEMETERY, STAINLAND.** Grave location:- 469. ROH:- St. Stephen's Church, Rashcliffe.

TAYLOR, HAROLD ERNEST. Corporal. No 2289. Household Battalion. Born Golcar. Son of Albert and Sarah Ann Taylor, Commercial Mills, Slaithwaite. Employed by Messrs Pogson and Company, Bridge Street Mills, Slaithwaite. Attended St. James's Church and Sunday School, Slaithwaite. Was a member of the Slaithwaite Conservative Club. Killed in action, 29.1.1918, aged 27 years. Buried **MONCHY BRITISH CEMETERY.** Grave location:- Plot 2, Row B, Grave 25. ROH:- St. James Church, Slaithwaite; Slaithwaite War Memorial.

TAYLOR, HARRY. Private. No 319629. 2nd Battalion Duke of Wellington's Regiment. Born Marsh 9.6.1891. Son of the late Charles E Taylor and Mrs Martha Taylor, 15 Zion Square, Lindley. Educated Oakes Board School. Employed as a teamer by Messrs J. W. Leech and Company, chemical manufacturers, of Milnsbridge. Single. Enlisted 3.2.1910. Had only been home from the annual training a fortnight when he was called upon to rejoin his Regiment. He embarked for France on 14.8.1914. Killed in action at Annequin on 13.10.1914, aged 23. Has no known grave. Commemorated **LE TOURET MEMORIAL TO THE MISSING.**

TAYLOR, HARRY. Corporal. No 25415. 10th Battalion West Yorkshire Regiment. Son of Joseph and Mary Ann Taylor, 26 Westgate, Honley. Educated Honley National School. Employed in the Honley Cooperative grocery department. Was a member of the local Wesleyan Society. Single. Killed in action at Bouzincourt Ridge on 30.3.1918, aged 25 years. Buried **BOUZINCOURT RIDGE CEMETERY.** Grave location:- Plot 1, Row B, Grave 22. ROH:- Honley War Memorial.

TAYLOR, HARRY. Corporal. No 6493. 2nd Battalion Duke of Wellington's Regiment. Born Ripponden, near Halifax, 23.3.1885. Son of Mr and Mrs Fred Taylor, 7 Bankfield Road, Huddersfield. Educated Zion Congregational Day School, Ripponden. Employed as a labourer. Married. Lived 383 Leeds Road, Huddersfield. Enlisted in May 1901. Was mobilised 5.8.1914. Killed in action at Hill 60 on 18.4.1915. Buried **RAILWAY DUGOUTS BURIAL GROUND (TRANSPORT FARM).** Grave location:- Plot 1, Row A, Grave 8.

TAYLOR, HENRY JOHN. Lance Corporal. No 203039. 1/4th Battalion King's Own Yorkshire Light Infantry. Formerly No 4308 Duke of Wellington's Regiment. Born Yew Green, Lockwood, Huddersfield. Son of David and Ada Taylor, 11 Bath Street, Lockwood. Educated Mount Pleasant Council School. Employed as a percher by Messrs Jennens, Welch and Company, cloth shrinkers of Springwood Works. Attended Mount Pleasant Wesleyan Church. Married, with one child. Lived Springdale Street, Huddersfield. Joined the local Territorials in 1913 and was mobilised with them at the outbreak of the war. Was afterwards transferred to the K.O.Y.L.I. Died of gas poisoning on 26.7.1917, aged 23 years. Buried **COXYDE MILITARY CEMETERY.** Grave location:- Plot 1, Row L, Grave 14. (Brother of Private **WILLIAM FERGUS TAYLOR,** who died at home, 15.5.1917, q.v.). ROH:- Emmanuel Church, Lockwood; Mount Pleasant Chapel, Lockwood.

TAYLOR, HERBERT. Private. No M/341414. Army Service Corps (Mechanical Transport Section). Born Meltham. Husband of Laura Ann Taylor, of Greensend, Meltham. Employed as a dyer's labourer by the Colne Valley Spinning Company, of Milnsbridge. Died of accidental injuries on 14.11.1918, aged 36 years. Buried **St. MARIE CEMETERY, LE HAVRE.** Grave location:- Plot 2, Row O, Grave 2. ROH:- St. Bartholomew's Church, Meltham.

TAYLOR, HUBERT HARRY. Private. No 17917. 9th Battalion Duke of Wellington's Regiment. Born 112 Rashcliffe Hill, Lockwood 8.1.1897. Son of Fred and Matilda Taylor, 112 Rashcliffe Hill, Lockwood. Educated Rashcliffe Church of England School. Employed as a woollen piecer by Messrs James Shires and Sons of Milnsbridge. Single. Enlisted 22.1.1916. Embarked for France on 18.5.1916. Killed in action at Delville Wood during the Battle of the Somme on 2.8.1916, aged 19 years. Has no known grave. Commemorated **THIEPVAL MEMORIAL TO THE MISSING.** ROH:- St. Stephen's Church, Rashcliffe.

TAYLOR, IRVIN. Private. No 102219. 166th Company, Machine Gun Corps. Formerly No 208601 Army Service Corps. Born Linthwaite. Son of A I and Mary Ellen Taylor, 32 Rufford Road, Scar lane, Milnsbridge. Attended Milnsbridge Wesleyan Sunday School. Reported missing, presumed killed, at the Battle of Cambrai on 30.11.1917, aged 20 years. Has no known grave. Commemorated **CAMBRAI MEMORIAL TO THE MISSING.** ROH:- St. John's Church, Golcar; Longwood War Memorial.

TAYLOR, JABEZ WILLIAM. Private. No 29986. 2/7th Battalion Duke of Wellington's Regiment. Born Meltham. Killed in action, 26.3.1918. Buried **POMMIER COMMUNAL CEMETERY.** Grave location:- Grave No 5. ROH:- St. Bartholomew's Church, Meltham; Huddersfield Drill Hall.

TAYLOR, JOE. Private. No 4925. 'A' Company, 2/5th Battalion Duke of Wellington's Regiment. Son of William Henry and Eleanor Taylor, 16 Spring Mill, Milnsbridge. Employed as a tailor's cutter by Messrs Bairstows, Sons and Company, of Fitzwilliam Street, Huddersfield. He formerly attended Thornton Lodge Wesleyan Church but, prior to enlistment, attended Lepton Wesleyan Church. Was a well known athlete, having won several prizes for running and walking. He also played as wing three-quarter with the Huddersfield A team. Enlisted 8.3.1916. Embarked for France on 10.1.1917. Killed by shell fire on 27.2.1917, aged 30. Has no known grave. Commemorated **THIEPVAL MEMORIAL TO THE MISSING**. ROH:- Milnsbridge War Memorial; Huddersfield Drill Hall.

TAYLOR, JOE. Gunner. No 84206. 238th Siege Battery, Royal Garrison Artillery. Born Slaithwaite. Son of George Edwin and Mary Ann Taylor, Lane, Lingards, Slaithwaite. Employed as a weaver by Mr John Ed Crowther at Bank Bottom Mills, Marsden. Attended Holthead General Sunday School. Was a member of Slaithwaite Cricket Club, Slaithwaite Socalist Club and Boothbanks Working Men's Club. Enlisted 24.5.1916. Embarked for France on 17.11.1916. Was dangerously wounded on 7.9.1917. Admitted to No 11 Casualty Clearing Station, where he died of his wounds on 13.9.1917. He was 33 years of age. Buried **GODEWAERSVELDE BRITISH CEMETERY**. Grave location:- Plot 1, Row B, Grave 34. ROH:- St. James Church, Slaithwaite; Slaithwaite War Memorial.

TAYLOR, JOE SYKES. Private. No 43063. 9th Battalion King's Own Yorkshire Light Infantry. Formerly No TR/5/60501 85th Territorial Reserve Battalion. Born Golcar, Huddersfield. Son of Edward and Florence Taylor. Husband of Elsie Taylor, 73 Scarborough Terrace, Town End, Golcar. Employed as a woollen teaser by Messrs T. W. Thorpe and Company, Heath House Mills, Golcar. Attended Golcar Parish Church. Enlisted 18.4.1916. Had been in hospital suffering from gas poisoning and shell shock. Died from gunshot wounds at No 29 Casualty Clearing Station on 1.9.1918, aged 24 years. Buried **BAGNEUX BRITISH CEMETERY**. Grave location:- Plot 5, Row F, Grave 4. ROH:- Longwood War Memorial; St. John's Church, Golcar.

TAYLOR, JOHN IRVIN. Private. No 17946. 9th Battalion Duke of Wellington's Regiment. Born 118 Victoria Road, Lockwood, Huddersfield. Son of James and Eliza Taylor, 11 Bentley Street, Lockwood. Educated Mount Pleasant Council School. Employed as an angora yarn spinner by Messrs Shires and Sons, George Street, Milnsbridge. Attended Lockwood Baptist Sunday School. Single. Enlisted 22.1.1916. In his last letter home before he left England he wrote, *'I mean to do my duty like a soldier and a man. I am able to hold my head up because I know that I am doing my duty and if I had known what I know now I should have joined long since.'* Killed by the bursting of a shell at Delville Wood on 2.8.1916, aged 21 years. Has no known grave. Commemorated **THIEPVAL MEMORIAL TO THE MISSING**. ROH:- St. Stephen's Church, Rashcliffe; Emmanuel Church, Lockwood; Mount Pleasant Chapel, Lockwood; memorial in Lockwood Cemetery.

TAYLOR, JOHN JAMES. Private. No 22313. 2/4th Battalion Duke of Wellington's Regiment. Born Netherton, Huddersfield. Son of Mr and Mrs Thomas H Taylor of Healey House, Netherton. Prior to enlistment, was employed at the Crosland Factory. Killed in action near Rheims on 20.7.1918, aged 19 years. Has no known grave. Commemorated **SOISSONS MEMORIAL TO THE MISSING**. ROH:- South Crosland and Netherton War Memorial.

TAYLOR, JOHN SAMSON. Sergeant. No 1088. 1/5th Battalion Duke of Wellington's Regiment. Born Netherton, Huddersfield, 16.8.1872. Son of the late James and Hannah Taylor. Educated Berry Brow Council School. Attended Berry Brow Wesleyan Church. Employed as a wool sorter by Messrs J. Brooke and Sons at Armitage Bridge Mills. Husband of Selina Taylor, Fair Hill, Berry Brow, Huddersfield. Enlisted 4.8.1914. Shot through the head by a sniper at 5.20am on 16.8.1915, aged 43 years, on his birthday. Has no known grave. Commemorated **MENIN GATE MEMORIAL TO THE MISSING**. ROH:- Lockwood Baptist Church; Armitage Bridge War Memorial; Armitage Bridge National School; Armitage Bridge Mills; Huddersfield Drill Hall.

TAYLOR, JOHN THOMAS. Private. No 790. 1/7th Battalion Duke of Wellington's Regiment. Eldest son of Mr Walter Taylor of Handel Street, Golcar. Was in the 1/7th Battalion prior to the outbreak of the war and had just finished his four years training but had not received his discharge papers. Was married before he embarked for France in April, 1915. Killed in action, 22.10.1915, aged 22 years. Buried **TALANA FARM CEMETERY**. Grave location:- Plot 4, Row C, Grave 18. His wife received the following letter from Lieutenant J W Tetlow, who wrote, *'I am more than sorry to have to tell you that your husband was killed this afternoon. He had gone down to the canal bank* *with me and a shell hit a tree and part of the dugout where he was and burst. He was killed at once and suffered no pain which was a blessing. He was my servant and was much more than that, he was a friend. We all felt his loss very much indeed and sympathise with you in your great sorrow. Yet there is one consolation – that he died a death which we should all wish to die if the time comes.'* ROH:- St. John's Church, Golcar; Huddersfield Drill Hall; Longwood War Memorial.

TAYLOR, JOHN WILLIAM. Private. No 242980. 1/5th Battalion King's Own Yorkshire Light Infantry. Born Golcar. Married, with one child. Lived 21 Scar House Fold, Golcar. Employed as a weaver by Messrs George Mallinson and Sons Limited, Linthwaite. Was a member of the Smith Ryding Working Men's Club. Enlisted 14.9.1916. Had been in France about eleven weeks when he was killed in action on 18.3.1917, aged 33 years. Buried **RUE-DU-BACQUEROT No 1 MILITARY CEMETERY.** Grave location:- Plot 3, Row A, Grave 2. (Brother of Private **EDGAR TAYLOR,** who died of wounds, 11.12.1917, q.v.). ROH:- Longwood War Memorial; St. John's Church, Golcar.

TAYLOR, LAMBERT. Gunner. No 342015. 1st Brigade, Canadian Field Artillery. Born Golcar. Son of Mr and Mrs H. Taylor, 24 Cliffe Ash, Golcar. Formerly worked as a pattern weaver by Messrs Charles Lockwood and Sons Limited, Blackrock Mills, Linthwaite. Attended Golcar Providence United Methodist Sunday School. Went to Canada in 1903. Was married there in January, 1917. Husband of Rose Taylor, 340 Pine Street, Jacksonville, Illinois, U.S.A. Enlisted in the Canadian Artillery in October, 1916. Whilst completing his training in England he visited his home in Golcar in May, 1917, and embarked for France a few days later. Died from wounds and gas poisoning, having been struck by a gas shell, on 26.8.1917, aged 34 years. Buried **LAPUGNOY MILITARY CEMETERY.** Grave location:- Plot 5, Row E, Grave 15. ROH:- St. John's Church, Golcar; memorial in Wellhouse Churchyard.

TAYLOR, LEONARD. 2nd Lieutenant. 2nd Battalion Manchester Regiment. Formerly 5th Battalion Duke of Wellington's Regiment. Born Golcar 1.9.1892. Son of Fred and Elizabeth Taylor, 20 Sunny Mead, Deighton. Educated St. Andrew's Church of England School, Leeds Road, Huddersfield. Employed as a mill tuner by Messrs Learoyd Brothers and Company Limited, Trafalgar Mills, Huddersfield. Single. Enlisted 8.8.1914. He was commissioned in April, 1918. Killed in action, 27.8.1918, aged 25 years. Has no known grave. Commemorated **VIS-en-ARTOIS MEMORIAL TO THE MISSING.** ROH:- Christ Church, Woodhouse Hill; Deighton United Methodist Chapel; St. Andrew's Church, Leeds Road, Huddersfield; Learoyd Brothers; Deighton War Memorial.

TAYLOR, MARMADUKE. Gunner. No 133485. 301st Battery, Royal Garrison Artillery. Born Meltham. Son of George and Mary Ann Oldfield Taylor, of Meltham. Husband of Elsie Taylor of Brechin Terrace, Meltham. Employed by the Meltham Spinning Company. Was a member of the Meltham Wesleyan Choir. Enlisted December 1916. Embarked for France in June, 1917. Killed in action, 31.7.1917, aged 27 years. Buried **YPRES TOWN CEMETERY EXTENSION.** Grave location:- Plot 3, Row B, Grave 12. ROH:- St. Bartholomew's Church, Meltham.

TAYLOR, NORMAN. Private. No 241546. 2/5th Battalion Duke of Wellington's Regiment. Lived with his Uncle and Aunt, Mr and Mrs George Roebuck, 68 Parkgate, Berry Brow. Employed as a cleaner in the Huddersfield Corporation Tramsheds. Embarked for France in January, 1917. Killed in action, 11.6.1917, aged 23 years. Buried **FLESQUIERES HILL BRITISH CEMETERY.** Grave location:- Plot 4, Row D, Grave 7. ROH:- Huddersfield Corporation; Huddersfield Drill Hall; Almondbury War Memorial.

TAYLOR, NORMAN STRINGER. Gunner. No 240308. 'D' Battery, 103rd Brigade, Royal Field Artillery. Born Lascelles Hall, Lepton, 29.9.1892. Son of Albert Edward and Alice Taylor, 16 North Street, Lockwood, Huddersfield. Educated Lepton Board School. Employed as a weaver by Messrs Walter Sykes Limited, Zetland Mills, Huddersfield. Single. Enlisted 23.5.1917. Killed in action in Italy on 15.6.1918, aged 25 years. Buried **GRANEZZA BRITISH CEMETERY, ITALY.** Grave location:- Plot 1, Row D, Grave 4. ROH:- Lockwood Baptist Church; Emmanuel Church, Lockwood; Mount Pleasant Chapel, Lockwood; Armitage

Bridge War Memorial; commemorated on headstone in Kirkheaton Cemetery.

TAYLOR, PERCY. Private. No 204164. 1/5th Battalion Duke of Wellington's Regiment. Fourth son of Mrs Atkinson, 3 Hanginroyd, Wellhouse, Golcar. Employed as a fettler by Messrs John Lockwood and Sons Limited, Milnsbridge. Was a member of the Wellhouse Liberal Club and of the Slaithwaite United Harriers. Attended the Wellhouse United Methodist Sunday School. Enlisted September, 1916, and embarked for France on 28.12.1916. Killed in action, 7.8.1917, aged 19 years. Buried **COXYDE MILITARY CEMETERY.** Grave location:- Plot 2, Row E, Grave 28. (Brother of Private **FRED TAYLOR**, died of wounds, 7.6.1917, q.v.). ROH:- St. John's Church, Golcar; Huddersfield Drill Hall.

TAYLOR, PERCY. Private. No M2/181210. Army Service Corps (Motor Transport Section). Born Cumberworth, near Huddersfield. Son of George William and Clarice Taylor, 170 Barton Road, Crosland Moor. Educated Shepley Council School. Assisted his father in the family motor haulage business. Married. His wife lived with her parents at Burdett House, Milnsbridge. Enlisted December 1915. Wounded on the Menin Road near Ypres on 17.8.1917. Admitted to No 44 Casualty Clearing Station, where he died of his wounds on 20.8.1917, aged 24 years. Buried **BRANDHOEK NEW MILITARY CEMETERY No 3.** Grave location:- Plot 1, Row B, Grave 27. ROH:- St. Barnabas Church, Crosland Moor.

TAYLOR, THOMAS CYRIL. Corporal. No 212076. Royal Air Force. Son of Charles Albert and Sarah Ann Taylor of Helme, Meltham. Died of meningitis on 29.11.1918, aged 26 years. Buried **MELTHAM METHODIST CHAPEL YARD.** Grave location:- Special Memorial, near main door of Chapel.

TAYLOR, VINCENT. Lance Corporal. No 18591. 8th Battalion Duke of Wellington's Regiment. Born Golcar, Huddersfield. Enlisted Huddersfield. Died of wounds at No 4 Casualty Clearing Station on 19.1.1917, aged 22 years. Buried **VARENNES MILITARY CEMETERY.** Grave location:- Plot 1, Row F, Grave 65. ROH:- St. Stephen's Church, Lindley; St. Philip's Church, Birchencliffe.

TAYLOR, WALTER. Private. No 7830. 'A' Company, 2nd Battalion The Yorkshire Regiment. Born Huddersfield. Brother of Mr G H Taylor of Chapel Hill, Huddersfield. Employed as a labourer. Lived with his sister, Ada Hyland, at 34 Blackmoorfoot Road, Crosland Moor, Huddersfield. Single. Was mobilised as a Reservist at the outbreak of the war. Died from wounds received at Neuve Chapelle on 29.3.1915. He was 32 years of age. Buried **RUE-DAVID MILITARY CEMETERY.** Grave location:- Plot 1, Row H, Grave 68.

TAYLOR, WILLIAM FERGUS. Sergeant. 1st Battalion Duke of Wellington's Regiment. Born Yew Green, Lockwood, Huddersfield. Son of David and Ada Taylor, 11 Bath Street, Lockwood. Educated Mount Pleasant Council School. Prior to enlistment, was employed as an iron moulder. Enlisted 4.1.1909. Went to India, where he was on the General Staff at Headquarters at Dehli and Simla. Whilst in India he contracted Enteric Fever, followed by tuberculosis. He arrived in England in April, 1917, and, after spending a month in a London hospital, was sent to Mill Hill Sanatorium, Huddersfield, for treatment for tuberculosis. Died at Mill Hill Sanatorium, Huddersfield on 15.5.1917, aged 25 years. (Brother of Private **HENRY JOHN TAYLOR**, died of wounds, 26.7.1917, q.v.). ROH:- Emmanuel Church, Lockwood; Mount Pleasant Chapel, Lockwood.

TAYLOR, WRIGHT. Private. No 59589. 1/9th Battalion Durham Light Infantry. Born Clay Well, Golcar 13.8.1899. Son of Fred and Hannah Ellen Taylor, 151 Fern Bank, Newsome Road, Huddersfield. Educated Stile Common Council School. Was in business with his brother, Mr F. Taylor, shoddy and waste dealer, of Aspley. Single. Enlisted 18.10.1917. Reported missing, presumed killed, near Rheims on 21.7.1918, aged 18 years. Has no known grave. Commemorated **SOISSONS MEMORIAL TO THE MISSING.** ROH:- St. John's Church, Newsome; St. John's Church, Golcar.

TEAL, WILFRED. Private. No 241529. 2/5th Battalion Duke of Wellington's Regiment. Born 31 Matthew's Buildings, Paddock Foot, Huddersfield, 10.7.1896. Younger son of Sarah Ellen Teale, 27 Matthew's Buildings, Paddock Foot, Huddersfield. Educated St. Thomas's School, Huddersfield. Employed as a fettler by Messrs B. Armistead and Sons, Longroyd Bridge, Huddersfield. Single. Enlisted 6.3.1916. Killed in action at Miraumont on 17.3.1917, aged 20 years. Buried **ADANAC MILITARY CEMETERY**. Grave location:- Plot 4, Row H, Grave 34. ROH:- New North Road Baptist Church; All Saints Church, Paddock; Huddersfield Drill Hall.

TEBB, JOHN LEONARD. Rifleman. No C/7403. 18th Battalion King's Royal Rifle Corps. Born 22 Wood Terrace, Primrose Hill, Huddersfield 13.11.1890. Son of John and Margaret Kilvington Tebb, 16 Manor Street, Huddersfield. Educated St. Paul's Church of England School, Huddersfield. Employed as a cashier and book-keeper by Messrs John Kaye and Son, Kings Mill, Huddersfield. Single. Enlisted 1.11.1915. Embarked for France on 1.5.1916. Reported wounded and missing during the Battle of Flers on 15.9.1916. Has no known grave. Commemorated **THIEPVAL MEMORIAL TO THE MISSING**. ROH:- St. Paul's Church, Southgate, Huddersfield; Almondbury War Memorial; memorial in Almondbury Cemetery.

TETLEY, GEORGE ERNEST. Lance Corporal. No 42361. 2/6th Battalion South Staffordshire Regiment. Born Bradford 25.10.1898. Son of Frederick and Henrietta Maude Tetley, 35 Thornton Lodge Road, Huddersfield. Educated Spring Grove Council School. Attended St. Thomas's Church, Longroyd Bridge. Employed as an assistant with Messrs. Jackson and Fitton, Market Place, Huddersfield. Single. Reported missing on 21.3.1918 and afterwards presumed to have been killed on that date, aged 19. Has no known grave. Commemorated **ARRAS MEMORIAL TO THE MISSING**. ROH:- St. Thomas's Church, Longroyd Bridge; memorial in Almondbury Cemetery.

THACKRA, ERNEST. Private. No 204478. 'A' Company, 9th Battalion Duke of Wellington's Regiment. Son of George and Ann Thackra, Wesley Terrace, Denby Dale. Employed by Messrs G. H. Norton of Nortonthorpe Mills, Scissett. Was a member of the local Territorials prior to the outbreak of the war. Embarked for France in 1916. Was wounded three times. Died of wounds received during the attack on the Canal du Nord on 21.10.1918, aged 24 years. Buried **ROCQUIGNY-EQUANCOURT ROAD BRITISH CEMETERY**. Grave location:- Plot 14, Row D, Grave 35. ROH:- G. H. Norton; Denby Dale and Cumberworth War Memorial.

THEWLIS, DAN. Private. No 28149. 7th Battalion Duke of Cornwall's Light Infantry. Formerly No 140550 Royal Field Artillery. Born Milnsbridge, Huddersfield. Son of Mr T. W. Thewlis, 23 Armitage Road, Milnsbridge. Married. Lived 18 Lowergate, Longwood. Employed as a labourer by Messrs Dempsters during the construction of the new works of the Longwood and Slaithwaite Gas Company. Had also been employed as a minder by Messrs John Crowther and Sons Limited, of Milnsbridge. Enlisted 10.4.1916. Embarked for France in September, 1916. Reported missing during an attack on Rainbow Trench, 8.10.1916, during the Battle of the Somme, and afterwards was presumed to have been killed on that date. Has no known grave. Commemorated **THIEPVAL MEMORIAL TO THE MISSING**. ROH- Longwood War Memorial.

THEWLIS, HAROLD. Private. No 59941. 'D' Company, 14th Battalion Leicestershire Regiment. Born Meltham. Son of Arthur and Annie Elizabeth Thewlis, 12 Sunny View, Deighton Road, Huddersfield. Employed by Messrs J. F. Siddal and Company, Thomas Street, Huddersfield. Enlisted in December 1917. Embarked for France in August, 1918. Died of illness at No 56 General Hospital on 12.9.1918, aged 18 years. Buried **ETAPLES MILITARY CEMETERY**. Grave location:- Plot 66, Row G, Grave 30. ROH:- Christ Church, Woodhouse Hill; St. Andrew's Church, Leeds Road, Huddersfield.

THEWLIS, HAROLD DARLING. Lieutenant. 'C' Company, 1/7th Battalion Manchester Regiment. Born 27.7.1890 in Manchester. Only son of Mr James Herbert Thewlis, umbrella manufactuer, of Daisy Mount, Victoria Park, Manchester, who was a member of a well known and respected old Huddersfield family and ex Lord Mayor of Manchester, and Isabella Thewlis. His brother, Mr Edgar Thewlis, was connected with the firm of Messrs Thewlis and Company, finishing machinery makers, of Folly Hall. Lieutenant Thewlis was educated at Manchester Grammar School and Manchester University, where he was awarded a BSc. degree.

At the outbreak of the war he was studying at the Cheshire Agricultural College at Holmes Chapel, as he was interested in agricultural research. Single. He was an active member of the OTC at University and was granted a commission in the 7th Battalion Manchester Regiment in 1912. When his Regiment proceeded to Khartoum in September, 1914, he was promoted to full Lieutenant. Killed in action at the Third Battle of Krithia, Gallipoli, on 4.6.1915, aged 24 years. Has no known grave. Commemorated **HELLES MEMORIAL TO THE MISSING.** *Lieutenant Thewlis' Will was administered by his father in London on December 23rd, 1915. His estate was valued at £181 16s 10d.*

THEWLIS, HENRY. Private. No 31311. 8th Battalion East Yorkshire Regiment. Formerly No 29137 The Yorkshire Regiment. Born Lascelles Hall, Kirkheaton, Huddersfield. Only son of Mr and Mrs Herbert Thewlis, of Lascelles Hall. Employed by Mr Ernest Priestley, boot and shoemaker, of Lepton. Enlisted March 1916. Reported missing, presumed killed, on 13.11.1916, aged 32 years. Buried **SERRE ROAD CEMETERY No 1**. Grave location:- Plot 1, Row C, Grave 32. ROH:- St. John's Church, Kirkheaton; Lepton Parish Church.

THEWLISS, HERBERT. Private. No 2211. 1/5th Battalion Duke of Wellington's Regiment. Born Kirkheaton, Huddersfield, 7.11.1893. Son of Eli and Annie E. Thewlis, 196 Kilner Bank, Moldgreen. Educated Moldgreen Church of England School. Employed as a cloth finisher by Messrs Pecketts of Lindley. Husband of Daisy Thewlis, 124 Bradford Road, Huddersfield. Enlisted 4.8.1914. Wounded at Thiepval during the Battle of the Somme on 7.9.1916. Died of his wounds at No 13 General Hospital on 11.9.1916, aged 23 years. Buried **BOULOGNE EASTERN CEMETERY**. Grave location:- Plot 8, Row C, Grave 136. ROH:- Huddersfield Drill Hall.

THEWLIS, JAMES SYKES. Lance Corporal. No 203011. 1/4th Battalion Duke of Wellington's Regiment. Born Holmfirth. Son of James and Ruth Hannah Thewlis of Upperthong, Holmfirth. Educated St. John's School and attended Upperthong Sunday School. Employed by Mr W. Hardy at Prickleden dyeworks. Enlisted at the outbreak of the war. Died of wounds, 20.10.1918, aged 32 years. Buried **TERLINCTHUN BRITISH CEMETERY**. Grave location:- Plot 6, Row A, Grave 51. ROH:- Upperthong War Memorial.

THEWLIS, WALTER. Gunner. No 152658. 'A' Battery, 71st Brigade, Royal Field Artillery. Born Thongsbridge. Son of Mr and Mrs Albert Thewlis, of West End, Wooldale. Husband of Ada Thewlis of Hollowgate, Thurstonland. Educated Lane Bottom School. Attended Wooldale Wesleyan Chapel, where he was a member of the choir. Was a keen athlete, a member of the Wooldale Association Football Club and the Thurstonland Cricket Club. Employed as a scourer by Messrs Lancaster and Sons, Mytholm Bridge Mills. Enlisted August 1916. Embarked for France on 28.3.1917. Killed in action, 22.3.1918, aged 28 years. Has no known grave. Commemorated **ARRAS MEMORIAL TO THE MISSING**. His wife received the following letter from Major Willett of the 71st Brigade R.F.A. who wrote, *'It is with the deepest regret that I have to inform you that your husband, Gunner Thewlis of this Battery, was killed in action on the 22nd of this month. He was hit by several pieces of shell while out mending telephone wires and you will be glad to hear that he was killed instantaneously and suffered no pain. Your husband is a very great loss to the Battery as he was good at any work he was given to do. He was an excellent gunner and when he began to learn signalling about four months ago he picked it up very quickly, so much so that after three months he was qualified as a first class signaller. In addtion he was a most gallant soldier and I shall find it most difficult to replace him in the Battery.'* ROH:- Wooldale War Memorial; Thurstonland War Memorial.

THOMAS, JAMES ALBERT. Private. No 5/2990. 1/5th Battalion Duke of Wellington's Regiment. Born 153 Rashcliffe Hill, Lockwood, Huddersfield, 2.10.1888. Son of Mr and Mrs Sam Thomas, 159 Rashcliffe Hill, Lockwood. Educated Rashcliffe Church of England School. Employed as a labourer. Married Nellie Holliday in 1910. Lived 143 Rashcliffe Hill, Lockwood. Was an old Volunteer and a member of the local Territorials prior to the outbreak of the war. Enlisted 6.8.1914. Was wounded three days before Christmas, 1915, and had only been back in France for seven weeks when he was killed in action during the Battle of the Somme on 4.7.1916. He was 27 years of age. Buried **CONNAUGHT CEMETERY, THIEPVAL.** Grave location:- Plot 4, Row M, Grave 8. ROH:- St. Stephen's Church, Rashcliffe; Huddersfield Drill Hall.

THOMAS, FRED. Artist's Rifles. Lodged with Mrs Fryer, James Street, Golcar. Employed at the London City and Midland bank, Milnsbridge. Attended Golcar Baptist Church. Was a member of the Christian Endeavour Society and teacher at the Sunday School. Killed in action. ROH:- Golcar Baptist Church.

THOMAS, REGINALD (REGGIE). Private. No 40857. 23rd (Tyneside Scottish) Battalion Northumberland Fusiliers. Formerly No 20310 Duke of Wellington's Regiment. Born Clifton Road Marsh 28.8.1894. Son of Mrs M. Thomas, 85 Cleveland Road, Marsh, Huddersfield. Educated Spring Grove Council School. Employed as a polisher by Messrs M. Darwent and Sons, french polishers of Rosemary Lane, Huddersfield. Was assistant secretary at the Highfield Congregational Church Sunday School, the secretary for the Highfield Band of Hope and a member of the Highfield Church Choir. Was a member of Marsh United Harriers. Single. Enlisted May 1916. Reported missing, presumed killed, 14.2.1917, aged 22 years. Buried **RUE-PETILLON MILITARY CEMETERY, FLEURBAIX.** Grave location:- Plot 2, Row A, Grave 26. ROH:- Marsh War Memorial.

THOMPSON, ALLAN LAW. Private. No 10874. 'A' Company, 2nd Battalion King's Own Yorkshire Light Infantry. Born Huddersfield. Brother of Mrs Dyson, 72 Upperhead Row, Huddersfield. Enlisted at the outbreak of the war. Died of Enteric Fever on 9.1.1915, aged 21 years. Buried **WIMEREUX COMMUNAL CEMETERY.** Grave location:- Plot 1, Row C, Grave 17a. (Brother of Private **TOM THOMPSON**, killed in action, 14.3.1915, q.v.).

THOMPSON, BROOKSBANK. Private. No 241361. 5/6th Battalion The Cameronians (Scottish Rifles). Born Crosland Moor 19.1.1883. Educated Crosland Moor Council School. Husband of Phillis Thompson, 11 Barton Road, Crosland Moor. Employed as an insurance agent by the Prudential Assurance Company Limited. Enlisted September 1916. Killed in action at Kemmel Hill on 8.5.1918, aged 35 years. Has no known grave. Commemorated **TYNE COT MEMORIAL TO THE MISSING.** ROH:- St. Barnabas Church, Crosland Moor; United Methodist Church, Crosland Moor.

THOMPSON, CHARLES. Driver. No 846518. 3rd Division Ammunition Column, Royal Field Artillery. Born Allerton Bywater, near Castleford, 31.5.1893. Son of Thomas and Mary Thompson, Woodman Terrace, Bradley, Huddersfield. Educated at Keighley Schools. Married. Lived at Longwood. Employed as a teamer. Died of wounds, 21.3.1918, aged 26 years. Buried **BUCQUOY ROAD CEMETERY.** Grave location:- Plot 2, Row E, Grave 26. ROH:- St. Thomas's Church, Bradley.

THOMPSON, ERNEST. Private. No 18/893. 'B' Company, 18th Battalion West Yorkshire Regiment (2nd Bradford Pals). Born Cliffe End, Longwood, Huddersfield. Son of William and Sarah Ann Thompson, 2 Bull Green Road, Longwood. Educated at Paddock Schools. Employed as a traveller by Messrs Fattorini and Sons of Bradford. Was formerly a tram driver in Halifax. Husband of Nora Elizabeth Thompson, 60 Newlands Place, Undercliffe, Bradford. Reported missing, 1.7.1916, on the first day of the Battle of the Somme and afterwards presumed to have been killed on that date, aged 30. Has no known grave. Commemorated **THIEPVAL MEMORIAL TO THE MISSING.** ROH:- St. Mark's Parish Church, Longwood.

THOMPSON, FRANK. Private. No 13979. 5th Battalion Duke of Wellington's Regiment. Born Scarborough. Son of James Richard Thompson of Greenside, Thurstonland and formerly of Birkby. Lived 7 Chadwick's Yard, Birkby. Employed as a finisher by Messrs Middlemost Brothers and Company Limited, of Birkby. Attended Highfield Congregational Church. Enlisted September 1914. Embarked for France in 1915. Killed in action during the Battle of Arras on 9.4.1917, aged 19 years. Buried **LEVEL CROSSING CEMETERY, FAMPOUX.** Grave location:- Plot 1, Row B, Grave 67. ROH:- Fartown and Birkby War Memorial.

THOMPSON, HARRY. Private. No 204737. 2/5th Battalion Duke of Wellington's Regiment. Born Fartown, Huddersfield, 18.9.1892. Son of John and Ellen Thompson, 8 Ballroyd Road, Fartown. Educated Hillhouse Council School. Employed as a tailor's presser by Messrs Edgerton, St. John's Road, Huddersfield. Was a member of Woodhouse Church Young Men's Bible Class. Single. Enlisted 10.2.1916. Wounded on the Somme in July, 1916. Was wounded near Bapaume on 19.7.1917 and died the same day, aged 25. Buried **VAULX AUSTRALIAN FIELD AMBULANCE CEMETERY.** Grave location:- Row A, Grave 20. ROH:- Fartown and Birkby War Memorial; Christ Church, Woodhouse Hill, Huddersfield; Huddersfield Drill Hall.

THOMPSON, HERBERT. Signaller. No 175749. 284th Siege Battery, Royal Garrison Artillery. Born Huddersfield 17.11.1882. Educated Crosland Moor Council Schools. Husband of Annie Greaves Thompson, 14 Cowlersley Lane, Milnsbridge. Was a partner in the firm of Messrs Wilkinson and Thompson, wholesale costumiers, of Market Street, Huddersfield. Wounded by a gas shell near Ham on 1.9.1918. Died of wounds on the same day at No 53rd Casualty Clearing Station, aged 35 years. Buried **DAOURS COMMUNAL CEMETERY EXTENSION.** Grave location:- Plot 4, Row F, Grave 6. ROH:- Milnsbridge War Memorial; St. Thomas's Church, Longroyd Bridge, Huddersfield.

THOMPSON, JOHN HENRY. Private. No 16489. 18th Battalion Lancashire Fusiliers. Born Almondbury 15.3.1896. Son of Christopher George and Margaret Louisa Thompson, 7a Sunny Bank, Longwood. Educated Lindley Church of England Schools. Employed as a woollen finisher by Messrs A. and T. Clay of Rastrick. Lived Regent Place, Rastrick. Single. Was a member of the Huddersfield troop of boy scouts. Enlisted 18.1.1915. Killed by a shell, 23.8.1916, during the Battle of the Somme. He was 20 years of age. Has no known grave. Commemorated **THIEPVAL MEMORIAL TO THE MISSING.** ROH:- St. Mark's Parish Church, Longwood; Almondbury War Memorial.

THOMPSON, JOHN WILLIAM. Gunner. No 174440. 'B' Battery, 68th Brigade, Royal Field Artillery. Born Halifax. Son of Fred Thompson, 50 Rock Street, Linthwaite. Lived 21 Height, Linthwaite. Employed by Mr Arthur Dawson, cotton spinner, of Huddersfield. Attended Linthwaite Parish Church. Enlisted at the outbreak of the war. Died of illness in Egypt on 24.4.1916, aged 27 years. Buried **HADRA WAR MEMORIAL CEMETERY, ALEXANDRIA.** Grave location:- Row F, Grave 131. ROH:- Linthwaite War Memorial.

THOMPSON, LAW NETHERWOOD. Private. No 302440. 2/7th Battalion Manchester Regiment. Born 69 Prospect Street, Huddersfield, 20.5.1884. Son of George Henry Thompson, 91 Brighton Street, Seacombe, Wallasey, Liverpool. Educated Hillhouse Board School. Employed as a cost clerk at Messrs Lever Brothers, Port Sunlight. Single. Enlisted 21.8.1916. Died of dysentery as a Prisoner of War on 4.6.1918 at Fins, France. He was 34 years of age. Buried **FINS NEW BRITISH CEMETERY.** Grave location:- Plot 4, Row H, Grave 12. ROH:- Fartown and Birkby War Memorial.

THOMPSON, TOM. Lance Corporal. No 9720. 'B' Company, 1st Battalion King's Own Yorkshire Light Infantry. Born Huddersfield. Brother of Mrs J. Dyson, 72 Upperhead Row, Huddersfield. Was serving in Singapore when the war broke out and reached England in November, 1914. His few days furlough were spent in Huddersfield and he embarked for France in January, 1915. Killed in action, 14.3.1915, aged 26 years. Buried **WULVERGHEM-LINDENHOEK ROAD MILITARY CEMETERY.** Grave location:- Plot 1, Row C, Grave 4. (Brother of Private **ALLEN LAW THOMPSON,** who died of Enteric Fever, 9.1.1915, q.v.).

THOMPSON, W. Private. No 268180. 6th Battalion Duke of Wellington's Regiment. Died at home, 18.9.1919. Buried **EDGERTON CEMETERY, HUDDERSFIELD.** Grave location:- 11B, 117.

THOMSON, JAMES ALBERT RAYMOND, DSO. Lieutenant-Colonel. 5th Battalion The Yorkshire Regiment. Croix-de-Guerre (French). Born Huddersfield. Son of the late James and Eliza Thomson. Husband of Ethel Norah Mayson Thomson of The Uplands, Malton, Yorkshire. Prior to the outbreak of the war was a partner in the firm of Messrs W. Metcalfe and Sons, millers, Malton. Was a member of the local Territorials before the war. Embarked for France in April, 1915. Was wounded on three occasions. Awarded the DSO in 1918. The following citation is from the London

Gazette, dated 16.9.1918, *'For conspicuous gallantry and devotion to duty. Throughout ten days fighting this Officer had rendered splendid service, inspiring the Brigade by his example of cheerfulness and leadership. When the enemy captured a village he established his Battalion on some high ground above it, holding on from 9am to 5pm although his right was in the air and he had neither orders or information. On a later occasion after encouraging his men throughout a day of intense shelling, he led a counter-attack in the evning to cover the withdrawal of another division. This was successful, as was also his rearguard action afterwards.'* Killed in action at Craonne, France, on 27.5.1918, aged 42 years. Buried **VENDRESSE BRITISH CEMETERY.** Grave location:- Plot 2, Row A, Grave 2. The following extract is taken from Volume 3 - 1918.- of the Official History of the Great War (Page 52), *'From his headquarters at Craonne, Lieutenant Colonel J. A. R Thomson (5th Green Howards) saw enemy troops on the southern edge of the Californie Plateau about 6am and, with his headquarters and the reserve Company of the 4th East Yorkshires, made a gallant attempt to dislodge them by counter-attack: but the ascent was steep and the effort failed with heavy casualties. A Company of the 4th Green Howards, the reserve battalion near La Hutte, about a mile south of Craonne, tried, by Brigadier-General Rees's orders, to join in this counter-attack, but was swept away by the terrific fire falling near La Hutte. A buried cable communicating with the 5th Green Howards being intact, Brigadier-General Rees ordered the survivors of the counter-attack to fight their way out but few succeeded in doing so, Lieutenant-Colonel Thomson being among the killed.'* ROH:- Commemorated in a memorial window at St. Leonard's Church, Malton; Sledmere War Memorial.

THORNTON, ALBERT. Private. No 52642. 10th Battalion West Yorkshire Regiment. Formerly No 205342 Duke of Wellington's Regiment. Born Kirkheaton, Huddersfield. Son of Walter and Betty Thornton of Junction Buildings, Kirkheaton. Killed in action, 20.9.1918, aged 25 years. Buried **GAUCHE WOOD CEMETERY, VILLERS-GUISLAIN.** Grave location:- Grave 38. ROH:- St. John's Church, Kirkheaton.

THORNTON, CHARLES WILLIAM. Rifleman. No C/8131. 16th Battalion King's Royal Rifle Corps. Born Huddersfield. Lived 2 Stock's Buildings, Upperhead Row, Huddersfield. Employed as a woollen warehouseman by Messrs J. Wilkinson and Son, St. George's Square, Huddersfield. Killed in action, 2.12.1917. Has no known grave. Commemorated **TYNE COT MEMORIAL TO THE MISSING.**

THORNTON, FRANK. 2nd Lieutenant. 'C' Company 7th Battalion East Yorkshire Regiment. Born Birkby, Huddersfield, 3.4.1893. Son of Mr and Mrs William Thornton, 'Ashfield', Fenay Bridge, Huddersfield, and later of 12 South Parade, Llandudno, North Wales. Educated Almondbury Grammar School and The Leys School, Cambridge, where he was in the Officers' Training Corps. Employed as a traveller in his father's business, Messrs Woodhead and Barker, woollen merchants, Dundas Street, Huddersfield. Was a playing member of the Huddersfield Old Boys Football Club and had been included in the County trial teams. Was recommended for a commission by the Huddersfield Town Council under a scheme arranged early in the war, and he was gazetted in November, 1914, and posted to the 7th Battalion East Yorkshire Regiment. Had been in France for six months and returned there for the last time on Whit Saturday, 1916, after a few days leave of absence. Killed in action at Fricourt on 1.7.1916, aged 23 years. Buried **FRICOURT NEW MILITARY CEMETERY.** Grave location:- Row B, Grave 5. ROH:- St. John's Church, Kirkheaton; Waterloo Rugby Union Football Club; Fartown and Birkby War Memorial. The following extract is taken from 'The East Yorkshire Regiment in the Great War' by Everard Wyrall:- (7th Battalion, 1.7.1916), *'At Zero hour – 7.30am – on 1st July, after smoke discharges at many points along the front, and the blowing of mines beneath the enemy's trenches, the assaulting troops advanced with the utmost steadiness to the attack despite the enemy's barrage which was falling very heavily on the line of advance across No Man's Land.*

The 50th Brigade of the 17th Division had been given the task of assaulting and clearing Fricourt village and wood, thus ensuring contact between the 7th Division on the right and the 21st Division on the left. The dispositions of the four battalions of the Brigade at Zero hour were: 7th Green Howards held trenches from the cemetery to the 'Tambour': this Battalion was to attack the village. The 10th West Yorkshires, detailed to form the defensive flank, were disposed in a line from the 'Tambour' to the apex at Purfleet: the 7th East Yorkshires were in Becordel and 'Bonte Redoubt' in support. The 6th Dorsets were in Brigade Reserve at Meaulte. The East Yorkshires and Dorsets were ready to follow up as the assault was delivered.

At 7.30am the assault was delivered. Two companies of the West Yorkshires got across No Man's Land and into the first German line with slight loss and reached their objective, but they had no support, for the two remaining Companies were met by a murderous machine-gun fire from Fricourt and were practically annihilated. The two forward Companies in the German line, left without assistance, were gradually overwhelmed and, being separated into small groups, were practically wiped out, only a few survivors getting back to the old British front line: one small detachment however, managed to effect a junction with troops of the 21st Division.

Machine gun and rifle fire prevented a further advance from the British line and the Battalions which had been ordered to follow in rear of the troops detailed for the initial assault were unable to move. 'C' and 'D' Companies of the 7th East Yorkshires were in South Avenue when, at 8.26am the last of the West Yorkshires 'went over.' By 9am 'A' and 'B' Companies from Bonte Redoubt had moved up to Kingston Road and held the front line with one platoon, two Lewis guns and a trench-mortar carrying party. 'D' Company was then in Surrey Street. At 10.06am the 7th Green Howards reported that their front Company had attacked and was in front of Fricourt and a little later 'A' Company of the East Yorkshires was ordered up in support. The Lewis-gun officers reported that it was impossible to mount a gun on the lip of the crater as long as the German machine guns remained active, though he had mounted a gun on the trench parapet. Just after 11am 'B' Company was moved up towards Rundel Avenue and 2nd Lieutenant Thomas with two other ranks was sent out from Purfleet to try and gain touch with the West Yorkshires. About an hour later he was brought back wounded by his servant. No West Yorkshiremen were found in the front German trench. Two other patrols sent out had not returned by 1.15pm, at which hour the 7th East Yorkshires were ordered to attack in support of the West Yorkshires at second Zero which was to be 2.30pm.

At 2.33.pm 'C' and 'D' Companies of the East Yorkshires advanced over the parapet towards Red Cottage. They were met at once by a murderous machine-gun and rifle fire and were unable to get on. 'B' Company, which had been detailed to support the attack did not get beyond the front line. Terrible casualities were suffered in this second attempt. The two attacking companies of the East Yorkshires, 'C' and 'D' were practically swept away when ever they set foot in No Man's Land, which was already thick with dead and wounded men. This second attempt also failed and during the night of 1/2nd July the 50th Brigade was relieved and marched back to Heilly and Meaulte to reorganise, though having to provide carrying parties for the 51st Brigade.

The 7th East Yorkshires lost on the 1st July 4 Officers killed and 1 Officer wounded:- in other ranks the losses were - killed 29, wounded 72 and missing 17: a total of 5 Officers and 118 other ranks'.

THORNTON, FRED. Private. No 242187. 9th Battalion Highland Light Infantry. Born 6 Folly Road, Cowcliffe, Huddersfield, 28.10.1897. Son of Brook and Alice Thornton, 65 Netheroyd Hill Road, Cowcliffe. Educated St. John's School, Hillhouse. Employed as a beamer by Mr D. J. Green, Bay Hall Mills, Birkby. Attended the Netheroyd Hill Congregational Sunday School and was a member of the Cowcliffe and Netheroyd Hill Liberal Club. Single. Enlisted 29.9.1916. Embarked for France 1.6.1917. Reported missing, presumed killed, on 26.9.1917, at Passchendaele, aged 19 years. Has no known grave. Commemorated **TYNE COT MEMORIAL TO THE MISSING.** ROH:- Fartown and Birkby War Memorial; Netheroyd Hill Methodist Church.

THORNTON, GILBERT KAYE. Private. No 68293. 'E' Company, 3rd Battalion King's Own Yorkshire Light Infantry. Born Hall Bower, Huddersfield, 3.3.1896. Son of William Robert and Ann Thornton, 31 Hall Bower, Huddersfield. Educated Berry Brow Council School and Huddersfield Technical College. Employed as an assistant in maker department. Single. Enlisted 3.10.1918. Died of pneumonia, 27.10.1918, at Patrington Hospital. He was 22 years of age. Buried **ALMONDBURY CEMETERY, HUDDERSFIELD.** Grave location:- 6, 'C', 20. ROH:- Almondbury War Memorial.

THORNTON, HERBERT. Private. No 241533. 'A' Company, 2/5th Battalion Duke of Wellington's Regiment. Born Fartown, Huddersfield, 26.6.1891. Son of Sam and Clara Thornton, 5 Pollard Street, Fartown. Educated Hillhouse Board School. Employed in a cloth warehouse. Single. Enlisted 9.3.1915. Reported missing, presumed killed, on 3.5.1917, at Bullecourt. Has no known grave. Commemorated **ARRAS MEMORIAL TO THE MISSING.** ROH:- Netheroyd Hill Methodist Church; Christ Church, Woodhouse Hill; Huddersfield Drill Hall; Fartown and Birkby War Memorial.

THORNTON, JOSEPH EDWIN HAROLD. Driver. No 27030. 'A' Battery, 86th Brigade, Royal Field Artillery. Born Huddersfield. Only son of the late Thomas and Elizabeth Thornton, 202 Manchester Road, Milnsbridge. He was apprenticed to Mr J. W. Thorpe, joiner, of Linthwaite and afterwards worked for Mr R. Quarmby, Triangle, Paddock. At the outbreak of war he worked at the Y.M.C.A. at Wrexham and Rhyl for a few months. Enlisted in January, 1915, and embarked for France in June, 1915. Died of wounds at No 11 Stationary Hospital, Rouen, on 16.10.1918. He was 25 years of age. Buried **St. SEVER CEMETERY EXTENSION.** Grave location:- Block S, Plot 2, Row M, Grave 2. ROH:- Milnsbridge War Memorial.

THORNTON, PERCY. Private. No 32135. 1/6th Battalion West Yorkshire Regiment. Born Low Row, Armitage Bridge, 31.1.1897. Son of Fred and Martha Thornton, 6 Conservative Buildings, Berry Brow, Huddersfield. Educated Armitage Bridge Church of England School. Employed as a textile worker in the scribbling department of Armitage Bridge Mills. Single. Enlisted 9.5.1916. Killed in action near Cambrai on 11.10.1918, aged 21 years. Buried **IWUY COMMUNAL CEMETERY.** Grave location:- Row C, Grave 5. ROH:- Armitage Bridge Mills; Armitage Bridge War Memorial; memorial in Armitage Bridge Churchyard.

THORPE, ERNEST. Private. No 3576. 'D' Company, 1/5th Battalion Duke of Wellington's Regiment. Born Filbert Street, Birkby, Huddersfield, 31.12.1895. Son of Joe and Florence Thorpe, 212 Olive Terrace, Bradford Road, Huddersfield, and later of Ettrick Cottages, Selkirk, Scotland. Employed as an iron turner by Messrs Hopkinsons, of Birkby. Prior to enlistment had lived for a time at Ptone, Wellington, New Zealand, and had undergone four years military training there. Enlisted in November, 1914, on returning to England. Died of wounds, 30.11.1915, aged 19 years. Buried **TALANA FARM CEMETERY.** Grave location:- Plot 4, Row F, Grave 1. His parents received a letter from Sergeant Howard, who wrote, *'It is with deep regret and heartfelt sympathy that I am writing to inform you of the death of your brave son Private E. Thorpe who was in my platoon. He died this morning of wounds which he received at about 11.30pm last night. We had just been relieved from our advanced trench and your son was one of a party of five who were carrying water to the platoon which had relieved us when he was hit by a stray bullet in the stomach. He seemed to bear up for an hour or two but must have had a relapse after getting to the field hospital. I am writing this letter on behalf of myself and all his comrades in the platoon.'* ROH:- Christ Church, Woodhouse Hill; Huddersfield Drill Hall; Fartown and Birkby War Memorial.

THORPE, FRANK. Private. No PLY/16054. Royal Marine Light Infantry. *HMS Exmouth*. Born Cowcliffe, Huddersfield, 27.9.1897. Son of George William and Maud Thorpe, Eastbank, 119 Cowcliffe Hill Road, Huddersfield. Educated Hillhouse Council School and Huddersfield Higher Elementary School. Employed as a clerk by Messrs Chiltern, Wrigley and Company, wholesale clothiers, Viaduct Street, Huddersfield. Attended Fartown Trinity Wesleyan Sunday School. Enlisted in January 1913. Was attached to *HMS Exmouth*. Took part in fleet operations in the North Sea, at the Dardenelles, and Salonica, Greece. Killed in action ashore at Athens, Greece, on 1.12.1916, aged 19 years. Buried **PIRAEUS NAVAL AND CONSULAR CEMETERY, GREECE.** Grave location:- Grave 19. ROH:- Cowcliffe Wesleyan Church; Fartown and Birkby War Memorial. (*Piraeus was the scene of fighting between Allied and Greek forces on 1st December 1916, which resulted in the recognition by the Allied Powers of the Revolutionary Government of M. Venizelos*).

THORPE, FRANK. Private. No 245441. 20th Battalion Manchester Regiment. Formerly No 205182 West Yorkshire Regiment. Born Huddersfield. Married. Lived 66 Leymoor Road,

Golcar. Employed in the finishing department at Messrs C. and J. Hirst and Sons, of Longwood. Attended Golcar Baptist Chapel and was formerly a member of the Reading Room. Enlisted April 1916. Embarked for France in July, 1916. Was transferred to Italy in November, 1916, and returned to France in September, 1918. Was seriously wounded by machine gun fire and died of his wounds on 23.10.1918, aged 33 years. Buried **HONNECHY BRITISH CEMETERY.** Grave location:- Plot 1, Row B, Grave 69/71. ROH:- Golcar Baptist Church.

THORPE, GEORGE HERBERT. Corporal. No 2787. 'A' Company, 1/5th Battalion Duke of Wellington's Regiment. Born Walton, Liverpool, 16.5.1893. Elder son of the late Thomas Henry Thorpe, Customs and Excise Officer, and Jane Middlebrook Thorpe, Cleveland Road, Edgerton, Huddersfield. Since his father's death had lodged with Mrs Haigh, of George Street, Huddersfield. Educated Oakes Council School, Huddersfield College and Municipal Secondary School. Employed as a bank clerk in the Huddersfield branch of the Yorkshire Penny Bank. Was one of three joint secretaries of the Gledholt Wesleyan Sunday School. Enlisted 4.9.1914. Was promoted Lance Corporal a year later. At the beginning of November, 1915, along with Private **FRANK DEAN**, (died of wounds, 13.11.1915), q.v., was recommended for the Distinguished Conduct Certificate for bomb throwing in an advanced sap on 26.9.1915. A member of the Battalion bombers, of whom Corporal Thorpe was in command, said that their position was about the worst on the front as regarded getting the water away and none of them had had dry clothes on for 12 days, *'We had November 5th in the trenches and the Boche were a bit lively. Bert Thorpe was recommended for the D.C.M. but they granted him a gallantry card and he was complimented by the Colonel. He is the Corporal of the bombers and we were called up to help another Regiment to bomb the Germans and we did very well. Indeed we did everything but go over to them so he was recommended. Bert is a trump and a champion to work under. The last time in the Germans started bombing us so we bombed them. Bert took his coat off and threw 70 bombs back. When things quietened down he said 'Come on lads, let us sing a bit.' He started us and then he was so tired that he fell in the bottom of the trench. He had fallen asleep stood up! We groped for him in the mud and picked him up and then had a good laugh and treated it as a joke.'* Killed in action, 17.11.1915, at Boesinghe near Ypres, aged 22. Buried **TALANA FARM CEMETERY.** Grave location:- Plot 3, Row E, Grave 1. ROH:- Gledholt Wesleyan Church; St. Stephen's Church, Lindley; Huddersfield Drill Hall.

THORPE, HAROLD. Private. No 18291. 8th Battalion Duke of Wellington's Regiment. Born Golcar 26.1.1895. Son of Albert and Emily Ann Thorpe, Park Cottage, 151 Acre Street, Lindley, Huddersfield. Educated Oakes Council School. Employed as a woollen weaver at Plover Mills, Lindley. Single. Enlisted on 26.1.1916 – his 21st birthday. Reported missing, presumed killed, 28.9.1916, during the action at Stuff Redoubt during the Battle of the Somme, aged 21. Has no known grave. Commemorated **THIEPVAL MEMORIAL TO THE MISSING.** ROH:- St. Stephen's Church, Lindley; Salendine Nook Baptist Church; commemorated in the Chapel yard, 505E.

THORPE, NED. Sergeant. No 240330. 2/5th Battalion Duke of Wellington's Regiment. Born Underbank, Holmfirth. Son of Mr and Mrs Sam Thorpe, of Underbank. Attended Holmfirth Parish Church Day and Sunday Schools. Was a member of the Underbank football club. Had been employed at Dover Mills, Washpit Mills and later at Neiley Mills, Honley. Enlisted at the outbreak of the war. Embarked for France in January, 1917. Killed in action at the Battle of Cambrai on 27.11.1917, aged 23 years. Has no known grave. Commemorated **CAMBRAI MEMORIAL TO THE MISSING.** ROH:- Underbank War Memorial; Huddersfield Drill Hall.

THORPE, SAM. Private. No 8147. 2nd Battalion King's Own Yorkshire Light Infantry. Born Rashcliffe, Huddersfield. Son of Tom and Ellen Thorpe, 34 Rashcliffe Hill, Lockwood, Huddersfield. Husband of Harriet Thorpe, 36 Rashcliffe Hill, Lockwood. Was called up as a Reservist at the outbreak of the war. Killed in action in the trenches at Richebourg l'Avoue on 28.10.1914, aged 29 years. Has no known grave. Commemorated **LE TOURET MEMORIAL TO THE MISSING.** ROH:- St. Stephen's Church, Rashcliffe.

THORPE, TURNER. Private. No 24793. 1/7th Battalion Duke of Wellington's Regiment. Born Holmfirth. Husband of Edith Thorpe, Dobb Lane, Hinchliffe Mill. Employed at Albert Mills, Holmfirth, by Messrs B. Mellor and Sons Limited. Enlisted at the outbreak of war. Twice wounded. Taken prisoner by the Germans on 13.4.1918. Died as a Prisoner of War of 'intestinal catarrh' on 16.7.1918, aged 29 years. Buried **CONDE-sur-L'ESCAUT COMMUNAL CEMETERY**. Grave location:- A 72. ROH:- Holme and Holmbridge War Memorial; Huddersfield Drill Hall.

THORPE, WALTER. Private. No 235827. 2/4th Battalion King's Own Yorkshire Light Infantry. Born 11 Fields Yard, West Street, Lindley 17.4.1897. Son of Allen and Annie Thorpe, 6 Fields Yard, West Street, Lindley. Educated Oakes Council School. Employed as a brass finisher by Messrs Hopkinsons of Birkby. Single. Enlisted October 1914. Killed in action near Havrincourt on 26.8.1918, aged 21 years. Buried **BUCQUOY ROAD CEMETERY**. Grave location:- Plot 6, Row C, Grave 13. ROH:- St. Stephen's Church, Lindley.

THORP, CHARLES MORTON. Lance Corporal. No 202630. 1/4th Battalion King's Own Yorkshire Light Infantry. Born Kirkburton. Lived Wood View, Bankside, Shelley. Killed in action, 22.9.1918. Has no known grave. Commemorated **VIS-en-ARTOIS MEMORIAL TO THE MISSING**. ROH:- Emmanuel Church, Shelley.

THORP, JOHN ERIC. 2nd Lieutenant. 7th Battalion Duke of Wellington's Regiment. Born Huddersfield 14.5.1890. Son of John William and Clara Thorp, 49 Grasmere Road, Marsh, Huddersfield. Educated Hillhouse Council School, the Higher Grade School and at the Huddersfield Technical College. Single. Employed as estate clerk at the Ramsden estate office. Had served for ten years in the local Territorial battalion and became Company Quartermaster Sergeant. Played football with the Territorials. Was gazetted in August 1915. Killed in action at Bullecourt on 3.5.1917, aged 26 years. Buried **QUEANT ROAD CEMETERY, BUISSY**. Grave location:- Plot 2, Row F, Grave 24. (Brother of Lance Corporal **WILLIAM THORP**, died of wounds, 19.5.1915, q.v.). ROH:- Huddersfield Parish Church; Marsh War Memorial.

THORP, WILLIAM. Lance Corporal. No 2985. 1/5th Battalion Duke of Wellington's Regiment. Born Huddersfield 24.7.1891. Son of John William and Clara Thorp, 49 Grasmere Road, Marsh, Huddersfield. Educated Hillhouse Council School and the Higher Grade School. Employed as a bank clerk by the Lancashire and Yorkshire Bank. Single. Enlisted 6.9.1914. Seriously wounded in the arm and thigh at Fleurbaix on 15.5.1915. Died of wounds at No 14 General Hospital on 19.5.1915, aged 23 years. Buried **WIMEREUX COMMUNAL CEMETERY**. Grave location:- Plot 1, Row H, Grave 8. (Brother of 2nd Lieutenant **JOHN ERIC THORP**, killed in action, 3.5.1917, q.v.). ROH:- Huddersfield Parish Church; Huddersfield Drill Hall.

THWAITES, WILLIAM HENRY. Chief Petty Officer. No 138012. Royal Navy. *HMS Hampshire*. Born Moldgreen 25.12.1870. Brother of John Thwaites, 23 Airedale Crescent, Otley Road, Bradford. Enlisted in the Navy in 1888. Killed by mine explosion off the Orkneys when *HMS Hampshire* was sunk on 5.6.1916. He was 44 years of age. Has no known grave. Commemorated **PORTSMOUTH NAVAL MEMORIAL TO THE MISSING**.

TIFFANY, CHARLES EDWARD, MC. Regimental Sergeant Major. No 240002. 1/5th Battalion Duke of Wellington's Regiment. Born Almondbury 8.7.1873. Father of Ernest Tiffany, 4 Colne Street, Paddock. Educated Paddock Board School. Employed as an engine packing maker. Married. (His only son had joined the local Territorial battalion, as a drummer, at the age of 13 and accompanied the 1/5th Battalion to the Western front). Had served in the local Volunteer and Territorial battalions for a period of 27 years and, during the whole of that time, never missed a single camp. When the Territorials were mobilised he was Colour Sergeant of 'G' (Kirkburton) Company, to which he was transferred from 'A' Company Headquarters when the formation of the new Company was sanctioned. Embarked for France in April, 1915, and was promoted C.S.M. He was awarded the Military Cross on 1.7.1916. for, *'conspicuous gallantry and devotion to duty at all times. His coolness under fire has been particularly valuable, a man of untiring energy.'* (London Gazette 19th August 1916). Killed in action at Nieuport on 7.8.1917. Buried **RAMSCAPELLE ROAD**

MILITARY CEMETERY. Grave location:- Plot 2, Row A, Grave 33. ROH:- All Saints Church, Paddock; All Hallows Parish Church, Kirkburton; Huddersfield Drill Hall.

TIFFANY, HAROLD. Private. No 30175. 'Y' Company, 8th Battalion Northumberland Fusiliers. Born Lockwood 15.3.1897. Son of Fred and Ada Tiffany, 14 Scar Top, Lockwood, Huddersfield. Educated Lockwood Council School. Employed by Messrs Cliffe and Company, machine makers, of Longroyd Bridge. Was a member of the Primrose Hill United Methodist Church Young Men's Class. Single. Enlisted 19.6.1916. Embarked for France in October, 1916. Killed by a fragment of a shell at Grandcourt on 23.11.1916, aged 19. Buried **GRANDCOURT ROAD CEMETERY.** Grave location:- Row B, Grave 51. ROH:- Emmanuel Church, Lockwood.

TINDALE, MATTHEW. Private. No 252722. 2/6th Battalion Manchester Regiment. Born Leeds. Lived Meltham, Huddersfield. Died of wounds, 23.4.1918. Buried **St. SEVER CEMETERY EXTENSION, ROUEN.** Grave location:- Block P, Plot 9, Row D, Grave 4B. ROH:- St. Bartholomew's Church, Meltham.

TINKER, FRED. Private. No 23602. 9th Battalion Duke of Wellington's Regiment. Born Ravensthorpe. Lived 16 Reins, Honley. Reported missing, presumed killed, at the Battle of Arras on 25.4.1917. He was 34 years of age. Has no known grave. Commemorated **ARRAS MEMORIAL TO THE MISSING.** ROH:- Honley War Memorial.

TINKER, FRED. Private. No 32104. 'D' Company, 2/5th Battalion Duke of Wellington's Regiment. Born Upperthong, Holmfirth. Son of Mr and Mrs Alfred Tinker, of Howood Farm, Holmbridge. Educated Park Head School. Attended Holmbridge Sunday School. Employed as a porter at Holmfirth railway station. Enlisted 1915. Embarked for France in August, 1917. Killed by a fragment of shell, 22.7.1918, near Rheims. He was 25 years of age. Has no known grave. Commemorated **SOISSONS MEMORIAL TO THE MISSING.** ROH:- Holme and Holmbridge War Memorial; Huddersfield Drill Hall.

TINKER, PERCY. Private. No 242008. 2/5th Battalion Duke of Wellington's Regiment. Born Hepworth, Holmfirth. Son of Mr and Mrs Fred Tinker of Whitewells Road, Scholes. Attended Scholes Primitive Methodist Sunday School. Employed at Holmfirth Mill. Was a keen cricketer. Reported missing, presumed killed, at the Battle of Bullecourt on 3.5.1917, aged 27 years. Has no known grave. Commemorated **ARRAS MEMORIAL TO THE MISSING.** ROH:- Hepworth and Scholes War Memorial; Hepworth Church; Huddersfield Drill Hall.

TINSLEY, HENRY HAYES. Private. No 235793. 9th (Yorkshire Hussars) Battalion West Yorkshire Regiment. Born Malton, Yorkshire. Son of the late Richard Tinsley, M.R.C.V.S. Husband of Eleanor A. Tinsley, 1 Lea Street, Hillhouse, Huddersfield. Killed in action, 3.12.1917, aged 34 years. Buried **St. PATRICK'S CEMETERY, LOOS.** Grave location:- Plot 2, Row B, Grave 10. ROH:- Fartown and Birkby War Memorial.

TINSLEY, SYDNEY FRANCIS. Private. No 10297. 9th (Yorkshire Hussars) Battalion West Yorkshire Regiment. Born Whitby. Lived Huddersfield. Killed in action at Gallipoli, 8.8.1915. Has no known grave. Commemorated **HELLES MEMORIAL TO THE MISSING.** ROH:- Fartown and Birkby War Memorial.

TIPTON, JAMES HENRY. Sergeant. No 550711. 16th (County of London) Battalion Queen's Westminster Rifles. Only son of Cornelius and Alice Tipton of Connecticut, U.S.A., and formerly of Oakes, Huddersfield. Died of wounds in Palestine on 1.12.1917, aged 32 years. Buried **JERUSALEM WAR CEMETERY.** Grave location:- Plot T, Grave 75.

TODD, NATHAN. Private. No 12547. 2nd Battalion York and Lancaster Regiment. Born Netherton, Huddersfield. Son of Edward and Martha Todd, 154 Birks Road, Lockwood, Huddersfield. Killed in action, 22.3.1918, aged 23 years. Has no known grave. Commemorated **ARRAS MEMORIAL TO THE MISSING.** ROH:- South Crosland and Netherton War Memorial; Emmanuel Church, Lockwood.

TODD, WILFRED. Private. No 40991. 10th Battalion Lincolnshire Regiment. Formerly No 32367 North Staffordshire Regiment. Born

Netherton, Huddersfield. Son of Mr and Mrs George Todd, The Fold, Netherton. Killed in action, 28.4.1917, at the Battle of Arras. He was 29 years of age. Has no known grave. Commemorated **ARRAS MEMORIAL TO THE MISSING**. ROH:- South Crosland and Netherton War Memorial.

TOLSON, DOUGLAS IRVINE. Cadet. No 177552. 2 Observer School. Royal Air Force. Second son of Walter and Kate Helena Tolson, Upperbridge, Holmfirth. Educated Holmfirth Secondary School. Prior to enlistment, was a student in the dyeing and chemistry department at the Huddersfield Technical College. Enlisted in Spring 1918. Died from pneumonia, 1.11.1918, whilst in training at Manston near Ramsgate. He was 19 years of age. Buried **HOLMFIRTH WESLEYAN BURIAL GROUND**. Grave location:- FO 7. ROH:- Holmfirth War Memorial; Holmfirth Secondary School; Huddersfield Corporation Roll.

TOLSON, HORACE. 2nd Lieutenant. 6th Battalion The Royal Warwickshire Regiment. Formerly 87th Field Ambulance, Royal Army Medical Corps. Son of Joah and Sarah Tolson, Ryefield, Holmfirth. Educated Holmfirth Wesleyan Day School. After training as a teacher at Westminster College, London, he took up a post at a large school in Liverpool. Enlisted September 1914. Served with the R.A.M.C in the Dardenelles. Was commissioned in November, 1917. Was in charge of machine guns at Demuin on 29.2.1918 when he was reported missing, presumed killed. He was 33 years of age. Has no known grave. Commemorated **POZIERES MEMORIAL TO THE MISSING**. ROH:- Holmfirth War Memorial; Holmfirth Secondary School.

TOLSON, JAMES MARTIN. 2nd Lieutenant. 'A' Battery, 74th Brigade, Royal Field Artillery. Born Oaklands, 1 Greenhead Lane, Dalton, Huddersfield 26.3.1898. Youngest son of Whiteley and Jessy Tolson. Educated at Bramcote, Scarborough, and Uppingham Public School, Rutland, which he left in December, 1915. He had been awarded a place at University College, Oxford. Single. Enlisted in the Honourable Artillery Company in April, 1916. Was commissioned into the R.F.A. on 20.2.1917. Was wounded in October, 1917, near Ypres. He was treated at Fazakerley Hospital. He returned to France and was gassed in June, 1918, near Adinfer. He rejoined his Battery in July, 1918. Was wounded, 20.10.1918, near Cambrai. Died of wounds, 20.10.1918, aged 20 years. Buried **QUIEVY COMMUNAL CEMETERY EXTENSION**. Grave location:- Row C, Grave 51. (Brother of Second Lieutenant **ROBERT HUNTRISS TOLSON**, killed in action, 1.7.1916, q.v.). ROH:- Huddersfield Parish Church; St. John's Church, Kirkheaton; The Tolson Memorial Museum.

TOLSON, ROBERT HUNTRISS. Lieutenant. 15th Battalion West Yorkshire Regiment (1st Leeds Pals). Born Elm Lea, Dalton, Huddersfield, 6.11.1884. Son of Whiteley and Jessy Tolson, Oaklands, 1 Greenhead Lane, Dalton. Educated Aysgarth School, near Newton le Willows, and King William's College, Castletown, Isle of Man. Employed at the Leeds branch of the Becketts Bank. On 9.10.1909 married Miss Zoe A. Stanley, 'Kirk Lea', Driffield. Enlisted as a Private in the Public Schools Battalion in September, 1914. Obtained a commission in the King's Own Yorkshire Light Infantry in January, 1915. Transferred to the 15th Battalion West Yorkshire Regiment in September, 1915. Went with them to Egypt in September, 1915. Returned to France in March, 1916. Killed in action at Serre, 1.7.1916, on the first day of the Battle of the Somme, aged 31. His father received a telegram informing him that his son had been wounded. Second Lieutenant Tolson's body was eventually found in March, 1917, and he is buried in **SERRE ROAD CEMETERY No 1**. Grave location:- Plot 1, Row B, Grave 52. (Brother of 2nd Lieutenant **JAMES MARTIN TOLSON**, died of wounds, 20.10.1918, q.v.). ROH:- Huddersfield Parish Church; St. John's Church, Kirkheaton; The Tolson Memorial Museum; commemorated on headstone in Kirkheaton Cemetery.

TOMLINSON, FRANCIS EDGAR. Lance Corporal. No 1257. 1/7th Battalion Duke of Wellington's Regiment, attached to the Machine Gun section. Born Linthwaite. Son of Ed and Clara Jane Tomlinson, of Flathouse, Linthwaite. Apprenticed to Mr J. G. Bamforth as a card nailer. Had served four years in the local Territorials. Enlisted at the outbreak of the war. Embarked for France in April 1915. Killed in action, 16.5.1915, aged 21 years. Buried **RUE-DAVID MILITARY CEMETERY, FLEURBAIX**. Grave location:- Plot 1, Row B,

Grave 25. ROH:- Linthwaite War Memorial; Huddersfield Drill Hall.

TOMLINSON, HUGH, MC. Captain. 57th Squadron, Royal Flying Corps. Born Huddersfield 1882. Son of the late G. W. Tomlinson, F.S.A., of Woodfield, Huddersfield, and Charlotte Tomlinson, 65 Iverna Court, Kensington, London. Educated at Lockers Park and Charterhouse Public School. Worked in Java as a tea planter. On the outbreak of war he came back to England to enlist. He joined the Red Cross as a motor ambulance driver and served in France. In April, 1915, he went to Hendon and was gazetted into the Royal Flying Corps in November, 1915. After being stationed at various places, he was put on the night defence of London and was up in several Zeppelin raids. Had a bad accident during one raid on 31.1.1916. He did a great deal of experimental night work and had another serious accident in May, 1916, due to engine failure. He was awarded the Military Cross in June, 1916, for, *'gallantry and devotion to duty. Captain Tomlinson has taken part in several raids. On two occasions he has had serious accidents at night flying, but he has not been in the least discouraged, and he has continued to do most valuable work.'* (London Gazette 27th July, 1916). Was Mentioned in Despatches in January, 1917. Involved in a battle over Oignies, France, and was seriously wounded. He was taken prisoner and died of his wounds in a German Field Hospital on 2.4.1917. He was 34 years of age. Buried **CABARET ROUGE BRITISH CEMETERY.** Grave location:- Plot 7, Row J, Grave 3. ROH:- Huddersfield Parish Church.

TOMLINSON, JACK, MM and Bar. Private. No PO/1222(S). 2nd Battalion Royal Marine Light Infantry. Born 9 Haigh's Yard, Huddersfield, 28.12.1889. Son of Harry and Sarah Jane Tomlinson, 30 High Street, Paddock. Educated Paddock Church of England School. Employed as a hairdresser at the Paddock Toilet Rooms. Was a member of the Paddock Church choir. Single. Awarded the Military Medal for 'bravery on the battlefield.' Died in No 6 Stationary Hospital from a shrapnel wound to the left leg on 27.3.1918, aged 28 years. Buried **St. HILAIRE CEMETERY, FREVENT.** Grave location:- Plot 5, Row E, Grave 9. ROH:- All Saints Church, Paddock.

TONG, ARTHUR CLIFFORD. Sergeant. No 240345. 1/5th Battalion Duke of Wellington's Regiment. Born Elland 21.1.1891. Son of John William and Sarah Elizabeth Tong, 43 Birch Road, Berry Brow, Huddersfield. Educated Berry Brow Board School. Was a fine athlete and played both cricket and football. Was a member of the Armitage Bridge Conservative Club and attended Armitage Bridge Church. Employed as an electrical engineer by Messrs Broadbents Limited, Central Ironworks, Huddersfield. Single. Was a member of the local Territorials before the war. Rejoined the colours in August, 1914. Reported missing, presumed killed, on 3.9.1916 during the attack on the Schwaben Redoubt, aged 25. Has no known grave. Commemorated **THIEPVAL MEMORIAL TO THE MISSING.** ROH:- Huddersfield Drill Hall; Armitage Bridge War Memorial.

TOPPING, HARRY. Lance Corporal. No 17929. 'B' Company, 13th Battalion Royal Welsh Fusiliers. Born Huddersfield 12.9.1885. Second son of Councillor T. Topping, 121 Cowcliffe Hill, Huddersfield. Educated Hillhouse Council Boys School, Huddersfield College Higher Grade School. Husband of Fanny Topping, 488 Bradford Road North, Huddersfield. Was a member of the staff of the Huddersfield Education Department from August, 1900, until July, 1911, when he became assistant secretary at the Huddersfield Technical College. Enlisted 18.11.1914. Embarked for France in December, 1915. Was mentioned in despatches in 1916. Severely gassed in July, 1917. Home on leave in December, 1917. Returned to France in January and was killed on 22.4.1918 during a heavy attack by a section of the Royal Welsh Fusiliers and the Durham Light Infantry at Bouzincourt, near Albert. Has no known grave. Commemorated **POZIERES MEMORIAL TO THE MISSING.** ROH:- Christ Church, Woodhouse Hill; Huddersfield Corporation Roll; Fartown and Birkby War Memorial.

TOPPING, TOM. Private. No 41854. 2nd Battalion South Staffordshire Regiment. Formerly No 50653 North Staffordshire Regiment. Born Marsden. Married, with one child. Lived Towngate, Marsden. Was in business on his own account as a plumber and glazier in Towngate, Marsden. He was a very clever comic singer and was in great demand at local concerts and entertainments. Enlisted April 1917. Embarked for France on 2.10.1917. Was seriously wounded in the head on 18.12.1917. Died of wounds at No 48 Casualty Clearing Station, 26.12.1917, aged 34 years. Buried **ROCQUIGNY-EQUANCOURT BRITISH CEMETERY.** Grave location:- Plot 8, Row C, Grave 15. ROH:- Marsden Liberal Club; Marsden War Memorial.

TOWLSON, THOMAS WILLIAM. Sergeant. No 10856. 4th Battalion (1st Central Ontario Regiment) Canadian Forces. Formerly 1st Battalion King's Own Yorkshire Light Infantry. Born Pontefract 29.6.1877. Son of Joseph and Jane Towlson, 195 Halifax Old Road, Grimscar, Huddersfield. Educated Hillhouse Board School, Fartown. Enlisted in the K.O.Y.L.I. on 3.1.1895 and served for eight years. Was in the South African War. Went out to Canada and lived at Emerald Street, Hamilton, Ontario, Canada. Was working as a stock-keeper in Hamilton when war was declared. Enlisted in August 1914. Killed in action at Langemarck, Belgium, on 23.4.1915. Has no known grave. Commemorated **MENIN GATE MEMORIAL TO THE MISSING.** ROH:- Fartown and Birkby War Memorial.

TOWLSON, WILLIAM HOLLAND. 2nd Lieutenant. 122nd Company, Machine Gun Corps. Formerly Private Royal Welsh Fusiliers. Born Huddersfield 16.2.1887. Son of Herbert and Mary Towlson, 4 Cobcroft Road, Fartown, Huddersfield. Educated Spring Grove Board School. Served his articles as a solicitor with Mr F. A. Reed of the firm of Messrs Learoyd and Company, Huddersfield, and on completion practiced for 12 months in Liverpool, 12 months in Staffordshire and 2 years in Aberdare, South Wales. Enlisted in the Royal Welsh Fusiliers as a Private in June, 1916, at Kinmel and had gained his first stripe as a Lance Corporal when he was recommended for a commission. He went through his course with a Cadet battalion at Bisley and was granted a commission into the Machine Gun Corps on 26.1.1917. Embarked for France in March, 1917. Suffered serious gunshot wounds on 31.7.1917 and underwent an emergency operation. He was gradually moved down the line and arrived at No 10 British Red Cross Hospital (Lady Murray's Hospital) on 26.8.1917. At 1.30pm on 28.9.1917 his parents received telegrams from the War Office and Lady Murray to say that their son's condition was critical after a serious operation, followed by a third telegram at 5.30pm containing the sad news of his death and conveying the sympathy of the Army Council. Died of wounds at 9am on 28.9.1917, aged 30 years. Buried **MONT HUON MILITARY CEMETERY.** Grave location:- Plot 4, Row O, Grave 2b. ROH:- Fartown and Birkby War Memorial.

TOWNEND, ASA, MM. Private. No 117469. 38th Field Ambulance, Royal Army Medical Corps. Born Golcar. Son of Joe and Christiana Townend, 2 Hollin Hall, Golcar. Educated Crow Lane Board School, Milnsbridge. Employed by Messrs John Crowther and Sons, of Milnsbridge. Died of bronchial-pneumonia at the 3rd Canadian Hospital, Boulogne, on 28.11.1918. He was 24 years of age. Buried **TERLINCTHUN BRITISH CEMETERY.** Grave location:- Plot 12; Row A; Grave 8. ROH:- St. John's Church, Golcar; Crow Lane Board School, Milnsbridge.

TOWNSEND, CHARLES WILLIAM. Private. No 40620. 8th Battalion Northumberland Fusiliers. Born Vicarage Road, Longwood, Huddersfield, 24.3.1883. Son of the late Oliver and Louisa Townend, 73 Thornhill Road, Longwood. Was in business on his own account as a rug manufacturer at Thornhill Road, Longwood. Single. Enlisted 24.5.1916. Killed in action, 16.8.1917, at the Battle of Langemarck. He was 34 years of age. Has no known grave. Commemorated **TYNE COT MEMORIAL TO THE MISSING.** ROH:- St. Mark's Parish Church, Longwood War Memorial.

TOWNEND, DONALD WHITELEY. Private. No 62300. 1/4th Battalion King's Own Yorkshire Light Infantry. Formerly No 93616 8th Territorial Reserve Battalion. Born 5 Hope Street, Milnsbridge, Huddersfield, 23.9.1899. Son of Josiah and Mary Ann Townend, 5 Hope Street, Milnsbridge. Educated Crow Lane Board School, Milnsbridge, where he won a scholarship to the Huddersfield Muncipal School. He attended there for six years. In 1917 he was awarded a local scholarship to Huddersfield Municipal School and later gained the Ackroyd Scholarship at Leeds University. Enlisted 23.10.1917. He was on the teaching staff at Brockton Camp prior to going to France on 11.4.1918. Single. Killed in action at Kemmel Hill on 26.4.1918.

He was 18 years of age. Has no known grave. Commemorated **TYNE COT MEMORIAL TO THE MISSING.** ROH:- Oakes Baptist Church; St. Mark's Parish Church, Longwood; Crow Lane Board School, Milnsbridge; commemorated in Salendine Nook Baptist Chapel yard, F282.

TOWNEND, FRANK. Guardsman. No 20375. Coldstream Guards. Born 71 Thornhill Road, Longwood, Huddersfield, 10.1.1888. Son of the late Andrew and Betsy Ellen Townend, 1 Rock Street, Spark Hall, Longwood. Educated at Longwood National School. Employed as a woollen spinner. Husband of Sarah H. Townend, 10 Lamb Hall Road, Longwood. Enlisted 20.11.1916. Killed in action, 30.11.1917, during the Battle of Cambrai. Has no known grave. Commemorated **CAMBRAI MEMORIAL TO THE MISSING.** ROH:- Longwood Wesleyan Chapel; St. Mark's Parish Church, Longwood.

TOWNEND, FRED. Private. No 46601. 15th Battalion Durham Light Infantry. Formerly No 367261 Northern Cyclist Battalion. Born Huddersfield. Son of William and Jane Townend, 6 Lower Slades, Linthwaite. As a boy, was a chorister in the Linthwaite Church Choir and attended the Sunday School up to the time of enlistment. Employed as a woollen piecer by Messrs Hirst and Mallinson of Milnsbridge. Enlisted May 1917. Embarked for France in April, 1918. Killed in action, 24.8.1918, aged 19 years. Has no known grave. Commemorated **VIS-en-ARTOIS MEMORIAL TO THE MISSING.** ROH:- Linthwaite War Memorial.

TOWNEND, GEORGE. Private. No 24719. 49th Battalion Machine Gun Corps. Formerly No 4041 Duke of Wellington's Regiment. Born Fartown 12.1.1900. Educated Hillhouse Council School. Employed as a cloth finisher. Enlisted February 1915. Killed in action on 13.10.1918, near Cambrai. He was 18 years of age. Buried **NAVES COMMUNAL CEMETERY EXTENSION.** Grave location:- Plot 5, Row A, Grave 14.

TOWNEND, HAROLD. Private. No 204526. 2nd Battalion Duke of Wellington's Regiment. Born Huddersfield. Son of Horace and Syble Townend, 20 Gelder Terrace, Moldgreen, Huddersfield. Husband of Lavinia Townend, 2 Gelder Terrace, Moldgreen. Had four children. Prior to enlistment, was employed as a collier by British Dyes Limited. Reported missing 15.4.1918 and afterwards presumed to have been killed on that date. He was 23 years of age. Has no known grave. Commemorated **PLOEGSTEERT MEMORIAL TO THE MISSING.** ROH:- Christ Church, Moldgreen.

TOWNEND, LEWIS. Private. No 242009. 2/5th Battalion Duke of Wellington's Regiment. Born Paddock 11.8.1892. Son of Benjamin and Annie Townend, 117 May Street, Crosland Moor, Huddersfield. Educated All Saints Church of England School, Paddock. Employed as a dyer's labourer by Messrs Tom Liversedge and Sons Limited, Canal Bank Works, Huddersfield. Was a member of the Paddock All Saints Church Choir, the Huddersfield and District Light Opera Society and the Huddersfield Amateur Operatic Society. Single. Enlisted 28.3.1916. Killed in action, 3.5.1917, at Bullecourt during the Battle of Arras, aged 24. Has no known grave. Commemorated **ARRAS MEMORIAL TO THE MISSING.** ROH:- All Saints Church, Paddock; St. Barnabas Church, Crosland Moor; Huddersfield Drill Hall.

TOWNSEND, JOHN. 2nd Lieutenant. 12th Battalion West Yorkshire Regiment. Formerly a Sergeant in the York and Lancaster Regiment. Only son of David F. and Mary Hannah Townsend, of Bradshaw Road, Honley. Educated Honley National School and Huddersfield College Higher Grade School. He then studied at Sheffield University, where he was awarded a BA degree. After holding a teaching post for a month he enlisted in the ranks of the York and Lancaster Regiment, in August, 1914. He went with his Regiment to Egypt from December, 1915, until March, 1916, when he was drafted to France. In June, 1916, he was gazetted Second Lieutenant and transferred to the West Yorkshire Regiment. He was an expert Scout and Signaller and was made Intelligence Officer. Killed in action on 14.7.1916 at Bazentin-le-Grand, during the Battle of the Somme. He was 23 years of age. Has no known grave. Commemorated **THIEPVAL MEMORIAL TO THE MISSING.** ROH:- Honley War Memorial.

TOWNSEND, JOHN ROBINSON. Private. No 15098. 10th Battalion Devonshire Regiment. Born Rastrick, Yorkshire. Lived Huddersfield. Died of wounds in Salonica, 18.9.1917. Buried **LEMBET ROAD MILITARY CEMETERY,**

SALONICA. Grave location:- No 1202. ROH:- St. Stephen's Church, Rashcliffe.

TOYNE, ALFRED. Private. No 32144. 2nd Battalion West Yorkshire Regiment. Born Horncastle, Lincolnshire. Had lived in Slaithwaite for four years. Employed as a baker by the Slaithwaite Equitable Industrial Society Limited. Attended St. James's Church, Slaithwaite. Enlisted May 1916. Embarked for France at the end of August, 1916. Killed by a sniper on 25.10.1916, during the Battle of the Somme. Has no known grave. Commemorated **THIEPVAL MEMORIAL TO THE MISSING.** ROH:- St. James Church, Slaithwaite; Slaithwaite War Memorial.

TRUEMAN, JOHN. Private. No 240725. 1/5th Battalion Duke of Wellington's Regiment. Born Huddersfield. Son of William and Myra Trueman, 30 Whiteley Street, Milnsbridge. Enlisted at the outbreak of the war. Had been wounded on 8.8.1915 and 5.8.1916. Reported wounded and missing after an attack on the Liepzig Salient, 16.9.1916, during the Battle of the Somme, aged 21. Has no known grave. Commemorated **THIEPVAL MEMORIAL TO THE MISSING.** ROH:- Milnsbridge War Memorial; Huddersfield Drill Hall.

TUCK, JOHN WILLIAM. Private. No 19897. 2nd Battalion Border Regiment. Born Salford, Manchester. Husband of Annie Tuck, 8 Bay Hall, Birkby, Huddersfield. Died on 28.10.1917 at No 10 Casualty Clearing Station as the result of severe head wounds. He was 32 years of age. Buried **LIJSSENTHOEK MILITARY CEMETERY.** Grave location:- Plot 21, Row G, Grave 17a.

TUCKER, HAROLD ALBERT EDWARD. Corporal. No L/25663. 168th (Huddersfield) Brigade H.Q., Royal Field Artillery. Born Norwich, Norfolk, 15.4.1891. Son of Alfred Edward and Ellen Tucker, 32 Water Street, Springwood, Huddersfield. Educated Rutherford College, Newcastle-on-Tyne. Served his apprenticeship with Peter Conacher and Company Limited, organ builders, and remained with them until he enlisted. Single. Was a member of the Y.M.C.A. Attended St. Thomas's Church. Enlisted 14.5.1915. Killed in action, 3.7.1916, aged 25. Buried **CONNAUGHT CEMETERY, THIEPVAL.** Grave location:- Plot 12, Row K, Grave 5. ROH:- Huddersfield Parish Church.

TUCKER, ROBERT BRUCE. Private. No 242927. 1/7th Battalion Duke of Wellington's Regiment. Youngest son of Mrs Tucker, of Damhouse, Holmfirth. Was born in the West of England where he was educated. Employed by Messrs Greenwoods at Digley Mills. Attended Hinchliffe Mill Wesleyan Chapel. Married, with three children. Enlisted 5.7.1916. Trained at Clipstone Camp and embarked for France in October, 1916. Killed in action in Belgium on 29.4.1918. Buried **KLEIN-VIERSTRAAT BRITISH CEMETERY.** Grave location:- Plot 5, Row C, Grave 2. ROH:- Holme and Holmbridge War Memorial; Huddersfield Drill Hall.

TUCKFIELD, ALBERT. Private. No 44991. 1st Battalion York and Lancaster Regiment. Born Llandudno, Carnaervon, North Wales. Youngest son of the late Mr Henry and Mrs Tuckfield, 25 Midland Street, Huddersfield. Employed by Messrs J. Hopkinson and Company Limited of Birkby. Died of dysentery in Malta on 21.10.1918, aged 26 years. Buried **PIETA MILTARY CEMETERY, MALTA.** Grave location:- Plot A, Row 20, Grave 7. ROH:- Fartown and Birkby War Memorial.

TUNNICLIFFE, ERIC. Private. No 38126. 2nd Battalion The Yorkshire Regiment. Born Skelmanthorpe. Son of Charlie and Cinderella Tunnacliffe, Fairmount, Huddersfield Road, Skelmanthorpe. Husband of Emily Tunnacliffe (later Emily Meachen, 16 Carr Hill, Balby, Doncaster). Employed as a butcher by Mr Robert Heaton, of Skelmanthorpe. Attended the Skelmanthorpe Primitive Methodist Chapel. Enlisted 18.9.1916. Embarked for France in January, 1917. Killed in an enemy air raid on 1.10.1917, aged 23 years. Buried **LONGUENESSE (St. OMER) SOUVENIR CEMETERY.** Grave location:- Plot 4, Row E, Grave 19. ROH:- St. Aidan's Church, Skelmanthorpe.

TUNNACLIFFE, HARRY. Private. No 202820. 1/4th Battalion King's Own Yorkshire Light Infantry. Born Lepton, Huddersfield. Husband of Janet Tunnacliffe, 10 Tandem, Kirkheaton. Employed by Mr C. H. Best, painter and decorator, of Moldgreen. Enlisted September 1916. Died from gas poisoning on 25.7.1917 at No 24 Casualty Clearing Station at Oosthoek, Belgium. He was 33 years of age. Buried **ADINKERKE CHURCHYARD EXTENSION.**

Grave location:- Grave No 848. ROH:- St. John's Church, Kirkheaton; Lepton Parish Church.

TUOHY, MICHAEL. Guardsman. No 11319. 1st Battalion Irish Guards. Born Scariff, County Clare, Eire. Lived Thurstonland. Killed in action, 30.4.1918. Buried **AYETTE BRITISH CEMETERY.** Grave location:- Row A, Grave 10. ROH:- Thurstonland War Memorial.

TURNER, FRANK. Private. No 13529. 2/5th Battalion Duke of Wellington's Regiment. Born 35 Manchester Street, Huddersfield, in May 1890. Educated St. Paul's Church of England School. Husband of Beatrice Turner, 15 St. Andrew's Road, Aspley, Huddersfield. Employed as a dyer's labourer by Messrs J. Mellor, dyers, Colne Road, Huddersfield. Enlisted September 1914. Killed in action, 29.3.1918. Has no known grave. Commemorated **ARRAS MEMORIAL TO THE MISSING.** ROH:- Huddersfield Drill Hall.

TURNER, GEORGE ARCHIE. Lance Corporal. No 267615. 1/6th Battalion Duke of Wellington's Regiment. Born Loughborough 1.9.1898. Son of Edmund and Elizabeth Turner, 15 Harriet Street, Derby. Educated Church Gate School, Loughborough. Employed in Huddersfield as a woollen fettler. Single. Enlisted 10.7.1916. Killed in action, 1.11.1918, near Valenciennes, aged 21. Buried **MAING COMMUNAL CEMETERY EXTENSION.** Grave location:- C.1. ROH:- St. Barnabas Church, Crosland Moor.

TURNER, HAROLD. Rifleman. No 205547. 2/7th Battalion West Yorkshire Regiment. Son of Job Turner, 115 Woodside, Slaithwaite. Husband of Maria Turner, 10 Holme Villas, Marsden. Killed in action, 27.3.1918, aged 30 years. Has no known grave. Commemorated **ARRAS MEMORIAL TO THE MISSING.** ROH:- Marsden War Memorial.

TURNER, JACK FOXHALL. Private. No 301990. 1/8th Battalion Durham Light Infantry. Formerly No 6269 Duke of Wellington's Regiment. Born Huddersfield. Son of Fred and Sarah Ann Turner, 102 Bradford Road North, Huddersfield. Employed as a machine mechanic by Messrs Bairstow, Sons and Company. Attended Hillhouse Congregational Church. Died of wounds at No 33 Casualty Clearing Station on 10.4.1918, aged 21 years. Buried **HAVERSKERQUE BRITISH CEMETERY.** Grave location:- Row C, Grave 6. ROH:- Fartown and Birkby War Memorial.

TURNER, JOSEPH HENRY. Private. No 17935. 9th Battalion Duke of Wellington's Regiment. Born Meltham, Huddersfield. Son of Joseph and Julia Turner, 27 New Street, Meltham. Killed in action, 25.4.1917, during the Battle of Arras. He was 20 years of age. Has no known grave. Commemorated **ARRAS MEMORIAL TO THE MISSING.** ROH:- St. Bartholomew's Church, Meltham.

TURNER, ARTHUR WIDDOWSON Private No. 55420 12/13th Battalion Northumberland Fusiliers. Lived with his brother at 5 Newland Avenue, Birkby. Prior to enlistment, was employed by Mr T. Hardcastle, Blacker Road, Birkby. Son of Ellis Turner, of The Moss, 67, Talbot St., Batley, Yorks. Killed in action 18.4.1918. He was 19 years of age. No known grave. Commemorated on Tyne Cot Memorial to the Missing. ROH:- Fartown and Birkby War Memorial.

TURTON, FRED. Private. No 32665. 2nd Battalion Durham Light Infantry. Born Holmfirth. Son of Mr and Mrs Joe Turton, Cinderhills, Holmfirth. Husband of Rosa Turton, 19 Greenfield Bank, New Mill. Killed in action, 15.10.1916, aged 34 years. Buried **BANCOURT BRITISH CEMETERY.** Grave location:- Plot 8, Row D, Grave 10. ROH:- New Mill Working Men's Club; Fulstone War Memorial; Messrs. Taylor and Littlewood, Newsome Mills.

TURTON, FRED. Private. No 28671 West Yorkshire Regiment, transferred to No 376845 Labour Corps. Son of John and Ellen Turton, Cinderhills Road, Holmfirth. Prior to enlistment, was employed by Messrs Taylor and Littlewood Limited, Newsome Mills. Enlisted May 1916. Had been serving in Belgium with the Labour Corps. Was taken to hospital at the beginning of March, 1919, suffering from influenza and pneumonia. Died at the Holmfirth Auxiliary Hospital on 10.3.1919, where he was the last patient. He was 39 years of age. Buried **LANE CONGREGATIONAL BURIAL GROUND.** Grave location:- J. 7. ROH:- Underbank War Memorial; Messrs. Taylor and Littlewood, Newsome Mills.

TURTON, WILSON. Private. No 5424. 22nd Battalion Australian Imperial Forces. Born Cinderhills, Holmfirth. Son of Joe and Mary Turton. Married, with three children. Died, 15.6.1918, aged 37 years. Buried **MERICOURT-L'ABBE COMMUNAL CEMETERY EXTENSION.** Grave location:- Plot 3, Row C, Grave 6.

TURVILLE, FRANK. Lance Corporal. No 241807. 2/5th Battalion York and Lancaster Regiment. Born Worksop, Nottinghamshire, 12.7.1887. Son of William Turville, 7 Greenhead Road, Huddersfield. Educated Melbourne Road Council School, Leicester: Wesleyan Higher Grade School, Skipton, Wesleyan School, Burnley, Council School, Tonbridge, Wesleyan School, Kettering. Employed as a compositor. Single. Enlisted March 1916. Reported missing, presumed killed, during the Battle of Cambrai on 27.11.1917. Has no known grave. Commemorated **CAMBRAI MEMORIAL TO THE MISSING.**

TYAS, ERNEST. Private. No 38512. 10th Battalion West Yorkshire Regiment. Born Brockholes, Huddersfield. Son of the late William and Ann Tyas, 6 Smithy Place, Brockholes. Husband of Edith Tyas. Employed by Messrs Robinsons, of Smithy Place Mills. Attended St. George's Church, Brockholes. Killed by a sniper in No Man's Land on 14.4.1917, aged 29 years. Has no known grave. Commemorated **ARRAS MEMORIAL TO THE MISSING.** ROH:- Honley War Memorial; Brockholes War Memorial.

TYAS, FRANK. Guardsman. No 30471. 1st Battalion Grenadier Guards. Born Cartworth, Holmfirth. Son of Charlie and Lydia Tyas of Longley, Holmfirth. Educated Hade Edge Council School. Attended Choppards Sunday School. Employed as a farm labourer by Mr W. H. Hinchliffe, of Longley. Killed in action, 12.9.1918, aged 21 years. Buried **VAULX HILL CEMETERY.** Grave location:- Plot 2, Row G, Grave 25. ROH:- Hade Edge War Memorial.

TYAS, FRED. Private. No 31985. 4th Battalion Special Reserve Battalion South Staffordshire Regiment. Born Huddersfield. Son of Mr and Mrs Herbert Tyas, 28 Salford, Lockwood. Employed as a cloth finisher by Messrs Kaye and Stewart. Enlisted November 1916. Killed in action, 24.3.1918, aged 18 years. Has no known grave. Commemorated **ARRAS MEMORIAL TO THE MISSING.** ROH:- Emmanuel Church, Lockwood.

TYAS, HERBERT. Rifleman. No 47210. 2/6th Battalion Durham Light Infantry. Formerly No 39461 York and Lancaster Regiment. Born Smithy Place, Brockholes 18.11.1899. Son of the late William and Hannah Tyas, 24 Storths, Moldgreen, Huddersfield. Educated Christ Church School, Moldgreen. Employed as a motor driver by Mr H. Roebuck, cabinet maker. Single. Enlisted 1.1.1918. Killed in action near Aubers Ridge on 6.10.1918, aged 19 years. Buried **RATION FARM MILITARY CEMETERY.** Grave location:- Plot 6, Row I, Grave 8. ROH:- St. Andrew's Church, Moldgreen; Christ Church, Moldgreen.

TYAS, HERBERT. Private. No 42118. 1/5th Battalion York and Lancaster Regiment. Born Skelmanthorpe. Married, with four children. Lived Cumberworth Road, Skelmanthorpe. Employed as a plush finisher by Messrs Field and Botterill. Enlisted April 1917. Killed in action, 15.4.1918, aged 32 years. Has no known grave. Commemorated **TYNE COT MEMORIAL TO THE MISSING.** ROH:- St. Aidan's Church, Skelmanthorpe.

TYAS, JAMES. Rifleman. No 242696. 1/5th Battalion King's Own Yorkshire Light Infantry. Formerly No 3874 3/7th Battalion Duke of Wellington's Regiment. Born Penistone 17.9.1891. Son of Walter and Martha Tyas, 20 Bentley Street, Lockwood. Educated at Penistone Schools. Employed as a shop assistant at the Maypole Dairy. Single. Enlisted June 1916. Reported missing at Nieuport on 23.7.1917 and afterwards presumed to have been killed on that date, aged 27. Has no known grave. Commemorated **NIEUPORT MEMORIAL TO THE MISSING.** ROH:- Emmanuel Church, Lockwood; St. Stephen's Church, Rashcliffe.

TYAS, NORMAN. Private. No 48416. 11th Battalion The Royal Scots (Lothian Regiment). Born Huddersfield 31.10.1887. Educated Thomas Street Board School. Was a widower, with two children. Lived with his sister, Mrs Cruise, at 5 Lily Street, Turnbridge, Huddersfield. Employed as a teamer by Messrs Eastwood at the Wholesale Market, Huddersfield. Killed in action, 12.10.1917, aged 29 years. Has no known grave.

Commemorated **TYNE COT MEMORIAL TO THE MISSING.** Commemorated on his parents' headstone in Edgerton Cemetery, Huddersfield.

TYAS, WILLIE. Private. No 17942. 1/6th Battalion Duke of Wellington's Regiment. Born Huddersfield 20.7.1894. Son of Lister and Mary Elizabeth Tyas, 8 Halifax Old Road, Huddersfield. Educated Hillhouse Council School. Employed as a dyer's labourer. Single. Enlisted 28.1.1916. Wounded 25.7.1918. Died of wounds on 26.7.1918, aged 22 years. Buried **HAGLE DUMP CEMETERY, ELVERDINGHE, BELGIUM.** Grave location:- Plot 2, Row B, Grave 4. ROH:- Fartown and Birkby War Memorial.

TYSON, JOHN. Private. No 200896. 2/4th Battalion Duke of Wellington's Regiment. Born Keighley. Lived Huddersfield. Killed in action, 17.3.1917. Buried **ACHIET-LE-GRAND COMMUNAL CEMETERY EXTENSION.** Grave location:- Plot 3, Row G, Grave 14.

TYSON, THOMAS. Driver. No 128062. 30th Battery, Royal Field Artillery. Born Meltham. Son of Robert and Elizabeth Tyson of Golcar Brow, Meltham. Employed at Lower Sunnybank Mills, Meltham. Attended Meltham Church Sunday School. Enlisted 1916. Went out to Mesopotamia and was later invalided to Bombay, India. Accidentally drowned in India on 24.9.1917, aged 21 years. Buried **TRIMULGHERRY CANTONMENT CEMETERY, INDIA.** Commemorated **MADRAS 1914-1918 WAR MEMORIAL, CHENNAI, INDIA.** ROH:- St. Bartholomew's Church, Meltham.

ULRICH, ERNEST WILLIAM. Private. No 49812. 1/5th Battalion The King's (Liverpool Regiment). Born Chorley, Lancashire, 11.9.1987. Son of Emma Ulrich and the late Frederick William Ulrich, 45 Wakefield Road, Moldgreen, Huddersfield. Educated Middleton Junction Church of England School, near Manchester. Was in business as a newsagent on his own account. Husband of Madeline Florence Ulrich, 45 Wakefield Road, Moldgreen. Enlisted 28.2.1917. Killed in action at St. Julien, near Ypres, on 20.9.1917. Has no known grave. Commerated **TYNE COT MEMORIAL TO THE MISSING.** ROH:- Fartown and Birkby War Memorial; Christ Church, Moldgreen.

UMPLEBY, GEORGE E. Private. No 68378, 186th Company, Machine Gun Corps. Born Shepley. Son of Edward Wright and Mary Umpleby. Husband of Mabel Umpleby, Lea Head, Shepley. Employed as a weaver at Messrs Armitage's Mill, The Knowle, Shepley. Died in Iran on 20.11.1918, aged 31 years. Buried **TEHRAN WAR CEMETERY.** Grave location:- Plot 4, Row B, Grave 2. ROH:- Shepley War Memorial.

UNDERWOOD, FRANCIS (FRANK) RICHARD. Private. No 25511. 7th Battalion East Yorkshire Regiment. Born Stepney, London. Came to Slaithwaite, Huddersfield, in 1912. Apprenticed to Mr Harry Walker, tailor, Hill Top, Slaithwaite. Reported missing, presumed killed, 8.11.1916. Has no known grave. Commemorated **THIEPVAL MEMORIAL TO THE MISSING.** ROH:- St. James Church, Slaithwaite; Slaithwaite War Memorial.

UTTLEY, SIDNEY. Corporal. No 1853. 1/7th Battalion Duke of Wellington's Regiment. Born Marsden, Huddersfield. Son of Emily Uttley and the late William Uttley, Bankfield, Manchester Road, Marsden. Employed as a weaver by Mr J. E. Crowther, Bank Bottom Mills, Marsden. Had served four years with the local Territorials. Enlisted at the outbreak of the war. On 21.9.1915 a trench mortar shell burst in the middle of a group of seven Territorials and Lance Sergeant Uttley was very seriously wounded. Within ten minutes his right leg had been amputated and the other leg was severely mutilated. He was admitted to No 10 Casualty Clearing Station, where he died of his wounds on 24.7.1915. He was 30 years of age. Buried **LIJSSENTHOEK MILITARY CEMETERY.** Grave location:- Plot 3, Row A, Grave 18. (*Both Lance Sergeant Uttley's father and grandfather died from gunshot wounds. His grandfather, who was a gamekeeper was killed accidentally by his gun discharging as he climbed a wall and his father was found murdered on the Marsden Moors on 9.9.1903*). ROH:- Huddersfield Drill Hall; Marsden War Memorial.

VALERIO, ALFRED. Driver. No 89791. 'C' Battery, 165th Brigade, Royal Field Artillery. Born Huddersfield. Son of Salvatore and Emily Harriet Valerio, Hawk Street, Huddersfield. One of five brothers serving in the war. Had 14 years service to his credit when he enlisted at the outbreak of the war. Died of wounds at No 6 British Red Cross Hospital on 27.9.1917, aged 35 years. Buried **ETAPLES MILITARY CEMETERY**. Grave location:- Plot 26, Row R, Grave 11a. (Brother of Private **SYLVESTER VALERIO**, died of wounds, 24.6.1918, q.v.).

VALERIO, SYLVESTER. Private. No 31558. 2nd Battalion Duke of Wellington's Regiment. Born Huddersfield. Son of Salvatore and Emily Harriet Valerio, Hawk Street, Huddersfield. Was in business with Valerio and Rushworth, hatters and hosiers, Market Street, Milnsbridge. Died of wounds at No 18 Casualty Clearing Station on 24.6.1918, aged 35 years. Buried **LAPUGNOY MILITARY CEMETERY**. Grave location:- Plot 10, Row B, Grave 7. (Brother of Private **ALFRED VALERIO**, died of wounds, 27.9.1917, q.v.).

VARLEY, GERALD. Lance Corporal. No 267957. 'C' Company, 2/5th Battalion Duke of Wellington's Regiment. Born 14 Holme Place, Marsh, Huddersfield ,27.3.1891. Son of Joseph and Sarah Eliza Varley, 4 Syringa Street, Marsh. Employed as a woollen warehouseman. Was a sidesman at Huddersfield Parish Church. Enlisted February 1916. Embarked for France on Christmas Day, 1916. Was wounded in March, 1917. After being in hospital in England for several months, he returned to France in September, 1917. Killed in action at Bourlon Wood on 27.11.1917, during the Battle of Cambrai, aged 26. Has no known grave. Commemorated **CAMBRAI MEMORIAL TO THE MISSING**. ROH:- Huddersfield Parish Church; Huddersfield Drill Hall; commemorated on his parents' headstone in Edgerton Cemetery, Huddersfield.

VARLEY, HARRY. Private. No 14892. 8th Battalion Duke of Wellington's Regiment. Born Ripponden near Halifax. Lived with his sister, Mrs Joe Johnson, 15 Station Road, Marsden. Employed by Messrs Robinson Brothers, Clough Lea Mills, Marsden. Was a member of Marsden Cricket Club. Was a keen football player and was one of the founders and chief supporters of the Marsden United Football Club. Enlisted November 1914. Went to the Dardenelles in August, 1915. Killed in action, 19.10.1915, aged 31 years. Has no known grave. Commemorated **HELLES MEMORIAL TO THE MISSING**. His sister received a letter from Private W R Cooper, of the same Battalion, who wrote, *'I am writing to tell you as a friend of Private Harry Varley to tell you he has unfortunately been killed whilst on duty. He was in the trenches putting up sandbags for cover when he put his head up rather too high and was shot right through the head. He only lived a few minutes and never spoke. The Sergeant Major dug his grave and took charge of his personal belongings. The whole Company send their sympathy to you in your sad trouble. He was my pal and it has given me a bad shock.'* ROH:- Marsden Liberal Club; Marsden War Memorial.

VARLEY, JAMES W. MM. Lance Sergeant. No 238031. 1/7th Battalion Duke of Wellington's Regiment. Born Marsden. Son of Luke and Agnes Varley, 28 Plains, Marsden. Husband of Charlotte Ann Varley, Oliver Lane, Marsden. Died at home of pneumonia on 6.5.1919, aged 26 years. Buried **St. BARTHOLOMEW'S CHURCHYARD, MARSDEN**. Grave location:- SW, 32, 1. (Brother of Lance Sergeant **JOE VARLEY**, killed in action, 20.9.1915, q.v.). ROH:- Huddersfield Drill Hall; Marsden War Memorial.

VARLEY, JOE. Lance Sergeant. No 1174. 1/7th Battalion Duke of Wellington's Regiment. Born Marsden. Second son of Luke and Agnes Varley, 28 Plains, Marsden. Employed as a spinner by Mr J. E. Crowther, of Marsden. Was a member of the Marsden Wesleyan Sunday School. Played the cornet in the Marsden Brass Band. Enlisted at the outbreak of the war. Embarked for France in April, 1915. Killed in action, 20.9.1915, aged 20 years. Buried **BARD COTTAGE CEMETERY, BOESINGHE, BELGIUM**. Grave Location:- Plot 1, Row H, Grave 22. (Brother of Private **JAMES W. VARLEY**, died at home, 6.5.1919, q.v.). His parents received a letter from their son, Private James W. Varley, who wrote, *'Yesterday afternoon about 3pm our Joe was hit by a bullet but mercifully he did not suffer a moment's pain as it at once made him unconscious. He lived about twenty minutes and passed away quite peacefully in my arms. Fortunately I was close to him at the time and I am thankful to say that everything was done that could be done for him both before and after he passed away by both Officers and men. He was buried in a graveyard about one and a half miles behind the firing line. Major Wilkinson completely broke down once reading the service.'* ROH:- Huddersfield Drill Hall; Marsden War Memorial.

VARLEY, LESLIE. Gunner. No 25483. 'A' Company, 168th (Huddersfield) Brigade, Royal Field Artillery. Born Marsden, Huddersfield. Son of William and Emma Varley, Grange Avenue, Marsden. Was head of the pattern department at Clough Lea Mills, Marsden. Was a member of the Wesleyan Adult Bible Class, secretary to the Old Folks Treat Committee, assistant secretary to the Marsden branch of the Sons of Temperance and played the violin with the Slaithwaite Philharmonic Band. Enlisted May 1915. Embarked for France on Boxing Day, 1915. Died from wounds at No 4 Casualty Clearing Station on 19.10.1917, aged 24 years. Buried **DOZINGHEM MILITARY CEMETERY.** Grave location:- Plot 11, Row G, Grave 3. ROH:- Marsden War Memorial.

VARLEY, WILLIAM. Fusilier. No 45796. 9th Battalion Northumberland Fusiliers. Born Huddersfield. Son of John and Hannah Varley, 55 Kings Mill Lane, Huddersfield. Husband of Elizabeth Varley, 33 George Street, Milnsbridge. Employed as a pattern weaver by Messrs Walter Sykes Limited, Zetland Mills, Huddersfield. Attended Milton Church Sunday School and formerly attended the P.S.A. there. Enlisted 6.7.1916. Embarked for France in December, 1916. Wounded 13.4.1918. Died of wounds at No 46 Stationary Hospital on 17.4.1918, aged 36 years. Buried **ETAPLES MILITARY CEMETERY.** Grave location:- Plot 29, Row F, Grave 5a. ROH:- Milnsbridge War Memorial; memorial in Almondbury Cemetery; commemorated in Salendine Nook Baptist Chapel yard, F189.

VARLEY, WILLIE. Private. No 11313. 8th Battalion Duke of Wellington's Regiment. Born Primrose Hill, Huddersfield, 1893. Son of William Henry and Emma Varley, 124 Albany Street, Lockwood Road, Huddersfield. Educated Primrose Hill School and the Huddersfield Parish Church School. Employed as a brass worker by Messrs J. Hopkinson and Company Limited, of Birkby. Single. Lived Moldgreen. Enlisted September 1914. Killed in action at Bouzincourt on 30.9.1916, aged 23 years. Has no known grave. Commemorated **THIEPVAL MEMORIAL TO THE MISSING.** ROH:- Northumberland Street Primitive Methodist Church and Sunday School.

VARLEY, WOOD. Private. No 26750. 2nd Battalion Duke of Wellington's Regiment. Born Golcar. Married. Lived 10 Grange Cottages, Marsden. Employed as a weaver by Messrs Crowther, Bruce and Company Limited, of Marsden. Was formerly a teacher at the Slaithwaite Zion Baptist Sunday School and a member of the Young Men's Class. Enlisted 5.10.1916. Reported missing, presumed killed, on 11.4.1917, during the Battle of Arras. He was 30 years of age. Buried **BROWN'S COPSE CEMETERY, ROEUX.** Grave location:- Plot 2, Row E, Grave 6. ROH:- St. James Church, Slaithwaite; Slaithwaite War Memorial; Longwood War Memorial.

VARO, CHARLES E. Driver. No 252314. 'D' Battery, 282nd Army Brigade, Royal Field Artillery. Born Huddersfield. Son of Charles Edward and Mary Ann Varo, 12 Stoney Battery, Crosland Moor, Huddersfield. Husband of Lizzie Varo, Lingards Buildings, Top o th' Hill, Marsden. Killed in action, 1.11.1918, aged 27 years. Buried **VERCHAIN BRITISH CEMETERY.** Grave location:- Row D, Grave 21.

VASEY, HARRY. Rifleman. No 31704. 15th Battalion Durham Light Infantry. Born Garforth, near Leeds, 5.6.1881. Educated Hillhouse Board School. Employed as a tailor's presser. Lived 48 Birkby Hall Road, Huddersfield. Single. Enlisted 17.3.1916. Killed in action at Croisilles on 23.8.1917, aged 36 years. Buried in **CROISILLES BRITISH CEMETERY.** Grave location:- Plot 1, Row E, Grave 28.

VAUGHAN, WALTER, R. Bombardier. No 12334. 'B' Battery, 66th Brigade, Royal Field Artillery. Born Crewe. Son of Edward and Alice Vaughan, 68 Stewart Street, Crewe. Lodged with Mr Chidlow in Bradford Road, Huddersfield. Employed as a butcher. Died of wounds in Mesopotamia on 15.12.1916, aged 22 years. Buried **AMARA WAR CEMETERY.** Grave location:- Plot 15, Row C, Grave 12. ROH:- Northumberland Street Primitive Methodist Church.

VAUSE, ARTHUR. Private. No 241455. 1/5th Battalion Duke of Wellington's Regiment. Born Selby. Lived Thurstonland. Killed in action, 3.9.1916, in the attack on the Schwaben Redboubt. Has no known grave. Commemorated **THIEPVAL MEMORIAL TO THE MISSING.** ROH:- Huddersfield Drill Hall; Thurstonland War Memorial.

VICKERMAN, FRANK. Private. No 23043. 8th Battalion Duke of Wellington's Regiment. Born Huddersfield. Married. Lived 8 Hill Top, Dalton, Huddersfield. Employed as a dyer's labourer by Messrs I. Robson and Sons. Played football for the Brighouse Rangers. Was a member of the Milton Church Brotherhood. Enlisted 5.7.1916. Embarked for France on 24.12.1916. Killed in action, 17.1.1917, aged 23 years. Buried **QUEENS CEMETERY, BUCQUOY.** Grave location:- Plot 1, Row E, Grave 6. ROH:- Milton Independent Church; St. Stephen's Church, Rashcliffe; Christ Church, Moldgreen.

VIGRASS, EDWIN. Corporal. No 36166. 9th Battalion King's Own Yorkshire Light Infantry. Formerly TR/5/56362 84th Training Reserve Battalion. Born Marsh, Huddersfield. Son of Mr and Mrs T H Vigrass, 19 Calton Street, Bradford Road, Huddersfield. Educated Spring Grove Council School. Was a Sunday School teacher at the Railway Mission. Employed as a heating engineer by Messrs T. A. Heaps and Company Limited. Enlisted April, 1916, in the 29th Reserve Battalion Northumberland Fusiliers and trained at Hornsea. Remained at Hornsea with the 84th Training Reserve Battalion as a Corporal and Machine Gun Instructor. Embarked for France at the beginning of 1917. He was posted as a reinforcement to the 9th (Service) Battalion King's Own Yorkshire Light Infantry. Reported missing, presumed killed, at Polygon Wood on 4.10.1917, aged 21 years. Has no known grave. Commemorated **TYNE COT MEMORIAL TO THE MISSING.** The following summary of the attack in which Corporal Vigrass was killed was written by Captains A E Day and J H Frank who were there, leading their Companies,
'On the night of the 2nd/3rd October the 9th Battalion moved from CLAPHAM JUNCTION and relieved the Leicesters in the front line in POLYGON WOOD. During the 24 hours that we spent in these trenches the Battalion suffered about 50 casualties. On the night of the 3rd/4th we took up battle positions and were in the assembly trenches by 5am. The 3rd/4th Queens were on our left, with the 2nd Duke of Cornwall's Light Infantry on our right. Twice during the night we were barraged at midnight and 5.30am.

We were in position by 5am with our leading waves 50yds. behind the road running north and south in J. 10.d. we were in touch with our flank battalions.

Just before 6am all was more or less quiet, at Zero the barrage opened with a fearsome noise and we leapt from our shell holes and went forward in snake formation. It was the darkness that preceeds the dawn and one could recognise nobody. We are thankful to say that we got away from our assembly positions before the full force of the German barrage descended, but we were immediately subjected to a withering machine gun fire, men were falling right and left, but who cared? Our one idea was to get forward. JOIST FARM proved to be our first stumbling block and was a tough nut to crack. Even when our left had reached the swamp, lights were being fired at us from this point which was eventually mopped up by two sections of D. Coy. under Captain SYKES, and one section of B. Coy. under Sgt. Pyott. This place was found to contain one officer, twelve men and four machine guns.

As soon as we left our assembly positions we found a party of D.C.L.I. crossing our front to the North, it is evident that this Battalion completely lost direction.

The swamp proved a veritable death trap, we were up to our knees in slush and at the same time subjected to enfilade machine gun fire from the right. A small strong point not concreted and immediately on the west bank of the swamp we took by surprise and the garrison surrendered without firing a shot. On this same bank were a considerable number of German bivouacs constructed of 'elephants' and filled with Germans, more of these had been blown in by our bombardment. The remainder containing Germans were bombed by our men and the Germans shot as they ran out. On the East side the ground rose rapidly and contained a number of concreted strong points two of which were in our area. These fired at us until we were within 50yds. The garrisons then surrendered, the majority of them being bombed and shot. The left strong point turned out to be Battalion H.Q. and was an elaborate concern. Each contained two machine guns.

JUNIPER TRENCH was strongly held but the garrison preferred to retire rather than fight. 2nd Lieut. Spicer, by a quick manoeuvre, cut off the majority of these who gave themselves up to him. On the right the garrison showed a little more pluck and attempted to counter-attack us. They were immediately squashed by D. Coy. After attacking these strong points we received little

opposition until our own objective was reached. All the troops of the Brigade were mixed up and we had a considerable number of Northumberland Fusiliers and Queen's with us. During the one hour and forty minutes bombardment we were considerably troubled by a strong point on the east edge of REUTEL which was eventually knocked out by a tank. It was at this time that we realised that our right flank was absolutely in the air. At the allotted time the remainder of the 10th and Northumberland Fusiliers attempted to go forward to the eastern extremity of the village. They were not successful and we dug in slightly in advance of our first objective i.e. 100yds in front of the road running N and S on the western extremity of the village. We were in touch with the Northumberland Fusiliers on our left. We were now joined by the remnants of one Coy. of the 15th Durham Light Infantry and one Coy. of the East Yorkshires. These we sent over to the right to form a defensive flank. It did not take the enemy long to realise our position because we were immediately subjected to a heavy bombardment which continued throughout the day.
About noon the enemy commenced to advance up the valley out of the village of GHELUVELT and massed about the road in front of POLDERHOEK CHATEAU. They continued until about 3 in the afternoon. We should say that at least 3 battalions left the village. We sent out a party under Lieut. Spicer with two Lewis guns and one Vickers to flank the advancing enemy and got enfilade fire to bear upon them. Later in the day this party disappeared and that evening we searched the ground both to the right of us and in front of the village for signs of them or their bodies but found nothing. We can only conclude that they were cut off and probably taken prisoner'. ROH:- Marsh War Memorial.

VIGUS, GEORGE ALBERT. Able Seaman. No KP/22. Royal Naval Volunteer Reserve. 'A' Company, 'Anson' Battalion Royal Naval Division. Born 14.8.1891. Son of Robert Edward Vigus, 105 Mayall Road, Herne Hill, Brixton, London. Had lived at Dearnecafe, Clayton West Road, Scissett, since 1906. Was employed as a miner. Was a member of the St. John Ambulance Association. On 5.9.1914, he enlisted as a Private (No 14034) in the King's Own Yorkshire Light Infantry but, on 10.9.1914, he transferred to the R.N.V.R. at Crystal Palace. Killed in action at the Third Battle of Krithia, Gallipoli, on 4.6.1915, aged 24 years. Has no known grave. Commemorated **HELLES MEMORIAL TO THE MISSING.** ROH:- Scissett War Memorial.

VOUTT, NORMAN. Private. No 52646. 1st Battalion West Yorkshire Regiment. Formerly No 268821 Duke of Wellington's Regiment. Born Marsden, Huddersfield. Married. Lived 15 Chapel Street, Slaithwaite. Attended Holthead General Sunday School, where he was a teacher for many years. Employed at Messrs Brook's dyeworks, Slaithwaite. Enlisted June 1917. Embarked for France in November, 1917. Was out with a working party when he was hit by a piece of shell on 14.2.1918 and death was instantenous. He was 30 years of age. Buried **FAVREUIL BRITISH CEMETERY.** Grave location:- Plot 2, Row E, Grave 11. ROH:- St. James Church, Slaithwaite; Slaithwaite War Memorial.

WADDINGTON, DOUGLAS. Rifleman. No 37629. 2nd Battalion King's Own Yorkshire Light Infantry. Formerly No 86691 Territorial Reserve Battalion. Born Slaithwaite. Son of Ernest and Elizabeth Waddington. 17 Netherend Road, Slaithwaite. Employed as head counterman at Messrs Wallace's grocery store at Slaithwaite. Attended the Young Men's Class at St. James's Church Sunday School. Killed in action, 11.8.1918, aged 19 years. Has no known grave. Commemorated **VIS-en-ARTOIS MEMORIAL TO THE MISSING.** ROH:- St. James Church, Slaithwaite; Slaithwaite War Memorial.

WADDINGTON, EDGAR. Ordinary Seaman. No Z/3634. Royal Naval Volunteer Reserve. *SS Wathfield*. Born New Hey Road, Oakes, Huddersfield, 20.4.1890. Son of Mr and Mrs Tom Waddington, 7 Weatherhill Road, Lindley, Huddersfield. Educated Oakes Board School. Employed in the scouring and milling department of Messrs Martin, Sons and Company Limited, Oakes, Huddersfield. Attended St. Stephen's Parish Church, Lindley. Married, with one child. Before the war was in the Army Service Corps, attached to the West Lancashire Regiment, for about two years. Enlisted in the Naval service on 14.8.1916. Reported missing, presumed killed, when the *SS Wathfield* was struck by two torpedoes from a submarine in the Mediterrean on 21.2.1917. He was 26 years of age. Has no known grave. Commemorated **PLYMOUTH NAVAL**

MEMORIAL TO THE MISSING. ROH:- St. Stephen's Church, Lindley.

WADE, ARTHUR. Private. No 62261. 15th/17th Battalion West Yorkshire Regiment. Born 5 Somerset Place, Mulberry Street, Moldgreen, Huddersfield, 21.3.1899. Son of Thomas H. and Laura J. Wade. Educated Moldgreen Board School. Employed as a number taker by the London and North Western Railway. Company at Hillhouse railway sheds. Single. Enlisted 16.4.1917. Killed in action, 19.7.1918, aged 19 years. Buried LE GRAND HASARD MILITARY CEMETERY, MORBECQUE. Grave location:- Plot 1, Row B, Grave 14. ROH:- Christ Church, Moldgreen; London and North Western Railway Company Roll.

WADE, DENNISON. Private. No TR/5/161043. 53rd Battalion Training Reserve. Son of Mrs Louisa Turner, 39 Boocock's Yard, Brook Street, Dalton, Huddersfield. Died of pneumonia, 23.10.1918, aged 18 years. Buried EDGERTON CEMETERY, HUDDERSFIELD. Grave location:- 11B, 78.

WADE, JOHN. Marconi Wireless Operator. Pilot Service, Liverpool. Born Cowcliffe, Huddersfield, 9.11.1897. Son of Mr R. Wade, Garden House, Heaton Lodge, Colne Bridge, Bradley, Huddersfield. Educated Hillhouse Church of England School. Was previously employed as a wireless operator by the Aberdeen Line, London, on SS Jukosi. Transferred to the Mersey Docks and Harbour Board, Liverpool. Was serving on board *HM Examining Vessel No 1* at Mersey Bar, Liverpool, when the vessel was either mined or torpedoed and he was killed on 27.12.1917, aged 20 years. His body was washed ashore at Formby, near Liverpool, on March 18th, 1918. Buried EDGERTON CEMETERY, HUDDERSFIELD.

WADE, JOHN THOMAS. Private. No 40992. 10th Battalion Lincolnshire Regiment. Formerly No 31832 North Staffordshire Regiment. Born Golcar. Son of William Henry and Charlotte Wade, 29 James Street, Golcar. Was in business as a greengrocer. Enlisted November 1916. Embarked for France in March, 1917. Died of wounds at No 30 Casualty Clearing Station on 29.4.1917, aged 33 years. Buried AUBIGNY COMMUNAL CEMETERY. Grave location:- Plot 2, Row G, Grave 82. ROH:- St. John's Church, Golcar.

WADE, THOMAS RUSSELL. Private. No 202368. 2/5th Battalion Manchester Regiment. Born Golcar. Son of John Alfred and Annice A. Wade, 1 Yew Tree Lane, Cowlersley, Milnsbridge. Educated Crow Lane Board School, Milnsbridge. Was a member of Milnsbridge Socalist Club. Attended the Milnsbridge Wesleyan Sunday School. Married, with two children. Lived Gorton, Manchester. Took over a business in Manchester in 1916. Enlisted October 1916. Killed in action by a shell whilst in a dugout on 14.4.1917, aged 23 years. Buried CAMBRIN MILITARY CEMETERY. Grave location:- Row J, Grave 10. ROH:- Linthwaite War Memorial; Crow Lane Board School, Milnsbridge.

WADSWORTH, EBBY. Acting Bombardier. No L/28096. 168th (Holme Valley) Battery, Royal Field Artillery. Born Holmfirth. Son of Ebby Wadsworth, Spring View, Malkinhouse, Holmfirth. Employed on his father's farm. Enlisted 27.5.1915. Embarked for France in January 1916. Killed in action, 3.7.1916, during the Battle of the Somme. Buried CONNAUGHT CEMETERY, THIEPVAL. Grave Location:- Plot 12, Row K, Grave 6. ROH:- Cartworth War Memorial.

WADSWORTH, EDGAR. Fusilier. No 40223. 10th Battalion Northumberland Fusiliers. Formerly No 32238 Durham Light Infantry. Born Bradley Mills 9.5.1881. Son of Herbert Wadsworth, 12 Fieldhouse Lane, off Leeds Road, Huddersfield. Educated St. Andrew's School, Leeds Road, Huddersfield. Employed as a cloth scourer. Lived 514 Carlton Terrace, Leeds Road, Huddersfield. Single. Enlisted 13.5.1916. Killed in action 23.9.1917. Buried YPRES RESERVOIR CEMETERY. Grave location:- Plot 9, Row D, Grave 4. (Brother of Private **WALTER WADSWORTH**, killed in action, 14.9.1916, q.v.). ROH:- Christ Church, Woodhouse Hill.

WADSWORTH, JIM. Private. No 269299. 2/4th Battalion Duke of Wellington's Regiment. Born Daisy Lea, Outlane, 11.9.1898. Son of Mr and Mrs Ben Wadsworth, 20 Hall Street, Longwood, Huddersfield. Educated Goitfield Schools, Longwood. Employed as a warehouseman. Single. Enlisted 19.7.1917.

Killed in action near Rheims, 20.7.1917, aged 19 years. Buried **MARFAUX BRITISH CEMETERY.** Grave location:- Plot 2, Row C, Grave 8. ROH:- Outlane Trinity Methodist Church; Longwood Wesleyan Chapel; St. Mark's Parish Church, Longwood.

WADSWORTH, WALTER. Private. No 16124. 8th Battalion Duke of Wellington's Regiment. Born Bradley Mills, Huddersfield, 12.9.1889. Son of Herbert Wadsworth, 12 Fieldhouse Lane, off Leeds Road, Huddersfield. Educated St. Andrew's School, Leeds Road, Huddersfield. Employed as a pit head worker at Messrs Brook's pottery, Leeds Road, Huddersfield. Married, with two children. Enlisted 28.5.1915. Served in Egypt and the Dardenelles. Embarked for France in June, 1916. Killed in action, 14.9.1916, during the Battle of the Somme. He was 33 years of age. Buried **HEATH CEMETERY, HARBONNIERES.** Grave location:- Plot 7, Row L, Grave 4. (Brother of Private **EDGAR WADSWORTH,** killed in action, 20.9.1917, q.v.).

WAGSTAFF, JOE. Private. No S/2784. 11th Battalion Argyll and Sutherland Highlanders. Born Holmfirth 12.8.1893. Second son of the late Mr and Mrs Jonathan, of Underbank, Holmfirth, and grandson of Mrs J. Lockwood, of Pog Ing, Holmfirth. Educated Holmfirth National School. Employed as a teamer. Husband of Mary Wagstaffe, Leeds Road, Huddersfield. Enlisted 2.9.1914. Killed in action, 31.7.1917, aged 24 years. Has no known grave. Commemorated **MENIN GATE MEMORIAL TO THE MISSING.** ROH:- St. Andrew's Church, Leeds Road, Huddersfield; Underbank War Memorial, Holmfirth.

WAGSTAFF, JOHN HERBERT. Fusilier. No 41062. 23rd (Tyneside Scottish) Battalion Northumberland Fusiliers. Formerly No 31834 Durham Light Infantry. Born Hepworth, Holmfirth. Son of George and Jemima Wagstaffe, of Barracks Fold, Hepworth. Educated Hepworth National School. Attended Hepworth Church, where he was a member of the Bible Class. Employed by the Hepworth Iron Company and later at the Shaley Wood Pit. Enlisted January 1916. Killed in action, 9.9.1917, aged 21 years. Buried **HARGICOURT BRITISH CEMETERY.** Grave location:- Plot 1, Row B, Grave 32. ROH:- Hepworth and Scholes War Memorial; memorial in Hepworth Churchyard.

WAGSTAFF, JOHN WILLIAM. Corporal. No 1147. 1/7th Battalion Duke of Wellington's Regiment. Born Huddersfield 5.11.1893. Son of Joseph and Emma Wagstaff, 33 Cliffe End, Longwood, Huddersfield. Educated Lindley Church of England School. Employed as a finisher by Messrs Crowther Brothers, Milnsbridge. Had been a member of the local Territorials since 10.7.1911. Single. Enlisted 23.10.1914. Embarked for France in April, 1915. Killed in action, 1.10.1915, aged 21 years. Buried **BARD COTTAGE CEMETERY, BOESINGHE, BELGIUM.** Grave location:- Plot 1, Row I, Grave 28. His parents received a letter from Major W U Rothery, who wrote on the 2.10.1915, 'I am extremely sorry to inform you that your son was killed yesterday. He was in charge of the bombers and after a successful sniping shot he received a bullet through the head. I saw him immediately afterwards and death was instantenous. He was buried in our cemetery last night by the Brigade Chaplain and his grave will be marked with a cross. His death is a blow to me as he was one of the very few old members of the Milnsbridge Company and I knew him intimately. He was a good soldier and will be a great loss to the Company. I am afraid I can say nothing which will comfort you but it will be some satisfaction to you to know that he gave his life whilst actually fighting for his country. My brother Officers and the whole Company join me in offering our deepest sympathy.' ROH:- St. Mark's Parish Church, Longwood; Salendine Nook Baptist Chapel; Huddersfield Drill Hall.

WAINWRIGHT, JOSEPH. Private. No 21666. 6th Battalion King's Own Scottish Borderers. Born Skelmanthorpe, Huddersfield. Son of Mr and Mrs Henry Wainwright. Husband of Annie Wainwright. Enlisted 28.9.1915. Embarked for France in February, 1916. Died at Fishponds War Hospital, Bristol, 16.8.1916, as a result of shell wounds sustained in France on 18.7.1916. He was 26 years of age. Buried **SKELMANTHORPE CEMETERY.** Grave location:- Plot 3, Row 'U', Grave 141. ROH:- St. Aidan's Church, Skelmanthorpe.

WAITE, HENRY. Private. No 241476. 1/5th Battalion Duke of Wellington's Regiment. Born

Acre Street, Lindley, 29.4.1890. Son of Mrs Mary Waite, 60 Eldon Road, Marsh, Huddersfield. Educated Lindley Church of England School. Was in business as a jobbing yarn merchant at the bottom of May Street, Crosland Moor. Attended the Buxton Road Wesleyan School. Single. Enlisted 17.2.1916. Reported missing, presumed dead, on 3.9.1916, during the attack on the Schwaben Redoubt. Has no known grave. Commemorated **THIEPVAL MEMORIAL TO THE MISSING.** ROH:- Marsh War Memorial; All Saints Church, Paddock, Huddersfield; Huddersfield Drill Hall.

WAITE, HORACE. Rifleman. No C/7654. 18th Battalion King's Royal Rifle Corps. Born Honley. Son of Luther and Lizzie Waite of Ainsgarth, Honley. Educated Almondbury Grammar School. Attended Honley Congregational Church where he was the Band of Hope secretary and a teacher at the Sunday School. Played cricket for the Honley Wesleyan Cricket Club. Worked in the family business in the manufacture of ruling machines. Enlisted 1915. Reported missing, presumed killed, on 15.9.1916 during the attack on Flers at the Battle of the Somme, aged 21. Has no known grave. Commemorated **THIEPVAL MEMORIAL TO THE MISSING.** ROH:- Honley War Memorial.

WALKDEN, JAMES. Private. No 31769. 2/4th Battalion Duke of Wellington's Regiment. Born Golcar, Huddersfield. Son of Charles and Emma Walkden, of Scar Bottom, Golcar. Husband of Maud Walkden, 173 Scar Lane, Milnsbridge. Employed as a spinner by Messrs Shaw and Shaw, Britannia Mills, Milnsbridge. Enlisted June 1917. Had been in France for six weeks when he was killed on 20.11.1917, aged 28, during the Battle of Cambrai. Has no known grave. Commemorated **CAMBRAI MEMORIAL TO THE MISSING.** ROH:- St. John's Church, Golcar; Longwood War Memorial

WALKER, CHARLIE. Private. No 20525. 9th Battalion Duke of Wellington's Regiment. Born Golcar, Huddersfield. Son of Mr Elliot Walker, Myrtle Road, Golcar. Employed as a weaver by Messrs Crowther and Nicholson Limited, Ashbrow Mills, Huddersfield. Attended St. John's Church, Golcar. Was a member of the Golcar Conservative Club. Enlisted May 1916. Embarked for France 29.8.1916. Reported missing, presumed killed, on 4.11.1916. He was 27 years of age. Has no known grave. Commemorated **THIEPVAL MEMORIAL TO THE MISSING.** ROH:- St. John's Church, Golcar.

WALKER, ERNEST. Private. No 205414. 1/7th Battalion Duke of Wellington's Regiment. Born Huddersfield. Son of Joe and Mary Elizabeth Walker, of Linthwaite. Husband of Annie Walker, 14 Lowestwood, Golcar. Employed by the Colne Valley Spinning Company, Linthwaite. Played cricket with the Helme and Linthwaite clubs. Died of wounds, 3.5.1918, aged 29 years. Buried **ESQUELBECQ MILITARY CEMETERY.** Grave location:- Plot 2, Row B, Grave 30. ROH:- St. John's Church, Golcar; Huddersfield Drill Hall.

WALKER, ERNEST DUNNING. Rifleman. No 81644. 15th Battalion Durham Light Infantry. Formerly No 38621 York and Lancaster Regiment. Born York 28.4.1898. Son of Ernest Edward and Emily Walker, 41 Lees Lodge, Dalton Bank, Huddersfield. Educated Hull Commercial School. Employed as a dentist. Prior to enlistment, was living at 59 Hexthorpe Road, Doncaster. Enlisted November 1916. Was wounded in July, 1917. Returned to France in March, 1918. Reported missing, presumed killed, on 29.5.1918. Has no known grave. Commemorated **SOISSONS MEMORIAL TO THE MISSING.**

WALKER, FRANK HERBERT. Gunner. No 89220. 253rd Siege Battery, Royal Garrison Artillery. Born Golcar. Son of Samuel Walker, Carlton Terrace, Golcar. Employed by Messrs C. and J. Hirst and Sons, Longwood. Attended St. John's Church, Golcar. Was a member of Golcar Conservative Club. Enlisted May 1916. Had served in France and Flanders for twelve months. Killed in action, 12.11.1917, aged 40 years. Buried **MENIN ROAD SOUTH MILITARY CEMETERY, YPRES.** Grave location:- Plot 3, Row M, Grave 12. ROH:- St. John's Church, Golcar.

WALKER, GEORGE WILLIAM QUARMBY. Lieutenant. 7th Battalion Duke of Wellington's Regiment. Youngest son of Benjamin Henry Sykes Walker and Hannah Walker, Croft House, Slaithwaite. Educated Neilds School, Slaithwaite; Longwood Grammar School; Devonport High School and New College, Harrogate. Was apprenticed to Messrs Pogson and Company, yarn spinners, of Slaithwaite, where he was learning the business of mill manager. Was gazetted Second Lieutenant on 14.10.1914 and was in training at Milnsbridge, Withernsea, Strensall and at Chelsea Barracks with the Grenadier Guards. Killed by the explosion of a shell on 7.7.1916 during the Battle of the Somme. He was 20 years of age. Buried **AUTHUILE MILITARY CEMETERY.** Grave location:- Row H, Grave 12. ROH:- St. James Church, Slaithwaite; Slaithwaite War Memorial; Huddersfield Drill Hall.

WALKER, HARRY. Private. No 241372. 1/5th Battalion Duke of Wellington's Regiment. Born Slaithwaite, Huddersfield. Son of the late Mr and Mrs Lister G. Walker, Wharf House, Carr Lane, Slaithwaite. Employed as a weaver by Messrs Hirst and Mallinson Limited, Milnsbridge. Was a member of the Slaithwaite Liberal Club and the Slaithwaite Y.M.C.A. Enlisted October 1915. Reported missing, presumed killed, on 3.9.1916 during the attack on the Schwaben Redoubt. He was 22 years of age. Has no known grave. Commemorated **THIEPVAL MEMORIAL TO THE MISSING.** ROH:- St. James Church, Slaithwaite; Slaithwaite War Memorial; Huddersfield Drill Hall.

WALKER, HERMAN. Private. No 203541. 1/4th Battalion Duke of Wellington's Regiment. Born Golcar. Youngest son of Mrs Martha Walker, 26 Parkwood Road, Leymoor, Golcar. Employed by Messrs Ben Hall and Sons, Milnsbridge. Was a member of the Thorpe Green Working Men's Club and the Leymoor Cricket Club. Attended Golcar Baptist Chapel and Sunday School. Enlisted August 1916. Killed in action, 13.3.1918, aged 20 years. According to an officer, Private Walker went out with raiding party on the 13.3.1918 and he was blown up by a shell. Has no known grave. Commemorated **TYNE COT MEMORIAL TO THE MISSING.** ROH:- Golcar Baptist Church.

WALKER, JAMES HENRY. Private. No 18036. 8th Battalion Loyal North Lancashire Regiment. Born Stalybridge. Husband of Mary E. Walker, 30 Deighton Road, Deighton, Huddersfield. Killed in action, 21.5.1916, aged 41. Has no known grave. Commemorated **ARRAS MEMORIAL TO THE MISSING.** ROH:- St. Stephen's Church, Rashcliffe.

WALKER, JOE. Private. No 301955. 11th Battalion The Royal Scots (Lothian Regiment). Born Slaithwaite, Huddersfield. Son of John and Sarah Jane Walker, Mill Moor, Meltham. Killed in action, 10.4.1918, aged 20 years. Has no known grave. Commemorated **TYNE COT MEMORIAL TO THE MISSING.** ROH:- St. Bartholomew's Church, Meltham.

WALKER, JOHN. Private. No 2007. 1/7th Battalion Duke of Wellington's Regiment. Son of John and Sarah Walker, Amber Hill, near Boston, Lincolnshire. Was married but lived apart from his wife. Had lodged with Mrs Casson, Bridge Street, Slaithwaite, for five years. (She was the guardian of his child). Employed as a teamer by Messrs Joseph Sykes and Sons, Slaithwaite. Enlisted at the outbreak of the war. Died from heart failure at No 2 West Riding Field Ambulance Dressing Station on 5.11.1915, aged 42 years. Buried **FERME-OLIVER CEMETERY, ELVERDINGHE, BELGIUM.** Grave location:- Plot 1, Row H, Grave 2. ROH:- St. James Church, Slaithwaite; Slaithwaite War Memorial; Huddersfield Drill Hall.

WALKER, JOHN. Private. No 300086. 2/6th Battalion Duke of Wellington's Regiment. Born Milnsbridge, Huddersfield. Son of Mrs Walker, 130 Lowergate, Longwood, Huddersfield. Educated Crow Lane Board School, Milnsbridge. Employed by Messrs C. and J. Hirst of Milnsbridge. Enlisted at the outbreak of the war. Was wounded on four occasions. Killed in action, 2.3.1917, aged 28 years. Has no known grave. Commemorated **THIEPVAL MEMORIAL TO THE MISSING.** ROH:- St. Mark's Parish Church, Longwood; Crow Lane Board School, Milnsbridge.

WALKER, JOSEPH ROBERTS. Private. No 28481. 40th General Hospital, Royal Army Medical Corps. Born New Mill, Holmfirth, 30.6.1883. Son of Thomas and Thirza Walker, Royde House, New Mill. Husband of Annie Elizabeth Walker, 106 Eldon Road, Marsh, Huddersfield. Educated at New Mill National School and Shepley Board School. Employed by the Pearl Assurance Company as an insurance agent. Was a member of the St. John Ambulance Brigade and the Crosland Moor Conservative Club. Sang in the choir at Crosland Moor Church. Enlisted 17.11.1914. Was stationed at Sheerness until July, 1916, when he went out to

India. Died from typhoid at the Victoria War Hospital, Bombay, on 24.10.1916, aged 33 years. Was originally buried in **SEWRI CEMETERY, BOMBAY, INDIA.** Grave Location:- Plot 15, Row C, Grave 11. Commemorated **KIRKEE 1914-1918 MEMORIAL, INDIA.** ROH:- Holy Trinity Church, Huddersfield; Marsh War Memorial.

WALKER, LEWIS. Lance Corporal. No 3006. 'A' Company, 1/5th Battalion Duke of Wellington's Regiment. Born Armitage Bridge, Huddersfield, 13.3.1892. Son of James and Catherine Mary Walker, School Lane, Armitage Bridge. Educated Armitage Bridge Church of England School and Huddersfield College Higher Grade School. Was a chorister at Armitage Bridge Church and a member of the choir at Huddersfield Parish Church. He was a baritone and soloist of great promise. Employed as an electrical engineer in the motor department of Messrs David Browns Limited, Lockwood. Enlisted 4.9.1914. Embarked for France in April, 1915. Killed in action at Fleurbaix on 15.5.1915, aged 23 years. Buried **RUE-DAVID MILIITARY CEMETERY.** Grave location:- Plot 1, Row B, Grave 20. His parents received a letter from Lieutenant Middlemost who stated that, *'Lance Corporal Walker was struck with shrapnel between the eyes and killed instantenously.'* ROH:- Huddersfield Parish Church; Huddersfield Drill Hall; Armitage Bridge War Memorial.

WALKER, LISTER WADE. Sergeant. No 203609. 1/5th Battalion West Yorkshire Regiment. Son of the late James Walker, of Slaithwaite. Husband of Sarah Louisa Walker, Pickle Top, Slaithwaite. Was a member of Slaithwaite Church gymnasium and won the Huddersfield and District championship for the high jump in 1901. Attended Slaithwaite Parish Church and was a member of the Slaithwaite Conservative Club. Employed by the Slaithwaite Spinning Company Limited and was a member of the fire brigade there. Was a National Reservist and was called up at the outbreak of the war. He was sent to York to guard prisoners, He was afterwards on duty at British Dyes Limited for 18 months. Embarked for France on 7.1.1917. Killed in action, 9.10.1917, at Passchendaele. He was 35 years of age. Has no known grave. Commemorated **TYNE COT MEMORIAL TO THE MISSING.** ROH:- St. James Church, Slaithwaite; Slaithwaite War Memorial.

WALKER, OSCAR. Lieutenant. 2/5th Battalion Duke of Wellington's Regiment. Born Lindley, Huddersfield, 15.5.1889. Son of Arthur Edward and Kate Walker, Ormesty House, Sunnybank Road, Edgerton, Huddersfield. Employed as a manufacturer by Messrs Broadbent and Graves of Kirkheaton. Enlisted as a Private on 6.8.1914 in the Duke of Wellington's Regiment. Killed in action at Bullecourt on 3.5.1917, aged 27 years. Has no known grave. Commemorated **ARRAS MEMORIAL TO THE MISSING.** ROH:- Oakes Baptist Church; St. Stephen's Church, Lindley; Huddersfield Drill Hall.

WALKER, PERCY. Rifleman. No S/34939. 2/10th Battalion London Regiment The Rifle Brigade. Formerly No 92955 Royal Flying Corps. Born Gomersal, Leeds, 18.3.1897. Son of Edwin and Ann Walker, Ravensmount, 96 Ravensknowle Road, Moldgreen, Huddersfield. Educated Almondbury Grammar School. Employed as a clerk in the buying department of Messrs J. Hopkinson and Company, Birkby. Was a member of Lascelles Hall Cricket Club. Single. Enlisted 27.8.1917. Reported wounded and missing on 24.4.1918 and afterwards presumed to have been killed on that date, aged 21. Buried **CRUCIFIX CORNER CEMETERY, VILLERS BRETONNEUX.** Grave location:- Plot 1, Row E, Grave 7. ROH:- St. John's Church, Kirkheaton.

WALKER, REGINALD. Private. No 260303. 2/8th Battalion Worcestershire Regiment. Born Lindley, Huddersfield, 21.4.1878. Son of the late Charles Henry and Mary Ann Walker, Lower Park House, Lindley. Educated Giggleswick Public School from May, 1894, to December, 1895. An estate agent. To New York, U.S.A. Enlisted in Canada and came over with the 1st Canadian contingent. Transferred to the Worcestershire Regiment. Killed in action, 27.8.1917, aged 38. Has no known grave. Commemorated **TYNE COT MEMORIAL TO THE MISSING.** ROH:- Oakes Baptist Church; Giggleswick School; commemorated in Salendine Nook Baptist Chapel yard, D308.

WALKER, REGINALD. Private. No 18832. 2nd Battalion Duke of Wellington's Regiment. Formerly No 8678 North Staffordshire Regiment. Born Honley. Lived West View, Bradshaw Lane, Honley, Huddersfield. Reported wounded and missing, presumed killed, 1.7.1916, during the first day of the Battle of the Somme. Has no known grave. Commemorated **THIEPVAL MEMORIAL TO THE MISSING.** ROH:- Honley War Memorial.

WALKER, SYKES. Private. No 14546. 10th Battalion Duke of Wellington's Regiment. Born Dalton, Huddersfield. Husband of Mary Walker, 45 Kirkgate, Huddersfield. Employed by Messrs John Kaye and Sons, Kings Mill, Huddersfield. Enlisted November 1914. Embarked for France in November, 1915. Killed in action at Munster Alley on 29.8.1916 during the Battle of the Somme, aged 40. Buried **PEAKE WOOD CEMETERY, FRICOURT.** Grave location:- Row B, Grave 24.

WALKER, THOMAS ARNOLD. Private. No 44650. 5th Battalion Lincolnshire Regiment. Born Moldgreen, Huddersfield, in 1899. Son of William G. and Alice Walker, 8 Wellington Street, Lindley. Educated Oakes Council School. Employed as a grocer's assistant at Messrs Wallace's Limited, Lindley. Single. Enlisted in 1915. Reported missing, presumed killed, 15.4.1918. Has no known grave. Commemorated **PLOEGSTEERT MEMORIAL TO THE MISSING.** ROH:- St. Stephen's Church, Lindley.

WALKER, THOMAS VINCENT. Private. No 204429. 2nd Battalion Duke of Wellington's Regiment. Elder son of Edward and Frances Walker, 5 Gordon Terrace, Linthwaite. Employed by the Globe Worsted Company Limited, Slaithwaite. Attended the Holthead General Sunday School. Enlisted at the outbreak of the war. Embarked for France on 10.1.1917. Twice wounded. Returned to France in January, 1918. Died of wounds, 16.4.1918, aged 23 years. Buried **LE VERTANNOY BRITISH CEMETERY, HINGES.** Grave location:- Row A, Grave 7. ROH:- Linthwaite War Memorial.

WALKER, WALTER PERCY. Sapper. No 82992. 170th Tunnelling Company, Royal Engineers. Formerly No 1179 King's Own Yorkshire Light Infantry. Born Flockton. Lived Church Street, Emley. Killed in action by a mine explosion on 6.8.1915. Buried **CAMBRIN MILITARY CEMETERY.** Grave location:- Row B, Grave 12. ROH:- Emley War Memorial.

WALLIS, JOHN WILLIAM. Private. No 14594. 2nd Battalion Duke of Wellington's Regiment. Born Milnsbridge. Son of Joseph Wallis, 133 Upper Brow Road, Paddock. Husband of Alice Wallis, 115 Upper Brow Road, Paddock. Employed by Mr Tom Dyson, Ballroyd, Longwood. Was a member of the Paddock Church Sunday School. Enlisted November 1914. Embarked for France in April, 1915. Reported missing, presumed killed, on 1.7.1916 during the first day of the Battle of the Somme. He was 32 years of age. Has no known grave. Commemorated **THIEPVAL MEMORIAL TO THE MISSING.** ROH:- All Saints Church, Paddock.

WALMSLEY, THOMAS RICHARDSON, DCM. Sergeant. No 49872. 'Y', 14th Trench Mortar Battery, Royal Field Artillery. Born Saddleworth. Eldest son of Police Sergeant and Mrs Walmsley, Station Road, Holmfirth. Attended Holmfirth Parish Church and was a member of the choir and of Mr Fletcher's bible class. He formerly worked for the firm of Messrs B. Mellor and Son Limited, Albert Mills, Holmfirth but at the outbreak of the war he was a tram driver employed by the Halifax Corporation Tramways Department. Engaged to Alice, who lived at West View, Lightcliffe Road, Brighouse. Enlisted at the outbreak of the war. Awarded the DCM 4.6.1917. Died of wounds, 3.12.1917, aged 24 years. Buried **OXFORD ROAD CEMETERY, YPRES.** Grave location:- Plot 5, Row E, Grave 6. His parents received a letter from the Lieutenant of the section of the Trench Mortar Battery of which Sergeant Walmsley was a member. He wrote, *'I am extremely sorry to have very bad news to report to you. Your son was killed in action at 10am yesterday, December 3rd, by an enemy shell. He was taken to a dressing station a few yards distant but died almost immediately. We have lost a good friend who was loved by everyone. He met his death as he was going to the help of comrades who were being shelled. We tender our heartfelt sympathy to his relatives who must feel his loss very keenly.'* ROH:- Wooldale War Memorial; Halifax Civic Book of Remembrance.

WALSHAW, GEORGE. Private. No S/2204. 8th Battalion Gordon Highlanders. Born Swinton 27.12.1891. Son of Charles Walshaw, 53 Leeds Road North, Huddersfield. Educated Thomas Street Board School. Employed as a toffee boiler by Messrs J. W. Seaton and Sons Limited, Bradford Road, Huddersfield. Single. Enlisted August 1914. Reported wounded and missing, presumed killed, 25.9.1915, during the Battle of Loos, aged 23. Has no known grave. Commemorated **LOOS MEMORIAL TO THE MISSING**. ROH:- St. Andrew's Church, Leeds Road, Huddersfield.

WALSHAW, GEORGE LIONEL. Private. No 45192. 13th Battalion York and Lancaster Regiment (1st Barnsley Pals). Born Rose Village, Alverthorpe, near Wakefield, 19.1.1884. Educated Wheelwright's Grammar School, Dewsbury, and Leeds University. Employed as a cloth designer. Husband of Ada Walshaw, 23 Ladyhouse Lane, Berry Brow, Huddersfield. Reported missing, presumed killed, on 12.4.1918 at Outtersteene near Bailleul, aged 34. Has no known grave. Commemorated **PLOEGSTEERT MEMORIAL TO THE MISSING**. ROH:- St. Thomas's Church, Longroyd Bridge; Armitage Bridge War Memorial.

WALSHAW, JOHN. Private. No M2/187879. 11th Divisional Supply Column, Army Service Corps. Born Denby Dale near Huddersfield. Son of Mr. J. Walshaw of Netherend, Denby Dale. Employed as a motor driver by Messrs Z. Hinchliffe and Sons, Hartcliffe Mills, Denby Dale. Was a scholar at the Primitive Methodist Sunday School. Enlisted in 1916. Embarked for France in June, 1916. Killed in action, 27.4.1917, aged 23 years. Buried **GREVILLERS BRITISH CEMETERY**. Grave location:- Plot 2, Row A, Grave 16. ROH:- Denby Dale and Cumberworth War Memorial.

WALSHAW, ROBERT ERNEST. Private. No 240132. 2/5th Battalion Duke of Wellington's Regiment. Born Sheepridge, Huddersfield, 17.2.1893. Son of Alfred and Mary Ann Walshaw, 17 Chestnut Street, Sheepridge. Educated Deighton Council School and Higher Grade School, New North Road, Huddersfield. Employed as a cloth finisher. Single. Was a member of the local Territorials prior to the outbreak of the war. Enlisted 21.5.1912. Wounded on 21.11.1917, during the Battle of Cambrai. Died of wounds at No 21 Casualty Clearing Station on 22.11.1917, aged 24. Buried **ROCQUIGNY-EQUANCOURT ROAD BRITISH CEMETERY**. Grave location:- Plot 2, Row B, Grave 23. ROH:- Sheepridge Providence United Methodist Church; Christ Church, Woodhouse Hill; Huddersfield Drill Hall.

WALTON, EDMUND REGINALD. Private. No 366768. 2nd/1st Northern Cyclist Battalion, attached Northumberland Fusiliers. Born 20 Pavement, York 6.1.1899. Son of Ernest Robert and Mary Ellen Walton. Educated Pannal Ash College, Harrogate. Employed as a draper's apprentice in Huddersfield. Lived 7 West Hill, Huddersfield. Attended Holy Trinity Church. Single. Enlisted 21.2.1917. Died of tuberculosis on 6.6.1917 at 4th Military Hospital, Lincoln, aged 18 years. Buried **YORK CEMETERY**. Grave location:- B1.3827. ROH:- Holy Trinity Church, Huddersfield.

WALTON, HARRY. Private. No 25441. 3rd Battalion East Yorkshire Regiment, transferred to No 36587, 12th Infantry Labour Company, Lincolnshire Regiment, re-transferred to No 30476, 51st Company, Labour Corps. Born Thurstonland, Brockholes, Huddersfield. Son of Andrew and Emily Walton, Bank Top, Thurstonland, Brockholes. Employed by Messrs T. and J. Tinker, Mytholm Bridge. Attended Thurstonland Wesleyan Chapel. Died of wounds at No 10 Casualty Clearing Station on 15.10.1917, aged 22 years. Buried **LIJSSENTHOEK MILITARY CEMETERY**. Grave location:- Plot 22, Row H, Grave 2A. ROH:- Thurstonland War Memorial.

WALTON, JOE. Private. No 305845. 2nd Battalion Duke of Wellington's Regiment. Was the adopted son of Mr and Mrs J Walton, Parkgate, Slaithwaite. Attended Lingards Wood Bottom Sunday School. Employed in the grocery department of the Marsden Cooperative Stores. Was a member of the Marsden Liberal Club. Enlisted November 1914. Embarked for France in April, 1915. Was seriously wounded in the thigh in 1917, but recovered and rejoined his Regiment in France. Killed in action, 10.5.1918, aged 26 years. Buried **CHOCQUES MILITARY CEMETERY**. Grave location:- Plot 3, Row D, Grave 9. ROH:- Marsden Liberal Club; St. James Church, Slaithwaite; Slaithwaite War Memorial.

WALTON, JOHN. Private. No 13448. 8th Battalion Duke of Wellington's Regiment. Born Huddersfield. Employed by Messrs Taylor and

Littlewood, Newsome Mills, Huddersfield. Died of wounds at the Dardenelles 28.10.15. Buried **HILL 10 CEMETERY, GALLIPOLI.** Grave location:- Plot 1, Row G, Grave 7. ROH:- Messrs. Taylor and Littlewood, Newsome Mills.

WALTON, L. Private. No 81704. 3rd Battalion Durham Light Infantry. Died at home, 5.6.1919. Buried **St. THOMAS' CHURCHYARD, THURSTONLAND, BROCKHOLES.** Grave location:- 197, (west). ROH:- Thurstonland War Memorial.

WARD, CHARLES. Private. No 300135. 1/6th Battalion Duke of Wellington's Regiment. Born Moores Yard, South Parade, Huddersfield, 21.12.1895. Son of Patrick Edward and Bridget Ward, 2 Ramsden's Yard, Charles Street, Huddersfield. Educated at St. Patrick's Roman Catholic School, New North Road, Huddersfield. Emloyed as a rag feeder by Messrs Alfred Sykes and Company, rug manufacturers, Viaduct Street, Huddersfield. Single. Was a drummer in the Huddersfield Territorials for 12 months prior to the outbreak of the war. Enlisted 4.8.1914. Was wounded on 13.4.1918 at Bailleul, France. Died of wounds on 30.6.1918 at King George's Hospital, Stamford Street, London. He was 22 years of age. Buried **EDGERTON CEMETERY, HUDDERSFIELD.** Grave location:- 63, RC, 88.

WARD, EDWARD ARTHUR HUNTER. Lieutenant and Flight Commander. 22nd Squadron, Royal Flying Corps. Formerly 2nd Lieutenant, 3/6th Battalion West Yorkshire Regiment. Born Leeds 2.10.1896. Son of John Henry Ward of Blundell Sands, Liverpool, formerly of Huddersfield and grandson of Mr John Ward, who was formerly Chief Constable of Huddersfield. Educated Spring Grove Council School and Huddersfield College, New North Road, Huddersfield. Obtained a scholarship to Hertford College, Oxford, just before the outbreak of the war. Single. Lived with George T. Lowe, Highfield Place, 74 New North Road, Huddersfield. Enlisted in the West Yorkshire Regiment and was transferred to the Royal Flying Corps in April, 1917. Killed in action over the German lines on 11.8.1917, aged 20 years. Buried **NOYELLES-GODAULT COMMUNAL CEMETERY.** Grave location:- Grave No 5. ROH:- Huddersfield Parish Church; Thurstonland War Memorial.

WARD, HARRY. Private. No 12072. 8th Battalion Duke of Wellington's Regiment. Born Longroyd Bridge, Huddersfield, 18.11.1893. Son of Mrs Ward, 20 Fisher's Yard, Longroyd Bridge. Educated St. Thomas's Church of England School, Longroyd Bridge. Employed as a teamer by Mr Henry Hanson, furniture remover. Enlisted at the outbreak of the war. Served in the Dardenelles, where he was killed in action on 29.8.1915 at Jephson's Post. He was 22 years of age. Has no known grave. Commemorated **HELLES MEMORIAL TO THE MISSING.** ROH:- St. Thomas's Church, Longroyd Bridge.

WARD, HENRY MICHAEL. Private. No 12891. 3rd Battalion Duke of Wellington's Regiment. Born Templemore, Ireland. Son of George and Sarah Ward. Husband of Ellen Ward, 17 Back Silver Street, Moldgreen, Huddersfield. Died on 13.1.1916 at the Royal Victoria Infirmary, Newcastle-on-Tyne, of sickness following an operation. He was 39 years of age. Buried **EDGERTON CEMETERY, HUDDERSFIELD.** Grave location:- 63, 135.

WARD, HERBERT. Guardsman. No 27792. 4th Company, 3rd Battalion Grenadier Guards. Born Lindley. Son of Mr and Mrs Arthur Ward, 26 New Hey Road, Huddersfield. Educated Oakes Board School. Was formerly a clerk in the employ of Isaac Robson and Sons Limited and was later on the postal staff at the G.P.O., Shrewsbury. Single. Attended Lindley United Methodist Church and was a local preacher. Enlisted on 4.11.1916 at Shrewsbury Barracks. Reported missing on 27.11.1917 at Fontaine-Notre-Dame and afterwards was presumed to have been killed on that date, aged 26. Buried **ANNEUX BRITISH CEMETERY.** Grave location:- Plot 2, Row F, Grave 3.

WARD, JAMES. Rifleman. No C/7620. 18th Battalion King's Royal Rifle Corps. Born Clayton West 15.12.1882. Son of the late William and Anna Ward of Clayton West. Educated at Clayton West Schools. Lodged with Mrs Lucy Fenwick, 17 Green Lane, Dalton, Huddersfield. Employed as a wool sorter. Single. Enlisted 15.11.1915. Reported missing, presumed killed, 11.8.1918, aged 35 years. Has no known grave. Commemorated **TYNE COT MEMORIAL TO THE MISSING.** ROH:- Clayton West and High Hoyland War Memorial.

WARD, JOHN THOMAS. Sergeant. No 3004. 1/5th Battalion Duke of Wellington's Regiment. Born 3 Lee Row, Thornbury, Bradford 20.8.1891. Son of Sarah Greenwood, 111 Dundas Street, Leeds Road, Bradford. Educated Thornbury Board School, Bradford. Employed as a sawyer by Messrs Jere Kaye and Company. Lodged at 24 Netheroyd Hill Road, Cowcliffe, Huddersfield. Single. Enlisted 3.9.1914. Killed in action, 2.7.1916, during the Battle of the Somme, aged 24. Has no known grave. Commemorated **THIEPVAL MEMORIAL TO THE MISSING.** ROH:- Huddersfield Drill Hall.

WARD, JOSEPH. Private. No 241253. 1/5th Battalion Duke of Wellington's Regiment. Born St. Andrew's Road, Huddersfield, 25.6.1894. Son of William Ward, 70 Castlegate, Huddersfield. Educated St. Patrick's Roman Catholic School. Was unemployed at the time of enlistment. Single. Enlisted May 1915. Reported missing, presumed killed, 3.9.1916, in the attack on the Schwaben Redoubt during the Battle of the Somme. Buried **MILL ROAD CEMETERY.** Grave location:- Plot 3, Row F, Grave 1. ROH:- Huddersfield Drill Hall.

WARD, ROBERT. Private. No 202223. 8th Battalion Seaforth Highlanders. Born Burley's Yard, Lowerhead Row, Huddersfield, 17.12.1892. Son of Thomas Ward, 27 York Street, Huddersfield. Educated Huddersfield Parish Church School. Employed as a painter's labourer by the London and North Western Railway. Single. Killed in action, 1.8.1917, aged 24 years. Has no known grave. Commemorated **MENIN GATE MEMORIAL TO THE MISSING.** (Brother of Private **THOMAS WARD**, died 22.8.1917, q.v.).

WARD, THOMAS. Private. No 17389. 10th Battalion Duke of Wellington's Regiment. Born Burley's Yard, Lowerhead Row, Huddersfield, 4.2.1895. Son of Thomas Ward, 27 York Street, Huddersfield. Educated Huddersfield Parish Church School. Employed as a platelayer by the London and North Western Railway. Single. Accidentally drowned, 22.8.1917, aged 23 years. Buried **LONGUENESSE (St. OMER) SOUVENIR CEMETERY.** Grave location:- Plot 4, Row D, Grave 45. (Brother of Private **ROBERT WARD**, killed in action, 1.8.1917, q.v.).

WARDLE, MARCUS. Sergeant. No 240427. 1/5th Battalion Duke of Wellington's Regiment. Born Leytonstone, Essex, 6.12.1891. Son of the late Gilbert and Emma Wardle and nephew of Alice Wardle, 25 Clifton Road, Gledholt, Huddersfield. Educated at Leytonstone schools. Lived 26 West View, Dalton, Huddersfield. Employed as a clerk in the counting house at Messrs Learoyd Brothers and Company Limited, Leeds Road, Huddersfield. Single. Enlisted 3.9.1914. Reported missing, presumed killed, 3.9.1916, during the attack on the Schwaben Redoubt during the Battle of the Somme. He was 24 years of age. Buried **MILL ROAD CEMETERY.** Grave location:- Plot 19, Row C, Grave 9. ROH:- Learoyd Brothers; Christ Church, Moldgreen; Huddersfield Drill Hall.

WAREY, CHARLES STUART. Air Mechanic 2nd Class. No 48537. Recruits Depot Royal Flying Corps. Born Kirkburton, Huddersfield. Son of David George and Mary Jane Warey. Husband of Elizabeth Warey, of Hallas, Kirkburton. Was treasurer of Dogley Lane Congregational Church and of the local Belgian Refugee Committee. He was a member of the Kirkburton Literary and Debating Society. Had taken over his father's jewellery business. Enlisted in the R.F.C. at Farnborough, Hampshire on Thursday, 28.10.1916. On Saturday, 30.10.1916, he was taken seriously ill and admitted to the Cambridge Hospital, Aldershot. He underwent an operation for a perforated gastric ulcer but he died the same day, 30.9.1916. His wife arrived at Aldershot too late to see him alive. He was 30 years of age. Buried with full military honours at **ALL HALLOWS CHURCHYARD, KIRKBURTON.** Grave location:- 23, 1788. ROH:- All Hallows Parish Church.

WARHURST, JAMES EWART. Private. No 241817. 2/5th Battalion Duke of Wellington's Regiment. Born Slaithwaite. Son of John William and Sarah Ann Warhurst, 8 Booth Banks, Slaithwaite. Attended the West Slaithwaite Sunday School and was a member of the choir. Employed by the Slaithwaite Spinning Company Limited. Enlisted March 1916. Embarked for France, 10.1.1917. Was wounded on one occasion and received treatment at the Norfolk Military Hospital. Returned to France in September, 1917. Reported missing, presumed killed, 27.11.1917, at the Battle of Cambrai, aged 24. Has no known grave. Commemorated **CAMBRAI MEMORIAL TO THE MISSING.** ROH:- St. James Church, Slaithwaite; Slaithwaite War Memorial; Huddersfield Drill Hall.

WARING, HARRY. Sapper. No 224405. 485th Field Company, Royal Engineers. Born Hillhouse Lane, Huddersfield. Son of Fred and Martha Ann Waring. 74 Hillhouse Lane, Huddersfield. Educated St. Andrew's Church of England School, Huddersfield. Employed as a joiner by British Dyes Limited. Husband of Edna Waring, 49 St. Andrew's Road, Turnbridge, Huddersfield. Died of heart disease on 12.12.1917 in hospital at Sheffield. He was 29 years of age. Buried **EDGERTON CEMETERY, HUDDERSFIELD.** Grave location:- 43, 121. ROH:- St. Andrew's Church, Leeds Road, Huddersfield.

WARING, JOHN WILLIE. Private. No 93766. 11th Battalion Sherwood Foresters. Born Huddersfield. Son of Mrs J. E. Waring, 10 Netheroyd Hill, Huddersfield. Killed in action, 5.10.1918. Buried **PROSPECT HILL CEMETERY, GOUY.** Grave location:- Plot 3, Row B, Grave 20. ROH:- Netheroyd Hill Methodist Chapel; St. Hilda's Church, Cowcliffe; Fartown and Birkby War Memorial.

WARING, NORMAN. Fusilier. No 45554. 20th (Tyneside Scottish) Battalion Northumberland Fusiliers. Formerly No 37472 Durham Light Infantry. Born Crown Street, Honley, 12.8.1897. Son of George and Ann Waring, 18 Lower Road, Berry Brow, Huddersfield. Educated Honley Church of England School. He was formerly assistant to Mr Albert Atkinson, butcher, of Honley but worked for the Argentine Meat Company, King Street, Huddersfield, prior to enlistment. Was a member of William Brook's bible class and was formerly in the Honley Parish Church choir. Enlisted 25.7.1916. Embarked for France at Christmas, 1916. Was killed by shrapnel whilst on the way to the trenches on 2.4.1917. He was 19 years of age. Buried **Ste. CATHERINE BRITISH CEMETERY.** Grave location:- Row A, Grave 19. ROH:- Honley War Memorial; Armitage Bridge War Memorial.

WARRENER, WALKER. Private. No 15990. 8th Battalion Duke of Wellington's Regiment. Born Oldham. Married, with two children. Lived 4 Outcote Bank, Huddersfield. Killed in action, 25.4.1917, aged 32 years. Buried **HERMIES BRITISH CEMETERY.** Grave location:- Row C, Grave 1.

WARRINGTON, CLINTON DRAKE. Private. No 10912. 2nd Battalion Hampshire Regiment. Born 18.5.1892. Son of George and Amy Warrington. Lived from infancy with Mr and Mrs J T Pentney, 6 South Parade, Huddersfield. Educated Spring Grove Council School and the Huddersfield Technical College. Attended St. Thomas's Church, Longroyd Bridge. Was a member of the Y.M.C.A. and its swimming club. Employed as a cutter by Mr Willis, wholesale clothier, John William Street, Huddersfield. Enlisted at the outbreak of the war. The following extract is taken from 'British Regiments at Gallipoli' by Ray Westlake, *'embarked at Avonmouth, Bristol for the Dardenelles on March 20th. Arrived at Lemnos on the 13th April. Transferred to 'River Clyde' on 24.4.1915 and sailed for Gallipoli. 'River Clyde' arrived off Cape Helles at dawn on 25.4.1915 and ran ashore on beach between Cape Helles and Sedd el Bahr. Heavy casualties on landing - many men were hit while wading ashore in shoulder-deep water, most of the wounded being drowned. On 27.4.1915 moved to positions astride Krithia Road. Advance continued on 28.4.1915. French on right counter attacked and retired. Whole line then withdrew to start positions. 3 Officers killed and 53 other ranks: 4 Officers and 246 other ranks wounded, 46 missing'.* Reported wounded and missing on 28.4.1915 and afterwards presumed to have been killed on that date, aged 22. Has no known grave. Commemorated **HELLES MEMORIAL TO THE MISSING.** ROH:- St. Thomas's Church, Longroyd Bridge.

WARWICK, GEORGE, MM. Sergeant. No7/417. 1/7th Battalion Duke of Wellington's Regiment. Born Woolwich, London. Employed by Messrs Crowther, Bruce and Company. Formerly lived in Brougham Road, Marsden, but, prior to enlistment, lived at Idle, Bradford. Married, with three children. Was a member of the local Territorial battalion prior to the war. Enlisted at the outbreak of the war. Killed by a bomb explosion in a dugout on 22.7.1916 during the Battle of the Somme. He was 36 years of age. Buried **CONNAUGHT CEMETERY, THIEPVAL.** Grave Location:- Plot 13, Row D, Grave 5. ROH:- Huddersfield Drill Hall.

WATERHOUSE, DANIEL. Private. No 4857. 1/5th Battalion Duke of Wellington's Regiment. Born Marsden. Son of the late James and of Alice Waterhouse, Woodside, Marsden. Employed as a weaver at Bank Bottom Mills, Marsden. Was a member of Marsden Conservative Club. Enlisted 17.2.1916. Embarked for France in July, 1916. Was seriously wounded in the shoulder at the beginning of September, 1916. After undergoing two operations he died of wounds at No 14 General Hospital, Wimereux, on 21.9.1916, aged 27 years. Buried **WIMEREUX COMMUNAL CEMETERY.** Grave location:- Plot 1, Row Q, Grave 15A. ROH:- Huddersfield Drill Hall; Marsden War Memorial; Marsden Conservative Club; memorial in Marsden Churchyard.

WATERHOUSE, JOE. Private. No 29408. 8th Battalion Duke of Wellington's Regiment. Born Leaches, Outlane, 22.6.1889. Son of the late Joseph and Mary Waterhouse of Outlane. Educated Outlane Board School. Employed as a woollen spinner by Messrs J. Sutcliffe and Sons. Married. Lived 51 Colne Head, Huddersfield. Enlisted 6.9.1916. Killed in action at Messines on 19.6.1917, aged 28 years. Buried **MESSINES RIDGE CEMETERY.** Grave location:- Plot 2, Row B, Grave 22. ROH:- Bethel United Methodist Chapel, Outlane.

WATERHOUSE, WILLIAM. Sergeant. No 240011. 2/5th Battalion Duke of Wellington's Regiment. Born Leeds 10.11.1882. Son of Charles Edward and Mary Ann Waterhouse. Educated Hillhouse Council School. Employed as a bookbinder by Messrs Alfred Jubb and Company Limited. Attended Kingscliffe United Methodist School, Hillhouse. Husband of Ada Waterhouse, 38 Corby Street, Birkby, Huddersfield. Was a well known fast bowler. Was an old Volunteer and enlisted at the outbreak of the war as a Stretcher-Bearer. Died of wounds at No 2 Canadian General Hospital on 6.4.1918, aged 36 years,. Buried **ETAPLES MILITARY CEMETERY.** Grave location:- Plot 33, Row D, Grave 6A. ROH:- Huddersfield Drill Hall; Fartown and Birkby War Memorial.

WATSON, ERNEST. Private. No 350284. 15th Battalion Highland Light Infantry. Formerly No 5203 King's Own Scottish Borderers. Born 246 Bradford Road North, Huddersfield, 23.8.1901. Son of Edwin and Mary Watson, 246 Bradford Road North. Educated St. John's Church of England School, Birkby and Huddersfield Higher Grade School. Was in business with his father as a grocer at 177 Bradford Road, Huddersfield. Enlisted March 1916. Was wounded in France in late 1917. Recovered and returned to France at the beginning of 1918. Killed in action, 16.5.1918, aged 26 years. Buried **BAC-du-SUD BRITISH CEMETERY, BAILLEULVAL.** Grave location:- Plot 2, Row D, Grave 12. ROH:- St. John's Church, Birkby; Fartown and Birkby War Memorial.

WATTHEWS, HAROLD. Lieutenant. 3rd, attached 10th, Battalion Duke of Wellington's Regiment. Third son of Doctor Herbert and Mrs Watthews of Hollybank, Holmfirth. Attended Lane Congregational Church. Educated Holmfirth Secondary School and George Watson's College, Edinburgh, where he was studying for the medical profession. Was a member of the Officers' Training Corps whilst at college. Embarked for France in February, 1917. Killed in action, 8.6.1917, aged 19 years. Has no known grave. Commemorated **MENIN GATE MEMORIAL TO THE MISSING.** ROH:- Holmfirth War Memorial; Holmfirth Secondary School.

WEAR, FRANK. Private. No 241690. 2/5th Battalion Duke of Wellington's Regiment. Born Huddersfield 1.4.1896. Son of Fred Wear, 4 Bath Street, St. John's Road, Huddersfield. Educated at St. John's School, Hillhouse. Employed as a fitter by Messrs J. Hopkinson and Company Limited, of Birkby. Single. Enlisted 6.3.1916. Reported missing, presumed killed, on 3.5.1917 at the Battle of Bullecourt. Has no known grave. Commemorated **ARRAS MEMORIAL TO THE MISSING.** ROH:- Huddersfield Drill Hall.

WEAVILL, JOHN MAUDE. Gunner. No 89648. 99th Siege Battery, Royal Garrison Artillery. Born Longwood Gate, Huddersfield. Eldest son of Mr and Mrs Tom Weavill and brother of Fred, Harry and John Weavill, 71 Cliffe End Hill, Longwood, Huddersfield. Educated Goitfield Council School. Employed as a woollen weaver. Enlisted June 1916. Was gassed and died from pneumonia at Boulogne Base Hospital on 5.7.1918. Buried **TERLINCTHUN BRITISH CEMETERY.** Grave location:- Plot 1, Row D, Grave 30. ROH:- Longwood Wesleyan Church; St. Mark's Parish Church, Longwood.

WEBB, CHARLES ARTHUR. Private. No 270304. 9th Battalion The Royal Scots (the Lothian Regiment). Formerly No 11375 The Royal Scots Fusiliers. Born Pontefract. Eldest son of Charles and Ada Webb, 58 Rock Terrace, Brockholes. Employed by Messrs T. Cresswell and Company Limited, woollen merchants, Lord Street, Huddersfield. Killed in action, 1.8.1918, aged 20 years. Buried **RAPERIE BRITISH CEMETERY.** Grave location:- Plot 2, Row E, Grave 6. ROH:- Brockholes War Memorial; Honley War Memorial.

WEBSTER, ARTHUR. Private. No 41447. 8th Battalion Leicestershire Regiment. Born Yeadon, Leeds. Son of William Henry and Betsy Webster, 19 Wood Terrace, Primrose Hill, Huddersfield. Employed in the finishing department of Messrs Taylor and Lodge, Folly Hall, Huddersfield. Died of wounds as a Prisoner of War in Stuttgart, Germany, on 7.7.1918. He was 19 years of age. Buried **NIEDERZWEHREN CEMETERY, CASSEL, GERMANY.** Grave location:- Plot 2, Row E, Grave 3. ROH:- Memorial in Lockwood Cemetery, Huddersfield.

WEBSTER, FRANK HARPER. Fusilier. No 46109. 22nd (Tyneside Scottish) Battalion Northumberland Fusiliers. Born 41 Bradford Road, Huddersfield, 26.11.1888. Educated Thomas Street Board School, Huddersfield. Employed as a weaver. Husband of Ada Webster, 26 Luck Lane, Marsh, Huddersfield. Enlisted 28.7.1916. Killed in action at Green Hill, Arras, on 5.6.1917, aged 28 years. Has no known grave. Commemorated **ARRAS MEMORIAL TO THE MISSING.** ROH:- Great Northern Street Congregational Chapel.

WEBSTER, JOHN. Private. No 14870. 2/6th Battalion Duke of Wellington's Regiment. Born Glasgow. Son of John Webster of Sheffield. Lived in Netherthong from 1910. Attended the Parish Church Sunday School. Was a member of the Netherthong Working Men's Club and the Netherthong Association football club. Employed as an apprentice by Mr B. Eastwood, brush manufacturer. Enlisted 24.11.1914. Was wounded on 2.7.1916 and invalided home. Returned to France some months later. Killed in action, 28.6.1917. Buried **QUEANT ROAD CEMETERY.** Grave location:- Plot 3, Row F, Grave 27.

In a letter, Second Lieutenant Thropler describes how Private Webster met his death, *'At the time of this sad happening we had just relieved a Company on the front line when a whizz-bang burst just a few yards away hitting Jack and another. The injuries he received were to the top of the head. He was unconscious immediately and in a few minutes he expired. His end was painless. He has a soldier's grave about two miles from the line, the service being conducted by our Chaplain.'* ROH:- Netherthong and Thongsbridge War Memorial; Netherthong Working Men's Club.

WEBSTER, RALPH. Private. No 57489. 2/7th Battalion West Yorkshire Regiment. Born Leeds 6.8.1896. Son of Joseph and Alice Webster, 78 Church Street, Paddock, Huddersfield. Educated at the National School, Burley, Leeds, and Knowle Bank School, Golcar. Was a member of the choir at the Paddock Congregational Church. Employed as a woollen piecer by Messrs Crowther Brothers of Milnsbridge. Single. Enlisted July 1917. Killed in action at Bucquoy, France, on 27.3.1918, aged 21 years. Has no known grave. Commemorated **ARRAS MEMORIAL TO THE MISSING.** ROH:- All Saints Church, Paddock; Shared Church, Paddock.

WELDRICK, ARTHUR. Private. No 8351. 2nd Battalion York and Lancaster Regiment. Born Barnsley. Son of Mr and Mrs Weldrick, 7 Castlereagh Street, Barnsley. Employed by Huddersfield Corporation Tramways Department. Killed in action, 18.2.1915, aged 30 years. Has no known grave. Commemorated **PLOEGSTEERT MEMORIAL TO THE MISSING.** ROH:- Huddersfield Corporation Roll.

WELLS, PERCY. Fusilier. No 56136. 15th Battalion Royal Welsh Fusiliers. Formerly No 32234 South Staffordshire Regiment. Born Marsden, Huddersfield. Son of William and Elizabeth Wells, 11 Spring Street, Marsden. Employed as a woollen piecer at Clough Lee Mill, Marsden. Was a member of Marsden Adult School. Enlisted April 1916. Embarked for France on 17.2.1917. Killed in action, 27.7.1917, aged 19 years. Buried **BARD COTTAGE CEMETERY, BOESINGHE,**

BELGIUM. Grave location:- Plot 3, Row F, Grave 8. ROH:- Marsden War Memorial.

WELSH, ROBERT GEORGE RAINSFORTH (RENNIE). Private. No 241884. 2/5th Battalion Duke of Wellington's Regiment. Born Ashbrook Cottage, Galashiels, Scotland, in 1877. Educated Stile Common Council School, Huddersfield. Lived 192 Moorbottom Road, Thornton Lodge, Huddersfield. Employed as a commercial traveller. Single. Enlisted March 1916. Killed in action, 27.4.1918, near Poperinghe, Belgium. Has no known grave. Commemorated **TYNE COT MEMORIAL TO THE MISSING.** ROH:- St. Stephen's Church, Rashcliffe; Huddersfield Drill Hall.

WEST, EDWIN. Lance Corporal. No 241526. 2/5th Battalion Duke of Wellington's Regiment. Born Towngate, Newsome, Huddersfield, 13.10.1896. Son of Mr and Mrs Arthur West, Weetwood House, Newsome. Educated Newsome Church of England School. Employed by his father as an assistant in the family grocery and drapery business at Newsome. Attended Newsome United Methodist Church. Enlisted 6.3.1916. Was wounded and taken prisoner by the Germans. Died of wounds on 12.6.1917, aged 20. Buried **MONS COMMUNAL CEMETERY.** Grave location:- Plot 6, Row E, Grave 7. *His family were informed both by the Record Office, York and the British Red Cross Society of his death in hospital at Mons. But in September, 1917, they received a postcard from him dated 2.8.1917 from Limburg, Germany, stating that he was well as can be expected under the circumstances. (According to the Huddersfield Examiner of 15.9.1917, this is one of three cases of men from Huddersfield who had been officially reported dead and who subsequently wrote to their families.)* ROH:- Newsome United Methodist Church; Huddersfield Drill Hall.

WHALLEY, JOHN ALDERSON. Fusilier. No 36311. 26th (Tyneside Irish) Battalion Northumberland Fusiliers. Born Halifax. Son of the late John and Alice Whalley, 12 Whitcliffe Lane, Cleckheaton. Husband of May Whalley, 29 Green View, Wellhouse, Golcar. Killed in action at the Battle of Arras on 5.6.1917, agd 26 years. Has no known grave. Commemorated **ARRAS MEMORIAL TO THE MISSING.** ROH:- St. John's Church, Golcar.

WHARF, JOE WILLIE. Private. No 1939. 1/7th Battalion Duke of Wellington's Regiment. Born 17 Prospect Place, Prospect Street, Huddersfield, 8.7.1896. Son of Inspector Percy Wharf and Mrs Ruth Wharf, The Fire Station, Princess Street, Huddersfield. Educated Hillhouse Elementary School. Employed as an apprentice at Messrs T. Broadbent of Huddersfield. Single. Enlisted 31.8.1914. Killed by a shell on 8.12.1915, aged 18. Buried **BARD COTTAGE CEMETERY, BOESINGHE, BELGIUM.** Grave location:- Plot 1, Row D, Grave 21. ROH:- St. Paul's Church, Southgate, Huddersfield.

WHARTON, GEORGE HENRY. Private. No 305279. 1/7th Battalion Duke of Wellington's Regiment. Born Marsden, Huddersfield, 20.9.1896. Son of Henry Hind Wharton and Jane Wharton, 29 Mark Street, Paddock, Huddersfield. Educated Paddock Council School. Attended Paddock United Methodist Church. Employed as a chain-maker. Single. Enlisted 4.8.1914. Killed in action, 17.9.1916, at Thiepval during the Battle of the Somme. He was 20 years of age. Has no known grave. Commemorated **THIEPVAL MEMORIAL TO THE MISSING.** ROH:- All Saints Church, Paddock, Shared Church, Paddock; Huddersfield Drill Hall.

WHEAWILL, EDWARD KILNER. Private. No 763219. 28th (County of London) Battalion (Artists Rifles). Born Huddersfield 6.10.1896. Son of Charles and Emily Wheawill, 104 Birkby Hall Road, Huddersfield. Educated at Huddersfield College School and the Leys School, Cambridge. Employed as an articled clerk with his father's firm of Wheawill, Son and Company. Enlisted November 1916. Embarked for France in September, 1917. Reported missing, presumed killed, on 30.10.1917, aged 21 years. Has no known grave. Commemorated **TYNE COT MEMORIAL TO THE MISSING.** ROH:- St. Cuthbert's Church, Birkby; Huddersfield College School; Fartown and Birkby War Memorial.

WHEELHOUSE, NORMAN. Private. No 240160. 2/5th Battalion Duke of Wellington's Regiment. Born Bradford Road, Huddersfield, 16.8.1896. Son of Fred Wheelhouse, 23 Clement Street, Birkby. Educated Thomas Street Board School. Employed as a labourer. Single. Had been a member of the local Territorials since 1912. Enlisted 4.8.1914. Reported missing, presumed killed, on 3.5.1917 at the Battle of Bullecourt. Has no known grave. Commemorated **ARRAS MEMORIAL TO THE MISSING.** ROH:- Great Northern Street Congregational Church; Huddersfield Drill Hall; Fartown and Birkby War Memorial.

WHELAN, STEPHAN. Lance Corporal. No 13195. 7th Battalion East Lancashire Regiment. Born Dewsbury. Husband of E. Whelan, 170 Albert Street, Lockwood, Huddersfield. Died of wounds at No 7 Casualty Clearing Station on 17.10.1915. Buried **MERVILLE COMMUNAL CEMETERY.** Grave location:- Plot 4, Row J, Grave 10.

WHITAKER, JOHN. Trumpeter. No 776147. 'D' Battery, 245th Brigade, Royal Field Artillery. Born Manchester. Lived Dalton, Huddersfield. Died of wounds, 13.5.1918. Buried **NINE ELMS BRITISH CEMETERY, POPERINGHE, BELGIUM.** Grave location:- Plot 14, Row D, Grave 5.

WHITE, EDWIN. Private. No 56896. 'A' Squadron, 3rd/1st Pembroke Yeomanry, attached as R.Q.M.S, 13th Battalion Welsh Regiment. Born South Street, Huddersfield, 23.2.1894. Son of Alfred and Anne White, 41 Maxwell Road, Bournemouth and formerly of 39 Grasmere Road, Huddersfield. Educated Oakes Council School, Huddersfield College School and Higher Grade School. Employed as Manager and cutter of the tailoring department of a firm in Swansea. Single. Enlisted 11.12.1915. Was attached to the 13th Battalion Welsh Regiment, 38th Division, as Regimental tailor. Was killed in his sleep by concussion of a bursting shell on 25.9.1918 at Lechelle, aged 24. Buried **FIVE POINTS CEMETERY, LECHELLE.** Grave location:- Row A, Grave 9.

WHITEHEAD, ARTHUR. Private. No 71001. Posted 2/2nd London Regiment, Royal Fusiliers. Formerly No 33960 3rd Reserve Cavalry Regiment. Born 5 Bombay Street, Bradford, 13.8.1896. Eldest son of Mr and Mrs H. Whitehead, 7 Back Union Street, Huddersfield. Educated Thomas Street Board School. Employed as a dyer's labourer by Mr. W. H. Murgatroyd, dyer, Leeds Road, Huddersfield. Single. Enlisted 1.5.1917. Reported missing, presumed killed, on 21.3.1918, aged 21 years. Has no known grave. Commemorated **POZIERES MEMORIAL TO THE MISSING.**

WHITEHEAD, ERNEST. Private. No 241275. 1/4th Battalion Duke of Wellington's Regiment. Married. Lived 10 Summer Street, Lockwood, Huddersfield. Employed as a woollen feeder by Messrs J. Crowther and Sons, Union Mills, Milnsbridge. Died of wounds at No 10 Casualty Clearing Station on 17.4.1918, aged 35 years. Buried **LIJSSENTHOEK MILITARY CEMETERY.** Grave location:- Plot 27, Row G, Grave 11.

WHITEHEAD, JOHN JOE. Private. No 38110. 6th Battalion The Yorkshire Regiment. Born Greenfield. Husband of Alice Ann Whitehead, 17 Royds Terrace, Marsden. Employed as a weaver at Bank Bottom Mills, Marsden. Was a member of Marsden Socalist Club. Enlisted September 1916. Embarked for France 31.12.1916. Killed in action, 21.4.1918, aged 35 years. Buried **DIVION COMMUNAL CEMETERY.** Grave location:- Grave No 3. ROH:- Marsden War Memorial.

WHITEHEAD, JOSEPH. Private. No 241640. 15th (Service) Battalion (1st Glasgow) Highland Light Infantry. Born Honley. Son of the late Mr Shaw Whitehead and Mrs Whitehead, 1 Scot Gate Road, Honley. Assisted in his fathers business as a plasterer. Was a member of the Holmfirth, Honley and Meltham Hunt and kept one of the hounds. Enlisted April 1915. Killed in action, 26.8.1918, aged 23 years. Buried **VILLERS-BRETONNEUX MILITARY CEMETERY.** Grave location:- Plot 14, Row F, Grave 9. ROH:- Honley War Memorial.

WHITEHEAD, LUKE. Lance Corporal. No 131738. 235th Army Troops Company, Royal Engineers. Born Honley, Huddersfield, 25.9.1880. Son of Vernal and Ann Whitehead, Victoria Road, Lockwood, Huddersfield. Educated Honley National School. Lived The Fold, Netherton. Married, with 8 children. Employed as a plasterer by Mr Edgar Jessop of Berry Brow. Attended Lockwood Wesleyan Chapel. Enlisted October 1915. Killed in action near Ypres on 20.8.1917, aged 33 years. Buried **BIRR CROSSROADS CEMETERY, ZILLEBEKE, BELGIUM.** Grave location:- Plot 3, Row D, Grave 2. ROH:- South

Crosland and Netherton War Memorial; Mount Pleasant Chapel, Lockwood.

WHITEHEAD, MILTON. Private. No 29191. 8th Battalion The Yorkshire Regiment. Born Paddock. Son of Mr and Mrs Fred Whitehead, 76 George Street, Milnsbridge. Employed by Mr Sam Hirst, cloth finisher, Bridge Croft Mills, Milnsbridge. Attended Milnsbridge Wesleyan Sunday School and Ramsden Street Chapel, Huddersfield. Was a member of the Longwood Harriers. Enlisted 31.3.1916. Was wounded on 13.3.1917 and was on the *Hospital Ship Lanfranc* on 17.4.1917 when it was torpedoed in the Channel when crossing to England. Killed in action, 28.9.1917, aged 22 years. Buried **TYNE COT CEMETERY.** Grave location:- Plot 63, Row F, Grave 4. ROH:- Milnsbridge; St. Mark's Parish Church, Longwood.

WHITEHEAD, PERCY. Sergeant. No 7610. 2nd Battalion Duke of Wellington's Regiment. Born Linthwaite. Son of George and Minnie Whitehead: Was married on Easter Monday, 1914, to Priscilla Whitehead, and lived West Mount, Linthwaite. Employed in the finishing department of Messrs Mallinsons, Spring Grove Mills, Linthwaite. Was a Reservist and had served six years in India, where he attained the rank of Lance Corporal. He had also fought in the Boer War. Recalled to the Colours on 5.8.1914 and sailed for France on 14.8.1914. After a brief rest, his Regiment had a two days march and then went straight into action at Mons. Was promoted to the rank of Sergeant on 23.11.1914 and was also in the fighting at the Aisne, Festubert, Ypres and La Bassee. During the winter he did duty in the trenches. During the last week in February he was granted a brief home leave where he saw his baby daughter, born eight weeks previously, for the first time. Killed in action in the attack on Hill 60 on 18.4.1915, aged 27. Has no known grave. Commemorated **MENIN GATE MEMORIAL TO THE MISSING.** ROH:- Linthwaite War Memorial; Golcar Baptist Church.

WHITEHEAD, TOM. Private. No 350211. 9th (Glasgow Highland) Battalion Highland Light Infantry. Formerly No 11395 Royal Scots Fusiliers. Born Huddersfield. Son of Mrs Emma Whitehead, 50 South View, Hilltop, Paddock. Employed by Messrs John Crowther and Sons, Milnsbridge. Was well known as a local concert artiste and contributed at many of the battalion concerts. Was a member of Paddock Socialist Club. Attended All Saints Church, Paddock. Killed in action, 28.11.1917, aged 32 years. Has no known grave. Commemorated **TYNE COT MEMORIAL TO THE MISSING.** ROH:- All Saints Church, Paddock.

WHITELEY, ARTHUR. Lance Corporal. No 45131. The Rifle Brigade, posted to 1st Battalion London Rifle Brigade. Born Linthwaite. Son of the late John Whiteley and Mrs Whiteley, Colne Terrace, Manchester Road, Linthwaite. Employed as a cotton twiner by the Slaithwaite Spinning Company Limited. Was a member of the Slaithwaite Conservative Club. Enlisted January 1917. Invalided home at the beginning of 1918 suffering from septic poisoning but returned to France on Good Friday, 1918. Killed in action, 26.8.1918, aged 28 years. Has no known grave. Commemorated **VIS-en-ARTOIS MEMORIAL TO THE MISSING.** ROH:- Linthwaite War Memorial; Fartown and Birkby War Memorial. (Brother of Private **HERBERT WHITELEY**, killed in action, 16.9.1916, q.v.).

WHITELEY, ARTHUR. Private. No 42060. 6th Battalion King's Own Scottish Borderers. Born Holmfirth. Son of Joshua and Eliza Whiteley, Carr Green, Holmfirth. Educated Netherthong National School. Employed in the receiving and delivery department of Messrs T. and J. Tinker, Bottom Mills, Holmfirth. Was a keen cyclist. Enlisted in the summer of 1916. Went into training in the South of England and then went to Ireland. After that he went to East Anglia and came home to Holmfirth on his draft leave. Had been in France for five weeks when he was killed in action on 26.7.1918. He was 30 years of age. Buried **LA KREULE MILITARY CEMETERY.** Grave location:- Plot 3, Row B, Grave 2. ROH:- Holme and Holmbridge War Memorial.

WHITELEY, CHARLES TAYLOR. Lieutenant. 2/8th Battalion, attached 14th Battalion Royal Warwickshire Regiment. Son of the late Tom and Ada Taylor of Huddersfield. Was a member of two old Huddersfield families. He was a grandson of the late William Whiteley, machine maker, of Lockwood, and of the late Joseph Taylor, iron and steel merchant, of Huddersfield. Educated Pembroke College, Harrogate, and later at the Bradford Grammar School.

He was an architect and surveyor and was engaged as assistant with Mr Rhodes Calvert of Forster Square, Bradford. Enlisted in 1915 in the Artist's Rifles. Later he was gazetted as a Second Lieutenant into the Royal Warwickshire Regiment. Died of wounds at No 39 Stationary Hospital on 1.7.1918. He was 32 years of age. Buried **AIRE COMMUNAL CEMETERY**. Grave location:- Plot 3, Row G, Grave 6.

WHITELEY, FRED. Private. No 24225. 2/7th Battalion Duke of Wellington's Regiment. Born Meltham, Huddersfield. Eldest son of Mr and Mrs Joe Whiteley of Hollingworth Green, Meltham. Husband of Alice Whiteley, Lower Foresters, Meltham, and later of 3 Fence Nook, Littleborough. Died of wounds, 4.12.1917, aged 24 years. Buried **HERMIES HILL BRITISH CEMETERY**. Grave location:- Plot 2, Row C, Grave 6. ROH:- St. Bartholomew's Church, Meltham; Huddersfield Drill Hall.

WHITELEY, HERBERT. Private. No 4691. 1/5th Battalion Duke of Wellington's Regiment. Born Halifax. Son of the late John Whiteley and Mrs Whiteley, Colne Terrace, Manchester Road, Linthwaite. Attended Slaithwaite United Methodist Church Young Men's Class. Acting as accompanist he was also a member of the choir. Enlisted February 1916. Was home on his last leave about Whitsuntide, returning on Whit Sunday to his duties. Embarked for France on 24.6.1916. Killed through the bursting of a shell on 16.9.1916 at the Leipzig Salient during the Battle of the Somme. He was 24 years of age. Has no known grave. Commemorated **THIEPVAL MEMORIAL TO THE MISSING**. (Brother of Private **ARTHUR WHITELEY**, killed in action, 26.8.1918, q.v.). ROH:- Linthwaite War Memorial; Huddersfield Drill Hall; Fartown and Birkby War Memorial.

WHITELEY, JAMES EDWARD. Private. No 20382. 1/4th Battalion Duke of Wellington's Regiment. Born Honley, Huddersfield. Son of the late William and Lydia Whiteley, Miner's Square, Netherton, Huddersfield. Killed in action, 10.4.1918 aged 28 years. Has no known grave. Commemorated **TYNE COT MEMORIAL TO THE MISSING**. ROH:- South Crosland and Netherton War Memorial.

WHITELEY, JOHN RICHARD. Private. No 202822. 1/4th Battalion King's Own Yorkshire Light Infantry. Born Linthwaite. Lived 75 Wood Top, Slaithwaite. Married, with one child. Employed as a weaver by Messrs Ben Hall and Sons, Milnsbridge. Was a chorister at Linthwaite Church. He was a member of the Slaithwaite Socalist Club. Enlisted in September 1916. Embarked for France in December, 1916. Died from gas poisoning at the 2nd Canadian Hospital, Le Treport, on 28.7.1917, aged 33 years. Buried **MONT HUON MILITARY CEMETERY**. Grave location:- Plot 4, Row H, Grave 1A. ROH:- St. James Church, Slaithwaite; Slaithwaite War Memorial.

WHITELEY, JOHN WILLIAM. Private. No 204534. 1/5th Battalion York and Lancaster Regiment. Born Emley. Son of Joseph and Eliza Ann Whiteley. Husband of Elizabeth Whiteley, of Church Street, Emley. Enlisted Wakefield. Killed in action, 9.10.1917, aged 29 years. Buried **TYNE COT CEMETERY**. Grave Location:- Plot 14, Row A, Grave 24. ROH:- Emley War Memorial.

WHITELEY, STANLEY. Rifleman. No B/203248. 13th Battalion The Rifle Brigade. Born 24 Church Lane, Moldgreen, Huddersfiel, 21.10.1889. Son of James William and Jessie Whiteley, 24 Church Lane, Moldgreen. Educated Moldgreen Church of England School. Employed as a hairdresser's assistant in the shop of Mr Fred Sykes, hairdresser, High Street, Huddersfield. Attended Moldgreen Church and Sunday School. Single. Enlisted 31.10.1915. Embarked for France in July, 1916. Killed in action at Monchy-le-Preux on 11.4.1917 during the Battle of Arras, aged 27. Buried **MONCHY BRITISH CEMETERY**. Grave location:- Plot 1, Row D, Grave 11. ROH:- Christ Church, Moldgreen; Moldgreen War Memorial; commemorated on headstone in Kirkheaton Cemetery.

WHITELEY, WILLIE DYSON. Private. No 267800. 1/7th Battalion West Yorkshire Regiment. Formerly No 5541 Duke of Wellington's Regiment. Born Cartworth, Holmfirth. Son of Albert and Lydia Ann Whiteley, Old Road, Hinchliffe Mill. Educated Dobb National School. Later he was a student at Dobb Evening School and the Holmfirth Technical College. Attended the Hinchliffe Mill Wesleyan Sunday School. Was an active member of the Cartworth Moor Cricket

Club. Employed as a weaver at Digley Mills. Enlisted March 1916. Captured by the Germans on 25.4.1918. Died on 19.10.1918, aged 23. Buried **COLOGNE SOUTHERN CEMETERY, GERMANY.** Grave location:- Plot 15, Row A, Grave 9. His parents received a letter from a Captain Rosier, who wrote, *'No doubt you will wonder who I am and for what reason I am taking the liberty of writing to you. First of all I can state that I am English interpreter in the same party as your son Willie. I had not the pleasure of knowing your son long, only about two months and during that short time I always found him a good colleague. Unfortunately the time came when him above called one of his children home. Your dear son was only ill a matter of four days and everything possible was done for him but he passed away on 19th October in Gelsenkirchen Hospital from lung trouble.'* ROH:- Holme and Holmbridge War Memorial.

WHITEMAN, DANIEL. Private. No 33291. 12/13th Battalion Northumberland Fusiliers. Born 78 Northumberland Street, Huddersfield, 15.2.1896. Son of William Henry and Catherine Whiteman, 78 Northumberland Street, Huddersfield. Educated St. Patrick's Roman Catholic School. Employed as a labourer by the Huddersfield Brick and Tile Company. Single. Enlisted August 1916. Killed in action, 8.10.1918, aged 22 years. Buried **PROSPECT HILL CEMETERY, GOUY.** Grave location:- Plot 4, Row F, Grave 12.

WHITTAKER, CHARLIE. Private. No 235316. 9th Battalion Duke of Wellington's Regiment. Born Lindley, Huddersfield, 18.2.1887. Son of Mrs Mary Whittaker, 15 Plover Road, Lindley. Employed as a foreman finisher by Messrs Smith and Calverley, Wellington Mills, Lindley. Was secretary of the Lindley Conservative Club and a member of the Oakes Working Men's Club. He was a well known runner. Single. Enlisted 17.11.1916. Was a Stretcher-Bearer. Died of wounds at No 3 Casualty Clearing Station on 23.3.1918, aged 31 years. Buried **DERNANCOURT COMMUNAL CEMETERY EXTENSION.** Grave location:- Plot 3, Row J, Grave 76. ROH:- St. Stephen's Church, Lindley.

WHITAKER, FRED. Private. No 208030. 704th Company, Labour Corps. Born Outlane. Eldest son of the late Mr Ernest Whittaker and of Mrs Whittaker, 30 New North Road, Crimble, Slaithwaite. Employed as a night feeder by Messrs Pogson and Company, Bridge Street Mills, Slaithwaite. Attended Crimble Congregational Mission. Enlisted at the outbreak of the war. Died of pneumonia at No 42 Casualty Clearing Station on 5.11.1918, aged 23 years. Buried **DOUAI BRITISH CEMETERY.** Grave location:- Row A, Grave 21. ROH:- St. James Church, Slaithwaite; Slaithwaite War Memorial.

WHITTAKER, R. HERBERT. Gunner. No 775972. 'B' Battery, 310th Brigade, Royal Field Artillery. Born Pontefract. Only son of Mr and Mrs Sam Whittaker, 56 George Street, Milnsbridge. Employed as an operator at the Star Picture House, Castleford, where the family lived before moving to Milnsbridge. Died of wounds on 5.5.1917, aged 20 years. Buried **ACHIET-LE-GRAND COMMUNAL CEMETERY EXTENSION.** Grave location:- Plot 1, Row E, Grave 21. ROH:- Milnsbridge War Memorial; Longwood War Memorial.

WHITTAKER, WALTER. Guardsman. No 17125. Coldstream Guards. Born Dalton Green, Huddersfield, 11.4.1897. Son of William and Sarah Whittaker, 20 Dalton Green Lane, Huddersfield. Educated at Kirkheaton National School and Moldgreen School. Employed as a painter and decorator for Messrs T. B. and W. Chekayne, of Sheffield, where he lived. Enlisted in Sheffield on 3.11.1915. Killed in action at Boesinghe near Ypres on 18.6.1917, aged 38 years. Buried **ARTILLERY WOOD CEMETERY.** Grave location:- Plot 7, Row E, Grave 19. ROH:- St. John's Church, Kirkheaton.

WHITTAKER, WILLIAM. Private. No 6662. 2nd Battalion Duke of Wellington's Regiment. Born Clayton West near Huddersfield. Lived Clayton West. Killed in action on 11.11.1914 during the 1st Battle of Ypres. Has no known grave. Commemorated **MENIN GATE MEMORIAL TO THE MISSING.** The following extract is taken from the diary of Colonel E. G. Harrison (who was in command of the 2nd Battalion Duke of Wellington's Regiment at the time), *'Wednesday 11th November. – Exceptionally heavy shelling started 7am, practically all shrapnel, covering the whole position from the firing line to the reserves, continuing the bombardment till 8am when it abated. At this* time a message came to me by an orderly from Lieut. R. O. D. Carey, saying, 'Am very hard pressed but will hang on as long as possible.' I then advanced with the remainder of my force. We found the Germans had advanced past the Veldhoek Chateau, but we managed to repulse them, gaining back the ground, being nearly as far as our old firing line, which Lieut. R .O. D. Carey, with D Company, had been driven out of. We could have actually regained these trenches if the troops on the right and left of us had been up, but in this position behind a small rise in the ground our right rested on the Ypres-Menin Road, the next troops being about 300 yards in rear on the south side of the road. On our left a company of the Zouaves occupied a position between us and the next British troops on our left, but immediately after the advance, in which they materially assisted, they vacated the position, thus leaving both our flanks exposed. At 10am I sent back a message saying I could retake my original trenches if I had another Company in support, but got no reply until 3pm. I also sent two more messages, which, however, were never received. By this time we had dug ourselves in under a small bank some 60 yards from the Germans, who were occupying our old trenches. Our losses during the day were 8 officers and about 300 men. ROH:- Clayton West and High Hoyland War Memorial.*

WHITTELL, JOSEPH HAROLD. Rifleman. No S/10326. 3rd Battalion The Rifle Brigade. Born Scissett. Only son of Mrs and the late Mr J. P. Whittell, Highbridge House, Scissett. Employed as a dyer's apprentice by Messrs Thornton of Honley. Enlisted May 1915. Was wounded shortly after going to France in July, 1915. He also contracted typhoid and he was unable to join his Regiment until April, 1916. Killed in action on 1.9.1916 in the attack on Orchard and Tea Trenches at High Wood during the Battle of the Somme. (211 casualties). Buried **LONDON CEMETERY AND EXTENSION, LONGUEVAL.** Grave location:- Plot 9, Row B, Grave 5 ROH:- Scissett War Memorial.

WHITTERON, ROBERT. Private. No 1379. 10th Battalion Duke of Wellington's Regiment. Born Huddersfield. Son of William Whitteron, Halifax Old Road, Fartown. Married. Employed in the grocery department of the Hillhouse Cooperative Society. Enlisted at the outbreak of the war. Killed in action on 29.7.1916 in the attack on Munster Alley during the Battle of the Somme. (205 casualties). He was 32 years of age. Has no known grave. Commemorated **THIEPVAL MEMORIAL TO THE MISSING.** ROH:- Fartown and Birkby War Memorial.

WHITTLES, FREDERICK. Gunner. No 71418. 'D' Battery, 23rd Brigade, Royal Field Artillery. Born Huddersfield. Lived Clayton West. Killed in action, 5.4.1918. Buried **MOREUIL COMMUNAL CEMETERY ALLIED EXTENSION.** Grave location:- Row D, Grave 27. ROH:- Clayton West and High Hoyland War Memorial.

WHITWAM, ALBERT. Private. No 22163. 2nd Battalion King's Own Scottish Borderers. Born Golcar. Son of Elizabeth A. Whitehead and the late Tom Whitwam, 2 Kiln Brow, Golcar. Educated Crow Lane Board School, Milnsbridge. Employed by Messrs B. and J. Whitwam and Sons Limited, Golcar. Attended the Golcar Providence United Methodist Church. Was a member of the Young Men's Reading Room and the bible class. Enlisted 5.11.1915. Trained in Scotland. Embarked for France on 10.8.1916. Killed in action on 3.9.1916 in attack on Falfemont Farm during the Battle of the Somme, aged 21. *'Assembled on slopes of the Leuze Wood spur, some 400 yards from objective. Attack commenced 8.50am. – Official History of the Great War recording the task as 'impossible'. Battalion swept by rifle and machine gun fire in front and flank. Casualties – almost 300.'* Buried **DELVILLE WOOD CEMETERY.** Grave location:- Plot 27, Row B, Grave 10. ROH:- St. John's Church, Golcar; Crow Lane Board School, Milnsbridge.

WHITWAM, ALBERT EDWARD. Private. No 36247. 1st Battalion Northumberland Fusiliers. Born Golcar. Eldest son of David and Mary Whitwam, 59 Handel Street, Golcar. Employed at Heath House Mills, Golcar. Attended Golcar Baptist Chapel and was a member of the Young Men's Class. Enlisted 1916. Severely wounded in the shoulder on 11.4.1918. Died of wounds and tuberculosis of the lungs on 16.10.1918 at Whitkirk V.A.D. Auxiliary Hospital. He was 29 years of age. Buried **GOLCAR BAPTIST CHAPEL YARD.** Grave location:- SE, G, 8. ROH:- Golcar Baptist Chapel; St. John's Church, Golcar.

WHITWAM, ALBERT WILLIAM. Private. No 32972. 13th Battalion Durham Light Infantry. Born Golcar. Son of Henry and Lavina Whitwam, 88 Swallow Lane, Golcar. Attended Golcar Baptist Chapel. Was a member of the Golcar Cricket and Bowling Club. Employed by Messrs Pearson Brothers, Victoria Mills, Golcar. Enlisted 30.5.1916. Embarked for France in September, 1916. He was expected home on leave when he was killed in action on 20.9.1917 during the Battle of Passchendaele. He was 39 years of age. Buried **TYNE COT CEMETERY.** Grave location:- Plot 59, Row F, Grave 34. (Brother of Private **JOHN HENRY WHITWAM,** killed in action, 27.9.1918, q.v.). ROH:- Golcar Baptist Chapel; St. John's Church, Golcar.

WHITWAM, ARTHUR EDWARD. Armourers Crew. No M/16731. Royal Navy. *HMS Champagne.* Born Golcar. Son of Sam Edwin and Harriet H. Whitwam, 26 The Avenue, Golcar. Employed as a tuner by Messrs Middlemost Brothers, of Birkby. Attended Golcar Baptist Chapel and was a member of the Young Men's Reading Room. Enlisted in the Navy in 1915. On 1.10.1917 *HMS Champagne* left port and shortly after 6am the following morning was attacked by an enemy submarine and hit by about four torpedoes. A terrific explosion occurred which killed many of the men at the guns including Armourer Whitwam. 56 of the crew were drowned, the total number on board being about 310. The boat sank in ten minutes after being attacked. Has no known grave. Commemorated **PLYMOUTH NAVAL MEMORIAL TO THE MISSING.** ROH:- Golcar Baptist Chapel; St. John's Church, Golcar.

WHITWAM, FRIEND. Private. No 320823. 12th (Norfolk Yeomanry) Battalion Norfolk Regiment. Born Huddersfield. Killed in action in Palestine on 9.3.1918. Buried **JERUSALEM WAR CEMETERY.** Grave location:- Row J, Grave 94.

WHITWAM, HAROLD. Private. No 332779. 9th (Glasgow Highland) Battalion Highland Light Infantry. Born Golcar. Eldest son of Henry and Lavina Whitwam, 1 Waterhouse Farm, Scapegoat Hill, Golcar. Employed as a spinner by Messrs Pearson Brothers, Victoria Mills, Golcar. Attended Scapegoat Hill Baptist Chapel and Sunday School. Was a member of the Thorpe Green Working Men's Club. Enlisted in 1916. Came home on leave in November, 1917, having served in France for 12 months. Killed in action, 26.2.1918, aged 23 years. Buried **TYNE COT CEMETERY.** Grave location: Special Memorial No 3. His parents received a letter from a chum of their son, who wrote, *'I write to convey to you the sad news that your son Harold was killed in action during our last tour of the trenches. He met his death when he was going out at about 11.30 on the morning of the 26th February. A shell landed about three yards in front of him, killing him instantenously and wounding two others. Your son was always cheery with a kind word for each. He was a most respected lad in the platoon and a great favourite with us all.'*

WHITWAM, HAROLD ERNEST. Captain. 7th Battalion Duke of Wellington's Regiment. Born Golcar. Elder son of Mr and Mrs Joe Whitwam, Clifton House, Golcar. Was a member of the firm of Messrs B. and J. Whitwam and Sons Limited, Stanley Mills, Golcar. Attended St. John's Parish Church, Golcar and was a teacher and organist in the Sunday School. Had served in the Colne Valley Territorials for five years prior to the war. Embarked for France in April, 1915, as a Lieutenant. After six months service was invalided home suffering from gas poisoning. He then acted as instructor in musketry at Strensall, York, for more than 12 months. Returned to France in September, 1917. Killed in action on 9.10.1917 at the Battle of Passchendaele. He was 27 years of age. Has no known grave. Commemorated **TYNE COT MEMORIAL TO THE MISSING.** ROH:- St. John's Church, Golcar.

WHITWAM, HARRY. Rifleman. No C/7432. 18th Battalion King's Royal Rifle Corps. Born Golcar. Son of Mr and Mrs Fred Whitwam, 9 Church Street, Golcar. Employed in the office of Messrs John Crowther and Sons of Milnsbridge. Attended Golcar Baptist Chapel and Sunday School. Was a member of the Golcar Liberal Club. Enlisted 5.11.1915. Severely wounded on 5.12.1916 and died the same day. He was 19 years of age. Buried **DICKEBUSCH NEW MILITARY CEMETERY, BELGIUM.** Grave location:- Row M, Grave 9. ROH:- St. John's Church, Golcar.

WHITWAM, HERBERT. Lance Corporal. No 14625. 2nd Battalion Duke of Wellington's Regiment. Born Meltham, Huddersfield. Eldest son of Mr and Mrs Arthur Whitwam, 3 Laneside, Linthwaite. Was a member of the Linthwaite Church Young Men's Bible Class. Employed as a piecer by Messrs Stead and Mallinson, Bootham Hall Mills, Milnsbridge. Enlisted at Halifax on 15.11.1914. Embarked for France in April, 1915. Took part in the fighting on Hill 60 in May, 1915. Died of wounds at No 3 Casualty Clearing Station on 13.6.1915, aged 19 years. Buried **BAILLEUL COMMUNAL CEMETERY EXTENSION**. Grave location:- Plot 1, Row E, Grave 118. His parents received a letter from the Rev. F R G Fletcher, Church of England Chaplain, who wrote, *'It is my painful duty to send you very bad news of your son, Lance Corporal Whitwam, No 14625, 2nd Battalion Duke of Wellington's Regiment. He received very severe wounds in both legs while in action last week and was brought into this hospital in a dying condition. Both his legs were practically shattered and soon gangrene set in. Everything possible was at once done for him by both Doctors and Nurses but in spite of all efforts he passed away on June 13th. This I know will be a very sad blow to you and I pray that God may comfort you. Your son died a noble death – he was bravely doing his duty and like our Master he gave his life for the sake of others. So great was the shock to his system he was practically unconscious and passed away very quietly. He was buried in Bailleul Military Cemetery in grave No 1298 on Monday June 14th. A cross is erected at the head of the grave bearing his name, number, Regiment, date of death and an intimation of the fact that he died of wounds received in action. In the course of the burial service I recited these words which may bring a message of comfort to you, 'Greater love hath no man than this that a man lay down his life for his friends.*" ROH:- Linthwaite War Memorial.

WHITWAM, JOHN HENRY. Private. No 40629. 8th Battalion Northumberland Fusiliers. Born Golcar. Second son of Henry and Lavinia Whitwam, 88 Swallow Lane, Golcar. Attended Golcar Baptist Chapel. Killed in action, 27.9.1918, aged 35 years. Buried **CHAPEL CORNER CEMETERY, SAUCHY-LESTREE**. Grave location:- Row C, Grave 10. (Brother of Private **ALBERT WILLIAM WHITWAM**, killed in action, 20.9.1917, q.v.). ROH:- Golcar Baptist Chapel; St. John's Church, Golcar.

WHITWAM, LEONARD. Private. No S/23983. 7th Battalion The Cameron Highlanders. Born Marsh, Huddersfield. Son of the late Joseph and Eliza Ann Whitwam, formerly of the 'Royal Oak Hotel', Paddock. Educated Paddock Council School. Employed as a pattern cutter by Messrs Martin, Sons and Company. Single. Enlisted 15.11.1915. Reported missing, presumed killed, on 24.8.1917 at Passchendaele. Has no known grave. Commemorated **TYNE COT MEMORIAL TO THE MISSING**. ROH:- Oakes Baptist Church; St. Mark's Parish Church, Longwood; St. Stephen's Church, Lindley; Salendine Nook Chapel yard, 70E.

WHITWAM, NELSON. Sergeant. No 1908. 1/7th Battalion Duke of Wellington's Regiment. Born Golcar. Son of Herbert and Ellen Whitwam, of Golcar. Husband of Annie Whitwam, 92 Croft Terrace, Townend, Golcar. Died of wounds at No 10 Casualty Clearing Station on 4.10.1915, aged 27 years. Buried **LIJSSENTHOEK MILITARY CEMETERY**. Grave location:- Plot 1, Row C, Grave 36. ROH:- St. John's Church, Golcar; Huddersfield Drill Hall; memorial in Golcar Churchyard.

WHITWAM, TITUS, T. Private. No D/387571. Remount Depot, Army Service Corps. Born Golcar. Son of Ben and Sarah Ann Whitwam, 96 James Street, Golcar. Employed at Victoria Mills, Golcar. Attended Golcar Baptist Chapel and Sunday School. Was formerly a member of the Boys Brigade and the Golcar Conservative Club. Enlisted at the end of 1917. Was stationed at Ormskirk, Liverpool. Had been home on leave on one occasion. Was admitted to the Sparrow Hall Military Hospital, Liverpool, on Saturday morning, 11.1.1919, suffering from diphtheria. Died just after midnight on 12.1.1919, aged 19 years. Buried **GOLCAR BAPTIST CHAPEL YARD**. Grave location:- SE, 253. ROH:- Golcar Baptist Chapel; St. John's Church, Golcar.

WHITHAM, TOM. Private. No 202616. 9th Battalion King's Own Yorkshire Light Infantry. Born Meltham. Died at home, 10.12.1918. Buried **MELTHAM METHODIST BURIAL GROUND**. Grave location:- 2, 94. ROH:- St. Bartholomew's Church, Meltham.

WHITWAM, WALTER. Private. No 24777. 147th Company, Machine Gun Corps. Formerly

No 1832 Duke of Wellington's Regiment. Born Golcar. Fourth son of Mrs Whitwam, 86 Handel Street, Golcar. Employed as a weaver by Mr J. E. Crowther, Bank Bottom Mills, Marsden. Attended Golcar Baptist Chapel and was a member of the Young Men's Bible Class. He was also a member of the Golcar Liberal Club. Enlisted December 1914. Embarked for France in April, 1915. Died of wounds at No 20 Casualty Clearing Station on 2.12.1916, aged 22 years. Buried **WARLINCOURT HALTE BRITISH CEMETERY.** Grave location:- Plot 3, Row G, Grave 1. ROH:- Golcar Baptist Chapel; St. John's Church, Golcar.

WHITWAM, WILFRED. Private. No 307860. 1/7th Battalion Duke of Wellington's Regiment. Born Golcar. Killed in action, 29.4.1918. Has no known grave. Commemorated **TYNE COT MEMORIAL TO THE MISSING.** ROH:- St. John's Church, Golcar; Huddersfield Drill Hall.

WHITWORTH, FRANK. Private. No 306034. 2/7th Battalion Duke of Wellington's Regiment. Son of the late Edwin and Harriet Whitworth, Ashworth Road, Dewsbury. Husband of Agnes Whitworth, 17 Chapel Lane, Milnsbridge. Killed in action on 3.5.1917 at the Battle of Bullecourt. He was 37 years of age. Has no known grave. Commemorated **ARRAS MEMORIAL TO THE MISSING.** ROH:- Huddersfield Drill Hall.

WHOWELL, LEVI. Corporal. No 812109. 49th Battalion Canadian Infantry (Alberta Regiment). Born Liverpool. Son of Jesse and Eliza Ann Whowell of Paddock. Educated Paddock Church of England School. Lived Church Street, Paddock. Attended Paddock United Methodist Church. Employed by Mr Joe Inman, woollen merchant, New Street, Huddersfield and later with Messrs Dugdale Brothers and Company. Emigrated to Canada in 1902. Married. Enlisted 16.3.1916. Killed in action, 30.10.1917, on Passchendaele Ridge, aged 51 years. Buried **POELCAPELLE BRITISH CEMETERY.** Grave location:- Plot 10, Row A, Grave 4. ROH:- Shared Church, Paddock.

WIBBERLEY, FRED. Private. No 5533. 1/5th Battalion Duke of Wellington's Regiment. Born Austenley, Holmfirth, 29.3.1897. Son of George Wibberley, Greengate Farm, Greengates, Holmbridge. Employed at Bent Ley Silk Mills, Meltham Mills. Attended Hall Sunday School. Enlisted 29.3.1916. and went into training at Clipstone Camp. Embarked for France in August, 1916, and took part in the attack on the Schwaben Redboubt on 3.9.1916. Was wounded by a shell on 11.3.1917. Died of wounds on 13.3.1917 at No 33 Casualty Clearing Station. He was 19 years of age. Buried **BETHUNE TOWN CEMETERY.** Grave location:- Plot 6, Row C, Grave 7. ROH:- Holme and Holmbridge War Memorial; Huddersfield Drill Hall.

WICKSTEAD, JOHN. Corporal. No TT/0899. Army Veterinary Corps. Born Barton-on-Humber, Lincolnshire. Son of Mr B. Wickstead, Manor Houses, Meltham Mills, Huddersfield. Died at home, 14.1.1917. Buried **St. JAMES'S CHURCHYARD, MELTHAM MILLS.** Grave location:- East, H, 36. ROH:- St. Bartholomew's Church, Meltham.

WIDDOWSON, CLARENCE. Private. No 14490. 10th Battalion Duke of Wellington's Regiment. Born Cumberworth near Huddersfield. Son of Mrs A J Widdowson, Hillside, Denby Dale. Employed at Messrs Stringer and Jagger's colliery at Emley Moor. Killed in action at Munster Alley on 29.7.1916 during the Battle of the Somme (Casualties - 205). He was 24 years of age. Has no known grave. Commemorated **THIEPVAL MEMORIAL TO THE MISSING.** ROH:- Denby Dale and Cumberworth War Memorial.

WIDER, ALBERT EDWARD. Private. No 32624. 15th/17th Battalion West Yorkshire Regiment (1st Leeds Pals). Born Marsden. Second son of William Wider. Lived Sandhurst Cottages, Marsden. Employed by Messrs J and J Bottomley, plasterers and painters, of Marsden. Enlisted May 1916. Embarked for France November, 1916. Killed in action on 25.3.1918, near St. Leger, by the bursting of a shell. He was 37 years of age. Has no known grave. Commemorated **ARRAS MEMORIAL TO THE MISSING.** ROH:- Marsden War Memorial.

WIGHTMAN, JOHN JOSEPH. Private. No 305810. 2/7th Battalion Duke of Wellington's Regiment. Born Marsden Road, Huddersfield, 27.8.1893. Son of Thomas James and Livey Wightman, 165 Marsden Road, Huddersfield. Educated Crosland Moor Council School.

Employed as a journeyman by Mr Allen Towlson, fishmonger and poulterer, Westgate, Huddersfield, and was previously apprenticed to Mr Robert Wynn, Victoria Street, Huddersfield. Attended the Brierley Wood Wesleyan Mission. Single. Enlisted 11.10.1914. Wounded at Bourlon Wood on 28.11.1917 during the Battle of Cambrai. Died of wounds at No 5 General Hospital, Rouen, on 5.12.1917, aged 28 years. Buried **St. SEVER CEMETERY EXTENSION, ROUEN.** Grave location:- Block P, Plot 5, Row 1, Grave 9A. ROH:- Huddersfield Drill Hall.

WILCOCK, LEONARD. Corporal. No 7871. Depot Battalion King's Own Scottish Borderers. Son of John and Hannah Wilcock, of Ovenden, Halifax. Husband of Annie Wilcock, 1 Club Row, Armitage Bridge, Huddersfield. Had served 16 years in the Army prior to the outbreak of the war. He saw six years in India and was engaged in the Boxer rebellion in China. Was employed at the G.P.O. in Huddersfield. As a Reservist he was called up in August, 1914, and was stationed at Berwick-on-Tweed, where he acted as military postman and orderly in camp. Whilst in India he had contracted tuberculosis and he died of this disease at Doncaster on 20.7.1915, aged 37 years. Buried **DONCASTER CEMETERY.** Grave location:- Row 15, Grave 139. ROH:- Huddersfield G.P.O.; Armitage Bridge War Memorial.

WILCOCK, WILLIE. Private. No 240989. 2/5th Battalion Duke of Wellington's Regiment. Lived Denby Dale. Killed in action on 3.5.1917 at the Battle of Bullecourt. Has no known grave. Commemorated **ARRAS MEMORIAL TO THE MISSING.** ROH:- Huddersfield Drill Hall; Denby Dale and Cumberworth War Memorial.

WILD, FREDERICK. Acting Bombardier. No 140991. 'C' Battery, 155th Brigade, Royal Field Artillery. Born Hopton, Mirfield, 30.11.1917. Son of Ambrose and Emma Wild, 27 Tanfield Terrace, Birkby. Educated Thomas Street Board School. Employed as a traveller by Messrs Netherwood, Dalton and Company, printers, of Folly Hall, Huddersfield. Lived 53 Hillhouse Road, Huddersfield. Single. Enlisted 6.5.1916. Died of wounds at No 10 Casualty Clearing Station on 17.7.1917, aged 39 years. Buried **LIJSSENTHOEK MILITARY CEMETERY.** Grave location:- Plot 16, Row D, Grave 3.

ROH:- St. John's Church, Birkby; St. Andrew's Church, Leeds Road, Huddersfield; Fartown and Birkby War Memorial.

WILDBLOOD, WILLIAM ARTHUR. Lieutenant. 24th Divisional Train, Army Service Corps (Horse Transport). Born Bridport, Dorset, 25.3.1889. Son of the Rev. Peter Charles Wildblood, Wesleyan Minister, of Grimsby and formerly of the Buxton Road circuit, Huddersfield, and Marion Wildblood. Educated Halifax Secondary School, left 1904, and Kingswood School, Bath. Was the holder of a Jones history scholarship at Manchester University, where he was awarded the M.A. (honours degree). Employed as a master at the Huddersfield Municipal Secondary School, Huddersfield, from October, 1912, until Easter, 1914. Played with the Huddersfield first team at cricket and rugby with the Waterloo Rugby Union Football Club. At the outbreak of the was was a master at Colston's School, near Bristol. Enlisted in October, 1914, as a Trooper in the Inns of Court Cavalry Squadron, Berkhamsted. Embarked for France in August, 1915. Killed in action on 16.6.1917 by shellfire at the military railhead near Ouderdom village, south of Ypres, Belgium. He was 28 years of age. Buried **RENINGHELST NEW MILITARY CEMETERY.** Grave location:- Plot 2, Row E, Grave 26. ROH:- Waterloo Rugby Union Football Club; Mount Pleasant Chapel, Lockwood; Halifax Civic Book of Remembrance; Halifax Secondary School.

WILDE, FREDERICK GEORGE. Air Mechanic 1st Class. No 43733. Air Supply Depot. Royal Flying Corps. Husband of Ann Wilde, 13 Heath House, Golcar. Died at home, 9.1.1918, aged 36 years. Buried **St. JOHN'S CHURCHYARD, GOLCAR.** Grave location:- A, (North-West), 79. ROH:- St. John's Church, Golcar.

WILDE, THOMAS. Private. No 265. 31st Battalion Australian Infantry. Born Linthwaite, Huddersfield. Son of Mr Jonas Wilde, Wilde Brow, Linthwaite. Before going out to Australia in 1913, was engaged in farming at Wood Nook, Meltham. In Australia he worked on a sheep station in Queensland. Enlisted in 1916 and arrived in France in November, 1916. Was over on leave at Linthwaite in the Spring of 1917, after being in hospital suffering from trench feet. Died of wounds at No 3 General Hospital, Le

Treport, on 2.10.1917, aged 25 years. Buried **MONT HUON MILITARY CEMETERY.** Grave location:- Plot 4, Row O, Grave 8A. ROH:- Linthwaite War Memorial; memorial in Christ Church, Linthwaite.

WILDS, FRANK. Private. No 23034. 13th Battalion The Yorkshire Regiment. Born Manchester 30.9.1893. Son of Frank and Annie Wilds, 18 Victoria Street, Lockwood, Huddersfield. Educated at Manchester schools. Employed as an iron fettler by Messrs Calvert and Company, Folly Hall. Single. Enlisted 25.7.1915. Killed in action, 26.5.1917, aged 24 years. Has no known grave. Commemorated **THIEPVAL MEMORIAL TO THE MISSING.** (Brother of Private **JAMES WILDS,** killed in action, 31.7.1917, q.v.). ROH:- St. Stephen's Church, Rashcliffe.

WILDS, FRANK. Private. No 240522. 2/5th Battalion Duke of Wellington's Regiment. Born Hampshire. Married. Lived 62 Wellington Street, Oakes, Huddersfield. Employed as a tram conductor by the Huddersfield Corporation Tramways Department. Killed in action on 3.5.1917 during the Battle of Bullecourt. He was 27 years of age. Has no known grave. Commemorated **ARRAS MEMORIAL TO THE MISSING.** ROH:- St. Stephen's Church, Lindley; Huddersfield Drill Hall; Huddersfield Corporation Roll.

WILDS, JAMES. Private. No 36121. 17th Battalion Manchester Regiment (2nd Manchester Pals). Born Manchester in 1897. Son of Frank and Annie Wilds, 18 Victoria Street, Lockwood, Huddersfield. Educated at Manchester schools. Employed as a warehouseman. Single. Enlisted May 1915. Reported missing, presumed killed, on 31.7.1917 near Stirling Castle during the Battle of Passchendaele. Has no known grave. Commemorated **MENIN GATE MEMORIAL TO THE MISSING.** (Brother of Private **FRANK WILDS,** killed in action, 26.5.1917, q.v.). ROH:- St. Stephen's Church, Rashcliffe.

WILES, THOMAS. Private. No 50778. 1/6th Battalion Lancashire Fusiliers. Formerly No 45195 York and Lancaster Regiment. Born Wakefield. Married. Lived 18 Fisher's Fold, Longroyd Bridge, Huddersfield. Employed as a fine dresser by Messrs W. C. Holmes and Company Limited of Turnbridge, Huddersfield. Died whilst a Prisoner of War in German hands on 1.4.1918. Buried **PREMONT BRITISH CEMETERY.** Grave location:- Plot 4, Row B, Grave 37.

WILKINSON, ALBERT. Private. No 29/354. 25th (Tyneside Irish) Battalion Northumberland Fusiliers. Born Huddersfield. Son of Mr S. Wilkinson, New Street, Netherton, Huddersfield. Employed as a teamer by the Anglo-American Oil Company Limited. Attended South Crosland Church. Killed in action, 12.10.1917, at Poelcapelle during the Battle of Passchendaele. Buried **CEMENT HOUSE CEMETERY, LANGEMARCK, BELGIUM.** Grave location:- Plot 1, Row K, Grave 3. ROH:- South Crosland and Netherton War Memorial.

WILKINSON, ALBERT. Private. No 2547. 2/8th Battalion The Royal Scots Fusiliers, transferred to No 147506 Labour Corps. Born Sowerby. Son of James and Mary A. Wilkinson. Husband of Rose A. Wilkinson, 333 Radcliffe Road, Crimble, Slaithwaite. Employed as a woollen spinner by Messrs W. and E. Crowther, Brook Mills, Crimble, Slaithwaite. Was a member of the Vineyard Working Men's Club. Enlisted November 2nd, 1916. Trained in various parts of England and Scotland. Had been in hospital in Glasgow since February, 1917, suffering from a tumour. Died on Sunday 10.6.1917 in Glasgow Military Hospital, aged 41 years. Buried **SLAITHWAITE CEMETERY.** Grave location:- B, 2, 158. ROH:- St. James Church, Slaithwaite; Slaithwaite War Memorial.

WILKINSON, ALBERT ERNEST. Private. No 37888. 10th Battalion York and Lancaster Regiment. Born Newsome, Huddersfield, 25.2.1898. Only son of Ruth Wilkinson, 66 Towngate, Newsome. Educated Newsome National School. Employed as a cloth finisher by Messrs Lockwood and Keighley, Upperhead Mills, Huddersfield. Was a member of Newsome Working Men's Club. Single. Enlisted 18.10.1916. Killed in action, 13.10.1917, during the Battle of Passchendaele. He was 19 years of age. Has no known grave. Commemorated **TYNE COT MEMORIAL TO THE MISSING.** ROH:- Newsome United Methodist Church; St. John's Church, Newsome.

WILKINSON, ARTHUR. Corporal. No 267618. 1/7th Battalion Duke of Wellington's Regiment. Born Slaithwaite, Huddersfield, in 1893. Second son of Mr and Mrs Clarence W. Wilkinson, Rose Cottage, Outlane. Educated Huddersfield College Secondary School. Was by profession a teacher of music and was organist at Salendine Nook Baptist Church. He was a Fellow of the Royal College of Organists and a L.R.C.M. Whilst in training he formed a concert party and also gave recitals in the vicinity of the camps. Single. Enlisted June 1917. Killed in action, 11.4.1918. Has no known grave. Commemorated **TYNE COT MEMORIAL TO THE MISSING.** (Brother of Lance Corporal **STANLEY WILKINSON**, died of wound,s 21.7.1918, q.v.). ROH:- Outlane Trinity Methodist Church; Salendine Nook Church; Huddersfield Drill Hall; memorial in Salendine Nook Churchyard; 423E. *'they fought, they died, they live.'* Plaque adjacent to the organ in the Chapel.

WILKINSON, DAVID. Private. No 14391. 'Y' Company, 8th Battalion Duke of Wellington's Regiment. Born Netherthong, Holmfirth. Lived with his sister, Mrs M. Hoyle at Deanhouse, Holmfirth. Employed as a millhand. Enlisted at the outbreak of the war. Died of wounds at Alexandria, Egypt, on 9.9.1915, received at Gallipoli. He was 29 years of age. Buried **CHATBY WAR MEMORIAL CEMETERY, ALEXANDRIA, EGYPT.** Grave location:- Row H, Grave 22. ROH:- Netherthong and Thongsbridge War Memorial; Netherthong Working Men's Club.

WILKINSON, FELIX. Private. No 32626. 15th Battalion West Yorkshire Regiment (Leeds Pals). Born Litton. Son of Mrs Jane Wilkinson, Park View, Kirkburton, Huddersfield. Killed in action on 3.5.1917 in the attack on Gavrelle during the Battle of Arras. Has no known grave. Commemorated **ARRAS MEMORIAL TO THE MISSING.** (Brother of Private **GEORGE EMSLEY WILKINSON, MM,** died of wounds, 26.7.1918, q.v.). ROH:- All Hallows Parish Church, Kirkburton; commemorated on headstone in Kirkburton Churchyard, and on a plaque in Conistone Church, Wharfedale.

WILKINSON, FRANK. Private. No 136997. 32nd Battalion Machine Gun Corps. Formerly No 60612 West Yorkshire Regiment. Born Marsden, Huddersfield. Only son of Mrs George Wilkinson, 'Junction Inn', Marsden. Employed as a carding engineer at Bank Bottom Mills, Marsden. In his leisure time was a keen student of natural history. Enlisted May 1917. Crossed to France eight weeks later. Suffered from a flesh wound in the arm on 3.6.1918. Was wounded again in the leg on 11.6.1918. Admitted to the Australian General Hospital, Rouen, where his leg was amputated. Died of wounds, 15.6.1918, aged 19 years. Buried **St. SEVER CEMETERY EXTENSION, ROUEN.** Grave location:- Block Q, Plot 2, Row G, Grave 22. His mother received a letter from a Major, who wrote, *'Your son passed away this evening. Amputation of his right leg had been done to try and save his life but unfortunately without avail. His end was painless and very peaceful. All who had anything to do with him feel keenly the loss of so fine a young man.'* ROH:- Marsden War Memorial; memorial in Marsden Churchyard.

WILKINSON, GEORGE. Private. No 32423. 2/4th Battalion South Lancashire Regiment. Born Cawthorne, Barnsley, 23.7.1889. Son of Walter and Frances E. Wilkinson, 6 Adelphi Road, Marsh, Huddersfield. Educated Cawthorne Church of England School and the New Higher Board School, Milnsbridge. Employed as a motor driver/mechanic by Mr F Thomas of Honley. Single. Enlisted May 1916. Killed in action near Langemarck on 6.11.1917, aged 28 years. Has no known grave. Commemorated **TYNE COT MEMORIAL TO THE MISSING.** ROH:- St. Stephen's Church, Lindley.

WILKINSON, GEORGE EMSLEY, MM. Sergeant. No 240112. 2/5th Battalion Duke of Wellington's Regiment. Born Litton. Son of Jane Wilkinson, Park View, Kirkburton. Employed by Messrs Taylor and Hobson, cabinet makers, of Huddersfield. Was mobilised with other Territorials at the outbreak of the war. Was awarded the Military Medal on 19.2.1917 for bravery in the field. Died of wounds on 26.7.1918, aged 23 years. Buried **VERTUS COMMUNAL CEMETERY.** Grave Location:- Grave No 79. (Brother of Private **FELIX WILKINSON,** killed in action, 3.5.1917, q.v.). ROH:- All Hallows Parish Church, Kirkburton; Huddersfield Drill Hall; commemorated on headstone in Kirkburton Churchyard, and on a plaque in Conistone Church, Wharfedale.

WILKINSON, GEORGE HENRY. Private. No 204391. 4th Battalion Bedfordshire Regiment. Born Folly Hall, Huddersfield, 10.12.1883. Son of Mr J. Wilkinson, 16 Rawthorpe Terrace, Dalton, Huddersfield. Educated Spring Grove Board School and Huddersfield Higher Grade School. Left Huddersfield in 1907 to work as an Insurance Superintendent for the London and Manchester Assurance Company, in Peterborough and Harwich. Was very well known in Peterborough musical circles. Married. His wife was the daughter of Mr Cartwright, grocer, of Moldgreen. Lived 250 Lincoln Road, Peterborough. Enlisted 7.1.1917. Killed in action near Arras on 7.7.1917. Buried **ALBUERA CEMETERY, BAILLEUL-SIRE-BERTHOULT.** Grave location:- Row A, Grave 18. ROH:- Christ Church, Moldgreen; Commemorated on his parents' headstone in Edgerton Cemetery, Huddersfield.

WILKINSON, HARRY. Private. No 58609. Royal Army Medical Corps, attached *HM Hospital Ship Galeka*. Born Brian Street, Lindley, 18.10.1885. Son of Mrs Wilkinson, 29 George Street, Lindley. Educated Oakes Council School. Employed as a weaver at Wellington Mills, Oakes, Huddersfield. Attended the Lindley Zion United Methodist Church. Husband of Annie Wilkinson, 13 Temple Street, Lindley. Enlisted 12.5.1915. Drowned at sea on 28.10.1916 when *HM Hospital Ship Galeka* was mined, five miles north west of Cape la Hague. He was 31 years of age. Buried **Ste. MARIE CEMETERY, LE HAVRE.** Grave location:- 'Galeka' Memorial. ROH:- Lindley Zion United Methodist Church; St. Stephen's Church, Lindley.

WILKINSON, HARRY. Private. No 45920. 12/13th Battalion Northumberland Fusiliers. Born Wibsey, Bradford. Married. Lived 36 Luck Lane, Marsh, Huddersfield. Employed as a hairdresser by Mr Barlow, Lion Arcade, Huddersfield. After enlisting he was engaged as a Company barber in his Regiment. Reported missing, presumed killed, on 4.10.1917. Has no known grave. Commemorated **TYNE COT MEMORIAL TO THE MISSING.**

WILKINSON, HARRY. Lance Corporal. No 32076. 8th Battalion York and Lancaster Regiment. Formerly No 3939 Yorkshire Dragoons. Lived 78 Norman Road, Birkby, Huddersfield. Killed in action, 7.6.1917. Has no known grave. Commemorated **MENIN GATE MEMORIAL TO THE MISSING.** ROH:- St. Hilda's Church, Cowcliffe; Fartown and Birkby War Memorial.

WILKINSON, NORMAN. Private. No 202960. 1/4th Battalion Duke of Wellington's Regiment. Born Lidget Street, Lindley, Huddersfield, 3.5.1892. Youngest son of Mr and Mrs F. Wilkinson, 59 Thorncliffe Street, Lindley. Married. Lived 72 Alder Street, Bradford Road, Huddersfield. Employed as a credit draper. Attended the Lindley Zion United Methodist Church. Enlisted July 1916. Killed in action near Ypres, Belgium, on 29.12.1917, aged 25 years. Buried **HOOGE CRATER CEMETERY.** Grave location:- Plot 4, Row A, Grave 10. ROH:- Lindley Zion United Methodist Church; St. Stephen's Church, Lindley.

WILKINSON, PERCY. Lieutenant. 6th Battalion Lancashire Fusiliers, attached 2/7th Battalion Royal Warwickshire Regiment. Was assistant master at the Neilds School, Slaithwaite. He was a member of the Slaithwaite Cricket Club, the Slaithwaite and District Golf Club and the Slaithwaite Y.M.C.A. Attended the Zion Baptist Church. Enlisted in the Durham Light Infantry as a Private in November, 1914. Was granted a commission in the Lancashire Fusiliers as a Second Lieutenant at Christmas, 1915, becoming a full Lieutenant in July 1917. He first embarked for France in July 1916. Married in 1917. His wife lived at 6 Brook Terrace, Slaithwaite. Killed in action, 4.12.1917, in the attack on La Vacquerie during the Battle of Cambrai. He was 27 years of age. Has no known grave. Commemorated **CAMBRAI MEMORIAL TO THE MISSING.** His wife received a letter from the Colonel of his Regiment, who wrote, *'The enemy made a determined attack on one trench about 2pm. That part of the line which was attacked was held by your husband's company. He organised a party to counter-attack and successfully led it, ejecting the enemy but whilst at the head of the party he was killed by bombs thrown by the enemy. Three bombs fell at his feet almost simultaneously and he appears to have been killed instantly. It was at the time impossible to recover his body and the following day the Regiment was relieved after a very hard fight over the same ground. I have hopes that we may be able to recover it for burial. The sympathy of the*

Regiment is with you in your great bereavement. Your husand was devoted to his men and beloved by them. He had only soldiered with me for a few weeks. I quickly picked him out for command of a Company and was never better served by any Company Commander. He was one of the best Officers I have ever served with - quiet, cool, brave and possessing my utmost confidence. His death is a great loss to the Regiment and to me a bitter blow. His gallantry during these recent operations was very fine.' ROH:- Carr Lane United Methodist Church, Slaithwaite; St. James Church, Slaithwaite; Slaithwaite War Memorial.

WILKINSON, STANLEY. Lance Corporal. No 241103. 2/5th Battalion Duke of Wellington's Regiment. Born Linthwaite, Huddersfield in 1888. Eldest son of Mr and Mrs C. W. Wilkinson, Rose Cottage, Outlane. Educated Huddersfield College Secondary School. Employed as a clerk by the Huddersfield Building Society. Single. Enlisted April 1915. Wounded on 20.7.1918 whilst tending the wounded on the battlefield. Died of wounds on 21.7.1918, aged 29. Buried **TERLINCTHUN BRITISH CEMETERY.** Grave location:- Plot 17, Row A, Grave 25. (Brother of Corporal **ARTHUR WILKINSON,** killed in action, 11.4.1918, q.v.). ROH:- Outlane Trinity Methodist Church; Huddersfield Drill Hall; memorial in Salendine Nook Churchyard. 423E – 'They fought, they died, they live.'

WILKINSON, STANLEY. Lance Corporal. No 2551. 2/5th Battalion Duke of Wellington's Regiment. Born Lockwood, Huddersfield. Son of Fred and Frances Wilkinson, 73 Woodfield Road, Lockwood. Was shot accidentally by a comrade and died at the Selby Cottage Hospital on 18.4.1915, aged 17 years. Buried **LOCKWOOD CEMETERY, HUDDERSFIELD.** Grave location:- A, 314. *It appears that Wilkinson was in the Guard Room on Monday night with the guard who was going off duty. One of them then unloaded his rifle which he placed on the guardroom table. Another soldier placed the unloaded rifle against the loaded one. The Commanding Officer was going to inspect the guard when the order 'Guard – turn out' was given the man who had placed the unloaded rifle on the table picked up what he thought was his own rifle. Noticing it was cocked he pulled the trigger with the result that the rifle which was loaded went off and the bullet, striking Wilkinson just above the thigh, inflicted a fatal wound.* ROH:- Emmanuel Church, Lockwood; Huddersfield Drill Hall; Armitage Bridge War Memorial.

WILKINSON, THOMAS. Gunner. No L/28038. 'A' Battery, 168th (Huddersfield) Brigade, Royal Field Artillery. Born Linthwaite. Married. Lived 9 Back Fold, Uppercloough, Linthwaite. Employed at Messrs James Dyson's dyeworks, Linthwaite. Was a member of the Hoyle Ing Working Men's Club. Killed in action, 24.10.1917, aged 30 years. Buried **St. JULIEN DRESSING STATION CEMETERY, BELGIUM.** Grave location:- Plot 1, Row D, Grave 9. ROH:- Linthwaite War Memorial.

WILKINSON, WALTER STERICKER. Private. No DM2/207407. 181st Mechanical Transport Company, Army Service Corps. Born Ravensknowle Road, Moldgreen, Huddersfield, 15.2.1885. Son of John William and Maria Wilkinson, of Dalton. Educated Moldgreen National School and Huddersfield Higher Grade School. Husband of Ethel Wilkinson, 22 Grange Avenue, Marsden. Employed as a textile instructor. Enlisted 28.8.1916. Killed by a landslide in a quarry near Bray on the 1.1.1917, aged 31 years. Buried **HEILLY STATION CEMETERY.** Grave location:- Plot 6, Row H, Grave 12. ROH:- Commemorated on headstone in Kirkheaton Cemetery.

WILKS, GEORGE ERNEST. Private. No 26477, 3rd Battalion York and Lancaster Regiment. Transferred to No 168615 Labour Corps. Born Huddersfield. Enlisted Halifax. Died at home, 3.11.1918. Buried **EDGERTON CEMETERY, HUDDERSFIELD.** Grave location:- 30, 168C. ROH:- St. Andrew's Church, Leeds Road, Huddersfield, Fartown and Birkby War Memorial.

WILLIAMS, FRED STANLEY. Rifleman. No C/12822. 21st Battalion King's Royal Rifle Corps. Born The Storth, Linthwaite, Huddersfield, 13.4.1888. Son of Mary Brook, 14 Dudley Road, Marsh. Educated Paddock Church of England School. Was a teacher at Paddock National School. He was a member of the Paddock Church choir. Had been a year at teacher training college in Leeds when he enlisted in December 1915. Killed in action on 15.9.1916 in the attack on Flers during the Battle of the Somme. Buried **A.I.F.**

BURIAL GROUND, FLERS. Grave location:- Plot 10, Row D, Grave 2. ROH:- Marsh War Memorial; All Saints Church, Paddock.

WILLIAMS, GEORGE. Private. No 21457. 1st Battalion Northumberland Fusiliers. Born Leeds. Son of Robert and Ann Williams of Leeds. Educated at Leeds schools. Husband of Lottie Williams, 212 Halifax Old Road, Birchencliffe, Huddersfield. Employed as a brick drawer by the Brick and Tile Company, Birchencliffe. Killed in action, 3.8.1915, aged 30 years. Buried **POTIJZE CHATEAU LAWN CEMETERY, BELGIUM.** Grave location:- Row E, Grave 38. ROH:- St. Philip's Church, Birchencliffe.

WILLIAMS, JOHN (JACK). Private. No 26754. 10th Battalion Duke of Wellington's Regiment. Born Farnworth, Bolton, 30.3.1898. Son of Elizabeth Williams, 103 Leeds Road, Bradley, Huddersfield. Educated St. Thomas's Church of England School, Bradley. Employed as a patent glazier. Single. Enlisted 8.10.1916. Died of wounds on 20.9.1917 at No 37 Casualty Clearing Station. He was 19 years of age. Buried **GODEWAERSVELDE BRITISH CEMETERY.** Grave location:- Plot 1, Row E, Grave 19. ROH:- St. Thomas's Church, Bradley.

WILLIAMSON, ARTHUR ERNEST. Lance Corporal. No 12959. 9th Battalion Duke of Wellington's Regiment. Born Crich, Derbyshire. Lodged with Mr Fenton-Smith of Highfield, Shepley. Employed by Mr Harris Wood at the Brick and Tile Works, Lower Cumberworth. Attended Birdsedge Wesleyan Reform Chapel and was a member of the choir. His fiancé lived in Birdsedge. Killed in action 2.3.1916. Has no known grave. Commemorated **MENIN GATE MEMORIAL TO THE MISSING.** ROH:- Shepley War Memorial; Denby Dale and Cumberworth War Memorial.

WILLIAMSON, GEORGE. Private. No 38456. 15th Battalion West Yorkshire Regiment (1st Leeds Pals). Born Lower Castle Hill, Almondbury, Huddersfield, 19.2.1884. Son of Harriet Williamson, 2 Bank Top, Lowerhouses Lane, Almondbury. Educated Lowerhouses Church of England School. Was in business on his own account as a stationer and newsagent at 10 Somerset Bridge, Moldgreen. Single. Enlisted October 1916. Killed in action on 3.5.1917 at Gavrelle during the Battle of Arras. Has no known grave. Commemorated **ARRAS MEMORIAL TO THE MISSING.** ROH:- Almondbury War Memorial; Lowerhouses War Memorial.

WILSON, ARTHUR. Private. No 126853. 7th Training Reserve Battalion, transferred to No 597002 Labour Corps. Born Huddersfield. Son of Charles Wilson. Husband of Florence Wilson (later Berry), 'Hazeldene', 10 Greenhead Lane, Dalton, Huddersfield. Died at home, 13.8.1918, aged 38. Buried **ALMONDBURY CEMETERY, HUDDERSFIELD.** Grave location:- 6, 'C', 46. ROH:- Almondbury War Memorial.

WILSON, ARTHUR LAWRENCE. Private. No 141862. 56th Company Machine Gun Corps. Formerly No 554110 London Regiment. Born Louth, Lincolnshire. Lived Clayton West near Huddersfield. Died of wounds, 28.3.1918. Has no known grave. Commemorated **ARRAS MEMORIAL TO THE MISSING.** ROH:- Clayton West and High Hoyland War Memorial; Scissett War Memorial.

WILSON, BERTIE. Gunner. No 140945. 1st Reserve Brigade, Royal Field Artillery. Born Lepton, Huddersfield, 12.4.1890. Educated Lepton Council School. Employed as a woollen spinner. Husband of E. E. Wilson, 20 Longwood Road, Huddersfield. Enlisted May 1916. Died on 23.10.1916 at Huddersfield Royal Infirmary. Buried **EDGERTON CEMETERY, HUDDERSFIELD.** Grave location:- 11B, 125. ROH:- St. John's Church, Kirkheaton; St. Mark's Parish Church, Longwood.

WILSON, CHARLES HENRY. Captain. 5th Battalion King's Own Yorkshire Light Infantry. Born Crosland Road, Crosland Moor, Huddersfield, 21.2.1894. Son of Herbert Henry and Jane Wilson, 2 Bland Street, Lockwood. Educated Mount Pleasant Council School, Almondbury Grammar School and Huddersfield Technical College, where he obtained a BA degree in art and literature, as an external student of London University, at the age of 19 years. Enlisted as a Private in the Royal Welsh Fusiliers on 13.11.1914. Obtained his commission in the K.O.Y.L.I. and served with them in France during the whole of 1917. After serving in Ireland for a few months he returned to France in June 1918. Was wounded on 29.10.1918 at Marcoing near Cambrai. Admitted into No 56 Casualty Clearing Station, where he died of wounds on 30.9.1918, aged 24 years. Buried **GREVILLERS BRITISH CEMETERY**. Grave location:- Plot 15, Row A, Grave 20. ROH:- St. Stephen's Church, Rashcliffe; Lockwood Baptist Church; memorial in Lockwood Cemetery.

WILSON, CLEMENT ARTHUR. Private. No 24990. 10th Battalion Duke of Wellington's Regiment. Born Launceston Street, Halifax, 5.10.1891. Son of Edwin and Annie Wilson, 107 North Street, Lockwood, Huddersfield. Educated Newsome Church of England School. Employed as a locomotive engineer by the London and North Western Railway Company. At the time of enlistment, was living at 45 Colne Road, Damside, Huddersfield. Single. Enlisted in the local Territorial battalion in June 1908. Wounded on two occasions. Reported missing, presumed killed, near Hooge on 20.9.1917, aged 25 years. Has no known grave. Commemorated **TYNE COT MEMORIAL TO THE MISSING**. ROH:- Spiritualist's National Church, Huddersfield; London and North Western Railway Company Roll.

WILSON, ERNEST. Private 2nd Class. No 234743 Marine Observer School. Royal Naval Air Service and Royal Air Force. Born Huddersfield. Youngest son of Frank H. and Annie Wilson, 'Hillthorpe', 78 Fitzwilliam Street, Huddersfield. Died on 10.10.1918 at the Royal Naval Hospital, Gillingham, Chatham, Kent, aged 23 years. Buried **EDGERTON CEMETERY, HUDDERSFIELD**. Grave location:- 48, 300C. ROH:- St. Paul's Church, Southgate, Huddersfield.

WILSON, FRANK HAYDN. Private. No 14900. 2nd Battalion Duke of Wellington's Regiment. Born 33 Nettleton Road, Dalton, Huddersfield, 29.8.1888. Son of Wright and Mary Wilson, 33 Nettleton Road, Dalton. Educated Kirkheaton National School. Employed as a warehouseman by Messrs R. Mitchell and Company, Spa Mills, Lepton. Was a member of the Dalton Liberal and Bowling Club. Single. Enlisted 29.11.1914. Was wounded in July, 1916, at the Battle of the Somme. He received treatment at a London hospital. Returned to France in March, 1917. Reported missing, presumed killed, on 3.5.1917, aged 29 years. Commemorated **FRANCE (1917–1918) MEMORIAL** (Brother of Private **JAMES SCHOFIELD WILSON**, died of wounds, 20.7.1917, q.v.). ROH:- St. John's Church, Kirkheaton.

WILSON, FRED. Private. No 32489. 8th Battalion York and Lancaster Regiment. Born Prospect Place, Huddersfield, 8.1.1898. Son of William Henry and Miranda Wilson, 17a Calton Street, Huddersfield. Educated Thomas Street Council School. Employed by his father as a wholesale fruiterer. Single. Enlisted 29.1.1917. Wounded near Ypres on 29.5.1917. Died of wounds on 30.5.1917, aged 19 years. Buried **BEDFORD HOUSE ENCLOSURE No 4**. Grave location:- Special Memorial 40. ROH:- Great Northern Street Congregational Chapel; Fartown and Birkby War Memorial.

WILSON, GILBERT. Private. No 50217. 2/5th Battalion West Yorkshire Regiment. Born Lowergate, Longwood, Huddersfield, 21.8.1887. Son of Harry and Elizabeth Wilson, 50 Broomfield Road, Marsh. Educated Paddock Council School. Employed by Messrs J Hopkinson and Company Limited of Birkby. Attended Queen Street Chapel. Husband of Edith Wilson, 334 Bradford Road North, Huddersfield. Enlisted 20.12.1916. Reported missing, presumed killed, on 22.11.1917 during the Battle of Cambrai, aged 30. Has no known grave. Commemorated **CAMBRAI MEMORIAL TO THE MISSING**. ROH:- Fartown and Birkby War Memorial.

WILSON, HARRY. Corporal. No 34804. 86th Brigade, Royal Field Artillery. Born Cowcliffe, Huddersfield, 9.4.1890. Son of John Richard and Sarah Ann Wilson, 9 Garden Street, Lockwood Road, Huddersfield. Educated Rashcliffe Church of England School. Employed as a mason's labourer by Messrs Radcliffe, St. John's Road, Huddersfield. Single. Enlisted 2.9.1914. Died of wounds on 3.5.1918, aged 28 years. Buried **CROUY BRITISH CEMETERY**. Grave location:- Plot 1, Row D, Grave 2. ROH:- St. Stephen's Church, Rashcliffe.

WILSON, HUBERT. Private. No 19681. 2nd Battalion Duke of Wellington's Regiment. Born Halifax. Lived Lepton, Huddersfield. Killed in action, 2.9.1916. Has no known grave. Commemorated **MENIN GATE MEMORIAL TO THE MISSING**. ROH:- Lepton Parish Church.

WILSON, JAMES SCHOFIELD. Private. No 241025. 'A' Company, 2/5th Battalion Duke of Wellington's Regiment. Born 33 Nettleton Road, Dalton, Huddersfield 21.10.1891. Son of Wright and Mary Wilson, 33 Nettleton Road, Dalton. Educated Kirkheaton National School. Employed as a power loom weaver by Messrs R. Mitchell and Company, Spa Mills, Lepton. Husband of May Wilson, Lascelles Hall, Kirkheaton. Was a member of the Dalton Liberal and Bowling Club. Enlisted 14.1.1915. Died of wounds on 18.7.1917, aged 25 years. Buried **FAVREUIL BRITISH CEMETERY.** Grave location:- Plot 1, Row A, Grave 18. (Brother of Private **FRANK HAYDN WILSON,** reported missing, 3.5.1917, q.v.). ROH:- St. John's Church, Kirkheaton; All Hallows Parish Church, Kirkburton; Huddersfield Drill Hall.

WILSON, JOHN EDWARD. Private. No 29486. 14th Battalion Highland Light Infantry. Formerly No 23464 The Yorkshire Regiment. Born London. Lived Kirkheaton, Huddersfield. Killed in action, 13.8.1916. Buried **VERMELLES BRITISH CEMETERY.** Grave location:- Plot 3, Row N, Grave 18. ROH:- St. John's Church, Kirkheaton.

WILSON, THOMAS JAMES. 2nd Lieutenant. 295th Brigade, Royal Field Artillery. Formerly Corporal Royal Engineers. Born 14 Easwold Bank, Kilbarchan, 8.5.1893. Educated Falkirk High School; Broughton Higher Grade School, Edinburgh; Herriott Watt College, Edinburgh. Employed as an analyst. Married. Enlisted 2.7.1915. Killed in action, 21.3.1918. Has no known grave. Commemorated **ARRAS MEMORIAL TO THE MISSING.** ROH:- St. James's Presbyterian Church, Huddersfield.

WILSON, WILLIAM CALVERT. Private. No 62346. 10th Battalion Royal Defence Corps. Born 4 Learoyd's Row, Leeds Road, Huddersfield, 21.3.1878. Son of Mrs Saville of Turnbridge, Huddersfield. Educated Thomas Street Board School. Husband of Annie Wilson, 4 Back Union Street, Huddersfield. Employed as a labourer. Enlisted 23.1.1915. Died at The Cameron Hospital, West Hartlepool, on 7.10.1917, aged 39. Buried **EDGERTON CEMETERY, HUDDERSFIELD.** Grave location:- 62, RC, 132.

WILTON, ERNEST PARKIN. Lieutenant. Royal Flying Corps and Royal Air Force. Born Roundhay Road, Leeds. Son of Ernest and Jane Ann Wilton, 'Studley', Westbourne Road, Marsh, Huddersfield. Educated Fartown Grammar School and Bradford Grammar School. Was in business with his father as a coal merchant at Gledholt, Huddersfield. Joined the local Territorials in 1907 and was in camp with them at the outbreak of the war. Enlisted in August, 1914, in the Army Service Corps as a Sergeant Major. In July, 1918, he obtained a commission in the Royal Flying Corps but met with a serious accident at Thetford, Norfolk. He was in hospital for nine weeks. After recovering he was on the staff of the Cadet School at Leigh. Died on 5.11.1918 in the Royal Herbert Hospital, Woolwich, of pneumonia following upon influenza. He was 27 years of age. Buried **EDGERTON CEMETERY, HUDDERSFIELD.** Grave location:- 49, 46G. ROH:- Gledholt Wesleyan Church; Longwood Methodist Church; Mount Pleasant Chapel, Lockwood.

WIMPENNY, FRED. Private. No 8587. 2nd Battalion Duke of Wellington's Regiment. Born Dewsbury. Lived Kirkheaton. Enlisted at the outbreak of the war. Killed in action near Ypres on 8.11.1914. Buried **RAILWAY DUGOUTS BURIAL GROUND. (TRANSPORT FARM).** Grave location:- Plot 6, Row S, Grave 26. ROH:- St. John's Church, Kirkheaton.

WIMPENNY, JOE. Private. No 307856. 1/7th Battalion Duke of Wellington's Regiment. Born Golcar. Lived Gladstone Buildings, Marsden. Married, with two children. Employed as a minder by Messrs J Pogson and Company, Bridge Street Mills, Slaithwaite. Attended Linthwaite Parish Church. Enlisted August 1916. Embarked for France in December, 1916. Killed in action, 21.11.1917, aged 30 years. Buried **DOCHY FARM NEW BRITISH CEMETERY.** Grave location:- Plot 3, Row B, Grave 23. (Brother of Private **JOHN WIMPENNY,** reported missing, presumed killed, 23.11.1916, q.v.). ROH:- Huddersfield Drill Hall; Marsden War Memorial.

WIMPENNY, JOHN. Private. No 305189. 1/7th Battalion Duke of Wellington's Regiment. Born Golcar. Son of Mrs B Wimpenny, Chain, Marsden. Employed as a teamer by Mr Albert Schofield. Was a member of the Colne Valley Territorials before the outbreak of the war. Enlisted August 1914. Embarked for France in April, 1915. Reported missing, presumed killed, on 23.11.1916, aged 20 years. Buried **SHRINE CEMETERY, BUCQUOY**. Grave location:- Plot 1, Row B, Grave 25. (Brother of Private **JOE WIMPENNY**, killed in action, 21.11.1917, q.v.). ROH:- Huddersfield Drill Hall; Marsden War Memorial.

WIMPENNY, JOHN. Private. No 13143. 'A' Company, 2nd Battalion Duke of Wellington's Regiment. Born Birch Road, Berry Brow, Huddersfield, 15.10.1889. Son of Tim and Mary Ann Wimpenny, 35 Back Lane, Berry Brow. Educated Berry Brow Council School. Employed as a fettler by Messrs John Brooke and Sons Limited, Armitage Bridge Mills. Single. Enlisted 7.9.1914. Killed in action at Fampoux on 3.5.1917 during the Battle of Arras. He was 27 years of age. Has no known grave. Commemorated **ARRAS MEMORIAL TO THE MISSING**. ROH:- Armitage Bridge Mills; Armitage Bridge War Memorial; Mount Pleasant Chapel, Lockwood.

WIMPENNY, JOSEPH TEDBAR. Private. No 21439. 1st Battalion Oxford and Bucks. Light Infantry. Formerly No 19542 Somerset Light Infantry. Born Holmfirth. Son of Samuel Shaw Wimpenny and Martha Amelia Wimpenny, The Masons Arms, Underbank, Holmfirth. Was a member of St. John's Church choir. Played halfback for the Underbank Rugby football club. Enlisted at the outbreak of the war. He was drafted into the Indian Expeditionary Force and left England on 10.12.1914. Killed in action in the Persian Gulf on 6.4.1916, aged 24 years. Has no known grave. Commemorated **BASRA MEMORIAL TO THE MISSING, IRAQ**. ROH:- Underbank War Memorial.

WIMPENNY, SAM. Lance Corporal. No 31251. 2nd Battalion Duke of Wellington's Regiment. Born Huddersfield. Son of Joseph Wimpenny, 43 Off Chapel Street, Berry Brow, Huddersfield. Employed by Messrs Taylor and Littlewood, Newsome Mills. Was a member of Berry Brow Conservative Club. Enlisted March 1918. Embarked for France in August, 1918. Killed in action, 10.10.1917, aged 31 years. Has no known grave. Commemorated **TYNE COT MEMORIAL TO THE MISSING**. Armitage Bridge War Memorial. ROH:- Messrs Taylor and Littlewood, Newsome Mills.

WINDLE, CHARLES. Private. No 6252. 'A' Company, 18th Battalion King's Royal Rifle Corps. Born Wellhouse Lane, Dalton, Huddersfield. Son of Harry and Emma Windle, 190 Kilner Bank, Moldgreen, Huddersfield. Educated Kirkheaton National School. Employed as a dyer by Messrs Heppinstall Brothers of Turnbridge, Huddersfield. Single. Enlisted June 1915. Embarked for France in April, 1916. Killed in action on 15.9.1916 in the attack on Flers during the Battle of the Somme. He was 36 years of age. Has no known grave. Commemorated **THIEPVAL MEMORIAL TO THE MISSING**. (Brother of Ordinary Seaman **SHEARD WINDLE**, drowned at sea, 12.12.1917, and Gunner **WILLIAM WINDLE**, killed in action, 7.6.1917, q.v.). ROH:- Moldgreen War Memorial; Christ Church, Moldgreen.

WINDLE, KEMPTON. Trooper. No 2279. Household Battalion. Born Shepley. Youngest son of Mr and Mrs Sam Windle, Lea Head, Shepley. Employed as a woollen piecer by Messrs Firth Brothers, of Shepley. Had only been in Belgium a few weeks when he was shot by a sniper whilst leaving the trenches on 8.10.1917. He was 19 years of age. Buried **BARD COTTAGE CEMETERY**. Grave location:- Plot 5, Row A, Grave 10. ROH:- Shepley War Memorial.

WINDLE, SHEARD. Ordinary Seaman. No J/75899. Royal Navy. *HMS Partridge*. Born Kirkheaton 4.8.1891. Son of Harry and Emma Windle, 190, Kilner Bank, Moldgreen, Huddersfield. Educated at Moldgreen Schools. Employed as a fettler by Messrs John Fenton and Sons, Bradley Mills. Husband of Edith Windle, 5 Tindall's Yard, Hawk Street, Huddersfield. Enlisted in the Royal Navy on 15.8.1917. Was drowned in the North Sea on 12.12.1917 when German destroyers raided a British convoy and *HMS Partridge* was sunk. His body was washed ashore at Cogsheim, Saellijornse, Norway on 21.12.1917. Buried **FITJAR CHURCHYARD** (which is on a large island south of Bergen, Norway. (Brother of Private **CHARLES WINDLE**, killed in action, 15.9.1916, and Gunner **WILLIAM WINDLE**, killed in action, 7.6.1917, q.v.). ROH:- Christ Church, Moldgreen. *(Three other men from Huddersfield were drowned aboard HMS Partridge. They were Ordinary Seaman **FRED DRANSFIELD**, Able*

Seaman **DONALD HAIGH** and Able Seaman **WALKER BAMFORTH**, q.v.).

WINDLE, WILLIAM. Gunner. No 59478. 180th Siege Battery, Royal Garrison Artillery. Born Wellhouse Lane, Dalton, Huddersfield. Son of Harry and Emma Windle, 190 Kilner Bank, Moldgreen, Huddersfield. Educated Kirkheaton National School. Employed as a cloth finisher by Messrs J. L. Walker and Sons Limited, of Deighton. Single. Enlisted October 1915. Embarked for France on Easter Sunday, 1917. Killed in action, 7.6.1917, aged 23 years. Has no known grave. Commemorated **MENIN GATE MEMORIAL TO THE MISSING.** (Brother of Private **CHARLES WINDLE**, killed in action, 15.9.1916, and Ordinary Seaman **SHEARD WINDLE**, drowned at sea, 12.12.1917, q.v.). ROH:- Moldgreen War Memorial; Christ Church, Moldgreen.

WINTERBOTTOM, LEWIS. Lance Corporal. No 11680. 2nd Battalion King's Own Scottish Borderers. Born Fartown Green Road, Fartown, Huddersfield. Son of Lucretia Winterbottom, Sour Milk Hall, Claremount, Halifax. Educated Hilhouse Board School. Single. Enlisted in the King's Own Scottish Borderers in September, 1913. Reported missing, presumed killed, on 4.10.1917 in the attack on Broodseinde during the Battle of Passchendaele, aged 21. Has no known grave. Commemorated **TYNE COT MEMORIAL TO THE MISSING.** ROH:- Fartown and Birkby War Memorial.

WINTERBOTTOM, NELSON. Lance Corporal. No 241012. 2/5th Battalion Duke of Wellington's Regiment. Born 22.8.1886. Educated Mount Pleasant Council School. Married. Lived 69 Swift's Buildings, Moorend, Lockwood, Huddersfield. Was a chimney sweep with his father at Yew Green, Lockwood. Enlisted 11.2.1915. Killed in action on 27.11.1917 at Bourlon Wood during the Battle of Cambrai. Has no known grave. Commemorated **CAMBRAI MEMORIAL TO THE MISSING.** ROH:- St. John's Church, Newsome; Emmanuel Church, Lockwood.

WINTERINGHAM, EDWIN. Private. No 11908. 'Y' Company, 8th Battalion Duke of Wellington's Regiment. Born Boroughbridge 12.9.1891. Son of Robert and Louisa Phillis Winteringham, 72 South Street, Huddersfield. Educated Boroughbridge National School. Along with his younger brother, Horace, was employed as a labourer at Messrs Hopkinsons of Birkby, Huddersfield. They enlisted together in August, 1914, and went out to the Dardenelles in August, 1915. Killed in action on 7.8.1915 at Suvla Bay, Gallipoli, aged 22. Has no known grave. Commemorated **HELLES MEMORIAL TO THE MISSING.** His parents received a letter from Horace (who survived the war); he wrote, *'I am just sending a line or two but I do not know how to put it together as we had it very hard. There are many of us left* (over the top of these words the censor had written ' quite a lot - cheer up'). *We have been fighting for four or five days and we have come for a rest at the back of the line. I am sorry to say that Ted got killed on August 8th. I was not with him at the time but not far off. He only lived about a minute. The Turks made us go back so I could not get to him but don't bother, he died doing his duty. Well I am living yet and we shall be going up again in a day or two. We had to go where there had been no fighting before so you can just tell how we had to do.'* ROH:- Holy Trinity Church, Huddersfield.

WINTOUR, CHARLES JOHN. Captain. Royal Navy. *HMS Tipperary*. Born High Hoyland 10.12..1871. Son of the Rev. Fitzgerald Wintour (former Vicar of Clayton West) and Mrs Wintour of High Hoyland. Husband of Katherine Mary Wintour, of Pickering Cottage, Loose, Maidstone, Kent. (Married 3.10.1900). Entered the Royal Navy on 15.11.1887 as a midshipman aboard *HMS Britannia*. Killed in action on 1.6.1916 at the Battle of Jutland. He was 44 years of age. Has no known grave. Commemorated **PORTSMOUTH NAVAL MEMORIAL TO THE MISSING.** Admiral Jellicoe, in a despatch dealing with the Battle of Jutland, paid a warm tribute to the Captain, *'During the night'* reads the despatch, *' the British heavy ships were not attacked but the 4th, 11th and the 12th Flotillas under Commodore Hawksley, Captain C. J. Wintour and Captain A. J. B. Stirling, delivered a series of very gallant and successful attacks on the enemy, causing him heavy losses. It was during these attacks that severe losses in the 4th Flotilla occurred, including that of the 'Tipperary' with the gallant leader of the flotilla, Captain Wintour. He had brought the flotilla to a high pitch of perfection and although suffering severely from the fire of the enemy a heavy toll of the enemy* *vessels was taken and many gallant actions were performed by the Flotilla.'* ROH:- Clayton West and High Hoyland War Memorial; memorial in Clayton West Parish Church.

WISEMAN, JOHN WALLACE. Sergeant. No 46443. 1st/1st Staffordshire Yeomanry. Formerly No 4982 19th Hussars. Born Almondbury 18.3.1881. Youngest son of Mr and Mrs J Wiseman, 5 Arnold Street, Birkby. Educated Huddersfield Higher Grade School, New North Road, Huddersfield. Employed by the London and North Western Railway Company as a railway shunter. Husband of Lizzie Wiseman, 182 Bradford Road North, Fartown, Huddersfield. Saw service in South Africa where he was wounded. He was awarded the King's Medal with four clasps. Enlisted 4.8.1914. Died of pneumonia on 27.12.1918 in Beirut, Lebanon, aged 37. Buried **BEIRUT BRITISH WAR CEMETERY.** Grave location:- Grave No 243. ROH:- Christ Church, Woodhouse Hill; Fartown and Birkby War Memorial; London and North Western Railway Company Roll.

WOFFENDEN, FRANCIS BERNARD (FRANK). Private. No 75688. 15th Battalion Durham Light Infantry. Born Gorton, Manchester, 4.6.1899. Son of Mr G H Woffenden, 68 Gledholt Road, Huddersfield. Educated at Hillhouse Council School and Almondbury Grammar School. Was employed as an apprentice in electrical engineering by Messrs Sykes and Sugden, of Huddersfield. Single. Died of wounds, 31.5.1918, aged 18 years. Has no known grave. Commemorated **SOISSONS MEMORIAL TO THE MISSING.** ROH:- St. John's Church, Birkby; Fartown and Birkby War Memorial.

WOFFINDIN, ERNEST. Gunner. No 185923. 306th Brigade, Royal Field Artillery. Born Barnsley. Son of William and Mary Woffenden, of High Hoyland. Died of wounds, 24.4.1918, aged 32 years. Buried **PICQUIGNY BRITISH CEMETERY.** Grave location:- Row D, Grave 4. ROH:- Clayton West and High Hoyland War Memorial.

WOMACK, JOE. Private. No 307685. 2nd Battalion Duke of Wellington's Regiment. Born Broken Cross, Almondbury, Huddersfield. Educated Almondbury National School. Employed as a tailor's presser by Messrs Haighs Limited, wholesale clothiers, St. John's Road, Huddersfield. Single. Enlisted 31.8.1916. Killed in action, 9.8.1918, aged 30. Buried **VIELLE-CHAPELLE NEW MILITARY CEMETERY.** Grave location:- Plot 9, Row C, Grave 9. ROH:- Almondbury War Memorial.

WOMERSLEY, BEN ABBOTT. Private. No 15603. 8th Battalion Duke of Wellington's Regiment. Born Huddersfield. Lived Lockwood. Killed in action, 14.9.1916. Has no known grave. Commemorated **THIEPVAL MEMORIAL TO THE MISSING.** The following extract is taken from the Official History, *'Advancing from Hindenburg Trench behind an excellent barrage at 6.30pm on the 14th September two Companies of the 8th Battalion Duke of Wellington's Regiment and two of the 9th Battalion West Yorkshires carried without a pause the German front line and then the Wonder Werk, together with the 250 yards of Hohenzollern Trench on the right: also the trench on the left as far as the Thiepval road.'* War Diary notes – Objectives reached – attacking Companies advanced 40 yards beyond and dug themselves in – communication trench to new position dug immediately. Counter attacks repulsed. 15.9.1916. Relieved at 4pm and to Hedauville. Casualties - 258. ROH:- St. Paul's Church, Southgate, Huddersfield.

WOMERSLEY, FRED RANDOLPH. Lance Sergeant. No 43077. 35th Company, Machine Gun Corps. Formerly No 4192 Shropshire Light Infantry. Born Deighton, Huddersfield. Son of Clifford and M A Womersley, of 'Highfield', Trinity Street, Shrewsbury, and formerly of Huddersfield. Attended Milton Church Sunday School. Enlisted at the age of 16 in August, 1914. Killed in action, 26.3.1918, aged 20 years. Has no known grave. Commemorated **POZIERES MEMORIAL TO THE MISSING.**

WOMERSLEY, IDO. Private. No 32322. 10th Battalion York and Lancaster Regiment. Born New Mill, Holmfirth. Son of Mr and Mrs Albert Womersley, 'The Junction Inn', Syke Bottom, New Mill. Educated New Mill National School and Snowgate Head Sunday School. Employed as a miner by Messrs Tinker Brothers at Woodpit Colliery. Enlisted 16.12.1916. Killed in action, 15.7.1917, aged 19 years. Buried **POND FARM CEMETERY, WULVERGHEM, BELGIUM.** Grave location:- Row N, Grave 5.

ROH:- New Mill Working Men's Club; Fulstone War Memorial; memorial in Christ Church Churchyard, New Mill.

WOMERSLEY, JAMES. Gunner. No 365782. 245th Siege Battery, Royal Garrison Artillery. Born Almondbury 15.10.1889. Educated Central School, Almondbury. Employed as a machine warper. Married. Lived 116 Bradley Mills Road, Huddersfield. Enlisted 20.7.1916. Died of wounds, 20.9.1917, aged 27 years. Buried **LARCH WOOD (RAILWAY CUTTING) CEMETERY, ZILLEBEKE, BELGIUM.** Grave location:- Plot 2, Row A, Grave 10.

WOMERSLEY, JOSEPH. Private. No 245310. 10th Battalion Durham Light Infantry. Born Leeds. Son of Alfred and Alice Ann Womersley, 4 St. Paul's Street, Huddersfield. Lived Denby Dale. Employed by Messrs J. Kitson and Sons at the brickworks, Denby Dale. Enlisted December 1914. Reported missing, presumed killed, 16.10.1917, aged 21 years. Has no known grave. Commemorated **TYNE COT MEMORIAL TO THE MISSING.** ROH:- Almondbury War Memorial; Denby Dale and Cumberworth War Memorial.

WOMERSLEY, JOSEPH WILLIAM. Private. No 18260. 2nd Battalion Highland Light Infantry. Born Wilson's Buildings, Great Northern Street, Huddersfield 14.9.1884. Educated Thomas Street Board School. Employed as a plasterer at Crosland Moor Workhouse. Husband of Hannah Womersley, 28 Cross Grove Street, Huddersfield. Enlisted 11.1.1915. Killed in action, 2.8.1916, during the Battle of the Somme. Has no known grave. Commemorated **THIEPVAL MEMORIAL TO THE MISSING.** ROH:- St. Paul's Church, Southgate, Huddersfield.

WOMERSLEY, WILLIAM. Private. No 3194. 1/5th Battalion Duke of Wellington's Regiment. Born 5 Aster Street, Turnbridge, Huddersfield. Educated St. Patrick's Roman Catholic School. Employed as a labourer. Husband of Mary Womersley, 3 Armitage Square, Quay Street, Huddersfield. Enlisted 21.10.1914. Killed in action, 17.7.1915. Has no known grave. Commemorated **MENIN GATE MEMORIAL TO THE MISSING.** ROH:- Huddersfield Drill Hall.

WOOD, A. Private. No 19781. 3rd Battalion Duke of Wellington's Regiment, transferred to No 237003 Labour Corps. Died at home, 3.4.1919. Buried **St. THOMAS'S CHURCHYARD, THURSTONLAND.** Grave location:- West.

WOOD, ALBERT. Private. No 18363. 10th Battalion Northumberland Fusiliers. Born Milnsbridge. Son of Mrs Wood and the late Mr Fred Wood, 130 Scar Lane, Milnsbridge. Husband of M. Wood of Manchester and formerly of 81 Station Road, Golcar. Attended Milnsbridge Baptist Sunday School. Employed by Messrs John Lockwood and Sons Limited. Enlisted August 1914. After serving in France for some time he was invalided home and was in hospital in Glasgow. He returned to France in October, 1916. Killed in action, 17.5.1917, aged 32 years. In the middle of a terrific bombardment a shell burst in the trench and killed him instantly. Buried **RAILWAY DUGOUTS (TRANSPORT FARM) BURIAL GROUND.** Grave location:- Special Memorial D 32. ROH:- St. John's Church, Golcar.

WOOD, ARCHIE. Private. No 59777. 2nd Battalion West Yorkshire Regiment. Born 168 Longwood Gate, Huddersfield, 26.3. 1899. Son of Fred and Mary Ann Wood, 18 Gilead Road, Longwood, Huddersfield. Educated Spark Hall Infants School and Goitfield Boys School. Employed as a woollen piecer. Single. Enlisted April 1916. Reported missing, presumed killed, on 23.5.1918 on the Chemin-des-Dames. He was 19 years of age. Has no known grave. Commemorated **SOISSONS MEMORIAL TO THE MISSING.** ROH:- Longwood Wesleyan Church. Extract from the CWGC Memorial Register, *'At the end of April 1918 five Divisions, forming 1X Corps, were transferred to the French Sixth Army to rest and refit. They were the 8th, 19th (Western), 21st, 25th and 50th (Northumbrian) Division. (The 2nd Battalion West Yorkshire Regiment was in the 8th Division). During the first fortnight in May the 21st, 8th and 50th Divisions were put into the line on a front of 24 kilometres running East and West between Reims and Soissons, with their left flank close to the Eastern end of the Chemin des Dames.*
Extract from The West Yorkshire Regiment in the War 1914–1918, Vol 2, by Everard Wyrall, *'The front held by the 8th Division was peculiar;*

it formed a right-angled salient pushed out into the German positions. The northern side was about seven thousand and the eastern side some three thousand yards in length. The Aisne and the Canal ran through Pontavert on the left, the village being roughly six thousand yards in rear of the front line trenches. On the right, the flank of the division rested on the Aisne itself at Berry au Bac. The river and the canal then swung forward and, running up along the eastern side of the salient, formed an obstacle both to the Germans and British so protected the front line trenches from surprise attacks.

The 8th Division had received strict orders that 'not one yard of ground must be lost,' and this necessitated the trenches being held in strength, the bulk of the infantry of the division being within range of the enemy's trench-mortars. Each night patrols crossed No Man's Land with the object of capturing a German prisoner for identification. On the night of 23rd May one of two patrols sent out bumped up against a strong German patrol and a fight ensued, during which seven of the enemy were accounted for, one being taken prisoner but afterwards killed in the fighting. Two men of the West Yorkshires were wounded and three were missing.

WOOD, ARNOLD. Corporal. No 18604. 2nd Battalion Duke of Wellington's Regiment. Born Golcar. Son of Charles and Mary Hannah Wood, 29 Green View, Wellhouse, Golcar. Killed in action on 10.10.1917 during the Battle of Passchendaele. He was 25 years of age. Has no known grave. Commemorated **TYNE COT MEMORIAL TO THE MISSING.** ROH:- St. John's Church, Golcar.

WOOD, ARNOLD. Private. No 46862. 8th Battalion The Yorkshire Regiment. Born Kirkheaton, Huddersfield. Son of Benjamin and Mary Jane Wood of Kirkheaton. Died of wounds on 29.6.1918 in Italy, aged 19 years. Buried **GRANEZZA BRITISH CEMETERY.** Grave location:- Plot 1, Row C, Grave 2. ROH:- St. John's Church, Kirkheaton.

WOOD, ARTHUR. Private. No 300139. 1/6th Battalion Duke of Wellington's Regiment. Born Leeds Road North, Huddersfield, 19.5.1890. Son of Frank Wood, 66 Hollybank Road, Lindley, Huddersfield. Educated Longwood Grammar School. In business as a music and piano dealer.

Single. Enlisted 1.8.1916. Killed in action 13.4.1918, aged 28. Buried **TROIS-ARBRES CEMETERY, STEENWERCK.** Grave location:- Plot 2, Row J, Grave 37.

WOOD, ARTHUR. Lance Corporal. No 45238. 14th Battalion Durham Light Infantry. Son of Alex and Ellen Wood, 27 Spring Grove Street, Huddersfield. Educated Spring Grove Council School. Employed as clerk by Messrs Dale and Sykes, accountants. Was a member of the choir at Milton Church. Single. Enlisted in 1916. Died of wounds at No 11 Stationary Hospital, Rouen, on 14.1.1918, aged 23 years. Buried **St. SEVER CEMETERY EXTENSION.** Grave location:- Block P, Plot 5, Row N, Grave 13B. ROH:- Milton Independent Church.

WOOD, ARTHUR JAMES. Lance Corporal. No 11122. 'Y' Company, 8th Battalion Duke of Wellington's Regiment. Born 12 Sunset Terrace, Birkby, Huddersfield 5.3.1895. Son of Emily Wood, 4 Blacker Road, Birkby, Huddersfield. Educated Hillhouse Board School. Employed as a clerk by Messrs J. Hopkinsons, of Birkby. Single. Enlisted September 1914. Went to the Dardenelles in July, 1915. Killed in action in the assault on Lala Baba, Suvla, Gallipoli, on 11.8.1915, aged 20 years. Has no known grave. Commemorated **HELLES MEMORIAL TO THE MISSING.** His mother received a letter from Corporal J Uttley who lived at 35 Netheroyd Hill Road, Cowcliffe, Huddersfield, and wrote, *'It is with deep regret that I write these few lines to tell you of your son's death. No doubt before you receive this letter you will have seen his name in the Roll of Honour but being his chum and sharing the trials of soldiering for 12 months together I thought it my duty to write you a short letter giving you an account of his death. On August 11th he went off with a small party after some snipers who were giving us a lot of trouble. They had located them near a house and they went out but failed to find them on three sides. On coming to the rear they were immediately fired upon, your son being killed immediately. At some future date, God willing, we may come across his grave which like every soldier's will bear his name on a small wooden cross and I am sure I and all his pals will see it suitably looked after while they are about the place where he is buried. Hoping that this letter will be a little consolation and also the knowledge that he died fighting for his King* *and Country.'* ROH:- St. John's Church, Birkby; Fartown and Birkby War Memorial.

WOOD, BEN. Private. No 241614. 2nd Battalion Duke of Wellington's Regiment. Born Huddersfield. Son of Mrs J W Wood, 14 Church Terrace, Longwood. Had been a chorister in the Longwood Parish Church choir and also a scholar at the Sunday School. Was an able pianist. Served his apprenticeship with Messrs Whitfield Brothers and Company Limited, tailors, Manchester Road, Huddersfield, and was a commercial traveller with with them at the time of his enlistment in 1915. Killed instantly by a machine gun bullet on 24.10.1918, aged 26 years. Buried **VERCHAIN BRITISH CEMETERY.** Grave location:- Row B, Grave 4. ROH:- St. Mark's Parish Church, Longwood.

WOOD, BENJAMIN. Guardsman. No 7463. 1st Battalion The Scots Guards. Born Huddersfield June, 1887. Employed as a tailor's presser. Lived Great Northern Street, Huddersfield. Single. Enlisted at the outbreak of the war. Killed in action, 26.10.1914. Has no known grave. Commemorated **MENIN GATE MEMORIAL TO THE MISSING.** The following extract from the 1st Battalion Scots Guards War Diary is taken from 'British Battalions in France and Belgium 1914' by Ray Westlake, *'Moved forward via Hooge (26th) and took up positions in front line near Gheluveldt. Took part in attack on Poezelhoek, advancing to within 200 yards of enemy's trenches then digging in. Captain Hamilton killed, 2 Officers wounded, approximately 130 other casualties. Later took over trenches from 2nd Bedfordshires on the Zandvoorde –Gheluveldt road near Zandvoorde Chateau.'*

WOOD, BERNAL. Bombardier. No L/25414. 'A' Battery, 168th (Huddersfield) Brigade, Royal Field Artillery. Born Huddersfield 22.8.1895. Son of Albert and Hannah Eliza Wood, 39 Church Lane, Moldgreen, Huddersfield. Educated Moldgreen Council School. Employed as a postman at Huddersfield General Post Office. Was a member of the Ramsden Street Men's Own Class. Single. Enlisted 28.4.1915. Killed in action, 20.10.1917, during the Battle of Passchendaele, aged 22. Buried **NEW IRISH FARM CEMETERY, St. JEAN-les-YPRES, BELGIUM.** Grave location:- Plot 10, Row D, Grave 19. ROH:- Huddersfield G.P.O; Christ Church, Moldgreen.

WOOD, BERTRAM BARRETT. Sergeant. No 6/1083. Canterbury Regiment, New Zealand Expeditionary Force. Born 59 West Parade, Huddersfield, 5.5.1891. Son of Arthur and Frances Wood. Educated Spring Grove Council School. Emigrated to New Zealand, where he was employed as a draper. Lived Ashburton, Canterbury, New Zealand. Single. Enlisted August 1914. Sailed for the Dardenelles. Wounded at Gallipoli on 30.4.1915. Died of wounds on 14.5.1915 at the Military Hospital, Ras-el-tin, Alexandria, Egypt. Buried **CHATBY WAR MEMORIAL CEMETERY, EGYPT.** Grave location:- Row E, Grave 95.

WOOD, CHARLIE. Ordinary Seaman. No J/77668. Royal Navy. *HMS Vehement.* Son of John and Ann Wood, Station Road, Clayton West. Killed in action by mine explosion in North Sea on 2.8.1918, aged 23 years. Has no known grave. Commemorated **PORTSMOUTH NAVAL MEMORIAL TO THE MISSING.** ROH:- Clayton West and High Hoyland War Memorial.

WOOD, CHARLIE. Rifleman. No R/19968. 16th Battalion King's Royal Rifle Corps. Born Slaithwaite. Son of Tom and Hannah Wood, 9 Lowestwood, Golcar. Killed in action at High Wood on 11.8.1916 during the Battle of the Somme. He was 31 years of age. Has no known grave. Commemorated **THIEPVAL MEMORIAL TO THE MISSING.** ROH:- St. John's Church, Golcar.

WOOD, DAVID. Private. No 32485. 2nd Battalion South Staffordshire Regiment. Born Cumberworth. Son of John and Mary Ann Wood of Croft Nook, Shepley. Husband of Mary Hannah Wood, Marsh Lane, Shepley. Employed as a merchant tailor. Died of wounds at No 7 Stationary Hospital on 9.5.1917, aged 32 years. Buried **BOULOGNE EASTERN CEMETERY.** Grave location:- Plot 4, Row B, Grave 9. ROH:- Shepley War Memorial.

WOOD, EDGAR. Gunner. No 241630. No 1 'A' Reserve Brigade, Royal Field Artillery. Son of William and Elizabeth Wood. Husband of Mary Wood, 6 Hudson Street, Hudson Road, Leeds, and formerly of Shepley. Was a foreman for Messrs Morton Joynt, wholesale clothiers, of Leeds. He learned the business with Mr Arthur Roebuck of Shepley. Had attended both the Thurstonland and Shepley Wesleyan Churches. Died in hospital at Newcastle on 17.3.1918 from injuries sustained from a fall from a hay wagon on 1.3.1918. He had been in training since September, 1917, and should have gone to the front the week he was injured. He was 29 years of age. Buried **SHEPLEY UNITED METHODIST CHAPEL YARD.** Grave location:- in North part, 106. ROH:- Shepley War Memorial.

WOOD, EDGAR. Private. No 45811. 12th/13th Battalion Northumberland Fusiliers. Born Huddersfield. Only son of Sarah Wood and the late William Wood, Daisy Lea, Outlane. Employed as a cloth finisher at Gosport Mills, Outlane. Was captured by the Germans on 27.5.1918 and died as a Prisoner of War on 19.10.1918 in Germany, aged 24. Buried **NIEDERZWEHREN CEMETERY, CASSEL, GERMANY.** Grave location:- Plot 4, Row J, Grave 10. ROH:- Pole Moor Baptist Church.

WOOD, ERNEST. Private. No 1616. 1/7th Battalion Duke of Wellington's Regiment, Born Marsden. Eldest son of Mr and Mrs John Henry Wood, 12 Royds Terrace, Binn Road, Marsden. Was a member of the local Territorials prior to the outbreak of the war. Enlisted in August 1914. Was seriously injured on 17.9.1916 in the attack on the Thiepval/Leipzig Salient (Casualities – 220). Both his thighs, sides and arm were very badly wounded and very little hope could be given for his recovery although he was quite conscious. Was admitted to the No 16 General Hospital, Le Treport, France. His parents were given permission to visit their son and arrived on Sunday, 23.9.1916, but he had just died. They were cared for by members of the Y.M.C.A. and attended their son's funeral the next day. Buried **MONT HUON MILITARY CEMETERY, LE TREPORT.** Grave Location:- Plot 2, Row E, Grave 8. ROH:- Huddersfield Drill Hall; Marsden War Memorial.

WOOD, FRANK. Private. No 17938. 9th Battalion Duke of Wellington's Regiment. Born 305 Leeds Road, Huddersfield, 21.5.1896. Only son of Albert Edward and Frances Amelia Wood, 83 Leeds Road North, Huddersfield. Educated St. Andrew's Church of England School, Leeds Road. Employed as a clerk by Messrs William White and Sons, silk throwsters, Fitzwilliam Street, Huddersfield. Attended the Brunswick Street United Methodist Chapel and Sunday School. Played football with the Brunswick Street and Woodhouse Clubs and cricket for the Bradley Mills team. Single. Enlisted January, 1916, and embarked for France in May, 1916. Killed in action on 4.8.1916 at Delville Wood during the Battle of the Somme, aged 20. Has no known grave. Commemorated **THIEPVAL MEMORIAL TO THE MISSING.** ROH:- St. Andrew's Church, Leeds Road, Huddersfield; Fartown and Birkby War Memorial.

WOOD, FREDERICK DOUGLAS. Private. No 14534. 10th Battalion Duke of Wellington's Regiment. Born Chapeltown, Leeds. Son of ex Police Sergeant Fred Wood and Therese Celestine Wood, 12 Council Terrace, New Mill Road, Honley. Employed as a joiner. Was a member of the Honley Parish Church choir. Enlisted at the outbreak of the war. Had been in France for one year when he was killed in action on 29.7.1916, at Munster Alley, during the Battle of the Somme, aged 25 (Casualties – 205). *According to five comrades who wrote to the parents he was carrying a bag of bombs to the front line when he was killed by a piece of shell.* Has no known grave. Commemorated **THIEPVAL MEMORIAL TO THE MISSING.** ROH:- Honley War Memorial.

WOOD, GEORGE. Sapper. No WR/501185. 3rd Port Construction Company, Inland Water Transport, Royal Engineers. Formerly 1/5th Battalion Duke of Wellington's Regiment. Born Bradford 22.7.1886. Son of Samuel and Annis Hirst Wood, Parkside House, Somerset Road, Huddersfield. Educated Stile Common Council School and Huddersfield Higher Grade School. Employed as a cabinet maker. Single. Enlisted in the local Territorial battalion at the outbreak of the war. Embarked for France in April, 1915. Was discharged as time expired and temporarily unfit due to trench feet and a shrapnel wound in the shoulder in April, 1916. He re-enlisted into the Royal Engineers, voluntarily, in July 1916. Accidentally killed on 9.1.1919, aged 32 years. *He was assisting in some repairs to the jetty at Dieppe when he slipped and fell a distance of twenty eight feet. He suffered multiple injuries including* *a fractured skull and died nine hours later in hospital without regaining consciousness.* Buried **JANVAL CEMETERY, DIEPPE.** Grave location:- Plot 2, Row C, Grave 5. ROH:- Huddersfield Parish Church; commemorated on his parents' headstone in Edgerton Cemetery, Huddersfield.

WOOD, GEORGE WALKER. Private. No G/20145. 1st Battalion Royal West Kent Regiment. Formerly No 33752 3rd Reserve Cavalry Regiment. Born Golcar. Son of Mr and Mrs Joseph Wood, 50 Upper Wellhouse, Golcar. Married, with one child. Had served in France and was seriously wounded in the spine. Was admitted to a military hospital at Chichester, where he died of his wounds on 16.11.1918, aged 25 years. Buried **WELLHOUSE METHODIST CHAPEL YARD.** Grave location:- A, 32. ROH:- St. John's Church, Golcar.

WOOD, GILBERT. Corporal. No 305472. 1/7th Battalion Duke of Wellington's Regiment. Born George Street, Lindley, Huddersfield, 25.3.1892. Son of Albert and Hetty Wood, 41 Quarmby Fold, Quarmby, Huddersfield. Educated Oakes Council School, Lindley. Employed as a woollen fettler by Messrs Seth Garside and Son, Temple Mills, Lindley. Single. Enlisted August 1914. Killed in action, 11.4.1918, aged 26. Has no known grave. Commemorated **TYNE COT MEMORIAL TO THE MISSING.** ROH:- Oakes Baptist Church; St. Stephen's Church, Lindley; Huddersfield Drill Hall; Longwood War Memorial.

WOOD, GILBERT HENRY. Gunner. No 29431. 'B' Battery, 168th (Huddersfield) Brigade, Royal Field Artillery. Born Heap Street, off South Street, Huddersfield, 29.11.1897. Son of Timothy and Miriam Wood, 15 Newland Avenue, Birkby, Huddersfield. Assisted in father's ironmongery business in Queen Street, Huddersfield. Attended Fartown Trinity Wesleyan Church. Single. Enlisted June 1915. Killed in action at Nieuport, Belgium on 12.9.1917, aged 19 years. Buried **COXYDE MILITARY CEMETERY.** Grave location:- Plot 2, Row G, Grave 14. ROH:- St. Cuthbert's Church, Birkby; Fartown and Birkby War Memorial.

WOOD, HAROLD. Private. No 67098. 29th Company, Machine Gun Corps. Formerly No 36174 York and Lancaster Regiment. Born East Street, Rastrick, 6.12.1891. Son of the late William and of Alice Wood, 17 Briar Lane, Birchencliffe, Huddersfield. Educated Lindley Church of England School. Employed as a labourer by Mr E. S. Dyson, plumber, of Lindley. Single. Enlisted September 1915. Died of wounds, 30.9.1918, aged 26 years. Has no known grave. Commemorated **TYNE COT MEMORIAL TO THE MISSING.** ROH:- War Memorial outside St. Philip's Church, Birchencliffe.

WOOD, HARRY. Ordinary Seaman. No J/74600. Royal Navy. *HMS Louvain.* Son of Matthew Henry Wood of Dunford Bridge, Holmfirth. Attended Townhead School. Employed by Mrs Jonas Wagstaffe, stone merchant. Enlisted 18.7.1917. After undergoing training he left Devonport on 1.1.1918. Killed in action involving a submarine in the Mediterrean on 20.1.1918. He was 19 years of age. Has no known grave. Commemorated **PLYMOUTH NAVAL MEMORIAL TO THE MISSING.** (Brother of Private **OLIVER WOOD**, died of pneumonia following wounds, 8.9.1917, q.v.).

WOOD, HARRY. Private. No 35709. 25th (Tyneside Irish) Battalion Northumberland Fusiliers. Formerly No 50241 West Yorkshire Regiment. Born Grasscroft Road, Honley, Huddersfield, 16.12.1897. Only son of Mr and Mrs George Wood, 37 Crosland Street, Crosland Moor, Huddersfield. Employed as a joiner's apprentice by Messrs George Ainley and Sons, Crosland Moor. Single. Enlisted 29.12.1916. Reported missing, presumed killed, on 28.4.1917. Has no known grave. Commemorated **ARRAS MEMORIAL TO THE MISSING.** ROH:- St. Barnabas Church, Crosland Moor.

WOOD, HARRY. Private. No 202542. 2/4th Battalion Duke of Wellington's Regiment. Born Huddersfield. Son of Eliza Ann Wood, of Burkinshaw Road, Outlane and the late Joseph Wood. Employed as a spinner by Messrs B. Crosland and Sons, Oakes, Huddersfield. Attended Outlane Wesleyan Sunday School. Was a member of the Outlane Bowling Club. Enlisted March 1916. Returned to France in March, 1918, after a spell of home leave. Died of gunshot wounds to the head on 2.4.1918, aged 29 years. Buried **ETAPLES MILITARY CEMETERY.** Grave location:- Plot 33, Row C, Grave 10. (Brother of Private **TEDDY WOOD**, reported

missing, presumed killed, 31.8.1917, q.v.). ROH:-
Outlane Trinity Methodist Church.

WOOD, HARRY. Private. No 203037. 1/4th
Battalion King's Own Yorkshire Light Infantry.
Born Marsden. Son of Abel and Betsy Wood,
8 Sandhurst Cottages, Marsden. Employed as
a scourer at Crimble Mills, Slaithwaite. Was
a member of the Marsden Conservative Club.
Attended Marsden Parish Church. Reported
missing, presumed killed, 10.10.1917, aged 22
years. Has no known grave. Commemorated
TYNE COT MEMORIAL TO THE MISSING.
ROH:- Marsden War Memorial; Marsden
Conservative Club.

WOOD, HARRY. Private. No 241580. 2/5th
Battalion Duke of Wellington's Regiment. Born
Kirkburton, Huddersfield. Elder son of Mr
and Mrs J. Wood, 129 Spa View, Linthwaite.
Employed by the Slaithwaite Spinning Company
Limited. Attended the Crimble Congregational
Mission. Enlisted March 1916. Embarked for
France on 11.1.1917. Seriously wounded in
the side on 22.11.1917. Admitted to the 48th
Casualty Clearing Station, where he died of
wounds on 23.11.1917. He was 26 years of
age. Buried **ROCQUIGNY-EQUANCOURT
ROAD BRITISH CEMETERY.** Grave location:-
Plot 1, Row E, Grave 29. ROH:- Linthwaite
War Memorial; St. James Church, Slaithwaite;
Huddersfield Drill Hall.

WOOD, HARRY. Private. No 29569. 7/8th
Battalion King's Own Scottish Borderers. Born
Lower Castle Hill, Huddersfield, 29.8.1892. Son
of William and Hannah Wood, 169 Longley,
Huddersfield. Educated at Lowerhouses School.
Employed as a weaver by Messrs B. Vickerman
and Sons Limited, Taylor Hill. Married. Lived
167 Longley, Huddersfield. Enlisted in 1916.
Wounded 28.7.1918. Died of wounds at No
2 British Red Cross Hospital on 30.7.1918,
aged 26 years. Buried **St SEVER CEMETERY
EXTENSION, ROUEN.** Grave location:- Block
Q, Plot 4, Row H, Grave 8. ROH:- Lowerhouses
War Memorial; Almondbury War Memorial.

WOOD, HUBERT. Private. No 47200. 9th
Battalion West Yorkshire Regiment. Formerly
No 29819 Northumberland Fusiliers. Born
Gomersal, Yorkshire. Married. Lived 22 Tandem,
Kirkheaton. Was the owner of a fish and chip
business at Kirkheaton. Enlisted in 1916.
Reported missing, presumed killed, on 27.8.1917
during the Battle of Passchendaele. Has no
known grave. Commemorated **TYNE COT
MEMORIAL TO THE MISSING.** The following
extract in taken from 'Passchendaele - the day
by day account' by Chris McCarthy, *'11th
Division (XV111 Corps). 32nd Brigade:- The
advance started well for the 9th West Yorkshires
but soon came under fire from Pheasant Trench
and Vancouver. However, they pressed on. The
right came under fire from Vieilles Maisons and
they seized the nearest concrete buildings. Two
platoons from the 6th York and Lancs. were
sent up to reinforce.'* ROH:- St. John's Church,
Kirkheaton; Lepton Parish Church.

WOOD, JESSE. Private. No 29008. 9th
Battalion The Yorkshire Regiment. Born Marsh,
Huddersfield. Lived with his sister, Mrs Joe
Lilley, at 22 Abbott Street, Marsh. Employed
by Messrs Joseph Sykes and Sons Limited, Acre
Mills, Lindley. Attended Holy Trinity Church,
Huddersfield. Killed in action, 13.10.1917, aged
30 years. Has no known grave. Commemorated
TYNE COT MEMORIAL TO THE MISSING.
ROH:- Holy Trinity Church, Huddersfield.

WOOD, JOE. Private. No 203085. 2/5th
Battalion Leicestershire Regiment. Born Kiln
Brow, Golcar 24.6.1898. Son of the late Truth
and Regina Wood, 29 Thornton Lodge Road,
Crosland Moor, Huddersfield. Educated Paddock
Church of England School. Employed as a garnet
feeder by his father's firm, Messrs Ephraim
Wood and Sons, waste pullers, of Crosland
Moor. Attended Paddock Church Sunday School.
Single. Enlisted September 1916. Killed in action,
26.9.1917, during the Battle of Polygon Wood.
He was 19 years of age. Buried **BRIDGE HOUSE
CEMETERY, LANGEMARCK, BELGIUM.**
Grave location:- Row A, Grave 5.

WOOD, JOE. Private. No 38145. 17th Battalion
West Yorkshire Regiment (2nd Leeds Pals). Born
Golcar. Son of Mr and Mrs Thomas William
Wood, Swallow Lane, Golcar. Husband of Lily
Wood, 106 Swallow Lane, Golcar. Employed
as a fettler by Messrs Joseph Dyson and Sons,
Milnsbridge. Attended Golcar Baptist Chapel
and was a member of the Young Men's Reading
Room. Enlisted October 1916. Embarked
for France in January, 1917. Killed in action,

15.4.1917, aged 25 years. Buried **BELLICOURT BRITISH CEMETERY.** Grave location:- Plot 4, Row F, Grave 5. His wife received a letter from her husband's chum, who wrote, *'The Germans had been shelling us very heavily during the day and after tea we were sitting together and laughing at Joe who was trying to mend his stocking. Joe and another fellow ran into the yard and were both hit by a bursting shell and killed instantly. We buried them both together in the little churchyard. The Company was engaged in road mending at the time.'* ROH:- St. John's Church, Golcar.

WOOD, JOHN HENRY, MM. Lance Corporal. No 38162. 15th Battalion Lancashire Fusiliers (1st Salford Pals). Formerly No 32232 South Staffordshire Regiment. Born Linthwaite. Lived 59 Roydhouse, Linthwaite. Attended Linthwaite Church School. Employed as a crane driver by Messrs J. W. Mallinson, contractors, of Lockwood. Was a member of the Upper Wellhouse Working Men's Club. Enlisted November 1916. Killed in action, 20.3.1918, aged 24 years. Has no known grave. Commemorated **TYNE COT MEMORIAL TO THE MISSING.** ROH:- Linthwaite War Memorial.

WOOD, JOHN HENRY. Acting Bombardier. No L/25794. 168th (Huddersfield) Brigade, Royal Field Artillery. Born 33 Whitehead Lane, Primrose Hill, Huddersfield. Son of James Frederick and Emily Jane Wood. Educated Stile Common Council School. Single. Enlisted 19.5.1915. Died at home, 33 Whitehead Lane, Primrose Hill, of Nephritis, on 16.7.1918, aged 22 years. Buried **LOCKWOOD CEMETERY, HUDDERSFIELD.** Grave location:- B, 27.

WOOD, JOHN HENRY. Company Quarter-Master Sergeant. No 11132. 'Y' Company, 8th Battalion Duke of Wellington's Regiment. Born Marsh, Huddersfield 29.9.1893. Son of John William and Eliza Jane Ward, 17 Grasscroft Road, Marsh. Educated Spring Grove Board School and Huddersfield Higher Grade School. Employed as a clerk. Single. Enlisted August 1914. Sailed for the Dardenelles aboard the *SS Aquitania* on 3.7.1915. Reported wounded and missing on 21.8.1915 in the attack on the village of Anafarta, Gallipoli, and afterwards presumed to have been killed on that date. Has no known grave. Commemorated **HELLES MEMORIAL TO THE MISSING.** ROH:- High Street United Methodist Church.

WOOD, JOHN WILLIAM. Private. No 82052. 23rd Company, Machine Gun Corps. Formerly No 29676 Duke of Wellington's Regiment. Born Slaithwaite. Married, with three children. Lived 28 Grange Cottages, Marsden. He formerly resided at Slaithwaite and attended Zion Baptist Church and Sunday School, Slaithwaite. Employed as a weaver by Messrs George Mallinson and Sons Limited, Linthwaite. Was a member of the Marsden Socalist Club. Played cricket with the Marsden Second Eleven. Enlisted 4.10.1916. Had only been in Belgium eight weeks when he was killed in action on 7.10.1917. He was 35 years of age. Buried **MOTOR CAR CORNER CEMETERY.** Grave location:- Row B, Grave 32. ROH:- Marsden War Memorial.

WOOD, JOSEPH WALKER (Served under the name of **SANDERSON**). Private. No 299. 1/5th Battalion Duke of Wellington's Regiment. Born Holmfirth. Husband of Edith Wood, 108 School Lane, Newtown, Holmfirth. Employed as a motor engineer's labourer by Messrs Coldwell Brothers, automobilists. Attended Cliffe Sunday School. Was a member of 'F' Company of the local Territorials before the outbreak of the war. Enlisted August 1914. Admitted to No 13 General Hospital, Boulogne, with serious head wounds. Died of wounds, 19.7.1915, aged 27 years. Buried **BOULOGNE EASTERN CEMETERY.** Grave location:- Plot 8, Row B, Grave 64. His wife received a letter from the Sister-in-charge, who wrote, *'Your husband, Drummer Sanderson passed away quietly at 4.10pm on July 19th. He has only been with us a few days but was dangerously ill when he came to hospital, the wounds in his head being very severe. He has never been conscious and so I do not think he has suffered any pain. The doctors did everything for him that could be done, you may be assured abour that.'* ROH:- Holmfirth War Memorial; Huddersfield Drill Hall.

WOOD, OLIVER. Lance Corporal. No 241042. 5th Battalion The Cameronians (Scottish Rifles). Formerly No 23398 York and Lancaster Regiment. Born Thurlstone. Son of Matthew Henry and Frances Revner Wood of Dunford Bridge. Employed by Mr Barger, Waterworks Manager, of the Dewsbury and Heckmondwike

Corporation Reservoir at Dunford Bridge. Attended Townhead Chapel, Dunford Bridge. Enlisted 4.3.1916. On 29.8.1917 the family received a field postcard from Oliver stating that: *he was wounded and was being sent down to the base*. In a letter which was received immediately afterwards he said that: *he had been operated upon and he had been shown a big piece of shrapnel which had been taken from him. He remarked that it was a big piece and that he was also gassed. This made it worse for him as he could feel his wound more when he coughed. 'However,'* he added, *'he could see plenty of lads worse than himself and now that it was done he would have to put up with it.'* The family received a telegram on the 8th inst. stating that: *Oliver was in a more serious condition and nobody could be allowed to visit him.* Died of pneumonia following wounds on 8.9.1917, aged 32 years. Buried **BOULOGNE EASTERN CEMETERY**. Grave location:- Plot 8, Row I, Grave 31. (Brother of Ordinary Seaman **HARRY WOOD**, killed in action, 20.1.1918, q.v.).

WOOD, PERCY. Lance Corporal. No 9/12654. 9th Battalion Duke of Wellington's Regiment. Born Great Northern Street, Huddersfield. Educated Thomas Street Council School. Employed as a tailor's presser by Messrs Bairstow and Sons and Company Limited. Husband of Mary Wood, 8 School Lane, Paddock, Huddersfield. Enlisted at the outbreak of the war. Suffered serious head wounds on 2.3.1916. Admitted to No 10 Casualty Clearing Station, where he died of wounds on 3.3.1916. He was 25 years of age. Buried **LIJSSENTHOEK MILITARY CEMETERY**. Grave location:- Plot 4, Row D, Grave 46. ROH:- All Saints Church, Paddock.

WOOD, ROBERT FREDERICK. Lance Corporal. No 2762. 1/5th Battalion Duke of Wellington's Regiment. Born Birkby, Huddersfield. Lived Primrose Hill, Huddersfield. Son of Fred and Annie Wood, Blidworth Road, Kirby in Ashfield, Nottinghamshire. Employed by Messrs Clayton and Company Limited, Karrier Car Works. Enlisted September 1914. Embarked for France in April 1915. Killed in action, 4.7.1916, during the Battle of the Somme. He was 21 years of age. Has no known grave. Commemorated **THIEPVAL MEMORIAL TO THE MISSING**. ROH:- Huddersfield Drill Hall.

WOOD, STANLEY DYSON. Private. No 202365. 15th (Service) Battalion (1st Glasgow) Highland Light Infantry. Born Marsden. Son of James and Sarah Wood. Husband of Mary Elizabeth Wood, 11 Grange Avenue, Marsden. Employed as a weaver by Messrs Crowther, Bruce and Company, New Mills. Enlisted October 1916. Embarked for France in August, 1917. Killed in action 11.4.1918, aged 40 years. Buried **BIENVILLERS MILITARY CEMETERY**. Grave location:- Plot 11, Row C, Grave 6. ROH:- Marsden War Memorial.

WOOD, STANLEY HERBERT. Private. No CH/ 21026. R.M. Depot (Deal), Royal Marine Light Infantry. Born Huddersfield. Son of Herbert Josiah and Sarah Ann Wood of 'Stanholme', 144 Newsome Road, Huddersfield. Lived 212 Leeds Road North, Huddersfield. Died at Deal Infirmary on 21.3.1917, aged 17 years. Buried **DEAL CEMETERY, KENT**. Grave location:- 2, 1264. ROH:- St. Andrew's Church, Leeds Road, Huddersfield.

WOOD, SYKES. Private. No 42002. 12th Battalion Manchester Regiment. Born Golcar 27.4.1890. Educated Knowle Bank School, Golcar. Married. Lived 15 Siggot Street. Longwood, Huddersfield. Employed as a woollen power loom tuner by Messrs C. and J. Hirst and Sons Limited, Longwood. Was a member of the choir at Golcar Providence Church. Enlisted 18.11.1916. Killed in action, 26.5.1917, during the Battle of Arras. He was 27 years of age. Has no known grave. Commemorated **ARRAS MEMORIAL TO THE MISSING**. ROH:- St. Mark's Parish Church, Longwood.

WOOD, TEDDY. Private. No 41531. 17th Battalion West Yorkshire Regiment (2nd Leeds Pals). Born Huddersfield. Son of Eliza Ann Wood, Burkinshaw Road, Outlane, and the late Joseph Wood. Employed as a night worker in the weaving department by Messrs Ben Hall and Sons, of Milnsbridge. Reported missing, presumed killed, 31.8.1917. Has no known grave. Commemorated **THIEPVAL MEMORIAL TO THE MISSING**. (Brother of Private **HARRY WOOD**, died of wounds, 2.4.1918, q.v.). ROH:- Outlane Trinity Methodist Chapel.

WOOD, TOM. Corporal. No 242571. 'C' Company, 1/5th Battalion Duke of Wellington's

Regiment. Born Golcar. Son of Samson and Miriam Wood, 61 Fern House, Golcar. Employed in the bootmaking department at the Golcar Cooperative Society, Brook Lane. Attended Golcar Baptist Sunday School. Was a member of the Golcar Central Liberal Club. Enlisted 3.4.1916. Embarked for France on Christmas Day, 1916. Killed in action by a sniper on 10.10.1917 during the Battle of Passchendaele. He was 20 years of age. Has no known grave. Commemorated **TYNE COT MEMORIAL TO THE MISSING.** ROH:- St. John's Church, Golcar; Golcar Baptist Church; Huddersfield Drill Hall.

WOOD, VERDI. Private. No 14832. 2nd Battalion Duke of Wellington's Regiment. Born Denby Dale near Huddersfield. Enlisted Huddersfield. Lived Moldgreen. Killed in action 12.10.1916, aged 39. *During the research for this book, I discovered that once again the Commonwealth War Graves Commision held no records for this soldier. After further investigation the CWGC have now engraved his name on the* **THIEPVAL MEMORIAL TO THE MISSING.**

WOOD, VERNON HAROLD. Sergeant. No 9391. 9th Battalion King's Royal Rifle Corps. Born Huddersfield. Son of Mr and Mrs F. Wood, 160 Bradford Road, Huddersfield. Joined the Regular Army in 1909 and gained his certificate as Instructor in Signalling prior to the outbreak of the war. Went out with a battalion of the K.R.R.C. in the British Expeditionary Force on 12.8.1914. He took part in the retreat from Mons and the battles of the Aisne and the Marne. Wounded on eight occasions. Reported missing, presumed killed, on 9.4.1917 during the Battle of Arras, aged 21. Has no known grave. Commemorated **ARRAS MEMORIAL TO THE MISSING.** ROH:- Fartown and Birkby War Memorial.

WOOD, WALKER. Gunner. No 47778. 'D' Battery, 186th Brigade, Royal Field Artillery. Born Huddersfield. Son of the late A. A. Wood and Betty Backhouse Wood, Union Street, Hill Top, Slaithwaite. Was in the Regular Army for three years before the outbreak of the war, being stationed in India. In December, 1914, he was sent to France where he served until December, 1915, when he was sent out to Salonica. Here he contracted Malaria and was invalided home, being sent to hospital at Stockport. He returned to France in February, 1917, and was wounded in the arm at Arras on 9.4.1917. Was sent to England to a hospital at Bradford. Returned to France at the beginning of July, 1917. Killed in action, 27.9.1917, aged 29 years. Buried **LA CLYTTE MILITARY CEMETERY.** Grave location:- Plot 3, Row C, Grave 4. ROH:- St. James Church, Slaithwaite; Slaithwaite War Memorial.

WOODALL, WILLIAM SHAW. Corporal. No S/21685. 5th Battalion The Cameron Highlanders. Formerly No 11423 The Royal Scots. (Lothian Regiment). Born Fartown, Huddersfield. Lived Huddersfield. Died of wounds at No 11 Stationary Hospital, Rouen, on 26.9.1917. Buried **St. SEVER CEMETERY EXTENSION, ROUEN.** Grave location:- Block P, Plot 3, Row I, Grave 11B.

WOODCOCK, GEOFFREY HERBERT. 2nd Lieutenant. 6th Battalion Royal Welsh Fusiliers, attached 4th Battalion. Formerly Private 1/5th Battalion Duke of Wellington's Regiment. Born Fartown, Huddersfield, 31.10.1892. Son of Herbert and Gertrude Woodcock, 'Lynwood', 8 Richmond Avenue, Huddersfield. Educated Fartown Grammar School. Employed as a clerk with Messrs Fishers and Company, merchants, of Upperhead Row, Huddersfield. Single. Enlisted in the local Territorial battalion on 3.9.1914. Embarked for France in April 1915. Was recommended for a commission and trained at Gailes, Ayrshire. Was gazetted to the Royal Welsh Fusiliers and returned to France in January, 1918. Killed in action at Aveluy Wood, near Albert, on 6.4.1918. He was 25 years of age. Buried **MARTINSART BRITISH CEMETERY.** Grave location:- Plot 1, Row F, Grave 23. ROH:- Fartown and Birkby War Memorial.

WOODHEAD, CHARLIE. Private. No 1331. 'Y Company, 8th Battalion Duke of Wellington's Regiment. Born Netherthong, Holmfirth. Son of Mr and Mrs Fred Woodhead, Cut Lane, Netherthong. For six years had played the clarinet in the band of the Huddersfield Battalion and was a former member of the Netherthong Philharmonic Band. Employed as a joiner at Holmfirth. Enlisted October 1914. Went out to the Dardenelles in July ,1915. Killed in action, 21.8.1915, aged 26 years. Has no known grave. Commemorated **HELLES MEMORIAL TO THE MISSING.** The following extract is taken from

'British Regiments at Gallipoli' by Ray Westlake, '21.8.1915. Official History of the Gallipoli campaign records that the Battalion, with the 9th Battalion West Yorkshires were hurried forward to capture first objective, but they swung left-handed, ending up in position north of Hetman Chair. An attempt was then made to assault a communication trench, but this turned out to be a heavily defended fire trench. 'The enemy's resistance could not be overcome and the troops fell back towards the southern slopes of Green Hill.' The War Diary rerecords, 'high casualties.' Held position under heavy artillery fire until relieved on 23.8.1915.' ROH:- Netherthong and Thongsbridge War Memorial; Netherthong Working Men's Club.

WOODHEAD, ERNEST. Lance Corporal. No 46427. 11th Battalion Leicestershire Regiment. Formerly No 140998 Royal Engineers. Born Paddock, Huddersfield 10.5.1889. Brother of Miss Woodhead, Croslands Crescent, Brow Road, Paddock. Educated Paddock Church of England School. Attended Paddock United Methodist Church. Employed as a clerk in the West Riding Police office at Keighley. Lived Keighley. Single. Enlisted 8.1.1915. Died of wounds at No 10 Casualty Clearing Station on 27.10.1917, aged 28 years. Buried **LIJSSENTHOEK MILITARY CEMETERY.** Grave location:- Plot 21, Row G, Grave 5. ROH:- All Saints Church, Paddock; Shared Church, Paddock.

WOODHEAD, HUBERT. Private. No 20390. 2nd Battalion Duke of Wellington's Regiment. Born Meltham. Son of Alfred and Elizabeth Ellen Woodhead, Green's End, Meltham. Killed in action on 12.10.1916 in the attack on Flers during the Battle of the Somme. He was 19 years of age. Buried **GUARDS' CEMETERY, (LESBOEUFS).** Grave location:- Plot 11, Row ZZ, Grave 4.

WOODHEAD, JAMES WILLIAM. Gunner. No 775766. Royal Field Artillery, attached 1034th Motor Transport Company, Army Service Corps. Born Leeds 4.8.1894. Son of Fred and Mary Annie Woodhead, 128 Somerset Road, Huddersfield. Educated Moldgreen School and Greenhead High School. Employed as a cashier. Single. Enlisted April 1915. Died of pneumonia following upon influenza on 17.3.1919 at 37th Stationary Hospital, Arquata Scrivia, Italy. He was 24 years of age. Buried **ARQUATA SCRIVIA COMMUNAL CEMETERY EXTENSION.** Grave location:- Plot 1, Row F, Grave 2. ROH:- Almondbury War Memorial; memorial in Almondbury Cemetery.

WOODHEAD, JOE. Private. No 46769. 'D' Company, 12th/13th Battalion Northumberland Fusiliers. Formerly No 31705 Durham Light Infantry. Born Holmfirth. Son of Alfred and Ellen Woodhead, East Bank, Station Road, Holmfirth. Attended the Holmfirth Wesleyan Day School. Was a member of the choir at Lane Chapel and secretary of the Sunday School. Was a painter and decorator, employed by Messrs Quarmby and Son, Upperbridge, Holmfirth. Enlisted in the Spring of 1916. Trained at Rugeley Camp, Staffordshire. Embarked for France in December, 1916. Killed in action, 18.4.1918, aged 35 years. Has no known grave. Commemorated **TYNE COT MEMORIAL TO THE MISSING.** ROH:- Holmfirth War Memorial.

WOODHEAD, LOUIS. Private. No 38162. 1st Battalion The Yorkshire Regiment. Born New Mill. Son of Mr and Mrs Walter Woodhead, Scar Hall, New Mill. Educated New Mill National Day School. Attended New Mill Parish Church Sunday School. As a boy, he was chorister in the Parish Church choir. Employed by Messrs Copley, Marshall and Company, Wildspur Mills. Married. Enlisted September 1916. Embarked for France at Christmas, 1916. Killed in action, 5.11.1918, aged 28 years. Buried **ROISIN COMMUNAL CEMETERY.** Grave location:- Row A, Grave 8. ROH:- New Mill Working Men's Club; Fulstone War Memorial; memorial in Christ Church Churchyard, New Mill. His wife received a letter from Private F Green, who wrote, *'Your husband has been killed in action. I know it is my duty to let you know otherwise you might have never know what has become of him. The poor lad must have been instantly killed by a shell during the recent advance for I came across his body two or three days after his Battalion went over the top and I may say I buried him on the field of battle as respectably as I could. I came across his body quite accidentally and I thought it my duty to let you know that he rests in peace.'*

WOODHEAD, NORMAN. Lance Corporal. No 14242. 2nd Battalion Duke of Wellington's Regiment. Born Holmfirth. Son of Mr Joshua

Woodhead, chemical manufacturer, of Upperthong, Holmfirth. Reported missing, 1.7.1916, during the 1st day of the Battle of the Somme, when he was lost sight of in a wood where there was some severe fighting and afterwards presumed to have been killed on that date. Has no known grave. Commemorated **THIEPVAL MEMORIAL TO THE MISSING.** The following extract is taken from 'British Battalions on the Somme' by Ray Westlake, *'2nd Battalion. 12th Brigade, 4th Division: From assembly trenches east of the sugar factory on Mailly-Maillet - Serre Road. moved forward 8.55am. in support of attack between Beaumont Hamel and Serre. Advancing on Brigade's left fought through into The Quadliteral - by nightfall holding Burrow, Wolf and Legend Trenches. Casualties – 323. Withdrew to Ellis Square in support'.* ROH:- Upperthong War Memorial.

WOODHEAD, WILLIE. Corporal. No 242037. 1/4th Battalion Leicestershire Regiment. Formerly No 1188 Duke of Wellington's Regiment. Born Golcar. Son of Herbert and Lizzie Woodhead, 105 Swallow Lane, Golcar. Died of wounds at No 11 Stationary Hospital, Rouen, on 5.11.1918, aged 22 years. Buried **St. SEVER CEMETERY EXTENSION.** Grave location:- Block S, Plot 2, Row Y, Grave 7. ROH:- St. John's Church, Golcar; memorial in Golcar Churchyard.

WOODHOUSE, HARRY LANCASTER. Private. No 40807. 2/5th Battalion South Staffordshire Regiment. Formerly No 31458 Duke of Wellington's Regiment. Born Thorncliffe Street, Lindley, Huddersfield. Son of Crosland and Elizabeth Woodhouse, 2 Croft House Lane, Marsh. Was employed for 23 years as a woollen warehouseman by Messrs Martin, Sons and Company Limited and afterwards by Messrs C. and J. Hirst Limited, of Longwood. Single. Enlisted in the local Territorials on 29.3.1907. Re-enlisted at the outbreak of the war. Killed in action, 26.9.1917, during the Battle of Passchendaele. He was 39 years of age. Buried **TYNE COT CEMETERY.** Grave location:- Plot 45, Row C, Grave 12. ROH:- Marsh War Memorial; Lindley Zion United Methodist Church; St. Stephen's Church, Lindley.

WOODHOUSE, HILDRED. Private. No 13559. 10th Battalion Duke of Wellington's Regiment. Born Almondbury, Huddersfield. Son of Arthur Woodhouse, 'The Commercial Inn', Cumberworth. Was a member of the choir at Cumberworth Parish Church. Employed by Messrs Hollingworth, contractors, of Cumberworth. Enlisted September 1914. Embarked for France in April, 1915. Died from injuries sustained on 4.11.1915, when his dugout collapsed. He was 19 years of age. Buried **ROYAL IRISH RIFLES GRAVEYARD, LAVENTIE.** Grave location:- Plot 4, Row K, Grave 11. ROH:- Denby Dale and Cumberworth War Memorial.

WOODHOUSE, JOE WILLIAM. Private. No 28784. 10th Battalion Duke of Wellington's Regiment. Born Paddock, Huddersfield. Son of Mr and Mrs Joe Woodhouse, 131 Upper Brow Road, Paddock. Married. Lived 174 Lowergate, Longwood. Employed by Messrs James Sykes, Stafford Mills, Milnsbridge. Attended Paddock United Methodist Church. Was a member of Paddock Socalist Club. Killed in action, 10.6.1917 aged 20 years. Has no known grave. Commemorated **MENIN GATE MEMORIAL TO THE MISSING.** ROH:- St. Mark's Parish Church, Longwood; All Saints Church, Paddock.

WOODHOUSE, JOSEPH. Private. No 24798. 8th Battalion Duke of Wellington's Regiment. Born Far End Lane, Honley, Huddersfield. Son of John Alfred and Sarah Jane Woodhouse, 9 Shore Bank, Ramsden Street, Huddersfield. Educated Honley National School. Employed as a woollen minder at Priestroyd Mills. Single. Enlisted 22.2.1916. Killed in action, 11.8.1917, aged 26 years. Has no known grave. Commemorated **MENIN GATE MEMORIAL TO THE MISSING.**

WOODHOUSE, JOSEPH. Private. No 3030509. 58th Battalion Canadian Infantry (2nd Central Ontario Regiment). Born Huddersfield. Lived Cliffe End, Longwood. Emigrated to America. After several futile attempts to join an American unit he travelled 600 miles and enlisted in a Canadian Regiment. Killed in action, 1.10.1918, aged 43 years. Buried **RAMILLIES BRITISH CEMETERY.** Grave location:- Row C, Grave 8. ROH:- St. Mark's Parish Church, Longwood.

WOODS, HAROLD SNELL. Guardsman. No 28113. 3rd Battalion Grenadier Guards. Born Grimsby. Lived Huddersfield. Employed by the

London and North Western Railway Company as a goods porter. Killed in action during the Battle of Cambrai on 27.11.1917, aged 20 years. Has no known grave. Commemorated **CAMBRAI MEMORIAL TO THE MISSING.** ROH:- Huddersfield Parish Church; London and North Western Railway Company Roll.

WOOLHOUSE, HIRAM. Private. No 204225. 1/4th Battalion Duke of Wellington's Regiment. Born Kirkheaton, Huddersfield, 1.10.1878. Son of the late Sykes and Mary Ann Woolhouse. Educated Kirkheaton National Schools. Employed as a weaver by Messrs B. Crosland and Sons, Oakes. Husband of Louisa Woolhouse, 111 Eldon Road, Marsh, Huddersfield. Enlisted 19.9.1916. Killed in action in Belgium on 26.4.1918, aged 39. Buried **GROOTEBEEK BRITISH CEMETERY, RENINGHELST, BELGIUM.** Grave location:- Row A, Grave 6. ROH:- Holy Trinity Church, Huddersfield.

WORSLEY, JOSEPH. Private. No 1854. 1/5th Battalion Duke of Wellington's Regiment. Born Holmfirth. Nephew of Mr and Mrs Albert Downes of Thongsbridge. Attended St. Andrew's Church, Thongsbridge, where he was a member of the choir and Young Men's Bible Class. He was also a member of the Free Gardener's Lodge and the cricket club. Enlisted at the outbreak of the war. Embarked for France in April, 1915. Killed in action, 28.9.1915. Has no known grave. Commemorated **MENIN GATE MEMORIAL TO THE MISSING.** His Uncle received a letter from Lieutenant Keith Sykes, who wrote, *'It is with the utmost grief and sorrow that I write to tell you that Joseph was killed early this morning. He has looked after me in every way and I shall ever hold his memory dear. He was a good soldier and you have the consolation of knowing that he has paid the supreme sacrifice of his patriotism and he has died nobly fighting for King and Country. The Officers of his Company and his many friends wish to sympathise with you in your great loss. May God comfort you and Mrs Downes in your great trial.'* ROH:- Netherthong and Thongsbridge War Memorial; Huddersfield Drill Hall.

WORTHINGTON, GEORGE. Private. No 204050. 1/4th Battalion Duke of Wellington's Regiment. Born Hillhouse Lane, Huddersfield, 15.3.1895. Son of Francis Herbert and Esther Worthington, 3 Hardy's Buildings, South Street, Huddersfield. Employed as a plasterer by Mr W E Jowett, Fitzwilliam Street, Huddersfield. Attended Queen Street Mission, Huddersfield. Single. Enlisted 4.8.1914. Killed in action, 12.4.1918, aged 22 years. Has no known grave. Commemorated **TYNE COT MEMORIAL TO THE MISSING.** ROH:- South Street Methodist Church.

WORTLEY, DAVID HENRY. Private. No 36310. 26th (Tyneside Irish) Battalion Northumberland Fusiliers. Born Shepley. Husband of Ellen Wortley, Greenside, Shepley. Employed as a painter at Kirkburton. Killed in action, 8.11.1917, aged 29 years. Buried **St. MARTIN CALVAIRE BRITISH CEMETERY.** Grave location:- Plot 1, Row D, Grave 5. ROH:- Shepley War Memorial.

WORTLEY, HARRY. Private. No 62411. 92nd Field Ambulance, Royal Army Medical Corps. Born Shepley. Youngest son of the late John Wortley of Lane Head, Shepley. Lived with his brother-in-law, Councillor Henry Tyas. Attended Shepley United Methodist School. Was a member of the Shepley Bowling Club and Conservative Club. Employed as a painter by Messrs Seth Senior and Sons Limited, Highfield Brewery, Shepley. Single. Enlisted September 1915. Was killed, 1.4.1917, whilst acting as a Stretcher-Bearer. A shell dropped on the party just as they arrived at a dressing station and only one of them escaped. He was 34 years of age. Buried **SAVY BRITISH CEMETERY.** Grave location:- Plot 1, Row I, Grave 22. ROH:- Shepley War Memorial.

WORTLEY, JOE. Gunner. No 77500. 262nd Siege Battery, Royal Garrison Artillery. Second son of Mr and Mrs Walter Wortley, of Highburton, near Huddersfield. Employed by Messrs B. H. Moxon and Sons Limited. Connected with the Kirkburton P.S.A. Brotherhood. Was married in October, 1916. Wounded in the thigh by the bursting of a shell. Died of wounds at No 26 General Hospital on 9.9.1917, aged 25 years. Buried **ETAPLES MILITARY CEMETERY.** Grave location:- Plot 25, Row P, Grave 8A. ROH:- All Hallows Parish Church, Kirkburton.

WRAGG, JOHN (JACK). Private. No 56158. 15th Battalion Royal Welsh Fusiliers. Formerly

No 32442 South Staffordshire Regiment. Born Huddersfield 3.6.1885. Educated Spring Grove Council School. Husband of Kate Wragg, 46 Dewhurst Road, Fartown, Huddersfield. Employed as a letterpress machine minder at the Borough Advertiser Office. Enlisted 23.11.1916. Wounded near Armentieres whilst on sentry duty on 26.12.1917. Died of wounds, 28.12.1917, aged 32 years. Buried **ESTAIRES COMMUNAL CEMETERY EXTENSION.** Grave location:- Plot 5, Row D, Grave 11. ROH:- Christ Church, Woodhouse Hill; Fartown and Birkby War Memorial.

WRAY, ALFRED. Private. No 43106. 10th Battalion King's Own Yorkshire Light Infantry. Formerly No 28891 Northumberland Fusiliers. Born Golcar, Huddersfield. Enlisted Huddersfield. Killed in action, 24.10.1917, at the Battle of Passchendaele. Buried **TYNE COT CEMETERY.** Grave location:- Plot 60, Row K, Grave 20.

WRAY, BENJAMIN. Gunner. No 127421. 156th Siege Battery, Royal Garrison Artillery. Born Golcar, Huddersfield. Husband of Sarah Alice Wray, 8 Royd Street, Slaithwaite. Employed as a weaver by Messrs Ben Hall and sons, Milnsbridge. Was a member of the Scapegoat Hill bandroom. Enlisted November 1916. Embarked for France in May, 1917. Was seriously wounded and gassed on 22.12.1917. Died of wounds at No 46 Casualty Clearing Station on 27.12.1917. He was 35 years of age. Buried **MENDINGHEM MILITARY CEMETERY.** Grave location:- Plot 6, Row BB, Grave 47. ROH:- St. James Church, Slaithwaite; Slaithwaite War Memorial.

WRAY, FRANK. Private. No 58110. 5th Battalion King's Own Yorkshire Light Infantry. Formerly No 32433 Duke of Wellington's Regiment. Born Denby Dale. Son of Mrs Martha Wray, Dearne Terrace, Denby Dale. Killed in action, 2.9.1918, aged 19 years. Buried **VAULX HILL CEMETERY.** Grave location:- Plot 1, Row K, Grave 18. ROH:- Denby Dale and Cumberworth War Memorial.

WRAY, HARRY. Private. No 325783. 1/9th Battalion Durham Light Infantry. Formerly No 7427 Duke of Wellington's Regiment. Born Shepley, Huddersfield. Son of Carter and Mary Wray, Bank End, Shelley. Husband of Ivy Wray, The Post Office, Townend, Shelley. Employed as a weaver by Messrs Firth Brothers of Shepley. Attended Shelley Congregational Church. Was a member of the Shelley Cricket Club first eleven. Enlisted July 1916. Embarked for France in November, 1916. Killed in action, 23.2.1917, aged 25 years. Buried **ASSEVILLERS NEW BRITISH CEMETERY.** Grave location:- Plot 2, Row A, Grave 5. ROH:- Emmanuel Church, Shelley.

WRAY, JAMES EDWARD. Private. No 5058. 1/4th Battalion Northumberland Fusiliers. Born Longwood, Huddersfield. Eldest son of Mr and Mrs Reuben Whitwam, of Scapegoat Hill, Golcar. Was a member of the Scapegoat Hill Brass Band. Enlisted in May 1916. Had only been in France a short time when he was killed in action on 28.10.1916, aged 38 years. Buried **WARLENCOURT BRITISH CEMETERY.** Grave location:- Plot 7, Row A, Grave 12. ROH:- St. John's Church, Golcar.

WRAY, WILLIE. Private. No 203931. 1/4th Battalion Duke of Wellington's Regiment. Born Golcar, Huddersfield. Enlisted Huddersfield. Killed in action, 16.4.1918. Buried **MONT NOIR MILITARY CEMETERY.** Grave location:- Plot 1, Row D, Grave 2.

WRIGHT, FRED STANLEY. Private. No5/4581. 1/5th Battalion Duke of Wellington's Regiment. Born Huddersfield 18.11.1889. Son of William Henry and Pamela Wright, 238 Halifax Old Road, Grimscar, Huddersfield. Educated Hillhouse Council School. Employed as a porter by Messrs Boots Limited, chemists. Single. Enlisted October 1915. Killed by a shell whilst on sentry duty on 12.8.1916 during the Battle of the Somme. He was 27 years of age. Buried **CONNAUGHT CEMETERY, THIEPVAL.** Grave location:- Plot 3, Row J, Grave 6. ROH:- Fartown and Birkby War Memorial; All Saints Church, Paddock; Huddersfield Drill Hall.

WRIGHT, JOHN WILLIAM. Private. No 82891. 230th Company, Machine Gun Corps. Formerly No 37891 York and Lancaster Regiment. Born Helmsley, Yorkshire. Married. Lived Lower Denby, Denby Dale, near Huddersfield. Employed as a gardener by Mr F. W. Sykes, Green Lea, Lindley, and then by Mr G. W. Wilby, of Norcroft, Denby Dale. Enlisted October 1916. Landed in Egypt on 1.6.1917. Killed in action in Palestine on 21.11.1917. Has no known grave. Commemorated **JERUSALEM MEMORIAL**

TO THE MISSING. ROH:- Denby Dale and Cumberworth War Memorial.

WRIGHT, STANLEY. Ordinary Seaman. No. J/22771 Royal Navy. *HMS Glory IV.* Born Huddersfield 31.10.1897. Brother of Annie Neatis, Union Street, Lindley and later of 482 New Hey Road, Salendine Nook, Huddersfield. Educated Spring Grove Board School. Employed as a butcher. Lodged with Mr Barraclough, Prospect Street, Huddersfield. Single. Enlisted in the Royal Navy, 31.12.1912. Killed in action on 14.9.1918 at Archangel, Russia, aged 20 years. Buried **SEMENOVKA (BEREZNIK) CHURCHYARD EXTENSION** and commemorated in **ARCHANGEL ALLIED CEMETERY, RUSSIA.** Grave Location:- Special Memorial, B 139, and on the **BROOKWOOD RUSSIA MEMORIAL IN BROOKWOOD CEMETERY, SURREY.** ROH:- St. Stephen's Church, Lindley.

WRIGHT, THOMAS EDWIN NEVILLE. Lance Corporal. No 240091. 1/5th Battalion Lincolnshire Regiment. Born Legborne, Lincolnshire 1.3.1895. Son of Edwin and Betsy Wright, 36 St. Helen's Lane, Almondbury, Huddersfield. Educated Alford Boys School, Lincolnshire. Employed as a dairyman. Single. Enlisted August 1914. Killed in action, 19.6.1917, at Lens, France, aged 22 years. Buried **LOOS BRITISH CEMETERY.** Grave location:- Plot 19, Row C, Grave 10. ROH:- Almondbury War Memorial.

WRIGLEY, BEN ALLEN. Private. No 203925. 1/5th Battalion Duke of Wellington's Regiment. Born Slaithwaite, Huddersfield. Lived 62 Spa Mill Terrace, Slaithwaite. Employed by Messrs John Haigh and Company, oil merchants, Slaithwaite. Enlisted July 1916. Embarked for France in November, 1916. Killed in action at Nieuport, Belgium, on 7.8.1917, aged 29 years. Buried **RAMSCAPELLE ROAD MILITARY CEMETERY.** Grave location:- Plot 2, Row A, Grave 26. ROH:- Carr Lane United Methodist Church, Slaithwaite; St. James Church, Slaithwaite; Slaithwaite War Memorial; Huddersfield Drill Hall.

WRIGLEY, CHARLIE. Private. No 224111. 243rd Divisional Employment Company, Labour Corps. Formerly No 305664., 7th Battalion Duke of Wellington's Regiment. Born Marsden. Son of Edward and Alice Wrigley, of Marsden. Husband of Mary Jane Wrigley, 23 Derby Terrace, Marsden. Father of five children. Employed as a cloth presser at Bank Bottom Mills, Marsden. Was a member of the Socalist Institute and the Marsden Brass Band. He was also a skilled violinist and, at the time of enlistment, played the double bass. Enlisted October 1914. Embarked for France in April, 1915. Killed in action on 19.3.1918 by shellfire. He was 42 years of age. Buried **THE HUTS CEMETERY, DICKEBUSCH, BELGIUM.** Grave location:- Plot 15, Row C, Grave 9. ROH:- Marsden War Memorial.

WRIGLEY, LEWIS. Private. No 306274. 2/7th Battalion Duke of Wellington's Regiment. Born Filbert Street, Birkby, Huddersfield, 20.7.1896. Son of Albert and Selina Wrigley, 62 Corby Street, Fartown. Educated Hillhouse Board School. Employed as a brass turner by Messrs J. Hopkinson and Company Limited, Birkby. Single. Enlisted 15.10.1915. Killed in action, 28.11.1917, at the Battle of Cambrai. Has no known grave. Commemorated **CAMBRAI MEMORIAL TO THE MISSING.** ROH:- Huddersfield Drill Hall; Fartown and Birkby War Memorial.

WRIGLEY, TOM. Pioneer. No 226830. 334th Road Construction Company, Royal Engineers. Born Crosland Moor, Huddersfield, 5.2.1888. Educated Crosland Moor Council School. Employed as an iron moulder. Husband of Jane Wrigley, 21 Charles Street, Crosland Moor. Enlisted 5.2.1917. Wounded on 10.7.1917 and died of wounds at Vlamertinghe, Belgium, on the same day, aged 28. Buried **HOP STORE CEMETERY, VLAMERTINGHE.** Grave location:- Plot 1, Row C, Grave 44. ROH:- St. Barnabas Church, Crosland Moor.

WRIGLEY, WILLIAM HENRY. Private. No 241612. 2/5th Battalion Duke of Wellington's Regiment. Born Crosland Hill, Huddersfield, 11.3.1896. Son of Joe and Elizabeth Wrigley, 33 Park Road West, Crosland Moor. Employed as a cloth finisher by Messrs John Crowther and Sons, Union Mills. Attended Crosland Moor Wesleyan Chapel. Single. Enlisted 13.3.1916. Killed in action, 25.11.1917, during the Battle of Cambrai. Has no known grave. Commemorated **CAMBRAI MEMORIAL TO THE MISSING.** ROH:- Crosland Moor Wesleyan Church; 'Rising

Sun' Public House, Crosland Hill; St. Barnabas Church, Crosland Moor; Huddersfield Drill Hall.

YATES, GEORGE HERBERT FOURTH. Lieutenant. 4th Army H.Q. Army Pay Corps. Born 229 Bradford Road North, Huddersfield, 11.9.1885. Son of William Pearson Yates and Mary Arabella Yates, 'Westholme', Tarraway Road, Preston, Paignton, South Devon. Educated Fartown Grammar School and King Edward's High School, Birmingham. Was a chartered accountant. Enlisted in the Royal Fusiliers in March, 1916. Wounded by shrapnel in December, 1916. Died of bronchial pneumonia at Boulogne on 15.2.1919, aged 33 years. Buried **TERLINCTHUN BRITISH CEMETERY.** Grave location:- Plot 13, Row D, Grave 15. ROH:- St. John's Church, Birkby; Fartown and Birkby War Memorial.

YATES, HARRY. Private. No 17607. 9th Battalion Duke of Wellington's Regiment. Born Rastrick. Married, with one child. Employed as a fettler by Messrs Pearson Brothers of Golcar. Embarked for France in January, 1916. Killed in action, 7.7.1916, aged 26 years. Has no known grave. Commemorated **THIEPVAL MEMORIAL TO THE MISSING.** ROH:- St. James Church, Slaithwaite; Slaithwaite War Memorial; Huddersfield Drill Hall.

YOUNG, NORMAN. Private. No 240669. 1/5th Battalion Duke of Wellington's Regiment. Born Marsden. Third son of Edwin and Sarah Young, 12 New Buildings, Hardend, Marsden. Employed as a piecer by Messrs Robinson Brothers, Clough Lea Mills, Marsden. Attended Marsden Wesleyan Church and Sunday School. Played football with the Marsden Villa football club. Enlisted November 1914. Embarked for France in June 1915. Killed in action, 12.9.1917, aged 22 years. Buried **COXYDE MILITARY CEMETERY.** Grave location:- Plot 2, Row G, Grave 9. ROH:- Huddersfield Drill Hall; Marsden War Memorial.

YOUNG, STEWART MOLSON. Private. No 202152. 4th Battalion Seaforth Highlanders. Born Glasgow 10.5.1898. Son of Andrew Herbert and Rose Emma Young, Gledholt Grove, Greenhead Road, Huddersfield. Attended New North Road Baptist Sunday School. Was a member of the Huddersfield Swimming Club. Employed as an assistant in the glass and china business of Messrs Andrew Young and Company. Single. Enlisted May 1916. Killed in action near Ypres on 31.7.1917. Buried **ARTILLERY WOOD CEMETERY.** Grave location:- Plot 4, Row B, Grave 15. ROH:- New North Road Baptist Church.

WAR MEMORIALS AND ROLLS OF HONOUR

Although individual memorials to soldiers and seamen have been placed in churches for hundreds of years and national memorials were erected at the end of the Napoleonic Wars, in particular to commemorate the Battle of Waterloo (such as at Pule Hill outside Halifax) it was not until the Boer War that these memorials were inscribed with names. The Duke of Wellington's Regiment erected a Boer War memorial in West End Park, inscribed with the names of those who had died, many from fever, during that conflict. In addition, a memorial plaque in Huddersfield Drill Hall lists the names of the town's Volunteers who had embarked with the Active Service Companies to bolster the Regulars in the Field in South Africa. Fortunately, very few of the Volunteers died of disease and only one was killed by enemy action.

However, during the Great War there was a desire to commemorate those who gave their lives, which permeated every facet of society. As a result, War Memorials were established in cities, towns and villages throughout the land during and just after the war. One of the earliest local examples is the Primrose Hill Memorial, unveiled on 20th January, 1917, at the Primrose Hotel, bearing 316 names of local men who had enlisted from the area since 1914, as announced in the *Huddersfield Examiner* on Monday 22nd January, 1917. Military garrisons were quick to commemorate those lost and Rolls of Honour were also placed in churches, work places and in many social venues. The result of this national fervour, headed by Sir Edwin Lutyens with his magnificent memorials, to those unfortunate men who have no known grave, at Ypres, Thiepval and Arras, is that, throughout this book, there are references to local servicemen being commemorated on local War Memorials and, among other places, Churches, Schools, Factories, Working Men's Clubs and Public Houses. The most outstanding example of a local family memorial is, of course, the Tolson Museum, which commemorates the Tolson brothers from Dalton.

In some cases, where there were smaller numbers of losses in local villages, the names are gathered together on one larger memorial such as that in Holmfirth. For example, the Rolls of Honour mentioned in the main text of the following villages and townships are incorporated on the Holme Valley War Memorial, situated in the grounds of the Home Valley Memorial Hospital in Holmfirth: Holme and Holmbridge – Plaques 1 & 2; Underbank – Plaque 2; Cartworth – Plaque 2; Holmfirth – Plaque 3; Upperthong – Plaque 4; Wooldale – Plaques 4 & 5; Netherthong and Thongsbridge – Plaque 5; Fulstone – Plaques 5 & 6; Hepworth and Scholes – Plaque 6; Hade Edge – Plaque 6.

Indeed, efforts are still being made to commemorate the fallen in this 100th anniversary year of the outbreak of the war and those listed on the new memorial at Farnley Tyas have been incorporated into this work.

In some cases servicemen are commemorated in several places but, in other cases, nowhere except in the pages of this book, fulfilling Margaret's wish that all those she was able to trace from Huddersfield and district would be remembered.

IN MEMORY OF MARGARET – A PERSONAL TRIBUTE

My friendship with Margaret did not start until she and Alan joined one of my tours of the First World War battlefields in France and Belgium in 1985. There turned out to be two Margarets. First there was the quiet, contemplative lady who listened carefully to everything I had to say and was completely cooperative and helpful. What shone out above all, was the compassion she had for the individual soldiers who died on the Western Front in 1914–18, particularly for those who came from her native Yorkshire, a county that had no less than six regiments, each with many battalions, 15 of them being the iconic 'Pals' raised by local initiative and serving together – at least until casualties whittled down the numbers of original members.

However, the 'after-dinner' Margaret was a very different person. After our evening meals there was always a group who would gather either in our hotel, or at some bar not too far away. Serious conversation soon gave way to jokes and sometimes to song. Our daytime pilgrimage to the battlefields had been serious, as had the service in the trenches for the soldiers we were honouring been serious. But those soldiers when 'out of the line' had done exactly the same – egg and chips usually, then jokes and songs. Margaret was often the main contributor to these evening parties, with a swift and piercing sense of humour and contributing alternative wording for otherwise well known songs. We enjoyed these evenings as part of the 'pilgrimage' aspect of the tours; we were doing exactly what the soldiers of 1914–18 had done.

Later, usually working from home, she became a seriously skilled researcher and archivist, helping anyone who needed help with their own work. I benefitted myself from her skill many times. All of this was done for devotion to the memory of the war, nothing for personal gain.

It did not surprise me when I was shown the contents of this publication. It reflects diligence, skill and sheer hard work so that the County Borough of Huddersfield can have, not just a comprehensive list of the names of the men who died in the First World War, but personal details of where, and often how, they died, where they are buried or are commemorated. There are 3,439 such entries, a significant number of which are for men and one woman who, for various reasons, had not been commemorated on the War Memorial in Greenhead Park.

How sad that Margaret died before she could see this marvelous work published.

Mr Martin Middlebrook

ACKNOWLEDGEMENTS

The original compilation of this Roll of Honour took Margaret Stansfield thirty years. During that time she was assisted by a huge number of people and, with the passage of time, it is now impossible to name all of them, however, their respective contributions have made this book possible. Some individuals were involved over an extended period and deserve individual mention: Kenneth Palmer, Ray Westlake, John Golding, Cyril Ford, and Kyle D Tallet as well as the late Phillip Gledhill, all of whom provided significant assistance with the research. The staff of Huddersfield Local History Library, in particular, came to know and respect Margaret for her knowledge and determination and provided her with great assistance over the years. Esther Barrett Page from the Commonwealth War Graves Commission was able to provide unique support in ironing out some of the inevitable anomalies Margaret discovered. Particular thanks are due to Martin Middlebrook, who fuelled Margaret's passion for this subject and shared many happy hours with Alan and Margaret visiting the battlefields and whose moving personal tribute to Margaret is included earlier in the book.

Both the Trustees of Huddersfield Drill Hall and the Trustees of the Duke of Wellington's Regiment Museum and Archives have been truly generous in providing access to original maps, diaries and documents, some of which are included in the book.

More recently, there are more people who have become involved who deserve thanks for their support in the final stages of the production of this book: Andrew Hirst from the *Huddersfield Examiner* is a passionate historian and journalist and, as well as supporting Margaret over the years, has helped to raise awareness among the local populace of those who lost their lives during the Great War. I would also like to thank Joe Hopkinson, a history student at the University, who undertook the initial proof checks, and also Sue White, Graham Stone and Lindsay Ince, from the University Computing and Library Services, for their advice in the production of the text. Finally, I am deeply grateful to Scott Flaving and Richard Harvey from the Duke of Wellington's Regimental Archives, Megan Beech, our Research Copywriter, and Andrea Wilcock, all of whom have worked tirelessly in checking details, sourcing images and, along with myself, laboured to try to ensure that this book truly reflects Margaret's ambition.

There remain two people to thank. First Alan Stansfield, who steadfastly supported his late wife's work for over thirty years, and, most importantly, Margaret herself. Without her vision, endeavours and tenacious quest to identify the fallen heroes from Huddersfield, this book could not have been written.

Reverend Paul Wilcock BEM
Huddersfield
November 2014